The Greek Testament

THE

GREEK TESTAMENT.

VOL III.

THE EPISTLES TO THE GALATIANS, EPHESIANS, PHILIPPIANS, COLOSSIANS, THESSALONIANS,—TO TIMOTHEUS, TITUS, AND PHILEMON

χριστῷ συνεσταύρωμαι· ζῶ δὲ οὐκ ἔτι ἐγώ, ζῇ δὲ ἐν ἐμοὶ χριστός.

GAL. ii. 20.

THE

GREEK TESTAMENT:

WITH A CRITICALLY REVISED TEXT: A DIGEST OF VARIOUS READINGS: MARGINAL REFERENCES TO VERBAL AND IDIOMATIC USAGE: PROLEGOMENA: AND A CRITICAL AND EXEGETICAL COMMENTARY.

FOR THE USE OF THEOLOGICAL STUDENTS AND MINISTERS.

BY

HENRY ALFORD, D.D.

DEAN OF CANTERBURY.

IN FOUR VOLUMES.

VOL. III.

CONTAINING

THE EPISTLES TO THE GALATIANS, EPHESIANS, PHILIPPIANS, COLOSSIANS, THESSALONIANS,—TO TIMOTHEUS, TITUS, AND PHILEMON.

FOURTH EDITION.

RIVINGTONS,
London, Oxford, and Cambridge.
DEIGHTON, BELL, AND CO.,
Cambridge.
1865.

LONDON
GILBERT AND RIVINGTON, PRINTERS,
ST. JOHN'S SQUARE.

CONTENTS OF THE PROLEGOMENA.

CHAPTER I

THE EPISTLE TO THE GALATIANS

SECTION		PAGE
I.	Its Authorship	1
II.	For what Readers it was written	2
III.	With what Object it was written	3
IV.	Its Matter and Style	ib.
V.	Time and Place of Writing	4

CHAPTER II.

THE EPISTLE TO THE EPHESIANS

I.	Its Authorship	6
II	For what Readers it was written	10
III.	Its Occasion, Object, and Contents	19
IV.	At what Time and Place it was written	20
V	Its Language and Style	23
VI.	Its Relation to the Epistle to the Colossians	26

CHAPTER III

THE EPISTLE TO THE PHILIPPIANS

I	Its Authorship and Integrity	26
II	For what Readers and with what Object it was written	28
III.	At what Place and Time it was written	30
IV.	Language and Style	32

CHAPTER IV.

THE EPISTLE TO THE COLOSSIANS

I.	Its Authorship	33
II.	For what Readers and with what Object it was written	34
III	Time and Place of Writing	39
IV.	Language and Style: connexion with the Epistle to the Ephesians	ib.

CHAPTER V.

THE FIRST EPISTLE TO THE THESSALONIANS

SECTION PAGE

I. Its Authorship 43
II. For what Readers and with what Object it was written 44
III. Place and Time of Writing 46
IV. Matter and Style 47

CHAPTER VI

THE SECOND EPISTLE TO THE THESSALONIANS

I Its Authorship 51
II. For what Readers and with what Object it was written 52
III Place and Time of Writing 53
IV. Style 54
V On the Prophetic Import of Ch. ii. 1—12 55

CHAPTER VII.

ON THE PASTORAL EPISTLES.

I Their Authorship 70
II. Time and Place of Writing 87

CHAPTER VIII.

ON THE FIRST EPISTLE TO TIMOTHEUS

I. To whom written 98
II. Occasion and Object 101

CHAPTER IX.

THE SECOND EPISTLE TO TIMOTHEUS.

I. To what Place written 101
II Occasion and Object 103

CHAPTER X.

THE EPISTLE TO TITUS.

I. To whom written 106
II. The Churches of Crete 108

CHAPTER XI.

THE EPISTLE TO PHILEMON.

I. Its Authorship 111
II. Place, Time, Occasion, and Object of Writing 113
III. To what Place addressed, &c . . . . ib.
IV. Character and Style 115

CHAPTER XII

APPARATUS CRITICUS.

I List of MSS containing the Epistles of St. Paul 116
II List, and Specification of Editions, of Books quoted, referred to, or made use of in this Volume 126

ADVERTISEMENT

TO THE

FOURTH EDITION.

This Volume was in the Third Edition made uniform with the rest of the work as regards the revision and augmentation of the references, and the re-writing of the critical digest and consequent occasional changes in the text. The notes were also in parts considerably modified and augmented.

In this Fourth Edition, the readings of the Codex Sinaiticus have been incorporated in the Digest, and some consequent alterations have been made in the text.

Some changes, but not many, have been made in the notes.

Deanery, Canterbury,
July, 1865

PROLEGOMENA.

CHAPTER I.

THE EPISTLE TO THE GALATIANS.

SECTION I

ITS AUTHORSHIP.

1. Of all the Epistles which bear the characteristic marks of St Paul's style, this one stands the foremost See below, on its style, § 4. So that, as Windischmann observes, whoever is prepared to deny the genuineness of this Epistle, would pronounce on himself the sentence of incapacity to distinguish true from false. Accordingly, its authorship has never been doubted.

2 But that authorship is also upheld by external testimony·

(α) Irenæus, adv. Hær iii. 7. 2, p. 182, quotes the Epistle by name: "Sed in ea quæ est ad Galatas, sic ait· Quid ergo lex factorum? posita est usque quo veniat semen, cui promissum est &c" (Gal. iii 19)

Many allusions to it are found

(β) Polycarp, ad Phil cap iii p 1008.

Παύλου . . ὃς καὶ ἀπὼν ὑμῖν ἔγραψεν ἐπιστολάς, εἰς ἃς ἐὰν ἐγκύπτητε, δυνηθήσεσθε οἰκοδομεῖσθαι εἰς τὴν δοθεῖσαν ὑμῖν πίστιν, ἥτις ἐστὶ μήτηρ πάντων ἡμῶν (Gal iv 26). And again, cap v, p 1009: εἰδότες οὖν, ὅτι θεὸς οὐ μυκτηρίζεται . . . . (Gal vi. 7.)

(γ) Justin Martyr, or whoever was the author of the Oratio ad Græcos, printed among his works, seems to allude to Gal iv. 12, in the words γίνεσθε ὡς ἐγώ, ὅτι κἀγὼ ἤμην ὡς ὑμεῖς· and to Gal v. 20, in these, ἔχθραι, ἔρεις, ζῆλος, ἐριθεῖαι, θυμοί, κ τὰ ὅμοια τούτοις, c. v., p. 5

(δ) Besides these, there are many more distant allusions in the works of Ignatius, Polycarp, and Justin, which may be seen cited in Lardner and Windischmann, and Davidson, Introd. to N. T. vol ii. pp 318-19

SECTION II

FOR WHAT READERS IT WAS WRITTEN.

1. This Epistle was written ταῖς ἐκκλησίαις τῆς Γαλατίας (ch. i. 2). GALATIA (Γαλλογραικία Strabo xii. 566, Gallogræcia Liv. xxxvii. 8, xxxviii. 12) was a district of Asia Minor (once part of Phrygia, Strabo xii. 571, ii. 130), bounded N. by Paphlagonia and Bithynia, E. by Pontus and Cappadocia (divided from both by the Halys), S. by Cappadocia and Phrygia, W. by Phrygia and Bithynia. Notwithstanding its mountainous character, it was fruitful, especially near the river Halys (Strabo xii. 567). The principal cities were Ancyra, Pessinus, and Tavium. Ancyra was declared the capital by Augustus. The inhabitants (Γαλάται, only a later form of Κέλται, Pausan. i. 3. 5,—also Gallogræci) were Gauls in origin. The Gallic tribes of the Trochmi and Tolistoboii, with the German tribe of Tectosagi (or Tectosages), crossed over from Thrace into Asia Minor, having formed part of the Gallic expedition which pillaged Delphi, in the third century B.C. (cir. 280). In Asia they at first became mercenary troops under Nicomedes, king of Bithynia, but soon overran nearly the whole of Asia Minor, till Antiochus Soter and Eumenes drove them into its central portion, afterwards called Galatia. There they were at first ruled by tetrarchs, and afterwards (when their real independence had been taken from them by the Consul Manlius Vulso, B.C. 189,—see Livy xxxviii. 16—27) by kings, of whom the two Deiotari, father and son, are known to us, the former as having been defended by Cicero in a speech still extant, the latter as also a friend of the great orator's (Epp. ad Attic. v. 17). Amyntas, the successor of this latter, was their last king: at his death (B.C. 26) Galatia was reduced to a Roman province. See for full accounts, Strabo, book xii. ch. 5: Livy, as above: the Introductions to this Epistle in Meyer, De Wette, and Windischmann: Winer's Realwörterbuch, art. Galatia: Conybeare and Howson, vol. i. p. 284 ff., edn. 2: and the learned dissertation on the question whether the Galatians were Teutons or Celts, appended to Prof. Lightfoot's edition of this Epistle.

2. The character of the people, as shewn in this Epistle, agrees remarkably with that ascribed to the Gallic race by all writers[1]. They received the Apostle at his first visit with extreme joy, and shewed him every kindness: but were soon shaken in their fidelity to him and the Gospel, and were transferring their allegiance to false teachers.

3. The Galatian churches were founded by St. Paul at his first visit,

[1] So Cæsar, B. G. iv. 5. "infirmitatem Gallorum veritus, quod sunt in consiliis capiundis mobiles, et novis plerumque rebus student, nihil his committendum existimavit." And Thierry, Hist. des Gaulois, Introd. "un esprit franc, impétueux, ouvert à toutes les impressions, éminemment intelligent: mais à côté de cela, une mobilité extrême, point de constance, . . . beaucoup d'ostentation, enfin une désunion perpétuelle, fruit d'excessive vanité." C. & H. i. 285, note.

when he was detained among them by sickness (ch iv. 13 see note and compare Acts xvi 6), during his second missionary journey, about A D 51 (see chronol table in Prolegg. to Acts, Vol II). Though doubtless he began his preaching as usual among the Jews (cf Jos Antt. xvi. 6. 2, for the fact of many Jews being resident in Ancyra), yet this Epistle testifies to the majority of his readers being Gentiles, not yet circumcised, though nearly persuaded to it by Judaizing teachers. At the same time we see by the frequent references to the O T. and the adoption of the rabbinical method of interpretation by allegory (ch. iv. 21—31), that he had to do with churches which had been accustomed to Judaizing teaching, and familiarized with the O T See Meyer, Einl p 3 In the manifold preparations for the Gospel which must have taken place wherever Jews were numerous, through the agency of those who had at Jerusalem heard and believed on Jesus, we need not wonder at any amount of judaistic influence apparent even in churches founded by St. Paul himself nor need any hypotheses respecting his preaching be invented to account for such a phænomenon.

SECTION III.

WITH WHAT OBJECT IT WAS WRITTEN

1. Judaizing teachers had followed, as well as preceded, the Apostle in Galatia, and had treated slightingly his apostolic office and authority (ch. i. 1, 11), giving out that circumcision was necessary (ch v 2; vi 12). Their influence was increasing, and the churches were being drawn away by it (i 6; iii 1, 3; iv 9—11; v 7—12) Against these teachers he had already testified in person (i 9, iv. 16, where see notes, and cf. Acts xviii. 23),—and now that the evil was so rapidly and seriously gaining ground, he writes this Epistle expressly to counteract it.

2 The object then of the Epistle was (1) to defend his own apostolic authority; and (2) to expose the judaistic error by which they were being deceived. Accordingly, it contains two parts, the apologetic (ch i ii) and the polemic (ch iii.—v 12) These are naturally followed by a hortatory conclusion (ch. v 13—end). See these parts subdivided into their minor sections in the notes.

SECTION IV

ITS MATTER, AND STYLE

1 The matter of the Epistle has been partly spoken of in the last section In the first, or apologetic portion, it contains a most valuable historical résumé of St. Paul's apostolic career, proving his independence of human authority, and confirming as well as illustrating the narrative in the Acts, by mentioning the principal occasions when he held intercourse with the other Apostles. relating also that remarkable interview

with St Peter, so important for its own sake, and giving rise to his own precious testimony to Christian truth in ch ii 14—21.

2 The polemical portion has much in common with the Epistle to the Romans But this difference is observable, that whereas in that Epistle, the whole subject is treated, as belonging to the great argument there handled, logically, and without reference to any special circumstances,—*here* all is strictly controversial, with immediate reference to the judaizing teachers

3 In style, this Epistle takes a place of its own among those of St Paul. It unites the two extreme affections of his remarkable character severity, and tenderness. both, the attributes of a man of strong and deep emotions Nothing can be more solemnly severe than its opening, and ch. iii. 1—5; nothing more touchingly affectionate than some of its appeals, e. g ch. iv 18—20 It is therefore quite a mistake to characterize its tone as altogether overpowering and intimidating[2] A half-barbarous people like the Galatians, known for their simplicity and impressibility, would be likely to listen to both of these methods of address. to be won by his fatherly pleading, as well as overawed by his apostolic rebukes and denunciations

4. There are several points of similarity in this Epistle to the peculiar diction of the Pastoral Epistles The student will find them pointed out in the reff., and for the most part remarked on in the notes They seem to indicate, in accordance with our interpretation of ch vi. 11, that he wrote this Epistle, as those, with his own hand, without the intervention of an amanuensis This matter will be found more fully treated below, ch vii. on the Pastoral Epistles, § i. 32

SECTION V.

TIME AND PLACE OF WRITING.

1. We have no date in the Epistle itself, which may enable us to determine the time when it was written This can only be gathered from indirect sources And consequently, the most various dates have been assigned to it: some, as Marcion in old times, and Michaelis, al, in modern, placing it *first* among St Paul's Epistles. and others, as Schrader and Kohler, *last* The following considerations will narrow our field of uncertainty on the point

2 If the reasoning in the note on the chronological table, Vol II. Prolegg pp 26, 27, be correct,—the visit to Jerusalem mentioned Gal ii 1 ff is identical with that in Acts xv 1 ff It will thence follow that the Epistle cannot have been written *before* that visit: i e (see Chron Table as above) not before A.D 50

3 I have maintained, in the note on Gal iv 16, that the words

[2] See Jowett, Epistles to the Romans, Thessalonians, and Galatians, vol i p. 191.

there used most naturally refer to the Apostle's second visit to the churches of Galatia, when Acts xviii 23, he went through τὴν Γαλατικὴν χώραν . . . στηρίζων πάντας τοὺς μαθητάς If so, this Epistle cannot date *before that visit*. i. e (Chron Table as above) not before the autumn of the year 54.

4 The first period then which seems probable, is the Apostle's stay at Ephesus in Acts xix, from autumn 54, till Pentecost 57. And this period is so considerable, that, having regard to the οὕτως ταχέως of ch. i 6, it must be regarded as quite possible that our Epistle may have been written during it The above is the view of Hug, De Wette, Olsh, Usteri, Winer, Neander, Greswell, Anger, Meyer, Wieseler, and many others

5. The next period during which it might have been written is, his stay at Corinth, Acts xx. 2, 3, where he spent the winter of the year 57-8, and whence he wrote the Epistle to the Romans This is the opinion of Conybeare and Howson (vol. ii. p. 162, edn 2) They support their view entirely by the similarity of this Epistle and that to the Romans "It is," they say (p. 165, note), "exactly that resemblance which would exist between two Epistles written nearly at the same time, while the same line of argument was occupying the writer's mind, and the same phrases and illustrations were on his tongue." It has also been maintained with much skill and learning, since the first edition of this volume appeared, by Prof Lightfoot, in an article in the Journal of Sacred and Classical Philology for Jan 1857: which article is reproduced in the Introduction to his edition of the Epistle, 1865. He traces the sequence of the lines of thought in the greater Epistles, and finds internal evidence enough to make him decide strongly that it is very improbable, that the two Epistles to the Corinthians intervened between those to the Galatians and Romans, or that to the Galatians between the second to the Thessalonians and the first to the Corinthians.

6 I own that these considerations seem to me weighty ones, and have caused me to modify the decided preference which I gave in my first edition to the earlier date Still, I do not feel Prof. Lightfoot's argument to have settled the question It might be that the elementary truths brought out amidst deep emotion, sketched, so to speak, in great rough lines in the fervent Epistle to the Galatians, dwelt long on St. Paul's mind (even though other subjects of interest regarding other churches intervened), and at length worked themselves out, under the teaching and leading of the Spirit, into that grand theological argument which he afterwards addressed, without any special moving occasion, but as his master-exposition of Christian doctrine, to the church of the metropolis of the world.

7. I think then that it must always remain a question between these two periods. In favour of the former of them it may be said that,

considering the οὕτως ταχέως[3], we can hardly let so long a time elapse as the second would pass over,—and that probability is in favour of strong emotion having, in the prompting of God's Spirit, first brought out that statement of Christian truth and freedom, which after-deliberation expanded, and polished, and systematized, in the Epistle to the Romans: and in favour of the latter may be alleged the interesting considerations respecting the grouping of St Paul's Epistles, and the parallels between 2 Corinthians, Galatians, and Romans, which Prof. Lightfoot has adduced.

8 Of course my objection to the date implied in the common subscription, ἐγράφη ἀπὸ Ῥώμης, adopted by Theodoret, Calov., Hammond, al, is even stronger than that stated above. Those who wish to see the matter discussed at more length, may refer to Davidson, Introd. ii p. 292 ff., and to Prof Lightfoot's edition of the Epistle, pp. 35—55.

CHAPTER II.

THE EPISTLE TO THE EPHESIANS.

SECTION I.

ITS AUTHORSHIP.

1. THE ancient testimonies to the Apostle Paul having been the author of this Epistle, are the following:

(α) Irenæus adv. Hær. v. 2. 36, p. 294

καθὼς ὁ μακάριος Παῦλός φησιν ἐν τῇ πρὸς Ἐφεσίους ἐπιστολῇ ὅτι μέλη ἐσμὲν τοῦ σώματος, ἐκ τῆς σαρκὸς αὐτοῦ, καὶ ἐκ τῶν ὀστέων αὐτοῦ (Eph. v. 30) Again i. 8 5, p. 12, τοῦτο δὲ καὶ ὁ Παῦλος λέγει· πᾶν γὰρ τὸ φανερούμενον, φῶς ἐστίν (Eph. v 13)

(β) Clem Alex. Strom. iv § 65, p 592 P.

διὸ καὶ ἐν τῇ πρὸς Ἐφεσίους γράφει (cf. supra, § 61, φησὶν ὁ ἀπόστολος, where 1 Cor xi 3, &c is quoted, § 62, ἐπιφέρει γοῦν, citing Gal v. 16 ff and infra, § 66, κἂν τῇ πρὸς Κολοσσαεῖς . . . from which it is evident that the subject of γράφει is 'St. Paul') ὑποτασσόμενοι ἀλλήλοις ἐν φόβῳ θεοῦ κ τ λ. Eph. v. 21—25.

(γ) ib Pæd. i § 18, p. 108 P.

ὁ ἀπόστολος ἐπιστέλλων πρὸς Κορινθίους φησίν, 2 Cor xi. 2. . . . . σαφέστατα δὲ Ἐφεσίοις γράφων ἀπεκάλυψε τὸ ζητούμενον ὧδέ πως λέγων· μέχρι καταντήσωμεν οἱ πάντες κ τ λ. Eph. iv. 13 – 15

[3] For I cannot accept the suggestion of Prof. Lightfoot, which would make ταχέως subjective to μετατίθεσθε, 'ye are so rapidly changing.' I have treated on this view in my note on Rev. i. 1, where much depends on it.

2. Further we have testimonies to the Epistle being received as canonical Scripture, and therefore, by implication, of its being regarded as written by him whose name it bears. as e g:

(δ) Polycarp, ad Philippenses, c xii, p 1013 ff.·
"Ut his scripturis dictum est, 'Irascimini et nolite peccare,' et 'Sol non occidat super iracundiam vestram'" Eph iv 26[3]

(ε) Tertullian adv Marcion. v 17, p 512 (see below, § ii 17 c).

(ζ) Irenæus several times mentions passages of this Epistle as perverted by the Valentinians · e g ch. i. 10 (Iren. i. 3. 4, p 16) iii 21 (Iren. i 3 1, p 14) v 32 (Iren i 8 4, p 40) and in many other places (see the Index in Stieren's edn.) cites the Epistle directly.

3. I have not hitherto adduced the testimony ordinarily cited from Ignatius, Eph. 12, p 656, on account of the doubt which hangs over the interpretation of the words[4]

πάροδός ἐστε τῶν εἰς θεὸν ἀναιρουμένων, Παύλου συμμύσται τοῦ ἡγιασμένου, τοῦ μεμαρτυρημένου, ἀξιομακαρίστου, οὗ γένοιτό μοι ὑπὸ τὰ ἴχνη εὑρεθῆναι ὅταν θεοῦ ἐπιτύχω, ὃς ἐν πάσῃ ἐπιστολῇ μνημονεύει ὑμῶν ἐν χριστῷ Ἰησοῦ.

I conceive however that there can be little doubt that these expressions are to be interpreted of the Epistle to the Ephesians First, the expression συμμύσται seems to point to Eph. i. 9, as compared with the rest of the chapter,—to ch iii 3—6, 9. And it would be the very perversity of philological strictness, to maintain, in the face of later and more anarthrous Greek usage, that ἐν πάσῃ ἐπιστολῇ must mean, 'in every Epistle,' and not 'in all his Epistle.' Assuming this latter meaning (see note on Eph ii 21), the expression finds ample justification in the very express and affectionate dwelling on the Christian state and privileges of those to whom he is writing—making mention of them throughout all his Epistle[5].

[3] Meyer, Einl. p 21, prefers to consider both these citations as made from the O T Ps iv. 4, and Deut. xxiv 15 (?), on the ground of the title 'Scripture' never occurring of the N. T in the apostolic fathers.

[4] The chapter itself is wanting in the ancient Syriac version published by Mr Cureton. But this will hardly be adduced as affecting its genuineness. Hefele's view, "pius ille monachus, qui versionem Syriacam elaboravit, omnia omisisse videtur quæ ipsi et usui suo ascetico minus congrua minusve necessaria putabat," seems to be the true one.

[5] Pearson's remarks on this point are worth transcribing. "Hæc a martyre non otiose aut frigide, sed vere, imo signanter et vigilanter dicta sunt Tota enim Epistola ad Ephesios scripta, ipsos Ephesios, eorumque honorem et curam maxime spectat, et summe honorificam eorum memoriam ad posteros transmittit In aliis epistolis apostolus eos ad quos scribit sæpe acriter objurgat aut parce laudat Hic omnibus modis perpetuo se Ephesiis applicat, illosque tanquam egregios Christianos tractat, evangelio salutis firmiter credentes, et Spiritu promissionis obsignatos, concives sanctorum, et domesticos Dei Pro iis sæpe ardenter orat, ipsos hortatur, obtestatur, laudat, utrumque sexum sedulo instruit, suum erga eos singularem affectum ubique prodit." Vindiciæ Ignatianæ, pt. ii ch. 10, end.

4 In the *longer* recension of this Epistle of Ignatius, the testimony is more direct: in ch vi, p 737, we read,

ὡς Παῦλος ὑμῖν ἔγραφεν ἓν σῶμα καὶ ἓν πνεῦμα κ τ λ (Eph. iv. 4—6)

And in ch ix., p. 741,

δι' οὓς ἀγαλλιώμενος ἠξιώθην δι' ὧν γράφω προσομιλῆσαι τοῖς ἁγίοις τοῖς οὖσιν ἐν Ἐφέσῳ, τοῖς πιστοῖς ἐν χριστῷ Ἰησοῦ

5 As we advance to the following centuries, the reception of the authorship of St Paul is universal[6] In fact, we may safely say that this authorship was never called in question till very recent times.

6. Among those critics who have repudiated our Epistle as not written by the Apostle, the principal have been De Wette and Baur The ground on which they build their reasoning is, for the most part, the same. De Wette holds the Epistle to be a verbose expansion of that to the Colossians. He describes it as entirely dependent on that Epistle, and as such, unworthy of a writer who always wrote in freshness and fulness of spirit, as did St Paul. He believes he finds in it every where expressions and doctrines foreign to his diction and teaching This being so, he classes it with the Pastoral Epistles and the first Epistle of Peter, and ascribes it to some scholar of the Apostles, writing in their name. He is not prepared to go so far as Baur, who finds in it the ideas and diction of Gnostic and Montanistic times. On this latter notion, I will treat below I now proceed to deal with De Wette's objections

7. First of all, I would take a general view of their character, and say that, on such a general view, they, as a whole, make *for*, rather than against, the genuineness of the Epistle. According to De Wette, a gifted scholar of the Apostles, in the apostolic age itself, writes an Epistle in imitation, and under the name, of St Paul Were the imitation close, and the imitator detected only by some minute features of inadvertent inconsistency, such a phænomenon might be understood, as that the Epistle found universal acceptance as the work of the Apostle but according to our objector, the discrepancies are wide, the inconsistencies every where abundant He is found, in his commentary, detecting and exposing them at every turn Such reasoning may prove a passage objectively (as in the case of Mark xvi 9—20, or John vii 53—viii 11) to be out of place among the writings of a particular author, all subjective considerations apart · but it is wholly inapplicable when used to account for the success of a forger among his contemporaries, and indeed acts the other way.

8. Let us view the matter in this light. Here is an Epistle *bearing the name* of St. Paul. Obviously then, it is no mere accidental inser-

[6] See Orig contra Celsum, iii. 20, vol i. p 158, Tert de Præscr Hær c 36, vol ii. p. 19, De Monog. c. 5, ib. p. 935, Cypr. Testim. iii. 7, p. 737, Ep. lxxv.

tion among his writings of an Epistle written by some other man, and on purely objective grounds requiring us to ascribe it to that other unknown author, but it is either a genuine production of the Apostle, or a *forgery*. Subjective grounds cannot be kept out of the question · it is a successful forgery: one which imposed on the post-apostolic age, and has continued to impose on the Church in every age We have then a right to *expect in it the phænomena of successful forgery* close imitation, skilful avoidance of aught which might seem unlike him whose name it bears,—construction, if you will, out of acknowledged pauline materials, but so as to shun every thing unpauline

9. Now, as has been seen above, the whole of De Wette's reasoning goes upon the exact opposite of all these phænomena. The Epistle is unpauline. strange and surprising in diction, and ideas Granting this, it might be a cogent reason for believing an *anonymous* writing *not to be* St Paul's · but it is no reason why a forgery bearing his name should have been successful,—on the contrary, is a very sufficient reason why it should have been immediately detected, and universally unsuccessful Let every one of De Wette's positions be granted, and carried to its utmost, and the more in number and the stronger they are, the more reason there will be to infer, that the only account to be given of a writing, so unlike St Paul's, obtaining universal contemporary acceptance as his, is, that it was his own genuine composition. Then we should have remaining the problem, to account for the Apostle having so far departed from himself a problem for the solution of which much acquaintance with himself and the circumstances under which he wrote would be required,—and, let me add, a treatment very far deeper and more thorough than De Wette has given to any part of this Epistle

10. But I am by no means disposed to grant any of De Wette's positions as they stand, nor to recognize the problem as I have put it in the above hypothetical form The relation between our Epistle and that to the Colossians, I have endeavoured to elucidate below (§ vi and Prolegg. to the Col., § iv.). The reasonings and connexions which he pronounces unworthy of the Apostle, I hold him, in almost every case, not to have appreciated. and where he has appreciated them, to have hastily condemned Here, as in the instance of 1 Tim, his unfortunate prejudgment of the spuriousness of the Epistle has tinged his view of every portion of it and his commentary, generally so thorough and able, so fearless and fair, is worth hardly more than those of very inferior men, not reaching below the surface, and unable to recognize the most obvious tendencies and connexions

11 The reader will find De Wette's arguments met in detail by Ruckert (Comm. p. 289 ff.), Hemsen (der Apostel Paulus, pp. 629—38), and touched upon by Harless (Comm. Einleit. p. lxvi ff.), Neander (in a note to his Pfl u Leit edn 4, p. 521 ff.), and Meyer (Einl

p 20 ff.) Davidson also treats of them in full (Introd to N. T. vol ii pp 352—60), and Eadie very slightly (Introd p xxx f)[7].

12 Baur's argument will be found in his 'Paulus, der Apostel Jesu Christi &c.' pp 417—57. It consists, as far as it is peculiar to him, mainly in an attempt to trace in our Epistle, and that to the Colossians (for he holds both to be spurious), expressions and sentiments known to be those of Gnosticism and Montanism. and in some few instances to shew that it is not probable that these heresies took their terms from the Epistles, but rather the Epistles from them This latter part, on which indeed the conclusiveness of the whole depends, is very slightly, and to me most inconclusively done. And nothing is said in Baur of the real account of the occurrence of such terms in the Epistle, and subsequently in the vocabulary of these heretics: viz that the sacred writer laid hold of them and employed them, so to speak, high up the stream of their usage, before they became polluted by heretical additions and misconceptions,—the heretics, lower down the same stream, when now the waters were turbid and noxious: his use of them having tended to impress them on men's minds, so that they were ready for the purpose of the heretics when they wanted them That those heretics used many other terms not known to these Epistles, is no proof that their account was the original one, and this of our Epistles borrowed from it, but simply proves nothing Some of these terms were suited to the Apostle's purpose in teaching or warning. these he was led to adopt: others were not so suitable,—those he left alone. Or it may be that between his writing and their development, the vocabulary had received additions, which consequently were never brought under his notice Eadie refers, for an answer to Baur, to Lechler, das apostolische u. nachapostolische Zeitalter, u s w Haarlem, 1852, a work which I have not seen.

13. Taking then the failure of the above objections into account, and strengthening it by anticipation with other considerations which will come before the reader as we advance, we see no reason whatever against following the universal view of the Church, and pronouncing St Paul to be, as he is stated to be (ch i 1), the author of our Epistle

SECTION II.

FOR WHAT READERS IT WAS WRITTEN

1. In treating of this part of our subject, that city and church seem first to deserve notice, to which the Epistle, according to our present text, is addressed. We will first assume, that it was an Epistle to the EPHESIANS

[7] See also "Ad Ephesios revera dabatur Epistola illa canonica, Paulo non Pseudopaulo auctore." a Prælectio which I read at Cambridge in 1849, the chronological view of which I have seen reason since to modify, but not its argument respecting this Epistle

2. EPHESUS, in Lydia, was situated in an alluvial plain (Herod ii 10) on the south side of and near the mouth of the Caÿstrus. "The city stood on the S of a plain about five miles long from E to W, and three miles broad, the N. boundary being Mount Gallesius, the E. Mount Pactyas, the S Mount Coressus, and on the W. it was washed by the sea The sides of the mountains were very precipitous, and shut up the plain like a stadium, or race-course." Lewin, i. p. 344. See his plan, p 362. and the view of the site of Ephesus in C and H vol ii p 83, edn 2 For its ancient history, see Lewin, and C and H ib, and the art. 'Ephesus,' in Smith's Dict of Geography. It was a place of great commerce (Strabo xiv 641), but was principally noted for its beautiful temple of Artemis (Herod i 26; ii. 148 Strabo, l c Plin v. 37. Pausan vii. 2 4; iv. 31. 6, &c), which was at the head of its harbour Panormus, and was from very ancient times the centre of the worship of that goddess. This temple was burnt down by Herostratus, in the night of the birth of Alexander the Great (B C 355; see Plut. Alex c. 3, Cicero de Nat. Deor ii 27), but rebuilt at immense cost (Strabo, l. c), and was one of the wonders of the ancient world. On the worship of Artemis there, &c, see Acts xix 24 ff. and notes, and Winer RWB. 'Ephesus. The present state of the site of the city, the stadium, theatre, supposed basement of the temple, &c, are described in Smith's Dict of Geogr., his Bible Dict, and in C and H, as above

3. St Paul's first visit to Ephesus is related Acts xviii. 19—21. It was very short, as he was hastening to reach Jerusalem by the next Pentecost The work begun by him in disputations with the Jews, was carried on by Apollos (ib 24—26), and by Aquila and Priscilla (ib 27). After visiting Jerusalem, and making a journey in the Eastern parts of Asia Minor, he returned thither (ib xix 1) and remained there τριετίαν (ib. xix; xx 31) during which period the founding of the Ephesian church must be dated. From what is implied in Acts xix and xx, that church was considerable in numbers and it had enjoyed a more than usual portion of the Apostle's own personal nursing and teaching It will be important to bear this in mind when we come to consider the question of this section.

4 On his last recorded journey to Jerusalem he sailed by Ephesus, and summoned the elders of the Ephesian church to meet him at Miletus, where he took what he believed to be his last farewell of them, in that most characteristic and wonderful speech, Acts xx 18—35.

5 At some subsequent time (see Prolegg to the Pastoral Epistles), he left Timotheus behind in Ephesus, at which place the first Epistle was addressed to him (1 Tim. i. 3), and perhaps (?) the second. The state of the Ephesian church at the time of these Epistles being written, will be found discussed in the Prolegomena to them

6 Ecclesiastical tradition has connected the Apostle John with

Ephesus, see Vol. I. Prolegg. ch. v. § i 9 ff., and his long residence and death there may with safety be assumed

7 To this church our Epistle is addressed, according to our present text And there is nothing in its contents inconsistent with such an address We find in it clear indications that its readers were mixed Jews and Gentiles[8],—that they were in an especial manner united to the Apostle in spiritual privilege and heavenly hope[9]—that they resided in the midst of an unusually corrupt and profligate people[1]

8 Nor are minor indications wanting, which possess interest as connecting our Epistle with the narrative in the Acts He had preached to them τὸ εὐαγγέλιον τῆς χάριτος τοῦ θεοῦ, Acts xx 24, and he commits them τῷ λόγῳ τῆς χάριτος αὐτοῦ, ib ver 32 In this Epistle alone, not in the contemporary and in some respects similar one to the Colossians, do we find such expressions as δόξης τῆς χάριτος αὐτοῦ, ch. i. 6,—τὸ πλοῦτος τῆς χάριτος αὐτοῦ, ib 7, and ii 7,—and an unusual recurrence of χάρις in all its forms and energies. If he preached among them 'the good tidings of the grace of God,' this may well be called 'the Epistle of the grace of God.' In no other of his writings, not even in the Epistle to the Romans, is grace so magnified and glorified. Again in Acts xx 22 f. we read δεδεμένος ἐγὼ τῷ πνεύματι πορεύομαι εἰς Ἱερουσαλήμ, τὰ ἐν αὐτῇ συναντήσοντά μοι μὴ εἰδώς, πλὴν ὅτι τὸ πνεῦμα τὸ ἅγιον κατὰ πόλιν διαμαρτύρεταί μοι λέγων ὅτι δεσμὰ καὶ θλίψεις με μένουσιν And accordingly, here only in his Epistles addressed to churches[2], and not in that to the Colossians, do we find him calling himself ὁ δέσμιος (ch iii 1; iv. 1)

He had not shrunk from declaring to them πᾶσαν τὴν βουλὴν τοῦ θεοῦ (Acts xx 27). and accordingly, in this Epistle alone is βουλή used by St Paul of the divine purpose,—κατὰ τὴν βουλὴν τοῦ θελήματος αὐτοῦ, ch i 11.

In Acts xx. 28 it is said of God and the church, ἣν περιεποιήσατο διὰ τοῦ αἵματος τοῦ ἰδίου and in Eph. i 14, we have the singular expression εἰς ἀπολύτρωσιν τῆς περιποιήσεως, i e of that which He περιεποιήσατο (see note there)

In Acts xx. 32, he commits them to God and the word of His grace, τῷ δυναμένῳ οἰκοδομῆσαι καὶ δοῦναι τὴν κληρονομίαν ἐν τοῖς ἡγιασμένοις πᾶσιν. Not to lay any stress on the frequent recurrence of the image of οἰκοδομή, as being common in other Epistles,—the concluding words can hardly fail to recall Eph. i. 18, τίς ὁ πλοῦτος τῆς δόξης τῆς κληρονομίας αὐτοῦ ἐν τοῖς ἁγίοις,—Eph i 14, ὅ ἐστιν ἀρραβὼν τῆς κληρονομίας ἡμῶν,—and v. 5, οὐκ ἔχει κληρονομίαν ἐν τῇ βασιλείᾳ (see Acts xix 8) τοῦ χριστοῦ καὶ θεοῦ.

9. I would not lay the stress which some have laid on the prevalence of the figure of 'the spiritual building' in this Epistle, as having any

[8] ch. ii 14 ff Compare Acts xix 10.

[9] ch i 3 ff. and passim.

[1] ch. iv. 17 ff, v 1—13

[2] The other cases are in those addressed to individuals, 2 Tim. i 8 Philem vv. 1, 9

connexion with the famous temple of Diana. We should, I think, be suspicious of such supposed local and temporal references (see on 1 Cor v 7), unless the context (as e. g in 1 Cor ix 24, 25) plainly points them out

10 But various objections have been brought against the view that this Epistle was really addressed to the Ephesians. I will take these as recently summed up by Conybeare and Howson, Life and Epistles of St Paul, vol ii. pp 486 ff

11. "*First, it would be inexplicable that St. Paul, when he wrote to the Ephesians, amongst whom he had spent so long a time, and to whom he was bound by ties of such close affection* (Acts xx 17, &c), *should not have a single message of personal greeting to send. Yet none such are found in this Epistle.*" It may be well, in dealing with this, to examine our Apostle's practice in sending these greetings. They are found in greatest abundance in the Epistle to the Romans, written to a church which, as a church, he had never seen, but which, owing to its situation in the great metropolis, contained many of his own friends and fellow-labourers, and many friends also of those who were with him at Corinth In 1 Cor, written to a church which he had founded, and among whom he had long resided (Acts xviii 11), there is not one person saluted by name[3],—and one salutation only sent, from Aquila and Priscilla. In 2 Cor., not one personal salutation of either kind. In Gal, not one · a circumstance commonly accounted for by the subject and tone of the Epistle and if there, why not here also? In Phil, not one though an approach may be said to be made to a personal greeting in μάλιστα οἱ ἐκ τῆς Καίσαρος οἰκίας In Col., the Epistle sent at the same time as this, and by the same messengers, several of both kinds In 1 Thess and 2 Thess, none of either kind In 1 Tim., *sent to Ephesus* (see Prolegg. to Pastoral Epistles), none: in 2 Tim., several of both kinds: in Philemon, salutations *from* brethren, but not *to* any.

The result at which we thus arrive, without establishing any fixed law as to the Apostle's practice, shews us how little weight such an objection as this can have. The Philippians were his dearly beloved, his joy and his crown yet not one of them is saluted The Galatians were his little children, of whom he was in labour till Christ should be formed in them · yet not one is saluted. The Thessalonians were imitators of him and of the Lord, patterns to all that believed in Macedonia and Achaia: yet not one of them is selected for salutation. The general salutations found in several of these cases, the total omission of all salutation in others, seem to follow no rule but the fervour of his own mind, and the free play of his feeling as he writes. The more general

[3] It is plain that the salutations sent *from persons who were with the Apostle,* would depend on his circumstances at the time, and on the connexion between those with him and the church to which he was writing. When he wrote from Corinth to Rome they were abundant.

and solemn the subject, the less he seems to give of these individual notices: the better he knows those to whom he is writing, as a whole, the less he seems disposed to select particular persons for his affectionate remembrance. May we not then conceive it to be natural, that in writing to a church with which he had been so long and intimately acquainted, in writing too on so grand and solemn a subject as the constitution and prospects of Christ's universal church, he should pass over all personal notices, referring them as he does to Tychicus, the bearer of the Epistle? I own I am unable to see any thing improbable in this:—but it seems to me, as far as we can trace his practice, to be in accordance with it.

12. "*Secondly, he could not have described the Ephesians as a church whose conversion he knew only by report*" (ch. i. 15).

The answer to this is very simple. First, he nowhere says that he knew their *conversion* only by report, but what he does say is, ἀκούσας τὴν καθ' ὑμᾶς πίστιν ἐν τῷ κυρίῳ Ἰησοῦ, καὶ τὴν [ἀγάπην τὴν] εἰς πάντας τοὺς ἁγίους: an expression having no reference whatever to their conversion, but pointing to the report which he had received of their abounding in Christian graces;—and perfectly consistent with, nay, explained as it seems to me most simply on, the hypothesis of his having known their previous circumstances well. Any supposition of allusion to their conversion robs the καθ' ὑμᾶς of its fine distributive force, and misses the point of the sentence. But, secondly, if there were any doubt on this point,—if any were disposed to charge us with thus understanding the words merely as a help out of the difficulty,—their meaning is decided for us by the Apostle himself. *Philemon* was his ἀγαπητός and συνεργός (Philem. 1). He was his son in the faith (ib. ver. 19). Yet he addresses him in almost the same words, and in the same connexion with εὐχαριστῶν κ.τ.λ. He says, ἀκούων σου τὴν ἀγάπην καὶ τὴν πίστιν ἣν ἔχεις εἰς τὸν κύριον Ἰησοῦν καὶ εἰς πάντας τοὺς ἁγίους. It is strange that after this had been pointed out, the objection should ever have been again raised.

13. "*Thirdly, he could not speak to them as only knowing himself* (*the founder of their church*) *to be an Apostle by hearsay* (ch. iii. 2), *so as to need credentials to accredit him with them*" (iii. 4).

This objection, as will be seen by the notes on iii. 2, is founded on inattention to the force of εἴ γε[4], and of the aorist ἠκούσατε. The meaning is not, as E. V., 'If ye have heard,' implying a doubt whether they ever had heard, but as given in my note in loc., 'If, that is, ye heard,'—i. e. 'assuming that, when I was with you, ye heard;' and the words convey a reminiscence of that which they did hear. The *cre-*

[4] In Conybeare's version he gives the force of εἴ γε, but, as so often, renders the aorist by a perfect, 'for I suppose that you have heard.'

dential view of ver 4 falls with this mistaken rendering of ver 2: not to mention that it could not for a moment stand, even were that other possible, the reference being to what was before written in ch i [5]

14. "*Fourthly, he could not describe the Ephesians as so exclusively Gentiles* (ch ii 11, iv 17), *and so recently converted*" (v. 8 i 13, ii 13).

To the former objection I reply, 1) that the Ephesian church, as other churches out of Judæa, would naturally be composed for the most part of Gentiles, and as such would be addressed in the main as Gentiles. so we have him writing to the Romans, xi 13, ὑμῖν δὲ λέγω τοῖς ἔθνεσιν. And if exception be taken to this reference, and it be understood as rather marking off the Gentile portion of those to whom he was then writing, the same exception cannot be taken to 1 Cor. xii 2, where, in writing to a mixed church (Acts xviii 4, 8), he says, almost in the same words as in Eph. ii 11, οἴδατε ὅτι ὅτε ἔθνη ἦτε, κ τ λ. · 2) that in this Epistle, of all others, we might expect to find the distinction between Jew and Gentile pass into the background, the subject being, the constitution and glories of the universal Church. 3) that, as before remarked (under 7), indications are not wanting of the mixed composition of the Ephesian Church. Surely the ἵνα τοὺς δύο κτίσῃ ἐν αὐτῷ εἰς ἕνα καινὸν ἄνθρωπον (ii 15) would not have been written to a Church exclusively Gentile

To the latter objection I answer, that in no one of the passages cited is there the slightest intimation of their having been recently converted; —but, if any temporal conclusion can be drawn from them, all three testify rather to a considerable period having elapsed since that event. In ch. v. 8 we have, ἦτε γάρ ποτε σκότος, νῦν δὲ φῶς ἐν κυρίῳ in i. 13, ἐν ᾧ καὶ πιστεύσαντες ἐσφραγίσθητε . . : in ii. 13, ὑμεῖς οἱ ποτὲ ὄντες μακρὰν ἐγενήθητε ἐγγύς

Of the first and third of these, we may observe that the same ποτέ designates *their* unconverted state, by which he designates *his own* in Gal i 13, 23 bis, Tit. iii 3 yet his conversion was by many years antecedent to that of the Ephesians. Of the second and third, that the aorists serve to remove both the things spoken out of the category of recent events. Had their conversion been recent, and its presence, as an act, still abiding, we should have read perfects here and not aorists[6].

15 Having endeavoured to give a reply to these internal objections to the *Ephesian* view of the Epistle, I go on to notice the *external* difficulties besetting the view which I have taken

[5] This indeed is confessed in Conybeare's note, in loc p 497

[6] The force of the former aorist is preserved in Conybeare's version, "you believed in him and received his seal " but the latter is made into a perfect, "ye who were once far off have been brought near," this not being one of those cases where νυνί makes such a rendering in English necessary. See note there.

16 They may be summed up in a discussion of the various reading in ch i 1 (see var readings), by which ἐν Ἐφέσῳ is omitted from the text Basil the Great, contra Eunom ii 19, vol i p. 254 f, says τοῖς Ἐφεσίοις ἐπιστέλλων ὡς γνησίως ἡνωμένοις τῷ ὄντι δι' ἐπιγνώσεως, ὄντας αὐτοὺς ἰδιαζόντως ὠνόμασεν εἰπών τοῖς ἁγίοις τοῖς οὖσιν καὶ πιστοῖς ἐν χριστῷ Ἰησοῦ οὕτω γὰρ οἱ πρὸ ἡμῶν παραδεδώκασι, καὶ ἡμεῖς ἐν τοῖς παλαιοῖς τῶν ἀντιγράφων εὑρήκαμεν From this we infer, that Basil received our Epistle as really written to the Ephesians, but read ch. i. 1 without the words ἐν Εφέσῳ, both traditionally, and because he had seen it so read in ancient MSS The testimony then *does not touch the recognition of the Epistle as written to the Ephesians*, but simply the insertion or omission of the words ἐν Ἐφέσῳ in the text, a matter with which we will deal below.

17. "*This assertion of Basil's is confirmed by Jerome, Epiphanius, and Tertullian*" C. and H vol. ii. p. 487

(a) Jerome: "Quidam . . putant . eos qui Ephesi sunt sancti et fideles essentiæ vocabulo nuncupatos, ut . ab eo qui EST, hi qui SUNT appellentur . . Alii vero simpliciter non ad eos qui sint (al sunt), sed qui Ephesi sancti et fideles sint, scriptum arbitrantur." Ad Eph. i 1, vol vii p 545 .

Doubtless this *may* point to the various reading, and I have allowed it in the Digest as a testimony that way: but it is by no means a decisive one. It may be fairly interpreted on the contrary hypothesis, as indeed Meyer takes it. "Eos qui Ephesi sunt sancti et fideles" represents τοῖς ἁγίοις τοῖς οὖσιν ἐν Ἐφέσῳ καὶ πιστοῖς. This he may be assumed to have read without dispute Then he proceeds to say, that τοῖς οὖσιν was interpreted in two ways: either as an *essentiæ vocabulum*, or as belonging to ἐν Ἐφέσῳ His whole sentence *need not point to any omission* of the words ἐν Ἐφέσῳ.

(b) "*Epiphanius quotes Eph. iv 5, 6, from Marcion's* πρὸς Λαοδικέας" C and H ib, note.

But to this I must demur, for Epiphanius in reality does no such thing Having cited the words, εἷς κύριος, μία πίστις κ τ λ, he proceeds, οὐ γὰρ ἔδοξε τῷ ἐλεεινοτάτῳ Μαρκίωνι ἀπὸ τῆς πρὸς Ἐφεσίους ταύτην τὴν μαρτυρίαν λέγειν, ἀλλ' ἀπὸ τῆς πρὸς Λαοδικέας (i 3 12, vol i. p 375) Therefore his testimony shews merely what we knew before, that Marcion, among his recognized Epistles of St. Paul, had καὶ πρὸς Λαοδικέας λεγομένης μέρη —that this passage was one of such μέρη,—and that Epiphanius blames him for not quoting it from the Epistle to the Ephesians, where accordingly we infer that he himself read it

(c) Tertullian His testimony is the following, contra Marcion v. 11, vol ii p 500,—" Prætereo hic et de alia epistola quam nos ad Ephesios præscriptam habemus, hæretici vero ad Laodicenos " and ib c 17, p 512,—" Ecclesiæ quidem veritate epistolam istam ad Ephesios habemus emissam, non ad Laodicenos, sed Marcion ei titulum aliquando interpolare gestit, quasi et in isto diligentissimus explorator: nihil autem de titulis interest, cum ad omnes apostolus scripserit, dum ad quosdam."

Hence it is commonly argued, and conceded even by Meyer (Einl p. 4), that Tertullian did not read the words ἐν Ἐφέσῳ, or he would have charged Marcion with endeavouring to falsify the *text* as well as to supply a new title. Certainly, it might be so: but it might also be, that he used the word *titulum* in a wide sense, including the title and the corresponding portion of the text. It might be again, since, as Epiphanius tells us (see above), Marcion acknowledged only fragments of an Epistle to the Laodiceans, that the beginning of our Epistle was not among them.

18. If it be thought necessary to deal with the fact of the omission of ἐν Ἐφέσῳ in B and other ancient MSS., we may find at least an illustration of it in the words ἐν Ῥώμῃ (Rom. i. 7) being omitted in G al. It seems to have been done with reference to the catholic subject of the Epistle, very possibly by churches among whom it was read, and with a view to generalize the reference of its contents[7].

19. It is necessary now to deal with two hypotheses respecting the readers to whom our Epistle was addressed, both obviously falling to the ground with the genuineness of the words ἐν Ἐφέσῳ, but requiring also separate treatment. The first of these is, that it was to the *Laodiceans*. So (see above) Marcion: so Grot., Hammond, Mill, Pierce, Wetst., Paley, and many more. But this idea has not even tradition to stand on. All the consensus of the ancient Church is against it. It has nothing to rest on but conjecture, arising out of the mention of an Epistle ἐκ Λαοδικείας, in Col. iv. 16, which seems to have induced Marcion to alter the title. No single MS fills in the gap produced by omitting ἐν Ἐφέσῳ with the words ἐν Λαοδικείᾳ. Again, if this had been really so, is it conceivable that the Laodicean church would without protest and without any remaining sign of their right to the Epistle, have allowed that right to be usurped by the Ephesians and universally acknowledged by the church as theirs? See other minor difficulties of the hypothesis alleged by Meyer, Einl pp. 9, 10, 19, and Harless, Einl p. xxxix. This failing, another way has been struck out, possessing much more plausibility, and gaining many more adherents[1]. It has been supposed that the Epistle was *encyclical*, addressed to more churches than Ephesus only. But I cannot help regarding this hypothesis as even less worthy

[7] See Meyer, Einl. p. 7.

[1] The hypothesis was started by Usher, in his Annals, on the year 64; and is upheld by Bengel, Benson, Michaelis, Schmidt, Eichhorn, Hug, Flatt, Hemsen, Schott, Feilmoser, Schrader, Guericke, Schneckenburger, Neander, Ruckert, Credner, Matthies, Harless, Olshausen, Stier, Conybeare and Howson, and many more, with various sub-hypotheses as to the central church to which it was sent and the means by which it was to be circulated.

of our acceptance than the other It has against it, 1) and chiefly, its total discrepancy with the spirit of the Epistle, which, to whomsoever sent, is clearly addressed to one set of persons throughout, coexisting in one place, and as one body, and under the same circumstances 2) the improbability that the Apostle, who in two of his Epistles (2 Cor , Gal) has so plainly specified their encyclical character, should have here omitted all such specification 3) the even greater improbability that he should have, as on this hypothesis must be assumed, written a circular Epistle to a district of which Ephesus was the commercial capital[2], addressed to various churches within that district, yet from its very contents (as by the opponents' hypothesis) not admitting of application to the church of that metropolis, in which he had spent so long a time, and to which he was so affectionately bound: 4) the inconsistency of this hypothesis with the address of the Epistle, and the universal consensus of the ancient church, who, however they read that address, had no doubt of its being properly entitled. Nor is this objection removed by the form of the hypothesis suggested by C and H , that copies were sent, differently superscribed, which superscriptions, perplexing the copyists, were left out, and then, as copies of the Epistle became spread over the world,—all imported from Ephesus, it was called 'the Epistle from Ephesus,' and so the name of Ephesus came into the text.—for this would, besides being very far-fetched and improbable, not account for the consensus throughout the church, in the Asiatic portion of which, at least, traces of the accurate addresses would be preserved. 5) Another objection, running counter to 1) but not therefore inconsistent with it, is that if it had been *encyclical*, some notice at least would have been found of special local (or rather *regional*) circumstances, as in those to the Corinthians and Galatians The absence of such notice might easily be accounted for, if it were indeed written to the Ephesians alone· but not, if to various Asiatic churches, some of which were so far from having the Ephesians' intimacy with the Apostle, that they had never even seen him There could be no reason for his addressing in common the churches of Laodicea, Hierapolis, Philadelphia, and others (I take the names from C. and H ii. 489), except the existence of some common special dangers, and need of some common special exhortation, of neither of which do we find any hint See various ramifications of this hypothesis dealt with and refuted in Meyer, Einl pp 11—13

20. I infer then, in accordance with the prevalent belief of the Church in all ages, that this Epistle was VERITABLY ADDRESSED TO THE SAINTS IN EPHESUS, and TO NO OTHER CHURCH.

[2] See C and H. ii. 489.

SECTION III

ITS OCCASION, OBJECT, AND CONTENTS

1 The contents of the Epistle afford no indication of its having sprung out of any *special circumstances* of the Ephesian church. Tychicus and Onesimus were being sent to Colossæ The former was charged with a weighty Epistle to the church there, arising out of peculiar dangers which beset them, the latter, with a private apostolic letter of recommendation to his former master, also a resident at Colossæ Under these circumstances, the yearning heart of St Paul went forth to his Ephesians He thought of them as a church in Christ of his own planting—as the mystic Body of Christ, growing onwards for an habitation of God through the Spirit. And, full of such thoughts, he wrote this Epistle to them at the same time with, or immediately subsequent to, his penning of that to the Colossians (on their relation, see below, § vi., and principally, Prolegg. to Col § iv. 4 ff).

2. This being so, the object of the Epistle is a general one—*to set forth the ground, the course, the aim and end, of the* CHURCH OF THE FAITHFUL IN CHRIST. He speaks to the Ephesians as a type or sample of the Church universal. He writes to them not as an ecclesiastical father, united with others, Timotheus or the like, directing and cautioning them,—but as their Apostle and prisoner in the Lord, bound for them, and set to reveal God's mysteries to them.

3 To this intent and this spirit the contents admirably correspond Through the whole Epistle, without one exception, we read of ἡ ἐκκλησία in the singular, never of ἐκκλησίαι in the plural. Of this Church, through the whole, he describes the origin and foundation, the work and course, the scope and end. Every where, both in its larger and smaller portions, this threefold division is found I have endeavoured, in the notes, to point it out, as far as my space would enable me and those who wish to see it traced yet further, will find this done even with more minuteness than I should be disposed in every particular to subscribe, in Stier's very elaborate and diffuse commentary But in fact, the *trichotomy* respecting the Church rests upon another, and sublimer yet Every where with him the origin and foundation of the Church is in the WILL OF THE FATHER, τοῦ τὰ πάντα ἐνεργοῦντος κατὰ τὴν βουλὴν τοῦ θελήματος αὐτοῦ,—the work and course of the Church is by the SATISFACTION OF THE SON, by our υἱοθεσίαν διὰ Ἰησοῦ χριστοῦ,—the scope and end of the Church is the LIFE IN THE HOLY SPIRIT,—δυνάμει κραταιωθῆναι διὰ τοῦ πνεύματος αὐτοῦ εἰς τὸν ἔσω ἄνθρωπον

4. The various sections will be found indicated in the notes. I will here give only a general summary of the Epistle —In ch i, after the introduction of the subject by an ascription of praise to the Father,

who chose us to be holy to Himself in Christ by the Spirit[3], he opens the counsel of the Father[4], whose will it was to sum up all things in Christ[5], and above all His Church[6], composed of Jews and Gentiles, believers in Christ, and sealed with His Spirit. Then with a sublime prayer, that the eyes of their hearts might be enlightened to see the magnitude of the matter[7], he brings in the PERSON OF CHRIST[8], exalted above all for His Church's sake, to which God hath given Him as Head over all things. Thence[9] he passes to the fact of their own vivification in and with Christ, and the fellowship of the mystery which he, the Apostle of the Gentiles, was set to proclaim to the world, viz that spiritual life, by which, rooted and grounded in love, they might come to know the knowledge-passing love of Christ, that they might be filled up to all the fulness of God. Thus having laid forth the ground, course, and scope of the Church, he ends this first part of his Epistle with a sublime doxology[1].

The rest from ch iv 1, is principally hortatory but here also we have the same tripartite division. For he begins by explaining[2] the constitution of the Church, in unity and charity and spiritual gifts, by Christ · then[3] he exhorts to all these graces which illustrate the Christian life,—laying the foundation of each in the counsel of God towards us,—and proposing to us their end, our salvation and God's glory And this he carries[4] into the common duties of ordinary life—into wedlock, and filial and servile relations After this, in a magnificent peroration[5], he exhorts to the putting on of the Christian armour, by which the great end of the militant Church may be attained, to withstand in the evil day, and having accomplished all things, to stand firm And most aptly, when this is concluded, he sums up all with the Catholic benediction and prayer of ch vi. 23, 24

SECTION IV.

AT WHAT TIME AND PLACE IT WAS WRITTEN.

1 When St. Paul wrote our Epistle, he was a PRISONER; ch. iii 1; iv 1, vi 20 This narrows our choice of time to two occasions, supposing it to have been written before the period when the history in the Acts terminates:

A) his imprisonment at Jerusalem and Cæsarea (Acts xxi 27—xxvi 32), from Pentecost 58, to the autumn of 60 (see Chronological Table in Vol II. Prolegg pp. 23—25) ·

B) his imprisonment at Rome, commencing in February 61, and lasting to the end of the history in the Acts, and probably longer.

[3] ver 3 ff. [4] ver 8 ff. [5] ver 10. [6] ver 11 ff
[7] ver. 15 ff. [8] ver. 20 ff. [9] ch ii 1 ff. [1] iii. 20 f.
[2] ch. iv. 1—16. [3] iv 17 v 21. [4] v. 22—vi 9 [5] vi 10—20

2. Further, the three Epistles, to the Colossians, Ephesians, and Philemon, it can hardly be questioned, were sent at one and the same time. The two former are connected as well by their great similarity of contents, as by the fact that Tychicus was the common bearer of both: the two latter, by the common mention of Onesimus as sent to Colossæ, and the common mention of Epaphras, Marcus, Aristarchus, Demas, Lucas, as sending salutations. In speaking therefore of the time and place of writing this Epistle, we are dealing with those others likewise.

3. The view (A) has been taken by some distinguished scholars of modern times in Germany; Schulz (Stud. u. Krit. 1829, p 612 f.), Schneckenburger (Beitr. p 144 f), Schott, Bottger, Wiggers (Stud. u. Krit. 1841, p 436 ff), Thiersch (die Kirche im apostol Zeitalter, 1852, p 176), and Meyer (Einl p 15 ff).

4. The arguments by which it is supported are best and most compendiously stated by Meyer, and are as follows:

a) Because it is more natural and probable that the slave Onesimus fled from Colossæ to Cæsarea, than that he undertook a long sea-voyage to Rome.

b) If our Epistle and that to the Colossians were sent from Rome, Tychicus and his fellow-traveller Onesimus would arrive first at Ephesus and then at Colossæ: in which case we might expect that St Paul would, in his notice of Tychicus to the Ephesians (ch vi 21, 22), have named Onesimus also, as he has done in Col iv 8, 9, to gain for his beloved Onesimus a good reception in Ephesus also. Whereas, if Tychicus and Onesimus travelled from Cæsarea, they would come first, according to the purpose of Onesimus's journey, to Colossæ, where the slave would be left with his master,—and thence to Ephesus: in which case Onesimus would naturally be named in the Epistle to the Colossians, and not in that to the Ephesians.

c) In Eph. vi. 21, ἵνα δὲ εἰδῆτε καὶ ὑμεῖς—καί shews that, when Tychicus should arrive at Ephesus, he would already have reported the affairs of the Apostle to some others. These others are the Colossians, whom Paul knew that he would visit *first*: which again speaks for Cæsarea, and not for Rome, as the place of writing. Had it been the latter, the καί would have appeared in Col iv. 8, not in Eph vi 21.

d) In Philem. 22, the Apostle begs Philemon to prepare him a lodging, and seems to anticipate occupying it soon; which assumes a direct journey to Phrygia after his liberation, which he would reach almost contemporaneously with the arrival of Onesimus. Now it appears from Phil ii 24, that on his liberation from his *Roman* imprisonment, he intended to go to Macedonia, which is inconsistent with visiting Philemon.

5. The view (B) has been the general belief from ancient times down-

wards Its upholders urge that every circumstance of the Epistle fits it, and reply to the considerations urged above,

a) That there is no weight in this a fugitive slave would be in fact more likely than otherwise to get on board ship and take refuge in the great metropolis. And there, notwithstanding what Meyer says to the contrary, he would be more likely to escape the search of the 'fugitivarii,' whose knowledge and occupation, we may presume, were principally local, hardly in strict organization over the whole empire

b) This evidently requires, to be good for any thing, the assumption. that it fell in with the Apostle's plan, to recommend Onesimus to the Ephesians But in the absence of any allusion to personal matters in this Epistle,—in the reference of all such things to Tychicus,—accordant with the very *general* purpose and subject of the Epistle itself, this assumption cannot be received Meyer argues that the *general* character of our Epistle cannot be pleaded with regard to the one passage in it which is individual and personal But surely, it is perfectly legitimate to say, even with regard to such a passage, that the same plan, which induced the Apostle to insert only one such passage in the Epistle would also induce him to insert one personal notice only in such passage To found an argument on any such omission in our Epistle, would be unsafe

c) This, it is maintained, falls entirely to the ground on the different rendering of καί, adopted in the following commentary (see note in loc),—viz referring it, not to another party who were to receive notices of the Apostle, besides those to whom he was writing, but to the reciprocal introduction of ὑμεῖς, 'you also concerning me, as I have been long treating concerning you.'

d) No argument can be raised on ground so entirely uncertain as this It is very possible that altered circumstances may from time to time have changed the Apostle's plans; and that, as we have some reason to believe his projected journey to Spain (Rom xv 22—24) to have been relinquished, or at all events postponed,—so also other projected journeys may have been, according as different churches seemed to require his presence, or new fields of missionary work to open before him Besides which, it may be fairly said, that there is nothing inconsistent in the two expressions, of Phil ii 23 and Philem 22, with the idea of the Apostle projecting a land journey through Greece to Asia Minor · or at all events a general visitation, by what route he may not as yet have determined, which should embrace both Philippi and Colossæ.

6 On the positive side of this view (B), it is alleged, that the circumstances of the Roman imprisonment suit those of these Epistles better than those of the Cæsarean From Eph vi 19, 20, we gather that he had a certain amount of freedom in preaching the Gospel, which is

hardly consistent with what we read in Acts xxiv. 23 of his imprisonment at Cæsarea, where, from the necessity of the case, a stricter watch was requisite (cf Acts xxiii. 21), and none but those ascertained to be his friends (οἱ ἴδιοι αὐτοῦ) were permitted to see him. Among any such multitude of Jews as came to his lodgings on the other occasion, Acts xxviii. 23 ff, might easily be introduced some of the conspirators, against whom he was being guarded.

Besides, we may draw some inference from his *companions*, as mentioned in these Epistles Tychicus, Onesimus, Aristarchus, Marcus, Jesus Justus, Epaphras, Lucas, Demas, were all with him. Of these it is very possible that Lucas and Aristarchus may have been at Cæsarea during his imprisonment, for we find them both accompanying him to Rome, Acts xxvii. 1, 2. But it certainly is not so probable that all these were with him at one time in Cæsarea The two, Lucas and Aristarchus, are confessedly common to both hypotheses. Then we may safely ask, In which of the two places is it more probable that six other of his companions were found gathered round him? In the great metropolis, where we already know, from Rom. xvi, that so many of the brethren were sojourning,—or at Cæsarea, which, though the most important place in Palestine, would have no attraction to gather so many of his friends, except the prospect of sailing thence with him, which we know none of them did?

Perhaps this is a question which never can be definitely settled, so as absolutely to preclude the Cæsarean hypothesis: but I own it appears to me that the whole weight of probability is on the Roman side. Those who firmly believe in the genuineness of this Epistle, will find another reason why it should be placed at Rome, at an interval of from three to five years after the Apostle's parting with the Ephesians in Acts xx., rather than at Cæsarea, so close upon that event In this latter case, the absence of all special notices would be far more surprising than it is at present

7. We may then, I believe, safely assume that our Epistle was written FROM ROME,—and that probably during the period comprised in Acts xxviii. 30, before St. Paul's imprisonment assumed that harsher character which seems to come before us in the Epistle to the Philippians (see Prolegg to that Epistle, § iii)

8 This would bring the time of writing it within the limits A D 61—63: and we should not perhaps be far wrong in dating it A.D. 62

SECTION V

ITS LANGUAGE AND STYLE.

1 As might be expected from the account given of the object of our

Epistle in § iii, the thoughts and language are elevated and sublime; and that to such a degree, that it takes, in this respect, a place of its own among the writings of St Paul. *ὑψηλῶν σφόδρα γέμει τῶν νοημάτων καὶ ὑπερόγκων ἃ γὰρ μηδαμοῦ σχεδὸν ἐφθέγξατο, ταῦτα ἐνταῦθα δηλοῖ,* Chrys, who subjoins examples of this from ch iii 10, ii 6, iii 5 Theophylact says, *ἐπεὶ οὖν δεισιδαίμων τε ἦν οὕτως ἡ πόλις, καὶ οὕτω σοφοῖς ἐκόμα, πολλῇ σπουδῇ κέχρηται Παῦλος πρὸς τοὺς τοιούτους γράφων, καὶ τὰ βαθύτερα δὲ τῶν νοημάτων καὶ ὑψηλότερα αὐτοῖς ἐπίστευσεν, ἅτε κατηχημένοις ἤδη.* So also Grotius, in his preface "Paulus jam vetus in apostolico munere, et ob Evangelium Romæ vinctus, ostendit illis quanta sit vis Evangelii præ doctrinis omnibus quomodo omnia Dei consilia ab omni ævo eo tetenderint, quam admiranda sit in eo Dei efficacia, rerum sublimitatem adæquans verbis sublimioribus quam ulla unquam habuit lingua humana." Witsius, in his Meletemata Leidensia (p 192; cited by Dr Eadie, Commentary on the Ephesians, Introd p xxxi) thus characterizes it "Ita vero universam religionis Christianæ summam divina hac epistola exponit, ut exuberantem quandam non sermonis tantum evangelici *παῤῥησίαν*, sed et Spiritus Sancti vim et sensum, et charitatis Christianæ flammam quandam ex electo illo pectore emicantem, et lucis divinæ fulgorem quendam admirabilem inde elucentem, et fontem aquæ vivæ inde scaturientem, aut ebullientem potius, animadvertere liceat: idque tanta copia, ut superabundans illa cordis plenitudo, ipsa animi sensa intimosque conceptus, conceptus autem verba prolata, verba denique priora quæque subsequentia, premant, urgeant, obruant"

2 These characteristics contribute to make our Epistle *by far the most difficult of all the writings of St Paul* Elsewhere, as in the Epistles to the Romans, Galatians, and Colossians, the difficulties lie for the most part at or near the surface: a certain degree of study will master, not indeed the mysteries of redemption which are treated of, but the contextual coherence, and the course of the argument: or if not so, will at least serve to point out to every reader where the hard texts lie, and to bring out into relief each point with which he has to deal. whereas here the difficulties lie altogether beneath the surface, are not discernible by the cursory reader, who finds all very straightforward and simple We may deduce an illustration from secular literature Every moderately advanced schoolboy believes he can construe Sophocles; he does not see the difficulties which await him, when he becomes a mature scholar, in that style apparently so simple. So here also, but for a different reason. All on the surface is smooth, and flows on unquestioned by the untheological reader but when we begin to enquire, why thought succeeds to thought, and one cumbrous parenthesis to another,—depths under depths disclose themselves, wonderful systems of parallel allusion, frequent and complicated underplots; every word, the more we search, approves itself as set in its exact logical place; we see every phrase contributing, by its

own similar organization and articulation, to the carrying out of the organic whole But this result is not won without much labour of thought, —without repeated and minute laying together of portions and expressions, —without bestowing on single words and phrases, and their succession and arrangement, as much study as would suffice for whole sections of the more exoteric Epistles.

3. The student of the Epistle to the Ephesians must not expect to go over his ground rapidly, must not be disappointed, if the week's end find him still on the same paragraph, or even on the same verse, weighing and judging,—penetrating gradually, by the power of the mind of the Spirit, through one outer surface after another,—gathering in his hand one and another ramifying thread, till at last he grasps the main cord whence they all diverged, and where they all unite,—and stands rejoicing in his prize, deeper rooted in the faith, and with a firmer hold on the truth as it is in Christ

4 And as the wonderful effect of the Spirit of inspiration on the mind of man is nowhere in Scripture more evident than in this Epistle, so, to discern those things of the Spirit, is the spiritual mind here more than any where required We may shew this by reference to De Wette, one of the ablest of Commentators I have mentioned above, § i. 6, that he approaches this Epistle with an unfortunate and unworthy prejudgment of its spuriousness He never thinks of applying to it that humble and laborious endeavour which rendered his commentary on the Romans among the most valuable in existence It is not too much to say, that on this account he has missed almost every point in the Epistle· that his Handbuch, in this part of it, is hardly better than works of third-rate or fourth-rate men. and just for this reason—that he has never come to it with any view of learning from it, but with the averted eyes of a prejudiced man. Take, as a contrast, the two laborious volumes of Stier Here, I would not deny, we have the opposite course carried into extreme but with all Stier's faults of too minute classification,—of wearisome length in exegesis,—of unwillingness to lose, and attempts to combine, every divergent sense of the same passage,—we have the precious and most necessary endowment of spiritual discernment,—acquaintance with the analogy of the faith. And in consequence, the acquisition to the Church of Christ from his minute dissection of this Epistle has been most valuable, and sets future students, with regard to it, on higher spiritual ground than they ever occupied before.

5 It is not to be wondered at, where the subject is *sui generis*, and treated of in a method and style unusually sublime, that the *ἅπαξ λεγόμενα* should be in this Epistle more in number than common, as well as the ideas and images peculiar to it. The student will find both these pointed out and treated of in the references and the notes I would again impress on him, as against De Wette and others, that all such

phænomena, instead of telling against its genuineness, are in its favour, and that strongly. Any skilful forger would not perhaps make his work a mere cento from existing undoubted expressions of St Paul, but at all events would write on new matter in the Apostle's well-known phraseology, avoiding all words and ideas which were in his writings entirely without example.

SECTION VI.

ITS RELATION TO THE EPISTLE TO THE COLOSSIANS.

1. I reserve the full discussion of this subject to the chapter on the Epistle to the Colossians. It would be premature, until the student is in full possession of the object and occasion of that Epistle, to institute our comparison between the two.

2. It may suffice at present to say what may be just enough, as regards the distinctive character of the Epistle to the Ephesians. And this may be done by remarking, that we have here, in the midst of words and images common to the two, an entire absence of all controversial allusion, and of all assertion as against maintainers of doctrinal error. The Christian state, and its realization in the Church, is the one subject, and is not disturbed by any looking to the deviations from that state on either hand, nor guarded, except from that fundamental and directly subversive error of impure and unholy practice.

CHAPTER III.

THE EPISTLE TO THE PHILIPPIANS.

SECTION I.

ITS AUTHORSHIP AND INTEGRITY.

1. It has been all but universally believed that this Epistle was written by St Paul. Indeed, considering its peculiarly Pauline psychological character, the total absence from it of all assignable motive for falsification, the spontaneity and fervour of its effusions of feeling, he must be a bold man who would call its authorship in question[1].

[1] Meyer quotes from Rilliet, Commentaire, Genève, 1841: "Si parmi les écrits de Paul il est vu, qui plus d'autres porte l'empreinte de la spontanéité, et repousse toute apparence de falsification motivée par l'intérêt d'une secte, c'est sans contredit l'épître aux Philippiens."

2. Yet this has been done, partially by Schrader (der Apost. Paulus, vol v see especially p 233, line 14 from bottom, and following), who supposed ch iii 1—iv 9 interpolated, as well as shorter passages elsewhere, conceding however the Pauline authorship in the main and entirely by Baur (Paulus Ap Jesu Christi u s.w., pp. 458—475), on his usual ground of later Gnostic ideas being found in the Epistle To those who would see an instance of the very insanity of hypercriticism, I recommend the study of these pages of Baur. They are almost as good by way of burlesque, as the "Historic Doubts respecting Napoleon Buonaparte" of Abp. Whately According to him, all *usual* expressions prove its spuriousness, as being taken from other Epistles all *unusual* expressions prove the same, as being from another than St. Paul. Poverty of thought, and want of point, are charged against it in one page in another, excess of point, and undue vigour of expression Certainly the genuineness of the Epistle will never suffer in the great common-sense verdict of mankind, from Baur's attack There is hardly an argument used by him, that may not more naturally be reversed and turned against himself

3 In external testimonies, our Epistle is rich.

(α) Polycarp, ad Philipp iii, p. 1008, testifies to the fact of St. Paul having written to them,

. Παύλου ὃς καὶ ἀπὼν ὑμῖν ἔγραψεν [2] ἐπιστολάς, εἰς ἃς ἐὰν ἐγκύπτητε, δυνηθήσεσθε οἰκοδομεῖσθαι εἰς τὴν δοθεῖσαν ὑμῖν πίστιν

(β) And ib xi, pp. 1013 f, he writes,

"Ego autem nihil tale sensi in vobis, vel audivi, in quibus laboravit beatus Paulus, qui estis (laudati) in principio epistolæ ejus. De vobis etenim gloriatur in omnibus ecclesiis quæ Deum solæ tunc cognoverant." Cf Phil i 5 ff

(γ) Irenæus, iv. 18. 4, p. 251.

"Quemadmodum et Paulus Philippensibus (iv 18) ait Repletus sum acceptis ab Epaphrodito, quæ a vobis missa sunt, odorem suavitatis, hostiam acceptabilem, placentem Deo"

(δ) Clement of Alexandria, Pædag i 6 [52], p 129 P .

αὐτοῦ ὁμολογοῦντος τοῦ Παύλου περὶ ἑαυτοῦ οὐχ ὅτι ἤδη ἔλαβον ἢ ἤδη τετελείωμαι κ.τ.λ. Phil iii 12—14.

In Strom iv. 3 [12], p 569 P., he quotes Phil ii 20 in id. 5 [19], p. 572, Phil i 13: in id 13 [94], p. 604, Phil i 29, 30; ii 1 ff., 17, i 7, and ii 20 ff, &c &c

(ε) In the Epistle of the Churches of Lyons and Vienne, in Euseb.

[2] Not necessarily to be understood of more than one Epistle. See Coteler and Hefele in loc.

H. E v. 2, the words ὃς ἐν μορφῇ θεοῦ ὑπάρχων οὐχ ἁρπαγμὸν ἡγήσατο τὸ εἶναι ἴσα θεῷ are cited. Cf Phil ii 6.

(ζ) Tertullian, de resurr. carnis, c 23, vol ii p. 826

"Ipse (Paulus, from the preceding sentence) cum Philippensibus scribit siqua, inquit, concurram in resuscitationem quæ est a mortuis, non quia jam accepi aut consummatus sum," &c &c Phil iii. 11 ff.

(η) The same author devotes the 20th chapter of his fifth book against Marcion (p 522 f) to testimonies from this Epistle, and shews that Marcion acknowledged it. And de præscr. c. 36, p. 49, among the places to which 'authenticæ literæ' of the Apostle's 'recitantur,' he says, 'habes Philippos'

(θ) Cyprian, Testt. iii 39, p. 756

"Item Paulus ad Philippenses Qui in figura Dei constitutus," &c. ch ii 6—11.

4. It has been hinted above, that Schrader doubted the *integrity* of our Epistle This has also been done in another form by Heinrichs, who fancied it made up of two letters,—one to the Church, containing chaps. i ii, to ἐν κυρίῳ iii 1, and iv. 21—23. the other to private friends, beginning at τὰ αὐτὰ γράφειν, iii 1, and containing the rest with the above exception. Paulus also adopted a modification of this view But it is hardly necessary to say, that it is altogether without foundation The remarks below (§ iv) on its style will serve to account for any seeming want of exact juncture between one part and another

SECTION II

FOR WHAT READERS AND WITH WHAT OBJECT IT WAS WRITTEN

1. The city of PHILIPPI has been described, and the πρώτη τῆς μερίδος τῆς Μακεδονίας πόλις, κολωνία discussed, in the notes on Acts xvi 12 ff, to which the student is referred. I shall now notice only the foundation and condition of the Philippian Church

2 The Gospel was first planted there by Paul, Silas, and Timotheus (Acts xvi. 12 ff.), in the second missionary journey of the Apostle, in A D 51. (See Chron Table in Prolegg. to Acts) There we read of only a few conversions, which however became a rich and prolific seed of future fruit He must have visited it again on his journey from Ephesus into Macedonia, Acts xx 1, and he is recorded to have done so (a third time), when, owing to a change of plan to avoid the machinations of his enemies, the Jews at Corinth, he returned to Asia through Macedonia, see Acts xx 6 But we have no particulars of either of these visits

3 The cruel treatment of the Apostle at Philippi (Acts xvi l c 1 Thess ii 2) seems to have combined with the charm of his personal fervour of affection to knit up a bond of more than ordinary love between him and the Philippian Church. They, alone of all churches, sent subsidies to relieve his temporal necessities, on two several occasions, immediately after his departure from them (Phil. iv. 15, 16, 1 Thess ii. 2) and they revived the same good office to him shortly before the writing of this Epistle (Phil iv 10, 18, 2 Cor xi 9)

4 This affectionate disposition may perhaps be partly accounted for by the fact of *Jews* being so few at Philippi. There was no synagogue there, only a προσευχή by the river side and the opposition to the Apostle arose not from Jews, but from the masters of the dispossessed maiden, whose hope of gain was gone. Thus the element which resisted St. Paul in every Church, was wanting, or nearly so, in the Philippian His fervent affection met there, and almost there only, with a worthy and entire return. And all who know what the love of a warm-hearted people to a devoted minister is, may imagine what it would be between such a flock and such a shepherd. (See below, on the style of the Epistle.)

5 But while this can hardly be doubted it is equally certain that the Church at Philippi was in danger from Jewish influence: not indeed among themselves[3], but operating on them from without (ch iii 2),—through that class of persons whom we already trace in the Epistle to the Galatians, and see ripened in the Pastoral Epistles, who insisted on the Mosaic law as matter of external observance, while in practice they gave themselves up to a life of lust and self-indulgence in depraved conscience.

6. The slight trace which is to be found in ch iv 2, 3, of the fact related Acts xvi 13, that the Gospel at Philippi was first received by female converts, has been pointed out in the notes there

7 The general state of the Church may be gathered from several hints in this Epistle and others They were *poor* In 2 Cor. viii 1, 2, we read that ἡ κατὰ βάθους πτωχεία αὐτῶν ἐπερίσσευσεν εἰς τὸ πλοῦτος τῆς ἁπλότητος αὐτῶν They were *in trouble*, and probably from persecution. compare 2 Cor viii 2 with Phil i 28—30. They were *in danger of*, if not already in, *quarrel and dissension* (cf. ch ii 1—4; and i 27, ii 12, 14, iv 2), on what account, we cannot say, it may be, as has been supposed by De W, that they were peculiarly given to spiritual pride and mutual religious rivalry and jealousy. This may have arisen out of their very progress and flourishing state as a Church engendering pride. Credner supposes (Davidson, p 381), that it may have

[3] This has been supposed, by Eichhorn, Storr, Flatt, &c, but certainly without reason De W and Dr. Davidson refer (ii. 380) with praise to Schinz, Die christliche Gemeinde zu Philippi, ein exegetischer Versuch, 1833, which I have not seen.

been a spiritual form of the characteristic local infirmity, which led them to claim the title πρώτη πόλις for their city; but this falls to the ground, if πρώτη be geographically explained see note Acts xvi. 12

8 The *object* of the Epistle seems to have been no marked and definite one, but rather the expression of the deepest Christian love, and the exhortation, generally, to a life in accordance with the Spirit of Christ Epaphroditus had brought to the Apostle the contribution from his beloved Philippians, and on occasion of his return, he takes the opportunity of pouring out his heart to them in the fulness of the Spirit, refreshing himself and them alike by his expressions of affection, and thus led on by the inspiring Spirit of God to set forth truths, and dilate upon motives, which are alike precious for all ages and for every Church on earth

SECTION III

AT WHAT PLACE AND TIME IT WAS WRITTEN

1 It has been believed, universally in ancient times (Chrys, Euthal, Athanas., Thdrt, &c), and almost without exception (see below) in modern, that our Epistle was written *from Rome*, during the imprisonment whose beginning is related in Acts xxviii 30, 31.

2. There have been some faint attempts to fix it at Corinth (Acts xviii 11, so Oeder, in Meyer), or at Cæsarea (so Paulus and Bottger, and Rilliet hesitatingly; see Meyer) Neither of these places will suit the indications furnished by the Epistle The former view surely needs no refuting And as regards the latter it may be remarked, that the strait between life and death, expressed in ch i 21—23, would not fit the Apostle's state in Cæsarea, where he had the appeal to Cæsar in his power, putting off at all events such a decision for some time Besides which, the Καίσαρος οἰκία, spoken of ch iv 22, cannot well be the πραιτώριον τοῦ Ἡρώδου at Cæsarea of Acts xxiii 35, and therefore it is by that clearer notice that the πραιτώριον of ch. i 13 must be interpreted (see note there), not vice versâ It was probably the barrack of the prætorian guards, attached to the palatium of Nero

3. Assuming then that the Epistle was written from Rome, and during the imprisonment of Acts xxviii ult, it becomes an interesting question, to *which part of that imprisonment* it is to be assigned

4 On comparing it with the three contemporaneous Epistles, to the Colossians, to the Ephesians, and to Philemon, we shall find a marked difference. In them we have (Eph vi. 19, 20) freedom of preaching the Gospel implied. here (ch i 13—18) much more stress is laid upon his bondage, and it appears that others, not he himself, preached the Gospel, and made the fact of his imprisonment known Again, from this same

passage it would seem that a considerable time had elapsed since his imprisonment: enough for "his bonds" to have had the general effects there mentioned. This may be inferred also from another fact: the Philippians had heard of his imprisonment,—had raised and sent their contribution to him by Epaphroditus,—had heard of Epaphroditus's sickness,—of the effect of which news on them he (Epaphroditus) had had time to hear, ch ii. 26, and was now recovered, and on his way back to them These occurrences would imply four casual journeys from Rome to Philippi Again (ch ii 19, 23) he is expecting a speedy decision of his cause, which would hardly be while he was dwelling as in Acts xxviii. ultt.

5. And besides all this, there is a spirit of anxiety and sadness throughout this Epistle, which hardly agrees with the two years of the imprisonment in the Acts, nor with the character of those other Epistles His sufferings are evidently not the chain and the soldier only Epaphroditus's death would have brought on him λύπην ἐπὶ λύπην (ch. ii 27): there was then a λύπη before He is now in an ἀγών—in one not, as usual, between the flesh and the spirit, not concerning the long-looked for trial of his case, but one of which the Philippians had heard (ch. i 29, 30), and in which they shared by being persecuted too. some change in his circumstances, some intensification of his imprisonment, which had taken place before this time

6. And if we examine history, we can hardly fail to discover what this was. and whence arising In February, 61, St Paul arrived in Rome (see Chron Table in Prolegg. to Acts, Vol II.). In 62[4], Burrus, the prætorian præfect, died, and a very different spirit came over Nero's government who in the same year divorced Octavia, married Poppæa[5], a Jewish proselytess[6], and exalted Tigellinus the principal promoter of that marriage, to the joint prætorian præfecture From that time, Nero began 'ad deteriores inclinare[7]·' Seneca lost his power· 'validior in dies Tigellinus[8]·' a state of things which would manifestly deteriorate the condition of the Apostle, and have the effect of hastening on his trial. It will not be unreasonable to suppose that, some little time after the death of Burrus (Feb., 63, would complete the διετία ὅλη of Acts xxviii 30), he was removed from his own house into the πραιτώριον, or barrack of the prætorian guards attached to the palace, and put into stricter custody, with threatening of immediate peril of his life Here it would be very natural that some of those among the prætorians who had had the custody of him before, should become agents in giving the publicity to "his bonds," which he mentions ch i 13. And

[4] Tacit Annal. xiv. 51 See Clinton's Fasti Romani, i. p. 44
[5] Tacit Annal xiv 60
[6] Jos. Antt. xx. 8 11.
[7] Tacit Annal xiv. 52
[8] Tacit. Annal. xiv. 57.

such a hypothesis suits eminently well all the circumstances of our Epistle

7 According to this, we must date it shortly after Feb., 63. when now the change was fresh, and the danger imminent. Say for its date then, the summer of 63

SECTION IV

LANGUAGE AND STYLE

1 The language of this Epistle is thoroughly Pauline. Baur has indeed selected some phrases which he conceives to savour of the vocabulary of the later Gnosticism, but entirely without ground All those which he brings forward, οὐχ ἁρπαγμὸν ἡγήσατο,—ἑαυτὸν ἐκένωσεν,—μορφὴ θεοῦ,—σχῆμα,—καταχθόνιοι,—may easily be accounted for without any such hypothesis. and, as has been already observed in Prolegg. to Ephesians, peculiar expressions may just as well be held to have descended from our Epistle to the Gnostics, as vice versâ

2 The mention of ἐπίσκοποι καὶ διάκονοι in ch i. 1, has surprised some. I have explained in the note there, that it belongs probably to the late date of our Epistle But it need surprise no one, however that may be for the terms are found in an official sense, though not in formal conjunction, in speeches made, and Epistles written long before this: e g in Acts xx 28; Rom. xvi 1.

3 In style, this Epistle, like all those where St. Paul writes with fervour, is discontinuous and abrupt, passing rapidly from one theme to another[1]; full of earnest exhortations[2], affectionate warnings[3], deep and wonderful settings-forth of his individual spiritual condition and feelings[4], of the state of Christians[5] and of the sinful world[6],—of the loving counsels of our Father respecting us[7], and the self-sacrifice and triumph of our Redeemer[8].

4. No epistle is so warm in its expressions of affection[9] Again and again we have ἀγαπητοί and ἀδελφοί recurring: and in one place, ch. iv. 1, he seems as if he hardly could find words to pour out the fulness of his love—ὥστε, ἀδελφοί μου ἀγαπητοὶ καὶ ἐπιπόθητοι, χαρὰ καὶ στέφανός

[1] e g, ch ii 18, 19,—21, 25,—30, iii 1,—2, 3, 4,—14, 15, &c.
[2] See ch. i 27, iii 16, iv. 1 ff, 4, 5, 8, 9
[3] See ch ii 3, 4, 14 ff, iii. 2, 17—19.
[4] See ch i 21—26, ii. 17, iii 4—14, iv 12, 13
[5] See ch. ii 15, 16, iii. 3, 20, 21.
[6] See ch iii 18, 19
[7] See ch. i. 6, ii. 13, iv. 7, 19.
[8] See ch. ii 4—11.
[9] See ch i. 7, 8, ii 1, 2, iv 1

μου, οὕτως στήκετε ἐν κυρίῳ, ἀγαπητοί. We see how such a heart, penetrated to its depths by the Spirit of God, could love We can see how that feeble frame, crushed to the very verge of death itself, shaken with fightings and fears, burning at every man's offence, and weak with every man's infirmity, had yet its sweet refreshments and calm resting-places of affection We can form some estimate,—if the bliss of reposing on human spirits who loved him was so great,—how deep must have been his tranquillity, how ample and how clear his fresh springs of life and joy, in HIM, of whom he could write, ζῶ δὲ οὐκ ἔτι ἐγὼ, ζῇ δὲ ἐν ἐμοὶ χριστός (Gal ii 20). and of whose abiding power within him he felt, as he tells his Philippians (ch iv. 13), πάντα ἰσχύω ἐν τῷ ἐνδυναμοῦντί με

CHAPTER IV.

THE EPISTLE TO THE COLOSSIANS.

SECTION I.

AUTHORSHIP.

1 THAT this Epistle is a genuine work of St Paul, was never doubted in ancient times · nor did any modern critic question the fact, until Schrader[1], in his commentary, pronounced some passages suspicious, and led the way in which Baur[2] and Meyerhoff[3] followed In his later work Baur entirely rejects it[4] The grounds on which these writers rest, are partly the same as those already met in the Prolegomena to the Ephesians The Epistle is charged with containing phrases and ideas derived from the later heretical philosophies,—an assertion, the untenableness of which I have there shewn as regards that Epistle, and almost the same words would suffice for this Even De Wette disclaims and refutes their views, maintaining its genuineness though as Dr Davidson remarks, "it is strange that, in replying to them so well, he was not led to question his own rejection of the authenticity of the Ephesian Epistle."

2 The arguments drawn from considerations peculiar to this Epistle, its diction and style, will be found answered under § iv

3 Among many external testimonies to its genuineness and authenticity are the following

(a) Justin Martyr, contra Tryph 85, p. 182, calls our Lord πρωτότοκος πάσης κτίσεως (Col i 15), and similarly § 84, p. 181; 100, p. 195

[1] Der Apost Paulus, v 175 ff
[2] Die sogenannt Pastoralbr p 79 Ursprung der Episcop p. 35.
[3] Der Br an die Col, &c Berlin, 1838
[4] Paulus, Apost. Jesu Christi, pp 417—57

(β) Theophilus of Antioch, ad Autolycum, ii 22, p 365, has τοῦτον τὸν λόγον ἐγέννησε προφορικόν, πρωτότοκον πάσης κτίσεως

These may perhaps hardly be conceded as direct quotations But the following are beyond doubt

(γ) Irenæus, iii. 14 1, p. 201:

"Iterum in ea epistola quæ est ad Colossenses, ait · 'Salutat vos Lucas medicus dilectus'" (ch. iv 14)

(δ) Clement of Alexandria, Strom. i. 1 [15], p. 325 P:

κἀν τῇ πρὸς Κολοσσαεῖς ἐπιστολῇ, "νουθετοῦντες," γράφει, "πάντα ἄνθρωπον καὶ διδάσκοντες κ τ λ" (ch i 28)

In Strom iv. 7 [56], p 588, he cites ch iii. 12 and 14:—in Strom v 10 [61, ff.], p. 682 f,—ch. i. 9—11, 28, ch ii 2 ff, ch iv 2, 3 ff. In id. vi. 8 [62], p 771, he says that Παῦλος ἐν ταῖς ἐπιστολαῖς calls τὴν Ἑλληνικὴν φιλοσοφίαν 'στοιχεῖα τοῦ κόσμου' (Col ii 8)

(ε) Tertullian, de præscr. hæret. c. 7, vol. ii. p 20:

"A quibus nos Apostolus refrænans nominatim philosophiam testatur caveri oportere, scribens ad Colossenses videte, ne quis sit circumveniens vos &c" (ch ii 8)

And de Resurr carnis, c 23, vol. ii. p. 825 f.

"Docet quidem Apostolus Colossensibus scribens " and then he cites ch. ii. 12 ff, and 20,—iii 1, and 3

(ζ) Origen, contra Cels v 8, vol. i. p. 583:

παρὰ δὲ τῷ Παύλῳ, ... τοιαῦτ' ἐν τῇ πρὸς Κολασσαεῖς λέλεκται· μηδεὶς ὑμᾶς καταβραβευέτω θέλων κ τ λ (ch ii 18, 19)

4 I am not aware that the integrity of the Epistle has ever been called in question. Even those who are so fond of splitting and portioning out other Epistles, do not seem to have tried to subject this to that process

SECTION II

FOR WHAT READERS AND WITH WHAT OBJECT IT WAS WRITTEN.

1 COLOSSÆ, or (for of our two oldest MSS,—ℵ writes one (α) in the title and subscription, and the other (ο) in ch i. 2, and B has α with ο written above by 1 m in the title and subscription, and ο in ch i. 2) COLASSÆ, formerly a large city of Phrygia (ἀπίκετο [Xerxes] ἐς Κολοσσάς, πόλιν μεγάλην Φρυγίας, Herod vii 30: ἐξελαύνει [Cyrus] διὰ Φρυγίας . . . . εἰς Κολοσσάς, πόλιν οἰκουμένην, εὐδαίμονα καὶ μεγάλην, Xen Anab i. 2 6) on the river Lycus, a branch of the Mæander (ἐν τῇ Λύκος ποταμὸς ἐς χάσμα γῆς ἐσβαλὼν ἀφανίζεται[5], ἔπειτα διὰ σταδίων ὡς μάλιστά κη

[5] See this chasm accounted for in later ages by a *Christian legend*, Conyb and Hows, edn 2, vol. ii. p. 480, note.

πέντε ἀναφαινόμενος, ἐκδιδοῖ καὶ οὗτος ἐς τὸν Μαίανδρον Herod. ibid.). In Strabo's time it had lost much of its importance, for he describes Apamea and Laodicea as the principal cities in Phrygia, and then says, περίκειται δὲ ταύταις καὶ πολίσματα, among which he numbers Colossæ. For a minute and interesting description of the remains and neighbourhood, see Smith's Dict. of Ancient Geography, sub voce. From what is there said it would appear, that Chonæ (*Khonos*), which has, since the assertion of Nicetas, the Byzantine historian who was born there[6], been taken for Colossæ, is in reality about three miles S. from the ruins of the city.

2. The Church at Colossæ consisted principally of Gentiles, ch. ii. 13. To whom it owed its origin, is uncertain. From our interpretation of ch. ii. 1 (see note there), which we have held to be logically and contextually necessary, the Colossians are included among those who had not seen St. Paul in the flesh. In ch. i. 7, 8, Epaphras is described as πιστὸς ὑπὲρ ἡμῶν διάκονος τοῦ χριστοῦ, and as ὁ καὶ δηλώσας ἡμῖν τὴν ὑμῶν ἀγάπην ἐν πνεύματι: and in speaking of their first hearing and accurate knowledge of the grace of God in truth, the Apostle adds καθὼς ἐμάθετε ἀπὸ Ἐπαφρᾶ τοῦ ἀγαπητοῦ συνδούλου ἡμῶν. As this is not[7] καθὼς καὶ ἐμάθετε, we may safely conclude that the ἐμάθετε refers to that first hearing, and by consequence that Epaphras was the founder of the Colossian Church. The time of this founding must have been subsequent to Acts xviii. 23, where St. Paul went καθεξῆς through Galatia and Phrygia, στηρίζων πάντας τοὺς μαθητάς: in which journey he could not have omitted the Colossians, had there been a Church there.

3. In opposition to the above conclusion, there has been a strong current of opinion that the Church at Colossæ *was founded by St. Paul.* Theodoret seems to be the first who took this view (Introd. to his Commentary). His argument is founded mainly on what I believe to be a misapprehension of ch. ii. 1[8], and also on a partial quotation of

[6] So also Theophylact on ch. i. 2, πόλις Φρυγίας αἱ Κολοσσαί, αἱ νῦν λεγόμεναι Χῶναι.

[7] The rec. has the καί: see var. readd. Its insertion would certainly primâ facie change the whole face of the passage as regards Epaphras, and make him into an accessory teacher, after the ᾗ ἡμέρᾳ ἠκούσατε. Still, such a conclusion would not be *necessary.* It might merely carry on the former καθὼς καί, or it might introduce a particular additional to ἐπέγνωτε, specifying the accordance of that knowledge with Epaphras's teaching.

[8] His words are: ἔδει δὲ συνιδεῖν τῶν ῥητῶν τὴν διάνοιαν. βούλεται γὰρ εἰπεῖν, ὅτι οὐ μόνον ὑμῶν ἀλλὰ καὶ τῶν μὴ τεθεαμένων με πολλὴν ἔχω φροντίδα. εἰ γὰρ τῶν μὴ ἑωρακότων αὐτὸν μόνον τὴν μέριμναν περιέφερε, τῶν ἀπολαυσάντων αὐτοῦ τῆς θέας καὶ τῆς διδασκαλίας οὐδεμίαν ἔχει φροντίδα. Leaving the latter argument to go for what it is worth, it will be at once seen that the οὐ μόνον view falls into the logical difficulty mentioned in the note in loc., and fails to account for the αὐτῶν.

Acts xviii 23, from which he infers that the Apostle must have visited Colossæ in that journey, adducing the words διῆλθε τὴν Φρυγίαν καὶ τὴν Γαλατικὴν χώραν, but without the additional clause στηρίζων πάντας τοὺς μαθητάς

4 The same position was taken up and very elaborately defended by Lardner, ch xiv. vol. ii p 172 His arguments are chiefly these·

1) The improbability that the Apostle should have been twice in Phrygia and not have visited its principal cities

2) The Apostle's assurance of the fruitful state of the Colossian Church, ch i. 6, 23; ii. 6, 7.

3) The kind of mention which is made of Epaphras, shewing him not to have been their first instructor· laying stress on the καθὼς καί in ch i. 7 (rec reading, but see above, par 2), and imagining that the recommendations of him at ch i 7, 8, iv 12, 13, were sent to prevent his being in ill odour with them for having brought a report of their state to St. Paul,—and that they are inconsistent with the idea of his having founded their Church

4) He contends that the Apostle does in effect say that he had himself dispensed the Gospel to them, ch. i 21—25

5) He dwells on the difference (as noted by Chrysostom in his Pref. to Romans, but not with this view) between St. Paul's way of addressing the Romans and Colossians on the same subject, Rom xiv 1, 2, Col. ii. 20—23, and infers that as the Romans were not his own converts, the Colossians must have been.

6) From ch ii 6, 7, and similar passages as presupposing his own foundership of their Church.

7) "If Epaphras was sent to Rome by the Colossians to enquire after Paul's welfare, as may be concluded from ch iv 7, 8, that token of respect for the Apostle is a good argument of personal acquaintance. And it is allowed, that he had brought St. Paul a particular account of the state of affairs in this Church Which is another argument that they were his converts"

8) Ch. i 8, "who declared unto us your love in the Spirit," is "another good proof of personal acquaintance."

9) Ch. iii 16, as shewing that the Colossians were endowed with spiritual gifts, which they could have received only from an Apostle

10) From ch ii 1, 2, interpreting it as Theodoret above.

11) From the ἄπειμι of ch ii 5, as implying previous presence.

12) From ch iv 7—9, as "full proof that Paul was acquainted with them, and they with him"

13) From the salutations in ch iv 10, 11, 14, and the appearance of Timotheus in the address of the Epistle, as implying that the Colossians were acquainted with St Paul's fellow-labourers, and consequently with himself

14) From the counter salutations in ch iv. 15.

15) From ch. iv 3, 4, and 18, as "demands which may be made of strangers, but are most properly made of friends and acquaintance."

16) From the Apostle's intimacy with Philemon an inhabitant of Colossæ, and his family; and the fact of his having converted him "Again, ver 22, St Paul desires Philemon to prepare him a lodging Whence I conclude that Paul had been at Colossæ before."

5. To all the above arguments it may at once be replied, that based as they are upon mere verisimilitude, they must give way before the fact of the Apostle never having once directly alluded to his being their father in the faith, as he does so pointedly in 1 Cor. iii. 6, 10; in Gal i. 11; iv 13· Phil ii 16, iii 17; iv 9. 1 Thess i 5; ii 1, &c Only in the Epistles to the Romans and Ephesians, besides here, do we find such notice wanting in that to the Romans, from the fact being otherwise. in that to the Ephesians, it may be from the general nature of the Epistle, but it may also be because he was not entirely or exclusively their founder: see Acts xviii 19—28.

6 Nor would such arguments from verisimilitude stand against the logical requirements of ch. ii. 1. In fact, all the inferences on which they are founded will, as may be seen, full as well bear turning the other way, and ranging naturally and consistently enough under the other hypothesis The student will find them all treated in detail in Dr Davidson's Introduction, vol. ii. pp. 402—406

7. It may be interesting to enquire, if the Church at Colossæ owed its origin not to St. Paul, but to Epaphras, why it was so, and at what period we may conceive it to have been founded Both these questions, I conceive, will be answered by examining that which is related in Acts xix, of the Apostle's long sojourn at Ephesus During that time, we are told, ver. 10,—*τοῦτο δὲ ἐγένετο ἐπὶ ἔτη δύο, ὥστε πάντας τοὺς κατοικοῦντας τὴν Ἀσίαν ἀκοῦσαι τὸν λόγον τοῦ κυρίου, Ἰουδαίους τε καὶ Ἕλληνας*·—and this is confirmed by Demetrius, in his complaint ver. 26,—*θεωρεῖτε καὶ ἀκούετε ὅτι οὐ μόνον Ἐφέσου, ἀλλὰ σχεδὸν πάσης τῆς Ἀσίας ὁ Παῦλος οὗτος πείσας μετέστησεν ἱκανὸν ὄχλον* So that we may well conceive, that during this time Epaphras, a native of Colossæ, and Philemon and his family, also natives of Colossæ, and others, may have fallen in with the Apostle at Ephesus, and become the seeds of the Colossian Church. Thus they would be dependent on and attached to the Apostle, many of them personally acquainted with him and with his colleagues in the ministry This may also have been the case with them at Laodicea and them at Hierapolis, and thus Pauline Churches sprung up here and there in Asia, while the Apostle confined himself to his central post at Ephesus, where, owing to the concourse to the temple, and the communication with Europe, he found so much and worthy occupation

8 I believe that this hypothesis will account for the otherwise strange phænomena of our Epistle, on which Lardner and others have laid stress, as implying that St Paul had been among them: for their personal regard for him, and his expressions of love to them. for his using, respecting Epaphras, language hardly seeming to fit the proximate founder of their Church·—for the salutations and counter salutations

9. The enquiry into the occasion and object of this Epistle will be very nearly connected with that respecting the state of the Colossian Church, as disclosed in it

10. It will be evident to the most cursory reader that there had sprung up in that Church a system of erroneous teaching, whose tendency it was to disturb the spiritual freedom and peace of the Colossians by ascetic regulations. to divide their worship by inculcating reverence to angels, and thus to detract from the supreme honour of Christ

11 We are not left to infer respecting the class of religionists to which these teachers belonged· for the mention of νουμηνία and σάββατα in ch ii 16, at once characterizes them as Judaizers, and leads us to the then prevalent forms of Jewish philosophy, to trace them Not that these teachers were *merely Jews*, they were Christians: but their fault was, the attempt to mix with the free and spiritual Gospel of Christ the theosophy and angelology of the Jews of their time, in which they had probably been brought up. Of such theosophy and angelology we find ample traces in the writings of Philo, and in the notices of the Jewish sect of the Essenes given us by Josephus[9].

12 It does not seem necessary to mark out very strictly the position of these persons as included within the limits of this or that sect known among the Jews they were infected with the ascetic and theosophic notions of the Jews of their day, who were abundant in Phrygia[10] and they were attempting to mix up these notions with the external holding of Christianity.

13 There must have been also mingled in with this erroneous Judaistic teaching, a portion of the superstitious tendencies of the Phrygian character, and, as belonging to the Jewish philosophy, much of that incipient Gnosticism which afterwards ripened out into so many strange forms of heresy

14 It may be noticed that the Apostle does not any where in this Epistle charge the false teachers with immorality of life, as he does the very similar ones in the Pastoral Epistles most frequently The infer-

[9] Cf B J. ii. 8. 2—13, where, beginning τρία γὰρ παρὰ Ἰουδαίοις εἴδη φιλοσοφεῖται, he gives a full account of the Essenes Among other things he relates that they took oaths συντηρήσειν τά τε τῆς αἱρέσεως αὐτῶν βιβλία, καὶ τὰ τῶν ἀγγέλων ὀνόματα

[10] See Jos. Antt. xii 3 4, where Alexander the Great is related to have sent, in consequence of the disaffection of Lydia and Phrygia, two thousand Mesopotamian and Babylonian Jews to garrison the towns

ence from this is plain. The false teaching was yet in its bud Later down, the bitter fruit began to be borne, and the mischief required severer treatment Here, the false teacher is εἰκῇ φυσιούμενος ὑπὸ τοῦ νοὸς τῆς σαρκὸς αὐτοῦ (ch. ii 18): in 1 Tim iv 2, he is κεκαυτηριασμένος τὴν ἰδίαν συνείδησιν. ib vi 5, διεφθαρμένος τὸν νοῦν, ἀπεστηρημένος τῆς ἀληθείας, νομίζων πορισμὸν εἶναι τὴν εὐσέβειαν. Between these two phases of heresy, a considerable time must have elapsed, and a considerable development of practical tendencies must have taken place

15 Those who would see this subject pursued further, may consult Meyer and De Wette's Einleitungen: Davidson's Introduction, vol. ii pp 407—424, where the various theories respecting the Colossian false teachers are mentioned and discussed · and Professor Eadie's Literature of the Epistle, in the Introduction to his Commentary.

16 The occasion then of our Epistle being the existence and influence of these false teachers in the Colossian Church, the object of the Apostle was, to set before them their real standing in Christ the majesty of His Person, and the completeness of His Redemption · and to exhort them to conformity with their risen Lord following this out into all the subordinate duties and occasions of common life.

SECTION III

TIME AND PLACE OF WRITING

1. I have already shewn in the Prolegg to the Ephesians that that Epistle, together with this, and that to Philemon, were written and sent at the same time · and have endeavoured to establish, as against those who would date the three from the imprisonment at Cæsarea, that it is much more natural to follow the common view, and refer them to that imprisonment at Rome, which is related in Acts xxviii ultt

2. We found reason there to fix the date of the three Epistles in A D. 61 or 62, during that freer portion of the imprisonment which preceded the death of Burrus such freedom being implied in the notices found both in Eph. vi 19, 20, and Col iv 3, 4, and in the whole tone and spirit of the three Epistles as distinguished from that to the Philippians

SECTION IV.

LANGUAGE AND STYLE: CONNEXION WITH THE EPISTLE TO THE EPHESIANS.

1. In both language and style, the Epistle to the Colossians is peculiar. But the peculiarities are not greater than might well arise from the fact, that the subject on which the Apostle was mainly writing was

one requiring new thoughts and words. Had not the Epistle to the Romans ever been written, that to the Galatians would have presented as peculiar words and phrases as this Epistle now does

2 It may be well to subjoin a list of the ἅπαξ λεγόμενα in our Epistle.

ἀρέσκεια, ch i 10	νουμηνία, ib 16
δυναμόω, ib 11	καταβραβεύω, ib 18
ὁρατός ib 16	ἐμβατεύω, ib. 18.
πρωτεύω, ib 18.	δογματίζω, ib 20.
εἰρηνοποιέω, ib 20	ἀπόχρησις, ib. 22.
μετακινέω, ib. 23.	λόγον ἔχειν, ib 23
ἀνταναπληρόω, ib 24	ἐθελοθρήσκεια, ib 23
πιθανολογία, ch. ii. 4.	ἀφειδία, ib. 23
στερέωμα, ib 5	πλησμονή, ib 23
συλαγωγέω, ib 8	αἰσχρολογία, ch iii 8
φιλοσοφία, ib 8	μομφή, ib. 13
θεότης, ib 9.	βραβεύω, ib 15.
σωματικῶς, ib 9	εὐχάριστος, ib 15
ἀπέκδυσις, ib. 11	ἀθυμέω, ib 21
χειρόγραφον, ib 14	ἀνταπόδοσις, ib 24.
προσηλόω, ib 14.	ἀνεψιός, ch iv 10
ἀπεκδύω, ch ii 15; ch iii 9	παρηγορία, ib 11.
δειγματίζω, ib 15 (?) (see Matt i 19.)	

3 A very slight analysis of the above will shew us to what they are chiefly owing. In ch. i we have *seven*. in ch ii, *nineteen* or *twenty*: in ch. iii., *seven*. in ch iv, *two* It is evident then that the nature of the subject in ch ii has introduced the greater number. At the same time it cannot be denied that St Paul does here express some things differently from his usual practice. for instance, ἀρέσκεια, δυναμόω, πρωτεύω, εἰρηνοποιέω, μετακινέω, πιθανολογία, ἐμβατεύω, μομφή, βραβεύω, all are peculiarities, owing not to the necessities of the subject, but to *style* to the peculiar frame and feeling with which the writer was expressing himself, which led to his using these unusual expressions rather than other and more customary ones And we may fairly say, that there is visible throughout the controversial part of our Epistle, a loftiness and artificial elaboration of style, which would induce precisely the use of such expressions It is not uncommon with St Paul, when strongly moved or sharply designating opponents, or rising into majestic subjects and thoughts, to rise also into unusual, or long and compounded words see for examples, Rom. i. 21—32; viii. 35—39; ix 1—5, xi 33—36, xvi 25—27, &c, and many instances in the Pastoral Epistles It is this σεμνότης of controversial tone, even more than the necessity of the subject handled, which causes our Epistle so much to abound with peculiar words and phrases.

4. And this will be seen even more strongly, when we turn to the Epistle to the Ephesians, sent at the same time with the present letter. In writing both, the Apostle's mind was in the same general frame—full of the glories of the Person of Christ, and the consequent glorious privileges of His Church, which is built on Him, and vitally knit to Him. This mighty subject, as he looked with indignation on the beggarly system of meats and drinks and hallowed days and angelic mediations to which his Colossians were being drawn down, rose before him in all its length and breadth and height; but as writing to *them*, he was confined to one portion of it, and to setting forth that one portion pointedly and controversially. He could not, consistently with the effect which he would produce on them, dive into the depths of the divine counsels in Christ with regard to them. At every turn, we may well conceive, he would fain have gone out into those wonderful prayers and revelations which would have been so abundant if he had had free scope: but at every turn, *οὐκ εἴασεν αὐτὸν τὸ πνεῦμα Ἰησοῦ*: the Spirit bound him to a lower region, and would not let him lose sight of the *βλέπετε μή τις*, which forms the ground-tone of this Colossian Epistle. Only in the setting forth of the majesty of Christ's Person, so essential to his present aim, does he know no limits to the sublimity of his flight. When he approaches those who are Christ's, the urgency of their conservation, and the duty of marking the contrast to their deceivers, cramps and confines him for the time.

5. But the Spirit which thus bound him to his special work while writing to the Colossians, would not let His divine promptings be in vain. While he is labouring with the great subject, and unable to the Colossians to express all he would, his thoughts are turned to another Church, lying also in the line which Tychicus and Onesimus would take: a Church which he had himself built up stone by stone; to which his affection went largely forth: where if the same baneful influences were making themselves felt, it was but slightly, or not so as to call for special and exclusive treatment. He might pour forth to his Ephesians all the fulness of the Spirit's revelations and promptings, on the great subject of the Spouse and Body of Christ. To them, without being bound to narrow his energies evermore into one line of controversial direction, he might lay forth, as he should be empowered, their foundation in the counsel of the Father, their course in the satisfaction of the Son, their perfection in the work of the Spirit.

6. And thus,—as a mere human writer, toiling earnestly and conscientiously towards his point, pares rigidly off the thoughts and words, however deep and beautiful, which spring out of and group around his subject, putting them by and storing them up for more leisure another day: and then on reviewing them, and again awakening the spirit which prompted them, playfully unfolds their germs, and amplifies their sug-

gestions largely, till a work grows beneath his hands more stately and more beautiful than ever that other was, and carrying deeper conviction than it ever wrought:—so, in the higher realms of the fulness of Inspiration, may we conceive it to have been with our Apostle. His Epistle to the Colossians is his caution, his argument, his protest is, so to speak, his working-day toil, his direct pastoral labour and the other is the flower and bloom of his moments, during those same days, of devotion and rest, when *he* wrought not so much in the Spirit, as the Spirit wrought in *him*. So that while we have in the Colossians, system defined, language elaborated, antithesis, and logical power, on the surface—we have in the Ephesians the free outflowing of the earnest spirit, —to the mere surface-reader, without system, but to him that delves down into it, in system far deeper, and more recondite, and more exquisite: the greatest and most heavenly work of one, whose very imagination was peopled with the things in the heavens, and even his fancy rapt into the visions of God.

7. Thus both Epistles sprung out of one Inspiration, one frame of mind. that to the Colossians first, as the task to be done, the protest delivered, the caution given. that to the Ephesians, begotten by the other, but surpassing it: carried on perhaps in some parts simultaneously, or immediately consequent. So that we have in both, many of the same thoughts uttered in the same words[11], many terms and phrases peculiar to the two Epistles; many instances of the same term or phrase, still sounding in the writer's ear, but used in the two in a different connexion. All these are taken by the impugners of the Ephesian Epistle as tokens of its spuriousness: I should rather regard them as psychological phænomena strictly and beautifully corresponding to the circumstances under which we have reason to believe the two Epistles to have been written: and as fresh elucidations of the mental and spiritual character of the great Apostle

[11] See reff. tables of these have been given by the Commentators I will not repeat them here, simply because to complete such a comparison would require far more room and labour than I could give to it, and I should not wish to do it as imperfectly as those mere formal tables have done it The student may refer to Davidson, vol ii p 391

CHAPTER V.

THE FIRST EPISTLE TO THE THESSALONIANS.

SECTION I

ITS AUTHORSHIP.

1 This Epistle has been all but universally recognized as the undoubted work of St Paul. It is true (see below) that no reliable citations from it appear in the Apostolic Fathers: but the external evidence from early times is still far too weighty to be set aside.

2. Its authorship has in modern times been called in question (1) by Schrader, and (2) by Baur, on internal grounds. Their objections, which are entirely of a subjective and most arbitrary kind, are reviewed and answered by De Wette, Meyer, and Dr. Davidson (Introd to N T vol ii. pp 454 ff)[1]: and have never found any acceptance, even in Germany.

3 The external testimonies of antiquity are the following

Irenæus adv Hær v 6 1, p 299 f. "Et propter hoc apostolus seipsum exponens, explanavit perfectum et spiritualem salutis hominem, in prima epistola ad Thessalonicenses dicens sic. Deus autem pacis sanctificet vos perfectos," &c (1 Thess v 23.)

[1] I must, in referring to Dr. Davidson, not be supposed to concur in his view of the Apostle's expectation in the words ἡμεῖς οἱ ζῶντες οἱ περιλειπόμενοι (1 Thess. iv. 15, 17). See my note there.

There is a very good statement of Baur's adverse arguments, and refutation of them, in Jowett's work on the Thessalonians, Galatians, and Romans, "Genuineness of the first Epistle," vol i 15—26 In referring to it, I must enter my protest against the views of Professor Jowett on points which lie at the very root of the Christian life views as unwarranted by any data furnished in the Scriptures of which he treats, as his reckless and crude statement of them is pregnant with mischief to minds unaccustomed to biblical research. Among the various phænomena of our awakened state of apprehension of the characteristics and the difficulties of the New Testament, there is none more suggestive of saddened thought and dark foreboding, than the appearance of such a book as Professor Jowett's Our most serious fears for the Christian future of England, point, it seems to me, just in this direction: to persons who allow fine æsthetical and psychological appreciation, and the results of minute examination of spiritual feeling and mental progress in the Epistles, to keep out of view that other line of testimony to the fixity and consistency of great doctrines, which is equally discoverable in them. I have endeavoured below, in speaking of the matter and style of our Epistle, to meet some of Professor Jowett's assertions and inferences of this kind

Clem. Alex. Pædag i. 5 [19], p 109 P : τοῦτό τοι σαφέστατα ὁ μακάριος Παῦλος ὑπεσημήνατο, εἰπών· δυνάμενοι ἐν βάρει εἶναι κ τ λ to ἑαυτῆς τέκνα (1 Thess. ii 6)

Tertullian de resurr carnis, § 24, vol ii p 828 "Et ideo majestas Spiritus sancti perspicax ejusmodi sensuum et in ipsa ad Thessalonicenses epistola suggerit: De temporibus autem . . quasi fur nocte, ita adveniet." (1 Thess. v. 1 f.)

SECTION II.

FOR WHAT READERS AND WITH WHAT OBJECT IT WAS WRITTEN

1. THESSALONICA was a city of Macedonia, and in Roman times, capital of the second district of the province of Macedonia (Liv. xlv. 29 f), and the seat of a Roman prætor (Cic Planc. 41) It lay on the Sinus Thermaicus, and is represented to have been built on the site of the ancient Therme (Θέρμη ἡ ἐν τῷ Θερμαίῳ κόλπῳ οἰκημένη, ἀπ' ἧς καὶ ὁ κόλπος οὗτος τὴν ἐπωνυμίην ἔχει, Herod vii 121), or peopled from this city (Pliny seems to distinguish the two 'medioque flexu littoris Thessalonica, liberæ conditionis Ad hanc, a Dyrrhachio cxv mil pas, Therme.' iv. 10) by Cassander, son of Antipater, and named after his wife Thessalonice, sister of Alexander the Great (so called from a victory obtained by his father Philip on the day when he heard of her birth)[2]. Under the Romans it became rich and populous (ἡ νῦν μάλιστα τῶν ἄλλων εὐανδρεῖ, Strab vii. 7. see also Lucian, Asin. c. 16, and Appian, Bell Civ iv 118), was an 'urbs libera' (see Pliny, above), and in later writers bore the name of "metropolis" "Before the founding of Constantinople it was virtually the capital of Greece and Illyricum, as well as of Macedonia and shared the trade of the Ægean with Ephesus and Corinth" (C and H edn 2, vol. i p. 380). Its importance continued through the middle ages, and it is now the second city in European Turkey, with 70,000 inhabitants, under the slightly corrupted name of Saloniki For further notices of its history and condition at various times, see C and H. i pp 378—83 Winer, RWB sub voce (from which mainly the above notice is taken) Dr Holland's Travels. Lewin, vol i p 252

2 The church at Thessalonica was founded by St Paul, in company with Silas and Timotheus[3], as we learn in Acts xvii. 1—9 Very little

[2] So Strabo, vii excerpt 10 μετὰ τὸν Ἄξιον ποταμόν, ἡ Θεσσαλονίκη ἐστὶν πόλις, ἡ πρότερον Θέρμη ἐκαλεῖτο κτίσμα δ' ἐστὶν Κασσάνδρου ὃς ἐπὶ τῷ ὀνόματι τῆς ἑαυτοῦ γυναικός, παιδὸς δὲ Φιλίππου τοῦ Ἀμύντου, ὠνόμασεν μετῴκισεν δὲ τὰ πέριξ πολίχνια εἰς αὐτήν οἷον Χαλάστραν, Αἰνείαν (see Dion. Hal, Antiq i. 49), Κίσσον, καί τινα καὶ ἄλλα.

[3] That this latter was with Paul and Silas, though not expressly mentioned in the

is there said which can throw light on the origin or composition of the Thessalonian church. The main burden of that narrative is the rejection of the Gospel by the Jews there It is however stated (ver 4) that some of the Jews believed, and consorted with Paul and Silas, and of the devout Greeks a great multitude, and of the chief women not a few

3 But some account of the Apostle's employment and teaching at Thessalonica may be gathered from this narrative, connected with hints dropped in the two Epistles. He came to them, yet suffering from his persecution at Philippi (1 Thess ii 2) But they received the word joyfully, amidst trials and persecutions (ib i 6; ii 13), and notwithstanding the enmity of their own countrymen and of the Jews (ii. 14 ff). He maintained himself by his labour (ib ii 9), although his stay was so short[4], in the same spirit of independence which characterized all his apostolic course. He declared to them boldly and clearly the Gospel of God (ii. 2). The great burden of his message to them was the approaching coming and kingdom of the Lord Jesus (i 10; ii 12, 19; iii 13, iv 13—18; v 1—11, 23, 24. Acts xvii 7 see also § iv below), and his chief exhortation, that they would walk worthily of this their calling to that kingdom and glory (ii 12; iv. 1; v 23)

4 He left them, as we know from Acts xvii. 5—10, on account of a tumult raised by the unbelieving Jews, and was sent away by night by the brethren to Berœa, together with Silas and Timotheus (Acts xvii. 10) From that place he wished to have revisited Thessalonica: but was prevented (1 Thess ii. 18), by the arrival with hostile purposes, of his enemies the Thessalonian Jews (Acts xvii 13), in consequence of which the brethren sent him away by sea to Athens.

5 Their state after his departure is closely allied with the enquiry as to the object of the Epistle. The Apostle appears to have felt much anxiety about them. and in consequence of his being unable to visit them in person, seems to have determined, during the hasty consultation previous to his departure from Berœa, to be left at Athens, which was the destination fixed for him by the brethren, alone, and to send Timotheus back to Thessalonica to ascertain the state of their faith[5].

Acts, is inferred by comparing Acts xvi. 3, xvii. 14, with 1 Thess. i. 1, 2 Thess. i. 1, 1 Thess iii. 1—6

[4] We are hardly justified in assuming, with Jowett, that it was only three weeks. For "three Sabbaths," even if they mark the whole stay, may designate four weeks and we are not compelled to infer that a Sabbath may not have passed at the beginning, or the end, or both, on which he did not preach in the synagogue. Indeed the latter hypothesis is very probable, if he was following the same course as afterwards at Corinth and Ephesus, and on the Jews proving rebellious and unbelieving, separated himself from them at which, or something approaching to it, the προσεκληρώθησαν τῷ Παύλῳ κ τῷ Σίλᾳ of Acts xvii. 4 may perhaps be taken as pointing.

[5] I cannot see how this interpretation of the difficulty as to the mission of Timotheus

6 The nature of the message brought to the Apostle at Corinth (Acts xviii 5) by Timotheus on his arrival there with Silas, must be inferred from what we find in the Epistle itself It was, in the main, favourable and consolatory (1 Thess. iii. 6—10) They were firm in faith and love, as indeed they were reputed to be by others who had brought to him news of them (i 7—10), full of affectionate remembrance of the Apostle, and longing to see him (iii 6). Still, however, he earnestly desired to come to them, not only from the yearnings of love, but because he wanted to fill up τὰ ὑστερήματα τῆς πίστεως αὐτῶν (iii. 10). Their attention had been so much drawn to one subject—his preaching had been so full of one great matter, and from the necessity of the case, so scanty on many others which he desired to lay forth to them, that he already feared lest their Christian faith should be a distorted and unhealthy faith. And in some measure, Timotheus had found it so They were beginning to be restless in expectation of the day of the Lord (iv 11 ff),—neglectful of that pure, and sober, and temperate walk, which is alone the fit preparation for that day (iv. 3 ff ; v. 1—9), —distressed about the state of the dead in Christ, who they supposed had lost the precious opportunity of standing before Him at His coming (iv 13 ff)

7. This being so, he writes to them to build up their faith and love, and to correct these defects and misapprehensions I reserve further consideration of the contents of the Epistle for § iv, 'On its matter and style.'

SECTION III

PLACE AND TIME OF WRITING.

1 From what has been said above respecting the state of the Thessalonian Church as the occasion for writing the Epistle, it may readily be inferred that no considerable time had elapsed since the intelligence of that state had reached the Apostle Silas and Timotheus were with him (i 1) : the latter had been the bearer of the tidings from Thessalonica

2 Now we know (Acts xviii 5) that they rejoined him at Corinth, apparently not long after his arrival there. That rejoining then forms

lies open to the charge of "diving beneath the surface to pick up what is really on the surface," and thus of "introducing into Scripture a hypercritical and unreal method of interpretation, which may be any where made the instrument of perverting the meaning of the text" (Jowett, i. p. 120) Supposing that at Berœa it was fixed that Timotheus should not accompany St Paul to Athens, but go to Thessalonica, and that the Apostle should be deposited at Athens and left there alone, the brethren returning, what words could have more naturally expressed this than διὸ μηκέτι στέγοντες εὐδοκήσαμεν καταλειφθῆναι ἐν Ἀθήναις μόνοι?

our *terminus a quo*. And it would be in the highest degree unnatural to suppose that the whole time of his stay at Corinth (a year and six months, Acts xviii 11) elapsed before he wrote the Epistle,—founded as it is on the intelligence which he had heard, and written with a view to meet present circumstances. CORINTH therefore may safely be assumed as the place of writing.

3. His stay at Corinth ended with his setting sail for the Pentecost at Jerusalem in the spring of 54 (see chron table in Prolegg to Acts, Vol. II.). It would begin then with the autumn of 52 And in the *winter of that year*, I should be disposed to place the writing of our Epistle.

4. It will be hardly necessary to remind the student, that this date places the Epistle *first*, in chronological order, *of all the writings of St. Paul* that remain to us.

SECTION IV.

MATTER AND STYLE

1. It will be interesting to observe, wherein the first-written Epistle of St Paul differs from his later writings. Some difference we should certainly expect to find, considering that we have to deal with a temperament so fervid, a spirit so rapidly catching the impress of circumstances, so penetrated by and resigned up to the promptings of that indwelling Spirit of God, who was ever more notably and thoroughly fitting His instrument for the expansion and advance of His work of leavening the world with the truth of Christ.

2 Nor will such observation and enquiry be spent in vain, especially if we couple it with corresponding observation of the sayings of our Lord, and the thoughts and words of his Apostles, on the various great departments of Christian belief and hope.

3 The faith, in all its main features, was delivered once for all The facts of Redemption,—the Incarnation, and the Atonement, and the glorification of Christ,—were patent and undeniable from the first. Our Lord's own words had asserted them. the earliest discourses of the Apostles after the day of Pentecost bore witness to them. It is true that, in God's Providence, the whole glorious system of salvation by grace was the gradual imparting of the Spirit to the Church by occasion here and there, various points of it were insisted on and made prominent. Even here, the freest and fullest statement did not come first "Repentance toward God, and faith toward our Lord Jesus Christ" was ever the order which the apostolic proclamation took The earliest of the Epistles are ever moral and practical, the advanced ones more

doctrinal and spiritual It was not till it appeared, in the unfolding of God's Providence, that the bulwark of salvation by grace must be strengthened, that the building on the one foundation must be raised thus impregnable to the righteousness of works and the law, that the Epistles to the Galatians and Romans were given through the great Apostle, reaching to the full breadth and height of the great argument Then followed the Epistles of the imprisonment, building up higher and higher the edifice thus consolidated and the Pastoral Epistles, suited to a more developed ecclesiastical condition, and aimed at the correction of abuses, which sprung up later, or were the ripened fruit of former doctrinal errors

4 In all these however, we trace the same great elementary truths of the faith Witness to them is never wanting nor can it be said that any change of ground respecting them ever took place The work of the Spirit as regarded them, was one of expanding and deepening, of freeing from narrow views, and setting in clearer and fuller light of ranging and grouping collateral and local circumstances, so that the great doctrines of grace became ever more and more prominent and paramount.

5 But while this was so with these 'first principles,' the very view which we have taken will shew, that as regarded other things which lay at a greater distance from central truths, it was otherwise In such matters, the Apostle was taught by experience, Christ's work brought its lessons with it · and it would be not only unnatural, but would remove from his writings the living freshness of personal reality, if we found him the same in all points of this kind, at the beginning, and at the end of his epistolary labours if there were no characteristic differences of mode of thought and expression in 1 Thessalonians and in 2 Timotheus if advance of years had brought with it no corresponding advance of standing-point, change of circumstances no change of counsel, trial of God's ways no further insight into God's designs

6 Nor are we left to conjecture as to those subjects on which especially such change, and ripening of view and conviction, might be expected to take place There was one most important point on which our Lord Himself spoke with marked and solemn uncertainty The TIME OF HIS OWN COMING was hidden from all created beings,—nay, in the mystery of his mediatorial office, from the Son Himself (Mark xiii 32). Even after his Resurrection, when questioned by the Apostles as to the time of his restoring the Kingdom to Israel, his reply is still, that "it is not for them to know the times and the seasons, which the Father hath put in his own power" (Acts i 7)

7 Here then is a plain indication, which has not, I think, been sufficiently made use of in judging of the Epistles The Spirit was to *testify of Christ* · to take of the things of Christ, and shew them unto them So that however much that Spirit, in His infinite wisdom, might be

pleased to impart to them of the details and accompanying circumstances of the Lord's appearing, we may be sure, that the truth spoken by our Lord, "Of that day and hour knoweth no man," would hold good with regard to them, and be traced in their writings If they were true men, and their words and Epistles the genuine production of inspiration of them by that Spirit of Truth, we may expect to find in such speeches and writings tokens of this appointed uncertainty of the day and hour: expectations, true in expression and fully justified by appearances, yet corrected, as God's purposes were manifested, by advancing experience, and larger effusions of the Spirit of prophecy.

8. If then I find in the course of St Paul's Epistles, that expressions which occur in the earlier ones, and seem to indicate expectation of His almost immediate coming, are gradually modified,—disappear altogether from the Epistles of the imprisonment,—and instead of them are found others speaking in a very different strain, of dissolving, and being with Christ, and passing through death and the resurrection, in the latest Epistles,—I regard it, not as a strange thing, not as a circumstance which I must explain away for fear of weakening the authority of his Epistles, but as exactly that which I should expect to find; as the very strongest testimony that these Epistles were written by one who was left in this uncertainty,—not by one who wished to make it appear that Inspiration had rendered him omniscient.

9 And in this, the earliest of those Epistles, I do find exactly that which I might expect on this head While every word and every detail respecting the Lord's coming is a perpetual inheritance for the Church, —while we continue to comfort one another with the glorious and heart-stirring sentences which he utters to us in the word of the Lord, —no candid eye can help seeing in the Epistle, how the uncertainty of "the day and hour" has tinged all these passages with a hue of near anticipation. how natural it was, that the Thessalonians receiving this Epistle, should have allowed that anticipation to be brought even yet closer, and have imagined the day to be actually already present

10. It will be seen by the above remarks, how very far I am from conceding their point to those who hold that the belief, of which this Epistle is the strongest expression, was an idle fancy, or does not befit the present age as well as it did that one It is God's purpose respecting us, that we should ever be left in this uncertainty, looking for and hasting unto the day of the Lord, which may be upon us at any time before we are aware of it. Every expression of the ages before us, betokening close anticipation, coupled with the fact that the day has not yet arrived, teaches us much, but unteaches us nothing does not deprive that glorious hope of its applicability to our times, nor the

Christian of his power of living as in the light of his Lord's approach and the daily realization of the day of Christ[6].

11. In style, this Epistle is thoroughly Pauline,—abounding with phrases, and lines of thought, which may be parallelled with similar ones in his other Epistles[7]: not wanting also in insulated words and sentiments, such as we find in all the writings of one who was so fresh in thought and full in feeling, such also as are in no way inconsistent with St. Paul's known character, but in every case finding analogical justification in Epistles of which no one has ever thought of disputing the genuineness

12. As compared with other Epistles, this is written in a quiet and unimpassioned style, not being occasioned by any grievous errors of doctrine or defects in practice, but written to encourage and gently to admonish those who were, on the whole, proceeding favourably in the Christian life. To this may be attributed also the fact, that it does not deal expressly with any of the great verities of the faith, rather taking them for granted, and building on them the fabric of a holy and pure life. That this should have been done until they were disputed, was but natural and in consequence not with these Epistles, but with that to the Galatians, among whom the whole Christian life was imperilled by Judaistic teaching, begins that great series of unfoldings of the mystery of salvation by grace, of which St. Paul was so eminently the minister.

[6] It is strange that such words as the following could be written by Mr. Jowett, without bringing, as he wrote them, the condemnation of his theory and its expression home to his mind: "*In the words which are attributed in the Epistle of St. Peter to the unbelievers of that day* (? surely it is to the unbelievers of *days to come*,—a fact which the writer, by altering the reference of the words, seems to be endeavouring to dissimulate), *we might truly say that, since the fathers fell asleep, all things remain the same from the beginning Not only do 'all things remain the same,' but the very belief itself (in the sense in which it was held by the first Christians) has been ready to vanish away.*" Vol i p. 97.

[7] Baur has most perversely adduced *both these* as evidences of spuriousness among the former he cites ch i 5, as compared with 1 Cor ii 4 i 6, with 1 Cor. xi. 1 . i. 8, with Rom. i 8: ii 4—10, with 1 Cor ii 4, iv. 3, 4, ix 15, 2 Cor ii 17, v 11, xi 9 for his discussion of the latter, see his "Paulus Apostel, u s.w ," pp 489, 490

CHAPTER VI.

THE SECOND EPISTLE TO THE THESSALONIANS.

SECTION I.

ITS AUTHORSHIP.

1 The recognition of this Epistle has been as general,—and the exceptions to it for the most part the same,—as in the case of the last.

2 The principal testimonies of early Christian writers are the following.

(α) Irenæus, adv Hær iii 7 2, p. 182

"Quoniam autem hyperbatis frequenter utitur Apostolus (Paulus, from what precedes) propter velocitatem sermonum suorum, et propter impetum qui in ipso est Spiritus, ex multis quidem aliis est invenire . Et iterum in secunda ad Thessalonicenses de Antichristo dicens, ait: Et tunc revelabitur," &c. ch. ii. 8, 9

(β) Clement of Alexandria, Strom. v. 3 [17], p. 655 P.:

οὐκ ἐν πᾶσι, φησὶν ὁ ἀπόστολος, ἡ γνῶσις, προσεύχεσθε δὲ ἵνα ῥυσθῶμεν ἀπὸ τῶν ἀτόπων καὶ πονηρῶν ἀνθρώπων οὐ γὰρ πάντων ἡ πίστις (2 Thess iii 1, 2)

(γ) Tertullian, de resurr carnis c 24, vol ii p 828 following on the citation from the first Epistle given above, ch v. § i 3, . . "et in secunda, pleniore sollicitudine ad eosdem: obsecro autem vos, fratres, per adventum Domini nostri Jesu Christi," &c (ch ii 1, 2)

3 The objections brought by Schmidt (Einl ii p 256 ff.), Kern (Tubing Zeitschrift für 1839, 2 heft.), and Baur (Paulus u.s w. p 488 ff) against the genuineness of the Epistle, in as far as they rest on the old story of similarities and differences as compared with St Paul's acknowledged Epistles, have been already more than once dealt with. I shall now only notice those which regard points peculiar to our Epistle itself

4 It is said that this second Epistle is not consistent with the first that directed their attention to the Lord's coming as almost immediate· *this* interposes delay,—the apostasy,—the man of sin, &c. It really seems as if no propriety nor exact fitting of circumstances would ever satisfy such critics It might be imagined that this very discrepancy, even if allowed, would tell most strongly in favour of the genuineness.

5 It is alleged by Kern, that the whole prophetic passage, ch. ii 1 ff,

does not correspond with the date claimed for the Epistle It is assumed, that the man of sin is Nero, who was again to return, Rev. xvii 10,—ὁ κατέχων, Vespasian.—the ἀποστασία, the falling away of Jews and Christians alike This view, it is urged, fits a writer in A D 68—70, between Nero's death and the destruction of Jerusalem But than this nothing can be more inconclusive Why have we not as good a right to say, that *this interpretation* is wrong, because it *does not correspond to the received date* of the Epistle, as vice versâ? To us (see below, § v) the interpretation is full of absurdity, and therefore the argument carries no conviction.

6 It is maintained again, that ch. iii. 17 is strongly against the genuineness of our Epistle· for that there was no reason for guarding against forgeries, and as for πάσῃ ἐπιστολῇ, the Apostle had written but one. For an answer to this, see note in loc., where both the reason for inserting this is adduced, and it is shewn, that almost all of his Epistles either are expressly, or may be understood as having been, thus authenticated

7 See the objections of Schmidt, Schrader, Kern, and Baur, treated at length in Lunemann's Einleitung to his Commentary, pp 161—167 and in Davidson, Introd vol ii. pp. 484, end.

SECTION II.

FOR WHAT READERS, AND WITH WHAT OBJECT IT WAS WRITTEN

1 The former particular has been already sufficiently explained in the corresponding section of the Prolegomena to the first Epistle But inasmuch as the condition of the Thessalonian Church in the mean time bears closely upon the object of the Epistle, I resume here the consideration of their circumstances and state of mind

2 We have seen that there were those among them, who were too ready to take up and exaggerate the prevalence of the subject of Christ's coming among the topics of the Apostle's teaching. These persons, whether encouraged by the tone of the first Epistle or not, we cannot tell (for we cannot see any reference to the first Epistle in ch. ii. 2, see note there), were evidently teaching, as an expansion of St Paul's doctrine, or as under his authority, or even as enjoined in a letter from him (ib note), the actual presence of the day of the Lord In consequence of this, their minds had become unsettled. they wanted directing into the love of God and the imitation of Christ's patience (ch iii 5). Some appear to have left off their daily employments, and to have been taking advantage of the supposed reign of Christ to be walking disorderly.

3 It was this state of things, which furnished the occasion for our Epistle being written. Its object is to make it clear to them that the day of Christ, though a legitimate matter of expectation for every Christian, and a constant stimulus for watchfulness, was not yet come that a course and development of events must first happen, which he lays forth to them in the spirit of prophecy: shewing them that this development has already begun, and that not until it has ripened will the coming of the Lord take place

4 This being the occasion of writing the Epistle, there are grouped round the central subject two other general topics of solace and confirmation. comfort under their present troubles (ch i.) exhortation to honesty and diligence, and avoidance of the idle and disorderly (ch. iii).

SECTION III

PLACE AND TIME OF WRITING

1 In the address of the Epistle, we find the same three, Paul, Silvanus, and Timotheus, associated together, as in the first Epistle This circumstance would at once direct us to Corinth, where Silas and Timotheus rejoined St Paul (Acts xviii 5), and whence we do not read that they accompanied him on his departure for Asia (ib xviii 18) And as we believe the first Epistle to have been written from that city, it will be most natural. considering the close sequence of this upon that first, to place the writing of it at Corinth, somewhat later in this same visit of a year and a half (Acts xviii 11).

2 *How long* after the writing of the first Epistle in the winter of A D 52 (see above, ch v § iii. 3) we are to fix the date of our present one, must be settled merely by calculations of probability, and by the indications furnished in the Epistle itself

3 The former of these do not afford us much help For we can hardly assume with safety that the Apostle had received intelligence of the effects of his first Epistle, seeing that we have found cause to interpret ch ii 2 not of that Epistle, but of false ones, circulated under the Apostle's name. All that we can assume is, that more intelligence had arrived from Thessalonica: how soon after his writing to them, we cannot say. Their present state, as we have seen above, was but a carrying forward and exaggerating of that already begun when the former letter was sent. so that a very short time would suffice to have advanced them from the one grade of undue excitement to the other.

4 Nor do any hints furnished by our Epistle give us much more assistance. They are principally these. (a) In ch i 4, the Apostle speaks of his ἐγκαυχᾶσθαι ἐν ταῖς ἐκκλησίαις τοῦ θεοῦ concerning the en-

durance and faith of the Thessalonians under persecutions It would seem from this, that the Achæan Churches (see 1 Cor i 2; 2 Cor. i 1; Rom. xvi. 1) had by this time acquired number and consistence This however would furnish but a vague indication it might point to any date after the first six months of his stay at Corinth (b) In ch iii 2, he desires their prayers *ἵνα ῥυσθῶμεν ἀπὸ τῶν ἀτόπων καὶ πονηρῶν ἀνθρώπων* It has been inferred from this, that the tumult which occasioned his departure from Corinth was not far off that the designs of the unbelieving Jews were drawing to a head. and that consequently our date must be fixed just before his departure But this inference is not a safe one for we find that his open breach with the Jews took place close upon the arrival of Silas and Timotheus (Acts xviii 5—7), and that his situation immediately after this was one of peril for in the vision which he had, the Lord said to him, *οὐδεὶς ἐπιθήσεταί σοι τοῦ κακῶσαί σε*

5 So that we really have very little help in determining our date, from either of these sources All we can say is, that it must be fixed, in all likelihood, between the winter of 52 and the spring of 54 and taking the medium, we may venture to place it somewhere about the middle of the year 53

SECTION IV

STYLE

1. The style of our Epistle, like that of the first, is eminently Pauline Certain dissimilarities have been pointed out by Baur, &c (see above, § i 3) · but they are no more than might be found in any one undoubted writing of our Apostle In a fresh and vigorous style, there will ever be, so to speak, librations over any rigid limits of habitude which can be assigned: and such are to be judged of, not by their mere occurrence and number, but by their subjective character being or not being in accordance with the writer's well-known characteristics Professor Jowett has treated one by one the supposed inconsistencies with Pauline usage (vol i p 139 f), and shewn that there is no real difficulty in supposing any of the expressions to have been used by St Paul. He has also collected a very much larger number of resemblances in manner and phraseology to the Apostle's other writings The student who makes use of the references in this edition will be able to mark out these for himself, and to convince himself that the style of our Epistle is so closely related to that of the rest, as to shew that the same mind was employed in the choice of the words and the construction of the sentences

2. One portion of this Epistle, viz. the prophetic section, ch. ii. 1—12,

as it is distinguished from the rest in subject, so differs in style, being, as is usual with the more solemn and declaratory paragraphs of St. Paul, loftier in diction and more abrupt and elliptical in construction The passage in question will be found on comparison to bear, in style and flow of sentences, a close resemblance to the denunciatory and prophetic portions of the other Epistles: compare for instance ver 3 with Col. ii. 8, 16; vv 8, 9 with 1 Cor. xv. 24—28, ver. 10 with Rom i. 18, 1 Cor. i 18, 2 Cor ii 15, ver 11 with Rom i 24, 26, ver 12 with Rom. ii 5, 9, and Rom. i. 32.

SECTION V.

ON THE PROPHETIC IMPORT OF CH. II 1—12.

1. It may be well, before entering on this, to give the passage, as it stands in our rendering in the notes[1]

"(1) But we entreat you, brethren, in regard of the coming of our Lord Jesus Christ, and our gathering together to Him,—(2) in order that ye should not be lightly shaken from your mind nor troubled, neither by spirit, nor by word, nor by epistle as from us, to the effect that the day of the Lord is present (3) Let no man deceive you in any manner for [that day shall not come] unless there have come the apostasy first, and there have been revealed the man of sin, the son of perdition, (4) he that withstands and exalts himself above every one that is called God or an object of adoration, so that he sits in the temple of God, shewing himself that he is God (5) . . (6) And now ye know that which hinders, in order that he may be revealed in his own time. (7) For the MYSTERY ALREADY is working of lawlessness, only until he that now hinders be removed: (8) and then shall be REVEALED the LAWLESS ONE, whom the Lord Jesus will destroy by the breath of His mouth, and annihilate by the appearance of His coming (9) whose coming is according to the working of Satan in all power and signs and wonders of falsehood, (10) and in all deceit of unrighteousness for those who are perishing, because they did not receive the love of the truth in order to their being saved (11) And on this account God is sending to them the working of error, in order that they should believe the falsehood, (12) that all might be judged who did not believe the truth, but found pleasure in iniquity."

[1] I must caution the reader, that the rendering given in my notes is not in any case intended for a polished and elaborated version, nor is it my object to put the meaning into the best idiomatic English: but I wish to represent, as nearly as possible, the construction and intent of the original The difference between a literal rendering, and a version for vernacular use, is very considerable, and has not been enough borne in mind in judging of our authorized English version

2 It will be my object to give a brief résumé of the history of the interpretation of this passage, and afterwards to state what I conceive to have been its meaning as addressed to the Thessalonians, and what as belonging to subsequent ages of the Church of Christ The history of its interpretation I have drawn from several sources principally from Lünemann's Schlussbemerkungen to chap ii of his Commentary, pp. 204—217

3 The first particulars in the history must be gleaned from the early Fathers. And their interpretation is for the most part well marked and consistent They all regard it as a prophecy of the future, as yet unfulfilled when they wrote They all regard the *παρουσία* as the personal return of our Lord to judgment and to bring in His Kingdom They all regard the adversary here described as an individual person, the incarnation and concentration of sin [2].

[2] The following citations will bear out the assertion in the text

IRENÆUS, adv hær. v 25 1, p 322 "Ille enim (Antichristus) omnem suscipiens diaboli virtutem, veniet non quasi rex justus nec quasi in subjectione Dei legitimus· sed impius et injustus et sine lege, quasi apostata, et iniquus et homicida, quasi latro, diabolicam apostasiam in se recapitulans. et idola quidem seponens, ad suadendum quod ipse sit Deus. se autem extollens unum idolum, habens in semetipso reliquorum idolorum varium errorem. ut hi qui per multas abominationes adorant diabolum, hi per hoc unum idolum serviant ipsi, de quo apostolus in Epistola quæ est ad Thessalonicenses secunda, sic ait" (vv 3, 4).

Again, ib 3, p 323 "'Usque ad tempus temporum et dimidium temporis' (Dan. vii 25), hoc est, per triennium et sex menses, in quibus veniens regnabit super terram. De quo iterum et apostolus Paulus in secunda ad Thess, simul et causam adventus ejus annuntians, sic ait" (vv 8 ff).

Again, ib. 30 4, p 330 "Cum autem devastaverit Antichristus hic omnia in hoc mundo, regnabit annis tribus et mensibus sex, et sedebit in templo Hierosolymis: tum veniet Dominus de cœlis in nubibus, in gloria Patris, illum quidem et obedientes ei in stagnum ignis mittens adducens autem justis regni tempora, hoc est requietionem, septimam diem sanctificatam, et restituens Abrahæ promissionem hæreditatis: in quo regno ait Dominus, multos ab Oriente et Occidente venientes, recumbere cum Abraham, Isaac et Jacob"

TERTULLIAN, de Resurr. c 24, vol ii. p 829, quoting the passage, inserts after *ὁ κατέχων*, "quis, nisi Romanus status? cujus abscessio in decem reges dispersa Antichristum superducet, et tum revelabitur iniquus." See also his Apol. c. 32, vol. i p 447.

JUSTIN MARTYR, dial. cum Tryph. c. 110, p 203 *δύο παρουσίαι αὐτοῦ κατηγγελμέναι εἰσί, μία μὲν ἐν ᾗ παθητὸς καὶ ἄδοξος καὶ ἄτιμος καὶ σταυρούμενος κεκήρυκται, ἡ δὲ δευτέρα ἐν ᾗ μετὰ δόξης ἀπὸ τῶν οὐρανῶν πάρεσται, ὅταν καὶ ὁ τῆς ἀποστασίας ἄνθρωπος, ὁ καὶ εἰς τὸν ὕψιστον ἔξαλλα λαλῶν, ἐπὶ τῆς γῆς ἄνομα τολμήσῃ εἰς ἡμᾶς τοὺς Χριστιανούς*

ORIGEN, contra Cels vi 45 f. vol i. p. 667 f: *ἔχρην δὲ τὸν μὲν ἕτερον τῶν ἄκρων, καὶ βέλτιστον, υἱὸν ἀναγορεύεσθαι τοῦ θεοῦ, διὰ τὴν ὑπεροχήν τὸν δὲ τούτῳ κατὰ διάμετρον ἐναντίον, υἱὸν τοῦ πονηροῦ δαίμονος, καὶ Σατανᾶ, καὶ διαβόλου . . λέγει δὲ ὁ Παῦλος, περὶ τούτου τοῦ καλουμένου ἀντιχρίστου διδάσκων, καὶ παριστὰς μετά τινος ἐπικρύψεως τίνα τρόπον ἐπιδημήσει, καὶ πότε τῷ γένει τῶν ἀνθρώπων, καὶ διὰ τί* He then quotes this whole passage.

4 Respecting, however, the minor particulars of the prophecy, they are not so entirely at agreement Augustine says (de civ. Dei, xx 19. 2, p 685 cf also Jerome in the note),—' in *quo templo* Dei sit sessurus, incertum est utrum in illa ruina templi quod a Salomone rege constructum est, an vero in Ecclesia. Non enim templum alicujus idoli aut dæmonis templum Dei Apostolus diceret [3].' And from this doubt about his 'session,' a doubt about his person also had begun to spring up, for he continues, ' unde nonnulli non ipsum principem sed universum quodammodo corpus ejus, id est, ad eum pertinentem hominum multitudinem simul cum ipso suo principe hoc loco intelligi Antichristum volunt '

5 The meaning of *τὸ κατέχον*, though, as will be seen from the note, generally agreed to be the Roman empire, was not by any means universally acquiesced in Theodoret says, *τινὲς τὸ κατέχον τὴν Ῥωμαικὴν ἐνόησαν βασιλείαν, τινὲς δὲ τὴν χάριν τοῦ πνεύματος. κατεχούσης γάρ, φησί, τῆς τοῦ πνεύματος χάριτος ἐκεῖνος οὐ παραγίνεται, ἀλλ' οὐχ οἷόν τε παύσασθαι παντελῶς τὴν χάριν τοῦ πνεύματος . . ἀλλ' οὐδὲ τὴν Ῥωμαικὴν βασιλείαν ἑτέρα διαδέξεται βασιλεία· διὰ γὰρ τοῦ τετάρτου θηρίου καὶ ὁ θειότατος Δανιὴλ*

CHRYSOSTOM in loc *τίς δὲ οὗτός ἐστιν, ἆρα ὁ Σατανᾶς, οὐδαμῶς ἀλλ' ἄνθρωπός τις πᾶσαν αὐτοῦ δεχόμενος τὴν ἐνέργειαν. καὶ ἀποκαλυφθῇ ὁ ἄνθρωπός, φησιν, ὁ ὑπεραιρόμενος ἐπὶ πάντα λεγόμενον θεὸν ἢ σέβασμα οὐ γὰρ εἰδωλολατρείαν ἄξει ἐκεῖνος, ἀλλ' ἀντίθεός τις ἔσται, καὶ πάντας καταλύσει τοὺς θεούς, καὶ κελεύσει προσκυνεῖν αὐτὸν ἀντὶ τοῦ θεοῦ, καὶ καθεσθήσεται εἰς τὸν ναὸν τοῦ θεοῦ, οὐ τὸν ἐν Ἱεροσολύμοις μόνον, ἀλλὰ καὶ εἰς τὰς πανταχοῦ ἐκκλησίας.*

And below . *καὶ τί μετὰ ταῦτα; ἐγγὺς ἡ παραμυθία. ἐπάγει γάρ· ὃν ὁ κύριος Ἰησοῦς κ τ λ. καθάπερ γὰρ κ τ λ* See the rest cited in the note on ver 8

CYRIL OF JERUS, Catech xv. 12, p 229. *ἔρχεται δὲ ὁ προειρημένος ἀντίχριστος οὗτος, ὅταν πληρωθῶσιν οἱ καιροὶ τῆς Ῥωμαίων βασιλείας, καὶ πλησιάζει λοιπὸν τὰ τῆς τοῦ κόσμου συντελείας. δέκα μὲν ὁμοῦ Ῥωμαίων ἐγείρονται βασιλεῖς, ἐν διαφόροις μὲν ἴσως τόποις, κατὰ δὲ τὸν αὐτὸν βασιλεύοντες καιρόν. μετὰ δὲ τούτους ἑνδέκατος ὁ Ἀντίχριστος ἐκ τῆς μαγικῆς κακοτεχνίας τὴν Ῥωμαικὴν ἐξουσίαν ἁρπάσας*

Theodoret's interpretation agrees with the above as to the personality of Antichrist and as to our Lord's coming. I shall quote some portion of it below, on *ὁ κατέχων*, and *τὸ μυστήριον*.

AUGUSTINE, de civ Dei, xx. 19. 4, vol. vii. p. 687. "Non veniet ad vivos et mortuos judicandos Christus, nisi prius venerit ad seducendos in anima mortuos adversarius ejus Antichristus."

JEROME, Epist cxxi, ad Algasiam, qu 11, vol i p. 887 f. "Nisi, inquit, venerit discessio primum . . . ut omnes gentes quæ Romano imperio subjacent, recedant ab his, et revelatus fuerit, id est, ostensus, quem omnia prophetarum verba prænunciant, homo peccati, in quo fons omnium peccatorum est, et filius perditionis, id est diaboli ipse est enim universorum perditio, qui adversatur Christo, et ideo vocatur Antichristus, et extollitur supra omne quod dicitur Deus, ut cunctarum gentium deos, sive probatam omnem et veram religionem suo calcet pede. et in templo Dei, vel Hierosolymis (ut quidam putant), vel in ecclesia, ut verius arbitramur, sederit, ostendens se, tanquam ipse sit Christus et filius Dei nisi, inquit, fuerit Romanum imperium ante desolatum, et Antichristus præcesserit, Christus non veniet · qui ideo ita venturus est, ut Antichristum destruat."

[3] Theodoret also · *ναὸν δὲ θεοῦ τὰς ἐκκλησίας ἐκάλεσεν, ἐν αἷς ἁρπάσει τὴν προεδρείαν, θεὸν ἑαυτὸν ἀποδεικνῦναι πειρώμενος*

τὴν Ῥωμαικὴν ᾐνίξατο βασιλείαν. ἐν δὲ τούτῳ τὸ μικρὸν κέρας ἐβλάστησε τὸ ποιοῦν πόλεμον μετὰ τῶν ἁγίων. αὐτὸς δὲ οὗτός ἐστι περὶ οὗ τὰ προῤῥηθέντα εἶπεν ὁ θεῖος ἀπόστολος οὐδέτερον τούτων οἶμαι φάναι τὸν θεῖον ἀπόστολον, ἀλλὰ τὸ παρ' ἑτέρων εἰρημένον εἶναι ἀληθὲς ὑπολαμβάνω ἐδοκίμασε γὰρ ὁ τῶν ὅλων θεὸς παρὰ τὸν τῆς συντελείας αὐτὸν ὀφθῆναι καιρόν. ὁ τοῦ θεοῦ τοίνυν ὅρος νῦν ἐπέχει φανῆναι. And so also Theodor-Mops[4] Another meaning yet is mentioned by Chrysostom, or rather another form of that repudiated above by Theodoret, viz, that the continuance of ἡ τοῦ πνεύματος χάρις, τουτέστι χαρίσματα, hindered his appearing And remarkably enough, he rejects this from a reason the very opposite of that which weighed with Theodoret,—viz, from the fact that spiritual gifts had ceased ἄλλως δὲ ἔδει ἤδη παραγίνεσθαι, εἴ γε ἔμελλε τῶν χαρισμάτων ἐκλειπόντων παραγίνεσθαι καὶ γὰρ πάλαι ἐκλέλοιπεν[5] Augustine's remarks (ubi supra) are curious: "Quod autem ait, et nunc quid detineat scitis, . quoniam scire illos dixit, aperte hoc dicere noluit. Et ideo nos, qui nescimus quod illi sciebant, pervenire cum labore ad id quod sensit Apostolus, cupimus, nec valemus præsertim quia et illa quæ addidit, hunc sensum faciunt obscuriorem Nam quid est, 'Jam enim,' &c. (ver 7)? Ego prorsus quid dixerit, fateor me ignorare" Then he mentions the various opinions on τὸ κατέχον, giving this as the view of some, that it was said "de malis et fictis qui sunt in ecclesia, donec perveniant ad tantum numerum qui Antichristo magnum populum faciat et hoc esse mysterium iniquitatis quia videtur occultum " then again quoting ver 7, adds, "hoc est, donec exeat de medio ecclesiæ mysterium iniquitatis, quod nunc occultum est"

6 This μυστήριον τῆς ἀνομίας was also variously understood Chrysostom says, Νέρωνα ἐνταῦθα φησίν, ὡσανεὶ τύπον ὄντα τοῦ Ἀντιχρίστου καὶ γὰρ οὗτος ἐβούλετο νομίζεσθαι θεός. καὶ καλῶς εἶπε τὸ μυστήριον οὐ γὰρ φανερῶς ὡς ἐκεῖνος, οὐδ' ἀπηρυθριασμένως εἰ γὰρ πρὸ χρόνου ἐκείνου ἀνειρέθη, φησίν, ὃς οὐ πολὺ τοῦ Ἀντιχρίστου ἐλείπετο κατὰ τὴν κακίαν, τί θαυμαστὸν εἰ ἤδη ἔσται; οὕτω δὴ συνεσκιασμένως εἶπε, καὶ φανερὸν αὐτὸν οὐκ ἠθέλησε ποιῆσαι, οὐ διὰ δειλίαν, ἀλλὰ παιδεύων ἡμᾶς μὴ περιττὰς ἔχθρας ἀναδέχεσθαι ὅταν μηδὲν ᾖ τὸ κατεπεῖγον. This opinion is also mentioned by Augustine, al, but involves of course an anachronism Theodoret, also mentioning it, adds: ἐγὼ δὲ οἶμαι τὰς ἀναφυείσας αἱρέσεις δηλοῦν τὸν ἀπόστολον δι' ἐκείνων γὰρ ὁ διάβολος πολλοὺς ἀποστήσας τῆς ἀληθείας, προκατασκευάζει τῆς ἀπάτης τὸν ὄλεθρον μυστήριον δὲ αὐτοὺς ἀνομίας ἐκάλεσεν, ὡς κεκρυμμένην ἔχοντας τῆς ἀνομίας τὴν πάγην . . . . ὃ κρύβδην ἀεὶ κατεσκεύαζε, τότε προφανῶς καὶ διαῤῥήδην κηρύξει

[4] It is decisive against this latter view, as Lunemann has observed, that if τὸ κατέχον be God's decree, ὁ κατέχων must be *God Himself*, and then the ἕως ἐκ μέσου γένηται could not be said

[5] An ingenuous and instructive confession, at the end of the fourth century, from one of the most illustrious of the fathers.

7[6] The view of the fathers remained for ages the prevalent one in the Church. Modifications were introduced into it, as her relation to the state gradually altered, and the Church at last, instead of being exposed to further hostilities from the secular power, rose to the head of that power, and, penetrating larger and larger portions of the world, became a representation of the kingdom of God on earth, with an imposing hierarchy at her head. Then followed, in the Church in general, and among the hierarchy in particular, a neglect of the subject of Christ's coming. But meanwhile, those who from time to time stood in opposition to the hierarchy, understood the Apostle's description here, as they did also the figures in the Apocalypse, of that hierarchy itself. And thus arose,—the παρουσία being regarded much as before, only as an event far off instead of near,—first in the eleventh century the idea, that the Antichrist foretold by St Paul is the *establishment and growing power of the Popedom.*

8 This view first appears in the conflict between the Emperors and the Popes, as held by the partisans of the imperial power but soon becomes that of all those who were opponents of the hierarchy, as wishing for a freer spirit in Christendom than the ecclesiastical power allowed. It was held by the Waldenses, the Albigenses, the followers of Wickliffe and Huss. The κατέχον, which retarded the destruction of the papacy, was held by them to be the *Imperial power*, which they regarded as simply a revival of the old Roman Empire.

9. Thus towards the time of the Reformation, this reference of Antichrist to the papal hierarchy became very prevalent: and after that event it assumed almost the position of a dogma in the Protestant Churches. It is found in Bugenhagen, Zwingle, Calvin, &c., Osiander, Baldwin, Aretius, Erasm.-Schmid, Beza, Calixtus, Calovius, Newton, Wolf, Joachim-Lange, Turretin, Benson, Bengel, Macknight, Zachariæ, Michaelis, &c.: in the symbolical books of the Lutheran Church, and in Luther's own writings and runs through the works of our English Reformers[7].

10 The upholders of this view generally conceive that the Papacy will go on bringing out more and more its antichristian character, till at last the παρουσία will overtake and destroy it. The ἀποστασία is the *fall from pure evangelical doctrine* to the traditions of men. The singular, ὁ ἄνθρωπος τῆς ἁμαρτίας, is taken collectively, to signify a '*series et successio hominum*,' inasmuch as it is a monarchical empire which is in question, which remains one and the same, though its individual

[6] What follows, as far as paragraph 24, is taken principally from Lunemann's Schlussbemerkungen, as above, with the exception of the citations made in full, and personal opinions expressed.

[7] See a very complete résumé of the passages on Antichrist in the Reformers, under the word, in the excellent Index to the publications of the Parker Society.

head may change. The godlessness of Antichrist, described in ver. 4, is justified historically by the Pope setting himself above all authority divine and human, the words πάντα λεγόμενον θεόν, &c. being, in accordance with Scriptural usage, taken to mean the princes and governments of the world, and an allusion being found in σέβασμα to σεβαστός, the title of the Roman Emperors The ναὸς τοῦ θεοῦ is held to be the *Christian Church*, and the καθίσαι to point to the tyrannical power which the Pope usurps over it By τὸ κατέχον is understood the *Roman Empire*, and by ὁ κατέχων the *Roman Emperor*,—and history is appealed to, to shew that out of the ruins of that empire the papacy has grown up. The declaration, τὸ μυστήριον ἤδη ἐνεργεῖται τῆς ἀνομίας, is justified by the fact, that the "semina erroris et ambitionis," which prepared the way for the papacy, were already present in the Apostle's time For a catalogue of the τέρατα ψεύδους, ver 9, rich material was found in relics, transubstantiation, purgatory, &c. The annihilation of Antichrist by the πνεῦμα τοῦ στόματος of the Lord, has been understood of the breaking down of his power in the spirits of men by the opening and dispersion of the word of God in its purity by means of the Reformation, and the καταργήσει τῇ ἐπιφανείᾳ τῆς παρουσίας αὐτοῦ, of the final and material annihilation of Antichrist by the coming of the Lord Himself

11. In the presence of such a polemical interpretation directed against them, it could hardly be expected that the Roman Catholics on their side would abstain from retaliation on their opponents. Accordingly we find that such writers as Estius, al., interpret the ἀποστασία of *the defection from the Romish Church and the Pope*, and understand by Antichrist the *heretics*, especially *Luther and the Protestant Church.*

12 Even before the reference to the papacy, the interpreters of the Greek Church took *Mohammed* to be the Antichrist intended by St. Paul, and the ἀποστασία to represent the *falling off* of many Oriental and Greek Churches *to Islamism* And this view so far influenced the Protestant Church, that some of its writers have held a double Antichrist,—an Eastern one, viz Mohammed and the Turkish power,—and a Western, viz the Pope and his power. So Melancthon, Bucer, Bullinger, Piscator, &c

13 Akin to this method of interpretation is that which in our own century has found the apostasy in the enormities of the French Revolution, Antichrist in *Napoleon*, and τὸ κατέχον in the *continuance of the German Empire:* an idea, remarks Lunemann, convicted of error by the termination of that empire in 1806.

14 One opinion of modern days has been, that it is objectionable to endeavour to assign closely a meaning to the single details of the imagery used by St Paul This has led to giving the whole description a general, ideal, or symbolic sense. So *Koppe*, who thinks that the Apostle

is only following the general import of the Jewish expectations, resting on the prophecy of Daniel, that there should be a season of godlessness before the time of the end, the full eruption of which he expects after his own death: he himself being ὁ κατέχων. Similarly *Storr*,—who sees in ἄνθρωπος τῆς ἁμαρτίας 'potestas aliqua, Deo omnique religioni adversaria, quæ penitus incognita et futuro demum tempore se proditura sit,' and in τὸ κατέχον, the 'copia hominum, verissimo amore inflammatorum in Christianam religionem.' *Nitzsch* again believes the 'man of sin to be the power of godlessness' come to have open authority, or the general contempt of all religion. *Pelt*, comm. in Thess. p. 204, sums up his view thus: "Mihi igitur cum Koppio adversarius ille *principium* esse videtur, sive vis spiritualis evangelio contraria, quæ huc usque tamen in Pontificiorum Romanorum operibus ac serie luculentissime sese prodiit, ita tamen, ut omnia etiam mala, quæ in ecclesiam compareant, ad eandem Antichristi ἐνέργειαν sint referenda. Ejus vero παρουσία, i. e. summum fastigium, quod Christi reditum, qui nihil aliud est nisi regni divini victoria[8], antecedet, futurum adhuc esse videtur, quum illud tempus procul etiam nunc abesse putemus, ubi omnes terræ incolæ in eo erunt ut ad Christi sacra transeant. κατέχον vero cum Theodoreto putarim esse Dei voluntatem illud Satanæ regnum cohibentem, ne erumpat, et si mediæ spectantur causæ, apostolorum tempore maxime imperii Romani vis, et quovis ævo illa resistentia, quam malis artibus, quæ religionem subvertere student, privati commodi et honoris augendorum cupiditas opponere solet." And Pelt thinks that the symptoms of the future corruption of the Christian Church were already discernible in the apostolic times, in the danger of falling back from Christian freedom into Jewish legality, in the mingling of heathenism with Christianity, in false γνῶσις and ἄσκησις, in angelolatry, in the "fastus a religione Christiana omnino alienus."

15. *Olshausen's* view is, that inasmuch as the personal coming of Christ is immediately to follow this revelation of Antichrist, such revelation cannot have yet taken place: and consequently, though we need not stigmatize any of the various interpretations as false, none of them has exhausted the import of the prophecy. The various untoward events and ungodly persons which have been mentioned, including the unbelief and godlessness of the present time, are all prefigurations of Antichrist, but contain only *some* of his characteristics, not *all*: it is the union of *all* in some one personal appearance, that shall make the full Antichrist, as the union in one Person, Jesus of Nazareth, of all the types and prophecies, constituted the full Christ. And the κατέχον is the *moral and conservative influence of political states*, restraining this great final outbreak. See more on this below.

[8] So again Pelt, p. 185: "Tenentes, illum Christi adventum a Paulo *non visibilem* habitum."

16 On the other hand, some have regarded the prophecy as one already fulfilled. So Grotius, Wetstein, Le Clerc, Whitby, Schottgen, Nosselt, Krause, and Harduin. All these concur in referring the παρουσία τοῦ κυρίου to the coming of Christ in the *destruction of Jerusalem*

17. *Grotius* holds Antichrist to be the godless *Caligula*, who (Suet Calig 22, 33) ordered universal supplication to himself as the High God, and (Jos. Antt xviii. 8 2 Philo, Leg ad Cai. § 31, vol ii. p 576) would have set up a colossal image of himself in the temple at Jerusalem · and in ὁ κατέχων he sees *L Vitellius*, the proconsul of Syria and Judæa, whose term of office delayed the putting up of the statue,—and in ὁ ἄνομος, *Simon Magus* This theory is liable to the two very serious objections, 1) that it makes ὁ ἄνθρ. τῆς ἁμαρτ and ὁ ἄνομος into two separate persons: 2) that it involves an anachronism, our Epistle having been written after Caligula's time.

18. According to *Wetstein*, the ἄνθρ τῆς ἁμαρτίας is *Titus*, whose army (Jos B. J vi. 6. 1), καιομένου αὐτοῦ τοῦ ναοῦ, καὶ τῶν πέριξ ἁπάντων, κομίσαντες τὰς σημαίας εἰς τὸ ἱερόν, καὶ θέμεναι τῆς ἀνατολικῆς πύλης ἄντικρυς, ἔθυσάν τε αὐταῖς αὐτόθι, καὶ τὸν Τίτον μετὰ μεγίστων εὐφημιῶν ἀπέφηναν αὐτοκράτορα. His κατέχων is *Nero*, whose death was necessary for the reign of Titus,—and his ἀποστασία, the *rebellion and slaughter of three princes*, Galba, Otho, and Vitellius, which brought in the Flavian family. But this is the very height of absurdity, and surely needs no serious refutation

19 *Hammond*[9] makes the *man of sin* to be *Simon Magus*, and *the Gnostics*, whose head he was. The ἐπισυναγωγὴ ἐπ' αὐτόν, ver. 1, he interprets as the "major libertas coeundi in ecclesiasticos cœtus ad colendum Christum:" the ἀποστασία, the falling off of Christians *to Gnosticism* (1 Tim iv 1): ἀποκαλυφθῆναι, the Gnostics "putting off their disguise, and revealing themselves in their colours, i e. cruel, professed enemies to Christ and Christians." ver 4 refers to Simon "making himself the supreme Father of all, who had created the God of the Jews" (Iren. i. 24 1, 2, p 100 f.). By τὸ κατέχον, he understands the *union* yet subsisting more or less *between the Christians and the Jews* in the Apostle's estimation, which was removed when the Apostles entirely separated from the Jews. and ὁ κατέχων he maintains to be virtually the same with τὸ κατέχον, but if any masculine subject must be supplied, would make it ὁ νόμος The μυστήριον τῆς ἀνομίας he refers to the *wicked lives* of these Gnostics, but mostly to their persecution of the Christians Ver 8 he explains of the *conflict at Rome* between Simon and the Apostles Peter and Paul, which ended in the death of the former. Lunemann adds, "The exegetical and historical monstrosity of this interpretation is at present universally acknowledged "

[9] On the New Test in loc.

20. *Le Clerc* holds the ἀποστασία to be the *rebellion of the Jewish people* against the yoke of Rome: the man of sin, the *rebel Jews*, and especially their leader *Simon, son of Giora*, whose atrocities are related in Josephus —πᾶς λεγόμ. θεὸς κ τ λ, denotes the *government* —τὸ κατέχον is *whatever hindered the open breaking out of the rebellion*,—partly the influence of those Jews in office who dissuaded the war,—partly fear of the Roman armies and ὁ κατέχων, on one side, the "*præses Romanus*,"—on the other, the "*gentis proceres, rex Agrippa et pontifices plurimi*." The μυστήριον τῆς ἀνομίας is the *rebellious ambition*, which under the cloke of Jewish independence and zeal for the law of Moses, was even then at work, and at length broke openly forth

21. *Whitby* takes the *Jewish people* for Antichrist, and finds in the apostasy the *falling away of the Jewish converts to their old Judaism*, alluded to in the Epistle to the Hebrews (iii. 12—14; iv. 11, vi. 4—6; x 26, 27 al fr) His κατέχων is "the *Emperor Claudius*, who will let till he be taken away, i e he will hinder the Jews from breaking out into an open rebellion in his time, they being so signally and particularly obliged by him, that they cannot for shame think of revolting from his government."

22 *Schöttgen* (vol i p. 861 ff) takes Antichrist to be the *Pharisees, Rabbis, and doctors of the law*, who set up themselves above God, and had impious stories tending to bring Him into contempt. the ἀποστασία, the *rebellion against Rome*: the κατέχον, "*Christiani*, qui precibus suis rem aliquando distulerunt, donec oraculo divino admoniti Hierosolymis abierunt, et Pellam secesserunt" the μυστήριον τῆς ἀνομίας, "*ipsa doctrina perversa*," referring to 1 Tim iii 16.

23 *Nosselt* and *Krause* understand by Antichrist the *Jewish zealots*, and by the κατέχον, *Claudius*, as Whitby Lastly, *Harduin* makes the ἀποστασία the *falling off of the Jews to paganism*,—the man of sin, the *High Priest Ananias* (Acts xxiii. 2),—the κατέχων, *his predecessor*, whose term of office must come to an end before he could be elected From the beginning of his term, the ἄνθρωπος τῆς ἁμαρτίας was working as a prophet of lies, and was destroyed at the taking of Jerusalem by Titus

24 All these *præterist* interpretations have against them one fatal objection.—that it is impossible to conceive of the destruction of Jerusalem as in any sense corresponding to the παρουσία in St Paul's sense of the term: see especially, as bearing immediately on this passage, 1 Thess ii. 19; iii. 13; iv. 15; v 23

25. A third class of interpretations is that adopted by many of the modern German expositors, and their followers in England. It is best described perhaps in the words of De Wette (Einl. Handb. ii 132): "He goes altogether wrong, who finds here any more than the Apostle's

subjective anticipation from his own historical position, of the future of the Christian Church," and expanded by Mr. Jowett (vol ii. p 178), "Such passages (Eph vi 12) are a much safer guide to the interpretation of the one we are considering, than the meaning of similar passages in the Old Testament. For they indicate to us the habitual thought of the Apostle's mind: 'a falling away first,' suggested probably by the wavering which he saw around him among his own converts, the grievous wolves that were entering into the Church of Ephesus (Acts xx 29). the turning away of all them of Asia (2 Tim i 15) When we consider that his own converts, and his Jewish opponents, were all the world to him,—that through them, as it were in a glass, he appeared to himself to see the workings of human nature generally, we understand how this double image of good and evil should have presented itself to him, and the kind of necessity which he felt, that Christ and Antichrist should alternate with each other It was not that he foresaw some great conflict, decisive of the destinies of mankind What he anticipated far more nearly resembled the spiritual combat in the seventh chapter of the Romans. It was the same struggle, written in large letters, as Plato might have said, not on the tables of the heart, but on the scene around the world turned inside out, as it might be described. evil as it is in the sight of God, and as it realizes itself to the conscience, putting on an external shape, transforming itself into a person"

26. This hypothesis is so entirely separate from all others, that there seems no reason why we should not deal with it at once and on its own ground, before proceeding further. It will be manifest to any one who exercises a moment's thought, that the question moved by it simply resolves itself into this *Was the Apostle, or was he not, writing in the power of a spirit higher than his own?* In other words, we are here at the very central question of *Inspiration or no Inspiration* · not disputing about any of its details, which have ever been matters of doubt among Christians. but just asking, for the Church and for the world, *Have we, in any sense, God speaking in the Bible, or have we not?* If we have,—then of all passages, it is in these which treat so confidently of futurity, that we must recognize His voice if we have it not in these passages, then where are we to listen for it at all? Does not this hypothesis, do not they who embrace it, at once reduce the Scriptures to books written by men,—their declarations to the assertions of dogmatizing teachers,—their warnings to the apprehensions of excited minds,—their promises to the visions of enthusiasts,—their prophecies, to anticipations which may be accounted for by the circumstances of the writers, but have in them no objective permanent truth whatever?

27 On such terms, I fairly confess I am not prepared to deal with a question like that before us. I believe that our Lord uttered the words ascribed to Him by St John (ch xvi 12, 13); I believe the

apostolic Epistles to be the written proof of the fulfilment of that promise, as the apostolic preaching and labours were the spoken and acted proof and in writing such passages as this, and 1 Thess iv 13—17, and 1 Cor xv, I believe St. Paul to have been giving utterance, not to his own subjective human opinions, but to truths which the Spirit of God had revealed to him: which he put forth indeed in writing and in speaking, as God had placed him, in a Church which does not know of the time of her Lord's coming,—as God had constituted his own mind, the vessel and organ of these truths, and gifted him with power of words,—but still, as being the truth for the Church to be guided by, not his own forebodings, for her to be misled by. What he may have meant by his expressions, is a question open to the widest and freest discussion: but that what he did mean, always under the above necessary conditions, is truth for us to receive, not opinion for us to canvass, is a position, the holding or rejecting of which might be very simply and strictly shewn to constitute the difference between one who receives, and one who repudiates, Christian revelation itself.

28. I now proceed to enquire, which, or whether any of all the above hypotheses, with the exception of the last, seems worthy of our acceptance. For the reason given above (24), I pass over those which regard the prophecy as fulfilled The destruction of Jerusalem is inadequate as an interpretation of the coming of the Lord here He has not yet come in any sense adequate to such interpretation: therefore the prophecy has yet to be fulfilled.

29. The interpretations of the ancient Fathers deserve all respect, short of absolute adoption *because they were* their interpretations We must always in such cases strike a balance In living near to the time when the speaking voice yet lingered in the Church, they had an advantage over us in living far down in the unfolding of God's purposes, we have an advantage over them. They may possibly have heard things which we have never heard: we certainly have seen things which they never saw In each case, we are bound to enquire, which of these two is likely to preponderate?

30. Their consensus in expecting a *personal* Antichrist, is, I own, a weighty point There was nothing in their peculiar circumstances or temperament, which prevented them from interpreting all that is here said as a personification, or from allegorizing it, as others have done since This fact gives that interpretation a *historical* weight, the inference from which it is difficult to escape The subject of the coming of Antichrist must have been no uncommon one in preaching and in converse, during the latter part of the first, and the second century That no echoes of the apostolic sayings on the matter should have reached thus far, no savour of the first outpouring of interpretation by

the Spirit penetrated through the next generation, can hardly be conceived So far, I feel, the patristic view carries with it some claim to our acceptance.

31. The next important point, the interpretation of τὸ κατέχον and ὁ κατέχων, rests, I would submit, on different grounds Let us for a moment grant, that by the former of these words was imported the *temporal political power*, and by the latter, *he who wielded it* Such being the case, the concrete interpretation most likely to be adopted by the Fathers would be, the *Roman Empire*, which existed before their eyes as that political power. But *we* have seen that particular power pass away, and be broken up: and that very passing away has furnished us with a key to the prophecy, which they did not possess

32 On the μυστήριον τῆς ἀνομίας, as has been seen, they are divided: but even were it otherwise, their concrete interpretations are just those things in which we are not inferior to them, but rather superior. The prophecy has since their time expanded its action over a wide and continually increasing historic field it is for us to observe what they could not, and to say what it is which could be thus described,—then at work, ever since at work, and now at work, and likely to issue in that concentration and revelation of evil which shall finally take place

33. On looking onward to the next great class of interpretations, that which makes the man of sin to be the *Papal power*, it cannot be doubted, that there are many and striking points of correspondence with the language of the prophecy in the acts and professions of those who have successively held that power. But on the other hand it cannot be disguised that, in several important particulars, the prophetic requirements are very far from being fulfilled. I will only mention two, one subjective, the other objective. In the characteristic of ver. 4, the Pope does not and never did fulfil the prophecy. Allowing all the striking coincidences with the latter part of the verse which have been so abundantly adduced, it never can be shewn that he fulfils the former part, nay so far is he from it, that the abject adoration of and submission to λεγόμενοι θεοί and σεβάσματα has ever been one of his most notable peculiarities[1] The second objection, of an external and historical character, is even more decisive. If the Papacy be Antichrist, then has the manifestation been made, and endured now for nearly 1500 years,

[1] It must be plain to every unbiassed mind, that the mere logical inference, that the Pope sets himself up above all objects of worship, because he *creates* objects of worship, and *the maker must be greater than the thing made*, is quite beside the purpose. It entirely fails in shewing *hostility to, and lifting himself above, every one that is called God or an object of worship.* The Pope is the *devoted servant* of the false gods whom he creates, not their antagonist and treader-down. I should not have noticed so irrelevant an argument, had it not been made much of as against my view.

and yet that day of the Lord is not come, which by the terms of our prophecy such manifestation is immediately to precede[2].

34. The same remarks will apply even more forcibly to all those minor interpretations which I have enumerated above. None of them exhausts the sense of the prophecy: and the taking any one of them to be that which is here designated, would shew the failure of the prophecy, not its fulfilment: for they have been and have passed away, and the Lord is not yet come.

35. We are thus directed to a point of view with regard to the prophecy, of the following kind. The ἄνομος, in the full prophetic sense, is not yet come. Though 1800 years later, we stand, with regard to him, where the Apostle stood: the day of the Lord not present, and not to arrive until this man of sin be manifested: the μυστήριον τῆς ἀνομίας still working, and much advanced in its working: the κατέχον still hindering. And let us ask ourselves, what does this represent to us? Is it not indicative of a state in which the ἀνομία is working on, so to speak, underground, under the surface of things,—gaining, throughout these many ages, more expansive force, more accumulated power, but still hidden and unconcentrated? And might we not look, in the progress of such a state of things, for repeated minor embodiments of this ἀνομία,—ἄνομοι, and ἀντίχριστοι πολλοί (1 John ii. 18) springing up here and there in different ages and countries,—the ἀποστασία going onward and growing,—just as there were of Christ Himself frequent types and minor embodiments before He came in the flesh? Thus in the Papacy, where so many of the prophetic features are combined, we see as it were a standing embodiment and type of the final Antichrist—in the remarkable words of Gregory the Great, the '*præcursor Antichristi*:' and in Nero, and every persecutor as he arose, and Mohammed, and Napoleon, and many other forms and agencies of evil, other more transient types and examples of him. We may, following out the parallelism, contrast the Papacy, as a type of Antichrist, having its false priesthood, its pretended sacrifices, its 'Lord God' the Pope, with that standing Jewish hierarchy of God's own appointing, and its High Priesthood by which our Lord was prefigured: and the other and personal types, with those typical persons, who appeared under the old covenant, and set forth so plainly the character and sufferings and triumphs of the Christ of God.

36. According then to this view, we still look for the man of sin, in the fulness of the prophetic sense, to appear, and that immediately before the coming of the Lord. We look for him as the final and central embodiment of that ἀνομία, that resistance to God and God's law, which has been for these many centuries fermenting under the crust of human society, and of which we have already witnessed so many

[2] For surely this is the only possible understanding of our ver. 8 on the ordinary acceptance of words.

partial and tentative eruptions. Whether he is to be expected personally, as one individual embodiment of evil, we would not dogmatically pronounce still we would not forget, that both ancient interpretation, and the world's history, point this way Almost all great movements for good or for ill have been gathered to a head by one central personal agency. Nor is there any reason to suppose that this will be otherwise in the coming ages. In proportion as the general standard of mental cultivation is raised, and man made equal with man, the ordinary power of genius is diminished, but its extraordinary power is increased, its reach deepened, its hold rendered more firm As men become familiar with the achievements and the exercise of talent, they learn to despise and disregard its daily examples, and to be more independent of mere men of ability; but they only become more completely in the power of gigantic intellect, and the slaves of pre-eminent and unapproachable talent So that there seems nothing improbable, judging from these considerations, and from the analogy of the partial manifestations which we have already seen, that the centralization of the antichristian power, in the sense of this prophecy, may ultimately take place in the person of some one of the sons of men

37 The great ἀποστασία again will receive a similar interpretation. Many signal apostasies the world and the Church have seen Continually, those are going out from us, who were not of us Unquestionably the greatest of these has been the Papacy, that counterfeit of Christianity, with its whole system of falsehood and idolatry But both it, and Mohammedanism, and Mormonism, and the rest, are but tentamina and foreshadowings of that great final apostasy (ἡ ἀποστασία), which shall deceive, if it were possible, even the very elect.

38 The particulars of ver. 4 we regard variously, according as the ἄνομος is a person or a set of persons, with however every inclination to take them literally of a person, giving out these things respecting himself, and sitting as described in the temple of God, whether that temple is to be taken in the strictly literal signification of the Jerusalem-temple (to which we do not incline), or as signifying a Christian place of assembly, the gathering-point of those who have sought the fulfilment of the divine promise of God's presence,—and so called the temple of God

39 The κατέχον and κατέχων, the one the *general hindrance*, the other the *person in whom that hindrance is summed up*, are, in this view, very plain. As the Fathers took them of the Roman Empire and Emperor, standing and ruling in their time, repressing the outbreak of sin and enormity,—so have we been taught by history to widen this view, and understand them of the *fabric of human polity*, and *those who rule that polity*, by which the great up-bursting of godlessness is kept down and hindered I say, we have been taught this by history seeing that as often as these outbursts have taken place, their course and devastations

have been checked by the knitting up again of this fabric of temporal power seeing that this power, wherever the seeds of evil are most plentiful, is strictly a *coercive* power, and that there only is its restraining hand able to be relaxed, where the light and liberty of the Gospel are shed abroad· seeing that especially has this temporal power ever been in conflict with the Papacy, restraining its pretensions, modifying its course of action, witnessing more or less against its tyranny and its lies.

40. The explanation of the μυστήριον τῆς ἀνομίας has been already anticipated. It, the ἀνομία, in the hearts and lives, in the speeches and writings of men, is and ever has been working in hidden places, and only awaits the removal of the hindering power to issue in that concentrated manifestation of ὁ ἄνομος, which shall usher in the times of the end

41 *When* this shall be, is as much hidden from us, as it was from the Apostles themselves This may be set, on the one hand, as a motive to caution and sobriety; while on the other let us not forget, that every century, every year, brings us nearer to the fulfilment,—and let this serve to keep us awake and watchful, as servants that wait for the coming of their Lord. We are not to tremble at every alarm; to imagine that every embodiment of sin is the final one, or every falling away the great apostasy· but to weigh, and to discern, in the power of Him, by whom the prince of this world is judged. that whenever the Lord comes He may find us ready,—ready to stand on His side against any, even the final concentration of His adversaries, ready, in daily intercourse with and obedience to Him, to hail His appearance with joy

42. If it be said, that this is somewhat a dark view to take of the prospects of mankind, we may answer, first, that we are not speculating on the phænomena of the world, but we are interpreting God's word: secondly, that we believe in One in whose hands all evil is working for good,—with whom there are no accidents nor failures,—who is bringing out of all this struggle, which shall mould and measure the history of the world, the ultimate good of man and the glorification of His boundless love in Christ: and thirdly, that no prospect is dark for those who believe in Him For them all things are working together for good; and in the midst of the struggle itself, they know that every event is their gain; every apparent defeat, real success, and even the last dread conflict, the herald of that victory, in which all who have striven on God's part shall have a glorious and everlasting share

CHAPTER VII.

ON THE PASTORAL EPISTLES.

SECTION I

THEIR AUTHORSHIP

1. THERE never was the slightest doubt in the ancient Church, that the Epistles to Timothy and Titus were canonical, and written by St Paul.

(α) They are contained in the Peschito Syriac version, which was made in the second century.

(β) In the fragment on the Canon of Scripture first edited by Muratori and thence known by his name, generally ascribed to the end of the second century or the beginning of the third (see Routh, Reliq Sacr i. pp 397 ff.), we read, among the Epistles of St Paul "verum ad Philemonem una, et ad Timotheum duas (duæ?) pro affectu et dilectione, in honore tamen Ecclesiæ catholicæ, in ordinatione ecclesiasticæ disciplinæ, sanctificatæ sunt."

(γ) Irenæus begins his preface, p. 1, with a citation of 1 Tim i. 4, adding καθὼς ὁ ἀπόστολός φησιν: in iv 16 3, p 246, cites 1 Tim i 9 in ii. 14. 7, p. 135, 1 Tim. vi 20. in iii. 14. 1, p. 201, quotes 2 Tim. iv. 9—11:

> "Lucas . . . quoniam non solum prosecutor, sed et co-operarius fuerit apostolorum, maxime autem Pauli, et ipse autem Paulus manifestavit in epistolis, dicens: Demas me dereliquit et abiit Thessalonicam, Crescens in Galatiam, Titus in Dalmatiam. Lucas est mecum solus"

In i 16 3, p. 83, quotes Titus iii. 10:

> οὓς ὁ Παῦλος ἐγκελεύεται ἡμῖν μετὰ μίαν καὶ δευτέραν νουθεσίαν παραιτεῖσθαι

And again, with ὡς καὶ Παῦλος ἔφησεν, iii. 3 4, p 177 In iii. 2. 3, p. 176, he says, τούτου τοῦ Λίνου Παῦλος ἐν ταῖς πρὸς Τιμόθεον ἐπιστολαῖς μέμνηται.

(δ) Clement of Alexandria, Strom. ii. 11 [52], p 457 P :

> περὶ ἧς ὁ ἀπόστολος γράφων, ὦ Τιμόθεε, φησιν, τὴν παρακαταθήκην φύλαξον ἐκτρεπόμενος τὰς βεβήλους κενοφωνίας κ τ λ 1 Tim. vi. 20

Strom iii 6 [51], p 534 P :

> αὐτίκα περὶ τῶν βδελυσσομένων τὸν γάμον Παῦλος ὁ μακάριος λέγει . . 1 Tim iv 1

Ib. [53], p 536 P :
ἴσμεν γὰρ καὶ ὅσα περὶ διακόνων γυναικῶν ἐν τῇ ἑτέρᾳ πρὸς Τιμόθεον ἐπιστολῇ ὁ γενναῖος διατάσσεται Παῦλος

Strom i 14 [59], p. 350 P :
τὸν δὲ ἕβδομον οἱ μὲν . . . οἱ δὲ Ἐπιμενίδην τὸν Κρῆτα . . οὗ μέμνηται ὁ ἀπόστολος Παῦλος ἐν τῇ πρὸς Τίτον ἐπιστολῇ λέγων οὕτως· Κρῆτες ἀεὶ κ τ λ (Tit. i. 12)

These are only a few of the direct quotations in Clement

(ε) TERTULLIAN.

De præscript hæret. c 25, vol. ii. p. 37. "Et hoc verbo usus est Paulus ad Timotheum O Timothee, depositum custodi (1 Tim vi. 20). Et rursum. Bonum depositum serva" (2 Tim i 14). And he further proceeds to quote 1 Tim i 18, vi 13 ff.; 2 Tim. ii. 2 (twice).

Ib c. 6, p. 18· "Nec diutius de isto, si idem est Paulus, qui et alibi hæreses inter carnalia crimina enumerat scribens ad Galatas, et qui Tito[3] suggerit, hominem hæreticum post primam correptionem recusandum, quod perversus sit ejusmodi et delinquat, ut a semetipso damnatus." (Tit iii 10, 11)

Adv Marcion v 21, p 524, speaking of the Epistle to Philemon "Soli huic epistolæ brevitas sua profuit, ut falsarias manus Marcionis evaderet. Miror tamen, cum ad unum hominem literas factas receperit, quod ad Timotheum duas et unam ad Titum de ecclesiastico statu compositas recusaverit."

(ζ) Eusebius includes all three Epistles among the universally confessed canonical writings (ὁμολογούμενα), H E iii 25

It is useless to cite further testimonies, for they are found every where, and in abundance

2 But we must notice various allusions, more or less clear, to these Epistles, which occur in the *earlier* Fathers

(η) CLEMENT OF ROME (end of Cent I): Ep. 1 ad Cor. ch 29, p 269 προσέλθωμεν οὖν αὐτῷ ἐν ὁσιότητι ψυχῆς, ἁγνὰς καὶ ἀμιάντους χεῖρας αἴροντες πρὸς αὐτόν. See 1 Tim ii 8[4].

(θ) IGNATIUS (beginning of Cent. II.): Ep to Polycarp, § 6, p 724: ἀρέσκετε ᾧ στρατεύεσθε. See 2 Tim. ii 4.

(ι) POLYCARP (beginning of Cent. II). Ep ad Philipp. ch 4, p 1008· ἀρχὴ δὲ πάντων χαλεπῶν φιλαργυρία εἰδότες οὖν ὅτι οὐδὲν εἰσηνέγκαμεν εἰς τὸν κόσμον, ἀλλ' οὐδὲ ἐξενεγκεῖν τι ἔχομεν, ὁπλισώμεθα τοῖς ὅπλοις τῆς δικαιοσύνης 1 Tim vi 7, 10

[3] Dr. Davidson, Introd iii. 109, omits the word 'Tito,' as it would appear, from inadvertency.

[4] Two other supposed references may be seen in Lardner, ii p 39, and Davidson, iii p. 101; but they are too slight to authorize their introduction here.

Ib ch. 9, p 1013: οὐ γὰρ τὸν νῦν ἠγάπησαν αἰῶνα See 2 Tim iv 10[6]

(κ) HEGESIPPUS (end of Cent. II), as cited by Eusebius (H E iii 32), says that, while the ἱερὸς τῶν ἀποστόλων χορός remained, the Church παρθένος καθαρὰ καὶ ἀδιάφθορος ἔμεινεν: but that, after their withdrawal, and that of those who had been ear-witnesses of inspired wisdom, ἡ σύστασις τῆς ἀθέου πλάνης began, διὰ τῆς τῶν ἑτεροδιδασκάλων ἀπάτης who, as no apostle was left, γυμνῇ λοιπὸν ἤδη τῇ κεφαλῇ τῷ τῆς ἀληθείας κηρύγματι τὴν ψευδώνυμον γνῶσιν ἀντικηρύττειν ἐπεχείρουν See 1 Tim. vi 3, 20[6]

(λ) ATHENAGORAS (end of Cent. II) · Legat pro Christianis 16, p. 291. πάντα γὰρ ὁ θεός ἐστιν αὐτὸς αὐτῷ, φῶς ἀπρόσιτον 1 Tim vi 16

(μ) THEOPHILUS OF ANTIOCH (end of Cent. II.). ad Autolyc. iii. 14, p. 389: ἔτι μὴν καὶ περὶ τοῦ ὑποτάσσεσθαι ἀρχαῖς καὶ ἐξουσίαις, καὶ εὔχεσθαι περὶ αὐτῶν, κελεύει ἡμᾶς θεῖος λόγος ὅπως ἤρεμον καὶ ἡσύχιον βίον διάγωμεν 1 Tim. ii 1, 2 Tit iii 1[7].

ii p. 95 (Lardner): διὰ ὕδατος καὶ λουτροῦ παλιγγενεσίας πάντας τοὺς προσιόντας τῇ ἀληθείᾳ

(ν) To these may be added Justin Martyr (middle of Cent. II.), Dial c. Tryph. c 47, p 143 ἡ χρηστότης καὶ ἡ φιλανθρωπία τοῦ θεοῦ. Tit. iii 4.

3 Thus the Pastoral Epistles seem to have been from the earliest times known, and continuously quoted, in the Church It is hardly possible to suppose that the above coincidences are all fortuitous The only other hypothesis on which they can be accounted for, will be treated further on

4 Among the Gnostic heretics, however, they did not meet with such universal acceptance Clement of Alexandria, Strom. ii 11 (p. 457 P.), after having quoted 1 Tim vi 20 ff, adds · ὑπὸ ταύτης ἐλεγχόμενοι τῆς φωνῆς, οἱ ἀπὸ τῶν αἱρέσεων τὰς πρὸς Τιμόθεον ἀθετοῦσιν ἐπιστολάς Tertullian (see above, under ε) states that Marcion rejected from his canon (recusaverit) the Epistles to Timothy and Titus And Jerome, Prol ad Titum, vol vii p 685, says: "Licet non sint digni fide qui fidem primam irritam fecerunt, Marcionem loquor et Basilidem et omnes hæreticos qui vetus laniant testamentum. tamen eos aliqua ex parte ferremus, si saltem in novo continerent manus suas, et non auderent Christi (ut ipsi jactitant) boni Dei Filii, vel Evangelistas violare, vel Apostolos . .. ut enim de cæteris Epistolis taceam, de quibus quicquid contrarium suo dogmati viderant, eraserunt, nonnullas integras repudiandas

[5] See other slighter parallels in Lardner and Davidson, ubi supra The μέγα τῆς θεοσεβείας μυστήριον, commonly adduced from Justin (in Eus H. E iii. 27), is not his, but forms part of the text of Eusebius See Huther, Einl. p. 35.

[6] See on Baur's attempt to meet this, below, par. 14 note.

[7] Lardner gives ὃς διδάσκει ἡμᾶς δικαιοπραγεῖν, καὶ εὐσεβεῖν καὶ καλοποιεῖν, as an allusion to Tit. ii. 11, 12 but it is far too slight

crediderunt, ad Timotheum videlicet utramque, ad Hebræos, et ad Titum, quam nunc conamur exponere . . Sed Tatianus, Encratitarum patriarches, qui et ipse nonnullas Pauli Epistolas repudiavit, hanc vel maxime, id est, ad Titum, Apostoli pronunciandam credidit, parvipendens Marcionis et aliorum, qui cum eo in hac parte consentiunt, assertionem" This last fact, Tatian's acceptance of the Epistle to Titus, Huther thinks may be accounted for by the false teachers in that Epistle being more expressly designated as *Jews*, ch i 10, 14; iii 9.

5 From their time to the beginning of the present century, the authenticity of the Pastoral Epistles remained unquestioned At that time, Schmidt (J E C) first, and afterwards Schleiermacher (in his Letters to Gass, 1807) attacked the genuineness of the first Epistle to Timothy · which on the other hand, was defended by *Planck*, *Wegscheider*, and *Beckhaus* It soon began however to be seen, that from the close relation of the three Epistles, the arguments which Schleiermacher had used against one, would apply to all. and accordingly first *Eichhorn*, and then not so decidedly *De Wette*, denied the genuineness of all three

6 The latter Commentator, in his Introduction (1826), combined the view of Schleiermacher, that 1 Tim was a compilation from the other two, with that of Eichhorn, that all three were not the genuine productions of St Paul but at the same time allowed to the consent of the Church in all ages so much weight, that his view influenced only the historical origin of the Epistles, not their credit and authority.

7 This mere negative ground was felt to be unsatisfactory: and Eichhorn soon put forth a positive hypothesis, that the Epistles were written by some disciple of St Paul, with a view of collecting together his oral injunctions respecting the constitution of the Church This was adopted by Schott, with the further conjecture that St. Luke was the author.

8 The defenders of the Epistles[8] found it not difficult to attack such a position as this, which was raised on mere conjecture after all: and Baur, on the other hand, remarked[9], "We have no sufficient resting-place for our critical judgment, as long as we only lay down that the Epistles are not Pauline: we must have established some positive data which transfer them from the Apostle's time into another age." Accordingly, he himself has laboured to prove them to have been written in the time of the Marcionite heresy, and their author to have been one who, not having the ability himself to attack the Gnostic positions, thought to uphold the Pauline party by putting his denunciations of it into the mouth of the Apostle

[8] Hug, Bertholdt, Feilmoser, Guerike, Bohl, Curtius, Kling, Heydenreich, Mack. See Huther, Einleitung, p 38, from which many of the particulars in the text are taken

[9] Die sogenn. Pastoralbriefe des Apostel Paulus aufs neue Kritisch untersucht, 1835.

9 This view of Baur's has been, however, very far from meeting with general adoption, even among the impugners of the genuineness of our Epistles. The new school of Tubingen have alone accepted it with favour. De Wette himself, in the later editions of his Handbuch (I quote from that of 1847), though he is stronger than ever against the three Epistles, does not feel satisfied with the supposed settling of the question by Baur He remarks, "According to Baur, the Epistles were written after the middle of the second century, subsequently to the appearance of Marcion and other Gnostics But, inasmuch as the allusions to Marcion, on which he builds this hypothesis, are by no means certain, and the testimonies of the existence of the Pastoral Epistles stand in the way (for it is hardly probable that the passage in Polycarp, c. 4 [see above, par. 2], can have been the original of 1 Tim. vi. 7, 10): it seems that we must assume an earlier date for the Epistles,—somewhere about the end of the first century[1]."

10. With this last dictum of De Wette's, adverse criticism has resumed its former uncertain footing, and is reduced to the mere negative complexion which distinguished it before the appearance of Baur's first work. We have then merely to consider it as a negation of the Pauline origin of the Epistles, and to examine the grounds on which that negation rests These may be generally stated under the three following heads

I The historical difficulty of finding a place for the writing of the three Epistles during the lifetime of St Paul

II The apparent contact with various matters and persons who belong to a later age than that of the Apostles: and

III. The peculiarity of expressions and modes of thought, both of which diverge from those in St. Paul's recognized Epistles

11. Of the first of these I shall treat below, in the section "On the times and places of writing" It may suffice here to anticipate merely the general conclusion to which I have there come, viz that they belong to the latest period of our Apostle's life, after his liberation from the imprisonment of Acts xxviii. Thus much was necessary in order to our discussion of the two remaining grounds of objection.

12 As regards objection II, three subordinate points require notice:

(a) *The heretics, whose views and conduct are opposed in all three Epistles*

It is urged that these belonged to later times, and their tenets to systems undeveloped in the apostolic age In treating of the various places where they are mentioned, I have endeavoured to shew that the tenets and practices predicated of them will best find their explanation by regarding them as the marks of a state of transition between Judaism,

[1] Handbuch · allgemeine Bemerkungen uber die Pastoralbriefe, p. 121.

through its ascetic form, and Gnosticism proper, as we afterwards find it developed[2].

13. The traces of Judaism in the heretics of the Pastoral Epistles are numerous and unmistakeable. They professed to be νομοδιδάσκαλοι (1 Tim i. 7): commanded ἀπέχεσθαι βρωμάτων (ib iv. 3): are expressly stated to consist of μάλιστα οἱ ἐκ περιτομῆς (Tit i 10): caused men προσέχειν Ἰουδαικοῖς μύθοις (ib. 14): brought in μάχας νομικάς (ib. iii. 9).

14. At the same time, the traces of incipient Gnosticism are equally apparent. It has been thought best, in the notes on 1 Tim i. 4, to take that acceptation of γενεαλογίαι, which makes it point to those lists of Gnostic emanations, so familiar to us in their riper forms in after history. in ch. iv. 3 ff, we find the seeds of Gnostic dualism, and though that passage is prophetic, we may fairly conceive that it points to the future development of symptoms already present. In ib vi. 20, we read of ψευδώνυμος γνῶσις, an expression which has furnished Baur with one of his strongest objections, as betraying a post-apostolic origin[3]. But, granted the reference to *gnosis*, Gnostically so called, neither Baur nor any one else has presumed to say, when the term began to be so used. For our present purpose, the reference is clear. Again in 2 Tim. ii. 17, 18, we read of some of them explaining away the resurrection of the body, saying that it has passed already,—a well-known error of the Gnostics (see note in loc.)

15. It remains that we should shew two important facts, which may influence the reader's mind concerning both the nature of these heretics, and date of our Epistles. First, they are not the Judaizers of the Apostle's earlier Epistles. These his former opponents were strong upholders of the law and its requirements: identify themselves plainly with the 'certain men from Judæa' of Acts xv. 1, in spirit and tenets: uphold circumcision, and would join it with the faith in Christ. Then as we proceed, we find them retaining indeed some of their former features, but having passed into a new phase, in the Epistle to the Colossians. There, they have added to their Judaizing tenets, various excrescences of will-worship and superstition. are described no longer as persons who would be under the law and Christ together, but as vain,

[2] See 1 Tim. i. 3, 4, 6, 7, 19; iv 1—7; vi. 3 ff; 2 Tim ii. 16—23, iii. 6—9, 13; iv 4; Titus i. 10, 11, 14, 16, iii. 9, 10,—and notes.

[3] Baur makes much of the passage of Hegesippus quoted above, par. 2, κ, in which he says that this ψευδών γνῶσις first became prevalent after the Apostles were removed from the Church. On this he founds an argument that our Epistle could not have appeared till that time. But the passage as compared with the Epistle proves the very reverse. The ψευδών. γν. was secretly working in the Apostles' time, and for that reason this caution was given: but after their time it began to be openly professed, and came forth, as Hegesippus says, with uncovered head.

puffed up in their carnal mind, not holding the Head (see Prolegg. to Col, § ii 10 ff).

16 The same character, or even a further step in their course, seems pointed out in the Epistle to the Philippians. There, they are not only Judaizers, not only that which we have already seen them, but *κύνες, κακοὶ ἐργάται, ἡ κατατομή*: and those who serve God in the power of His Spirit are contrasted with them. And here (Phil iii. 18), we seem to find the first traces becoming perceptible of the heresy respecting the resurrection in 2 Tim ii 18, just as the preliminary symptoms of unsoundness on this vital point were evident in 1 Cor xv.

17 If now we pass on to our Epistles, we shall find the same progress from legality to superstition, from superstition to godlessness, in a further and riper stage. Here we have more decided prominence given to the abandonment of the foundations of life and manners displayed by these false teachers They had lost all true understanding of the law itself (1 Tim i. 7) · had repudiated a good conscience (ib 19) · are hypocrites and liars (ib iv. 2), branded with the foul marks of moral crime (ib) · are of corrupt minds, using religion as a means of bettering themselves in this world (ib vi. 5 Tit i. 11) · insidious and deadly in their advances, and overturning the faith (2 Tim. ii. 17). proselytizing and victimizing foolish persons to their ruin (ib iii 6 ff) polluted and unbelieving, with their very mind and conscience defiled (Tit i. 15) confessing God with their mouths, but denying Him in their works, abominable and disobedient, and for every good work worthless (ib i 16)

18 I may point out to the reader, how well such advanced description of these persons suits the character which we find drawn of those who are so held up to abhorrence in the later of the Catholic Epistles, and in the Epistle to the Hebrews how we become convinced, as we pass down the apostolic age, that all its heresies and false teachings must be thought of as gradually converging to one point,—and that point, godlessness of life and morals Into this, Judaism, once so rigid, legality, once so apparently conscientious, broke and crumbled down I may state my own conviction, from this phænomenon in our Pastoral Epistles, corroborated indeed by all their other phænomena, that we are, in reading them, necessarily placed at a point of later and further development than in reading any other of the works of St Paul

19. The *second* important point as regards these heretics is this as they are not the Judaizers of former days, so *neither are they the Gnostics of later days* Many minor points of difference might be insisted on, which will be easily traced out by any student of church history I will only lay stress on one, which is in my mind fundamental and decisive

20 The Gnosticism of later days was eminently *anti-judaistic*. The Jewish Creator, the Jewish law and system, were studiously held in con-

tempt and abhorrence The whole system had migrated, so to speak, from its Jewish standing-point, and stood now entirely over against it And there can be little doubt, whatever other causes may have co-operated to bring about this change, that the great cause of it was the break-up of the Jewish hierarchy and national system with the destruction of Jerusalem and the temple The heretical speculations had, so to speak, no longer any mooring-place in the permanence of the old law, and thus, rapidly drifting away from it, soon lost sight of it altogether, and learned to despise it as a thing gone by. Then the oriental and Grecian elements, which had before been in a state of forced and unnatural fusion with Judaism, cast it out altogether, retaining only those traces of it which involved no recognition of its peculiar tenets.

21 The false teachers then of our Epistles seem to hold a position intermediate to the Apostle's former Judaizing adversaries and the subsequent Gnostic heretics, distinct from both, and just at that point in the progress from the one form of error to the other, which would suit the period subsequent to the Epistle to the Philippians, and prior to the destruction of Jerusalem There is therefore nothing in them and their characteristics, which can cast a doubt upon the genuineness of the Epistles

22 (b) [See above, par 12], *the ecclesiastical order subsisting when they were written.* Baur and De Wette charge the author of these Epistles with hierarchical tendencies. They hold that the strengthening and developing of the hierarchy, as we find it aimed at in the directions here given, could not have been an object with St. Paul De Wette confines himself to this general remark. Baur goes further into detail In his earlier work, on the Pastoral Epistles, he asserts, that in the genuine Pauline Epistles there is found no trace of any official leaders of the Churches (it must be remembered that with Baur, the genuine Epistles are only those to the Galatians, Corinthians, and Romans): whereas here those Churches are found in such a state of organization, that ἐπίσκοποι, πρεσβύτεροι, and διάκονοι are significantly put forward. πρεσβύτεροι according to him being the name for the collective body of church-rulers, and ἐπίσκοπος for that one of them who was singly entrusted with the government In his later work ('Paulus u s.w.'), he maintains that the Gnostics, as the first heretics proper, gave the first occasion for the foundation of the episcopal government of the Churches But even granting this, the very assumption would prove the earlier origin of our Epistles for in them there is not the slightest trace of episcopal government, in the later sense. Baur's own explanation of ἐπίσκοπος differs entirely from that later sense.

23 The fact is, that the form of Church government disclosed in our Epistles is of the simplest kind possible. The diaconate was certainly, in some shape or other, coæval with the very infancy of the Church:

and the presbyterate was almost a necessity for every congregation No Church could subsist without a government of some kind and it would be natural that such an one as that implied in the presbyterate should arise out of the circumstances in every case.

24. The directions also which are here given, are altogether of an ethical, not of an hierarchical kind. They refer to the selection of men, whose previous lives and relations in society afford good promise that they will discharge faithfully the trust committed to them, and work faithfully and successfully in their office. The fact that no such directions are found in the other Epistles, is easily accounted for: partly from the nature of the case, seeing that he is here addressing persons who were entrusted with this selection, whereas in those others no such matter is in question · partly also from the late date of these letters, the Apostle being now at the end of his own course,—seeing dangerous heresies growing up around the Church, and therefore anxious to give those who were to succeed him in its management, direction how to consolidate and secure it.

25 Besides which, it is a pure assumption that St. Paul could not, from his known character, have been anxious in this matter In the Acts, we find him ever most careful respecting the consolidation and security of the churches which he had founded: witness his journeys to inspect and confirm his converts (Acts xv 36, xviii. 23), and that speech uttered from the very depth of his personal feeling and desire, to the presbytery of the Ephesian Church (ib. xx 18—38).

26. We must infer then, that there is nothing in the hints respecting Church-government which these Epistles contain, to make it improbable that they were written by St. Paul towards the close of his life

27 (c) [See above, par. 12] *The institution of widows*, referred to 1 Tim. v. 9 ff., is supposed to be an indication of a later date. I have discussed, in the note there, the description and standing of these widows holding them to be not, as Schleiermacher and Baur, deaconesses, among whom in later times were virgins also, known by the name of χῆραι (τὰς παρθένους τὰς λεγομένας χήρας, Ign ad Smyrn c 13, p. 717), but as De W., al, an especial band of real widows, set apart, but not yet formally and finally, for the service of God and the Church In conceiving such a class to have existed thus early, there is no difficulty: indeed nothing could be more natural we already find traces of such a class in Acts ix. 41; and it would grow up and require regulating in every portion of the Church. On the ἑνὸς ἀνδρὸς γυνή, which is supposed to make another difficulty, see note, 1 Tim iii 2

28 Other details belonging to this objection II. are noticed and replied to in treating of the passages to which they refer. They are founded for the most part in unwarranted assumptions regarding the apostolic age and that which followed it: in forgetting that there

must have been a blending of the one age into the other during that later section of the former and earlier section of the latter, of both of which we know so little from primitive history that the forms of error which we find prevalent in the second century, must have had their origin and their infancy in an age previous: and that here as elsewhere, 'the child is father of the man' the same characteristics, which we meet full-grown both in the heretics and in the Church of the second century, must be expected to occur in their initiative and less consolidated form in the latter days of the Apostles and their Church[1]

29 We come now to treat of objection III,—*the peculiarity of expressions and modes of thought, both of which diverge from those in St Paul's recognized Epistles* There is no denying that the Pastoral Epistles do contain very many peculiar words and phrases, and that the process of thought is not that which the earlier Epistles present. Still, our experience of men in general, and of St Paul himself, should make us cautious how we pronounce hastily on a phænomenon of this kind Men's method of expression changes with the circumstances among which they are writing, and the persons whom they are addressing Assuming the late date for our Epistles which we have already mentioned, the circumstances both of believers and false teachers had materially changed since most of those other Epistles were written And if it be said that on any hypothesis it cannot have been many years since the Epistles of the imprisonment, we may allege on the other hand the very great difference in subject, the fact that these three are addressed to his companions in the ministry, and contain directions for Church management, whereas none of the others contain any passages so addressed or of such character

30. Another circumstance here comes to our notice, which may have modified the diction and style at least of these Epistles Most of those others were written by the hand of an amanuensis, and not only so, but probably with the co-operation, as to form of expression and putting out of the material, of either that amanuensis or some other of his fellow-helpers The peculiar character of these Pastoral Epistles forbids us from imagining that they were so written Addressed to dear friends and valued colleagues in the ministry, it was not probable that he should have written them by the agency of others Have we then, assuming that he wrote them with his own hand, any points of comparison in the other Epistles? Can we trace any resemblance to their peculiar diction in portions of those other Epistles which were undoubtedly or probably also autographic?

[1] See the objection regarding the *youth of Timotheus* assumed in these Epistles, treated below in § ii, 'On the places and times of writing.'

31 The first unquestionably autographic Epistle which occurs to us is that to Philemon which has also this advantage for comparison, that it is written to an individual, and in the later portion of St. Paul's life And it must be confessed, that we do not find here the resemblance of which we are in search The single word *εὔχρηστος* is the only point of contact between the unusual expressions of the two It is true that the occasion and subject of the Epistle to Philemon were totally distinct from those of any of the Pastoral Epistles almost all their *ἅπαξ λεγόμενα* are from the very nature of things excluded from it Still I must admit that the dissimilarity is striking and not easily accounted for I would not disguise the difficulty which besets this portion of our subject I would only endeavour to point out in what direction it ought to guide our inference from the phænomena.

32. We have found reason to believe (see note on Gal. vi. 11) that the Epistle to the Galatians was of this same autographic character. Allowing for the difference of date and circumstances, we may expect to find here some points of peculiarity in common In both, false teachers are impugned in both, the Apostle is eager and fervent, abrupt in expression, and giving vent to his own individual feelings And here we do not seek in vain[5] We find several unusual words and phrases common only to the two or principally occurring in them Here again, however, the total difference of subject throughout a great portion of the Epistle to the Galatians prevents any very great community of expression

33 We have a very remarkable addition to the Epistle to the Romans in the doxology, ch xvi 25, 26, appended to it as we have there in-

[5] I set down a list of the principal similarities which I have observed between the diction of the Gal and the Pastoral Epp

1 *τοῦ δόντος ἑαυτὸν περὶ κ τ λ*, Gal i 4 · compare *ὁ δοὺς ἑαυτὸν ἀντίλυτρον ὑπὲρ κ τ λ*, 1 Tim ii 6, *ὃς ἔδωκεν ἑαυτὸν ὑπὲρ ἡμῶν*, Tit ii. 14 These are the only places where this expression is used of our Lord

2 *εἰς τοὺς αἰῶνας τῶν αἰώνων*, Gal. i. 5 : compare the same expression in 1 Tim i 17, 2 Tim iv 18 The only other places where it occurs is in the last Epistle of the imprisonment, Phil iv. 20

3. *προέκοπτον*, Gal i 14, found in 2 Tim ii 16, iii 9, 13, and Rom xiii 12 only in St Paul.

4. *ἰδοὺ ἐνώπιον τοῦ θεοῦ*, Gal. i 20 the expression *ἐν τ θ* occurs elsewhere frequently in St Paul but in this asseverative sense is found only in the Past. Epp 1 Tim. v 21, vi 13, 2 Tim. ii. 14 (*κυρίου*), iv 1.

5. *στύλος*, Gal ii 9 : in St. Paul, 1 Tim iii 15 only.

6 *ἀνόητοι*, Gal iii 1 : in St Paul (Rom i 14), 1 Tim vi 9, Tit iii 3 only

7. *μεσίτης*, Gal. iii. 20 in St Paul (three times in Hebrews), 1 Tim. ii. 5 only.

8 *ἐλπίς*, objective, Gal v 5 · compare Tit ii 13

9. *πνεύματι ἄγεσθε*, Gal. v. 18 construction, with *ἄγομαι* (Rom. viii. 14), 2 Tim iii. 6 only

10 *καιρῷ ἰδίῳ*, Gal vi 9 found 1 Tim ii. 6, vi. 15, Tit i 3 only

ferred, in later times by the Apostle himself, as a thankful effusion of his fervent mind That addition is in singular accordance with the general style of these Epistles. We may almost conceive him to have taken his pen off from writing one of them, and to have written it under the same impulse[6]

34 There remain, however, many expressions and ideas not elsewhere found Such are πιστὸς ὁ λόγος, 1 Tim. i. 15, iii 1; iv. 9. 2 Tim ii 11 Tit iii 8,—a phrase dwelling much at this time on the mind of the writer, but finding its parallel at other times in his favourite πιστὸς ὁ θεός, and the like: cf 1 Cor. i 9; x. 13: 2 Cor i 18 1 Thess. v 24: 2 Thess iii 3:—εὐσέβεια, εὐσεβῶς,.1 Tim. ii. 2, iii. 16; iv. 7, vi. 11. 2 Tim. iii. 5, 12· Tit. i. 1; ii 12,—of which we can only say that occurring as it does in this peculiar sense only here and in 2 Peter, we should be disposed to ascribe its use to the fact of the word having at the time become prevalent in the Church as a compendious term for the religion of Christians.—σώφρων and its derivatives, 1 Tim ii. 9, 15; iii 2· 2 Tim i 7 Tit i. 8, ii. 2, 4 ff, 12,—a term by no means strange to the Apostle's other writings, cf Rom xii 3: 2 Cor. v 13, but probably coming into more frequent use as the necessity for the quality itself became more and more apparent in the settlement of the Church (cf. also 1 Pet iv 7) —ὑγιής, ὑγιαίνειν, of right doctrine, 1 Tim. i 10; vi. 3: 2 Tim. i. 13; iv. 3. Tit i 9, 13, ii. 1 f, 8,—one of the most curious peculiarities of our Epistles, and only to be ascribed to the prevalence of the image in the writer's mind at the time, arising probably from the now apparent tendency of the growing heresies to corrupt the springs of moral action —μῦθοι, 1 Tim i 4; iv 7 2 Tim. iv. 4: Tit. i. 14,—to be accounted for by the fact of the heretical legends having now assumed such definite shape as to deserve this name, cf also 2 Pet. i.

[6] The actual verbal accordances are frequent, but even less striking than the general similarity

ver. 25. εὐαγγέλιόν μου. (Rom. ii. 16) 2 Tim. ii. 8 only.

κήρυγμα (1 Cor. i 21, ii 4, xv. 14): 2 Tim. iv. 17, Tit. i. 3 only.

χρόνοις αἰωνίοις. 2 Tim. i 9, Tit i. 2 only.

ver. 26 φανερωθέντος in this sense, St. Paul elsewhere, but also 1 Tim. iii. 16, 2 Tim. i 10, Tit i 3

κατ' ἐπιταγὴν . . . θεοῦ, (1 Cor. vii 6, 2 Cor. viii 8,) 1 Tim. i 1, Tit. i 3 only

μόνῳ σοφῷ θεῷ 1 Tim. i. 17, var. readd

I may add to these instances, those of accordance between the Pastoral Epistles and the speech of St. Paul in Acts xx. viz.

δρόμος, found only Acts xiii. 25, xx. 24, 2 Tim. iv 7.

περιποιεῖσθαι, Paul, only Acts xx. 28, 1 Tim. iii 13

ἱματισμός, Paul, only Acts xx. 33, 1 Tim. ii. 9

ἐπιθυμέω, with a gen, only Acts xx. 33, 1 Tim. iii. 1.

λόγοι τοῦ κυρίου, Acts xx 35, 1 Tim. vi. 3.

ἀντιλαμβάνεσθαι, Paul, only Acts xx. 35, 1 Tim vi 2.

for προσέχειν, with a dative, see next paragraph.

16 —ζητήσεις, 1 Tim. i 4, vi 4: 2 Tim. ii. 23: Tit iii. 9,—which expression, if not exactly applied to erroneous speculations, is yet used elsewhere of disputes about theological questions; cf. Acts xv 2; xxv. 20 (John iii 25); the difference of usage is easily accounted for by the circumstances:—ἐπιφάνεια, instead of παρουσία, 1 Tim vi 14 2 Tim iv. 1, 8 Tit. ii. 13,—which has a link uniting it to 2 Thess ii 8, and may have been, as indeed many others in this list, a word in familiar use among the Apostle and his companions, and so used in writing to them —δεσπότης, for κύριος, in the secular sense of *master*, 1 Tim. vi. 1, 2: 2 Tim ii 21 Tit ii. 9,—which is certainly remarkable, St. Paul's word being κύριος, Eph vi. 5, 9 Col. iii 22; iv 1,—and of which I know no explanation but this possible one, that the Eph and Col. being written simultaneously, and these three also near together, there would be no reason why he might not use one expression at one time and the other at another, seeing that the idea never occurs again in his writings.—ἀρνεῖσθαι, 1 Tim. v. 8: 2 Tim. ii. 12 f., iii 5: Tit. i. 16, ii 12,—common to our Epistles with 2 Pet, 1 John, and Jude, but never found in the other Pauline writings; and of which the only account that can be given is, that it must have been a word which came into use late as expressing apostasy, when the fact itself became usual, being taken from our Lord's own declarations, Matt x 33, &c —παραιτεῖσθαι, 1 Tim. iv. 7; v. 11· 2 Tim ii. 23: Tit. iii 10,—a word the links of whose usage are curious It is confined to St. Luke and St. Paul and the Epistle to the Hebrews. We have it thrice in the parable of the great supper, Luke xiv. 18, 19· then in the answer of Paul to Festus, in all probability made by himself in Greek, Acts xxv 11: and Heb. xii 19, 25 bis We may well say of it, that the *thing* introduced the word had the Apostle had occasion for it in other Epistles, he would have used it but he has not (the same may be said of γενεαλογίαι, 1 Tim i 4 Tit. iii 9;—ματαιόλογος, -γία, 1 Tim i. 6 Tit. i 10;—κενοφωνίαι, 1 Tim vi. 20. 2 Tim. ii. 16;—λογομαχίαι, -εῖν, 1 Tim vi 4: 2 Tim ii 14;—παραθήκη, 1 Tim vi 20: 2 Tim. i 12, 14):—σώτηρ, spoken of God,—1 Tim i. 1, ii 3, iv 10. Tit i 3; ii. 10, common also to Luke (i. 47) and Jude (25): the account of which seems to be, that it was a purely Jewish devotional expression, as we have it in the Magnificat,—and not thus absolutely used by the Apostles, in their special proclamation of the Son of God in this character;—we may observe that St Jude introduces it with the limitation διὰ Ἰησοῦ χρ τοῦ κυρίου ἡμῶν,—but in familiar writing one to another, when there was no danger of the mediatorship of Jesus being forgotten, this true and noble expression seems still to have been usual —βέβηλος, 1 Tim i 9, iv 7; vi. 20 2 Tim. ii. 16,—common only to Heb (xii. 16),—an epithet interesting, as bringing with it the fact of the progress of heresy from doctrine to practice, as also does ἀνόσιος, 1 Tim. i. 9;

2 Tim iii 2 —διαβεβαιοῦσθαι, 1 Tim. i. 7: Tit iii. 8, a word but slightly differing in meaning, and in its composition with διά (a natural addition in later times), from βεβαιοῦν, which is a common expression with our Apostle, Rom. xv. 8: 1 Cor i. 6, 8 2 Cor i 21: Col ii 7 (Heb. ii. 3, xiii. 9) —προσέχειν, with a dat, 1 Tim. i 4; iii. 8; iv. 1, 13: Tit. i. 14,—found also frequently in St Luke, Luke xii 1; xvii. 3, xxi 34. Acts v 35; viii. 6, 10, 11; xvi 14: xx. 28 (Paul), and Heb. ii. 1; vii. 13. 2 Pet i 19.—a word testifying perhaps to the influence on the Apostle's style of the expressions of one who was so constantly and faithfully his companion —ὑπομιμνήσκειν, 2 Tim. ii 14 Tit. iii 1 (2 Pet. i. 12: 3 John 10. Jude 5):—a word naturally coming into use rather as time drew on, than "in the beginning of the Gospel:" —ἀποτρέπεσθαι, ἐκτρ, 2 Tim iii. 5 1 Tim i 6; v. 15; vi 20 2 Tim. iv. 4 (Heb. xii 13),—words owing their use to the progress of heresy; which may be said also of ἀστοχεῖν, 1 Tim. i. 6, vi. 21 2 Tim. ii. 18,—and of τυφοῦσθαι, 1 Tim iii. 6; vi. 4 2 Tim iii. 4:—&c &c

35 There seems no reason why any of the above peculiarities of diction should be considered as imperilling the authenticity of our Epistles The preceding paragraph will have shewn, that of many of them, some account at least may be given: and when we reflect how very little we know of the circumstances under which they were used, it appears far more the part of sound criticism to let such difficulties stand unsolved, under a sense that we have not the clue to them, than at once and rashly to pronounce on them, as indicative of a spurious origin.

36 Another objection brought by De Wette against our Epistles seems to me to make so strikingly and decisively *for* them, that I cannot forbear giving it in his own words before commenting upon it: "In the composition of all three Epistles we have this common peculiarity,—that from that which belongs to the object of the Epistle, and is besides for the most part of general import, the writer is ever given to digress to general truths, or so-called common-places (1 Tim. i 15, ii 4—6; iii 16, iv 8—10 2 Tim. i 9 f, ii 11—13, 19—21, iii 12, 16: Tit ii. 11—14; iii 3—7), and that even that which is said by way of contradiction or enforcing attention, appears in this form (1 Tim. i. 8—10, iv. 4 f.; vi 6—10 2 Tim. ii. 4—6 Tit. i. 15) With this is combined another peculiarity common to them, that after such digressions or general instructions, the writer's practice is to recur, or finally to appeal to and fall back on previous exhortations or instructions given to his correspondent (1 Tim. iii 14 f.; iv. 6, 11; vi 2, 5 [rec.]: 2 Tim ii. 7, 14, iii. 5: Tit. ii. 15; iii. 8)" In commenting on this, I would ask, what could be more natural than both these phænomena, under the circumstances, supposing St Paul their author? Is it not the tendency of an instructor writing to his pupil to make these compendious references to truths well known and established between them? Would not

this especially be the case, as age drew on, and affectionate remembrance took the place of present and watchful instruction? We have hardly a stronger evidence for the authenticity of our Epistles, than our finding them so exactly corresponding with what we might expect from Paul the aged towards his own sons in the faith His restless energies are still at work. we see that the ἐνδυνάμωσις will keep him toiling to the end in his οἰκονομία. but those energies have changed their complexion they have passed from the dialectic character of his former Epistles, from the wonderful capacity of intricate combined ratiocination of his subsequent Epistles, to the urging, and repeating, and dilating upon truths which have been the food of his life there is a resting on former conclusions, a stating of great truths in concentrated and almost rhythmical antithesis, a constant citation of the '*temporis acti*,' which lets us into a most interesting phase of the character of the great Apostle We see here rather the succession of brilliant sparks, than the steady flame: burning words indeed and deep pathos, but not the flower of his firmness, as in his discipline of the Galatians, not the noon of his bright warm eloquence, as in the inimitable Psalm of Love (1 Cor. xiii.).

37. We may also notice, as I have pointed out in the notes on 1 Tim i 11 ff., a habit of going off, not only at a word, or into some collateral subject, as we find him doing in all his writings, but on the mention of any thing which reminds him of God's mercies to himself, or of his own sufferings on behalf of the Gospel, into a digression on his own history, or feelings, or hopes See 1 Tim. i 11 ff ; ii. 7: 2 Tim. i 11 ff, 15 ff ; ii. 9, 10, iii. 10 f., iv 6 ff. These digressions do not occur in the Epistle to Titus, perhaps on account of the less intimate relation which subsisted between him and the Apostle I cannot help considering them also as deeply interesting, betokening, as I have there expressed it in the note, advancing age, and that faster hold of individual habits of thought, and mannerisms, which characterizes the decline of life.

38 De Wette brings another objection against our Epistles, which seems to me just as easily to bear urging on the other side as the last. It is, the constant *moral* reference of all that is here said respecting the faith the idea that error is ever combined with evil conscience, the true faith with good conscience From what has been already said, it will be seen how naturally such a treatment of the subject sprung out of the progress of heresy into ethical corruption which we have traced through the later part of the apostolic age: how true all this was, and how necessary it was thus to mark broadly the line between that faith, which was the only guarantee for purity of life, and those perversions of it, which led downwards to destruction of the moral sense and of practical virtue.

39. When however in his same paragraph (Allgem. Bemerkungen üb. die Pastoralbriefe, p 117 c) he assumes that the writer gives a validity to *moral desert*, which stands almost in contradiction to the Pauline doctrines of grace, and cites 1 Tim. ii. 15; iii. 13; iv. 8, vi 18 ff: 2 Tim iv 8, to confirm this,—I own I am quite unable to see any inconsistency in these passages with the doctrine of grace as laid down, or assumed, in the other Epistles. See Rom ii 6—10: 1 Cor. iii. 14; ix. 17, 25; xv. 58. Phil. i. 19, and many other places, in which the foundation being already laid of union with Christ by faith, and salvation by His grace, the carrying on and building up of the man of God in good works, and reward according to the measure of the fruits of the Spirit, are quite as plainly insisted on as any where in these Epistles.

40 De Wette also finds what he calls, 'an *apology for the law*, and an admission of its possessing an ethical use,' in 1 Tim. i. 8. In my notes on that passage, I have seen reason to give it altogether a different bearing: but even admitting the fact, I do not see how it should be any more inconsistent with St. Paul's measure of the law, than that which he says of it in Rom vii And when he objects that the *universalism* of these Epistles (1 Tim. ii. 4, iv. 10; Tit ii. 11), although in itself Pauline, does not appear in the same polemical contrast, as e. g. in Rom. iii 29,—this seems very trifling in fault-finding nothing on the contrary can be more finely and delicately in accordance with his former maintenance against all impugners of God's universal purpose of salvation to all mankind, than that he should, even while writing to one who did not doubt of that great truth, be constant to his own habit of asserting it.

41. There are many considerations pressed by the opponents of the Pauline authorship, which we can only mention and pass by. Some of them will be found incidentally dealt with in the notes: with others the student, who has hitherto followed the course of these remarks, will know how himself to deal As usual, the similarities to, as well as discrepancies from, the other Epistles, are adduced as signs of spuriousness[7]. The three Epistles, and especially the first to Timothy, are charged with poverty of sentiment, with want of connexion, with unworthiness of the Apostle as author. On this point no champion of the Epistles could so effectually defeat the opponents, as they have defeated themselves. Schleiermacher, holding 1 Tim. to be compiled out of the other two, finds it in all these respects objectionable and below the mark: Baur will not concede this latter estimate, and De Wette charges Schleier-

[7] Huther gives a list of parallels against which this objection has been brought, and I transcribe it, that the reader may judge and refute for himself 1 Tim. i 12—14, as compared with 1 Cor. xv. 9, 10. 1 Tim. ii. 11, 12, with 1 Cor xiv 34, 35 2 Tim. i. 3—5, with Rom. i 8 ff.: ii. 5, with 1 Cor. ix. 24 ii 6, with 1 Cor ix 7 ff ii. 8, with Rom i. 3: ii. 11, with Rom vi 8 ii 20, with Rom ix. 21: iii. 2 ff., with Rom. i. 29 ff.: iv. 6, with Phil. ii. 17: Tit. i. 1—4, with Rom. i 1 ff.

macher with having failed to penetrate the sense of the writer, and found faults, where a more thorough exposition must pronounce a more favourable judgment. These differences may well serve to strike out the argument, and indeed all such purely subjective estimates, from the realms of biblical criticism.

42. A word should be said on the smaller, but not less striking indications of genuineness, which we here find. Such small, and even trifling individual notices, as we here meet with, can hardly have proceeded from a forger Of course a careful *falsarius* may have taken care to insert such, as would fall in with the known or supposed state of the Apostle himself and his companions at the time a shrewd and skilful one would invent such, as might further any views of his own, or of the Churches with which he was connected · but I must say I do not covet the judgment of that critic, who can ascribe such a notice as that of 2 Tim iv. 13, τὸν φελόνην ὃν ἀπέλιπον ἐν Τρωάδι παρὰ Κάρπῳ ἐρχόμενος φέρε, καὶ τὰ βιβλία, μάλιστα τὰς μεμβράνας, to either the caution or the skill of a forger What possible motive there could be for inserting such minute particulars, unexampled in the Apostle's other letters, founded on no incident in history, tending to no result,—might well baffle the acutest observer of the phænomena of falsification to declare

43. A concession by Baur himself should not be altogether passed over St Paul in his farewell discourse, Acts xx 29, 30, speaks thus · ἐγὼ οἶδα ὅτι εἰσελεύσονται μετὰ τὴν ἄφιξίν μου λύκοι βαρεῖς εἰς ὑμᾶς μὴ φειδόμενοι τοῦ ποιμνίου, καὶ ἐξ ὑμῶν αὐτῶν ἀναστήσονται ἄνδρες λαλοῦντες διεστραμμένα τοῦ ἀποσπᾶν τοὺς μαθητὰς ὀπίσω ἑαυτῶν Baur confesses that here the defenders of the Epistles have firm ground to stand on "Here we see," he continues, "the Apostle anticipating just what we find more in detail in the Pastoral Epistles" But then he proceeds to set aside the validity of the inference, by quietly disposing of the farewell discourse, as written "post eventum." For those who look on that discourse very differently, his concession has considerable value

44 I would state then the general result to which I have come from all these considerations.

1. External testimony in favour of the genuineness of our Epistles is so satisfactory, as to suggest no doubt on the point of their universal reception in the earliest times
2. The objections brought against the genuineness by its opponents, on internal grounds, are not adequate to set it aside, or even to raise a doubt on the subject in a fair-judging mind

45. I therefore rest in the profession of the Epistles themselves, and the universal belief of Christians, that they were VERITABLY WRITTEN BY ST PAUL[8]

[8] I have preferred in this section giving those considerations which influence most

SECTION II

TIME AND PLACE OF WRITING.

1 A difficult problem yet remains: to assign, during the life of the Apostle, a time for the writing, which will suit the phænomena of these Epistles.

2 It will have been abundantly seen by what has preceded, that I cannot consent to place them in any portion of St Paul's apostolic labours recorded in the Acts All the data with which they themselves furnish us, are against such a supposition. And most of all is the state of heresy and false teaching, as indicated by their common evidence No amount of ingenuity will suffice to persuade us, that there could have been during the long sojourn of the Apostle at Ephesus in Acts xix., such false teachers as those whose characters have been examined in the last section No amount of ingenuity again will enable us to conceive a state of the Church like that which these Epistles disclose to us, at any time of that period, extending from the year 54 to 63, during which the other Epistles were written Those who have attempted to place the Pastoral Epistles, or any of them, in that period, have been obliged to overlook all internal evidence, and satisfy themselves with fulfilling the requirements of external circumstances

3. It will also be seen, that I cannot consent to separate these Epistles widely from one another, so as to set one in the earlier, and the others in the later years of the Apostle's ministry. On every account, they must stand together Their style and diction, the motives which they furnish, the state of the Church and of heresy which they describe, are the same in all three and to one and the same period must we assign them.

4 This being so, they necessarily belong to the latest period of the Apostle's life. The concluding notices of the Second Epistle to Timotheus forbid us from giving an earlier date to that, and consequently to the rest. And no writer, as far as I know, has attempted to place that Epistle, supposing it St Paul's, at any date except the end of his life [9].

my own mind, to entering at full length on all the bearings of the subject The reader will find a very good and terse compendium of the objections and their answers in Conybeare and Howson, vol ii pp. 657—660, edn 2: and a full and elaborate discussion of both in Dr. Davidson's Introduction to the N. T vol iii pp 100—153 That portion of Dr Davidson's work is very well and thoroughly done, in which he shews the insuperable difficulties which beset the hypothesis of a scholar of St Paul having forged the Epistles at the end of the first century, as De Wette supposes. Huther's and Wiesinger's Einleitungen also contain full and able discussions of the whole question, especially the latter.

[9] De Wette has fallen into a curious blunder in carrying out his own hypothesis. He argues that 1 Tim. must have been written after 2 Tim, because we find Hyme-

5. The question then for us is, What was that latest period of his life? Is it to be placed at the end of the first Roman imprisonment, or are we to conceive of him as liberated from that, and resuming his apostolic labours?

6. Let us first try the former of these hypotheses. It has been adopted by chronologers of considerable note: lately, by Wieseler and Dr. Davidson. We approach it, laden as it is with the weight of (to us) the insuperable objection on internal grounds, stated above. We feel that no amount of chronological suitableness will induce us complacently to put these Epistles in the same age of the Church with those to the Ephesians, Colossians, and Philippians. But we would judge the hypothesis here on its own merely external grounds.

7. In order for it to stand, we must find some occasion, *previous to the imprisonment*, when St. Paul may have left Timotheus at Ephesus, himself proceeding to Macedonia. And this time must of course be subsequent to St. Paul's first visit to Ephesus, Acts xviii. 20, 21, when the Church there was founded, if indeed it can be said to have been then founded. On his departure then, he did not go into Macedonia, but to Jerusalem; which alone, independently of all other considerations, excludes that occasion [1].

8. His second visit to Ephesus was that long one related in Acts xix., the τριετία of Acts xx. 31, the ἔτη δύο of xix. 10, which latter, however, need not include the whole time. When he left Ephesus at the end of this time, after the tumult, ἐξῆλθε πορευθῆναι εἰς τὴν Μακεδονίαν, which seems at first sight to have a certain relation to πορευόμενος εἰς Μακεδονίαν of 1 Tim. i. 3. But on examination, this relation vanishes: for in Acts xix. 22, we read that, intending to go to Jerusalem by way of Macedonia and Achaia, he sent off from Ephesus, before his own departure, Timotheus and Erastus: so that he could not have left Timotheus behind in Ephesus. Again, in 1 Tim. iii. 14, he hopes to return to Ephesus shortly. But we find no trace of such an intention, and no attempt to put it in force, in the history. And besides, even if Timotheus, as has sometimes been thought from 1 Cor. xvi. 11, did return to Ephesus before the Apostle left it, and in this sense might have been left there on his departure, we must then suppose him to have almost immediately deserted the charge entrusted to him; for he is again, in the autumn of

næus, who is mentioned with reprobation, apparently for the first time, in 2 Tim. ii. 17 f.,—in a further stage of reprobation, judged and condemned, in 1 Tim. i. 20. He forgets that, the two Epistles being according to him forgeries, with no real circumstances whatever as their basis, such reasoning is good for nothing. He is in fact arguing from their genuineness to their spuriousness.

[1] This was however supposed by Calvin to have been the time of writing 1 Tim.: on ch. iii. 14,—"omnino enim sperabat se venturum: ut venisse probabile est, si hanc epistolam scripsit quo tempore Phrygiam peragrabat: sicuti refert Lucas Act. xviii. 23."

57, with St Paul in Macedonia in 2 Cor i. 1, and in Corinth in the winter (Rom. xvi. 21), and returned to Asia thence with him, Acts xx. 4: and thus, as Wieseler remarks, the whole scope of our Epistle, the ruling and ordering of the Ephesian Church during the Apostle's absence, would be defeated. Grotius suggested, and Bertholdt adopted, a theory that the Epistle might have been sent on St. Paul's return from Achaia to Asia, Acts xx. 4, and that Timotheus may, instead of remaining in Troas on that occasion, as related Acts xx 5, have gone direct to Ephesus, and there received the Epistle. But, apart from all other difficulties[2], how exceedingly improbable, that such an Epistle should have preceded only by a few weeks the farewell discourse of Acts xx 18—35, and that he should have sent for the elders to Miletus, though he himself had expressed, and continually alluded to in the Epistle, an intention of visiting Ephesus shortly!

9. These difficulties have led to a hypothesis that the journey from Ephesus is one unrecorded in the Acts, occurring during the long visit of Acts xix. That during that time a journey to Corinth did take place, we have inferred from the data furnished in the Epistles to the Corinthians: see Prolegg to Vol II. ch. iii § v During that journey, Timotheus may have been left there. This conjecture is at least worthy of full discussion: for it seems to fulfil most of the external requirements of the first Epistle.

10 Mosheim, who was its originator, held the journey to Greece to have taken place very early in the three years' visit to Ephesus, and to have lasted nine months,—thus accounting for the difference between the *two years and three months* of Acts xix 8, 10, and the *three years* of Acts xx. 31. Wieseler[3], however, has so far regarded the phænomena of the Epistle itself, as to shew that it would be very unlikely that the false teachers had early in that visit assumed such consistency and acquired such influence: and besides, we must assume, from the intimation in 1 Tim i 3 ff, that the false teachers had already gained some notoriety, and were busy in mischief, *before* the Apostle's departure

11 Schrader[4], the next upholder of the hypothesis, makes the Apostle remain in Ephesus up to Acts xix 21, and then undertake the journey there hinted at, through Macedonia to Corinth, thence to Crete (where he founded the Cretan Churches and left Titus), to Nicopolis in Cilicia (see below, in the Prolegg. to Titus: sending from thence the first Epistle to Timotheus and that to Titus), Antioch, and so through Galatia back to Ephesus. The great and fatal objection to this hypothesis is, the insertion in Acts xix 21—23 of so long a journey, lasting, according to

[2] See Wieseler, Chronologie, vol ii p 291 ff.
[3] Ib. p, 296 f.
[4] Der Apostel Paulus, vol. i. pp. 100 ff.

Schrader himself[5], two years (from Easter 54 to Easter 56), not only without any intimation from St Luke, but certainly against any reasonable view of his text, in which it is implied, that the intention of ver 21 was not then carried out, but afterwards, as related in ch. xx 1 ff

12. Wieseler himself has adopted, and supported with considerable ingenuity, a modified form of Schrader's hypothesis. After two years' teaching at Ephesus, the Apostle, he thinks, went, leaving Timotheus there, on a visitation tour to Macedonia, thence to Corinth, returning by Crete, where he left Titus, to Ephesus. During this journey, either in Macedonia or Achaia, he wrote 1 Tim,—and after his return to Ephesus, the Epistle to Titus: 2 Tim falling towards the end of his Roman imprisonment, with which, according to Wieseler, his life terminated. This same hypothesis Dr Davidson adopts, rejecting however the unrecorded visit to Corinth, which Wieseler inweaves into it: and placing the voyage to Crete during the same Ephesian visit, but separate from this to Macedonia

13. It may perhaps be thought that some form of this hypothesis would be unobjectionable, if we had *only the first Epistle to Timotheus* to deal with But even thus, it will not bear the test of thorough examination. In the first place, as held by Davidson, in its simplest form, it inserts into the Apostle's visit to Ephesus, a journey to Macedonia and back entirely for the sake of this Epistle[6] Wieseler's form of the hypothesis avoids, it is true, this gratuitous supposition, by connecting the journey with the unrecorded visit to Corinth: but is itself liable to these serious objections (mentioned by Huther, p. 17), that 1) it makes St Paul write the first Epistle to the Corinthians a very short time after the unrecorded visit to Corinth, which is on all accounts improbable. And this is necessary to his plan, in order to give time for the false teachers to have grown up at Ephesus —2) that we find the Apostle, in his farewell discourse, prophetically anticipating the arising of evil men and seducers among the Ephesians· whereas by any placing of this Epistle during the three years' visit, such must have already arisen, and drawn away many[7] 3) The whole character of the first Epistle shews that it belongs, not to a very brief and casual absence of this kind, but to one originally intended to last some time, and not unlikely to be prolonged beyond expectation. The hope of returning very soon (iii 14)

[5] See his Chronological Table at the end of his Apostel Paulus, vol i

[6] "Why the Apostle went into Macedonia from Ephesus, cannot be discovered." Davidson, vol. iii. p 13

[7] Dr Davidson (iii. p 14) refers for a refutation of this objection, to his subsequent remarks (pp. 32 f) on the state of the Ephesian Church But no sufficient refutation is there found Granting the whole account of the Ephesian Church there given, it would be quite impossible to conceive that subsequently the Apostle should have spoken of the λύκοι βαρεῖς as altogether future.

is faint: the provision made, is for a longer absence. Had the Apostle intended to return in a few weeks to Ephesus and resume the government of the Church there, we may safely say that the Epistle would have presented very different features. The hope expressed in ch iii 14, quite parenthetically, must not be set against the whole character of the Epistle[8], which any unbiassed reader will see provides for a lengthened superintendence on the part of Timothy as the more probable contingency.

14. Thus we see that, independently of graver objections, independently also of the connexion of the three Epistles, the hypothesis of Wieseler and Davidson does not suit the requirements of this first Epistle to Timotheus. When those other considerations come to be brought again into view,—the necessarily later age of all three Epistles, from the heresies of which they treat, from the Church development implied by them, from the very diction and form of thought apparent in them,—the impossibility, on any probable psychological view of St Paul's character, of placing writings, so altogether diverse from the Epistles to the Corinthians, in the same period of his life with them,—I am persuaded that very few students of Scripture will be found, whose mature view will approve any form of the above hypothesis.

15 It will not be necessary to enter on the various other sub-hypotheses which have been made such as that of Paulus, that the first Epistle was written from Cæsarea; &c &c. They will be found dealt with in Wieseler and Davidson, and in other introductions.

16. Further details must be sought in the following Prolegomena to each individual Epistle. I will mention however two decisive notices in 2 Tim, which no advocate of the above theory, or of any of its modifications, has been able to reconcile with his view. According to that view, the Epistle was written at the end of the first (and only) Roman imprisonment. In ch iv. 13, we have directions to Timotheus to bring a cloak and books which the Apostle left at Troas. In ib. ver. 20 we read "*Erastus remained in Corinth, but Trophimus left I in Miletus sick.*" To what these notices point, I shall consider further on: I would now only call the reader's attention to the following facts. Assuming as above, and allowing only the two years for the Roman imprisonment,—the last time he was at Troas and Miletus was *six years before* (Acts xx 6, 17), on that occasion *Timotheus was with him:* and he had repeatedly seen Timotheus since: and, what is insuperable, even supposing these difficulties overcome, *Trophimus did not remain there*, for he was at Jerusalem with St. Paul at the time of his apprehension, Acts xxi. 29. It will be easily seen by reference to any of the supporters of the one imprisonment, how this point presses them Dr Davidson tries to account for it by supposing Trophimus to have sailed with St Paul from Cæsarea in Acts xxvii., and to have been left at Myra, with the

[8] See Davidson, ib. vol. iii p 14.

understanding that he should go forward to Miletus, and that under this impression, the Apostle could say Trophimus I left at Miletus (ἀπέλιπον ἐν Μιλήτῳ) sick. Any thing lamer, or more self-refuting, can hardly be conceived: not to mention, that thus also some years had since elapsed, and that the above insuperable objection, that Timotheus had been with him since, and that Trophimus *the Ephesian* must have been talked of by them, remains in full force.

17. The whole force then of the above considerations, as well of the internal character of the Epistles, as of their external notices and requirements, compels us to look, for the time of their writing, to a period subsequent to the conclusion of the history in the Acts, and consequently, since we find in them the Apostle at liberty, ***subsequent to his liberation from the imprisonment with which that history concludes***. If there were no other reason for believing that he was thus liberated, and undertook further apostolic journeyings, the existence and phænomena of these Epistles would enforce such a conclusion upon us. I had myself, some years since, on a superficial view of the Pauline chronology, adopted and vindicated the one-imprisonment theory[9]: but the further study of these Epistles has altogether broken down my former fabric. We have in them, as I feel satisfied any student who undertakes the comparison will not fail to discover, a link uniting St. Paul's writings with the Second Epistle of Peter and with that of Jude, and the Epistles of St. John: in other words, with the later apostolic age. There are *two ways only* of solving the problem which they present: one of these is, by believing them to be spurious; the other, by ascribing them to a period of St. Paul's apostolic agency subsequent to his liberation from the Roman imprisonment of Acts xxviii. ult.

18. The whole discussion and literature of this view, of a liberation and second imprisonment of our Apostle, would exceed both the scope and the limits of these Prolegomena. It may suffice to remind the reader, that it is supported by an ancient tradition by no means to be lightly set aside: and to put before him the principal passages of early ecclesiastical writers in which that tradition is mentioned.

19. Eusebius, H. E. ii. 22, relates thus:

καὶ Λουκᾶς δὲ ὁ τὰς πράξεις τῶν ἀποστόλων γραφῇ παραδούς, ἐν τούτοις κατέλυσε τὴν ἱστορίαν, διετίαν ὅλην ἐπὶ τῆς Ῥώμης τὸν Παῦλον ἄνετον διατρίψαι, καὶ τὸν τοῦ θεοῦ λόγον ἀκωλύτως κηρύξαι ἐπισημηνάμενος. τότε μὲν οὖν ἀπολογησάμενον, αὖθις ἐπὶ τὴν τοῦ κηρύγματος διακονίαν λόγος ἔχει στείλασθαι τὸν ἀπόστολον, δεύτερον δ' ἐπιβάντα τῇ αὐτῇ πόλει, τῷ κατ' αὐτὸν τελειωθῆναι μαρτυρίῳ. ἐν ᾧ δεσμοῖς ἐχόμενος τὴν πρὸς Τιμόθεον δευτέραν ἐπιστολὴν συντάττει κ.τ.λ.

20. Clement of Rome, Ep. i. ad Corinth. c. 5, p. 17 ff (the lacunæ in the text are conjecturally filled in as in Hefele's edition):

[9] In pp. 5—7 of the Prælectio referred to above, ch. ii. § i. 11 note.

διὰ ζῆλον [καὶ ὁ] Παῦλος ὑπομονῆς βραβεῖον ὑ[πέσχ]εν, ἑπτάκις δεσμὰ φορέσας, φ[υγα]δευθείς, λιθασθείς. κῆρυξ γ[ενό]μενος ἔν τε τῇ ἀνατολῇ καὶ ἐν [τῇ] δύσει, τὸ γενναῖον τῆς πίστεως αὐτοῦ κλέος ἔλαβεν, δικαιοσύνην διδάξας ὅλῳ τῷ κόσμῳ, κα[ὶ ἐπὶ] τὸ τέρμα τῆς δύσεως ἐλθών, καὶ μαρτυρήσας ἐπὶ τῶν ἡγουμένων οὕτως ἀπηλλάγη τοῦ κόσμου, καὶ εἰς τὸν ἅγιον τόπον ἐπορεύθη, ὑπομονῆς γενόμενος μέγιστος ὑπογραμμός[1].

21. The fragment of Muratori on the canon contains the following passage[2]:

"Lucas optime Theophile comprehendit quia sub præsentia ejus singula gerebantur, sicuti et semote passionem Petri evidenter declarat, sed profectionem Pauli ab urbe ad Spaniam proficiscentis . ."

This passage is enigmatical, and far from easy to interpret But all that we need dwell on is, that *the journey of St Paul into Spain is taken as a fact;* and in all probability, the word 'omittit' being supplied, the writer means to say, that St. Luke in the Acts does not relate that journey.

22. This liberation and second imprisonment being assumed, it will naturally follow that the First Epistle to Timotheus and that to Titus were written during the interval between the two imprisonments;—the second to Timotheus during the second imprisonment. We shall now proceed to enquire into the probable assignment and date of each of the three Epistles.

23. The last notice which we possess of the first Roman imprisonment, is the Epistle to the Philippians There (i. 26) the Apostle evidently intends to come and see them, and (ii. 24) is confident that it will be before long The same anticipation occurred before in his Epistle to Philemon (ver. 22). We may safely then ascribe to him the intention, in case he should be liberated, of visiting the Asiatic and the Macedonian Churches.

24 We suppose him then, on his hearing and liberation, which cannot have taken place before the spring of A D. 63 (see chronological table in Prolegg. to Acts), to have journeyed Eastward · visiting perhaps Philippi, which lay on the great Egnatian road to the East, and passing into Asia There, in accordance with his former desires and intentions, he would give Colossæ, and Laodicea, and Hierapolis, the benefit of his apostolic counsel, and confirm the brethren in the faith And there perhaps, as before, he would fix his head-quarters at Ephesus I would not however lay much stress on this, considering that there might well

[1] By some of those who deny a second imprisonment, *τὸ τέρμα τῆς δύσεως* is interpreted as if the gen were one of apposition, '*his τέρμα, which was ἡ δύσις*,' by others it is rendered the *goal* or *centre* of the West: by others, the *Eastern* boundary of the West: and by all it is taken to mean *Rome*. By those who hold a second imprisonment, it is taken to mean *Spain* or even *Britain*.

[2] See Routh, Reliq Sacr. iv. p. 4.

have been a reason for his not spending much time there, considering the cause which had driven him thence before (Acts xix.) But that he did *visit* Ephesus, must on our present hypothesis be assumed as a certain fact, notwithstanding his confident anticipation expressed in Acts xx 25 that he should never see it again It was not the first time that such anticipations had been modified by the event [8].

25. It would be unprofitable further to assign, except by the most distant indications, his course during this journey, or his employment between this time and that of the writing of our present Epistles One important consideration, coming in aid of ancient testimony, may serve as our guide in the uncertainty. The contents of our Epistles absolutely require as late a date as possible to be assigned them. The same internal evidence forbids us from separating them by any considerable interval, either from one another, or from the event which furnished their occasion.

26 Now we have traditional evidence well worthy of note, that our Apostle suffered martyrdom in the last year, or the last but one, of Nero Euseb, Chron. anno 2083 (commencing October A D 67) says, "Neronis 13°. Nero ad cætera scelera persecutionem Christianorum primus adjunxit sub quo Petrus et Paulus apostoli martyrium Romæ consummaverunt."

And Jerome, Catalog. Scriptorum Ecclesiasticorum (c. 5, vol ii p 838), under Paulus, "Hic ergo, *decimo quarto* Neronis anno, eodem die quo Petrus, Romæ pro Christo capite truncatus, sepultusque est in via Ostiensi, anno post passionem Domini tricesimo septimo."

27. I should be disposed then to agree with Conybeare and Howson in postponing both the occasions and the writing of the Pastoral Epistles to very near this date. The interval may possibly have been filled up, agreeably to the promise of Rom xv 24, 28, and the tradition of Clement of Rome (quoted above, par 20), by a journey to Spain, the τέρμα τῆς δύσεως or it may have been spent in Greece and Asia and the interjacent islands

As we approach the confines of the known ground again furnished by our Epistles, we find our Apostle again at Ephesus. However the

[8] Compare 2 Cor. v 4, 5, with Phil i. 23. Dr. Davidson (iii pp. 16 ff.) lays great stress on the **οἶδα** of Acts xx 25, as implying certain apostolic foresight in the power of the Spirit, and argues thence that a subsequent visit to Ephesus cannot have taken place. For argument's sake, let it be so, and let us turn to Phil i. 25, written, according to Dr. Davidson, at the close of the Roman imprisonment, from which he was not liberated but by death. There we read, **οἶδα** ὅτι μενῶ καὶ παραμενῶ πᾶσιν ὑμῖν εἰς τὴν ὑμῶν προκοπὴν καὶ χαρὰν τῆς πίστεως, ἵνα τὸ καύχημα ὑμῶν περισσεύῃ ἐν χριστῷ Ἰησοῦ ἐν ἐμοὶ **διὰ τῆς ἐμῆς παρουσίας πάλιν πρὸς ὑμᾶς** Surely what is good on one side is good on the other and I do not see how Dr. Davidson can escape the force of his own argument. He must take his choice, and give up one **οἶδα** or the other. He has surrendered the latter · why may not we the former?

intervening years had been spent, much had happened which had wrought changes on the Church, and on himself, since his last visit Those heresies which were then in the bud, had borne bitter fruit. He had, in his own weak and shattered frame, borne about, for four or five more years of declining age, the dying of the Lord Jesus. Alienation from himself had been spreading wider among the Churches, and was embittering his life Supposing this to have been in A D. 66 or 67, and the 'young man Saul' to have been 34 or 35 at his conversion, he would not now be more than 64 or 65: but a premature old age would be every way consistent with what we know of his physical and mental constitution. Four years before this he had affectionately pleaded his advancing years in urging a request on his friend Philemon (Philem 9)

28 From Ephesus, leaving Timotheus there, he went into Macedonia (1 Tim. i. 3) It has been generally assumed, that the first Epistle was written from that country. It may have been so; but the words παρεκάλεσά σε προσμεῖναι ἐν Ἐφέσῳ πορευόμενος εἰς Μακεδονίαν, rather convey to my mind the impression that he was *not in Macedonia* as he was writing He seems to speak of the whole occurrence as one past by, and succeeded by other circumstances. If this impression be correct, it is quite impossible to assign with any certainty the place of its being written Wherever it was, he seems to have been in some field of labour where he was likely to be detained beyond his expectations (1 Tim iii. 14, 15): and this circumstance united with others to induce him to write a letter full of warning and exhortation and direction to his son in the faith, whom he had left to care for the Ephesian Church.

29. Agreeably with the necessity of bringing the three Epistles as near as may be together, we must here place a visit to Crete in company with Titus, whom he left there to complete the organization of the Cretan Churches. From the indications furnished by that Epistle, it is hardly probable that those Churches were now founded for the first time. We find in them the same development of heresy as at Ephesus, though not the same ecclesiastical organization (cf. Tit i 10, 11; 15, 16, iii 9, 11, with i. 5). Nor is the former circumstance at all unaccountable, even as combined with the latter. The heresy, being a noxious excrescence on Judaism, was flourishing independently of Christianity,—or at least required not a Christian Church for its place of sustenance When such Church began, it was at once infected by the error So that the Cretan Churches need not have been long in existence. From Tit i. 5, they seem to have sprung up σποράδην, and to have been on this occasion included by the Apostle in his tour of visitation: who seeing how much needed supplying and arranging, left Titus there for that purpose (see further in Prolegg to Titus, § ii.).

30 The Epistle to Titus, evidently written very soon after St. Paul left Crete, will most naturally be dated from Asia Minor. Its own

notices agree with this, for we find that he was on his way to winter at Nicopolis (ch. iii. 12), by which it is most natural to understand the well-known city of that name in Epirus[4]. And the notices of 2 Tim. equally well agree with such an hypothesis. for there we find that the Apostle had, since he last communicated with Timotheus, been at Miletus and at Troas, probably also at Corinth (2 Tim iv 13, 20) That he again visited Ephesus, is on every account likely indeed, the natural inference from 2 Tim i 18 is, that he had spent some time (possibly of weakness or sickness—from the expression ὅσα διηκόνησεν but this inference is not necessary, see note there) at that city in the companionship of Timotheus, to whom he appeals to confirm what he there says of Onesiphorus.

31 We may venture then to trace out this his last journey as having been from Crete by Miletus, Ephesus, Troas, to Corinth (?) · and thence (or perhaps direct by Philippi without passing up through Greece: or he may have gone to Corinth from Crete, and thence to Asia) to Nicopolis, where he had determined to winter (Tit. iii 12). Nicopolis was a Roman colony (Plin. iv. 1 or 2. Tacit Ann. v. 10), where he would be more sure against tumultuary violence, but at the same time more open to direct hostile action from parties plotting against him in the metropolis. The supposition of Mr. Conybeare (C. and H. ii. 573, edn. 2), that being known in Rome as the leader of the Christians, he would be likely, at any time after the fire in 64, to be arrested as implicated in causing it, is not at all improbable. In this case, as the crime was alleged to have been committed at Rome, he would be sent thither for trial (C. and H ib note) by the duumviri of Nicopolis.

32 Arrived at the metropolis, he is thrown into prison, and treated no longer as a person charged with matters of the Jewish law, but as a common criminal κακοπαθῶ μέχρι δεσμῶν ὡς κακοῦργος, 2 Tim ii. 9. All his Asiatic friends avoided him, except Onesiphorus, who sought him out, and was not ashamed of his chain (2 Tim. i. 16). Demas,

[4] See a complete account of Nicopolis in Wordsworth's Pictorial Greece, pp. 310—312; Conybeare and Howson, vol ii p 572, edn. 2, Smith's Dict. of Geography, sub voce.

It is very improbable that any of the comparatively insignificant places elsewhere called by this name is here intended An enumeration of them will be found in Smith's Dict of Geogr as above. The only two which require mention are, 1) Nicopolis in *Thrace*, on the Nessus (Νικόπολις ἡ περὶ Νέσσον, Ptol iii. 11, 13), supposed by Chrysostom and Theodoret (ἡ δὲ Ν. τῆς Θρᾴκης ἐστί, Chrys.: τῆς Θρᾴκης ἐστὶν ἡ Ν, τῇ δὲ Μακεδονίᾳ πελάζει, Thdrt.) to be here intended This certainly *may* have been, for this Nicopolis is not, as some have objected, the one founded by Trajan, see Schrader, vol. i. p. 117 but it is hardly likely to have been indicated by the word thus absolutely put: 2) Nicopolis in *Cilicia*, which Schrader holds to be the place, to suit his theory of the Apostle having been (at a totally different time, see above, par 11) on his way to Jerusalem.

I may mention that both Winer (RWB.) and Dr Smith (Dict of Geogr as above · not in Bibl Dict) fall into the mistake of saying that *St Paul dates the Epistle from Nicopolis* No such inference can fairly be drawn from ch. iii 12.

Crescens, and Titus had, for various reasons, left him Tychicus he had sent to Ephesus Of his usual companions, only the faithful Luke remained with him. Under these circumstances he writes to Timotheus a second Epistle, most likely to Ephesus (ii. 17, iv 13), and perhaps by Tychicus, earnestly begging him to come to him before winter (iv. 21) If this be the winter of the same year as that current in Tit iii 12, he must have been arrested immediately on, or perhaps even before, his arrival at Nicopolis And he writes from this his prison, expecting his execution (ἐγὼ γὰρ ἤδη σπένδομαι, καὶ ὁ καιρὸς τῆς ἐμῆς ἀναλύσεως ἐφέστηκεν, 2 Tim iv 6)

33 We hear, 2 Tim iv. 16, 17, of his being brought up before the authorities, and making his defence If in the last year of Nero, the Emperor was absent in Greece, and did not try him in person To this may perhaps point the μαρτυρήσας ἐπὶ τῶν ἡγουμένων of Clement of Rome (see above, par. 20) but it would be manifestly unwise to press an expression in so rhetorical a passage. At this his hearing, none of his friends was bold enough to appear with or for him: but his Christian boldness was sustained by Him in whom he trusted.

34 The second Epistle to Timotheus dates after this his first apology. How long after, we cannot say probably some little time, for the expression does not seem to allude to a *very recent* occurrence.

35. After this, all is obscurity. That he underwent execution by the sword, is the constant tradition of antiquity, and would agree with the fact of his Roman citizenship, which would exempt him from death by torture. We have seen reason (above, par. 26) to place his death in the last year of Nero, i e late in A D. 67, or A D 68 And we may well place the Second Epistle to Timotheus a few months at most before his death [5].

[5] One objection which is brought against the view taken above of the date of the Pastoral Epistles, is drawn from 1 Tim iv 12, μηδείς σου τῆς νεότητος καταφρονείτω. It is argued (recently by Dr. Davidson, vol. iii. p. 30 f.) that supposing Timotheus to have been twenty when the Apostle first took him for his companion,—at the date which we have assigned to the first Epistle, he would not be less than thirty-four or thirty-five when the Epistle was written, "an age," adds Dr Davidson, "at which it was not likely he should be despised for his youth." But surely such an age would be a very early one at which to be set over such a Church as that of Ephesus: and at such an age, an ecclesiastical officer whose duty was to rebuke elders, unless he comported himself with irreproachable modesty and gravity, would be exceedingly liable to be slighted and set aside for his youth The caution seems to me quite to stand in its place, and to furnish no valid objection whatever to our view.

CHAPTER VIII.

ON THE FIRST EPISTLE TO TIMOTHEUS.

THE AUTHORSHIP, and TIME AND PLACE OF WRITING, have been already discussed. and much has been said on the style and diction of this in common with the other Pastoral Epistles. It only remains to consider, 1. The person to whom the Epistle was written: 2. Its especial occasion and object.

SECTION I.

TO WHOM WRITTEN.

1 TIMOTHEUS is first mentioned Acts xvi 1 ff as dwelling either in Derbe or Lystra (ἐκεῖ, after both places have been mentioned), but probably in the latter (see on Acts xx 4, where Δερβαῖος cannot be applied to Timotheus): at St Paul's second visit to those parts (Acts ib. cf. xiv. 6 ff.). He was of a Jewish mother (Euniké, 2 Tim. i. 5) and a Gentile father (Acts xvi. 1, 3): and had probably been converted by the Apostle on his former visit, for he calls him his γνησίον τέκνον ἐν πίστει (1 Tim. i. 2). His mother, and his grandmother (Lois, 2 Tim. i. 5), were both Christians,—probably also converts, from having been pious Jewesses (2 Tim iii 14, 15), during that former visit

2 Though as yet young, Timotheus was well reported of by the brethren in Lystra and Iconium (Acts xvi. 2), and hence, forming as he did by his birth a link between Jews and Greeks, and thus especially fitted for the exigencies of the time (Acts ib. ver 4), St. Paul took him with him as a helper in the missionary work He first circumcised him (ib 3), to remove the obstacle to his access to the Jews.

3 The next time we hear of him is in Acts xvii 14 ff., where he with Silas remained behind in Berœa on occasion of the Apostle being sent away to Athens by sea. From this we infer that he had accompanied him in the progress through Macedonia His youth would furnish quite a sufficient reason why he should not be mentioned throughout the occurrences at Philippi and Thessalonica. That he had been at this latter place, is almost certain · for he was sent back by St Paul (from Berœa, see Prolegg to 1 Thess. § ii. 5 f) to ascertain the state of the Thessalonian Church (1 Thess. iii. 2), and we find him rejoining the Apostle, with Silas, at Corinth, having brought intelligence from Thessalonica (1 Thess. iii. 6).

4 He remained with the Apostle at Corinth, and his name, together with that of Silas (Silvanus), appears in the addresses of both the Epistles

to the Thessalonians, written (see Prolegg to 1 Thess. § iii) at Corinth. We have no express mention of him from this time till we find him "ministering" to St. Paul during the long stay at Ephesus (Acts xix. 22): but we may fairly presume that he travelled with him from Corinth to Ephesus (Acts xviii 18, 19), either remaining there with Priscilla and Aquila, or (which is hardly so probable) going with the Apostle to Jerusalem, and by Antioch through Galatia and Phrygia. From Ephesus (Acts xix 22) we find him sent forward with Erastus to Macedonia and Corinth (1 Cor. iv. 17; xvi 10: see on this whole visit, Vol. II Prolegg to 2 Cor. § ii 4) He was again with St. Paul in Macedonia when he wrote the Second Epistle to the Corinthians (2 Cor i. 1. Vol II Prolegg. ibid.). Again, in the winter following we find him in his company in Corinth, where he wrote the Epistle to the Romans (Rom. xvi. 21): and among the number of those who, on his return to Asia through Macedonia (Acts xx. 3, 4), went forward and waited for the Apostle and St. Luke at Troas.

5 The next notice of him occurs in three of the Epistles of the first Roman imprisonment He was with St Paul when he wrote to the Colossians (Col i 1), to Philemon (Philem 1), and to the Philippians (Phil. i 1) How he came to Rome, whether with the Apostle or after him, we cannot say. If the former, we can only account for no mention of him being made in the narrative of the voyage (Acts xxvii, xxviii) by remembering similar omissions elsewhere when we know him to have been in company, and supposing that his companionship was almost a matter of course.

6 From this time we know no more, till we come to the Pastoral Epistles[1] There we find him left by the Apostle at Ephesus to take care of the Church during his absence: and the last notice which we have in 2 Tim makes it probable that he would set out (in the autumn of A.D. 67?), shortly after receiving the Epistle, to visit St. Paul at Rome.

7. Henceforward, we are dependent on tradition for further notices In Eus. H. E. iii. 42, we read Τιμόθεός γε μὴν τῆς ἐν Ἐφέσῳ παροικίας ἱστορεῖται πρῶτος τὴν ἐπισκοπὴν εἰληχέναι. an idea which may well have originated with the Pastoral Epistles, and seems inconsistent with the very general tradition, hardly to be set aside (see Prolegg Vol I ch. v. § i. 9 ff.), of the residence and death of St John in that city. Nicephorus (H. E. iii. 11) and the ancient martyrologies make him die by martyrdom under Domitian See Winer, sub voce: Butler's Lives of the Saints, Jan 24.

8. We learn that he was set apart for the ministry in a solemn manner by St Paul, with laying on of his own hands and those of the presbytery (1 Tim iv 14; 2 Tim i 6), in accordance with prophetic utterances of the Spirit (1 Tim. ib and i 18): but at what time this

[1] On the notice of him in Heb. xiii 23, see Proleg. to Vol IV. ch. i. § i 160; ii. 34.

took place, we are not informed: whether early in his course, or in Ephesus itself, as a consecration for his particular office there. This latter seems to me far the more probable view.

9. The character of Timotheus appears to have been earnest and self-denying. We may infer this from his leaving his home to accompany the Apostle, and submitting to the rite of circumcision at his hands (Acts xvi. 1 ff.),—and from the notice in 1 Tim. v. 23, that he usually drank only water. At the same time it is impossible not to perceive in the notices of him, signs of backwardness and timidity in dealing with the difficulties of his ministerial work. In 1 Cor. xvi. 10 f., the Corinthians are charged, *ἐὰν δὲ ἔλθῃ Τιμόθεος, βλέπετε ἵνα ἀφόβως γένηται πρὸς ὑμᾶς· τὸ γὰρ ἔργον κυρίου ἐργάζεται ὡς κἀγώ· μήτις οὖν αὐτὸν ἐξουθενήσῃ, προπέμψατε δὲ αὐτὸν ἐν εἰρήνῃ.* And in the notes to the two Epistles the student will find several cases, in which the same traits seem to be referred to[2]. They appear to have increased, in the second Epistle[3], where the Apostle speaks earnestly, and even severely, on the necessity of Christian boldness in dealing with the difficulties and the errors of the day.

10. I subjoin a chronological table of the above notices in the course of Timotheus, arranging them according to that already given in the Prolegg. to Acts, and to the positions taken in the preceding chapter:

A.D.	
45.	Converted by St. Paul, during the first missionary journey, at Lystra.
51. Autumn.	Taken to be St. Paul's companion and circumcised (Acts xvi. 1 ff.).
	Sent from Berœa to Thessalonica (Acts xvii. 14; 1 Thess. iii. 2).
52.	With Silas, joins St. Paul at Corinth (Acts xviii. 5; 1 Thess. iii. 6).
Winter, see above, ch. v. § iii.	With St. Paul (1 Thess. i. 1; 2 Thess. i. 1).
57. Spring.	With St. Paul at Ephesus (Acts xix. 22): sent thence into Macedonia and to Corinth (Acts ib.; 1 Cor. iv. 17, xvi. 10).
Winter.	With St. Paul (2 Cor. i. 1).
58, beginning.	With St. Paul (Rom. xvi. 21).
Spring.	Journeying with St. Paul from Corinth to Asia (Acts xx. 4).
62 or 63.	With St. Paul in Rome (Col. i. 1; Philem. 1; Phil. i. 1).
63—66.	Uncertain.
66 or 67.	Left by St. Paul in charge of the Church at Ephesus. (**First Epistle.**)
67 or 68.	(**Second Epistle.**) Sets out to join St. Paul at Rome.
Afterwards.	Uncertain.

[2] See notes on 1 Tim. v. 23; 2 Tim. i. 5, 7; iii. 10; and cf. besides 1 Tim. iv. 12.

[3] It is possible that there may have been a connexion between these indications and the tone of the message in Rev. ii. 1—6: see note there.

SECTION II.

OCCASION AND OBJECT.

1 The Epistle declares its own occasion The Apostle had left the Ephesian Church in charge to Timotheus and though he hoped soon to return, was apprehensive that he might be detained longer than he expected (1 Tim. iii 14, 15) He therefore despatched to him these written instructions

2 The main object must be described as personal · to encourage and inform Timotheus in his superintendence at Ephesus But this information and precept regarded two very different branches of his ecclesiastical duty

3 The first was, the making head against and keeping down the growing heresies of the day These are continually referred to. again and again the Apostle recurs to their mention. they evidently dwelt much on his mind, and caused him, in reference to Timotheus, the most lively anxiety. On their nature and characteristics I have treated in the preceding chapter.

4. The other object was, the giving directions respecting the government of the Church itself. as regarded the appointing to sacred offices, the selection of widows to receive the charity of the Church, and do service for it,—and the punishment of offenders.

5. For a compendium of the Epistle, and other details connected with it, see Davidson, vol. iii.

CHAPTER IX.

THE SECOND EPISTLE TO TIMOTHEUS.

SECTION I.

TO WHAT PLACE WRITTEN.

1. It has been very generally supposed, that this Epistle was written to Timotheus while the latter was still at Ephesus

2. The notices contained in it seem partially to uphold the idea In ch i. 16—18, Onesiphorus is mentioned as having sought out the Apostle

at Rome, and also having ministered to him at Ephesus: and in ch iv. 19, the household of Onesiphorus is saluted. Such a notice, it is true, *decides* nothing: but comes in aid of the supposition that St Paul was writing to Ephesus. Our impression certainly is, from ch. i. 18, that Onesiphorus resided, when living, at Ephesus.

3. Again, in ch. ii 17, we find Hymenæus stigmatized as a teacher of error, who can hardly be other than the Hymenæus of 1 Tim. i. 20 (see notes there) Joined with this latter in 1 Tim. appears an Alexander. and we again have an Alexander ὁ χαλκεύς mentioned as having done the Apostle much mischief in our ch. iv. 14: and there *may be* a further coincidence in the fact that an Alexander is mentioned as being put forward by the Jews during the tumult at Ephesus, Acts xix 33[1]

4. Besides, the whole circumstances, and especially the character of the false teachers, exactly agree It would be very difficult to point out any features of difference, such as change of place would be almost sure to bring out, between the heretical persons spoken of here, and those in the first Epistle

5. The *local* notices come in aid, but not with much force Timotheus is instructed to bring with him matters which the Apostle had left at *Troas* (ch iv 13), which he would pass in his journey from Ephesus to Rome. Two other passages (ch iv. 12, 20) present a difficulty and Michaelis, who opposes this view, urges them strongly. St. Paul writes, Τυχικὸν δὲ ἀπέστειλα εἰς Ἔφεσον. This could hardly have been so written, as a simple announcement of a fact, if the person to whom he was writing was himself in that city. This was also felt by Theodoret,—δῆλον ἐντεῦθεν ὡς οὐκ ἐν Ἐφέσῳ διῆγεν ἀλλ' ἑτέρωθί που κατὰ τουτονὶ τὸν καιρὸν ὁ μακάριος Τιμόθεος. The only answer that I can give, may be derived from the form and arrangement of the sentence. Several had been mentioned, who had left him of their own accord: then, with δέ, introducing a contrast, he states that *he had sent* Tychicus to Ephesus. If any stress is meant to be laid on this circumstance, the notice might still consist with Timotheus himself being there: "but do not wonder at Tychicus being at Ephesus, for I sent him thither" This however is not satisfactory: nor again is it, to suppose with Dr Davidson (iii. 63) that for some reason Tychicus would not arrive in Ephesus so soon as the Epistle He also writes, Τρόφιμον δὲ ἀπέλιπον ἐν Μιλήτῳ ἀσθενοῦντα. This would be a strange thing to write from Rome to Timotheus in Ephesus, within a few miles of Miletus itself, and respecting Trophimus, who was an Ephesian (Acts xxi. 29). It certainly may be said that there might be reasons why the notice should be sent. It might

[1] See note there The latter hypothesis mentioned in it, that he was put forward to clear the Jews, is at least possible. and then he might well have been an enemy of the Apostle.

be intended to clear Trophimus from the charge which appears to be laid against Erastus, that he had remained behind of his own accord in his native land. With the Apostle's delicate feeling for all who were connected with him, he might well state this (again with a δέ) respecting Trophimus, though the fact of his remaining at Miletus might be well known to Timotheus, and his own profession of sickness as the reason.

6 There is a very slight hint indeed given in ch. iv. 11, which may point the same way. Timotheus was to take up Mark and bring him to Rome. The last notice we have had of Mark, was a recommendation of him to the Colossian Church (Col iv 10), and that in a strain, which *may* import that he was to be a resident labourer in the Gospel among them. If Mark was at Colossæ, he might be easily sent for from Ephesus to accompany Timotheus.

SECTION II.

OCCASION AND OBJECT.

1. It only remains to enquire respecting this Epistle, what special circumstances occasioned it, and what objects are discernible in it

2 The immediately moving occasion seems to have been one personal to the Apostle himself. He was anxious that Timotheus should come to him at Rome, bringing with him Mark, as soon as possible (ch i 4; iv 9, 11, 21).

3. But he was uncertain how it might be with himself: whether he should live to see his son in the faith, or be 'offered up' before his arrival. He sends to him therefore, not merely a message to come, but a letter full of fatherly exhortations and instructions, applicable to his present circumstances. And these seem not to have been unneeded. Many of his former friends had forsaken him (ch. i 15; iv 10), and the courage and perseverance of Timotheus himself appeared to be giving way (see above, Prolegg to 1 Tim § i 9) The letter therefore is calculated in some measure to supply what his own mouth would, if he were permitted to speak to him face to face, still more fervently urge on him. And thus we possess an Epistle calculated for all ages of the Church: in which while the maxims cited and encouragements given apply to all Christians, and especially ministers of Christ in their duties and difficulties,—the affecting circumstances, in which the writer himself is placed, carry home to every heart his earnest and impassioned eloquence.

4 For further notices, I again refer to Dr. Davidson, vol. iii. pp 48—75.

EXCURSUS ON PUDENS AND CLAUDIA

1. In 2 Tim iv 21, we read as follows:

ἀσπάζεταί σε Εὔβουλος καὶ Πούδης καὶ Λῖνος καὶ Κλαυδία καὶ οἱ ἀδελφοὶ πάντες.

2. Martial, lib. iv. Epigr. 13, is inscribed 'ad Rufum, de nuptiis Pudentis et Claudiæ peregrinæ' and the first lines run thus.

> "Claudia, Rufe, meo nubit peregrina Pudenti·
> Macte esto tædis, o Hymenæe, tuis."

3. An inscription was found at Chichester in the early part of the last century, and is now in a summer-house in the gardens at Goodwood, running thus, the lacunæ being conjecturally filled in.—

> [N]eptuni et Minervæ templum
> [pr]o salute d[omu]s divinæ
> [ex] auctoritat[e Tib.] Claud
> [Co]gidubni r leg aug in Brit.
> [colle]gium fabror et qui in eo
> [a sacris] sunt d. s. d. donante aream
> [Pud]ente Pudentini fil.

4. Now in Tacitus, Agricol. 14, we read, "quædam civitates (in Britain) Cogidubno regi donatæ (is ad nostram usque memoriam fidissimus mansit) vetere ac jampridem recepta populi R consuetudine, ut haberet instrumenta servitutis et reges" From this inscription these 'civitates' appear to have constituted the kingdom of Sussex. We also gather from the inscription that Cogidubnus had taken the name of his imperial patron, [Tiberius] Claudius and we find him in close connexion with a Pudens

5. It was quite natural that this discovery should open afresh a point which the conjectures of British antiquarians appeared before to have provisionally closed It had been imagined that Claudia, who was identified with the Claudia Rufina of Martial, xi. 53 ('Claudia cæruleis quum sit Rufina Britannis Edita, quam Latiæ pectora plebis habet!'), was a native of *Colchester*, and a daughter of Caractacus, whom they supposed to have been admitted into the Claudian gens.

6. A new fabric of conjecture has been now raised, more ingenious and more probable[2]. The Pudens of Martial is (i 32) a centurion, aspiring to the "meriti præmia pili," i. e. to be made a primipilus· which ambition we find accomplished in lib. v. 48. and his return to Rome from the North to receive the honour of equestrian rank is anticipated in lib vi. 58 He may at some time have been stationed in Britain—possibly attached in capacity of adjutant to King Cogidubnus. His presentation of an area for a temple to Neptune and Minerva may have been occasioned by escape from shipwreck, the college of carpenters (shipbuilders) being commissioned to build it to their patrons, Neptune and Minerva, or, as Archdn Williams (p 24) seems to think, by a desire to introduce Roman arts among the subjects of the client king. If the British maiden Claudia was a daughter of King Tiberius Claudius Cogidubnus, there would be no great wonder in her thus being found mentioned with Pudens

7. But conjecture is led on a step further by the other notices referred to above. Claudia is called *Rufina*. Now Pomponia, the wife of the late commander in Britain,

---

[2] In Archdeacon Williams's pamphlet on Pudens and Claudia I have also consulted an article in the Quarterly Review for July, 1855, entitled "the Romans at Colchester," in which Archdeacon Williams's view is noticed.

Aulus Plautius, belonged to a house of which the Rufi were one of the chief branches If she were a Rufa, and Claudia were her protégée at Rome (as would be very natural, seeing that her father was received into alliance under Aulus Plautius), the latter would naturally add to her very undistinguishing appellation of Claudia the cognomen of Rufina. Nor is the hypothesis of such a connexion purely arbitrary A very powerful link appears to unite the two ladies—viz. that of Christianity Pomponia, we learn from Tacitus (Ann xii 32), was (in the year 57) 'superstitionis externæ rea,' and being 'mariti judicio permissa,' was by him tried, 'prisco instituto, propinquis coram,' and pronounced innocent. Tacitus adds, that after many family sorrows, 'per XL annos non cultu nisi lugubri, non animo nisi mæsto, egit. Idque illi imperitante Claudio, impune, mox ad gloriam vertit.' Now it is not at all an improbable explanation of this, that Pomponia may have been a Christian. and the remarkable notice with which our citation from Tacitus concludes may point to the retirement of a Christian life, for which the garb of sorrow would furnish an excuse and protection [3].

8. If then such a connexion as this subsisted, it would account for the conversion of the British maiden to Christianity and the coincidences are too striking to allow us to pass over the junction of Pudens with her in this salutation They apparently were not married at this time, or the Apostle would hardly have inserted a third name, that of Linus, between theirs And this is what we might expect: for the last year of Nero, which is the date we have assigned to the Epistle, is the earliest that can be assigned to any of Martial's pieces, being the year in which he came to Rome.

9. Two of the Epigrams of Martial, i 32 and v. 48, mention facts which involve Pudens in the revolting moral licence of his day. But there is no reason for supposing them to refer to dates subsequent to his conversion and marriage. Martial's Epigrams are by no means in chronological order, and we cannot gather any indications of this fact with certainty from them.

10. Again, a difficulty has been found in the heathen invocation in the marriage epigram. But, as remarked in the article referred to in the note, we have no allusion to Christian marriage rites during the first three or four centuries, and it is not at all improbable that the heathen rites of the *confarreatio* may, at this early period at least, have been sought by Christians to legalize their unions. When we do find a Christian ceremonial, it is full of the symbolism of the confarreatio And it seems to be shewn that this was so in the case before us, by the epithet of *sancto*, (in the line 'Di bene, quod sancto peperit fecunda marito,' Mart. xi 53,) implying that all rites had been duly observed [4]

11. If the above conjectural but not purely arbitrary fabric of hypothesis is allowed to stand, we have the satisfaction of knowing that Claudia was a woman not only of high character, but of mental acquirement ('Romanam credere matres Italides possint, Atthides esse suam,' Mart ib), and the mother of a family of three sons, and possibly daughters as well (Mart ib).

---

[3] Archdeacon Williams (p. 38) fancies he sees in this *cultus lugubris* and *animus mæstus* signs that she gave way in the trial, and thus saved herself, and that the same circumstance may account for so noble a lady not being mentioned by St. Paul.

[4] This '*sancto*' Archdeacon Williams thinks represents ἁγίῳ, and implies the Christianity of Pudens. Surely this is very improbable

CHAPTER X.

THE EPISTLE TO TITUS.

SECTION I.

TO WHOM WRITTEN.

1. THE time and place of writing this Epistle have been before discussed (see above, ch. vii § ii. 29 f.). It appears to have been sent from Ephesus, or perhaps from Macedonia, during the last year of the Apostle's life (A D. 67), to Titus, who was left in charge with the Churches in the island of Crete. We shall now gather up the notices which remain to us respecting Titus himself.

2. It is by no means easy to construct an account of Titus. At first sight, a strange phænomenon presents itself. The narrative in the Acts never once mentions him. And this is the more remarkable, because of all the companions of St Paul he seems to have been the most valued and trusted. No adequate reason has ever been given for this omission. There must be some, it is thought, which we cannot penetrate Was he identical with some one or other of St Paul's companions, known to us in the Acts under another name? None seems to satisfy the conditions Or are we to regard the notice in 2 Tim iv. 10 as indicative of his ultimate desertion of the Apostle, and thus to seek for a solution of the problem? But even with such a supposition, we shall not touch the narrative of the Acts, which we believe to have been published some years previous to the writing of that Epistle. So that we must be content to leave the problem unsolved, and to put together the few notices which we possess, as given of a person distinct from any mentioned in the Acts.

3 The first notice of Titus, in respect of time, occurs in Gal ii. 1, 3 We there learn that he was of Gentile origin, and that he was taken by Paul and Barnabas to the council of the Apostles and elders which was convened at Jerusalem to consider of the question of the obligation of the Mosaic law. The narrative in the Acts speaks merely of τινὲς ἄλλοι being sent with the two Apostles. But we see clearly the reason why Titus should be marked out in Gal ii for separate mention He was an uncircumcised Gentile, and the independence of action of St Paul is shewn by his refusing to listen for a moment to the proposal, which appears to have been urged, for his circumcision In the Acts, no such reason for special mention of him existed And this considera-

tion will shew, that we are perhaps not justified in assuming from this incident that Titus held any position of high confidence or trust *at this time.* We find him in close companionship with the Apostles, but that is all we can say. He was certainly converted by means of St Paul himself, from the γνησίῳ τέκνῳ of Tit i 4.

4. Our next notice of him is found in 2 Cor., where it appears (ch. xii 18) that he, with two other brethren, whose names are not mentioned, was sent forward by St Paul from Ephesus, during his long visit there, to Corinth, to set on foot a collection (ch viii. 6) for the poor saints at Jerusalem, and also to ascertain the effect of the first Epistle on the Corinthians St Paul, on his departure from Ephesus, waited at Troas, where great opportunities of usefulness were opening before him (ch ii. 12). but so anxious was he for the return of Titus (Τίτον τὸν ἀδελφόν μου), that he "left them and passed into Macedonia" (ib. 13) There he met with Titus, who brought him a satisfactory account of the effect of the first Epistle (ch vii 6—15). and from that which St. Paul there says of him, his effective zeal and earnestness in the work of the Gospel is sufficiently shewn. Further proof of these is given in his undertaking of his own accord the delicate task of completing the collection (ch. viii 6, 16, 17 ff) and proof also of the Apostle's confidence in him, in the terms in which he commends him to the Corinthians. He calls him his own κοινωνός (ch. viii. 23): appeals to his integrity, and entire unity of action with himself (ch xii. 18)

5 From this time (A D 57 see Vol II. Prolegg. to 2 Cor. § ii 3), to the notices furnished by our Epistle (A D. 67), we know nothing of Titus At this latter date we find him left in Crete by St Paul, obviously for a temporary purpose viz to "carry forward the correction of those things which are defective" (ch i. 5), and among these principally, to establish presbyteries for the government of the various Churches, consisting of ἐπίσκοποι (ib ver 7). His stay there was to be very short (ch iii 12), and he was, on the arrival of Tychicus or Artemas, to join the Apostle at Nicopolis. Not the slightest trace is found in the Epistle, of any intention on the part of St Paul to place Titus permanently over the Cretan Churches indeed, such a view is inconsistent with the date furnished us in it.

6. Titus appears to have accordingly rejoined the Apostle, and afterwards to have left him for Dalmatia (2 Tim iv. 10). Whether from this notice we are to infer that he had been with him in Rome, is quite uncertain. It would seem more probable that he had gone from Nicopolis, or at all events from some point on the journey We can hardly, on mature consideration of the expressions in 2 Tim iv 10, entirely get rid of the impression, that Titus had left the Apostle of his own accord. There is, as has been above observed, an apparent contrast intended between those who are classed with Demas,—they being even included

under his ἐπορεύθη, without another verb expressed—and Tychicus, who had been sent on a mission by the Apostle Still, it would be unfair to lay any stress on this, in a matter so well admitting of charitable doubt: and we may be well permitted, with Mr. Conybeare, to "hope that his journey to the neighbouring Dalmatia was undertaken by desire of St. Paul"

7. The traditionary notices of the after life of Titus are too evidently grounded on a misunderstanding of our Epistle, to be worth much. Eus H E. iii 4, says, Τιμόθεός γε μὴν τῆς ἐν Ἐφέσῳ παροικίας ἱστορεῖται πρῶτος τὴν ἐπισκοπὴν εἰληχέναι (see on this above, Prolegg to 1 Tim. § i. 7), ὡς καὶ Τίτος τῶν ἐπὶ Κρήτης ἐκκλησιῶν. And so Theodoret assumes, on 1 Tim iii 1.

8. Butler informs us (Lives of the Saints, Jan 4) that Titus is honoured in Dalmatia as its principal Apostle· that he again returned from Dalmatia to Crete, and finished a laborious and holy life by a happy death in Crete, in a very advanced old age, some say in his 94th year that he is looked on in Crete as the first archbishop of Gortyna, which metropolitical see is now fixed at Candia, the new capital, built by the Saracens after the destruction of Gortyna But all this fabric too manifestly bears the appearance of having been raised on the above misapprehension, to possess any traditional worth.

SECTION II

THE CHURCHES OF CRETE.

1 When, and by whom, these Churches were founded, is quite uncertain. Crete abounded with Jews of wealth and influence We find proof of this in Jos. Antt. xvii. 12 1, Κρήτῃ προσενεχθεὶς (the Pseudo-Alexander) Ἰουδαίων ὁπόσοις εἰς ὁμιλίαν ἀφίκετο, ἐπήγαγεν εἰς πίστιν, καὶ χρημάτων εὐπορηθεὶς δόσει τῇ ἐκείνων ἐπὶ Μήλου διῇρεν· and again B J. ii 7. 1, τοὺς ἐν Κρήτῃ Ἰουδαίους ἐξαπατήσας καὶ λαμπρῶς ἐφοδιασθείς, διέπλευσεν εἰς Μῆλον: Philo, leg. ad Caium, § 36, vol ii. p. 587,—οὐ μόνον αἱ ἤπειροι μεσταὶ τῶν Ἰουδαϊκῶν ἀποικιῶν εἰσιν, ἀλλὰ καὶ νήσων αἱ δοκιμώταται Εὔβοια, Κύπρος, Κρήτη In Acts ii 11 Cretans are named among those who heard the utterance of the Spirit on the day of Pentecost It is probable therefore, that these Churches owed their origin to the return of individuals from contact with the preaching of the Gospel, and had therefore as yet been unvisited by an Apostle, when they first come before us towards the end of St Paul's ministry.

2. It is plain that no certain evidence can be deduced, as to the existence of these Churches, from no mention being made of them when St Paul passed by Crete on his voyage to Malta in Acts xxvii. We have no reason to suppose that he was at liberty to go where he pleased

while remaining in port, nor can we reason, from the analogy of Julius's permission at Sidon, that similar leave would be given him where perhaps no personal relation subsisted between him and the inhabitants. Besides which, the ship was detained by a contrary wind, and probably expecting, during a good part of the time, to sail every day.

3. The next point requiring our attention is, the state of those Churches at the date of our Epistle. If it appear, on comparison, that the false teachers in them were more exclusively Jewish than those at Ephesus, it must be remembered, that this would be a natural consequence, the origin of the Churches being that which we have supposed. And in that case the Apostle's visit, acting as a critical test, would separate out and bring into hostility this Judaistic element, and thus lead to the state of things which we find in this Epistle.

4. Various objections are brought by De Wette against the Epistle, as not corresponding with the facts, in its assumptions and expressions. The first of them, that "it professes to have been written shortly after the founding of the Churches, but sets forth a ripeness and abundance of heretical teaching quite inconsistent with such recent foundation," falls to the ground on our hypothesis of their origin. They were old in actual date of existence, but quite in their infancy of arrangement and formal constitution.

5. With our hypothesis also falls his second objection: viz. that "the great recent success of the Apostle there makes the severity of his characterization of the inhabitants, and that upon another's testimony (ch. i. 12), quite inexplicable. We should rather have looked for thankful recognition, as in other Epistles." But, supposing Christianity to have grown up there in combination with the national vices, and a thorough work of purification to be wanted, then we need not be surprised at the Apostle reminding Titus of the character of those with whom he had to deal, appealing to the testimony of their own writers to confirm the fact.

6. His *third* objection, that "the heretical teachers must have grown up under the eyes of Titus since the Apostle's absence, and thus must have been better known to him than to St. Paul, whereas here we have St. Paul informing him about them,"—is grounded on pure assumption, arising from mistake. The false teachers had been there throughout, and, as we have said, had been awaked into activity by the Apostle's presence and teaching. He knew, from long and bitter experience, far more of them than Titus could do: and his notices and warnings are founded on this longer experience and more thorough apostolic insight.

7. His *fourth*, that "in relation to the moral and ecclesiastical state of the Cretan Christians, as disclosed in the Epistle, a duration of the Gospel among them of some length must be assumed,—from the stress laid on previous purity of character in those to be chosen to church-

offices,"—also falls to the ground on our hypothesis of the origin and previous duration of the Churches.

8. The *fifth* is,—that "it is most unnatural and startling to find not one reference to what the Apostle had taught and preached in Crete, when in 1 Thess., an Epistle written under similar circumstances, we find so many." But we entirely deny the parallelism. The Thessalonian Church had been founded by himself, he was torn away from it in the midst of his teaching every reason existed for constantly recalling what he had said to them, either to enforce it, or to guard it from misunderstanding Such was not the case here. He was writing of a Church which he had not himself founded. whose whole situation was different and writing not to the Church itself, but to one whom he had commissioned to set it in order, and who knew, and needed not reminding of, what he had preached there.

9 It only remains under this head, that we should say something of the character of the Cretans which St. Paul has quoted from Epimenides, ch. i 12,—Κρῆτες ἀεὶ ψεῦσται, κακὰ θηρία, γαστέρες ἀργαί.

10. Meursius, in his very complete and elaborate treatise on Crete, has accumulated nearly all the testimonies of the ancients respecting them From his pages I take a few, that the student may be able to illustrate the character by them.

11. On their *avarice*, we have the testimony of Livy, xliv. 45, "Cretenses spem pecuniæ secuti: et quoniam in dividendo plus offensionum quam gratiæ erat, quinquaginta talenta iis posita sunt in ripa diripienda."—of Plutarch, Paul Æmil c. 23, τῶν δὲ στρατιωτῶν, ἐπηκολούθησαν οἱ Κρῆτες, οὐ δι' εὔνοιαν, ἀλλὰ τοῖς χρήμασιν, ὥςπερ κηρίοις μέλιτται, προςλιπαροῦντες:—of Polybius, vi. 46. 3, ὁ περὶ τὴν αἰσχροκέρδειαν καὶ πλεονεξίαν τρόπος οὕτως ἐπιχωριάζει παρ' αὐτοῖς, ὥςτε παρὰ μόνοις Κρηταιεῦσι τῶν ἁπάντων ἀνθρωπων μηδὲν αἰσχρὸν νομίζεσθαι κέρδος.

12. On their *ferocity and fraud*, Polybius vi 46 9, Κρηταιεῖς ἐν πλείσταις ἰδίᾳ τε καὶ κατὰ κοινὸν στάσεσι καὶ φόνοις καὶ πολέμοις ἐμφυλίοις ἀναστρεφομένους: and iv. 8. 11, Κρῆτες δὲ καὶ κατὰ γῆν καὶ κατὰ θάλατταν πρὸς μὲν ἐνέδρας καὶ λῃστείας καὶ κλοπὰς πολεμίων, καὶ νυκτερινὰς ἐπιθέσεις καὶ πάσας τὰς μετὰ δύλου καὶ κατὰ μέρος χρείας ἀνυπόστατοι, πρὸς δὲ τὴν ἐξ ὁμολόγου καὶ κατὰ πρόςωπον φαλαγγηδὸν ἔφοδον, ἀγεννεῖς καὶ πλάγιοι ταῖς ψυχαῖς —Strabo, x. c. 4, περὶ δὲ τῆς Κρήτης ὁμολογεῖται διότι . . . ὕστερον πρὸς τὸ χεῖρον μετέβαλεν ἐπὶ πλεῖστον. μετὰ γὰρ τοὺς Τυῤῥηνούς, οἳ μάλιστα ἐδῄωσαν τὴν καθ' ἡμᾶς θάλατταν, οὗτοι εἰσὶν οἱ διαδεξάμενοι τὰ λῃστήρια —an Epigram of Leonides, Anthol. iii. 22,—αἰεὶ λῃσταὶ καὶ ἁλιφθόροι οὔτε δίκαιοι Κρῆτες· τίς Κρητῶν οἶδε δικαιοσύνην,

13. On their *mendacity*, Polybius vi. 47. 5, καὶ μὴν οὔτε κατ' ἰδίαν ἤθη δολιώτερα Κρηταιέων εὕροι τις ἄν, πλὴν τελείως ὀλίγων, οὔτε καθόλου ἐπιβουλὰς ἀδικώτερας —again, the proverb, Κρὴς πρὸς Αἰγινήτην, is thus

explained by Diogenianus, Cent. v. prov 92,—ἐπὶ τῶν πανούργοις χρωμένων πρὸς ἀλλήλους λέγεται —Psellus, de operat. Dæm , πλὴν ἴσθι μηδ' αὐτὸν ἐρραψῳδηκέναι με ταῦτα τερατευόμενον, κατὰ τοὺς Κρῆτας καὶ Φοίνικας. And the word κρητίζειν was an expression for 'to lie' Suidas has κρητίζειν πρὸς Κρῆτας, ἐπειδὴ ψεῦσται καὶ ἀπατεῶνές εἰσι: see also Polyb. viii 21. 5 And their *general depravity* was summed up in the proverb, quoted by Constant Porphyrogen de them. lib. i., τρία κάππα κάκιστα· Καππαδοκία, Κρήτη, Κιλικία.

CHAPTER XI.

THE EPISTLE TO PHILEMON.

SECTION I

ITS AUTHORSHIP.

1. THE testimonies to the Pauline authorship of this Epistle are abundant.

(α) Tertullian, in enumerating the Epistles of St. Paul with which Marcion had tampered, concludes his list thus (adv. Marc. v. 21, vol. ii. p. 524):

"Soli huic epistolæ brevitas sua profuit ut falsarias manus Marcionis evaderet. Miror tamen, cum ad unum hominem litteras factas receperit, quod &c" (see the whole passage cited above, ch. vii § i 1. ε)

(β) Origen, Hom xix in Jer. 2: vol iii. p. 263:

ὅπερ καὶ ὁ Παῦλος ἐπιστάμενος ἔλεγεν ἐν τῇ πρὸς Φιλήμονα ἐπιστολῇ τῷ Φιλήμονι περὶ Ὀνησίμου· ἵνα μὴ κατ' ἀνάγκην τὸ ἀγαθὸν ᾖ, ἀλλὰ καθ' ἑκούσιον (Philem ver 14).

And again in Matth. Comm series, § 72, p 889:

"Sicut Paulus ad Philemonem dicit Gaudium enim magnum habuimus et consolationem in caritate tua, quia viscera sanctorum requieverunt per te, frater" (Philem. ver 7.)

And again in id. § 66, p 884·

"A Paulo autem dictum est ad Philemonem: hunc autem ut Paulus senex, &c" (ver. 9.)

(γ) Eusebius, H. E iii. 25, reckons this Epistle among the ὁμολογούμενα.

(δ) Jerome, procem. in Philem. vol vii pp. 743, 4, argues at some length against those who refuse to acknowledge this Epistle for St. Paul's because it was simply on personal matters and contained nothing for edification

2 That neither Irenæus nor Clement of Alexandria cites our Epistle, is easily accounted for, both by its shortness, and by the fact of its containing nothing which could illustrate or affirm doctrinal positions. Ignatius seems several times to allude to it

Eph c. ii, p 645, *ὀναίμην ὑμῶν διὰ παντός, ἐάνπερ ἄξιος ὦ* (Philem ver 20).

Magnes. c xii, p 672, the same expression; which also occurs in the Ep to Polycarp, c. i., p 720, and c vi, p 725

3. The internal evidence of the Epistle itself is so decisive for its Pauline origin,—the occasion and object of it (see below, § ii.) so simple, and unassignable to any fraudulent intent, that one would imagine the impugner of so many of the Epistles would at least have spared this one, and that in modern times, as in ancient, according to Tertullian and Jerome, "sua illam brevitas defendisset." But Baur has rejected it, or, which with him is the same thing practically, has placed it in his second class, of *antilegomena*, in common with the other Epistles of the imprisonment.

4 In doing so, he confesses ("Paulus, u.s.w" pp 475 ff) to a feeling of subjecting himself to the imputation of hypercritical scepticism as to authenticity· but maintains that the Epistle must stand or fall with those others and that its very insignificance, which is pleaded in its defence, all the more involves it in their fate Still, he professes to argue the question on the ground of the Epistle itself

5. He finds in its diction several things which strike him as unpauline[1]: several which establish a link between it and those other Epistles The latter position we should willingly grant him, and use against him. But the former is here, as so often, taken up by him in the merest disregard to common sense and probability Such expressions, occurring in a familiar letter, such as we do not elsewhere possess, are no more than are perfectly natural, and only serve to enlarge for us the Apostle's vocabulary, instead of inducing doubt, where all else is so thoroughly characteristic of him.

6. The contents also of the Epistle seem to him objectionable. The incident on which it is founded, he says, of itself raises suspicion He then takes to pieces the whole history of Onesimus's flight and conversion and the feeling shewn to him by the Apostle, in a way which, as I observed before (ch iii § i 2) respecting his argument against

[1] I subjoin Baur's list *συνστρατιώτης*, ver. 2 *ἀνῆκον, ἐπιτάσσειν*, ver. 8: *πρεσβύτης*, ver 9. *ἄχρηστος* and *εὔχρηστος*, ver. 11 *ἀπέχω* in the sense of '*receive back*' (but see note there), ver 15 *ἀποτίω, προσοφείλω*, ver. 19 *ὀνίνασθαι*, ver. 20. *ξενία*, ver 22: the *frequent recurrence* (vv. 7, 12, 20) of the expression *σπλάγχνα*, not otherwise unpauline.

the Epistle to the Philippians, only finds a parallel in the pages of burlesque so that, I am persuaded, if the section on the Epistle to Philemon had been first published separately and without the author's name, the world might well have supposed it written by some defender of the authenticity of the Epistle, as a caricature on Baur's general line of argument.

7. On both his grounds of objection—the close connexion of this with the other Epistles of the imprisonment, and its own internal evidence,—fortified as these are by the consensus of the ancient Church, we may venture to assume it as certain that this Epistle was written by St. Paul.

SECTION II.

THE PLACE, TIME, OCCASION, AND OBJECT OF WRITING.

1. The Epistle is connected by the closest links with that to the Colossians It is borne by Onesimus, one of the persons mentioned as sent with that Epistle (Col. iv 9). The persons sending salutation are the same, with the one exception of Jesus Justus In Col iv. 17, a message is sent to Archippus, who is one of those addressed in this Epistle. Both Epistles are sent from Paul and Timotheus, and in both the Apostle is a prisoner (Col iv. 18; Philem vv 1, 9)

2. This being so, we are justified in assuming that it was written at the same place and time as the Epistles to the Colossians and Ephesians, viz. at Rome, and in the year 61 or 62

3 Its occasion and object are plainly indicated in the Epistle itself Onesimus, a native of Colossæ[2], the slave of Philemon, had absconded, after having, as it appears, defrauded his master (ver 18). He fled to Rome, and there was converted to Christianity by St. Paul Being persuaded by him to return to his master, he was furnished with this letter to recommend him, now no longer merely a servant, but a brother also, to favourable reception by Philemon This alone, and no didactic or general object, is discernible in the Epistle.

SECTION III

TO WHAT PLACE ADDRESSED, &c

1 From comparing Col. iv. 9, with ib 17 and Philem 2, we infer that Philemon was a resident at Colossæ. The impression on the

[2] ἐξ ὑμῶν can hardly in Col. iv 9 bear any other meaning he could surely not be described, under the circumstances, as "belonging to the Colossian Church," as supposed by Dr. Davidson, Introd ii. p. 138. The case of Epaphras in Col iv 12 is not strictly parallel, but even there, there is no reason why the words should not bear their proper sense

reader from Philem. 1, 2, is that Apphia was his wife, and Archippus (a minister of the church there, Col iv. 17), their son, or some near relative dwelling with them under the same roof A letter on a matter so strictly domestic would hardly include strangers to the family in its address

2 An hypothesis has been advanced, recently by Wieseler, that our present Epistle is alluded to in Col iv 16, as ἡ ἐκ Λαοδικείας, and that the message to Archippus in the next verse favours the view that he, and consequently Philemon, dwelt at Laodicea. And this is corroborated, by Archippus being called bishop of Laodicea in the Apostolic Constitutions (vii. 46, p. 1056, Migne).

3. The objection to this hypothesis is not so much from any evidently false assumption or inference in the chain of facts, all of which may have been as represented, but from the improbability, to my view, that by the latter limb of the parallelism—"*this Epistle*," "*that from Laodicea*,"—can be meant a private letter, even though it may have regarded a member of the Colossian church We seem to want some Epistle corresponding in weight with that to the Colossians, for such an order, in such a form, to receive its natural interpretation [3].

4. Of Onesimus we know nothing for certain, except from the notices here and in Col. iv. 9. Tradition reports variously respecting him. In the Apostolical Canons (73) he is said to have been emancipated by his master, and in the Apostolical Constitutions (vii 46, p 1056) to have been ordained by St Paul himself bishop of Berœa in Macedonia, and to have suffered martyrdom in Rome, Niceph. H. E. iii 11. In the Epistle of Ignatius to the Ephesians, we read, cap i, p 645, ἐπεὶ οὖν τὴν πολυπληθίαν ὑμῶν ἐν ὀνόματι θεοῦ ἀπείληφα ἐν Ὀνησίμῳ, τῷ ἐν ἀγάπῃ ἀδιηγήτῳ, ὑμῶν δὲ ἐν σαρκὶ ἐπισκόπῳ· ὃν εὔχομαι κατὰ Ἰησοῦν χριστὸν ὑμᾶς ἀγαπᾶν, καὶ πάντας ὑμᾶς ἐν ὁμοιότητι εἶναι· εὐλογητὸς γὰρ ὁ χαρισάμενος ὑμῖν ἀξίοις οὖσι τοιοῦτον ἐπίσκοπον κεκτῆσθαι [4]. It is just possible that this may be our Onesimus. The earliest date which can be assigned to the martyrdom of Ignatius is A D 107, i e thirty-five years after the date of this Epistle Supposing Onesimus to have been thirty at this time, he would then have been only sixty-five. And even setting Ignatius's death at the latest date, A D. 116, we should still be far within the limits of possibility It is at least singular that in ch ii, p 645 immediately after naming Onesimus, Ignatius proceeds ὀναίμην ὑμῶν διὰ παντός (cf. Philem. ver. 20; and above, § i 2).

[3] In the Prælectio above referred to, Prolegg to Eph., § i. 11, note, I had adopted Wieseler's hypothesis Maturer consideration led me to abandon it, solely on the ground of the improbability stated in the text. We must regard the Epistle to the Laodiceans as one now lost to us (see Prolegg to Vol. II ch iii. § iv. 3)

[4] See also id. chapters ii., vi., pp. 645, 649.

SECTION IV.

CHARACTER AND STYLE.

1. This Epistle is a remarkable illustration of St. Paul's tenderness and delicacy of character. Dr. Davidson well remarks, "Dignity, generosity, prudence, friendship, affection, politeness, skilful address, purity, are apparent. Hence it has been termed with great propriety, *the polite Epistle.* The delicacy, fine address, consummate courtesy, nice strokes of rhetoric, render the letter an unique specimen of the epistolary style." Introd vol. iii p. 160.

2 Doddridge (Expositor, introd to Philem) compares it to an Epistle of Pliny to Sabinianus, ix. 21, written as an acknowledgment on a similar occasion of the reception of a libertus by his master[5]: and justly gives the preference in delicacy and power to our Epistle The comparison is an interesting one, for Pliny's letter is eminently beautiful, and in terseness, and completeness, not easy to surpass.

3. Luther's description of the Epistle is striking, and may well serve to close our notice of it, and this portion of our prolegomena to the Epistles.

"This Epistle sheweth a right noble lovely example of Christian love. Here we see how St. Paul layeth himself out for the poor Onesimus, and with all his means pleadeth his cause with his master; and so setteth himself, as if he were Onesimus, and had himself done wrong to Philemon Yet all this doeth he not with power or force, as if he had right thereto, but he strippeth himself of his right, and thus enforceth Philemon to forego his right also. Even as Christ did for us with God the Father, thus also doth St. Paul for Onesimus with Philemon. for Christ also stripped Himself of His right, and by love and humility enforced the Father to lay aside His wrath and power, and to take us to His grace for the sake of Christ, who lovingly pleadeth our cause, and with all His heart layeth Himself out for us. For we are all His Onesimi, to my thinking."

[5] The Epistle runs thus.

"C. Plinius Sabiniano suo S.

"Bene fecisti quod libertum aliquando tibi charum, reducentibus epistolis meis, in domum, in animum recepisti Juvabit hoc te. me certe juvat. primum quod te talem video, ut in ira regi possis deinde, quod tantum mihi tribuis, ut vel autoritati meæ pareas, vel precibus indulgeas. Igitur et laudo et gratias ago. simul in posterum moneo, ut te erroribus tuorum, etsi non fuerit qui deprecetur, placabilem præstes. Vale"

CHAPTER XII.

APPARATUS CRITICUS.

SECTION I

LIST OF MSS CONTAINING THE EPISTLES OF ST. PAUL.

NOTE.—It is intended to include in this Table the mention of those MSS. only which contain, and of those particulars which concern, the portion of the N. T. comprehended in this Volume.

	Designation	Date	Name of Collator and other information	Gosp.	Cath	Apoc.
A	Alexandrinus	V	*See Vol I*	A	A	A
B	Vatican 1209.	IV	*See Vol. I*	B	B	—
C	Ephraemi.	V.	*See Vol. I*	C	C	C
D	Claromontanus	VI.	*See Vol II.*	—	—	—
E	Sangermanensis.	IX	A faulty transcript of D	—	—	—
F	Augiensis	IX	*See Vol II*	—	—	—
G	Boernerianus	IX	Cited only when it differs from F.	Δ	—	—
H	Paris, Coisl 202, A.	VI	Only fragments. *See Vol II.*	—	—	—
I_b	Frag Tischendorf.	V.	*See Vol I.*	—	I_b	—
K	Moscow Synod, 98	IX.	*See Vol. II.*	—	K	—
L	Passionei	IX	*See Vol II.*	—	L	—
ℵ	Sinaiticus.	IV.	*See Vol. I.*	ℵ	ℵ	ℵ
a	Lambeth 1182	XII.	Scrivener	—	a	—
b	Lambeth 1183	1358	Scrivener	—	b	—
c	Formerly Lambeth 1184.	XV.	Sanderson in Scrivener.	—	c	—
d	Lambeth 1185.	XV.	Scrivener	—	d	—
e	Lambeth 1186	XI	Scrivener	—	—	a
f	Theodori	1295	Scrivener.	q	f	—
g	Wordsworth.	XIII	Scrivener	l	g	—
[h]	*See* 101 *below.*	1357	*Cited as* h *in this edition.*	m	h	b
k	Trin Coll. Camb., B. x 16.	1316	Scrivener	w	k	—
[l]	*See* 29 *below.*	—	*Cited as* l	—	—	—
[m]	*See* 37 *below.*	—	*Cited as* m *Acts Epp*, 69 *in the Gospels.*	—	—	—
[n]	*See* 30 *below.*	—	*Cited as* n *in this edition.*	—	—	—
[o]	*See* 61 *below.*	—	*Cited as* o *in this edition*	—	—	—
1	Basle, K iii. 3 (late B. vi 27)	X.	Tregelles and Roth in Gosp.	1	1	—
2	Basle (late B. ix. ult.)	XV	Mill (*B.* 2) Belonged to Amerbach Mutilated	—	2	—
3	Vienna, Theol 5 (Kol)	XII.	Alter. Known as Corsendoncensis.	3	3	—
4	Basle (late B. x. 20)	XV.	Mill's *B* 3. Wetstein, throughout Epp.	—	4	—
5	Paris 106.	XII	Stephens' δ'. Scholz	5	5	—
6	Paris 112.	XIII	Stephens' ϵ' [Def Tit ii. 1—Philem. 12]	6	6	—
7	Basle (late B vi. 17).	X. ?	Readings given in Wetstein Text surrounded by various scholia from Thdrt, Gennad, Œc, Sevrn, &c On parchment.	—	—	—

	Designation	Date	Name of Collator and other information	Gosp	Cath	Apoc
[8]	. . . .	—	Stephens' ζ'. *Identified by some with 132 below.*	—	50	—
9	Paris 102.	X.	Stephens' ι' No lacunæ	—	7	—
[10]	*Not identified.*	—	Stephens' ια'.	—	8	—
11	Univ. Lib Camb, MS Kk 6. 4.	XI	Stephens' ιγ' [Def 1 Tim iv 12—2 Tim. iv 3]	—	9	—
12	Paris 237.	X.	Stephens (ιε'). Wetstein, "de integro" Scholia	—	10	2
[13]	. . . .	—	*See note* [a]			
[14]	Jacobi Fabri Daventriensis.	XVI.	*See note* [b].	90	47	—
[15]	Amandi.	—	*See note* [c].	—	—	—
16	Paris 219.	XI.	Wetstein. Variorum scholia. Inspected by Reiche. Belonged to J Lascaris.	—	12	4
17	Paris 14. (Colb 2844.)	XI	Tregelles *See 33, Vol I.*	33	13	—
18	Paris, Coisl. 199.	XI.	Wetstein.	35	14	17
19	Paris, Coisl. 26	XI.	Wetstein. Variorum comm.	—	16	—
20	Paris, Coisl. 27.	X.	Wetstein. Variorum comm. Mutilated	—	—	—
21	Paris, Coisl. 205.	XI	Wetstein.	—	17	19
22	Paris, Coisl. 202, A	XIII.	Wetstein. Variorum comm.	—	18	18
23	Paris, Coisl. 200	XIII	Wetstein. Stephens' θ "Continet totum N. T praeter Apoc [nam in Catalogo hujus Bibliothecæ Apoc per errorem pro Ep Paul ponitur.]" Wetstein.	38	19	—
24	Bodleian, Misc. 136	XII.	Cited by Wetstein on Joh vii Ebnerianus.	105	48	—
25	Brit. Mus, King's Lib. 1 B. 1	XIV	Wetstein (Westmonasteriensis 935). Mutilated	—	20	—
26	Camb Univ. Lib., MS Dd. 11. 90.	XIII	[Def 2 Tim i 1—ii 4, Tit i. 9—ii 15. Ends Philem ver 2]	—	21	—
27	Camb Univ Lib., MS. Ff I 30.	XI	The following portions were supplied in XIIth century. Gal i. 1—8; Eph i. 1—13, Col i 1, 2, 2 Thess iii 16—end, 1 Tim i 1—4; Philem. 24, 25 Of these Gal (or Eph.?) i 1—4, Col.			

[a] Jacobus Faber Stapulensis, i e. Jacques le Fevre d'Estaples, a native of Etaples in Picardy, collated five Greek MSS. of St Paul's Epistles which he sometimes appeals to in his Commentary (Paris, 1512). These citations, whenever it is necessary to refer to them, should not be quoted as if they came from some one MS distinct from the others in the list, but as "var read in comm Fab. Stap" or the like.

[b] A ms which once belonged to J C. Wolf of Hamburg It was procured by Wetstein from Wolf's library, and collated by him. It consists of two square paper volumes, containing the whole N. T. exc. Apoc., copied by Jas. Faber, of Daventer (a brother scholar of Erasmus), from a ms. written A D. 1293 on Mt Athos, by the scribe Theodore, who wrote also Gosp 74, and Scrivener's Gosp q Epp. f. The Epistle of St Jude occurs twice, the 2nd copy is entered as Cath 55.

[c] "We know nothing more of it than that Amandus, who lived at Louvain, had it in his possession, that Zegers appealed to it," on Rom. i 32 (as reading ου συνηκαν), "and that Erasmus supposed it to be a latinizing manuscript. How many books of the N. T. it contains, where it is at present preserved, whether it has been used in modern times under another name, are questions which I am unable to answer." (Michaelis.)

	Designation	Date	Name of Collator and other information	Gosp	Cath	Apoc
			i. 1, 2, are also found in the older portion. Catena chiefly from Photius.	—	—	—
28	Bodleian, Baroc. 3.	XI.	Mill (*Baroc*). Scholia	—	23	6
29	Chr Coll Camb. F. i 13	XII.	Mill (*Cant* 2). Scrivener (l, *so cited in this ed*).	—	24	—
30	Em Coll. Camb i 4 35	XII.	Mill (*Cant.* 3). Scrivener (n, *so cited in this ed*).	—	53	—
31	Brit Mus., Harl 5537.	1087	Mill (*Cov* 2).	—	25	7
32	Brit Mus., Harl. 5557.	XII.	Mill (*Cov.* 3).	—	26	—
33	Brit Mus., Harl 5620.	XV.	Mill (*Cov* 4). No lacuna (Griesb. Symb. Crit.).	—	27	—
34	Brit Mus, Harl. 5778	XIII	Mill (*Sin.*). Very much mutilated	—	28	8
35	Geneva 20.	XII.	Mill (*Genev*).	—	29	—
36	Bodleian, Misc. 74.	XIII.	Mill (*Hunt.* 1). Formerly known as Huntingdon 131. "Perlegi . . Gal. i, ii." (Griesbach)	—	30	9
37	The Leicester MS	XIV	Scrivener. *Cited as* "m" *in this vol.,* "f" *in Apoc*, 69 *in the Gospels. See* 69, *Vol. I.*	69	31	14
38	Bodleian, Laud. 31.	XIII.	Mill (*Laud.* 2)	51	32	—
39	Linc. Coll. Oxf 82.	XI.	Mill (*Lin.* 2).	—	33	—
40	Dublin, Montfort MS.	XVI	Barrett and Dobbin.	61	34	92
41	Magd. Coll Oxf. 9.	XI.	Mill (*Magd.* 1).	57	35	—
43	New Coll. Oxf 59	XIII	Mill (*N.* 2).	—	37	—
44	Leyden, Voss. 77.	XIII.	Sarrau. Mill's *Pet.* 1 Wetstein, Dermout.	—	38	—
[d][45]	*Situation unknown.*	—	Sarrau Mill's *Pet* 2 Belonged (with *Pet* 1 and 3) to Paul Petavius	—	39	11
46	Vatican, Alex. 179.	XI.	Zacagni. Mill's *Pet.* 3 Birch [Def Tit. iii 3 to end of Philem.]	—	40	12
47	Bodleian, Roe 16	XII.	Mill (*Roe* 2) Marginal scholia	—	—	—
48	Frankfort on Oder, Seidel MS.	XI	Middeldorpf.	—	42	13
49	Vienna, Theol. 300 (Nessel).	XII	Alter. Mill's *Vien*	76	43	—
[d][50]	*Situation unknown*	—	A MS brought from Rhodes, occasionally referred to by Stunica, one of the Complutensian editors	—	52	—
[51]	. . . .	—	*See note* [e].	—	—	—
[d][52]	Hamburg.	XV.	Bengel's Uffenbachianus	—	45	16
[53]	*See* M *in Vol. II.*					
55	Munich 375.	XI	Bengel (*Augsburg*, 6) Œc.-comm	—	46	—
[f][56]						

[d] These numbers are bracketed because it is perfectly possible that the MSS. denoted by them may be entered in the list under other numbers.

[e] Under this number Wetstein and succeeding editors have entered "*Codices Laur Vallæ.*" "Laurentius Valla, a learned Roman, who was born in 1417, and died in 1467, published in 1440, *Annotationes in N. T*, in which he collected the readings of three Greek and three Latin MSS, and took particular pains to amend the Latin version. The book was published at Paris in 1505, and gave occasion to the Complutensian Polyglott." (Michaelis' Introductory Lectures, 4to, London, 1761, p 66)

[f] Under this number Wetstein and succeeding editors have entered a Zurich MS,

	Designation.	Date	Name of Collator and other information	Gosp	Cath	Apoc.
57	Vienna, Theol 23 (Nessel).	XIII	Edited by Alter.	218	65	33
58	Vatican 165.	XII	Edited by Zacagni. Called Cryptoferratensis	—	—	—
59	Paris, Coisl 204.	XI.	Inspected. Catena.	—	—	—
[g][60]						
61	Camb. Univ Lib., MS Mm. 6 9	XII.	Mill's *Hal*, identified by Scrivener with 221 below. *Cited as* "o" from Scrivener's Collation.	140	61	—
62	Brit Mus, Harl. 5588	XIII.	Eph. collated by Griesbach.	—	59	—
63	Brit Mus, Harl 5613	1407	Eph collated by Griesbach.	—	60	29
[64]	*See* M *in Vol II.*					
65	Paris 60.	XIV.	Inspected by Griesbach.	—	62	—
[h][66]						
67	Vienna, Theol 302 (Nessel).	XII.	Alter and Birch. The readings inserted by a corrector (67[2]) are very valuable.	—	66	34
68	Vienna, Theol. 313 (Nessel)	XIII.	Alter and Birch.	—	63	—
69	Vienna, Theol. 303 (Nessel)	XIII.	Alter and Birch.	—	64	—
70	Vienna, Theol. 221 (Nessel).	1331	Alter and Birch	—	67	—
71	Vienna, Theol. 10 (Kollar).	XII.	Alter and Birch.	—	—	—
72	Copenhagen 1.	1278	Hensler. Cited by Bengel and Birch.	234	57	—
73	Upsala, Sparwenfeld, 42	XI.	Aurivilius Catena. (Part of this MS. is XIIth cent)	—	68	—
74	Wolfenbuttel xvi. 7.	XIII.	Knittel (collation given in Matthæi).	—	69	30
75	Brit. Mus., Addl. MS 5115-7.	1326?	(Epp Cent xii. Scrivener) "Lectt. ex 1 Tim mecum communicavit Rev. Paulus" (Griesbach)	109	22	—
76	Bibl. Paul. Leipsic.	XIII.	Readings of Gal Eph. given by Matthæi, p. 203	—	—	—
77	Vatican 360	XI.	Birch (cursorily inspected)	131	70	66
78	Vatican 363	XI.	Inspected by Birch and Scholz.	133	71	—
79	Vatican 366.	XIII.	Birch (cursorily)	—	72	37
80	Vatican 367.	XI.	Birch "per omnia contuli."	—	73	—
81	Vatican 761.	XII.	Inspected by Birch Œc-comm.	—	—	—
83	Vatican 765.	XI	Inspected by Birch Comm. on marg	—	—	—
84	Vatican 766	XII.	Ditto ditto	—	—	—
85	Vatican 1136.	XIII.	Epp. inspected by Birch. [Def. from 1 Tim vi. 5] Apoc bef. Epp.	—	—	39
86	Vatican 1160.	XIII.	Inspected by Birch and Scholz.	141	75	40
87	Vatican 1210.	XI.	1, 2 Thess; 1, 2 Tim Tit Philem. "exacte contuli" Birch	142	76	—
88	Vatican, Palat. 171.	XIV.	Zacagni	149	77	25

which consists merely of the Epistles of St. Paul, transcribed for his own benefit by the reformer Zwingle from Erasmus' 1st edition.

[g] Under this number Wetstein cites "Codices Græci, quorum fit mentio in *Correctorio* Bibliorum Latinorum seculo xiii. scripto."

[h] Another transcript of Erasmus' 1st edition, Harl. 5552 in the British Museum Griesbach copied certain various readings found on the margin.

	Designation.	Date	Name of Collator and other information	Gosp	Cath	Apoc
89	Vatican, Alex 29	XII	Birch "accurate exam" Contains Gal, Eph i 1—9 only of this vol	—	78	—
90	Vatican, Urb 3	XI	Inspected by Birch	—	79	—
91	Vatican, Pio 50	XII	Birch "per omn diligenter his coll"	—	80	42
92	Propaganda Lib. Rome 250	1274	Engelbreth in Birch (once *Bory* 1)	180	82	44
93	Naples i B 12	XI.	1 Tim collated by Birch	—	83	—
94	Laur Lib Florence iv 1	X.	Inspected by Birch Mutilated at end. Marginal commentary	—	84	—
95	Laur Lib Florence iv 5	XIII.	Inspected by Birch. Thl's comm	—	85	—
96	Laur Lib. Florence iv 20	XI.	Inspected by Birch. Marg comm	—	86	75
97	Laur Lib. Florence iv 29	X.	Inspected by Birch.	—	87	—
98	Laur Lib Florence iv 31	XI	Inspected by Birch.	—	88	—
99	Laur Lib. Florence iv 32	XI	Inspected by Birch.	—	89	45
100	Laur Lib Florence x 1.	XII	Inspected by Birch Comm	—	—	—
101	Laur Lib. Florence x 6	XI.	Inspected by Birch. Comm	—	—	—
102	Laur Lib. Florence x 7.	XI.	Inspected by Birch Var comm	—	—	—
103	Laur. Lib Florence x 19	XII	Inspected by Birch. Catena	—	—	—
104	Brit Mus Addl 11837	1357	Scrivener *Cited as* "h"	201	91	—
105	Bologna Can. Reg, 640.	XI	Inspected by Scholz	204	92	—
106	St. Mark's Venice, 5	XV.	Rinck	205	93	88
107	St Mark's Venice, 6	XV.	Rinck	206	94	—
108	St Mark's Venice, 10	XV.	Rinck.	209	95	46
109	St Mark's Venice, 11	XI	Rinck. [Philem wanting.]	—	96	—
110	St Mark's Venice, 33	XI	Rinck Comm	—	—	—
111	St Mark's Venice, 34	XI	Rinck Comm	—	—	—
112	St Mark's Venice, 35	XI	Rinck Comm [Def. 1 Thess iv 13—2 Thess ii. 14]	—	—	—
[1]113	(Moscow?)	XI	Matthæi (a). Belonged to Matthæi himself	—	98	—
114	Moscow Synod, 5	1445	Matthæi (c)	—	99	—
115	Moscow Synod, 334.	XI	Matthæi (d) Thl.'s comm.	—	100	—
116	Moscow Synod, 333.	XIII	Matthæi (f). Scholia	—	101	—
[117]	*The MS called* "K" *above.*					
118	Moscow Synod, 193.	XII	Matthæi (h)	—	103	—
120	Dresden, Cod Matth	XI	Matthæi (k)	241	104	47
121	Moscow Synod, 380	XII	Matthæi (l)	242	105	48
122	Moscow Synod, 328	XI	Matthæi (m)	—	106	—
123	Moscow Synod, 99	XI	Matthæi (n) Scholia	—	—	—
125	Munich 504	1387	Inspected by Scholz Philem. wanting	—	—	—
126	Munich 455.	XIV	Inspected by Scholz Philem. wanting Prob copied from same MS as preceding	—	—	—
128	Munich 211.	XI	Inspected by Scholz	—	179	82

[1] Rinck uses this number for St. Mark's Venice 36.

	Designation.	Date	Name of Collator and other information	Gosp	Cath	Apoc.
129	Munich 35.	XVI	Inspected by Scholz. Thl.'s comm. (So Hardt.)	—	—	—
130	Paris, Bibl. de l'Arsenal 4.	XI.	Inspected by Scholz.	43	54	—
131	Paris, Coisl. 196.	XI.	Inspected by Scholz	330	132	—
132	Paris 47.	1364	Reiche	18	113	51
133	Paris 56.	XII	Inspected by Scholz.	—	51	52
134	Paris 57	XIII	Reiche.	—	114	—
135	Paris 58.	XIII.	Inspected by Scholz [Def 2 Tim ii. to end, Tit.]	—	115	—
136	Paris 59	XVI.	Inspected by Scholz.	—	116	53
137	Paris 61.	XIII.	Reiche [Def Philem. 21—25.]	263	117	—
138	Paris 101.	XIII	Coll. 1 Tim.; 1 and 2 Thess by Scholz	—	118	55
139	Paris 102 A.	X.	Reiche.	—	119	56
140	Paris 103.	X	Reiche (in Epp. Paul) Marginal Schol.	—	11	—
141	Paris 103 A.	XI.	Inspected by Scholz. [Def Phil i 5 — end; Col; 1 Thess i. 1 —iv 1, v. 26—end, 2 Thess i 1—11.]	—	120	—
142	Paris 104.	XIII	Inspected by Scholz	—	121	—
143	Paris 105.	XI.	Inspected by Scholz. Contains Gal i 1—10, ii 4—end, Eph i 1—18, 1 Tim i. 14—v 5	—	122	—
144	Paris 106 A.	XIV.	Inspected by Scholz.	—	123	—
145	Paris 108.	XVI.	Inspected by Scholz Contains Phil, Col., Thess, Tim	—	—	—
148	Paris 111.	XVI.	Inspected by Scholz. Contains Tit, Philem.	—	—	—
149	Paris 124.	XVI.	Inspected by Scholz	—	124	57
150	Paris 125.	XIV.	Inspected by Scholz	—	125	—
151	Paris 126.	XVI.	Inspected by Scholz	—	—	—
153	Paris 216.	X.	Reiche. Scholia	—	126	—
154	Paris 217.	XI.	Inspected by Scholz and Reiche Thdrt.'s Comm. on Epp. Paul.	—	127	—
155	Paris 218.	XI	Inspected by Scholz. Catena	—	128	—
156	Paris 220.	XIII.	Inspected by Scholz. Comm, txt often omitted	—	129	—
157	Paris 222	XI	"Coll. magna codicis pars" Scholz [Def. Col. i 1—6.]	—	—	—
158	Paris 223	1045	Inspected by Scholz and Reiche. Catena.	—	131	—
159	Paris 224	XI.	Inspected by Scholz. Catena.	—	—	61
160	Paris 225	XVI.	Inspected by Scholz Fragments w Thl.'s comm.	—	—	—
161	Paris 849.	XVI.	Inspected by Scholz Thdrt.'s comm. w. txt on marg	—	—	—
165	Turin, C I 39	XVI	Inspected by Scholz Contains 1 and 2 Thess, Tim., Tit., Philem.	—	—	—
166	Turin, C I 40	XIII.	Scholz "accurate coll."	—	133	—
167	Turin, C II 17 (19)	XI.	Inspected by Scholz.	—	134	—
168	Turin, C II 38 (325)	XII.	Inspected by Scholz. Comm.	—	—	—
169	Turin, C II 31 (1)	XII.	Inspected by Scholz.	—	136	—
170	Turin, C II. 5 (302)	XIII.	Inspected by Scholz.	339	135	83
171	Ambros Lib Milan 6	XIII	Inspected by Scholz.	—	—	—
172	Ambros Lib Milan 15	XII.	Inspected by Scholz. Comm. after Chr	—	—	—
173	Ambros Lib Milan 102.	XIV.	Inspected by Scholz.	—	138	—

	Designation.	Date.	Name of Collator and other information.	Gosp.	Cath.	Apoc.
174	Ambros. Lib. Milan 104.	1434	Inspected by Scholz.	—	139	—
175	Ambros. Lib. Milan 125.	XV.	Inspected by Scholz. Continuous comm.	—	—	—
176	Ambros. Lib. Milan 97.	XI.	"Coll. loca Ep. Paul. plurima." Scholz.	—	137	—
177	Modena 14 (Ms. II. A. 14).	XV.	"Coll. cod. integer." Scholz.	—	—	—
178	Modena 243 (Ms. III. B. 17).	XII.	"Coll. cod. integer." Scholz under Paul.	—	142	—
[179]	Cursive portion of H of the Acts.	XII.	Scholz. *Cited as* H[r].	—	H	—
180	Laur. Lib. Florence vi. 13.	XIII.	Inspected by Scholz.	363	144	—
181	Laur. Lib. Florence vi. 36.	XIII.	Inspected by Scholz.	365	145	—
182	Laur. Lib. Florence 2708 (?).	1332	Inspected by Scholz.	367	146	—
183	Laur. Lib. Florence iv. 30.	XII.	Inspected by Scholz.	—	147	76
184	Laur. Lib. Florence 2574 (?).	984	Inspected by Scholz.	—	148	—
185	Vallicella Lib. Rome, E. 22.	XVI.	Inspected by Scholz.	393	167	—
186	Vallicella Lib. Rome, F. 17.	1330	Inspected by Scholz.	394	170	—
188	Vatican 1430.	XII.	Inspected by Scholz.	—	155	—
189	Vatican 1649.	XIII.	Inspected by Scholz. Thdrt.'s comm.	—	—	—
190	Vatican 1650.	1073	Inspected by Scholz. Comm. on Epp. Paul.	—	156	—
192	Vatican 1761.	XI.	Inspected by Scholz. Past. Epp. edited by Mai, as supplementary to B.	—	158	—
193	Vatican 2062.	XI.	Inspected by Scholz. Scholia.	—	160	24
194	Vatican 2080.	XII.	Inspected by Scholz.	175	41	20
195	Vatican, Ottob. 31.	X.	Inspected by Scholz.	—	—	—
196	Vatican, Ottob. 61.	XV.	Inspected by Scholz.	—	—	—
197	Vatican, Ottob. 176.	XV.	Inspected by Scholz.	—	—	78
198	Vatican, Ottob. 258.	XIII.	Inspected by Scholz. Latin version.	—	161	69
199	Vatican, Ottob. 66.	XV.	Inspected by Scholz.	386	151	70
200	Vatican, Ottob. 298.	XV.	Inspected by Scholz. Latin version.	—	162	—
201	Vatican, Ottob. 325.	XIV.	Inspected by Scholz.	—	163	—
203	Vatican, Ottob. 381.	1252	Inspected by Scholz.	390	164	71
204	Vallicella Lib. Rome, B. 86.	XIII.	Inspected by Scholz.	—	166	22
205	Vallicella Lib. Rome, F. 13.	XIV.	Inspected by Scholz.	—	168	—
206	Ghigi Lib. Rome, R. v. 29.	1394	Inspected by Scholz.	—	169	—
207	Ghigi Lib. Rome, R. v. 32.	XV.	Inspected by Scholz. Comm.	—	—	—
208	Ghigi Lib. Rome, R. viii. 55.	XI.	Inspected by Scholz. Thdrt.'s comm.	—	—	—
209	Two MSS. in the Library of the Col-	XVI.	Inspected by Scholz.	—	171	—
210	legio Romano.	XVI.	Inspected by Scholz.	—	172	—

	Designation.	Date.	Name of Collator and other information.	Gosp.	Cath.	Apoc.
[211]	Naples (no number).	XI.	Inspected by Scholz. *Apparently the same as 93 above.*	—	[173]	—
212	Naples 1 C. 26.	XV.	Inspected by Scholz.	—	174	—
213	Barberini Lib. Rome 29.	1338	Inspected by Scholz. Scholia.	—	—	—
215	Venice 546.	XI.	(Part Cent. XIII.) Inspected by Scholz. Comm.	—	140	74
216	Mon. of S. Bas. Messana 2.	XII.	Inspected by Münter.	—	175	—
217	Palermo.	XII.	Inspected by Scholz. [Def. 2 Tim. i. 8—ii. 14.]	—	—	—
218	Syracuse.	XII.	Inspected by Münter.	421	176	—
219	Leyden, Meerm. 116.	XII.	Dermout.	122	177	—
220	Berlin, Diez. 10.	XV.	[Def. 1 Tim. iv. 1—end.]	400	181	—
[k][221]	*The same MS. as* 61 *above.*					
[k][222]	Camb. Univ. Lib., MS. Nn. 5. 27.	—	A folio copy of the Greek Bible, printed "Basileæ per Joan. Hervagium 1545." A few notes are written on the margin.	441	110	—
[k][223]	Camb. Univ. Lib., MS. Nn. 3. 20, 21.	—	A copy of the Greek Test., 8vo., London, 1728, interleaved and bound up in two volumes. Contains MS. notes by John Taylor.	442	152	—
224	Bodleian, Clarke 9.	XIII.	On parchment. Inspected by Scholz.	—	58	—
[k][225]	*The same MS. as* 11 *above.*					
[k][226]	*The same MS. as* 27 *above.*					

[k] Scholz has run into great confusion with the manuscripts in the Cambridge University Library from not understanding the signs in his memoranda respecting them. The following explanation may be sufficient to clear up the matter. All the MSS. in the Library have since 1753 been denoted by a double-letter class mark, a number for the shelf, and a number for the volume. Nasmith, in writing out a list of the MSS. as thus arranged, added numbers on the margin to indicate merely the position which each MS. held in his catalogue. Nasmith's classified index contains references to this catalogue by these marginal numbers, ψ being prefixed if the reference is to a printed book with MS. notes, an asterisk if to a Greek MS. Similar marginal numbers have been inserted in the printed catalogue now in course of publication; they are not the same as Nasmith's, and it is as misleading to refer to MSS. by these numbers without stating what catalogue is meant, as to the pages of a book more than once edited, without stating the edition used. This may be seen in the following examples:—

MS. Ff. 1. 30, is 1152 on Nasmith's margin, and 1163 on that of the new Printed Catalogue.

MS. Kk. 6. 4, is 2068 on Nasmith's margin, and 2084 on that of the new Printed Catalogue.

MS. Mm. 6. 9, is 2423 on Nasmith's margin, and 2468 on that of the new Printed Catalogue.

MS. Nn. 3. 20, is ψ 2537 in Nasmith's index.

MS. Nn. 5. 27, is ψ 2622 in Nasmith's index.

It is right to prefix MS. to the double letter to indicate that the volumes meant belong to the Cases so marked in the Library, and to prevent any confusion with the classes of Printed Books alone known by the same letters.

	Designation	Date	Name of Collator and other information	Gosp	Cath	Apoc
227	Bodleian, Clarke 4	XII.	On parchment Inspected by Scholz	—	56	—
228	Escurial χ iv 17	XI	Moldenhauer. (See Birch, Gospels)	226	108	—
229	Escurial χ iv 12	XIV.	Moldenhauer (See Birch, Gospels)	228	109	—
230	Riccardi Lib. Florence 84	XV	Inspected by Scholz. (= lect.-37)	368	150	84
231	Gr Mon Jerusalem 8	XIV.	Inspected by Scholz.	—	183	—
232	Gr Mon. Jerusalem 9	XIII	Inspected by Scholz.	—	184	85
233	Mon S Saba, nr Jerus 1	XI	Inspected by Scholz.	—	185	—
234	Mon S Saba, nr Jerus 2	XIII.	Inspected by Scholz.	457	186	—
235	Mon S Saba, nr Jerus 10	XIII	Inspected by Scholz.	462	187	86
236	Mon S Saba, nr Jerus 15.	XII.	Inspected by Scholz.	—	188	—
237	Mon S Saba, nr Jerus 20.	XIII	Inspected by Scholz	466	189	89
238	Strasburg, Molsheimensis	XII.	Various readings of Gospels given by Arendt in the German Theol quarterly for 1833 Those of Acts and Epp communicated to Scholz	131	180	—
239	Laur Lib. Florence vi 27.	XII.	Inspected by Scholz.	189	141	—
240	Brit. Mus, Harl 5796	XV	Inspected by Scholz.	144	153	—
241	Wolfenbuttel, Gud 104	XII	(Inspected by Scholz ?) Scholia.	—	97	—
242	Middlehill Worcestersh 1461	XI	(Inspected by Scholz ?) Once Meermann 118.	—	178	87
243 } 243ª }	Two MSS in a monastery in the Island of Patmos	XII. XIII.	Inspected by Scholz.	—	182	—
244	Ch Ch Oxf, Wake 34	XI.	Inspected by Scholz	—	190	27
245	Ch Ch Oxf, Wake 38	XI	(Inspected by Scholz ?) Catena	—	191	—
246	Ch Ch Oxf, Wake 37	XI	(Inspected by Scholz ?)	—	192	—
8-pe	St Petersburgh xi. 1 2. 230.	XII	Muralto.	8 pe	8-pe	—

The following is a List of Lectionaries

	Designation	Date	Name of Collator and other information
lect-1	Leyden 243 Scaliger.	XI	Wetstein and Dermout Contains Col. i 12–23, 1 Thess iv 13–v 10; 1 Tim. iv 9–v. 10 [= ev-6]
lect-2	Brit Mus, Cotton Vesp B 18	XI.	"Contains the portions of Acts and Epp. appointed to be read throughout the whole year Casley collated it in 1735, and Wetstein inserted his extracts." (Michaelis) Mutilated at beg. and end
lect 3	Bodleian, Baroc 202 ?	995	(Quoted by Mill Heb x 22, 23 qu ?)
lect-4	Brit Mus., Harl. 5731.	XIV	Griesbach Contains the following fragments —Gal iii. 23–29, iv 4–7, id. 22–27; v 22–vi 2, Phil ii 5–

	Designation	Date.	Name of Collator and other information
			11; Col ii. 8—12; iii. 4—11; id 12—16, 2 Tim ii 1—10. [= Gosp. 117]
lect-5	Bodleian, Cromwell 11 [Olim 296] A liturgy book, containing 5thly (pp. 149—290), εὐαγγελοαποστόλων τῶν μεγάλων ἑωρτῶν	1225	Griesbach, who says "Variantes lectiones collegi e . . . Gal iv 4—7, Phil iv. 4—9, Col ii. 8, 9 . . ."
lect-6	Gottingen (C. de Missy).	XV	Matthæi (v) See his appendix to Thess Contains a large number of the usual lections
lect-7	Copenhagen 3	XV	Hensler in Birch. [= ev-44]
lect-8	Propaganda Lib Rome 287	XI	Birch [= ev-37]
lect-9	Paris 32	XII.	Inspected by Scholz. [= ev-84]
lect-10	Paris 33.	XII	Inspected by Scholz [= ev-85]
lect-11	Paris 34	XII	Inspected by Scholz
lect-12	Paris 375.	1022	Scholz An important MS. [= ev-60]
lect-13	Moscow Synod, 4	X	Matthæi (b)
lect-14	Moscow Synod, 291	XII.	Matthæi (e)
lect-16	Moscow Synod, 266.	XV	Matthæi (ξ). [= ev-52]
lect-17	Moscow Synod, 267	XV.	Matthæi (χ). [= ev-53]
lect-18	Moscow Synod, 268	1470	Matthæi (ψ) [= ev-54]
lect-19	Moscow Typogr, 47.	XVII	Matthæi (ω) [= ev-55]
lect 20	Moscow Typogr, 9.	XVI	Matthæi (16). Contains 2 Tim ii 1—10 [= ev-56]
lect-21	Paris 294	XI	Inspected by Scholz. [= ev-83]
lect-22	Paris 304.	XIII	Inspected by Scholz
lect-23	Paris 306	XII	Inspected by Scholz.
lect-24	Paris 308	XIII	Mostly O T. lections; only a few from N T.
lect-25	Paris 319	XI	Inspected by Scholz
lect-26	Paris 320	XII.	Inspected by Scholz Mutilated.
lect-27	Paris 321	XIII	Inspected by Scholz. Defective
lect-28	Bodleian, Selden 2.	XV	Griesbach [= ev-26]
lect-29	Paris 370	XII.	Some lections from Gospp. and Epp. [= ev-94]
lect 30	Paris 373	XIII.	
lect-31	Paris 276	XV	Inspected by Scholz [= ev-82]
lect-32	Paris 376.	XIII	Entered in list of MSS of Gospels as 324 [Lections in] 1 and 2 Tim. collated by Scholz
lect-33	Paris 382	XIII	"Cursim coll magna codicis pars" Scholz
lect-34	Paris 383.	XV.	Inspected by Scholz
lect-35	Paris 324.	XIII	Inspected by Scholz [ev-92]
lect-36	Paris 326	XIV.	Inspected by Scholz [ev-93]
lect-37	Riccardi Lib. Florence 84	XV.	*See* ms 230 *above*
lect-38	Vatican 1528	XV	
lect-39	Vatican, Ottob. 416.	XIV	[ev-133]
lect-40	Barberini Lib Rome 18	XIV	Some parts of Cent. X
lect-41	Barberini Lib Rome (no number)	XI	The first 114 leaves are lost.
lect-42	Vallicella Lib. Rome, C 16	XVI.	
lect-43	Riccardi Lib. Florence 2742	?	(Inspected by Scholz ?)
lect-44	Glasgow (Missy BB)	?	Manuscript collations by Missy were once in Michaelis' possession.
lect-45	Glasgow (Missy CC)	1199	
lect-46	Ambros Lib. Milan 63	XIV	Inspected by Scholz
lect-47	Ambros Lib Milan 72	XII	Inspected by Scholz. [ev-104]
lect-48	Laur. Lib Florence 2742.	XIII	Inspected by Scholz. [ev-112]
lect-49	Mon. St. Saba, nr. Jerus	XIV.	(Inspected by Scholz ?)

	Designation	Date	Name of Collator and other information
lect-50	St. Saba 18	XV.	Inspected by Scholz.
lect-51	St Saba 26	XIV	Inspected by Scholz
lect-52	St Saba (no number)	1059	Inspected by Scholz.
lect-53	St Saba (no number)	XIV	Inspected by Scholz. [ev-160]
lect-54	St Saba (no number)	XIII.	
lect-57	Ch Ch Oxf, Wake 1	XI	(26 Apoc)
lect-58	Ch. Ch Oxf., Wake 4	1172	

For VERSIONS *and* FATHERS, *see Vol II.*

SECTION II.

LIST, AND SPECIFICATION OF EDITIONS, OF BOOKS QUOTED, REFERRED TO, OR MADE USE OF IN THIS VOLUME

(Works mentioned in the lists given in the Prolegg. to Vols. I. and II. are not here again noticed.)

BAUR, Paulus, der Apostel Jesu Christi, u.s w , Stuttgart, 1845.

Ditto, Die sogenannte Pastoral-briefe u s w. (this latter work is quoted second hand)

BISPING, Erklarung der Briefe an die Epheser, Philipper, Colosser, u des ersten Briefes an d. Thessalonicher, Münster 1855. (Rom Catholic.)

DAVIDSON, DR S, Introduction to the New Testament, vol iii : 1 Timothy—Revelation, Lond. 1851.

DE WETTE, Exegetisches Handbuch, u s w : Gal and Thess., 2nd ed , Leipzig 1845 Eph , Phil , Col , Philem , 2nd ed , Leipzig 1847 : 1 Tim., 2 Tim , and Titus, 2nd ed , Leipzig 1847.

EADIE, PROF., Commentary on the Epistle to the Ephesians, Lond. and Glasgow 1854

Ditto, Commentary on the Epistle to the Colossians, Lond. and Glasgow 1856.

ELLICOTT, C. J (now Bishop of Gloucester and Bristol), a Critical and Grammatical Commentary on St Paul's Epistle to the Galatians, &c , London 1854. 2nd edition, 1859.

Ditto, on the Epistle to the Ephesians, London 1855 2nd edition, 1859

Ditto, on the Pastoral Epistles, London 1856 2nd edition, 1861

Ditto, on the Epistles to the Philippians, Colossians, and Philemon, London 1857

Ditto, on the Epistles to the Thessalonians, London 1858[1]

[1] I cannot forbear recording my very deep sense of the service rendered by Bishop Ellicott to students of the Greek Testament by these laborious, conscientious, and

FRITZSCHE, Pauli ad Romanos Epistola, 3 voll, Hal Sax. 1836.
FRITZSCHIORUM Opuscula Academica, Lipsiæ 1838
HARLESS, Commentar uber den Brief Pauli an die Ephesier, Erlangen 1834
HEFELE, Patrum Apostolicorum Opera, ed 3, Tubingen 1847.
HOFMANN, Der Schriftbeweis, 2 voll, Nordlingen 1855.
JOWETT, PROF., the Epistles of St. Paul to the Thessalonians, Galatians, Romans · with critical Notes and Illustrations, Lond. 1856.
KRUGER, Griechische Sprachlehre fur Schulen, Berlin 1852
MACK, Commentar uber die Pastoralbriefe des Apostels Paulus, Tübingen 1836. (Rom Catholic.)
MEYER, H. A. W., Kritisch-exegetischer Commentar uber das neue Testament.—Gal., 2nd ed, Gottingen 1851. Eph., Gottingen 1853. Col, and Philem., Gottingen 1848: Thess., continuation by Lünemann, Gottingen 1850: 1 Tim, 2 Tim., and Titus, continuation by Huther, Gottingen 1850
PASSOW, Handworterbuch der Griechischen Spiache: neu bearbeitet und zeitgemäss umgestaltet von Dr. Rost u. Dr. Palm, Leipzig 1841—1857 [2]
PELT, Epist Pauli Ap ad Thessalonicenses &c, Griefswald 1830.
STIER, DR RUDOLF, Die Gemeinde in Christo Jesu: Auslegung des Briefes an die Epheser, 2 voll, Berlin 1848.
USTERI, der Paulinische Lehrbegriff, Zurich 1851.
WINDISCHMANN, Erklarung des Briefes an die Galater, Mainz 1843. (Rom. Catholic.)
WINER, Pauli ad Galatas Epistolam latine vertit et perpetua annotatione illustravit Dr. G. B Winer, ed. tertia, Lips. 1829.

scholarlike volumes They have set the first example in this country of a thorough and fearless examination of the grammatical and philological requirements of every word in the sacred text I do not know any thing superior to them, in their own particular line, in Germany: and they add what, alas, is so seldom found in that country, profound reverence for the matter and subjects on which the author is labouring. Nor is their value lessened by Bishop Ellicott having confined himself for the most part to one department of a Commentator's work—the grammatical and philological. No student ought to be without these books, nor ought he to spare himself in making them his own by continual study

[2] This Lexicon (which has now all appeared) is as superior to all other editions of Passow, German and English, as Passow was to all that went before A comparison of any important words will shew the difference at once. The immense labour requisite will, it is to be feared, deter our lexicographers from giving the English public a translation but it would be a great boon to the scholarship of our country. [It is understood that a new edition of Liddell and Scott's Lexicon, now long promised, will contain all the valuable improvements and additions from Rost and Palm. A translation was in progress, but was broken off by the lamented death of Dr. Donaldson in the spring of 1861]

ERRATA.

Page 9, text, last line, *dele* ρ before ἕτερον, and transfer the reference to next page
— 88, reference o, *for* Rom. viii. 1, 4 *read* Rom viii 4.
— 111, reference o, *for* Rom xi. 30 *read* Rom. xi 33
— 192, reference l, *for* iii 14 *read* iii. 16
— 215, reference r, *dele* (bis).
— 289, reference g, *after* 2 Cor xii. 7 *insert* [bis].
— 292, reference u, *for* Rom ii 18 *read* Rom i 18.
— 295, reference k, *for* Matt xvii 43 *read* Matt xxvii 43.

Readings of the Codex Vaticanus (B) in the text of this volume, which have been ascertained by the Editor's personal inspection of the MS. at Rome, February, 1861.

Gal i. 4. του ενεστωτος, not ενεστωτος as Bentley

5 των αιωνων as in Mai ed 1, not τω αι. as in ed 2

15 αφωρισας is in codex.

ii. 4. καταδουλουσουσιν is 1. m.

14 Κηφα is in codex.

iii 16. ερρεθησαν is 1 m

21. οντως εν νομω, not εν ν οντως as Bentley.

iv. 4 ο θεος is in codex, not omitted as in Bentley.

15 ουν μακαρισμος as in ed. 2, not ουν ο μακ as in ed 1.

17. υμας θελουσιν is in codex without correction, not ημας.

25 το δε αγαρ, not το αγαρ as Bentley.

v. 11 π ηλικοις is in codex, all from 1. m

Eph. i. 1 ουσιν is at the end of a line, and εν εφεσω in margin, but it is very doubtful whether it is 2. m, and not rather 1 m, as some of its letters seem to have the double ink of 1. and 2. m.

23. του τα παντα, not του παντα as Bentley and Birch.

iv. 2. εν αγαπη, not αγαπη as Bentley.

—

20. εμαθετε as Mai ed. 1, not εμαθητε as ed. 2.

23. δε is not omitted as in Bentley

32. ημιν is not "added by another hand" as Bentley asserts, but in the codex, 1. m.

Phil i 22. αιρησωμαι as Bentley, not -σομαι as Mai.

ii 9 αυτω το ονομα is in codex

30. παρακολευσαμενος, not -βολ-.

ο

Col Title κολασσαεις, both letters being 1. m

i 2 κολοσσ- is 1 m.

4 εις παντας, not τη εις as Muralto

16 εν τοις, not τα εν τοις as Muralto.

18 η αρχη, not αρχη as Muralto

20 επι γης, not επι της γης as Muralto.

27 ο εστιν, not ος εστιν as Muralto

ii. 1 and 2 Vercellone's marginal notes are right: cod has εωρ-, and του θεου χριστου εορ- is 1 m. in ver. 18.

iii. 8 νυνει 1 m.

end. κολλασσ. is here plainly 1 m.

1 Thess i 2 1st υμων is not omitted as in Bentley.

iii 8 στηκετε as in Mai ed. 2, not -ητε as in ed 1

iv 1. λοιπον αδελφοι is 1. m.: το λ. ουν αδ 2. m.

[4 "ειδεναι ends a line, and is followed by ενα written by the 2da manus." — Mr. Cure, April, 1862.]

v. 13. ηγεισθε is in codex.

2 Thess ii. 3 η αποστασ. is in codex.

iii. 14. συναναμιγνυσθαι as Bentley, not -σθε as Mai

EPISTLES

TO

THE GALATIANS, EPHESIANS, PHILIPPIANS, COLOSSIANS, THESSALONIANS,—TO TIMOTHEUS, TITUS, AND PHILEMON

ΠΡΟΣ ΓΑΛΑΤΑΣ.

ABDF KLℵab cdefg hklm no17 I. [1] Παῦλος ἀπόστολος οὐκ [a] ἀπ' ἀνθρώπων οὐδὲ [b] δι' ἀνθρώπου, ἀλλὰ διὰ Ἰησοῦ χριστοῦ καὶ [c] θεοῦ [c] πατρὸς

a = Ro. xiii 1 so ἐκ, Matt xxi 25 b = 1 … 2 Co … c Eph vi 23 1 Thess i 1 2 Thess i. 1, 2 1 Pet i. 2. 2 John 3 Jude 1 see 1 Cor viii 6.

TITLE. rec η προς γαλατας επιστολη παυλου· elz παυλου του αποστολου η προς γαλατας επιστολη· του αγιου και πανευφημου αποστολου παυλου επ προ γαλ I πρ γαλ επ τ. αγ απ παυλ. h. επ. πρ. γαλ k l. txt ABKℵ m n o 17, and (prefixing αρχεται) DF.

CHAP. I 1—5] ADDRESS AND GREETING πολλοῦ τὸ προοίμιον γέμει θυμοῦ κ μεγάλου φρονήματος· οὐ τὸ προοίμιον δὲ μόνον, ἀλλὰ καὶ πᾶσα, ὡς εἰπεῖν, ἡ ἐπιστολή. Chrys In the very opening sentence of the Epistle, we see the fervour of the Apostle's mind and the weightiness of his subject betraying themselves The vindication of his own apostolic calling,—and the description of the work and purpose of Christ towards us, shew him to be writing to those who had disparaged that apostleship, and were falling from their Saviour. 1] It is better not to join ἀπόστολος (here of course used in its strict and highest sense see Ellicott, and an interesting note in Jowett) with ἀπ', but to let it stand by itself, and take the two prepositions as indicating, ἀπό the remote originating cause, διά the nearer instrumental one. In St. Paul's case, neither of these was merely human; the Lord Jesus was both the original Sender, and Himself the Announcer of the mission. Perhaps however the prepositions must not be so strictly pressed,—see ref 1 Cor,—and observe that the following διά belongs to θεοῦ πατρός as well as to Ἰησοῦ χριστοῦ—ἀνθρώπου is perhaps (as Mey, De W, Ellic, al) singular, for the sake of contrast to Ἰησ χρ following, but more probably for solemnity's sake, the singular making even a more marked exclusion of human agency than the plural. Luther's view of the sentence is: "The Judaizing teachers could shew their credentials as disciples of Apostles or messengers of churches and despised Paul as having none such To this he answers that he had not indeed any commission from men, but derived his authority from a higher source" But (1) this was not the fact, for he had a regular mission from the church at Antioch: (2) the words do not express this. κ θεοῦ πατρός] If by Jesus Christ, then also by God the Father, in and by whose appointment all the mediatorial acts of Christ in the Headship of His Church are done The inferences of Chrys. al as to the equality of the Father and the Son from this juxtaposition, appear far fetched, and according to "the mind, not of the apostolic, but of the Nicene age," as Jowett but we may say at least this, that the strongest possible contrast is here drawn between man, in the ordinary sense, on the one side, and Jesus Christ, and God the Father, on the other. Had not the Apostle regarded Jesus Christ as one with the Father in the Godhead, he never could have written thus On the use of διά here where ἀπό might be expected, see Ellicott's note He refers it to the brevity with which St Paul ex-

τοῦ ^{d} ἐγείραντος αὐτὸν ^{d} ἐκ νεκρῶν, 2 καὶ οἱ σὺν ἐμοὶ
πάντες ἀδελφοί, ταῖς ἐκκλησίαις τῆς Γαλατίας. 3 ^{e} χάρις
ὑμῖν καὶ ^{e} εἰρήνη ἀπὸ ^{c} θεοῦ ^{c} πατρὸς καὶ κυρίου ἡμῶν
Ἰησοῦ χριστοῦ, 4 τοῦ ^{f} δόντος ἑαυτὸν ^{g} περὶ τῶν ἁμαρτιῶν

ABDF KLℵ a b c d e f g h k l m n o 17

vi. 9. 7. 22. 9. 17. Acts. al. Rom. 24 and passim. Heb xi 19. 1 Pet i 21. e Rom i 7 al. f = 1 Tim ii 6. Tit ii 14. 1 Macc vi 44 (= παραδ., ch ii 20 reff.) g = Rom viii 3. Heb x 6, from Ps xxxix 6.

3 ημων bef και κυριου (*as in Rom* i 7, 1 *Cor* i. 3, 2 *Cor* i 2, *&c*) Aℵ d 17 fuld(with demid hal) Chr-txt lat-ff · om ημων a l (not 67): ins in both places copt æth.
4. rec (for περι) υπερ, with Bℵ[3] rel Chr Thdrt Damasc Œc-comm: txt ADFKℵ[1]

presses himself: I should rather say that he states our Lord Jesus and God the Father to have been the *causa medians*, in bringing down divine agency even to the actual *fact* of his mission—and leaving it therefore to be inferred à fortiori that the *causa principalis* was the will of God It is important to remember that the mission of Paul to the actual work of the ministry was by the command of the *Holy Spirit*, Acts xiii. 2,—proceeding from, and expressing the will of, the Father and the Son. πατρός is better taken generally, as in reff, the Father, than supplied with ἡμῶν (as De W. al) or αὐτοῦ (as Meyer al) τοῦ ἐγ αὐτ.] Why specified here? Not, I think, because (Meyer) Paul was called to be an Apostle *by the risen Saviour*,—nor merely (De W) to identify the Father as the Originator of the Son's work of Redemption (which is so in Rom. iv. 24,—but here would not immediately concern Paul's calling to be an Apostle),—nor (Calvin, al) to meet the objection that he had never seen Christ, and turn it into an advantage, in that (Aug [but cf. his Retractations], Erasm., Beza, al.) he alone was commissioned by the already risen and ascended Jesus,—for in this case we should not find τοῦ ἐγείραντος κ τ λ. stated as a predicate of the Father, but τοῦ ἐγερθέντος κ τ λ as one of the Son,—nor as asserting the Resurrection against the Jews and Judaizing Galatians (Chrys, Luther), which is far-fetched,—nor again (Jowett) as expressing an attribute of the Father, without which He can hardly be thought of by the believer,—for this is too loose a relevancy for a sentence so pointed as the present. but because the Resurrection, including and implying the Ascension, was the Father's bestowal on Christ of gifts for men, by virtue of which (ἔδωκεν τοὺς μὲν ἀποστόλους, κ τ λ Eph iv 11) Paul's *Apostleship had been received*. Cf. a similar sentiment in Rom. i 4, 5 ἐκ νεκρῶν = ἐκ τῶν ν.,—see note on Rom iv. 24. In Matt xiv 2; xxvii. 64; xxviii. 7, Eph v. 14, Col. i. 18 (ii 12?); 1 Thess. i 10, the article is expressed: otherwise it is always omitted 2 ἀδελφοί] Who these were, may best be inferred by the Apostle's usage in the addresses of other Epistles, where we have Σωσθένης ὁ ἀδελφός (1 Cor i 1), Τιμόθεος ὁ ἀδ (2 Cor. i. 1. Col. i 1. Philem 1). They were his colleagues in the work of the Gospel, his companions in travel, and the like (not all the members of the church where he was, as Erasm, Grot, Jowett, al., who would hardly be specified as being σὺν αὐτῷ,—besides that such an address would be unprecedented): and their unanimity (πάντες) is here stated, as Chrys., Luther, al., to shew that he was not alone in his doctrine, but joined by all the brethren who were present. At the same time πάντες would seem to imply that just now he had many of these ἀδελφοί with him. But we cannot draw any inference from this as to the date of our Epistle for we do not know who were his companions on many occasions. At Ephesus, where probably it was written, we hear only of Gaius and Aristarchus (Acts xix 29), but we cannot say that there were not others in all likelihood, several more of those mentioned Acts xx. 4, were with him. ταῖς ἐκκλ] πανταχοῦ γὰρ εἷρψεν ἡ νόσος. Thdrt The principal cities of Galatia were Pessinus and Ancyra. but this plural seems to imply more than two such churches. See 1 Cor. xvi. 1, and Acts xvi. 6; xviii. 23. That we have here barely ταῖς ἐκκλ, without any honourable adjunct (as in 1 Cor., 2 Cor., 1 Thess., 2 Thess, &c.), must be explained as Chrys. al. θέα δέ μοι καὶ ἐνταῦθα τ. πολλὴν ἀγανάκτησιν οὐ γὰρ εἶπε Τοῖς ἀγαπητοῖς, οὐδὲ Τοῖς ἡγιασμένοις, ἀλλὰ Τ. ἐκκλ. τ Γαλ. Meyer denies this, alleging (carelessly, which is not usual with him) 1 Thess. and 2 Thess as addressed barely τῇ ἐκκλησίᾳ, whereas in both we have added ἐν θεῷ πατρὶ κ. κυρίῳ Ἰησ. χρ. 3] See introductory note on Rom i 1—7. 4] He thus *obiter* reminds the Galatians, who wished to return to the bondage of the law, of the

ημων ἡμῶν, ὅπως [g] ἐξέληται ἡμᾶς ἐκ τοῦ [h] αἰῶνος τοῦ [i] ἐνεστῶτος
ABDF KLℵ a d e f n k l n o 17 πονηροῦ κατὰ τὸ θέλημα τοῦ [j] θεοῦ καὶ [j] πατρὸς ἡμῶν,
5 [k] ᾧ ἡ [k] δόξα εἰς τοὺς [l] αἰῶνας τῶν αἰώνων. ἀμήν.
6 [m] Θαυμάζω ὅτι οὕτως ταχέως [n] μεταπίθεσθε ἀπὸ τοῦ

g = Acts vii 10 xii 11. xxiii 27 xxvi 17 only Exod iii 8 Polyb xv 22 4, ἐξελούμενοι τοὺς κιανοὺς ἐκ τῶν περιεστώτων κακῶν h = Matt xii 32 xiii 40 Rom xii 2 1 Cor i 20 al i = Rom viii 38 1 Cor vii 26 al 1 Macc xii 44 j Phil iv 20 1 Thess i 3 iii 11, 13 see Isa lxiii 16. k ellips, Rom xi 36 Eph iii 21 l Phil iv 20 1 Tim i. 17 2 Tim iv 18 Dan vii 18. see Ps. cx 10 m = Mark vi 6 John vii 21 1 John iii. 13 Eccl v 7 Demosth 349 3 w ὅτι, Luke xi 38 John iii 7 iv. 27 n Acts vii 16 (Heb vii. 12 xi 5 pass) Jude 4 only Deut xxvi 17 (= 2 Macc. vii 24 Polyb xvii 13 5, μετατιθέναι τὰς ἐκείνων πατρίδας ἀπὸ τινων ὑποκειμένων εἰς ἑτέρας συμμαχίας).

a c e f m n Orig Thl (67[2] is given on difft sides by Bch and Alter) rec *ενεστωτος* bef *αιωνος* (omg 3rd *του*), with DFHKLℵ[3] rel latt goth Orig$_1$ Chr Thdrt Œc-comm Victorin om *αιωνος* e[1] txt ABℵ[1] 17 æth Orig$_3$ Did. om *το* ℵ[1].
6 om *ουτως* F al$_2$.

great object of the Atonement, which they had forgotten Ch iii. 13 is but a restatement, in more precise terms, of this. **δόντος ἑαυ.**] viz. as an offering, unto death: an expression only found (in N T.) here and in the Pastoral Epistles Several such will occur; see the inference, in Prolegomena to Past. Epistles, § i. 32, note. **περί**, in this connexion, has much the same sense as *ὑπέρ* see reff, and note on Eph. vi 19; also Ellic.'s note here. **ὅπ ἐξέληται**] *ἐξαιρεῖσθαι* is the very word used by the Lord of St. Paul's own great deliverance, see reff. **τ αἰῶνος τ ἐνεστ πονηροῦ**] the present (not, as Mey, '*coming*' The word will not bear this meaning in 1 Cor. vii 26, nor apparently [see note] in 2 Thess. ii. 2, much less in Rom. viii 38) evil age (state of things; i e the course of this present evil world,—and, as understood, make us citizens and inheritors of a better *αἰῶνος, τοῦ μέλλοντος*. So Luther: "vocat hunc totum mundum, qui fuit, est et erit, præsens seculum, ad differentiam futuri et æterni sæculi." The allusion (Jowett) to the Jewish expressions, "the present age," "the age to come," as applying to the periods before and after the Messiah's coming, is very faint,—indeed hardly traceable, in the change which the terms had undergone as used in a spiritual sense by Christians. See however the rest of his note, which is full of interest) **κατὰ τὸ θέλημα . .**] And this, (1) not according to our own plan, in proportion to our legal obedience or any quality in us, but according to the Father's sovereign will, the prime standard of all the process of redemption and (2) not so that we may trifle with such rescuing purpose of Christ by mixing it with other schemes and fancies, seeing that it is according to a procedure prescribed by Him, who doeth all things after the counsel of His own will. And this, not as the lord merely of His works, but as *πατρὸς ἡμῶν*, bound to us in the ties of closest love—for our good, as well as to fulfil His own eternal purpose On the question, whether the genitive *ἡμῶν* depends on both, or only on the latter of the two nouns *θεοῦ κ. πατρός*, I agree in Ellicott's conclusion, that as *πατρός* is regularly anarthrous, and thus purely grammatical considerations are confounded,—as *θεός* conveys one absolute idea, while *πατήρ* might convey many relative ones, it is natural to believe that the Apostle may have added a defining genitive to *πατήρ*, which he did not intend to be referred to *θεός*. Render therefore, **God and our Father**, not '*our God and Father*' **5 ᾧ ἡ δόξ.**] So (reff) on other occasions, when speaking of the wonderful things of God, St. Paul adds a doxology. "In politeia, quando regum aut principum nomina appellamus, id honesto quodam gestu, reverentia, et genuflexione facere solemus. Multo magis cum de Deo loquimur, genu cordis flectere debemus" Luther. In *ἡ δόξα*,—the **glory** *κατ' ἐξοχήν*, or 'the glory which is His,'—the article is probably inserted for solemnity. "In this and similar forms of doxology,—excepting the angelic doxology, Luke ii. 14, and that of the multitude, Luke xix. 38,—*δόξα* regularly takes the article when used alone see Rom xi. 36; xvi 27, Eph iii 21; Phil iv 20, 2 Tim iv. 18, Heb. xiii 21, 2 Pet. iii. 18 When joined with one or more substantives, it appears sometimes with the article (1 Pet iv. 11; Rev i 6; vii 12) sometimes without it (Rom ii 10; 1 Tim. i 17; Jude 25)." Ellicott **τοὺς αἰῶν. τ αἰών.**] See note on Eph. iii. 21. **6—10**] ANNOUNCEMENT OF THE OCCASION OF THE EPISTLE, IN HIS AMAZEMENT AT THEIR SPEEDY FALLING AWAY FROM THE GOSPEL. ASSERTION OF THAT GOSPEL'S EXCLUSIVE CLAIM TO THEIR ADHESION, AS PREACHED BY HIM, WHO SERVED GOD IN

[o] καλέσαντος ὑμᾶς [p] ἐν [q] χάριτι [q] χριστοῦ εἰς [r] ἕτερον εὐαγ-
γέλιον· 7 ὃ οὐκ ἔστιν ἄλλο, [s] εἰ μή τινές εἰσιν οἱ [t] τα-

ABDF HKLℵ a b c d e f g h k l m n o 17

o = ver. 15. Rom. viii. 30. ix. 24 al. fr. p 1 Cor. vii. 15. Eph. iv. 4. 1 Thess. iv. 7. q Rom. v. 15. Acts xv. 11. r = 2 Cor. xi. 4 al. s see note. t = Acts xv. 24. constr. w. art., Luke xviii. 9. Col. ii. 8. Ps. xxi. 11. Xen. Anab. vi. 5. 9.

ins ιυ̅ bef χυ̅ D al[1] vss. om χριστου F Tert[2] Cypr[2] Lucif.

CHRIST, AND NOT POPULARITY AMONG MEN. We have none of the usual expressions of thankfulness for their faith, &c.; but he hurries vehemently into his subject, and, as Chrys. says, *σφοδρότερον τῷ μετὰ ταῦτα κέχρηται λόγῳ, καθάπερ πυρωθεὶς σφοδρῶς ὑπὸ τῆς ἐννοίας τῶν εὐεργεσιῶν τοῦ θεοῦ.* 6.] **θαυμάζω** in this sense (see reff.) is a word of mildness, inasmuch as it imports that better things were expected of them,—and of condescension, as letting down the writer to the level of his readers and even challenging explanation from them. Still, like many other such mild words, it carries to the guilty conscience even sharper rebuke than a harsher one would. **οὕτως ταχέως**] either (1) '*so soon after your conversion*' (Calv., Olsh., Meyer, &c.), or (2) '*so quickly,'—'after so little persuasion,' when the false teachers once came among you* (Chr., De W., &c.), or (3) '*so soon after my recent visit among you*' (Bengel, &c.). Of these I prefer (1), as more suiting the dignity of the passage, and as the more general and comprehensive reason. But it does not exclude (2) and (3): 'so soon,' might be, and might be intended to be, variously supplied. See Prolegomena, on the time and place of writing this Epistle. **μετατίθ.**] **are passing over**, pres.: not as E. V. '*are removed*,' which is doubly wrong, for *μετ.* is not passive but *middle*, in the common usage of the word, according to which the Galatians would understand it. So Plat. Theog. 122 c, *σμικρὸν γάρ τι μετατίθεμαι*, 'I am beginning somewhat to change my opinion:' see also Gorg. 493 c: Demosth. 379. 10: *Ἴβηρες, ὅσοι . . . ἐς Ῥωμαίους μετέθεντο*, Appian, Hisp. c. 17; &c. See also examples in Wetst. Chrys. says well, *οὐκ εἶπε Μετέθεσθε, ἀλλὰ Μετατίθεσθε· τουτέστιν, οὐδέπω πιστεύω, οὐδὲ ἡγοῦμαι ἀπηρτισμένην εἶναι τὴν ἀπάτην· ὃ καὶ αὐτὸ πάλιν ἐστὶν ἀνακτωμένου.* It is interesting to notice, in connexion with *οὕτως ταχέως μετατίθεσθε*, the character given by Cæsar of the Gauls: "ut ad bella suscipienda Gallorum alacer ac promtus est animus: sic mollis ac minime resistens ad calamitates mens ipsorum est." B. G. iii. 19:—"Cæsar . . . infirmitatem Gallorum veritus, quod sint in consiliis capiendis mobiles, et novis plerumque rebus student:" ib. iv. 5: see also ib. ii. 8; iii. 10. **τοῦ καλέσ. ὑμ.**] not to be taken with *χριστοῦ*, as Syr., Jer., Luth. (gives both constructions, but prefers this), Calv., Grot., Bengel, &c., nor understood of Paul, as al. and recently by Bagge,—but, as almost always with the Apostle (see note on Rom. i. 6), of GOD the Father (see ver. 15; and cf. Rom. viii. 30; ix. 24, 25: 1 Cor. i. 9; vii. 15, 17: 1 Thess. ii. 12: 2 Thess. ii. 14: 2 Tim. i. 9. Also 1 Pet. v. 10). **ἐν χάρ. χρ.**] **in** (as the *element*, and hence the *medium*; not **into**, as E. V.; see for construction 1 Cor. vii. 15. In the secondary transferred sense of local prepositions, so often found in later Greek, it is extremely difficult to assign the precise shade of meaning: see Jowett's and Ellic.'s notes here. But we may safely lay down two strongly marked regions of prepositional force, which must never be confounded, that of *motion*, and that of *rest*. *ἐν*, for example, can never be strictly rendered '*into*,' nor *εἰς*, '*in*.' Where such appears to be the case, some logical consideration has been overlooked, which if introduced would right the meaning) **the grace of Christ.** Christ's grace is the elementary medium of our 'calling of God,' as is set forth in full, Rom. v. 15, *ἡ δωρεὰ (τοῦ θεοῦ) ἐν χάριτι τῇ τοῦ ἑνὸς ἀνθρ. Ἰησ. χρ.*:—see also Acts xv. 11. And '*Christ's grace*' is the sum of all that He has suffered and done for us to bring us to God;—*whereby* we come to the Father,—*in* which, as its element, the Father's calling of us has place. **εἰς ἕτερ. εὐαγγ.**] **to a different** (*in kind:* not *ἄλλο*, *another of the same kind*, which title he denies it, see below) **gospel** (so called by its preachers; or said by way of at once instituting a comparison unfavourable to the new teachers, by the very etymology of *εὐαγγέλιον*). 7.] Meyer's note appears to me well to express the sense: "the preceding *εἰς ἕτερον εὐαγγέλιον* was a paradoxical expression, there being in reality *but one Gospel.* Paul appeared by it to admit the existence of *many Gospels*, and he therefore now explains himself more accurately, how he wishes to be understood—*ὃ οὐκ ἔστιν ἄλλο, εἰ μή* &c.," i. e. **which** "different Gospel," whereto you are falling away, **is not another**, not a second, besides the one Gospel (*ἄλλο*, not *ἕτερον* again; see above), **except that there are some who trouble you &c.** That

ράσσοντες ὑμᾶς καὶ θέλοντες [u] μεταστρέψαι τὸ εὐαγγέλιον
τοῦ χριστοῦ. 8 ἀλλὰ [q] καὶ ἐὰν ἡμεῖς ἢ ἄγγελος ἐξ
οὐρανοῦ [v] εὐαγγελίζηται ὑμῖν [w] παρ' ὃ [v] εὐηγγελισάμεθα

u Acts ii 20 (from Joel ii 31) James iv 9 only Deut xxiii 5 1 Kings x 9 Sir xl 31

v absol w dat, ch iv 13 Luke iv 18, from Isa lxi 1 Rom i 15 (1 Cor xv 1) pass, 1 Pet iv 6
w = Acts xviii 13 Rom i 26 iv 18 xvi 17 al

7. om και θελοντες ℵ[1] · ins ℵ-corr[1] obl

8. καν B Dial Chr Thl. ευαγγελιζεται K c d k n al Thdrt-ms Œc : ευαγγελισηται Aℵ æth Eus Ath Cyr-jer Cyr Thdrt$_1$ Procl, *evangelizaverit* latt Tert$_2$ Cypr. υμιν bef ευαγγ. BH Chr Archel Aug : om υμιν Fℵ[1] Dial Eus Damasc Tert$_2$(elsw$_1$ om 2nd υμ) Cypr Lucif. for υμιν, υμας D[1] f l Cyr-jer Chron ευαγγελισαμεθα D(ed Tischdf) FH.

is: 'This ἕτερον εὐαγγ is *only in so far another*, that there are certain, who &c.' Notice that the stress is on οὐκ; so that Paul, though he had before said εἰς ἕτερον εὐαγγ, yet *guards the unity* of the Gospel, and explains what he meant by ἕτερον εὐαγγέλιον to be *nothing but a corruption and perversion of the one Gospel of Christ*. Others, as Chrys., Œc, Thdrt, Luther, De Wette, &c, take ὃ οὐκ ἔστιν ἄλλο as all referring to εὐαγγέλιον, "*which is* (admits of being) *no other*" (= μὴ ὄντος ἄλλου) and then εἰ μή is merely adversative, '*but*,' or '*only*,' a meaning which it will hardly bear, but which, as De W. remarks, is not necessarily involved in his interpretation 'except that' answering for it quite as well. The objection to his view is (1) that the meaning assigned to ὃ οὐκ ἔστιν ἄλλο is very harsh, taking the relative from its application to the concrete (ἕτερον εὐαγγ), and enlarging it to the abstract (τὸ εὐαγγ. in general) (2) that the juxtaposition of ἕτερον and ἄλλο in one sentence seems to require, as in 1 Cor xv 40, 41, that the strict meaning of each should be observed. Others again (Winer, Olsh, &c) refer the ὃ to the whole sentence from ὅτι &c to εὐαγγέλιον—'*which* (viz your falling away) *is nothing else but* (has no other cause, but that) *&c*' To this the objection (2) above applies, and it is besides very unlikely that St. Paul would thus have shifted all blame from the Galatians to their false teachers ('hanc culpam non tam vobis imputo quam perturbatoribus illis,' &c Luther), and, as it were, wiped out the effect of his rebuke just after uttering it. Lastly, Schott., and Cornel. a Lapide, take ὃ οὐκ ἔστ. ἄλλο as a parenthesis, and refer εἰ μή to θαυμάζω, which should thus have been ἐθαύμαζον (ἄν). This would besides make the sentence a very harsh and unnatural one. The nature of this 'different Gospel,' as gathered from the data in our Epistle, was (1), though recognizing Jesus as the Christ, it insisted on circumcision and the observance of the Mosaic ordinances as to times, &c. (2) it professed to rest on the authority of some of the other Apostles see Chrys. quoted below. οἱ ταρ.] The article points out in a more marked manner the (notorious) occupation of these men, q d. '*certain your disturbers, &c*' Add to reff, Herodot. ix. 70, τὴν σκηνὴν τ. Μαρδονίου οὗτοι ἔσαν οἱ διαρπάσαντες. Xen. An ii. 4. 5, ὁ ἡγησόμενος οὐδεὶς ἔσται. and compare the common expression εἰσὶν οἱ λέγοντες τὸ εὐαγγ τ. χρ.] perhaps here not '*Christ's Gospel*,' but the Gospel of (i e relating to, preaching) Christ. The context only can determine in such expressions whether the genitive is subjective or objective

8] **But** (no matter who they are οἱ ταρ. &c.) **even though** (in καὶ εἰ, καὶ ἐάν, &c., the force of the καί is distributed over the whole supposition following, see Hartung, Partikell. i 139; and ἐάν is distinguished from εἰ, in supposing a case which has never occurred, see 1 Cor xiii. 1, and a full explanation in Herm. on Viger, p 832) **we** (i e usually, '*I, Paul*:' but perhaps *used* here on account of οἱ σὺν ἐμοὶ πάντες ἀδελφοί, ver 2) **or an angel from heaven** (ἄγγ ἐξ οὐρ to be taken together, not ἐξ οὐρ. εὐαγγ. introduced here as the highest possible authority, next to a divine Person · even were this possible, were the highest rank of created beings to furnish the preacher, &c See 1 Cor. xiii 1. Perhaps also, as Chrys, there is a reference to the new teachers having sheltered themselves under the names of the great Apostles μὴ γάρ μοι Ἰάκωβον εἴπῃς, φησί, καὶ Ἰωάννην· κἂν γὰρ τῶν πρώτων ἀγγέλων ᾖ τις τῶν ἐξ οὐρανοῦ διαφθειρόντων τὸ κήρυγμα κ τ λ. Then he adds ταῦτα δὲ οὐχ ὡς καταγινώσκων τ. ἀποστόλων φησίν, οὐδὲ ὡς παραβαινόντων τὸ κήρυγμα, ἄπαγε εἴτε γὰρ ἡμεῖς, εἴτε ἐκεῖνοι, φησίν, οὕτω κηρύσσομεν· ἀλλὰ δεῖξαι βουλόμενος ὅτι ἀξίωμα προσώπων οὐ προσίεται, ὅταν περὶ ἀληθείας ὁ λόγος ᾖ), **preach** (evangelize · it is impossible to preserve in English the εὐαγγέλιον, and

ὑμῖν, [x] ἀνάθεμα ἔστω. 9 ὡς [y] προειρήκαμεν, καὶ ἄρτι
πάλιν λέγω, εἴ τις ὑμᾶς [z] εὐαγγελίζεται [w] παρ' ὃ [a] παρελάβετε, [x] ἀνάθεμα ἔστω. 10 ἄρτι γὰρ ἀνθρώπους [b] πείθω
ἢ τὸν θεόν; ἢ ζητῶ ἀνθρώποις [c] ἀρέσκειν; εἰ ἔτι ἀνθρώποις [c] ἤρεσκον, [d] χριστοῦ [d] δοῦλος οὐκ ἂν [e] ἤμην.
11 [f] Γνωρίζω γὰρ ὑμῖν, ἀδελφοί, τὸ εὐαγγέλιον τὸ εὐ-

...πειθω. 11. ABDF KLℵ a b c d e f g h k l m n o 17

x Acts xxiii. 14. Rom. ix. 3. 1 Cor. xii. 3. xvi. 22 only. Deut. vii. 26. (-ατιζειν, Acts xxiii. 12, &c.)
y Matt. xxiv. 25. 2 Cor. vii. 3 al.? 2 Macc. ii. 32 al.
z w. acc., Luke iii. 18. Acts viii. 25. xiv. 15, 21. xvi. 10. 1 Pet. i. 12. Paul, here only. a = 1 Cor. xi. 23. xv. 1, 3 al. b = Matt. xxviii. 14. Acts xii. 20. 2 Cor. v. 11. 2 Macc. iv. 45. c = Rom. xv. 1, 2. P. only, exc. Matt. xiv. 6 || Mk. Acts vi. 5. Sir. xx. 28. d = Rom. i. 1. Phil. i. 1. (Tit. i. 1.) James i. 1. 2 Pet. i. 1. Jude 1. e Gospp. & Acts, passim. Paul, 1 Cor. xiii. 11. ver. 22 only. Neh. ii. 13. ἤμεθα, Matt. xxiii. 30 bis. Acts xxvii. 37. Eph. ii. 3. f = Luke ii. 15. Acts i. 23. 1 Cor. xv. 1 al. Ezek. xliv. 23.

9. προειρηκα ℵ[1] k.

10. rec aft ει ins γαρ (*for connexion*), with D[2.3]KL rel syrr Chr Thdrt Thl Œc: om ABD[1]Fℵ 17. 67[2] latt copt arm Cyr[2] Damasc lat-ff.

11. rec (for γαρ) δε, with AD[2.3]KLℵ[1.3] d(in red) rel syrr copt Chr Cyr[2] Thdrt Ambrst: om æth: txt BD[1]F ℵ-corr[1] 17 latt Damasc Jer Aug.

in it the reference back to vv. 6, 7) **to you other than what** (*παρά* [reff.] as in *παρὰ δόξαν, παρὰ τοὺς ὅρκους, παραβαίνειν,* &c. not merely '*against,*' nor merely '*besides,*' but indicating '*beyond,*' in the sense of overstepping the limit into a new region, i. e. it points out *specific difference.* The preposition is important here, as it has been pressed by Protestants in the sense of '*besides,*' against Roman Catholic tradition, and in consequence maintained by the latter in the sense of '*against.*' It in fact includes both) **we preached** (evangelized) **to you, let him be accursed** (*of God:* no reference to ecclesiastical excommunication: for an *angel* is here included. See note, Rom. ix. 3, and compare ch. v. 10: also Ellic.'s and Bagge's notes here). **9.**] **As we said before** (referring, not to ver. 8 as most Commentators; for the word more naturally, as in 2 Cor. xiii. 2 [so προείπαμεν, 1 Thess. iv. 6], relates to something said on a former occasion,—and the plural seems here to bind it to εὐηγγελισάμεθα,—but to what he had said during his presence with them: see a similar reference, ch. v. 3, 21), **I also now say again,—If any one is** (no longer now a supposition, but an assumption of the fact: see Hermann, ut supra; and Ellic.'s note) **evangelizing you** (reff.) **other** (with another gospel) **than that which ye received** (from us), **let him be accursed** (see above). **10.**] **For** (accounting for, and by so doing, softening, the seeming harshness of the last saying, by the fact which follows) **am I** NOW (ἄρτι takes up the ἄρτι of the last verse, having here the principal emphasis on it,—q. d. 'in saying this,'—'in what I have just said;' 'is this like an example of men-pleasing?') **persuading** (seeking to win over to me, ζητῶ ἀρέσκειν nearly; see reff.) MEN (see 1 Cor. iv. 3; 2 Cor. v. 11: not, as Erasm. al. [not Luther], 'num res humanas suadeo, an divinas?'—nor as Calvin, 'suadeone secundum homines an secundum Deum?') **or** (**am I conciliating**) (πείθω losing its more proper meaning, as of course, when thus applied) **God? or am I seeking to please** MEN (a somewhat wider expression than the other, embracing his whole course of procedure)? (**Nay**) **if I any longer** (implying that such is the course of the world before conversion to Christ; not necessarily referring back to the time before his own conversion, any more than that is contained by implication in the words, but rather perhaps to the accumulated enormity of his being, after all he had gone through, a man-pleaser) **were pleasing men** (either (1) imperf., = 'seeking to please:' so that the fact, of being well-pleasing to men, does not come into question; or (2) as Mey., 'the fact of pleasing, *result* of *seeking* to please:' 'if I were popular with men:' the construction will bear both), **I were not** (ἤμην is a late form, found however in Xen. Cyr. vi. 1. 9: see Ellic. here) **the** (or **a**, but better 'the') **servant of Christ.** Some interpret χρ. δοῦ. οὐκ ἂν ἤμην as Chr., ἔτι μετὰ Ἰουδαίων ἤμην, ἔτι τὴν ἐκκλησίαν ἐδίωκον. But this would more naturally be expressed by οὐκ ἂν ἐγενόμην, and, as Mey. remarks, would give a very flat and poor sense: it is better therefore to take δοῦλος in its ethical, not its historical meaning.

11—CHAP. II. 21.] FIRST, OR APOLOGETIC PART OF THE EPISTLE; *consisting in an historical defence of his own teaching, as not being from men, but revealed to him by the Lord,—nor influenced even by the chief Apostles, but of independent authority.* **11, 12.**] *Enunciation of this subject.* **γν. γάρ**] The γάρ

αγγελισθὲν ὑπ᾽ ἐμοῦ, [g] ὅτι οὐκ ἔστιν [h] κατὰ ἄνθρωπον·
12 [i] οὐδὲ [i] γὰρ ἐγὼ παρὰ ἀνθρώπου [a] παρέλαβον αὐτό,
οὔτε ἐδιδάχθην, ἀλλὰ δι᾽ [j] ἀποκαλύψεως Ἰησοῦ χριστοῦ.
13 [k] ἠκούσατε γὰρ τὴν ἐμὴν [l] ἀναστροφήν [m] ποτε ἐν τῷ
[n] Ἰουδαϊσμῷ, ὅτι [o] καθ᾽ [op] ὑπερβολὴν [q] ἐδίωκον τὴν [r] ἐκκλησίαν τοῦ [r] θεοῦ καὶ [s] ἐπόρθουν αὐτήν, 14 καὶ [t] προέκοπτον

g constr, 1 Cor xvi 15 al see Winer, edn 6, § 60 5 a
h Rom iii 5 1 Cor iii 3 ix 8 xv 32 ch iii 15 1 Pet iv 6
i John v 22 vii 5 viii 42 Rom viii 7
j ch ii 2 1 Cor xiv 6, 26 2 Cor xii 1, 7 Rev i 1
k = Matt xi 2 Luke xxiii 6 Acts xvii 32 3 Kings x 1
l = Eph iv 22 reff
m = John ix 13 Rom vii 9 xi 30 al
n here only † 2 Macc viii 1 al (ιζειν, ικῶς, ch ii 14)
o Rom vii 13 1 Cor xii 31 2 Cor i 8, iv 17 only
p as above (o) 2 Cor iv 7 xii 7 only †
q = Matt v 10, 11, &c Ps vii 1 2 Macc v 8
r 1 Cor i 2 al (xv 9 exp)
s Acts ix 21 ver 23 only †
t Luke ii 52. Rom xiii 12 2 Tim ii 16 iii 9, 13 only see Sir li 17 Jos Vit § 2, εις μεγάλην παιδειας προὔκοπτον επιδοσιν

12 for ουτε, ουδε (*mechanical repetition*) AD[1]Fℵ m Eus Chr Cyr$_1$: txt BD[3]KL rel Œc for δι', δια A a[2].
13. for εποργθ, επολεμ F, *expugnabam* latt lat-ff(exc Aug). (here and in ver 23)

seems to have been corrected to δέ, as not applying immediately to the foregoing,—or perhaps in reminiscence of 1 Cor. xv 1, 2 Cor. viii 1 It refers back to vv. 8, 9. On γνωρ., see note, 1 Cor. xv 1. **κατὰ ἄνθρωπον**] **according to man**, as E. V. (see reff.) i e. measured by merely human rules and considerations, as it would be were it of human origin: so *βελτίονος ἢ κατ' ἄνθρωπον νομοθέτου*, Xen. Mem. iv. 4. 24, *κατά* cannot itself express the *origin* (as Aug., a Lapide, Est., al), though it is included by implication: see note ver. 4, on *κατὰ τὸ θέλημα*. 12] *proof of this*. **For neither** (*οὐδὲ γάρ* in negative sentences, answers to *καὶ γάρ* in positive, e. g. in Herod i 3, *ἐπιστάμενον πάντως ὅτι οὐ δώσει δίκας οὐδὲ γὰρ ἐκείνους διδόναι*.—omit the *οὐ*, and substitute *καί* for *οὐδέ*, and the sentence becomes affirmative. So that *οὐδέ* has nothing to do, except in ruling the negative form of the clause, with *οὔτε* following, but belongs to this clause only. See on the whole, Ellic.'s note) **did I** (*ἐγώ* strongly emphatic, —see example from Herodot. above: '*neither did I, any more than the other Apostles.*' Thus this clause stands alone; the '*neither*' is exhausted and does not extend to the next clause) **receive it** (historically) **from man** (i. e. 'any man;' not '*a man*,' but generic, the article being omitted after the preposition as in ver 1), **nor was taught it** (dogmatically), but **through revelation of** (i. e. **from**, genitive subjective · see reff. Thdrt. [but not altogether: for he subjoins, *αὐτὸς αὐτὸν ἔσχε διδάσκαλον*] al take the genitive as objective, '*revelation of*,' i. e *revealing*) **Jesus Christ** WHEN did this revelation take place?—clearly, soon after his conversion, imparting to him as it did the knowledge of the Gospel which he afterwards preached; and therefore in all probability it is to be placed during that sojourn in Arabia referred to in ver. 17. It cannot be identical with the visions spoken of 2 Cor xii. 1 ff.,—for 2 Cor. was written in A D 57, and fourteen years before that would bring us to A D. 43, whereas his conversion was in 37 (see Chron. Table in Prolegomena, Vol II), and his subsequent silence, during which we may conceive him to have been under preparation by this apocalyptic imparting of the Gospel, lasted but three years, ver 18 Nor can it be the same as that appearance of the Lord to him related Acts xxii. 18,—for that was not the occasion of any revelation, but simply of warning and command He appears to refer to this special revelation in 1 Cor. xi. 23 (where see on the supposed distinction between *ἀπό* and *παρά*), xv 3 1 Thess iv 15, see notes in those places.

13—II. 21.] *historical working out of this proof* · and first (vv. 13, 14) by *reminding them of his former life in Judaism*, during which he certainly received no instruction in the Gospel from men. 13 **ἠκούσ**] **ye heard**, viz. when I was among you from myself · not as E. V., '*ye have heard*.' **γάρ** binds the narrative to the former verses, as in the opening of a mathematical proof. **ἀναστρ.**] Wetst cites Polyb iv. 82 1, *κατά τε τὴν λοιπὴν ἀναστροφὴν καὶ τὰς πράξεις τεθαυμασμένος ὑπὲρ τὴν ἡλικίαν*. This meaning of the word seems (Mey) to belong to post-classical Greek There is no article before nor after *ποτε*, perhaps because the whole, *ἀναστ.-ποτε-ἐν-τῷ-'Ιουδ*, is taken as one, q d. *τὸν ἐμόν ποτε 'Ιουδαϊσμόν* or better, as Donaldson in Ellicott, "the position of *ποτε* is due to the verb included in *ἀναστροφήν*. As St Paul would have

ἐν τῷ ° Ἰουδαϊσμῷ ὑπὲρ πολλοὺς [u] συνηλικιώτας ἐν τῷ
[v] γένει μου, [w] περισσοτέρως [x] ζηλωτὴς [y] ὑπάρχων τῶν
[z] πατρικῶν μου [a] παραδόσεων.
15 ὅτε δὲ [b] εὐδόκησεν ὁ
[c] ἀφορίσας με [d] ἐκ κοιλίας μητρός μου καὶ [e] καλέσας
[f] διὰ τῆς χάριτος αὐτοῦ
16 [g] ἀποκαλύψαι τὸν υἱὸν αὐτοῦ
ἐν ἐμοί, ἵνα εὐαγγελίζωμαι αὐτὸν ἐν τοῖς ἔθνεσιν, εὐθέως
οὐ [h] προσανεθέμην [i] σαρκὶ καὶ [i] αἵματι,
17 οὐδὲ ἀπῆλθον

ABDF KLℵa b c d e f g h k l m n o 17

u here only † Dion Hal Antt x 49 (-λικος, Dan i 10 Theod) v = Acts xviii 2 2 Cor xi 26 al Esth ii 10 w 2 Cor i 12 a 6 Phil i 14 1 Thess ii 17 Heb ii 1 xiii 19 (Mark xv 14 v r) only † x = Tit ii 14 (reff). y = Acts viii 16 xvi 3, 20, 37 Rom iv 19 al z here only Gen l 8 Levit xxii 13 al a = Matt xv 2 1 Mk 1 Cor xi 2 2 Thess ii 15, iii 6 1 Jer xxxix (xxxii) 4 xli (xxx v) 2 only b constr., Luke xii 32 Rom xv 26 1 Cor i 21 1 Macc xiv 46 c Acts xiii 2 Rom i 1 Levit xx 26 d Matt xix 12 Luke i 15 Isa xlix 1 see Jer i 5 e ver 6 f = Rom xii 3 g Matt xi 25 1 Cor ii 10 Phil iii 15. 1 Pet i 12 1 Kings iii 21 h ch ii 6 only † Diod Sic xvii 116, τοῖς μάντεσι προσαναθέμενος περὶ τοῦ σημείου Lucian Jup Trag § 1, ἐμοὶ προσανάθου, λαβέ με σύμβουλον πόνων i Matt xvi 17 1 Cor xv 50 Eph vi 12 Heb ii 14 only Sir xiv 18

15 rec aft ευδοκησεν ins ο θεος, with ADKLℵ rel syr-w-ast copt Orig$_1$ Chr$_1$ Thdrt$_2$ Iren-lat$_1$ Aug om BF vulg Syr Chr$_1$ Thdrt$_2$ Iren-lat$_1$ Orig-lat Faust(in Aug) Ambrst Jer αφωρισας B(ita cod see table at end of prolegg to this vol) D[1] m n.

17. rec (for 1st απηλθον) ανηλθον, with AKLℵ rel latt syr copt Chr Thdrt · txt BDF

said ἀνεστρεφόμην ποτέ, he allows himself to write τὴν ἐμ. ἀναστροφήν ποτε." Mey. cites as a parallel construction, ἡ τῆς Τροίας ἅλωσις τὸ δεύτερον, Plat. Legg. iii. 685 D. τ ἐκκλ τ. θεοῦ] for solemnity, to set himself in contrast to the Gospel, and shew how alien he then was from it (1 Cor xv 9). ἐπόρθ] τουτέστι, σβέσαι ἐπεχείρει τ ἐκκλησίαν, καταστρέψαι κ καθελεῖν, ἀφανίσαι τοῦτο γὰρ πορθοῦντος ἔργον Chrys. But more than the *mere attempt* is to be understood . he was verily *destroying* the Church of God, as far as in him lay. Nor must we think of merely *laying waste;* the verb applies to *men*, not only to cities and lands, cf. Acts ix 21,—κεῖνος γὰρ ἔπερσεν ἀνθρώπους, Soph Aj 1177, and σὲ παρακαλῶ, μὴ ἡμῖν ὁ Πρωταγόρας τὸν Σιμωνίδην ἐκπέρσῃ, Plat Protag , p 340. 14. **συνηλικιώτας**] "The compound form (compare συμμέτοχος, Eph iii 6; v. 7 συγκοινωνός, 1 Cor ix 23 al) is condemned by the Atticists Attic writers using only the simple form " Ellicott **ἐν τ. γένει μ**, in my nation, see reff. **περισσ**] viz than they **ζηλ. τ π μ. παρ**] a zealous assertor (or defender) of my ancestral traditions (i. e those handed down in the sect of the Pharisees, Paul being Φαρισαῖος, υἱὸς Φαρισαίων, Acts xxiii 6,—not, the law of Moses This meaning is given by the μου without it the παραδόσεις of the whole Jewish nation handed down from οἱ πατέρες, might be meant cf Acts xxvi 5). 15–17] *After his conversion also, he did not take counsel with* MEN 15] It was God's act, determined at his very birth (cf especially Acts xiii. 2), and effected by a special calling · viz , that on the road to Damascus, carried out by the instrumentality of Ananias To understand καλέσας of an act in the divine Mind, as Ruckert, is contrary to our Apostle's usage of the word, cf ver 6, Rom viii 30 al. This calling first took place, then the revelation, as here 16] **ἀποκαλ** belongs to εὐδόκησεν, not to καλ (Erasm.), nor to ἀφορ and καλ (Est , al),—to reveal his Son (viz by that subsequent revelation, of which before, ver. 12 not by his *conversion*, which, as above, answers to καλέσας) in me (strictly *'within me,'* τῆς ἀποκαλύψεως καταλαμπούσης αὐτοῦ τὴν ψυχήν, Chrys · not *'through me'* (Jer , Erasm., Grot , &c), which follows in ἵνα εὐαγγ. κ τ λ , nor *in my case* (Ruckert, al), as manifested by me as an example to myself or to others, as in 1 John iv. 9 the context here requires that his own personal illumination should be the point brought out ;—nor *'to me'* (Calv , al), which though nearly equivalent to *'in me,'* weakens the sense), &c. Notice the *present* εὐαγγελίζωμαι, the ministry being not a single act, but a lasting occupation. **ἐν τ. ἔθν.**] the main object of his Apostleship see ch ii. 7, 9. 'εὐθέως is really connected with ἀπῆλθον · but the Apostle, whose thoughts outrun his words, has interposed the negative clause, to anticipate his purpose in going away.' Jowett **προσανεθ**] See reff The classical sense is, *'to lay on an additional burden '* and in middle voice, *'on oneself '* cf Xen. Mem ii 1. 8. The later sense, *'to impart to,'* τινί τι, either, as here, with the view of *getting*, or as in ch ii 6, with that of *conferring*. The πρός in composition does not signify *addition*, but *direction :* see Acts xxvii. 7, note **σαρκὶ κ αἱμ**] i. e. with man-

εἰς Ἱεροσόλυμα πρὸς τοὺς πρὸ ἐμοῦ ἀποστόλους, ἀλλὰ
ἀπῆλθον εἰς Ἀραβίαν καὶ πάλιν [k] ὑπέστρεψα εἰς Δα-
μασκόν. 18 ἔπειτα μετὰ ἔτη τρία [l] ἀνῆλθον εἰς Ἱεροσόλυμα [m] ἱστορῆσαι Κηφᾶν, καὶ [n] ἐπέμεινα [o] πρὸς αὐτὸν
ἡμέρας δεκαπέντε· 19 [p] ἕτερον δὲ τῶν ἀποστόλων οὐκ

k Luke chiefly, i 56 Acts viii 25 al fr elsw Heb vii 1 2 Pet ii 21 (Matt viii 13 Mark xiv 40 v r) Gen xliii 10 1 John vi 3 only 3 Kings xiii 12 Judg xxi. 8 Ald only (?)

m here only † Esdr i 33 (31) bis 42 (40) only ἀνὴρ ὃν ἐγὼ ἱστόρησα, Jos B J vi 1 8. ἱστόρησα γὰρ τινα Ἐλεάζαρον, Antt viii 2 5 (see Ellicott's note) n Acts x 48. xii 16 al L P [John viii 7] Exod xii 39 vat w πρός, 1 Cor xvi 7 o — Matt xiii 56. John i 1, 2 1 Cor xvi 6, 7 al. p Matt xii 4 1 Cor viii. 4 see ver 7

a Syr syr-marg Bas Thl-marg. [αλλα, so ABDFLℵ.]

18. τρια bef ετη Aℵ a b o 17 Syr copt Chr Damasc. rec (for κηφαν) πετρον, with DFKLℵ[1] rel latt syr-txt: txt ABℵ[1] 17 67[2] Syr syr-marg coptt æth. (Cf ch ii. 11, 14) 19. for ουκ ειδον, ειδον ουδενα D[1]F latt lat-ff (exc Aug Sedul).

kind, "generally with the idea of weakness and frailty," Ellic. whose note see, and also reff 17.] ἀπῆλθον both times refers to his departure from Damascus: q d 'when I left Damascus, I did not go . . . . . but when I left Damascus, I went' The repetition of ἀπῆλθον is quite in the Apostle's manner; Meyer adduces as examples Rom. viii. 15 [Heb xii. 18, 22 We may add Heb ii. 16] εἰς Ἀραβ] On the place which this journey holds in the narrative of Acts ix, see notes on vv. 19, 22 there Its object does not seem to have been (as Chrys, al, Meyer, al) the preaching of the gospel, —nor are the words ἵνα εὐαγγελ. κ τ λ necessarily to be connected with it,—but preparation for the apostolic work, though of course we cannot say, that he did not preach during the time, as before and after it (Acts ix. 20, 22) in the synagogues at Damascus. Into *what part* of Arabia he went, we have no means of determining. The name was a very vague one, sometimes including Damascus ('Damascus Arabiæ retro deputabatur, antequam transcripta erat in Syrophœnicem ex distinctione Syriarum' Tert adv. Marcion, iii. 13, vol. ii p 339: so also (verbatim) adv Judæos 9, p. 619 ὅτι δὲ Δάμασκος τῆς Ἀραβικῆς γῆς ἦν κ. ἔστιν, εἰ καὶ νῦν προσνενέμηται τῇ Συροφοινίκῃ λεγομένῃ, οὐδ' ὑμῶν τινες ἀρνήσασθαι δύνανται, Justin Mart. c. Trypho, 78, p 176),—sometimes extending even to Lebanon and the borders of Cilicia (Pliny, Hist. Nat vi. 32). It was however more usually restricted to that peninsula now thus called, between the Red Sea and the Persian Gulf. Here we must apparently take it in the wider sense, and understand that part of the Arabian desert which nearly bordered on Damascus (From C and H edn 2, i. p 117, f) *How long* he remained there we are equally at a loss to say. Hardly for any considerable portion of the three years Acts ix 23 will scarcely admit of this for those ἡμέραι ἱκαναί were manifestly passed at Damascus. The journey is mentioned here, to account for the time, and to shew that he did not spend it in conferring with *men*, or with the other Apostles. καὶ πάλ ὑπέστρ] cf. Acts ix. 22, 25 18—24] *But after a very short visit to Peter at Jerusalem, he retired to Syria and Cilicia* 18] At first sight, it would appear as if the three years were to be reckoned from his *return to Damascus*: but on closer examination we see that μετὰ ἔτη τρ stands in opposition to εὐθέως above, and the ἀνῆλθον κ τ λ. here answers to ἀπῆλθον κ τ λ. there. So that we must reckon them from his *conversion* ὅτε δὲ εὐδόκησεν κ τ λ ruling the whole narrative. See also on ch ii. 1. This is the journey of Acts ix. 26,—where see note There is no real discrepancy between that account and this. The incident which led to his leaving Damascus (Acts ix 25. 2 Cor xi 32, 33) has not necessarily any connexion with his purpose in *going to Jerusalem*. a purpose which may have been entertained before, or determined on after, that incident. To this visit must be referred the vision of Acts xxii. 17, 18 ἱστορ Κηφ] to make the acquaintance of Cephas —not to get information or instruction from him: see reff, and Ellic. here Peter was at this early period the prominent person among the Apostles, see note on Matt xvi. 18. ἐπέμ. πρός] originally a pregnant construction, but from usage become idiomatic. See reff. ἡμέρ δεκαπ] mentioned to shew how little of his institution as an Apostle he could have owed to Peter. *Why no longer*, see in Acts ix. 29, xxii. 17—21. 19] This verse admits of two interpretations, between which other considerations must decide. (1) That

q constr., Luke xxi. 6. 2 Cor. xii. 17. r = 1 Tim. v. 21. vi. 13. 2 Tim. ii. 14. iv. 1. s Rom. ix. 1. 2 Cor. xi. 31. 1 Tim. ii. 7. Prov. xiv. 5. t Rom. xv. 23. 2 Cor. xi. 10 only. (Judg. xx. 2 F.?)

εἶδον, [p] εἰ μὴ Ἰάκωβον τὸν ἀδελφὸν τοῦ κυρίου. 20 [q] ἃ
δὲ γράφω ὑμῖν, ἰδοὺ [r] ἐνώπιον τοῦ θεοῦ ὅτι οὐ [s] ψεύδομαι.
21 ἔπειτα ἦλθον εἰς τὰ [t] κλίματα τῆς Συρίας καὶ τῆς Κιλι- C επειτα
κίας. 22 [u] ἤμην δὲ [v] ἀγνοούμενος τῷ [w] προςώπῳ ταῖς ABCDF
ἐκκλησίαις τῆς Ἰουδαίας ταῖς [x] ἐν χριστῷ, 23 μόνον δὲ KLℵ a b c d e f g
[v] ἀκούοντες ἦσαν ὅτι ὁ [y] διώκων ἡμᾶς [z] ποτὲ νῦν [a] εὐαγ- h k l m n o 17

u ver. 10. v constr., Luke i. 10, 20 al. fr. Prov. vi. 3. ἀγν., Paul, Acts xiii. 27. xvii. 23. Rom. i. 13 al[8]. Mark ix. 32 ‖ L. Heb. v. 2. 2 Pet. ii. 12. Lev. iv. 13. w dat., see 1 Thess. ii. 17. x Rom. xvi. 7. Eph. i. 15 al. y = ver. 13 reff. partic., Eph. iv. 28 al. fr. z ver. 13. a here only. w., = Rom. i. 5. ch. iii. 25, 26. pres., Matt. ii. 22. John i. 46. ii. 9. iv. 1. Acts viii. 18 al. fr. Winer, Engl. trans. p. 383, § 40. 2. c.

21. om 2nd της ℵ[1]: ins ℵ-corr[1 obl].
22. om τω F al$_1$. for 2nd ταις, της D[1](not lat), της εκ . . . της εν χῶ d.

James, the Lord's brother, was one of the Twelve, and the only one besides Peter whom Paul saw at this visit: (2) that he was one τῶν ἀποστόλων, but not necessarily of the Twelve. Of these, (1) apparently cannot be: for after the choosing of the Twelve (John vi. 70), the **ἀδελφοί** of our Lord did not believe on Him (John vii. 5): an expression (see note there) which will not admit of *any* of His brethren having then been His disciples. We must then adopt (2): which is besides in consonance with other notices respecting the term ἀπόστολος, and the person here mentioned. I reserve the subject for full discussion in the prolegomena to the Ep. of James. See also notes, Matt. x. 3; xiii. 55; John vii. 5. **20.**] This asseveration (cf. 2 Cor. xi. 31) applies most naturally to the important fact just asserted—his short visit to Jerusalem, and his having seen only Peter and James, rather than to the whole subject of the chapter. If a report had been spread in Galatia that after his conversion he spent years at Jerusalem and received regular institution in Christianity at the hands of the Apostles, this last fact would naturally cause amazement, and need a strong confirmatory asseveration. As regards the construction, **ἃ . . . . . ὑμῖν** stands alone, (**with regard to) the things which I am writing to you,**—and the word necessary to be supplied to carry on the sense from ἰδοὺ ἐνώπ. τ. θεοῦ to ὅτι, lies under the ἰδού, which here answers to such words as διαμαρτύρομαι, 1 Tim. v. 21; 2 Tim. ii. 14; iv. 1,—παραγγέλλω, 1 Tim. vi. 13. Meyer would supply γράφω, which seems harsh: others take ὅτι as '*for*,' which is worse still (cf. 2 Cor. xi. 21, ὁ θεὸς οἶδεν . . . . **ὅτι** οὐ ψεύδομαι),—and this too, understanding ἐστίν after θεοῦ (Bengel). **21.** The beginning only of this journey is related in Acts ix. 30, where see note. Mr. Howson suggests (edn. 2, i. p. 129, f.) that he may have gone at once from Cæsarea to Tarsus by sea, and Syria and Cilicia may afterwards have been the field of his activity,—these provinces being very generally mentioned together, from their geographical affinity, Cilicia being separated from Asia Minor by Mount Taurus. (See also note on Luke ii. 1, 2.) Winer, al. have understood by Syria here, Phœnicia: but as Meyer has shewn, inconsistently with usage. In Acts xv. 23, 41, we find churches in Syria and Cilicia, which may have been founded by Paul on this journey. The supposition is confirmed by our ver. 23: see below. **22, 23.**] 'So far was I from being a disciple of the Apostles, or tarrying in their company, that the churches of Judæa, where they principally laboured, did not even know me by sight.' **τῷ προςώπῳ**, the referential, or adverbial dative: Donalds., Gramm. § 457. **τῆς Ἰουδαίας** excludes Jerusalem, where he *was known*. Jowett doubts this: but it seems to be required by Acts ix. 26—29. Chrys. seems to mistake the Apostle's purpose, when he says, ἵνα μάθῃς, ὅτι τοσοῦτον ἀπεῖχε τοῦ κηρύξαι αὐτοῖς περιτομήν, ὅτι οὐδὲ ἀπὸ ὄψεως γνώριμος ἦν αὐτοῖς: and Olshausen, in supposing him to be refuting the idea that he had learned the Gospel from other Christians in Palestine. **23. ἀκ. ἦσαν**] They (the members of the churches: cf. Eurip. Hec. 39, πᾶν στράτευμ' Ἑλληνικόν, πρὸς οἶκον εὐθύνοντας ἐναλίαν πλάτην) **heard reports** (not '*had heard*,' as Luth.: the resolved imperfect gives the sense of *duration*: see reff. and passim) **that** (not the recitative ὅτι, but the explicative, following ἀκ. ἦσαν. Mey. remarks that no example is found of the former use of ὅτι by St. Paul, except in O. T. citations, as ch. iii. 8) **our** (better taken as a change of person into the *oratio directa*, than with Mey. to understand ἡμᾶς as '*us Christians*,' the Apostle including himself as he writes) **former persecutor** (not, as Grot., for διώξας, but as ὁ πειράζων, taken as a

γελίζεται τὴν [a] πίστιν ἥν ποτὲ [b] ἐπόρθει. 24 καὶ [c] ἐδόξαζον
[d] ἐν ἐμοὶ τὸν θεόν. II. 1 ἔπειτα [e] διὰ δεκατεσσάρων ἐτῶν
πάλιν [f] ἀνέβην εἰς Ἱεροσόλυμα μετὰ Βαρνάβα, [g] συνπαρα-

b ver 13 Acts ix 21 only † c — Matt v 16 w ἐν John xiii 31, 32 x v 13 xvii 10 d — 1 Cor iv 2, 6 e — Matt xxvi 61 | Mk Acts xxiv 17 al Deut ix 11 xv 1 f Matt xx 18 Acts xv 2 al Ezra vii 6, 7 g Acts xii 25 xv 37, 38 only Gen xix. 17. Job i 4 only

24. εν εμοι bef εδοξαζον DF latt goth Victorin Ambrst

Chap. II 1 ανεβην bef παλιν DF goth om παλιν copt Chr Iren-lat. ανηλθον (*from ch* i. 18) C Chron

substantive see reff) is **preaching the faith** (objective, as in reff, and 1 Tim i. 19 b, iii. 9, iv 1, &c.; but not = the doctrine of the Gospel) **which he once was destroying** (see on ver. 13) **And they glorified God in me** ('in my case.' i.e. my example was the cause of their glorifying God·—not, '*on account of me*,' see reff., and cf. ἐν ἀρεταῖς γέγαθε, Pind. Nem. iii. 56,—ἐν σοὶ πᾶσ' ἔγωγε σώζομαι, Soph Aj. 519. Bernhardy, Syntax, p. 210). By thus shewing the spirit with which the churches of Judæa were actuated towards him, he marks more strongly the contrast between them and the Galatian Judaizers. Thdrt. says strikingly. μανθάνοντες γὰρ τὴν ἀθρόαν μεταβολήν, κ ὅτι ὁ λύκος τὰ ποιμένων ἐργάζεται, τῆς εἰς τὸν θεὸν ὑμνῳδίας τὰ κατ' ἐμὲ πρόφασιν ἐλάμβανον. II. 1—10.] *On his subsequent visit to Jerusalem, he maintained equal independence, was received by the Apostles as of co-ordinate authority with themselves, and was recognized as the Apostle of the uncircumcision.* 1 διὰ δεκατ ἐτῶν] First, *what does this διά imply?* According to well known usage, διά with a genitive of time or space signifies 'through and beyond' thus, ὁ μὲν χρόνος δὴ διὰ χρόνου προὔβαινέ μοι, Soph. Philoct 285, —διὰ δέκα ἐπάλξεων πύργοι ἦσαν μεγάλοι, Thuc iii 21, and then τῶν πύργων ὄντων δι' ὀλίγου see reff., and Bernhardy, Syntax, p 235 Winer, Gramm edn. 6, § 51 (The *instrumental* usage, διὰ δακρύων, διὰ νυκτὸς, &c is derived from this, the instrument being regarded as the means, passed through before the end is attained but obviously has no place here, where a *definite* time is mentioned) See more in Ellic. **διὰ δεκ. ἐτ.** then is **after fourteen years**, δεκατεσσάρων παρελθόντων ἐτῶν, Chrys. Next, *from what time* are we to reckon? Certainly at first sight it would appear,—*from the journey last mentioned* And Meyer maintains that we are bound to accept this first impression without enquiring any further But why? Is the *prima facie* view of a construction always right? Did we, or did he, judge thus in ch i. 18? Are we not bound, in all such cases, should any reason *ab extra* exist for doing so, to re-examine the passage, and ascertain whether our *prima facie* impression may not have arisen from neglecting some indication furnished by the context? That this is the case here, I am persuaded. The ways of speaking, in ch i. 18, and here, are very similar. The ἔπειτα in both cases may be well taken as referring back to the same *terminus a quo*, διά being used in this verse as applying to the *larger* interval, or even perhaps to prevent the fourteen years being counted from the event last mentioned, as they would more naturally be, had a second μετά been used What would there be forced or unnatural in a statement of the following kind? "After my conversion (ὅτε δέ, &c ch. i 15) my occasions of communicating with the II other Apostles were these (1) after three years I went up, &c. (2) after fourteen years had elapsed, I again went up, &c?" This view is much favoured, if not rendered decisive, by the change in position of ἐτῶν and the numeral, in this second instance In ch i. 18, it is μετὰ ἔτη τρία ἔτη, in the first mention of the interval, having the emphatic place. But now, it is not δι' ἐτῶν δεκατεσσάρων, but διὰ δεκατεσσάρων ἐτῶν—ἐτῶν now passing into the shade, and the numeral having the emphasis—a clear indication to me that the ἔτη have the same reference as before, viz to the *time of his conversion.* A list, and ample discussion, of the opinions on both sides, will be found in Anger, de ratione temporum, ch iv. This (cf. Chronol. Table in Prolegg. Vol II) would bring the visit here related to the year 50· see below **πάλιν ἀνέβην] I again went up** but nothing is said, and there was no need to say any thing, of another visit during the interval It was the object of the Apostle to specify, *not all his visits to Jerusalem*, but *all his occasions of intercourse with the other Apostles:* and it is mere trifling, when Meyer, in his love of creating discrepancies, maintains that in such a narration as this, St. Paul

λαβὼν καὶ Τίτον· 2 [f] ἀνέβην δὲ [h] κατὰ ἀποκάλυψιν, καὶ
[i] ἀνεθέμην [j] αὐτοῖς τὸ εὐαγγέλιον ὃ [k] κηρύσσω ἐν τοῖς ἔθνεσιν,

ABCDF KL‎ℵ a b c d e f g h k l m n o 17

h = (Rom. xvi. 25.) Eph. iii. 3 only. κατά = Phil. iv. 11. ἀποκ. = 1 Cor. xiv. 6, 26 al.) (1 Kings xx. 29 al.) i Acts xxv. 14 only. 2 Macc. iii. 9. j so Matt. iv. 23. 2 Cor. ii. 13. v. 19 al. k = Matt. iv. 23. ix. 35 al. Acts viii. 5. xx. 25.

2. for ανεθεμην (contuli D-lat vulg[and lat col of F]), ανεβαλομην exposui F.

would be putting a weapon into the hands of his opponents by omitting his second journey. That journey was undertaken (Acts xi. 30) in pursuance of a mission from the church at Antioch, to convey alms to the elders of the suffering church at Jerusalem. It was at a period of persecution, when James the son of Zebedee and Peter were under the power of Herod, —and in all probability the other Apostles were scattered. Probably Barnabas and Saul did not see any of them. They merely (Acts xii. 25) fulfilled their errand, and brought back John Mark. If in that visit he had no intercourse with the Apostles, as his business was not with them, the mention of it here would be irrelevant: and to attempt, as Mey., to prove the Acts inaccurate, because that journey is not mentioned here, is simply absurd. That the visit here described is in all probability the THIRD related in the Acts (A.D. 50) on occasion of the council of Apostles and elders (Acts xv.), I have shewn in a note to the chronological table, Prolegomena to Acts, Vol. II. The various separate circumstances of the visit will be noticed as we proceed.

συνπ. καὶ Τίτον] In Acts xv. 2, *ἔταξαν ἀναβαίνειν Π. κ. Βαρν. καί τινας ἄλλους ἐξ αὐτῶν.* Titus is here particularized by name, on account of the notice which follows, ver. 3: and the **καί** serves to take him out from among the others. On Titus, see Prolegg. to Ep. to Titus. **2.**] **δέ** not only carries on the narrative, emphatically repeating the verb (Mey.), but carries on the refutation also—**but I went up** (not for any purpose of learning from or consulting others, but) **&c.**:—So Il. ω. 484, *ὡς Ἀχιλεὺς θάμβησεν ἰδὼν Πρίαμον θεοειδέα· θάμβησαν δὲ καὶ ἄλλοι*,—and other examples in Hartung, i. p. 168. Of his undertaking the journey *κατ' ἀποκάλυψιν*, nothing is said in the Acts, all that is related there being, the appointment by the church of Paul and Barnabas and others to go. What divine intimation Paul may have received, inducing him to offer himself for the deputation, we cannot say: that some such occurred, he here assures us, and it was important for him to assert it, as shewing his dependence only on divine leading, and independence of any behests from the Jerusalem church. Meyer well remarks that the history itself of the Acts furnishes an instance of such a double prompting: Peter was induced by a vision, and at the same time by the messengers of Cornelius, to go to Cæsarea. Schrader would give a singular meaning to **κατ' ἀποκάλυψιν**; that his visit was *for the purpose of making known* the Gospel which he preached, &c. Hermann (de ep. ad Gal. trib. prim. capp., cited by Meyer) agrees; "*explicationis causa, i.e. ut pateferet inter ipsos quæ vera esset Jesu doctrina.*" But it is against this sense, that (1) the N. T. usage of **ἀποκάλυψις** always has respect to *revelation from above*, and (2) this very phrase, *κατ' ἀποκάλυψιν*, is found in ref. Eph. used absolutely as here, undoubtedly there signifying **by revelation.** Hermann's objection that for this meaning, *κατά τινα ἀποκ.* would be required, is nugatory: not the particular revelation (concrete) which occasioned the journey, but merely the fact that it was by (abstract) revelation, is specified.

ἀνεθέμην] (reff.): so Aristoph. Nub. 1436, *ὑμῖν ἀναθεὶς ἅπαντα τἀμὰ πράγματα.* See more examples in Wetst. **αὐτοῖς**] to the Christians at Jerusalem, implied in Ἱεροσόλ. above: see reff. This wide assertion is limited by the next clause, **κατ' ἰδ.** &c. Œc., Calv., Olsh., al. take **αὐτοῖς** to mean *the Apostles*: in which case, the stress by and by must be on *κατ' ἰδίαν*,—*I communicated it* (*indeed*,—*μέν* would more naturally stand here on this interpretation) *to them, but privately* (i.e. *more confidentially*,—but how improbable, that St. Paul should have thus given an exoteric and esoteric exposition of his teaching) *τοῖς δοκοῦσιν.* Chrys. is quoted for this view by Mey., but not quite correctly; *ἐπειδὴ γὰρ ἐν τοῖς Ἱεροσολύμοις πάντες ἐσκανδαλίζοντο, εἴ τις παραβαίη τὸν νόμον, εἴ τις κωλύσειε χρήσασθαι τῇ περιτομῇ . . . . παῤῥησίᾳ μὲν παρελθεῖν κ. τὸ κήρυγμα ἀποκαλύψαι τὸ ἑαυτοῦ οὐκ ἠνείχετο, κατ' ἰδίαν δὲ τοῖς δοκοῦσιν ἀνέθετο ἐπὶ Βαρνάβα κ. Τίτου, ἵνα οὗτοι μάρτυρες ἀξιόπιστοι γένωνται πρὸς τοὺς ἐγκαλοῦντας, ὅτι οὐδὲ τοῖς ἀποστόλοις ἔδοξεν ἐναντίον εἶναι, ἀλλὰ βεβαιοῦσι τὸ κήρυγμα τὸ τοιοῦτον.* Estius, characteristically enough, as a Romanist; 'publice ita contulit, ut ostenderet gentes non debere circumcidi et servare legem Mosis,—privato autem et secreto colloquio cum apostolis habito placuit ipsos quoque Ju-

[l] κατ' ἰδίαν δὲ τοῖς [m] δοκοῦσιν, [n] μή [n] πως [o] εἰς κενὸν [p] τρέχω
ἢ [p] ἔδραμον. 3 [q] Ἀλλ' [q] οὐδὲ Τίτος ὁ σὺν ἐμοὶ Ἕλλην
ὢν [r] ἠναγκάσθη [s] περιτμηθῆναι· 4 διὰ [t] δὲ τοὺς [u] παρεισ-

l Matt xiv 13, 23 xvii 1 al + 2 Macc. iv 5 m — ver 6 b only ‡ Eur Hec. 292 see vv 6 a, 9 Mark x 42 n Rom xi 21 al[9] Paul (Acts xxvii 29 rec) only o 2 Cor vi 1 Phil ii 16 bis 1 Thess. iii 5 Isa lxv 23 ϰ, 1 Thess ii 1 reff p — ch v 7 Phil ii 16 see 1 Cor ix 24—26 Ps cxviii 32 q Luke xxiii 15 Acts xix 2 r — Acts xxvi 11 xxviii 19 ver 14 ch vi 12 ‡ (Prov vi. 4) 1 Macc ii 25 al. s Luke i. 59 al fr L P, exc. John vii 22 Gen xvii 10 t so ver 2 Rom iii 22. Phil. ii 8 u here only †. (-αγειν, 2 Pet ii 1 see also Jude 4)

3 om ὁ B.

dæos ab observantia Mosaicæ legis . . esse liberandos' κατ ἰδ. δέ] but (limits the foregoing *αὐτοῖς*, q d., "when I say 'to them,' I mean" Ellic. ed 2, questions this, and understands δέ to introduce *another* conference, more private than that just mentioned) **in private** (in a private conference . not to be conceived as separate from, but as specifying, the former ἀνεθέμην) **to those that were eminent** (more at length ver. 6, *οἱ δοκοῦντες εἶναί τι*. These were James, Cephas, and John, ver 9,—who appear to have been the only Apostles then at Jerusalem. Olsh supposes the words to imply *blame*, not in the mind of the Apostle himself, but as reflecting on the unworthy exaltation of these Apostles by the Judaizing teachers He illustrates this by *οἱ ὑπερλίαν ἀπόστολοι*, 2 Cor xi 5, but an expression of such feeling here seems out of place, and it is better to understand *οἱ δοκοῦντες* as describing mere matter of fact, see examples in Kypke and Elsner), **lest by any means I should** (seem to) **be running, or** (to) **have run, in vain.** *οὐ περὶ ἑαυτοῦ τέθεικεν, ἀλλὰ περὶ τῶν ἄλλων τουτέστιν, ἵνα μάθωσιν ἅπαντες τὴν τοῦ κηρύγματος συμφωνίαν, κ ὅτι κ τοῖς ἄλλοις ἀρέσκει τὰ ὑπ' ἐμοῦ κηρυττόμενα*, Thdrt.. so also Chrys, Thl, Calv., al The construction of two moods after the same conjunction is found elsewhere in Paul: cf 1 Thess iii 5 The present subjunctive *τρέχω* implies continuance in the course; the 2 aorist indicative *ἔδραμον*, the course already run It is quite out of the question, that this last clause should express a bonâ fide fear, lest his ministry should really be, or have been, in vain, without the recognition of the church at Jerusalem (De W, al.): such a sentiment would be unworthy of him, and, besides, at variance with the whole course of his argument here The reference must be (as Thdrt above) to the *estimation* in which his preaching would be held by those to whom he imparted it When we consider the very strong prejudices of the Jerusalem church, this feeling of anxiety, leading him to take measures to prevent his work from being tumultuously disowned by them, is surely but natural On *εἰς κενόν* and *τρέχω*, see reff. (The grammatical difficulty is well discussed in Ellicott's note)

3] **But** (so far were they from regarding my course to have been in vain, that) **neither** (ἀλλ' οὐδέ introduces a climax, see reff) **was Titus, who was with me, being a Greek** (i e though he was a Gentile, and therefore liable to the demand that he should be circumcised), **compelled to be circumcised** (i e we did not allow him to be thus compelled the facts being, as here implied, that the church at Jerusalem [and the Apostles? apparently not, from Acts xv 5] demanded his circumcision, but on account of the reason following, the demand was not complied with, but resisted by Paul and Barnabas So Meyer, with Piscator and Bengel, and I am persuaded, rightly, from what follows But usually it is understood, that the circumcision of Titus was *not even demanded*, and that Paul alleged this as shewing his agreement with the other Apostles. So Chrys : *ἀκρόβυστον ὄντα οὐκ ἠνάγκασαν περιτμηθῆναι οἱ ἀπόστολοι, ὅπερ ἀπόδειξις ἦν μεγίστη τοῦ μὴ καταγινώσκειν τῶν ὑπὸ τοῦ Παύλου λεγομένων ἢ πραττομένων*· so also Thdrt., Thl., Œc, &c, and Winer and De W. Had this been so, besides that the following could not have stood as it does, not the strong word *ἠναγκάσθη*, but the weakest possible word would have been used—'*the circumcision of Titus was not even mentioned*'):

4] but (i e '*and this*'—the construction of the sentence is [against Ellic] precisely as ver. 2 this *δέ* restricts and qualifies the broader assertion which went before '*Titus was not compelled . . . . and that,*' &c. To connect this with ver 2, supposing ver 3 to be parenthetical, as Mr. Bagge, seems harsh, and unnecessary. A second *δέ* would hardly be found in the same sentence in this restrictive sense) **on account of the false brethren who had been foisted in** among us (the Judaizers in the church at Jerusalem, see Acts xv. 1. The word *παρείσακτος* is not found elsewhere It

άκτους ψευδαδέλφους, οἵτινες παρεισῆλθον κατασκο-
πῆσαι τὴν ἐλευθερίαν ἡμῶν ἣν ἔχομεν ἐν χριστῷ Ἰησοῦ,
ἵνα ἡμᾶς καταδουλώσουσιν, 5 οἷς οὐδὲ πρὸς ὥραν
εἴξαμεν τῇ ὑποταγῇ, ἵνα ἡ ἀλήθεια τοῦ εὐαγγελίου
διαμείνῃ πρὸς ὑμᾶς. 6 ἀπὸ δὲ τῶν δοκούντων εἶναί

ABCDF KLℵ a b c d e f g h k l m n o 17

v 2 Cor. xi. 26 only†. w = Acts x. 41, 47. xiii. 31, 43. Rom. i. 25 al. x Rom. v. 20 only†. y here only. 2 Kings x. 3. 1 Chron. xix. 3. Ezek. xxi. 21 vat. (-πεύειν, Josh. ii. 2, 3. -πος, Heb. xi. 31.) z = 1 Cor. x. 29. ch. v. 1, 13. a 2 Cor. xi. 20 only. Gen. xlvii. 21. constr., see note. b = 1 Cor. v. 1. xiv. 21 al. c John v. 35. 2 Cor. vii. 8. Philem. 15 only. (1 Thess. ii. 17.) d here only†. Wisd. xviii. 25 only. e 2 Cor. ix. 13. 1 Tim. ii. 11. iii. 4 only†. (-τάσσειν, Eph. v. 21, 22.) f ver. 14. Col. i. 5. g Luke i. 22. xxii. 28. Heb. i. 11 (from Ps. ci. 26). 2 Pet. iii. 4 only. Jer. xxxix. (xxxii.) 14. h = ch. i. 18 reff. i = here bis. Mark x. 42. Susan. 5. see ver. 2.

4. aft ινα ins μη F. (not F-lat.) rec καταδουλωσωνται, with K rel Chr(δουλωσωντ.) Thdrt, -σονται L al: txt AB[1]CDℵ; -σωσιν B[2]F 17 Damasc.

5. om οις ουδε D[1] Iren-lat Tert(who attributes "*nec*" to Marcion) Ambrst (*Græci e contra: "nec . . ."*) Victorin Primas: om ουδε hal, latt mss mentioned by Jer and Sedul: ins ABCD[3]FKLℵ rel vulg syrr copt goth gr-mss-in-Jer-Ambrst Orig Epiph Chr Thdrt Mcion-t Ambr Aug_2. for διαμεινη, διαμενη F. (C defective.)

occurs in the title of the "prologus incerti auctoris" to Sirach: πρόλογος παρείσακτος ἀδήλου. It is found however in the lexicons of Hesych., Photius, and Suidas, and interpreted ἀλλότριος. The verb παρεισάγειν is common in Polybius, without any idea of surreptitious introduction: see Schweigh.'s Index: but such an idea certainly seems here to be attached to it, by the repetition of παρεισ-, in **παρεισῆλθον** immediately after), **men who** (οἵτινες classifies) **crept in to spy out** (in a hostile sense: so Chrys.,—ὁρᾷς πῶς καὶ τῇ τῶν κατασκόπων προσηγορίᾳ ἐδήλωσε τὸν πόλεμον ἐκείνων,—reff., and Eur. Helen. 1607, ὅποι νοσοῖεν ξυμμάχων κατασκοπῶν) **our freedom** (from the ceremonial law: to see whether, or how far, we kept it) **which we have in Christ Jesus, with intent to enslave us utterly** (the future after ἵνα is found John xvii. 2; Rev. iii. 9; viii. 3; xxii. 14. Hermann, on Œd. Col. 156, says—"futuro non jungitur ἵνα, *ut*." The construction of the future with ὅπως and ὅπως μή is common enough in the classics. Winer remarks, Gr. edn. 6, § 41. b. 1. b, that it denotes continuance, whereas the aorist subjunctive is used of something transitory: but qu.? I should rather say that it signifies the certain sequence, in the view of the agent, of that which follows, not merely that it is his intent,—and that it arises from the mingling of two constructions, beginning as if ἵνα with the subjunctive were about to be used, and then passing off to the direct indicative); **to whom not even for one hour** (reff.) **did we** (Barnabas, Titus, and myself) **yield with the subjection required of us** (dative of the manner: the article giving the sense, '*with the subjection claimed*.' Fritzsche takes it, 'yield by complying with the wish of the *Apostles*:' but this is manifestly against the context: Hermann, and similarly Bretschneider, '*quibus ne horæ quidem spatium Jesu obsequio segnior fui*,'—absurdly enough, against the whole drift of the passage, and the Apostle's usage of ὑποταγή abstractedly), **that the truth of the Gospel** (as contrasted with the perverted view which they would have introduced: but not to be confounded with τὸ ἀληθὲς εὐαγγέλιον. Had they been overborne in this point, the verity of the Gospel would have been endangered among them,—i. e. that doctrine of justification, on which the Gospel turns as the truth of God) **might abide** (reff.: and note on ch. i. 18) **with you** ('*you Galatians*:' not, '*you Gentiles in general*:' the fact was so,—the Galatians, specially, not being in his mind at the time: it is only one of those cases where, especially if a rhetorical purpose is to be served, we apply home to the particular what, as matter of fact, it only shares as included in the general).

The omission of οἷς οὐδέ in this sentence (see var. readd.) has been an attempt to simplify the construction, and at the same time to reconcile Paul's conduct with that in Acts xvi. 3, where he circumcised Timothy on account of the Jews. But the circumstances were then widely different: and the whole narrative in Acts xv. makes it extremely improbable that the Apostle should have pursued such a course on this occasion. **6.**] He returns to his sojourn in Jerusalem, and his intercourse with the δοκοῦντες. The construction is difficult, and has been very variously given. It seems best (and so most Commentators) to regard it as an anacoluthon. The Apostle begins with ἀπὸ δὲ τῶν δοκούντων εἶναί τι, having it in his

[k] τι, [l] ὁποῖοί ποτε ἦσαν [m] οὐδέν μοι [m] διαφέρει· [n] πρόσωπον
θεὸς ἀνθρώπου οὐ [n] λαμβάνει·) ἐμοὶ γὰρ οἱ [o] δοκοῦντες
οὐδὲν [p] προσανέθεντο, 7 ἀλλὰ [q] τοὐναντίον ἰδόντες ὅτι
[r] πεπίστευμαι τὸ εὐαγγέλιον τῆς [s] ἀκροβυστίας καθὼς

k — Acts v 36. 1 Cor iii 7. x 19. ch vi 3, 15. Demosth. 582 27. l Acts xxvi 29. 1 Cor iii 13. 1 Thess i 9. James i 24 only† m — here (ch iv 1) only. διαφ, see 1 Cor xv 41. n Luke xx 21. Ps lxxxi 2 (see Acts x 34. Eph vi 9). o — ver. 2 only ‡. Eur Hec 292. p ch i 16 only†. q 2 Cor ii 7. 1 Pet iii 9 only†. 3 Macc iii 22. r — Rom. iii 2. 1 Cor ix 17. constr, Acts xxi 3. s Rom iii 30 al17. Paul only, exc Acts xi 3. Gen xvii 11.

6 ποτ ℵ[1]. ins ο bef θεος Aℵ 17. θεος ανθρωπου bef προσωπον D[1.3]F Victorin Aug. aft δοκουντες ins τι ειναι (*repetition of foregoing*) F vulg(ed, agst am Jer) Ambrst Pelag.
7 for ιδοντες, ειδοτες C f 17 al Œc-txt, ιδοτες m n.

mind to add οὐδὲν προσελαβόμην or the like but then, going off into the parenthesis ὁποῖοί ποτε ἦσαν &c, he entirely loses sight of the original construction, and proceeds with ἐμοὶ γάρ &c., which follows on the parenthesis, the γάρ rendering a reason [this is still my view, against Ellic whose note see] for the οὐδέν μοι διαφέρει &c De Wette and others think that the parenthesis ends at λαμβάνει, and the construction is resumed from ἀπὸ δέ &c. in an active instead of in a passive form · but it seems better, with Meyer, to regard the parenthesis as never formally closed, and the original construction not resumed. Other ways are; (1) most of the Greek Fathers (Chrys hardly says enough for this to be inferred as his opinion), and others (e. g. Olsh, Ruckert) take ἀπό as belonging to διαφέρει, as if it were περί so Thl, οὐδεμία μοι φροντὶς περὶ τῶν δοκούντων, &c. The preposition seems capable, if not exactly of this interpretation, of one very nearly akin to it, as in βλέπετε ἀπό and the like expressions: but the objection is, that it is unnatural to join διαφέρει with ἀπό which lies so far from it, when ὁποῖοί ποτε ἦσ. so completely fills up the construction. (2) Homberg (Parerg. p 275: Meyer) renders,—'*ab illis vero, qui videntur esse aliquid, non differo.*' But as Meyer remarks, though διαφέρω ἀπό τινος may bear this meaning, certainly διαφέρει μοι ἀπό τινος cannot. (3) Hermann assumes an aposiopesis, and understands '*what should I fear?*' but an aposiopesis seems out of place in a passage which does not rise above the fervour of narrative. See other interpretations in Meyer and De Wette. οἱ δοκοῦντ. εἶναί τι may be either subjective ('*those who believe themselves to be something*'), or objective ('*those who have the estimation of being something*') The latter is obviously the meaning here ποτε is understood by some to mean '*once,*' '*olim.*' 'whatever they once were, when Christ was on earth.' so vulg ('*quales aliquando fuerint*'), Pelag, Luth, Beza, al. But this is going out of the context, and unnecessary. The emphasis is on μοι, and is again taken up by the ἐμοὶ γάρ below Phrynichus (p 384) condemns τίνι διαφέρει as not used by the best writers, but Lobeck (note, ibid) has produced examples of it, as well as of the more approved construction τί διαφέρει, from Xenophon, Plato, and Aristotle πρόσωπ . . . λαμβ] q d. 'I wish to form all my judgments according to *God's* rule—which is that of strict unbiassed justice' See Eph. vi. 9 προσανέθεντο] as in ch i. 16, —imparted. As I, at my first conversion, did not impart it to flesh and blood, so they now imparted nothing to me · we were independent the one of the other. The meaning '*added*' (οὐκ ἐδίδαξαν, οὐ διώρθωσαν, οὐδὲν προσέθηκαν ὧν ᾔδειν, Chrys; so Thdrt., and most Commentators, and E V. '*in conference added*') is not justified by the usage of the word: see note, as above. Ruckert, Bretschneider, Olsh., al. explain it: '*laid on no additional burden.*' But this is the active, not the middle, signification of the verb see Xen. Mem. ii. 1. 8, where προσαναθέσθαι is not 'to impose on another additional duties,' but 'to take them on a man's self.' 7.] Not only did they impart nothing to *me*, but, on the contrary, they gave in their adhesion to the course which I and Barnabas had been (independently) pursuing. "In what does this opposition (ἀλλὰ τοὐναντίον) consist? Apparently in this, that instead of strengthening the hands of Paul, they left him to fight his own battle [practically but they added the weight of their approval: see Ellic]. They said, 'Take your own course preach the Gospel of the uncircumcision to Gentiles, and we will preach the Gospel of the circumcision to Jews'" Jowett ἰδόντες, viz. by the communication mentioned ver 2, coupled with the now manifest results of

Πέτρος τῆς [t] περιτομῆς (8 ὁ γὰρ [u] ἐνεργήσας Πέτρῳ
[v] εἰς [w] ἀποστολὴν τῆς [t] περιτομῆς, [u] ἐνήργησεν καὶ ἐμοὶ
εἰς τὰ ἔθνη) 9 καὶ γνόντες τὴν [x] χάριν τὴν [x] δοθεῖσάν μοι
Ἰάκωβος καὶ Κηφᾶς καὶ Ἰωάννης, οἱ [i] δοκοῦντες [y] στύλοι
εἶναι, [z] δεξιὰς [z] ἔδωκαν ἐμοὶ καὶ Βαρνάβᾳ [a] κοινωνίας, ἵνα
ἡμεῖς εἰς τὰ ἔθνη, αὐτοὶ δὲ εἰς τὴν [b] περιτομήν, 10 [c] μόνον
τῶν πτωχῶν [d] ἵνα [e] μνημονεύωμεν, ὃ καὶ [f] ἐσπούδασα [g] αὐτὸ

H και βαρναβα ... ABCDF HKLℵ a b c d e f g h k l m n o 17

t = Rom. iii. 30. see Phil. iii. 3. u w. dat., here only. Prov. xxxi. 12. w. ἐν, Rom. vii. 5. 1 Cor. xii. 6. Phil. ii. 13 al. (Isa. xli. 4.) (-γεῖν w. εἰς, of the object, Philem. 6.) v = 2 Cor. ii. 12. Col. i. 29. w Acts i. 25. Rom. i. 5. 1 Cor. ix. 2 only. Deut. xxii. 7. x = (Paul) Rom. xii. 3, 6. xv. 15. 1 Cor. i. 4. iii. 10. 2 Cor. viii. 1. Eph. iii. 2, 8. iv. 7 (29). 2 Tim. i. 9. (James iv. 6. 1 Pet. v. 5.) y = here only. 1 Tim. iii. 15. Rev. iii. 12 x. 1 only. 3 Kings vii. 41. z here only. 1 Macc. xi. 62. xiii. 45, 50 only. Jos. Antt. xviii. 9. 3. a = Acts ii. 42. Levit. vi. 2. arrangt. of words, 1 Thess. ii. 13. b = ver. 7. ellips., ch. v. 13. Rom. iv. 16. c 1 Cor. vii. 39. ch. i. 23. v. 13 al. d inversion of words, John xiii. 29. Acts xix. 4. Rom. xi. 31. 1 Cor. ix. 15. xiv. 9. 2 Cor. ii. 4. e = Col. iv. 18. 1 Macc. xii. 11. f Eph. iv. 3 reff. g Acts xxiv. 15, 26. 2 Cor. ii. 3. vii. 11 al.

8. om ο γαρ to περιτομης (homœot) ℵ[1]: ins ℵ-corr[1a]. καμοι ACD[1]F a f k m 17 Chr$_2$ Damasc: txt BD[3]KLℵ rel Chr Thl Œc.

9. for ιακωβ. κ. κηφας, πετρος κ. ιακωβ. DF fuld goth Thdrt$_1$ Nyssen Iren-lat Tert: ιακωβος (omg και κηφ.) A Epiph: txt BCKLℵ rel vulg syrr copt Ath Chr Thdrt$_2$ Damasc Aug Pelag Bede. aft ημεις ins μεν (*to correspond to δε follg*) ACD ℵ-corr[1 9&1] a b d[2] f h o 67[2] syr copt Naz Bas Chr$_2$ Thdrt$_2$ Damasc: om BFHKLℵ[1] rel latt goth Orig$_2$ Chr Thl Œc lat-ff.

10. ινα bef των πτωχων DF vss lat-ff.

his preaching among the Gentiles. Compare Acts xv. 12. **πεπίστ.** (for construction see reff. Acts and 1 Cor. and other examples in Winer, Gram., § 39. 1. a) has the emphasis: **they saw that I was** (lit. **am**: the state being one still abiding) ENTRUSTED **with the Gospel of the uncircumcision, as Peter with that of the circumcision**; therefore they had only to accede to the appointment of God. **τῆς ἀκροβ.**] i. e. belonging to, addressed to, the uncircumcised (*οὐ τὰ πράγματα λέγων αὐτά, ἀλλὰ τὰ ἀπὸ τούτων γνωριζόμενα ἔθνη*, Chrys.). Peter was not the Apostle of the circumcision *only*, for he had opened the door to the Gentiles (Acts x., to which he refers, ib. xv. 7), but in the ultimate assignment of the apostolic work, he wrought less among the Gentiles and more among the Jews than Paul: see 1 Pet. i. 1, and note. But his own Epistles are sufficient testimonies that, in his hands at least, the Gospel of the circumcision did not differ in any essential point from that of the uncircumcision. Cf., as an interesting trait on the other side, Col. iv. 11. **8.**] Parenthetic explanation of *πεπίστευμαι κ.τ.λ.* *Πέτρῳ* and *ἐμοί* are datives commodi, not governed by the *ἐν* in *ἐνεργ.*, the meaning of this preposition being already expressed in the word *ἐνεργεῖν*, and having therefore no force to pass on: cf. ref. Prov. **ἐνήργ.** applies to the *ἀπακολουθοῦντα σημεῖα* with which the Lord accompanied His word spoken by them, and to the power with which they spoke that word. The agent in *ἐνεργ.* is GOD,—the Father: see 1 Cor. xii. 6; Phil. ii. 13; Rom. xv. 15, 16. **εἰς ἀποστ.**] towards, with a view to, **the Apostleship**,—reff. **εἰς τὰ ἔθνη**] The fuller construction would be, *εἰς ἀποστολὴν τ. ἐθνῶν*: so *τάων οὔτις ὁμοῖα νοήματα Πηνελοπείῃ | ᾔδη*, Od. β. 120: and frequently. **9.**] resumes the narrative after the parenthesis. **Ἰάκωβος**] placed first, as being at the head of the church at Jerusalem, and presiding (apparently) at the conference in Acts xv. **δοκοῦντες** alludes to vv. 2 and 6; see there. **στύλοι**] pillars, i. e. principal supporters of the church, men of distinction and weight; see reff., and examples in Wetst.: and Suicer, sub voce. Clem.-rom. ad Cor. i. 5, p. 217, uses the word directly, without metaphor: *οἱ δικαιότατοι στύλοι ἐδιώχθησαν*. **δεξ. ἔδωκ. κοιν.**] On the separation of the genitive from its governing noun, see Winer, § 30. 3, note 2. It is made here, because what follows respects rather *κοινωνίας* than *ἔδωκαν*. **ἵνα κ.τ.λ.**] There is an ellipsis of some verb; *πορευθῶμεν* and *-θῶσιν*, or perhaps *εὐαγγελιζώμεθα*, *-ζωνται*, which might connect with *εἰς* (see 1 Thess. ii. 9; 1 Pet. i. 25. But Meyer objects that it is not found with *εἰς* in St. Paul): or as Beza, *ἀπόστολοι γενώμεθα*. Similar ellipses occur Rom. iv. 16; ch. v. 13. This division of labour was not, and could not be, strictly observed. Every where in the Acts we find St. Paul preaching 'to the Jews first,' and every where the Judaizers followed on his track: see Jowett's note.

10. μόν. τ. πτ. ἵνα μν.] The genitive is put before the conjunction for emphasis: see reff., and 2 Thess. ii. 7, and

τοῦτο ποιῆσαι. 11 ὅτε δὲ ἦλθεν Κηφᾶς εἰς Ἀντιόχειαν, [h]
[i] κατὰ πρόσωπον αὐτῷ [j] ἀντέστην, ὅτι [k] κατεγνωσμένος ἦν.

h Luke ii 31 Acts iii 13 xxv 16. 2 Cor x 1 2 Chron xiii 8 20, 21 only i Deut vii 24 Deut xxv 1 j Acts vi 10 xiii 8 Job xli 2 al. k 1 John iii

11 rec (for κηφας) πετρος, with DFKL rel demid goth Chr Thl Œc Tert *petrus cephas* fuld. txt ABCHℵ 17. 67² vulg Syr syr-marg coptt Clem(in Eus) Chron Damasc Pelag Ambrst

John xiii. 29, where remarkably enough it is the same word which precedes ἵνα, . τοῖς πτωχοῖς ἵνα τὶ δῷ The construction is complete without supplying any participle (αἰτοῦντες or παρακαλοῦντες), depending upon ἔδωκαν ὃ καὶ ἐσπ αὐτὸ τ ποι] **which was the very thing that I also was anxious to do,**—viz, then and always. it was my habit So that ἐσπούδασα has not a pluperfect sense. He uses the singular, because the plural could not correctly be predicated of the whole time to which the verb refers for he parted from Barnabas shortly after the council in Acts xv Meyer understands ἐσπούδ of the time subsequent to the council only: but this does not seem necessary The proofs of this σπουδή on his part may be found, Rom. xv 25—27; 1 Cor xvi 1—4, 2 Cor. viii ix; Acts xxiv 17 which, though they probably happened after the date of our Epistle, yet shewed the bent of his habitual wishes on this point **αὐτὸ τοῦτο** is not merely redundant, as in ἧς εἶχεν τὸ θυγάτριον αὐτῆς πνεῦμα ἀκάθαρτον, Mark vii 25,—but is an emphatic repetition of that to which ὃ refers, as in the version above So that ὃ ἐσπ. αὐτὸ τοῦτο ποι = καὶ ἐσπ. τὸ αὐτὸ τοῦτο ποι. Cf Thuc i 10,—Ἀθηναίων δὲ τὸ αὐτὸ τοῦτο παθόντων. Cf Ellicott's note. 11—17.] *He further proves his independence, by relating how he rebuked Peter for temporizing at Antioch.* This proof goes further than any before: not only was he not taught originally by the Apostles,—not only did they impart nothing to him, rather tolerating his view and recognizing his mission,—but he on one occasion stood aloof from and reprimanded the chief of them for conduct unworthy the Gospel · thus setting his own Apostleship in *opposition* to Peter, for the time. 11 **ὅτε δὲ ἦλθ**] This visit of Peter to Antioch, not related in the Acts, will fall most naturally (for our narrative follows the order of time) in the period described, Acts xv 35, seeing that (ver 13) Barnabas also was there See below. **Κηφᾶς**] ἡ ἱστορία παρὰ Κλήμεντι κατὰ τὴν πέμπτην τῶν ὑποτυπώσεων, ἐν ᾗ καὶ Κηφᾶν, περὶ οὗ φησὶν ὁ Παῦλος Ὅτε δὲ ἦλθ. Κ. εἰς Ἀντ κατ. πρ. αὐτ ἀντέστην, ἕνα φησὶ γεγονέναι τῶν ἑβδομήκοντα μαθητῶν, ὁμώνυμον Πέτρῳ τυγχάνοντα τῷ ἀποστόλῳ Eus H E. i 12. This story was manifestly invented to save the credit of St. Peter. See below **κατὰ πρόσωπον**] **to the face,**—see reff not '*before all*,' which is asserted by and by, ver 14 One of the most curious instances of ecclesiastical ingenuity on record has been afforded in the interpretation of this passage by the fathers. They try to make it appear that the reproof was only an apparent one—that ὁ θεῖος Πέτρος was entirely in the right, and Paul withstood him, κατὰ πρόσωπον, '*in appearance merely*,' because he had been blamed by others So Chrys so Thdrt. also and Jerome,—"Paulus . . nova usus est arte pugnandi, ut dispensationem Petri, qua Judæos salvari cupiebat, nova ipse contradictionis dispensatione corrigeret, et resisteret ei in facie, non arguens propositum, sed quasi in publico contradicens, ut ex eo quod Paulus eum arguens resistebat, hi qui crediderant e gentibus servarentur." In Ep ad Gal. ad loc. This view of his met with strong opposition from Augustine, who writes to him, nobly and worthily, Ep. 40 3, vol ii p 155, ed Migne "In expositione quoque Ep. Pauli ad Gal., invenimus aliquid, quod nos multum moveat Si enim ad Scripturas sanctas admissa fuerint velut officiosa mendacia, quid in eis remanebit auctoritatis? Quæ tandem de Scripturis illis sententia proferetur, cujus pondere contentiosæ falsitatis obteratur improbitas? Statim enim ut protuleris. si aliter sapit qui contra nititur, dicet illud quod prolatum erit honesto aliquo officio scriptorum fuisse mentitum. Ubi enim hoc non poterit, si potuit in ea narratione, quam exorsus Apostolus ait, *Quæ autem scribo vobis, ecce coram Deo quia non mentior*, credi affirmarique mentitus, eo loco ubi dixit de Petro et Barnaba, *cum viderem, quia non recte ingrediuntur ad veritatem Evangelii*? Si enim recte illi ingrediebantur, iste mentitus est. si autem ibi mentitus est, ubi verum dixit? Cur ibi verum dixisse videbitur, ubi hoc dixerit quod lector sapit; cum vero contra sensum lectoris aliquid occurrerit, officioso mendacio deputabitur? . . . . Quare arripe, obsecro te, ingenuam et vere Christianam cum caritate severitatem, ad illud opus corrigendum et emendandum, et παλινῳδίαν, ut

12 πρὸ τοῦ γὰρ ἐλθεῖν τινας ἀπὸ Ἰακώβου μετὰ τῶν ABCDF
ἐθνῶν [l] συνήσθιεν· ὅτε δὲ ἦλθον, [m] ὑπέστελλεν καὶ [n] ἀφ- HKLℵ a b c d e f
ώριζεν ἑαυτόν, φοβούμενος τοὺς [o] ἐκ περιτομῆς, 13 καὶ g h k l m n o 17
[p] συνυπεκρίθησαν αὐτῷ καὶ οἱ λοιποὶ Ἰουδαῖοι, ὥςτε καὶ

l Luke xv 2. Acts x 41. xi 3. 1 Cor v 11 only. Gen xliii 32. m — but mid, Heb x 38, from Hab ii 4 (Acts xx 20, 27 only. Deut i 17) see 2 Thess iii 6. Demosth 54 ult. n — Acts xix 9. 2 Cor vi 17, from Isa lii 11 (ch i 15) al. o Acts x 45. xi 2. Rom iv 12. Col iv 11. Tit i 10 only. p here only †. Polyb iii. 92 5, Φυβιος . . . συνυπεκρινετο τοις φ λοκινδυνως διακειμενοις & al.

12. ηλθεν BD[1]Fℵ e k Orig(ελθοντος ιακωβου), *venisset* D-lat G-lat some mss of vulg: txt ACD[2] [3]HKL rel vss gr-lat-ff, *venissent* am(with fuld F-lat), *venirent* vulg-ed(and demid).

13. om 2nd και B 67[2] vulg(and F-lat) copt goth. aft ιουδαιοι ins παντες ℵ[1](ℵ[3]

dicitur, cane Incomparabiliter enim pulchrior est veritas Christianorum, quam Helena Græcorum. . . ." (Similarly in several other Epistles in vol ii ed Migne, where also Jerome's replies may be seen.) Afterwards, Jerome abandoned his view for the right one · 'Nonne idem Paulus in faciem Cephæ restitit, quod non recto pede incederet in Evangelio ?' Apol. adv. Ruf. iii. 2, vol ii p 532 · see also cont. Pelag i 22, p 718. Aug. Ep. 180 5, vol. ii p 779. **ὅτι κατεγνωσμένος ἦν]** (not, as vulgate, *quia reprehensibilis erat* ['because he was to be blamed,' E. V.. similarly Calv., Beza, al.]. no such meaning can be extracted from the perfect participle passive, nor can Hebrew usage be alleged for such a meaning in Greek The instance commonly cited from Lucian de saltat, p. 952, ἀληθῶς, ἐπὶ μανίᾳ κατεγνωσμένος, is none whatever, nor is Iliad, α 388, ὃ δὴ τετελεσμένος ἐστί the perfect participle having in both its proper sense Nor again is ψηλαφωμένῳ (ὄρει), Heb xii 18, at all to the purpose · see note there) **because he was condemned** ('a condemned man,' as we say by whom, does not appear: possibly, *by his own act*. or, *by the Christians in Antioch* · but St. Paul would hardly have waited for the prompting of others to pronounce his condemnation of him I therefore prefer the former **he was [self] convicted** convicted of inconsistency by his conduct) **12**] These τινες ἀπὸ Ἰακώβου have been softened by some Commentators into persons who merely *gave themselves out* as from James (Winer, &c and even Ellicott, edn. 2), or who merely came from Jerusalem where James presided (Beza, Grot, Olsh., &c.) But the candid reader will I think at once recognize in the words a *mission* from James (so Thl., Œc, Estius [doubtfully], Ruckert, Meyer, De W) and will find no difficulty in believing that that Apostle, even after the decision of the council regarding the Gentile converts, may have retained (characteristically, see his recommendation to St Paul, in Acts xxi 18 ff) his strict view of the duties of Jewish converts,—for that is perhaps all that the present passage requires. And this mission may have been for the very purpose of admonishing the Jewish converts of *their* obligations, from which the Gentiles were free. Thus we have no occasion to assume (with De W) that James had in the council been over-persuaded by the earnestness and eloquence of Paul, and had afterwards undergone a reaction · for his course will be consistent throughout. And my view seems to me to be confirmed by his own words, Acts xv. 19, where the emphatic τοῖς ἀπὸ τῶν ἐθνῶν ἐπιστρέφουσιν tacitly implies, that the Jews would be bound as before. **συνήσθιεν**] As he had done, Acts x, on the prompting of a heavenly vision, and himself defended it, Acts xi. See below. **ὑπέστελλεν**] as well as ἀφώριζεν, governs ἑαυτόν: **withdrew himself.** So Polyb i. 16 10, ὁ δὲ βασιλεὺς Ἱέρων, ὑποστείλας ἑαυτὸν ὑπὸ τὴν Ῥωμαίων σκέπην, and al. freq. The imperfects express that there were more cases than one where he did this—it was the course he took **φοβούμενος**] **being afraid of.** Chrys, to bear out his interpretation of the whole incident, says, οὐ τοῦτο φοβούμενος, μὴ κινδυνεύσῃ· ὁ γὰρ ἐν ἀρχῇ μὴ φοβηθεὶς (witness his denial of his Lord), πολλῷ μᾶλλον τότε· ἀλλ' ἵνα μὴ ἀποστῶσιν. ἐπεὶ καὶ αὐτὸς λέγει Γαλάταις, φοβοῦμαι ὑμᾶς μή πως εἰκῇ κεκοπίακα κ.τ.λ. And so Piscator, Grot., Estius, al. The whole incident is remarkably characteristic of Peter—ever the first to recognize, and the first to draw back from, great principles and truths. see this very ably enlarged on in Jowett's note on ver 11 **13 συνυπεκρ**] **were guilty of like hypocrisy.** The word is not (as De W.) too strong a one to describe their conduct They were aware of the liberty in Christ which allowed them to eat with Gentiles, and had practised it. and now, being still aware of it, and not *convinced* to the contrary, from mere fear of man they adopted a contrary course The case here

Βαρνάβας [q] συναπήχθη αὐτῶν τῇ [r] ὑποκρίσει. 14 ἀλλ᾽
ὅτε εἶδον ὅτι οὐκ [s] ὀρθοποδοῦσιν [t] πρὸς τὴν [u] ἀλήθειαν
τοῦ [u] εὐαγγελίου, εἶπον τῷ Κηφᾷ [v] ἔμπροσθεν πάντων Εἰ

ι αλη-θειαν II. ABCDF KLℵ a b d e f g h k l m n o 17

q Rom xii 16. 2 Pet iii 17 only. Exod xiv 6 only constr, John iii 16 only see Winer, § 41 5, note 1 r Matt xxiii 28 Mark xii 15 Luke xii 1 1 Tim iv 2 (James v 12 v r) 1 Pet ii 1 only † 2 Macc vi 25 only s here only † pres., John i 40 ii 9 Acts iv 13 al Winer, § 11 2 c t = Luke xii 47 2 Cor v 10 u ver 5 v = Matt v 16 al 2 Kings iii 31 F see 1 Tim v 20

disapproving) συνυπηχθη partly written by ℵ[1] συνυπαχθηναι a τη υποκρ. bef αυτων DFH b m o 17 latt txt ABCKL rel Chr Damasc.

14 for ειδ., ιδον AD[2]FL m. rec (for κηφα) πετρω, with DFKL rel fuld-vict syr goth Chr Victorin txt ABCℵ 17. 67[2](Bch) vulg Syr coptt æth arm Clem(in Eus) Ps-Ath

but very little likeness to that discussed in 1 Cor viii—x; Rom. xiv There, it was a mere matter of *licence* which was in question · here, the very foundation itself. It was not now a question of using a liberty, but of asserting a truth, that of justification by the faith of Christ, and not by the works of the law ὥστε . . . συναπήχθη] The indicative usually follows ὥστε, when the result is matter of fact · the infinitive usually, when it is matter of course as well So Herod vi. 83,—Ἄργος δὲ ἀνδρῶν ἐχηρώθη οὕτω, ὥστε οἱ δοῦλοι αὐτέων ἔσχον πάντα τὰ πρήγματα, where it was not a necessary consequence of the depopulation, but a result which followed as matter of fact (so also John iii 16, where the sending the Son to be the Saviour of the world was not a necessary consequence of the Father's love, but followed it as its result in fact. so that it is [against Ellic edn. 1] an instance in point). Plat. Apol 37 c,—οὕτως ἀλόγιστός εἰμι, ὥστε μὴ δύνασθαι λογίζεσθαι, where the degree of ἀλογία supposed involves the result of not being able to reason at all. See Kruger, Gram. § 65, 3. 1, Kuhner, ii. p. 563 But the distinction does not seem always to be accurately observed. On συναπ., see ref. Rom, and note. Understand αὐτοῖς after συναπ., and take τῇ ὑπ. as the instrumental dative '*was carried away* (*with them*) *by their hypocrisy*' or possibly the dative of the state *into* which &c · see 2 Pet. iii 17. but this construction seems questionable. see Ellic. edn 2. Fritz. cites Zosimus, Hist. v. 6, καὶ αὐτὴ δὲ ἡ Σπάρτη συναπήγετο τῇ κοινῇ τῆς Ἑλλάδος ἁλώσει: add Clem. Alex. Strom. i 17, p. 368 P., τῇ ἡδονῇ συναπαγόμενος (Ellicott). "Besides the antagonism in which this passage represents the two great Apostles, it throws an important light on the history of the apostolic church in the following respects —1] As exhibiting Peter's relation to James, and his fear of those who were of the circumcision, whose leader we should have naturally supposed him to have been. 2] Also, as pourtraying the state of indecision in which all, except St. Paul, even including Barnabas, were in reference to the observance of the Jewish law." Jowett

14] ὀρθοποδεῖν apparently not occurring elsewhere, its meaning must be got from cognate words We have ἀτραπὸν ὀρθοβατεῖν, Anthol. ix 11, ὀρθοπραγεῖν, Arist Eth. Eud iii 2, and ὀρθοτομέω, ὀρθοδρομέω, &c. to walk straight is therefore undoubtedly its import, and metaphorically (cf περιπατεῖν, στοιχεῖν frequently in Paul), to behave uprightly

πρός] It is best, with Meyer, to take ἀλήθεια as in ver 5, and render, connecting πρός with ὀρθοποδοῦσιν, towards (with a view to) maintaining and propagating the truth (objectively, the unadulterated character) of the Gospel Others (De W, al) render πρός '*with reference to*,' ('*according to*,' E V,) and take τ. ἀλήθ τ εὐ to mean '*the truth* (*-fulness of character*) *required by the Gospel*' Mey remarks, that St. Paul does not express *nouns* after verbs of motion by πρός, but by κατά, cf Rom viii 4; xiv 15, 1 Cor iii. 3. Ellic however answers, that in all these instances, περιπατέω, St. Paul's favourite verb of moral motion, is used, and that ὀρθοποδέω does not so plainly express motion as περιπατέω. Still, I prefer the former meaning, as better suiting the expression ἡ ἀλήθεια τ εὐαγγ cf. ver 5 ἔμπρ. πάντ] 'before the church assembled The words require this, and the reproof would otherwise have fallen short of its desired effect on the Jewish converts The speech which follows, and which I believe to extend to the end of the chapter, must be regarded as a compendium of what was said, and a free report of it, as we find in the narratives by St Paul himself of his conversion. See below. If thou, being (by birth, originally, cf Acts xvi 20 and note) a Jew, livest (as thy usual habit. As Neander [Pfl. u. Leit., p 111] remarks, these words shew that Peter had long been himself convinced of the truth on this matter, and lived according to it · see further on ver 18) as a Gentile (*how*, is shewn by μετὰ τῶν ἐθνῶν συνήσθιεν

w = ch. i. 14 reff. x here only †. (-κός, Matt. v. 47.) y here only †. (-κός, Tit. i. 14.) z = Rom. vi. 2. 1 Cor. xv. 12. ch. iv. 9. a = ver. 3 reff.

σὺ Ἰουδαῖος [w] ὑπάρχων [x] ἐθνικῶς καὶ οὐκ [y] Ἰουδαϊκῶς ζῇς,
[z] πῶς τὰ ἔθνη [a] ἀναγκάζεις [b] Ἰουδαΐζειν; 15 ἡμεῖς [c] φύσει
Ἰουδαῖοι καὶ οὐκ [d] ἐξ [d] ἐθνῶν [e] ἁμαρτωλοί, 16 εἰδότες δὲ
ὅτι οὐ [f] δικαιοῦται ἄνθρωπος [f] ἐξ ἔργων νόμου, [g] ἐὰν
μὴ διὰ [h] πίστεως [h] Ἰησοῦ χριστοῦ, καὶ ἡμεῖς εἰς χριστὸν

ABCDF KLℵ a b c d e f g h k l m n o 17

b here only. Esth. viii. 17 (ix. 4) only. (-σμός, ch. i. 13, 14.) c Rom. ii. 14. ch. iv. 8. Eph. ii. 3 only. (-σις, Rom. i. 26 al.† Wisd. vii. 20 only.) d Acts xv. 14, 23. Rom. ix. 24. e = Tobit xiii. 6. see Rom. ii. 12. 1 Cor. vi. 1. ix. 21. Eph. ii. 12. 1 Kings xv. 18. f Rom. iii. 20. iv. 2. James ii. 21, 24, 25. g = εἰ μή, Matt. xii. 4. Rev. ix. 4. ἐὰν μή, = here only. see note. h obj. gen., Rom. iii. 22, 26 al.

Did₂ Thdrt Dial-trin Philo-carp Pelag. for υπαρχ., ων D¹. rec ζῃς bef και ουκ ιουδαικως, with DKL rel syrr goth Chr Thdrt Damasc Thl Œc: txt ABCFℵ m 17 am(with [besides F-lat] demid fuld) arm Orig Philo-carp lat-ff(but D-lat Ambrst Sedul Agap om και ουκ ιουδ.).—ουχ ABCℵ¹ m 17 Chr₁: ουχι D³ℵ³ d² l Damasc: om ουκ c d¹.—om και a. rec (for πως) τι, with KL rel syr Chr Thdrt Thl Œc: txt ABCDFℵ m 17 latt Syr copt æth Orig Damasc lat-ff.

16. rec om δε, with AD³K rel vss gr-ff: ins BCD¹FLℵ latt goth Cyr Thdrt₁ lat-ff, ουν f. χριστου bef ιησ. AB 17 Victorin Aug$_{sl}$: txt CDFKLℵ rel vss Chr Cyr Thdrt

above) **and not as a Jew, how** (is it that [reff.]) **thou art compelling the Gentiles** (i. e. virtually and ultimately; for the high authority of Peter and Barnabas would make the Gentile converts view their course as necessary to all Christians. There is no need, with De W. and Wieseler, to suppose that the τινες ἀπὸ Ἰακ. actually compelled the Gentile converts to Judaize, as necessary to salvation, and Peter upheld them: nor is there any difficulty in the expression: the present may mean, as it often does, '*art compelling to the best of thy power,*' '*doing thy part to compel,*'—for such certainly would be the *ultimate result*, if Jews and Gentiles might not company together in social life—"his principle logically involved this, or his influence and example would be likely to effect it." Jowett) **to Judaize** (observe the ceremonial law)!

15.] Some (Calv., Beza, Grot., Hermann, al.) think that the speech ends with ver. 14: Calov., al., with ver. 15: Luther, al., with ver. 16: Flatt, Neander, al., with ver. 18: Jowett, that the conversation gradually passes off into the general subject of the Epistle. "Ver. 14," he says, "is the answer of St. Paul to St. Peter: what follows, is more like the Apostle musing or arguing with himself, with an indirect reference to the Galatians." But it seems very unnatural to place any break before the end of the chapter. The Apostle recurs to the Galatians again with ὦ ἀνόητοι Γαλάται, ch. iii. 1: and it is harsh in the extreme to suppose him to pass from his speech to Peter into an address to them with so little indication of the transition. I therefore regard the speech (which doubtless is freely reported, and gives rather the bearing of what was said, than the words themselves, as in Acts xxii. and xxvi.) as continuing to the end of the chapter, as do Chr., Thdrt., Jer., Est., Beng., Rosenm., Winer, Rückert, Usteri, Olsh., B.-Crus., Meyer, De W. **We** (thou and I) **by nature** (birth) **Jews and not sinners from among the Gentiles** (he is speaking to Peter from the common ground of their Judaism, and using [ironically?] Judaistic language, in which the Gentiles were ἄθεοι, ἄνομοι, ἄδικοι, ἁμαρτωλοί [reff.]. The putting a comma after ἐθνῶν, and taking ἁμαρτωλοί with ἡμ. φύσ. Ἰουδ. [Prim. in Est., Elsner, Er.-Schmid, al.], '*We, by birth Jews, and, though not from the Gentiles, yet sinners,*' is absurd), **knowing nevertheless** (this seems, against Ellic. ed. 2, the proper force of **δέ** here, and is the same in sense as his "*but as we know,*" but clearer) **that a man is not justified by** (as the ground of justification: see Ellic.'s note on the sense of ἐκ) **the works of the law** (not, '*by works of law,*' or '*on the score of duty done*' [Peile]: this, though following as an inference, and a generalization of the axiom, was not in question here. '*The works of the law,*' just as 'the faith of Jesus Christ;' the genitives in both cases being objective—the works which have the law [ceremonial and moral] for their object,—which are wrought to fulfil the law: Meyer compares ἁμαρτήματα νόμου, Wisd. ii. 12,—faith which has Jesus Christ for its object,—which is reposed in or on Him. On δικαιόω, see note, Rom. i. 17),—(supply, nor is any man justified, and see reff.) **except by** (as the medium of justification. Ellic. observes that two constructions seem to be mixed: οὐ δικ. ἄνθ. ἐξ ἔργ. ν., and οὐ δικ. ἄνθ. ἐὰν μὴ διὰ π. Ἰ. χ. ἐὰν μή in this elliptical construction is not elsewhere found; but εἰ μή repeatedly [reff.]. The ἐάν seems to remove further off the

Ἰησοῦν [i] ἐπιστεύσαμεν, ἵνα [f h] δικαιωθῶμεν [h] ἐκ [h] πίστεως
[h] χριστοῦ καὶ οὐκ [i] ἐξ ἔργων νόμου, ὅτι [f] ἐξ ἔργων
νόμου οὐ [f] δικαιωθήσεται [l] πᾶσα σάρξ. 17 εἰ δὲ ζητοῦντες
δικαιωθῆναι [m] ἐν χριστῷ [n] εὑρέθημεν καὶ αὐτοὶ ἁμαρτωλοί,
[o] ἆρα χριστὸς ἁμαρτίας [p] διάκονος; [q] μὴ γένοιτο. 18 εἰ

i aor., — Acts xix 2 Rom xiii 11 1 Cor iii 5 πιστ εις, John i 12 and passim Acts x 43 xix 4 Rom x 14 al. k Rom iii 30 v 1 ch iii 8, 24 l constr, Rom iii 20 Matt xxiv 22 Acts x 14 Exod xv 26 m = Col i 16 reff n = Matt i 18 Rom vii 10 Neh ix 8 o Luke xviii 8 Acts viii 30 only Gen xxvi 9 vat (ἄρα F) p see Rom xv 8 2 Cor xi 15. q Gospp., Luke xx 16 only Rom iii 4, 6, 31 al6 1 Cor vi 15 only L P. Josh xxii 29

Ambr Jer Aug₂. ιησουν bef χριστον B a¹ 17 syr copt æth Thdrt₁ Aug₂ · om ιησ d¹ l om 2nd χριστου F Thdrt₁ Tert Tisch (*see Rom* iii 28 *al*). ιησ χ K syr-w-ast. rec διοτι, with CD³KL rel · txt ABD¹Fℵ 17 67² Damasc. rec ου δικαιωθησεται bef εξ εργων, with KL rel goth Thdrt₁ Thl Œc. ουκ εξ εργ ν δικ a: txt ABCDFℵ m 17 latt syrr copt arm Thdrt₁ Damasc₂ lat-ff.

hypothesis, which arises in the mind, of the two being united) **the faith of** (see above) **Jesus Christ,—we also** (as well as the Gentile sinners, q. d., casting aside our legal trust) **believed** (reff) **on Christ Jesus** (notice Ἰησ. χρ above, χρ. Ἰησ here This is not arbitrary. In the general proposition above, Ἰησ χρ, as the name of Him on whom faith is to be exercised here, when Jews receive Him as their Messiah, χρ. Ἰησ, as bringing that Messiahship into prominence Perhaps, however, such considerations are but precarious For example, in this case, the readings are in some confusion It may be remarked, that the Codex Sinaiticus agrees throughout with our text) **that we might be justified by** (this time, faith is the *ground*) **the faith of Christ, and not by the works of the law: because** (it is an axiom in our theology that) **by the works of the law shall all flesh find no justification** (Angl. · '*shall no flesh be justified*' our language not admitting of the logical form of the Greek: but by this transposition of the negative, the sense is not accurately rendered). There is a difference between Commentators in the arrangement of the foregoing sentence. Meyer follows Lachmann in placing a period after χριστοῦ, and understanding ἐσμέν at Ἰουδ. or ἁμαρτωλοί. Beza, Hermann, Ruckert, Usteri, Ellicott, al., begin a new sentence at εἰδότες δέ, also understanding ἐσμέν. But it seems much better, as above (with De W, al), to carry on the sentence throughout Meyer's objection, that thus it would not represent the matter of fact, for Peter and Paul were not converted as εἰδότες κ τ λ., would apply equally to his own arrangement, for they were not converted ἵνα δικαιωθῶσιν κ τ λ

17] Continues the argument. **But if, seeking** (put first for emphasis—in the course of our earnest endeavour) **to be justified in Christ** (as the element—the Body, comprehending us the members This is lost sight of by rendering '*through* Christ'), **we ourselves also** (you and I, addressed to Peter) **were found to be sinners** (as we should be, if we regarded the keeping of the law as necessary, for we should be just in the situation of those Gentiles who in the Judaistic view are ἁμαρτωλοί, faith having failed in obtaining righteousness for us, and we having cast aside the law which we were bound to keep), **is therefore Christ the minister of sin** (i e are we to admit the consequence which would in that case be inevitable, that Christ, having failed to obtain for his own the righteousness which is by faith, has left them sinners, and so has done all His work only to minister to a state of sin)? Whether we read ἄρα or ἆρα matters little; either will express the meaning, but the latter more pungently than the former The clause must be interrogative, as μὴ γένοιτο always follows a question in St. Paul; see reff. Those who would take ἆρα for ἆρ' οὐ [qu. can it ever be so taken, in spite of Matthiæ (Gr Gr § 611), Winer (comm. h. l, but not in Gr. ed 6, § 57 2, where he allows the translation given above), Monk (on Eur Alcest. 353), and Porson (pref. to Hec. p. x)?] seem to me to miss altogether the fine irony of the question, which, as it stands, presupposes the ἆρ' οὐ question already asked, the inevitable answer given, and now puts the result, 'Can we believe, are we to hold henceforth, such a consequence?' The same might be said of all the passages alleged by the above scholars in support of their view. Theodoret expresses well the argument εἰ δὲ ὅτι τὸν νόμον καταλιπόντες τῷ χριστῷ προσεληλύθαμεν, διὰ τῆς ἐπ' αὐτὸν πίστεως τῆς δικαιοσύνης ἀπολαύσασθαι προσδοκήσαντες, παράβασις τοῦτο νενόμισται, εἰς αὐτὸν ἡ αἰτία χωρήσει τὸν δεσπότην χριστόν αὐτὸς γὰρ ἡμῖν τὴν

r = Matt xxvi 61 Acts vi 14 2 Cor v 1 James ii 12 s = Rom xv 20 t Rom ii 25, 27 James ii 9, 11 only † Ps xvi 4 Symm u = Paul only, Rom iii 5 v 8. 2 Cor vi 4 Susann 61 Theod

γὰρ ἃ ʳκατέλυσα, ταῦτα πάλιν ˢοἰκοδομῶ, ᵗπαραβάτην ABCDF
ἐμαυτὸν ᵘσυνιστάνω. 19 ἐγὼ γὰρ διὰ νόμου ᵛνόμῳ ʷἀπ- KLℵ a b
έθανον, ἵνα ᵛθεῷ ζήσω. 20 χριστῷ ˣσυνεσταύρωμαι· ζῶ c d e f g
δὲ οὐκ ἔτι ἐγώ, ζῇ δὲ ἐν ἐμοὶ χριστός· ʸὃ δὲ νῦν ζῶ ᶻἐν h k l m
σαρκί, ἐν πίστει ζῶ τῇ τοῦ ᵃυἱοῦ τοῦ θεοῦ τοῦ ἀγαπή- n o 17
σαντός με καὶ ᵇᶜπαραδόντος ᵇἑαυτὸν ὑπὲρ ἐμοῦ. 21 οὐκ

ἀνέστ 2 Cor iii 1 v 12 x 12, 18 only. v dat., = Rom vi 2, 11 w = Col ii 20 x Matt xxvii 44 | Mk | J Rom vi 6 only † y accus of object Rom vi 10 z = 1 Tim iii 16 reff a gen, ver 16 b Eph v 25 only παρ., = Rom iv 25 Isa liii 12. c 1 Cor i 19 ch. iii 15 Isa xxxi 2 see 1 Thess iv 8

18. rec συνιστημι, with D³KL rel: txt ABCD¹Fℵ 17. 67² Cyr
20 ins ο bef χριστος F Ign om 3rd ζω A for του υι. τ. θ., του θεου κ. χριστου BD¹F txt ACD²·³KLℵ rel vulg(and F-lat) syrr copt goth Clem Dial Chr Cyr₄ Thdrt Damasc Ambrst.

καινὴν ὑπέδειξε διαθήκην ἀλλὰ μὴ γένοιτο ταύτην ἡμᾶς τολμῆσαι τὴν βλασφημίαν

18] **For** (substantiates the *μὴ γένοιτο*, and otherwise deduces the *εὑρέθημεν ἁμαρτωλοί*) **if the things which I pulled down, those very things** (and no others) **I again build up** (which thou art doing, who in Cæsarea didst so plainly announce freedom from the law, and again here in Antioch didst practise it thyself. The *first person* is chosen *clementiæ causa*; the *second* would have placed Peter, where the first means that he should place *himself*), **I am proving** (reff) **myself a transgressor** (*παραβάτης* is the species, bringing me under the genus *ἁμαρτωλός*. So that *παραβ. ἐμ. συνιστ.* is the explanation of *ἁμαρτωλοὶ εὑρέθημεν*). The *force* of the verse is,—'You, by now reasserting the obligation of the law, are proving (*quoad te*) that your former step of setting aside the law was in fact a *transgression* of it:' viz. in that you neglected and set it aside,—not, as Chrys., Thl., and Meyer (from ver. 19), because the law itself was leading you on to faith in Christ: for (1) that point is not yet raised, not belonging to this portion of the argument, and (2) by the hypothesis of this verse the *ἐγώ* has *given up* the faith in Christ, and so cannot be regarded as acknowledging it as the end of the law. See against this view, but to me not convincingly, Ellicott, ed. 2.

19] **For** (the *γάρ* [agst Ellic.] retains, on our view of *παραβάτης*, its full exemplifying force) **I** (*ἐγώ*, for the first time expressed, is marked and emphatic. The first person of the *last* verse, serves as the transition point to treating, as he now does, of HIS OWN state and course. And this *ἐγώ*, as that in Rom. vii., is purely and bona fide 'I Paul;' not 'I and all believers') **by means of the law died to the law** (Christ was the end of the law for righteousness: the law itself, properly apprehended by me, was my *παιδαγωγός* to Christ: and in Christ, who fulfilled the law, I died to the law: i. e. satisfied the law's requirements, and passed out of its pale: the dative, as Ellic. remarks, is a sort of dativus commodi, as also in *ζῆν θεῷ*) **that I should live to God** (the end of Christ's work, LIFE unto God. *ζήσω* is 1 aor. subj. in subordination to the aor. preceding: not fut., as stated in former edd. See Ellic.). Many of the Fathers (some as an *alternative*), Luther, Bengel, al., take the first *νόμος* here to mean the Gospel (the *νόμος τοῦ πνεύματος τῆς ζωῆς* of Rom. viii. 2); but it will be manifest to any who follow the argument, that this cannot be so. This *διὰ νόμου νόμῳ ἀπέθανον* is in fact a compendium of his expanded experience in Rom. vii.: and also of his argument in ch. iii. iv. below.

20] **I am** ('*and have been*,' perf.) **crucified with Christ** (specification of the foregoing *ἀπέθανον*: the way in which I died to the law was, by being united to, and involved in the death of, that Body of Christ which was crucified): **but it is no longer I that live, but** (it is) **Christ that liveth in me** (the punctuation—*χρ. συνεσταύρωμαι, ζῶ δέ· οὐκέτι ἐγώ, ζῇ δὲ ἐν ἐμ. χρ.*,—as in E. V., &c.—is altogether wrong, and would require *ἀλλά* before *οὐκέτι*. The construction is one not without example, where the emphatic word is repeated in two parallel clauses, each time with *δέ*. Thus Eur. Iph. Taur. 1367, *φιλεῖς δὲ καὶ σὺ τὸν κασίγνητον, θεά· φιλεῖν δὲ κἀμὲ τοὺς ὁμαίμονας δόκει*. Xen. Cyr. vi. 2. 22, *ἔνθα πολὺς μὲν οἶνος, πολλὰ δὲ σῦκα, πολὺ δὲ ἔλαιον, θάλαττα δὲ προσκλύζει*. So that our second *δέ* is not *sondern*,—'*not I, but*,'—but *aber*, as the first—q. d. 'but the life is not mine,—but the life is Christ's within me.' Notice, not *ὁ ἐν ἐμοὶ χρ.*. Christ is the vine, we the branches. He lives, He, the same Christ, through and in every one of His believing

[c] ἀθετῶ τὴν χάριν τοῦ θεοῦ· εἰ γὰρ διὰ νόμου [d] δικαιοσύνη,
ἄρα χριστὸς [e] δωρεὰν ἀπέθανεν.
III. 1 Ὦ [f] ἀνόητοι Γαλάται, τίς ὑμᾶς [g] ἐβάσκανεν,
οἷς [h] κατ' [i] ὀφθαλμοὺς Ἰησοῦς χριστὸς [j] προεγράφη

d ellips., ch iii 21 e = John xv 25, from Ps xxxiv 19 (Matt x 8 Rom iii 24 al) f Luke xxiv 25 Rom i 14 1 Tim vi 9 Tit iii 3 only L P Prov xvii 28 Sir xiv 6, 8 only g here only Deut xxviii 54, 56 h = ch ii 11 reff i here only see note Eph iii 3 Jude 4 only † 1 Macc x 36 Esdr vi 31 F only j Rom xv 4

CHAP. III. 1 rec aft εβασκανεν add τη αληθεια μη πειθεσθαι (*from ch* v 7), with CD³KL rel vulg syr goth æth arm Ath Cyr₁ Thdrt₂ Damasc: om ABD¹FN 17¹. 67² fuld Syrr coptt Orig(in Jer) Chr₂ Cyr₁ Thdrt₁ lat-ff. rec aft προεγραφη ins εν υμιν, with DFKL rel vulg syr goth Ath Chr Thdrt₂ Damasc lat-ff: om ABCN 17¹ am (with tol F-lat) Syr coptt æth arm Cyr₂ Thdrt₁ Eus-int Archel Aug.

people)—**but** (taken up again, parallel with ζῶ δὲ . . ζῇ δέ) **that which** (i. e. 'the life which,' as E. V.) **I now** (since my conversion, as contrasted with the time before: not, as Rück., al., the *present* life contrasted with the *future*) **live in the flesh** (in the fleshly body,—which, though it appear to be a mere animal life, is not. So Luth. "in carne quidem vivo, sed ego hanc vitam quantulacunque est, quæ in me agitur, non habeo pro vita. Non enim est vere vita, sed tantum larva vitæ, sub qua vivit alius, nempe Christus, qui est vere vita mea") **I live in** (not '*by*,' as E. V., Chr [διὰ τὴν πίστιν], Œc., Thl., Thdrt. [διὰ τῆς πίστεως]: ἐν π. corresponds to ἐν σαρκί *faith*, and *not the flesh*, is the real element in which I live) **faith, viz that** (the article particularizes, what sort of faith) **of** (having for its object, see on ver. 16) **the Son of God** (so named for solemnity, and because His eternal Sonship is the source of His life-giving power, cf. John v. 25, 26) **who loved me** (the link, which binds the eternal Son of God to me) **and** (proved that love, in that He) **gave Himself up** (to death) **for me** (on my behalf) 21] **I do not** (as thou [Peter] art doing, and the Judaizers) **frustrate** (reff.: not merely '*despise*,' as Erasm., al.) **the grace of God: for** (justification of the strong expression ἀθετῶ) **if by the law** (comes) **righteousness** (not *justification*—but *the result of justification*), **then Christ died without cause** (not '*in vain*,' with reference to the *result* of His death [for which meaning Lidd. and Scott's Lex. refers to LXX: but it does not appear to occur in that sense], but *gratuitously, causelessly* (reff.);—'*Christ need not have died*.' εἰ γὰρ ἀπέθανεν ὁ χριστός, εὔδηλον ὅτι διὰ τὸ μὴ ἰσχύειν τὸν νόμον ἡμᾶς δικαιοῦν· εἰ δὲ ὁ νόμος δικαιοῖ, περιττὸς ὁ τοῦ χριστοῦ θάνατος. Chr.).
οὕτω ταῦτα διεξελθὼν ἐκ τῆς πρὸς τὸν τρισμακάριον (truly so in this case, in having found such a faithful reprover) Πέτρον διαλέξεως, πρὸς αὐτοὺς λοιπὸν ἀποτείνεται, κ. βαρυθυμῶν ἀποφθέγγεται. Thdrt.

CH. III. 1—V. 12.] SECOND, OR POLEMICAL PART OF THE EPISTLE. 1.] The Apostle exclaims indignantly, moved by the fervour and truth of his rebuke of Peter, against the folly of the Galatians, for suffering themselves to be bewitched out of their former vivid apprehension of Christ's work and Person. **ἀνόητοι** must not, with Jer., be taken as an allusion to any supposed national stupidity of the Galatians (Wetst. on ch. i. 6, cites from Themistius a very different description: οἱ ἄνδρες . . ὀξεῖς κ. ἀγχίνοι κ. εὐμαθέστεροι τῶν ἄγαν Ἑλλήνων): it merely springs out of the occasion: see ref. Luke. **ὑμᾶς** has the emphasis—'you, to whom,' &c. **ἐβάσκανεν**] Not with Chr. al., '*envied*,' in which sense the verb usually takes a dative: so Thom. Mag., βασκαίνω, οὐ μόνον ἀντὶ τοῦ φθονῶ, ὅπερ πρὸς δοτικὴν συντάσσεται, ἀλλὰ καὶ ἀντὶ τοῦ μέμφομαι κ. διαβάλλω παρὰ τοῖς παλαιοῖς εὕρηται, κ. συντάσσεται πρὸς αἰτιατικήν (not always, cf. Sir. xiv. 6); but, as E. V. **bewitched,—fascinated**: so Aristot. Probl. xx. 34, διὰ τί τὸ πήγανον βασκανίας φασὶ φάρμακον εἶναι; ἢ διότι βασκαίνεσθαι δοκοῦσι λάβρως ἐσθίοντες; . . . ἐπιλέγουσι γοῦν, ὅταν τῆς αὐτῆς τραπέζης ἰδίᾳ τι προσφέρωνται, μεταδιδόντες, "ἵνα μή βασκάνῃς με." **κατ' ὀφθ.**] **openly,—before your eyes**: so ἵνα σοι κατ' ὀφθαλμοὺς λέγῃ, Aristoph. Ran. 625, cf. κατ' ὄμμα, Eur. Androm. 1010, κρυπτὸς καταστάς, ἢ κατ' ὄμμ' ἐλθὼν μάχῃ; **προεγράφη**] **was described before**, as in reff. It has been variously explained, (1) '*depicted before you*.' So Œc., Thl. (Chrys ?), Erasm., Luth., Calv., Winer, Rückert, Jowett, &c. But προγράφειν cannot be shewn to have any such meaning; nor [see below] is it required [as Jow.] by the context. (2) '*palam scriptus est*,' so Estius, Elsner, Bengel, al. But this, although an allowable meaning (τῆς δίκης προγεγραμμένης αὐτῷ, διὰ πένθος

ἐσταυρωμένος; 2 τοῦτο μόνον θέλω [k] μαθεῖν ἀφ' ὑμῶν, ABCDF
[l] ἐξ ἔργων νόμου τὸ [m] πνεῦμα [m] ἐλάβετε ἢ ἐξ [n] ἀκοῆς KLℵab
πίστεως; 3 [o] οὕτως [l] ἀνόητοί ἐστε; [p] ἐναρξάμενοι [q] πνεύ- cdefg
ματι νῦν [q] σαρκὶ [r] ἐπιτελεῖσθε; 4 τοσαῦτα [s] ἐπάθετε [t] εἰκῇ; hklm no17

k = Acts xxiii 27. Esth iv 5. 2 Macc vii 2. l = ch ii 16 reff. m Acts viii 15, 17, 19 xix 2 al. n = Rom x 16 (from Isa liii 1), 17. 1 Thess ii 13 al. o = Heb xii 21. p Phil i 6 only. Deut ii 24, 25, 31. q dat of manner, 1 Cor ix 7. xi 5 al. Winer, § 31. 7. r Rom xv 28. 2 Cor vii 1. Phil i 6 al. 1 Kings iii 12. s Paul, 1 Cor xii 26. 2 Cor i 6. Phil i 29. 1 Thess ii 14. 2 Thess i 5. 2 Tim i 12 only. see note. t ch iv 11. Matt v 22. Rom xiii 4. 1 Cor xv 2. Col ii 18 only. Prov xxviii 25 only.

2 μαθειν bef θελω D[1] [3]F.

οἰκούρει, Plut. Camill 11), would not suit ἐν ὑμῖν (see below) (3) '*proscriptus est.*' So Vulg, Ambr, Aug, Lyra (προὔγραφεν αὐτοὺς φυγάδας, Polyb xxxii. 21. 12; οἱ προγεγραμμένοι, ib 22. 1) But this is quite irrelevant to the context It is best therefore to keep to St Paul's own meaning of προγράφειν, and understand it to refer to the time when he preached Christ among them, which he represents as a previous description in writing of Christ, in their hearts and before their eyes Jerome, Hermann, al, understand it as above, '*olim scriptus est,*' interpreting it, however, of the prophecies of the O T But not to mention that no prophecy sets Him forth as ἐσταυρωμένος, the whole passage (cf. vv. 2—5) evidently refers to the time when the Apostle preached among them. (See more in De W and Meyer, from whom the above is mainly taken) [The ἐν ὑμῖν of the rec could hardly belong to ἐσταυρωμένος; for if so, it would more naturally be ἐσταυρ ἐν ὑμῖν, the emphasis, as it now stands, being on ἐν ὑμῖν but it must belong to προεγράφη, as above, and as in 2 Cor iii 2,—'in animis vestris' So Mey Among the various meanings proposed,—'among you' (E V, &c., De W, Ruck), 'on account of you' (Koppe, but wrongly, see ch i. 24, note),—Luther's is the most remarkable "jam non solum abjecistis gratiam Dei, non solum Christus frustra vobis mortuus est, sed turpissime in vobis crucifixus est Ad eum modum loquitur et Epistola ad Ebr. vi 6 denuo crucifigentes sibimetipsis filium Dei, &c." This again is condemned by the context, and indeed by the aor προεγράφη.] ἐσταυρωμένος, as expressing the whole mystery of redemption by grace, and of freedom from legal obligation. 'It has an echo of συνεσταύρωμαι in ch. ii 20.' Jowett 2] τ. μόνον,—not to mention all the *other* grounds on which I might rest my argument, '*this only,*' &c διὰ συντόμου λόγου κ. ταχίστης ἀποδείξεως ὑμᾶς πεῖσαι βούλομαι Chr. μαθεῖν, be informed: not to be pressed, as Luther, al ("Agite nunc, respondete mihi discipulo vestro, tam subito enim facti estis docti, ut mei jam satis præceptores et doctores"), but taken in its ordinary sense, see reff. **Did ye from** (as its ground, see ch ii 16) **the works of the Law** (not a Law) **receive the Spirit** (evidently here to be taken as including *all His gifts,* spiritual and external not as Chr, Thl, Jer, χαρίσματα only: for the two are distinguished in ver 5), **or from the hearing of faith** (meaning either, '*that preaching which proclaimed faith,*' or '*that hearing, which received* (*the*) *faith*' The first is preferable, because (1) where their first receiving the Gospel is in question, the *preaching* of it would probably be hinted at, as it is indeed taken up by the οὖν below, ver 5 · (2) where the question is concerning the power of faith as contrasted with the works of the law, faith would most likely be *subjective* But certainly we must not understand it '*obedience* [ὑπακ Rom i. 5, xvi 26 See 1 Kings xv 22] *to the faith,*' as Wahl, al, which would spoil the contrast here)? 3] **Are ye so** (to such an extent, emph) **foolish** (as viz. the following fact would prove)? **Having begun** (see Phil i 6, where the same two verbs occur together, and 2 Cor. viii 6, where προενήρξατο is followed by ἐπιτελέσῃ Understand, 'the Christian life') **in the Spirit** (dative of the manner in which, ref. The Spirit, i. e the Holy Spirit, guiding and ruling the spiritual life, as the 'essence and active principle' [Ellic.] of Christianity,—contrasted with the flesh,—the element in which the law worked), **are ye now being completed** (passive here, not mid., cf Phil i 6, where the active is used and for the passive, Luke xiii 32 The middle does not appear to occur in the N. T, though it does in classical Greek, e. g. Polyb ii. 58 10, μηθὲν ἀσεβὲς ἐπιτελεσαμένοις. Diod Sic xii. 54, μεγάλας πράξεις ἐπιτελεσάμενοι) **in** (dative, as above) **the flesh?**
4] **Did ye suffer** (not, '*have ye suffered,*' as almost all Commentators, E V, &c,—i e πεπόνθατε, Heb ii. 18, Luke xiii 2) **so many things in vain?** There is much controversy about the meaning. (1) Chrys., Aug, and the ancients, Grot, Wolt, Ruck, Olsh., &c., understand it of the sufferings

[u] εἴ γε καὶ [t] εἰκῇ. 5 ὁ οὖν [v] ἐπιχορηγῶν ὑμῖν τὸ πνεῦμα
καὶ [w] ἐνεργῶν [x] δυνάμεις ἐν ὑμῖν [l] ἐξ ἔργων νόμου ἢ ἐξ
[m] ἀκοῆς πίστεως; 6 καθὼς Ἀβραὰμ [y] ἐπίστευσεν τῷ θεῷ,

u = 2 Cor v 3 Col i 23
v 2 Cor ix 10 Col ii 19 2 Pet i 5, 11 only † Sir xxv 22 only (-γία, Eph iv 16 Phil i 19)
w ch ii 8 reff
x = Matt. vii 22 Acts ii 22 xix 11 1 Cor xii 10, 28 ‡
y w dat, Gen xv 6. John v. 24 Acts xvi 34

5. aft νομου ins (see ver 2) το πνευμα ελαβετε A.
6. καθως γεγραπται Επιστευσεν αβρ F.

which the Galatians underwent at the time of their reception of the Gospel And, I believe, rightly For (a) πάσχω occurs (see reff.) seven times in St. Paul, and always in the strict sense of '*suffering*,' by persecution, or hardship (similarly in Heb, 1 Pet, &c) · (b) the historic aorist here marks the reference to be to some definite time Now the time referred to by the context is that of their conversion to the Gospel, cf τὸ πν ἐλάβετε,—ἐναρξάμενοι πνεύματι above Therefore the meaning is, **Did ye undergo all those sufferings** (not specially mentioned in this Epistle, but which every convert to Christ must have undergone as a matter of course) **in vain** (Schomer first, and after him many, and Winer, B-Crus, De Wette, understand παθεῖν here in a *good sense*, in reference to divine grace bestowed on them. But πάσχω seems never to be thus used in Greek without an indication in the context of such a meaning, e g εὖ πάσχειν, or as in Jos. Antt. iii. 15 1, ὅσα παθόντες ἐξ αὐτοῦ κ πηλικῶν εὐεργεσιῶν μεταλαβόντες, where the added clause defines the παθόντες, and never in N. T., LXX nor Apocrypha at all. (3) Bengel refers it to their patience with Paul [*patientissime sustinuistis pertulistisque me*]; but this, as Meyer remarks, would be expressed by ἀνέχειν, hardly by πάσχειν. (4) Meyer, to the troubles of their bondage introduced by the false and judaizing teachers. But not to dwell on other objections, it is decisive against this, (a) that it would thus be *present*, πάσχετε [see ch iv. 10], not *past* at all, and (b) that even if it might be past, it must be the perfect and not the aorist. I therefore hold to (1); οὐ γὰρ ὑπὲρ τοῦ νόμου ἀλλ' ὑπὲρ τοῦ χριστοῦ τὰ παθήματα, Thdrt.. πάντα γὰρ ἐκεῖνα, φησίν, ἅπερ ὑπεμείνατε, ζημιῶσαι ὑμᾶς οὗτοι βούλονται, κ τὸν στέφανον ὑμῶν ἁρπάσαι. Chrys. [So Ellic. ed 2] When Meyer says that this meaning is ganz isolirt vom Contert, he is surely speaking at random. see above [Ellic. ed. 1 took ἐπάθετε in a neutral sense, as applying to both persecutions and blessings, and nearly so Jowett. 'Had ye all these experiences in vain?' objecting to (1) that it is unlike the whole spirit of the Apostle. But we find surely a trace of the same spirit in Phil. i 29, 30; as there suffering is represented as a special grace from Christ, so here it might well be said, 'let not such grace have been received in vain']) **? if it be really in vain** (on εἴ γε καί, see note on 2 Cor v 3 the construction is, 'if, as it must be, what I have said, εἰκῇ, is really the fact' The Commentators all take it as a supposition,—some, as Chr, &c., E V, 'if it be yet in vain,' as a softening of εἰκῇ, others, as Meyer, De W, al, as an intensification of it, 'if it be only in vain [and not something worse]')

5] **οὖν** takes up again the question of ver 2, and asks it in another form There is a question whether the participles **ἐπιχορηγῶν** and **ἐνεργῶν** are present, referring to things done among them while the Apostle was *writing*, or imperfect, still spoken of the time when he was with them? Chrys., Thdrt, &c, and Bengel, al, maintain the latter. Luth, Calv, Ruck, Meyer, De W, &c, the former It seems to me, that this question must be settled by first determining who is the agent here spoken of Is it the Apostle? or is it not rather God, and is not this indicated by the reference to Abraham's faith in the next verse, and the taking up the passive ἐλογίσθη by δικαιοῖ ὁ θεός in ver 8? If it be so, then the participles here must be taken as present, but indefinite, in a substantive sense (Winer), as ὁ διώκων ἡμᾶς ποτέ, ch. i. 23. And certainly God alone can be said (and so in ref 2 Cor) ἐπιχορηγεῖν τὸ πνεῦμα, and ἐνεργεῖν (ch. ii 8) δυνάμεις ἐν ὑμῖν (see below). **ἐπιχορ.**] The ἐπί does not imply *addition*, but as so often with prepositions of motion in composition, the *direction* of the supply: see notes on Acts xxvii. 7; Rom. viii. 16.

δυνάμεις] here, not merely *miracles* or χαρίσματα, though those are included: nor is ἐν ὑμῖν, '*among you*;' but δυν. are the wonders wrought by divine Power **in you** (cf θεὸς ὁ ἐνεργῶν τὰ πάντα ἐν πᾶσιν, 1 Cor xii 6 θεὸς γάρ ἐστιν ὁ ἐνεργῶν ἐν ὑμῖν τὸ θέλειν κ τ λ. Phil. ii. 13. Eph ii. 2, also Matt. xiv. 2), viz at your conversion and since. **ἐξ ἔργ**] (supply **does He it**) **in consequence of** ("as the originating or moving cause," Ellic) **the works of the law, or in consequence of the hearing** (see above, ver. 2) **of faith?**

6—9] *Abraham's faith was his entrance into righteous-*

καὶ [z] ἐλογίσθη αὐτῷ [a] εἰς δικαιοσύνην. 7 γινώσκετε ἄρα
ὅτι οἱ [b] ἐκ πίστεως, οὗτοί εἰσιν υἱοὶ Ἀβραάμ. 8 [c] προ-
ϊδοῦσα δὲ ἡ [d] γραφὴ ὅτι [e] ἐκ πίστεως [e] δικαιοῖ τὰ ἔθνη ὁ
θεός, [f] προευηγγελίσατο τῷ Ἀβραὰμ ὅτι [g] ἐνευλογηθήσονται ἐν σοὶ πάντα τὰ ἔθνη. 9 ὥςτε οἱ [b] ἐκ πίστεως [h] εὐλο-

ABCDF KLℵab cdefg hklm no17

z = Rom ii 26 al Prov xvii 28 only = Ps cxxxviii 3 Wisd xix 1 see Gen xxxvii 18.
a = Acts x 4 xix 27 Rom ix 8 & passim Wisd ix 6
b Rom ii 8 iii 26 iv 12, 14 al
c Acts ii 31 only
d γρ., personified, Rom iv 3 ix 17 John vii 38 al
e ch ii 16 reff
f here only † see note
g Acts iii 25 only Gen xii 3 vat. xxii 18 xxvi 4
h = Acts iii 26 Eph. i 3 Heb vi 14 al Gen xii 3

7. om οἱ C[1](appy). υιοι bef εισιν BN[1] Chr Thdrt Iren-int[1] Ambr
8. τα εθνη bef δικαιοι ℵ m προευηγγελισται D[1] 67[2] elz (for ενευλ.) ευλογηθ., with F h n: txt ABCDKLℵ rel Cyr Thdrt Damasc Œc

ness before God and Scripture, in recording this, records also God's promise to him, by virtue of which all the faithful inherit his blessing 6.] The reply to the foregoing question is understood: it is ἐξ ἀκοῆς πίστεως And then enters the thought of God's ἐνεργεῖν as following upon Abraham's faith. The fact of justification being now introduced, whereas before the ἐπιχορηγεῖν τὸ πνεῦμα was the matter enquired of, is no real departure from the subject, for both these belong to the ἐνάρξασθαι of ver. 3,—are concomitant, and inseparable. On the verse, see note, Rom. iv 3. 7.] **γινώσκ** is better taken indicatively, with Jer., Ambr, Beza, Rück, al, than imperatively, with most Commentators (and Mey, De W., Olsh, Ellic). It is no objection to the indicative that such knowledge could not well be predicated of the Galatians it is not so predicated, but is here set before them as a thing which they ought to be acquainted with—**from this then you know** (q d. 'omnibus patet' The imperative seems to me to lose the fine edge of the Apostle's argumentative irony besides that the usage of that mood with ἄρα is not frequent: indeed apparently only to be found in Homer, cf. Il κ 249, ω. 522. See on the other side, Ellicott's note here). **οἱ ἐκ πίστεως**] see Rom ii. 8, iii. 26, and notes, **those who are of faith**, as the origin and the ἀφορμή of their spiritual life. **οὗτοι**] emphatic, **these**, and these only (see Rom viii. 14), not οἱ ἐξ ἔργων. Chrys. says οὐχ οἱ τὴν φυσικὴν ἔχοντες πρὸς αὐτὸν συγγένειαν: but this point is not here raised: besides, they might be, as well as others, if they were ἐκ πίστεως, see Rom iv 16 **υἱοὶ Ἀβρ**] see Rom iv. 11–17, and notes 8] **But** (transitional [see Ellicott's note]) **the Scripture** (as we say, Nature meaning, the Author of the Scripture, see reff.) **foreseeing** (Schöttgen, Hor Hebr. i. 732, gives examples of 'quid vidit Scriptura?' and the like, as common sayings among the Jews) **that of faith** (emphatic,—'*and not of works*') **God justifieth** (present, not merely as Mey, De W, al., because the time foreseen was regarded as present, nor 'respectu Pauli scribentis,' as Bengel,—but because it was God's *one* way of justification—He never justified in any other way—so that it is the normal present, q d 'is a God that justifieth') **the Gentiles** (observe, there is no *stress* here on τὰ ἔθνη,—it is not ἐκ πίστεως καὶ τὰ ἔθνη δικαιοῖ ὁ θ so that, as is remarked above, no question is raised between the carnal and spiritual seed of Abraham,—nor, as Bengel, 'δέ vim argumenti extendit etiam ad *gentes*.' the question is between those who were ἐκ πίστεως, and those who wanted to return to the ἔργα νόμου, whether Jews or Gentiles So that in fact τὰ ἔθνη must be here taken in its widest sense, as in the Abrahamic promise soon to be quoted) **announced the good news beforehand** (the word is found only in Philo, and in this sense — ἑσπέρα τε καὶ πρωΐα, ὧν ἡ μὲν προευαγγελίζεται μέλλοντα ἥλιον ἀνίσχειν, de Mundi Opif § 9, vol. i. p 7, and de mut. nom. § 29, p. 602, ὃς (viz ὁ νεοττὸς) . . . . τοὺς ταρσοὺς διασείειν φιλεῖ, τὴν ἐλπίδα τοῦ πέτεσθαι δυνήσεσθαι προευαγγελιζόμενος) **to Abraham:** (ὅτι recitative) **In thee** (not, '*in thy seed*,' which is a point not here raised, but strictly **in thee**, as followers of thy faith, it having first shewn the way to justification before God. That the words will bear that other reference, does not shew that it must be introduced here) **shall all the Gentiles** (see above not to be restricted with Meyer, al., to its narrower sense, but expressing, from Gen. xviii. 18; xxii 18, in a form suiting better the Apostle's present argument, the πᾶσαι αἱ φυλαὶ τῆς γῆς of Gen xii. 3) **be blessed** 9.] Consequence of ἐνευλογηθήσονται above, substantiated

γοῦνται σὺν τῷ [i] πιστῷ Ἀβραάμ. 10 ὅσοι γὰρ [b] ἐξ ἔργων
νόμου εἰσίν, [k] ὑπὸ [l] κατάραν [k] εἰσίν· γέγραπται γὰρ ὅτι
[m] ἐπικατάρατος πᾶς ὃς οὐκ [n] ἐμμένει ἐν πᾶσιν τοῖς γεγραμμένοις ἐν τῷ βιβλίῳ τοῦ νόμου, [o] τοῦ ποιῆσαι αὐτά.
11 [p] ὅτι δὲ [q] ἐν νόμῳ οὐδεὶς [q] δικαιοῦται [r] παρὰ τῷ θεῷ
[p] δῆλον, ὅτι [s] ὁ δίκαιος ἐκ πίστεως ζήσεται· 12 ὁ δὲ νόμος
οὐκ ἔστιν ἐκ πίστεως. ἀλλ' [t] ὁ ποιήσας αὐτὰ ζήσεται ἐν
αὐτοῖς. 13 χριστὸς ἡμᾶς [u] ἐξηγόρασεν ἐκ τῆς [v] κατάρας

i = John xx 27 so δίκαιον Λωτ, 2 Pet ii 7 only. k w dat, Acts xiv 22 absol., Acts xxviii 30 only h Rom iii 9 1 Cor ix 20 l ver 13 bis Heb vi 8 James iii 10 2 Pet ii 14 only Gen xxvii 12, 13 m Deut xxvii. 26 (John vii 49 v r) ver 13 only n constr, Heb viii 9, from Jer xxxviii (xxxi) 32 Acts xiv 22 o constr, Matt xxi 32 Acts iii 12 vii 19 al 3 Kings xvi 19 Winer, § 44 4 p 1 Cor xv 27 only δῆλ, Matt xxvi 73 only Num xxiii 21 q = Acts xiii 39 Rom v 9 1 Cor vi 11 r = Rom ii 13 1 Cor iii 19 al s Hab ii 4 t Levit xviii 5 u = ch iv 5 only (Eph. v 16 Col iv 5 only Dan ii 8 only) v ver 10.

10. rec om οτι, with KL rel vulg syrr Chr Thdrt. ins ABCDFℵ 17 arm Cyr Damasc. om 1st εν Bℵ[1] m 17. 67[2] Damasc. ενγεγραμμενοις B

11. om τω bef θεω D[1]F. om δηλον F. ins γεγραπται γαρ bef 2nd οτι D[1]F.

12. αλλα D[1]ℵ rec aft αυτα ins ανθρωπος, with D[3]KL rel om A(appy) BCD[1]Fℵ 17 67[2] latt syrr copt æth arm Marcion-e Chr Cyr Damasc Ambrst Aug Jer. εν αυτω F. (not F-lat)

by ver. 10 below. A share in Abraham's *blessing* must be the accompaniment of faith, not of works of the law. πίστεως has the emphasis σύν, to shew their community with him in the blessing τῷ πιστῷ, to shew wherein the community consists, viz FAITH.

10] substantiation of ver. 9: they *ἐξ ἔργων νόμου* cannot be sharers in the blessing, for they are accursed, it being understood that they do not and cannot *ἐμμένειν ἐν πᾶσιν* &c: see this expanded in Rom. iii 9—20. The citation is freely from the LXX On *τοῦ ποιῆσαι*, not a Hebraism, but a construction common in later Greek, see Ellic.'s note.

11, 12.] 'contain a perfect syllogism, so that *ὁ δίκ ἐκ πίστ ζήσεται* is the major proposition, ver. 12 the minor, and *ἐν νόμῳ οὐδ. δικ. παρὰ τ. θεῷ* the consequence' Meyer. It is inserted to strengthen the inference of the former verse, by shewing that not even could a man keep the law, would he be justified—the *condition* of justification, as revealed in Scripture, being that it is *by faith*. **But** (= moreover) **that in** (not merely the *elemental* in, but the *conditional* as well: 'in and by' not '*through*') **the law no man is justified** (the *normal* present is, in God's order of things) **with God** (not emphatic as Bengel, 'quicquid sit apud homines' this would require *οὐδεὶς παρὰ τῷ θεῷ δικαιοῦται* but *δικαιοῦται-παρὰ-τῷ-θεῷ* is simply predicated of *οὐδείς*) **is evident, for** (it is written, that) **the just by faith shall live** (not '*the just shall live by his faith*,' as Winer, De W., al. The order of the words would indeed suggest this rendering, seeing that *ὁ ἐκ π δ ζ* would properly represent the other. but we must regard St Paul's logical use of the citation and I think, with Meyer, that he has abstained from altering the order of the words as being well known He is not seeking to shew *by what* the righteous shall live, but the *ground itself* of *that righteousness* which shall *issue in life*, and the contrast is between *ὁ δίκαιος ἐκ πίστεως* and *ὁ ποιήσας αὐτά* [It is right to say that Ellic (both edd) prefers the other rendering, and supports it by the fact that the original Hebrew will not bear this one, and that St Paul adopts the words of the LXX as they stand; and by the contrast between *ζήσεται ἐκ πίστεως*, and *ζήσεται ἐν αὐτοῖς* Jowett doubts whether *ζήσεται* could be used absolutely· but see Heb xii 9. I still however prefer rendering as above. The construction desiderated by Bp Middleton to suit our rendering,—*ὁ δίκαιος ὁ ἐκ π*,—would stultify the sentence, by bringing into view other *δίκαιοι*, who were not *ἐκ πίστεως*]) **but** (logical, introducing the minor of the syllogism see above) **the law** (not 'law, as such,' Peile: no such consideration appears here, nor any where, except in so far as the law of Moses is treated of as possessing the qualities of law in general) **is not of** (does not spring from nor belong to 'non agit fidei partes,' Beng) **faith** **but** (sondern) (its nature is such that) **he who has done them** (viz *πάντα τὰ προστάγματά μου κ. π*

w – John vi 51 xviii 19 Rom v 6
x (Deut xxi. 23, κεκατηραμένος ὑπὸ θεοῦ) ver 10, from Deut xxvii 26
y Acts v 30 x 39 only

τοῦ νόμου, γενόμενος ʷ ὑπὲρ ἡμῶν ᵛ κατάρα, ὅτι γέγραπ- ABCDF
ται ˣ Ἐπικατάρατος πᾶς ὁ ʸ κρεμάμενος ἐπὶ ʸ ξύλου, 14 ἵνα KLℵ a b c d e f g
ᶻ εἰς τὰ ἔθνη ἡ ᵃ εὐλογία τοῦ ᵃ Ἀβραὰμ ᵇ γένηται ἐν h k l m n o 17
χριστῷ Ἰησοῦ, ἵνα τὴν ᶜ ἐπαγγελίαν τοῦ πνεύματος λά-
βωμεν διὰ τῆς πίστεως.

Gen xl 19 κρ, – Luke xxiii 39 (Matt xviii 6, xxii 40 Acts xxviii 4 only) z – Rom iii 22 2 Cor viii 14 (see Acts xxi 17 xxv 15) a Gen xxviii 4 εὐλ, 1 Cor x 16 Heb. vi 7 al gen obj, Rom xv 8. b – 2 Cor viii 14 Matt xviii 19 c Luke xxiv 49 Acts i 4. ii 33, 39 al fr. Amos ix 6

13 rec (for οτι γεγρ) γεγρ. γαρ, with D³KLℵ rel syrr copt Iren-gr Did Chr Cyr Thdrt · txt ABCD¹F 17 latt Eus Damasc Iren-int Jer Ambrst Hil Aug.
14 ιησ. bef χρ. Bℵ Syr for επαγγ, ευλογιαν D¹F k Tert Ambrst Vig (not F-lat)

τὰ κρίματά μου of Levit. xviii 5) shall live in (conditional element) them (see Rom. x 5). 13] But this curse has been removed by the redemption of Christ. The joyful contrast is introduced abruptly, without any connecting particle · see an asyndeton in a similar case in Col iii 4 The ἡμᾶς is emphatic, and applies solely to the Jews They only were under the curse of ver. 10,—and they being by Christ redeemed from that curse, the blessing of Abraham (justification by faith), which was always destined by God to flow through the Jews to the Gentiles, was set at liberty thus to flow out to the Gentiles This, which is Meyer's view, is certainly the only one which suits the context. To make ἡμᾶς refer to Jews and Gentiles, and refer ἡ κατ. τοῦ νόμ. to the law of conscience, is to break up the context altogether ἐξηγόρ] See, besides reff., 1 Cor. vi 20, vii 23; 2 Pet ii 1, Rev. v 9 Ellicott remarks, 'the ἐξ- need not be very strongly pressed, see Polyb. iii. 42 2, ἐξηγόρασε παρ' αὐτῶν τά τε μονόξυλα πλοῖα κ τ.λ . The tendency,' he continues, 'to use verbs compounded with prepositions without any obvious increase of meaning, is one of the characteristics of later Greek so Thiersch, de Pentat. vers. alex ii 1, p 83.' The form of the idea is,—the Law (personified) held us (Jews) under its curse, (out of this) Christ bought us, BECOMING (emphatic, standing first) a curse (not ἐπικατάρατος, concrete, but κατάρα, abstract, to express that he became not only accursed, but the curse, coextensive with the disability which affected us) for us (the Jews again Not, as many older Commentators, and Rück., Olsh, Peile, &c, '*instead of us*,' but '*on our behalf*' It *was* in our stead, but that circumstance is not expressed by ὑπέρ used of Christ's death for us—see reff and Ellic's note, and Usteri, Paulin. Lehrbegriff, p 115 ff). ὅτι γέγρ κ τ λ is a parenthesis, justifying the formal expression γενόμ. ὑπ. ἡμ κατάρα The citation omits the words ὑπὸ θεοῦ of the LXX. They were not to the point here, being understood as matter of course, the law being *God's* law The article ὁ is not in the LXX The words are spoken of hanging *after death by stoning*, and are given in l c as a reason why the body should not remain on the tree all night, because one hanging on a tree is accursed of God. Such formal curse then extended to Christ, who *died* by hanging on a tree

14] in order that (the intent of γενόμ. ὑπ. ἡμ κατάρα) the blessing of Abraham (promised to Abraham i e justification by faith; ver 9) might be (come) upon the Gentiles (not, all nations, but strictly the Gentiles · see above on ver. 13) in (in and by, *conditional element*) Jesus the Christ, that (*ἵνα*, parallel with, not dependent on and included in, the former ἵνα for this clause has no longer to do with τὰ ἔθνη, see below. We have a second ἵνα co-ordinate with a first in Rom vii 13, 2 Cor ix 3, Eph. vi 19, 20) we (not emphatic, nor is ἡμεῖς expressed. no longer the Jews, as Beza and Bengel, but all Christians see Jowett's note, which perhaps is too finely drawn) might receive (in full, as fulfilled, aor.) through the (or, but not so usually, *our*) faith (as the subjective medium but rendered objective by the article, as so often by St Paul. no *stress* on διὰ τ π) the promise of the Spirit (viz. that made Joel ii 28 See Acts ii. 17, 33, Luke xxiv. 49, THE PROMISE of the new covenant) The genitive τοῦ πν. is objective, —the Spirit being the thing promised. But let me guard tiros against the old absurdity, "ἐπαγγελία τοῦ πνεύματος pro τὸ πνεῦμα τὸ ἐπηγγελμένον," which would destroy, here and every where else, the logical form of the sentence This 'receiving the promise of the Spirit' distinctly refers back to ver. 2, where he asked them whether they received the

15 Ἀδελφοί, [d] κατὰ ἄνθρωπον [d] λέγω· [e] ὅμως ἀνθρώπου
[f] κεκυρωμένην [g] διαθήκην οὐδεὶς [h] ἀθετεῖ ἢ [i] ἐπιδιατάσσεται.
16 τῷ δὲ Ἀβραὰμ [k] ἐρρέθησαν αἱ [l] ἐπαγγελίαι καὶ τῷ
[m] σπέρματι αὐτοῦ. οὐ [n] λέγει Καὶ τοῖς σπέρμασιν, ὡς
[o] ἐπὶ πολλῶν, ἀλλ' ὡς [o] ἐφ' ἑνός Καὶ τῷ σπέρματί σου,

d Rom. iii. 5. 1 Cor. ix. 8 (κ. ἄνθ.). ch. i. 11. e (—) John xii. 42. 1 Cor. xiv. 7 only. 2 Macc. xv. 5. f 2 Cor. ii. 8 only. Gen. xxiii. 20. Levit. xxv. 30 only. g 1 Cor. xi. 25 al. fr. Deut. ix. 5 al. h ch. ii. 20 reff. i here only †. k Matt. v. 21, &c. l plur., = Rom. ix. 4. xv. 8. 2 Cor. i. 20. vii. 1. Heb. vi. 13 al5. m Acts iii. 25. Gen. xiii. 15. xvii. 8. n = Rom. xv. 10 [11]. see 1 Cor. vi. 16. o = Heb. vii. 11 (?) only (see 2 Cor. vii. 14). = w. acc., Mark ix. 12.

15. κατα ανθρωπον λεγω bef αδελφοι A arm Damasc. προκεκυρωμενην (see ver 17) C 17 Chr-ms. επιτασσεται D[1].
16. om δε D[1]F latt Chr lat-ff. [ερρεθησαν, so AB[1](ita cod) CD[1]FℵE c (d) e f h 17 Cyr$_2$ Thdrt$_3$ Damasc.] aft σπερμασιν ins σου D[1]. αλλα B.

Spirit by the works of the law, or by the hearing of faith? "Here is a pause, at which the indignant feeling of the Apostle softens, and he begins the new train of thought which follows with words of milder character, and proceeds more quietly with his argument." Windischmann.

15—18.] But what if the law, coming after the Abrahamic promise, *abrogated* that promise? These verses contain the refutation of such an objection: *the promise was not abrogated by the law*.

15.] τί ἐστι κατ' ἄνθρ. λέγω; ἐξ ἀνθρωπίνων παραδειγμάτων. Chrys. But (see 1 Cor. xv. 32) the expression refers not only to the character of the example chosen, but to the temporary standing-point of him who speaks: I put myself for the time on a level with ordinary men in the world. ὅμως is out of its logical place, which would be after οὐδείς; see on ref. 1 Cor. To make it '*even*' and take it with ἀνθρώπου, is contrary to its usage. **A (mere) man's covenant** (not 'testament,' as Olsh., after Aug., al.; for there is here no introduction of that idea: the promise spoken to Abraham was strictly a *covenant*, and designated διαθήκη in the passages which were now in the Apostle's mind, see Gen. xv. 18, xvii. 7. On the general meaning, see Mr. Bagge's note) **when ratified** (reff.), **no one notwithstanding** (that it is merely a human covenant) **sets aside or supplements** (with new conditions, Jos. Antt. xvii. 9. 4 describes Archelaus as ὁ ἐν ταῖς ἐπιδιαθήκαις ὑπὸ τοῦ πατρὸς ἐγγεγραμμένος βασιλεύς,—'in his father's subsequent testament:' and again says of Antipas, B. J. ii. 2. 3, ἀξιῶν τῆς ἐπιδιαθήκης τὴν διαθήκην εἶναι κυριωτέραν, ἐν ᾗ βασιλεὺς αὐτὸς ἐγέγραπτο. Nothing is implied as to the nature of the additions, whether consistent or inconsistent with the original covenant: the simple fact that *no additions are made*, is enounced).

16.] This verse is not, as commonly supposed, the minor proposition of the syllogism, applying to Abraham's case the general truth enounced in ver. 15: for had it been so, (1) we should certainly find ὑπὸ θεοῦ contrasted with the ἀνθρώπου before, and (2) the parenthesis οὐ λέγει . . . . χριστός would be a mere irrelevant digression. This minor proposition does not follow till ver. 17. What is *now* said, in a parenthetical and subsidiary manner, is this: The covenant was not merely nor principally made with Abraham, but with Abraham *and* HIS SEED, and that seed referred, not to the Jewish people, but to CHRIST. The covenant then was not fulfilled, but awaiting its fulfilment, and He to whom it was made was yet to appear, when the law was given. **αἱ ἐπ.**] because the promise was many times repeated: e. g. Gen. xii. 7; xv. 5, 18, xvii. 7, 8, xxii. 18. **κ. τῷ σπ. αὐ.**] These words, on which, from what follows, the stress of the whole argument rests, are probably meant to be a formal quotation. If so, the promises quoted must be Gen. xiii. 15, xvii. 8 [Jowett supposes xxi. 12, but qu.?], where the words occur as here. **οὐ λέγει**] viz. He who gave the promises—God. **ἐπὶ πολ., ἐφ' ἑνός**] **of one, of many**, as E. V. Plato has very nearly this usage, βούλομαι δέ μοι μὴ ἐπὶ θεῶν (de diis) λέγεσθαι τὸ τοιοῦτον, Legg. p. 662 d. See also Rep. 521 e. Cf. Ellic.'s note. **τοῖς σπέρμασιν . . . τῷ σπέρματι**] The central point of the Apostle's argument is this: The seed to whom the promises were made, was Christ. To confirm this position,—see Gen. xvii. 17, 18, where the collective σπέρμα of ver. 17 is summed up in the individual σπέρμα of ver. 18, he alleges a philological distinction, recognized by the Rabbinical schools (see Wetst. and Schöttgen ad loc.). This has created considerable difficulty: and all sorts of attempts have been made to evade the argument, or to escape standing committed to the distinction. Jerome (ad loc.), curiously and characteristically, applies the κατὰ ἄνθρω-

p ὅς ἐστιν χριστός. 17 q τοῦτο δὲ λέγω, διαθήκην r προ- ABCDF KLℵ a b c d e f g h k l m n o 17

p attr., Mark xv. 16. Eph i. 14. 1 Tim. iii. 16 al. Winer, § 24. 3. q 1 Cor. i. 12. x. 29. see 1 Cor. vii. 29. xv. 50. r here only †.

for ὅς, ο D[1]F[2], *quod* Iren-int Tert: ου F[1]G, *quo* G-lat. (*qui* D-lat F-lat.)

πον λέγω to this distinction especially, and thinks that the Apostle used it as adapted to the calibre of those to whom he was writing: "Galatis, quos paulo ante stultos dixerat, factus est stultus." The Roman-Catholic Windischmann, one of the ablest and most sensible of modern expositors, says, "Our recent masters of theology have taken up the objection, which is as old as Jerome, and forgetting that Paul knew Hebrew better than themselves, have severely blamed him for urging the singular σπέρματι here, and thus justifying the application to Christ, seeing that the word זֶרַע, which occurs here in the Hebrew text, has no plural (Wind. is not accurate here: the plur. זְרָעִים is found 1 Sam. viii. 15, in the sense of 'grains of wheat'), and so could not be used. Yet they are good enough to assume, that Paul had no fraudulent intent, and only followed the arbitrary exegesis of the Jews of his time (Rückert). The argument of the Apostle does not depend on the grammatical form, by which Paul here only puts forth his meaning in Greek,—but on this, that the Spirit of God in the promise to Abraham and the passage of Scripture relating that promise, has chosen a word which implies a collective unity, and that the promise was not given to Abraham *and his children*. Against the prejudice of the carnal Jews, who held that the promise applied to the plurality of them, the individual descendants of the Patriarch, as such,—the Apostle maintains the truth, that only the Unity, Christ, with those who are incorporated in Him, has part in the inheritance." On these remarks I would observe, (1) that the Apostle's argument is independent of his philology: (2) that his philological distinction must not be pressed to mean more than he himself intended by it: (3) that the *collective and individual* meanings of σπέρμα are both undoubted, and must have been evident to the Apostle himself, from what follows, ver. 29. We are now in a position to interpret the words **ὅς ἐστιν χριστός**. Meyer says 'χριστός is the personal Christ Jesus, not, as has been held (after Aug.), Christ and His Church.' This remark is true, and untrue. χρ. certainly does not mean 'Christ *and* His Church:' but if it imports only the personal Christ Jesus, why is it not so expressed, χριστὸς Ἰησοῦς? For the word does not here occur in passing, but is the predicate of a very definite and important proposition. The fact is, that we must place ourselves in St. Paul's position with regard to the idea of Christ, before we can appreciate all he meant by this word here. Christians are, not by a figure, but really, the Body of Christ: Christ contains His people, and the mention even of the personal Christ would bring with it, in the Apostle's mind, the inclusion of His believing people. This seed is, Christ: not merely in the narrower sense, the man Christ Jesus, but Christ the Seed, Christ the Second Adam, Christ the Head of the Body. And that this is so, is plain from vv. 28, 29, which are the key to ὅς ἐστιν χριστός: where he says, **πάντες γὰρ ὑμεῖς ΕΙ'Σ ἐστε ἐν χριστῷ Ἰησοῦ** (notice Ἰησοῦ here carefully inserted, where the Person is indicated). **εἰ δὲ ὑμεῖς χριστοῦ, ἄρα τοῦ Ἀβραὰμ ΣΠΕ'ΡΜΑ 'ΕΣΤΕ', κατ' ἐπαγγελίαν κληρονόμοι.** So that while it is necessary for the form of the argument here, to express Him to whom the promises were made, and not the aggregate of his people, afterwards to be identified with Him (but not here in view), yet the Apostle has introduced His name in a form not circumscribing His Personality, but leaving room for the inclusion of His mystical Body.

17.] Enthymematical inference from vv. 15, 16, put in the form of a restatement of the argument, as applying to the matters in hand. **This however I say** (this is my meaning, the drift of my previous statement): **the covenant** (better than *a* covenant, as most Commentators; *even* Meyer and De W.: the emphatic substantive is often anarthrous: cf. the different arrangement in ver. 15) **which was previously ratified by God** (εἰς χρ. being inserted by some to complete the correspondence with ver. 16: the *fact was so*, it was '*to Christ*,' as its second party, that the covenant was ratified by God), **the Law, which took place** (was constituted) **four hundred and thirty years after, does not abrogate, so as to do away the promise.** As regards the interval of 430 years, we may remark, that in Exod. xii. 40, it is stated, "The sojourning of the children of Israel who dwelt in Egypt, was four hundred and thirty years." (In Gen. xv. 13, Acts vii. 6, the period of the oppression of Israel in Egypt is roundly stated at 400 years.) But to this, in order to obtain

κεκυρωμένην ὑπὸ τοῦ θεοῦ ὁ μετὰ τετρακόσια καὶ τριά-
κοντα ἔτη γεγονὼς νόμος οὐκ [s] ἀκυροῖ [t] εἰς τὸ [u] καταρ-
γῆσαι τὴν [v] ἐπαγγελίαν. 18 εἰ γὰρ [w] ἐκ νόμου ἡ [x] κληρονομία, [y] οὐκ ἔτι [w] ἐξ ἐπαγγελίας· τῷ δὲ Ἀβραὰμ [z] δι'
ἐπαγγελίας [a] κεχάρισται ὁ θεός. 19 [b] τί οὖν ὁ νόμος;

s Matt xv 6 | Mk only † Esdr vi 32 only (ἄκυρον ποιεῖν, Prov i 25 v 7) t Acts iii 19 vii 19 al u Rom iii 3 iv 14 1 Cor xiii 8 P only, exc Luke xiii 7 Heb ii 14 Ezra iv 21, 23 v 5 vi 8 only v ver 14 w ver ? x Acts vii 5 xx 32 al Isa liv 17 y — Rom vii 17, 20 xi 6 z — Rom xii 3. a act signif & — Acts xxvii 24 (2 Cor ii 10) 2 Macc iii 33 b so ταῦτα τί ἐστιν, Æschin Ctes p 77

17. rec aft θεου ins εις χριστον, with DFKL rel syr1 arm(ed ven) Chr Thdrt Chron Ambrst om ABCℵ 17 67² vulg copt æth Cyr$_2$ Damasc Jer Aug$_{saepe}$ Pelag Bede rec ετη bef τετρ κ τρ., with KL rel Thdrt Chron txt ABCDFℵ a m 17 latt syrr copt Chr Cyr Damasc Ambrst Jer.

the entire interval between the covenant with Abraham and the law, must be added the sojourning of the patriarchs in Canaan,—i. e. to the birth of Isaac, 25 years (Gen xii 4, xxi 5),—to that of Jacob, 60 more (Gen xxv. 26),—to his going down into Egypt, 130 more (Gen. xlvii 9), in all = 215 years So that the time really was 645 years, not 430. But in the LXX (and Samaritan Pentateuch) we read, Exod xii 40, ἡ δὲ κατοίκησις (παροίκ, F) τῶν υἱῶν Ἰσραήλ, ἣν κατῴκησαν (παρῴκ, F.) ἐν γῇ Αἰγύπτῳ καὶ ἐν γῇ Χαναάν (F adding, from the Cod. Alex, αὐτοὶ καὶ οἱ πατέρες αὐτῶν) ἔτη τετρακόσια τριάκοντα·—and this reckoning St. Paul has followed We have instances of a similar adoption of the LXX text, in the apology of Stephen: see Acts vii. 14, and note. After all, however, *the difficulty* lies in the 400 years of Gen. xv. 13 and Acts vii 6 For we may ascertain thus the period of the sojourn of Israel in Egypt· Joseph was 39 years old when Jacob came into Egypt (Gen. xli. 46, 47, xlv. 6). therefore he was born when Jacob was 91 (91 + 39 = 130 see Gen xlvii. 9) But he was born 6 years before Jacob left Laban (compare ib xxx 25 with xxxi. 41), having been with him 20 years (ib xxxi. 38, 41), and served him 14 of them for his two daughters (xxxi 41) Hence, seeing that his marriage with Rachel took place when he was 78 [91—20—7, the marriages with Leah and Rachel being contemporaneous, and the second seven years of service occurring *after*, not, as I assumed in the first edition, before, the marriage with Rachel], Levi, the *third* son of Leah, whose *first* son was born after Rachel's marriage [xxix 30—32], must have been born not earlier than Jacob's 81st year,—and consequently was about 49 [130—81] when he went down into Egypt Now (Exod. vi. 16) Levi *lived in all* 137 years· i e., about 88 [137—49] years in Egypt. But (Exod. vi. 16, 18, 20) Amram, father of Moses and Aaron, married his father Kohath's sister, Jochebed, who was therefore, as expressly stated Num. xxvi. 59, 'the daughter of Levi, whom *her mother* bare to Levi in Egypt.' Therefore Jochebed must have been born within 88 years after the going down into Egypt. And seeing that Moses was 80 years old at the Exodus (Exod vii. 7),—if we call x his mother's age when he was born, we have $88 + 80 + x$ as a maximum for the sojourn in Egypt, which clearly therefore cannot be 430 years, or even 400, as in the former case x would $= 262$,—in the latter 232 If we take $x =$ cir. 47 (to which might be added in the hypothesis any time which 88 and x might have had in common) we shall have the sojourn in Egypt = 215 years, which added to the previous 215, will make the required 130 Thus it will appear that the LXX, Samaritan Pent., and St. Paul, have the right chronology,—and as stated above, the difficulty lies in Gen xv. 13 and Acts vii 6,—and in the Hebrew text of Exod xii 40 18] See Rom iv 14. **For if the inheritance** (the general term for all the blessings promised to Abraham, as summed up in his Seed who was to inherit the land,—in other words, for the Kingdom of Christ· see 1 Cor. vi 9, 10) **is of the law** (i e by virtue of the law, having as its ground the covenant of the law) **it is no more** (οὐκ ἔτι, as νῦν in argumentative passages, not of time, but logical—the *οὐκ follows* on the hypothesis) **of** (by virtue of) **promise: but** (the 'but' of a demonstration, appealing to a well-known fact) **to Abraham by promise hath God granted** [it] (and therefore it is not of the Law) 19—24] *The use and nature of the Law* **What** (ref) **then** [is] **the Law** ('ubi audimus Legem nihil valere ad conferendam justitiam, statim obrepunt

τῶν [c] παραβάσεων [d] χάριν [e] προσετέθη, [f] ἄχρις οὗ ἔλθῃ | ABCDF KLℵ a b
τὸ σπέρμα ᾧ [g] ἐπήγγελται, [h] διαταγεὶς δι' ἀγγέλων [i] ἐν | c d e f g h k l m n o 17

c absol., Rom. iv. 15. v. 14. 1 Tim. ii. 14. Heb. ii. 2. ix. 15. Ps. c. 3. Wisd. xiv. 31 only. w. gen., Rom. ii. 23. 2 Macc. xv. 10 only. d Eph. iii. 1 reff. e Acts ii. 41 al. fr. Paul, here only. Heb. xii. 19. Deut. iv. 2. f constr., Rom. xi. 25. 1 Cor. xi. 26. g pass. sign., here only. 2 Macc. iv. 27. act., Rom. iv. 21. Heb. xii. 26. h = Acts vii. 44 (-γή, Acts vii. 53). i Levit. xxvi. 46.

19. for παραβασ., παραδοσεων D[1]: πραξεων F, *factorum* D-lat Iren-int$_2$ Ambrst, *prævaricationum aut factorum* G-lat. (*propter transgressionem* F-lat.) om χαριν F Iren-int$_2$ Ambrst. for προσετ., ετεθη D[1]F (*posita est* latt) Clem Orig Eus.
for οὗ, αν B 17 Clem. for αγγελων, αγγελου C[1](appy) d Thdrt$_1$-ms.

variæ cogitationes: aut igitur esse inutilem, aut contrariam fœderi Dei, aut tale quippiam.' Calv.)? **For the sake of the transgressions** [**of it**] (the words τῶν παραβάσεων . χάριν have been variously understood. (1) Aug., Calv., Beza, Luth., al., explain it of the *detection* of transgressions, as in Rom. vii. (2) Chrys., Œc., Thl., Jer., Erasm., Grot., Rück., Olsh., B.-Crus., De Wette, al., of their *repression*; μὴ ἐξῇ Ἰουδαίοις ἀδεῶς ζῆν . . . . ἀλλ' ἀντὶ χαλινοῦ ὁ νόμος αὐτοῖς ἐπικείμενος ᾖ, παιδεύων, ῥυθμίζων, κωλύων παραβαίνειν. Chrys. (3) Luth., Est., Bengel, al., combine (1) and (2). But it is hardly possible that either of these should be the true explanation. For the Apostle is not now treating of the detection of sin, or of the repression of sin [which latter was besides *not the office* of the Law, see Rom. v. 20], but of the Law as a preparation for Christ, vv. 23, 24: and therefore it must be regarded in its propædeutic office, not in its detective or (?) repressive. Now this propædeutic office was, to *make sin into* TRANSGRESSION,—so that what was before not a transgression might now become one. The law then was added [to the promise, which had no such power], for the sake of [in order to bring about *as transgressions*] the transgressions [of it] which should be, and thus [ver. 23] to shut us up under sin, viz. the transgression of the law. This is nearly Meyer's view, except that he makes this the exclusive meaning of χάριν, which usage will not sustain, cf. 1 John iii. 12. Ellic.'s view is very close to mine, which he has mistaken) **it was superadded** ("προσετέθη does not contradict the assertion of ver. 15, οὐδεὶς . . . . ἐπιδιατάσσεται. For the Law was not given as an ἐπιδιαθήκη, but came in as another institution, additional to that already existing." Meyer) **until the seed shall have come** (he places himself at the giving of the law and looks on into the future: hence the subjunctive, not the optative: and without ἄν, because the time is a certain and definite one), **to whom** (ver. 16) **the promise has been** (see above) **made** (the vulgate renders ἐπήγγελται *promiserat*, sc. Deus: and so Bengel prefers, from reff. active. But the passive suits ver. 16 [ἐρρέθησαν] better, and is justified by reff. Macc. Bretschneider understands it *cui demandatum est*, viz. *to put an end to the law*: but this is against N. T. usage of ἐπαγγέλλω, and absurd, where ἐπαγγελίαι is so often used in the context. This Seed is of course Christ), **being enjoined** (the aorist participle does not here denote previous occurrence, but is merely part of an aorist sentence: so Herod. i. 14, Γύγης δὲ τυραννεύσας ἀνέπεμψεν ἀναθήματα . . .: Diod. Sic. xi. 31, γενναίως ἀγωνισάμενος πολλοὺς ἀνεῖλε τῶν Ἑλλήνων. See Hermann on Viger, pp. 772-3. For διατάσσω, cf. note on Acts vii. 53, and Hesiod, Op. 274, τόνδε γὰρ ἀνθρώποισι νόμον διέταξε Κρονίων: it is not *promulgate*, as Winer) **by means of** (not, *under the attestation of*, as Peile, nor *in the presence of*, as Calov., al.) **angels** (angels were, according to the Rabbinical view, the enactors and enjoiners of the Law: so Jos. Antt. xv. 5. 3, ἡμῶν τὰ κάλλιστα τῶν δογμάτων κ. τὰ ὁσιώτατα τῶν ἐν τοῖς νόμοις **δι' ἀγγέλων παρὰ τοῦ θεοῦ μαθόντων**: see also the citations in Wetst.: Heb. ii. 2; and note on Col. ii. 15. Of course no explaining away of ἄγγελοι into men [Moses, Aaron, &c.] as Chrys. [altern.: ἢ τοὺς ἱερέας ἀγγέλους λέγει, ἢ καὶ αὐτοὺς τοὺς ἀγγέλους ὑπηρετήσασθαί φησι τῇ νομοθεσίᾳ], al., can be allowed. Observe, the angels are not the *givers* of the Law, but its *ministers*, and *instrumental enactors*: the Law, with St. Paul, is always *God's* Law; see especially Rom. vii. 22) **in the hand of a mediator** (viz. MOSES, who came from God to the people with the tables of the law in his hands. Cf. his own words, Deut. v. 5, κἀγὼ εἱστήκειν **ἀναμέσον κυρίου κ. ὑμῶν** ἐν τῷ καιρῷ ἐκείνῳ ἀναγγεῖλαι ὑμῖν τὰ ῥήματα κυρίου, ὅτι ἐφοβήθητε ἀπὸ προσώπου τοῦ πυρὸς κ. οὐκ ἀνέβητε εἰς τὸ ὄρος, λέγων . . .: Philo, vit. Mos. iii. 19, vol. ii. p. 160, οἷα **μεσίτης** κ. διαλλακτὴς οὐκ εὐθὺς ἀνεπήδησεν, ἀλλὰ πρότερον τὰς ὑπὲρ τοῦ ἔθνους ἱκεσίας κ. λιτὰς ἐποιεῖτο. Schöttgen gives numerous examples from the Rabbinical books, in which

χειρὶ [k] μεσίτου. 20 ὁ δὲ [k] μεσίτης [l] ἑνὸς οὐκ ἔστιν, ὁ δὲ

k 1 Tim ii 5 Heb viii 6 ix 15 xii 24 only. Job ix 33 (only?)
l gen, — Rom iii 29.

the name *Mediator* is given to Moses.—But most of the Fathers (not Thdrt), Bede, Lyra, Calvin, Calov, al, understand *Christ* to be meant: Schmieder and Schneckenburger, *the Angel of the Covenant*,—the Metatron Neither of these interpretations however will hold against the above evidence). *Why* does the Apostle add this last clause? I am inclined to think with Meyer that it is,—not to disparage the Law in comparison with the Gospel (as Luth., Elsn, Flatt, Ruck., Jowett, &c. &c) or with the promise (Estius, Schneckenb., De Wette), but to enhance the solemnity of the giving of the law as a preparation for Christ, in answer to the somewhat disparaging question *τί οὖν ὁ νόμος*, If the *δι' ἀγγέλων* had been here disparaging, as in Heb. ii. 2, *διὰ τοῦ κυρίου* or the like must have been expressed, as there, on the other side And *ἐν χειρὶ μεσίτου* is certainly no disparagement of the old covenant in comparison with the new, for this it has in common with the other The fact is (see below on ver 20), that no such comparison is in question here. 20] "The explanations of this verse, so obscure from its brevity, are so numerous (Winer counted 250 Jowett mentions 430) that they require a bibliography of their own" De Wette. I believe we shall best disentangle the sense as follows (1) Clearly, *ὁ μεσίτης* and *ὁ θεός* are opposed (2) As clearly, *ἑνὸς οὐκ ἔστιν* and *εἷς ἐστιν* are opposed (3) From this contrast arises an apparent opposition between the law and the promises of God, which (not alone, but as the conclusion of the whole *τί οὖν* to *εἷς ἐστιν*) gives occasion to the question of ver 21 Taking up therefore again (1),—*ὁ μεσίτης*, by whose hand the law was enacted, stands opposed to *ὁ θεός*, the giver of the promises And that, in this respect (2),—(a) *ὁ μεσίτης* is not *ἑνός*, but (b) *ὁ θεός* is *εἷς* And herein lies the knot of the verse; that is, in (b), for the meaning of (a) is pretty clear on all hands, viz that *ὁ μεσίτης* (generic, so ref Job, 'quæ multa sunt cunctis in unum colligendis,' Hermann ad Iph. in Aul p 15, præf cited by Meyer) does not belong to *one party* (masculine) (but to *two*, as going between one party and another) Then to guide us to the meaning of (b), we must remember, that the numerical contrast is the primary idea · *ὁ μεσίτης* belongs not to *one*, but *ὁ θεός is one*. Shall we then say, that all reference of *εἷς* (as applied to *ὁ θεός*) beyond this numerical one is to be repudiated? I cannot think so. The proposition *ὁ θεὸς εἷς ἐστιν* would carry to the mind of every reader much more than the mere *numerical* unity of God—viz His Unity as an *essential attribute*, extending through the whole divine Character And thus, though the proposition *ὁ μεσίτης ἑνὸς οὐκ ἔστιν* would not, by itself, convey any meaning but that a mediator belongs to more than one, it would, when combined with *ὁ θεὸς εἷς ἐστιν*, receive a shade of meaning which it did not bear before,—of a state of things involved in the fact of a *μεσίτης* being employed, which was not according to the *ἑνότης* of God, or, so to speak, in the main track of His unchanging purpose And thus (3), the law, administered by the *μεσίτης*, belonging to a state of *οὐχ εἷς*, two at variance, is apparently opposed to the *ἐπαγγελίαι*, belonging entirely to *ὁ εἷς*, the one (faithful) God And observe, that the above explanation is deduced entirely from the *form of the sentence itself*, and from the idea which the expression *ὁ θεὸς εἷς ἐστιν* must necessarily raise in the mind of its reader, accustomed to the proposition as the foundation of the faith,—not from any preconceived view, to suit which the words, or emphatic arrangement, must be forced. Notice by the way, that the objection, that the Gospel too is *ἐν χειρὶ μεσίτου*, does not apply here · for (α) there is no question here of the *Gospel*, but only of the *promises*, as direct from God (β) the *μεσίτης* of the Gospel is altogether different, and His work different He has absolutely reconciled the parties at variance, and MADE THEM ONE in Himself Remember St Paul's habit of *insulating* the matter in hand, and dealing with it irrespective of all such possible objections. To give even an analysis of the various opinions on this verse would far exceed the limits of this commentary. I will only take advantage of Meyer's long note, and of other sources, to indicate the main branches of the exegesis. (1) The Fathers, for the most part, pass lightly over it, as easy in itself,—and do not notice its pragmatic difficulty Most of them understand by the *μεσίτης*, Christ, the mediator between God and man In interpreting *ἑνὸς οὐκ ἔστιν* and *εἷς ἐστιν*, they go in omnia alia It may suffice to quote one or two samples Chrys says, *τί ἂν ἐνταῦθα εἴποιεν αἱρετικοί, εἰ γὰρ τὸ "μόνος ἀλη-*

m = Matt. xii. 30. Rom. viii. 31. ch. v. 23. n plur., ver. 16.

θεὸς εἷς ἐστιν. 21 ὁ οὖν νόμος m κατὰ τῶν n ἐπαγγελιῶν

ABCDF KLℵ a b c d e f g h k l m n o 17

θινός," οὐκ ἀφίησι τὸν υἱὸν εἶναι θεὸν ἀληθινόν, οὐκ ἄρα οὐδὲ θεόν, διὰ τὸ λέγεσθαι "ὁ δὲ θεὸς εἷς ἐστιν." ..... ὁ δὲ μεσίτης, φησί, δύο τινῶν γίνεται μεσίτης. τίνος οὖν μεσίτης ἦν ὁ χριστός; ἢ δῆλον ὅτι θεοῦ κ. ἀνθρώπων; ὁρᾷς πῶς δείκνυσιν ὅτι καὶ τὸν νόμον αὐτὸς ἔδωκεν; εἰ τοίνυν αὐτὸς ἔδωκε, κύριος ἂν εἴη καὶ λῦσαι πάλιν. And Jerome, 'manu mediatoris potentiam et virtutem ejus debemus accipere, qui cum secundum Deum unum sit ipse cum patre, secundum mediatoris officium alius ab eo intelligitur.' Theodoret, having explained the μεσίτης of Moses, proceeds, on ὁ δὲ θεὸς εἷς ἐστιν,—ὁ καὶ τὴν ἐπαγγελίαν τῷ Ἀβραὰμ δεδωκώς, καὶ τὸν νόμον τεθεικώς, καὶ οὖν τῆς ἐπαγγελίας ἡμῖν ἐπιδείξας τὸ πέρας. οὐ γὰρ ἄλλος μὲν ἐκεῖνα θεὸς ᾠκονόμησεν, ἄλλος δὲ ταῦτα. (II) The older of the modern Commentators are generally quite at fault: I give a few of them: Grotius says, 'Etsi Christus mediator Legem Judæis tulerit, ut ad agnitionem transgressionum adduceret, eoque ad fœdus gratiæ præpararet, non tamen unius est gentis Judaicæ mediator, sed omnium hominum: quemadmodum Deus unus est omnium.' Luther (1519), 'Ex nomine mediatoris concludit, nos adeo esse peccatores, ut legis opera satis esse nequeant. Si, inquit, lege justi estis, jam mediatore non egetis, sed neque Deus, cum sit ipse unus, secum optime conveniens. Inter duos ergo quæritur mediator, inter Deum et hominem; ac si dicat, impiissima est ingratitudo, si mediatorem rejicitis, et Deo, qui unus est, remittitis, &c.' Erasmus, in his paraphrase: 'Atqui conciliator, qui intercedit, inter plures intercedat oportet, nemo enim secum ipse dissidet. Deus autem unus est, quocum dissidium erat humano generi. Proinde tertio quopiam erat opus, qui naturæ utriusque particeps utramque inter sese reconciliaret, &c.' Calvin, as the preferable view, 'diversitatem hic notari arbitror inter Judæos et Gentiles. Non unius ergo mediator est Christus, quia diversa est conditio eorum quibuscum Deus, ipsius auspiciis, paciscitur, quod ad externum personam. Verum Paulus inde æstimandum Dei fœdus negat, quasi secum pugnet, aut varium sit pro hominum diversitate.' (III) The later moderns begin to approach nearer to the philological and contextual requirements of the passage, but still with considerable errors and divergences. Bengel, on the first clause, 'Medius terminus est in syllogismo, cujus major propositio et minor exprimitur, conclusio subauditur. *Unus non utitur mediatore illo*: atqui *Deus est unus.* Ergo Deus non prius sine mediatore, deinde per mediatorem egit. Ergo is cujus erat mediator non est unus idemque cum Deo sed diversus a Deo, nempe ὁ νόμος, Lex..... ergo mediator Sinaiticus non est Dei sed legis: Dei autem, promissio.' Locke (so also Michaelis): "God is but one of the parties concerned in the promise: the Gentiles and Israelites together made up the other, ver. 14. But Moses, at the giving of the law, was a mediator only between the Israelites and God: and therefore could not transact any thing to the disannulling the promise, which was between God and the Israelites and Gentiles together, because God was but one of the parties to that covenant: the other, which was the Gentiles as well as Israelites, Moses appeared or transacted not for." (IV) Of the recent Commentators, Keil (Opusc. 1809—12) says: 'Mediatorem quidem non unius sed duarum certe partium esse, Deum autem qui Abrahamo beneficii aliquid promiserit, unum modo fuisse: hincque apostolum id a lectoribus suis colligi voluisse, in lege ista Mosaica pactum mutuum Deum inter atque populum Israeliticum mediatoris opera intercedente initum fuisse, contra vero in promissione rem ab unius tantum (Dei sc. qui solus eam dederit) voluntate pendentem transactam,—hincque legi isti nihil plane cum hac rei fuisse, adeoque nec potuisse ea novam illius promissionis implendæ conditionem constitui, eoque ipso promissionem omnino tolli.' And similarly Schleiermacher (in Usteri's Lehrbegriff, p. 186 ff.), but giving to εἷς the sense of freedom and independence;—and Meyer, only repudiating the second part of Keil's explanation from 'hincque,' as not belonging to an abstract sentence like this, but being historical, as if it had been ἦν, and besides contrary to the Apostle's meaning, who deduces from our verse a consequence the contrary to this ('hincque ..... fuisse'), and obviates it by the question in ver. 21. For the numerous other recent interpretations and their refutations I must refer the reader to Meyer's note [as also to Ellicott's (in his ed. 1: see his present view in his ed. 2), who preferred Windischmann's interpretation of εἷς, 'One, because He was both giver and receiver united: giver, as the Father;

τοῦ ° θεοῦ; ᵖ μὴ γένοιτο. εἰ γὰρ ᑫ ἐδόθη νόμος ʳ ὁ δυνάμενος ˢ ζωοποιῆσαι, ᵗ ὄντως ἐκ νόμου ἂν ἦν ἡ δικαιοσύνη·
22 ἀλλὰ ᵘ συνέκλεισεν ἡ γραφὴ ᵛ τὰ πάντα ὑπὸ ἁμαρτίαν,

o ellips, ch ii 21. p ch ii 17 reff. q = John i 17 vii 19, 22 Acts vii 8 Ezek xx 11 al. r so Acts iv 12 x 41 (μάρτ. τοῖς προκεχ.) Winer, § 20 4. s John v 21 Rom iv 17 1 Pet iii 18 al Eccl vii 13 only. t Mark xi 32 Luke xxiii 47 1 Cor xiv 25 al Num xxii. 37. u Luke v 6 Rom. xi 32 only Josh vi 1 al. v (= τοὺς πάντας, Rom xi 32) so neut, 1 Cor i 27, 28. Heb vii. 7 al Winer, § 27 5.

21. om του θεου B D-lat Ambrst-ed for οντως, αληθεια F. rec αν bef εκ νομου, with D²·³KL rel Chr Thdrt: om αν D¹ Damasc: om ην a om αν ην F txt ABCℵ 17 (but ην bef αν ℵ 17) Cyr.
22 om τα FK Damasc υφ AD¹F m Damasc.

receiver, as the Son, the σπέρμα ᾧ ἐπήγγελται.' But this seems going too deep—almost, we may say, arriving at the conclusion by a *coup de main*, which would not have borne any meaning to the readers]: see also Jowett's note, which seems to me further to complicate the matter by introducing into it God's unity of dealing with man, and man's unity with God in Christ. (V) We may profitably lay down one or two canons of interpretation of the verse (α) Every interpretation is wrong, which understands *Christ* by ὁ μεσίτης. The context determines it to be abstract, and its reference to be to Moses, the mediator of the Law. (β) Every interpretation is wrong, which makes εἷς mean 'one party' in the covenant. ὁ θεὸς εἷς ἐστιν itself confutes any such view, being a well known general proposition, not admitting of a concrete interpretation. (γ) Every interpretation is wrong, which confines εἷς (as Meyer) to its mere numerical meaning, and does not take into account the ideas which the general proposition would raise. (δ) Every interpretation is wrong, which deduces from the verse the *agreement* of the law with the promises because the Apostle himself, in the next verse, draws the very opposite inference from it, and refutes it on other grounds. (ε) Every attempt to set aside the verse as a gloss is utterly futile. **21.**] The Law being thus set over against the promises,—being given through a mediator between two,—the promises by the one God,—it might seem as if there were an inconsistency between them The nature of the contrariety must not (as De W) be deduced from the following disproof of it: this disproof proceeds on τῶν παραβάσεων χάριν προσετέθη, which is *not* the ground of the apparent contrariety, but its explanation The appearance of inconsistency lay in the whole paragraph preceding—the οὐκ ἀκυροῖ of ver. 17, the εἰ ἐκ νόμου, οὐκέτι ἐξ ἐπαγγελίας of ver. 18,—and the contrast between the giving of the two in ver 20. "τοῦ θεοῦ is not without emphasis the promises which rest immediately on God, and were attested (? sic still in ed. 2) by no mediator" Ellic. **εἰ γάρ**] Notwithstanding all the above features of contrast between the Law and the prophets, it is not against them, for it does not pretend to perform the same office; *if it did*, then there would be this rivalry, which now does not exist **νόμος ὁ δυν.** is best expressed in English, as in E. V., **a law which could** . . for the article circumscribes the νόμος to some particular quality indicated in the defining participle which follows: see reff. Peile's rendering, "if that which (ὁ δυνάμενος!) should have power to give life had been given in the form of law," is in the highest degree ungrammatical. **ζωοποιῆσαι** takes for granted that we by nature are *dead* in trespasses and sins. **ὄντως** has the emphasis. **in very truth,** and not only in the fancy of some, **by the law** (as its ground) **would have been righteousness** (which is the condition of life eternal,—ὁ δίκαιος . . ζήσεται If life, the result, had been given by the law, then righteousness, the *condition* of life, must have been by it also reasoning from the whole to its part). **22.**] **But on the contrary** (**ἀλλά**, not δέ comp Ellic. This not being the case,—no law being given out of which could come righteousness) **the Scripture** (not the Law, as Chrys and most of the Fathers, also Calv, Beza, al, but as in ver. 8, the Author of Scripture, speaking by that His witness) **shut up** (not subjective as Chrys, ἤλεγξεν . . κ ἐλέγξας κατεῖχεν ἐν φόβῳ,—for it is then objective state of incapacity to attain righteousness which is here brought out —nor 'conclusit omnes simul,' as Bengel, al.: the preposition enhances the force of κλείειν, as in 'contraho,' συμπνίγειν, &c see note Rom xi. 32, where the same expression occurs "The word συγκλείειν is beautifully chosen, to set off more clearly the idea of Christian freedom by and by." Windischmann: cf. ch. v. 1. Nor has

ἵνα ἡ [w] ἐπαγγελία ἐκ [x] πίστεως [x] Ἰησοῦ χριστοῦ δοθῇ τοῖς
πιστεύουσιν. 23 πρὸ τοῦ δὲ [y] ἐλθεῖν τὴν [z] πίστιν, ὑπὸ
νόμον [a] ἐφρουρούμεθα [u] συγκλειόμενοι [b] εἰς τὴν [c] μέλλουσαν [z] πίστιν [d] ἀποκαλυφθῆναι. 24 ὥςτε ὁ νόμος [e] παιδ-

ABCDF KLℵ a b c d e f g h k l m n o 17

w ver. 14 reff. x gen., = ch. ii. 16. Rom. iii. 22, 26. y = Rom. vii. 9. z = ch. i. 23. Rom. i. 5. Jude 3. a 2 Cor. xi. 32. Phil. iv. 7. 1 Pet. i. 5 only†. Judith iii. 6. b see Wisd. xvii. 16. c transp. of words, Rom. viii. 18. 1 Cor. xii. 22. d = Matt. xi. 25. Rom. i. 17. 1 Cor. ii. 10. Isa. lvi. 1. e 1 Cor. iv. 15 only†.

23. rec *συγκεκλεισμενοι*, with CD[3]KL rel Clem[1] Cyr[2] Thdrt Thl Œc: txt ABD[1]Fℵ 17 Clem[1] Chr[2] Cyr[2].

συγκλ. merely a declaratory sense, as Bull, Examen Censuræ xix. 6, 'conclusos involutos declaravit,' al.) **all** (neuter, as indicating the entirety of mankind and man's world: 'humana omnia,' as Jowett: cf. reff. I think [against Ellic. ed. 2] that we must hold fast this) **under sin, in order that** (the *intention* of God, as in Rom. xi. 32: *not the mere result*, here or any where else. Beware of such an assertion as Burton's, quoted also by Peile;—"*ἵνα* here implies, not the cause, but the consequence, as in many places." *ἵνα* never implies any thing of the sort; nor does any one of the examples he gives bear him out) **the promise** (i. e. the things promised—the *κληρονομία*, cf. vv. 16, 18) (which is) **by** (depends upon, is conditioned by) **faith of** (which has for its object and its Giver—is a matter altogether belonging to) **Jesus Christ** (q. d. *ἡ ἐπαγγ. ἡ ἐκ π.*: but the article in such sentences is frequently omitted, especially where no distinction is intended between the subject and another of the same kind: cf. *τῆς πίστεως ἐν χρ. Ἰησ.* below, ver. 26,—*τοῖς κυρίοις κατὰ σάρκα*, Eph. vi. 5, &c. The words *ἐκ πίστ.* cannot well be taken with *δοθῇ* without harshness, especially as *Ἰησοῦ χριστοῦ* intervenes, and *τοῖς πιστεύουσιν* is already expressed. Besides, in this case they would most naturally come first,—*ἵνα ἐκ πίστεως Ἰ. χρ. ἡ ἐπαγγ. δοθῇ τ. π.*) **might be given** (be a *free gift*—*δοθῇ* has the emphasis) **to them that believe** (*δοθῇ* having the emphasis, *τοῖς πιστ.* does no more than take up *ἐκ πίστ.* above; q. d. 'to those who fulfil that condition').

23.] **But** (*δέ* carries us on to a further account of the rationale and office of the law. "When the noun, to which the particle is attached, is preceded by a preposition, and perhaps the article as well, *δέ* may stand the third or fourth word in the sentence. So *ἐν τοῖς πρῶτοι δὲ Ἀθηναῖοι*, Thuc. i. 6: *οὐχ ὑπὸ ἐραστοῦ δέ*, Plat. Phædr. 227 d, &c." Hartung, Partikell. i. 190) **before** (this) **faith** (not, *the faith*, in the sense of *the objects of faith*, but the faith just mentioned, viz. *πίστις Ἰησοῦ χρ.*, which did not exist until Christ) **came** (was found, or was possible, in men: cf. ref., where however it is more entirely subjective), **we** (properly, we Jewish believers—but not here to be pressed, because he is speaking of the divine dealings with men generally—the Law was for *τὰ πάντα*, the only revelation) **were kept in ward** (not simply '*kept*' as E. V., but as Chrys., *ὥσπερ ἐν τειχίῳ τινί*,—though not as he proceeds, *τῷ φόβῳ κατεχόμενοι*—for, as above, our objective state is here treated of: see Rom. vii. 6. But we must not yet, with Chrys., al., introduce the *παιδαγωγός*, or understand *ἐφρουρ.* as conveying the idea of '*safely kept*' [*οὐδὲν ἕτερον δηλοῦντός ἐστιν, ἢ τὴν ἐκ τῶν ἐντολῶν τοῦ νόμου γενομένην ἀσφάλειαν*]: *συγκλειόμενοι* is quite against this, and the pædagogic figure does not enter till the next verse, springing out of the preparation implied in *εἰς*, joined to the fact of our sonship, see below. Our present verse answers to ch. iv. 2, where we find *ἐπίτροποι* and *οἰκονόμοι*, not the *παιδαγωγός*. See Jowett's beautiful illustration), **shut up under the law, in order to** (*εἰς* of the preparatory *design*, not merely of the *result*, or the arrival of the time: and it may belong either to *συγκλειόμ.* [not to *συγκεκλεισμένοι*, if that be read, as that would betoken the act completed when the Law was given], or to the imperfect *ἐφρουρούμεθα*) **the faith** (as in ver. 22) **about to be revealed** (on the order of the words see on ref. Rom. "As long as there was no such thing as faith in Christ, this faith was *not yet revealed*, was as yet an element of life hidden in the counsel of God." Meyer). **24.**] **So that** (taking up the condition in which the last verse left us, and *adding to it the fact* that we are the sons of God, cf. *γάρ*, ver. 26) **the Law has become** (has turned out to be) **our tutor** (pedagogue, see below) **unto** (ethically; for) **Christ** (the *παιδαγωγός* was a faithful slave, entrusted with the care of the boy from his tender years till puberty, to keep him from evil physical and moral, and accompany him to his amusements and studies. See Dict. of Gr. and Rom. Antt. sub voce. The E. V. '*schoolmaster*' does not express the mean-

αγωγὸς ἡμῶν γέγονεν εἰς χριστόν, ἵνα [f] ἐκ πίστεως [f] δι-
καιωθῶμεν· 25 [y] ἐλθούσης δὲ τῆς [z] πίστεως οὐκ ἔτι ὑπὸ
[e] παιδαγωγόν ἐσμέν. 26 πάντες γὰρ [g] υἱοὶ θεοῦ ἐστε διὰ
τῆς [h] πίστεως [h] ἐν χριστῷ Ἰησοῦ· 27 ὅσοι γὰρ [i] εἰς
χριστὸν [i] ἐβαπτίσθητε, χριστὸν [k] ἐνεδύσασθε. 28 οὐκ
[l] ἔνι [m] Ἰουδαῖος οὐδὲ [m] Ἕλλην, οὐκ [l] ἔνι [n] δοῦλος οὐδὲ

f ch ii 16 reff. g Matt. v 9 Luke (vi 35) xx 36 Rom viii 14, 19 h Eph i 15 Col i 4 1 Tim iii 13. 2 Tim iii 15. i Matt xxviii 19 Acts xix 5. Rom vi 3 1 Cor x 2 xii 13 k = Rom xiii 14 Eph iv 24 Col iii 10 Ps cxxxi 9 Luke xi 41 l 1 Cor vi 5 Col iii 11. James i 17 only see m see Rom i 16 n Eph vi 8 al

24. for γεγονεν, εγενετο B Clem[1]. aft χρ ins ιησουν D[1](and lat) F fuld(and F-lat) Ambrst.
26 aft υιοι ins οι ℵ[1]: but marked for erasure by ℵ[1] or ℵ-corr.
28. for 2nd ουδε, η D[1] και lect[1]. (not D-lat)

ing fully. but it disturbs the sense less than those have done, who have selected one portion only of the pedagogue's duty, and understood by it, '*the slave who leads a child to the house of the school-master*' [οἷόν τινι σοφῷ διδασκάλῳ προσφέρει τῷ δεσπότῃ χριστῷ, Thdrt. so also Thl: see Suicer, νόμος, b], thus making Christ the schoolmaster, which is inconsistent with the imagery On the contrary, the whole schoolmaster's work is included in the παιδαγωγός, and Christ represents the ἐλευθερία of the grown-up son, in which he is no longer guarded or shut up, but justified by faith, the act of a free man, and to Christ *as a Teacher* there is here no allusion), **in order that by faith we might be justified** (which could only be done when Christ had come) **but** (adversative) **now that the faith** (see above) **has come, we are no longer under a tutor** (pedagogue). **26.**] *Reason of the negation in last verse* **For ye all** (Jews and Gentiles alike) **are** SONS (no longer παῖδες, requiring a παιδαγωγός) **of God by means of the** (or, but not so well, your) **faith in Christ Jesus** (some [Usteri, Windisch, al] would join ἐν χρ Ἰησ. with υἱοὶ θεοῦ ἐστε, but most unnaturally,—and unmeaningly, for the idea of ἐν χρ Ἰησ in that case has been already given by διὰ τῆς πίστεως The omission of τῆς before ἐν will stagger no one see Col i 4, where the same expression occurs). **27**] **For** (substantiates and explains the assertion of ver 26. see below) **as many of you as were baptized into** (see Rom vi 3 and notes) **Christ, put on Christ** (at that time, compare the aorists in Acts xix. 2· not "*have been baptized*," and "*have put on*," as E. V, which leaves the two actions only concomitant· the aorists make them identical as many as were baptized into Christ, did, in that very act, put on, clothe yourselves with, Christ see Ellicott's note) **The force of the argument is well given by Chrys.**· τίνος ἕνεκεν οὐκ εἶπεν, ὅσοι γὰρ εἰς χριστὸν ἐβαπτίσθητε, ἐκ τοῦ θεοῦ ἐγεννήθητε; τὸ γὰρ ἀκόλουθον τοῦ δεῖξαι υἱοὺς τοῦτο ἦν. ὅτι πολὺ φρικωδέστερον αὐτὸ τίθησιν εἰ γὰρ ὁ χριστὸς υἱὸς τοῦ θεοῦ, σὺ δὲ αὐτὸν ἐνδέδυσαι, τὸν υἱὸν ἔχων ἐν ἑαυτῷ κ πρὸς αὐτὸν ἀφομοιωθεὶς, εἰς μίαν συγγένειαν κ μίαν ἰδέαν ἤχθης Observe here how boldly and broadly St Paul asserts the effect of Baptism on all [πάντες γὰρ . and ὅσοι ἐβαπτ] the baptized Luther remarks " Hic locus diligenter observandus est contra fanaticos spiritus, qui majestatem baptismi extenuant, et scelerate et impie de eo loquuntur. Paulus contra magnificis titulis baptismum ornat, appellans lavacrum regenerationis ac renovationis Sp. sancti (Tit. iii 5), et hic dicit omnes baptisatos Christum induisse, quasi dicat non accepistis per baptismum tesseram, per quam adscripti estis in numerum christianorum, ut nostro tempore multi fanatici homines senserunt, qui ex baptismo tantum tesseram fecerunt, hoc est, breve et inane quoddam signum, sed 'quotquot' inquit etc id est, estis extra legem rapti in novam nativitatem, quæ facta est in baptismo" But we may notice too, as Meyer remarks, that the very putting on of Christ, which as matter of standing and profession is done in baptism, forms a subject of exhortation to those already baptized, in its ethical sense, Rom xiii 14

28] The absolute equality of all in this sonship, to the obliteration of all differences of earthly extraction or position. See Col. iii. 11; Rom. x 12, 1 Cor. xii 13 οὐκ ἔνι = οὐκ ἔνεστιν—'il n'y a pas' De Wette quotes Plat Gorg. 507, ὅτῳ δὲ μὴ ἔνι κοινωνία, φιλία οὐκ ἂν εἴη Buttmann (ii 299), Kuhner (i 671), Winer (§ 14 2, note), maintain ἔνι to be a form of the preposition ἐν, and the same of ἔπι, πάρα, &c But Meyer replies, that all those passages are against this view, where ἔνι and ἐν occur together, as 1 Cor. vi. 5, Xen. Anab v. 3.

o Matt xix 4 (Mk), from Gen i 27. Rom i 27 only. p as above (o) Luke ii 23. Rev xii 5 only. q as above (o) Rom i 26 only. r gen, Rom xiv 8. 1 Cor i. 12. iii 22, 23 al

ABCDF KLℵ a b c d e f g h k l m n o 17

ⁿ ἐλεύθερος, οὐκ ˡ ἔνι ᵒᵖ ἄρσεν καὶ ᵒᵠ θῆλυ· ἅπαντες γὰρ
ὑμεῖς εἷς ἐστε ἐν χριστῷ Ἰησοῦ. 29 εἰ δὲ ὑμεῖς ʳ χριστοῦ,
ˢ ἄρα τοῦ ᵗ Ἀβραὰμ ᵗ σπέρμα ἐστέ, ᵘ κατ᾽ ᵘ ἐπαγγελίαν
ᵛ κληρονόμοι.
IV. 1 ʷ Λέγω δέ, ˣ ἐφ᾽ ὅσον ˣ χρόνον ὁ ᵛ κληρονόμος
ʸ νήπιός ἐστιν, οὐδὲν ᶻ διαφέρει δούλου κύριος πάντων ὤν,

s 1 Cor xv 14. 2 Cor v 15. see Rom viii 3, 25. t John viii 33. Rom ix 7. Isa xli 8. u Acts xiii 23 (Paul). 2 Tim i 1 only. v Rom iv 13, 14. viii 17. Heb i 2 al. Micah i 15. w Rom xv 8. ch v 16. x Rom vii 1. 1 Cor vii 39. see 2 Pet i 13. Deut xii 19. y = 1 Cor xiii 11 (5 times). Ps viii 2. z = and constr, 1 Cor xv 41 only‡. Dan vii 3 (Theod.)

αρσεν ℵ. rec παντες (*from ver 26, where there is no variation · Ellic wrong*), with B¹CDFKL rel Clem₂ Orig Chr Thdrt Damasc: txt AB²ℵ. om εἷς Aℵ¹. for εἷς, ἕν F 17 latt copt goth Orig Ath₁ Ps-Ath Dial-trin Thdrt₁ Philo-carp lat-ff. for εν χρ. ιησ., χριστου ιησου A, so ℵ¹, εν having been written before χῡ, and marked for erasure: the marks have been removed by ℵ³ which reads as text: om ιησ c.

29. for χριστου, εις εστε ἐν χῷ ιῦ D¹F (with [besides F-lat] harl) Ambrst. aft αρα ins ουν D¹F. σπερματος B copt. rec ins και bef κατ᾽, with DKL rel syrr goth Chr Thdrt: om ABCDℵ 17 vulg copt arm Thdor-mops Damasc Ambrst Victorin Aug. κατα ℵ.

11. Observe, Ἰουδ. οὐδὲ Ἑλλ., δοῦλος οὐδὲ ἐλεύθ.,—but ἄρσεν καὶ θῆλυ: the two former being accidental distinctions which may be entirely put off in falling back on our humanity,—but the latter a necessary distinction, absorbed however in the higher category: q. d. "there is no distinction into male and female." ἄρσεν κ. θῆλυ, generalized by the neuter, as being the only gender which will express both. γάρ, reason why there is neither, &c.—viz. our unity in Christ. On the unavoidable inference from an assertion like this, that Christianity did alter the condition of women and slaves, see Jowett's note. εἷς, more forcible and more strict than ἕν: for we are one, *in Him*, εἷς καινὸς ἄνθρωπος, as he says in Eph ii 15, speaking on this very subject. 29.] Christ is '*Abraham's seed*' (ver. 16): ye are one in and with Christ, have put on Christ; therefore *ye* are Abraham's seed, consequently heirs by promise, for to Abraham and his seed were the promises made. The stress is on ὑμεῖς, τοῦ Ἀβραάμ, and κατ᾽ ἐπαγγελίαν, especially on the latter,—carrying the conclusion of the argument, as against inheritance *by the law*. See on this verse, the note on ver. 16 above. "The declaration of ver 7 is now substantiated by 22 verses of the deepest, the most varied, and most comprehensive reasoning that exists in the whole compass of the great Apostle's writings." Ellicott.

IV. 1—7.] The Apostle shews the *correspondence between our treatment under the law and that of heirs in general*: and thus, *by God's dealing with us, in sending forth His Son, whose Spirit of Sonship we have received*, confirms (ver 7) the conclusion that WE ARE HEIRS. 1.] λέγω δέ refers to what follows (reff), and does not imply, 'What I mean, is.' ὁ κληρ., generic, as ὁ μεσίτης, ch. iii. 20. The question, whether the *father* of the κληρονόμος here is to be thought of as dead, or absent, or living and present, is in fact one of no importance: nor does it belong properly to the consideration of the passage. The fact is, the antitype breaks through the type, and disturbs it: as is the case, wherever the idea of *inheritance* is spiritualized. The supposition in our text is, that a father (from what reason or under what circumstances matters not. Mr Bagge quotes from Ulpian, speaking of the right of a testator appointing guardians, "Tutorem autem et a certo tempore dare et usque ad certum tempus licet." Digest xxvi 2. 8) has preordained a time for his son and heir to come of age, and till that time, has subjected him to guardians and stewards. In the *type*, the reason might be absence, or decease, or even high office or intense occupation, of the father: in the *antitype*, it is the Father's sovereign will: but the *circumstances* equally exist. οὐδὲν διαφ. δούλου] διὰ τοῦτο γὰρ κ. παίειν κ. ἄγχειν κ. στρεβλοῦν, κ. ἃ τῶν δεσποτῶν πρὸς τοὺς οἰκέτας, ταῦτα τῶν υἱέων τοῖς ἐφεστῶσιν ἀξιοῦσιν ὑπάρχειν. Libanius (Wetst.). See below on ver 3: and Plato, Lysis, pp 207, 8, cited at length in Bagge. κύριος πάντων ὤν must be understood *essentially*, rather than prospectively. It is said of him in virtue of his rank, rather than of his actual estate: *in posse*, rather than *in*

2 ἀλλὰ ὑπὸ [a] ἐπιτρόπους ἐστὶν καὶ [b] οἰκονόμους [c] ἄχρι τῆς
[d] προθεσμίας τοῦ πατρός. 3 οὕτως καὶ ἡμεῖς ὅτε ἦμεν
[y] νήπιοι, ὑπὸ τὰ [e] στοιχεῖα τοῦ κόσμου ἦμεν [f] δεδουλω-
μένοι· 4 ὅτε δὲ ἦλθεν τὸ [g] πλήρωμα τοῦ χρόνου, [h] ἐξαπέστειλεν ὁ θεὸς τὸν υἱὸν αὐτοῦ, [i] γενόμενον ἐκ γυναικός,

a Matt xx 8 Luke viii 3 only† 2 Macc xi 1. xiii 2 xiv 2. b Luke xii 42 xvi 1, 3, 8 1 Cor iv 1, 2 al 3 Kings iv 6 c Rom viii 22 1 Cor iv 11 2 Cor iii 14 al d here only† Job xxxviii 3 Symm Jos Antt xii 4 7, τῆς προθ. ἐνισταμένης, καθ' ἣν ἔδει e ver 9 Col ii 8, 20 Heb v 12 2 Pet iii 10, 12 only† Wisd vii 17 xix 18 only f Acts vii 6 Rom vi 18, 22 1 Cor vii 15 ix 19 Ilt ii 3 2 Pet ii 19 only Gen xv 13. g = Eph i 10 only (comp Luke i 57 ix 51 Acts ii 1 Ezek. v 2) h Paul, here (bis) only Luke i 53 xx 10, 11 Acts vii 12 al[6] L P Mal iii 1 i see Matt xi 11 Job xiv 1 ἐξ ἧς σὺ ἐγένου, Xen Cyr viii 5 19

CHAP IV. 2. ins της bef του πατρος B
3 for ημεν, ημεθα D[1]F ℵ 17.
4 for 1st γενομ., γενωμενον k[1]. γεννομενον K al[4] γεννωμενον a d e f g (26 others and correctors of 4 more in Reiche) æth Clem-ms Eus Ath[1] Thdrt[3] Damasc Phot, *natum* fuld(with demid tol harl[2]) Iren-lat[1] Cypr txt ABCDFLℵ rel syrr copt goth Clem Orig Eus Ath[1] Ps-Ath Method Cyr jer Chr Cyr[2] Thdrt, *factum* latt Iren-lat[3] Tert Victorin Hil.

esse. 2] **ἐπιτρόπους**, overseers of the person; **guardians**· **οἰκονόμους**, overseers of the property, **stewards** See Ellicott's and Bagge's notes. **προθεσμία**, **the time (previously) appointed.** The word (an adjective used substantively scil. ἡμέρα or ὥρα. See for the classical meaning, 'the time allowed to elapse before bringing an action,' Smith's Dict. of Antt sub voce) is a common one· Wetst. gives many examples The following clearly explain it. ὁρίσαι προθεσμίαν, ἐν ᾗ τὸ ἱερὸν συντελεσθήσεται, Polyæn p. 597:— εἰ δὲ ὁ τῆς ζωῆς τῶν ἀνθρώπων χρόνος εἰκοσαετὴς ἦν . . τὴν δὲ τῶν κ ἐτῶν προθεσμίαν ἐκπληρώσαντα, Plut ad Apollon. p. 113 e It is no objection to the view that the father is dead, that the time was *fixed by law* (Hebrew as well as Greek and Roman) nor on the other hand any proof of it, that **προθεσμία** will hardly apply to a living man's arrangement see on the whole, above.

3] **ἡμεῖς**—are Jews only here included, or Jews and Gentiles? Clearly, *both*· for ἵνα τ. υἱοθεσ. ἀπολάβωμεν is spoken of all believers in Christ He regards the Jews as, for this purpose, including all mankind (see note on ch. iii 23), God's only positive dealings by revelation being with them—and the Gentiles as partakers both in their infant-discipline, and in their emancipation in Christ **ὅτε ἦμεν νήπιοι** refers, not to any immaturity of capacity in *us*, but to the lifetime of the church, as regarded in the προθεσμία τοῦ πατρός· see below on ver. 4

τὰ στοιχεῖα τοῦ κόσμου] Aug interprets this physically, of the worship of the elements of nature by the Gentiles Chrys, Thdrt, al, of the Jewish new moons and sabbaths Neander (Pfl u Leit. p. 370), of a religion of sense as opposed to that of the spirit But it is more natural to take στοιχεῖα in its simpler meaning, that of *letters* or symbols of the alphabet, and τοῦ κόσμου not in its worst sense, but as in Heb ix. 1, ἅγιον κοσμικόν,—'belonging to the unspiritual outer world.' Thus (as in reff Col) the words will mean, the **elementary lessons of outward things** (as Conybeare has rendered it in his note: 'outward ordinances,' in his text, is not so good) Of this kind were all the enactments peculiar to the Law, some of which are expressly named, ver 10 See στοιχεῖα well discussed in Ellicott's note; and some useful remarks in Jowett, in loc.

Meyer prefers taking ἦμεν and δεδουλωμένοι separate. 'we were under the elements of the world, enslaved.' as answering better to ὑπὸ ἐπιτρόπους ἐστίν above. 4] **τὸ πλήρωμα τ. χρόνου** ('that whereby the time was filled up:' see note on Eph. i. 23,—Fritzsche's note on Rom. xi 12, and Stier's, Eph. i. p 199 ff for a discussion of the meanings of πλήρωμα) answers to the προθεσμία τ. πατρός, ver. 2 see reff The Apostle uses this term with regard not only to the absolute will of God, but to the preparations which were made for the Redeemer on this earth partly as Thl, ὅτε πᾶν εἶδος κακίας διεξελθοῦσα ἡ φύσις ἡ ἀνθρωπίνη ἐδεῖτο θεραπείας, partly as Bengel, 'suas etiam ecclesia ætates habet' The manifestation of man's guilt was complete —and the way of the Lord was prepared, by various courses of action which He had brought about by men as his instruments **ἐξαπέστ.** cannot,—however little, for the purposes of the present argument, the divine side of our Lord's mission is to be pressed,—mean any thing less than **sent forth from Himself** (reff.).

γενόμ. ἐκ γυν will not bear being pressed, as Calv, Grot, Estius, al., have done ("discernere Christum a reliquis voluit hominibus: quia ex semine matris creatus sit, non viri et mulieris coitu,"

k ver. 21. Rom. vi. 14, 15. 1 Cor. ix. 20.
l = ch. iii. 13 only. (Eph. v. 16. Col. iv. 5 only. Dan. ii. 8 only.)
m Rom. viii. 15, 23. ix. 4. Eph. i. 5 only †. (not found elsw.)
n = Luke (vi. 34) xvi. 25. Num. xxxiv. 14.
o so 1 Cor. xii. 15.

γενόμενον [k] ὑπὸ νόμον, 5 ἵνα τοὺς [k] ὑπὸ νόμον [l] ἐξ- ABCDF
αγοράσῃ, ἵνα τὴν [m] υἱοθεσίαν [n] ἀπολάβωμεν. 6 [o] ὅτι δέ KLℵ a b
ἐστε υἱοί, [h] ἐξαπέστειλεν ὁ θεὸς τὸ πνεῦμα τοῦ υἱοῦ αὐτοῦ c d e f g h k l m n o 17

6. aft υιοι add του θεου DF fuld(with [besides F-lat] demid hal tol) goth lat-ff(not Aug$_1$). om ο θεος B.

Calv.) it is Christ's HUMANITY which is the point insisted on, not His being born of a virgin. On the other hand, the words cannot for an instant be adduced as *inconsistent* with such birth: they state generically, what all Christians are able, from the Gospel record, to fill up specifically. **γενόμ. ὑπὸ νόμον**] '*born of a woman*,' identified Him with all mankind: **born under** (the idea of motion conveyed by the accusative after ὑπό is accounted for by the transition implied in γενόμενος) **the law**, introduces another condition, in virtue of which He became the Redeemer of those who were under a special revelation and covenant. A Gentile could not (humanly speaking, as far as God has conditioned His own proceedings) have saved the world: for the Jews were the representative nation, to which the representative man must belong. γενόμ. is both times emphatic, and therefore not to be here rendered 'legi subjectum,' as Luther, 'unter das Gesetz gethan.' 5] See above. Christ, being born under the law, a Jewish child, subject to its ordinances, by His perfect fulfilment of it, and by enduring, as the Head and in the root of our nature, its curse on the tree, bought off (from its curse and power, but see on ch. iii. 13) those who were under the law: and if them, then the rest of mankind, whose nature He had upon Him. Thus in buying off τοὺς ὑπὸ νόμον, He effected that ἡμεῖς, all men, τὴν υἱοθεσίαν ἀπολάβωμεν—**should receive** (not '*recover*,' as Aug., al., and Jowett ['receive back']: there is no allusion to the innocence which we lost in Adam, nor was redemption by Christ in any sense a *recovery* of the state before the fall, but a far more glorious thing, the bestowal of an adoption which Adam never had. Nor is it, as Chrys., καλῶς εἶπεν, ἀπολάβωμεν, δεικνὺς ὀφειλομένην: it is true, it *was* the subject of promise, but it is the mere act of *reception*, not how or why it was received, which is here put forward. Nor again, with Rückert and Schott, must we render ἀπο—'*therefrom*,' as a fruit of the redemption. This again it *is*, but it is not expressed in the word) **the adoption** (the place, and privileges) **of sons**. The word υἱοθεσία occurs only in the N. T. In Herod. vi. 57 we have θετὸν παῖδα ποιέεσθαι, and the same expression in Diod. Sic. iv. 39. 6] Meyer interprets this verse with Chrys.: καὶ πόθεν δῆλον ὅτι γεγόναμεν υἱοί, φησίν, εἶπε τρόπον ἕνα, ὅτι τὸν χριστὸν ἐνεδυσάμεθα τὸν ὄντα υἱόν· λέγει κ. δεύτερον, ὅτι τὸ πνεῦμα τῆς υἱοθεσίας ἐλάβομεν· οὐ γὰρ ἂν ἐδυνήθημεν καλέσαι πατέρα, εἰ μὴ πρότερον υἱοὶ κατέστημεν. And so Thdrt., Thl., Ambr., Pel., al., Koppe, Flatt, Rückert, Schott., and Ellicott. [Jowett combines both interpretations: but this can hardly be.] If so, we must assume a very unusual ellipsis after ὅτι δέ ἐστε υἱοί,—one hardly justified by such precedents as Rom. xi. 18,—εἰ δὲ κατακαυχᾶσαι, οὐ σὺ τ. ῥίζαν βαστάζεις, κ.τ.λ., Rom. xi. 15, and supply, 'God hath given you this proof, that . .' Meyer urges in defence of his view the emphatic position of ἐστε, on which see below. I prefer the ordinary rendering because it suits best (1) the simplicity of construction,—the causal ὅτι thus beginning a sentence followed by an apodosis, as in ref.,—whereas we have no example of the demonstrative ὅτι followed by the ellipsis here supposed: cf. ch. iii. 11, where δῆλον follows.—(2) the context,—it is not in *corroboration* of the fact that we are sons, but as a *consequence* of that fact, that the Apostle states what follows: to shew the completeness of the state of sonship. In Rom. viii. 16, the order of these is inverted, and the witness of the Spirit *proves* our sonship: but that does not affect the present passage, which must stand on its own ground. (3) The aorist ἐξαπέστειλεν is against Meyer's view—it would be in that case ἐξαπεσταλκεν. It is now used of the time of the gift of the Spirit. Render then **Because moreover ye are sons** (the stress on ἐστε is hardly to be urged: υἱοί ἐστε would certainly give a very strong emphasis on the *noun*: all we can say of ἐστε υἱοί, where so insignificant a word as a verb substantive is concerned, is that there is now no such strong stress on υἱοί, but that the *whole fact*, of the state of sonship having been brought in, and actually existing, is alleged) **God sent forth** (not, '*hath sent forth*'—see above) **the Spirit of His Son** (you being now fellows with that Son in the communion of the Spirit, won for you as a consequence of His atonement: called,

εἰς τὰς καρδίας ἡμῶν, [p] κρᾶζον [pq] Ἀββᾶ ὁ [pq] πατήρ.
7 ὥςτε οὐκ ἔτι εἶ δοῦλος, ἀλλὰ υἱός· εἰ δὲ υἱός, καὶ [r] κληρονόμος διὰ θεοῦ. 8 ἀλλὰ τότε μὲν οὐκ [s] εἰδότες θεὸν
[t] ἐδουλεύσατε τοῖς [u] φύσει μὴ οὖσιν θεοῖς· 9 νῦν δὲ [v] γνόντες [v] θεόν, [w] μᾶλλον δὲ [x] γνωσθέντες ὑπὸ θεοῦ, [y] πῶς [z] ἐπι-

p Rom viii 15 κρ. Mark x 48 | L Ps cvi 6
q Rom, as above Mark xiv 36 only
r ver 1
s 1 Thess iv 5 2 Thess i 8 (Exod v 2)
t Matt vi 24 Acts xx 19 al Ps ii 11
u Rom ii 14 ch ii 15 (reff) Eph ii 3 only
v Rom i 21 1 Cor i 21 1 John iv 6, 7 (Jer xxxviii [xxxi] 34)
w = Rom viii 34 Eph iv 28 v 11
x 1 Cor viii 3 2 Tim ii 19, from Num xvi 5 see Matt vii 23
y = Rom vi 2 1 Cor xv 12 ch ii 14
z = 2 Pet ii 22 Jer xi 10

rec υμων, with D³KL rel vulg syrr copt Chr Cyr Thdrt Aug txt ABCD¹FN c l n am(with [besides F-lat] flor hal) Ps Justin Ath_2(and elsw-mss_2) Bas Did Ps-Ath Tert Hil Ambrst Jer.

7. om ει F copt. [αλλα, so ABCD¹FLN b g n o 17.] rec (for δια θεου) θεου δια χριστου (*see note*), with C³DKLN³ rel goth Chr $Thdrt_4$ Œc Damasc. txt ABC¹N¹ 17 vulg copt Clem Ath Bas_{expr} Cyr_2 Did Ambrst Aug Ambr Pelag Bede, δια θεον F.

8. rec μη bef φυσει, with D³FL rel syr Chr Cyr_1 Dial-trin Thdrt Ps-Ath: om φυσει K D-lat lat-mss-in-Ambr Iren-lat Ambrst om μη o: txt ABCD¹·³N k 17 vulg Syr copt goth Ath_4 Bas_2 $Nyssen_4$ $Cyr_{sæpe}$ Damasc Jer. εδουλευσατε at end of ver D¹F latt goth. txt ABCD²·³KLN rel Ambr Jer.

9. νυνει D F. ins τον bef θεον F aft υπο ins του K Orig Dial-trin

Rom. viii. 15, πνεῦμα υἱοθεσίας, and ib 9, πνεῦμα χριστοῦ, where participation in Him is said to be the necessary condition of belonging to Christ at all) into our hearts (as he changed from the third person to the first in the foregoing verse, so now from the second both times from the fervour of his heart, wavering between logical accuracy and generous largeness of sympathy), crying (in Rom. viii 15, it is ἐν ᾧ κράζομεν. Here the Spirit being the main subject, is regarded as the agent, and the believer merely as His organ) **Abba Father** ὁ πατήρ is not a mere Greek explanation of Ἀββᾶ, but an address by His name of relation, of Him to whom the term Ἀββᾶ was used more as a token of affection than as conveying its real meaning of 'my father' see notes on Mark xiv. 36, Rom viii. 15. Aug gives a fanciful reason for the repetition: "Eleganter autem intelligitur non frustra duarum linguarum verba posuisse idem significantia propter universum populum, qui de Judæis et de Gentilibus in unitatem fidei vocatus est ut Hebræum verbum ad Judæos, Græcum ad gentes, utriusque tamen verbi eadem significatio ad ejusdem fidei spiritusque unitatem pertineat." And so Luther, Calvin, and Bengel

7] Statement of the conclusion from the foregoing, and corroboration, from it, of ch iii. 29. The second person singular individualizes and points home the inference. Meyer remarks that this individualization has been gradually proceeding from ver. 5—ἀπολάβωμεν,—ἔστε,—εἶ

διὰ θεοῦ] The rec θεοῦ διὰ χριστοῦ seems to have been an adaptation to the similar passage, Rom. viii. 17. On the text, Windischmann remarks, "διὰ θεοῦ combines, on behalf of our race, the whole before-mentioned agency of the Blessed Trinity the Father has sent the Son and the Spirit, the Son has freed us from the law, the Spirit has completed our sonship, and thus the redeemed are heirs through the tri-une God Himself, not through the law, nor through fleshly descent"

8—11] *Appeal to them*, as the result of the conclusion just arrived at, *why, having passed out of slavery into freedom, they were now going back again*

8] **τότε** refers back for its time, not to ver 3, as Windischmann, but to οὐκέτι εἶ δοῦλος, ver 7. In οὐκ εἰδότ. θ., there is no inconsistency with Rom. i 21 there it is the knowledge which the Gentile world might have had here, the matter of fact is alleged, that they *had it not*

τοῖς φύσει μὴ οὖσιν θ.] to gods, which by nature exist not: see 1 Cor viii. 4; x. 19, 20 and note The rec. would be, "*to those which are not by nature gods*," i e. only made into gods by human fancy but this is not the Apostle's way of conceiving of the heathen deities Meyer compares 2 Chron xiii 9, ἐγένετο εἰς ἱερέα τῷ μὴ ὄντι θεῷ. Notice μή—giving the Apostle's judgment of their non existence —and see 2 Cor v. 21 note, where however I cannot hold with Ellic, that μὴ γνόντα expresses '*God's judgment*' (?).

9] "The distinction which Olsh. attempts to set up between εἰδότες as the mere outward, and γνόντες as the inner knowledge, is mere arbitrary fiction. see John vii 26, 27, viii 55, 2 Cor v 16" Meyer

μᾶλλον δὲ γν. ὑπ. θ.] See note on 1 Cor viii 3 Here the propriety

στρέφετε πάλιν ἐπὶ τὰ [a] ἀσθενῆ καὶ [b] πτωχὰ [c] στοιχεῖα,
οἷς [d] πάλιν [d] ἄνωθεν [t] δουλεύειν θέλετε; 10 ἡμέρας [e] παρα-
τηρεῖσθε καὶ [f] μῆνας καὶ [g] καιροὺς καὶ ἐνιαυτούς. 11 [h] φοβοῦμαι ὑμᾶς, [h] μή πως [i] εἰκῇ [j] κεκοπίακα [j] εἰς ὑμᾶς.

ABCDF KLℵ a b c d e f g h k l m n o 17

a — Heb vii 18. (so εἶν, Rom viii 3) b — here only c ver 3. d Wisd xix 6. e — here only (Luke vi 7 Mk iii 2 xx 20 Acts ix. 24 only) ὁ δὲ τέταρτος, παρατηρεῖν τὰς ἑβδομάδας, Jos Antt iii 5 5. f Levit xxiii 24 g absol, Acts xvii 26 Gen i 14 h 2 Cor xi 3 xii 20 constr, Col iv 17 i ch iii 4 reff j Rom xvi 6 Indic, see Col ii 8 1 Thess iii 5 Winer, Engl transl p 525, § 56 2 b a

Ps-Ath επιστρεφεσθαι D[1] επιστρεφεται F. δουλευσαι Bℵ.
10 transp ενιαυτους and καιρους DF Aug.

of the expression is even more strikingly manifest than there. the Galatians did not so much acquire the knowledge of God, as they were taken into knowledge, recognized, by Him,—*προσληφθέντες ὑπὸ θεοῦ*, Thl. *οὐδὲ γὰρ ὑμεῖς καμόντες εὕρετε τὸν θεόν, . . . αὐτὸς δὲ ὑμᾶς ἐπεσπάσατο*, Chrys And thus made their fall from Him the more matter of indignant appeal, as being a resistance of His will respecting them No change of the meaning of **γνωσθ.** must be resorted to, as '*approved*,' '*loved*' (Grot., al see others in De W. and Mey) cf Matt xxv 12, 2 Tim ii. 19 Cf also Phil. iii 12 **πῶς**] how is it that . . . ? see reff **ἀσθ**] so the *προάγουσα ἐντολή* is called in Heb vii 18, *ἀσθενὲς κ. ἀνωφελές* Want of power to *justify* is that to which the word points here. **πτωχ**] in contrast with the riches which are in Christ Or both words may perhaps refer back to the state of childhood hinted at in ver 6, during which the heir is *ἀσθενής*, as immature, and *πτωχός*, as not yet in possession. But this would not strictly apply to the elements as the Gentiles were concerned with them. see below On *στοιχεῖα*, see note, ver. 3 **πάλιν**] These Galatians had never been *Jews* before but they had been before under the *στοιχεῖα τοῦ κόσμου*, under which generic term both Jewish and Gentile cultus was comprised so that they were turning back again to these elements. **ἄνωθεν**] from the beginning,—**afresh**; not a repetition of **πάλιν** Mey. quotes **πάλιν** *ἐξ ἀρχῆς*, Barnab Ep 16, p 773 Migne and Wetstein gives, from Plautus, Cas. Prol 33, '*rursum denuo*' **θέλετε**, as in E V, **ye desire** · but if thus expressed here by our translators, why not also in John v 40, where it is still more emphatic?

10] The affirmative form seems best, as (see Ellic) supplying a verification of the charge just brought against them interrogatively explaining *τίς τῆς δουλείας τρόπος*, Thdrt Wishing to shew to them in its most contemptible light the unworthiness of their decadence, he puts the *observation of days* in the front of his appeal, as one of those things which they already practised Circumcision he does not mention, because they were not yet drawn into it, but only in danger of being so (ch v 2, al) —nor abstinence from meats, to which we do not hear that they were even tempted

ἡμέρας, emphatic, as the first mentioned, and also as a more general predication of the habit, under which the rest fall The days would be sabbaths, new moons, and feast days. see Col. ii 16, where these are specified **παρατηρ**] There does not seem to be any meaning of superstitious or inordinate observance (as Olsh., Winer, &c), but merely a statement of the fact · see ref Joseph, where, remarkably enough, the word is applied to the very commandment [the fourth] here in question. "When *παρά* is ethical, i e when the verb is used in a bad sense, e.g. *ἐνεδρεύειν κ. παρατηρεῖν*, Polyb. xvii. 3. 2, the idea conveyed is that of *hostile observation*" Ellicott **μῆνας**] hardly new moons, which were *days* but perhaps the seventh month, or any others which were distinguished by great feasts.

καιρούς] any festal seasons so Levit. xxiii. 4, *αὗται αἱ ἑορταὶ τῷ κυρίῳ κληταὶ ἅγιαι, ἃς καλέσετε αὐτὰς ἐν τοῖς καιροῖς αὐτῶν* **ἐνιαυτούς**] can hardly apply to the sabbatical or jubilee years, on account of their rare occurrence, unless indeed with Wieseler, Chron der Apost. Zeitalt. p 286 note, we are to suppose that they were then celebrating one perhaps those observations may be intended which especially regarded the *year*, as the *new* year But this is not likely (see above on *μῆνας*) · and I should much rather suppose, that each of these words is not minutely to be pressed, but all taken together as a rhetorical description of those who observed times and seasons. Notice how utterly such a verse is at variance with any and every theory of a *Christian sabbath*, cutting at the root, as it does, of ALL obligatory *observance of times as such* · see notes on Rom xiv. 5, 6, Col. ii 16 "These periodical solemnities of the

12 Γίνεσθε ὡς ἐγώ, ὅτι κἀγὼ ὡς ὑμεῖς, ἀδελφοί, δέομαι
ὑμῶν. οὐδέν με ἠδικήσατε· 13 οἴδατε δὲ ὅτι δι᾽ ἀσθένειαν

law shewed, by the fact of their periodical repetition, the imperfection of the dispensation to which they belonged typifying each feature of Christ's work, which, as one great and perfect whole, has been performed once for all and for ever,—and were material representations of those spiritual truths which the spiritual Israel learn in union with Christ as a risen Lord To observe periods then, now in the fulness of time, is to deny the perfection of the Christian dispensation, the complete and finished nature of Christ's work to forsake Him as the great spiritual teacher of His brethren, and to return to carnal pædagogues to throw aside sonship in all its fulness, and the spirit of adoption and to return to childhood and the rule of tutors and governors." Bagge who however elsewhere maintains the perpetual obligation of the Sabbath 11] There is no attraction in the construction (φοβ ὑμᾶς, μή πως . .), as Winer (comm in loc) holds in that case ὑμεῖς must be the subject of the next clause (so in Diod Sic iv 40 [Meyer], τὸν ἀδελφὸν εὐλαβεῖσθαι, μή ποτε . . . ἐπίθηται τῇ βασιλείᾳ) but φοβ ὑμᾶς stands alone, and the following clause explains it So Soph. Œd Tyr. 760, δέδοικ᾽ ἐμαυτὸν . μὴ πόλλ᾽ ἄγαν εἰρημέν᾽ ᾖ μοι. The indicative assumes the fact which μή πως deprecates·—see reff 12—16] *Appeal to them to imitate him, on the ground of their former love and veneration for him.* 12] This has been variously understood. But the only rendering which seems to answer the requirements of the construction and the context, is that which understands εἰμι or γέγονα after ἐγώ, and refers it to the Apostle having in his own practice cast off Jewish habits and become as the Galatians i e a Gentile see 1 Cor ix. 20, 21 And so Winer, Neander, Fritz , De W., Meyer, Jowett (alt.), &c. (2) Chrys., Thdrt., Thl , Erasm -par., al., regard it as said to Jewish believers, and explain,—τοῦτον εἶχον πάλαι τὸν ζῆλον· σφόδρα τὸν νόμον ἐπόθουν· ἀλλ᾽ ὁρᾶτε πῶς μεταβέβλημαι ταύτην τοίνυν καὶ ὑμεῖς ζηλώσατε τὴν μεταβολήν (Thdrt) But to this Meyer rightly objects, that ἤμην, which would in this case have to be supplied, must have been *expressed*, as being emphatic, and cites from Justin ad Græcos, c 2, where however I cannot find it, γίνεσθε ὡς ἐγώ, ὅτι κἀγὼ ἤμην ὡς ὑμεῖς. (3) Jerome, Erasm.-not , Corn.-a-lap., Estius, Michaelis, Ruckert, Olsh , '. . . . as also I have accommodated myself to you' But thus the second member of the sentence will not answer to the first (4) Luther, Beza, Calvin, Grot , Bengel, Morus, Peile, al , would understand it, 'love me, as I love you' ("accipite hanc meam objurgationem eo animo quo vos objurgavi sit in nobis is affectus erga me, qui est in me erga vos," Luth). But nothing has been said of a want of *love*· and certainly had this been meant, it would have been more plainly expressed. The words ἀδελφοί, δέομαι ὑμῶν are by Chrys , Thdrt , al , Luther, Koppe, al , joined to the following . but wrongly, for there is no δέησις in what follows οὐδέν με ἠδικήσατε] The key to rightly understanding these words is, their apposition with ἐξουθενήσατε, . . . ἐξεπτύσατε . ἐδέξασθε below. To that period they refer viz. to the time when he first preached the Gospel among them, and the first introduction of this period seems to be in the words, ὅτι κἀγὼ ὡς ὑμεῖς. Then I became as you and at that time you did me no wrong, but on the contrary shewed me all sympathy and reverence Then comes in the inference, put in the form of a question, at ver. 16,—I must then have *since* become your enemy by telling you the truth The other explanations seem all more or less beside the purpose: δηλῶν ὅτι οὐ μίσους, οὐδὲ ἔχθρας ἦν τὰ εἰρημένα . . Chrys., and similarly Thl , Aug , Pel , Luth , Calv. ('non excandesco mea causa, nec quod vobis sim infensus'), Estius, Winer, al., which would be irrelevant, and indeed preposterous without some introduction after the affection of the foregoing words '*ye have done me no wrong*,' i. e. 'ex animo omnia condonabat si resipiscerentur,' Beza · so Bengel, Ruckert, al.,—which is refuted by the aorist ἠδικήσατε, of some definite *time*. The same is true of 'ye have wronged not me but yourselves' (Ambr , Corn -a-lap., Schott), —'. . . not me, but God, or Christ' (Grot. al.) 13] δι᾽ ἀσθένειαν τῆς σαρκός can surely bear but one rendering,—on account of bodily weakness· all others (e.g. '*in weakness*,' as E. V., μετὰ ἀσθενείας, as Œc., Thl., '*per infirmitatem*,' as vulg , Luth , Beza, Grot , Estius, Jowett [comparing Phil. i. 15, where see note], '*during a period of sickness*,' as Mr Bagge) are ungrammatical, or irrelevant, as '*on account of the infirmity of (your) flesh*' (Jer , Estius, Hig , Rettig), which would require some qualifying adverb such as οὕτως with εὐηγγελισάμην, and would be-

της σαρκὸς [k] εὐηγγελισάμην ὑμῖν [l] τὸ πρότερον, 14 καὶ
τὸν [m] πειρασμὸν ὑμῶν [n] ἐν τῇ σαρκί μου οὐκ [o] ἐξουθενήσατε οὐδὲ [p] ἐξεπτύσατε, ἀλλὰ ὡς ἄγγελον θεοῦ
[q] ἐδέξασθέ με, ὡς χριστὸν Ἰησοῦν. 15 ποῦ οὖν ὁ [r] μακα-
ρισμὸς ὑμῶν; [s] μαρτυρῶ γὰρ ὑμῖν ὅτι εἰ δυνατὸν τοὺς

ABCDF KLℵ a b c d e f g h k l m n o 17

k constr., ch. i. 8. Rom. i. 15. pass., 1 Pet. iv. 6. l John vi. 62. ix. 8. 1 Tim. i. 13 only. Gen. xiii. 3. m Luke xxii. 28. Acts xx. 19. 1 Cor. x. 13 al. Deut. iv. 34.
n see 2 Cor. xii. 7. o Rom. xiv. 3. 1 Cor. i. 28. vi. 4 al. Prov. i. 7. p here only †.
q = Matt. x. 14, 40. Luke ix. 53. 2 Cor. vii. 15. Wisd. xix. 14. r Rom. iv. 6, 9 only †.
s constr., Acts xxii. 5. Rom. x. 2. Col. iv. 13.

13. om δε D[1]F goth Damasc Aug. om της F a.

14. rec (for *υμων*) *μου τον*, with D[3]KL rel syr Chr Thdrt Damasc Œc: *τον* ℵ[3] m Syr goth arm Bas Thl: txt ABD[1]Fℵ[1] 17. 67[2](Bch) latt copt Cyr latt-ff, *υμων τον* C[2]. (C[1] illegible.) om *ουκ* ℵ[1]: ins ℵ-corr[1 obl]. [αλλα, so BF.]

15. rec (for *που*) *τις*, with DKL rel syr goth æth-rom Thdor-mops Thl Œc Aug$_2$ Ambrst: txt ABCFℵ 17. 67[2] vulg Syr syr-marg copt arm Damasc Jer Pelag Bede. ("τὸ τίς ἀντὶ τοῦ ποῦ τέθεικεν" Chr Thdrt.) rec aft *ουν* ins *ην*, with DK vss Chr; *η* F: *fuit aut est* G-lat; *εστιν* al$_1$ vulg Jer Sedul; *νυν* al$_1$: om ABCLℵ m o 17. 67[2]

sides be wholly out of place in an Epistle in which he is recalling them to the substance of his first preaching. The meaning then will be, that it was *on account of an illness* that he first preached in Galatia: i. e. that he was for that reason detained there, and preached, which otherwise he would not have done. On this, see Prolegomena, § ii. 3: the fact itself, I cannot help thinking, is plainly asserted here. Beware of conjectural emendation, such as δι' ἀσθενείας of Peile, for which there is neither warrant nor need. **τὸ πρότερον** may mean 'formerly,' but is more probably 'the first time,' with reference to that second visit hinted at below, ver. 16, and ch. v. 21. See Prolegomena, § v. 3. **14.**] I had in some former editions retained the rec., feeling persuaded that out of it the other readings have arisen. The whole tenor of the passage seeming to shew that the Apostle's weakness was spoken of as a trial to the Galatians, *μου* appeared to have been altered to *ὑμῶν*,—or to have been omitted by some who could not see its relevance, or its needfulness. But the principles of sounder criticism have taught me how unsafe is such ground of arguing, and have compelled me to adopt the text of the most ancient MSS. The **temptation** seems to have been the 'thorn in the flesh' of 2 Cor. xii. 1 ff., whatever that was: perhaps something connected with his sight, or some nervous infirmity: see below, and notes on Acts xiii. 9; xxiii. 1. **ἐξεπτύσατε**] "expresses figuratively and in a climax the sense of *ἐξουθ.* Cf. the Latin *despuere, respuere.* In other Greek writers we have only *καταπτύειν τινός, ἀποπτύειν τινά* (Eur. Troad. 668; Hec. 1265. Hes. *ἔργ.* 724), and *διαπτύειν τινά* in this metaphorical sense,—but *ἐκπτύειν* always in its literal sense (Hom. Od. ε. 322), as also *ἐμπτύειν τινί*. Even in the passage cited by Kypke from Plut., Alex. i. p. 328, it is in its literal sense, as *ὥσπερ χαλινόν* follows. We must treat this then as a departure from Greek usage, and regard it as occasioned by *ἐξουθ.*, as Paul loves to repeat the same prepositions in composition (Rom. ii. 17; xi. 7 al.), not without emphasis." Meyer.

ὡς ἄγγελ. θ., ὡς χρ. Ἰησ.] a climax:—besides the freedom of angels from fleshly weakness, there is doubtless an allusion to their office as messengers—and to His saying, who is above the angels, Luke x. 16. No inference can be drawn from *these expressions* being used of *the Galatians' reception* of him, that they were already Christians when he first visited them: the words are evidently not to be pressed as accurate in point of chronology, but involve an *ὕστερον πρότερον*: not, 'as you *would have* received,' &c., but 'as you would (now) receive.' **15.**] **Where then** (i. e. where in estimation, holding what place) **(was) your congratulation** (of yourselves)? i. e. considering your fickle behaviour since. "Quæ causa fuit gratulationis, si nos nunc pœnitet mei?" Bengel. Various explanations have been given: '*quæ* (reading *τίς*) *erat beatitudo vestra*,' neglecting the *οὖν*, and making *μακαρισμός* into *beatitudo*, which it will not bear: so Œc., Luth., Beza, &c. All making the words into an *exclamation* (even if *τίς* be read) is inconsistent with the context, and with the logical precision of *οὖν*, and *ὥστε* below. '*Where is then the blessedness ye spake of?*' (E. V.) is perhaps as good a rendering as the words will bear. **μαρτυρῶ γὰρ . . .**] a proof to what lengths this *μακαρισμός*, and consequently their high value for St. Paul ran, at his first visit. In seeking for a reference for this expression, **τ. ὀφθ. ὑμῶν**

ὀφθαλμοὺς ὑμῶν ᵗ ἐξορύξαντες ᵘ ἐδώκατέ μοι. 16 ὥστε
ᵛ ἐχθρὸς ὑμῶν γέγονα ʷ ἀληθεύων ὑμῖν; 17 ˣ ζηλοῦσιν
ὑμᾶς οὐ ʸ καλῶς, ἀλλὰ ᶻ ἐκκλεῖσαι ὑμᾶς θέλουσιν, ἵνα

t — here (Mark ii 4) only Judg xvi 21 F 1 Kings xi 2 (Prov xix 22 only) see note u ἄν omitted John ix 33 xv 22 xix 11 Rom vii 7 Winer, § 42 2 v — Rom xi 28 w Eph iv 15 only Gen xlii 16 x = 2 Cor xi 2 Zech i 14 pass, see Xen Mem ii 1 19, ἐπαινούμενος κ ζηλούμενος ὑπὸ τ ἄλλων y John xviii 23 1 Cor vii 37 ch v 7 al 2 Macc xv 38 z Rom iii 27 only Exod xxiii 2 Vat 2 Macc xiii 21 Ald only

æth Thdrt-ms Damasc Thl. rec ins αν bef εδωκατε, with D³KLℵ³ rel και, F; add *et* latt. om ABCD¹ℵ¹ 17 Damasc

16 aft ωστε add εγω D¹F D-lat Cypr.

17 elz (for 2nd υμας) ημας, with none of our mss (*Apparently, from a conjecture of Beza's*)

ἐξορ. ἐδώκ. μοι, the right course will be, not at once to adopt the conclusion, that they point to ocular weakness on the part of the Apostle, nor because they form a trite proverb in many languages, therefore to set down (as Meyer, De W., Windischmann, al, have done) at once that no such allusion can have been intended, but to judge from the words themselves and our information from other sources whether such an allusion is likely. And in doing so I may observe that a proverbial expression so harsh in its nature, and so little prepared by the context, would perhaps hardly have been introduced without some particle of climax Would not the Apostle have more naturally written, ὅτι εἰ δυνατόν, **καὶ** τοὺς ὀφθ. ὑμ ...? Had the **καί** been inserted, it would have deprived the words of all reference to a matter of fact, and made them purely proverbial. At the same time it is fair to say that the order τοὺς ὀφθ ὑμῶν rather favours the purely proverbial reference. Had the Apostle's eyes been affected, and had he wished to express "You would, if possible, have pulled out *your own* eyes, and have given them to *me*," he would certainly have written ὑμῶν τοὺς ὀφθ, not τοὺς—ὀφθ. ὑμῶν. In other words, the more emphatic τοὺς ὀφθαλμούς is, the more likely is the expression to be proverbial merely the less emphatic τ. ὀφθ is, the more likely to refer to some fact, in which the eyes were as matter of notoriety concerned. The inference then of any ocular disease from these words themselves seems to me precarious. Certainly Acts xxiii. 1 ff. receives light from such a supposition; but with our very small knowledge on the subject, many conjectures may be hazarded with some shew of support from Scripture, while none of them has enough foundation to make it probable on the whole. The proverb is abundantly illustrated by Wetst **ἐξορύσσω** is the regular classic word. cf Herod. viii. 116 this however is doubted by Ellic. See on the whole passage, Jowett's most interesting "fragment on the character of St. Paul," Epp. &c vol. i. pp. 290—303. **16.]** **So that** (as things now stand, an inference derived from the contrast between their former love and their present dislike of him See Klotz, Devar. ii. 776) **have I become your enemy** ('hated by you;'—ἐχθρ in passive sense: or perhaps it may be active, as Ellic.) **by speaking the truth** (see Eph iv. 15 note) **to you?** *When* did he thus incur their enmity by speaking the truth? Not *at his first visit*, from the whole tenor of this passage. nor *in this letter*, as some think (Jer, Luther, al), which they had *not yet read*, but at his *second visit*, see Acts xviii 23, when he probably found the mischief beginning, and spoke plainly against it. Cf. similar expressions in Wetst · especially 'obsequium amicos, veritas odium parit,' Ter Andr. i 1 40. ὀργίζονται ἅπαντες τοῖς μετὰ παῤῥησίας τ' ἀληθῆ λέγουσι, Lucian, Abdic 7.
17.] 'My telling you the truth may have made me seem your enemy. but I warn you that these men who court you so zealously (see ref. 2 Cor., and cf Plut. vii. 762, cited by Fritz ὑπὸ χρείας τὸ πρῶτον ἕπονται κ. ζηλοῦσιν, ὕστερον δὲ καὶ φιλοῦσιν) have no honourable purpose in so doing it is only in order to get you away from the community as a separate clique, that you may court them' Thus the verse seems to fit best into the context. As regards particular words, **ἐκκλείω** must bear the meaning of exclusion from a larger and attraction to a smaller, viz. their own, party. (Our very word 'exclusive' conveys the same idea) I have therefore not adopted Mey's rendering, '*from all other teachers*,'—nor that of Luther (1538), Calv, Grot, Beng, Ruck, Olsh, Winer, al., '*from me and my communion*,'—nor that of Chrys, Œc, Thl, τῆς τελείας γνώσεως ἐκβαλεῖν,—nor that of Erasm., Corn.-a-lap, '*from Christian freedom*'
The mood of **ζηλοῦτε** has been disputed: and it must remain uncertain here, as in 1 Cor. iv 6, where see note. Here as

αὐτοὺς ˣᵃ ζηλοῦτε. 18 καλὸν δὲ ˣ ζηλοῦσθαι ἐν καλῷ
πάντοτε, καὶ μὴ μόνον ᵇ ἐν τῷ ᶜ παρεῖναί με ᶜ πρὸς ὑμᾶς.
19 ᵈ τεκνία μου, οὓς πάλιν ᵉ ὠδίνω, ᶠ ἄχρις οὗ ᵍ μορφωθῇ

ABCDF KLℵ a b c d e f g h k l m n o 17

a indic (?) pres, 1 Cor iv 6 (see Rev iii 9 al) b Matt xiii 4 al Ezek ix 8 c here bis Acts xii 20 2 Cor xi 8 d Paul, here only John xiii 33 al6 only† e constr, here only (ver 27 Rev xii 2 only Isa xxiii 4 al) ἡ πρὶν ὠδίνουσ' ἐμέ, Iph Aul 1234 ὠδίνουσα καλὰς πράξεις, Philo, Deus immut 29, vol i p 293 f constr, Rom xi 25. 1 Cor xi 26 g here only Isa. xliv 13 F only

at end ins ζηλουτε δε τα κρειττω χαρισματα (*see* 1 *Cor* xii. 31) D¹F Victorin Ambrst Sedul.

18. for δε, γαρ 17 : *quoque* F-lat · om D¹F h Victorin Ambr₂. rec ins το bef ζηλουσθαι, with DFKL rel Chr Thdrt Thl Œc : om ABCℵ 17 Damasc.—ζηλουσθε (*itacism*) Bℵ 17 vulg(and F-lat) Damasc Jer Ambrst : txt ACDFKL rel Chr Thdrt Thl Œc Aug Ambr. for εν καλ. παν., παν. εν τω αγαθω F. (not F-lat.) for μη, ου DF.

19. for τεκνια, τεκνα B D¹(sic) Fℵ¹ Eus Marcell · txt ACD²·³KLℵ³ rel Clem Method Bas₂ Chr Cyr Thdrt₄ Damasc Phot for αχρ., μεχρις Bℵ¹ m.

there Meyer would give ἵνα the meaning of '*in which case :*' but it is surely far better where the sentence so plainly requires ἵνα of the purpose, to suppose some peculiar usage or solœcism in formation of the subjunctive on the part of the Apostle.

18.] Two meanings are open to us · (1) as E. V. (apparently but perhaps 'zealously affected' may be meant for the passive—for 'earnestly courted') and many Commentators taking ζηλοῦσθαι as middle—or passive with a signification nearly the same, '*it is good to be zealously affected in a good cause, and not only during my presence with you* ' in which case the sense must be referred back to vv 13—15, and the allusion must be to their zeal while he was with them. But, considering that this context is broken at ver. 17,—that the words ζηλοῦσθαι ἐν καλῷ are an evident reference to ζηλοῦσιν ὑμ οὐ καλῶς, and that the wider context of the whole passage adduces a contrast between their conduct when he was with them and now, I think it much better (2) to explain thus 'I do not mean to blame them in the abstract for τὸ ζηλοῦν ὑμᾶς : any teacher who did this καλῶς, preaching Christ, would be a cause of joy to me (Phil. i. 15—18) · and it is an honourable thing (for you) to be the objects of this zeal ('ambiri') ἐν καλῷ, in a good cause (I still cannot see how this rendering of ἐν καλῷ '*alters the meaning of the verb*' [Ellic.] : it rather seems to me that the non-use of καλῶς, while the paronomasia is retained, leads to this meaning), at all times and by every body, not only when I am (or was) present with you ' q d 'I have no wish, in thus writing, to set up an exclusive claim to ζηλοῦν ὑμᾶς—whoever will really teach you good, at any time, let him do it and welcome.' Then the next verse follows naturally also, in which he narrows the relation between himself and them, from the wide one of a mere ζηλωτής, to the closer one of their parent in Christ, much as in 1 Cor iv. 14 f.,—ὡς τέκνα μου ἀγαπητὰ νουθετῶ ἐὰν γὰρ μυρίους παιδαγωγοὺς ἔχητε ἐν χριστῷ, ἀλλ' οὐ πολλοὺς πατέρας ἐν γὰρ χρ. Ἰησοῦ διὰ τ. εὐαγγελίου ἐγὼ ὑμᾶς ἐγέννησα On other interpretations, I may remark, (α) that after ζηλοῦσιν, the strict passive meaning is the only suitable one for ζηλοῦσθαι, as it is indeed the only one justified by usage : (β) that ζηλόω must keep its meaning throughout, which will exclude all such renderings as '*invidiose tractari*' here (Koppe). (γ) that all applications of the sentence to the Apostle himself as its object (ἐν καλῷ, in the matter of a good teacher, as Estius, Corn.-a-lap , al.) are beside the purpose.

19] belongs to what follows, not to the preceding. Lachmann, (I suppose on account of the δέ following, but see below,) with that want of feeling for the characteristic style of St. Paul which he so constantly shews in punctuating, has attached this as a flat and irrelevant appendage to the last verse (so also Bengel, Knapp, Ruckert, al) and has besides tamed down τεκνία into τέκνα, thus falling into the trap laid by some worthless corrector. **My little children** (the diminutive occurs only here in St Paul, but is manifestly purposely, and most suitably chosen for the propriety of the metaphor It is found [see reff] often in St John, while our Apostle has τεκνον, 1 Tim. i 18 ; 2 Tim ii 1), **whom** (the change of gender is common enough. Meyer quotes an apposite example from Eur. Suppl. 12, θανόντων ἑπτὰ γενναίων τέκνων . οὕς ποτ' . . . . ἤγαγε) **I again** (a second time, the former was ἐν τῷ παρεῖναί με, ver. 18) **travail with** (bear, as a mother, with pain and anxiety, till the time of birth) **until Christ shall have been fully formed within you** (for Christ dwelling in a man is the secret and principle of his new life, see ch ii. 20),

χριστὸς ἐν ὑμῖν, 20 [h] ἤθελον δὲ [c] παρεῖναι [c] πρὸς ὑμᾶς ἄρτι
καὶ [i] ἀλλάξαι τὴν φωνήν μου, ὅτι [k] ἀπορουῦμαι ἐν ὑμῖν.
21 Λέγετέ μοι οἱ [l] ὑπὸ νόμον θέλοντες εἶναι, τὸν νόμον
οὐκ [m] ἀκούετε; 22 [n] γέγραπται γὰρ ὅτι Ἀβραὰμ δύο
υἱοὺς ἔσχεν, ἕνα ἐκ τῆς [o] παιδίσκης καὶ ἕνα ἐκ τῆς [p] ἐλευθέρας. 23 ἀλλ' ὁ μὲν ἐκ τῆς [o] παιδίσκης κατὰ [q] σάρκα
γεγέννηται, ὁ δὲ ἐκ τῆς [p] ἐλευθέρας [r] διὰ τῆς ἐπαγγελίας.
24 [s] ἅτινά ἐστιν [t] ἀλληγορούμενα· αὗται γάρ [u] εἰσιν δύο

h imperf. — Acts xxv 22 Rom ix 3 Winer, § 41 a 2
i Acts vi 14 Rom i 23 1 Cor xv 51, 52. Heb. i 12, from Ps ci 26 only Levit xxvii 33.
k Luke xxiv 4 John xiii 22 Acts xxv 20 2 Cor iv 8 Gen xxxii 7
l vv 4, 5

m — Matt x 14 Luke xvi 29 Isa xlviii 18 n Gen xvi. 15 xxi 1, 2 o — Matt xxvi 69 Acts xii. 13 al Gen xvi 1 xx 17. p = 1 Cor vii 21 Neh xiii 17
q — Rom ix 8 κ σ, Rom i 3 iv 1 ix 35 1 Cor x 18 al P see John viii 15 r = Rom xii 3. s = Col ii 23. t here only + (see note) u = Matt xxvi 26 xiii 38. John xv 1 1 Cor x. 4 Gen xli. 26, 27

21 for ακουετε, αναγινωσκετε DF latt coptt arm Orig$_1$ Cyr Jer$_1$ Ambr$_1$ Ambrst Bede.
23. om μεν B vulg Tert Hil. γεγενηται D[1] m[1] 17 Orig$_2$. ελευθεριας(sic) ℵ. δι' επαγγ., omg της, ACℵ b[1] o 17 Cyr$_2$ Damasc Thdrt$_1$.
24. for αυται, αυτα F. rec ins αι bef δυο, with ℵ[1] 67 om ABCDFKLℵ[3] rel

20] yea, I could wish (see note on Rom. ix. 3 There is a contrast in the δέ between his present anxiety in absence from them and his former παρεῖναι ver 18. similar constructions with δέ are frequent, especially after vocatives, when some particular is adduced more or less inconsistent with the *address* which has preceded thus Hom Il. ο. 244, Ἕκτορ, υἱὲ Πριάμοιο, τίη δὲ σὺ νόσφιν ἀπ' ἄλλων | ἧσ' ὀλιγηπελέων, Eur. Hec. 372, μῆτερ, σὺ δ' ἡμῖν μηδὲν ἐμποδὼν γένῃ . . . al. freq) **to be present with you now, and to change my voice** (from what, to what? Some say, from mildness to severity. But surely such a change would be altogether beside the tone of this deeply affectionate address. I should rather hold, with Meyer, —from my former severity, when I became your enemy by ἀληθεύων ὑμῖν, to the softness and mildness of a mother, still ἀληθεύων, but in another tone The great majority of Commentators understand ἀλλάξαι as Corn.-a-lap. [Mey.]: 'ut scilicet quasi mater nunc blandirer, nunc gemerem, nunc obsecrarem, nunc objurgarem vos' But so much can hardly be contained in the mere word ἀλλάξαι without some addition, such as πρὸς τὸν καιρόν, πρὸς τὸ συμφέρον [1 Cor. xii. 7], or the like). **for I am perplexed about you** (not '*I am suspected among you*,' but ἐν ὑμῖν as in 2 Cor vii 16, θαῤῥῶ ἐν ὑμῖν,—the element in which the other is irrelevant, and inconsistent with the N. T. usage of ἀποροῦμαι· see reff. The verb is passive: Meyer quotes Demosth. p 830 2, πολλὰ τοίνυν ἀπορηθεὶς περὶ τούτων κ καθ' ἕκαστον ἐξελεγχόμενος, and Sir xviii 7, ὅταν παύσηται, τότε ἀπορηθήσεται). 21—30] *Illustration of the relative positions of the law and the promise, by an allegorical interpretation of the history of the two sons of Abraham* · "intended to destroy the influence of the false Apostles with their own weapons, and to root it up out of its own proper soil" (Meyer). 21. θέλοντες] καλῶς εἶπεν **οἱ θέλοντες**, οὐ γὰρ τῆς τῶν πραγμάτων ἀκολουθίας, ἀλλὰ τῆς ἐκείνων ἀκαίρου φιλονεικίας τὸ πρᾶγμα ἦν. Chrys. τ. νόμον οὐκ ἀκούετε] **do ye not hear (heed) the law,** listen to that which the law imparts and impresses on its hearers? Meyer would understand, 'do ye not hear the law read?' viz in the synagogues, &c. But the other seems to me more natural. 22] γάρ answers to a tacit assumption of a negative answer to the foregoing question—'nay, ye do not: *for,*' &c. Phrynichus says on **παιδίσκη**, τοῦτο ἐπὶ τῆς θεραπαίνης οἱ νῦν τιθέασιν, οἱ δ' ἀρχαῖοι ἐπὶ τῆς νεάνιδος, οἷς ἀκολουθητέον 23] **κατὰ σάρκα, according to nature,** in her usual course. **δι' ἐπαγγελίας, by virtue of (the) promise,** as the efficient cause of Sara's becoming pregnant contrary to nature. see Rom. iv. 19. 24] **which things** (on ὅς and ὅστις see Ellic's note. here ἅτινα seems to enlarge the allegory beyond the mere births of the two sons to all the circumstances attending them) **are allegorical:** i e. to be understood otherwise than according to their literal sense So Suidas ἀλληγορία, ἡ μεταφορά, ἄλλο

v ch iii 15, 17 reff   v διαθῆκαι· μία w μὲν ἀπὸ ὄρους Σινᾶ, εἰς x δουλείαν ABCDF KLℵ a b c d e f g h k l m n o 17

w μεν solitarium, Col ii 23 reff   x ch v 1 reff

λέγον τὸ γράμμα, κ. ἄλλο τὸ νόημα. Hesych, ἀλληγορία, ἄλλο τι παρὰ τὸ ἀκουόμενον ὑποδεικνύουσα: and gloss. N. T, ἀλληγορούμενα, ἑτέρως κατὰ μετάφρασιν νοούμενα, καὶ οὐ κατὰ τὴν ἀνάγνωσιν The word is often used, as the thing signified by it is exemplified, by Philo. It was the practice of the Rabbinical Jews to allegorize the O T. history "Singula fere gesta quæ narrantur, allegorice quoque et mystice interpretantur Neque hac in parte labores ipsorum plane possumus contemnere. Nam eadem Paulus habet, qualia sunt de Adamo primo et secundo, de cibo et potu spirituali, de Hagare, etc Sic Joannes memorat Sodomum et Ægyptum mysticam, plagas item Ægyptias per revelationem hostibus Ecclesiæ immittendas prædicit," Schottgen. How various persons take this allegorical comment of the Apostle, depends very much on their views of his authority as a Scripture interpreter To those who receive the law as a great system of prophetic figures, there can be no difficulty in believing the events by which the giving of the law was prepared to have been prophetic figures also not losing thereby any of their historic reality, but bearing to those who were able to see it aright, this deeper meaning. And to such persons, the fact of St Paul and other sacred writers adducing such allegorical interpretations brings no surprise and no difficulty, but only strong confirmation of their belief that there are such deeper meanings lying hid under the O T. history. That the Rabbis and the Fathers, holding such deeper senses, should have often missed them, and allegorized fancifully and absurdly, is nothing to the purpose it is surely most illogical to argue that because they were wrong, St Paul cannot be right. The only thing which really does create any difficulty in my mind, is, that Commentators with spiritual discernment, and appreciation of such a man as our Apostle, should content themselves with quietly casting aside his Scripture interpretation wherever, as here, it passes their comprehension On their own view of him, it would be at least worth while to consider whether his knowledge of his own Scriptures may not have surpassed ours But to those who believe that he had the Spirit of God, this passage speaks very solemnly; and I quite agree with Mr Conybeare in his note, edn 2, vol. ii p 178, "The lesson to be drawn from this whole passage, as regards the Christian use of the O T., is of an importance which can scarcely be overrated" Of course no one, who reads, marks, learns, and inwardly digests the Scriptures, can subscribe to the shallow and indolent dictum of Macknight, 'This is to be laid down as a fixed rule, that *no ancient history is to be considered as allegorical, but that which inspired persons have interpreted allegorically*. but at the same time, in allegorizing Scripture, he will take care to follow the analogy of the faith, and proceed soberly, and in dependence on that Holy Spirit, who alone can put us in possession of His own mind in His word' Calvin's remarks here are good "Quemadmodum Abrahæ domus tunc fuit vera Ecclesia ita minime dubium est quin præcipui et præ aliis memorabiles eventus qui in ea contigerunt, nobis totidem sint typi Sicut ergo in circumcisione, in sacrificiis, in toto sacerdotio levitico allegoria fuit sicuti hodie est in nostris sacramentis, ita etiam in domo Abrahæ fuisse dico Sed id non facit ut a literali sensu recedatur Summa perinde est ac si diceret Paulus, figuram duorum testamentorum in duabus Abrahæ uxoribus, et duplicis populi in duobus filiis, veluti in tabula, nobis depictam." As to the objection of Luther, repeated by De Wette, that this allegory shews misapprehension of the history (die Allegorie von Sara und Hagar, welche .... zum Stich zu schwach ist, denn sie weichet ab vom historischen Verstand. Luth., cited by De W), because Ishmael had nothing to do with the law of Moses, the misapprehension is entirely on the side of the objectors Not the bare literal historical fact is in question here, but the inner character of God's dealings with men, of which type, and prophecy, and the historical fact itself, are only so many exemplifications The difference between the children of the bond and the free, of the law and the promise, has been shewn out to the world before, by, and since the covenant of the law See an excellent note of Windischmann's ad loc, exposing the shallow modern critical school See also Jowett's note, on the other side and while reading it, and fearing the consequences which will follow from adopting his view, bear in mind that the question between him and us is not affected by any thing there said on the similarity between St. Paul and the Alexandrians as interpreters of Scripture,—

ʸ γεννῶσα, ᶻ ἥτις ἐστὶν Ἄγαρ· 25 τὸ *γὰρ Ἄγαρ Σινᾶ ʸ Luke i 13 al fr Prov xvii 17.
ὄρος ἐστὶν ἐν τῇ Ἀραβίᾳ· ᶻ συστοιχεῖ δὲ τῇ νῦν Ἱερου- ᶻ here only† Polyb x 21 7
σαλήμ, ᵃ δουλεύει γὰρ μετὰ τῶν τέκνων αὐτῆς. 26 ἡ δὲ ᵃ absol., 1 Tim vi. 2

25. *δὲ ABD m copt Cyr₁ : *γαρ* CFKLℵ vulg syrr æth arm Epiph Chr Cyr Thdrt Damasc Orig-lat Jer.—om *αγαρ* CFℵ vulg æth arm Epiph Cyr_{abc} Damasc Orig-int Jer —om *το γαρ αγαρ* 17 (*The variation appears to have sprung from the juxtaposition of γαρ αγαρ hence one or other was omd, and δε insd for connexion*) aft *εστιν* ins *ον* ℵ for *συστοιχ. δε*, [*ἡ*] *συνστοιχουσα* D¹F latt goth. (om *ἡ* D¹) rec (for 2nd *γαρ*) *δε*, with D³KL rel syr-marg goth . *et servit* vulg(and F-lat) Syr Jer Aug_3 · txt ABCD¹Fℵ 17 copt Cyr Orig-lat Aug_4.

but remains as it was before,—was the O. T dispensation a system of typical events and ordinances, or is all such typical reference fanciful and delusive? **For these** (women [*αὗται*], not as Jowett, Ishmael and Isaac, which would confuse the whole the mothers are the covenants,—the sons, the children of the covenants) **are** (import in the allegory, see reff) **two covenants** (not '*revelations*,' but literally covenants between God and men): **one** (covenant) **indeed from Mount Sina** (taking its origin from,—or having Mount Sina as its centre, as *ὁ ἐκ Πελοποννήσου πόλεμος*) **gendering** (bringing forth children · De W. compares *υἱοὶ τῆς διαθήκης*, Acts iii 25) **unto** (with a view to) **bondage, which one is** (identical in the allegory with) **Agar**

25] (No parenthesis **συστοιχεῖ δέ** begins a new clause) **For the word Agar** (when the neuter article precedes a noun of another gender, not the *import* of that noun, but the *noun itself*, is designated,—so Demosth. p 255. 4, *τὸ δ' ὑμεῖς ὅταν εἴπω, τὴν πόλιν λέγω*. Kuhner ii 137) **is** (imports) **Mount Sina, in Arabia** (i e. among the Arabians This rendering, which is Chrysostom's,—*τὸ δὲ Σινὰ ὄρος οὕτω μεθερμηνεύεται τῇ ἐπιχωρίῳ αὐτῶν γλώττῃ* [so also Thl , Luther], is I conceive necessitated by the arrangement of the sentence, as well as by *τὸ Ἄγαρ*. Had the Apostle intended merely to localize *Σινᾶ ὄρος* by the words *ἐν τῇ Ἀρ*, he could hardly but have written *τὸ ἐν τῇ Ἀρ*, or have placed *ἐν τ Ἀρ* before *ἐστιν*. Had he again, adopting the reading *τὸ γὰρ Σινᾶ ὄρος ἐστὶν ἐν τῇ Ἀραβίᾳ*, intended to say [as Windischmann], '*for Mount Sina is in Arabia, where Hagar's descendants likewise are*,' the sentence would more naturally have stood *τὸ γὰρ Σινᾶ ὄρ. ἐν τῇ Ἀρ ἐστίν*, or *καὶ γὰρ Σινᾶ ὄρ ἐν τ. Ἀρ ἐστίν* As it is, the law of emphasis would require it to be rendered, '*For Sina is a mountain in Arabia*,' information which the judaizing Galatians would hardly require As to the fact itself, Meyer states, "حجر in Arabic, is a stone and though we have no further testimony that Mount Sina was thus named *κατ' ἐξοχήν* by the Arabians, we have that of Chrysostom, and Busching, Erdbeschreibung, v. p 535, adduces that of the traveller Haraut, that they to this day call Sinai, *Hadschar* Certainly we have *Hagar* as a geographical proper name in Arabia Petræa · the Chaldee paraphrast always calls the wilderness of Shur, חגרא" So that Jowett certainly speaks too strongly when he says, "the old explanations, that Hagar is the Arabic word for a rock or the Arabic noun for Mount Sinai, are destitute of foundation." As to the improbability at which he hints, of St Paul quoting Arabic words in writing to the Galatians, I cannot see how it is greater than that of his making the covert allusion contained in his own interpretation. We may well suppose St. Paul to have become familiarized, during his sojourn there, with this name for the granite peaks of Sinai), **but** (*δέ* marks the latent contrast that the addition of a new fact brings with it · so Ellic.) **corresponds** (viz. Agar, which is the subject, not Mount Sina, see below. "*συστοιχεῖν* is '*to stand in the same rank*' hence '*to belong to the same category*,' '*to be homogeneous with*' see Polyb. xiii 8 1, *ὅμοια κ. σύστοιχα*." Mey., Chrys., all., and the Vulg. [*conjunctus est*], take it literally, and understand it, *γειτνιάζει, ἅπτεται*, 'is joined, by a continuous range of mountain-tops,' understanding *Sina* as the subject) **with the present Jerusalem** (i. e Jerusalem under the law, the Jerusalem of the Jews, as contrasted with the Jerusalem of the Messiah's Kingdom), **for she** (*ἡ νῦν Ἱερουσ*, not *Ἄγαρ*) **is in slavery with her children**

26] **But** (opposes to the last sentence, not to *μία μέν*, ver 21, which, as Meyer observes, is left without an apodosis, the reader supplying that the other covenant is Sina, &c) **the Jerusalem above** (i e.

b Phil. iii. 14. Col. iii. 1.
c Isa. liv. 1. Luke xv. 23. Acts ii. 26. Rom. xv. 10 al.
d Luke i. 7. xxiii. 29 only. Gen. xi. 30.
e = here only. (Matt. vii. 6. ix. 17 ‖. Mark ix. 18 ‖ L. only.) see Isa. xlix. 13. lii. 9.
f ver. 19.
g = here only.
h w. posit., Mark ix. 42. Acts xx. 35. 1 Cor. ix. 15 (xii. 22) only. l. c. only.
i = John iv. 17, 18.
k = Eph. iv. 24. Col. iii. 10. 1 Pet. i. 15. Lam. i. 12.
l Rom. ix. 8.

ABCDF KLℵ a b c d e f g h k l m n o 17

[b] ἄνω Ἱερουσαλὴμ ἐλευθέρα ἐστίν, [a] ἥτις ἐστὶν μήτηρ
ἡμῶν· 27 γέγραπται γὰρ [c] Εὐφράνθητι [d] στεῖρα ἡ οὐ
τίκτουσα, [e] ῥῆξον καὶ βόησον ἡ οὐκ [f] ὠδίνουσα, ὅτι πολλὰ
τὰ τέκνα τῆς [g] ἐρήμου [h] μᾶλλον ἢ τῆς [i] ἐχούσης τὸν [i] ἄνδρα.
28 ὑμεῖς δέ, ἀδελφοί, [k] κατὰ Ἰσαὰκ [l] ἐπαγγελίας [l] τέκνα

26. om ητις εστιν (*homœot*) ℵ[1]: ins ℵ-corr[1]. rec ins παντων bef ημων, with AC[3]KLℵ[3] rel Mac Cyr-jer Thdrt$_{\text{persæpe}}$ Damasc Iren-int Jer Aug$_2$: om BC[1]DFℵ[1] 17 67[2] latt syrr coptt goth æth-mss Orig$_{\text{sæpe}}$ Eus$_2$ Chr Cyr Thdrt$_1$(mss vary) Isid Tert Hil Ambrst Aug$_{\text{sæpe}}$.
27. for ου, μη DF.
28. rec ημεις and εσμεν (*from ver* 26), with ACD[3]KLℵ rel vulg(and F-lat) syrr copt goth æth-pl Chr Cyr Thdrt Aug: txt BD[1]F 17. 67[2] sah æth Orig(in Jer) Iren-int Victorin Ambrst Tich Ambr. (Υμεις [Υ in red] k o.)

the heavenly Jerusalem = Ἱερ. ἐπουράνιος Heb. xii. 22, ἡ καινὴ Ἱερ. Rev. iii. 12; xxi. 2, and see reff. on ἄνω. Michaelis, al., suppose *ancient Jerusalem* [Melchisedek's] to be meant. Vitringa, al., *Mount Zion*, as ἡ ἄνω πόλις means the Acropolis. But Rabbinical usage, as Schöttgen has abundantly proved in his Dissertation de Hierosolyma cœlesti [Hor. Heb. vol. i. Diss. v.], was familiar with the idea of a Jerusalem in heaven. See also citations in Wetst. This latter quotes a very remarkable parallel from Plato, Rep. ix. end, —ἐν ᾗ νῦν δὴ διήλθομεν οἰκίζοντες πόλει λέγεις, τῇ ἐν λόγοις κειμένῃ, ἐπεὶ γῆς γε οὐδαμοῦ οἶμαι αὐτὴν εἶναι. Ἀλλ, ἦν δ' ἐγώ ἐν οὐρανῷ ἴσως παράδειγμα ἀνάκειται τῷ βουλομένῳ ὁρᾷν καὶ ὁρῶντι ἑαυτὸν κατοικίζειν. διαφέρει δὲ οὐδὲν εἴτε που ἔστιν εἴτε ἔσται· τὰ γὰρ ταύτης μόνης ἂν πράξειεν, ἄλλης δὲ οὐδεμιᾶς. Εἰκός γ', ἔφη. The expression here will mean, "the *Messianic Theocracy*, which before the παρουσία is the *Church*, and after it Christ's Kingdom of glory." Mey.) **is free, which** (which said city, which heavenly Jerusalem) **is our mother** (the emphasis is not on ἡμῶν as Winer: nay rather it stands in the least emphatic place, as indicating a relation taken for granted by Christians. See Phil. iii. 20. The rendering adopted by Mr. Bagge, "*which* [Jerusalem the free] *is* [answers to, as ἥτις ἐστὶν Ἄγαρ above] *our mother* [viz. Sarah]," is untenable from the absence of the article before μήτηρ, besides that it would introduce confusion, and a *double* allegory). 27.] *Proof of this relation from prophecy.* The portion of Isaiah from which this is taken, is directly Messianic: indicating in its foreground the reviviscence of Israel after calamity, but in language far surpassing that event. See Stier, Jesaias nicht pseudo-Jesaias, vol. ii. p. 512. The citation is from the LXX, verbatim. **ῥῆξον**] sc. φωνήν: cf. many examples in Wetst. Probably the rule of supplying ellipses from the context (following which Kypke and Schött. here supply εὐφροσύνην, from εὐφράνθητι, and Isa. xlix. 13; lii. 9; cf. also 'erumpere gaudium,' Ter. Eun. iii. 5. 2 [Ellic.]) need hardly be applied here; the phrase with φωνήν was so common, as to lead at last to the omission of the substantive. The Hebrew רִנָּה, 'into joyful shouting,' seems not to have been read by the LXX. St. Paul here interprets the barren of Sara, who bore not according to the flesh (= the promise), and the fruitful of Agar (= the law). Clem. Rom., Ep. ii. ad Cor. 2, p. 333, takes the στεῖρα of the Gentile Church, ἐπεὶ ἔρημος ἐδόκει εἶναι ἀπὸ τοῦ θεοῦ, ὁ λαὸς ἡμῶν, νυνὶ δὲ πιστεύσαντες πλείονες ἐγενόμεθα τῶν δοκούντων ἔχειν θεόν (the Jewish church), and similarly Origen (in Rom., lib. vi. 7, vol. iv. p. 578), . . . 'quod multo plures ex gentibus quam ex circumcisione crediderint.' And this has been the usual interpretation. It only shews how manifold is the 'perspective of prophecy:' this sense neither is incompatible with St. Paul's, nor surely would it have been denied by him. (So Chrys., al., in *this* passage, which is clearly wrong: for ἡμῶν, even without πάντων, must apply to *all* Christians for the argument to hold.) **ὅτι πολ.**] not, as E. V., "*many more* &c.," which is inaccurate: but, **many are the children of the desolate, more than** (rather than; both being numerous, hers are the *more* numerous) **of her, &c.** **τὸν ἄνδρα**] The E. V. has perhaps done best by rendering '*an husband*,' though thus the force of the Greek is not given. 'The husband' would mislead, by pointing at

ἐστέ. 29 ἀλλ' ὥςπερ τότε ὁ [m] κατὰ σάρκα γεννηθεὶς
[n] ἐδίωκεν τὸν [o] κατὰ πνεῦμα, οὕτως καὶ νῦν. 30 ἀλλὰ [p] τί
λέγει ἡ γραφή; [q] Ἔκβαλε τὴν [r] παιδίσκην καὶ τὸν υἱὸν
αὐτῆς. οὐ γὰρ μὴ [s] κληρονομήσῃ ὁ υἱὸς τῆς [r] παιδίσκης
μετὰ τοῦ υἱοῦ τῆς [r] ἐλευθέρας. 31 [t] διό, ἀδελφοί, οὐκ

m ver 23
n — Matt v 10, 11, 12 Ps vii 1
o Rom i 4
p so Rom iv 3 x 8 xi 2, 4
q Acts xvi 37 Gen xxi 10
r ver 22
s absol, here only (Matt v 5 al) Numb xviii 24
t see Rom ii 1 Eph ii 11 al.

30. aft παιδισκην ins ταυτην (*from* LXX) A. om μη F m. κληρονομησει (*so* LXX) BDℵ k[1] m n 17 om του υιου ℵ[1]. ins ℵ-corr[1] ins υιου ℵ[3]. for της ελευθ, μου ισαακ (*from* LXX) D[1]F demid Ambrst Jer Aug_{aliq}

31. rec (for διο) αρα, with KL rel syr Chr Thl Œc αρα ουν F Thdrt. ημεις δε (*see ver* 28 *var read*) AC copt Cyr_1 Damasc Jer_1 Aug_3 txt BD[1]ℵ 17. 67[2] (sah goth) Cyr_1, *itaque* latt Ambrst Jer_1

the one husband (Abraham) who was common to Sara and Agar, which might do in this passage, but would not in Isaiah whereas ἐχ. τὸν ἄνδρα means, 'her (of the two) who has (the) husband,' the other having none a fineness of meaning which we cannot give in English.

28] **But** (transitional: or rather perhaps adversative to the children of her who had an husband, which were last mentioned With ἡμεῖς, it would be resumptive of ver. 26) **ye** (see var readd.), **brethren, like** (the expression in full, κατὰ τ. ὁμοιότητα Μελχισεδέκ, occurs Heb. vii. 15. Wetst. quotes from Galen, ὁ ἄνθρωπος οὐ κατὰ λέοντά ἐστι τὴν ῥώμην, and from Arrian, Hist Gr. ii, τιμώμενος ὑπὸ τοῦ δήμου κατὰ τὸν πατέρα Ἄγνωνα· see also reff.) **Isaac, are children of** PROMISE (ἐπαγγ. emphatic —are children, not κατὰ σάρκα, but διὰ τῆς ἐπαγγελίας, see ver. 23, and below, ver. 29)

29] ὁ κατ σάρ γεν, see ver 23 It has been thought that there is nothing in the Hebrew text to justify so strong a word as **ἐδίωκεν**. It runs, 'and Sarah saw the son of Hagar .. מְצַחֵק' (παίζοντα μετὰ Ἰσαὰκ τοῦ υἱοῦ αὐτῆς, LXX), and some deny that צָחַק ever means 'he mocked.' But certainly it does see Gen xix 14 And this would be quite ground enough for the ἐδίωκεν, for the spirit of persecution was begun. So that we need not refer to tradition, as many have done (even Ellic., whom see; Jowett, as unfortunately usual with him when impugning the accuracy of St Paul, asserts rashly and confidently, that the sense in which the Apostle takes the Hebrew is inadmissible), to account for St. Paul's expression **τὸν κατὰ πνεῦμα**, sc. γεννηθέντα, **him that was born after the Spirit**, i. e. in virtue of the promise, which was given by the Spirit. Or, '*by virtue of the Spirit's agency*:' but the other is better. **οὕτως καὶ νῦν**] "nec quicquam est quod tam graviter animos nostros vulnerare debeat, quam Dei contemptus, et adversus ejus gratiam ludibria· nec ullum magis exitiale est persequutionis genus, quam quum impeditur animæ salus" Calv.

30] **ἀλλά**, as in E V, '*nevertheless*:' notwithstanding the fact of the persecution. just mentioned. The quotation is adapted from the LXX, where μου Ἰσαάκ stands for τῆς ἐλευθέρας We need hardly have recourse (with Ellic.) to the fact that God confirmed Sarah's words, in order to prove this to be *Scripture* the Apostle is allegorizing the whole history, and thus every part of it assumes a significance in the allegory. **κληρονομήσῃ**] See Judg xi. 2 (LXX), κ. ἐξέβαλον τὸν Ἰεφθάε, κ εἶπον αὐτῷ, οὐ κληρονομήσεις ἐν τῷ οἴκῳ τοῦ πατρὸς ἡμῶν, ὅτι υἱὸς γυναικὸς ἑταίρας σύ. "The distinction drawn by Hermann on Œd Col 853, between οὐ μή with future indicative (duration or futurity) and with aorist subjective (speedy occurrence), is not applicable to the N T on account of (1) various readings (as here)· (2) the decided violations of the rule where the MSS are unanimous, as 1 Thess iv. 15. and (3) the obvious prevalence of the use of the subjunctive over the future, both in the N T. and 'fatiscens Græcitas' see Lobeck Phryn p 722" Ellicott.

31.] I am inclined to think, against Meyer, De W., Ellic, &c, that this verse is, as commonly taken, the conclusion from what has gone before: and that the διό is bound on to the κληρονομήσῃ preceding. For that we are κληρονόμοι, is an acknowledged fact, established before, ch iii 29; ver 7 And if we are, we are not the children of the handmaid, of whom it was said οὐ μὴ κληρονομ., but of the freewoman, of whose son the same words asserted that he should inherit. Observe in the first clause παιδίσκης is anarthrous most likely because emphatically prefixed

ἐσμὲν ʳ παιδίσκης τέκνα, ἀλλὰ τῆς ʳ ἐλευθέρας. [V.] 1 τῇ
ᵘ ἐλευθερίᾳ ἡμᾶς χριστὸς ᵛ ἠλευθέρωσεν. ʷ στήκετε οὖν,
καὶ μὴ πάλιν ˣ ζυγῷ ʸ δουλείας ᶻ ἐνέχεσθε. 2 ἴδε ᵃ ἐγὼ
ᵃ Παῦλος λέγω ὑμῖν ὅτι ἐὰν ᵇ περιτέμνησθε χριστὸς ὑμᾶς
οὐδὲν ᶜ ὠφελήσει. 3 ᵈ μαρτύρομαι δὲ πάλιν παντὶ ἀνθρώπῳ

ABCDF KLℵ a b c d e f g h k l m n o 17

u = 1 Cor. x. 29. ch. ii. 4 al. v John viii. 32, 36. Rom. vi. 18, 22. viii. 2, 21 only †. (Sir. l. 21 Ald.) 2 Macc. i. 27. ii. 22 only. w Mark iii. 31. xi. 25. Rom. xiv. 4. 1 Cor. xvi. 13. Phil. i. 27. iv. 1. 1 Thess. iii. 8. 2 Thess. ii. 15 only. Exod. xiv. 13 F. constr., 2 Cor. i. 24. x = Matt. xi. 29, 30. Acts xv. 10. 1 Tim. vi. 1 (Rev. vi. 5) only. Jer. xxxv. (xxviii.) 14. y Rom. viii. 15, 21. ch. iv. 24. Heb. ii. 15 only. Exod. xx. 2 al. z = here (Mark vi. 19. Luke xi. 53) only. (Gen. xlix. 23. Ezek. xiv. 4 only.) Herod. ii. 121, τῇ παγῇ ἐνέχεσθαι. Plut. Symp. ii. 3, ἐνέχεσθαι δόγμασιν Πυθαγορικοῖς. a 2 Cor. x. 1. Eph. iii. 1. Col. i. 23. 1 Thess. ii. 18. Philem. 19. b Luke i. 59. ch. ii. 3 al. fr. Gen. xvii. 10. c = 1 Cor. xiv. 6. Heb. iv. 2. Prov. x. 2. d constr., Acts xx. 26. -ομαι, Acts xxvi. 22. Eph. iv. 17. 1 Thess. ii. 12 only †.

Chap. V. 1. rec aft ελευθερια ins ουν, omg it aft στηκετε, with C³KL rel Damasc Thl Œc: om D m latt syr Thdrt₂ Jer Ambrst: txt ABC¹Fℵ 17. 67² (Syr) goth copt Cyr Aug. (*An eccles. lect. ended with ἠλευθέρωσεν, C³ marks this by insg τελος.*) rec ins ῃ bef ημας, with D²·³(F)KL rel Marc Chr Cyr Thdrt₂ Thl Œc (ῃ ἐλευθερίᾳ ἡμ. F latt Syr lat-ff): om ABCD¹ℵ m 17 copt. rec χριστος bef ημας, with CKLℵ³ rel vss (Chr) Thdrt Damasc₁ Mcion-t Victorin: txt ABDFℵ¹ 17 am goth Cyr Damasc₁ (Orig-int). δουλειας bef ζυγω DF goth Aug. ανεχεσθε D¹·³ (1?) m Thdrt-ms Œc.

2. om παυλος ℵ¹: ins ℵ-corr¹ obl. περιτεμησθε B n¹.

3. om παλιν D¹F a goth Chr Thl Jer Aug Ambrst. om οτι ℵ¹: ins ℵ³.

to its governing noun (cf. ἐθνῶν ἀπόστολος, Rom. xi. 13): but possibly, as indefinite, q. d. we are the children of no bondwoman, but of the freewoman. I prefer the former reason, as most consonant to N. T. diction. V. 1—12.] De W. calls this the *peroration* of the whole second part of the Epistle. It consists of *earnest exhortation to them, grounded on the conclusion of the foregoing argument, to abide in their evangelical liberty, and warning against being led away by the false teachers.*

1.] It is almost impossible to determine satisfactorily the reading (see var. readd.). I have in this Edition adopted that in the text, as being best attested by the most ancient authorities. **With liberty did Christ make you free** (i. e. ἐλεύθεροι is your rightful name and ought to be your estimation of yourselves, seeing that ἐλευθερία is your inheritance by virtue of Christ's redemption of you). **Stand fast, therefore** (reff. στήκω is unknown in classical Greek), **and be not again** (see note on ch. iv. 9: in fact, the whole world was under the law in the sense of its being God's only revelation to them) **involved** (reff.) **in the yoke of bondage** (better than '*a* yoke;' an anarthrous noun or personal pronoun following another noun in the genitive often deprives that other noun of its article: e. g., τίς ἔγνω νοῦν κυρίου; 1 Cor. ii. 16: see numerous instances in Cant. v. 1. Cf. Winer, § 19. 2, most of whose examples however are after prepositions. Wetst. quotes from Soph. Aj. 944, πρὸς οἷα δουλείας ζυγὰ χωροῦμεν). 2.] ἴδε, not ἰδέ, in later Greek: see Winer, § 6. 1. a:—it draws attention to what follows, as a strong statement. **ἐγὼ Παῦλος**] ἄντικρυς ὑμῖν λέγω κ. διαῤῥήδην, κ. τὸ ἐμαυτοῦ προστίθημι ὄνομα, Thdrt. τὴν τοῦ οἰκείου προσώπου ἀξιοπιστίαν ἀντὶ πάσης ἀποδείξεως τίθησι, Theophyl., and so Chrys. There hardly seems to be a reference (as Wetst. "ego quem dicunt circumcisionem prædicare") to his having circumcised Timothy. Calvin says well: "Ista locutio non parvam emphasin habet; coram enim se opponit, et nomen dat, ne videatur causam dubiam habere. Et quanquam vilescere apud Galatas cœperat ejus auctoritas, tamen ad refellendos omnes adversarios sufficere asserit." The *present*, **ἐὰν περιτέμνησθε**, implies the continuance of a habit, q. d. **if you will go on being circumcised.** He does not say, '*if you shall have been circumcised*:' so that Calv.'s question, 'quid hoc vult? Christum non profuturum omnibus circumcisis?' does not come in. On **χρ. ὑμ. οὐδ. ὠφελήσει,** Chrys. remarks: ὁ περιτεμνόμενος ὡς νόμον δεδοικὼς περιτέμνεται, ὁ δὲ δεδοικὼς ἀπιστεῖ τῇ δυνάμει τῆς χάριτος, ὁ δὲ ἀπιστῶν οὐδὲν κερδαίνει παρὰ τῆς ἀπιστουμένης. Nothing can be more directly opposed than this verse to the saying of the Judaizers, Acts xv. 1. The exception to the rule in Paul's own conduct, Acts xvi. 3, is sufficiently provided for by the *present tense* here: see above. 3.] δέ, moreover, introduces an addition, and a slight contrast—'not only will Christ not profit . . . . . but

ᵇ περιτεμνομένῳ ὅτι ᵉ ὀφειλέτης ἐστὶν ὅλον τὸν νόμον
ποιῆσαι. 4 ᵗ κατηργήθητε ᶠ ἀπὸ [τοῦ] χριστοῦ ᵍ οἵτινες
ʰ ἐν νόμῳ ʰ δικαιοῦσθε, ⁱ τῆς χάριτος ᵏ ἐξεπέσατε. 5 ἡμεῖς
γὰρ ˡ πνεύματι ᵐ ἐκ πίστεως ⁿ ἐλπίδα δικαιοσύνης ᵒ ἀπεκδεχόμεθα. 6 ἐν γὰρ χριστῷ Ἰησοῦ οὔτε ᵖ περιτομή
τι ᵠ ἰσχύει οὔτε ʳ ἀκροβυστία, ἀλλὰ πίστις δι' ἀγάπης
ˢ ἐνεργουμένη. 7 ᵗ ἐτρέχετε ᵘ καλῶς· τίς ὑμᾶς ᵛ ἐνέκοψεν

e Matt vi 12 xviii 24 Luke xiii 4 Rom i 14 viii 12 xv 27 only † Soph Aj 590
f Rom vii 2, 6 see 2 Cor xi. 3 κατ ch iii 17 reff
g = Acts x 41, 47 al
h ch iii 11 reff
i = Rom v 2 Jude 4
k = 2 Pet iii 17 (Acts xii 7 1 Pet i 24, from Isa xl 8 al) l = ch iii 3 ver 16 1 Cor ii 4
m ch ii 16 iii 8, 22 n = Col i 5 Tit ii 13 Heb vi 18 o Rom viii 19, 23, 25 1 Cor i 7 Phil iii 20 Heb ix 28 1 Pet iii 20 only † p John vii 22, 23 Rom ii 25 al tr Exod iv 26 q = Heb ix 17 James v 16 — ἐστιν, 1 Cor vii 19 ch vi 15
r Rom iv 9, &c. 1 Cor vii 19 Col iii 11 P only, exc Acts xi 3. Gen xvii 11 s mid., Rom vii 5 2 Cor i 6. iv 12 Eph iii 20 (ch ii 8 reff) t ch ii 2 reff Rom xi 16.
u = 1 Cor vii 37 John xviii 23 al Prov xxiii 24 v Acts xxiv 4 Rom xv 22 1 Thess ii 18 1 Pet iii 7 Dan ix 26 Theod Ald only (F vat ἐκκόπτ)

4 om του BCD¹Fℵ Thl· ins AD³KL rel Chr Thdrt Damasc. εξεπεσετε D³ a b² c d e f g h k m.
5. εκδεχ. ℵ¹. txt ℵ³ 6 om ιησου B copt.

. . . . .' On **μαρτύρομαι** (usually, in this sense, -ροῦμαι,— -ρομαι having an accusative, whence Bretschn, al, supply τὸν θεόν here, but wrongly), see reff. **πάλιν, once more:** applies to the verb, not to the μαρτυρία which follows, for that is not a repetition. Thus it will refer to παντὶ ἀνθρ as 'a more extended application of ὑμῖν' (Ellic), not, as Meyer, to a former inculcation of this by word of mouth at his second visit. **περιτεμνομένῳ**, not -τμηθέντι, see above—**to every man who receives circumcision,**—'submits to be circumcised,' as Ellic The emphasis is on **παντί**, substantiating, and carrying further, the last verse. **ὅλον** has the stress The circumcised man became a 'proselyte of righteousness,' and bound to keep the whole law. "This true and serious consequence of circumcision the false Apostles had probably at least dissembled" Mey. 4] Explains and establishes still further the assertion of ver 2. **Ye were annihilated from Christ** (literally· the construction is a pregnant one, 'ye were cut off from Christ, and thus made void' see ref. 2 Cor '*were*,' viz. at the time when you began your course of ἐν νόμῳ δικ), **ye who are being justified** ('endeavouring to be justified,' 'seeking justification.' such is the force of the subjective *present* So Thl ὡς ὑπολαμβάνετε) **in** (not 'by' it is the element in which, as in the expression ἐν κυρίῳ) **the law,—ye fell from** (reff. see 1 Cor. xiii. 8, note Wetst quotes from Plut, Agis and Cleom. p. 796, τῶν πλείστων ἐξέπεσεν ἡ Σπάρτη καλῶν· Gracch. p 834, ἐκπεσεῖν κ στέρεσθαι τῆς πρὸς τὸν δῆμον εὐνοίας 'So Plato, Rep vi 496, ἐκπεσεῖν φιλοσοφίας: Polyb xii. 14. 7, ἐκπίπτειν τοῦ καθήκοντος,' Ellic) **grace** 5.] Proof (hence γάρ) of ἐξεπ. τ. χάρ., by statement e contrario of the condition and hope of *Christians* Emphasis (1) on **ἡμεῖς**, as opposed to οἵτινες ἐν νόμῳ δικαιοῦσθε,—(2) on **πνεύματι** (not '*mente*' [Fritz.], nor '*spiritually*' Middleton, al, but by the [Holy] Spirit, reff), as opposed to σαρκί, the fleshly state of those under the law, see ch. iv 29,—(3) on **ἐκ πίστεως**, as opposed to ἐν νόμῳ, which involves ἐξ ἔργων.
ἐλπίδα δικαιοσύνης] Is this genitive *objective*, the hope of righteousness, i e. the hope whose object is perfect righteousness, —or *subjective*, the hope of righteousness, i e the hope which the righteous entertain—viz that of eternal life? Certainly I think the *former*. for this reason, that ἐλπίδα has the emphasis, and ἐλπίδα δικ ἀπεκδεχ. answers to δικαιοῦσθε above —'*Ye* think ye *have* your righteousness in the law *we*, on the contrary, anxiously wait for the hope of righteousness (full and perfect)' The phrase ἀπεκδέχεσθαι ἐλπίδα may be paralleled, Acts xxiv. 15, Tit ii. 13, Eur. Alcest 130, τίν' ἔτι βίου ἐλπίδα προσδέχωμαι, Polyb viii. 21. 7, ταῖς προσδοκωμέναις ἐλπίσιν. 6] Confirmation of the words ἐκ πίστεως, ver. 5 **ἐν χριστῷ**, in Christ, as an element, in union with Christ, = in the state of a Christian notice χρ Ἰησ, not Ἰησ χρ —in Christ, and that Christ, Jesus of Nazareth **ἐνεργουμένη**, not passive, but middle, as always in N T. See reff and notes on those places also Fritzsche's note on Rom. vii 5. "ἐνεργεῖν, *vim exercere* de *personis*, ἐνεργεῖσθαι, *ex se* (aut *suam*) *vim exercere* de *rebus* collocavit, Gal v 6, Col. i. 29, 1 Thess.

[τῇ] [w] ἀληθείᾳ μὴ [x] πείθεσθαι; 8 ἡ [y] πεισμονὴ οὐκ ἐκ τοῦ
[z] καλοῦντος ὑμᾶς. 9 μικρὰ [abc] ζύμη ὅλον τὸ [ad] φύραμα
[ae] ζυμοῖ. 10 ἐγὼ πέποιθα [f] εἰς ὑμᾶς ἐν κυρίῳ ὅτι οὐδὲν

ABCDF KLℵ a b c d e f g h k l m n o 17

w — Rom. ii. 8. 1 Pet. i. 22.
x Acts xxviii. 24. Rom. ii. 8.
y here only†. only used by Chrys. on 1 Thess. i. 3 (De W.), and Eustath. (see Wetst.)
z ch. i. 6 reff. particip., as 1 Thess. v. 24.
a 1 Cor. v. 6. b 1 Cor. as above. Matt. xiii. 3 ‖. c as above (a, b). Matt. xvi. 6 ‖, 11, 12. Luke xii. 1. 1 Cor. v. 7, 8 only. Exod. xii. 15.
d Rom. ix. 21. xi. 16. 1 Cor. v. 6, 7 only. Exod. xii. 34.
e as above (b) only—always w. ὅλον. Exod. xii. 39.
f 2 Cor. ii. 9, 12. viii. 22. ix. 8. (ἐπί, 2 Cor. ii. 3. 2 Thess. iii. 4.)

7. rec ανεκοψε, with none of our mss: txt ABCDFKLℵ rel. om τη ABℵ[1]: ins CDFKLℵ[3] rel. at end add μηδενι πειθεσθαι F lat-mss-in-Jer vulg-sixt(with demid hal) Victorin Lucif Ambrst-comm Pelag Bede. (*Gloss to account for η πεισμονη follg.*)

8. om ουκ D[1] al$_3$ lat-mss in Jer(who says "*abstulerunt* non") in Sedul(who says *male*) Orig$_1$ Lucif. καλουντας(sic) ℵ.

9. for ζυμοι, δολοι D[1] vulg(and F-lat) lat-mss('*male*') in Jer and Sedul Mcion-e Constt Bas-mss Lucif Ambrst Pelag: *corrumpit fermentat* G-lat.

10. aft εγω ins δε C[1]F demid syr arm Damasc Œc-comm. om εν κυριω B Chr

ii. 13 al., ut h. l. Passivo (cf. ἐνεργεῖται πόλεμος, Polyb. i. 13. 5; Jos. Antt. xv. 5. 3) nunquam Paulus usus est." The older Romanist Commentators (Bellarm., Est.) insisted on the passive sense as favouring the dogma of *fides formata*, for which it is cited by the Council of Trent, sess. vi. cap. 7, de justific. And the modern Romanist Commentators, though abandoning the passive sense, still claim the passage on their side (e. g. Windischmann); but without reason; love is the *modus operandi* of faith, *that which justifies*, however, is *not love*, but *faith*; nor can a passage be produced, where St. Paul says we are justified by 'faith working by love,' but it is ever by faith only. One is astonished at the boldness of such a generally calm and fair writer as Windischmann, in claiming the passage for the Tridentine doctrine, even when the passive interpretation, which was all it had to lay hold on, is given up. As parallels to our passage, see Rom. xiv. 17; 1 Cor. vii. 19.

7—12.] *He laments their deflexion from their once promising course, and denounces severely their perverters.* **Ye were running well** ('hoc est, omnia apud vos erant in felici statu et successu, vivebatis optime, contendebatis recta ad vitam æternam quam vobis pollicebatur verbum,' &c. Luther): **who** (see ch. iii. 1, the question expresses astonishment) **hindered you** (Polyb. xxiv. 1. 12, uses ἐγκόπτειν with a dative, διὰ τὸ τὸν Φίλιππον ἐγκόπτειν τῇ δικαιοδοσίᾳ: Ellic. quotes, in connexion with the view of the primary notion being that of hindering by breaking up a road,—Greg. Naz. Or. xvi. p. 260, ἡ κακίας ἐγκοπτομένης δυσπάθεια τῶν πονηρῶν, ἡ ἀρετῆς ὁδοποιουμένης εὐπάθεια τῶν βελτιόνων) **that ye should not** (μή before πείθεσθαι is not pleonastic, but the construction, so often occurring, of a negative after verbs of hindering, is in fact a pregnant one, μὴ πείθεσθαι being the *result* of the hindrance: q. d. ὥστε μὴ π. or καὶ ἐποίησε μὴ π. See Bernhardy, Syntax, ix. 6 b, who quotes one example very apposite to this,—ἐμποδὼν ἡμῖν γένηται τὴν θεὸν μὴ 'ξελκύσαι, Aristoph. Pac. 315) **obey the truth** (i. e. submit yourselves to the true Gospel of Christ. These words, which Chrys. omits here, have been transferred hence to ch. iii. 1. See var. readd. there. On that account they are certainly genuine here)?

8.] **The persuasion** (to which you are yielding—active; not *your persuasion*, passive. πεισμονή may mean either. Ellic. says: "As the similar form πλησμονή means both *satietas* (the state) and also *expletio* (the act), Col. ii. 23; Plato, Sympos. 186 c. πλ. καὶ κένωσις,—so πεισμονή may mean the state of being persuaded, i. e. conviction, or the act of persuading, 'persuadendi sollertia' (Schött.): cf. Chrys. on 1 Thess. i. 3, οὐ πεισμονὴ ἀνθρωπίνη . . . ἦν ἡ πείθουσα." But here, ἡ πεισμ. being connected with ὁ καλῶν ὑμᾶς, and answering to the act of ἐγκόπτειν in the last verse, is better taken actively) **is not from** (does not come from, is not originated by) **Him who calleth you** (i. e. God: see ch. i. 6 and note).

9.] **ζύμη** may allude either to men (Jer., Aug., Grot., Est., Beng., De W., al.), or to doctrine. In the parallel place in 1 Cor. v. 6, it is moral influence; so also where our Lord uses the same figure, Matt. xvi. 12, where ζύμη = διδαχή. Nor can there be any objection to taking it as abstract, and φύραμα concrete:—a little false doctrine corrupts the whole mass (of Christians). So Chrys. (οὕτω καὶ ὑμᾶς ἰσχύει τὸ μικρὸν τοῦτο κακόν, μὴ διορθωθέν, καὶ εἰς τέλειον ἰουδαϊσμὸν ἀγαγεῖν), Thl., Luth., Calv., all.

10.] "After the warning of vv. 8, 9, Paul assures his readers that he has confidence in them,

ἄλλο [g] φρονήσετε· ὁ δὲ [h] ταράσσων ὑμᾶς [i] βαστάσει τὸ
[k] κρίμα, ὅςτις ἐὰν ᾖ. 11 ἐγὼ δέ, ἀδελφοί, εἰ [p] περιτομὴν
ἔτι [l] κηρύσσω, [m] τί ἔτι [n] διώκομαι; ἄρα [o] κατήργηται τὸ
[p] σκάνδαλον τοῦ [q] σταυροῦ. 12 [r] ὄφελον καὶ [s] ἀποκόψονται οἱ [t] ἀναστατοῦντες ὑμᾶς.

g = Acts xxviii 22 Rom xii 3 al 2 Macc xiv 26
h = Acts xv 24 ch i 7 1 Chron ii 7 Ald particip, 2 Cor xi 4 ver 8 al
i = Luke xiv 27 John xix 17 Acts xv 10 ch vi 2, 5 al 4 Kings xviii 14
k = 1 Cor xi 29 1 Tim v 12 James iii 1 2 Pet ii 3
l constr, Mark i 4 Luke iv 49 (from Isa lxi 1) al
m Rom iii 7 ix 19
n = ch iv 29 reff
o ch iii 17 reff
p Rom xiv 13 1 Cor i 23 Rev ii 14 al[1] 1 Kings xxv 31
q = 1 Cor i 17 ch vi 12, 14. Phil iii 18
r 1 Cor iv 8 2 Cor xi 1 Rev iii 15 only 4 Kings v 3 Job xiv 13 Ps cxviii 5 only
s Mark ix 43, 45 John xviii 10, 26 Acts xxvii 32 only. = (see note) Deut xxiii 1
t Acts xvii 6. xxi 38 only L P Dan vii 23 LXX only Ps x 1 Aq

(in Niceph; elsw has it εν χριστω Chr-txt). rec (for εαν) αν, with CDFKL rel Dial txt ABℵ b o 17. 67[2] Damasc

11 om 1st ετι D[1]F f 67[2] demid goth arm Jer Ambrst. [ἆρα D[3].] aft σταυρου ins του χριστου AC copt æth.

12. ωφελον D[3]KL l n αποκοψωνται DF Œc.

but that their perverters shall not escape punishment *Divide et impera!*" Meyer. **ἐγώ**, emphatic, **I, for my part**; 'quod ad me attinet, . .' **εἰς, with regard to**, see reff, and Bernhardy, p. 220. On **ἐν κυρίῳ**, see 2 Thess iii. 4:—it is the element or sphere in which his confidence is conditioned **οὐδὲν ἄλλο φρον.**] See *ἑτέρως*, Phil iii. 15: of which this ἄλλο is a kind of softening We take the meaning here to be, **ye will be of no other mind than this**, viz. which I enjoin on you,—not in vv 8, 9 only, but in this Epistle, and in his preaching generally. **ὁ δὲ ταράσσων** need not be interpreted as referring necessarily to any one *ἐπίσημος* among the Judaizers (as Olsh, al), but simply as individualizing the warning, and carrying home the denunciation to each one's heart among the perverters. Cf *οἱ ἀναστατοῦντες* below, and ch. i. 7, iv. 17. **τὸ κρῖμα, the sentence**, understood to be unfavourable, is a burden laid on the judged person, which he *βαστάζει*, bears The **ὅςτις ἐὰν ᾖ** generalizes the declaration to the fullest extent: see ch i 8, 9

11] The connexion appears to be thus the Apostle had apparently been charged with being a favourer of circumcision in other churches, as shewn e. g. by his having circumcised Timothy After the preceding sharp denunciation of *ὁ ταράσσων ὑμᾶς*, and *ὅστις ἐὰν ᾖ*, it is open to the adversaries to say, that Paul himself was one of their *ταράσσοντες*, by his inconsistency. In the abruptness then of his fervid thoughts he breaks out in this self-defence **ἐγώ**, emphatic as before **περιτομήν** has the chief emphasis, as the new element in the sentence, and not **κηρύσσω**, as Chrys (*οὐ γὰρ εἶπεν ὅτι περιτομὴν οὐκ ἐργάζομαι, ἀλλά, οὐ κηρύσσω, τουτέστιν, οὐχ οὕτω κελεύω πιστεύειν*), al,—its position not allowing this The first **ἔτι** is best understood, as referring, not to any change in his preaching as an Apostle (for he appears always to have been of the same mind, and certainly was from the first persecuted by the Jews), but to the change since his conversion, before which he was a strenuous fautor of Judaism. Olsh objects to this, that *κηρύσσω* could not be used of that period But this (even if it be necessary to press *κηρύσ.* so far into matter of fact) cannot be said with any certainty—the course of Saul as a zealot may have often led him even to preach, if not circumcision in its present debated position, yet that strict Judaism of which it formed a part. **τί ἔτι διώκ**] **ἔτι** is logical, as in reff (De W.): i e, **what further excuse is there for my being** (as I am) **persecuted** (by the Jews)? **For**, if this is so, if I still preach circumcision, **ἄρα, then is brought to nought**, is done away, **the** OFFENCE (reff. stumbling-block, *σκάνδ* has the emphasis) **of the cross**—because, if circumcision, and not faith in Christ crucified, is the condition of salvation, then the Cross has lost its offensive character to the Jew *οὐδὲ γὰρ οὕτως ὁ σταυρὸς ἦν ὁ σκανδαλίζων τοὺς Ἰουδαίους, ὡς τὸ μὴ δεῖν πείθεσθαι τοῖς πατρῴοις νόμοις καὶ γὰρ τὸν Στέφανον προσενέγκοντες, οὐκ εἶπον ὅτι οὗτος τὸν ἐσταυρωμένον προσκυνεῖ, ἀλλ' ὅτι κατὰ τοῦ νόμου κ τοῦ τόπου λέγει τοῦ ἁγίου* Chrys.

12] The *καί* introduces a climax—**I would** (reff) **that they who are unsettling you would even** As to **ἀποκόψονται**, (1) it cannot be passive, as E V., '*were even cut off*' (2) It can hardly mean '*would cut themselves off from your communion*,' as the **καί** is against so mild a wish, besides that this sense of the word is unexampled. (3) There is certainly an allusion to *ἐνέκοψεν* in ver. 7, so that in *reading aloud*

13 Ὑμεῖς γὰρ ^u ἐπ' ^v ἐλευθερίᾳ ἐκλήθητε, ἀδελφοί· ^w μόνον μὴ ^x τὴν ^v ἐλευθερίαν εἰς ^y ἀφορμὴν τῇ σαρκί, ἀλλὰ
^z διὰ τῆς ἀγάπης ^a δουλεύετε ἀλλήλοις. 14 ^b ὁ γὰρ ^b πᾶς
νόμος ἐν ἑνὶ ^c λόγῳ ^d πεπλήρωται, ἐν ^e τῷ ^f Ἀγαπήσεις

ABCDF KLℵ a b c d e f g h k l m n o 17

u = Eph ii 10 1 Thess iv 7 v = ver 1 reff w ch ii 10 Phil i 27 x ellips, ch ii 9 Matt xxvi 5 al y Rom vii 8, 11 2 Cor v 12 xi 12 bis 1 Tim v 14 only P Ezek v 7 only z so ver 6 a see Rom vi 18, 22 1 Cor ix 19 b order, Acts xix 7 xxvii 37 c Rom xiii 9 d = Matt iii 15 Acts xii 25 xiv 26 al Ps xix 4 e Matt xix 18 Rom xiii 9 bis f Levit xix 18

13 for γαρ, δε F al Chr Aug₁ Pac της σαρκος D¹ 17 vulg copt goth Ambr Aug Ambrst Pelag for δια τ. αγαπ, τη αγαπη του πνευματος DF vulg-ed copt goth Bas Ambrst

14 for νομος, λογος KL ins εν υμιν bef εν ενι λογω (*to refer the sentence to the Galatians*) D¹F Ambrst υμιν Meion-e *in paucis* syr(but txt in marg) rec πληρουται (*corrn, in ignorance of true sense of perfect*), with DFKL rel Chr Thdrt Damasc₁ Jer txt ABCℵ m 17 Meion-e Damasc₂ Aug om εν τω D¹F

the Greek, the stress would be, ὄφελ κ ἀποκόψονται οἱ ἀν ὑμ But (4) this allusion is one only of sound, and on account of the και, all the more likely to be to some well-known and harsh meaning of the word, *even as far as to which* the Apostle's wish extends. And (5) such a meaning of the word is that in which (agreeably to its primitive classical sense, of hewing off limbs, see Lidd and Scott) it is used by the LXX, ref Deut, by Arrian, Epict ii 20, by Hesych, ὁ ἀπόκοπος, ἤτοι ὁ εὐνοῦχος—by Philo, de legg special ad vi vii. dec cap § 7, vol. ii p 306, τὰ γεννητικὰ προσαπέκοψαν, —de vict. offerent. § 13, p 261, θλαδίας κ ἀποκεκομμένος τὰ γεννητικά (Wetst.). It seems to me that this sense *must be adopted*, in spite of the protests raised against it; e. g that of Mr. Bagge recently, who thinks it "involves a positive insult to St Paul" (?). And so Chrys, and the great consensus of ancient and modern Commentators and, as Jowett very properly observes, "the common interpretation of the Fathers, confirmed by the use of language in the LXX, is not to be rejected only because it is displeasing to the delicacy of modern times"

ὄφελον is used in the N T as a mere particle see reff: also Hermann on Viger, p. 756-7, who says "omnino observandum est, ὤφελον nonnisi tunc adhiberi, quum quis optat ut fuerit aliquid, vel sit, vel futurum sit, quod non fuit aut est aut futurum est" The construction with a future is very unusual, in Lucian, Solœc. 1, ὄφελον καὶ νῦν ἀκολουθῆσαι δυνήσῃ is given as an example of a solœcism I need hardly enter a caution against the punctuation of a few mss and editions, by which ὄφελον is taken alone, and the following future supposed to be assertive, as βαστάσει above, ver 10. The reff will shew, how alien such an usage is from the usage of the N T. ἀναστατοῦντες, ἀνατρέποντες, Hesych It belongs to later Greek · the classical expression is ἀνάστατον ποιεῖν, Polyb iii 81. 6 al or τιθέναι, Soph Antig. 670. and it is said to belong to the Macedonian dialect. Ellic, referring to Tittmann, p 266 where however I can find no such assertion

13—CH VI 5] THE THIRD OR HORTATORY PORTION OF THE EPISTLE, not however separated from the former, but united to it by the current of thought—and, 13—15] *Though free, be one another's servants in love* **γάρ** gives the reason why the Apostle was so fervent in his denunciation of these disturbers; because they were striking at the very root of their Christian calling, which was for (on condition of, hardly, for the purpose of, see reff) **freedom. Only (make not)** (so μή with the verb omitted and an accusative in μή 'μοιγε μύθους, Aristoph Vesp 1179; μὴ τριβὰς ἔτι, Soph. Antig 577, μή μοι μυρίους μηδὲ δισμυρίους ξένους, Demosth Phil i § 19 See more examples in Hartung, ii. 153) **your liberty into** (or, use it not for) **an occasion** (opportunity) **for the flesh** (for giving way to carnal passions), **but by means of (your) love, be in bondage** (opposition to ἐλευθερία) **to one another** Chrys. remarks, πάλιν ἐνταῦθα αἰνίττεται, ὅτι φιλονεικία κ στάσις κ φιλαρχία κ ἀπόνοια ταύτης αἰτία τῆς πλάνης αὐτοῖς ἐγένετο ἡ γὰρ τῶν αἱρέσεων μήτηρ ἡ τῆς φιλαρχίας ἐστὶν ἐπιθυμία 14] See Rom. xiii. 8, 9

The rec reading πληροῦται would mean merely '*is in course of being fulfilled*,' whereas now it is, 'is fulfilled' not '*comprehended*' (Luth, Calv, Olsh, Winer, al) "The question, how the Apostle can rightly say of the *whole* law, that it is fulfilled by loving one's neighbour, must not be answered by understanding νόμος of the *Christian* law (Koppe), or of the *moral* law only (Estius, al), or of the *second* table of the decalogue (Beza, al),

τὸν πλησίον σου ὡς σεαυτόν.
15 εἰ δὲ ἀλλήλους [g] δά-
κνετε καὶ [h] κατεσθίετε, [i] βλέπετε μὴ ὑπὸ ἀλλήλων [j] ἀνα-
λωθῆτε.
16 [k] Λέγω δέ, πνεύματι [l] περιπατεῖτε, καὶ [m] ἐπιθυμίαν
[m] σαρκὸς οὐ μὴ [n] τελέσητε.
17 ἡ γὰρ σὰρξ [o] ἐπιθυμεῖ [p] κατὰ
τοῦ πνεύματος, τὸ δὲ πνεῦμα [p] κατὰ τῆς σαρκός· ταῦτα

g here only = Heb ii 7. h Mark xii 40 L 2 Cor xi 20 Rev xi 5 only Isa ix 12. i = Matt xxiv 4 1 Cor viii 9 x 12 al. j Luke ix 54 (2 Thess ii 8 v r) only Joel ii 3.

k ch iv 1 Rom xv 8 l constr, Acts (ix 31) xxi 21 2 Cor xii 18 m (Rom xiii 14) Eph ii 3 2 Pet ii 18 1 John ii 16 see 1 Pet ii 11 n = Rom ii 27 James ii 8 o absol, James iv 2 2 Kings xxiii 15 p = ch iii 21 reff

latt arm Mcion-e Ambrst Jer Pelag (not Aug$_3$). rec (for σεαυτον) εαυτον, with FL rel Chr Thl Œc: txt ABCDKℵ b c g h n o 17 Mcion-e Thdrt Damasc. (*Simly Rom* xiii. 9)

15 δακ κ. κατεσθ bef αλληλους, and αναλωθ bef υπ. αλληλ D[1] [3]F Cypr$_2$ Victorin. υπ' BDFℵ[1] a g m Bas Chr Thl txt ACD[2.3]Lℵ[3] rel Thdrt Damasc Œc

or of every divinely revealed law in general (Schott); – for ὁ πᾶς νόμος cannot, from the circumstances of the whole Epistle, mean any thing but '*the whole law of Moses*'—but by placing ourselves on the lofty spiritual level from which St Paul looked down, and saw all other commands of the law so far subordinated to the law of love, that whoever had fulfilled *this* command, must be treated as having fulfilled the whole." Meyer who also remarks that τὸν πλησίον σου applies to fellow-Christians, cf ἀλλήλους below

15.] **ἀλλήλους** has both times the emphasis. The form of the sentence is very like Matt xxvi. 52, — πάντες οἱ λαβόντες μάχαιραν, ἐν μαχαίρᾳ ἀπολοῦνται, except that there λαβόντες, as having the stress, precedes Chrys. says, ταῖς λεξεσιν ἐμφαντικῶς ἐχρήσατο οὐ γὰρ εἶπε **δάκνετε** μόνον, ὅπερ ἐστὶ θυμουμένου, ἀλλὰ καὶ **κατεσθίετε**, ὅπερ ἐστὶν ἐμμένοντος τῇ πονηρίᾳ ὁ μὲν γὰρ δάκνων, ὀργῆς ἐπλήρωσε πάθος ὁ δὲ κατεσθίων, θηριωδίας ἐσχάτης παρέσχεν ἀπόδειξιν, δήγματα δὲ κ βρώσεις οὐ τὰς σωματικάς φησιν, ἀλλὰ τὰς πολὺ χαλεπωτέρας οὐ γὰρ οὕτως ὁ ἀνθρωπίνης ἀπογευσάμενος σαρκὸς ἔβλαψεν, ὡς ὁ δήγματα εἰς τὴν ψυχὴν πηγνύς ὅσον γὰρ ψυχὴ τιμιωτέρα σώματος, τοσούτω χαλεπωτέρα ἡ ταύτης βλάβη

ἀναλωθ] The literal sense must be kept, —**consumed** (by one another), — your spiritual life altogether annihilated · ἡ γὰρ διάστασις κ ἡ μάχη φθοροποιὸν κ ἀναλωτικὸν καὶ τῶν δεχομένων αὐτὴν κ τῶν εἰσαγόντων, καὶ σητὸς μᾶλλον ἅπαντα ἀνατρώγει Chrys

16—26] *Exhortation to a spiritual life, and warning against the works of the flesh.*

16.] **λέγω δέ** refers to ver. 13—repeating, and explaining it—q d, 'What I mean, is this' **πνεύματι**, the *normal* dative, of the rule, or manner, after or in which: Meyer quotes Hom. Il. ο 194, οὔτι Διὸς βέομαι φρεσίν:—**by the Spirit** But πν is not man's '*spiritual part*,' as Beza, Ruck., De W., al.; nor is **πνεύματι** '*after a spiritual manner*,' Peile,—nor will ἡ ἐνοικοῦσα χάρις give the force of πνεῦμα (Thdrt.) it is (as in ver. 5) **the Holy Spirit of God**: this will be clear on comparing with our vv 16 – 18, the more expanded parallel passage, Rom vii 22—viii 11 The history of the verbal usage is, that πνεῦμα, as χριστός and θεός, came to be used as a proper name. so that the supposed distinction between τὸ πν as the objective (the Holy Ghost), and πν as the subjective (man's spirit), does not hold

σαρκός] **the natural man**:—that whole state of being in the flesh, out of which spring the practices and thoughts of ver 19

οὐ μὴ τελέσητε] Is this (1) merely *future* in meaning, and a sequence on πνεύματι περιπ, 'and ye shall not fulfil,'—or is it (2) *imperative*, 'and fulfil not?' Ellic in his note has shewn that this latter meaning is allowable, it being doubtful even in classical Greek whether there are not some instances of οὐ μή with the second person subjunctive imperatively used, and the tendency of later Greek being rather to use the subjunctive aorist for the future And Meyer defends it on exegetical grounds. But surely (1) is much to be preferred on these same grounds For the next and following verses go to shew just what this verse will then assert, viz, that the Spirit and the flesh *exclude one another*

17] *Substantiation of the preceding,*—that *if ye walk by the Spirit, ye shall not fulfil the lusts of the flesh* The second **γάρ** (see var readd) gives a reason for the continual ἐπιθυμεῖν of these two against one another viz, that they are opposites

ἵνα] not '*so that*'—this is the

q Luke xiii. 17. xxi. 15. 1 Cor. xvi. 9. Phil. i. 28. 2 Thess. ii. 4. 1 Tim. i. 10. v. 14 only. L.P. Zech. iii. 1.
r = 1 Thess. v. 4. (see note.)
s constr., Rom. vii. 15.

γὰρ ἀλλήλοις ᵍ ἀντίκειται, ʳ ἵνα μὴ ˢ ἃ ἐὰν θέλητε ˢ ταῦτα ABCDF KLℵ a b
ποιῆτε. 18 εἰ δὲ ᵗ πνεύματι ᵗ ἄγεσθε, οὐκ ἐστὲ ᵘ ὑπὸ νόμον. c d e f g
19 ᵛ φανερὰ δέ ἐστιν τὰ ʷ ἔργα τῆς σαρκός, ˣ ἅτινά ἐστιν h k l m n o 17
ʸ πορνεία, ᶻ ἀκαθαρσία, ᵃᵇ ἀσέλγεια, 20 ᶜ εἰδωλολατρεία,
ᵈ φαρμακεία, ᵉ ἔχθραι, ᵇᶠ ἔρις, ᵇᵍ ζῆλος, ᵇʰ θυμοί, ᵇⁱ ἐριθεῖαι,

t Rom. viii. 14. constr., 2 Tim. iii. 6. u ch. iv. 4, 5 reff. v Rom. i. 19 al.
w see Rom. xiii. 12. x = ch. iv. 24. Col. ii. 23. y Matt. v. 32 al. fr. Gen. xxxviii. 24
z Rom. i. 24. vi. 19 al. P, exc. Matt. xxiii. 27. Prov. vi. 16. y z a 2 Cor. xii. 21. y a m Mark vii. 21, 22. z a Eph. iv. 19. a 2 Pet. ii. 2. Jude 4 al.† Wisd. xiv. 26 only. b Rom. xiii. 13.
a c o 1 Pet. iv. 3. c 1 Cor. x. 14. Col. iii. 5. 1 Pet. iv. 3 only †. d here (-ια, Rev. xviii. 23) only. Exod. vii. 11, 22. Isa. xlvii. 9, 12. e Eph. ii. 15 reff. f 1 Cor. i. 11. Tit. iii. 9 † Sir. xxviii. 11 al. f g 1 Cor. iii. 3. f g h i 2 Cor. xii. 20. (Sir. xl. 5.) f i m Rom. i. 29.
h plur., 2 Cor. xii. 20. (Wisd. vii. 20.) i Rom. ii. 8. 2 Cor. xii. 20. Phil. i. 17. ii. 3. James iii. 14, 16 only †.

17. rec for (2nd) γαρ, δε (*prob to avoid recurrence of γαρ which introduced the former clause: the recurrence of δε would not be simly felt*), with ACD^{3}KLℵ^3 rel Chr Thdrt Damasc: txt BD^{1}Fℵ^1 17 latt copt lat-ff. rec αντικειται bef αλληλοις, with KLℵ rel syrr copt: txt ABCDF m 17 latt goth Damasc$_1$ lat-ff. for ἃ, ὃ D^{1}F goth: οσα 31. rec (for εαν) αν, with C^{2}DF K(e sil) L rel Clem Chr Thdrt Damasc$_2$: om C^1: txt ABℵ a.
18. aft ουκ ins ετι Cℵ^3 syr Aug$_1$.
19. rec ins μοιχεια bef πορνεια (*from places such as Mt* xv. 19, *Mk* vii. 21, *cf Hos* ii. 2), with DFKLℵ^3 rel syr gr-lat-ff: om ABCℵ^1 17 vulg Syr copt æth Clem Mcion-e Cyr Eph Damasc$_1$ Tert Jer$_{expr}$ Aug Fulg Pelag.
20. rec ερεις (*the mss vary much between the sing and plur forms*), with CD$^{2\cdot3}$FKL rel latt Justin: txt ABD^{1}ℵ b f g h k o. rec ζηλοι, with CD$^{2\cdot3}$KLℵ rel vss gr-lat-ff: txt BD^1 17 goth Justin Damasc Concil-Carthag-in-Cypr, ζηλους F. (A defective.)

result: but more is expressed by ἵνα. Winer gives the meaning well: "Atque hujus luctæ hoc est consilium, *ut* &c. Scil. τὸ πν. impedit vos, quo minus perficiatis τὰ τῆς σαρκός (ea, quæ ἡ σάρξ perficere cupit), contra ἡ σάρξ adversatur vobis ubi τὰ τοῦ πνεύματος peragere studetis;" and Bengel: "Spiritus obnititur carni et actioni malæ: caro, Spiritui et actioni bonæ, *ut* (ἵνα) neque illa neque hæc peragatur." The necessity of supposing an ecbatic meaning for ἵνα in theology is obviated by remembering, that with God, results are all purposed. See this verse expanded in Rom. vii. viii. as above: in vii. 20 we have nearly the same words, and the same construction. It is true that θέλειν there applies only to one side, the better will, striving after good: whereas here it must be taken 'sensu communi,' for 'will' in general, to whichever way inclined. So that our verse requires expansion, both in the direction of Rom. vii. 15—20,—and in the other direction, οὐ γὰρ ὃ θέλω (after the natural man) ποιῶ κακόν· ἀλλ' ὃ οὐ θέλω ἀγαθόν, τοῦτο ποιῶ,—to make it logically complete. **18.**] By this verse, the locus respecting the flesh and the Spirit is interwoven into the general argument, thus (cf. ver. 23): the law is made for the flesh, and the works of the flesh: the Spirit and flesh ἀντίκεινται: **if** (δέ bringing out the contrast between the treatment of *both* in ver. 17, and the selection of *one side* in this verse) **then ye are led by** (see Rom. ref., ὅσοι . . . . πνεύματι θεοῦ ἄγονται, οὗτοι υἱοί εἰσιν θεοῦ) **the Spirit, ye are not under the law.** This he proceeds to substantiate, by specifying the works of the flesh and of the Spirit. This interpretation is better than the merely practical one of Chrys., al., ὁ γὰρ πνεῦμα ἔχων ὡς χρή, σβέννυσι διὰ τούτου πονηρὰν ἐπιθυμίαν ἅπασαν· ὁ δὲ τούτων ἀπαλλαγεὶς οὐ δεῖται τῆς ἀπὸ τοῦ νόμου βοηθείας, ὑψηλότερος πολλῷ τῆς ἐκείνου παραγγελίας γενόμενος,—for it is a very different thing οὐ δεῖσθαι νόμου, from οὐκ εἶναι ὑπὸ νόμον.
19—23.] *substantiates* (see above) *ver.* 18. **19.**] **φανερά** (emphatic), **plain to all**, not needing, like the more hidden fruits of the *Spirit*, to be educed and specified: and therefore more clearly amenable to law, which takes cognizance of τὰ φανερά. **ἅτινά ἐστιν**] almost = 'for example:' 'qualia sunt:' see on ch. iv. 24. **ἀκαθ., impurity** in general. **ἀσέλγ.**, ἑτοιμότης πρὸς πᾶσαν ἡδονήν, Etym. Mag. It does not seem to include necessarily the idea of lasciviousness: "Demosthenes, making mention of the blow which Meidias had given him, characterizes it as in keeping with the well-known ἀσέλγεια of the man (Meid. 514). Elsewhere he joins δεσποτικῶς and ἀσελγῶς and προπετῶς." Trench, New Test. Synonyms, p. 64. The

[j] διχοστασίαι, [k] αἱρέσεις, 21 [l] φθόνοι, [[m] φόνοι,] [n] μέθαι, [bo] κῶ-
μοι, καὶ τὰ ὅμοια τούτοις, ἃ [p] προλέγω ὑμῖν καθὼς καὶ
[q] προεῖπον, [r] ὅτι οἱ τὰ [s] τοιαῦτα [s] πράσσοντες [t] βασιλείαν
θεοῦ οὐ [t] κληρονομήσουσιν. 22 ὁ δὲ [u] καρπὸς τοῦ πνεύματός ἐστιν ἀγάπη, χαρά, εἰρήνη, [vwx] μακροθυμία, [vwy] χρηστότης, [z] ἀγαθωσύνη, πίστις, 23 [va] πραΰτης, [b] ἐγκράτεια·

j Rom xvi 17 (1 Cor iii 3 v r) only † 1 Macc iii 29
k 1 Cor xi 19 Acts v 17 al5. 2 Pet ii 1 only 1 Macc. viii 30.
l m see above, with y a and f
n Luke xxi 34 Rom xiii 13 only L P Hag i 6 Judith xiii 15
o Rom xiii 13 1 Pet iv 3 only † Wisd xiv 23 2 Macc vi 4 only
p 2 Cor xiii 2 1 Thess iii 4 only Isa xli 26 only
q Acts i 16 1 Thess iv 6 only †
r constr, John viii 54 ix 19 x 36
s Rom i 32 ii 2, 3.
t 1 Cor vi 9, 10 xv 50 (see Eph v 5 James ii 5)
u — Rom xv 28 Eph v 9 Heb xii 11 James iii 18 Prov xi 30
v Col iii 12
w as above (v) Rom ii 4 2 Cor vi 6
x as above (v w) Rom ix 22 1 Tim i 16 Heb vi. 12 James v 10 al Prov xxv 15.
y as above (v w) Rom iii 12 xi 22(3ce) Eph ii 7 Tit iii. 4 only Ps xiii 1, 3
z Rom xv 14 Eph v 9 2 Thess i 11 only Neh. ix 35
a Paul, 1 Cor iv 21 al7 James i 21 iii 13 1 Pet iii 15 only Ps xliv 4
b Acts xxiv 25 2 Pet i 6(bis) only † Sir xviii. 30(title) only

21. om φονοι (*prob from homœotel, but see Rom* i 29) Bℵ 17 demid F-lat[1] Clem Marc-e Iren-int Cypr Jer$_2$(and elsw expressly) Ambrst Aug ins ACDFKL rel Chr Thdrt$_2$ Damasc lat-mss-in-Jer Lucif. om 2nd και BFℵ[1] 67[2] vulg æth Chr$_1$ Tert Lucif ins ACDKLℵ[3] rel vss Clem Chr$_{hl}$ Thdrt Damasc Iren-int Jer for προειπ, ειπον ℵ[1]: προειρηκα D[1]F.

23 rec πραοτης, with DFKL rel: txt ABCℵ 17 Cyr-jer aft εγκρατ. ins αγνεια D[1]F latt(not am harl) Bas Pallad Iren-int Cypr Ambrst Pelag Sedul (not Jer Aug).

best word for it seems to be **wantonness**, '*protervitas*' 20] **εἰδωλ** in its proper meaning of **idolatry**. not, as Olsh, '*sins of lust*,' because of the unclean orgies of idolatry **φαρμ**, either '*poisonings*,' or '*sorceries*.' The latter is preferable, as more frequently its sense in the LXX and N. T (reff), and because (Mey) Asia was particularly addicted to sorceries (Acts xix. 19) **θυμοί**] **passionate outbreaks**. *θυμὸς μέν ἐστι πρόσκαιρος, ὀργὴ δὲ πολυχρόνιος μνησικακία*, Ammonius. *διαφέρει δὲ θυμὸς ὀργῆς, τῷ θυμὸν μὲν εἶναι ὀργὴν ἀναθυμιωμένην κ ἔτι ἐκκαιομένην, ὀργὴν δὲ ὄρεξιν ἀντιτιμωρήσεως.* Orig sel in Ps. ii, vol. ii. 541. both cited by Trench, Syn p 146. **ζῆλος**, **jealousy** (in bad sense)—reff **ἐριθεῖαι**] not '*strife*,' as E V. and commonly, in error. see note on Rom ii. 8,—but **cabals**, unworthy compassings of selfish ends 21.] Wetst N T ii. p. 147, traces in a note the later meanings of **αἵρεσις** Here *διχοστ*, **divisions**, seems to lead to *αἱρέσ*, **parties**, composed of those who have *chosen* their self-willed line and adhere to it. Trench quotes Aug. (cont Crescon Don ii 7 (9), vol. ix. p 471) "*Schisma* est recens congregationis ex aliquâ sententiarum diversitate dissensio *hæresis* autem schisma inveteratum" But we must not think of an ecclesiastical meaning only, or chiefly here **φθόν**, (**φόν**)] see Rom. i 29, where we have the same alliteration **ἃ προλ**] The construction of **ἃ** is exactly as John viii. 54, *ὃν ὑμεῖς λέγετε ὅτι θεὸς ὑμῶν ἐστιν*—it is governed, but only as matter of reference, by *προλέγω*,—not to be joined by attraction with *πράσσοντες*, as Olsh, al **προλ κ προεῖπον**] **I forewarn you** (now), **and did forewarn you** (when I was with you) the *προ-* in both cases pointing on to the great day of retribution. **τὰ τοιαῦτα**] The article generalizes *τοιαῦτα*, **the things of this kind, i. e all such things** See Ellic.'s note **βασ θ. οὐ κλ**] See reff 22] **καρπός**, not **ἔργα, τοῦ πνεύματος**. The works of the flesh are no *καρπός*, see Rom vi 21. These are the only real *fruit* of men: see John xv 1—8: compare also John iii. 20, note. They *are*, or are manifested in, **ἔργα** but they are much more whereas those others are nothing more, as to any abiding result for good. **ἀγάπη**—at the head, as chief—1 Cor. xiii. See Rom xii. 9. **χαρά**, better merely **joy**, than as Winer, al, '*voluptas ex aliorum commodis percepta*,' as opposed to *φθόνος*. We must not seek for a detailed logical opposition in the two lists, which would be quite alien from the fervid style of St Paul. **χρηστότης, ἀγαθωσ.**] Jerome, comm. in loc., says, "Benignitas sive suavitas, quia apud Græcos *χρηστότης* utrumque sonat, virtus est lenis, blanda, tranquilla, et omnium bonorum apta consortio invitans ad familiaritatem sui, dulcis alloquio, moribus **temperata**. Non multum bonitas (*ἀγαθωσύνη*) a benignitate diversa est, quia et ipsa ad benefaciendum videtur exposita Sed in eo differt, quia potest bonitas esse tristior, et fronte severis moribus irrugata bene quidem facere et præstare quod poscitur non

c ch iii 21 ver 17 d gen, 1 Cor iii 22, 23 al e = ch vi 14 see Rom vi 6 f = Rom vii 5 (viii 18 al7, Paul Heb ii 9, 10 x 32 1 Pet i 11 al3) only † g = ver 16 reff Rom i 24 al Sus 11, &c h dat, Rom xii 12 al Winer, § 31 6 7 i (=) Acts xxi 24 Rom iv 12 ch vi 16 Phil iii 16 only (Eccles xi 6 only) j = ch iv. 12 Eph v 17 al k here only † (-ξια, Phil ii 3) l here only †. m here only † Tobit iv 16 only

ABCDF KLℵ a b c d e f g h k l m n o 17

[c] κατὰ τῶν τοιούτων οὐκ ἔστιν νόμος. 24 οἱ δὲ τοῦ
[d] χριστοῦ Ἰησοῦ τὴν σάρκα [e] ἐσταύρωσαν σὺν τοῖς [f] παθήμασιν καὶ ταῖς [g] ἐπιθυμίαις. 25 εἰ ζῶμεν [h] πνεύματι, πνεύματι καὶ [i] στοιχῶμεν. 26 μὴ [j] γινώμεθα [k] κενόδοξοι, ἀλλήλους [l] προκαλούμενοι, ἀλλήλοις [m] φθονοῦντες. VI. 1 ἀδελ-

24 ins *κυριου* bef *χριστου* ℵ[1](but erased). rec om *ιησου*, with DFKL rel latt syrr Chr Thdrt Ps-Ath Cypr Jer ins ABCℵ 17 coptt æth $Cyr_{persæpe}$ Bas Procop Damasc Aug. aft *σαρκα* ins *αυτων* F vulg Cypr.
25 *πνευματι* bef *ζωμ* DF latt(not am demid al) Aug *ζ. ουν εν πν. κ πν. στοιχ* syrr Chr om *και* F Ambrst-ed *στοιχουμεν* D[3]KL e 67[2].
26. *αλληλους* BG[1] c d k l Chr $Thdrt_1$-ms_1 Œc: *αλληλοιυς*(*sic*) a txt ACDFKLℵ rel $Clem_2$ $Thdrt_2$ Damasc.

tamen suavis esse consortio, et sua cunctos invitare dulcedine." Plato, deff. 412 e, defines **χρηστότης**, *ἤθους ἀπλαστία μετ' εὐλογιστίας.* **ἀγαθωσ** is a Hellenistic word, see reff Perhaps **kindness** and **goodness** would best represent the two words. **πίστις**, in the widest sense. **faith**, towards God and man of love it is said, 1 Cor xiii. 7, *πάντα πιστεύει.*

23] **πραΰτης** seems to be well represented by **meekness,—again**, towards God and man and **ἐγκρ** by **temperance**,—the *holding in* of the lusts and desires. *τῶν τοιούτ* answers to *τὰ τοιαῦτα* above, and should therefore be taken as neuter, not masculine, as Chrys, al. This verse (see above on ver 18) substantiates *οὐκ ἐστὲ ὑπὸ νόμον*—for if you are led by the Spirit, these are its fruits in you, and against these the law has nothing to say see 1 Tim i 9, 10 **24**] *Further confirmation of this last result, and transition to the exhortations of vv 25, 26* **But** (contrast, the *one universal choice* of Christians, in distinction from the *two* catalogues) **they who are Christ's crucified** (when they became Christ's,—at their baptism, see Rom vi 2· not so well, '*have crucified*,' as E V) **the flesh, with its passions and its desires**,—and therefore are entirely severed from and dead to the law, which is for the fleshly, and those passions and desires—on which last he founds,— **25**] **If** (no connecting particle—giving more vividness to the inference) **we** LIVE (emphatic—if, as we saw, having slain the flesh, our life depends on the Spirit) **in** (said to be a species of instrumental dative, but such usage is of very rare occurrence, and hardly ever undoubted Here the dative is probably employed more as corresponding to the dative in the other member, than with strict accuracy But it may be justified thus our inner life, which is hid with Christ in God, Col. iii. 3, is lived *πνεύματι* [normal dative], the Spirit being its generator and upholder) **the Spirit,—in the Spirit** (emphatic) **let us also walk** (in our conduct in life. let our practical walk, which is led *κατὰ προαίρεσιν* of our own, be in harmony with that higher life in which we live before God by faith, and in the Spirit). **26.**] connected with *στοιχῶμεν* above, by the *first person*,—and with ch vi. 1, by the *sense*, and so forming a transition to the admonitions which follow **μὴ γινώμ**, **let us not become**—*efficiamur*, vulg, Erasm,—a mild, and at the same time a solemn method of warning For while it seems to concede that they were not this as yet, it assumes that the process was going on which would speedily make them so '*Let us not be*,' of the E V, misses this **κενόδοξοι** would include, as De W. observes, all worldly honour, as not an object for the Christian to seek, 1 Cor. i 31, 2 Cor x. 17 **ἀλλήλ. προκαλ**] *εἰς φιλονεικίας κ ἔρεις*, Chrys So *ἐς δίκας προκαλουμένων τῶν Ἀθηναίων*, Thuc vii 18: *εἰς μάχην προὐκαλεῖτο*, Xen (Wetst) "**φθονεῖν** is the correlative act on the part of the weak, to the *προκαλεῖσθαι* on the part of the strong The strong vauntingly challenged their weaker brethren. they could only reply with *envy*." Ellicott These words are addressed to *all* the Galatians —the danger was common to both parties, the obedient and disobedient, the orthodox and the Judaizers.

VI. 1—5] *Exhortation to forbearance and humility.* **Brethren** (bespeaks their attention by a friendly address, marking also the opening of a new subject, con-

φοί, ἐὰν καὶ ⁿ προλημφθῇ ° ἄνθρωπος ἐν τινὶ ᵖ παραπτώ-
ματι, ὑμεῖς οἱ ᵠ πνευματικοὶ ʳ καταρτίζετε ˢ τὸν ˢ τοιοῦτον
ἐν ᵗ πνεύματι ᵘ πραΰτητος, ᵛ σκοπῶν σεαυτόν, μὴ καὶ σὺ
ʷ πειρασθῇς. 2 ἀλλήλων τὰ ˣ βάρη ʸ βαστάζετε, καὶ
ᶻ οὕτως ᵃ ἀναπληρώσατε τὸν ᵇ νόμον τοῦ χριστοῦ. 3 εἰ

n = here only (Mark xiv 8 1 Cor xi 21 only †) Wisd xvii 17 only
o = 1 Cor iv 1 xi 28
p Matt vi 14 Rom iv 25 al Ps xviii 12 Ezek xviii 26
q = 1 Cor iii 1 xiv 37 al †
r 1 Cor i 10 Matt iv 21 al Ezra iv 13
s Acts xxii 22 1 Cor v 5, 11 2 Cor ii 6, 7 x 11 Tit iii 11
t Rom viii 15 bis xi 8 (from Isa xxix 10) 2 Cor iv 13 Eph i 17 al πν πρ, 1 Cor iv 21
u ch v 23 reff
v = & constr, Luke xi 35 (Rom xvi 17 2 Cor iv 18 Phil ii 4 iii 17 only † 2 Macc iv 5 only)
w = 1 Cor vii 5 1 Thess iii 5 James i 13 al
x Matt xx 12 Acts xv 28 2 Cor iv 17 1 Thess ii 6 Rev ii 24 only Sir xiii 2
y = Rom xv 1 (ch v 10 reff)
z = Acts xvii 33 1 Cor xi 28 xiv 25 al
a Matt xiii 14 1 Cor xiv 16 xvi. 17 Phil ii 30 1 Thess ii 16 only Gen xxix 28 imper aor, John xiv 15 1 Cor vi 20
b see Rom viii 2. 1 Cor ix 21

Chap. VI 1 om 1st *και* K o. *forsan* arm. προκαταληφθη K. rec πραοτ, with ACDFKL rel txt Bℵ 17. (*See ch* v. 23) for *συ*, *αυτος* D¹ —σκ εκαστος σεαυτ μη κ αυτος πειρασθη F

2 *βαστασετε* ℵ¹: txt ℵ³. *αναπληρωσετε* (*prob corrn, the imper aor being unusual see reff*) BF latt Syr sah æth Thdrt-ms Procl lat-ff. txt ACDKLℵ rel syr Clem Ath Chr Thdrt Damasc, *impletis* goth.

nected however with the foregoing: see above), **if a man be even surprised** (προλημφθῇ has the emphasis, on account of the καί. This makes it necessary to assign a meaning to it which shall justify its emphatic position. And such meaning is clearly not found in the ordinary renderings. E. g. Chrysostom,—*ἐὰν συναρπαγῇ*,—so E. V. *'overtaken,'* and De Wette, al, which could not be emphatic, but would be palliative. Grotius,—'*si quis antea* [h. e. antequam hæc ep. ad vos veniat] *deprehensus fuerit.*' Winer,—'*etiam si* [si vel] *quis antea deprehensus fuerit in peccato, eum tamen* [iterum peccantem] *corrigite.*' Olsh., who regards the προ- almost as expletive, betokening merely that the λαμβάνεσθαι comes in time before the καταρτίζειν. The only meaning which satisfies the emphasis is that of being caught in the fact, '*flagrante delicto,*' before he can escape: which, though unusual, seems justified by ref. Wisd. and so Meyer, Ellic, al) **in any transgression** (with the meaning 'overtaken' for προλημφθῇ, falls also that of '*inadvertence*' for **παράπτωμα**. The stronger meaning of '*sin*' is far commoner in St. Paul: see ref. Rom. and ib. v. 15, 16, 20, 2 Cor. v. 19, Eph. i 7, ii. 1, 5, Col. ii 13 bis), **do ye, the spiritual ones** (said not in irony, but *bonâ fide* referring not to the clergy only, but to every believer), **restore** (Beza, Hammond, Bengel, al, have imagined an allusion to a dislocated limb being reduced into place but the simple ethical sense is abundantly justified by examples. see Herodot., cited on 1 Cor. i. 10, Stob. i. 85, *καταρτίζειν φίλους διαφερομένους* [Ellic.]) **such a person** (see especially 1 Cor v 5, 11) **in the spirit of meekness** (beware of the silly *hendiadys*. Chrys gives the right allusion,—*οὐκ εἶπεν "ἐν πραότητι," ἀλλ' "ἐν πνεύματι πραότητος" δηλῶν ὅτι καὶ τῷ πνεύματι ταῦτα δοκεῖ, καὶ τὸ δύνασθαι μετ' ἐπιεικείας διορθοῦν τοὺς ἁμαρτάνοντας, χαρίσματός ἐστι πνευματικοῦ* and Ellic, "*πν.* here seems *immediately* to refer to the state of the inward Spirit as wrought upon by the Holy Spirit, and *ultimately* to the Holy Spirit, as the in-working power. Cf. Rom. i 4, viii 15; 2 Cor. iv 13; Eph. i 17: in all of which cases *πν* seems to indicate the Holy Spirit, and the abstract genitive the specific *χάρισμα*"),—**looking to thyself** (we have the same singling out of individuals from a multitude previously addressed in Thucyd. i 42, *ὧν ἐνθυμηθέντες, καὶ νεώτερός τις παρὰ πρεσβυτέρου μαθών, ἀξιούτω* . . *ἡμᾶς ἀμύνεσθαι*. See more examples in Bernhardy, p. 421), **lest thou also be tempted** (on a similar occasion: notice the aorist).

2] **ἀλλήλων**, prefixed and emphatic, has not been enough attended to. You want to become disciples of that Law which imposes heavy burdens on men: if you will bear burdens, **bear** ONE ANOTHER'S **burdens, and thus fulfil** (see var readd.: notice aorist. by this act fulfil) **the law of Christ**,—a far higher and better law, whose only burden is love. The position of **ἀλλήλων** I conceive fixes this meaning, by throwing **τὰ βάρη** into the shade, as a term common to the two laws. As to the **βάρη**, the more general the meaning we give to it, the better it will accord with the sense of the command. The matter men-

γὰρ [c] δοκεῖ τις [d] εἶναί τι μηδὲν ὤν, [e] φρεναπατᾷ ἑαυτόν. ABCDF
4 τὸ δὲ [f] ἔργον ἑαυτοῦ [g] δοκιμαζέτω ἕκαστος, καὶ τότε [h] εἰς KLℵ a b c d e f g
ἑαυτὸν μόνον τὸ [i] καύχημα [i] ἕξει, καὶ οὐκ [h] εἰς [j] τὸν ἕτερον· h k l m n o 17
5 ἕκαστος γὰρ τὸ ἴδιον [k] φορτίον [y] βαστάσει. 6 [l] κοινω-
νείτω δὲ ὁ [m] κατηχούμενος τὸν λόγον τῷ [m] κατηχοῦντι ἐν

c Phil iii 4 reff
d ch ii 6 reff ἐὰν δοκῶσι τι εἶναι, μηδὲν ὄντες, Plato, Apol Socr p 41, § 33
e here only † (-της, Tit i 10)
f = Rom ii 6 1 Pet i 17. Rev xxii 12 Ps xxvii 4 g = Luke xiv 19 1 Cor iii 13 xi 28 2 Cor viii 8 Prov viii 10 h = Luke xii 21 xvi 8 Eph i 5 i Rom iv 2 καυχ, 1 Cor v 6 al[8], Paul Heb iii 6 Deut x 21 al j Rom ii 1 viii 8 1 Cor iv 6 vi 1 x 24, 29 al Exod xvi 15 k Matt xi 30 xxiii 4 Luke xi 46 (bis). Acts xxvii 10 only 2 Kings xix 35 l Rom xii 13 xv 27 Phil iv 15 1 Tim v 22 Heb ii 14 1 Pet iv 13 2 John 11 Eccl ix 4 m Luke i 4 Acts xviii 25 xxi 21, 24 Rom ii 18 1 Cor xiv 19 only †

3 rec ἑαυτον bef φρεναπατα, with DFKL rel latt gr-lat-ff: txt ABCℵ m 17 coptt Chr.
4 om ἑκαστος B sah.

tioned in the last verse led on to this: but this grasps far wider, extending to *all* the burdens which we can, by help and sympathy, bear for one another. There are some which we *cannot*: see below. **ἀναπληρ., thoroughly fulfil**: Ellic quotes Plut Poplicol. ii, *ἀνεπλήρωσε τὴν βουλὴν ὀλιγανδροῦσαν*, 'filled up the Senate.' **3**] The chief hindrance to sympathy with the burdens of others, is self-conceit: that must be got rid of. **εἶναί τι**, see reff. **μηδὲν ὤν**] there is (perhaps: but this must not be over-pressed, see Ellic.) a fine irony in the subjective *μηδέν*—'being, if he would come to himself, and look on the real fact, nothing'—whereas *οὐδὲν ὤν* expresses more the objective fact,—his real absolute worthlessness. See examples of both expressions in Wetst h. l. **φρεναπατᾷ**] not found elsewhere: see ref and James i. 26. The word seems to mean just as *ἀπατῶν καρδίαν αὐτοῦ* there. I should hardly hold Ellic.'s distinction: both are subjective deceits, and only to be got rid of by testing them with plain matter of fact. **4**] *The test applied*: emphasis on **τὸ ἔργον**, which (as Mey.) is the complex, the whole practical result of his life, see reff. **δοκ.**] **put to the trial** (reff) not '*render δόκιμον*,' which the word will not bear. **κ. τότε**] **And then** (after he has done this) **he will have his matter of boasting** (the article makes it subjective: the *καύχημα*, **that whereof to boast**, not without a slight irony,—whatever matter of boasting he finds, after such a testing, will be) **in reference to himself alone** (**εἰς ἑαυ. μόν.** emphatic—corresponds to **εἰς τὸν ἕτ.** below), **and not** (as matter of *fact*: not *μή*) **in reference to the other,** (or, **his neighbour**—the man with whom he was comparing himself: general in its meaning, but particular in each case of comparison). **5**] And this is the more advisable, because in the nature of things, **each man's own load** (of infirmities and imperfections and sins: not of '*responsibility*,' which is alien from the context) **will** (*in ordinary life*: not '*at the last day*,' which is here irrelevant, and would surely have been otherwise expressed: the **βαστάσει** must correspond with the *βαστάζετε* above, and be a taking up and carrying, not an ultimate bearing the consequences of) **come upon himself to bear.** **φορτίον** here, hardly with any allusion to Æsop's well-known fable (C and H ii. 182, edn. 2),—but,—as distinguished from *βάρος*, in which there is an idea of grievance conveyed,—the load imposed on each by his own fault. The future, in this sense of that which must be in the nature of things, is discussed by Bernhardy, pp. 377-8. **6—10**] *Exhortation* (in pursuance of the command in ver 2, see below), *to liberality towards their teachers, and to beneficence in general.*

6] **κοινωνείτω** most likely intransitive, as there does not appear to be an instance of its transitive use in the N. T. (certainly not Rom xii 13). But the two senses come nearly to the same: he who shares in the necessities of the saints, can only do so by making that necessity partly his own, i. e., by depriving himself to that extent, and communicating to them. On *κατηχούμ.* and *κατηχῶν*, see Suicer, Thes. sub voce. This meaning, of '*giving oral instruction*,' is confined to later Greek: see Liddell and Scott. **δέ**, as bringing out a contrast to the individuality of the last verse. **τὸν λόγον**, in its very usual sense of **the Gospel,—the word of life.** It is the accusative of reference or of second government, after *κατηχούμενος*, as in Acts xviii. 25. **ἐν πᾶσ. ἀγ.**] **in all good things**: *the things of this life* mainly, as the context shews. Nor does this meaning produce an abrupt break between vv. 5 and 6, and 6 and 7, as Meyer (who understands **ἀγαθά** of moral

πᾶσιν ἀγαθοῖς. 7 [n] μὴ [n] πλανᾶσθε, θεὸς οὐ [o] μυκτηρίζεται.
ὃ γὰρ ἐὰν [p] σπείρῃ ἄνθρωπος, τοῦτο καὶ [p] θερίσει· 8 ὅτι ὁ
[p] σπείρων εἰς τὴν σάρκα ἑαυτοῦ ἐκ τῆς σαρκὸς [p] θερίσει
[q] φθοράν· ὁ δὲ [p] σπείρων εἰς τὸ πνεῦμα ἐκ τοῦ πνεύματος
[p] θερίσει ζωὴν αἰώνιον. 9 [r] τὸ δὲ [r] καλὸν ποιοῦντες μὴ
[s] ἐγκακῶμεν· [t] καιρῷ γὰρ [t] ἰδίῳ θερίσομεν μὴ [u] ἐκλυ-

n 1 Cor vi 9 xv 33 James i 16 Isa xliv 8. πλ., Matt xxii 29 al
o here only — Prov i 30 xv 20 al
p Matt vi 26 ‖ xxv 24 ‖ John iv 36, 37 al Job iv 8
q Rom viii 21 1 Cor xv 42, 50 Col ii 22 2 Pet i 4 ii 12 (bis), 19 only Micah ii 10
r Rom vii 18, 21 2 Cor xiii 7
s Eph iii 13 reff
t 1 Tim ii 6 vi 15 Tit i 3 only
u Matt xv 32 ‖ Mk Heb xii 3, 5 (from Prov iii 31) only — Deut xx 3 2 Kings iv 1

7 for εαν, αν BD¹F m Dial Thl · txt ACD³KLℵ rel Clem Chr Thdrt Damasc for τουτο, ταυτα D¹F (latt)

8 τη σαρκι F · *in carne* latt. for εαυτου, αυτου D¹F a¹ Thdrt Thl: txt ABCD³KLℵ rel. aft σαρκος ins αυτου DF copt æth Chr Thdrt Zeno. θερισισει(sic) ℵ¹(corrd by ℵ-corr¹). for εις τ. πν. (*in spiritu* latt), εκ του πν D¹ sah

9 rec εκκακ, with CD³KL rel Clem Chr Thdrt, εκκακησωμεν F txt ABD¹ℵ m 17 Chr-wlf θερισωμεν CFLℵ d h¹ k m 17.

good, '*share with your teachers in all virtues*' i.e. '*imitate their virtues*') maintains From the mention of bearing one another's burdens, he naturally passes to one way, and one case, in which those burdens may be borne—viz by relieving the necessities of their ministers (thus almost all Commentators), and then,

7.] regarding our good deeds done for Christ as a seed sown for eternity, he warns them not to be deceived in this, as in other seed-times, God's order of things cannot be set at nought whatever we sow, that same shall we **reap** **οὐ μυκτηρ.**] **is not mocked**—though men subjectively mock God, this mocking has no objective existence there is no such thing as mocking of God in reality. μυκτηρίζειν λέγομεν τοὺς ἐν τῷ διαπαίζειν τινὰς τοῦτό πως τὸ μέρος (μυκτῆρα) ἐπισπῶντας, Etym. Mag. (cited by Ellic) Pollux quotes the word from Lysias in medicine it is used for bleeding at the nose (Hippocrat. p 1240 D). **γάρ**, 'and in this it will be shewn.' **σπείρῃ**, present subjunctive (cf. σπείρων below). **τοῦτ κ θ.**] **this** (emphatic, this and nothing else) **shall he also** (by the same rule) **reap**, viz eventually, at the great harvest The final judgment is necessarily *now* introduced by the similitude (ὁ θερισμὸς—συντέλεια αἰῶνός ἐστιν, Matt xiii 39), but does not any the more belong to the context in ver 5. **8**] **ὅτι**, **for**—i.e. and this will be an example of the universal rule. **ὁ σπείρων, he that** (now) **soweth,—is now sowing.** **εἰς, unto,—with a view to**—not local, '*drops his seed into*,' 'tanquam in agrum,' Bengel this in the N. T is given by ἐν (Matt xiii. 24, 27. Mark iv. 15), or ἐπί (Matt. xiii. 20, 23 Mark iv 16, 20, 31) εἰς τὰς ἀκάνθας (Matt xiii 22. Mark iv. 18) rather being '*among the thorns*' (see Ellic). **ἑαυτοῦ**, not apparently with any *especial* emphasis—**to his own flesh.** **φθοράν**] (not ἀπώλειαν—as Phil. iii. 19) **corruption**—because the flesh is a prey to corruption, and with it all fleshly desires and practices come to nothing (De W) see 1 Cor. vi. 13, xv. 50.—or perhaps in the *stronger* sense of φθορά (see 1 Cor. iii. 17, 2 Pet. ii 12), **destruction** (Meyer) **ἐκ τ πν**] See Rom. viii. 11, 15—17. **9.**] **But** (in our case, let there be no chance of the alternative. see Hartung, Partikell. i. 166) **in well-doing** (stress on **καλόν**) **let us not be faint-hearted** (on **ἐγκ** and **ἐκκ.**, see note, 2 Cor. iv. 1. It seems doubtful, whether such a word as ἐκκακέω exists at all in Greek, and whether its use by later writers and place in lexicons is not entirely due to these doubtful readings See Ellic.'s note). **for in due time** (an expression of the pastoral Epistles, see reff,—and Prolegomena to those Epistles, § i. 32, and note) **we shall reap, if we do not faint** (so reff., and Isocr, p 322 a ἵν' οὖν μὴ παντάπασιν ἐκλυθῶ, πολλῶν ἔτι μοι λεκτέων ὄντων) Thdrt, al, join μὴ ἐκλ. with θερίσομεν,—πόνου δίχα θερίσομεν τὰ σπειρόμενα . . ἐπὶ μὲν γὰρ τῶν αἰσθητῶν σπερμάτων καὶ ὁ σπόρος ἔχει πόνον, κ ὁ ἀμητὸς ὡσαύτως· διαλύει γὰρ πολλάκις τοὺς ἀμῶντας κ. τὸ τῆς ὥρας θερμόν ἀλλ' ἐκεῖνος οὐ τοιοῦτος ὁ ἀμητός πόνου γάρ ἐστι κ. ἱδρῶτος ἐλεύθερος But though such a rendering would be unobjectionable (not requiring οὐ for μή, as Rück., al, for as Mey. rightly, the particle being subjective, μή would be in place), it would give a very vapid sense · whereas the other eminently suits the exhortation

όμενοι. 10 [v]ἄρα [v]οὖν [w]ὡς [x]καιρὸν ἔχομεν, [y]ἐργαζώμεθα
[z]τὸ ἀγαθὸν πρὸς πάντας, μάλιστα δὲ πρὸς τοὺς [a]οἰκείους
τῆς πίστεως.
11 Ἴδετε [b]πηλίκοις ὑμῖν [c]γράμμασιν [d]ἔγραψα [de]τῇ ἐμῇ
[e]χειρί. 12 ὅσοι θέλουσιν [f]εὐπροσωπῆσαι ἐν [g]σαρκί,
οὗτοι [h]ἀναγκάζουσιν ὑμᾶς [i]περιτέμνεσθαι, μόνον ἵνα τῷ
[k]σταυρῷ τοῦ χριστοῦ μὴ [l]διώκωνται. 13 οὐδὲ γὰρ οἱ

ABCDF KLℵ a b c d e f g h k l m n o 17

v Rom. v. 18 al[10]. P. w = Luke xii. 58. John xii. 35. Rev. xxii. 12. x = Acts xxiv. 25. 1 Cor. vii. 29. Eccl. iii. 1, &c. y Rom. ii. 10. Eph. iv. 28. z Rom. ii. 10. vii. 13. xiii. 3, 4. 1 Thess. v. 15. a Eph. ii. 19. 1 Tim. v. 8 only. Isa. iii. 6. 2 Macc. xv. 12 vat. οἰκεῖοι φιλοσοφίας, Strab. i. p. 13. οἰκεῖος γεωγραφίας, ib. p. 25. (Wetst.) b Heb. vii. 4 only. Zech. ii. 2. c see note and Acts xxviii. 21. 1 Macc. v. 10. dat., Matt. viii. 8. d Philem. 19. e 1 Cor. xvi. 21. Col. iv. 18. 2 Thess. iii. 17. f here only †. (-πος, Gen. xii. 11. Xen. Mem. i. 3. 10. -πίζειν, Ps. cxl. 6 Symm.) g Rom. ii. 28. 1 Tim. iii. 16 reff. h = ch. ii. 3 reff. i Luke i. 59 al. Gen. xvii. 10. k = ch. v. 11 reff. dat., Rom. xi. 20. 2 Cor. ii. 13. Bernhardy, p. 370. l ch. iv. 29 reff.

10. εχωμεν B[1]ℵ. εργαζομεθα AB[2]L c d m n goth Œc: txt B[1]CDFℵ rel vss Clem, -σωμεθα K al_3.

11. γραμμασιν bef υμιν DF Ang.

12. rec μη bef τω στ. τ. χρ., with FKL rel Chr Thdrt Ambrst: txt ABCDℵ 17 vulg Syr goth Victorin Ang Jer Pelag. διωκονται ACFKL a d f k m: txt BDℵ rel.

μὴ ἐγκ. **10.**] **ἄρα οὖν, so then**: "the proper meaning of ἄρα, '*rebus ita comparatis*,' is here distinctly apparent: its weaker ratiocinative force being supported by the collective power of οὖν." Ellic. **ὡς**] not '*while*' (Olsh., al.), nor, '*according as*,' i. e. '*quotiescunque*,' nor, 'since,' causal (De W., Winer, al.),—but **as**, i. e. **in proportion as**: let our beneficence be in proportion to our καιρός—let the seed-time have its καιρὸς ἴδιος, as well as the harvest, ver. 9. Thus καιρός is a common term between the two verses. **τὸ ἀγ.**] **the good thing**: as we say, 'he did the right thing:' that which is (in each case) good. **τ. οἰκείους τ. πίστ.**] **those who belong to the faith**: there does not seem to be any allusion to a household, as in E. V. In Isa. lviii. 7 'thy fellow-men' are called οἱ οἰκεῖοι τοῦ σπέρματός σου: so also in the examples from the later classics in Wetst., οἰκεῖοι φιλοσοφίας, — γεωγραφίας, — ὀλιγαρχίας, τυραννίδος,—τρυφῆς.

11—end.] Postscript and Benediction. **11.**] **See in how large letters** (in what great and apparently unsightly characters: see note on next verse. **πηλίκοις** will not bear the rendering (1) '*how many*,' πόσοις,—or (2) '*what sort*,' ποίοις:—but only (3) **how great** [reff.]. Nor can (3) be made to mean (1) by taking γράμματα for 'Epistle,' a sense unknown to St. Paul) **I wrote** (not strictly the epistolary *scribebam*, nor referring to the following verses only: but the aorist spoken as at the time when they would receive the Epistle, and referring I believe to the whole of it, see also below) **with my own hand**. I do not see how it is possible to avoid the inference that these words apply to the whole Epistle. If they had reference only to the passage in which they occur, would not γράφω have been used, as in 2 Thess. iii. 17? Again, there is no break in style here, indicating the end of the dictated portion, and the beginning of the written, as in Rom. xvi. 25; 2 Thess. iii. 17 al. I should rather believe, that on account of the peculiar character of this Epistle, St. Paul wrote it all with his own hand,—as he did the pastoral Epistles: and I find confirmation of this, in the partial resemblance of its style to those Epistles. (See Prolegomena, as above on ver. 9.) And he wrote it, whether from weakness of his eyes, or from choice, in large characters. **12.**] As my Epistle, so my practice: I have no desire to make a fair show outwardly: my γράμματα are not εὐπρόσωπα (is there a further allusion to the same point in ὅσοι τῷ **κανόνι** τούτῳ στοιχήσουσιν, and even in **στίγματα**, below?) and I have no sympathy with these θέλοντες εὐπροσωπῆσαι ἐν σαρκί. The word εὐπροσωπεῖν occurs only here: but we have φαινοπροσωπεῖν, Cic. Att. vii. 21; xiv. 21: σεμνοπροσωπεῖν, Aristoph. Nub. 363. **ἐν σαρκί**, not merely '*in the flesh*,' but **in outward things**, which belong to man's natural state: see ch. v. 19. **οὗτοι**, **it is these who**: see ver. 7. **ἀναγκάζουσιν**] **are compelling**:—**go about to compel**. **τῷ σταυρῷ**] dative of the cause, see reff. Winer would understand '*should be persecuted with the Cross* (i. e. with sufferings like the Cross) *of Christ*.' But apart from other objections (which I do not feel, however, so strongly as Ellic.), surely this would have been otherwise expressed—by

περιτεμνόμενοι αὐτοὶ [m] νόμον [m] φυλάσσουσιν, ἀλλὰ θέλουσιν ὑμᾶς περιτέμνεσθαι, ἵνα [n] ἐν τῇ ὑμετέρᾳ σαρκὶ
[n] καυχήσωνται. 14 [o] ἐμοὶ δὲ μὴ [o] γένοιτο [n] καυχᾶσθαι, εἰ
μὴ [n] ἐν τῷ σταυρῷ τοῦ κυρίου ἡμῶν Ἰησοῦ χριστοῦ, δι'
οὗ [p] ἐμοὶ κόσμος [q] ἐσταύρωται κἀγὼ κόσμῳ. 15 οὔτε γὰρ
[rs] περιτομή [t] τι [s] ἔστιν οὔτε [rs] ἀκροβυστία, ἀλλὰ [u] καινὴ
[u] κτίσις. 16 καὶ ὅσοι τῷ [v] κανόνι τούτῳ [w] στοιχήσουσιν,

m Acts vii 53 xxi 24 Rom ii 26
n Rom ii 17 v 3 2 Cor x 15 al Jer ix 23, 24
o Mark v 16 Acts xx 16 Gen xliv 7, 17
p dat, Heb vi 6
q — ch v 24 see Rom vi 6
r ch v 6 reff
s 1 Cor vii 19
t ch ii 6 reff
u 2 Cor v 17
v 2 Cor x 13, 15, 16 (Phil iii 16 v r.) only Micah vii 4 Judith xiii 6 only — Job xxxviii 5 Aq (σπαρτίον LXX)
w dat, ch v 16 Phil iii 16. w & constr, ch v 25 (reff)

13 περιτετμημενοι BL rel 67[2] copt goth lat-ff: txt ACDKℵ d h l 17 syrr Marcion-e Chr Thdrt Damasc Bede. for θελουσιν, βουλονται AC. περιτεμεσθαι B. καυχησονται DG[1] c d.

14. καυχησασθαι AD[1]. ins ο bef κοσμος F (Clem Bas$_4$) Thl. rec ins τω bef κοσμω, with C[3]D[3]KL rel Clem Orig$_7$ Ath$_1$ Mac Bas$_5$ Epiph Chr Cyr Thdrt Damasc om ABC[1]D[1]Fℵ 17 Orig$_3$ Ath$_1$

15 rec (for ουτε γαρ) εν γαρ χ. ιησ. ουτε (*from ch v 6*), with ACDFKLℵ rel latt syr-w-ast(εν to ιησ) copt æth-pl Thdrt Damasc Victorin Ambrst · txt B 17 Syr syr(altern) sah goth æth arm(ed 1805) Chr Sync Jer Aug rec (for εστιν) ισχυει (*from ch* v. 6), with D[3]KLℵ[3] rel vulg Chr Thdrt txt ABCD[1]Fℵ[1] 17. 67[2] Syr syr-marg coptt æth Orig Thl$_{alic}$ Sync Jer Aug Ambrst.

16 στοιχουσιν (*corrn to pres, as more usual and simpler. No reason can be given why the fut should have been* substituted, *and it belongs to the nervous style of this conclusion*) AC[1]DF syrr copt(appy) goth arm Chr Cyr Victorin Jer Aug$_2$ Ambrst Ruf

τοῖς παθήμασιν or the like 13.] **For** (proof that they wish only to escape persecution) **not even they who are being circumcised** (who are the adopters and instigators of circumcision, cf ἀναγκάζουσιν above) **themselves keep the law** (**νόμον** emphatic the words contain a matter of fact, not known to us otherwise,—that these preachers of legal conformity extended it not to the whole law, but selected from it at their own caprice), **but wish you** (emphatic) **to be circumcised, that in your** (emphatic) **flesh they may make their boast** (ἵνα ἐν τῷ κατακόπτειν τὴν ὑμετέραν σάρκα καυχήσωνται ὡς διδάσκαλοι ὑμῶν, i. e, μαθητὰς ὑμᾶς ἔχοντες, Thl In this way they escaped the scandal of the Cross at the hands of the Jews, by making in fact their Christian converts into Jewish proselytes). 14.] **But to me let it not happen to boast** (on the construction, see reff. Meyer quotes Xen Cyr. vi. 3 11,—ὦ Ζεῦ μέγιστε, λαβεῖν μοι γένοιτο αὐτόν), **except in the Cross** (the atoning death, as my means of reconcilement with God) **of our Lord Jesus Christ** (the full name for solemnity, and ἡμῶν to involve his readers in the duty of the same abjuration), **by means of whom** (not so well, 'of *which*' [τοῦ σταυροῦ] as many Commentators; the greater antecedent, **τοῦ κυρ ἡμ. Ἰ χ**, coming after the σταυρῷ, has thrown it into the shade. Besides, it could hardly be said of the Cross, **δι' οὗ**) **the world** (the whole system of unspiritual and unchristian men and things Notice the absorption of the article in a word which had become almost a proper name · so with ἥλιος, γῆ, πόλις, &c.) **has been** (and **is**) **crucified** (not merely '*dead*·' he chooses, in relation to σταυρός above, this stronger word, which at once brings in his union with the death of Christ, besides his relation to the world) **to me** (**ἐμοί**, dative of ethical relation: so μόνῳ Μαικήνᾳ καθεύδω, Plut Erot p 760 A · see other examples in Bernhardy, p 85), **and I to the world.** Ellic. quotes from Schott., 'alter pro mortuo habet alterum' 15.] See ch. v. 6. *Confirmation of last verse* · so far are such things from me as a ground of boasting, that they are *nothing* the new birth by the Spirit is all in all **κτίσις** (see note on 2 Cor. v. 17), **creation:** and therefore the result, as regards an individual, is, that he is **a new creature:** so that the word comes to be used in both significations 16.] **And as many** (reference to the ὅσοι of ver. 12; and in κανόνι to the εὐπροσωπ and πηλίκοις γράμμ ? see above) **as shall walk by this rule** (of ver 15 κανών is a 'straight rule,' to detect crookedness hence a *norma vivendi* The dative is *normal*), **peace be** (not '*is*.' it is the apostolic blessing,

εἰρήνη [x] ἐπ' αὐτοὺς καὶ ἔλεος, [y] καὶ [x] ἐπὶ τὸν [z] Ἰσραὴλ ABCDF KLℵ a b
τοῦ θεοῦ. 17 [a] τοῦ λοιποῦ [b] κόπους μοι μηδεὶς [b] παρεχέτω· c d e f g
ἐγὼ γὰρ τὰ [c] στίγματα τοῦ Ἰησοῦ ἐν τῷ σώματί μου h k l m
[d] βαστάζω. n o 17
18 Ἡ χάρις τοῦ κυρίου ἡμῶν Ἰησοῦ χριστοῦ μετὰ τοῦ
[e] πνεύματος ὑμῶν, ἀδελφοί. ἀμήν.

ΠΡΟΣ ΓΑΛΑΤΑΣ. ...C.

x = Rom. ii. 9, 6. y = 1 Cor. iii. 5. viii. 12. xv. 38. z = Rom. ix. 6. a gen. of time, John iii. 2. χειμῶνος, Thuc. iii. 104, & passim. b Matt. xxvi. 10 || Mk. Luke xviii. 5. Sir. xxix. 4. c here only. Cant. i. 11 only. d = (1) ver. 2. Rom. xi. 18. xv. 1. or (2) Acts ix. 15. εἰκόνα θεοῦ βαστάζειν, Clem. Rom. (Coteler. i. 692—Ellic.) e Phil. iv. 23. 2 Tim. iv. 22. Philem. 25.

txt BC²KLℵ rel vulg(and F-lat) Chr Thdrt Hil Bede. om 3rd και D³. for θεου, κυριου D¹F (G-lat has both).

17. το λοιπον D¹. μηδεις μοι κοπους D. rec ins κυριου bef ιησου, with C³D³KL rel vulg D-lat syrr goth æth-pl: του χρ. Euthal-ms al: τ. κυ ιυ χυ ℵ: του κυρ. ημων ιησ. χρ. D¹F: alii aliter: txt ABC¹ 17 am(with demid F-lat) Petr-alex Dial Euthal Epiph.

18. om ημων ℵ m. om αμην G Victorin Ambrst.

Subscription. rec adds εγραφη απο ρωμης, with B²K(L) rel syrr copt Thdrt Euthal Jer, απο εφεσου Thl₁ (Ec: some add δια τιτου, or δια τιτ. κ. λουκα, or δια τυχικου: δια χειρος παυλου al₁: l has no subscr: τελος της επ. πρ. γαλ. L (d): txt AB¹C¹ℵ(adding στιχ τιβ') 17, and D(addg επληρωθη) F(prefixing ετελεσθη).

so common in the *beginnings* of his Epistles: see also Eph. vi. 23) **upon them** (come on them from God; reff, and Luke ii. 25, 40 al. freq.) **and** (and indeed, 'und zwar:' the καί explicative, as it is called: see reff.) **upon the Israel of God** (the subject of the whole Epistle seems to have given rise to this expression. Not the Israel after the flesh, among whom these teachers wish to enrol you, are blessed: but the Israel of God, described ch. iii. ult., εἰ δὲ ὑμεῖς χριστοῦ, ἄρα τοῦ Ἀβραὰμ σπέρμα ἐστέ. Jowett compares, though not exactly parallel, yet for a similar apparent though not actual distinction, 1 Cor. x. 32). 17.] **τοῦ λοιποῦ**, as E. V., **henceforth**: scil., χρόνου. So Herod. iii. 15, ἔνθα τοῦ λοιποῦ διαιτᾶτο:—see numerous other examples in Wetstein. "**τὸ λοιπόν** continuum et perpetuum tempus significat, ut apud Xen. Cyr. viii. 5. 24; **τοῦ λοιποῦ** autem repetitionem ejusdem facti reliquo tempore indicat, ut apud Aristoph. in Pace, v. 1684 [1050 Bekk.]." Hermann ad Viger., p. 706. But the above example from Herod. hardly seems to bear this out. Rather is a thing happening in time regarded as *belonging* to the period including it, and the genitive is one of possession. Against this Ellic., viewing the gen. as simply partitive, refers to Donalds. Gram. § 451: who however defines his meaning by saying "partitive, or, what is the same thing, possessive." This indeed must be the clear and only account of a partitive genitive. **κόπ. παρεχ.**] How? Thdrt. (hardly Chrys.), al., understand it of the trouble of writing more epistles—οὐκέτι, φησί, γράψαι τι πάλιν ἀνέξομαι· ἀντὶ δὲ γραμμάτων τοὺς μώλωπας δείκνυμι, κ. τῶν αἰκισμῶν τὰ σημεῖα. But it seems much more natural to take it of giving him trouble by rebellious conduct and denying his apostolic authority, seeing that it was stamped with so powerful a seal as he proceeds to state. **ἐγὼ γάρ**] **for it is I** (not the Judaizing teachers) **who carry** (perhaps as in ver. 5, and ch. v. 10,—bear, as a burden: but Chrys.'s idea seems more adapted to the 'feierlich' character of the sentence: οὐκ εἶπεν, ἔχω, ἀλλά, βαστάζω, ὥσπερ τις ἐπὶ τροπαίοις μέγα φρονῶν ἢ σημείοις βασιλικοῖς: see reff. [2]) **in** (on) **my body the marks of Jesus.** **τὰ στίγματα,**—the marks branded on slaves to indicate their owners. So Herod. vii. 233, τοὺς πλεῦνας αὐτέων, κελεύσαντος Ξέρξεω, ἔστιζον στίγματα βασιλήϊα: and in another place (ii. 113) is a passage singularly in point: ὅτεῳ ἀνθρώπων ἐπιβάληται στίγματα ἱρά, ἑωυτὸν διδοὺς τῷ θεῷ, οὐκ ἔξεστι τούτου ἅψασθαι. See many more examples in Wetst. These marks, in St. Paul's case, were of course the *scars of his wounds received in the service of his Master*—cf. 2 Cor. xi. 23 ff. **Ἰησοῦ** is the genitive of possession,—answering to the possessive βασιλήϊα in the extract above There is no allusion whatever to any similarity between himself and our Lord, 'the marks which Jesus bore,' such an allusion would be quite irrelevant and with its irrelevancy falls a whole fabric of Romanist superstition which has been raised on this verse, and which the fair and learned Windischmann, giving as he does the honest interpretation here, yet attempts to defend in a supplemental note. Neither can we naturally suppose any comparison intended between these his στίγματα as Christ's servant, and *circumcision* · for he is not now on that subject, but on his *authority as sealed by Christ* · and such a comparison is alien from the majesty of the sentence 18.] THE APOSTOLIC BLESSING. No special intention need be suspected in πνεύματος (ἀπάγων αὐτοὺς τῶν σαρκικῶν, Chrys.), as the same expression occurs at the end of other Epistles (reff). I should rather regard it as a deep expression of his Christian love, which is further carried on by ἀδελφοί, the last word,—parting from them, after an Epistle of such rebuke and warning, in the fulness of brotherhood in Christ.

ΠΡΟΣ ΕΦΕΣΙΟΥΣ.

a Rom. xv. 32. 1 Cor. i. 1. 2 Cor. i. 1. viii. 5. Col. i. 1. 2 Tim. i. 1 only.

I. 1 Παῦλος ἀπόστολος χριστοῦ Ἰησοῦ [a] διὰ θελήματος ABDF
θεοῦ, τοῖς [b] ἁγίοις τοῖς οὖσιν [ἐν Ἐφέσῳ] καὶ [c] πιστοῖς ἐν KLℵ a b c d e f g h k l m n o 17

b = Acts ix. 13, 32, 41. Rom. i. 7 al. fr. Dan. vii. 18. c = Acts x. 45. 1 Tim. v. 16. Rev. xvii. 14. Wisd. iii. 9.

TITLE. elz παυλου του αποστολου η προς εφεσιους επιστολη: Steph προς εφεσιους επιστολη παυλου, with al: προς εφ. επ. του αγιου αποστολου παυλου h: του αγ. απ. π. επιστ. πρ. εφ. L: τοις εφεσιοις μυσταις ταυτα διδασκαλος εσθλος f: αρχεται προς εφεσιους DF: *incipit epistula ad ephesios* am: πρ. εφ. επ. k.: επ. πρ. εφ. l: txt ABKℵ m n o 17.

CHAP. I. 1. rec ιησ. bef χρ., with AFKLℵ rel vulg-ed(with fuld F-lat) Syr gr-lat-ff: txt BD 17 am syr copt goth Orig-cat Damasc Ambrst. aft αγιοις ins πασιν Aℵ[3] vulg copt Cyr Jer-txt. om 2nd τοις D. om εν εφεσω B[1]ℵ[1] 67[2]. (supplied in margin B[1][? see table][2], so also ℵ[3].) Basil says, οὕτω γὰρ καὶ οἱ πρὸ ἡμῶν παραδεδώκασι καὶ ἡμεῖς ἐν τοῖς παλαιοῖς τῶν ἀντιγράφων εὑρήκαμεν: Marcion is accused by Tert of inserting *ad Laodicenos*, and so does not seem to have read εν εφ. here. Also Tert and Jerome seem to have found it omd in other MSS. "quidam . . . putant . . . eos qui Ephesi sunt sancti et fideles essentiæ vocabulo nuncupatos ut . . . ab Eo qui EST, hi qui SUNT appellentur . . . Alii vero simpliciter non ad eos qui sint(*al* sunt), sed qui Ephesi sancti et fideles sint, scriptum arbitrantur." Jerome ad Eph. i. 1, vol. vii. p. 545. (*See prolegomena*, § ii. 17 a.)

CHAP. I. 1, 2.] ADDRESS AND GREETING. 1.] **χρ. Ἰησ.**, as in the case of δοῦλος Ἰησ. χρ., seems rather to denote possession, than to belong to ἀπόστολος and designate the person from whom sent. **διὰ θελ. θεοῦ**] See on 1 Cor. i. 1. As these words there have a special reference, and the corresponding ones in Gal. i. 1 also, so it is natural to suppose that here he has in his mind, hardly perhaps the especial subject of vv. 3–11, the will of the Father as the ground of the election of the church, but, which is more likely in a general introduction to the whole Epistle, the great subject of which he is about to treat, and himself as the authorized expositor of it. **τ. οὖσιν ἐν Ἐφ.**] On this, and on Ephesus, see Prolegomena. On ἁγίοις, see Ellicott's note. It is used here in its widest sense, as designating the members of Christ's visible Church, presumed to fulfil the conditions of that membership: cf. especially ch. v. 3. **καὶ πιστοῖς ἐν χ. Ἰ.**] These words follow rather unusually, separated from τ. ἁγ. by the designation of abode: a circumstance which might seem to strengthen the suspicion against ἐν Ἐφέσῳ, were not such transpositions by no means unexampled in St. Paul. See the regular order in Col. i. 2. The omission of the article before **πιστ.** shews that the *same persons* are designated by *both* adjectives. Its insertion would not, however, prove the contrary. **ἐν χρ. Ἰησ.** belongs only to πιστοῖς: see Col. i. 2: **faithful**, i. e. **believers, in** (but ἐν does not belong to πιστός, as it often does to πιστεύω: see also Col. i. 4)

χριστῷ Ἰησοῦ. 2 [d] χάρις ὑμῖν καὶ εἰρήνη ἀπὸ θεοῦ
πατρὸς ἡμῶν καὶ κυρίου Ἰησοῦ χριστοῦ.
3 [e] Εὐλογητὸς ὁ θεὸς καὶ πατὴρ τοῦ κυρίου ἡμῶν
Ἰησοῦ χριστοῦ, ὁ [f] εὐλογήσας ἡμᾶς [g] ἐν πάσῃ [h] εὐλογίᾳ

d Gal i 3 al. e Mark xiv 61 Luke i 68 Rom i 5 ix 5 2 Cor i 3 xi 31 1 Pet i 3 only Gen ix 26 f = Acts iii 26 Gal iii 9 Heb vi 14 al Gen xxii 17 g constr, here only see James iii 9 h = Rom xv 29 Heb vi 7 Ps xxiii 5

2 χρ bef ιησ. B
3 om και πατηρ B. aft κυριου ins και σωτηρος (*completing the familiar phrase* · *see* 2 *Pet* i. 11, ii. 20, iii 2) א¹(א³ disapproving) om ημας א¹ · ins א-corr¹

Christ Jesus. This, in its highest sense, '*qui fidem præstant*,' not mere *truth*, or *faithfulness*, is imported · see reff The ἁγίοις and πιστοῖς denote their spiritual life from its two sides—that of God who calls and sanctifies,—that of themselves who believe So Bengel, 'Dei est, sanctificare nos et sibi asserere; nostrum, ex Dei munere, credere' Stier remarks that by πιστ ἐν χ Ἰ.,—ἁγίοις gets its only full and N T. meaning. He also notices in these expressions already a trace of the two great divisions of the Epistle—God's grace towards us, and our faith towards Him **2.**] After **χάρις ὑμ. κ εἰρ** supply rather εἴη than ἔστω, see 1 Pet. i. 2, 2 Pet. i. 2, Jude 2 On the form of greeting, cf Rom. i 7; 1 Cor. i. 3, 2 Cor. i. 2, Gal. i. 3, &c. The Socinian perversion of the words, '*from God, who is the Father of us and of our Lord Jesus Christ*,' is decisively refuted by Tit. i 4, not to mention that nothing but the grossest ignorance of St Paul's spirit could ever allow such a meaning to be thought of We must not fall into the error of refining too much, as Stier, on χάρις and εἰρήνη, as referring respectively to ἁγίοις and πιστοῖς see || above, where these last epithets do not occur

3—III 21] **FIRST PORTION OF THE EPISTLE · THE DOCTRINE OF THE CHURCH OF CHRIST** And herein, I **3—23**] GROUND AND ORIGIN OF THE CHURCH, IN THE FATHER'S COUNSEL, AND HIS ACT IN CHRIST, BY THE SPIRIT And herein again, (A) *the preliminary* IDEA OF THE CHURCH, *set forth in the form of an ascription of praise* vv 3—11·—thus arranged·—vv 3—6] The FATHER, in His eternal Love, has *chosen us to holiness* (ver 4),—*ordained us to sonship* (ver. 5),—*bestowed grace on us in the Beloved* (ver. 6)·—vv. 7—12] In the SON, we have,—*redemption according to the riches of His grace* (ver. 7), *knowledge of the mystery of His will* (vv 8, 9),—*inheritance under Him the one Head* (vv 10—12)·—vv. 13, 14] through the SPIRIT we are *sealed*,—by *hearing the word of salvation* (ver. 13),—by *receiving the earnest of our inheritance* (ver. 14),—to the *redemption of the purchased possession* (ib).

3] **Blessed** (see note on Rom ix 5 Understand εἴη (Job i 21, Ps cxii. 2, or ἔστω, 2 Chron. ix. 8 Ellicott)—'Be He praised' See a similar doxology, 2 Cor i 3 Almost all St. Paul's Epistles begin with some ascription of praise. That to Titus is the only exception [not Gal cf Gal. i. 5] See also 1 Pet i. 3) **be the God and Father of our Lord Jesus Christ** (cf Rom. xv. 6, 2 Cor i 3; xi. 31, Col i. 3—also 1 Cor. xv. 24. Such is the simplest and most forcible sense of the words—as Thl, ἰδοὺ κ θεὸς κ πατὴρ τοῦ αὐτοῦ κ ἑνὸς χριστοῦ θεὸς μέν, ὡς σαρκωθέντος· πατὴρ δέ, ὡς θεοῦ λόγου. See John xx. 17, from which saying of our Lord it is not improbable that the expression took its rise. Meyer maintains, 'God who is also the Father of . ' on the ground that only πατήρ, not θεός, requires a genitive supplied But we may fairly reply that, if we come to strictness of construction, his meaning would require ὁ θεός, ὁ καὶ πατήρ Harless's objection, that on our rendering it must be ὁ θεός τε καὶ π, is well answered by Meyer from 1 Pet ii 25, τὸν ποιμένα κ. ἐπίσκοπον τῶν ψυχῶν ἡμῶν Ellicott prefers Meyer's view, but pronounces the other both grammatically and doctrinally tenable), **who blessed** (aor not '*hath* blessed·' the historical fact in the counsels of the Father being thought of throughout the sentence. εὐλογητός—εὐλογήσας —— εὐλογία—such was the ground-tone of the new covenant As in creation God blessed them, saying, 'Be fruitful and multiply,'—so in redemption,—at the introduction of the covenant, "all families of the earth shall be BLESSED,"—at its completion,—"Come ye BLESSED of my Father" But *God's* blessing is in *facts*—ours in words only) **us** (whom? not the Apostle only · nor Paul and his fellow-Apostles —but, ALL CHRISTIANS—all the members of Christ. The καὶ ὑμεῖς of ver. 13 perfectly agrees with this see there · but the κἀγώ of ver 15 does not agree with the other views) **in** (instrumental or medial, the element in

[l] πνευματικῇ ἐν τοῖς [k] ἐπουρανίοις [l] ἐν χριστῷ, 4 καθὼς
[m] ἐξελέξατο ἡμᾶς [l] ἐν αὐτῷ [n] πρὸ [n] καταβολῆς κόσμου,

ABDF KLℵab cdefg hklm no17

i = Rom i 11 1 Cor ix 11 Col i 9 1 Pet. ii 5+ k = ver 20 ch ii 6. iii 10 vi 12 only 2 Macc. iii 39 (Matt xviii 35 al fr Ps. lxvii 14 only Dan iv 23 Theod, Compl Ald Cod Alex (F vat οὐραν.)) l = Col i 16 reff see Acts xv 7. m Mark xiii 20 John vi. 70 xiii 18 al (1 Cor i 27 bis, 28. James ii 5 only in e p) Deut vii 7. n John xvii 24 1 Pet i 20 only απο, Matt xiii 35 al κατ, 2 Macc ii 29 only †

υμας c d. aft χριστω ins ιησου D[2 3] syr æth Thl
4 for εν αυτω, εαυτω F Did

which, and means by which, the blessing is imparted) all (i e all possible—all, exhaustive, in all richness and fulness of blessing cf. ver 23 note) **blessing of the Spirit** (not merely, '*spiritual* [inward] *blessing*' πνευματικός in the N T. always implies the working of the Holy Spirit, never bearing merely our modern inaccurate sense of spiritual as opposed to bodily. See 1 Cor. ix 11, which has been thus misunderstood) **in the heavenly places** (so the expression, which occurs five times in this Epistle [see reff], and nowhere else, can only mean · cf. ver 20 It is not probable that St Paul should have chosen an unusual expression for the purposes of this Epistle, and then used it in several different senses. Besides, as Harless remarks, the preposition ἐπί in composition with adjectives gives usually a local sense e g. in ἐπίγειος, ἐπιχθόνιος, ἐπουράνιος, as compared with γήϊνος, χθόνιος, οὐράνιος. Chrys., al., would understand it '*heavenly blessings*,' in which case the Apostle would hardly have failed to add χαρίσμασιν, or ἀγαθοῖς, or the like.
But, with the above rendering, *what is the sense?* Our country, πολίτευμα, is *in heaven*, Phil iii 20 · there our High Priest stands, blessing us. There are our treasures, Matt. vi 20, 21, and our affections to be, Col. iii. 1 ff.. there our hope is laid up, Col i. 5 our inheritance is reserved for us, 1 Pet i 4. And there, in that place, and belonging to that state, is the εὐλογία, the gift of the Spirit, Heb. vi 4, poured out on those who τὰ ἄνω φρονοῦσιν Materially, we are yet in the body · but in the Spirit, we are in heaven —only waiting for the redemption of the body to be entirely and literally there.
I may once for all premise, that it will be impossible, in the limits of these notes, to give even a synopsis of the various opinions on the rich fulness of doctrinal expressions in this Epistle I must state in each case that which appears to me best to suit the context, and those variations which must *necessarily* be mentioned, referring to such copious commentaries as Harless or Stier for further statement) **in Christ** ("the threefold ἐν after εὐλογήσας, has a meaning ever deeper and more precise: and should therefore be kept in translating. The blessing with which God has blessed us, consists and expands itself in all *blessing of the Spirit*—then brings in *Heaven*, the heavenly state in us, and us in it—then finally, CHRIST, *personally*, He Himself, who is set and exalted into Heaven, comes by the Spirit down into us, so that He is in us and we in Him of a truth, and thereby, and in so far, we are with Him in heaven" Stier). 4.] **According as** (καθώς explains and expands the foregoing—shewing wherein the εὐλογία consists as regards us, and God's working towards us Notice, that whereas ver 3 has summarily included in the work of blessing the Three Persons, the FATHER bestowing the SPIRIT in CHRIST,—now the threefold cord, so to speak, is unwrapped, and the part of each divine Person separately described cf argument above) **He selected us** (reff I render *selected*, in preference to *elected*, as better giving the middle sense,—'chose for himself,'—and the ἐξ, that it is a choosing *out of* the world The word [ref. Deut.] is an O. T word, and refers to the spiritual Israel, as it did to God's elect Israel of old. But there is no *contrast* between their election and ours it has been but one election throughout—an election in Christ, and to holiness on God's side—and involving accession to God's people [cf πιστεύσαντες, ver 13, and εἴγε ἐπιμένετε τῇ πίστει, Col. i. 23] on ours. See Ellicott's note on the word, and some excellent remarks in Stier, p 62, on the divine and human sides of the doctrine of election as put forward in this Epistle) **in Him** (i. e. in Christ, as the second Adam [1 Cor. xv 22], the righteous Head of our race. In Him, in one wide sense, were all mankind elected, inasmuch as He took their flesh and blood, and redeemed them, and represents them before the Father. but in the proper and final sense, this can be said only of His faithful ones, His Church, who are incorporated in Him by the Spirit But in any sense, all God's election is *in* Him only) **before the foundation of the world** (πρὸ κατ κ only here in St. Paul we have ἀπὸ κατ. κ. in Heb iv. 3, his expressions elsewhere are πρὸ

[o] εἶναι ἡμᾶς ἁγίους καὶ [p] ἀμώμους [q] κατενώπιον αὐτοῦ ἐν

o constr, Col i 10, 22 p ch v 27 Col i 22 Phil ii 15. Heb ix 24 1 Pet i 19 Jude 24 Rev xiv 5 only 2 Kings xxii 24 q Col i 22 Jude 24 only (both times w ἀμωμ.) Josh xxi 42 (44) Levit iv 17 vat

τῶν αἰώνων, 1 Cor. ii 7,—ἀπὸ τ αἰ., Eph iii 9 Col i 26,—πρὸ χρόνων αἰωνίων, 2 Tim i 9,—χρόνοις αἰωνίοις, Rom xvi. 25,—ἀπ' ἀρχῆς, 2 Thess ii 13 Stier remarks on the necessary connexion of the true doctrines of creation and redemption how utterly irreconcileable pantheism is with this, God's election before laying the foundation of the world, of His people in His Son), **that we should be** (infinitive of the purpose, see Winer, edn. 3, p 267, § 45 3. [In edn 6, the treatment of the inf of the purpose without the art. τοῦ, seems to have been inadvertently omitted] The Apostle seems to have Deut. vii 6; xiv 2, before his mind, in both which places the same construction occurs) **holy and blameless** (the positive and negative sides of the Christian *character*—ἅγιοι, of the general positive category,—ἄμωμοι, of the non-existence of any exception to it So Plut Pericl., p 173 [Mey.], βίος καθαρὸς κ. ἀμίαντος. This holiness and unblameableness must not be understood of that justification by faith by which the sinner stands accepted before God · it is distinctly put forth here [see also ch v 27] as an ultimate *result* as regards us, and refers to that sanctification which follows on justification by faith, and which is the will of God respecting us, 1 Thess. iv. 7. See Stier's remarks against Harless, p 71) **before Him** (i e. in the deepest verity of our being—throughly penetrated by the Spirit of holiness, bearing His searching eye, ch. v 27 but at the same time implying an especial nearness to His presence and dearness to Him—and bearing a foretaste of the time when the elect shall be ἐνώπιον τοῦ θρόνου τοῦ θεοῦ, Rev vii. 15 Cf Col i. 22, note) **in love.** There is considerable dispute as to the position and reference of these words Three different ways are taken (1) Œcum, &c., join them with ἐξελέξατο. I do not see, with most Commentators, the extreme improbability of the qualifying clause following the verb after so long an interval, when we take into account the studied solemnity of the passage, and remember that ἐν χριστῷ in the last verse was separated nearly as far from its verb εὐλογήσας My objection to this view is of a deeper kind see below. (2) The Syr, Chrys, Thdrt, Thl, Bengel, Lachm, Harless, Olsh., Mey., De W., Stier, Ellic, all, join them with προορίσας in the following verse To this, in spite of all that has been so well said in its behalf, there is an objection which seems to me insuperable. It is, that in the whole construction of this long sentence, the verbs and participles, as natural in a solemn emphatic enumeration of God's *dealings* with His people, *precede* their qualifying clauses e. g. εὐλογήσας ver. 3, ἐξελέξατο ver. 4, ἐχαρίτωσεν ver. 6, ἐπερίσσευσεν ver. 8, γνωρίσας ver. 9, προέθετο ib, ἀνακεφαλαιώσασθαι ver 10. In no one case, except the necessary one of a *relative* qualification (ἧς ver 6, and again ver. 8), does the verb *follow* its qualifying clause. and for this reason, that the verbs themselves are emphatic, and not the conditions under which they subsist. "Blessed be God who DID all this, &c." He may have fore-ordained, and did fore-ordain, *in love* and this is implied in what follows, from κατὰ τ εὐδ to ἠγαπημένῳ but the point *brought out*, as that for which we are to bless Him, is not that *in love* He fore-ordained us, but the *fact* of *that fore-ordination itself* not His attribute, but His act It is evidently no answer to this, to bring forward sentences elsewhere in which ἐν ἀγάπῃ stands first, such as ch iii 18, where the spirit of the passage is different. (3) The vulg, Ambrst, Erasm, Luth, Castal, Beza, Calvin, Grot, all, join them, as in the text, with εἶναι . . ἀμώμους κατ. αὐτοῦ This has been strongly impugned by the last-mentioned set of Commentators mainly on the ground that the addition of ἐν ἀγάπῃ to ἁγ κ ἀμώμ κατ αὐτοῦ, is ungrammatical,—is flat and superfluous,—and that in neither ch v. 27, nor Col i 22, have these adjectives any such qualification But in answer, I would submit, that in the first place, as against the *construction* of ἐν ἀγ with ἀμώμ, the objection is quite futile, for our arrangement does not thus construct it, but adds it as a qualifying clause to the whole εἶναι . . . . αὐτοῦ. Next, I hold the qualification to be in the highest degree solemn and appropriate ἀγάπη, that which man lost at the Fall, but which God is, and to which God restores man by redemption, is the great element in which, as in their abode and breathing-place, all Christian graces subsist, and in which, emphatically, all perfection before God must be found. And so, when the Apostle, ch iv 16, is describing the glorious building up of the body, the Church,

r ver. 11 reff. s Rom. viii. 15, 23. ix. 4. Gal. iv. 5 only†. t = Col. i. 20.

ἀγάπῃ,
5 [t] προορίσας ἡμᾶς εἰς [s] υἱοθεσίαν διὰ Ἰησοῦ
χριστοῦ [t] εἰς αὐτόν, κατὰ τὴν [u] εὐδοκίαν τοῦ θελήματος

ABDF KLℵ a b c d e f g h k l m n o 17

u Matt. xi. 26. Luke ii. 14. x. 21. Phil. i. 15. ii 13. 2 Thess. i. 11. Ps. v. 12.

5. προωρισας D[1], προωρησας d. (simly D[1] d m in ver 11.) χριστου bef ιησου B: om χρ. e.

he speaks of its increasing εἰς οἰκοδομὴν ἑαυτοῦ ἐν ἀγάπῃ. And it his practice, in this and the parallel Epistle, to add ἐν ἀγάπῃ as the completion of the idea of Christian holiness—cf. ch. iii. 18; Col. ii. 2, also ch. iv. 2; v. 2. With regard to the last objection,—in both the places cited, the adjectives are connected with the verb παραστῆσαι, expressed therefore in the abstract as the ultimate result of sanctification in the sight of the Father, not, as here, referring to the *state* of sanctification, as consisting and subsisting in love. 5.] **Having predestined us** (subordinate to the ἐξελέξατο: see Rom. viii. 29, 30, where the steps are thus laid down in succession;—οὓς προέγνω, καὶ προώρισεν—οὓς προώρισεν, τούτους καὶ ἐκάλεσεν. Now the ἐκλογή must answer in this rank to the προέγνω, and precede the προώρισεν. Stier remarks well, "In God, indeed, all is one; but for our anthropomorphic way of speaking and treating, which is necessary to us, there follows on His first decree to adopt and to sanctify, the nearer decision, how and by what this shall be brought about, because it *could* only thus be brought about." προ,—as Pelagius [in Harless],—"ad eos refertur qui antea non fuerunt, et priusquam fierent, de his cogitatum est et postea substiterunt") **unto adoption** (so that we should become His sons, in the blessed sense of being reconciled to Him and having a place in His spiritual family,—should have the remission of our sins, the pledge of the Spirit, the assurance of the inheritance) **through Jesus Christ** (THE SON of God, in and by whom, elementally and instrumentally, our adoption consists, cf. Rom. viii. 29, προώρισεν συμμόρφους τῆς εἰκόνος τ. υἱοῦ αὐτοῦ, εἰς τὸ εἶναι αὐτὸν πρωτότοκον ἐν πολλοῖς ἀδελφοῖς) **to Him** (the Father: see Col. i. 20, δι' αὐτοῦ [Christ] ἀποκαταλλάξαι τὰ πάντα εἰς αὐτόν [the Father]. So Thdrt., all., Harl., Olsh., Meyer, Stier: and rightly, for the Son could not be in this sentence the *terminus ultimus* [the whole reference being to the work and purpose of the Father]; and had this been intended, as Harl. remarks, we must have had καὶ εἰς αὐτόν. De W., who, after Anselm, Tho.-Aq., Castal., all., refers it to the Son, fails to answer this objection of Harl.'s. But now arise two questions: (1) the meaning. Does it merely represent ἑαυτῷ, a dativus commodi? So Grot., al., but it cannot be, after the insertion of the *special* διὰ 'Ι. χ., that the sentence should again return to the general purpose. It seems much better, to join it with διὰ 'Ι. χ. as in Col. i. 20, above: and so Harl., but too indefinitely, taking it only as a phrase common with the Apostle and not giving its full import. As in Col. i. 20, the εἰς αὐτόν, though thus intimately connected with δι' αὐτοῦ, depends on ἀποκαταλλάξαι, so here it must depend on υἱοθεσίαν, and its import must be '*to* [*into*] *Himself*,'—i. e. so that we should be partakers of the divine nature: cf. 2 Pet. i. 4. (2) Should we read αὐτόν or αὑτόν? It will depend on whether we refer this clause, from διά to κατά, to the Father as its subject, or consider it as a continuation of the Apostle's thanksgiving. And the latter is much the most likely; for had the former been the case, we should probably have had, instead of διὰ 'Ιησ. χριστοῦ, διὰ τοῦ υἱοῦ αὐτοῦ 'Ι. χρ., so that reference to the Father might still be kept up. I decide therefore for αὐτόν, as Thdrt. certainly read, or his remark, τὸ δὲ εἰς αὐτόν, τὸν πατέρα λέγει, would have been needless. And so Erasm., Wetst., Lachm., Harl., Olsh., Meyer. Then αὐτοῦ in ver. 6 naturally takes it up again) **according to** (in pursuance of) **the good pleasure** (it is disputed whether εὐδοκία has here merely this general meaning of *beneplacitum*, or that of *benevolentia*. Harl. [see also Ellicott] examines thoroughly the use of the word by the LXX, and decides in favour of the *latter*, alleging especially, that a mere assertion of doctrine would be out of place in an ascription of thanksgiving. But surely this is a most unfortunate position. The facts on which doctrines rest are here the very subjects of the Apostle's thanksgiving: and the strict parallels of Matt. xi. 26, Luke x. 21, should have kept him from adducing it. Granting, as we must, *both senses* to εὐδοκεῖν and εὐδοκία, the context must in each case determine which is meant. And its testimony here is clear. It is, as De W. remarks, not in προωρισμένοι, but in προορίσας, that the object, to which εὐδοκία refers, is to be sought: and the subsequent recurrences to the same idea in ver. 9 and ver. 11 point out that it is not the Father's

αὐτοῦ, 6 εἰς ᵛ ἔπαινον ʷ δόξης τῆς χάριτος αὐτοῦ, ˣ ἧς
ʸ ἐχαρίτωσεν ἡμᾶς ᶻ ἐν τῷ ἠγαπημένῳ, 7 ᵃ ἐν ᾧ ἔχομεν

v Phil i 11 1 Pet i 7 Sir xxxix 10 Col i 27 see Ps cxliv 12. w = ver 18. x constr, 2 Cor i 4 ch iv 1 Winer, § 24 1. y Luke i 28 only † Sir xviii 17 only Ps xvii 25 Symm. z vv 3, 4 reff. a Col i 14 1 Cor i 30.

6. ins της bef δοξης D rec (for ἧς) εν η, with DFKLℵ[3] rel latt syr goth arm Bas Chr$_{h\,l}$ Thdrt Damasc Jer Aug. txt ABℵ[1] 17. 67[2] Syr æth Orig-cat Chr$_1$ η Thl Ambrst. aft ηγαπημενω ins υιω αυτου (*explanatory addition*) D[1]F vulg(but not am al) syr-w-ast goth æth Dial lat-mss-in-Jer Aug Oros Ambrst Pelag

7. εσχομεν D[1](not D lat) ℵ[1] copt (*accepimus*)Iren-int.

benevolentia, but His *beneplacitum*, which is in the Apostle's mind And so Meyer, De W., Stier, and Ellic This *beneplacitum* WAS *benevolentia*, ver 6; but that does not affect the question. See, besides Harl, a long note in Fritz on Romans ii p. 369) **of His will,** 6] **to** (with a view to, as the purpose of the predestination) **the praise** (by men and angels—all that can praise) **of the glory of His grace** (beware of the miserable hendiadys, '*His glorious grace*,' by which all the richness and depth of meaning are lost. The end, God's end, in our predestination to adoption, is, that the glory,—glorious nature, brightness and majesty, and kindliness and beauty,—of His grace might be an object of men and angels' praise both as it is in HIM, ineffable and infinite,—and exemplified in *us*, its objects, see below, ver. 12. "Owing to the defining genitive, the article (before δόξης) is not indispensable: see Winer, edn 6, § 19. 2, b · compare Madvig, Synt. § 10. 2." Ellic) **which** (there is some difficulty in deciding between the readings, ἐν ᾗ, and ἧς. The former would be the most naturally substituted for an attraction found difficult and the existence of ᾗ, as a reading, seems to point this way The latter, on the other hand, might perhaps be written by a transcriber carelessly, χάριτος having just preceded But I own this does not seem to me very probable A relative following a substantive, is as often in a different case, as in the same and there could be no temptation to a transcriber to write ἧς here, which could hardly occur at all unless by attraction, a construction to which transcribers certainly were not prone I therefore, with Lachm, Mey., Rück, al, adopt ἧς Considerations of the exigencies of the sense, alleged by Harl, al, do not come into play unless where external authorities are balanced [which *is* the case here], and probabilities of alteration also [which *is not*]) **He bestowed upon us** (the meaning of χαριτόω is disputed The double meaning of χάρις,—*favour*, *grace bestowed*, and *that which ensures favour*, viz *grace inherent*, *beauty*,—has been supposed to give a double meaning to the verb also,—to *confer grace*, and to *render gracious*, or *beautiful*, or *acceptable* And this latter sense is adopted, here and in Luke i. 28 [where see note], by many,—e g by Chrys, τουτέστιν, οὐ μόνον ἁμαρτημάτων ἀπήλλαξεν, ἀλλὰ καὶ ἐπεράστους ἐποίησε,—Erasm, Luth, all. But the meaning of χάρις, on which this is founded, does not seem to occur in the N T, certainly not in St Paul. And χαριτόω, both here and in l c, according to the analogy of such verbs, will be 'to bestow grace' Another reason for this sense is the indefinite aorist, referring to an act of God once past in Christ, not to an abiding state which He has brought about in us This, as usual, has been almost universally overlooked, and the perfect sense given Another still is, the requirement of the context Harl. well remarks, that, according to the sense '*bestowed grace*,' ver. 7 is the natural answer to the question, '*How* hath He bestowed grace?' whereas, on the other rendering, it has only a mediate connexion with this verse. Stier would unite both meanings, but surely this is impossible The becoming χαρίεντες may be a *consequence* of being κεχαριτωμένοι, but must be quite independent of its verbal meaning. Conyb. remarks that it may be literally rendered '*His favour, wherewith He favoured us*' but '*favour*' would not reach deep enough for the sense) **in** (see above on ἐν χριστῷ, ver 3. Christ is our Head and including Representative) **the Beloved** (i e Christ: = υἱὸς τῆς ἀγάπης αὐτοῦ, Col i. 13. He is God's ἠγαπημένος κατ' ἐξοχήν,—cf Matt iii. 17, John iii. 16, 1 John iv 9—11). 7] Now the Apostle passes, with ἐν ᾧ, to the consideration of *the ground of the church in the* SON (7—12) see the synopsis above But the Father still continues the great subject of the whole,—only the *reference* is now to the Son **In whom** (see on ἐν χρ ver 3—cf. Rom iii. 24) **we have** (objective—'*there is for us*' But

τὴν ^b ἀπολύτρωσιν διὰ τοῦ αἵματος αὐτοῦ, τὴν ^c ἄφεσιν
τῶν ^c παραπτωμάτων, κατὰ τὸ ^d πλοῦτος τῆς χάριτος
αὐτοῦ, 8 ^e ἧς ^f ἐπερίσσευσεν εἰς ἡμᾶς ^g ἐν πάσῃ σοφίᾳ καὶ

ABDF KLℵ a b c d e f g h k l m n o 17

b Luke xxi 28. Rom iii 24 1 Cor i 30 Col i 14 Heb ix 15 xi 35 Dan ii 32 (LXX) only (-τρουν, Exod xxi 8 Zeph iii 1 see also Ps lxviii 18 Isa lxiii 4) c here only see Col i 14. παρ Gal vi 1 reff d neut, ch ii 7 iii 8, 16 Phil iv 19 Col i 27 ii 2 e attr, ver 6 reff f trans, 2 Cor iv 15 ix 8 (a) 1 Thess iii 12 only † g = ver 17 Col i 9, 28

rec τον πλουτον, with D³KLℵ³ rel Orig-cat Cyr-jer Cyr: txt ABD¹(F)ℵ¹ 67².—το πληθος 17. for χαριτος, χρηστοτητος A copt

not without a subjective implied import, as spoken of those who truly *have* it—have laid hold of it. "are ever needing and ever having it," Eadie) **the Redemption** (from God's wrath—or rather from that which brought us under God's wrath, the guilt and power of sin, Matt. i. 21. The article expresses notoriety—'of which we all know,'—'of which the law testified, and the prophets spoke') **through** (as the instrument·—a further fixing of the *ἐν ᾧ*) **His blood** (which was the price paid for that redemption, Acts xx 28; 1 Cor. vi 20, both the ultimate climax of His obedience for us, Phil ii 8, and, which is most in view here,—the *propitiation*, in our nature, for the sin of the world, Rom. iii 25, Col. i 20 It is a noteworthy observation of Harless here, that the choice of the word, the BLOOD of Christ, is of itself a testimony to the idea of *expiation* having been in the writer's mind Not the *death* of the victim, but its BLOOD, was the typical instrument of expiation And I may notice that in Phil ii. 8, where Christ's *obedience*, not His atonement, is spoken of, there is no mention of His shedding His Blood, only of the act of His Death), **the remission** (not "*overlooking*" [*πάρεσιν*]; see note on Rom. iii. 25) **of** (our) **transgressions** (explanation of *τ. ἀπολύτρωσιν* not to be limited, but extending to all riddance from the practice and consequences of our transgressions at least equipollent with *ἀπολύτρωσις*.—so Thdrt., *δι' ἐκείνου γὰρ τὰς τῶν ἁμαρτημάτων ἀποθέμενοι κηλῖδας, κ τῆς τοῦ τυράννου δουλείας ἀπαλλαγέντες, τοὺς τῆς εἰκόνος τῆς θείας ἀπελάβομεν χαρακτῆρας* This against Harless), **according to the riches** (Ellic. compares Plato, Euthyphr 12 A, *τρυφᾷς ὑπὸ πλούτου τῆς σοφίας*) **of His grace** (this alone would prevent *ἄφεσις* applying to merely the *forgiveness* of sins. As Passavant [in Stier], "We have in this grace not only redemption from misery and wrath, not only forgiveness,—but we find in it the liberty, the glory, the inheritance of the children of God,—the crown of eternal life cf 2 Cor viii 9"), 8] **which he shed abundantly** ('caused to abound' *ἀφθόνως ἐξέχεε*, Thl. · Thdrt has the same idea, *ἀναβλύζει γὰρ τὰς τοῦ ἐλέους πηγάς, κ τούτοις ἡμᾶς περικλύζει τοῖς ῥεύμασιν* The E V is wrong, '*wherein He hath abounded*' no such construction of attraction of a dative being found in the N. T. Calvin and Beza would take *ἧς* not as an attraction, but as the genitive after *ἐπερίσ* as in Luke xv 17, 'of which He was full, &c' But this does not agree well with the *γνωρίσας*, &c below As little can the '*quæ superabundavit*' of the Vulg. [and Syr.] stand the attraction of the nominative being scarcely possible, and this being still more inconsistent with *γνωρίσας*) **forth to us in all** (possible) **wisdom and prudence** (with E. V, De Wette, &c, I would refer these words to God On the other hand, Harless [with whom are Olsh, Stier, Ellic, al.] maintains, that neither *πάσῃ* nor *φρονήσει* will allow this "*πᾶς*," he says, "never = *summus*,—never betokens the *intension*, but only the *extension*, never the power, but the frequency,—and answers to our 'every,' i e all possible,—so that, when joined to abstracts, it presents them to us as concrete *πᾶσα δύναμις*, 'every power that we know of,' 'that exists,'—*πᾶσα ὑπομονή*, every kind of endurance that we know of,—*πᾶσα εὐσέβεια*, &c Now it is allowable enough, to put together all excellences of one species, and allege them as the motive of a human act, because we can conceive of *men* as wanting in any or all of them but not so with God, of whom the Apostle, and all of us, conceive as the Essence of all perfection. We may say of God, '*in Him is all wisdom*,' but not, '*He did this or that in all wisdom*'" "Again," he continues, "*φρόνησις* cannot be ascribed to God." And this he maintains,—not by adopting the view of Wolf, al, that it is *practical knowledge*, which suits neither the context nor usage,—nor that of Anselm, Bengel, al, that *σοφ* is '*de præsentibus*,' *φρον* '*de futuris*,'—but by understanding *σοφία* of the normal collective state of the spirit, with reference especially to the *intelligence*, which last is expressed accord-

[h] φρονήσει 9 [i] γνωρίσας ἡμῖν τὸ [j] μυστήριον τοῦ θελήματος αὐτοῦ, κατὰ τὴν [k] εὐδοκίαν αὐτοῦ, ἣν [l] προέθετο
[m] ἐν αὐτῷ 10 [n] εἰς [o] οἰκονομίαν τοῦ [p] πληρώματος τῶν [q] και-

h Luke i 17 only 3 Kings iii 28 iv 7, 9 Ezek xliv 23
i John xvii 26 ch iii 3, 5. vi 19 Col i 26 al
j Mark iv 11 Rom xi 25 xvi 25 1 Cor ii 7 Dan ii 39 al
k ver 5 reff
l Rom i 13 iii 25 only † Exod xl 4
m vv 3, 4 reff
n = Matt x 18
o ch iii 2, 9. Luke xvi 2, 3, 4 1 Cor ix 17 Col i 25 1 Tim i 4 only Isa xxii 19, 21 only
p = Gal iv 4 only
q see note, and Mark i 15 1 Thess v 1

9 γνωρισαι F latt goth Hil lat-ff (not Jer) om 2nd αυτου DF goth copt Tert Hil Victorin.

ing to its various sides, by the words so often found conjoined with σοφία,—σύνεσις, φρόνησις, γνῶσις. So that φρόνησις, as a one-sided result of σοφία, cannot be predicated of God, but only of men According to this then, ἐν πάσ σ. κ φρ. must refer to that *in the bestowal of which on us* He hath made His grace to abound, so that *we should thereby become* σοφοὶ κ φρόνιμοι:—as Olsh , ἵνα ἐν πάσῃ σοφίᾳ κ. φρονήσει περιπατῶμεν. Chrys. joins the words with γνωρίσας, understanding them, however, of *us*, not of God ἐν π σοφ. κ φρ., φησί, γνωρίσας ἡμ τὸ μ. τ θ αὐτ τουτέστι, σοφοὺς κ. φρονίμους ποιήσας τὴν ὄντως σοφίαν, τὴν ὄντως φρόνησιν But see, on such arrangement, the note on ἐν ἀγάπῃ ver. 4

Stier quotes from Passavant. 'In the living knowledge of the thoughts and ways of God we first get a sure and clear light upon ourselves and our ways, a light cast from above upon the import and aim of this our earthly life in the sight of God and His eternity. Here is the true wisdom of the heart, the true prudence of life." But against this view, De W alleges, (1) that φρόνησις can be as well predicated of God as γνῶσις, Rom. xi 33, and is actually thus predicated, Prov. iii. 19; Jer x. 12 LXX, of His *creative* wisdom, which is analogous to His *redemptive* wisdom. (2) that God's *absolute* wisdom is not here treated of, but His relative wisdom, as apparent in the use of means subservient to its end so that ἐν πάσῃ would mean 'in all wisdom thereto belonging,' as Jer 'Deus in omni sapientia sua atque prudentia, juxta quod consequi poterant, mysterium revelavit' And he compares ἡ πολυποίκιλος σοφία τ θ ch iii 10 These last arguments are weighty, as shewing the *legitimacy* of the application to God · but even beyond them is that which construction and usage furnish It would be hardly possible, did no other consideration intervene, to refer this ἐν π σ. κ φρ to other than the subject of the sentence,—cf ἧς ἐχαρ ἡμᾶς ἐν τῷ ἠγαπ above. I therefore decide [still, after reconsideration of Ellicott's note] for the application to God, not to us It was in His manifold wisdom and prudence, manifested in all ways possible for us, that He poured out His grace upon us: and this wisdom and prudence was especially exemplified in that which follows, the notification to us of His hidden will, &c In Col. i 9, the reference is clearly different see note there), **having made known** (γνωρίσας is explicative of ἐπερίσσευσεν, just as προορίσας is of ἐξελέξατο above:—'in that He made known.' This 'making known' is not merely the information of the understanding, but the revelation, in its fulness, to the heart) **to us** (not, the Apostles, but Christians in general, as throughout the passage) **the mystery** (reff. and Rom xvi 25. St. Paul ever represents the redemptive counsel of God as a mystery, i. e *a design hidden in His counsels*, until revealed to mankind in and by Christ So that his use of μυστήρ. has nothing in common, except the facts of concealment and revelation, with the mysteries of the heathen world, nor with any secret tradition over and above the gospel as revealed in the Scriptures All who vitally know that, i e. all the Christian church are the initiated and all who have the word, read or preached, *may vitally* know it Only the *world* without, the unbelieving, are the uninitiated) **of** (objective genitive, 'the material of which mystery was, &c') **His will** (that which He purposed), **according to His good pleasure** (belongs to γνωρίσας, and specifies it not to θελήμ [τοῦ κατὰ τ ε αὐ]: i. e. so that the revelation took place in a time and manner consonant to God's eternal pleasure—viz εἰς οἰκον., &c On εὐδοκ, see above ver. 5) **which He purposed** (reff) **in Himself** (ἐν αὐτῷ is read, and referred (1) to *Christ*, by Chrys and the ff, Anselm, Bengel, Luther, all. But this is impossible, because ἐν τῷ χριστῷ is introduced with the proper name below, which certainly would not occur on the *second* mention after ἐν αὐτῷ, in the same reference (2) to *the Father*, by Harless But this is equally impossible. For αὐτῷ to refer to the subject of the sentence, we must have the mind of the reader removed one step from that subject by an

r Rom xiii 9 only† Ps lxxi 20 Theod

ρῶν, ʳ ἀνακεφαλαιώσασθαι τὰ πάντα ἐν τῷ χριστῷ, τὰ

ABDF KLℵ a b c d e f g h k l m n o 17

10 for εις, κατα την A εις is written twice, but the first marked for erasure, by ℵ[1]. rec aft 2nd τα ins τε, with ℵ[3] m Epiph: om ABDFKLℵ[1] rel vss Eus Cyr

intermediate idea supervening, as in κατὰ τὴν εὐδοκίαν αὐτοῦ. Had this been κατὰ τ. πρόθεσιν αὐτοῦ, the reference would have been legitimate. But when, as here, no such idea intervenes,—ἣν προέθετο ἐν αὐτῷ—the subject is directly before the mind, and αὐτός, not being reflective but demonstrative, must point to some other person, who in this case can only be Christ Our only resource then is to read αὐτῷ) **in order to** (belongs to προέθετο, not to γνωρίσας Very many ancient Commentators and the Vulg. and E V., take εἰς wrongly as = ἐν, by which the whole sense is confused Hardly less confusing is the rendering of Erasm, Calv, Est, al, *usque ad tempus dispensationis*, thereby introducing into προέθετο the complex idea of *decreed and laid up*, instead of the simple one which the context requires) **the œconomy of the fulfilment of the seasons** (after long and careful search, I am unable to find a word which will express the full meaning of οἰκονομία The difficulty of doing so will be better seen below, after τὸ πλήρ τῶν καιρ has been dealt with This expression is by no means = τὸ πλ τοῦ χρόνου in Gal iv 4, nor to be *equalized* with it, as Harl attempts to do, by saying that many καιροί make up a χρόνος. The mistake which has misled almost all the Commentators here, and which as far as I know Stier has been the only one to expose, has been that of taking τ. πλ τῶν καιρῶν as a fixed terminus a quo, = the coming of Christ, as Gal iv 4,—whereas usage, and the sense, determine it to mean, the whole duration of the Gospel times, cf especially ch ii 7, ἐν τοῖς αἰῶσιν τοῖς ἐπερχομένοις. 1 Cor x 11, τὰ τέλη τῶν αἰώνων, and Luke xxi. 24, καιροὶ ἐθνῶν, Acts i 7, iii 19, 21; 1 Tim ii 6 Thus τ. πλ τ καιρῶν will mean, the filling up, completing, fulfilment, of the appointed seasons, carrying on during the Gospel dispensation. Now, belonging to, carried on during, this fulfilling of the periods or seasons, is the οἰκονομία here spoken of And, having regard to the derivation and usage of the word, it will mean, *the giving forth of the Gospel under God's providential arrangements* First and greatest of all, He is the οἰκονόμος: then, above all others, His divine Son and as proceeding from the Father and the Son, the Holy Spirit—and then in subordinate degrees, every one who οἰκονομίαν πεπίστευται, i. e all Christians, even to the lowest, as οἰκονόμοι ποικίλης χάριτος θεοῦ, 1 Pet. iv 10 So that our best rendering will be, **œconomy**, leaving the word to be explained in teaching The genitive καιρῶν is one of *belonging* or *appurtenance* as in κρίσις μεγάλης ἡμέρας, Jude 6), **to sum up** (the infinitive belongs to and specifies εὐδοκίαν,—ἣν . . καιρῶν having been logically parenthetical,—and explains what that εὐδοκία was. The verb, here as in the only other place in the N. T. where it occurs [ref], signifies *to comprehend, gather together, sum up*. As there the whole law is comprehended in one saying, so here all creation is comprehended, summed up, in Christ. But it can hardly be supposed that the ἀνακεφαλαιώσασθαι has express reference here to Him as the κεφαλή for 1) this is not predicated of Him till below, ver 22,—2) the verb is from κεφάλαιον, not from κεφαλή; so that such reference would be only a play on the word —3) the compound verb, as here, is used in Rom. l c in the simple ordinary sense The ἀνα- applies to the gathering of all individuals, not to any *restoration* [Syr, vulg, Olsh (Ellic in part), al.], in which τὰ ἐπὶ τοῖς οὐρανοῖς would have no share See more below and cf the ||, Col i 19, 20, and note there) **all things** (neuter, and to be literally so taken not as a masculine, which, when a neuter is so understood, must be implied in the context, as in Gal. iii 22:—*the whole creation*, see Col i 20) **in the Christ** (q d, His Christ The article is not expressed with χριστός after a preposition, unless with some such special meaning see below ver 12), **the things in** (lit *on*; see below) **the heavens** (universal—not to be limited to the *angels* [Chrys., &c.], nor *spirits of the just* [Beza, al], still less to be understood of the *Jews*, τὰ ἐπὶ τ γῆς being the Gentiles [Locke, &c] Chrys.'s words are so far true, μίαν κεφαλὴν ἅπασιν ἐπέθηκε τὸ κατὰ σάρκα χριστόν, κ ἀγγέλοις κ. ἀνθρώποις· . . τοῖς μὲν τὸ κατὰ σάρκα, τοῖς δὲ τὸν θεὸν λόγον—but the Apostle's meaning extends much further. The rec. ἐν τ. οὐρ seems to have been adopted from Col i. 20 There also ἐπί is read, but by L and a few mss only, and evidently from our passage The construction is a common one cf. ἐπὶ χθονί Il γ 195, ἐπὶ πύλησι, ib. 149. It is strange

ἐπὶ τοῖς οὐρανοῖς καὶ τὰ ἐπὶ τῆς γῆς· 11 ἐν αὐτῷ, ἐν ᾧ
καὶ [s] ἐκληρώθημεν [t] προορισθέντες [u] κατὰ [v] πρόθεσιν τοῦ
τὰ πάντα [w] ἐνεργοῦντος κατὰ τὴν [x] βουλὴν τοῦ θελήμα-

s here only 1 Kings xiv 41 (only ?) only + t Acts iv 28 Rom viii 29, 30 1 Cor ii 7 ver 5 u v = Phil ii 3 reff u = Rom viii 28 ix 11 ch iii 11 2 Tim i 9 Acts xxvii 13 ‡ 2 Macc iii 8 w Gal ii 8 reff x = Acts ii 23 iv 28 xiii 36 Heb vi 17 Ps xxxii 11

rec (for 1st επι) εν, with AFKℵ[3] rel copt Orig-cat $Epiph_2$ Chr Cyr Thdrt Thl Iren-int Victorin txt BDLℵ[1] a c d e h l n goth Thdrt Œc Tert

11 for εκληρωθημεν, εκληθημεν (*gloss*) ADF syr txt BKLℵ rel vulg(and F-lat) syr-w-ob goth Chr Thdrt Damasc Ambrst Jer. ins την bef προθεσιν D[1]F l. aft προθεσιν ins του θεου DF copt goth æth Ambrst om τα D[1]F. for τα παντα, παντας d

to find in Ellicott a defence of the rec. ἐν, grounded on the fact that "ἐπί is never joined in the N T with οὐρανός or οὐρανοί, and that ἐν οὐρανῷ and ἐπὶ γῆς are invariably found in antithesis" Such an argument would sweep away all ἅπαξ λεγόμενα of construction, and break down the significance of all exceptional usage) **and the things on the earth** (general, as before τὰ πάντα All creation is summed up in Christ it was all the result of the Love of the Father for the Son [see my Doctrine of Divine Love, Serm. i.], and in the Son it is all regarded by the Father The vastly different relation to Christ of the different parts of creation, is no objection to this union in Him it affects, as Beng. on Rom viii. 19, "pro suo quodque genus captu" The Church, of which the Apostle here mainly treats, is subordinated to Him in the highest degree of conscious and joyful union those who are not His spiritually, in mere subjugation, yet consciously; the inferior tribes of creation, unconsciously. but objectively, all are summed up in Him), 11] **in Him** (emphatic repetition, to connect more closely with Him the following relative clause), **in whom we** (Christians, *all*, both Jews and Gentiles, who are resolved below into ἡμεῖς and ὑμεῖς see on ver 12) **were also** (besides having, by His purpose, the revelation of His will, ver. 9 Not '*we also*,' καὶ ἡμεῖς, as vulg. "*in quo etiam nos* . . ," nor as E. V. '*in whom also*') **taken for His inheritance** (κληρόω, in its ordinary meaning, '*to appoint by lot*,'—then '*to appoint*' generally· κληροῦμαι, mid. '*to get*, or *possess* any thing *by* such *appointment*.' The aorist passive, if ever taken in a middle sense, cannot be thus understood here, on account of εἰς τὸ εἶναι following. Confining ourselves therefore to the strict passive sense, we have three meanings apparently open to us (1) '*we were appointed by lot*' So Chrys., Thl, vulg [*sorte vocati sumus*], Erasm. [*sorte electi sumus*]. Chrys. supposes this apparently fortuitous choice to be *corrected* by προορ. κ τ.λ following. 'we were allotted, yet not by chance·' others justify it, as Estius, 'quia in ipsis electis nulla est causa cur eligantur præ aliis' But to this Meyer properly opposes the fact, that we are never by St Paul said to be chosen by any such θεία τύχη, but only by the gracious purpose of God. cf Plato, Legg. vi p. 759 c· κληροῦν οὕτω τῇ θείᾳ τύχῃ ἀποδιδόντα. (2) '*we were made partakers of the inheritance*,' i e of the Kingdom of God, as Israel of Canaan,—Acts xxvi 18 Col i. 12. This is adopted by Harl, and Mey, and many others. But it seems without authority from usage: the instance which Mey quotes from Pind., Ol viii. 19, κληροῦν τινι, not bearing this rendering And besides, the context is against it. ἐκληρώθημεν being followed, as Stier observes, not by εἰς τὸ ἔχειν ἡμ, but by εἰς τὸ εἶναι ἡμ, and thus pointing at something which 'we' are to *become*, not to *possess*. Another reason, see below. (3) '*we were made an* (God's) *inheritance*' This (Grot, Beng., Olsh, De W., Stier, Ellic, al) seems to me the only rendering by which philology and the context are alike satisfied We thus take the ordinary meaning of κληρόω, to assign as a κλῆρος and the prevalent idea of Israel in the O. T. is as a people whom the Lord chose *for His inheritance*, cf Deut iv 20, ὑμᾶς ἔλαβεν ὁ θεὸς . . . . εἶναι αὐτῷ λαὸν ἔγκληρον ib ix. 29, xxxii. 9, 3 Kings viii 51, al. Flatt cites from Philo (qu ref ?), ᾧ προσκεκλήρωνται, διότι τοῦ σύμπαντος ἀνθρώπων γένους ἀπενεμήθη οἷα τις ἀπαρχὴ τῷ ποιητῇ κ. πατρί Olsh calls this 'the realization *in time* of the ἐκλογὴ ἐν χριστῷ spoken of before,' viz by God taking to Himself a people out of all nations for an inheritance —first in type and germ in the O. T., then fully and spiritually in the N. T. This interpretation will be further substantiated by the note on ver 12 below), **having been predestined** (why mention this again ? Harl maintains that it here applies to the

y Acts iii. 19 vii. 10. Rom. i. 11, 20 al. z ver. 6 reff. a here only †. b 1 Cor. xv. 19. Ps. xxxii. 21.

τος αὐτοῦ, 12 y εἰς τὸ εἶναι ἡμᾶς εἰς z ἔπαινον δόξης αὐτοῦ
τοὺς a προηλπικότας b ἐν τῷ χριστῷ. 13 ἐν ᾧ καὶ ὑμεῖς,

ABDF KLℵ a b c d e f g h k l m n o 17

12. rec ins της bef δοξης, with A h Chr Thdrt Œc: om BDFKLℵ rel Eus Cyr Damasc Thl. om αυτου D[1]F flor Tert (not F-lat.)

Jews only, and refers to their selection [according to him to *possess* the inheritance] by God: but this cannot be, because as remarked above, ἡμᾶς, which first brings up the difference, does not occur yet. The true answer to the question lies in this,—that here first the Apostle comes to the idea of the universal Church, the whole Israel of God, and therefore here brings forward again that fore-ordination which he had indeed hinted at generally in ver. 5, but which properly belonged to Israel, and is accordingly predicated of the Israel of the Church) **according to** (in pursuance of) **the purpose** (repeated again [see above] from ver. 9: cf. also ch. iii. 11) **of Him who works** (energizes; but especially in and among material previously given, as here, in His material creation, and in the spirits of all flesh, also His creation) **all things** (not to be restricted, as Grot., to the matter here in hand, but universally predicated) **according to the counsel of His will** (the βουλή here answers to the εὐδοκία ver. 5, —the definite shape which the will assumes when decided to action—implying in this case the union of sovereign will with infinite wisdom), 12] **in order that we** (here first expressed, as distinguished from ὑμεῖς, ver. 13: see below) **should be to the praise of His glory** (see on ver. 6 and ver. 11 below), **namely, we who have before hoped in the Christ** (we Jewish-Christians, who, before the Christ came, looked forward to His coming, waiting for the consolation of Israel: cf. especially Acts xxviii. 20, ἕνεκεν γὰρ τῆς ἐλπίδος τοῦ Ἰσραὴλ τὴν ἅλυσιν ταύτην περίκειμαι—and xxvi. 6, 7. The objection, that *so few* thus looked, is fully met by the largeness of St. Paul's own expression in this last passage. But this whole interpretation requires defending against opponents. First, the verse is variously punctuated: Harl., and Olsh. even more decidedly, read it εἰς τὸ εἶναι ἡμᾶς, εἰς ἔπαινον δόξ. αὐ., τοὺς προηλπ. ἐν τ. χρ. But to this it may be objected, (1) that εἰς ἔπ. δόξης αὐ., occurring as it does again at the end of the whole passage as the final aim of all, cannot with any probability be here merely parenthetical: (2) that above, ver. 6, and below, ver. 14, it, as well as the predestination, has reference to the fulness of the Gospel, not to incomplete prefatory hope in Christ [this would be no objection to De W.'s view: see below]: (3) that thus we should require some demonstrative expression preceding, to mark out these ἡμᾶς, such as ἐν ᾧ καὶ ἐκληρώθημεν ἡμεῖς οἱ προορισθέντες. The objections which Harl. brings against the ordinary construction are implicitly answered in this exposition. They rest mainly on the mistake of referring ἐκληρώθ. προορισθέντες to the Jewish Christians: see above. De W. denies all reference to Jews and Gentiles,—(1) from the analogy of words compounded with προ- [προ-ακούειν Col. i. 5, προλέγειν Gal. v. 21; 1 Thess. iii. 4, προγράφειν Rom. xv. 4, προεπαγγέλλεσθαι Rom. i. 2], which he says indicate always priority as to the thing spoken of [in his idea here merely, 'hope previous to the fulfilment of that hope,' i. e. προ- has no meaning, for all hope must be this], not in comparison with other persons: but (a) this is not true—cf. προελθόντες Acts xx. 13, προέχεσθαι, προηγεῖσθαι, προτιθέναι, προάγειν, προπορεύεσθαι,—and (b) if it were, it does not touch our interpretation—hoped before [Christ's coming]: —(2) from ver. 13 saying nothing peculiar to Gentile Christians [but see there]: (3) from καὶ ὑμᾶς, in ch. ii. 1, and Col. i. 21, not meaning Gentile Christians, but being merely addressed to the readers generally. But in both these places it is so, merely because other things or persons have just been treated of: whereas here he would understand this ἡμᾶς as including the ὑμεῖς, thus depriving it of the force which it has there).

13] What is the construction? Have we but one sentence, ἐν ᾧ . . . . ἐσφραγίσθητε, the two participial clauses being parallel, and both belonging to the verb? so the ff., Beng., De W., Ellic., [by whom the view is well defended and explained,] &c. But this seems to me impossible, from the arrangement. It would require the omission of the second ἐν ᾧ, or the placing of the καὶ ὑμεῖς after ἀκούσαντες. As the sentence now stands, the second ἐν ᾧ καί must begin a new sentence, and surely cannot be the mere rhetorical repetition of the first. This being so, we must un-

ἀκούσαντες τὸν [c] λόγον τῆς [c] ἀληθείας, τὸ εὐαγγέλιον
τῆς σωτηρίας ὑμῶν, ἐν ᾧ καὶ πιστεύσαντες [d] ἐσφραγίσθητε
τῷ [e] πνεύματι τῆς [e] ἐπαγγελίας τῷ ἁγίῳ, 14 ὅ ἐστιν

c 2 Cor vi 7. 2 Tim ii 15. James i 18.
d = 2 Cor i 22. ch iv 30. see Rev vii 4 al.
e here only. see Rom i 4. viii 15. xi 8. 2 Cor iv 13. 2 Tim i 7. Heb x 29.

13. ημεις AKLℵ³(but υ restored) c f g¹ h k l n o Thl-ms. om 2nd και DF copt Did, Iren-int Tert Pelag Aug. εσφραγισθη B.
14. rec (for ὅ) ος, with DKℵ rel Chr-comm Thdrt Damasc Thl Œc: οστις, omg εστιν,

derstand some verb to complete ἐν ᾧ καὶ ὑμεῖς. Nothing can be more usual or more simple than to supply ἐστέ: nothing commoner than ἐν χριστῷ εἶναι: nothing better suited to the context than, after putting forward the Jewish believers, to turn to the Gentiles, 'Ye also have your part in Christ—our prominence does not exclude you.' Some supply ἠλπίκατε (Erasm.-ver., Calv., Est., al.), some ἐκληρώθητε (Erasm.-par., Harl., Olsh., al.); but the other is far simpler; and I cannot see how it deserves the charge which Ellicott brings against it, of being "a statement singularly frigid and out of harmony with the linked and ever-rising character of the context." It is quite accounted for as above, as forming a link in the context, whose character is well thus described. **In whom are ye also** (ye Gentile believers) **since ye heard** (from the time when .... Their *hearing* was the *terminus a quo*) **the word of the truth** (the word whose character and contents are the truth of God: "quasi extra ipsum nulla esset proprie veritas," Calv. see reff. This word is the instrument of the new birth, James i 18. See Col i 5, and, above all, John xvii 17), (viz.) **the Gospel of your salvation** (the Gospel whose contents, whose good tidings are your salvation: not a genitive of apposition, as Harl.,—cf. the expressions εὐαγγ. τῆς χάριτος τ. θεοῦ, Acts xx 24,—τῆς εἰρήνης, ch vi 15,—τ. βασιλείας, Matt ix 35,—Ἰησοῦ χριστοῦ, Mark i 1), **in whom** (belongs to *Christ*, as the former ἐν ᾧ—not to λόγον nor to εὐαγγέλιον,—nor is ἐν ᾧ to be taken with πιστεύσαντες, see below: but with ἐσφραγίσθητε—in whom ye not only are, but were sealed. The ἐν ᾧ καὶ . . . ἐσφραγίσθητε answers exactly to ἐν ᾧ καὶ ἐκληρώθημεν above; πιστεύσαντες not being by this construction rendered superfluous [Mey.]; see below) **also** (belongs to πιστεύσαντες ἐσφραγίσθητε, not to either word alone) **on your believing** (*terminus a quo*, as ἀκούσαντες above. Not to be taken with ἐν ᾧ [as = εἰς ὅν, an usage unknown to St Paul], for see Acts xix 2, εἰ πνεῦμα ἅγ. ἐλάβετε πιστεύσαντες;—'did ye receive the Holy Ghost when ye believed?'—and Rom xiii. 11 νῦν . . . ἐγγύτερον ἡμῶν ἡ σωτηρία ἢ ὅτε ἐπιστεύσαμεν: see also 1 Cor. iii. 5; xv 2, 11, Heb. iv 3. This use of the aorist marks the time when the act of belief first took place—and it must naturally therefore stand absolutely) **ye were sealed** (the fact followed on baptism, which was administered on belief in Christ. See the key-passage Acts xix. 1—6. πιστεύσαντες is, and is not, contemporaneous with ἐσφραγίσθητε: it is not, inasmuch as in strict accuracy, faith preceded baptism, and baptism preceded the gift of the Spirit: but it is, inasmuch as on looking back over a man's course, the period of the commencement of his faith includes all its accidents and accompaniments. See Ellic.'s note. The figure of *sealing* is so simple and obvious, that it is perhaps mere antiquarian pedantry, with Schottgen, Grot., and Wetst., to seek for an explanation of it in Gentile practices of branding with the names of their deities, or even in circumcision itself. The sealing was objective, making manifest to others [ὥστε εἶναι δῆλον, ὅτι θεοῦ ἐστε λάχος κ. κλῆρος, Thl., so Chr., al.]: see John iii 33, Rev. vii. 3,—but also subjective, an approval and substantiation of their faith [τὴν βεβαίωσιν ἐδέξασθε, Theod. Mops.], see Rom viii 16, 2 Cor. i 22, 1 John iii. 24 b) **by the spirit of the promise** (i. e. who was ἡ ἐπαγγελία τοῦ πατρός, Luke xxiv 49; Acts i 4, Gal iii 14, 22, and I therefore insert the article. This, and not the other alternative, that the Spirit confirms God's promises to us, is the true rendering: He was the promise of the O. T. as well as of the N. T.: as Chr.: δύο εἰσὶν ἐπαγγελίαι, μία μὲν διὰ τῶν προφητῶν, ἑτέρα δὲ ἀπὸ τοῦ υἱοῦ. To unite together both alternatives as Stier does, weakens the force of the reference of ἐπαγγελίας back to God, so necessary to the context. The fact, that the Spirit is *to us* the Spirit of promise, is abundantly expressed in the following clause), **the Holy One** (I have preferred giving the ἁγίῳ separately, feeling with Meyer that there is an emphatic pathos in it which

f 2 Cor i 22 v 5 only Gen xxxviii 17, 18, 20 only
g = Acts xx 32 Col iii 24 1 Pet i 4 14 Heb x 39 1 Pet ii 9 only 2 Chron xiv 13 Mal iii 17 only
h ver 7 reff
i 1 Thess v 9. 2 Thess ii
j ver 6 reff

[f] ἀρραβὼν τῆς [g] κληρονομίας ἡμῶν εἰς [h] ἀπολύτρωσιν τῆς [i] περιποιήσεως, εἰς [j] ἔπαινον τῆς δόξης αὐτοῦ.

ABDF KLℵ a b c d e f g h k l m n o 17

d: txt ABFL 67[2] Ath Euthal Chr-txt. om last της ℵ

should not be lost in the usual prefix, 'the Holy Spirit.' The Spirit with whom He sealed you is even *His own* Holy Spirit—what grace, and mercy, and love, is here!) **which** (if the ὅς of the rec. be retained, it is not for a moment to be referred to Christ,—nor to be insisted on as agreeing with the understood gender of the personal πνεῦμα,—but as so very often, a relative agreeing in gender with the subject [ἀῤῥαβών] of the relative clause: see ch. iii. 13 reff and many more examples in Bruder) **is the** (not 'an') **earnest** ("the word signifies the first instalment paid as a pledge that the rest will follow It is used by the Greek orators, and by the earlier Latin writers, especially Plautus and Terence. A Gellius [xvii 2] speaks of it as a word considered in his time [A D 120—50] to be vulgar, and superseded by 'arra,' which is the substitute for it in later Latinity It is remarkable that the same word עֵרָבוֹן is used in the same sense in Hebrew, Gen. xxxviii 17, 18, from עָרַב, to *mix* or *exchange*, and thence to *pledge*, as Jer. xxx 21; Neh v. 3. It was therefore probably derived by the Greeks from the language of Phenician traders, as *tariff, cargo*, are derived, in the English and other modern languages, from Spanish traders" Stanley, on 2 Cor. i. 22 And so here—the Spirit is the ἀπαρχή, Rom viii 23,—the μέρος τοῦ παντός, as Chrys, or πρόδομα, as Hesych the pledge and assurer to us of τὰ ὑπὸ τοῦ θεοῦ χαρισθέντα ἡμῖν, 1 Cor ii. 12, which eye hath not seen, &c.) **of our inheritance** (here the first person comes in again, and not without reason. The inheritance [see above on ἐκληρώθημεν, which involved the converse idea] belongs to both Jew and Gentile—to all who are the children of Abraham by faith, Gal iii. 28, 29), **for** ('in order to,'—not '*until*,' as E. V; nor in ch iv. 30 nor does εἰς belong to ὅ ἐστιν . ., but to ἐσφραγίσθητε. These two final clauses express the great purpose of all—not any mere intermediate matter—nor can the Holy Spirit be said to be any such intermediate gift) **the full redemption** (ἀπολ is often used by the Apostle in this sense. e g ch iv. 30, Rom viii 23, of the full and exhaustive accomplishment of that which the word imports) **of His purchased possession** (the sense of περιποίησις has been much disputed, and many ungrammatical and illogical renderings of the words given A full discussion may be seen in Harless's note The senses to be avoided are, (1) the nonsensical *antiptosis*, that ἀπολ τ. περιπ = περιποίησιν τῆς ἀπολυτρώσεως (2) the equally absurd hendiadys, taking τ περιποιήσεως for τὴν περιποιηθεῖσαν, which fits neither the true sense of εἰς, nor the context (3) the taking περιποιήσεως as *active* in meaning —'redemptio qua contingat certa vitæ possessio.' Bucer. But this it could not convey to the Apostle's readers, unless constructed with some substantive to indicate such a meaning, as in 1 Thess. v 9, where see note. A variety of this is proposed by Grot —'rescuing,' i. e. salvation—and defended by Heb. x 39, where περιποίησις ψυχῆς is opposed to ἀπώλεια. But besides that there the genitive ψυχῆς fixes the meaning,—the article τῆς here, in my view, is an insuperable objection. (4) the taking περιπ in a *passive* sense, as *res acquisita*—making it therefore = κληρονομία, and giving to ἀπολύτρωσις the sense of *entire bestowal*, which it cannot have It remains then, that we seek some technical meaning of περιποίησις, since the obvious etymological ones fail And such a meaning is found by considering its uses in the O T It, and its cognate word περίειμι, are found applied to the people of God, in the sense of a people whom He preserves for Himself as His possession. So Exod xix 5, ἔσεσθέ μοι λαὸς περιούσιος ἀπὸ πάντων τῶν ἐθνῶν, Deut. vii 6, xiv. 2, xxvi 18,—Ps cxxxiv. 4, τὸν Ἰακὼβ ἐξελέξατο ὁ κύριος, Ἰσραὴλ εἰς περιουσιασμὸν ἑαυτῷ,—Isa xliii 21, λαόν μου ὃν περιεποιησάμην τὰς ἀρετάς μου διηγεῖσθαι,—Mal iii 17, ἔσονταί μοι, λέγει κύριος παντοκρ, εἰς ἡμέραν, ἣν ἐγὼ ποιῶ, εἰς περιποίησιν, κ αἱρετιῶ αὐτοὺς. κ τ λ In ref 2 Chron. we have the wider meaning of a *remnant* generally The above sense as applied to the people of the Lord, was adopted by the N. T. writers e g St Paul, Acts xx 28, τὴν ἐκκλησίαν τ. θεοῦ, ἣν περιεποιήσατο διὰ τ. αἵματος τ ἰδίου,—St Peter, 1 Pet ii 9, ὑμεῖς . . . λαὸς εἰς περιποίησιν And such seems to be the meaning here though no other case can be alleged in which the word stands so absolutely We must suppose, that it would explain itself to the

15 Διὰ τοῦτο κἀγώ, [k] ἀκούσας τὴν [l] καθ' ὑμᾶς [m] πίστιν
[m] ἐν τῷ κυρίῳ Ἰησοῦ καὶ τὴν [[n] ἀγάπην τὴν] [n] εἰς πάντας
τοὺς [o] ἁγίους, 16 οὐ [p] παύομαι [q] εὐχαριστῶν ὑπὲρ ὑμῶν,
[r] μνείαν [r] ποιούμενος [s] ἐπὶ τῶν [s] προσευχῶν μου, 17 ἵνα

k constr, Matt xi 2 Acts xxiii 16 Gal i 13 Col i 4 Philem 5. l constr, Acts xvii 28 xviii 15 xxvi 3

m Gal iii 26. Col i 4 1 Tim. iii 13 2 Tim iii 15 P n Rom v 8. Col i 4 1 Pet ii 8 = ἀγ ἐν, 1 John iv 16 o = ver 1 reff p = Acts vi 13 xiii 10 xx 31 Col i 9 al Isa xxxviii 20 q = John xi 41 Rom i 8 1 Cor i 4 al fr + Judith viii 25 Wisd xviii 2 2 Macc i 11 only r Rom i 9 1 Thess i 2 Philem 4 only Job xiv 13 μν, Phil i 3 1 Thess iii 6 2 Tim i 3 (Rom xii 13 v r) only P s Rom i 10 1 Thess i 2 Philem 4 only

15. aft ιησ ins *χριστω* D[1]F vss (χῦ D[1]) om *αγαπην την* (*possibly from homœotel?*) ABℵ[1] 17 Cyr Jer Aug$_{alic}$ · om *την* D[1]F ins KLℵ[3] rel latt syrr copt goth Chr Cyr$_1$ Thdrt Damasc Ambrst Aug$_1$ —κ. τ. ε. π. αγαπην τ. αγιους n[1]. κ. τ. ε. π. τ. αγ. αγαπ m 80.

16 *παυσομαι* D Victorin rec (aft *μνειαν*) ins *υμων*, with D[3]KL rel vulg syrr copt Chr Thdrt Damasc Jer Ambrst aft *ποιουμ* F · om ABDℵ[1] m 17 goth Hil.

readers, from their familiarity with O. T expressions, or with the Apostle's own use of it. This view is taken by the Syr, Œc., Erasm, Calv., Grot, and most Commentators, also by De Wette, Harless, Olsh, Meyer, Stier, Ellic Stier endeavours, as so often, to unite the meanings regarding God, and ourselves,—for that we in being God's possession, reserved for survivorship to others, do, in the root of the word, thus survive, are thus saved · and undoubtedly this is so, but is not the leading idea) **for the praise of His glory** (as before, ver. 6 but as Stier well remarks, *χάριτος* does not appear here, grace having *done its work*. **αὐτοῦ** is the Father cf. ver. 17, ὁ πατὴρ τῆς δόξης This, the thorough and final redemption of the Church which He hath acquired to Himself, is the greatest triumph of His glory. as Grot. well says, 'Plus aliquanto est in voce *περιποιήσεως* quam in voce *κλήρου* quam antea habuimus κλῆρος, sors, jus proprium perpetuumque significat περιποίησις, acquisitio, et hoc, et modum acquirendi gravem et laboriosum. Solemus autem plurimi ea facere quæ magno nobis constant') See the typico-historical connexion of this wonderful passage with the patriarchal, legal, and prophetic periods, unfolded in Stier, i. pp 129—136 I would not be understood to subscribe to all there advanced but though his parallelism sometimes borders on the fanciful, the connexion is too striking to be altogether set aside by the real student of Scripture

(B) vv. **15—23.**] *The* IDEA OF THE CHURCH *carried forward, in the form of a prayer for the Ephesians, in which the fulfilment of the Father's counsel through the Son and by the Spirit, in His people, is set forth, as consisting in the* KNOWLEDGE *of the hope of His calling, of the riches of His promise, and the power which He exercises on His saints as first wrought by Him in Christ, whom He has made Head over all to the Church.*

15, 16.] INTRODUCTION TO THE PRAYER. **Wherefore** (i e., on account of what has gone before since ver 3. but especially of what has been said since ver 13, where καὶ ὑμεῖς first came in —because ye are in Christ, and in Him were sealed, &c) **I also** (κἀγώ, either as resuming the first person after the second, going back to the ἐκληρώθημεν ver 11,—or as corresponding to καὶ ὑμεῖς above —not, as Mey., al, because he is sensible that in thus praying for them he is helping *their* prayers for themselves) **having heard of** (on the indication supposed to be furnished by this respecting the readers, see Prolegg § ii. 12) **the faith among you in the Lord Jesus** (καθ' ὑμᾶς is not = ὑμετέραν, as ordinarily rendered [even by Meyer], either here or any where else · cf the example which Mey. quotes from Thuc vi. 16, τῷ κατ' αὐτοὺς βίῳ, 'the life which prevails among them.' Ellic. compares, for the distinction, τῷ νόμῳ τῷ ὑμετέρῳ, addressed to Pharisees, John viii. 17, with νόμου τοῦ καθ' ὑμᾶς, said with reference to Jews in Achaia, Acts xviii. 15 nor is 'among you' merely local [*chez vous*], but is *partitive*, implying the possibility of some not having this faith, and thus intensifying the prayer which follows) **and [your love which is] towards all the saints** (on the reading, see digest Taking the bracketed words as genuine, *τήν specifies τὴν ἀγ* which might be general · τ καθ' ὑμ πίστιν wants no such specification, *all our faith* being ἐν τ κυρ Ἰησ, grounded in Him Chrys remarks πανταχοῦ συνάπτει κ. συγκολλᾷ τ. πίστιν κ τ. ἀγάπην

t here only w πατήρ, ver 3 Rom xv 6 2 Cor i 3 xι 31 Col ι 3 1 Pet ι 3 only

ὁ [t] θεὸς [t] τοῦ κυρίου ἡμῶν Ἰησοῦ χριστοῦ, ὁ [u] πατὴρ
τῆς [v] δόξης, [w] δῴη ὑμῖν [x] πνεῦμα [x] σοφίας καὶ [y] ἀποκαλύψεως [z] ἐν [a] ἐπιγνώσει [b] αὐτοῦ,
18 [c] πεφωτισμένους τοὺς

ABDF KLℵ a b c d e f g h k l m n o 17

u = 2 Cor ι 3 James i 17 v Acts vii 2 Ps xxiii 9, 10 w (form) Rom xv 5 2 Tim i 16, 18 al Gen xxvii 28 see Winer, edn 6, § 14 1 g x Exod xxviii 3 vat Isa xi 2 πν, Gal vi 1 reff y = ch iii 3 z = ver 8 reff a = ch iv 13. Col i 9, 10. ii 2 1 Tim ii 4 al 2 Pet i 2, 3, 8 ii 20 Paul & 2 Pet only exc Heb x 26. Prov ii 5. b obj gen aft επ always c = ch iii 9 Heb vi 4 x 32 Ps xviii 8

17. δῳ B

θαυμαστήν τινα ξυνωρίδα) cease not giving thanks for you, making mention (of them,—viz. your faith and love) in (see reff 'In ἐπί with a genitive, the apparent *temporal* reference partakes somewhat of the *local* reference of juxtaposition' Bernhardy, p. 216) my (ordinary, see Rom. i. 9 note) prayers 17.] *purpose* (including also the *purport*, see note on 1 Cor. xiv. 13, and Ellicott's note here) *of the prayer*:—that (depends on the sense of μνείαν ποι. ἐπ τ. προσευχῶν, implying that a *prayer for them* took place) the God of our Lord Jesus Christ (see on ver. 3. The appellation is here solemnly and most appropriately given, as leading on to what is about to be said in vv 20 ff of God's *exaltation of Christ* to be Head over all things to His Church. To His God, Christ also in the days of His Flesh prayed, πάτερ, δόξασόν σου τὸν υἱόν: and even more markedly in that last cry, θεέ μου, θεέ μου), the Father of glory (not merely the *auctor*, *fons*, of glory, Grot, Olsh: still less = πατὴρ ἔνδοξος: nor with Chrys to be explained ὁ μεγάλα ἡμῖν δεδωκὼς ἀγαθά· ἀπὸ γὰρ τῶν ὑποκειμένων ἀεὶ αὐτὸν καλεῖ, ὡς, ὅταν λέγῃ ὁ πατὴρ τῶν οἰκτιρμῶν. nor is δόξης to be understood of the divine nature of Christ, as Thdrt · θεὸν μὲν ὡς ἀνθρώπου, πατέρα δὲ ὡς θεοῦ, δόξαν γὰρ τὴν θείαν φύσιν ὠνόμασεν for this would require τ. δόξης αὐτοῦ but God is the Father,—by being the God and Father of our Lord Jesus Christ,—of that glory, the true and all-including glory, and *only glory*, of the Godhead, which shone forth in the manhood of the only-begotten Son [John i 14],—the true Shechinah, which His saints beheld in the face of Christ, 2 Cor. iv. 4, 6, and into which they are changed by the Lord the Spirit, ib iii 18. In fact, 2 Cor. iii 7—iv 6, is the key to this sublime expression), would give (the account of the optative after ἵνα, when a present [παύομαι] has preceded, is very simple. It is used when the purpose is not that of the writer *as he is writing*, but is described as that of himself or some one else *at another time*. Thus Herod. ii 93, καταπλώουσι ἐς θάλασσαν, κ ἀναπλώοντες ὀπίσω τῆς αὐτῆς ἀντέχονται, ... ἵνα δὴ μὴ ἁμάρτοιεν τῆς ὁδοῦ διὰ τὸν ῥόον See Klotz, Devar p 622) to you the Spirit (certainly it would not be right to take πνεῦμα here as solely the Holy Spirit, nor as solely the spirit of man · rather is it the complex idea, of the spirit of man indwelt by the Spirit of God, so that as such, it is His special gift, see below) of wisdom (not, which *gives* wisdom, but which possesses it as its character— q d to which appertains wisdom) and of revelation (i. e. that revelation which belongs to *all Christians* · see 1 Cor ii. 10 ff . not the χαρίσματα of the early Church, as Olsh.,—nor could the Apostle be alluding to any thing so trivial and fleeting, see 1 Cor. xiii xiv To those who are taught of God's Spirit, ever more and more of His glories in Christ are revealed, see John xvi 14, 15) in (belongs to δῴη · as the element and sphere of the working of this gift of the Spirit) the full knowledge (for the distinction between γνῶσις and ἐπίγνωσις, see 1 Cor xiii. 12) of Him (Chr , Thl , Olsh., al , strangely connect ἐν ἐπιγνώσει αὐτοῦ with the following sentence, πεφωτισμ κ.τ λ The whole parallelism is against this, in which πνεῦμ σοφ. κ ἀποκ is || πεφωτ. τ ὀφθ. τ κ ὑμ. and ἐν ἐπιγνώσ. αὐτοῦ is || εἰς τὸ εἰδέναι κ τ λ.;—and the object being to exalt the gifts of the Spirit, ἐν ἐπ αὐτ would hardly come first in the sentence, and thus monopolize the emphasis. See also on a similar proposal, ver. 4, end αὐτοῦ [not αὑτοῦ] refers to the Father,—not to Christ, as Beza, Calv , al.; cf. αὐτοῦ four times in vv 18, 19 · Christ first becomes thus designated in ver 20), having the eyes of your heart enlightened (the construction is as in Soph Electr 479, ὕπεστί μοι θράσος ἁδυπνόων κλύουσαν ἀρτίως ὀνειράτων,—Æsch Choeph 396, πεπάλται δ' αὖτέ μοι φίλον κέαρ τόνδε κλύουσαν οἶκτον see also Acts xxvi 3,—Kuhner ii. p. 381 so that πεφωτισμένους belongs to ὑμῖν, and τοὺς ὀφθαλμούς is the accusative of reference So Beza, Beng , Koppe, Meyer, Ellic . and such is the simpler and more forcible construction. But Grot , Ruck , Harl , Olsh , De W.,

[d] ὀφθαλμοὺς τῆς [d] καρδίας ὑμῶν, [e] εἰς τὸ εἰδέναι ὑμᾶς τίς ἐστιν ἡ [f] ἐλπὶς τῆς [fg] κλήσεως [g] αὐτοῦ, τίς ὁ [h] πλοῦτος τῆς [i] δόξης τῆς [j] κληρονομίας [j] αὐτοῦ ἐν τοῖς [k] ἁγίοις,

d here only see Matt xiii 15. e ver 12 reff f ch iv 4 only constr, see Col i 23 g Rom xi. 29 Phil iii 14 h i Rom ix 23 ch iii 16. Col i 27 see Phil iv. 19 h Rom ii 4 ch iii 8 al i ver 6 j ver 14 reff constr., here only, k ver 1 reff

18 rec (for καρδιας) διανοιας, with d Cyr-jer Thdrt Œc: txt ABDFKLℵ rel. om υμων B 17 for εις το υμας, ινα οιδατε F for 1st τις, τι F Ephr. rec (aft αυτου) ins και, with D³KLℵ³ rel vulg(not am fuld tol) syr copt Orig-cat Chr Thdrt Damasc Ambrst-ms Jer om ABD¹Iℵ¹ 17 goth Ambrst-ed Victorin. κληρον της δοξης ℵ.

Stier, all., take πεφ. τ. ὀφθ together, and govern it by δῴη, to which the article before ὀφθ. is no objection [as Beng.], but the logic of the passage is. The *enlightening as regards* [or *of*] *the eyes of the heart*, is a *condition, subordinate* to the πνεῦμα σοφ. κ. ἀποκ., not another gift, correlative with it. Besides which, the sentence, even after all the grammatical vindications of Harl., al,—δῴη ὑμῖν . . . . πεφωτισμένους τοὺς ὀφθ. τῆς καρδίας ὑμῶν, is clumsy and unpauline in the last degree. On πεφωτισμ., cf. Matt. iv. 16. ch. iii. 9 [v 14]: Harl gives an elaborate analysis, as usual, of the meaning, and remarks well that φωτίζω has the double meaning of 'belehren und beleben'—'*enlightening and enlivening.*' He cites from Greg. Naz.: φῶς ὡς λαμπρότης ψυχῶν κ. λόγῳ κ. βίῳ καθαιρομένων εἰ γὰρ σκότος ἡ ἄγνοια κ ἡ ἁμαρτία, φῶς ἂν εἴη ἡ γνῶσις κ. ὁ βίος ὁ ἔνθεος. The expression τ. ὀφ. **τῆς καρδίας** is somewhat unusual. The καρδία of Scripture is, as Harl., the Mittelpunkt des Lebens, the very core and centre of life, where the intelligence has its post of observation, where the stores of experience are laid up, and the thoughts have their fountain. Similarly the Homeric κραδίη, see Damm. Lex: the Latin '*cor*'—cf Cic Tusc i. 9,—'alius cor ipsum animus videtur, ex quo excordes, vecordes, concordesque dicuntur' Thus the ὀφθ. τῆς καρδίας would be those pointed at in Matt. vi. 22, 23,—that inner eye of the heart, through which light is poured in on its own purposes and motives, and it looks out on, and perceives, and judges things spiritual: the eye, as in nature, being both receptive and contemplative of the light), **that you may know** (purpose of the πεφωτισμ, not of the πνεῦμ. σοφ. κ. ἀποκ. This which is now to be described, to the end of the chapter, is *involved in* the πν. σοφ κ ἀποκ, not its *object*: but it is the object of the *enlightening*, which will endue us with the knowledge) **what** (the dispute among the Commentators, whether τίς implies *quality* or *quantity*, seems hardly worth entering into. The fulness of the simple meaning, '*what*,' embraces all categories under which the things mentioned can be contemplated In the passage to which both sides appeal, ch. iii 18, τί τὸ πλάτος κ τ λ of course implies, '*how great is the breadth*, &c ' but it implies this by the simple meaning '*what* is the breadth, &c,' not by making τί = quantum, quantity being already involved in the substantives) **is the hope** (again, it is mere trifling to enquire whether ἐλπίς is the hope [subjective] or the thing hoped for [objective], in this case. For the τίς involves in itself both these. If I know WHAT the hope is, I know both its essence and its accidents. Undoubtedly such an objective sense of ἐλπίς does occur,—see on Col. i. 5; but certainly the meaning here is far wider than in that passage. As well might the subjective sense of Col. i 23, be alleged on that side) **of** (belonging to, see on ch. iv. 4) **His calling** (i e the calling wherewith He called us All the matters mentioned, κλῆσις, κληρονομία, δύναμις, are αὐτοῦ, *His*,—but not all in the same sense: see below. On κλῆσις, see notes, Rom viii 28—30), **what the riches of the glory of His inheritance** ("what a rich, sublime cumulation, setting forth in like terms the weightiness of the matters described;—and not to be weakened [verwässert] by any resolution of the genitives into adjectives" Mey. See Col. i 27) **in** (in the case of, as exemplified in; not so weak as '*among*,'—nor merely '*in*,' so as to refer to its subjective realization in them) **the saints** (much dispute has arisen on the construction of ἐν τ ἁγ Koppe and Winer [Gram §19 2 b, edn. 3 not appy in edn. 6], with whom Meyer and De Wette agree, connect it with ἐστίν understood, so as to mean 'what the richness of, &c is among the saints.' To mention no other objection to this awkward construction, the context and sense are decisive against it. As Stier well says, 'Paul does not pray for their eyes to be enlightened, to see what great and rich things are already among Christians.' No: nor is it easy to conceive how any

19 καὶ τί τὸ [l] ὑπερβάλλον [m] μέγεθος τῆς δυνάμεως αὐτοῦ ABDF KLℵ a b
[n] εἰς ἡμᾶς τοὺς πιστεύοντας [o] κατὰ τὴν [p] ἐνέργειαν τοῦ c d e f g h k l m
[q] κράτους τῆς [q] ἰσχύος αὐτοῦ, 20 ἣν [r] ἐνήργηκεν ἐν τῷ n o 17

l 2 Cor. iii. 10. ix. 14. ch. ii. 7. iii. 19 only †. P. 2 Macc. iv. 13 al. (-λόντως, 2 Cor. xi. 23.) m here only. Exod. xv. 16. n = 2 Cor. ix. 13. ch. iii. 2. see ἐφ', ch. ii. 7. o = ver. 5. Col. i. 11. p ch. iii. 7. iv. 16. Phil. iii. 21. Col. i. 29. ii. 12. 2 Thess. ii. 9, 11. P.† Wisd. vii. 17, 26 al. q ch. vi. 10 only. Isa. xl. 26. Dan. iv. 27 (30 Theod. F.) see Col. i. 11. 2 Thess. i. 9. r ver. 11 reff.

19. om υπερβαλλον F. εις υμας D[1]F d m 17 Ambrst.
20. rec ενηργησεν, with DFKLℵ rel (vss and lat-ff ambiguous) Eus Cyr Chr Thdrt

intelligent reader of the Epistle could ever maintain such a rendering. The other construction is, to take ἐν τ. ἁγ. as belonging either to πλοῦτος, or to δόξης, or to κληρονομίας, as if it had been ὁ (or τῆς) ἐν τοῖς ἁγ. And this is the only one allowed by the context: cf. vv. 19, 20, where εἰς ἡμᾶς, ἐν χριστῷ, form objects of reference precisely similar. Again there is manifestly a distinction between οἱ ἅγιοι here, and ἡμεῖς οἱ πιστεύοντες in the next verse: the former being the *perfected*, the latter the *militant* saints. And this decides for the joining ἐν τ. ἁγ. to κληρονομίας αὐτοῦ,—'*His inheritance in*, whose example and fulness, and embodying is in *the saints*.' The objection to this is supposed to be the want of the article before ἐν, which is urged by Meyer [see also Ellicott's note here], because αὐτοῦ has intervened, thereby preventing κληρ. ἐν τ. ἁγ. being considered as one idea. But surely this is not so. If, *before* αὐτοῦ *was inserted*, ἡ κληρ. ἐν τ. ἁγίοις was sufficiently *one* to prevent the necessity of a *specification* of the genus κληρονομία that it was *the* κληρ. which was ἐν τ. ἁγ. [for such is the force of the inserted article], how can this logical fact be altered by the insertion of Him, *whose* κληρ. it is,—who originated and bestowed it,—and who is therefore necessarily *prior* to the κληρονομία, not intervening between it and its example? I therefore join it to κληρ., and so Rück., Harless, Olsh., Stier, al. This latter, as usual, combines the senses of κληρ. αὐτοῦ, including the inheritance which *God* has in *His people*, and that which they have in Him. His whole note is well worth attention), 19.] **and what the surpassing** (a word only pauline in N. T., see reff.) **greatness of His power to usward who believe** (construction as before, ver. 18, τῆς δυνάμ. αὐτ. εἰς ἡμ., not τί τὸ ὑπ. . . . . [ἐστὶν] εἰς ἡμ. Not His future power in the actual resurrection only is spoken of, but THE WHOLE of His energizing to usward from first to last, principally however His *present* spiritual work, cf. **πιστεύοντας**, not, as in 2 Thess. i. 10, **πιστεύσασιν**: see also Col. ii. 12, and 1 Pet. i. 3—5. This power is exerted to *usward*, which expression of the E. V. I retain as giving better the prominence to *us* in the fact of its *direction*, than the more usual but tamer '*toward us*.' But it is not, as Matth., Flatt, the power which works faith in us, except in so far indeed as faith is a portion of its whole work: here, the **πιστεύοντες** are the material on which the power works), **according to** (in proportion to,—as might be expected from: but more than this—His power to usward is a part of, a continuation of, or rather included as a consequence in, the other. All the shallower interpretations must be avoided here:—Grot., 'rei similitudinem significat:' Van Ess., gleich der Werkung: nor must we join, as Erasm. al., **κατὰ τ. ἐν.** with **πιστεύοντας**, which is beside the Apostle's purpose: nor, with Mey., understand it as a qualification of **εἰς τὸ εἰδέναι** [Erkenntnißgrund des vorherigen Momentes]: nor, with Harless, refer it to all three, **ἐλπίς, πλοῦτος, μέγεθος**: but with Chrys., Calv., Est., Grot., De W., Ellic., take it as an amplification, or grounding, of—τὸ ὑπερβ. . . . to πιστεύοντας) **the working** (putting forth in action, in an object) **of the strength of His might** (**κράτος** the actual measure of **ἰσχύς**, His might. The latter is the attribute, subjectively considered: the former the weight of that attribute, objectively esteemed: the **ἐνέργεια**, the operation, in matter of fact, of the strength of that might. Calvin's distinction, though not quite accurate, is worth noting: "Inter tria nomina quæ hic posuit, hoc interest: quod *robur* est quasi radix, *potentia*, autem, arbor (*qu. vice versâ?*): *efficacia*, fructus, est enim extensio divini brachii, quæ in actum emergit"). **which** (viz. ἐνέργειαν: *cf. ver.* 6, *note*) **He hath wrought in Christ** (our ἀπαρχή, as Œc.: nor only this, but our Head, in virtue of God's ἐνέργεια in whom, His power to usward is made possible and actual. No shallower view, such as that of Grot. that 'Deus oculis humanis quantum posset, in Christo, capite et duce nostro, *ostendit*,' must be for a moment admitted) **in that He raised**

χριστῷ, [s] ἐγείρας αὐτὸν [s] ἐκ νεκρῶν, καὶ [t] καθίσας [u] ἐν δεξιᾷ
αὐτοῦ ἐν τοῖς [v] ἐπουρανίοις 21 [w] ὑπεράνω πάσης [x] ἀρχῆς
καὶ [y] ἐξουσίας καὶ [z] δυνάμεως καὶ [a] κυριότητος καὶ παντὸς
[b] ὀνόματος [c] ὀνομαζομένου οὐ μόνον ἐν τῷ [d] αἰῶνι [d] τούτῳ

s Paul, 1 Cor xv 12, 20 al fr Matt xvii 9 Luke ix 7 John ii 22 al
t trans, Acts ii 30 1 Cor vi 4 only 1 Kings xxx 21 intrans, 2 Thess ii 4 reff
u = Rom viii 34 Col iii 1 Heb i 3 viii 1 x 12 xii 2 1 Pet iii 22 only Ps xv 11 see Mark xvi 5
v ver 3 reff
w ch iv 10 Heb ix 5 only Deut xxvi 19
x y = Luke xii 11 ch vi 12. 1 Cor xv 24 Col i 16 ii 15 Tit iii 1 ἐξ, Rom xiii 1
x z Rom viii 38
y z 1 Pet iii 22
a Col i 16 2 Pet ii 10 Jude 8 only †
b = Acts iv 12 Phil ii 9 Heb i 4 Rev iii 5
c Luke vi. 13, 14 Acts xix 13 Rom xv 20. 1 Cor v 11 ch iii 15 v 3 2 Tim ii 19 only Josh xxiii 7 al
d Matt xii 32 αἰ. οὗ. Mt L (Mark iv 19 v r) not John Rom xii 2 al fr αἰ μελ. Heb vi 5 only Isa ix 6 F

Damasc txt AB Procop rec (for *καθισας*) *εκαθισεν*, with DFKL rel copt goth Chr Thdrt Damasc Thl Œc · txt ABℵ 17 Eus Cyr Procop Tert Jer Ambr Pelag
ins *αυτον* bef *εν δεξια* Aℵ d 17 67² copt Eus Procop lat-ff —(for *εκ δεξιας*, *εν*[*sic*, altered to *εκ* quite recently] *δεξιων* A.) for *επουρ*, *ουρανοις* B Hil.
21 *εξουσιας και αρχης* B.

(as *γνωρίσας* above, ver 9) **Him from the dead** (the resurrection of Christ was not a mere bodily act, an earnest of our bodily resurrection, but was a spiritual act, the raising of His humanity [which is ours], consisting of body and soul, from infirmity to glory, from the curse to the final triumph. In that He died, He died unto sin once, but in that He liveth, He liveth unto God And so *ἡμεῖς οἱ πιστεύοντες*, knit to Him, have died unto sin and live unto God It is necessary to the understanding of the following, thoroughly to appreciate this—or we shall be in danger of regarding, with the shallower expositors, Christ's resurrection as merely a *pledge* of our *bodily* resurrection, or as a mere *figure representing* our *spiritual* resurrection,—not as *involving* the resurrection of the Church in both senses), **and setting Him at His right hand** (see especially Mark xvi. 19) **in the heavenly places** (see on ver. 3. and Matt vi 9, note. But the fact of the universal idea, of God's dwelling being in heaven, being only a symbolism common to all men, must not for a moment induce us to let go the verity of Christ's bodily existence, or to explain away the glories of His resurrection into mere spiritualities As Stephen saw Him, so He veritably is. in human form, locally existent) **over above** (not, as in my former editions, '*far above*' Ellicott says, "The intensive force which Chrys. and Thl find in this word, *ἵνα τὸ ἀκρότατον ὕψος δηλώσῃ*, and which has recently been adopted by Stier and Eadie, is very doubtful: as is also the assertion [Eadie] that this prevails in the majority of passages in the LXX. cf. Ezek i. 26; viii 2, x. 19, xi. 22, xliii 15; and even Deut. xxvi. 19, xxviii. 1 Such distinct instances as Ezek. xliii. 15, and in the N T, Heb ix. 5, the similarly unemphatic use of the antitheton *ὑποκάτω*, John i. 51, Luke viii 16, and the tendencies of Alexandrian and later Greek to form duplicated compounds, make it highly probable that *ὑπεράνω*, both here and ch iv. 10, implies little more than simple local elevation So too Syr and apparently all the ancient versions") **all government** (cf Matt xxviii 18) **and power and might and lordship** (see similar combinations in reff The most reasonable account of the four words seems to be this *ὑπ πάσ ἀρχῆς* gives the highest and fullest expression of exaltation · **κ. ἐξουσίας** is added as filling out *ἀρχῆς* in detail *ἐξουσία* being not only government, but every kind of official power, primary and delegated cf Matt viii 9, x. 1, xxi. 23 ff, Luke xx. 20, xxiii 7 Then in the second pair, **δύναμις** is mere *might*, the raw material, so to speak, of power **κυριότης** is that pre-eminence or lordship, which *δύναμις* establishes for itself. So that in the first pair we descend from the higher and concentrated to the lower and diffused in the second we ascend from the lower and diffused to the higher and concentrated The following shews that in this enumeration not only earthly, nor only heavenly authorities are meant to be included, but both together,—so as to make it perfectly general. That the *evil spirits* are included, is therefore manifest see also ch. vi. 12, 1 Cor xv. 24—26) **and every name that is named** (further generalization indicating not merely titles of honour [cf. *ὀνομαζομ.*], nor persons, but, as Stier, a transition from the *ἀρχαί*, &c to *πάντα* below answering to *οὔτε τις κτίσις ἑτέρα*, cf. Rom. viii. 39. And this transition passes into still wider meaning in the following words) **not only in this present state, but also in that which is to come** (= *ἐνεστῶτα* and

ἀλλὰ καὶ ἐν τῷ [d] μέλλοντι· 22 καὶ πάντα [e] ὑπέταξεν ὑπὸ
τοὺς πόδας αὐτοῦ, καὶ αὐτὸν [f] ἔδωκεν [g] κεφαλὴν ὑπὲρ πάντα
τῇ [h] ἐκκλησίᾳ, 23 ἥτις ἐστὶν τὸ [i] σῶμα αὐτοῦ, τὸ [j] πλήρωμα
τοῦ τὰ πάντα [k] ἐν πᾶσιν [j] πληρουμένου.

ABDF KLℵ a b c d e f g h k l m n o 17

e Luke ii 51 1 Cor xv 27, 28 Heb ii 5, 8 al fr Psa viii. 6 f John iii 16, 35 ch iv 11 Heb viii 10 x 16 Rev passim g = 1 Cor xi 3 ch iv 15 v 23 Col i 18. ii 10, 19 only h absol, Acts viii 3. see Matt xvi 18 epp passim i = Rom xii 5 1 Cor xii 27 ch iv 4, &c Col i 18 al j see notes k = ch v 18 Col i 9 (note) Gal v 14

23. rec om τα, with e · ins ABDFKLℵ rel

μέλλοντα of Rom. viii. 38—not only *time* present and to come, but the present [earthly] condition of things, and the future [heavenly] one. And forasmuch as that heavenly state which is for us *future*, is now, to those in it, present, *it* is by the easiest transition denoted by the μέλλων αἰών. cf Luke xx. 35, and especially Heb. ii. 5, τὴν οἰκουμένην τ. μέλλουσαν. So that the meanings seem combined,—'every name now named in earth and heaven' and, 'every name which we name,—not only now, but hereafter' And in this last view Thdrt.: προστέθεικεν, ὅτι καὶ εἴ τινας τούτων ἀγνοοῦμεν, μετὰ δὲ ταῦτα γνωσόμεθα ἐν τῷ μέλλοντι βίῳ. Chrys.: ἄρα ἐστὶ δυνάμεών τινων ὀνόματα ἡμῖν ἄσημα κ οὐ γνωριζόμενα. Grot., 'quæ noscemus in altero sæculo:' Beng., 'quamvis non omnes nominare possumus.' Wesley, beautifully expanding Bengel (Stier, p. 183) 'We know that the king is above all, though we cannot name all the officers of his court. So we know that Christ is above all, though we are not able to name all His subjects'), 22] **and subjected all things under His feet** (from the Messianic Ps viii., not without an allusion also in καθίσας, &c above to Ps cx. 1 not merely cited, as Thdrt, καὶ τ προφητικὴν ἐπήγαγε μαρτυρίαν, but interwoven into the context, πάντα being a summing up of all mentioned before), **and gave** ('*presented*,' keep the literal sense not '*appointed*;' see below) **Him** (emphatic, from its position Him, thus exalted, thus glorified, the Father not only raised to this supereminence, but gave Him to His redeemed as their Head, &c) **as Head over all things to the Church** (not as Chrys,—in either of his alternatives. ἢ τὸν ὄντα ὑπὲρ πάντα τὰ ὁρώμενα κ τὰ νοούμενα χριστόν [which would be τὴν κεφ, or τὸν ὑπὲρ πάντα], ἢ ὑπὲρ πάντα τὰ ἀγαθὰ τοῦτο πεποίηκε, τὸ τὸν υἱὸν δοῦναι κεφαλήν,—which is beside the context, in which no comparison is made between the gift of Christ and other blessings nor as Beng, 'Ecclesia, super omnia, super imperia, &c., quorum caput (?) Christus est, potest dicere, Christus est caput meum. ego sum corpus ejus,'—for this sense cannot possibly be extracted out of the words themselves ὑπὲρ πάντα nor as Baumgarten, ὑπὲρ πάντα = μάλιστα πάντων, *præcipue, potius quam cæteris*,—for, not to mention other objections, πάντα must surely be the same in meaning as πάντα before nor can πάντα be masculine, as Jer, Anselm, al, and Wahl nor, as Calv, 'quia *simul* plena rerum omnium potestas et administratio illi sit commissa·' nor, with Harl, does πάντα find its limitation within the Church, so as not to apply to other things without it nor is ὑπὲρ πάντα to be taken with κεφ, *summum caput*, as Olsh, all. nor as Meyer, Stier, and Ellicott [edn. 1 in edn. 2, he interprets nearly as below], is another κεφαλήν to be supplied before τῇ ἐκκλ, 'gave Him, as Head over all things, as Head to the Church:' nor is the dative a dat commodi, as De W. but the meaning is thus to be gained, from what follows CHRIST is Head over all things the Church is the BODY of Christ, and as such is the fulness of Him who fills all with all the Head of such a Body, is Head over all things, therefore when God gives Christ as *Head* to the church, He gives Him as *Head over all things* to the church, from the necessity of the case Thus what follows is epexegetical of this), **which same** (Church, '*quæ quidem*,' hardly '*ut quæ*,' "in virtue of her being," as Meyer) **is His BODY** (not in a figure merely. it is veritably His Body: not that which in our glorified humanity He personally bears, but that in which He, as the Christ of God, is manifested and glorified by spiritual organization He is its Head, from Him comes its life; in Him, it is exalted· in it, He is lived forth and witnessed to, He possesses nothing for Himself,—neither His communion with the Father, nor His fulness of the Spirit, nor His glorified humanity,—but all for His Church, which is in the innermost reality, HIMSELF; His flesh and His bones—and therefore) **the fulness** (πλήρ is in apposition with τὸ σῶμα αὐτ,

II. [1] Καὶ ὑμᾶς ὄντας [l] νεκροὺς τοῖς [m] παραπτώμασιν

l = John v 25 Rom xi 15 Col ii 13 Rev iii 1 m here only παρ, Gal vi 1 reff

and is a fresh description of ἡ ἐκκλησία. It would pass my limits, even to notice summarily what has been written on πλήρωμα I will endeavour to give an account of the word itself Like other derivatives in -μα from the perfect passive, it would appear primarily to designate either (1) concrete, that thing on which the action denoted by the verb has passed: e g ποίημα, the thing made, πρᾶγμα, the thing done, σπέρμα, the thing sown, πλήρωμα, *the thing filled*. or (2) abstract, that occurrence whereby the action denoted has been exemplified · e. g τρῶμα, the effect of τιτρώσκειν, not the thing wounded, but the wound inflicted so κλάσμα, ἀρίθμημα, and the like, πλήρωμα, *the fulness.* From this latter, the transition is very easy to the meaning the *thing whereby* the effect is produced, as where πλήρωμα is used for the crew of a ship [see also Matt. ix 16 ||, Mark vi 43; 1 Cor. x 26, Gal. iv. 4, ver. 10], ζεῦγμα for a bridge or yoke, &c. Hence arises the *so-called active* sense of such nouns, which is not in fact an active sense at all, but a logical transference from the effect to that which exemplifies the effect. Here, the simple and primary meaning is by far the best,—'*the thing filled,*'—"*the filled up receptacle*" [cf. κατοικητήριον, ch ii 22], as Eadie expresses it [see also Ellicott], the meaning being, that the church, being the Body of Christ, is dwelt in and filled by God it is His πλήρωμα in an especial manner—His fulness abides in it, and is exemplified by it The nearest approach to any one word in English which may express it, is made by fulness, though it, as well as πλ, requires explaining, as importing not the inherent plenitude of God Himself, but that communicated plenitude of gifts and graces wherein He infuses Himself into His Church. I would refer those who wish to enter more fully into this matter, to the long and laboured notes of Harless, and Stier · and to Fritzsche on Rom vol ii pp. 169 ff.) **of Him who filleth** (it is doubted whether πληρουμένου is passive, or middle in an active sense. Those who take πλήρωμα above, actively, "*the filling up,*" generally [Harless is an exception] defend the passive sense here, "of Him who is [being] filled, &c." So Chrys πλήρωμα, φησίν οἷον κεφαλὴ πληροῦται παρὰ τοῦ σώματος . . . διὰ πάντων οὖν πληροῦται τὸ σῶμα αὐτοῦ. τότε πληροῦται ἡ κεφαλή, τότε τέλειον σῶμα γίνεται, ὅταν ὁμοῦ πάντες ὦμεν συνημμένοι κ συγκεκολλημένοι Jer "Sicut adimpletur imperator, si quotidie ejus augeatur exercitus, et fiant novæ provinciæ, et populorum multitudo succrescat, ita et Christus, in eo, quod sibi credunt omnia, ipse adimpletur in omnibus," and Estius "Qui secundum omnia, sive quoad omnia in omnibus sui corporis membris adimpletur. Nisi enim essent hic quidem pes ejus, ille vero manus, alius autem aliud membrum . . non perficeretur Christus secundum rationem capitis." But to this it is difficult to assign any satisfactory sense, especially on account of τὰ πάντα ἐν πᾶσιν. It certainly cannot be said that Christ awaits His completion, in any such meaning as this, by the completion of his Church And it is not probable that if such had been the meaning, τὰ πάντα ἐν πᾶσιν would have thus barely and emphatically preceded the participle which itself conveyed so new and startling an idea We should have had some such arrangement as this—τὸ πλήρωμα τοῦ καὶ αὐτοῦ τὰ πάντα [κ] ἐν πᾶσιν πληρουμένου If now we take πληρουμένου in an active reflective sense, both meaning and arrangement will be satisfactory—'*the fulness* [receptacle, filled and possessed] *of Him who filleth*' τὰ πάντα ἐν πᾶσιν But are we justified in thus taking it? It seems so, from Xen. Hell vi. 2 14, ὁ στρατηγὸς μάλα ὀξέως τὰς ναῦς ἐπληροῦτο κ τοὺς τριηράρχους ἠνάγκαζε See likewise Plato, Gorg. § 106; Xen Hell. v 4. 56; vi 2. 35 Demosth p. 1208 14 Plut Alcib. 35 Pollux i 99: in all of which the 1 aor middle is thus used. Having then this authority as far as grammatical usage is concerned, we are further inclined to this rendering by ch iv 10, where it is said of Christ, ὁ ἀναβὰς ὑπεράνω πάντων τῶν οὐρανῶν, ἵνα πληρώσῃ **τὰ πάντα**, and the Apostle proceeds to enumerate the various gifts bestowed by Him on His Church See further in note there) **all things** (the whole universe not to be restricted in meaning. The Church is the special receptacle and abiding-place—the πλήρωμα κατ' ἐξοχήν, of Him who fills all things) **with all things** (i e who is the bestower of all, wherever found ἐν πᾶσιν has been rendered '*every where*' [B.-Crus.]. '*in every way*' [De W] '*in every case*' [Harl] and al: but the Apostle's own usage is our best guide,—πληροῦσθε ἐν πνεύματι, ch v. 18, and other reff., and directs us to the *in-*

n — Gal i 13 reff o w ἐν, ver 10 reff w κατά, Rom viii 1, 4 xiv 15. 1 Cor iii 3. 2 John 6 al

καὶ ταῖς [m] ἁμαρτίαις [ὑμῶν], 2 ἐν αἷς [n] ποτὲ [o] περιεπατή-

ABDF KLℵ a b c d e f g h k l m n o 17

CHAP II. 1 for αμαρτιαις, επιθυμιαις B   rec om υμων, with KL rel Chr-comm Damasc Thl Œc   ins BDFℵ m 17 67[2] vss Thdrt Lucif Victorin, εαυτων A.

strumental or elemental meaning—the thing with, or by, or in which as an element, the filling takes place. So that the expression will mean, *with all*, not only gifts, not only blessings, but *things* who fills all creation with whatever it possesses—who is the Author and Giver of all things The reference is, I think, to the Father, not to Christ The latter has been imagined [see especially Ellicott], principally from strictly parallelizing the two clauses,—τὸ σῶμα | αὐτοῦ ||, τὸ πλήρωμα | τοῦ τ. π. ἐν π. πληρουμένου ||. But this is by no means conclusive · the second definitive clause may assert more than the first,—may be, not subordinate to the first, but inclusive of it. In ch. iv 10, where Christ's filling all things is spoken of, we have the active voice, denoting the bare objective fact whereas here the reciprocal middle implies a filling for Himself, which can hardly be predicated of any but the Father, for whom are all things, even the Son himself)

II 1—22.] (See on ch i 3) COURSE AND PROGRESS OF THE CHURCH THROUGH THE SON; consisting mainly in the receiving of believers in the new man Christ Jesus—setting forth on one side the death and ruin in which they were,—on the other, the way to life opened to them by the finished work of Christ This throughout the chapter, which is composed (as ch. i) of two parts—the first, more doctrinal and assertive (vv 1—10), the second more hortative and reminiscent (vv 11—22) In both, the separate cases of Gentiles and Jews, and the present union in Christ, are treated of And herein

A 1—10] THE POWER OF THE FATHER IN QUICKENING US, BOTH GENTILES AND JEWS, IN AND WITH CHRIST (1—6), —HIS PURPOSE IN MANIFESTING THIS POWER (7), — INFERENCE RESPECTING THE METHOD OF OUR SALVATION (8—10)

1, 2] *Actual state of the Gentiles —dead in trespasses and sins, living under the power of the devil.* 1] **You also** (καί is much more than merely copulative. It selects and puts into prominence ὑμᾶς, from among the recipients of God's grace implied in vv 19—23 of the former chapter See below), **who were** ("ὄντας clearly marks the state in which they were at the time when God quickened them this in ver 5 is brought prominently forward by the καί here however καί is joined with and gives prominence to ὑμᾶς. A simple indication, then, of their state, without any temporal or causal adjunct, '*when*,' '*whereas*,' &c, seems in the present case most satisfactory, as less calling away the attention from the more emphatic ὑμᾶς" Ellicott, edn 1) **dead** (certainly not, as Meyer, '*subject to* [physical] *death* ' the whole of the subsequent mercy of God in His quickening them is *spiritual*, and therefore of necessity the death also. That it *involves* physical death, is most true; but as I have often had occasion to remark [see e g on John xi 25, 26], this latter is so subordinate to spiritual death, as often hardly to come into account in Scripture) **in** (not exactly as in Col ii. 13, νεκροὺς ὄντας ἐν τοῖς παραπτώμασιν, where the *element* is more in view, whereas here it is the causal dative—we might render, were the expression good in serious writing, 'dead *of* your trespasses,' as we say 'he lies dead of cholera' I use 'in' as giving nearly the same causal sense: we say, indiscriminately, 'sick *of* a fever,' and 'sick *in* a fever') [**your**] **trespasses and sins** (it seems difficult to establish universally any distinction such as has been attempted, e g by Tittm. Synon. p 47,—"licet non satis vera Hieronymi distinctio videntur, qui παράπτωμα primum ad peccatum lapsum esse dicit, ἁμαρτίαν, quum ad ipsum facinus perventum est; tamen in v παράπτωμα proprie inest notio peccati quod temere commissum est, i e a nolente facere injuriam, sed in ἁμαρτία et ἁμάρτημα cogitatur facinus quod, qui fecit, facere voluit, sive imprudens erraverit, recte se facere existimans, sive impetu animi et libidine obreptus fecerit . . . Levius est παράπτωμα quam ἁμαρτία, si ἁμαρτία de singulo peccato dicitur" Where however, as here, the two occur together, it may be accepted as correct. If we take merely that of Ellicott, al, that "παραπτώματα are the particular, special acts of sin,—ἁμαρτίαι the more general and abstract, viz all forms, phases, and movements of sin, whether entertained in thought or consummated in act," we shall not provide for the whole case for ἁμαρτίαι are unquestionably used for special acts [= ἁμαρτήματα] · and we want a distinction which shall embrace

σατε κατὰ τὸν [p] αἰῶνα τοῦ [p] κόσμου τούτου, [o] κατὰ τὸν [q] ἄρχοντα τῆς [r] ἐξουσίας τοῦ [s] ἀέρος, τοῦ [t] πνεύματος τοῦ

p here only see Gal i 4 q = John xii 31 xiv 30 xvi 11 r ch i 21 reff s Acts xxii 23. 1 Cor ix 26 xiv 9 1 Thess iv 17 Rev ix 2 xvi 17 only Ps xvii 11. t = Luke ix 55 Rom viii 15 1 Cor iv 21 2 Tim i 7 1 John iv 1 ff

this case Another question concerns the construction of this accusative clause Some [Beng., Lachm, Harl] consider it as a continuation of ch i 23, and place a comma only at πληρουμένου But [see our division of the sense] the sentence evidently finishes with πληρουμένου, and a new subject is here taken up. The simplest view seems to be the usual one, that the Apostle began with the accusative, intending to govern it by συνεζωοποίησεν τῷ χριστῷ, but was led away by the relative clauses, ἐν αἷς ποτὲ . . , ἐν οἷς καὶ ἡμεῖς . . , and himself takes up the dropped thread of the construction by ὁ δὲ θεὸς , ver 4 So Erasm "hyperbati longioris ambitum ipse correxit Apostolus dicens 'Deus autem qui dives est' . . ." At all events, the clause should be left, in translation, pendent, as it stands, and not filled in conjecturally), 2] in which (ἁμαρτίαις, the last substantive, but applying in fact to both) ye once walked (we hardly need, as Eadie, al, go back every time to the figure in περιπατεῖν—the word has become with the Apostle so common in its figurative sense See Fritzsche's note, Rom vol iii p 140) according to (after the leading of, conformably to) the course (so E V . the very best word, as so often The meaning of αἰών here is compounded of its temporal and its ethical sense it is not exactly '*lifetime*,' 'duration,' nor again 'fashion,' 'spirit,' but some common term which will admit of being both temporally and ethically characterized,—'career' or 'course' Beware 1) of taking αἰῶνα and κόσμου as synonymous, and the expression as a pleonasm [" utrumque nominat, seculum et mundum, cum sufficeret alterum dixisse," Estius], 2) of imagining, as Michaelis and Baur, that the expression is a gnostic one, the æon being *the devil* for, as Meyer remarks, the ordinary sense of αἰών gives a good meaning, and one characteristic of St Paul. See Gal. i 4, for a use of αἰών—somewhat similar, but more confined to the temporal meaning) of this world (St. Paul generally uses ὁ κόσμος, but has ὁ κ. οὗτος in 1 Cor iii. 19; v. 10, vii 31. It designates the present system of things, as alien from God, and lying in the evil one), according to the ruler of the power of the air (the devil—the θεὸς τοῦ αἰῶνος τούτου, 2 Cor. iv 4, is clearly meant. but it is difficult exactly to dissect the phrase, and give each word its proper meaning ἐξουσία appears to be used here as ὁμηλικίη in Homer, ἡλικία, ἑταιρία, δουλεία, ὑπηρεσία, συμμαχία, and the like, to represent *the aggregate* of those in power: as we say, 'the government' So that all such renderings as 'princeps potentissimus' are to be at once dismissed So also is every explanation which would ascribe to the Apostle a polemical, or distantly allusive tendency, in an expression which he manifestly uses as one of passage merely, and carrying its own familiar sense to his readers This against Michaelis, and all who have imagined an allusion to the gnostic ideas — and Wetst, who says, " Paulus ita loquitur ex principiis philosophiæ Pythagoreæ, quibus illi ad quos scribit imbuti erant " Not much better are those who refer the expression to Rabbinical ideas for its source The different opinions and authorities [which would far exceed the limits of a general commentary] may be seen cited and treated in Harless, Stier, and Eadie. I am disposed to seek my interpretation from a much more obvious source viz the persuasion and common parlance of mankind, founded on analogy with well-known facts. [Ellic, edn. 2, disapproves this, but without sufficiently attending to my explanation which follows, which, as in so many cases where he imagines a difference between our interpretations, is practically the same as his own] We are tempted by evil spirits, who have access to us, and suggest thoughts and desires to our minds We are surrounded by the air, which is the vehicle of speech and of all suggestions to our senses Tried continually as we are by these temptations, what so natural, as to assign to their ministers a dwelling in, and power over that element which is the vehicle of them to us ? And thus our Lord, in the parable of the sower, when He would represent the devil coming and taking away the seed out of the heart, figures him by τὰ πετεινὰ τοῦ οὐρανοῦ. The Apostle then, in using this expression, would be appealing to the common feeling of his readers, not to any recondite or questionable system of dæmonology. That traces are found in such systems, of a belief agreeing with this, is merely a proof that they have embodied the same general feeling, and may be used

νῦν ᵘ ἐνεργοῦντος ἐν τοῖς ᵛ υἱοῖς τῆς ᵛ ἀπειθείας, 3 ἐν οἷς
καὶ ἡμεῖς πάντες ʷ ἀνεστράφημέν ποτε ἐν ταῖς ˣ ἐπιθυμίαις

ABDF KLℵ a b c d e f g h k l m n o 17

u ch i. 11 reff. v ch v. 6 (Col iii. 6 v. r.) only. vi.—John xvii. 12. 2 Thess ii. 3. see Isa. lvii. 4. uπ., Rom xi. 30, 32. Heb iv. 6, 11 † w = Matt xvii. 22. 2 Cor i. 12 (& constr.). 1 Tim iii. 15. 1 Pet i. 17. 2 Pet ii. 18. Ezek xix. 6. see Heb x. 33. x (Rom xiii. 14.) Gal v. 16. 2 Pet ii. 18. 1 John ii. 16. see 1 Pet ii. 11.

in illustration, not as the ground, of the Apostle's saying All attempts to represent ἀήρ as meaning '*darkness*,' or '*spirit*,' are futile, and beside the purpose The word occurs (see reff) six more times in the N T and nowhere in any but its ordinary meaning), of the spirit (τῆς ἐξουσίας being used as designating [see above] the personal aggregate of those evil ones who have this power, τοῦ πνεύματος, in apposition with it, represents their aggregate character, as an influence on the human mind, a spirit of ungodliness and disobedience,—the πνεῦμα τοῦ κόσμου of 1 Cor ii. 12,—the aggregate of the πνεύματα πλάνα of 1 Tim iv 1 So that [against Harless] the meaning of πνεύματος, though properly and strictly objective, almost passes into the subjective, when it is spoken of as ἐνεργοῦντος ἐν κ τ λ And this will account for the otherwise harsh conjunction of ἄρχοντα τοῦ πνεύματος As he (the devil) is the ruler of τὰ πνεύματα, whose aggregate τὸ πνεῦμα is,—so he is the ἄρχων of the thoughts and ways of the ungodly,—of that πνεῦμα which works in them. The genitive, πνεύματος, must not be taken, as by many Commentators and by Ruckert, as in apposition with ἄρχοντα, by the Apostle's negligence of construction No such assumption should ever be made without necessity, and there is surely none here) which is now (i e '*still*' contrast to ποτέ,—to *you*, who have escaped from his government no allusion need be thought of to the interval before the παρουσία being that of the hottest conflict between the principles [2 Thess ii. 7 Rev. xii 12], as De W) working in the sons of (the expression is a Hebraism, but is strictly reproduced in the fact that of which they are sons, is the source and spring of their lives, not merely an accidental quality belonging to them) disobedience (the vulg renders it *diffidentia*, but unfortunately, as also Luther Unglaube; for both here and in ch v 6, it is practical conduct which is spoken of. Doubtless unbelief is the root of disobedience. but it is not here expressed, only implied. In Deut. ix 23, ἠπειθήσατε τῷ ῥήματι κυρίου τ θεοῦ ὑμῶν, and the allusion to it in Heb. iv 6, οἱ πρότερον εὐαγγελισθέντες οὐκ εἰσῆλθον δι' ἀπείθειαν, we have the disobedience in its root—here, in its fruits—cf. ver. 3, ποιοῦντες τὰ θελήματα κ τ λ). 3] among whom (the υἱοὶ τ ἀπειθείας not merely local, but 'numbered among whom,'—ὧν καὶ αὐτοὶ ὄντες, as Ruckert. not '*in which*,' viz. παραπτώμασιν, as Syr, Jer, Grot, Bengel, al, and Stier, who would divide off ἁμαρτίαι, allotting them to the Gentiles, and to ver. 2,—and παραπτώματα, assigning them to the Jews, and to ver. 3. See further on this below but meantime, besides its very clumsy treatment of the ἁμαρτ. and παραπτ. which both belong to ὑμεῖς in ver 1, it ascribes to the Apostle an unusual and unnatural precision in distinguishing the two words which he had used without any such note of distinction, such as τε—καί) we also all (WHO? The usage of ἡμεῖς πάντες by St. Paul must decide. It occurs Rom. iv. 16, ὅς ἐστιν πατὴρ πάντων ἡμῶν, undeniably for Jews and Gentiles included [for the slight difference arising from πάντων being first, and therefore emphatic, need not be insisted on]. viii 32, ὑπὲρ ἡμῶν πάντων παρέδωκεν αὐτόν, where the universal reference is as undeniable 1 Cor xii. 13, where it is still more marked: ἡμεῖς πάντες· . . . . εἴτε Ἰουδαῖοι εἴτε Ἕλληνες, εἴτε δοῦλοι εἴτε ἐλεύθεροι· 2 Cor. iii. 18, equally undoubted. It can hardly then be that here he should have departed from his universal usage, and placed an unmeaning πάντες after ἡμεῖς merely to signify, 'we Jews, every one of us.' I therefore infer that by ἡμεῖς πάντες, he means, we all, Jews and Gentiles alike; all, who are now Christians) lived our life (reff especially 2 Cor.) once, in (as in ref. 1 Pet, of the element, in which in 2 Cor i 12, the same double use of ἐν, of the place, and the element, is found) the desires of our flesh (of our unrenewed selves, under the dominion of the body and the carnal soul. See a contrast, Gal v 16), doing the wishes (the instances in which τὸ θέλημα manifested itself see reff.) of our flesh and of our thoughts (the plural use is remarkable There appears to be a reference to Num xv 39, οὐ διαστραφήσεσθε ὀπίσω τῶν διανοιῶν ὑμῶν In Isa lv 9, a distinction is made, ἀπέχει . . τὰ διανοήματα ὑμῶν ἀπὸ τῆς διανοίας μου, which is useful here, as pointing to διάνοιαι as an improper use for διανοήματα,

τῆς [x] σαρκὸς ἡμῶν, ποιοῦντες τὰ [y] θελήματα τῆς [y] σαρκὸς καὶ τῶν [z] διανοιῶν, καὶ ἤμεθα [a] τέκνα [b] φύσει ὀργῆς ὡς

y John i. 13 only. θελ. plur., Acts xiii. 22 (from Isa. xliv. 28?) only. Jer. xxiii. 26 al. z = ch. iv. 18. Col. i. 21. plur., here (Heb. x. 16 v. r.) only. see note. a = Matt. xi. 19. Rom. ix. 8. ch. v. 8. 1 Pet. i. 14. 2 Pet. ii. 14. Isa. lvii. 4. b Rom. ii. 14. Gal. ii. 15. iv. 8 only. (-σις, Rom. i. 26 al.)

3. om και ημεις FL: for ημ., υμ. A(but nearly erased) D[1]. rec (for ημεθα) ημεν, with ADFKL rel Clem Did Chr Thdrt Damasc: txt Bℵ 17 $Orig_4$. φυσει bef τεκνα ADFL m latt arm $Orig_1$ Did Thdrt lat-ff: om φυσει 109 æth Clem: txt BKℵ rel $Orig_3$ Chr Thl Œc.

—the instrument for its results. Thus '*thoughts*' will be our nearest word—those phases of mind which may or may not affect the will, but which then in our natural state we allowed to lead us by the desires they excited), **and were** (the change of construction has been remarked by the best Commentators as intentional, not of negligence,—"to give emphasis to the weighty clause that follows, and to disconnect it from any possible relation to present time, 'we *were* children of wrath by nature,—it was once our state and condition, it is now so no longer.'" Ellicott. And Eadie remarks: "Had he written καὶ ὄντες, as following out the idea of ποιοῦντες, there might have been a plea against the view of innate depravity [see below]—'fulfilling the desires of the flesh and of the mind, and being,' or 'so being, children of wrath.' But the Apostle says, καὶ ἤμεθα—'and we were,' at a point of time prior to that indicated in ποιοῦντες") **children** (not = υἱοί, but implying closer relation. The effect of the expression is to set those of whom it is predicated, beneath, in subjection to, as it were, the products of, ὀργή. So in the passages adduced by Harl.;—Deut. xxv. 2, אִם־בִּן הַכּוֹת, 'if he be the son of stripes,' i. e. not as LXX and E. V. ἄξιος πληγῶν, but actually beaten:—1 Sam. xx. 31, בֶּן־מָוֶת הוּא, 'he is the son of death,'—i. e. as we express it, 'he is a dead man,' anticipating the effect of that which seems to be certain) **by nature** (the meaning of φύσει is disputed. Some of the ancients [Cyr., Œc., Thl.], and Grot. took it as = ὄντως, ἀληθῶς, which meaning it never bears; see on Gal. iv. 8. Others [Holzhausen, Hoffm.] would join it with ὀργῆς,—'anger, which arises from the ungodly natural life:' but as Mey. remarks, even granting this use of φύσις, this would require τῆς τῇ φύσει ὀργῆς or τῆς ἐκ τῆς φύσ. ὀργῆς. It can then only mean, 'by nature.' And what does this imply? Harl., in loc., seems to have given the distinctive sense well: "φύσις, in its fundamental idea, is that which has *grown* as distinguished from that which has been *effected* [das Gewordene in Gegensatz zum Gemachten], i. e. it is that which according to our judgment has the ground of its existence in individual development, not in accessory influence of another. Accordingly, φύσις, in its concrete idea, as the sum total of all growth, is 'rerum natura:' and in its abstract philosophical idea, φύσις is the contrast to θέσις. The φύσις of an individual thing denotes the peculiarity of its being, which is the result of its being, as opposed to every accessory quality: hence φύσει εἶναι or ποιεῖν τι means, '*sua sponte facere, esse aliquid*' and '*natura esse aliquid:*' *to be and do any thing by virtue of a state* [εἶναι] or an *inclination* [ποιεῖν], *not acquired, but inherent:* ἐξοιδα καὶ φύσει σε μὴ πεφυκότα | τοιαῦτα φωνεῖν, μηδὲ τεχνᾶσθαι κακά, Soph. Philoct. 80." If this be correct, the expression will *amount to* an assertion on the part of the Apostle of the doctrine of original sin. There is from its secondary position [cf. Plutarch de frat. am. p. 37, in Harl., ὀργάνων φύσει τοιούτων ἔτυχεν] no emphasis on φύσει: but its doctrinal force as referring to a fundamental truth otherwise known, is not thereby lessened. And it is not for Meyer to argue against this by assuming original sin not to be a pauline doctrine. If the Apostle asserts it here, this place must stand on its own merits, not be wrested to suit an apparent preconceived meaning of other passages. But the truth is, he cites those other passages in a sense quite alien from their real one. It would be easy to shew that every one of them [Rom. i. 18; ii. 8, 9; v. 12; vii. 9; xi. 21. Gal. ii. 15] is consistent with the doctrine here implied. The student will do well to read the long notes in Harl., De W., Stier, and Eadie) **of wrath** (WHOSE wrath, is evident: the meaning being, we were all concluded under and born in sin, and so actual objects of that wrath of God which is His mind against sin. **ὀργή** must not be taken as = τιμωρία, κόλασις, as Chrys., Thdrt., Basil, Thl., al.: this would in fact make the expression mean, *actually punished:* see above on τέκνα;—just as it now means, the

c 1 Thess iv 13 v 6 1 Tim v 20 Rev xi 13 al
d = James ii 5 only see ch i 7, 18

καὶ ^c οἱ λοιποί· 4 ὁ δὲ θεός, ^d πλούσιος ὢν ^e ἐν ^f ἐλέει, διὰ
τὴν πολλὴν ^g ἀγάπην αὐτοῦ ^g ἣν ^g ἠγάπησεν ἡμᾶς, 5 καὶ
ὄντας ἡμᾶς ^h νεκροὺς τοῖς ^h παραπτώμασιν ^i συνεζωποί-

ABDF KLℵ a b c d e f g h k l m n o 17

e = 1 Tim vi 18 James ii 5 f Luke i 50, &c Rom ix 23 1 Pet i 3 Isa liv 7, 8 g John xvii 26 2 Kings xiii 15. h ver 1 i Col ii 13 only †

4. ο is written twice in ℵ, but the first partly rubbed out. om εν ℵ[1]: ins ℵ[3] om αυτου D[1]F.

5 ins εν bef τοις παραπτωμασιν B syr copt om ℵ &c. for τοις παραπτ., ταις αμαρτιαις D[1] τη αμαρτια F. aft παραπτωμασιν ins και επιθυμιαις (see ver 1,

actual objects of God's wrath against sin), **as also are** (not, were) **the rest** (of mankind not Gentiles, as those hold who take the ἡμεῖς πάντες of Jews,—see above nor, as Stier, the rest of the Jews who disbelieved. but, *all others, not like us, Christians*). 4] The construction is resumed, having been interrupted (see above on ver 1) by the two relative sentences, **ἐν αἷς** . **ἐν οἷς** **But** (contrast to the preceding verse,—the ἔλεος and ἀγάπη, to the ὀργή just mentioned δέ is, however, often used after a parenthesis, where no such logical contrast is intended, the very resumption of the general subject being a contrast to its interruption by the particular clauses. see examples in Klotz, Devarius, II 376, 7) **God, being rich** (the participial clause states the general ground, and the following διὰ τ. πολλ ἀγ, the special or peculiar motive, of συνεζωοπ, De W) **in compassion** (for ἐν, see reff οὐχ ἁπλῶς ἐλεήμων, ἀλλὰ πλούσιος· καθάπερ καὶ ἐν ἑτέρῳ [Ps. v. 7; lxxiii 13] φησὶν Ἐν τῷ πλήθει τοῦ ἐλέους σου κ πάλιν [Ps l 1] Ἐλέησόν με κατὰ τὸ μέγα ἔλεός σου, Chrys ἔλεος, properly, as applying to our wretchedness before cf. Ezek xvi 6),—**on account of His great love wherewith** (the construction may be attractive but it would appear from ref 2 Kings, to be rather a Hellenistic idiom) **He loved us** (the clause belongs, not to πλού ὢν ἐν ἐλ, as Calv., al, and E V necessarily, by '*hath quickened*' following, but to the verb below ἡμᾶς are *all Christians*, = ἡμεῖς πάντες in the last verse) **even when we were dead** (the καί belongs to, and intensifies, the *state predicated by* **ὄντας νεκρούς**; and is therefore placed before the participle. It is not to be taken as a mere resumption of ver 1 [Rück, al.], nor as the copula only [Meyer] His objection to the above rendering, that a quickening to life can happen only in and from a state of death, and therefore no emphasis on such a state is required, is entirely removed by noticing that the emphasis is not on the mere fact ἐζωοποίησεν,—but on **συνεζ τῷ χριστῷ**, with all its glorious consequences) **in our** (**τοῖς**, the π which we committed) **trespasses** (see on ver 1), **vivified** (not '*hath vivified*'—a definite act in time, not an abiding consequence is spoken of) **us together with Christ** (the reading ἐν τ χρ [see var. readd] seems to have arisen either from repetition of the -εν in συνεζωοποίησεν, or from conformation to ver 6 It is clearly not allowable to render χριστῷ, *in Christ*, as Beza,—without the preposition It is governed by the συν-, and implies not exactly as Chrys, ἐζωοποίησε κἀκεῖνον καὶ ἡμᾶς,—but that Christ was THE RESURRECTION and the Life, and we follow in and because of Him. The disputes about the meaning of ἐζωοποίησεν have arisen from not bearing in mind the relation in N. T. language between natural and spiritual death We have often had occasion to observe that spiritual death in the N T. includes in it and bears with it natural death as a consequence, to such an extent that this latter is often not thought of as worth mentioning see especially John xi 25, 26, which is the key-text for all passages regarding life in Christ So here—God vivified us together with Christ in the one act and fact of His resurrection He raised all His people—to spiritual life, and in that to victory over death, both spiritual, and therefore necessarily physical also To dispute therefore whether such an expression as this is past [spiritual], or future [physical], is to forget that the whole includes its parts Our *spiritual life* is the primary subject of the Apostle's thought. but this includes in itself our share in the resurrection and exaltation [ver 6] of Christ The three aorists, συνεζωοποίησεν, συνήγειρεν, συνεκάθισεν, are all proleptical as regards the actuation in each man, but equally describe a past and accomplished act on God's part when He raised up Christ)—**by grace ye are saved** (this insertion in the midst of the mention of such great unmerited mercies to us sinners, is meant emphatically to call the reader's attention to so cogent a proof of that which the Apostle ever preached as the great foundation truth of the

ησεν τῷ χριστῷ (ʲ χάριτί ἐστε σεσωσμένοι) 6 καὶ ᵏ συνήγειρεν καὶ ˡ συνεκάθισεν ἐν τοῖς ᵐ ἐπουρανίοις ἐν χριστῷ
Ἰησοῦ, 7 ἵνα ⁿ ἐνδείξηται ἐν τοῖς ᵒ αἰῶσιν τοῖς ᵒ ἐπερχομέ-
νοις τὸ ᵖ ὑπερβάλλον ᵠ πλοῦτος τῆς χάριτος αὐτοῦ ἐν
ʳ χρηστότητι ˢ ἐφ' ἡμᾶς ἐν χριστῷ Ἰησοῦ. 8 τῇ γὰρ

j = Rom iii 24, and Paul passim k (=) Col ii 12 iii 1 only (Exod xxiii 5 F) Isa xiv 9 only l trans., here only: intr., Luke xxii 55 only Exod xviii 13 m ch i 3 reff n Paul (Rom ix 17, from Exod ix 16 1 Tim i 16 al) only, exc Heb vi 10, 11 o here only (see Mark x 30 ‖ L) ἐπ., = Luke xxi 26 James v 1 p ch i 19 reff q ch i 7 reff r Gal v 22 reff P Ps xxx 19 s Rom xi 22 see εις ἡμ, ch i 19

var read) B aft συνεζ. ins εν (see note) B 17. 118 vulg(not am demid al) G-lat(altern) copt Chr Damasc lat-ff. ins ου τη bef χαριτι D¹; ου F latt(not am) Aug

6 om εν χ ι F Hil Aug₂(ins₁) Victorin.

7 om ver (homœotel) ℵ¹: ins ℵ-corr¹. rec τον υπερβαλλοντα πλουτον, with D³KL rel. txt ABD¹Fℵ corr¹ 17 67² Orig₁ Eus. ins τη bef χρηστοτητι D. om ιησου D¹F æth-rom. (not F-lat)

Gospel Notice the perf '*are* saved,' not σώζεσθε, 'are *being* saved,' because we have passed from death unto life salvation is to the Christian not a future but a past thing, realized in the present by faith)—**and raised us together with Him** (the Resurrection of Christ being the next event consequent on His vivification in the tomb) **and seated us together with Him** (the Ascension being the completion of the Resurrection. So that all three verbs refer strictly to the same work wrought on Christ, and in Christ on all His mystical Body, the Church) **in the heavenly places** (see on ch i 3, 20 "Obiter observa, non dixisse Apostolum '*et consedere fecit ad dexteram suam*,' sicut superiori capite de Christo dixerat: sedere enim ad dexteram Patris Christo proprium est, nec cuiquam alteri communicatur tametsi in throno Christi dicantur sessuri qui vicerint, Apoc iii in fine." Estius. and so Bengel) **in Christ Jesus** (as again specifying the element in which, as united and included in which, we have these blessings which have been enumerated—ἐν χρ as in ch i 3, does not [Eadie] belong to τ ἐπουρ. but to the verb, as an additional qualification, and recalling to the fact of our union in Him as the medium of our resurrection and glorification. The disputes as to whether these are to be taken as present or future, actual or potential, literal or spiritual, will easily be disposed of by those who have apprehended the truth of the believer's union in and with Christ. All these we have, in fact and reality [see Phil iii. 20], in their highest, and therefore in all lower senses, in Him they were ours, when they were His but for their fulness in possession we are waiting till He come, when we shall be like and with Him),

7] **that He might shew forth** (see Rom ix. 23. and for ἐνδείξηται, reff The middle voice gives the reference which the English sentence itself implies, that the exhibition is for His own purpose, for His own glory [see ch. i. 6, 12, 14] —see note on Col ii 15. This meaning of *præ se ferre* is illustrated by Liddell and Scott sub voce or far better by Palm and Rost, Lex. Beware of the rendering 'might give a specimen of' [Ruckert, Eadie], which the word will not bear either here or in reff) **in the ages which are hereafter to come** (what are they? the future periods of the Church's earthly career,—or the ages of the glorified Church hereafter? The answer must be given by comparing this with the very similar expression in Col. i. 26, 27, ... *τὸ μυστήριον τὸ ἀποκεκρυμμένον ἀπὸ τῶν αἰώνων κ ἀπὸ τῶν γενεῶν, νυνὶ δὲ ἐφανερώθη τοῖς ἁγίοις αὐτοῦ, οἷς ἠθέλησεν ὁ θεὸς γνωρίσαι τίς ὁ πλοῦτος τῆς δόξης αὐτοῦ κ τ λ.* Here it is manifest (1) that the αἰῶνες from which the mystery was hidden are the past ages of this world; (2) that those to whom, as here, God will make known the riches of His glory, are His saints, i e His church on earth Therefore I conceive we are compelled to interpret analogously viz. to understand the αἰῶνες ἐπερχόμενοι of the coming ages of the church, and the persons involved in them to be the future members of the church Thus the meaning will be nearly as in ch i 12 The supposed reference to the future state of glory seems not to agree with αἰῶνες, nor with ἐπερχόμενοι —nor with the fact that the second coming and future kingdom of Christ are hardly ever alluded to in this Epistle) **the exceeding riches of His grace in** (of the material of which this display of His grace will consist, the department in which it will find its exercise) **goodness** (see especially Rom. ii 4) **towards us in** (not '*through*,' as E. V)

t ver. 5 reff.
u Rom. iii. 22, 30. 2 Cor. v. 7. Gal. ii. 16. iii. 26. Phil. iii. 9. Col. ii. 12 al., Paul. 1 Pet. i. 5.
π., — Acts xv. 9.
v Rom. xiii. 11. 1 Cor. vi. 6, 8. Phil. i. 28. 3 John 5.

[t] χάριτί ἐστε σεσωσμένοι [u] διὰ [τῆς] [u] πίστεως, [v] καὶ ABDF KLℵ a b c d e f g h k l m n o 17
[v] τοῦτο οὐκ [w] ἐξ ὑμῶν, θεοῦ τὸ [x] δῶρον· 9 οὐκ [w] ἐξ ἔργων,
ἵνα μή τις [y] καυχήσηται. 10 αὐτοῦ γάρ ἐσμεν [z] ποίημα,
[a] κτισθέντες ἐν χριστῷ Ἰησοῦ [b] ἐπὶ [c] ἔργοις [c] ἀγαθοῖς, [d] οἷς
[e] προητοίμασεν ὁ θεὸς ἵνα [f] ἐν αὐτοῖς [f] περιπατήσωμεν.

w 1 Cor. i. 30. 2 Cor. iii. 5. x = (& Paul) here only. (Matt. ii. 11 al. Rev. xi. 10.) δωρεά, John iv. 10. 2 Cor. ix. 15 al. y Paul (Rom. ii. 17 al[33], not Col.) only, exc. James i. 9, iv. 16. (so also καύχημα & καύχησις, exc. Heb. iii. 6. James iv. 16.) Jer. ix. 23, 24. z Rom. i. 20 only. Eccl. viii. 17. a = ch. iii. 9. iv. 24. Col. i. 16, iii. 10 al. b = Gal. v. 13. 1 Thess. iv. 7. c Paul (Rom. ii. 7. xiii. 3 al[13].) only, exc. Acts ix. 36. Heb. xiii. 21. d attr., ch. i. 6 reff. e Rom. ix. 23 only. Isa. xxviii. 24. Wisd. ix. 8 only. f Rom. vi. 4. 2 Cor. iv. 2. x. 3. ch. v. 2. Col. iii. 6, iv. 5. 1 John i. 6, 7 al. Prov. viii. 20.

8. *αυτου χαριτι σεσ. εσμεν* D[1] Syr copt æth. om *της* bef *πιστεως* BD[1]Fℵ 17. 67[2] Chr: ins AD[3]KL rel Thdrt[2] Damasc Thl-comm Œc. *ημων* DF d (Chrys Thl Œc in comm) Damasc.

9. *καυχησεται* B(Mai) F.

10. for *αυτου*, *θεου* ℵ[1]: txt ℵ-corr[1]. for *χ. ιη.*, *κυριω* F. for *επι*, *επ* F a c g k m Chr[1] Thdrt Damasc: *εν* 73. 74. 109 latt Aug lat-ff.

Christ Jesus (again and again he repeats this "*in Christ Jesus*:" HE is the great centre of the Epistle, towards whom all the rays of thought converge, and from whom all blessings flow; and this the Apostle will have his readers never forget).

8.] **For by grace** (the article shews us the import of the sentence—to take up and expand the parenthetic clause *χάριτί ἐστε σεσωσμένοι* above: but not barely so: that clause itself was inserted on account of the matter in hand being a notable example of the fact, and this *γάρ* takes up also that matter in hand—the *ὑπερβάλλον πλοῦτος κ.τ.λ.*) **ye are** (perf.) **saved, through [your]** (or [*the*], but the possessive article is preferable, see below: 'the' would make both objective. The abstract, '*through faith*,' must be the rendering if the article be omitted) **faith** (the dative above expressed the objective instrumental condition of your salvation,—this **διά** the subjective medial condition: it has been effected by grace and apprehended by faith): **and this** (not *your faith*, as Chrys. *οὐδὲ ἡ πίστις, φησίν, ἐξ ὑμῶν*: so Thdrt., al., Corn.-a-lap., Beza, Est., Grot., Beng., all.;—this is precluded [not by the gender of *τοῦτο*, but] by the manifestly parallel clauses *οὐκ ἐξ ὑμῶν* and *οὐκ ἐξ ἔργων*, of which the latter would be irrelevant as asserted of *πίστις*, and the reference of ver. 9 must therefore be changed:—but, as Calv., Calov., Rück., Harl., Olsh., Mey., De W., Stier, al., 'your salvation;' *τὸ σεσωσμένοι εἶναι*, as Ellic.) **not of yourselves**, (GOD's (emphatic) **is the gift** (not, as E. V. '*it is the gift of God*' [*θεοῦ δῶρον*],—*τὸ δῶρον*, viz. of your salvation:—so that the expression is pregnant—q. d., '*but it is a gift, and that gift is God's*.' There is no occasion, as Lachm., Harl., and De W., to parenthesize these words: they form a contrast to *οὐκ ἐξ ὑμ.*, and a quasi-parallel clause to *ἵνα μή τις καυχήσ.* below): **not of works** (for *ἐξ ἔργων*, see on Rom. iii. iv., and Gal. ii. 16), **that no man should boast** (on the proposition implied, see on Rom. iv. 2. **ἵνα** has in matter of fact its strictest telic sense. With God, results are all purposed; it need not be understood, when we predicate of Him a purpose in this manner, that it was His *main* or *leading* aim;—but it was one of those things included in His scheme, which ranked among His purposes).

10.] **For** (substantiates vv. 8, 9. The English reader is likely to imagine a contrast between 'not of *works*' and 'for we are His *work*manship,' which can hardly have been in the mind of the Apostle) **his handywork are we** (**ποίημα**, not, as Tert. and al., of our *original creation*: "quod vivimus, quod spiramus, quod intelligimus, quod credere possumus, ipsius est, quia ipse conditor noster est," Pelagius, in Harl.: this is clearly refuted by the defining clause below, *κτισθ. κ.τ.λ.*, and the *ποίημα* shewn to be the spiritual creation treated of in vv. 8, 9), **created in Christ Jesus** (see ver. 15, *ἵνα τοὺς δύο* **κτίσῃ ἐν αὐτῷ** *εἰς ἕνα καινὸν ἄνθρωπον*, and cf. Tit. iii. 5, where the beginning of this new life is called *παλιγγενεσία*. See also 2 Cor. v. 17; Gal. vi. 15) **for** (see reff.: so Xen. Anab. vii. 6. 3, *καλεῖ αὐτοὺς ἐπὶ ξενίᾳ*. See Winer, edn. 6, § 48, c. e; Phrynichus, ed. Lobeck, p. 475) **good works** (just as a tree may be said to be created for its fruit: see below), **which** (attraction for *ἅ*: not 'for which,' which would require *ἡμᾶς* after the verb) **God before prepared** ('ante paravit, quam conderet,' Fritz. in Ellic. So Philo, de Opif. 25, vol. i. p. 18,

11 Διὸ [g] μνημονεύετε ὅτι [h] ποτὲ ὑμεῖς τὰ ἔθνη [i] ἐν σαρκί,
οἱ [k] λεγόμενοι [l] ἀκροβυστία ὑπὸ τῆς [k] λεγομένης [m] περιτομῆς [i] ἐν σαρκὶ [n] χειροποιήτου, 12 ὅτι ἦτε τῷ καιρῷ ἐκείνῳ
[o] χωρὶς χριστοῦ [p] ἀπηλλοτριωμένοι τῆς [q] πολιτείας τοῦ

g w ὅτι, Paul only Acts xx 31 2 Thess ii 5
h = John ix 13. Rom vii 9 xi 30 al
i 1 Tim iii 16 reff
k Matt x 2 Acts iii 2 1 Cor viii 5 2 Thess ii 4 al
l Paul (Rom ii 25, &c, 1 Cor vii 17 al) only, exc Acts xi 3 Gen. xvii. 11, &c.
m Paul (Rom, as above (l)), 1 Cor vii. 19 al) only, exc John vii 22, 23. Acts vii 8 x. 45 xi. 2. Exod iv 26.
n Mark xiv 58 Acts vii 48 xvii 24 Heb ix 11, 24 only. Isa ii 18, of idols.
o John xv 5 Rom iii 21 al
p ch. iv. 18 Col i. 21 only Ps. lxviii. 8
q — here (Acts xxii, 28) only †. 2 Macc. iv. 11.

11. *δια τουτο μνημονευοντες υμ οι ποτε κ τ.λ* F Dial$_1$. rec *υμεις* bef *ποτε* (*for euphony*), with D³KLℵ³ rel vss ff. txt ABD¹ℵ¹ m 17 vulg Dial$_1$ Cyr Did Ambr Jer.
12 rec ins *εν* bef *τω καιρω* (*explanatory*), with D³KL rel vulg copt goth Orig-cat Dial Tert. om ABD¹Fℵ 17 tol(and F-lat) Chr-comm Epiph Cyr Victorin Jer Aug.

ὁ θεὸς τὰ ἐν κόσμῳ πάντα προητοίμασεν Wisd ix 8, *μίμημα σκηνῆς ἁγίας ἣν προητοίμασας ἀπ' ἀρχῆς* The sentiment is the same as that in John v 36, *τὰ ἔργα ἃ ἔδωκέν μοι ὁ πατὴρ ἵνα τελειώσω αὐτά* To recur to the similitude used above, we might say of the trees,—they were created for fruits which God before prepared that they should bear them: i. e defined and assigned to each tree its own, in form, and flavour, and time of bearing. So in the course of God's providence, our good works are marked out for and assigned to each one of us See the doctrine of præ-existence in God explained in Delitzsch's biblische Psychologie, p. 23 ff. Stier's view, after Bengel, is that the verb **προητ** is *neuter*, having no accusative after it,—'*for which God made preparation*, &c.' but this usage of the compound verb wants example) **that we should walk in them** Thus the truth of the maxim "bona opera non præcedunt justificandum, sed sequuntur justificatum" (see Harl) is shewn. The sentiment is strictly pauline (against De W and Baur),—in the spirit of Rom. xii, Gal v 22, 25, &c.

B. 11—22.] HORTATORY EXPANSION OF THE FOREGOING INTO DETAIL. REMINDING THEM, WHAT THEY ONCE WERE (vv 11, 12), WHAT THEY WERE NOW IN CHRIST (vv. 13—22). **11.] Wherefore** (since so many and great blessings are given by God to His people, among whom ye are) **remember, that once ye, the** (i. e. who belonged to the category of the) **Gentiles in the flesh** (i e in their corporeal condition of uncircumcision 'præputium profani hominis indicium est,' Calv.—construction see below), **who are called (the) uncircumcision by that which is called (the) circumcision in the flesh wrought by hands** (this last addition **ἐν σαρκὶ χειρ** seems made by the Apostle, not to throw discredit on circumcision, but as a reserve, *περιτομή* having a higher and spiritual application q d —'but they have it only in the flesh, and not in the heart' As Ellic well states the case—"The Gentiles were called, and *were* the *ἀκροβυστία* the Jews were called, but were not truly the *περιτομή*." See Col ii 11), **12] that ye were** (the **ὅτι** takes up again the *ὅτι* in ver. 11, after the relative clause,—and the **τῷ κ ἐκείνῳ** takes up the *ποτέ* there. It is not a broken construction, but only a repetition, 'that, I say . ') **at that time** (when ye were,—not *τὰ ἔθνη ἐν σαρκί*, which ye are now, and which is carefully divided from *ποτέ* above by *ὑμεῖς*,—but that which is implied in *ποτέ*,—heathens, before your conversion to Christ On the dative of time without the preposition *ἐν*, see Kuhner, vol ii. § 569, and remarks on its difference from the genitive and accusative) **without Christ** (separate from, having no part in, the promised Messiah That this is the sense, is evident from ver 13 see below. The words **χωρ χρ.** are not a defining clause to *ἦτε ἀπηλλοτρ*, as Lachmann points them, and De W. and Eadie render 'that ye were, being without Christ, &c.' The arrangement would thus be harsh and clumsy beyond all precedent) **alienated from** (*οὐκ εἶπε, κεχωρισμένοι . . πολλὴ τῶν ῥημάτων ἡ ἔμφασις, πολὺν δεικνῦσα τὸν χωρισμόν ἐπεὶ καὶ Ἰσραηλῖται τῆς πολιτείας ἦσαν ἐκτός, ἀλλ' οὐχ ὡς ἀλλότριοι ἀλλ' ὡς ῥᾴθυμοι, κ τῶν διαθηκῶν ἐξέπεσον, ἀλλ' οὐχ ὡς ξένοι, ἀλλ' ὡς ἀνάξιοι*, Chr Gentiles and Jews were once united in the hope of redemption—this was constituted, on the apostasy of the nations, into a definite *πολιτεία* for the Jews, from which and its blessings the Gentiles were alienated) **the commonwealth** (*πολιτεία* is both *polity, state* [objective],—*τῶν τὴν πόλιν οἰκούντων τάξις τις*, Aristot. Polit. iii. 1,—and *right of citizenship*, ref. Acts. The former appears best here, on account of

Ἰσραὴλ καὶ [r] ξένοι τῶν [s] διαθηκῶν τῆς [t] ἐπαγγελίας, ABDF KLℵa b
ἐλπίδα μὴ ἔχοντες καὶ [u] ἄθεοι ἐν τῷ κόσμῳ. 13 [v] νυνὶ δὲ c d e f g
[w] ἐν χριστῷ Ἰησοῦ ὑμεῖς οἵ [x] ποτε ὄντες [y] μακρὰν ἐγενή- h k l m n o 17
θητε [z] ἐγγὺς [a] ἐν τῷ αἵματι τοῦ χριστοῦ. 14 αὐτὸς γάρ

r — & constr., here only. Soph. Œd. Tyr. 219, 220. s Acts iii. 25. Heb. vii. 22 al. fr. Ezek. xxxiv. 25. plur., Rom. ix. 4. Gal. iv. 24 only. t Gal. iv. 23. Heb. iv. 1 al. Amos ix. 6. u here only †. v Paul (Acts xxii. 1. xxiv. 13. Rom. vi. 22 al.) only, exc. Heb. viii. 6. Deut. x. 22. w Rom. xvi. 7. Gal. i. 22. x ver. 11 reff. y ver. 17. Matt. viii. 30. Luke xv. 20. Acts ii. 39. xvii. 27. xxii. 21 (Paul). Isa. lvii. 19. Dan. ix. 7 Theod. z abs., John xix. 42. Phil. iv. 5. Jer. xxxii. (xxv.) 26. a Luke xxii. 20. Rom. iii. 25. v. 9. Heb. x. 19. Rev. i. 5. v. 9.

13. rec εγγυς bef εγενηθητε, with DFKL rel Chr Thdrt Damasc: txt ABℵ m 17 vulg(and F-lat) goth Dial Epiph Iren-int Tert.

ἀπηλλοτρ., which seems to require as its reference an objective external reality) **of Israel** (either as synonymous genitive, 'that commonwealth which is designated by the term Israel,' or possessive [as Ellic.], 'that commonwealth which Israel possessed.' I prefer the former, as more simple) **and strangers from** (so Soph. Œd. Tyr. 219, *ἁ'γὼ ξένος μὲν τοῦ λόγου τοῦδ' ἐξερῶ, ξένος δὲ τοῦ πραχθέντος*. The genitive may be explained either 1) as one of the quality, as in *μέλεος ἥβης, εὐδαίμων μοίρας*,—or as 2) one of privation = negative of possession, *ξένος* being resolved into *οὐ μέτοχος*. This latter is perhaps the best. See Bernhardy, p. 171 ff.; Kühner, ii. 163) **the covenants of the promise** (*τίνες ἦσαν αἱ δ. τ. ἐπ.; "Σοὶ κ. τῷ σπέρματί σου δώσω τ. γῆν ταύτην," κ. ὅσα ἕτερα ἐπηγγείλατο*, Chrys. See note on Rom. ix. 4. The meaning here, as there, has been mistaken [Calv. al.] to be 'the two tables of the law.' Cf. Wisd. xviii. 22; Sir. xliv. 11), **not having** (**μή** on account of the subjective colouring given to the whole sentence by *μνημονεύετε*. So in *ἀπιστοῦντες αὐτὸν μὴ ἥξειν*, Thuc. ii. 101: *ὃ ἂν γνῶσι δυνάμενον μὲν χάριν ἀποδιδόναι, μὴ ἀποδιδόντα δέ*, Xen. Cyr. i. 2. 7: *ψυχὴν σκοπῶν φιλόσοφόν τε καὶ μή*, Plat. Rep. p. 486 B. See Winer, § 55. 5; Kühner, ii. § 715. 3) **hope** (not 'covenanted hope' [*τὴν ἐλπ.*],—but 'hope' at all. The emphatic position of **ἐλπίδα** makes this the more necessary) **and without God** (this is the best rendering, as it leaves *ἄθεος* in its latitude of meaning. It may be taken either 1) actively, '*denying God*,' '*atheist*,' 2) in a neuter sense [see Ellic.]—'*ignorant of God*' [*ἔρημοι θεογνωσίας*, Thdrt.: see Gal. iv. 8; 1 Thess. iv. 5, where the Gentiles are described as *οὐκ εἰδότες τ. θεόν*], or 3) passively, '*forsaken of God*' [so Soph. Œd. Tyr. 661, *ἐπεὶ* **ἄθεος** *ἄφιλος ὅ τι πύματον ὀλοίμαν*: ib. 254, *τῆσδέ τε γῆς, ὧδ' ἀκάρπως* **κἀθέως** *ἐφθαρμένης*]. This latter meaning is best here, on account of the passive character of the other descriptive clauses) **in the world** (contrast to the *πολιτεία τοῦ Ἰσρ.* "He subjoins to the godless 'How,' the godless 'Where,'" Mey. Olsh. understands, 'in this wicked world, in which we have so much need of divine guidance,' which is hardly in the simple words: Rück., 'in God's world,' contrast to *ἄθεοι*. These words must not be separated, as some, from *ἄθεοι*). 13.] **But now** (contrast to *ἐν τῷ καιρῷ ἐκείνῳ*) **in Christ** (not merely *ἐν χριστῷ* as you were *χωρὶς χριστοῦ*, but more—in a personal Messiah, whom you know as) **Jesus** (there is hardly a reference to the *meaning* of *Jesus*—much rather to its *personal* import—q. d. 'Now in Jesus the Christ') **ye who once were far off were brought** (keep the historic tense: it is the effect of a definite event of which he is speaking. The passive *sense* of the passive form *ἐγενήθητε* is well kept where the context justifies it, but must not always be pressed: see Ellic.'s note on ch. iii. 7) **near** (it was a common Jewish way of speaking, to designate the Gentiles as '*far off*.' So Bereshith rabba, in Schöttg., Hor. Heb. in locum, 'Quicunque gentilem appropinquare facit, eumque ad religionem Judaicam perducit, idem est ac si creasset ipsum.' See also reff. Isa. and Dan.) **in** (or the instrument by which, but more—the symbol of a fact *in* which—the seal of a covenant *in* which,—your nearness to God consists. I prefer 'in' to 'by,' as wider, and better representing the Apostle's idea. The difference between *ἐν* here and *διά* in ch. i. 7 is, that there the blood of Christ is spoken of specifically, as the medium of our *ἀπολύτρωσις*—here inclusively, as *representing* the *ἀπολύτρωσις*. *ἐν* would have served there, and *διά* here, but the logical exactness of both would have been weakened by the change) **the blood of Christ** (see remarks on ch. i. 7). 14.] **For He** (there certainly is an emphasis on **αὐτός**, as Rück., Harl., Mey., Ellic., Eadie, 'He and none other.' This can hardly be denied by any one who will read through the whole from

ἐστιν ἡ [b] εἰρήνη ἡμῶν, ὁ ποιήσας τὰ ἀμφότερα ἓν καὶ
τὸ [c] μεσότοιχον τοῦ [d] φραγμοῦ [e] λύσας, 15 τὴν [f] ἔχθραν,
ἐν τῇ σαρκὶ αὐτοῦ, τὸν [g] νόμον τῶν [g] ἐντολῶν ἐν [h] δόγ-

b = here only see Rom v 1
c here only †
d Matt xxi 33 Mk Luke xiv 23 only Num xxii 24
e = John ii 19 2 Pet. iii 10, 11, 12 1 Esdr i 55 (52)
f ver 16 Luke xxiii 12 Rom viii 7 Gal v 20 James iv 4 only Gen iii 15
g here only see Rom iii 27 vii 2 viii 2 Sir xxxix 8
h Luke ii 1 Acts xvi 4 xvii 7 Col ii 14 only Ezek xx 26 vat (but appy error) only Dan vi 9 al Theod

ver 11, and mark the repetitions, χριστοῦ—χριστῷ Ἰησοῦ—τοῦ χριστοῦ, which this *αὐτός* takes up) **is our peace** (not by metonymy for *εἰρηνοποιός*, but in the widest and most literal sense, our peace He did not make our peace and then retire, leaving us to enjoy that peace,—but is Himself its medium and its substance, His making both one was no external reconciliation, but the taking both, their common nature, on and into Himself,—see ver 15. Bear in mind the multitude of prophetic passages which connect peace with Him, Isa. ix 5, 6; lii. 7, liii. 5; lvii. 19; Micah v 5; Hag ii. 9; Zech ix 10 also Luke ii 14, John xiv. 27, xx. 19, 21, 26. And notice that already the complex idea of the whole verse, that of uniting both Jews and Gentiles in one reconciliation to God, begins to appear: for He is our Peace, not only as reconciling Jew to Gentile, not as bringing the far-off Gentile near *to* the Jew, but as reconciling both, united, to God; as bringing the far-off Gentile, and the near Jew, both into peace with God. For want of observing this the sense has been much obscured see below) **who made** (specification, *how* He is our peace Better 'made,' than '*hath made*.' the latter is true, but it is the historic fact which is here brought out) **both** (Jews and Gentiles, not '*man* and God,' as Stier cf vv 15, 16 Neuter, as abstract,—both things, both elements) **one, and** (epexegetic—'namely, in that he) **threw down the middle wall of the fence** (i. e the middle wall which belonged to—was a necessary part of the carrying out of—the *φραγμός* The primary allusion seems to be, to the rending of the veil at the crucifixion. not that that veil separated Jew and Gentile, but that it, the chief symbol of separation from God, included in its removal the admission to Him of that one body into which Christ made Jew and Gentile This complex idea is before the Apostle throughout the sentence and necessarily, for the reconciliation which Christ effected between Jew and Gentile was in fact only a subordinate step of the great reconciliation of both to God, which He effected by His sacrifice in the flesh,—and in speaking of one he speaks of the other also. The **φραγμός**, from what has been said above, is more general in sense than the **μεσότοιχον**, is in fact the whole arrangement, of which that was but an instrument—the separation itself, consequent on a system of separation it = therefore the whole legal system, ceremonial and moral, which made the whole separation,—of Jew from Gentile,—and in the background, of both from God), **the enmity** (not, of Jew and Gentile so strong a term is not justified as applying to their separation, nor does such a reference satisfy ver 16,—see there;—but, the enmity in which both were involved against God, see Rom viii. 7. **τὴν ἔχθ** is in apposition with **τὸ μεσότ.** This enmity was the real cause of separation from God, and in being so, was the inclusive, mediate cause of the separation between Jew and Gentile Christ, by abolishing the first, abolished the other also see below) **in His flesh** (to be joined not with **καταργήσας**, as most Commentators, which is very harsh, breaking the parallelism, and making the instrumental predication precede the verb, which is not the character of this passage,—but with **λύσας** Christ destroyed the *μεσ*, i e. the *ἔχθρα*, in, or by, His flesh, see on ver. 16, where the same idea is nearly repeated It was in His crucified flesh, which was *ἐν ὁμοιώματι σαρκὸς ἁμαρτίας*, that He slew this enmity The rendering, 'the enmity which was in His flesh,' would certainly in this case require the specifying article *τήν*, besides being very questionable in sense), — **having done away the law of decretory commandments** (this law was the *φραγμός*,—the great exponent of the *ἔχθρα* Its specific nature was that it consisted in commandments, decretorily or dogmatically expressed, — in *ἐντολαὶ-ἐν-δόγμασιν*. So that we do not require *τὸν ἐν δόγ* or *τῶν ἐν δόγ*. This law, moral and ceremonial, its decalogue, its ordinances, its rites, was entirely done away in and by the death of Christ. See Col ii. 13—15 notes And the end of that *κατάργησις* was) **that He might create the two** (Jew and Gentile) **in Him** (it is somewhat difficult to decide

μασιν ⁱ καταργήσας, ἵνα τοὺς δύο ᵏ κτίσῃ ˡ ἐν ˡ αὐτῷ ᵐ εἰς
ἕνα ⁿ καινὸν ⁿ ἄνθρωπον, ᵖ ποιῶν εἰρήνην, 16 καὶ ᵠ ἀπο-
καταλλάξῃ τοὺς ἀμφοτέρους ἐν ʳ ἑνὶ σώματι τῷ θεῷ ˢ διὰ
τοῦ σταυροῦ, ᵗ ἀποκτείνας τὴν ᵘ ἔχθραν ἐν αὐτῷ. 17 καὶ
ᵛ ἐλθὼν ʷ εὐηγγελίσατο ʷ εἰρήνην ὑμῖν τοῖς ˣ μακρὰν καὶ

ABCDF KLℵ a b c d e f g h k l m n o 17

i Luke xiii 7 but — Paul (Rom iii 3 al fr) only, exc Heb ii 14 Ezra iv 21, 23 v 5 vi 8 only. k ver 10 reff l — ch i 11 al fr m — Matt xxvii 51 ‖ Mk. Rev xvi 19 Judg ix 43 o ch iv 24 only see 2 Cor v 17 Gal vi 15 p James iii 18 only Isa xlv 7 see Matt v 9. q Col i 20, 21 only † r Rom xii 4 5 1 Cor x 17 al s Col i 20 t = here only u ver 15 reff v = Matt ii 8 9 23 iv 13 al Prov xxiii 35 w Acts x 36 [Rom x 15 (from Isa lii 7)] only x ver 13 reff

15 rec εαυτω, with DKLℵ³ rel Eus Epiph Ath$_2$ Chr Cyr$_2$ Thdrt Damasc Thl Œc txt ABFℵ¹ m 17 Procop

16. εν εαυτω F 115 lat mss-in-Jer latt syr (Syr om) lat-ff (not Tert Jer al).

17. rec om 2nd ειρηνην (*as superfluous*), with KL rel syrr Dial$_2$ Constt Eus Chr Thdrt Tert: ins ABDFℵ 17 latt copt æth arm Eus Procop Cypr Hil.

between ἑαυτῷ and **αὐτῷ** On the one hand, **αὐτῷ** is the *harder* reading on the other, we have the constant confusion of *αὐτ*, *αὑτ*, and *ἑαυτ*., complicating the question Whichever be read, the reference clearly must be to Christ, which, with *αὑτῷ*, is, to say the least, a harsh recurrence to the *αὐτός* of ver. 11) **into one new man** (observe, not that He might reconcile the two *to each other* only, nor is the Apostle speaking merely of any such reconciliation: but that He might incorporate the two, reconciled in Him to God, into one *new* man,—the old man to which both belonged, the enemy of God, having been slain in His flesh on the Cross Observe, too, ONE new man: we are all in God's sight but one in Christ, as we are but one in Adam), **making peace** (not, between Jew and Gentile: He is *ἡ εἰρήνη ἡμῶν*, of us all see below on ver. 17), **and** (parallel with the former purpose not '*second* purpose' [Ellic, De W.], which yet must thus be the *first*. The *καί* is in fact just as in ver. 14) **might reconcile again** (most likely this is implied in the **ἀπο**. We have it only in Col. i 20, 21, where the same sense, of *reinstating* in the divine favour, seems to be intended) **both of us in one body** (not His own human body, as Chrys. [who however seems to waver,—cf. *ἕως ἂν μένωμεν ἐν τῷ σώματι τοῦ χριστοῦ*, —between this and His mystical body], al.—but the Church, cf the same expression Col iii 15) **to God** (if this had not been here expressed, the *whole* reference of the sentence would have been thought to be to the uniting Jews and Gentiles. That it is expressed, now shews that throughout, that union has been thought of only as a subordinate step in a greater reconciliation) **by means of the cross** (the cross regarded as the symbol of that which was done on and by it), **having slain the enmity** (**ἔχθρα** has been taken here to mean the enmity between Jew and Gentile. But see on ver 15 and let us ask here, was this the enmity which Christ slew at His death? Was this the *ἔχθρα*, the slaying of which brought in the *ἀποκατάλλαξις*, as this verse implies? Does such a meaning of *ἔχθρα* at all satisfy the solemnity of the sentence, or of the next two verses? I cannot think so and must maintain *ἔχθρα* here [and if here, then in ver. 15 also] to be that between man and God, which Christ did slay on the cross, and which being brought to an end, the separation between Jew and Gentile, which was a result of it, was done away Ellicott, who maintained the above opinion in his 1st edn, now agrees with that here insisted on) **on it** (on the cross compare Col ii. 15, notes not in His body see above) **and having come, He preached** (how? when? Obviously after his death, because by that death the peace was wrought. We seek in vain for any such announcement made by Him in person after his resurrection. But we find a key to the expression in John xiv 18, *οὐκ ἀφήσω ὑμᾶς ὀρφανούς· ἔρχομαι πρὸς ὑμᾶς* see also ver. 28. And this coming was, by his Spirit poured out on the Church. There is an expression of St. Paul's, singularly parallel with this, and of itself strongly corroborative of the genuineness of our Epistle, in Acts xxvi. 23, *εἰ παθητὸς ὁ χριστός, εἰ πρῶτος ἐξ ἀναστάσεως νεκρῶν φῶς μέλλει καταγγέλλειν τῷ τε λαῷ κ τοῖς ἔθνεσιν* This coming therefore is by His Spirit [see on ver 18], and ministers, and ordinances in the Church) **peace to you who were far off, and peace to those** (not "*to us*," for fear of still upholding the distinction where he wishes to merge it altogether) **that were nigh** (this **εἰρήνη** is plainly then not mere mutual reconciliation, but that

ʷ εἰρήνην ʸ τοῖς ˣʸ ἐγγύς, 18 ὅτι δι' αὐτοῦ ἔχομεν τὴν ᶻ προσαγωγὴν οἱ ἀμφότεροι ἐν ᵃ ἑνὶ πνεύματι πρὸς τὸν ᵇ πατέρα.
19 ᶜ ἄρα ᶜ οὖν οὐκέτι ἐστὲ ᵈ ξένοι καὶ ᵉ πάροικοι, ἀλλὰ ἐστὲ
ᶠ συμπολῖται τῶν ᵍ ἁγίων καὶ ʰ οἰκεῖοι τοῦ θεοῦ, 20 ⁱ ἐποικο-

[margin: 18. οἱ αμφοτεροι — ABCDF KLℵ a b d e f g h k l m n o 17]

y here only. Esth i. 14. z Rom v. 2. ch iii. 12 only †. a ch iv. (3) 4. Phil i. 27. b = Rom viii. 15. 1 Cor viii. 6. John, passim. c Rom v. 18. vii. 3. viii. 12. ix. 16, 18. Gal vi. 10 al. P. d = Matt xxv. 35 &c. xxvii. 7. Acts xvii. 21. Heb xi. 13. 3 John 5 only. Ruth ii. 10. e Acts vii. 6, 29. 1 Pet ii. 11 only. Gen xxiii. 4. f here only †. Jos. Antt. xix. 2. 2. g ch i. 1 reff. h (=) Gal vi. 10. 1 Tim v. 8 only. Isa iii. 6. i 1 Cor iii. 10, &c. Col ii. 7. Jude 20 only. Num. xxxii. 38 Ald. only.

19. aft *αυτου* ins *οι αμφοτεροι εν ενι* ℵ[1] (marked for erasure by ℵ-corr[1]). *εσχομεν* ℵ-corr[1]. rec om 2nd *εστε* (*as superfluous*), with D[3]KL rel syrr copt gr-ff Tert Jer Ambr; ins ABCD[1]Fℵ 17 latt goth Bas Victorin.

far greater peace which was effected by Christ's death, peace with God, which necessitated the union of the far off and the near in one body in Him. This is shewn especially by the repetition of *εἰρήνην*. See Isa lvii. 19. Then follows the empowering reason, why He should preach *peace* to us both: and it is this ver. 18 especially which I maintain cannot be satisfied on the ordinary hypothesis of mere reconciliation between Jew and Gentile being the subject in the former verses. Here clearly the union [not reconciliation, nor is enmity predicated of them] of Jew and Gentile is subordinated to the blessed fact of an access TO GOD having been provided for both through Christ by the Spirit); for (not epexegetic of *εἰρήνην*, 'viz. that . . ,' as Baumg.-Crus.) through Him we have our access (I prefer this intransitive meaning to that maintained by Ellic., al., '*introduction*,'—some [Mey.] say, by Christ [1 Pet iii. 18] as our *προσαγωγεύς* [*admissionalis*, a word of Oriental courts],—not as differing much from it in meaning, but as better representing, both here and in Rom. v. 2, and ch. iii. 12, the *repetition*, the *present* liberty of approach, which *ἔχομεν* implies, but which '*introduction*' does not give), both of us, in (united in, 1 Cor. xii. 13) one Spirit (not '*one frame of mind*' [Anselm, Koppe, al.]: the whole structure of the sentence, as compared with any similar one, such as 2 Cor. xiii. 13, will shew what spirit is meant, viz. the Holy Spirit of God, already alluded to in ver. 17; see above. As a parallel, cf. 1 Cor. xii. 13) to the Father. 19.] So then (*ἄρα οὖν* is said by Hermann [Viger, art. 292] not to be classical Greek. It is frequent in St. Paul, but confined to him: see reff. Cf. on Gal. vi. 10) ye no longer are strangers and sojourners (see ref. Acts, where certainly this is the sense: "*πάροικος* is here simply the same as the classic *μέτοικος* [a form which does not occur in the N. T., and only once, Jer. xx. 3, in the LXX], and was probably its Alexandrian equivalent. It is used frequently in the LXX,—in eleven passages as a translation of גֵּר, and in nine of תּוֹשָׁב." Ellicott. 'Sojourners,' as dwelling among the Jews, but not numbered with them. Bengel opposes *ξένοι* to 'cives' and *πάροικοι* to 'domestici,'—and so Harless: but this seems too artificial), but are fellow-citizens with the saints (*συμπολίτης* is blamed by Phrynichus [ed. Lob. p. 172: see Lobeck's note] and the Atticists as a later word. But it occurs in Eur. Heraclid. 821, and the compound verb *συμπολιτεύω* is found in pure Attic writers: see Palm and Rost's Lex. *πολῖται* would not here express the meaning of *comrades*, *co-citizens*, of the saints: οἱ ἅγιοι are not *angels*, nor *Jews*, nor *Christians then alive* merely, but the saints of God in the widest sense,—all members of the mystical body of Christ,—the commonwealth of the spiritual Israel) and of the household (*οἰκεῖοι*, not as Harl., 'stones of which the house is built,' which is an unnatural anticipation here, where all is a political figure, of the material figure in the next verse: but 'members of God's family,' in the usual sense of the word) of God,—having been built (we cannot express the *ἐπ-*: the '*superædificati*' of the Vulg. gives it: we have the substantive 'superstructure,' but no verb corresponding. There is, though Harl. [see above] denies it, a transition from one image, a political and social, to another, a material) upon the foundation (dative as *resting upon*: in 1 Cor. iii. 12, where we have *εἴ τις ἐποικοδομεῖ ἐπὶ τὸν θεμέλιον* . . . , the idea of *bringing and laying upon* is prominent, and therefore the case of motion is used. Between the genitive and dative of rest with *ἐπί* there is the distinction, that the genitive implies more partial overhanging, looser connexion,—the dative, a connexion of close fitting attach-

k = Rom xv 20. 1 Cor iii 10, 11. 2 Tim ii 19. Heb vi 1.

δομηθέντες ἐπὶ τῷ [k] θεμελίῳ τῶν [l] ἀποστόλων καὶ [lm] προφητῶν, ὄντος [n] ἀκρογωνιαίου αὐτοῦ χριστοῦ Ἰησοῦ, 21 ἐν

ABCDF KLℵ a b c d e f g h k l m n o 17

l Luke xi 49. 1 Cor xii 28, 29. ch iii 5. iv 11. Rev xviii 20. 1 xv 32. xxi 10. 1 Cor xiv 29, &c only.

m = as above (l). Acts xi 27. xiii 1. n 1 Pet ii 6 only, from Isa xxviii 16 (only).

20. aft ακρογωνιαιου ins λιθου DF Orig$_1$ Eus Chr-txt. for αυτου, του ℵ[1]: om Syr Orig$_{abc}$ Chr-comm: txt ℵ corr[1]. rec ιησ. bef χρ., with CDFKL rel syrr Ps-Just Orig$_1$ Eus Victorin Jer$_2$: om ιησου (ℵ[1]) in Chr-txt: txt ABℵ-corr 17 vulg (and F-lat) copt goth Orig$_2$ Thl Ambrst Jer$_2$ Aug$_{saepe}$.

ment. So in Xen we have, ἐπὶ τῆς κεφαλῆς τὰ ὅπλα ἔφερον, partial, '*over*,'—οἱ Θρᾷκες ἀλωπεκίδας ἐπὶ ταῖς κεφαλαῖς φοροῦσι, close, '*on*.' see Donaldson's Greek Gr. § 483) **of the Apostles and Prophets** (how is this genitive to be understood? Is it a genitive of apposition, so that the Apostles and Prophets themselves *are* the foundation? This has been supposed by numerous Commentators, from Chrys to De Wette. But, not to mention the very many other objections which have been well and often urged against this view, this one is to my mind decisive,—that it entirely destroys the imagery of the passage. The temple, into which these Gentiles were built, is the mystical body of the Son, in which the Father dwells by the Spirit, ver. 22. The Apostles and Prophets [see below], yea, Jesus Christ Himself, as the great inclusive Head Corner Stone [see again below], are also built into this temple. [That He includes likewise the *foundation*, and is the foundation, is true, and must be remembered, but is not prominent here.] Clearly then the Apostles and Prophets cannot *be* the foundation, being here spoken of as parts of the building, together with these Gentiles, and with Jesus Christ Himself. But again, does the genitive mean, the foundation which the Apostles and Prophets *have laid?* So also very many, from Ambrst, to Rück., Harl., Mey., Stier, Ellic., both edd. As clearly,—not thus. To introduce them here as *agents*, is as inconsistent as the other. No agents are here spoken of, but merely the fact of the great building in its several parts being built up together. The only remaining interpretation then is, to regard the genitive as simply possessive: '*the foundation of the Apostles and Prophets*,' = '*the Apostles' and Prophets' foundation*'—that upon which they as well as yourselves are built. This exegesis, which I find ascribed to Bucer only (in De W.), seems to me beyond question the right one. See more below. But (2) *who are* **προφῆται**? They have commonly been taken, without enquiry, as the *O. T. Prophets*. And certainly, the sense, with some little straining, would admit of this view. They may be said to be built upon Christ, as belonging to that widest acceptation of His mystical body, in which it includes all the saints, O. T. as well as N. T. But there are several objections: first, formal: the *order of the words* has been urged against this view, in that προφ should have come first. I should not be inclined to lay much weight on this, the Apostles might naturally be spoken of first, as nearest, and the Prophets second—'the Apostles, yea and of the Prophets also.' A more serious formal objection is, the omission of the article before προφ., thereby casting τῶν ἀποστόλων κ. προφητῶν together as belonging to the same class. But weightier objections are behind. In ch iii 5, we have ὃ ἑτέραις γενεαῖς οὐκ ἐγνωρίσθη τοῖς υἱοῖς τῶν ἀνθρώπων, ὡς νῦν ἀπεκαλύφθη τοῖς ἁγίοις ἀποστόλοις αὐτοῦ κ. προφήταις ἐν πνεύματι, where unquestionably the προφῆται are N. T. Prophets, and again ch iv 11, καὶ αὐτὸς ἔδωκεν τοὺς μὲν ἀποστόλους, τοὺς δὲ προφήτας. And it is difficult to conceive that the Apostle should have used the two words conjoined here, in a different sense. Even stronger is the consideration arising from the whole sense of the passage. All here is strictly Christian,—post-Judaic,—consequent on Christ's death, and triumph, and His coming preaching peace by the Spirit to the united family of man. So that we must decide for προφ being *N. T. Prophets*: those who ranked next to the Apostles in the government of the church: see Acts xi 27, note. They were not in every case distinct from the Apostles: the apostleship probably always including the gift of *prophecy* (so that all the Apostles themselves might likewise have been προφῆται), **Christ Jesus Himself** (the **αὐτοῦ** exalts the dignity of the temple, in that not only it has among its stones Apostles and prophets, but the Lord Himself is built into it. The attempt of Bengel, al., to render **αὐτοῦ**, '*ils*,' and refer it to θεμελίῳ, will be seen, by what has been said, to be foreign to

ᾧ πᾶσα ° οἰκοδομὴ ᵖ συναρμολογουμένη ᵍ αὔξει εἰς ναὸν
ἅγιον ʳ ἐν κυρίῳ, 22 ἐν ᾧ καὶ ὑμεῖς ˢ συνοικοδομεῖσθε ᵗ εἰς
ᵘ κατοικητήριον τοῦ θεοῦ ᵛ ἐν πνεύματι.

o — Matt xxiv 1 || Mk 1 Cor iii 9 2 Cor v 1 (ch ii 20 al) Ezek xvii 17
p ch iv 16 only †
q (ξεν) Col ii 19 only Isa lxi 11
r Rom xvi 11, 12 al fr P 1 Cor viii 10 18 vi 18 Col i 8 1 Pet i 12 Jude 20
s here only † Esdr v 68 (65)
t — Matt x 18 al fr see
u Rev xviii 2 only Ps lxxv 2
v Rom ix 1, ch iii 5 v
w εἰς, ch iv 15 Gen xxx 30

21 rec aft πασα ins η (*see note*), with ACℵ-corr Thl · om BDFKLℵ[1] rel Ps-Just Clem
22 for θεου, χριστου B.

the purpose. Besides, it would more naturally be ὄντος αὐτοῦ ἀκρογ. . . . . Bengel's idea, that on our rendering, it must be αὐτοῦ τοῦ, is refuted by such passages as καὶ αὐτὸς Δαυείδ, Luke xx 42) **being the Head corner stone** (see, besides reff, Ps. cxvii. 22; Jer. xxviii. (li.) 26; Matt xxi. 42, Acts iv. 11. The reference here is clearly to that Headstone of the Corner, which is not only the most conspicuous but the most important in the building: "qui, in extremo angulo [fundamenti, but qu ?] positus, duos parietes ex diverso venientes conjungit et continet," Est. Builders set up such a stone, or build such a pillar of brick, before getting up their walls, to rule and square them by. I must again repeat, that the fact of Jesus Christ being Himself the *foundation*, however it underlies the whole, is not to be brought in as interfering with this portion of the figure),

21.] **in whom** (ὁ τὸ πᾶν συνέχων ἐστὶν ὁ χριστός, Chr : not only so, but He is in reality the inclusive Head of the building. it all ἐν αὐτῷ συνέστηκεν, is squared and ruled by its unity to and in Him) **all the building** (more properly πᾶσα ἡ οἰκοδ.. and to a *classical Greek ear*, any other rendering of πᾶσα οἰκ than '*every building*,' seems preposterous enough. But 'every building' here is quite out of place, inasmuch as the Apostle is clearly speaking of but one vast building, the mystical Body of Christ · and πᾶσα οἰκ cannot have Meyer's sense 'every congregation thus built in ' nor would it be much better to take refuge in the proper sense of οἰκοδομή, and render 'all building,' i. e. 'every process of building,' for then we should be at a loss when we come to αὔξει below. Are we then to render ungrammatically, and force words to that which they cannot mean ? Certainly not but we seem to have some light cast here by such an expression as πρωτότοκος πάσης κτίσεως, Col. i 15, which though it may be evaded by rendering 'of every creature,' yet is not denied by most Commentators to be intended to bear this sense 'of all creation:' cf also ib. ver 23, ἐν πάσῃ κτίσει τῇ ὑπ' οὐρανόν. The account to be given of such later usages is, that gradually other words besides proper names became regarded as able to dispense with the article after πᾶς, so that as they said first πᾶσα Ἱεροσόλυμα [Matt. ii 3], and then πᾶς οἶκος Ἰσραήλ [Acts ii 36], so they came at length to say πᾶσα κτίσις [as we ourselves 'all creation,' for 'all *the* creation'] and πᾶσα οἰκοδομή, when speaking of one universal and notorious building Ellic adds to the examples, πᾶσα γῆ, Thucyd ii 43, πᾶσα ἐπιστολή, Ignat Eph § 12, p 656 **οἰκοδομή** itself is a late form, censured by Phryn [Lob. p. 421] and the Atticists) **being framed exactly together** (the verb [= συναρμόζω] sufficiently explains itself, being only found in these two places [ref.]. Wetst. quotes ἡρμολόγησε τάφον from Anthol. iii. 32. 4, and Palm and Rost refer for ἁρμολογέω to Philip of Thessalonica, Ep 78) **is growing** (there seems no reason why the proper sense of the present should not be retained Both participle and verb imply that the fitting together and the growing are still going on · and the only way which we in English have to mark this so as to avoid the chance of mistake, is by the auxiliary verb substantive, and the participle. The bare present, 'groweth,' is in danger of being mistaken for the abstract quality, and the temporal development is thus lost sight of: whereas the other, in giving prominence to that temporal development, also necessarily implies the 'normal, perpetual, unconditioned nature of the organic increase' [Ellic]) to (so 'crescere in cumulum,' Claudian in Piscator) **an holy temple in the Lord** (i e according to apostolic usage, and the sense of the whole passage, '*in Christ*' The ἐν ᾧ—ἐν κυρίῳ, —ἐν ᾧ,—like the frequent repetitions of the name χριστός in vv. 12, 13, are used by the Apostle to lay all stress on the fact that Christ is the inclusive Head of all the building, the element in which it has its being and its growth. I would join

III. 1 Τούτου [w] χάριν [x] ἐγὼ [x] Παῦλος ὁ [y] δέσμιος τοῦ

w Luke vii 47 Gal iii. 19 ver 14 Tit i 5, 11 1 John iii 12 Jude 16 only Prov xvii 17 x Gal v 2 reff y Acts xxiii 18 2 Tim i. 8 Philem 1, 9 Heb xiii 3 Zech ix 12

ἐν κυρίῳ with ναὸν ἅγιον, as more accordant with the Apostle's style than if it were joined with αὔξει [αὔξει ἐν κυρ. εἰς ναὸν ἅγ.], or with ἅγιον [εἰς ναὸν ἐν κυρίῳ ἅγ.]. The increase spoken of will issue in its being a holy temple in Christ), 22.] in whom (not '*in which*,' viz. the temple—it is characteristic [see above] of this part of the epistle to string together these relative expressions, all referring to the same) ye also (not, as Eadie, '*even you*.' there is no depreciation here, but an exaltation, of the Gentiles, as living stones of the great building) are being built in together (with one another, or with those before mentioned. An imperative sense ['Ephesios hortatur ut crescant in fide Christi magis et magis postquam in ea semel fuerunt fundati,' Calv.] is not for a moment to be thought of the whole passage is descriptive, not hortatory) for (Griesb. parenthesizes with two commas, ἐν ᾧ . . . συνοικοδομεῖσθε, and takes this εἰς as parallel with the former εἰς But this unnecessarily involves the sentence, which is simple enough as it stands) an habitation of God (the only true temple of God, in which He dwells, being the Body of Christ, in all the glorious acceptation of that term) in the Spirit (it is even now, in the state of imperfection, by the Spirit, dwelling in the hearts of believers, that God has His habitation in the Church. and then, when the growth and increase of that Church shall be completed, it will be still in and by the Holy Spirit fully penetrating and possessing the whole glorified Church, that the Father will dwell in it for ever. Thus we have the true temple of the Father, built in the Son, inhabited in the Spirit the offices of the Three blessed Persons being distinctly pointed out: God, THE FATHER, in all His fulness, dwells in, fills the Church. that Church is constituted an holy Temple to Him in THE SON,—is inhabited by Him in the ever-present indwelling of the HOLY SPIRIT The attempt to soften away ἐν πνεύματι into πνευματικῶς [ναὸς πνευματικός, Chrys, and so Thl, Œc, al, and even Olsh.] is against the whole sense of the passage, in which not the present spiritual state of believers, but their ultimate glorious completion [εἰς] is spoken of See reff)

III. 1—21.] AIM AND END OF THE CHURCH IN THE SPIRIT. And herein, *the revelation to it of the mystery of Christ, through those ministers who wrought in the Spirit: primarily, as regarded the Ephesians, through* himself. *Thus first, of* HIS OFFICE AS APOSTLE OF THE GENTILES (1—13) *secondly*, under the form of a prayer for them, THE AIM AND END OF THAT OFFICE AS RESPECTED THE CHURCH · *its becoming strong in the power of the Spirit* (14—19). Then (20, 21) *doxology*, concluding this first division of the Epistle 1—13] (See above) On this account (in order to explain this, something must be said on the construction. (a) Chrys. says ·—εἶπε τοῦ χριστοῦ τὴν κηδεμονίαν τὴν πολλήν· ἐκβαίνει λοιπὸν κ ἐπὶ τὴν ἑαυτοῦ, μικρὰν μὲν οὖσαν κ. σφόδρα οὐδὲν πρὸς ἐκείνην, ἱκανὴν δὲ καὶ ταύτην ἐπισπάσασθαι. διὰ τοῦτο καὶ ἐγὼ δέδεμαι, φησίν. This supplying of εἰμί after ὁ δέσμιος, and making the latter the predicate, is the rendering of Syr., and adopted by very many. It has against it, 1) that thus τούτου χάριν and ὑπὲρ ὑμῶν become tautological 2) that thus ver. 2 and the following are unconnected with the preceding, serving for no explanation of it ['legationis, non vinculorum rationem explicat,' Castalio in Harl] 3) that the article ὁ with the predicate δέσμιος gives it undue prominence, and exalts the Apostle in a way which would be very unnatural to him,—'sum captivus *ille* Christi,' as Glass,—and inconsistent with εἴ γε ἠκούσατε, &c. following. (b) Erasm.-Schmidt, Hammond, Michael, Winer [and so E. V.] regard the sentence, broken at ἐθνῶν, as resumed at ch iv 1. Against this is the decisive consideration, that ch iii. is no parenthesis, but an integral and complete portion of the Epistle, finished moreover with the doxology vv. 20, 21, and altogether distinct in subject and character from ch. ii. (c) Œc. says [and so Estius and Grot]· ἀνταπόδοσίς ἐστι τούτου χάριν, οἷον τούτου χ. ἐμοὶ τῷ ἐλ π ἁγ ἐδόθ. κ τ λ (ver 8) σκόπει δὲ ὅτι ἀρξάμενος τῆς περιόδου κατὰ τὸ ὀρθὸν σχῆμα ἐν τῇ ἀποδόσει ἐπλαγίωσε, σχηματίσας τ ἀνταπόδοσιν πρὸς τὸν περιβολῶν τύπον. But as Harl remarks, this deprives τούτου χάριν of meaning for it was not *because they were built in*, &c, that this grace was given to him and, besides, thus the leading thought of the antapodosis in ver 8 is clumsily forestalled in vv. 6, 7. (d) The idea that ver. 13 resumes the sentence [Cameran., Cramer, al] is refuted by the

χριστοῦ [Ἰησοῦ] ὑπὲρ ὑμῶν τῶν ἐθνῶν, 2 [z] εἴ γε [a] ἠκούσατε τὴν [b] οἰκονομίαν τῆς [c] χάριτος τοῦ θεοῦ τῆς [c] δοθείσης
μοι [d] εἰς ὑμᾶς, 3 ὅτι [e] κατὰ [e] ἀποκάλυψιν [f] ἐγνωρίσθη μοι
τὸ [g] μυστήριον, καθὼς [h] προέγραψα [i] ἐν [i] ὀλίγῳ, 4 [k] πρὸς

.. της d ABCDF KLℵ a b c e f g h k l m n o 17

z Col i 23. ch iv 21 2 Cor v 3 Gal iii 4 only P. a ch i 15 reff b — 1 Cor ix 17 (ch i 10 reff) c Gal ii 9 reff d — ch i 19 reff e — Gal ii 2 only (Rom xvi 25) f g ch i 9 reff h — here only Rom xv 4 Gal iii 1 Jude 4 only† Esdr vi 31 F 1 Macc x. 36 only i = here only (Acts xxvi 28, 29.) see 1 Pet v 12 k — Luke xii 47 2 Cor v 10 Gal ii 14

Chap. III 1. for χριστ, κυριου C. om ιησου D^1Fℵ^1 o D-lat G-lat æth: ins ABC$D^{2,3}$KL ℵ-corr rel vulg ιησ. bef χρ. Syr. aft εθνων add πρεσβευω D 10 Ambrst-comm, *postulo* D-lat something erased in 67.

2. for τ θεου, αυτου A του θεου bef της χαριτος $D^{1,2}$F. om τ. θ 115 Ambrst-txt Thl

3. om οτι B D-lat Ambrst: κατ. απ. γαρ F goth. rec εγνωρισε (*connecting with τ. θεου above*), with D^3KL rel æth Damasc-txt Thl Œc: txt ABCD^1Fℵ 17. 67^2 latt syrr copt goth Clem Chr Cyr Damasc-comm Jer Ambrst Pelag.

insufficiency of such a secondary sentiment as that in ver. 13 to justify the long parenthesis full of such solemn matter, as that vv 2—12, and by the improbability that the Apostle would resume *τούτου χάριν* by *διό*, with *τούτου χάριν* occurring again in the next verse, and not rather have expressed this latter in that case by *καί*. (e) It remains that with Thdrt [on ver. 1, *βούλεται μὲν εἰπεῖν ὅτι ταύτην ὑμῶν τὴν κλῆσιν εἰδὼς κ τ.λ. δέομαι κ ἱκετεύω τὸν τῶν ὅλων θεόν, βεβαιῶσαι ὑμᾶς τῇ πίστει κ τ λ*, then on ver 14, *ταῦτα πάντα ἐν μέσῳ τεθεικὼς ἀναλαμβάνει τὸν περὶ προσευχῆς λόγον*], Luth, Pisc, Corn-a-lap, Schottg, Beng, Ruck, Harl, De W, Stier, Ellic, al, we consider ver 14 as taking up the sense, with its repetition of **τούτου χάριν**, and the weighty prayer which it introduces, and which forms a worthy justification for so long and solemn a parenthesis. **τούτου χάριν** will then mean, 'seeing ye are so built in,'—stand in such a relation to God's purposes in the church) **I Paul** (he mentions himself here, as introducing to them the agent in the Spirit's work who was nearest to themselves, and setting forth that work as the carrying on of his enlightenment on their behalf, and the subject of his earnest prayer for them · see argument to this chapter above), **the prisoner** (but now without any prominence, or the very slightest cf *Τιμόθεος ὁ ἀδελφός* it is rather generic, or demonstrative, than emphatic) **of Christ** [**Jesus**] (see ref, *χρ* first, because it is not so much personal possession, as the fact of the Messiahship of Jesus having been the cause and origin of his imprisonment, which is expressed by the genitive) **on behalf of you Gentiles** (see ver. 13, where this *ὑπὲρ ὑμῶν* is repeated The matter of fact was so — his preaching to Gentiles aroused the jealousy of the Jews, and led to his imprisonment But he rather thinks of it as a result of his great office and himself as a sacrifice for those whom it was his intent to benefit),—**if, that is** (*εἴ γε*, 'assuming that·' see note on 2 Cor. v. 3. The Ephesians *had heard* all this, and St Paul was now delicately reminding them of it. So that to derive from *εἴ γε ἠκούσατε* an argument against the genuineness of the Epistle, as De Wette does, is mere inattention to philology), **ye heard of** (when I was among you · his whole course there, his converse [Acts xx. 18—21], and his preaching, were just the imparting to them his knowledge) **the œconomy** (see note on ch i 10. It is not the apostolic office,—but the dispensation—*munus dispensandi*, in which he was an *οἰκονόμος*, of that which follows) **of the grace of God which was given me** (the *χάρις δοθεῖσα* [beware of joining *δοθείσης* with *οἰκονομίαν* by any of the so-called figures] was the material with respect to which the dispensation was to be exercised so that the genitive is objective as in ch i 10) **towards you** (to be dispensed in the direction of, to, you) 3.] **that** (epexegesis of the fact implied in *ἠκούσατε τὴν οἰκ* 'viz of the fact that' as we say, 'how that') **by revelation** (see reff; the stress is on these words, from their position) **was made known to me the mystery** (viz of the *admission of the Gentiles* [ver 6] to be fellow-heirs, &c See ch i 9, directly referred to below) **even as I before wrote** (not, 'have before written,' though this perhaps better marks the reference 'Before wrote,' viz in ch. i 9 ff) **briefly** (*διὰ βραχέων*, Chrys "Habet locutionem hanc Aristoteles rhet iii. 2, p. 716, ubi de acuminibus orationis, quæ ex unius aut plurium vocum similium oppositione oriuntur, dicit, ex tanto ele-

ὃ δύνασθε [l] ἀναγινώσκοντες [m] νοῆσαι τὴν [n] σύνεσίν μου
[o] ἐν τῷ [g] μυστηρίῳ τοῦ χριστοῦ, 5 ὃ ἑτέραις [p] γενεαῖς
οὐκ [f] ἐγνωρίσθη τοῖς [q] υἱοῖς τῶν ἀνθρώπων, ὡς νῦν [r] ἀπεκαλύφθη τοῖς [s] ἁγίοις [tt] ἀποστόλοις αὐτοῦ καὶ [t] προφήταις [u] ἐν πνεύματι, 6 εἶναι τὰ ἔθνη [v] συγκληρονόμα καὶ
[w] σύνσωμα καὶ [x] συμμέτοχα τῆς [y] ἐπαγγελίας ἐν χριστῷ

ABCDF KLℵ a b c e f g h k l m n o 17

l Matt xii 3. 2 Cor i 13 al fr Isa xxxvii 14. m Matt xxiv 15. Rom i 20. 1 Tim i 7. 2 Tim ii 7. Prov i 2. n = Luke ii 47. 1 Cor i 19 (from Isa xxix 14). Col i 9. ii 2. 2 Tim ii 7 (Mark xii 33) only. o constr., 2 Chron xxxiv 12. Neh xiii 7. Esdr i 33 (31). p Acts xiv 16. xv 21. ver 21. Col i 26. Isa xli 4. q here only. Ps xxxv 7 al. r & constr., Matt xi 25. 1 Cor ii 10. Phil iii 15. 1 Pet i 12. 1 Kings iii 7. s Rev xviii 21 v. r. only. t 1 Cor xii 28. Rev xviii 20. ch ii 20. iv 11. u ch ii 22 reff. v Rom viii 17. Heb xi 9. 1 Pet iii 7 only † (-μεῖν, Sir xxii 20). w here only †. x ch v 7 only †. y Gal iii 14 reff.

5. rec ins εν bef ετεραις (*on account of the double dative*), with (none of our mss) syr copt: om ABCDFKLℵ rel latt Syr goth arm Clem$_2$ Orig Cyr-jer Chr Cyr$_2$ Jer. αυτου bef αποστολοις DF copt Thl Hil. ins τω bef πνευματι F Chr. aft πν ins αγιω D a b c o æth Vig: pref g.

6. rec aft επαγγελιας ins αυτου, with D[2] [3]FKL rel syr Thdrt Damasc Hil: om ABCD[1]ℵ 17 demid(with tol) D-lat Syr copt arm Orig$_3$ Chr Cyr Jer Pelag Sedul. rec ins τω bef χριστω, with DFKL rel. om ABCℵ 17 vulg syr-w-ast copt goth Ambrst Pelag.

gantiora esse, ὅσῳ ἂν ἐλάττονι, quanto brevius proferantur, et id ideo dicit sic se habere, ὅτι ἡ μάθησις, διὰ μὲν τὸ ἀντικεῖσθαι μᾶλλον, διὰ δὲ τὸ ἐν ὀλίγῳ θᾶττον γίνεται, quoniam ea ob oppositionem eo magis, ob brevitatem vero eo celerius percipiantur." Kypke, obss sacræ, ii p 293). **4**] **by** (or, '*in accordance with*,' perhaps '*at*' is our word nearest corresponding. The use of πρός is as in πρὸς τὸ ἀδόκητον τεταραγμένους) **which** (viz., *that which I wrote*: not the fact of my having written briefly, as Kypke) **ye can, while reading** (ἀναγ absolute), **perceive** (aorist, because the act is regarded as one of a series, each of which, when it occurs, is sudden and transitory) **my understanding in** (construction see reff, and compare σύνεσιν ἐν πάσῃ σοφίᾳ, Dan. i 17, also Dan. x 1, LXX and Theod) **the mystery of Christ** (by comparing Col i 27, it will clearly appear that this genitive is one of apposition—the mystery is Christ in all His fulness; not of the object, '*relating to Christ*'), **5**] **which in other generations** (dative of time: so Luke xii 20, ταύτῃ τῇ νυκτὶ τὴν ψυχήν σου ἀπαιτοῦσιν ἀπὸ σοῦ,—Matt xvi. 21 al: for the temporal meaning of γενεά, see reff) **was not made known to the sons of men** ('latissima appellatio, causam exprimens ignorantiæ, ortum naturalem, cui opponitur Spiritus,' Beng., and to which, remarks Stier, ἁγίοις and αὐτοῦ are further contrasted) **as** (ἐγνωρίσθη μὲν τοῖς πάλαι προφήταις, ἀλλ' οὐχ ὡς νῦν· οὐ γὰρ τὰ πράγματα εἶδον, ἀλλὰ τοὺς περὶ τῶν πραγμάτων προέγραψαν λόγους, Thdrt) **it has been now revealed** (we are compelled in the presence of νῦν, to desert the aorist rendering 'was revealed,' which in our language cannot be used in reference to present time. The Greek admits of combining the two. We might do it by a paraphrastic extension of νῦν,—'as in this present age it was revealed') **to His holy** (see Stier's remark above. Olshausen says, "It is certainly peculiar, that Paul here calls the Apostles, and consequently himself among them, 'holy Apostles.' It is going too far when De W. finds in this a sign of an unapostolic origin of the Epistle: but still the expression remains an unusual one. I account for it to myself thus,—that Paul here conceives of the Apostles and Prophets, as a corporation (cf. ch iv 11), and as such, in their official character, he gives them the predicate ἅγιος, as he names believers, conceived as a whole, ἅγιοι or ἡγιασμένοι, but never an individual") **Apostles and Prophets** (as in ch. ii 20, the N. T. Prophets—see note there) **in** (as the conditional element; in and by) **the Spirit** (Chrys remarks, ἐννόησον γάρ· ὁ Πέτρος, εἰ μὴ παρὰ τοῦ πνεύματος ἤκουσεν, οὐκ ἂν ἐπορεύθη εἰς τὰ ἔθνη. ἐν πν. must not be joined with προφ as Koppe, al [not Chrys, as the above citation shows]; for, as De W. remarks, the words would thus either be superfluous, or make an unnatural distinction between the Apostles and Prophets)—**that** ('namely, that'—giving the purport of the mystery) **the Gentiles are** (not, '*should be*:' a mystery is not a secret design, but a secret fact) **fellow-heirs** (with the Jews) **and fellow-members**

Ἰησοῦ διὰ τοῦ εὐαγγελίου, 7 οὗ ἐγενήθην [z] διάκονος κατὰ
τὴν [a] δωρεὰν τῆς [b] χάριτος τοῦ θεοῦ τῆς δοθείσης μοι
κατὰ τὴν [c] ἐνέργειαν τῆς [c] δυνάμεως αὐτοῦ. 8 ἐμοὶ τῷ
[d] ἐλαχιστοτέρῳ πάντων [e] ἁγίων ἐδόθη ἡ χάρις αὕτη, τοῖς
ἔθνεσιν [f] εὐαγγελίσασθαι τὸ [g] ἀνεξιχνίαστον [h] πλοῦτος
τοῦ χριστοῦ, 9 καὶ [i] φωτίσαι πάντας τίς ἡ [k] οἰκονομία

z = 1 Cor iii 5. 2 Cor iii 6. Col i 7, 23, 25 al. a John iv 10. Acts viii 20. Wisd xvi 25. b Gal ii 9 reff. c here only. ἐνεργ., ch i 19 reff. d here only†. δ χ., Rom i 15. μειζότερος, 3 John 4 only. Job v 9. ix 10. xxxiv 24 only. e ch i 1 reff. f ch ii 17 reff. g Rom xi 33. h neut., ch i 7 reff. i John i 9. ch i 18 reff. k ch i 10 reff.

7 rec εγενομην (*more usual form*), with CD³KL rel. txt ABD¹Fℵ 17. rec την δοθεισαν, with D³KL rel syrr goth Chr Thdrt Damasc Thl Œc txt ABCD¹Fℵ 17 latt copt lat-ff

8 rec aft παντων ins των, with (none of our mss) goth Cyr Thdrt Thl om ABCDFKLℵ rel Orig. aft αυτη ins του θεου F rec ins εν bef τοις εθνεσι (*from* ||, *Gal* i. 16, *where none omit it*), with DFKL rel latt syrr goth Dial Chr Cyr Did Thdrt Damasc lat-ff om ABCℵ o copt. rec τον α πλουτον, with D³KLℵ³ rel Dial Cyr: txt ABCD¹Fℵ¹ 17 67²

9 om παντας Aℵ¹ 67² Cyr Hil Jer Aug (not Tert all). rec (for οικονομια) κοινωνια (*explanatory gloss*), with e · txt ABCDFKLℵ rel vss gr-lat-ff

(of the same body) **and fellow-partakers of the promise** (in the widest sense; the *promise of salvation*—the complex, including all other promises, even that chief promise of the Father, the promise of the Spirit itself) **in** (not to be referred to **τῆς ἐπαγγ.**, which would be more naturally, though not necessarily, **τῆς ἐν**,—but to the three foregoing adjectives,—**in Christ Jesus**, as the conditional element in which their participation consisted) **Christ Jesus** (see above on ch ii. 13) **through the Gospel** (He Himself was the *objective ground* of their incorporation; the **εὐαγγέλιον**, the joyful tidings of Him, the *subjective medium* by which they apprehended it) **of which** (Gospel) **I became** (a reference to the event by which "The passive form, however, implies no corresponding difference of meaning [Rück., Eadie] γίγνομαι in the Doric dialect was a deponent passive ἐγενήθην was thus used for ἐγενόμην, and from thence occasionally crept into the language of later writers See Buttm., Irregular Verbs, s. v ΓΕΝ—, Lobeck, Phryn. pp 108-9" Ellic) **a minister** (see the parallel, Col. i 23 and the remarks in Mey., and Ellic on **διάκονος** and **ὑπηρέτης**) **according to** (in consequence of and in analogy with) **the gift of the grace** (genitive of apposition, as clearly appears from the definition of the grace given in the next verse the grace *was* the gift) **of God which was given to me** (**δοθ.** not tautological, or merely pleonastic after **δωρεάν**, but to be joined with what follows) **according to the working in me of his power** (because, and in so far as, His Almighty power wrought in me, was this gift of the *χάρις*, the *ἀποστολή*, the office of preaching among the Gentiles, &c., bestowed upon me)

8] Instead of going straight onward with *ἐν τοῖς ἔθνεσιν κ τ λ*, he calls to mind his own (not past, but present and inherent, see 1 Tim i 15) unworthiness of the high office, and resumes the context with an emphatic declaration of it **To me, who am less than the least** (thus admirably rendered by E V. Winer, edn 6, § 11 2 b, adduces *ἐλαχιστότατος* from Sext. Empir ix 406, and *μειότερος* from Apoll Rhod iii 368—and Wetst. *χερειότερος* from Il *β*. 218, and other examples [Ellic remarks that Thuc iv 118 must be removed from Wetst.'s examples, as the true reading is *κάλλιον*]) **of all saints** (*οὐκ εἶπε, τῶν ἀποστόλων*, Chrys. and herein this has been regarded as an expression of far greater depth of humility than that in 1 Cor xv 8 but each belongs to the subject in hand—each places him far below all others with whom he compared himself), **was given this grace** (viz) **to preach to the Gentiles** (**τ. ἔθν.** is emphatic, and points out *his* distinguishing office There is no parenthesis of *ἐμοί* to *αὕτη* as Harl has unnecessarily imagined) **the unsearchable** (reff., "in its nature, extent, and application." Ellic) **riches of Christ** (i e the fulness of wisdom, righteousness, sanctification, and redemption—all centred and summed up in Him)

9] **and to enlighten** (reff; not merely externally to teach, referred to *his work*,—

τοῦ [l] μυστηρίου τοῦ [m] ἀποκεκρυμμένου ἀπὸ τῶν [n] αἰώνων
[o] ἐν τῷ θεῷ τῷ τὰ πάντα [p] κτίσαντι, 10 ἵνα [q] γνωρισθῇ νῦν
ταῖς [r] ἀρχαῖς καὶ ταῖς [r] ἐξουσίαις ἐν τοῖς [s] ἐπουρανίοις διὰ

ABCDF KLℵ a b c e f g h k l m n o 17

l ch i 9 reff. m (Matt xi 25 xxv 18 v r) Luke x 21 1 Cor ii 7 Col i 26 only 4 Kings iv 27 n Col i 26 plur, Rom i 25 ix 5 1 Cor ii 7 x 11 ch ii 7 1 Tim i 17 Heb i. 2 xi 3 al. fr Ps cxliv 13 o Col iii 3 p ch ii 10 reff q ch i 9 reff r ch i 21 reff s ch i 3 reff

aft των αιωνων ins και απο των γενεων F syr om εν ℵ[1] om τα D[1]F Chr-ms rec aft κτισαντι ins δια ιησου χριστου, with D[3]KL rel syr-w-ast Chr Thdrt Thl Œc om ABCD[1]Fℵ 17 latt Syr copt æth arm Dial Bas Cyr Tert Jer Ambr Aug Ambrst Vig Pelag.
10 om νυν F vulg D-lat Syr Orig Meion-t Victorin.

but internally to enlighten the hearers, referred to *their apprehension:* as when the Apostles gave witness *with great power* of the resurrection of the Lord Jesus, Acts iv 33. On St. Paul's mission to enlighten, see especially Acts xxvi. 18) **all** (no emphasis on *πάντας*, as Harl —"not the Gentiles only, but all men,"—or as Mey. observes it would be *πάντας* [or *τοὺς π.*?] *φωτίσαι*) **what** (the ellipse is supplied by *εἰς τὸ εἰδέναι* in ch. i. 18) **is the œconomy** (see on ch. i 10) **of the mystery** ("the dispensation [arrangement, regulation] of the mystery [the union of Jews and Gentiles in Christ, ver 6] was now to be humbly traced and acknowledged in the fact of its having secretly existed in the primal counsels of God, and now having been revealed to the heavenly powers by means of the Church" Ellicott) **which has been hidden from** (the beginning of) **the ages** (**ἀπὸ τ αἰώνων** gives the temporal limit from which the concealment dated so *χρόνοις αἰωνίοις σεσιγημένου*, Rom xvi 25 The decree itself originated *πρὸ καταβολῆς κόσμου*, ch. i 4, *πρὸ τῶν αἰώνων* 1 Cor. ii. 7. the *αἰῶνες* being the spaces or reaches of *time* necessary for the successive acts of created beings, either physical or spiritual) **in** (join with **ἀποκεκρ.** —hidden within,—humanly speaking, 'in the bosom or the mind of') **God who created all things** ("rerum omnium creatio fundamentum est omnis reliquæ œconomiæ, pro potestate Dei universali liberrime dispensatæ." Beng. The stress is on **τὰ πάντα**—this concealment was nothing to be wondered at—for God of His own will and power created ALL THINGS, a fact which involves His perfect right to adjust all things as He will. **τὰ π**, in the widest sense, embracing physical and spiritual alike), **10.**] **that** (general purpose of the whole more properly to be referred perhaps to **ἐδόθη** than to any other one word in the last two verses For this sublime cause the humble Paul was raised up,—to bring about,—he, the least worthy of the saints,—that to the heavenly powers themselves should be made known, by means of those whom he was empowered to enlighten, &c. Cf. Chrys · *καὶ τοῦτο δὲ χάριτος ἦν, τὸ τὸν μικρὸν τὰ μείζονα ἐγχειρισθῆναι, τὸ γενέσθαι τούτων εὐαγγελιστήν*) **there might be made known** (emphatic, as opposed to **ἀποκεκρ** above—'no longer hidden, but . . .') **now** (has the secondary emphasis · opposed to *ἀπὸ τῶν αἰώνων*) **to the governments and to the** (Stier notices the repetition of the article. It perhaps here does not so much separate the two **ἀρχαί** and **ἐξ** as different classes, as serve to elevate the fact for solemnity's sake) **powers** (see ch. i. 21 and note) **in the heavenly places** (see ch i. 3 note. The **ἀρχ** and **ἐξ** are those of the holy angels in heaven, not, as has been vainly imagined, *Jewish rulers* [Locke, Schottg] *Christian rulers* [Pel] *good and bad angels* [Beng, Olsh]. These are excluded, not by *ἐν τοῖς ἐπουρανίοις*, see ch. vi. 12, but by the general tenor of the passage, as Ellic., who adds well. "evil angels more naturally recognize the *power*, good angels the *wisdom* of God") **by means of the Church** (*ὅτε ἡμεῖς ἐμάθομεν, τότε κἀκεῖνοι δι' ἡμῶν*, Chrys. See also Luke xv. 10, 1 Pet. i 12. and cf Calvin's note here. "That the holy angels are capable of a specific increase of knowledge, and of a deepening insight into God's wisdom, seems from this passage clear and incontrovertible." Ellic. "Vide, quantus honos hominum, quod hæc arcana consilia per ipsos, maxime per apostolos, Deus innotescere angelis voluit Ideo angeli post hoc tempus nolunt ab apostolis coli tanquam in ministerio majore collocatis, Apoc. xix 10, et merito." Grot But as Stier well notices, it is not by the Apostles directly, nor by human preaching, that the Angels are instructed in God's wisdom, but by the Church,—by the fact of the great spiritual body, constituted in Christ, which they contemplate, and which is to them the *θέατρον τῆς δόξης τοῦ θεοῦ*) **the manifold** (*πολυποίκιλος*, so far from

τῆς [t] ἐκκλησίας ἡ [u] πολυποίκιλος [v] σοφία τοῦ θεοῦ, 11 κατὰ
[w] πρόθεσιν τῶν [x] αἰώνων ἣν ἐποίησεν [y] ἐν τῷ χριστῷ Ἰησοῦ
τῷ κυρίῳ ἡμῶν, 12 ἐν ᾧ [z] ἔχομεν τὴν [a] παῤῥησίαν καὶ

t ch i 22 reff. u here only † v = Rom xi 33. 1 Cor i 21, 24. Rev v 12 al. Dan v 11 Theod.-compl. w ch i 11 reff. x gen — here only, see note. y = Col i 10 reff. ἐν τ. χρ., 2 Cor ii 14. ch. i 12, 20. z Paul, here only. Heb x 19. 1 John ii 28. iii 21. iv 17. v 14. Prov xiii 5. a Acts ii 29 al[1]. 2 Cor iii 12. vii 4. ch vi 19. Phil i 20. Col ii 15. 1 Tim iii 13. Philem 8. Heb iii 6 al[3]. 1 John ii 28 al, as above. adverbially only in Gospels.

11. rec om 1st τω, with C[3]DKIℵ[1] [3] rel Ath Chr Thdrt Damasc: ins ABC[1]ℵ-corr[1] m 17.—om τω χριστω ιησου F.

being a word found only here [Harl., Stier], occurs in Eur., Iph. Taur. 1149, πολυποίκιλα φάρεα: in a fragment of Eubulus, Ath. xv. 7, p. 679, στέφανον πολυποίκιλον ἀνθέων, and twice in the Orphic hymns, in this figurative sense: πολυποίκιλος τελετή, v. 11, π. λόγος, lx. 4) **wisdom of God** (*how* is the wisdom of God **πολυποίκιλος**? It is all *one* in sublime unity of truth and purpose: but cannot be apprehended by finite minds in this its unity, and therefore is by Him variously portioned out to each finite race and finite capacity of individuals—so that the Church is a mirror of God's wisdom, —chromatic, so to speak, with the rainbow colours of that light which in itself is one and undivided. Perhaps there was in the Apostle's mind, when he chose this word, an allusion to the πτέρυγες περιστερᾶς περιηργυρωμέναι καὶ τὰ μετάφρενα αὐτῆς ἐν χλωρότητι χρυσίου, the adornment of the ransomed church, in Ps. lxvii. 13. See Heb. i. 1, 1 Pet. iv. 10).

11.] **according to** (depends on γνωρισθῇ—this imparting of the knowledge of God's manifold wisdom was in accordance with, &c.) **the** (not, '*a*:' after a preposition, especially when a limiting genitive, as here, follows, the omission of the article can hardly be regarded as affecting the sense) **purpose of (the) ages** (the genitive is apparently one of time, as when we say, 'it has been an opinion of years:' the duration all that time giving the αἰῶνες a kind of possession. If so, the sense is best given in English by '*eternal*' as in E. V.), **which** (πρόθεσιν) **He made** (constituted, ordained. So Calv., Beza, Harl., Rück. On the other hand, Thdrt., Grot., Koppe, Olsh., Mey., De W., Stier, Ellic., would apply it to the *carrying out, executing, in its historical realization.* I can hardly think that so indefinite a word as ποιέω would have been used to express so very definite an idea, now introduced for the first time, but believe the Apostle would have used some word like ἐπετέλεσεν. Further, we should thus rather expect the perfect, whereas the aorist seems to refer back the act spoken of to the origination of the design. Both senses of ποιέω are abundantly justified: see, for our sense, Mark xv. 1, Isa. xxix. 15: for the other, ch. ii. 3, Matt. xxi. 31; John vi. 38; 1 Thess. v. 24 al.) **in Jesus our Lord the Christ** (or, '*in the Christ*, [namely] *Jesus our Lord.*' The former is official, the latter personal. It was in his Christ that He made the purpose: and that Christ is Jesus our Lord. The words do not necessarily refer ἐποίησεν to the *carrying out* of the design. They bind together God's eternal purpose and our present state of access to Him by redemption in Christ, and so close the train of thought of the last eleven verses, by bringing us again home to the sense of our own blessedness in Christ. That he says, ἐν τ. χριστῷ Ἰησ., does not, as Olsh. and Stier, imply that the act spoken of must necessarily be subsequent to the Incarnation: see ch. i. 3, 4: it is the complex personal appellation of the Son of God, taken from, and familiar to us by His incarnation, but applied to Him in His præexistence also).

12.] **in whom** (for the connexion, see note on last verse: in whom, as their element and condition) **we have our boldness** (not '*freedom of speech*' merely, nor boldness *in prayer*: **παῤῥησία** is used in a far wider sense than these, as will appear by the reff.: viz., that of the state of mind which gives liberty of speech, cheerful boldness, 'Freimüthigkeit,' Palm and Rost's lex.) **and [our] access** (see note on ch. ii. 18: here the intransitive sense is even more necessary, from the union with παῤῥησίαν. We may confidently say, that so important an objective truth as our *introduction to God by Christ* would never have been thus coupled to a mere subjective quality in ourselves. Both must be subjective if one is: the second less purely so than the first—but both referring to our own feelings and privileges) **in confidence** (τουτέστι, μετὰ τοῦ θαῤῥεῖν, Chrys. Meyer remarks what a noble example St. Paul himself has given of this πεποίθησις in Rom. viii. 38 f. πεποίθησις is a word of late Greek, see Lobeck's Phrynichus, p. 294) **through the faith**

[τὴν] ᵇ προςαγωγὴν ἐν ᶜ πεποιθήσει ᵈ διὰ τῆς πίστεως ABCDF
ᵉ αὐτοῦ. 13 διὸ ᶠ αἰτοῦμαι μὴ ᵍ ἐγκακεῖν ʰ ἐν ταῖς ⁱ θλίψεσίν KLℵ a b
μου ὑπὲρ ὑμῶν, ᵏ ἥτις ἐστὶν ˡ δόξα ὑμῶν. 14 τούτου ᵐ χάριν c e f g
ⁿ κάμπτω τὰ ᵒ γόνατά μου ᵖ πρὸς τὸν πατέρα, 15 ᵠ ἐξ οὗ h k l m
πᾶσα ʳ πατριὰ ἐν οὐρανοῖς καὶ ἐπὶ γῆς ˢ ὀνομάζεται, 16 ἵνα n o 17

b ch ii 18 reff c 2 Cor i 15 iii 4 viii 22 x 2 Phil iii 4 only P 4 Kings xviii 19 only d ch ii 8 reff e obj gen, Acts iii 16 Gal ii 16 al ff ver 20 Col i 9 1 John v 14 &c Ps xxvi 4 g Luke xviii 1 2 Cor iv 1 16 Gal vi 9 2 Thess iii 13 only 1 P + Prov iii 11 Theod h = John v 35 Rom ii 23 1 Thess iii 3 al i = Rom v 3 2 Cor vi 4 Phil iv 14 Ps xix 1 k attr, Mark xv 16 Gal iii 16 ch vi 17 Phil i 20 al fr l = 1 Cor ii 7 xi 15 Phil iii 19 1 Thess ii 20 Prov xx 29 m ver 1 reff n (in N T always w γονυ) Rom xi 4 xiv 11 Phil ii 10 only Isa xlv 24 o Mark xv 19 Heb xii 12 al p = Luke xii 3 1 Cor xiii 12 q = here only Xen Mem iv 5 12 r Luke ii 4 Acts iii 25 only Num i 18 s ch i 21 reff

12. om 2nd την ABℵ[1] 17 ins CDFKLℵ[3] rel Ath Chr Thdrt Damasc. for εν πεποιθησει, εν τω ελευθερωθηναι D[1].

13. rec εκκακειν, with CD[3]FKL rel txt ABD[1]ℵ m 17. (*See note on Gal* vi. 9.) for last υμων, ημων C c 17 71 72 80 copt arm

14. rec aft πατερα ins του κυριου ημων ιησ χριστου (*from ch* i. 3, *and simr passages, cf* θεον και *above It wd hardly have been erased, as De W., as coming between* πατ. *and* πατρια), with DFKLℵ[3] rel latt syrr goth Ps-Just Chr Thdrt Damasc$_{al}$ Phot Tert Victorin Lucif. om ABCℵ[1] 17 67[2] demid copt æth Thdot Orig Did Method Synod-ancyr in-Epiph Cyr-jer$_2$ Cyr$_2$ Damasc Elias-cret Thl comm$_{appy}$ Jer$_{expr}$("non, ut in latinis codd. additum est, '*ad Patrem Dom. nostri J. C.*'—sed simpliciter '*ad Patrem*' legendum") Aug$_1$ Cassiod comm Vig.

"**ἐν χρ** points to the objective ground of he possession, **διὰ τῆς πίστ**, the subective medium by which, and **ἐν πεποιθ** he subjective state in which, it is appreended" Ellic) **of** (objective. = '*in*' of which He is the object see reff) **Him.**

13] **Wherefore** ('quæ cum ita sint,' iz. the glorious things spoken of vv 1—2 · and especially his own personal part in hem, *ἐγὼ π., ἐμοὶ ἐδόθη, ἐγενήθην διάκονος*:—since I am the appointed minister f so great a matter) **I beseech you** (not, eseech *God*,—which would awkwardly ecessitate a new subject before *ἐγκακεῖν* · ce below) **not to be dispirited** (not, '*that may not be dispirited*,' as Syr., Thdrt, Beng., Rück, Harl., Olsh. Such a reference is quite refuted by the reason renered below, *ἥτις ἐσ* **δόξα ὑμῶν**, and by he insertion of *μου* after *θλ*, which in this ase would be wholly superfluous not to mention its inconsistency with all we know t the Apostle himself) **in** (of the element r sphere, in which the faint-heartedness ould be shewn '*in the midst of*') **my ribulations for you** (the grammatical ommentators justify the absence of the rticle before **ὑπέρ** by the construction λίβομαι ὑπέρ τινος. This surely is not ecessary, in the presence of such expressons as *τοῖς κυρίοις κατὰ σάρκα*, ch vi. 5 he strange view of Harl, that *ὑπὲρ ὑμῶν* to be joined with *αἰτοῦμαι*, needs no efutation), **seeing that they are** (not *which is*,' **ἥτις** is not = *ἥ*, but = quippe qui,' 'utpote qui' see examples n Palm and Rost's Lex. *ὅς*, p. 517) **your glory** (*πῶς ἐστι δόξα αὐτῶν; ὅτι οὕτως αὐτοὺς ἠγάπησεν ὁ θεός, ὥστε καὶ τ. υἱὸν ὑπὲρ αὐτῶν δοῦναι, κ τοὺς δούλους κακοῦν. ἵνα γὰρ αὐτοὶ τύχωσι τοσούτων ἀγαθῶν*, Παῦλος *ἐδεσμεῖτο*, Chrys Bengel compares *ὑμεῖς ἔνδοξοι, ἡμεῖς δὲ ἄτιμοι*, 1 Cor. iv 10: and this certainly seems against Stier's notion that *δόξα ὑμῶν* means 'your *glorification*,' 'the glory of God in you').

14—19] *His prayer for them, setting forth the aim and end of the ministerial office as respected the Church, viz. its becoming strong in the power of the Spirit*

14.] **On this account** (resumes the *τούτου χάριν* of ver. 1 [see note there] ·—viz. 'because ye are so built in, have such a standing in God's Church') **I bend my knees** (scil. in prayer: see reff, and cf 3 Kings xix 18) **towards** (directing my prayer to Him. see Winer, § 49, h) **the Father** (on the words here interpolated, see var readd), **from whom** (as the source of the name· so Hom. Il κ 68, *πατρόθεν ἐκ γενεῆς ὀνομάζων ἄνδρα ἕκαστον*:—Soph, Œd. Tyr. 1036, *ὥστ' ὠνομάσθης ἐκ τύχης ταύτης, ὃς εἶ* —Xen. Mem. iv. 5. 8, *ἔφη δὲ καὶ τὸ διαλέγεσθαι ὀνομασθῆναι ἐκ τοῦ συνιόντας κοινῇ βουλεύεσθαι διαλέγοντας*.—Cic de Amicitia, 8, 'amor, ex quo amicitia nominata') **every family** (not '*the whole family*' [*πᾶσα ἡ πα ἡ*, or, less strictly, *πᾶσα πατρ ἡ*], as E V. The sense, see below) **in the heavens and on earth is named** (it is difficult to convey in another language any trace of the deep

t δῷ ὑμῖν κατὰ τὸ uv πλοῦτος τῆς v δόξης αὐτοῦ w δυνάμει x κραταιωθῆναι y διὰ τοῦ πνεύματος αὐτοῦ z εἰς τὸν a ἔσω

t = Matt. xiii 11 Acts ii 4 al
u neut, ch i 7 reff
v ch i 18 reff
w = Col i 11 v 5 1 Cor ii 10 al.
x Luke i 80 ii 40 1 Cor xvi 13 only Neh ii 18
y Acts xxi 4 Rom
z = ch ii 21 al
a Rom vii 22 see 2 Cor iv 16

16 rec (for δω) δωη, with DKL rel Valent Ps-Just Orig-cat$_1$ Ath Mac Chr Cyr$_2$ Thdrt Damasc Thl Œc. txt ABCFℵ m 17 Orig-cat$_1$ Method Bas Cyr$_1$. rec τον πλουτον, with D³KL rel Ps-Just Cyr$_2$ txt ABCD¹Fℵ 67² Ath-ms Eph, το πληθος 17. ins εν bef δυναμει F copt

connexion of **πατήρ** and **πατριά** here expressed Had the sentence been 'the *Creator*, after whom every *creature* in heaven and earth is named,' all would be plain to the English reader But we must not thus render, for it is not in virtue of God's creative power that the Apostle here prays to Him, but in virtue of His adoptive love in Christ It is best therefore to keep the simple sense of the words, and leave it to exegesis to convey the idea **πατριά** is the *family*, or in a wider sense the *gens*, named so from its all having one **πατήρ** Some [Est, Grot, Wetst., al] have supposed St Paul to allude to the rabbinical expression, 'the family of earth and the family of heaven.' but as Harl observes, in this case he would have said π. ἡ πατρ, ἡ ἐν οὐρ κ ἡ ἐπὶ γ. Others [Vulg, Jer, Thdrt,—ὃς ἀληθῶς ὑπάρχει πατήρ, ὃς οὐ παρ' ἄλλου τοῦτο λαβὼν ἔχει, ἀλλ' αὐτὸς τοῖς ἄλλοις μεταδέδωκε τοῦτο,—Corn.-a-lap] have attempted to give **πατριά** the sense of *paternitas*, which it can certainly never have. But it is not so easy to say, to what the reference is, or why the idea is here introduced. The former of these will be found very fully discussed in Stier, pp 487—99 and the latter more shortly treated. The Apostle seems, regarding God as the Father of us His adopted children in Christ, to go forth into the fact, that He, in this His relation to us, is in reality the great original and prototype of the paternal relation, wherever found And this he does, by observing that every **πατριά**, *compaternity*, body of persons, having a common father, is thus named [in Greek], *from that father*, —and so every earthly [and heavenly] family reflects in its name [and constitution] the being and sonship of the great Father Himself But then, what are **πατριαί** *in heaven*? Some have treated the idea of paternity *there* as absurd but is it not necessarily involved in *any* explanation of this passage? He Himself is the Father of spirits, Heb. xii 9, the Father of lights, James i. 17 — may there not be fathers in the heavenly Israel, as in the earthly? May not the holy Angels be bound up in spiritual *πατριαί*, though they marry not nor are given in marriage? Observe, we must not miss the sense of **ὀνομάζεται**, nor render, nor understand it, as meaning '*is constituted*' This is the fact, but not brought out here), **16**] **that** (see on **ἵνα** after words of beseeching, &c, note, 1 Cor, xiv 13. The purpose and purport of the prayer are blended in it) **He may give you, according to the riches of His glory** (specifies **δῷ**, not what follows give you, in full proportion to the abundance of His own glory—His own infinite perfections), **to be strengthened with might** (the dative has been taken in several ways 1) adverbially, '*mightily*,' as βίᾳ εἰς οἰκίαν παριέναι, Xen Cyr i 2 2,—to which Meyer objects, that thus **δύναμις** would be strength on the side of the bestower rather than of the receiver, whereas the contrast with ἐγκακεῖν (?) requires the converse This hardly seems sufficient to disprove the sense 2) dative of the *form* or *shape* in which the κρατ was to take place (Harl, al), as in χρήμασι δυνατοὶ εἶναι, Xen. Mem ii. 7. 7,—to which Meyer replies that thus the κραταιωθῆναι would only apply to one department of the spiritual life, instead of to all But this again seems to me not valid for '*might*,' '*power*,' is not one faculty, but a qualification of all faculties. Rather I should say that such a meaning would involve a tautology—'strengthened in strength' 3) the instrumental dative is maintained by Mey, De W, al, and this view seems the best: '*with* [His] *might*,' imparted to you) **by His Spirit** (as the instiller and imparter of that might) **into** (not merely 'in,' but '*to and into*,' as Ellic importing "the direction and destination of the prayed for gift of infused strength" κραταιοῖ, κατοικίζων εἰς τὸν χωροῦντα ἔσω ἄνθρωπον τὸν χριστόν, Schol in Cramer's Catena Similarly Orig, ὥστε εἰς τ. ἔσ ἄνθ. κατοικῆσαι τ. χριστὸν διὰ τῆς πίστεως, ib Both rightly, as far as the idea of infusing into is concerned. but clearly wrong, as are the Gr -ff in general, in taking **εἰς τ ἔσ ἄνθ** with what follows,

b Col i 19 ii 9 c ch iv 2 Col ii 2 d Col ii 7 only Isa xl 24 e Matt vii 25 (Luke vii 48 v r) Col i 23. Heb i 10, from Ps ci 25 1 Pet v 10 only

[a] ἄνθρωπον, 17 [b] κατοικῆσαι τὸν χριστὸν διὰ τῆς πίστεως
ἐν ταῖς καρδίαις ὑμῶν, 18 [c] ἐν ἀγάπῃ [d] ἐρριζωμένοι καὶ
[e] τεθεμελιωμένοι, ἵνα [f] ἐξισχύσητε [g] καταλαβέσθαι [h] σὺν
πᾶσιν τοῖς [i] ἁγίοις τί τὸ [kl] πλάτος καὶ [km] μῆκος καὶ [kn] ὕψος

ABCDF KLℵ a b c e f g h k l m n o 17

f here only†. Sir vii 6 vat only. g Acts iv 13 x 34 xxv 25. Phil iii 12, 13. Obad 6. h = Acts x 2 xiv 13 al fr. i = ch i 1 reff. k Rev xxi 16. Gen vi 15. l Rev xx 9 xxi 16 bis only. m Rev xxi 16 bis only. n Luke i 78 xxiv 49. ch iv 8 (from Ps lxvii 19). James i 9. Rev xxi 16 only. n o see Rom viii 39.

18. rec *βαθος και υψος*, with AKLℵ rel syr Orig Mac Chr Thdrt Jer: txt BCDF m 17 latt Syr copt æth arm Ath Cyr Lucif Ambrst Pelag Jer. (Tischdf states the readings vice versa, appy by mistake.)

thus making **ἐν ταῖς καρδ ὑμ** tautological, or giving to **διὰ τῆς πίστεως ἐν ταῖς καρδίαις ὑμῶν** the meaning, '*through the faith which is in your hearts*,' which it cannot bear) **the inner man** (the spiritual man—the noblest portion of our being, kept, in the natural man, under subjection to the flesh [reff.], but in the spiritual, renewed by the Spirit of God)—**that** (continuation, not of the prayer merely,—not from **δῷ**,—as the strong word **κατοικῆσαι**, emphatically placed, sufficiently shews,—but from **κραταιωθῆναι**,—and that as its result [see Orig. above not its purpose,—*τοῦ κατ.*]. See a similar construction Col i 10) **Christ may dwell** (emphatic, abide, take up His lasting abode 'summa sit, non procul intuendum esse Christum fide, sed recipiendum esse animæ nostræ complexu, ut in nobis habitet,' Calv.) **by your faith** (apprehending Him, and opening the door to Him,—see John xiv 23; Rev iii. 20—and keeping Him there) **in your hearts** ("partem etiam designat ubi legitima est Christi sedes, nempe cor ut sciamus, non satis esse, si in lingua versetur, aut in cerebro volitet" Calv),—**ye having been** (Beza, Grot, al, and Meyer [and so E V], join the participles with the following **ἵνα**, justifying the trajection by Gal ii 10, 2 Thess ii 7; Acts xix 4 al But those cases are not parallel, as in every one of them the prefixed words carry especial emphasis, which here they cannot do. We must therefore regard the clause as an instance of the irregular nominative [see ch. iv. 2, Col ii 2, and reff there] adopted to form an easy transition to that which follows Meyer strongly objects to this, that the participles are *perfect*, not present, which would be thus logically required. But surely this last is a mistake It is upon the completion, not upon the progress, of their rooting and grounding in love, that the next clause depends. So Orig., Chrys, all, and Harl., De W, and Ellic.) **rooted and grounded** (both images, that of a tree, and that of a building, are supposed to have been before the Apostle's mind. But *ῥιζόω* was so constantly used in a figurative sense [see examples in Palm and Rost sub voce] as hardly perhaps of necessity to suggest its primary image. Lucian uses both words together, de Saltat 34 [Wetst],—*ὥσπερ τινὲς ῥίζαι κ. θεμέλιοι τῆς ὀρχήσεως ἦσαν*) **in love** (love, generally—not merely *αὐτοῦ*, as Chrys, nor '*qua diligimur a Deo*,' Beza, nor need we supply 'in Christ' after the participles, thus disconnecting them from *ἐν ἀγ*, as Harl., but as Ellic. well says, "This [love] was to be their basis and foundation, in (on?) which alone they were to be fully enabled to realize all the majestic proportions of Christ's surpassing love to man"),—**that ye may be fully able** (ref.: *ἡ ἐπιμέλεια πολλάκις καὶ τῆς φύσεως ἐξίσχυσεν ἐπιλειπούσης*, Strabo, xvii. p. 788 [417 Tauchn]) **to comprehend** (reff. "many middle forms are distinguished from their actives only by giving more the idea of earnestness or spiritual energy *ἠριθμοῦντο πολλοὶ ἅμα τὰς ἐπιβολάς*, Thucyd iii. 20 *οὕτω δεῖ περὶ παντὸς σκοπεῖν ὅταν γάρ τι ταύτῃ σκοπούμενος ἕλῃς, οὕτως ἔμφρων περὶ τοῦτο γέγονας* Plato." Kruger, griech. Sprachlehre, § 52 1) **with all the saints** (all the people of God, in whom is fulfilled that which is here prayed for) **what is the breadth and length and height and depth** (all kinds of fanciful explanations have been given of these words One specimen may be enough: *ἐσχημάτισεν ὥσπερ τυπικώτερον εἰς σταυροῦ τύπον.* **βάθος γὰρ καὶ ὕψος καὶ μῆκος καὶ πλάτος**, *τί ἕτερον ἂν εἴη, ἢ τοῦ σταυροῦ φύσις, διπλοῦν δέ που ἔοικε τὸν σταυρὸν λέγειν, οὐχ ἁπλῶς ἀλλ' ἐπειδὴ ἡ μὲν τοῦ κυρίου οἰκονομία θεότης ἐστὶν ἄνωθεν, καὶ ἀνθρωπότης κάτωθεν, τὸ δὲ κήρυγμα ἀποστολικὸν διετεινεν ἀπὸ ἄρκτου εἰς μεσημβρίαν καὶ ἀπὸ ἀνατολῆς εἰς δύσιν, συναγαγὼν καὶ κυρίου τὴν οἰκονομίαν καὶ τῶν ἀποστόλων ὑπηρεσίαν τὸ διπλοῦν τῆς οἰκονομίας, ὡς ἐν διπλῷ*

καὶ ° βάθος, 19 γνῶναί τε τὴν ᵖ ὑπερβάλλουσαν τῆς ᵠ γνώσεως ʳ ἀγάπην τοῦ ʳ χριστοῦ, ἵνα ˢ πληρωθῆτε ᵗ εἰς πᾶν τὸ
ᵘ πλήρωμα τοῦ θεοῦ. 20 τῷ δὲ δυναμένῳ ᵛ ὑπὲρ πάντα
ποιῆσαι ʷ ὑπερεκπερισσοῦ ὧν ˣ αἰτούμεθα ἢ ʸ νοοῦμεν κατὰ
τὴν δύναμιν τὴν ᶻ ἐνεργουμένην ἐν ἡμῖν, 21 ᵃ αὐτῷ ἡ ᵃ δόξα

o = Rom xi. 30
p ch i 19 reff
q = 1 Cor viii 1. xiii 2, 8 Hos iv 6 (see 1 Tim vi 20)
r = Rom viii 35 2 Cor v 14
s = Rom i 29 xv 13 2 Cor vii 4 al
t = ch ii 21 al
u = Rom xv 29 Col i 19 ii 9
v = Philem 21
w 1 Thess iii 10 only † Dan iii 22 Theod.-Ald compl (σφόδρα, 1 Thess v 13)
x ver 13 reff
y ver 4 reff
z = Matt xiv 2 || Rom vii 5 1 Cor xii. 6 2 Cor i 6 iv 12. Gal ii 8 iii 5 al, Paul chiefly
a Rom xi 36 2 Pet iii 18 Rev i 6

19 om τε D¹F copt. αγαπην bef της γνωσεως A a 115 syr Jer(*scientiam caritatis* Aug)₁. πληρωθη, omg εις B 17 73 116.
20. om υπερ DF latt lat-ff (exc Jer).

τῷ σταυρῷ ἐπιδεικνύμενος, οὕτως εἶπεν. Severianus, in Cramer's Catena Similarly Origen, ib., Jer, Aug., Anselm, Aquin, Est. ('longitudo temporum est, latitudo locorum, altitudo gloriæ, profunditas discretionis') Numerous other explanations, geometrical, architectural, and spiritual, may be seen in Corn.-a-lap, Pole's Synops, and Eadie The latter, as also Bengel and Stier, see an allusion to the Church as the temple of God—Chandler and Macknight to the temple of Diana at Ephesus. Both are in the highest degree improbable. Nor can we quite say that the object of the sentence is *the love of Christ* [Calv., Mey., Ellicott, al.]: for that is introduced in a subordinate clause by and by [see on **τε** below] rather, with De W, that the genitive **after** these nouns is left indefinite—that you may be fully able to comprehend every dimension—scil, of all that God has revealed or done in and for us [= τὸ μυστήριον τ. θεοῦ, Col ii 2]—though this is not a genitive *to be supplied*, but lying in the background entirely) **and** (**τε** introduces not a parallel, but a subordinate clause. Of this Hartung, i. p 105, gives many examples. Eur. Hec 1186,—δτ' ευτύχει | Τροία, πέριξ δὲ πύργος εἶχ' ἔτι πτόλιν, | ἔζη τε Πρίαμος, Ἕκτορός τ' ἤνθει δόρυ: Med. 642, ὦ πατρίς, δῶμά τ' ἐμόν So that the knowledge here spoken of is not identical with the **καταλαβέσθαι** above, but forms one portion of it, and by its surpassing excellence serves to exalt still more that great whole to which it belongs) **to know the knowledge-passing** (**τῆς γνώσεως**, genitive of comparison after ὑπερβ, as in διπλήσιος ἑωυτοῦ, Herod viii. 137,—οὐδενὸς ὕστερος, Plat. Tim p. 20 A. See Kuhner, ii. § 540 **γνῶναι . . . γνώσεως** are chosen as a paradox, **γνώσεως** being taken in the sense of '*mere*,' '*bare*' *knowledge* [ref], and **γνῶναι** in the pregnant sense of that knowledge which is rooted and grounded in love, Phil i 9) **Love of Christ** (subjective genitive, *Christ's Love to us*—see Rom. v. 5 note, and viii. 35—39—not '*our love to Christ.*' Nor must we interpret with Harl [and Olsh.], "*to know the Love of Christ more and more as an unsearchable love.*" It is not this *attribute* of Christ's Love, but the Love itself, which he prays that they may know), **that ye may be filled even to all the fulness of God** (πᾶν τὸ πλήρωμα τῆς θεότητος abides in Christ, Col. ii. 9. Christ then abiding in your hearts, ye, being raised up to the comprehension of the vastness of God's mercy in Him and of His Love, will be filled, even as God is full—each in your degree, but all to your utmost capacity, with divine wisdom and might and love. Such seems much the best rendering and so Chrys [altern.], ὥστε πληροῦσθαι πάσης ἀρετῆς ἧς πλήρης ἐστὶν ὁ θεός. **τοῦ θ** then is the possessive genitive. The other interpretation taking **θεοῦ** as a genitive of origin, and **πλήρωμα** for **πλῆθος**, 'ut omnibus Dei donis abundetis,' Est., is not consistent with **εἰς** [see above], nor with the force of the passage, which having risen in sublimity with every clause, would hardly end so tamely).

20, 21] Doxology, arising from the contemplation of the faithfulness and power of God with regard to His Church 20] **But to Him** (δέ brings out a slight contrast to what has just preceded—viz *ourselves*, and our need of strength and our growth in knowledge, and fulness) **who is able to do beyond all things** (ὑπέρ is not adverbial, as Bengel, which would be tautological), **far beyond** (reff **ὧν** is not governed by **πάντα** but this second clause repeats the first in a more detailed and specified form. "It is noticeable that **ὑπέρ** occurs nearly thrice as many times in St. Paul's Epistles and the Epistle to the Hebrews as in the rest of the N. T., and that, with a few exceptions [Mark vii 37 Luke vi 38, &c.], the compounds of ὑπέρ are all found in St. Paul's Epistles." Ellic.) **the things which** (genitive as γνώσεως above, ver. 19) **we ask or think** ('*cogitatio* latius

[b] ἐν τῇ ἐκκλησίᾳ [καὶ] ἐν χριστῷ Ἰησοῦ εἰς [c] πάσας τὰς
[c] γενεὰς τοῦ [d] αἰῶνος τῶν [d] αἰώνων, ἀμήν.
IV. 1 [e] Παρακαλῶ οὖν ὑμᾶς ἐγὼ ὁ [f] δέσμιος ἐν κυρίῳ,
[g] ἀξίως [h] περιπατῆσαι τῆς [ih] κλήσεως [l] ἧς [k] ἐκλήθητε,
2 [m] μετὰ πάσης [n] ταπεινοφροσύνης καὶ [o] πρᾳύτητος, μετὰ

ABCDF KLℵ a b c e f g h k l m n o 17

b 1 Cor xiv 19, 28 c Luke i 48 (ver 5 reff) d here only Dan vii 18 e = Matt viii 5 Rom xii 1 al fr Prov viii 4 f ch iii 1 reff g & constr, Rom xvi 2 Phil i 27 Col i 10 1 Thess. ii 12 Paul only, exc 3 John 6† Wisd vii 15 (xvi 1 Sir xiv 11) only h = Acts xxi 21 al fr prine Paul (31) & John (19) i Rom xi 29 1 Cor i 26 ch i 18 al (6) Paul only, exc Heb iii 1 2 Pet i 10 k 1 Cor vii 20 l attr, ch i 7 reff m = Matt xxviii 8 1 Chron xxix 22 al fr n Acts xx 19 (Paul) Phil ii 3 Col ii 18 23. iii 12 Paul only, exc 1 Pet v 5† (-φρων, 1 Pet iii 8 -φρονεῖν, Ps cxxx 2) o Gal v 23 vi 1 reff

21 om και D²KL rel syrr goth Chr Thdrt Thl Œc Vig ins ABC(D¹F)ℵ 17 vulg copt arm Damasc-comm lat-ff.—εν χ ι. και τη εκκλ. D¹F Victorin Ambrst om του αιωνος F tol.

Chap IV 1. for κυριω, χριστω ℵ
2. rec πραοτητος, with ADFL rel υπακοης K · txt BCℵ 17.

patet quam preces: gradatio' Beng) **according to the power which is working** (not passive see on Gal. v 6. the power is the might of the indwelling Spirit, see Rom. viii. 26) **in us,** 21] **to Him** (solemn and emphatic repetition of the personal pronoun) **be the glory** (the whole glory accruing from all His dealings which have been spoken of His own resulting glory) **in the Church** (as its theatre before men, in which that glory must be recognized and rendered) **[and] in Christ Jesus** (as its inner verity, and essential element in which it abides If the καί be omitted, beware of rendering '*in the Church which is in Christ Jesus,*' which would not only require the article [cf Gal i. 22, ταῖς ἐκκλ. τῆς Ἰουδαίας ταῖς ἐν χριστῷ], but would make **ἐν χριστῷ Ἰησοῦ** superfluous. As the text stands, we need not say that **ἐν χρ. Ἰησ** is a second independent clause: it belongs to **ἐν τῇ ἐκκ** as inclusive of it, though not as descriptive of ἐκκλ 'in the Church and [thus] in Christ Jesus') **to all the generations of the age of the ages** (probably as Grot, 'augendi causa duas locutiones Hebraicas miscuit Apostolus, quarum prior est ἀπὸ γενεᾶς εἰς γενεάν, לְדֹר וָדֹר, Ps. x 6, altera ἕως τοῦ αἰῶνος עוֹלְמֵי עַד, Isa xlv 17' Probably the account of the meaning is, that the *age of ages* [eternity] is conceived as containing ages, just as our 'age' contains years and then those ages are thought of as made up, like ours, of generations. Like the similar expression, αἰῶνες τῶν αἰώνων, it is used, by a transfer of what we know in time, to express, imperfectly, and indeed improperly, the idea of Eternity).

IV 1 VI 20] Second (hortatory) portion of the Epistle. and herein [A] (IV 1-16) *ground of the Christian's duties as a member of the Church,* viz *the unity of the mystical Body of Christ* (vv. 1—6) *in the manifoldness of grace given to each* (7—13), *that we may come to perfection in Him* (14—16). 1] **I exhort** (see reff παρακαλῶ, τὸ προτρέπω, ὡς ἐπὶ τὸ πολύ. Thom-Mag in Ellic) **you therefore** (seeing that this is your calling an inference from all the former part of the Epistle, as in Rom xii. 1, but here perhaps also a resumption of τούτου χάριν of ch iii. 1, 14, and thus carried back to the contents of ch. i ii.),—**the prisoner in the Lord** (who am, as regards, and for the sake of the cause, of the Lord, a prisoner, so that my captivity is *in the Lord*, as its element and sphere, and therefore to be regarded as an additional inducement to comply with my exhortation "Num quicquid est Christi, etiamsi coram mundo sit ignominiosum, summo cum honore suscipiendum a vobis est" Calv τοῖς διὰ τὸν χριστὸν δεσμοῖς ἐναβρύνεται μᾶλλον ἢ βασιλεὺς διαδήματι Thdrt Beware of joining **ἐν κυρ** with **παρακαλῶ**, as in 2 Thess iii 12 [see ver 17], which the arrangement of the words here will not permit), **to walk worthily of the calling** (see ch i 18, and note Rom viii 28, 30) **wherewith** (see ch. i 6 The attracted genitive may stand either for the dative ᾗ or the accusative ἥν Both constructions are legitimate attractions cf for the dative, Xen. Cyr. v 1 39, ἦγετο δὲ καὶ τῶν ἑαυτοῦ τῶν τε πιστῶν, οἷς ἥδετο, κ ὧν ἠπίστει πολλούς —ὧν, for ἐκείνων, οἷς; and for the accusative, ch i 6, and Hom Il χ 619,—τιμῆς ἧστέ μ' ἔοικε τετιμῆσθαι De W denies the legitimacy of **κλῆσιν καλεῖν**, but Raphel produces from Arrian, Epict p 122, καταισχύνειν τὴν κλῆσιν ἣν κέκληκεν) **ye were called, with** (not '*in*,' as Conyb, which, besides not expressing **μετά**, the association of certain dispositions to an act,—confuses

[p] μακροθυμίας, [q] ἀνεχόμενοι ἀλλήλων ἐν ἀγάπῃ, 3 [r] σπουδάζοντες [s] τηρεῖν τὴν [t] ἑνότητα τοῦ πνεύματος ἐν τῷ
[u] συνδέσμῳ τῆς εἰρήνης. 4 [v] ἓν σῶμα καὶ [w] ἓν πνεῦμα,

p Rom ii 4 (al8 Paul). Heb vi 12 James v 10 1 Pet iii 20. 2 Pet iii 15 Prov xxv 15

n o p Col iii 12 o p Gal v 22, 23 q & constr, Matt xvii 17 ‖ Acts xviii 14 1 Cor iv 12 2 Cor xi 1, &c Col iii 13 (al7 Paul) Isa lxiii 15 r Gal ii 10 1 Thess ii 17 (al4 Paul) Heb iv 11 2 Pet i 10, 15 iii 14 Isa xxi 3 s — (Paul) 2 Tim iv 7 only t ver 13 only † u Acts viii 23 Col ii 19 iii 14 only Isa lviii 6 v ch ii 16 reff w ch ii 16, 18 reff

3 for ειρηνης, αγαπης K 1: αγαπης ειρηνης a[1].

the ἐν which follows) all (see on ch. i. 8) **lowliness** (read by all means Trench's essay on **ταπεινοφροσύνη** and **πραότης**, in his N T Synonymes [xlii]. I can only extract one sentence here, to put the reader on his guard "Chrys is in fact bringing in pride again under the disguise of humility, when he characterizes it as a making of ourselves small *when we are great* [**ταπεινοφροσύνη** *τοῦτό ἐστιν, ὅταν τις μέγας ὤν, ἑαυτὸν ταπεινοῖ* and he repeats this often see Suicer, Thes s v] it is rather the esteeming ourselves small, *inasmuch as we are so* the thinking truly, and because truly, lowlily of ourselves") **and meekness** (before God, accepting His dealings in humility, and before men, as God's instruments, 2 Sam. xvi. 11: resting therefore on *ταπεινοφρ.* as its foundation See Trench, as above), **with long-suffering** (**μακροθυμία** consists in not taking swift vengeance, but leaving to an offender a place for repentance. From this, its proper meaning, it is easily further generalized to forbearance under all circumstances of provocation Some, as Est, Hail, Olsh, al, join these words with **ἀνεχόμενοι** But thus (1) we should have an emphatic tautology—for how could the **ἀνέχεσθαι** be otherwise than **μετὰ μακροθυμίας**? and (2) the parallelism, *μετὰ πάσης ταπ. κ πραΰτ, μετ μακρ*,—would be destroyed Still less should we, with Thdrt, Œc, and Bengel, make all one sentence from *μετὰ πάσ* to *ἀγάπ* for thus [Mey] we should lose the gradual transition from the general *ἀξίως περιπ τ. κλ.* to the special *ἀνεχ ἀλλ.*),—**forbearing** (see reff and Rom. ii 4, on the nom part, see ch. iii. 18) **one another in love** (it is very unnatural, as Lachm and Olsh. have done, to join *ἐν ἀγ* with *σπουδάζοντες*, making thereby an exceedingly clumsy clause of the following), **earnestly striving** (reff) **to maintain the unity of the Spirit** (that unity, in which God's Holy Spirit in the Church *τοὺς γένει κ τρόποις διαφόροις διεστηκότας ἑνοῖ*, as Chr not *animorum inter vos conjunctionem*, as Est,—and so Ambr, Anselm, Erasm, Calv, al. The genitive is *in fact* a possessive—*the Spirit's unity*, that unity which the Spirit brings about, *ἣν τὸ πν ἔδωκεν ἡμῖν*, Thl) **in** (united together by: *within*) **the bond of peace** (again Lachm. joins the qualifying clause to the following sentence: here again most unnaturally, both as regards what has preceded, and the general truths which are afterwards enounced. see below. The *σύνδ* is *εἰρήνη*, not *that which brings about εἰρήνη*, 'vinculum quo pax retinetur, id est, *amor*.' Beng. So Thl, Ruck., Hail, Stier. Col iii 14, which is quoted to support this meaning, is not applicable, because love there is *expressly named*, whereas here it certainly would not occur to any reader, especially after *ἐν ἀγάπῃ* has just occurred. The genitive of apposition is the simplest—peace binds together the Church as a condition and symbol of that inner unity which is only wrought by the indwelling Spirit of God).

4] Lachm, joining **ἓν σῶμα** *κ.τ.λ* as far as *ἐν* **πᾶσιν**, with what has gone before, makes these words hortatory. 'as one Body and one Spirit, even as, &c' Certainly the reference to *ἡ κλῆσις ὑμῶν* seems to tell for this But, on the other hand, it is very unlikely that the Apostle should thus use *ἓν σῶμα* and *ἓν πνεῦμα*, and then go on in the same strain, but with a different reference. I therefore prefer the common punctuation and rendering. **(There is)** (better than '*ye are*,' which will not apply to the following parallel clauses The assertion of the unity of the Church, and of our Lord in all His operations and ordinances, springs immediately out of the last exhortation, as following it up to its great primal ground in the verities of God. To suppose it connected by a *γάρ* understood [Eadie] is to destroy the force and vividness with which the great central truth is at once introduced without preface) **one Body** (reff. viz. Christ's mystical Body. *τί δ' ἐστιν, ἓν σῶμα, οἱ πανταχοῦ τῆς οἰκουμένης πιστοί, καὶ ὄντες κ γενόμενοι κ ἐσόμενοι. πάλιν καὶ οἱ πρὸ τῆς τοῦ χριστοῦ παρουσίας εὐηρεστηκότες, ἓν σῶμά εἰσι* Chrys.

x 1 Cor vii 15. Gal i 6. 1 Thess iv 7. y ch i 18. z 1 Cor viii 6 (1 Tim ii 5.) a Rom ix 5 al. b — Acts ix 32. 2 Cor viii 5. c ver 16 reff. d Gal ii 9 reff.

καθὼς καὶ ἐκλήθητε [x] ἐν μιᾷ [y] ἐλπίδι τῆς [y] κλήσεως ὑμῶν· ABCDF
5 [z] εἷς [z] κύριος, μία πίστις, ἓν βάπτισμα, 6 [z] εἷς [z] θεὸς καὶ KLℵ a b c e f g
[z] πατὴρ πάντων, ὁ [a] ἐπὶ πάντων καὶ [b] διὰ πάντων καὶ ἐν h k l m n o 17
πᾶσιν. 7 [c] ἑνὶ δὲ ἑκάστῳ ἡμῶν [d] ἐδόθη [ἡ] [d] χάρις κατὰ

4 om 2nd και B k 114 vulg(not fuld tol) syr goth Chr, Ambrst
6 om 3rd και B 114. rec aft πασιν ins υμιν (*the pronouns appear to be mere glosses to confine the assertion to Christians*), with k Chr-comm Thdrt ημιν DFKL rel latt syr goth Did Damasc Iren-lat: om ABCℵ 17. 67[2] copt æth Ign Eus Ath Naz Epiph Cyr Jer Victorin Ambr Aug Sedul.
7 υμων B k 120 Thdrt om η BD[1]FL k Damasc ins ACD[3]Kℵ rel Chr Thdrt —aft η χαρις ins αυτη C[4] 31 Cyr (*The art was prob absorbed by the precedg η, or omitted as superfluous*)

But these last hardly *sensu proprio* here) **and one Spirit** (viz. the Holy Spirit, who dwells in, and vivifies, and rules that one body see ch. ii. 18, 22, 1 Cor. xii. 13 al not as Chrys., ἓν πν καλῶς εἶπε, δεικνὺς ὅτι ἀπὸ τοῦ ἑνὸς σώματος ἓν πνεῦμα ἔσται, ἢ ὅτι ἐστὶ μὲν σῶμα εἶναι ἕν, οὐχ ἓν δὲ πνεῦμα ὡς ἂν εἴ τις καὶ αἱρετικῶν φίλος εἴη ἢ ὅτι ἀπ' ἐκείνου δυσωπεῖ, τουτέστιν, οἱ ἓν πνεῦμα λαβόντες, καὶ ἐκ μιᾶς ποτισθέντες πηγῆς οὐκ ὀφείλετε διχονοεῖν ἢ πν ἐνταῦθα τὴν προθυμίαν φησίν), as also (τὸ καθὰ οἱ Ἀττικοὶ χρῶνται, τὸ δὲ καθὼς οὐδέποτε, ἀλλ' ἡ τῶν Ἀλεξανδρέων διάλεκτος, καθ' ἣν ἡ θεία γραφὴ γέγραπται Emm Moschop a Byzantine grammarian, cited by Fabricius, vi 191 See also Phryn p. 426, and Lobeck's note and Ellic on Gal. iii 6) **ye were called in** (elemental—the condition and sphere in which they were called to live and move, see reff. Mey. referring to Gal. i 6, takes the instrumental sense · see there) **one hope of** (belonging to you were called *in it* as the element, see above · it is then an accident of the κλῆσις Or perhaps it may be the genitive of the *causa efficiens*, 'which the calling works,' as Ellic Cf. 1 Thess i 6, μετὰ χαρᾶς πνεύματος ἁγίου) **your calling:** 5.] **one Lord** (as the Head of the Church in this verse he grounds the co-existence of the ἓν σῶμα κ ἓν πνεῦμα in the three great facts on which it rests—the first objective,—**εἷς κύριος**—the second subjective,—**μία πίστις**—the third compounded of the two,—**ἓν βάπτισμα**), **one faith** (in that one Lord the subjective medium by which that one Lord is apprehended and appropriated not 'fides *quæ* creditur,' but 'fides *quâ* creditur' but it is necessarily understood, that this subjective faith has for its object the One Lord just mentioned) **one baptism** (the objective seal of the subjective faith, by which, as a badge, the members of Christ are outwardly and visibly stamped with His name. The other sacrament, being a matured act of subsequent participation, a function of the incorporate, not a seal of incorporation [a symbol of *union*, not of *unity* so Ellicott], is not here adduced In 1 Cor x. 17, where an act was in question which was a clear breach of union, it forms the rallying-point),
6] **one God** (the unity is here consummated in its central Object 'hoc est præcipuum, quia inde manant reliqua omnia,' Calv. But we must not miss the distinct witness to the doctrine of the Holy Trinity in these verses —going upwards, we have 1st, the One Spirit dwelling in the one body —2nd, the One Lord appropriated by faith and professed in baptism —3rd, One God and Father supreme, in whom all find their end and object) **and Father of all** (masculine · 'of all within the Church,' for so is clearly the *primary* meaning, where he is speaking distinctly of the Church:—of all (Mey) who have the υἱοθεσία. But it can hardly be doubted, that there is a further reference—to the universal Fathership of all men—which indeed the Church only inherits in its fulness, others having fallen out of it by sin,—but which nevertheless is just as absolutely true), **who is over all** (men, primarily, and from the following,—men only, in this place. He is over all, in his *sovereignty as the* FATHER), **and through all** (men in the co-extensiveness of Redemption by the Son with the whole nature of man see on ver. 10 below, and ch. ii. 20, 21) **and in all** (men · by the indwelling of the Spirit, see ch ii 22 So that I cannot but recognize, in these three carefully chosen expressions, a distinct allusion again to the Three Persons of the blessed Trinity. All these are the work of the Father:—it is He who in direct sovereignty is over all

τὸ [e] μέτρον τῆς [f] δωρεᾶς τοῦ χριστοῦ. 8 διὸ [g] λέγει
[h] Ἀναβὰς εἰς [i] ὕψος [k] ᾐχμαλώτευσεν [l] αἰχμαλωσίαν καὶ

e Rom xii 3. 2 Cor x 13. vv 13, 16. — Paul only.
f ch iii 7 reff.
g Gal iii 16. James iv 6. Heb x 5. see 1 Cor vi 16.
h John iii 13. Psa lxvii 18.
i = Luke i 78. xxiv 49. (ch iii 18 reff.)
k here only. Amos i 6. (-τίζειν, 2 Tim iii 6.)
l = Rev xiii 10 bis only. Num xxi 1. Judg v 12. 2 Chron xxviii 17. Diod Sic xvii 70, τ. αἰχμαλωσίαι δουλαγωγοῦντες.

8 ηχμαλωτευσας AL a[1] c k 114 æth. om και (see LXX) AC[2]D[1]Fℵ[1] 17 latt copt Iren-int Tert Hil Jer Ambrst ins BC[1,3]D[3]KLℵ[3] rel syrr goth Orig Chr Thdrt Cyr Victorin.

—He who is glorified in the filling of all things by the Son —He who is revealed by the witness of the indwelling Spirit. Many Commentators deny such a reference Almost all agree in ἐν πᾶσιν representing the indwelling of the Spirit the διὰ πάντων has been the principal stumbling block and is variously interpreted —by some, of God's Providence,—τουτέστιν, ὁ προνοῶν καὶ διοικῶν, Chrys, al · by others, of His pervading presence by the Spirit,—'Spiritu sanctificationis diffusus est per omnia ecclesiæ membra,' Calv by others, to the creation by the Son, 'per quem omnia facta sunt' [Aquin in Ellic] · but this seems to be a conversion of διὰ πάντων into δι' οὗ πάντες, as indeed Olsh expressly does, 'als Werkzeug, durch das die sind' Irenæus, v 18 2, p 315, gives the meaning thus, adopting the Trinitarian reference, but taking the πάντων both times as *neuter*, and reading ἐν πᾶσιν ἡμῖν · 'super omnia quidem Pater, et ipse est caput Christi: per omnia autem verbum, et ipse est caput ecclesiæ · in omnibus autem nobis Spiritus, et ipse est aqua viva,' &c). 7.] **But** (the contrast is between ἐν πᾶσιν and ἑνὶ ἑκάστῳ—the general, and the particular. And the connexion is—as a motive to keep the unity of the Spirit—'none is overlooked —each has his part in the distribution of the gifts of the One Spirit, which part he is bound to use for the well-being of the whole') **to each one of us was given** (by Christ, at the time of His exaltation—when He bestowed gifts on men) **[the] grace** (which was then bestowed. *the* unspeakable gift,—or, if the art. be omitted, grace, absolutely,—was distributed to each κατά &c) **according to the measure of** (subjective genitive the amount of cf Rom xii 3, ἑκάστῳ ὡς ὁ θεὸς ἐμέρισεν μέτρον πίστεως) **the gift of Christ** ('*Christ's gift*,'—the gift bestowed by Christ, 2 Cor. ix 15: not, 'the gift which Christ received,'—for He is the subject and centre here—so Calv ,—'porro Christum facit auctorem, quia sicut a Patre fecit initium, ita in ipsum vult nos et nostra omnia colligere.' Still less must we with Stier, suppose both senses of the genitive included) 8.] **Wherefore** ('quæ cum ita sint ' viz.—the gift bestowed by Christ on different men according to measure) **He** (viz God, whose word the Scriptures are See reff. and notes not merely 'it,' es heißt, as De W al nor, ἡ γραφή had it been the subject, it must have been expressed, as in Rom iv 3; ix 17 al) **says** (viz. in Ps. lxviii 18, see below not, in some Christian hymn, as Flatt and Storr,—which would not agree with λέγει, nor with the treatment of the citation, which is plainly regarded as carrying the weight of Scripture With the question as to the occasion and intent of that Psalm, we are not here concerned It is a song of triumph, as ver 1 [cf. Num x 35] shews, at some bringing up of the ark to the hill of Zion. It is *therefore* a Messianic Psalm Every part of that ark, every stone of that hill, was full of spiritual meaning Every note struck on the lyres of the sweet singers of Israel, is but part of a chord, deep and world-wide, sounding from the golden harps of redemption The partial triumphs of David and Solomon only prefigured as in a prophetic mirror the universal and eternal triumph of the Incarnate Son of God. Those who do not understand this, have yet their first lesson in the O T. to learn With this caution let us approach the difficulties of the citation in detail) **He ascended up on high** (viz. Christ, at His Ascension · not '*having* ascended ' the aorist participle denotes an action not preceding, but parallel to, that expressed in the finite verb which it accompanies see Bernhardy, Synt. p. 383. The ascending in the Psalm is that of God, whose presence was symbolized by the ark, to Zion. The Apostle changes the words from the 2nd person to the 3rd, the *address* asserting a *fact*, which fact he cites), **he led captive a captivity** (i. e. 'those who *suffer* captivity .' a troop of captives such is the constant usage of the abstract αἰχμαλωσία for the concrete in LXX cf. reff. and it is never put for *captivatores*, 'those who *cause* captivity,' as some would interpret it. In the Psalm, these would be, the captives from the then war, what-

m Matt vii 11 Luke xi 13. Phil iv 17 only Gen xxv 6. n — Rom x 7 Ps lxxxviii 8. o here only Ps lxii 9 (but superl.)

ἔδωκεν ᵐ δόματα τοῖς ἀνθρώποις. 9 τὸ δὲ ἀνέβη, τί ἐστιν
εἰ μὴ ὅτι καὶ ⁿ κατέβη εἰς τὰ ᵒ κατώτερα μέρη τῆς γῆς;

ABCDF KLℵ a b c e f g h k l m n o 17

9. rec aft κατεβη ins πρωτον, with BC³KLℵ³ rel vulg(and F-lat) syr goth Eus Thdrt Damasc Ambrst-ms Œc-comm: om AC¹DIℵ¹ 17 67² am¹ coptt æth Thdrt Chr-comm Cyr Iren-int Lucif Hil Jer Aug. om μερη D¹F Syr Thdot Orig₁ Eus₁ Iren₂-int Tert Lucif Hil Ambrst Jer Avit.: ins ABCD³KLℵ rel vulg(and F-lat) Orig₁ Eus₁ Cyr Aug₂.

ever it was in the interpretation, they were God's enemies, Satan and his hosts, as Chr., *ποίαν αἰχμαλωσίαν φησί, τὴν τοῦ διαβόλου αἰχμάλωτον τὸν τύραννον ἔλαβε, τὸν διάβολον καὶ τὸν θάνατον καὶ τὴν ἀρὰν καὶ τὴν ἁμαρτίαν*), **he gave gifts to mankind** (Heb לָקַחְתָּ מַתָּנוֹת בָּאָדָם,—LXX, *ἔλαβες δόματα ἐν ἀνθρώπῳ* [-ποις F]. The original meaning is obscure. There seems to be no necessity to *argue for* a sense of **ἔλαβες**—'thou receivedst in order to give,' as the qualifying **ἐν ἀνθρώποις** will shew for what purpose, in what capacity, the receipt took place. But certainly such a sense of לָקַח seems to be substantiated: see Eadie's note here, and his examples, viz Gen xv 9; xviii 5 [where the sense is very marked, E. V. 'I will fetch'],—xxvii 13 [ib 'fetch me them'], xlii. 16,—Exod xxvii. 20 ['that they bring thee'],—1 Kings xvii. 10 ['fetch me,' *λαβὲ δή μοι*], al. Then, what is בָּאָדָם? First, אָדָם is clearly used in a collective sense: we have Jer. xxxii 20, יִשְׂרָאֵל וּבָאָדָם, 'Israel and the rest of mankind,' see also Isa. xliii 4 al. In Prov. xxiii. 28, we have בְּאָדָם used for 'inter homines,' which is evidently its simplest meaning. If then we render here, 'hast taken gifts among men,' hast, as a victor, surrounded by thy victorious hosts, brought gifts home, spoils of the enemy,—the result of such reception of gifts would be naturally stated as the distribution of them among such hosts, and the people,—as indeed ver 12 of the Psalm has already stated. And so the Chaldee paraphrast [and Syr and Arabic vss: but their testimony, as Christian, is little worth] understood the words, interpreting the passage *of Moses* [which does not invalidate his testimony, against Harl.]: 'thou hast given gifts to the sons of men.' The literature of the passage may be seen in De W. and Meyer: and more at length in Stier, Eadie, and Harless. To give even a synopsis of it here would far exceed our limits). 9.] Further explanation of this text. **But that He ascended** (**τὸ ἀν.** does not here mean, '*the word*' ἀνέβη, which does not occur in the text cited), **what is it** (does it imply) **except that he also** (as well) **descended to the lower parts of the earth** (the argument seems to be this: the Ascension here spoken of was not a first exaltation, but a *return* to heaven of one who dwelt in heaven—*οὐδεὶς ἀναβέβηκεν εἰς τὸν οὐρανόν*, **εἰ μὴ ὁ ἐκ τοῦ οὐρανοῦ καταβάς**, *ὁ υἱὸς τ. ἀνθρώπου ὁ ὢν ἐν τῷ οὐρανῷ*, John iii 13, which is in fact the key to these verses. The *ascent* implied a previous *descent*. This is the leading thought. But it is doubted *how far* the words **κατώτερα μέρη τῆς γῆς** carry that descent, whether to *earth* merely, so that **τῆς γῆς** is the genitive of apposition,—or to *Hades*, so that it is genitive of possession. Usage will not determine—for 1) it is uncertain whether the Apostle meant any allusion to the corresponding Hebrew expression: 2) that expression is used both for *Hades*, Ps. lxiii 9, and for *earth* [*θεμελια*, LXX], Isa xliv 23 [and for the *womb*, Ps cxxxix 15]. Nor can it be said [as Harl., Mey.] that the descent into hell would be irrelevant here—or that our Lord ascended not from Hades but from the earth: for, the *fact of descent* being the primary thought, we have only to ask as above, *how far* that descent is carried in the Apostle's mind. The greater the descent, the greater the ascent: and if the *αἰχμαλωσία* consisted of Satan and his powers, the warfare in which they were taken captive would most naturally be contemplated in all its extent, as reaching to their habitation itself: 'this ascent, what does it imply but a descent, and that even to the lower parts of the earth from which the spoils of victory were fetched?' And this meaning seems to be upheld by the **ἵνα πληρώσῃ τὰ πάντα** which follows, as well as by the contrast furnished by **ὑπεράνω πάντων τῶν οὐρανῶν**. This interpretation is upheld by most of the ancients, Iren., Tert., Jer., Pelag., Ambrst., also by Erasm., Est., Calov., Bengel, Ruck., Olsh., Stier, Baur [uses it as a proof of the gnostic origin of the Epistle], Ellicott, al.: that of the Incarnation merely, *descent on earth*,

10 ὁ καταβὰς αὐτός ἐστιν καὶ ὁ ἀναβὰς [p] ὑπεράνω πάντων
τῶν οὐρανῶν, ἵνα [q] πληρώσῃ τὰ πάντα. 11 καὶ αὐτὸς
[r] ἔδωκεν τοὺς μὲν [st] ἀποστόλους, τοὺς δὲ [st] προφήτας, τοὺς
δὲ [u] εὐαγγελιστάς, τοὺς δὲ [v] ποιμένας καὶ [tw] διδασκάλους,
12 πρὸς τὸν [x] καταρτισμὸν τῶν ἁγίων, εἰς [y] ἔργον [yz] διακονίας, εἰς [a] οἰκοδομὴν τοῦ [b] σώματος τοῦ [b] χριστοῦ,

p ch i 21 reff. q = ch iii 19 reff (Acts ii 2 v 28). r ch i 22 reff. s ch iii 5 reff. t 1 Cor xii 28. u Acts xxi 8. 2 Tim iv 5 only†. v John x 2 &c but = here only see Jer iii 15 Ezek xxxiv passim. w Acts xiii 1 1 Cor xii 28, 29 2 Tim iv 8 Heb v 12 James iii 1. x here only† (τισις -τίζειν, 2 Cor xiii 9, 13). y here only. z = Acts i 17, 25 Rom xi 13 al fr† (1 Macc xi 58 only). a = (Paul only) Rom xiv 19 xv 2 al[9] (ch ii 12 al). b = 1 Cor xii 27 Col ii 17.

by Beza, Calv., Grot, Schöttg, Mich, Stier, Winer, Harl., B-Crus, Meyer, De W, al that of Christ's *death* [and burial], by Chr, Thdrt, Œc, al. that corresponding to Ps cxxxix 15, by Beza [alt], Witsius, al)[1] 10] **He that descended, He** (and no other *οὐ γὰρ ἄλλος κατελήλυθεν κ. ἄλλος ἀνελήλυθεν*, Thdrt. *αὐτός* is the subject, and not the predicate [*ὁ αὐτός*]) **is also he that ascended** (see again John iii 13) **up above** (reff) **all the heavens** (cf Heb vii. 26, *ὑψηλότερος τῶν οὐρανῶν γενόμενος* and ib. iv. 14, *διεληλυθότα τοὺς οὐρανούς* It is natural that one who, like St. Paul, had been brought up in the Jewish habits of thought, should still use their methods of speaking, according to which the heaven is expressed in the plural, '*the heavens.*' And from such an usage, *πάντες οἱ οὐρανοί* would naturally flow See, on the idea of a threefold, or sevenfold division of the heavens, the note on 2 Cor xii 2 Ellicott quotes from Bishop Pearson,—'whatsoever heaven is higher than all the rest which are called heavens, into that place did he ascend' Notice the subjunctive after the aorist participle, giving the present and enduring sense to the verb: used, when "res ita comparata est, ut actione præterita tamen eventus nondum expletus sit, sed etiam nunc duret. .. Eur. Med. 215, *Κορίνθιαι γυναῖκες, ἐξῆλθον δόμων μή μοί τι μέμφησθ'*" Klotz, Devar. ii 618), **that He may fill** (not as Anselm, al, '*fulfil*') **all things** (the whole universe see ch i. 23, note with His presence, His sovereignty, His working by the Spirit not, with His glorified Body, as some have thought "Christ is perfect God, and perfect and glorified man as the former He is present every where, as the latter He can be present any where" Ellicott)

11] Resumption of the subject—the diversity of gifts, all bestowed by Him, as a motive to unity. **And HE** (emphatic, 'it is He, that') **gave** (not for *ἔθετο*, any more than in ch i 22·—*the gifts which He gave* to His Church are now enumerated. "The idea is, that the men who filled the office, no less than the office itself, were a divine gift" Eadie) **some as Apostles** (see 1 Cor xii 28, and note; and a good enumeration of the essentials of an Apostle, in Eadie's note here), **some as prophets** (see on 1 Cor. xii. 10 and cf ch. ii. 20, iii 5, notes), **some as evangelists** (not in the narrower sense of the word, writers of gospels, but in the wider sense, of itinerant preachers, usually sent on a special mission *οἱ μὴ περιιόντες πανταχοῦ, ἀλλ' εὐαγγελιζόμενοι μόνον, ὡς Πρίσκιλλα κ 'Ακύλας* Chr. See note on Acts xxi 8), **some as pastors and teachers** (from these latter not being distinguished from the pastors by the *τοὺς δέ*, it would seem that the two offices were held by the same persons. The figure in **ποιμένες**, if to be pressed, would imply that they were entrusted with some special flock, which they tended, *καθήμενοι καὶ περὶ ἕνα τόπον ἠσχολημένοι*, as Chr, and then the *διδασκαλία* would necessarily form a chief part of their work. If this view be correct, this last class includes all the stationary officers of particular Churches), **in order to** (ultimate aim of these offices, see below) **the perfecting of the saints,—for** (immediate object, see below) **(the) work of (the) ministry** (of *διάκονοι* in God's Church The articles give completeness in English, but do not affect the sense),**—for building up of the body of Christ** (the relation of these three clauses has been disputed Chr, al, regard them as parallel *ἕκαστος οἰκοδομεῖ, ἕκαστος καταρτίζει, ἕκαστος διακονεῖ* but this is to confound the distinct prepositions, **πρός** and **εἰς**, after the unsupported notion that St Paul uses prepositions almost indifferently Others, as De W., regard **εἰς** . **εἰς** as dependent on **πρός**, and thus are obliged to give to *διακονία* a wider sense [*genus omnium functionum in ecclesia*] than it will bear The best way certainly seems to be, with Mey. and Ellic, to regard **πρός** as the ultimate end, **εἰς** as the immediate use, as in Rom. xv. 2, *ἕκαστος ἡμῶν τῷ πλησίον ἀρεσκέτω εἰς τὸ ἀγαθὸν* **πρὸς** *οἰκοδομήν*), **until** (marks

13 c μέχρι d καταντήσωμεν e οἱ e πάντες d εἰς τὴν f ἑνότητα ABCDF
τῆς πίστεως καὶ τῆς g ἐπιγνώσεως τοῦ υἱοῦ τοῦ θεοῦ, εἰς KLℵ a b c e f g h k l m
h ἄνδρα h τέλειον, εἰς i μέτρον h ἡλικίας τοῦ l πληρώματος n o 17

c constr., here only. see Mark xiii. 30. d Acts xvi. 1 al6. 1 Cor. xiv. 36. Phil. iii. 11 only. L.P. (2 Kings iii. 29.) 2 Macc. iv. 21. e 1 Cor. x. 17. 2 Cor. v. 10. Phil. ii. 21. ὁ πᾶς, Gal. v. 14. τὰ πάντα passim. f ver. 3 only †. g ch. i. 17 reff. h James iii. 2. 2 Kings xxii. 36. see Col. i. 28. iv. 12. i ver. 7 reff. k = Luke ii. 52. xix. 3 only. Ezek. xiii. 18. (see Matt. vi. 27 note. John ix. 21. Heb. xi. 11.) l ch. i. 23 note.

13. om οἱ D[1]F Clem[1] Orig[1]. om τ. υἱου F Clem[1] Lucif.

the duration of the offices of the ministry) **we** (being thus *κατηρτισμένοι* by virtue of the *ἔργον διακονίας* and the *οἰκοδομή*) **arrive** (see reff.: no sense of 'meeting,' but simply of 'attaining.' Ellicott well remarks, that we must be careful of applying to later Greek the canons of the grammarians respecting the omission of ἄν, as giving an air of less uncertainty to subjunctives in such constructions as this; and he adds, "the use of the subjunctive [the mood of conditioned but objective possibility], not future [as Chrys.], shows that the καταντᾶν is represented, not only as the eventual, but as the expected and contemplated result of the ἔδωκεν"), **all of us** (Christians, Jews as well as Gentiles: first person, because he himself was among the number. The article brings out the *πάντες*, as belonging to one class), **at the unity of the faith** ("How so? have not all Christians the same faith? . . No doubt they have, as regards its substance, but not as regards clearness and purity; because the object of faith may be diversely *known*, and knowledge has ever such a powerful influence on faith. Therefore he adds to this unity of faith *καὶ τῆς ἐπιγνώσεως κ.τ.λ.*: true and full unity of faith is then found, when all thoroughly know Christ, the object of faith, alike, and that in His highest dignity as the Son of God." De Wette) **and of the knowledge** (further result of the faith, ch. iii. 17, 19, 2 Pet. i. 5) **of the Son of God** (this objective genitive belongs to both **τῆς πίστεως** and *τῆς ἐπιγνώσεως*), **at a perfect man** (an awkwardness is given by the coupling of an abstract [**εἰς ἑνότητα**] to a concrete [**εἰς ἄνδρα τέλειον**]. The singular not only denotes unity [Beza], but refers to the summation of us all in the one perfect Man Christ Jesus. The maturity of the *ἀνὴρ τέλειος* is contrasted with the *νηπιότης* which follows. Among curiosities of exegesis may be adduced that which Aug. mentions, de Civ. Dei xxii. 17, vol. vii. p. 778: "Nonnulli, propter hoc quod dictum est, Eph. iv. 13, nec in sexu fœmineo resurrecturas fœminas credunt, sed in virili omnes aiunt") **to the measure of the stature** (or, '*age*:' this is doubtful. The similitude in *ἄνδρα τέλειον* seems to be derived from *age*: that in ver. 16, from *stature*. The fact seems to be, that **ἡλικία** is a comprehensive word, including both ideas—answering to the German 'Erwachsenheit,' but having no corresponding word in our language. We have *μέτρον ἥβης* in Hom. Il. λ. 225, Od. λ. 317, σ. 217. The expression itself occurs in Lucian, Imag. 7 [Wetst.], *τῆς ἡλικίας δὲ τὸ μέτρον, ἡλίκον ἂν γένοιτο κατὰ τὴν ἐν Κνίδῳ ἐκείνην μάλιστα . . μεμετρήσθω*,—and Philostratus, vit. Sophist. p. 513, *τὸ δὲ μέτρον τῆς ἡλικίας ταῖς μὲν ἄλλαις ἐπιστήμαις γήρως ἀρχή*. Clearly, none of these passages settles the question. In Homer, the meaning is 'the measure of youth,'—the size and ripeness of youth: in Lucian, as decidedly '*the measure of the stature*,' as in Philostr., '*the ripeness of manly age*.' The balance must here be inclined by the prevalence of the image of growth and extension, which can hardly be denied as pervading the passage) **of the fulness of Christ** (see note on ch. i. 23, iii. 19: χρ. is a genitive subjective,—the fulness which Christ has: '*Christ's fulness*.' Cf. Gal. iv. 19),—**that** (apparently *another*, and subordinate, *aim* of the bestowal of gifts on the church is here adduced. For we cannot *go forward* from the finished growth of ver. 13, and say that *its* object is *ἵνα μηκ. ὦμεν νήπιοι*, but must go back again to the growth itself and its purpose, that purpose being mainly the terminal one of ver. 13, and subordinately the intermediate one of our ver. 14. See Meyer's note) **we be no more** (having been so once: *τὸ μηκέτι δείκνυσι πάλαι τοῦτο παθόντας*. Chr.) **children, tossed** (like waves: see James i. 6. Jos. Antt. ix. 11. 3, *ἔσται Νινευὴ κολυμβήθρα ὕδατος κινουμένη, οὕτως κ. ὁ δῆμος ἅπας ταρασσόμενος κ. κλυδωνιζόμενος οἰχήσεται φεύγων*) **and borne about by every wind of teaching** (*τῇ τροπῇ ἐμμένων καὶ ἀνέμους ἐκάλεσε τὰς διαφόρους διδασκαλίας*. Thl. Wetst. quotes from Plut. de Audiend. Poetis, p. 28 D, *μὴ παντὶ λόγῳ πλάγιον, ὥσπερ πνεύματι, παραδιδοὺς ἑαυτόν*. The article before διδασκαλίας gives a greater definiteness to the abstract word, but cannot be ex-

τοῦ χριστοῦ, 14 ἵνα μηκέτι ὦμεν [m] νήπιοι, [n] κλυδωνιζόμενοι
καὶ [o] περιφερόμενοι παντὶ [p] ἀνέμῳ τῆς [q] διδασκαλίας ἐν τῇ
[r] κυβείᾳ τῶν ἀνθρώπων, ἐν [s] πανουργίᾳ πρὸς τὴν [t] μεθο-
δείαν τῆς [u] πλάνης, 15 [v] ἀληθεύοντες δὲ ἐν ἀγάπῃ [w] αὐξήσωμεν [w] εἰς αὐτὸν τὰ πάντα, ὅς ἐστιν ἡ [x] κεφαλή,

m Matt xi 25. xxi 16 from Ps viii 2. 1 Cor iii 1. xiii 11 (5 times) al3, Paul (1 Thess ii 7 v r). Ps xviii 7.
n here only. Isa lvii 20 only. Jos Antt. ix 11 3.
o = here only. [Heb xiii 9 v r. Jude 12 v r.] Eccl. vii 8. (Mark vi 55. 2 Cor iv 10 only.)
p Matt xi. 7. Jude 12.
q 1 Tim i 10 reff. Paul only, exc. Matt xv 9 || Mk. Prov ii. 17.
r here only †.
s (=) Luke xx 23. 1 Cor iii 19. 2 Cor iv 2. xi 3 only. Josh ix 4.
t ch vi 11 only †. (-δος 2 Macc xiii 18. -δευειν, 2 Kings xix 27. Polycarp ad Phil § 7, p 1012.)
u Matt xxvii 64. Rom i 27 al7. Prov xiv 8.
v Gal iv 16 only. Gen xlii 16.
w ch ii 21.
x ch i 22 reff.

14. for νηπ., ηπιοι A. την μεθοδιαν D[1]FKLℵ c m n. την μεθοδον 17: τας μεθοδιας A: *remedium* old-lat Lucif Ambrst Pelag-comm. aft πλανης ins του διαβολου A.

15. for αληθευοντες δε, αληθειαν δε ποιουντες F. om η D[1]F Clem. rec

pressed in English. So ἅπαξ προσουρήσαντα τῇ τραγῳδίᾳ, Aristoph. Ran. 95) in (elemental: "the evil atmosphere, as it were, in which the varying currents of doctrine exist and exert their force." Ellic. This is better than *instrumental*, which, as we have just had παντὶ ἀνέμῳ, would be a repetition) the **sleight** ('*dice-playing*,' from κύβος. The word, as well as κυβεύω, was naturally and constantly used to signify 'entrapping by deceit:' κυβείαν τὴν πανουργίαν καλεῖ· πεποίηται δὲ ἀπὸ κύβων τὸ ὄνομα· ἴδιον δὲ τῶν κυβευόντων, τὸ τῇδε κἀκεῖσε μεταφέρειν τὰς ψήφους, καὶ πανούργως τοῦτο ποιεῖν. Thdrt. See examples in Wetst. The word was borrowed by the Rabbinical writers, and used in this sense: see Schottg. h. l.) **of men** (as contrasted with τοῦ χριστοῦ, ver. 13), **in craftiness** (reff.) **furthering** (tending or working towards: or perhaps, but not so well,—*after, according to*, gemäß) **the system** (see reff. and especially ch. vi. 11, note, and Chr.'s explanation) **of error** (not, *deceit*, though in fact the sense is so: πλάνη, even in the passages generally alleged for this active meaning, is best taken as 'error.' The genitive πλάνης is subjective—the plans are those which error adopts. τῆς πλ., as τῆς διδασκαλίας: see above),

15.] **but** (opposition to the *whole* last verse, introducing as it does, not only ἀληθεύοντες ἐν ἀγάπῃ, but the αὐξήσωμεν below) **being followers of truth** (ἀληθεύειν cannot here mean merely to *speak the truth*, as the whole matter dealt with is more general; the particular follows, ver. 25. The verb has the widest meaning of *being* ἀληθής—and [as Stier remarks] not without a certain sense of effort, '*sectari veritatem*.' The Vulg gives it well, but perhaps with too exclusively practical a bearing, '*veritatem facientes*.' Bengel, '*verantes*.' the old English versions, '*folowe the truth*,' which gives too much the objective sense to truth. It is almost impossible to express it satisfactorily in English. I have somewhat modified this last rendering, restoring the general sense of 'truth.' The objection to 'followers of truth' is that it may be mistaken for 'searchers after truth'—but I can find no expression which does not lie open to equal objection) **in love** (must be joined with ἀληθεύοντες, not with αὐξήσωμεν. For 1) the mere participle with δέ would stand most feebly and awkwardly at the beginning of the sentence: and 2) we have already observed the habit of the Apostle to be, to subjoin, not to prefix, his qualifying clauses. ἐν ἀγάπῃ is added, as the element in which the Christian ἀληθεύειν must take place: it is not and cannot be an ἀληθεύειν at all hazards—a 'fiat justitia, ruat cœlum' truthfulness: but must be conditioned by love: a true-seeking and true-being with loving caution and kind allowance—not breaking up, but cementing, brotherly love by walking in truth) **may grow up into** (increase towards the measure of the stature of,—to the perfect man in Him. Again an allusion to the incorporation of all the Church in Christ: see below) **Him in all things** (accusative of reference; the article implying, in every department of our growth, 'in all things wherein we grow,' as Meyer) **who is the Head** (see ch. i. 22), **namely, Christ** (the nominative is best regarded as an attraction to the *foregoing* relative, just as in 'urbem quam statuo vestra est' the substantive is attracted to the *following* relative. So we have, Eur. Hecub. 754, πρὸς ἄνδρ', ὃς ἄρχει τῆσδε Πολυμήστωρ χθονός: and Plat. Apol. p. 41 A, εὑρήσει τοὺς ὡς ἀληθῶς δικαστάς, οἵπερ κ. λέγονται ἐκεῖ δικάζειν, Μίνως τε καὶ Ῥαδάμανθυς κ. Αἰακός. In the face of

χριστός, 16 ἐξ οὗ πᾶν τὸ [y] σῶμα [z] συναρμολογούμενον καὶ
[a] συμβιβαζόμενον διὰ πάσης [b] ἁφῆς τῆς [c] ἐπιχορηγίας
[d] κατ' [d] ἐνέργειαν ἐν [e] μέτρῳ [f] ἑνὸς [f] ἑκάστου [g] μέρους τὴν
[h] αὔξησιν τοῦ σώματος [i] ποιεῖται εἰς [k] οἰκοδομὴν ἑαυτοῦ ἐν
ἀγάπῃ.
17 Τοῦτο οὖν λέγω καὶ [l] μαρτύρομαι [m] ἐν κυρίῳ, μηκέτι

αγαπη C

ABDF KLℵ a b c e f g h k l m n o 17

y ch i 23 reff. z ch ii 21 only †. a Acts ix 22 xvi 10 (xix 33 v r) 1 Cor ii 16, from Isa xl 14 Col ii 2, 19 only. b Col ii 19 only † (Lev xiii 2 al fr = נֶגַע, plague) c Phil i 19 only † (χεῖ, Gal iii 5) d ch i 19 (reff) iii 7 Phil iii 21 Col i 29 2 Thess ii 9 only e ver 7 reff f Luke iv 40 Acts ii 3, 6 ver 7 Col iv 6 1 Thess ii 11 al 1 Kings xiii 20 Ald g Luke xi 36 Plat Legg vii p 795 e, ἐλαφρότητός τε ἕνεκα κ κάλλους τῶν τοῦ σώματος αὐτοῖ μελῶν κ μερῶν h Col ii 19 only † 2 Macc v 16 only i constr Luke v 33 Phil i 4 1 Tim ii 1 al k ver 12 reff l = Gal v 3 1 Thess ii 12 Acts xx 26 xxvi 22 (Paul only) † m 1 Thess iv 1 al fr P

ins ο bef χριστος, with DFKLℵ[3] rel: om ABCℵ[1] 17. 67[2] Bas Cyr Did Damasc.

16 om κατ' ενεργειαν F D-lat arm(not ed-1805) Iren-lat Lucif for μερους, μελους (corrn to suit τ σωματος) AC vulg Syr copt arm Chr Cyr Jer Pelag. txt BDFKLℵ rel syr goth Bas-mss Thdrt Iren-int Lucif Victorin. for εαυ., αυτου D[1]Fℵ a m.

these examples, there is no occasion, with De W and Ellic., to suppose that the Apostle places χρ at the end to give force to ἐξ οὗ which follows Beware of Eadie's rendering, 'who is the Head, the [ὁ χρ] Christ,' as alien from any design apparent in the argument, or indeed in the Epistle).

16] **from whom** (see Col. ii 19, an almost exact parallel, from which it is clear that ἐξ οὗ belongs to τὴν αὔξησιν ποιεῖται—He being the source of all growth) **all the body** (see on Col), (**which is**) **being closely framed together** (note the present participle—the framing is not complete but still proceeding For the word, see on ch. ii. 21) **and compounded** ('notat simul firmitudinem et consolidationem,' Bengel), —**by means of every joint** (to be joined, not with the participles preceding, but [see below] with τ. αὔξ ποι, as Chr , Thdrt , Beng , Mey , except that they understand ἁφή to mean αἴσθησις—the perception of the vital energy imparted from the head [τὸ πνεῦμα τὸ ἀπὸ τ ἐγκεφάλου καταβαῖνον, τὸ διὰ τῶν νεύρων], which is the cause of all growth to the body But it seems hardly controvertible that ἁφή does signify '*joint*' [συναφή] in the parallel Col ii 19, it is there [see note] joined with συνδεσμῶν so closely, as necessarily to fall into the same class of anatomical arrangements, and cannot mean αἴσθησις. Also in Damoxenus in Athenæus, iii. 102 F, we have it in this sense—καὶ συμπλεκομένης οὐχὶ συμφώνους ἁφάς Indeed the meaning Berührung, '*point d'appui*,' would naturally lead to that of *joint*) **of the** (article just as παντὶ ἀνέμῳ τῆς διδασκ. above: see note there) **supply** (the joints are the points of union where the supply passes to the different members, and by means of which the body derives the supply by which it grows The genitive, as σῶμα τῆς ἁμαρτίας, σκεύη τῆς λειτουργίας· "a kind of genitive *definitivus*, by which the predominant use, purpose, or destination of the ἁφή is specified and characterized " Ellic),—**according to vital working in the measure of each individual part,—carries on** (remark the intensive middle ποιεῖται, denoting that the αὔξησις is not carried on ab extra, but by functional energy within the body itself) **the growth of the body** (I thus render, preferring to join as well διὰ π. ἁφ τ. ἐπιχ. as κατ' ἐν κ τ λ with τ. αὔξ. ποιεῖται rather than with the preceding participles, 1) to avoid the very long awkward clause encumbered with qualifications, πᾶν τὸ σῶμα σ κ σ διὰ πάσ ἁφ τῆς ἐπιχ. κατ' ἐνέργ ἐν μέτρ ἐν ἑκ μέρους 2) because the repetition of τοῦ σώματος is much more natural in a cumbrous apodosis, than in a simple apodosis after a cumbrous protasis 3) for perspicuity the whole instrumentality and modality here described belonging to the growth [ἐπιχορ , ἐνέργ , ἐν μέτρῳ], and not merely to the compaction of the body. τοῦ σώματος is repeated, rather than ἑαυτοῦ used, perhaps for solemnity, perhaps [which is more likely] to call back the attention to the subject σῶμα after so long a description of its means and measure of growth) **for the building up of itself in love** (Meyer would join ἐν ἀγ with τ αὔξ τ σώμ ποι as suiting better ver 15. This is hardly necessary, and encumbers still further the already sufficiently qualified αὔξ ποιεῖται Love is just as much the element in which the edification, as that in which the growth, takes place).

[B] (See on ver 1) IV **17—VI 9**] *Exhortations to a course of walking and conversation, derived from the ground just*

ὑμᾶς [n] περιπατεῖν καθὼς καὶ τὰ ἔθνη [n] περιπατεῖ ἐν [o] ματαιότητι τοῦ νοὸς αὐτῶν, 18 [p] ἐσκοτωμένοι τῇ [q] διανοίᾳ
ὄντες, [r] ἀπηλλοτριωμένοι τῆς [s] ζωῆς τοῦ [s] θεοῦ, διὰ τὴν
[t] ἄγνοιαν τὴν οὖσαν ἐν αὐτοῖς διὰ τὴν [u] πώρωσιν τῆς

n ver 1 reff o Rom viii 20 2 Pet ii 18 only Ps xxx 6 p Rev ix 2 xvi 10 only Jer xiv 2 (-τίζειν, Matt xxiv 29 ‖ Mk Luke xxiii 45 Rom i 21 xi 10, from Ps lxviii 23 Rev viii 12 only) q ch ii 3 reff r ch ii 12 reff s here only t Acts iii 17 xvii 30 1 Pet i 14 Lev xxii 14 u Mark iii 5 only ϖ Rom xi 25 only †

17. rec ins λοιπα bef εθνη (*see note*), with D[3]KL א[3] rel syrr goth Chr Damasc Thdrt Thl Œc. om ABD[1]F א[1] 17. 67[2] latt coptt æth Clem Cyr lat-ff
18. rec εσκοτισμενοι, with DFKL rel Clem Chr Thdrt. txt ABא 17 Ath. om οντες F Thl

laid down, and herein (iv. 17—v. 21) *general duties of Christians as united to Christ their Head* 17.] This (which follows) then (resumptive of ver 1; as Thdrt, πάλιν ἀνέλαβε τῆς παραινέσεως τὸ προοίμιον This is shewn by the fact that the μηκέτι περιπατ here is only the negative side of, and therefore subordinate to, the ἀξίως περιπ of ver. 1 Vv. 1—16 form a digression arising out of τ ἑνότητα τ. πν in ver 3. Still this must not be too strictly pressed the digression is all in the course of the argument, and μηκέτι here is not without reference to μηκέτι in ver. 14 The fervid style of St Paul will never divide sharply into separate logical portions—each runs into and overlaps the other) I say (see Rom. xii 3. There is no need to understand δεῖν before the infinitive which follows The μηκ. ὑμ περιπατεῖν is the object of λέγω expressed in the infinitive, just as regularly as in βούλομαί σε λέγειν That an imperative sense is involved, lies in the context) and testify (see reff cf Plat Phileb. p. 47 D, ταῦτα δὲ τότε μὲν οὐκ ἐμαρτυράμεθα, νῦν δὲ λέγομεν Thuc. vi. 80, viii 53, Dnk) in the Lord (element; not 'formula jurandi,' see 1 Thess iv 1, note), that ye no longer ('*as once*' implied also by καί below) walk as also (besides yourselves though the Ephesians did not walk so now, their returning to such a course is made the logical hypothesis) the Gentiles (ye being now distinguished from them by being members of God's church, though once Gentiles according to the flesh Perhaps from this not being seen, λοιπά was inserted) walk in (element) vanity (see Rom i 21 they ἐματαιώθησαν in their downward course from God But we must not restrict the word to idolatry: it betokens the *waste* of the whole rational powers on worthless objects See also on Rom viii 20) of their mind (their rational part), being (beware of referring ὄντες to ἀπηλλ with Eadie Besides its breaking the force of the sentence, I doubt if such an arrangement is ever found) darkened (see again Rom i. 21, and the contrast brought out 1 Thess v 4, 5, and ch v. 8) in (the dative gives the sphere or element in which The difference between it and the accusative of reference [τὴν διάνοιαν ἐσκοτισμένους, Jos Antt ix. 4 3] is perhaps this, that the dative is more subjective—The man is dark — wherein? in his διάνοια the accusative more objective—Darkness is on the man·—in him, whereon? on his διάνοια) their understanding (perceptive faculty · intellectual discernment see note, ch ii 3), alienated (reff. objective result of the subjective 'being darkened') from the life of God (not 'modus vivendi quem Deus instituit,' as the ancients [Thdrt., Thl, and Grot, al.], for ζωή in N T never has this meaning [see the two clearly distinguished in Gal. v 25], but always *life*, as opposed to death. Thus '*the life of God*' will mean, as Beza beautifully says, 'vita illa qua Deus vivit in suis' for, as Beng, 'vita spiritalis accenditur in credentibus ex ipsa Dei vita.' Stier makes an important remark. "The Apostle is here treating, not so much of the life of God in Christ which is regenerated in believers, as of the original state of man, when God was his Life and Light, before the irruption of darkness into human nature") on account of the ignorance (of God see ref. 1 Pet) which is in them (not, by nature cf. Rom i 21–28 they did not *choose to retain* God in their knowledge, and this loss of the knowledge of Him alienated them from the divine Life), on account of (second clause, subordinate to ἀπηλλ not subordinate to and rendering a reason for τὴν ἄγν τ. οὖσαν, as Meyer, which would be awkward, and less like St Paul) the hardening ('πώρωσις est obduratio, callus Rem quæ hac voce significatur, eleganter describit Plutarchus, *de auditione* p. 46, ubi nullo monitorum ad vitam emendandam sensu duci, negotium esse dicit ἀνελευθέρου τινὸς δεινῶς κ.

[u] καρδίας αὐτῶν, 19 [v] οἵτινες [w] ἀπηλγηκότες ἑαυτοὺς [x] παρ-
έδωκαν τῇ [yz] ἀσελγείᾳ εἰς [a] ἐργασίαν [zb] ἀκαθαρσίας πάσης
ἐν [c] πλεονεξίᾳ. 20 ὑμεῖς δὲ οὐχ οὕτως [d] ἐμάθετε τὸν

ABDF KLℵ a b c e f g h k l m n o 17

v = Rom i 25. vi 2 2 Cor viii 10 al fr
w here only †
x = Rom i 24, &c 1 Cor v 5 1 Tim i 20 2 Pet ii 4
y Mark vii 22 Rom xiii 13 al † Wisd xiv 26 only
z 2 Cor xii 21 Gal v 19
a = here only (Luke xii 58 Acts xvi 16, 19 xix 24, 25 only Jonah i 8.)
b Rom i 24 al(7) Paul only, exc Matt xxiii 27 Prov vi 16
c Col iii 5 reff
d constr, Matt xxiv 32 | Mk Rom xvi 17 1 Cor xiv 35 Phil iv 9 Rev xiv 3 Isa xxvi 9, 10

19. for απηλγ., απηλπικοτες D αφηλπ. F *desperantes* latt Syr arm Iren-in-Epiph Iren-int Jer(notices the variation) Ambrst Gild Pelag   ε[ις ακα]θαρσιαν A   for εν πλ, και πλεονεξιας DF Clem Ambrst Aug Gild Sedul Pelag-comm

ἀπαθοῦς πρὸς τὸ αἰδεῖσθαι νέου διὰ συνήθειαν ἁμαρτημάτων κ συνέχειαν, ὥσπερ ἐν σκληρᾷ σαρκὶ κ τυλώδει τῇ ψυχῇ, μώλωπα μὴ λαμβάνοντος' Kypke The sense '*blindness*' is said by Fritzsche, on Rom xi. 7, to be invented by the grammarians Thdrt says πώρωσιν τὴν ἐσχάτην ἀναλγησίαν λέγει καὶ γὰρ αἱ τῷ σώματι ἐγγινόμεναι πωρώσεις οὐδεμίαν αἴσθησιν ἔχουσι διὰ τὸ παντελῶς νενεκρῶσθαι) **of their heart,**   19] **who as** (οἵτινες, see ch i 23 note) **being past feeling** (ὥσπερ τῶν ἀπὸ πάθους τινὸς μέρη πολλάκις τοῦ σώματος νενεκρωμένων οἷς οὐ μόνον ἄλγος οὐδὲν ἐκεῖθεν ἐγγίνεται, ἀλλ' οὐδὲ ἡ τοῦ μέρους ἀφαίρεσις αἴσθησιν ἐμποιεῖ Theod. Mops. in Stier. From the '*desperatio*' of the Vulg Syr, seems to have come the reading ἀπηλπικότες, see var. readd The obduration described may spring in ordinary life from despair —so Cicero, Ep fam ii 16, in Bengel, 'diuturna desperatione rerum obduruisse animum ad dolorem novum,'—and Polyb ix. 40. 9, ἀπαλγοῦντες ταῖς ἐλπίσι [where see Ernesti's note], but may also result from other reasons Certainly despair has nothing to do with the matter here, but rather the carrying on of the πώρωσις to positive ἀπάλγησις by the increasing habit of sin) **gave up themselves** ("ἑαυτ, with terrific emphasis. It accorded here with the hortatory object of the Apostle to bring into prominence that which happened on the side of their own free will It is otherwise in Rom. i. 24, παρέδωκεν αὐτοὺς ὁ θεός and the two treatments of the fact are not inconsistent, but parallel, each having its vindication and its full truth in the pragmatism of the context" Meyer) **to wantonness** (see Gal. v. 19 note) **in order to** (conscious aim, not merely incidental result of the παραδοῦναι —see below) **the working** (yes and more—the being ἐργάται—the working as at a trade or business—but we have no one word for it cf Chrys, ὁρᾷς πῶς αὐτοὺς αποστερεῖ συγγνώμης ἐργασίαν ἀκαθαρσίας εἰπών, οὐ παραπεσόντες, φησίν, ἥμαρτον, ἀλλ' εἰργάζοντο αὐτὰ τὰ δεινά, κ μελέτῃ τῷ πράγματι ἐκέχρηντο) **of impurity of every kind** (see Rom i 24—27 Ellic remarks, "As St Paul nearly invariably places πᾶς before, and not as here after the abstract [anarthrous] substantive, it seems proper to specify it [that circumstance] in translation") **in greediness** (such is the meaning, and not '*with greediness*,' i e greedily, as E V, Chr. [appy], Thdrt, Œc, Erasm., Calv, Est, al, nor '*certatim*, quasi agatur de lucro, ita ut alius alium superare contendat,' as Beza, nor as Harl '*in gluttony*' [which meaning his citation from Chrys does not bear out].   **πλεονεξία,** the desire of having more, is obviously a wider vice than mere covetousness, though this latter is generally its prominent form It is self-seeking, or *greed* in whatever direction this central evil tendency finds its employment So that it may include in itself as an element, as here, lustful sins, though it can never actually mean 'lasciviousness.' In 1 Cor. v. 10 it [πλεονέκταις] is disjoined from πόρνοις by ἤ, and joined by καί to ἅρπαξιν —clearly therefore meaning covetous persons See also ch v 3, and Col iii. 5. and compare Ellicott's note here).   20] **But YOU** (emphatic) **did not thus** (οὐκ ἐπὶ τούτοις, Chr.—not on these conditions, nor with such prospects Beza suggests that a stop might be put at οὕτως—'ye are not thus ye learned,' &c but the sense is altogether marred by it) **learn Christ** (Christ personal—not to be explained away into ὀρθῶς βιοῦν, as Chr., or any thing else cf. 1 Cor i 23, ἡμεῖς κηρύσσομεν χριστόν· Phil i 15—18, Col ii. 6 CHRIST Himself is the subject of all Christian preaching and all Christian learning — τὸ γνῶναι αὐτόν [Phil. iii 10] is the great lesson of the Christian life, which these Ephesians began to learn at their conversion see next verse), **if, that is** (see ch iii 2 note, and 2 Cor. v. 3 He does not *absolutely* assume the fact, but implies that he then believed and still trusts it was so), **it was**

[d] χριστόν, 21 [e] εἴ γε αὐτὸν [f] ἠκούσατε καὶ [g] ἐν αὐτῷ
ἐδιδάχθητε καθώς ἐστιν [h] ἀλήθεια [i] ἐν τῷ [i] Ἰησοῦ, 22 [k] ἀποθέσθαι ὑμᾶς [l] κατὰ τὴν προτέραν [m] ἀναστροφὴν τὸν
[n] παλαιὸν [n] ἄνθρωπον τὸν [o] φθειρόμενον κατὰ τὰς [p] ἐπι-

e ch iii 2 reff. f ch i 15 reff. g = ch i 15. h = John viii 44. Rom ix 1. i see 1 Thess iv 14. 2 Cor iv 11. k ver 25. Acts vii 58. Rom xiii 12. Col iii 8. Heb xii 1. James i 21. 1 Pet ii 1 only. 2 Chron xviii 26. l = Rom ix 3, 5. m Gal i 13. 1 Tim iv 12. Heb xiii 7. James iii 13. 1 Pet i 15 al(7)+. Tobit iv 14. 2 Macc v 8 vat only. n Rom vi 6. Col iii 9. o = 1 Cor xv 33. 2 Cor xi 3. Jude 10. Gen vi 11. p Mark iv 19 al fr.

Him that ye heard (if ye really heard at your conversion the voice of the Shepherd Himself calling you as his sheep —*τὰ πρόβατα τὰ ἐμὰ τῆς φωνῆς μου ἀκούει*, John x. 27, see also John v. 25) **and in Him that ye were taught** (if it was in vital union with Him, as members of Him, that ye after your conversion received my teaching. Both these clauses are contained in *ἐμάθετε τὸν χρ.*,—the first hearing of the voice of the Son of God, and growing in the knowledge of Him when awakened from spiritual death), **as is truth in Jesus** (the rendering and connexion of this clause have been much disputed. I will remark, 1) that it seems by its form to be subordinate to **ἐν αὐτῷ ἐδιδάχθητε**, and the **καθώς** to express the quality of the **διδαχή** 2) that in this case we have **ἐστιν ἀλήθεια ἐν τῷ Ἰησ** answering to **ἐν αὐτῷ ἐδιδάχθητε** 3) to take the easier members first, **ἐν τῷ Ἰησοῦ** is a closer personal specification of **ἐν αὐτῷ**—in Jesus—that one name recalling their union in both in His Person, and, which is important here, in His example also 4) **καθώς ἐστιν ἀλήθεια** expands **ἐδιδάχθητε**—if the nature of the teaching which you received was according to that which is truth [in Him] So that the meaning will amount to this—if ye were taught in Him according to that which is truth in Jesus;—if you received into yourselves, when you listened to the teaching of the Gospel, that which is true [respecting you—and Him] in your union with and life in Jesus, the Son of God manifest in the flesh. See Ellicott's note), 22] **namely** (the infinitive depends on **ἐδιδάχθητε** [not on *λέγω*, ver. 17, as Bengel and Stier], and carries therefore [not in itself, but as thus dependent] an imperative force—see on ver. 17) **that ye put off** (cf *ἐνδύσασθαι* ver 24: aorist, because the act of putting off is one and decisive, so also of *ἐνδύσασθαι* below but *ἀνανεοῦσθαι*, because the renewal is a gradual process Beware of rendering, with Eadie and Peile, '*that ye have put off*,' which is inconsistent with the context [cf. ver. 25], and not justified by *ὑμᾶς* being expressed This latter is done merely to resume the subject after the parenthetical ver 21), **as regards your former conversation** (explains the reference of *ἀποθέσθαι* q d [for you were clothed with it in your former conversation] and must not, as by Œc, Jer, Grot, Est, al, be joined with *τὸν παλ ἄνθρ.*. on **ἀναστρ**, see note, Gal. i 13), **the old man** (your former unconverted selves, see note on Rom vi 6) **which is** ("almost, '*as it is, &c*,' the participle having a slight causal force, and serving to superadd a further motive" Ellic) **being corrupted** (inasmuch as the whole clause is subjectively spoken of the *παλ ἄνθρ*, it is better to take **φθ** [as usually] of inward '*waxing corrupt*,' as in reff [especially Jude], than of *destination to perdition*, as Mey, which would be introducing an outward objective element) **according to** (in conformity with; as might be expected under the guidance of) **the lusts of deceit** (**ἡ ἀπάτη** is personified —the lusts which are the servants, the instruments of deceit cf *ἐκ χειλέων ἀπάτης μου*, Judith ix 10 Beware of the unsatisfactory hendiadys, '*deceitful lusts*,' E V, which destroys the whole force and beauty of the contrast below to *ὁσιότητι τῆς ἀληθείας*), 23] **and undergo renewal** (both should be marked,—the gradual process implied in the *present*, and the *passive* character of the verb Of this latter there can be no doubt. the middle **ἀνανεοῦσθαι** having always an active force: so we have *ἀνανεοῦσθαι τ συμμαχίαν*, Polyb xxiii 1. 5 see many more examples in the Lex. Polybianum, and in Harl's note here: and we have even, in Antonin. iv 3 [Harl], *ἀνανέου σεαυτόν*. Stier's arguments in favour of the middle sense seem to me to be misplaced **ἐνδύσασθαι** is middle, but that refers to a direct definite reflexive act; whereas the process here insisted on is one carried on by the Spirit of God, not by themselves And it is not to the purpose to ask, as Stier does, 'How can the Apostle say and testify by way of exhortation, that they should *be* renewed as they *ought to* walk?' for we have perpetually this seeming paradox, of *God's work* encouraged or checked by man's cooperation or counteraction The distinction between **ἀνακαίνωσις** and **ἀνανέωσις**

θυμίας τῆς [q] ἀπάτης,
23 [r] ἀνανεοῦσθαι δὲ τῷ [s] πνεύματι

ABDF KLℵ a b c e f g h k l m n o 17

q Matt xiii 22 || Mk Col ii 8 2 Thess ii 10 Heb iii 13 2 Pet ii 13 (Jude 12 v r) only † Judith ix 10, 13 xvi 8 only constr., 2 Pet ii 10
r here only Job xxxiii 24
s here only ν = Rom i 28. vii 23 xii 2 al

23 for δε, εν B om F.

is not [as Olsh.] beside the purpose here, but important The reference in **καινός** [*novus*] to the objective is prominent, in **νέος** [*recens*] to the subjective The **καινός** is used as opposed to the former self, the **νέος**, as regards the new nature and growth in it cf Col iii. 10, *τὸν νέον, τὸν ἀνακαινούμενον* Thus in Rom xii 2 it would not be said *μεταμορφ. τῇ ἀνανεώσει τ νοός*, because it is not by nor in the *ἀνανέωσις*, but by or in the *ἀνακαίνωσις*, that the *μεταμορφ* takes place Whereas here, where a process of growing up in the state of **ἀνακαίνωσις** is in question, **ἀνανεοῦσθαι** is properly used. **ἀνακαινοῦσθαι** is more 'renewal from the age of the old man,' **ἀνανεοῦσθαι**, 'renewal in the youth of the new man.' See Tittmann, Syn p 60 ff.) **by** (though [see more below] the expression **τῷ πν. τοῦ νοὸς ὑμ.** stands contrasted with *ἐν ματαιότητι τοῦ νοὸς αὐτῶν*, ver. 17, yet the omission of *ἐν* here serves to mark that not merely the sphere in which, but the agency by which, is now adduced) **the Spirit of** ***your*** (emphatic) **mind** (the expression is unusual, and can only be understood by reference to the N T. meaning of **πνεῦμα**, as applied to men First, it is clearly here not exclusively nor properly 'the Holy Spirit of God,' because it is called *τὸ πν* **τοῦ νοὸς ὑμῶν** It is a **πνεῦμα**, in some sense belonging to, not merely indwelling in, **ὑμεῖς** The fact is, that in the N T the *πνεῦμα* of man is only then used 'sensu proprio,' as worthy of its place and governing functions, when it is one Spirit with the Lord We read of no *πνεῦμα παλαιόν* the *πνευματικός* is necessarily a man dwelt in by the Spirit of God · the *ψυχικός* is the 'animal' man led by the *ψυχή*, and *πνεῦμα μὴ ἔχων*, Jude 19 Thus then the disciples of Christ are *ἀνανεούμενοι*, undergoing a process of renewal in the life of God, by the agency of the **πνεῦμα** of their minds, the restored and divinely-informed leading principle of their **νοῦς**, just as the children of the world are walking in the *ματαιότης* of *their* minds **νοῦς**, see above, ver 17), 24] **and put on** (see on *ἀποθέσθαι* above) **the new man** (as opposed to *παλαιόν*; not meaning *Christ*, any further than as He is its great Head and prototype, see on **κτισθ**), **which was created** (mark the aorist, as historical fact, once for all, in Christ In each individual case, it is not created again, but put on cf. Rom xiii 14) **after God** (= *κατ' εἰκόνα τοῦ κτίσαντος αὐτόν*, Col iii 10 · also *κατ' εἰκόνα θεοῦ ἐποίησεν αὐτόν*, Gen i 27: so 1 Pet i. 15, *κατὰ τὸν καλέσαντα ὑμᾶς ἅγιον καὶ αὐτοὶ ἅγιοι κ τ λ* The doctrine of the restoration to us of the divine image in Christ, as here implied, is not to be overlooked Muller, 'Lehre von der Sunde,' ii p. 485 ff, denies any allusion to it here, but on insufficient grounds, as indeed he himself virtually allows Not the bare fact of Gen i 27, but the great truth which that fact represents, is alluded to. The image of God in Christ is a far more glorious thing than Adam ever had, or could have had but still the *κατ' εἰκόνα θεοῦ*, = *κατὰ θεόν*, is true of both and, as Muller himself says, 'jenes ist erst die wahrhafte Erfullung von diesem') **in** (element, or sphere, of the character of the new man) **righteousness and holiness of truth** (again, beware of '*true holiness*,' E V —as destroying the whole antithesis and force of the words. The genitive, too, belongs to both substantives

ἡ ἀλήθεια, God's essence, John iii 33, Rom i. 25; iii. 7, xv. 8, opposed to *ἡ ἀπάτη* above "*δικαιοσύνη* and *ὁσιότης* occur together, but in contrary order, in ref Luke, and Wisd ix. 3. The adjectives and adverbs are connected, 1 Thess. ii 10 Tit i. 8 *δικαιοσύνη* betokens a just relation among the powers of the soul within, and towards men and duties without But *ὁσιότης*, as the Heb. תָּמִים [Prov ii 21 Amos v. 10], betokens the integrity of the spiritual life, and the piety towards God of which that is the condition Hence both expressions together complete the idea of moral perfection [Matt v 48]. As here the *ethical side* of the divine image is brought out, Col iii. 10 brings out the *intellectual* The new birth alone leads to *ἐπίγνωσις*. all knowledge which proceeds not from renewal of heart, is but outward appearance and of this kind was that among the false Colossian teachers On the other hand, in Wisd ii. 23 [*ὁ θεὸς ἔκτισεν τὸν ἄνθρωπον ἐπ' ἀφθαρσίᾳ, καὶ εἰκόνα τῆς ἰδίας ἰδιότητος* (*ἀιδιότ.* F. [not A]) *ἐποίησεν αὐτόν*] the physical side of the divine image is brought out" Olsh. Stier suggests that there is perhaps a slight contrast in **δικαιοσύνη** to **πλεο-**

τοῦ [s] νοὸς ὑμῶν [24] καὶ [t] ἐνδύσασθαι τὸν [u] καινὸν [u] ἄνθρωπον τὸν [v] κατὰ [v] θεὸν [w] κτισθέντα ἐν δικαιοσύνῃ καὶ [x] ὁσιότητι τῆς ἀληθείας.
[25] Διὸ [y] ἀποθέμενοι τὸ [z] ψεῦδος [a] λαλεῖτε [a] ἀλήθειαν [b] ἕκαστος μετὰ τοῦ [b] πλησίον αὐτοῦ, ὅτι ἐσμὲν ἀλλήλων [c] μέλη.
[26] [d] ὀργίζεσθε καὶ μὴ ἁμαρτάνετε. ὁ ἥλιος μὴ [e] ἐπιδυέτω
ἐπὶ [τῷ] [f] παροργισμῷ ὑμῶν, [27] μήδε [g] δίδοτε [g] τόπον τῷ
[h] διαβόλῳ. [28] ὁ [i] κλέπτων μηκέτι [i] κλεπτέτω, [k] μᾶλλον

t = Rom xiii. 12, 14 1 Cor xv 53, 54 Col iii 10 Ps cxxxi 9
u ch ii 15 reff
v Rom viii 27. 2 Cor vii 9, 10, 11 1 Pet. iv 6 only see note
w ch ii 10 reff
x Luke i 75 only Deut ix 5 al
y ver 22 reff
z John viii 44 Rom i 25 al Ps v 6

a John viii 40 only (elsw λεγειν, John viii 45, 46, ἐρεῖν, 2 Cor xii 6 only) Zech viii 16 b Rom xv 2 Heb viii 11 Micah vii 2 c = Rom xii 5 1 Cor xii 27 d Matt v 22 xviii 24 xxii 7 Luke xiv 21 xv 28. Rev xi 18 only Psa iv 4 e here only Deut xxiv 15 Josh viii 29 Jer xv 9 only, always w ἥλιος f here only 3 Kings xv 30 4 Kings xix 3 al see note g Luke xiv 9 Rom xii 19 Sir iv 5 xxxviii 12 τοπ, = Heb xii 17 h = Matt iv 1, &c ½ L al fr Job i 6, &c (adj, 1 Tim iii 11 2 Tim iii 3 Tit ii 3 only) i particip., Gal i 23 Rev xv 2 al fr κλ, Matt vi 19 Rom ii 21 al Obad 5 k Gal. iv 9 reff

24. ενδυσασθε ℵK k m οσιοτ και δικαιοσ ℵ[1] for της αλ, και αληθεια D[1]F Cypr Hil Lucif (not Tert).
25. εκαστος bef αληθειαν ℵ[1]. for μετα του, προς τον (LXX) ℵ[1]: txt ℵ-corr[1 3]
26 aft οργ ins δε F. for επι, εν D. om τω ABℵ[1] ins DFKLℵ[3] rel Clem Ath Ps-Ath Chr Thdrt$_2$ Damasc.
27 rec μητε, with rel Chr$_1$ Thdrt txt ABDFKLℵ e f g h k l m n o 17 Clem.

νεξία ver 19, and in **ὁσιότης** [τὸ καθαρόν, Chr.] to **ἀκαθαρσία**) 25.] **Wherefore** (because of the general character of the *καινὸς ἄνθρωπος* as contrasted with the *παλαιός*, which has been given *εἰπὼν τὸν παλαιὸν ἄνθρωπον καθολικῶς, λοιπὸν αὐτὸν κ. ὑπογράφει κατὰ μέρος*, Chr) **having put off** (the aorist should be noticed here it was open to the Apostle to write **ἀποτιθέμενοι**, but he prefers the past—because the man must have once for all put off falsehood as a characteristic before he enters the habit of speaking truth) **falsehood** (abstract, see reff), **speak truth each one with his neighbour** ('sciamus de Zacharia propheta sumptum,' Jer see ref 'We allow ourselves the remark, hoping it may not be over-refining, that the Apostle instead of **πρὸς τὸν πλησίον** with the LXX, prefers following the Hebrew text and writing *μετά*, to express by anticipation our inner connexion with one another as *ἀλλήλων μέλη*' Stier) **for we are members of one another** (Rom xii 5. The **ἀλλήλων** brings out the relation between man and man more strongly than if he had said, *of one body* at the same time it serves to remind them that all mutual duties of Christians are grounded on their union to and in Christ, and not on mere ethical considerations). 26.] **Be ye angry and sin not** (citation see ref Psa and that from the LXX, not from the Hebrew, which [see Hupfeld on the Psalms in loc.] means '*tremble* ['stand in awe,' E V.] and sin not' The first imperative, although jussive, is so in a weaker degree than the other it is rather assumptive, than permissive. 'Be angry [if it must be so]' as if he had said, 1 Cor vii. 31, *χρᾶσθε τῷ κόσμῳ τούτῳ* [for that must be], *καὶ μὴ καταχρᾶσθε* As Chr, *εἴ τις ἐμπέσοι ποτὲ εἰς τὸ πάθος, ἀλλὰ μὴ εἰς τοσοῦτον*. Thus Tholuck's question, Bergpred, p 186, is answered —"If Paul speaks of culpable anger, how can he distinguish sinning from being angry? If of allowable anger, how can he expect not to retain it over the night?"—the answer being, that he speaks of anger which *is* an infirmity, but by being cherished, may become a sin) **let the sun not set upon** (so Thuc has, *νὺξ ἐπεγένετο τῷ ἔργῳ*) **your irritation** (i e set to your wrath with a brother [in every case the omission of the art gives the sense '*upon any παροργισμός*'] a speedy limit, and indeed that one which nature prescribes—the solemn season when you part from that brother to meet again perhaps in eternity The Commentators quote from Plut de am frat., p 488 B, a custom of the Pythagoreans, *εἴποτε προσαχθεῖεν εἰς λοιδορίας ὑπ' ὀργῆς, πρὶν ἢ τὸν ἥλιον δῦναι, τὰς δεξιὰς ἐμβάλλοντες ἀλλήλοις κ. ἀσπασάμενοι διελύοντο* **παροργισμός** is a late word, apparently not found beyond the N T and LXX the verb **-ίζω** occurs ch vi. 4, where see note The **παρ-** implies, irritation *on occasion given*, as in *παρορμάω, παροξύνω*). 27.] **nor again** (there is a slight climax see below The rec *μήτε* would require that *μή* before should be capable of being taken as

δὲ [l] κοπιάτω [mn] ἐργαζόμενος ταῖς χερσὶν τὸ [n] ἀγαθόν, ἵνα
ἔχῃ [o] μεταδιδόναι τῷ [p] χρείαν ἔχοντι. 29 πᾶς λόγος
[q] σαπρὸς ἐκ τοῦ [r] στόματος ὑμῶν μὴ [r] ἐκπορευέσθω, ἀλλ'
[s] εἴ τις ἀγαθὸς πρὸς [t] οἰκοδομὴν τῆς [u] χρείας, ἵνα [v] δῷ
χάριν τοῖς ἀκούουσιν. 30 καὶ μὴ [w] λυπεῖτε τὸ [x] πνεῦμα τὸ
[x] ἅγιον τοῦ [x] θεοῦ, ἐν ᾧ [y] ἐσφραγίσθητε [z] εἰς [a] ἡμέραν [a] ἀπο-

ABDF KLℵ a b c e f g h k l m n o 17

l Paul, Rom. xvi 6 al[12] Matt vi 28 al Jer xvii 16 m Matt vii 23 xxvi 10 Acts x 35 Ps xiv 2 n Rom ii 10 Gal vi 10 o Luke iii 11 Rom i 11 xii 8 1 Thess ii 8 only Job xxxi 17 p Matt iii 14 Gospels pass 1 Cor xii 21 bis, 24 1 Thess i 8 (al[3] Paul) Heb v 12 bis x 36 1 John ii 27 iii 17 Rev iii 17 al Prov xviii 2 q Matt vii 17, 18 xii 33 bis xiii 48 Luke vi 43 bis only † r Matt iv 4 (from Deut viii 3) xv 11, &c Luke iv 22 Rev passim Paul, here only Numb xxxii 24 s = Phil iv 8 t = ver 12 reff u abs, Acts xxviii 10 Sir xxxix 33 see Phil ii 25 iv 16 v = James iv 6 1 Pet v 5 see Exod iii 21 (Ps lxxxiv 12) w = Rom xiv 15 ii. act, 2 Cor ii 2, 5 bis vii 8 bis only Job xxxi 39 x here only. ch i 7 reff y ch i 13 reff z = Phil ii 16 b 2 Tim i 12 a here only ως,

28 rec το αγαθον bef ταις χερσιν, with L rel Chr Damasc Thl Œc: om ταις χερσιν 17 67[2] Clem$_{2}$: το αγ. τ. ιδ. χ. K a f 71. 72. 80 syr Thdrt: ταις ιδιαις χ. το αγαθ (see 1 *Cor* iv. 12) ADFℵ[1] m latt coptt goth æth arm Bas Naz Epiph Damasc Jer Aug Pelag: txt Bℵ[3] am Ambrst. εχηται ℵ[1]. μεταδουναι D[1]F.

29 for χρειας, πιστεως D[1]F latt lat-mss-in-Jer Bas$_{sæpe}$ Naz Anton-and-Max Tert Cypr Hil Aug Ambrst Pelag. for δω, δοι D[1]F. μεταδιδω K: εχει L.

30 το αγ. πν. D[1 3]F goth.

μήτε, which it clearly cannot, on account of its position after ὁ ἥλιος) **give scope** (opportunity of action, which you would do by continuing in a state of *παροργισμός*) **to the devil** (not, *to the slanderer*, as Erasm., al. **διάβολος** as a substantive *always* has this personal meaning in the N. T.; see reff.). **28.] Let him that stealeth** (not '*that stole*,' as E. V., '*qui furabatur*,' Vulg.: cf. reff., and Winer, § 15. 7. Stier remarks well, that the word lies between *κλέψας* and *κλέπτης*—the former would be too mild, the latter too strong) **steal no longer, but rather** (οὐ γὰρ ἀρκεῖ παύσασθαι τῆς ἁμαρτίας, ἀλλὰ καὶ τὴν ἐναντίαν αὐτῆς ὁδὸν μετελθεῖν, Thl.: similarly Chr.) **let him labour, working** (cf. besides reff., John vi 27 and note) **with his hands** (contrast to his former idleness for good, and bad use of those hands) **that which is good** (τὸ ἀγ.: 'antitheton ad furtum prius manu piceata commissum.' Beng.), **in order that** (as a purpose to be set before every Christian in his honest labour) **he may have to impart to him that has need. 29.] Let every worthless** (ὃ μὴ τὴν ἰδίαν χρείαν πληροῖ, Chr. [in Mey. not in Hom. h. l.]: not so much '*filthy*,'—see ch. v. 4) **saying not come forth from your mouth,—but whatever (saying) is good for edification of the (present) need** (the **χρεία** is *the deficiency*—the part which needs *οἰκοδομεῖσθαι*,—the defect to be supplied by edification, and so is the regular objective genitive after **οἰκοδομήν**, which has no article, because it has a more general reference than merely to *τῆς χρείας*, which afterwards limits it. The renderings '*quâ sit opus*' [Erasm., Peile, al.], '*use of edifying*' [Syr., Beza, E. V.], are manifestly wrong), **that it may give grace** (minister spiritual benefit: be a means of conveying through you the grace of God. Such, from the context [cf. **οἰκοδ. τῆς χρ.**], must be the meaning, and not '*may give pleasure*,' as Thdrt., Kypke, al.) **to them that hear: 30.] and** (Thl. finely gives the connexion: ἐὰν εἴπῃς ῥῆμα σαπρὸν κ. ἀνάξιον τοῦ χριστιανοῦ στόματος, οὐκ ἄνθρωπον ἐλύπησας, ἀλλὰ τὸ πν. τ. θεοῦ) **grieve not** (the expression is anthropopathic,—but as Meyer remarks, truly and touchingly sets forth the *love* of God, which [Rom. v. 5] is shed abroad in our hearts by His Spirit) **the Holy Spirit of God** (the repetition of the articles gives solemnity and emphasis), **in whom** (as the element, condition, of the sealing: not *by* whom,—the sealing, both of the Lord and of us His members, is the act of the Father, John vi. 27: the Spirit *being the seal*, ch. i. 13) **ye were sealed unto** (in reservation for) **the day of redemption** (the day when redemption shall be complete in glory—see again ch. i. 13. On the genitive, see Winer, § 30. 2,—so ἡμέρα ὀργῆς, Rom. ii. 5, &c. So far from the doctrine of final perseverance, for which Eadie more sharply than reasonably contends, being involved here, there could hardly be a plainer denial of it by implication. For in what would issue the *grieving* of the Holy Spirit, if not in quenching His testimony and causing Him to depart from them? The caution of Thl., μὴ λύσῃς τὴν σφραγῖδα, is a direct inference

λυτρώσεως. 31 πᾶσα [b] πικρία καὶ [c] θυμὸς καὶ [c] ὀργὴ καὶ
[d] κραυγὴ καὶ [ce] βλασφημία [f] ἀρθήτω ἀφ' ὑμῶν σὺν πάσῃ
[g] κακίᾳ, 32 γίνεσθε δὲ εἰς ἀλλήλους [h] χρηστοί, [i] εὔσπλαγχνοι, [kl] χαριζόμενοι [lm] ἑαυτοῖς καθὼς καὶ ὁ θεὸς ἐν χριστῷ [k] ἐχαρίσατο * ὑμῖν.

b Acts viii 23 Rom iii 14, from Ps ix 7 (28) Heb xii 15 only c Col iii 8. d = Acts xxiii 9 (Matt xxv 6 Heb v 7 Rev xiv 18 xxi 4) only Isa v 7 (-γάζειν, Matt xii 19) e = Col iii 8 1 Tim vi 4 f = (in epp) 1 Cor vi 15 Col ii 14 only Matt xiii 12 & Gospp passim Acts xxii 22 Isa v 23 g Rom i 29 Tit iii 3 1 Pet ii 1 al Gen xxxi 52 h of men, here only (Matt xi 30 Luke v 39 vi 35 Rom ii 4 1 Cor xv 33 1 Pet ii 3 [from Ps xxxiii 8] only) Ps cxi 5 (-ότης, ch ii 7 reff) i 1 Pet iii 8 only † see note k = Luke vii 42, 43 2 Cor ii 7, 10 xii 13 Col ii 13 I P † (Sir xii 3 al) l Col iii 13 m = 1 Cor vi 7 see note, Col iii 13

31 οργη και θυμος DF latt copt Clem Ps-Ath Cypr.
32 om δε B k 177 Clem Damasc$_2$ Œc: for δε, ουν D[1]F 111 txt AD[3]KLℵ rel vulg(and F-lat) syr coptt Chr Thdrt Damasc Thl Tert Jer * ημιν B(sic 1. m, see table) DKL rel am syrr Orig-cat Chr-comm Thdrt Thl υμιν AFℵ d h m latt coptt goth Clem Cyr Thl-marg Œc Tert Ambrst.

from the passage) 31] Let all bitterness (οἱ δὲ πικροὶ δυσδιάλυτοι, κ πολὺν χρόνον ὀργίζονται, κατέχουσι γὰρ τὸν θυμόν, Aristot. Eth. Nic iv 11 ὁ τοιοῦτος κ βαρύθυμός ἐστι κ οὐδέποτε ἀνίησι τὴν ψυχήν, ἀεὶ σύννους ὢν κ σκυθρωπός, Chrys So that it is not only of speech, but of disposition) and wrath and anger (θυμὸς μέν ἐστι πρόσκαιρος, ὀργὴ δὲ πολυχρόνιος μνησικακία, Ammon Both are effects of πικρία, considered as a rooted disposition. See Trench, Synon, § 37) and clamour ('in quem erumpunt homines irati,' Est. Chrys. quaintly says, ἵππος γάρ ἐστιν ἀναβάτην φέρων ἡ κραυγὴ τὴν ὀργήν συμπόδισον τὸν ἵππον, κ. κατέστρεψας τὸν ἀναβάτην His reproofs to the ladies of Constantinople on this head give a curious insight into the domestic manners of the time) and evil speaking (the more chronic form of κραυγή—the reviling another not by an outbreak of abuse, but by the insidious undermining of evil surmise and slander. Chrys. traces a progress in the vices mentioned ὅρα πῶς πρόεισι τὸ κακόν. ἡ πικρία τὸν θυμὸν ἔτεκεν, ὁ θ. τὴν ὀργήν, ἡ ὀρ τὴν κραυγήν, ἡ κρ. τὴν βλασφημίαν, τουτέστι τὰς λοιδορίας) be put away from you, with all malice (the inner root, out of which all these spring ἢ οὐκ οἶδας, ὅτι αἱ πυρκαιαὶ μάλιστά εἰσι χαλεπώταται, αἵπερ ἂν ἔνδον τρεφόμεναι μὴ φαίνωνται τοῖς περιεστηκόσιν ἐκτός, Chrys): 32] but be ye (it is very difficult to mark the distinction between γίνεσθε and ἐστέ in a translation Become ye [Ellic] is certainly too far off the time present, be ye, too immediately belonging to it. The difficulty is best seen in such a command as that in John xx 27, μὴ γίνου ἄπιστος ἀλλὰ πιστός) towards one another kind (see note, Gal v 22), tender-hearted ("εὔσπλ. profanis animosum, fortem, cordatum notat [see Eurip Rhes 192] At res ipsa docet h l. esse, misericordem, benignum [ref] In testament xii. patriarch p. 644, de Deo dicitur ἐλεήμων ἐστὶ καὶ εὔσπλαγχνος, ibid paulo post; piis ἴασις κ εὐσπλαγχνία, 'salus et misericordia futura' dicitur, ibid p. 641, ἔχετε εὐσπλαγχνίαν κατὰ παντὸς ἀνθρώπου." Kypke So also in the prayer of Manasseh, 6, εὔσπλαγχνος, μακρόθυμος κ πολυέλεος, see also the parallel, Col iii 12), forgiving (see Luke vii 42 Bengel notices that the three, **χρηστοί, εὔσπλαγχνοι, χαριζόμενοι ἑαυτοῖς** are opposed respectively to **πικρία, θυμός**, and **ὀργή**) each other (this idiom is found in classical Greek—καθ' αὑτοῖν δικρατεῖς λόγχας στήσαντ' ἔχετον κοινοῦ θανάτου μέρος ἄμφω, Soph Antig 145. See Matthiæ, Gr. § 489 See remarks on its especial propriety as distinguished from ἀλλήλοις, on ref Col), even as (argument from His example whom we ought to resemble—also from the mingled motives of justice and gratitude, as Matt. xviii. 33, οὐκ ἔδει καί σε ἐλεῆσαι τὸν σύνδουλόν σου, ὡς κἀγώ σε ἠλέησα,) God in Christ (not '*for Christ's sake*,' as E. V., see 2 Cor. v. 19, 20. God IN Christ, manifested in Him, in all He has done, and suffered: Christ is the sphere, the conditional element in which this act took place Chrys. appears to take ἐν as '*at the cost of*,' as (?) Josh vi. 26, Matt xvii 21 for he says, ἵνα σοι συγγνῷ, τὸν υἱὸν ἔθυσε) forgave you (not '*hath forgiven*' [κεχάρισται], as E V It is the historical fact of Christ once for all putting away sin by the sacrifice of Himself, which is alluded to. So that we are not 1) to attempt to change the meaning into a future ["even as thou, Lord for

1 Cor. iv. 16. xi. 1. 1 Thess. i. 6. ii. 14. Heb. vi. 12 only †. 1 Cor. iv. 14, 17. 2 Tim. i. 2. see Phil. ii. 15. ch. ii. 10 reff. Gal. ii. 20. ver. 25 only. (=) Acts xxi.

ABDF KLℵ a b c e f g h k l m n o 17

V. 1 Γίνεσθε οὖν ⁿ μιμηταὶ τοῦ θεοῦ ὡς ᵒ τέκνα ᵒ ἀγα-
πητά, 2 καὶ ᵖ περιπατεῖτε ᵖ ἐν ἀγάπῃ, καθὼς καὶ ὁ χριστὸς ἠγάπησεν ὑμᾶς καὶ ᑫ παρέδωκεν ᑫ ἑαυτὸν ὑπὲρ ὑμῶν
ʳˢ προσφορὰν καὶ ˢᵗ θυσίαν τῷ θεῷ ᵘ εἰς ᵛʷ ὀσμὴν ᵛˣ εὐωδίας.
3 ʸ πορνεία δὲ καὶ ʸ ἀκαθαρσία πᾶσα ᶻ ἢ ʸᶻ πλεονεξία μηδὲ

26. xxiv. 17. Rom. xv. 16. Heb. x. 5, &c. only. s Heb. x. 5, from Ps. xxxix. 6. t Matt. ix. 13 al. fr. esp. Heb. u ch. ii. 22 reff. v Phil. iv. 18 only. Gen. viii. 21. Levit. i. 9. w John xii. 3. 2 Cor. ii. 14, 16 bis. Phil as above only. Exod. v. 21. x 2 Cor. ii. 15. Phil. as above only. Ezra vi. 10. Col. iii. 5 (reff.). Gal. v. 19. 2 Cor. xii. 21. z see 1 Cor. v. 10. ver. 5.

Chap. V. 2. rec ημας, with DFKLℵ[3] rel vss Chr Thdrt lat-ff: txt ABℵ[1] m sah æth Clem$_2$ Thl Victorin Ambr-ms. rec ημων, with ADFKLℵ rel Clem (Orig): txt B 116 spec sah æth Victorin Ambr-ms.—προσφοραν bef υπ. ημ. D: om υπ. υμ. 115 Chr-omm$_1$ Thl Leo$_1$. θυσιαν και προσφοραν ℵ.

3. rec πασα bef ακαθαρσια (see ch iv. 31), with DFKL rel latt Clem$_1$ Chr Thdrt$_1$ Jer: om πασα m Thdrt$_2$ Thl-ms: txt ABℵ 17 copt Clem$_1$ Ephr Tert.

hrist's sake, hast promised to forgive s." Family Prayers by Bishop Blomfield, . 43]: nor 2) to render **χαριζόμενοι** and **(αρίσατο**, with Erasmus, '*largientes*' nd '*largitus est*,' a meaning clearly at ariance with the context). V. 1, 2.] hese verses are best taken as transitional, -the inference from the exhortation which as immediately preceded, and introduc-on to the dehortatory passage which llows. Certainly Stier seems right in ewing the *περιπατεῖτε* as resuming *περι-πατῆσαι* ch. iv. 1, and indicating a begin-ing, rather than a close, of a paragraph. **e ye** (**γίνεσθε**, see on last verse) **there-re** (seeing that God forgave you in Christ, e next verse) **imitators of God** (viz. in alking in love, see below), **as children loved** (see next verse: and 1 John iv. 19, *μεῖς ἀγαπῶμεν, ὅτι αὐτὸς πρῶτος ἠγά-πησεν ἡμᾶς*) **and** (shew it by this, that) **walk in love, as Christ also** (this mes even nearer: from the love of the ather who gave His Son, to that of the on, the Personal manifestation of that ve in our humanity) **loved** (not, '*hath ved*' as E. V.) **you** (the *ὑμᾶς . . . ὑμῶν* more a personal appeal: the *ἡμᾶς . . . ἡμῶν* of the rec. is a general one, deduced om the universal relation of us all to hrist), **and gave up Himself** (absol.: not be joined with *τῷ θεῷ*) **for you** (see ote on Gal. iii. 13:—'*on your behalf*:' fact, but not necessarily here implied, *n your stead*') **an offering and a sa-ifice** (beware of **προσφ. κ. θυσ.** = *σίαν προσφερομένην* [Conyb.]: it is our ity, in rendering, to preserve the terms upled, even though we may not be able ecisely to say wherein they differ. The dinary distinction, that **προσφορά** is unbloody offering, **θυσία** a slain victim, nnot be maintained, see Heb. x. 5, 18; . 4. I believe the nearest approach to e truth will be made by regarding **προσφ.** as the more general word, including all kinds of offering,—**θυσία** as the more spe-cial one, usually involving the death of a victim. The great prominent idea here is the *one* sacrifice, which the Son of God made of Himself in his redeeming Love, in our nature—bringing it, in Himself, near to God—offering Himself as our repre-sentative Head: whether in perfect righte-ousness of life, or in sacrifice, properly so called, at his Death) **to God** (to be joined, as a dat. commodi, with **πρ. κ. θυσ.**: not with *παρέδωκεν* [as De W. and Mey.], from which it is too far removed: still less [as Stier, who would apply the clause *τῷ θ. . . . . εὐωδίας*, to *us*] with what follows) **for an odour of sweet smell** (the question so much discussed, whether these words can apply to a sin-offering strictly so called, is an irrelevant one here. It is not [see above] the death of Christ which is treated of, but the whole process of His redeeming Love. His death lies in the background as one, and the chief, of the acknowledged facts of that process: but it does not give the character to what is here predicated of Him. The allusion primarily is to ref. Gen., where after Noah had brought to God a sacrifice of every clean beast and bird, *ὠσφράνθη κύριος ὁ θεὸς ὀσμὴν εὐωδίας*,—and the promise followed, that He would no more destroy the earth for man's sake). 3—21.] *Dehortation* (for the most part) *from works unbecoming the holiness of the life of children and imitators of God.* 3.] **But** (not tran-sitional merely: there is a contrast brought out by the very mention of **πορνεία** after what has just been said) **fornication and all impurity or** (see ch. iv. 19 note) **covet-ousness** (ib.), **let it not be even named** ('ne nomen quidem audiatur.' Calv. So Dio Chrys. p. 360 B [Mey.], *στάσιν δὲ οὐδὲ ὀνομάζειν ἄξιον παρ' ὑμῖν*: Herod. i. 138, *ἅσσα δέ σφι ποιέειν οὐκ ἔξεστι, ταῦτα*

[a] ὀνομαζέσθω ἐν ὑμῖν, καθὼς [b] πρέπει [c] ἁγίοις, 4 καὶ [d] αἰσ-
χρότης καὶ [e] μωρολογία, ἢ [f] εὐτραπελία ἃ οὐκ [g] ἀν-
ῆκεν, ἀλλὰ μᾶλλον [h] εὐχαριστία. 5 τοῦτο γὰρ [i] ἴστε

a ch. i. 21 reff. b constr., 1 Tim. ii. 10. Tit. ii. 1. Heb. ii. 10. vii. 26 only. Ps. xxxii. 1. Sir. xxx. (xxxiii.) 28. c ch. i. 1 reff. d here only †. see ver. 12. Col. iii. 8. e here only †. see Isa. xxxii. 6. f here only †. see note. g Col. iii. 18. Philem. 8 only †. 1 Macc. xi. 35 (See) al. but not =. h = Acts xxiv. 3. Phil. iv. 6. Col. ii. 7 al. Luke & Paul only, exc. Rev. iv. 9. vii. 12 †. Wisd. xvi. 28. Sir. xxxviii. 11. 2 Macc. ii. 28 only. i Acts xxvi. 4. Heb. xii. 17. James i. 19 only.

4. for 1st and 2nd και, η (*to suit η before*) AD¹Fℵ¹(2nd) latt sah Bas Ephr Antch Iren-lat Orig-lat: transp 2nd και and η c: txt BD³KLℵ-corr¹ rel copt Clem Chr Thdrt Damasc Jer. rec (for ἃ ουκ ανηκεν) τα ουκ ανηκοντα, with DFKL rel (Clem,) Chr Thdrt Damasc: txt ABℵ 17(omg ἃ) 67² Clem, Ephr Antch Cyr.

5. rec (for ιστε) εστε, with D³KL rel syr Thdrt Damasc Thl: txt ABD¹Fℵ h 17

οὐδὲ λέγειν ἔξεστι. Cf. Ps. xv. 4) **among you, as becometh saints** (meaning, that if it were talked of, such conversation would be *unbecoming* the holy ones of God): **and obscenity** (not in word only [αἰσχρολογία, ref. Col.]: cf. Plat. Gorg. p. 525 A, ὑπὸ ἐξουσίας κ. τρυφῆς κ. ὕβρεως κ. ἀκρατίας τῶν πράξεων ἀσυμμετρίας τε καὶ **αἰσχρότητος** γέμουσαν τὴν ψυχὴν εἶδεν) **and foolish talking** ('stultiloquium,' Vulg. Wetst. quotes from Antigonus de Mirabilibus, 126, τὰ μεγάλα κ. ἐπανεστηκότα μωρολογίας κ. ἀδολεσχίας. Trench well maintains, Syn. § 34, that in Christian ethics, it is more than mere 'random talk:' it is that talk of fools, which is folly and sin together: including not merely the πᾶν ῥῆμα ἀργόν of our Lord [Matt. xii. 36], but in good part also the πᾶς λόγος σαπρὸς of his Apostle [Eph. iv. 29]) **or** (disjunctive, marking off **εὐτραπελία** as **πλεονεξία** before) **jesting** (much interest attaches to this word, which will be found well discussed in Trench, as above. It had at first a *good* signification: Aristot. Eth. Nic. iv. 8, deals with the **εὐτράπελος**—οἱ ἐμμελῶς παίζοντες εὐτράπελοι προσαγορεύονται,—and describes him as the mean between the βωμολόχος and ἄγροικος. So too Plato, Rep. viii. p. 563 A,—οἱ δὲ γέροντες ξυγκαθιέντες τοῖς νέοις εὐτραπελίας τε κ. χαριεντισμοῦ ἐμπίπλανται, . . . ἵνα δὴ μὴ δοκῶσιν ἀηδεῖς εἶναι μηδὲ δεσποτικοί. But Trench remarks that there were indications of a *bad* sense of the word: e. g. Pind. Pyth. i. 178,—μὴ δολωθῇς, ὦ φίλε, κέρδεσιν εὐτραπέλοις, where he quotes from Dissen—'primum est de facilitate in motu, tum ad mores transfertur, et indicat hominem temporibus inservientem, diciturque tum de sermone urbano, lepido, faceto, imprimis cum levitatis et assentationis, simulationis notione.' I may add, as even more apposite here, Pyth. iv. 185, οὔτε ἔργον οὔτ' ἔπος εὐτράπελον κείνοισιν εἰπών. Aristotle himself, Rhet. ii. 12 end, defines it as πεπαιδευμένη ὕβρις. "The profligate old man in the 'miles gloriosus' of Plautus, iii. 1. 42—52, who at the same time prides himself, and with reason, on his wit, his elegance, and his refinement [cavillatus, lepidus, facetus], is exactly the εὐτράπελος: and remarkably enough, when we remember that εὐτραπελία being only expressly forbidden once in Scripture, is forbidden to *Ephesians*, we find him bringing out, that all this was to be expected from him, seeing that he was an Ephesian: 'Post Ephesi sum natus: non enim in Apulis, non Animulæ.'" Trench: whose further remarks should by all means be read), **which are not becoming** (the reading τὰ οὐκ ἀνήκοντα has perhaps come into the text from the τὰ μὴ καθήκοντα of Rom. i. 28, the οὐκ of the text being preserved through inadvertence. If, however, the participial clause be retained in the text, it may be grammatically justified by remembering that, where the various objects are specified which as matter of fact are οὐκ ἀνήκοντα, the objective negative particle οὐκ may be used: whereas in Rom. i. 28, where no such objects are specified, we have ποιεῖν τὰ μὴ καθήκοντα, 'si quæ essent indecora,' as Winer, § 59. 3: see Hartung, vol. ii. p. 131): **but rather thanksgiving** (not, as Jer., Calv., al., '*sermo qui* gratiam apud audientes habet,' which the word cannot mean. It is a question, what verb is to be supplied: Beng. supposes ἀνήκει, which is perhaps most likely, as suiting the simplicity of the construction of these hortatory verses better than going back to ὀνομαζέσθω [De W., Mey., al.],—and as finding a parallel in ch. iv. 29, where the ellipsis is to be supplied from the sentence itself. There is a play perhaps on the similar sound of εὐτραπελία and εὐχαριστία, which may account for the latter not finding so complete a justification in the sense as we might expect: the connexion being apparently, 'your true cheerfulness and play of fancy will be found, not in buffoonery, but in the joy of a heart overflowing with a sense of God's mercies').

[h] γινώσκοντες, ὅτι πᾶς [l] πόρνος ἢ [m] ἀκάθαρτος ἢ [n] πλεονέκτης, [o] ὅ ἐστιν [p] εἰδωλολάτρης, οὐκ ἔχει [q] κληρονομίαν ἐν
τῇ βασιλείᾳ τοῦ [r] χριστοῦ καὶ [r] θεοῦ. 6 μηδεὶς ὑμᾶς
[s] ἀπατάτω [t] κενοῖς λόγοις· διὰ ταῦτα γὰρ ἔρχεται ἡ
ὀργὴ τοῦ θεοῦ ἐπὶ τοὺς [u] υἱοὺς τῆς [u] ἀπειθείας. 7 μὴ

ABDF KLℵ a b c e f g h k l m n o 17

h constr, here only see Luke iv 44 & pass in Gospp Gen i 0 l 1 Cor v 9, 10, 11 vi 10 1 Tim i 10 Heb xii 16 xiii 4. Rev xxi 8 xxii 15 † Sir xxiii 16, 17 only m = Rev xvii 4 only in Gospp, only with πνεῦμα so also Acts v 16 viii 7 Rev xvi 13 xviii 2 a legal, Acts x 14, 28 xi 8 1 Cor vii 14 2 Cor vi 17 Rev xviii 2 b n 1 Cor v 10, 11 vi 10 only † Sir xiv 9 only o constr (see note), Mark xii 42 xv 42 John i 42, 43 Acts iv 36 p 1 Cor v 10, 11 vi 9 x 7 Rev xxi 8 xxii 15 only † q ch i 14 reff r Rev xx 6 see 1 Tim v 21 Rev xi 15 s 1 Tim ii 14 James i 26 only Isa xxxvi 14 t 1 Cor xv 10, 14, 58 Col ii 8 James ii 20. Exod v 9 Job vi 6 u ch ii 2 reff

latt goth coptt arm Clem Chr Cyr Œc Suid Cypr Jer Vig Pelag rec (for ὅ) ὅς (*cf constr in the* ‖ *Col* iii. 5, *where* ητις *follows the gender of* πλεονεξιαν· *the readg of* F &c *is another form of the same corrn, retaining the origl* ὅ), with ADKL rel syr copt Clem Chr Thdrt$_2$. txt Bℵ 17 67[2] Cyr Jer$_2$, also with ιδωλολατρια F latt Cypr Victorin Jer Ambrst.

6. καινοις (*itacism*) ℵ. om γαρ ℵ[1] ins ℵ-corr[1].

5] *Appeal to their own knowledge that such practices exclude from the kingdom of God* see below **For this ye know** (indicative, not imperative this to my mind is decided 1) by the context, in which an appeal to their own consciousness of the fact is far more natural than a communication of the fact to them 2) by the position of the words, which in the case of an imperative would more naturally be ἴστε γὰρ τοῦτο γινώσκοντες 3) by the use of the construction **ἴστε γινώσκοντες**, which almost necessitates a matter of fact underlying γινώσκοντες —ἴστε γιν. is not an example of the γινώσκων γνώσῃ [Gen. xv 13 al] of Hebrew usage, the two verbs being different) **being aware that every fornicator or** (ἢ now, not καί, for individualization of each) **unclean man, or covetous man, which is** (i e 'that is to say,'—'quod;' meaning, *the word* πλεονέκτης. This reading necessarily confines the reference to *that one word*) **an idolater** (cf Col iii 5, which shews that even ὅς ἐστιν would apply to the πλεονέκτης only, not, as Stier, al., to the *three* see Job xxxi. 24, Ps lii 7, Matt vi 24 Mey. remarks well, that it was very natural for St Paul, whose forsaking of all things (2 Cor vi 10, xi 27) so strongly contrasted with selfish greediness, to mark with the deepest reprobation the sin of πλεονεξία), **hath not inheritance** (the *present* implying more the fixedness of the exclusion, grounded on the eternal verities of that Kingdom,—than mere future certainty see 1 Cor xv 25) **in the Kingdom of Christ and God** (not '*and of God*' [κ. τοῦ θ] as E. V. No *distinction* is to be made, **χριστοῦ καὶ θεοῦ** being in the closest union Nor is any specification needed that the Kingdom of Christ is also the Kingdom of God, as would be made with the second article. This follows as matter of course and thus the words bear no legitimate rendering, except on the substratum of our Lord's Divinity But on the other hand, we cannot safely say here, that the same Person is intended by χριστοῦ κ θεοῦ, merely on account of the omission of the article. For 1) any introduction of such a predication regarding Christ would here be manifestly out of place, not belonging to the context 2) θεός is so frequently and unaccountably anarthrous, that it is not safe to ground any such inference from its use here) **6] Let no one deceive you with vain** (empty—not containing the kernel of truth, of which words are but the shell—words with no underlying facts Æschines, de Corona, p 288, says that Demosthenes had drawn up a decree, κενώτερον τῶν λόγων οὓς εἴωθε λέγειν, κ τοῦ βίου ὃν βεβίωκε See other examples in Kypke h. l) **sayings** (the persons pointed at are heathen, or pretended Christian, palliators of the fore-mentioned vices The caution was especially needed, at a time when moral purity was so generally regarded as a thing indifferent Harl quotes from Bullinger,—"Erant apud Ephesios homines corrupti, ut hodie apud nos plurimi sunt, qui hæc salutaria Dei præcepta cachinno excipientes obstrepunt humanum esse quod faciant amatores, utile quod fœneratores, facetum quod joculatores, et idcirco Deum non usque adeo graviter animadvertere in istiusmodi lapsus"), **for** (let them say what they will, it is a fact, that) **on account of these things** (the above-mentioned crimes, see Col. iii 6, δι' ἃ ἔρχεται ἡ ὀργ. κ.τ λ.: not the ἀπάτη just spoken of, to which the objection is not so much the plural ταῦτα, as the τοὺς υἱοὺς τ. ἀπειθείας which follows, shewing that the carrying out of their ἀπείθεια are the ταῦτα spoken

οὖν γίνεσθε [v] συμμέτοχοι αὐτῶν. 8 [w] ἦτε γάρ ποτε [x] σκό- v ch. iii 6 only†
τος, νῦν δὲ [x] φῶς ἐν κυρίῳ· ὡς [y] τέκνα φωτὸς [z] περι- w Rom vi 17 x Acts xxvi 18 Rom ii 19 xiii 12
πατεῖτε 9 (ὁ γὰρ [a] καρπὸς τοῦ φωτὸς ἐν πάσῃ [b] ἀγαθωσύνῃ 2 Cor iv 6
καὶ δικαιοσύνῃ καὶ ἀληθείᾳ), 10 [b] δοκιμάζοντες τί ἐστιν al Isa ix 2 y ch ii 3 reff
[c] εὐάρεστον τῷ κυρίῳ· 11 καὶ μὴ [d] συγκοινωνεῖτε τοῖς z ch iv 1 reff a Gal v 22 reff

b Rom xv 14 Gal v 22 2 Thess i 11 only Neh ix 35 constr, Rom xii 2 δοκ, 1 Thess ii 4 reff
c Rom xii 1, 2. Phil iv 18 Col iii 20 al[3] only P II + Wisd iv 10 ix 10 only (-τως, Heb xii 28 -τεῖν, Heb xi 5)
d Phil iv 14 Rev xviii 4 only † (-ος, Phil i 7)

9 rec (for φωτος) πνευματος (*from Gal* v 25), with D[3]KL rel syr Chr Thdrt Damasc txt ABD[1]Fℵ 17. 67[2] latt Syr coptt æth arm Mcion lat-ff.
10 for κυριω, θεω D[1]F latt lat-ff(exc Aug).

of, and the μὴ οὖν γίν. κ. τ λ. of ver. 7) **cometh** (present, as ἔχει, ver 5) **the wrath of God** (not merely, or chiefly, His ordinary judgments, 'quorum exempla sunt ante oculos,' as Calv. nor the 'antitheton reconciliationis,' as Beng, for that is on all who are not in Christ [John iii. 36]. but His *special* wrath, His vengeance *for these sins*, over and above their state of ἀπείθεια) **on the sons of** (see on ch ii. 2) **disobedience** (the active and practical side of the state of the ἀπειθῶν [John iii 36] is here brought out. The word is a valuable middle term between unbelief and disobedience, implying their identity in a manner full of the highest instruction)

7] **Be not** (the distinction '*Become not*' ['nolite effici,' Vulg · so Stier, Ellic., al] is unnecessary and indeed unsuitable it is not a gradual 'becoming,' but 'being,' like them, which he here deborts from See on γίνεσθε not bearing the meaning "*become*," note, ch. iv ult) **therefore** (since this is so—that God's wrath comes on them) **partakers** (see ch. iii. 6) **with them** (the υἱοὶ τ. ἀπ., not the *sins* —sharers in that which they have in common, viz. these practices their *present* habitude, not, *their punishment*, which is future. nor can the two senses be combined, as Stier characteristically tries to do).

8.] **For** (your state [present, see above] is a totally different one from theirs—*excluding* any such participation) **ye** WERE (emphatic, see ref) **once** (no μέν. "The rule is simple: if the first clause is intended to stand in connexion with and prepare the reader for the opposition to the second, μέν is inserted if not, not see the excellent remarks of Klotz, Devar. ii p 356 sq: Fritz, Rom. x 19, vol ii p 423" Ellic.) **darkness** (stronger than ἐν σκότει, Rom. ii 19; 1 Thess v 4: they were *darkness itself*—see on φῶς below), **but now** (the ἐστέ is not expressed—perhaps, as Stier suggests, not only for emphasis, but to carry a slight tinge of the coming exhortation, by shewing them what they *ought* to be, as well as were by profession) **light** (not πεφωτισμένοι—light has an active, illuminating power, which is brought out in ver. 13) **in** ('*in union with*'—conditioning element—not '*by*'—διὰ τῆς θεοῦ χάριτος, Chr) **the Lord** (Jesus): **walk** (the omission of οὖν makes the inference rhetorically more forcible) **as children of light** (not τοῦ φωτός, as in Luke xvi. 8, where τὸ φῶς is contrasted with ὁ αἰὼν οὗτος, and in next verse, where τοῦ φωτός is the figurative φῶς—q d 'the light of which I speak' here it is light, *as light*, which is spoken of The omission of the article *may* be merely from the rules of correlation, as Ellic but I much prefer here to treat it as significant),

for (gives the reason of the introduction of the comparison in the context, connecting this with the moral details which have preceded) **the fruit of the light** (τοῦ, see above) **is in** (is borne within the sphere of, as its condition and element) **all goodness and righteousness and truth** (in all that is good [Gal. v. 22], right, and true. As Harl. observes, the opposites are κακία, ἀδικία, ψεῦδος) **proving** (to be joined with περιπατεῖτε as its modal predicate, ver 9 having been parenthetical The Christian's whole course is a continual proving, testing, of the will of God in practice · investigating not what pleases himself, but what pleases Him) **what is well-pleasing to the Lord**;

11.] **and have no fellowship with** (better than '*be not partakers in*,' as De W, which would require a genitive, see Demosth p 1299. 20, συγκεκοινωνήκαμεν τῆς δόξης ταύτης οἱ κατεστασιασμένοι whereas the person *with whom*, is regularly put in the dative, e g. Dio Cass xxxvii 41, συγκοινωνήσαντός σφισι τῆς συνωμοσίας,—ib lxxvii 16, συνεκοινώνησαν αὐτῇ κ. ἕτεραι τρεῖς τῆς καταδίκης. And Phil iv. 14 furnishes no objection to this rendering) **the unfruit-**

e Rom xiii 12 only see 1 Cor iv 5 Isa xxix 15
f Matt xiii 22 || Mk 1 Cor xiv 14 Tit iii 14 2 Pet i 8 Jude 12 only Jer ii 6 Wisd. xv 4 only
g Gal iv 9 reff

[e] ἔργοις τοῖς [f] ἀκάρποις τοῦ [e] σκότους, [g] μᾶλλον δὲ καὶ
[h] ἐλέγχετε. 12 τὰ γὰρ [i] κρυφῇ γινόμενα ὑπ' αὐτῶν [k] αἰσχρόν ἐστιν καὶ λέγειν· 13 τὰ δὲ πάντα [h] ἐλεγχόμενα ὑπὸ
τοῦ φωτὸς [l] φανεροῦται· πᾶν γὰρ τὸ [l] φανερούμενον φῶς
ἐστιν. 14 διὸ [m] λέγει [no] Ἔγειρε ὁ [op] καθεύδων καὶ [q] ἀνάστα

ABDF KLℵ a b c e f g h k l m n o 17

h = John iii 20 1 Cor xiv 24 2 Tim iv 2 Tit i 9, 13 ii 15 Ps xlix 21 Xen Symp viii 43 i here only 1 Kings xix 2 k 1 Cor xi 6 xiv 35. Tit i 11 only P Gen xli 3, &c only
l Mark iv 22 John iii 21 Paul, Rom i 19 al fr Jer xl (xxxiii) 6 only m ch iv 8 reff
n Isa lx 1 Heb Rom xiii 11 Isa xxvi 19 o Dan xii 2 Theod p 1 Thess v 6 reff
q Mark vi 14 ix 9, 10 xii 25. Luke xvi 31 John xx 9 Acts x 41 xvii 3

13. *φανερουνται* AK²L c m

ful works of darkness (see Gal. v. 19, 22; on which Jer, vol vii p 505, says 'vitia in semetipsa finiuntur et pereunt, virtutes frugibus pullulant et redundant' See also the distinction in John iii. 20, 21; v 29, between τὰ φαῦλα πράσσειν and τὰ ἀγαθὰ or τὴν ἀλήθειαν ποιεῖν), **but rather even reprove them** (see reff,—*in words*. not only abstain from fellowship with them, but attack them and put them to shame). **12.**] **For** (the connexion seems to be, 'reprove them—this they want, and this is more befitting you—for to have the least part in them, even in speaking of them, is shameful') **the things done in secret by them, it is shameful even to speak of** (so καί in Plat. Rep v p 465 B, τά γε μὴν σμικρότατα τῶν κακῶν δι' ἀπρέπειαν ὀκνῶ καὶ λέγειν, see Hartung ii p. 136 Klotz, Devar ii p 633 f the connexion being—'I mention not, and you need not *speak of*, these deeds of darkness, much less have any fellowship with them—your connexion with them must be only that which the act of ἔλεγξις necessitates') **13**] **but** (opposition to τ. κρυφῇ γιν) **all things** (not only, all the κρυφῇ γινόμενα, as Ellic. after Jer al. the Apostle is treating of the *general detecting power of light*, as is evident by the resumption of the πᾶν in the next clause) **being reproved, are made manifest by the light: for every thing which is made manifest is light** (the meaning being, 'the light of your Christian life, which will be by your reproof shed upon these deeds of darkness, will bring them out of the category of darkness into light' [ἐπειδὰν φανερωθῇ, γίνεται φῶς, Chr] They themselves were thus 'once darkness,' but having been 'reproved' by God's Spirit, had become 'light in the Lord' There is in reality no difficulty, nor any occasion for a long note here The only matters to be insisted on are, 1) ὑπὸ τοῦ φωτός belongs to φανεροῦται, not to ἐλεγχόμενα for it is not the fact of φανεροῦται that he is insisting on, but the fact that if they reproved the works of darkness, these would become *no longer works of darkness*, but would be ὑπὸ τοῦ φωτὸς φανερούμενα. And 2) φανερούμενον is *passive*, not middle, in which sense it is never used in N. T.; 'every thing which is made manifest, is no longer darkness, but light, and thus you will be, not compromised to these works of darkness, but making an inroad upon the territory of darkness with the ὅπλα τοῦ φωτός.' And thus the context leads on easily and naturally to the next verse The objection to this [Eadie] that 'light does not always exercise this *transforming* influence, for the devil and all the wicked are themselves condemned by the light, without becoming themselves light,' is null, being founded on misapprehension of the φῶς ἐστιν. Objectively taken, it is universally true · *every thing shone upon* IS LIGHT Whether this tend to condemnation or otherwise, depends just on whether the transforming influence takes place. The key-text to this, is John iii 20, πᾶς γὰρ ὁ φαῦλα πράσσων μισεῖ τὸ φῶς, κ οὐκ ἔρχεται πρὸς τὸ φῶς, ἵνα μὴ ἐλεγχθῇ τὰ ἔργα αὐτοῦ,—His works being thus brought into the light,—made light, and he being thus put to shame Notice also φανερωθῇ in the next verse, which is the desire of him who ποιεῖ τὴν ἀλήθειαν The E. V. is doubly wrong—1) in '*all things that are reproved*' [π τὰ ἐλεγχόμενα]. 2) in '*whatsoever doth make manifest is light*' [πᾶν τὸ φανεροῦν] besides that such a proposition has absolutely no meaning in the context. The meaning is discussed at length in Harl, Eadie, who however fall into the error of rendering φανερούμενον *active* [not middle],—Stier, Ellicott,—and best of all, Meyer) **14.**] **wherefore** (this being so—seeing that every thing that is made manifest becomes light,—is shone upon by the detecting light of Christ,—objectively,—it only remains that the man should be shone upon *inwardly* by the same Christ revealed in his awakened heart We have then in Scripture an

ἐκ τῶν q νεκρῶν, r καὶ s ἐπιφαύσει σοι ὁ χριστός. 15 t βλέπετε οὖν u πῶς v ἀκριβῶς περιπατεῖτε, μὴ ὡς w ἄσοφοι,
ἀλλ' ὡς σοφοί, 16 x ἐξαγοραζόμενοι τὸν y καιρόν, ὅτι αἱ
a ἡμέραι ab πονηραί εἰσιν. 17 διὰ τοῦτο μὴ γίνεσθε c ἄφρονες,

r = John ii 19. James iv 8 Rev ii 10
s here only Job xxv 5 xxxi 6 xli 9 vat only
t = Matt xxiv 4 1 Cor iii 10 viii 9 x 12 xvi 10 Gal v 15 Col ii 8 Heb iii 12 xii 25
u = (see note) Luke viii 18 1 Cor iii 10
v = here (1 Thess v 2 reff) only (-ής, Acts xxvi 5)
w here only +
x Gal iii 13 iv 5 Col iv 5 only Dan ii 8 only
y Col Dan as above
z = 2 Tim iii 1 Heb x. 32 1 Pet iii 10.
a Ps xl 1
b = Gal i 4 ch vi 13
c Luke xi 40 xii 20 Rom ii 20 al6 L P., exc 1 Pet. ii 15 Job v 3

14 rec εγειραι, with rel txt ABDFKLℵ e n επιψαυσεις του χριστου continges *Christum* D[1] mss-in-Chr-Jer Thdrt(who however cites txt from ἔνια τῶν ἀντιγρ with approval) Orig-int Ambrst txt ABD[3]FKLℵ rel Clem $Orig_2$ Ath Chr Damasc (Archel) Jer Ambr Aug_{aliq} Vig Pelag

15 aft ουν ins αδελφοι Aℵ[3] vulg copt Pelag. ακριβως bef πως Bℵ[1] 17 copt Chr_1.

exhortation to that effect) **He** (viz God, in the Scripture see ch iv 8 note· all other supplies, such as *'the Spirit in the Christian'* [Stier],—*'the Christian speaking to the Heathen'* [Flatt],—*'one may say'* [Bornemann], &c are mere lame helps out of the difficulty:—as are all ideas of St. Paul having quoted *a Christian hymn* [some in Thdrt], *an apocryphal writing* [some in Jer, Epiph, al], *a baptismal formula* [Michaelis],—*one of our Lord's unrecorded sayings* [Rhenferd],—or that he means, *'thus saith the Lord'* [some in Jer. al], or alludes to the *general tenor of Scripture* [Wesley],—or *does not quote at all* [Barnes], &c. &c) **saith, Awake, thou that sleepest, and arise from the dead, and Christ shall shine upon thee** (*where is this citation to be found?* In the first place, by the introduction of **ὁ χριστός**, it is manifestly a *paraphrase, not an exact citation* The Apostle cites, and had a perfect right to cite, the language of prophecy in the light of the fulfilment of prophecy: and that he is here doing so, the bare word *'Christ'* shews us beyond dispute. I insist on this, that it may be plainly shewn to be no shift in a difficulty, no hypothesis among hypotheses,—but the *necessary* inference from the form of the citation This being so,—of what passage of the O T. is this a paraphrase? I answer, of Isa lx 1, 2 There, the church is set forth as being in a state of darkness and of death [cf lix 10], and is exhorted to awake, and become light, for that her light is come, and the glory of Jehovah has arisen upon her Where need we go further for that of which we are in search? It is not true [as Stier], that there is *'no allusion to sleep or death'* in the prophet. nor is it true again, that ἐπὶ σὲ φανήσεται κύριος κ ἡ δόξα αὐτοῦ ἐπὶ σὲ ὀφθήσεται is not represented by **ἐπιφαύσει σοι ὁ χριστός.** The fact is, that Stier has altogether mistaken the context, in saying,—"The Apostle quotes here, not to justify the exhortation—'convict, that they may become light,'—but to exhort—'Become light, that ye may be able to convict [shine]'" the refutation of which see above, on ver. 13). **15.**] He now resumes the hortative strain, interrupted by the digression of vv. 12—14. **Take heed then** (there is not any immediate connexion with the last verse but the **οὖν** resumes from the περιπατεῖτε in ver 8, and that which followed it there) **how ye walk strictly** (the construction is exactly as in ref 1 Cor, ἕκαστος δὲ **βλεπέτω πῶς** ἐποικοδομεῖ 'Take heed, of what sort your ἀκριβῶς περιπατεῖν is'—the implication being, 'take heed not only that your walk be exact, strict, but also *of what sort* that strictness *is*—not only that you *have* a rule, and *keep to it*, but that that rule be the *best* one' So that a double exhortation is involved. See Ellic here · and the Fritzschiorum Opuscula, pp 208 f, note), (namely) **not as unwise, but as wise** (qualification of the **ἀκριβῶς περιπατεῖτε**, and expansion of the **πῶς** [μή, subj] no περιπατοῦντες need be supplied after μή, as Harl), **buying up for yourselves (the) opportunity** (viz of good, whenever occurring, let it not pass by, but as merchants carefully looking out for vantages, make it your own · see Col iv 5 The compound ἐξ- does not suggest the question *'from whom'* it is to be bought, as Beng, Calv., al, nor imply mere *completeness*, as Mey, but rather refers to the *'collection out of'* [see reff Gal], the buying *up*, as we say, culling your times of good out of a land where there are few such flowers. The middle gives the reflexive

ἀλλὰ [d] συνίετε τί τὸ [e] θέλημα τοῦ [e] κυρίου. 18 καὶ μὴ
[f] μεθύσκεσθε οἴνῳ, ἐν ᾧ ἐστιν [g] ἀσωτία, ἀλλὰ [h] πληροῦσθε
[i] ἐν πνεύματι, 19 λαλοῦντες [k] ἑαυτοῖς [ἐν] [km] ψαλμοῖς καὶ

ABDF KLℵ a b c e f g h k l m n o 17

d Rom iii 11, from Ps xiii 2, al fr. e Acts xxi 14 only elsw (ch vi 6 al fr) τοῦ θεοῦ f Prov xxiii 30 Luke xii. 45 1 Thess v 7 only (θύειν, 2 Cor xi 21) Prov iv 17 g Tit i 6 1 Pet iv 4 only Prov xxviii 7 2 Macc iv 6 only (-τος, Prov vii 11 -τως, Luke xv 13) h = Acts xiii 52 Rom i 29 xv 13 al i constr, Rom x 20 k Col iii 16 l = ch iv 32 reff m = 1 Cor xiv 26 Col as above (Luke xx 42 xxiv 44 Acts i 20 xiii 33) only. Isa lxvi 20

17. rec συνιεντες, with D³KL rel Chr Thdrt Damasc$_{hl}$: συνιοντες D¹F latt syr goth Lucif: txt ABℵ 17. 67² Chr-ms Damasc$_1$ Jer for θελημα, φρονημα ℵ¹. for κυριου, θεου A 115 D-lat F-lat Syr Thl Jer Aug Pelag Gild.—B adds ημων.

19 rec om 1st εν, with ADFKLℵ rel Cyr-jer Thdrt Damasc: ins B 17 67² vulg

sense: cf. ref Dan), **because the days** (of your time,—in which you live) **are evil** (see above: ὁ ἐξαγοραζόμενος τὸν ἀλλότριον δοῦλον, ἐξαγοράζεται κ. κτᾶται αὐτόν. ἐπεὶ οὖν ὁ καιρὸς δουλεύει τοῖς πονηροῖς, ἐξαγοράσασθε αὐτόν, ὥστε καταχρήσασθαι αὐτῷ πρὸς εὐσέβειαν. Severianus, in Cramer's Catena). 17] **On this account** (because ye have need so prudently to define your rule of life, and so carefully to watch for opportunities of good: not, because the ἡμέραι are πονηραί [Œc., Thl., De W., Olsh.], which would fritter down the context) **be not** (better than 'do not become,' which though more strictly the literal sense of **μὴ γίνεσθε**, puts the *process of degeneracy* too strongly in English) **senseless** (Tittmann, Syn. p. 143, has discussed the meaning of **ἄφρων**, 'qui mente non recte utitur'), **but understand** (**συνιέναι**, to know intelligently,—**γινώσκειν** merely to know as matter of fact, as the servant who knew his lord's will and did it not, Luke xii. 47) **what is the will of the Lord**. 18] The connexion seems to be after the general antithesis in ver. 17, **μὴ ἄφρονες, ἀλλὰ συνίετε** κ.τ.λ., he proceeds to give one prominent instance, in the same antithetical shape. **And** (**καί** is subordinate, introducing a particular after a general: so Herod. i. 73, τῶνδε εἵνεκα καὶ γῆς ἱμέρῳ . . . see Hartung i. 145) **be not intoxicated with wine, in which practice** (not, ἐν οἴνῳ, but ἐν τῷ μεθύσκεσθαι οἴνῳ—the crime is not in *God's gift*, but in the *abuse* of it: and the very arrangement of the sentence, besides the spirit of it, implies the lawful use of wine—see 1 Tim. v. 23) **is profligacy** (**ἀσωτία**, not from **ἀ—σώζεσθαι**,—as Clem. Alex. Pædag. ii. 1, p. 167 P. [ἀσώτους αὐτοὺς οἱ καλέσαντες πρῶτον εὖ μοι δοκοῦσιν αἰνίττεσθαι τὸ τέλος αὐτῶν, ἀσώστους αὐτοὺς κατὰ ἔκθλιψιν τοῦ σ στοιχείου νενοηκότες], al., but from **ἀ-σώζειν**. **ἀσωτία** ἐστὶν ὑπερβολὴ περὶ χρήματα, Aristot. Eth. Nic. iv. 1. 3. But as spendthrifts are almost of necessity self-indulgent and reckless, the word comes to have the meaning of '*dissoluteness*,' '*debauchery*,' '*profligacy*,'—see Eth. Nic. iv. 1. 36, Tittmann, p. 152, and Trench, N. T. Syn. § 16. Theodotion renders Isa. xxviii. 7 by ἐν τῇ μέθῃ ἠσωτεύθησαν ὑπερόγκως) **but** (contrast, see above) **be filled** (antith. to **μεθύσκεσθε οἴνῳ**,—not to **μεθύσκεσθε** alone, so that ἐν πνεύματι should be opposed to οἴνῳ: see below) **with** (ἐν, as ch. i. 23, but also '*in*:' let this be the region in, and the ingredient with which you are filled) **the Spirit** (the ambiguity in the preposition is owing to the peculiar meaning of **πνεῦμα** as applied to the Christian:—viz. *his own spirit, dwelt in and informed by the Holy Spirit of God*, see note on ch. iv. 23. If this is so, if you are full of the Spirit, full in Spirit, there will be a joy indeed, but not that of ἀσωτία: one which will find its expression not in drunken songs, but in Christian hymns, and continual thankfulness), **speaking to one another** (ch. iv. 32, see also the ||, Col. iii. 16. It is perhaps too much to find in this the practice of antiphonal chanting: but it is interesting to remember that in Pliny's letter the Christians are described as 'soliti stato die ante lucem convenire, *carmenque* Christo quasi Deo *dicere secum invicem*:' and that Nicephorus, Hist. xiii. 8 [cited by Eadie], says τὴν τῶν ἀντιφώνων συνήθειαν ἄνωθεν ἀποστόλων ἡ ἐκκλησία παρέλαβε. Conyb. places a full stop at ἑαυτοῖς: but surely both style and sense are thus marred) **in** (this must be the rendering, whether the preposition is inserted or not) **psalms** (not to be confined, as Olsh. and Stier, to O. T. hymns; see 1 Cor. xiv. 26, James v. 13. The word properly signified those sacred songs which were performed with musical accompaniment [so Basil, Hom. in Ps. xxix. 1, vol. i. p. 121, ὁ ψαλμὸς λόγος ἐστὶ μουσικός, ὅταν εὐρύθμως κατὰ τοὺς ἁρμονικοὺς λόγους πρὸς τὸ ὄργανον κρού-

[ko] ὕμνοις καὶ [ko] ᾠδαῖς [[kp] πνευματικαῖς], [kq] ᾄδοντες καὶ
[r] ψάλλοντες [ἐν] τῇ [ks] καρδίᾳ ὑμῶν τῷ κυρίῳ, 20 [tu] εὐχαριστοῦντες [tv] πάντοτε ὑπὲρ [tv] πάντων ἐν ὀνόματι τοῦ κυρίου
ἡμῶν Ἰησοῦ χριστοῦ [w] τῷ θεῷ καὶ πατρί, 21 [x] ὑποτασσόμενοι ἀλλήλοις ἐν φόβῳ χριστοῦ 22 αἱ γυναῖκες τοῖς

n Col as above only Neh xii 46 (-ειν Acts xvi 25) o Col as above Rev v 9 xiv 3 bis xv 3 only Exod xv 1 al p Rom i 11

al21 Paul only, exc 1 Pet. ii 5 bis † q Col Rev as above (o) only Jer xxxvii (xxx) 19 r Rom xv 9, from Ps xvii 49 1 Cor xiv 15 bis James v 13 only 1 Kings xvi 16. s = Acts vii 54 Rom ii 15, 29 x 6 1 Cor vii 37 al t 1 Cor i 4 1 Thess i 2 2 Thess i 3 P u = Luke xvii 16 xviii 11 John xi 41 Paul, Rom i 8 & freq Rev xi 17 † Judith viii 25 Wisd xviii 2 2 Macc i 11 only v 2 Cor ix 3 Phil i 4 1 Thess i 2 P w James i 27 x ch i 22 reff

D-lat Chr Ambrst Jer Pelag. om πνευματικαις B D-lat Ambrst-ed (*it prob came from Col* iii 16, *where* none omit it. *In* such a case, *the evidence of* B *might be sufficient, were it not for the possibility of omn by homœotel*). aft πνευμ ins εν χαριτι A om 2nd εν BN for τη καρδια, ταις καρδιαις (*see Col* iii. 16) ADFN³ latt Syr syr-marg copt goth Bas Chr_2 lat-ff txt BKLN¹ rel syr æth Chr-txt Thdrt Damasc Thl Œc.

20 for παντων, υμων F. om ημων N. χρ bef ιησ. B πατρι και θεω D¹F m D-lat G-lat goth Victorin Vig

21 rec (for χριστου) θεου (*φοβ θεου being the more usual expression*), with rel Clem Thdrt κυριου K · txt ABDFLN c f k m 17.—D adds, F(not F-lat) pref ιησου.

ηται—and Greg Nyss in Psal lib ii 3, vol i p. 493, Migne, **ψαλμός** ἐστιν ἡ διὰ τοῦ ὀργάνου τοῦ μουσικοῦ μελῳδία],—as **ὕμνοι** without it but the two must evidently here not be confined strictly to their proper meaning) **and hymns** (see above) **and** [**spiritual**] **songs** (ᾠδή being the general name for all lyrical poetry, and applying especially to such effusions as persons used in the state of drunkenness, the Christian's ᾠδή is to be spiritual [Chr opposes *αἱ σατανικαὶ ᾠδαί*], inspired by that fulness of the Spirit which is in him), **singing and playing** (as well as λαλοῦντες, not explanatory of it **ᾄδοντες** and **ψάλλοντες** corresponding to **ὕμνοις** and **ψαλμοῖς** above) **in your hearts** (Harl remarks that **ἐν καρδίᾳ** cannot, being joined with ὑμῶν, represent the abstract '*heartily*,' as Chr., Thdrt, Pelag, &c, but must be rendered as Bullinger, 'canentes intus in animis et cordibus vestris') **to the Lord** (i. e. Christ —cf Pliny's letter above),—**giving thanks** (another additional, not explanatory, clause) **always for all things** (see Phil. iv 6: not only for blessings, but for every dispensation of God: Ellic. quotes from Thl.,—*οὐχ ὑπὲρ τῶν ἀγαθῶν μόνον, ἀλλὰ καὶ τῶν λυπηρῶν, κ ὧν ἴσμεν, κ ὧν οὐκ ἴσμεν· καὶ γὰρ διὰ πάντων εὐεργετούμεθα κἂν ἀγνοῶμεν*) **in the name** (the element in which the **εὐχαριστοῦντες** must take place. "The name of the Lord is there, where He is named How He is named, depends on the particular circumstances it is one thing to be reproached [1 Pet. iv 14], another to be saved [Acts iv. 12], another to be baptized [Acts x. 48], another to command [2 Thess. iii 6], another to pray [John xiv 13], another to give thanks [cf. Col. iii 17] in the name of the Lord. . The Apostle says, that all the Christian would do, he must do *in the name of Christ* [Col iii 17]" Harl the rest of the note is well worth consulting) **of our Lord Jesus Christ to God and the Father** (see on ch i 3),—**being subject to one another** (a fourth additional, not subordinate clause λαλοῦντες,—ᾄδοντες κ ψάλλοντες, — εὐχαριστοῦντες, — ὑποτασσόμενοι ἀλλήλοις and then out of this last general injunction are unfolded all the *particular applications to the relations of life*, ver 22—ch vi 9. It is not so easy to assign precisely its connexion with those which have preceded. It is hardly enough to say that as the first three name three special duties in regard to God, so this last a comprehensive moral duty in regard to man [Ellic] for the question of the *connexion* is still unanswered. I would rather regard it [as I see Eadie also does], as a thought suggested by the μὴ μεθ κ τ λ with which the sentence began—that as we are otherwise to be filled, otherwise to sing and rejoice, so also we are otherwise to behave—not blustering nor letting our voices rise in selfish vaunting, as such men do,—but subject to one another, &c) **in the fear of Christ** ('rara phrasis,' Beng: of Him, whose members we all are, so that any displacement in the Body is a forgetfulness of the reverence due to Him)

22—VI 9.] The Church, in her relation to Christ, comprehending and hallowing those earthly relations on which all social unity (and hers also) is founded, the Apostle proceeds to treat of the *three*

[y] ἰδίοις [y] ἀνδράσιν ὡς τῷ κυρίῳ, 23 ὅτι ἀνήρ ἐστιν [z] κεφαλὴ
τῆς γυναικὸς ὡς καὶ ὁ χριστὸς [z] κεφαλὴ τῆς [a] ἐκκλησίας,
αὐτὸς [b] σωτὴρ τοῦ σώματος. 24 ἀλλὰ ὡς ἡ [a] ἐκκλησία
[x] ὑποτάσσεται τῷ χριστῷ, οὕτως καὶ αἱ γυναῖκες τοῖς
ἀνδράσιν [c] ἐν παντί. 25 οἱ ἄνδρες, ἀγαπᾶτε τὰς γυναῖκας,

y 1 Cor vii 2 xiv 35. z = 1 Cor xi 3. ch i 22. iv 15. Col i 18. ii 10, 19 only P. Isa vii 8, 9. x. a ch i 22 reff. b = John iv 42. 1 Tim iv 10. 1 John iv 14. c Phil iv 6, 12. 1 Thess v 18.

ABDF KLℵ a b c e f g h k l m n o 17

22 rec aft *ανδρασιν* ins *υποτασσεσθε* (*prob supplementary gloss, as also υποτασσεσθωσαν*), with KL rel Chr, and, bef *ιδ*, DF Syr; *υποτασσεσθωσαν* Aℵ 17 67[2] vulg copt Clem, Bas Thdrt Damasc lat-ff om B and Greek MSS in Jerome[" *Hoc quod in lat exx additum est*, subditæ sint, *in gr edd non habetur . . . Sed hoc magis in græco intelligitur quam in latino*"]

23 rec ins *ο* bef *ανηρ*, with b l o Clem · om ABDFKLℵ rel Damasc. 1st *κεφαλη* bef *εστιν* B m vulg (and F-lat) lat-ff rec ins *και* bef *αυτος* and adds *εστιν*, with D[2] [3]KLℵ[3] rel (17 has *ὁ* instead of *αυτος*) · om ABD[1]Fℵ[1] latt Clem Ambrst. ins *ο* bef *σωτηρ* Aℵ[1] Clem

24 [*αλλα*, so BD[1]] rec (for *ως*) *ωσπερ*, with D[3]KL rel Thdrt Damasc, : om B Ambrst-ed txt AD[1]Fℵ 17. 67[2] Clem Chr Damasc. for *χρ*, *κυριω* D[1]-gr Chr rec ins *ιδιοις* bef *ανδρασιν* (*from ver* 22), with AD[3]KL rel. om BD[1]Fℵ 17 67[2].

25. rec aft *γυναικας* ins *εαυτων* (*see below, ver* 28), with DKL rel Chr_1 $Thdrt_2$ Damasc, *υμων* F $Thdrt_1$: om ABℵ 17 Clem (citing vv 21 to 25) Orig Chr_4 Cyr.

greatest of those that of *husband and wife* (vv 22—33), that of *parent and child* (ch vi. 1—4), that of *master and servant* (vi 5—9) See this expanded by Stier, in his very long note, ii 316—329.

22—33] *Mutual duties of wives and husbands*, arising from the relation between Christ and the Church

22] **Wives** (supply, as rec has inserted, *ὑποτάσσεσθε*, seeing that the subsequent address to husbands is in the 2nd person), **to your own husbands** (**ἰδίοις**, as we often use the word [e g 'He murdered his own father'], to intensify the recognition of the relationship and suggest its duties. see 1 Cor. vii. 2. also John v 18), **as to the Lord** ('quasi Christo ipsimet, cujus locum et personam viri repræsentant.' Corn.-a-lap. in Ellic. i e. 'in obeying your husbands, obey the Lord:' not merely as in all things we are to have regard to Him, but because, as below expanded, the husband stands peculiarly in Christ's place. But he is not thus identified in power with Christ, nor the obedience, in its nature, with that which is owed to Him) **for a husband** (any husband, taken as an example the same in sense would be expressed by *ὁ ἀνήρ*, the husband in each case, generic sing of *οἱ ἄνδρες*) **is head of his wife, as also** (**καί**, introducing identity of category) **Christ is Head of the church** (see for the sentiment, 1 Cor xi. 3 note), (*being*, in His case—see below) **Himself Saviour of the Body** (i. e. 'in Christ's case the Headship is united with, nay gained by, His having SAVED the body in the process of Redemption. so that I am not alleging Christ's Headship as one entirely identical with that other, for He has a claim to it and office in it peculiar to Himself' 'Vir autem non est servator uxoris, in eo Christus excellit: hinc *sed* sequitur' Bengel Stier remarks the apparent play on **σωτήρ—σώματος**, in reference to the supposed derivation of *σῶμα* from *σάω* (*σώζω*); and has noticed that in the only other place [except the pastoral Epistles] where St. Paul uses **σωτήρ**, Phil iii 20, 21, it is also in connexion with **σῶμα**) but (what I do say is, that thus far the two Headships are to be regarded as identical, in the *subjection of the body* to the Head) **as the church is subjected to Christ, so also** (again, identity of category in the **ὑποτάσσ**) **let the wives be to their husbands** (not *ἰδίοις* now, as it would disturb the perspicuity of the comparison) **in every thing** (thus only, with Calv, Beng, Mey., Ellic, can I find any legitimate meaning or connexion in the words All attempts 1) to explain **σωτὴρ τοῦ σώμ** also of the marriage state [Bulling., Beza, 'viri est quærere quod mulier conservet'], or 2) to deprive **ἀλλά** of its adversative force [Rück, Harl, al], or 3) refer it to something other than the preceding clause [De W, Eadie] seem to me unsatisfactory)

25] I cannot refrain from citing Chrys.'s very beautiful remarks on this next passage,—*εἶδες μετρον ὑπακοῆς, ἄκουσον καὶ μέτρον ἀγάπης. βούλει σοι τὴν γυναῖκα ὑπακούειν, ὡς τῷ χριστῷ*

καθὼς καὶ ὁ χριστὸς ἠγάπησεν τὴν ἐκκλησίαν καὶ [d] ἑαυτὸν
[d] παρέδωκεν ὑπὲρ αὐτῆς, 26 ἵνα αὐτὴν [e] ἁγιάσῃ [f] καθαρίσας
τῷ [g] λουτρῷ τοῦ ὕδατος [h] ἐν [i] ῥήματι, 27 [k] ἵνα παραστήσῃ

d ver. 2 reff. e = John xvii. 17, 19. Rom. xv. 16. 1 Cor. vi. 11. 1 Thess. v. 23. Rev. xxii. 11 al.
f = Tit. ii. 14. Heb. x. 2. g Tit. iii. 5 only. Cant. iv. 2. Sir. xxxi. (xxxiv.) 25 only.
h ch. iv. 19. vi. 2. i (without art.) Rom. x. 17. ch. vi. 17. Heb. vi. 5. xi. 3. P.H. k = (L. P. only, see Matt. xxvi. 53.) 2 Cor. xi. 2. Luke ii. 22. Acts i. 3. ix. 41. xxiii. 33. Rom. vi. 13 bis al.

τὴν ἐκκλησίαν, προνόει καὶ αὐτὸς αὐτῆς, ὡς ὁ χριστὸς τῆς ἐκκλησίας· κἂν τὴν ψυχὴν ὑπὲρ αὐτῆς δοῦναι δέῃ, κἂν κατακοπῆναι μυριάκις, κἂν ὁτιοῦν ὑπομεῖναι καὶ παθεῖν, μὴ παραιτήσῃ· κἂν ταῦτα πάθῃς, οὐδὲν οὐδέπω πεποίηκας, οἷον ὁ χριστός· σὺ μὲν γὰρ ἤδη συναφθεὶς ταῦτα ποιεῖς, ἐκεῖνος δὲ ὑπὲρ ἀποστρεφομένης αὐτὸν καὶ μισούσης ὥσπερ οὖν αὐτὸς τὴν ἀποστρεφομένην αὐτὸν καὶ μισοῦσαν καὶ διαπτύουσαν καὶ θρυπτομένην, περὶ τοὺς πόδας αὐτοῦ τῇ πολλῇ ἤγαγε τῇ κηδεμονίᾳ, οὐκ ἀπειλαῖς, οὐδὲ ὕβρεσιν, οὐδὲ φόβῳ, οὐδὲ ἑτέρῳ τινὶ τοιούτῳ οὕτω καὶ σὺ πρὸς τὴν γυναῖκα ἔχε τὴν σήν· κἂν ὑπερορῶσαν, κἂν θρυπτομένην, κἂν καταφρονοῦσαν ἴδῃς, δυνήσῃ αὐτὴν ὑπὸ τοὺς πόδας ἀγαγεῖν τοὺς σοὺς τῇ πολλῇ περὶ αὐτὴν προνοίᾳ, τῇ ἀγάπῃ, τῇ φιλίᾳ. οὐδὲν γὰρ τούτων τυραννικώτερον τῶν δεσμῶν, καὶ μάλιστα ἀνδρὶ κ. γυναικί. οἰκέτην μὲν γὰρ φόβῳ τις ἂν καταδῆσαι δυνήσεται, μᾶλλον δὲ οὐδὲ ἐκεῖνον ταχέως γὰρ ἀποπηδήσας οἰχήσεται· τὴν δὲ τοῦ βίου κοινωνόν, τὴν παίδων μητέρα, τὴν πάσης εὐφροσύνης ὑπόθεσιν, οὐ φόβῳ καὶ ἀπειλαῖς δεῖ καταδεσμεῖν, ἀλλ' ἀγάπῃ καὶ διαθέσει. **Husbands, love your wives, as also** (see above) **Christ loved the church and gave Himself for her** (better than 'it,' the comparison is thus brought out as in the original κἂν πάθῃς τι ὑπὲρ αὐτῆς, μὴ ὀνειδίσῃς οὐδὲ γὰρ ὁ χρ. τοῦτο ἐποίησε Chr.) **that** (intermediate purpose, as regarded *her*; see below, ver. 27) **He might sanctify her, having purified her** (**ἁγιάσῃ** and **καθαρίσας** might be contemporaneous, and indeed this is the more common usage of past participles with past finite verbs in the N. T. [see ch. i. 9 note]. But here, inasmuch as the sanctifying is clearly a gradual process, carried on till the spotless presentation [ver. 27], and the washing cannot be separated from the introductory rite of baptism, it is best to take the **καθαρίσας** as antecedent to the **ἁγιάσῃ**) **by the laver** (not '*washing*,' as E. V.: a meaning the word never has) **of the water** (of which we all know, viz. the *baptismal water*, see ref. Tit. We can hardly set aside the reference to the purifying bath of the bride previous to marriage:—see below on ver. 27, and cf. Rev. xxi. 2) **in the word** (*what word?* ἐν ὀνόματι πατρὸς κ. υἱοῦ κ. ἁγίου πνεύματος, says Chrys. alluding to the formula in Baptism: and so many fathers:—the '*mandatum divinum*' on which Baptism rests [Storr, Peile]:—the '*invocatio divini nominis*' which gives Baptism its efficacy [Erasm.]:—the preached *word of faith* [Rom. x. 8] of which confession is made in baptism, and which carries the real cleansing [John xv. 3; xvii. 17] and regenerating power [1 Pet. i. 23; iii. 21 (?)]—so Aug. Tract. 80 in Joan. 3, vol. iii. p. 1840, Migne, where those memorable words occur, "Detrahe verbum, et quid est aqua nisi aqua? Accedit verbum ad elementum, et fit sacramentum, etiam ipsum tanquam visibile verbum." And this certainly seems the sense most analogous to St. Paul's usage, in which ῥῆμα is confined to the *divine* word. But we must not join **ἐν ῥήματι** with τῷ λουτρῷ nor with τοῦ ὕδατος, for the former would require τῷ ἐν ῥήματι,—the latter, τοῦ ἐν ῥήματι,—there being no such close connexion as to justify the omission of the article, indeed the specification being here absolutely required, after so common a term as τὸ λοῦτρον τοῦ ὕδατος. So that we are referred back to the verb [**ἁγ.**] and participle [**καθαρίσας**] preceding. The former connexion is not probable, on account of the participle intervening: see also below. The latter is on all accounts the most likely. Thus, *the word*, preached and received, is the conditional element of purification,—the real water of spiritual baptism;—that wherein and whereby alone the efficacy of baptism is conveyed—that wherein and whereby we are regenerated, the process of sanctification being subsequent and gradual),

27.] **that** (further purpose of ἑαυτ. παρέδωκεν ὑπὲρ αὐτῆς) **He might Himself present to Himself** (as a bride, see reff. 2 Cor.: not as a sacrifice [Harl.], which is quite against the context. The expression sets forth that the preparation of the Church for her bridal with Christ is exclusively by His own agency) **the church glorious** (the prefixed adjective is emphatic, which we lose in translation), **not having spot** (a late word—τοῦτο φυλάττου, λέγε δὲ κηλίς—Phryn. Lobeck 28, where see note. It is found in Dion

αὐτὸς ἑαυτῷ ˡἔνδοξον τὴν ἐκκλησίαν μὴ ἔχουσαν ᵐσπίλον
ἢ ⁿῥυτίδα ἤ τι ᵒτῶν τοιούτων, ἀλλ' ἵνα ᾖ ἁγία καὶ
ᵖἄμωμος. 28 οὕτως ᑫὀφείλουσιν καὶ οἱ ἄνδρες ἀγαπᾷν
τὰς ἑαυτῶν γυναῖκας ὡς τὰ ἑαυτῶν σώματα. ὁ ἀγαπῶν
τὴν ἑαυτοῦ γυναῖκα ἑαυτὸν ἀγαπᾷ. 29 οὐδεὶς γάρ ποτε τὴν
ἑαυτοῦ σάρκα ἐμίσησεν, ἀλλὰ ʳἐκτρέφει καὶ ˢθάλπει αὐτήν,
καθὼς καὶ ὁ χριστὸς τὴν ἐκκλησίαν. 30 ὅτι μέλη ἐσμὲν

ABDF KLℵ a b c e f g h k l m n o 17

l Luke vii 25 xiii 17 1 Cor iv 10 only 1 Kings ix 8 al. m 2 Pet ii 13 only † Jos Ant xiii 11. 3 (-λας, Jude 12). n here only † Aristoph Plut 1051 Plat Symp p 191 A. o Rom i 32 (al fr Paul) John 8 4 only 3 Kings xii 8, 10 al. p ch i 4 reff. q = Luke xvii 10 John xiii 14 1 Cor xi 10 al ‡. r ch vi 4. s 1 Thess ii 7 only Deut xxii 6.

27. rec (for *αυτος*) *αυτην*, with D³K rel syrr Chr Thdrt₁, *εαυτην* m¹ *αυτο* 67² txt ABD¹FLℵ 17 latt copt goth gr-lat-ff. for *εαυτω*, *αυτω* ℵ¹. om *η τι* ℵ¹: ins ℵ-corr¹ ᵒᵇˡ.

28 rec om *και*, with KLℵ rel syrr Method Chr Thdrt Damasc. ins ABDF 17 latt syr copt goth Clem lat-ff.—[*και*] *οι ανδρες* bef *οφειλουσιν* ADF latt copt goth Clem txt BKLℵ rel syrr Method Chr Thdrt Damasc. for *σωματα*, *τεκνα* ℵ¹.

29. for *εαυτου σ.*, *σαρκα αυτου* ℵ¹ [*αλλα*, so ABD³L a b e h l n o.] rec (for *χριστος*) *κυριος*, with D³KL rel Œc. txt ABD¹Fℵ b¹ k m o 17 latt syrr coptt gr-lat-ff.

Hal., Plut., Lucian, &c. The proper accentuation seems to be as in text, not *σπῖλος*. In Anthol vi 252, we have *ἄσπιλον, ἀῤῥυτίδωτον*, beginning a hexameter) or **wrinkle** (*ῥυτίς, ἡ συγκεκλυσμένη σάρξ*, Etym. Mag.: from [*ἐ*]*ρύω*, see Palm and Rost, Lex. A classical word, see reff.), **or any of such things, but that she may be holy** (perfect in holiness) **and blameless** (see on both, note, ch. i. 4). The *presentation* here spoken of is clearly, in its full sense, that future one at the Lord's coming, so often treated under the image of a marriage (Matt xxii 1 ff; xxv 1 ff; Rev xix 7 ff; xxi 2 al fr), not any progress of sanctification here below, as Harl., Beng., al., maintain [and Calv., commonly quoted on the other side: for he says on **παραστήσῃ**, 'finem baptismi et ablutionis nostræ declarat: ut sancte et inculpate Deo vivamus'] however the progress towards this state of spotlessness in this life may sometimes be spoken of in its fulness and completion, or with reference to its proper qualities, not here found in their purity. Schottgen quotes a rabbinical comment on Cant i 5—'Judæi de synagoga intelligunt, et sic explicant: nigra sum in hoc sæculo, sed decora in sæculo futuro.' **28.**] **Thus** (two ways of understanding this **οὕτως** are open to us: 1) as referring back to Christ's love for the church,—'Thus,' 'in like manner,' &c., as [being] 'their own bodies:' and 2) as referring forward to the *ὡς* below, as very frequently [though Eadie calls it contrary to grammatical law] in St Paul [cf. 1 Cor iii. 15; iv. 1, ix. 26, al., and ver. 33 below, where Eadie himself renders, '*so . . . as himself*'],—'*Thus*,' '*so*,' &c., '*as* [they love] *their own bodies*.' After weighing maturely what has been said on one side and the other, I cannot but decide for the *latter*, as most in accordance with the usage of St Paul and with ver. 33: also as more simple. The sense [against Ellic.] remains substantially the same, and answers much better to the comment furnished by the succeeding clauses—husbands ought to love their own wives as they love their own bodies [= themselves: for their wives are in fact part of their own bodies, ver 31]: this being illustrated by and referred to the great mystery of Christ and His church, in which the same love, and the same incorporation, has place) **ought the husbands also** (as well as Christ in the archetypal example just given) **to love their own** (emphatic: see above on ver. 22) **wives, as** (with the same affection as) **their own bodies. He that loveth his own** (see above) **wife, loveth himself** (is but complying with that universal law of nature by which we all love ourselves. The best words to supply before the following *γάρ* will be, "And this we all do") **for** (see above) **no man ever hated his own flesh** (= *ἑαυτόν*, but put in this form to prepare for *εἰς σάρκα μίαν* in the Scripture proof below. Wetst. quotes from Seneca, Ep. 14, 'fateor, insitam nobis esse corporis nostri caritatem'), **but nourishes it up** (through all its stages, to maturity: so Aristoph. Ran. 1189, of Œdipus, *ἵνα μὴ 'κτραφεὶς γένοιτο τοῦ πατρὸς φονεύς*: and ib. 1127, *οὐ χρὴ λέοντος σκύμνον ἐν πόλει τρέφειν* [at all]: *ἢν δ' ἐκτραφῇ τις* [have been brought up], *τοῖς τρόποις ὑπηρετεῖν*) **and cherishes** (ref. 1 Thess. It is certainly not necessary to confine the meaning to

τοῦ [t] σώματος αὐτοῦ[, ἐκ τῆς σαρκὸς αὐτοῦ, καὶ ἐκ τῶν
[u] ὀστέων αὐτοῦ]. 31 [v] ἀντὶ [v] τούτου [w] καταλείψει ἄνθρωπος πατέρα καὶ μητέρα, καὶ [x] προςκολληθήσεται πρὸς
τὴν γυναῖκα αὐτοῦ, καὶ ἔσονται οἱ δύο [y] εἰς σάρκα μίαν.
32 τὸ [z] μυστήριον τοῦτο μέγα ἐστίν, ἐγὼ δὲ λέγω [a] εἰς

t ch i 23 reff u Matt xxiii 27 Luke xxiv 39 John xix 36, from Num ix 12 Heb xi 22 only v here only see Luke xii. 3 w Matt xix 5 ‖, from Gen ii 24 1 Thess iii 1 al x Matt ‖ as above, from l c Acts v 36 only y Matt ‖ as above, xx 42 Luke iii 5. Rom ii 26 Gen xv 6 z = Paul, Rom xi 25 1 Cor xv 51 1 Tim iii 9, 16. a = Acts ii 25 Heb vii 14. 1 Pet i 11

30 om *εκ της σαρκος αυτου και εκ των οστεων αυτου* (*prob from homœotel · had the words been insd from* LXX, *οστ would prob have come first. See note*) ABℵ[1] 17 67[2] copt æth Method Ambrst ins DFKLℵ[3] rel vss Iren-gr-lat Chr Thdrt Damasc Jer

31 rec ins *τον* bef *πατερα* and *την* bef *μητερα* (*from* LXX), with AD[3]KLℵ rel Method Tit-bostr · om BD[1]F rec aft *πατερα* ins *αυτου* (*from* LXX), with AD[3]KLℵ[3] rel Mcion-e om BD[1]Fℵ[1] 17 67[2] Orig Thdrt$_1$ Thl-ms Jer(expr after Orig). for *προς την γυναικα*, *τη γυναικι* (*so also in Gen* ii 24, *A al Method Ath Epiph lat ff*) AD[1]Fℵ[1] m 17 latt lat-ff Method Epiph txt BD[3]KLℵ[3] rel Orig$_2$ Chr Thdrt$_2$. om *αυτου* ℵ[1] ins ℵ-corr[1,3]

'*warming*,' as Beng. ['*id spectat amictum*'], Mey, al for it is very forced to apply the feeding and clothing to the other member of the comparison [as Grot : 'nutrit eam verbo et spiritu, vestit eam virtutibus'], as must then be done [against Mey i]) it, **as also** (does) **Christ** (nourish and cherish) **the church** 30] **For** (again a link is omitted, 'the church, which stands in the relation of marriage to Him for, &c.') **members we are of His Body** [,—(**being**) **of His flesh, and of His bones** (see Gen ii 23 As the woman owed her natural being to the man, her source and head, so we owe our entire spiritual being to Christ, our source and head and as the woman was one flesh with the man in this natural relation, so we in our entire spiritual relation, body, soul, and Spirit, are one with Christ, God manifested in our humanity,—parts and members of His glorified Body Bengel well remarks, that we are not, as in Gen, l c *ὀστοῦν ἐκ τῶν ὀστέων αὐτοῦ, καὶ σὰρξ ἐκ τῆς σαρκὸς αὐτ* —'non ossa et caro nostra, sed *nos* spiritualiter propagamur ex humanitate Christi, carnem et ossa habente')] **wherefore** (the allusion, or rather free citation, is still carried on · cf. Gen ii. 24:—i. e because we are members of Him in the sense just insisted on. This whole verse is said [see on ver 32 below] not of human marriages, but of Christ and the church He is the **ἄνθρωπος** in the Apostle's view here, the Church is the **γυνή**. But for all this, I would not understand the words, as Meyer, in a prophetical sense of the future coming of Christ — the omission of the article before **ἄνθρωπος** sufficiently retains the general aphorismatic sense —but would regard the saying as applied to that, past, present, and future, which constitutes Christ's Union to His Bride the Church His leaving the Father's bosom, which is *past*—His gradual preparation of the union, which is *present*. His full consummation of it, which is *future* This seems to me to be necessary, because we are as truly now **εἰς σάρκα μίαν** with Him, as we shall be, when heaven and earth shall ring with the joy of the nuptials,—and hence the exclusive future sense is inapplicable In this allegorical sense [see below], Chrys, Jer, and most of the ancients Beng, Grot, Mey [as above], al, interpret and Eadie would have done well to study more deeply the spirit of the context before he characterized it as 'strange romance,' 'wild and visionary,' and said, 'there is no hint that the Apostle intends to allegorize.' That allegory, on the contrary, is the *key to the whole*) **shall a man leave father and mother and shall be closely joined to his wife, and they two shall become** (see Matt xix 5, note) **one flesh** ('non solum uti antea, respectu ortus sed respectu novæ conjunctionis' Beng) 32] **This mystery is great** (viz the matter mystically alluded to in the Apostle's application of the text just quoted · the mystery of the spiritual union of Christ with our humanity, typified by the close conjunction of the marriage state This meaning of **μυστήριον**, which is strictly that in which St Paul uses the word [see reff],—as something passing human comprehension, but revealed as a portion of the divine dealings in Christ,—is, it seems to me, required by the next words It is irksome, but necessary, to notice the ridiculous perversion of this text by the Romish church, which from the Vulgate rendering, 'sacramentum hoc magnum est, ego autem dico in Christo et in Ecclesia,' deduces that 'marriage is a great sacrament in Christ

b = always in Paul 1 Cor xi 11 al[3] & in Matt & Luke (Gosp vi 21 (ll3)) Rev ii 25 Judg iv 9 in Mark (xii 32) [John viii 10 rec], & Acts viii 1 al[3], with gen 'except.'

χριστὸν καὶ [[a] εἰς] τὴν ἐκκλησίαν. 33 [b] πλὴν καὶ ὑμεῖς
οἱ [c] καθ᾽ ἕνα ἕκαστος τὴν ἑαυτοῦ γυναῖκα [d] οὕτως ἀγαπάτω
[d] ὡς ἑαυτόν, ἡ δὲ γυνὴ [e] ἵνα φοβῆται τὸν ἄνδρα.
VI. 1 τὰ τέκνα [f] ὑπακούετε τοῖς γονεῦσιν ὑμῶν [[g] ἐν
κυρίῳ]· τοῦτο γάρ ἐστιν δίκαιον. 2 [h] Τίμα τὸν πατέρα

ABDF KIℵab cefg hklm no17

c Acts xxi 19 1 Cor xiv 31 see Mark xiv 19. [John viii 9] d 1 Cor iii 15. iv 1 ix 26 bis e constr., Mark v 23 f Matt viii 27 al Ir g ch iv 17 reff h Matt xv 4 || al from Exod xx 12 Deut v 16

32 om 2nd εις BK b g h k o Iren-gr-lat Tert : ins ADFLℵ rel latt Orig$_2$ Method Tit-bostr Chr Sevrn-cat Thdrt Chron Cypr Victorin Hil.
33 ins ινα bef εκαστος D[1]ℵ[3] εκαστον F. ως εαυ. bef αγαπ. DF

Chap. VI 1 om εν κυριω (*prob as appearing irrelevant, had it been inserted from ch v 22 it wd have been ως τω κ, if from Col iii 20, it wd have stood aft* δικαιον · *so Mey, and Harless*) BD[1]F Cyr-jer Cypr Ambrst ins AD[2,3]KLℵ rel vss Orig-cat Chr$_{expr}$ Thdrt Damasc Jer

and in His Church' [Encyclical letter of 1832 cited by Eadie] It will be enough to say that this their blunder of 'sacramentum' for 'mysterium,' had long ago been exposed by their own Commentators, Cajetan and Estius) · but I (emphatic) say (allege) it with reference to Christ, and [with reference to] the church (i e *my* meaning, in citing the above text, is to call your attention, not to mere human marriage, but to that high and mysterious relation between Christ and His Church, of which that other is but a faint resemblance). 33] **Nevertheless** (not to go further into the mystical bearings of the subject—so Meyer) **you also** (as well as Christ) **every one** (see ref and 1 Cor. xiv 27, Acts xv 21; Heb. ix 25), **let each** (the construction is changed and the verb put into concord with **ἕκαστος** instead of **ὑμεῖς** . so Plat Gorg. p. 503, *ὥσπερ κ. οἱ ἄλλοι πάντες δημιουργοὶ βλέποντες πρὸς τὸ ἑκάστου ἔργον ἕκαστος οὐκ εἰκῇ ἐκλεγόμενος προσφέρει κ τ λ.*; Rep p. 346, *αἱ ἄλλαι πᾶσαι [τέχναι] οὕτω τὸ αὑτῆς ἑκάστη ἔργον ἐργάζεται, κ τ λ.* Cic. de Off. i 41, 'poetæ suum quisque opus a vulgo considerari vult') **so love his own wife as himself, and the wife** (best taken as a nominative absolute, as Mey. Otherwise we should rather expect *ἵνα δὲ ἡ γυνὴ κ τ λ* It is no objection to this [Eadie] that in the resolution of the idiom a verb must be supplied:—but the wife, for her part,—'*I order*,' or, '*let her see*,' cf note on 2 Cor viii 7), **that she fear** (*ὡς πρέπει γυναῖκα φοβεῖσθαι, μὴ δουλοπρεπῶς*, Œc) **her husband** Ch VI. 1–4] See on ch v 22 *Duties of children and parents* **Children, obey your parents [in the Lord** (i e Christ the sphere in which the action is to take place, as usual **ἐν κυρίῳ** belonging to **ὑπακούετε τ γον** , not to **τοῖς γον.**, as if it were *τοῖς ἐν κυρίῳ γον* , nor can this be combined, as a second reference, with the other, as by Orig in Cramer's Catena, understanding 'your fathers in the faith, *ὁποῖος ὁ Παῦλος ἦν Κορινθίων*.' I should venture however to question whether the Apostle's view was to hint at such commands of parents as might not be according to the will of God, as is very generally supposed ['quia poterant parentes aliquid imperare perversum, adjunxit in Domino' Jer.] · for cf Col iii. 20, **ὑπακούετε** *τοῖς γονεῦσιν* **κατὰ πάντα.** I should rather believe, that he regards both parents and children as *ἐν κυρίῳ*, and the commands, as well as the obedience, as having that sphere and element How children were to regard commands *not answering to this description*, would be understood from the nature of the case. but it seems to violate the simplicity of this **ὑποτασσόμενοι ἀλλήλοις** passage, to introduce into it a by-thought of this kind)] · **for this is right** (Thdrt , Harl., De W , Mey , al , regard **δίκαιον** as explained by the next verse, and meaning *κατὰ τὸν θεοῦ νόμον* But it seems rather an appeal to the first principles of natural duty, as Est , 'ut a quibus vitam accepimus, iis obedientiam reddamus.' So Beng. Stier, as usual, combines both senses—just, according to the law both of nature and of God Surely it is better to regard the next verse as an additional particular, not the mere expansion of this). 2] **Honour thy father and thy mother, for such is** ('*seeing it is*,' as Ellic , is rather too strong for **ἥτις**, throwing the motive to obedience too much on the fact of the promise accompanying it. Whereas the obedience rests on the fact implied in *ἐντολή*, and the promise comes in to shew its special acceptableness to God) **the first commandment** (in the deca-

σου καὶ τὴν μητέρα, ἥτις ἐστὶν ἐντολὴ πρώτη [l] ἐν ἐπαγ-
γελίᾳ, 3 ἵνα [k] εὖ σοι [k] γένηται καὶ ἔσῃ [l] μακροχρόνιος ἐπὶ
τῆς γῆς. 4 καὶ οἱ πατέρες, μὴ [m] παροργίζετε τὰ τέκνα
ὑμῶν, ἀλλὰ [n] ἐκτρέφετε αὐτὰ ἐν [o] παιδείᾳ καὶ [p] νουθεσίᾳ
κυρίου.

i = ch v 26 reff. k here only. Gen xli 13 al. εὖ Matt xxv 21, 23 Mark xiv 7 (Luke xix 17) Acts xv 29 only. l here only. ll cc Deut xvii 20 F only. m Rom x 19 (Col iii 21 v r) only, from Deut xxxii 21 (-σμος, ch iv 26) n ch v 29 only. Prov xxiii 24 o 2 Tim iii 16 Heb xii 5, 7, 8, 11 only. Prov i 2, 7 Isa liii 5 p 1 Cor x 11 Tit iii 10 only † Judith viii 27 (23) Ald (τησις, F. vat) Wisd xvi 6 only

2 aft την μητερα ins σου F m. om εστιν B 46 ins τη bef επαγγελια DF.
3. א[1] has written the ver twice א corr has marked it for erasure.
4. [αλλα, so ABD[1]א]

logue, which naturally stands at the head of all God's other commandments, and which, though not formally binding on us as Christians, is quoted, in matters of eternal obligation [not of positive enactment], as an eminent example of God's holy will) with a promise (i e. with a special promise attached 'in respect of promise' is too vague, and does not convey any definite meaning in English. The fact certainly is so, and the occurrence of the description of God as 'shewing mercy unto thousands, &c' after the second commandment, does not, as Jer., al., have thought, present any difficulty—for that is no special promise attached to the commandment Nor does the fact that no other commandment occurs in the *decalogue* with a promise see above. The ἐν, as in reff —in the sphere or department of—characterized by—accompanied with), that it may be well with thee, and thou be long-lived upon the earth (he paraphrases the latter portion of the commandment, writing for ἵνα μακρ. γένῃ, ἔσῃ μ.,—and omitting after γῆς, [τῆς ἀγαθῆς, so in Exod., but not in Deut.] ἧς κύριος ὁ θεός σου δίδωσίν σοι. thus adapting the promise to his Christian readers, by taking away from it that which is special and peculiar to the Jewish people It is surely a mistake, as Jer., Aq., Est., Olsh., to spiritualize the promise, and understand by τῆς γῆς the heavenly Canaan. The very fact of the omission of the special clause removes the words from the region of type into undoubted reality and when we remember that the persons addressed are τὰ τέκνα, we must not depart from the simplest sense of the words. For the future after ἵνα, see 1 Cor ix. 18, note and John vii 3, Rev xxii 14 To consider it as such, is far better than to suppose a change of construction to the direct future—'and thou shalt be, &c').

4] And ye, fathers (the mothers being included, as ὑποτασσόμεναι τοῖς ἰδίοις ἀνδράσιν—they being the fountains of domestic rule: not for any other less worthy reason, to which the whole view of the sexes by the Apostle is opposed), irritate not (οἷον, says Chrys., οἱ πολλοὶ ποιοῦσιν, ἀποκληρονόμους ἐργαζόμενοι, καὶ ἀποκηρύκτους ποιοῦντες, καὶ φορτικῶς ἐπικείμενοι, οὐχ ὡς ἐλευθέροις ἀλλ' ὡς ἀνδραπόδοις But the Apostle seems rather to allude to provoking by vexatious commands, and unreasonable blame, and uncertain temper, in ordinary intercourse cf Col iii. 21) your children, but bring them up (see on ch v 29, where it was used of physical fostering up· and cf Plato, Rep p 538 c, περὶ δικαίων κ καλῶν, ἐν οἷς ἐκτεθράμμεθα ὡς ὑπὸ γονεῦσι) in (as the sphere and element. see Plato above) the discipline and admonition ('παιδεία hic significare videtur institutionem per pœnas· νουθεσία autem est ea institutio quæ fit verbis' Grot. Such indeed is the general sense of παιδεία in the LXX and N. T., the word having gained a deeper meaning than mere 'eruditio,' by the revealed doctrine of the depravity of our nature see Trench, Syn. § 32. Ellic. remarks, that this sense seems not to have been unknown to earlier writers, e. g Xen. Mem i. 3 5, διαίτῃ τήν τε ψυχὴν ἐπαίδευσε κ τὸ σῶμα . . . , he *disciplined* &c, but not Polyb ii 9 6, where it is ἀβλαβῶς ἐπαιδεύθησαν πρὸς τὸ μέλλον νουθεσία [a late form for νουθέτησις see Phryn Lob. p. 512] is as Cicero, '*quasi lenior objurgatio*' 'the training by word—by the word of encouragement, when no more is wanted,—of remonstrance, reproof, or blame where these are required' Trench, ubi supra) of the Lord (i e Christ either objective,—'*concerning the Lord*'—so Thdrt and very many of the ancients, and Erasm., Beza [not Est], &c, or sub-

q (Acts ii. 30 v. r.) Rom i. 3. iv. 1. ix. 3 al. Paul only. = σαρκι, or ἐν σ., 1 Pet iii. 18 al. r = ch. ii. 2 reff. s 1 Cor ii. 3. 2 Cor vii. 15. Phil ii. 12 only. Ps liv. 5. t as above (s). Mark xvi. 8 only. u Col iii. 22 al[6] only. P. 1 Chron. xxix. 17. v Col iii. 22 only †. w Col iii. 22 only. Ps lii. 5 only. x 1 Cor vii. 22. y Matt vii. 21. xii. 50. John ix. 34 (ch. ii. 3). Heb. x. 7, from Ps xxxix. 8. 1 John ii. 17 al. z Col iii. 23 only. Ezek xxv. 15. see Mark xii. 30, 33. a here only †. 1 Macc xi. 53 al.

ABDF KLℵ a b c e f g h k l m n o 17

5 Οἱ δοῦλοι, ὑπακούετε τοῖς κυρίοις [q] κατὰ σάρκα [r] μετὰ
[s] φόβου καὶ [st] τρόμου, ἐν [u] ἁπλότητι τῆς καρδίας ὑμῶν, ὡς
τῷ χριστῷ, 6 μὴ κατ' [v] ὀφθαλμοδουλείαν ὡς [w] ἀνθρωπάρεσκοι, ἀλλ' ὡς [x] δοῦλοι [x] χριστοῦ, [y] ποιοῦντες τὸ
[y] θέλημα τοῦ θεοῦ, 7 ἐκ [z] ψυχῆς μετ' [a] εὐνοίας δουλεύοντες

5. κατα σαρκα bef κυριοις (*see Col* iii. 22) ABℵ m 17 Clem Chr_1 Damasc Thl: txt DFKL rel Chr_2 Thdrt Œc. om της ℵ 72. 114. 115. 122. for χριστω, κυριω AL 17 copt Chr_1.

6. rec ins του bef χριστου, with D[3]KL rel Chr Thdrt. om ABD[1]Fℵ 1 n[1] 17 Damasc Thl-ms Œc.

jective—'*such as the Lord approves* and dictates by His Spirit,'—so De W., Harl., Olsh., Mey., Stier. Conyb. renders '*such training and correction as befits the servants of Christ*,' which surely the words can hardly contain). **5—9.**] See on ch. v. 22. *Duties of masters and slaves.* **Slaves** (or as Conyb., '*Bondsmen.*' There is no reason to render **οἱ δοῦλοι** *servants*, as in E. V., for by this much of the Apostle's exhortation is deprived of point), **obey your lords according to the flesh** (= τοῖς κατὰ σάρκα κυρίοις, Col iii. 22: not to be joined with **ὑπακούετε**: nor can it be here said as so often, that κύριος-κατὰ-σάρκα is united in one idea: for in the context, another description of κύριος is brought forward, viz. ὁ χριστός. Chrys. sees in **κατὰ σάρκα** a consolatory hint that the δεσποτεία is πρόσκαιρος καὶ βραχεῖα. Calv., that their real liberty was still their own. Ellic. in citing these, rightly observes, that however they may be doubted, still both, especially the latter, are obviously *deductions* which must have been, and which the Apostle *might* have intended to have been, made) **with fear and trembling** (see reff., and note on 1 Cor ii. 3: whence it appears that the **φόβος κ. τρόμος** was to be not that of dread, arising from their condition as slaves, but that of *anxiety* to do their duty,—'sollicita reverentia, quam efficiet cordis simplicitas.' Calv.), **in** (as its element) **simplicity** (singleness of view: "so Pind., Nem. viii. 61, speaks of κελεύθοις ἁπλόαις ζωᾶς in contrast with **πάρφασις**, treachery: in Aristoph. Plut. 1159, it is opposed to δόλιος: in Philo, Opif. 36, 39 [§ 55, 61, vol. i. pp. 38, 41], it is classed with ἀκακία," Harl.) **of your heart, as to Christ** (again—He being the source and ground of all Christian motives and duties), **not in a spirit of** (according to, measuring your obedience by) **eye-service** (τὴν οὐκ ἐξ εἰλικρινοῦς καρδίας προσφερομένην θεραπείαν, ἀλλὰ τῷ σχήματι κεχρωσμένην, Thdrt. Xen. Œc. xii. 20, βασιλεὺς ἵππου ἐπιτυχὼν ἀγαθοῦ παχῦναι αὐτὸν ὡς τάχιστα βουλόμενος ἤρετο τῶν δεινῶν τινα ἀμφ' ἵππους δοκούντων εἶναί τι τάχιστα παχύνει ἵππον· τὸν δὲ εἰπεῖν λέγεται ὅτι δεσπότου ὀφθαλμός) **as men-pleasers** (on **ἀνθρωπάρεσκοι**, see Lob. on Phryn., p. 621, who, while disapproving of forms such as εὐάρεσκος and δυσάρεσκος, allows ἀνθρωπάρεσκος), **but as slaves of Christ** (ὁ ἄρα ἀνθρωπάρεσκος, οὐ δοῦλος τοῦ χριστοῦ· ὁ δὲ δοῦλος τοῦ χριστοῦ, οὐκ ἀνθρωπάρεσκος· τίς γὰρ θεοῦ δοῦλος ὤν, ἀνθρώποις ἀρέσκειν βούλεται, τίς δὲ ἀνθρώποις ἀρέσκων, θεοῦ δύναται εἶναι δοῦλος; Chrys. The contrast is between **κατ' ὀφθαλμοδουλείαν** and **ὡς δοῦλοι χρ.**, and **ποιοῦντες κ τ λ** is a qualification of **δοῦλοι χριστοῦ**. This is much more natural, than, with Rückert, to make ποιοῦντες κ τ λ carry the emphasis, and ὡς δοῦλ. χρ. to be merely subordinate to it), **doing the will of God** (serving not a *seen* master only [ὀφθαλμοδουλ.], but the great invisible Lord of all, which will be the surest guarantee for your serving your earthly masters, even when unseen), **from your soul with good will doing service** (this arrangement, which is that of Syr., Chr., Jer., Beng., Lachm., Harl., De Wette, seems to me far better than the other [Tischdf., Mey., Ellic., al.] which joins **ἐκ ψυχῆς** to **ποιοῦντες τὸ θέλ. τοῦ θεοῦ**. For 1) these words need here no such qualification as ἐκ ψυχῆς: if the will of God be the real object of the man's obedience, the μὴ κατ' ὀφθαλμοδουλ. will be sufficiently answered: and 2) were it so, it would be more natural to find **ἐκ ψυχῆς** preceding than following the clause,—ἐκ ψυχῆς ποιοῦντες τὸ θέλ. τοῦ θεοῦ, or ἐκ ψυχῆς τὸ θέλ. τοῦ θεοῦ ποιοῦντες, or τὸ θέλ. τοῦ θεοῦ ἐκ ψυχῆς ποιοῦντες, whereas 3) the double qualification, ἐκ ψυχῆς μετ' εὐνοίας, attached to δουλεύοντες, describes beautifully the source in

ὡς τῷ κυρίῳ καὶ οὐκ ἀνθρώποις· 8 εἰδότες ὅτι ἕκαστος
ἐάν τι ποιήσῃ ἀγαθόν, τοῦτο ᵇ κομίσεται παρὰ κυρίου, εἴτε
ᶜ δοῦλος εἴτε ᶜ ἐλεύθερος. 9 καὶ οἱ κύριοι, τὰ αὐτὰ ποιεῖτε
πρὸς αὐτούς, ᵈ ἀνιέντες τὴν ᵉ ἀπειλήν, εἰδότες ὅτι καὶ
αὐτῶν καὶ ὑμῶν ὁ κύριός ἐστιν ἐν οὐρανοῖς καὶ ᶠ προσωποληψία οὐκ ἔστιν ᶠ παρ' αὐτῷ.
10 Τοῦ ᵍ λοιποῦ, ʰ ἐνδυναμοῦσθε ἐν κυρίῳ καὶ ἐν τῷ

b = 2 Cor v 10 Col iii 25 al Ps xxxix 15. c 1 Cor xii 13 Gal iii 28 Col iii 11 Rev vi 15 xiii 16 xix 18. d Acts xvi 26 xxvii 40 Heb xiii 5 (from Deut xxxi 6) only. e Acts iv [17]. 29 ix 1 only Job xxiii 6 f Rom ii 11 only. πρ., Col iii 25 James ii 1 only † g 2 Cor xiii 11 Phil iv 8 1 Thess iv 1 2 Thess iii 1 — Paul only h Paul (Rom iv 20 al⁵) only, exc Acts ix 22 (of Paul) and Heb xi 34 Ps li 7 (9)

7 μετα B rec om ως, with D³KL rel Thdrt ins ABDFℵ b c l² m o 17. 67² vss Constt Bas Chr Damasc Antch Thl-ms Ambrst-ed Pelag ανθρωπω B Damasc

8 rec (ὁ) εαν τι bef εκαστος, with L(Kℵ) rel syrr Chr Thdrt Damasc$_{hl}$ Thl Œc. txt ABDF m 17 latt Bas Damasc.—om ὁ BLℵ¹ g k¹ Thl-mss —εαν (ο εαν ℵ³) ποιηση bef εκαστος ℵ¹ —for εαν, αν D¹F a Chr$_1$: om K n¹.—om τι AD¹FKℵ m n¹ 17 Bas ins BD² or ³ L rel rec κομιειται (see Col iii. 25), with D³KLℵ³ rel Bas Chr Thdrt Damasc: txt ABD¹Fℵ¹ Petr-alex. rec ins του bef κυριου, with KL rel Chr Thdrt om ABDFℵ 17 Petr-alex Damasc$_2$.

9. rec (for αυτων κ. υμων) υμων αυτων (the sense of Col iv. 1 helping the omn of κ. αυτων by homœotel: cf varr), with K rel D-lat Syr ff και αυτ υμ. D³F αυτων κ ημων 13. ημων αυτων 26. 109 κ υμ κ αυτ. L 67². 115 syr Petr-alex Antch Cypr Ambrst εαυτ κ. υμων ℵ¹ υμων κ. εαυτ. ℵ³ txt ABD¹ m 17 vulg(and F-lat) copt goth arm Clem Jer ουρανω ℵ for παρ' αυτω, παρα θεω D¹ spec demid(and F-lat) Ambrst-ed Pelag: π τω θεω F εν αυτω b m o 118 syr-marg

10. rec το λοιπον (see Phil iii 1, iv. 8, 2 Thess iii. 1; 2 Cor xiii 11), with DFKLℵ³ rel Chr Thdrt Thl Œc txt ABℵ¹ 17. 67² Cyr Procop Damasc. rec ins αδελφοι μου bef ενδυναμ (see Phil &c. as above), with KLℵ³ rel(a in red), and (omg μου) F 71. 109 vulg syr Thdrt Aug Pelag om A(insg αδελφ aft ενδ) BDℵ¹ 17 æth arm Cyr Damasc Lucif Jer Ambrst. δυναμουσθε B 17 ins τω bef κυριω ℵ¹ 91 om ℵ corr¹(?) ³.

himself [ἐκ ψυχῆς] and the accompanying feeling towards another [μετ' εὐνοίας] of Christian service On εὔνοια in this sense, cf. Eur. Androm. 59, εὔνους δὲ καὶ σοί, ζῶντι δ' ἦν τῷ σῷ πόσει· Xen. Œcon. xii 5, εὔνοιαν πρῶτον . δεήσει αὐτὸν ἔχειν σοι καὶ τοῖς σοῖς . . .; ἄνευ γὰρ εὐνοίας τί ὄφελος ἐπιτρόπου ἐπιστήμης γίνεται; and the other examples in Wetst) **as to the Lord and not to men,** 8.] **knowing** (as ye do, i e seeing that ye are aware) **that each man if he shall have done** (at Christ's coming) **any good thing** (the reading is in some doubt. If we take the rec, or that of A, &c we must render '*whatsoever good thing* each man *shall have done*,' and take ὃ ἐάν τι for ὅτι ἄν, so Plat. Legg ix p. 864 E, ἥν ἄν τινα καταβλάψῃ: and Lysis p 160, ὃς ἄν τις ὑμᾶς εὖ ποιῇ [cited in Mey] On ἐάν, see Winer, § 42 6 obs), **this** (emphatic 'this in full,' 'this exactly') **he shall receive** (see reff where the same expression occurs—this he shall then receive in its value as then estimated,—changed, so to speak, into the currency of that new and final state) **from the Lord** (Christ), **whether he be slave or free** (Chrys. beautifully gives the connexion of thought. ἐπειδὴ γὰρ εἰκὸς ἦν πολλοὺς τῶν δεσποτῶν ἀπίστους ὄντας μὴ αἰσχύνεσθαι μηδὲ ἀμείβεσθαι τοὺς οἰκέτας τῆς ὑπακοῆς, ὅρα πῶς αὐτοὺς παρεμυθήσατο ὥστε μὴ ὑποπτεύειν τὴν ἀνταπόδοσιν, ἀλλὰ σφόδρα θαῤῥεῖν ὑπὲρ τῆς ἀμοιβῆς καθάπερ γὰρ οἱ καλῶς πάσχοντες, ὅταν μὴ ἀμείβωνται τοὺς εὐεργέτας, τὸν θεὸν αὐτοῖς ὀφειλέτην ποιοῦσιν· οὕτω δὴ καὶ οἱ δεσπόται, ἂν παθόντες εὖ παρὰ σοῦ μή σε ἀμείψωνται, μᾶλλον ἠμείψαντο, τὸν θεὸν ὀφειλέτην σοι καταστήσαντες): 9] **and ye masters, do the same things** ('jus analogum, quod vocant.' as *they* are to remember one whom they serve, so [below] are *ye*—and, 'mutatis mutandis,' to act to them as they to you. This wider sense is better than that of Chrys., τὰ αὐτὰ ποῖα; μετ' εὐνοίας δουλεύετε) **with regard to them, forbearing your** (usual) **threatening** (τήν, 'quemadmodum vulgus dominorum solet,' Erasm. par in Mey), **knowing** (as ye do see ver 8) **that both of them and of yourselves the Master is in the heavens, and respect of persons** (warping of justice from regard to any man's individual pre eminence, see reff)

i ch. i. 19 reff. k ch. iv. 24 reff. l ver. 13. Luke xi. 22 only. 2 Kings ii. 21. m = Matt. v. 28. vi. 1 al. n ch. iv. 14 only (reff.) o here only † (λαίειν, Job xxxviii. 8 Aq.) q ch. i. 21 reff.

[i] κράτει τῆς [i] ἰσχύος αὐτοῦ. 11 [k] ἐνδύσασθε τὴν [l] πανοπλίαν τοῦ θεοῦ, [m] πρὸς τὸ δύνασθαι ὑμᾶς στῆναι πρὸς τὰς
[n] μεθοδείας τοῦ διαβόλου. 12 ὅτι οὐκ ἔστιν * ἡμῖν ἡ [o] πάλη
πρὸς [p] αἷμα καὶ [p] σάρκα, ἀλλὰ πρὸς τὰς [q] ἀρχάς, πρὸς
τὰς [q] ἐξουσίας, πρὸς τοὺς [r] κοσμοκράτορας τοῦ [s] σκότους

ABDF KLℵ a b c e f g h k l m n o 17

p Matt. xvi. 17. 1 Cor. xv. 50. Gal. i. 16. Heb. ii. 14 only. Sir. xiv. 18. xvii. 31. r here only †. s = Col. i. 13. Luke xxii. 53.

11. aft ενδυσασθαι ins υμας F. for 1st προς, εις DF. στηναι bef υμας D. αντιστ K Orig. μεθοδιας A B[1](Rl) D FKLℵ e m 17.

12. * ὑμῖν BD[1]F a e Syr Lucif Ambrst: ημιν AD[3]KLℵ rel vulg copt syr Thdrt Clem Orig Method Cypr Hil Jer Aug Ambr. om 2nd προς τας F: for π. τ., και D vulg lat-ff. rec ins του αιωνος bef τουτου, with D[3]KLℵ[3](but rubbed out) rel syr-w-ast Mac Ath-ms Chr Thdrt: om ABD[1]Fℵ[1] 17 67[2] latt copt goth Clem Orig$_{saepe}$ Ath Eus Bas Nyssen Cyr$_{aliq}$ Cypr Lucif Hil Ambrst Jer Tert Ors.

exists not with Him (Wetst. quotes the celebrated lines of Seneca, Thyest. 607, 'vos quibus rector maris atque terræ | jus dedit magnum necis atque vitæ, | ponite inflatos tumidosque vultus | quicquid a vobis minor extimescit, | major hoc vobis dominus minatur | omne sub regno graviore regnum est'). **10–20**] *General exhortation to the spiritual conflict and to prayer.* **Henceforward** (cf. Gal. vi. 17, note: τοῦ λοιποῦ [see var. readd.] would be '*finally*.' Olsh.'s remark, that the Apostle never addresses his readers as ἀδελφοί in this Epistle, is perfectly correct: the ἀδελφοῖς in ver. 23 does not contravene it [as Eadie], but rather establishes it. He there sends his apostolic blessing τοῖς ἀδελφοῖς, but does not directly address them) **be strengthened** (passive, not middle, see reff.—and Fritz. on Rom. iv. 20) **in the Lord** (Christ), **and in the strength of His might** (see on **κράτος τῆς ἰσχύος**, note, ch. i. 19). **Put on the entire armour** (emphatic: repeated again ver. 13: offensive, as well as defensive. It is probable that the Apostle was daily familiarized in his imprisonment with the Roman method of arming) **of God** (Harl. maintains that the stress is on **τοῦ θεοῦ**, to contrast with **τοῦ διαβόλου** below: but there is no distinction made between the armour of God and any other spiritual armour, which would be the case, were this so. τοῦ θεοῦ, as supplied, ministered, by God, who ἅπασι διανέμει τὴν βασιλικὴν παντευχίαν, Thdrt.), **that ye may be able to stand against** (so Jos. Antt. xi. 5. 7, θαῤῥεῖν μὲν οὖν τῷ θεῷ πρῶτον, ὡς καὶ πρὸς τὴν ἐκείνων ἀπέχθειαν στησομένῳ: see Kypke, ii. p. 301, and Ellicott's note here) **the schemes** (the instances [concr.] of a quality [abstr.] of **μεθόδεια**. τί ἐστι μεθόδεια; μεθοδεῦσαί ἐστι τὸ ἀπατῆσαι, κ. διὰ συντόμου ἑλεῖν, Chrys.:—the word is however sometimes used in a good sense, as Diod. Sic. i. 81, ταύτας δὲ οὐ ῥᾴδιον ἀκριβῶς ἐξελέγξαι, μὴ γεωμέτρου τὴν ἀλήθειαν ἐκ τῆς ἐμπειρίας μεθοδεύσαντος,—'if the geometrician had not investigated, &c.' The bad sense is found in Polyb. xxxviii. 4. 10, πολλὰ δή τινα πρὸς ταύτην τὴν ὑπόθεσιν ἐμπορεύων κ. μεθοδευόμενος, ἐκίνει κ. παρώξυνε τοὺς ὄχλους. See Ellic. on ch. iv. 14) **of the devil**. **12**] **For** (confirms τ. μεθ. **τοῦ διαβ.** preceding) **our** (or, '*your*:' the ancient authorities are divided) **wrestling** (**πάλη** must be literally taken—it is a hand to hand and foot to foot 'tug of war'—that in which the combatants close, and wrestle for the mastery) **is not** (Meyer well remarks, that the negative is not to be softened down into *non tam*, or *non tantum*, as Grot., &c.—the conflict which the Apostle means [qu.? better, **ἡ πάλη**, the only conflict which can be described by such a word—our life and death struggle, there being but *one* such] is absolutely *not* with men but &c. He quotes from Aug., "Non est nobis colluctatio adversus carnem et sanguinem, i. e. adversus homines, quos videtis sævire in nos. Vasa sunt, alius utitur: organa sunt, alius tangit") **against blood and flesh** (i. e. men: see reff.), **but** (see above) **against the governments, against the powers** (see note on ch. i. 21), **against the world-rulers** (*munditenentes*, as Tert. c. Marc. v. 18, vol. ii. p. 58. Cf. John xii. 31 note, xiv. 30, xvi. 11, 2 Cor. iv. 4, 1 John v. 19. The Rabbis [see Schottg.] adopted this very word קוסמוקרטור, and applied it partly to earthly kings [as on Gen. xiii.], partly to the Angel of Death, 'quamvis te feci κοσμοκράτορα super homines, &c.' So that the word must be literally understood, as in the places cited. Cf. Ellicott's note) **of this** (state of) **darkness** (see ch. ii. 2, v. 8, 11),

τούτου, πρὸς τὰ [t] πνευματικὰ τῆς [u] πονηρίας ἐν τοῖς
[v] ἐπουρανίοις. 13 διὰ τοῦτο [w] ἀναλάβετε τὴν [x] πανοπλίαν
τοῦ θεοῦ, ἵνα δυνηθῆτε [y] ἀντιστῆναι ἐν τῇ [z] ἡμέρᾳ τῇ [z] πο-
νηρᾷ καὶ ἅπαντα [a] κατεργασάμενοι στῆναι. 14 στῆτε οὖν

t ch v 19 reff constr see note, here only u Matt. xxii 18 Mark vii 22 Luke xi 39 Acts iii 26 Rom i 29 1 Cor v 8 only Ps cxl 4 v ch i 3 reff w Acts vii 43 xx 13, 14 xxiii 31 2 Tim iv 11 Deut i 41 Jer xxvi (xlvi) 3 x ver 11 reff y Matt v 39 al Paul, Rom ix 19 al6 abs, here only Esth ix 2 Nah i 6 z ch v 16 reff a = Rom vii 15, 17, &c xv 18 al Paul only, exc James i 3 (20 v r). 1 Pet iv 3.

13. κατεργασμενοι A om στηναι and ουν ver 14 D¹F Cypr

against the spiritual (armies) (so we have [Mey] τὸ πολιτικόν [Herod. vii. 103], τὸ ἱππικόν [Rev. ix 16], τὰ λῃστρικά [Polyæn v 14], τὰ δοῦλα, τὰ αἰχμάλωτα &c. Winer, Gr § 34, note 3, compares τὰ δαιμόνια, originally a neuter-adjective form See Bernhardy, Synt. p. 326, for more examples Stier maintains the abstract meaning, '*the spiritual things*' but as Ellic. remarks, the meaning could not be '*spiritales malignitates*,' as Beza, but '*spiritualia nequitiæ*,' as the Vulg, i. e '*the spiritual elements*,' or '*properties*,' '*of wickedness*,' which will not suit here) **of wickedness in the heavenly places** (but *what is the meaning?* Chrys connects **ἐν τοῖς ἐπουρανίοις** with ἡ πάλη ἐστὶν—ἐν τοῖς ἐπ ἡ μάχη κεῖται . . . . ὡς ἂν εἰ ἔλεγεν, ἡ συνθήκη ἐν τίνι κεῖται; ἐν χρυσῷ. And so Thdrt, Phot., Œc., al. But it is plain that ἐν will not bear this [Chrys says, τὸ ἐν, ὑπέρ ἐστι, καὶ τὸ ἐν, διά ἐστι], though possibly the order of the sentence might Ruckert, Matth, Eadie, al, interpret of the *scene of the combat*, thus also joining ἐν τ ἐπ. with ἔστ ἡμ ἡ πάλη The objection to this is twofold. 1) that the words thus appear without any sort of justification in the context · nay rather as a weakening of the following διὰ τοῦτο, instead of a strengthening. and 2) that according to Eadie's argument, they stultify themselves. He asks, "How can they [the heavenly places, the scenes of divine blessing, of Christ's exaltation, &c] be the seat or abode of impure fiends?" But if they are "*the scene of*" our "*combat*" with these fiends, how can our enemies be any where else but in them? Two ways then remain to join **ἐν τοῖς ἐπουρ.** a) with **τὰ πνευματικὰ τῆς πονηρίας**—b) with **τῆς πονηρίας** only The absence of an article before **ἐν** forms of course an objection to both but not to both equally. Were b) to be adopted, the specifying **τῆς** would appear to be required – because the sense would be, '*of that wickedness*,' viz, the rebellion of the fallen angels, '*which was* (or is) *in the heavenly places*' If a), we do not so imperatively require the τά before ἐν, because ἐν τοῖς ἐπουρ only specifies the locality,—does not distinguish τὰ πνευματικὰ τῆς πονηρ ἐν τοῖς ἐπουρ from any other πνευματικὰ τῆς πονηρίας elsewhere So that this is in grammar the least objectionable rendering And in sense it is, notwithstanding what Eadie and others have said, equally unobjectionable. That habitation of the evil spirits which in ch ii 2 was said, when speaking of mere matters of fact, to be in the ἀήρ, is, now that the difficulty and importance of the Christian conflict is being forcibly set forth, represented as ἐν τοῖς ἐπουρανίοις—over us, and too strong for us without the panoply of God Cf. τὰ πετεινὰ τοῦ οὐρανοῦ, Matt vi 26, and reff) **13**] **Wherefore** (since our foes are in power too mighty for us,—and in dwelling, around and above us) **take up** (i e not 'to the battle,' but 'to put on:' 'frequens est ἀναλαμβάνειν de armis,' Kypke in loc He refers to Diod Sic. xx 33, ἕκαστοι τὰς πανοπλίας ἀνελάμβανον ἐπὶ τὴν τοῦ φονεύσαντος τιμωρίαν,—and many places in Josephus. See also Wetst) **the entire armour of God** (see on ver. 11) **that ye may be able to withstand in the evil day** (not as Chrys., ἡμέραν πονηρὰν τὸν παρόντα βίον φησί – for then the evil day would be upon the Christian before he has on the armour; the ἀεὶ ὁπλίζεσθε of Chr, if taken literally, would be but a poor posture of defence. Nor again can his view stand, ἀπὸ τοῦ χρόνου παραμυθεῖται· βραχύς, φησίν, ὁ καιρός—evidently no such point is raised in the following exhortations, but rather the contrary is implied—a long and weary conflict. The right interpretation is well given by Bengel—"Bellum est perpetuum. pugna alio die minus, alio magis fervet *Dies malus*, vel ingruente morte, vel in vita longior, brevior, in se ipso sæpe varius, ubi Malus vos invadit, et copiæ malignæ vos infestant, ver 12"), **and having accomplished all things** (requisite to the combat being fully equipped and having bravely fought. The words

[bc] περιζωσάμενοι τὴν [bd] ὀσφὺν ὑμῶν [e] ἐν ἀληθείᾳ, καὶ [f] ἐν- ABDF KLℵ a b c e f g h k l m n o 17
δυσάμενοι τὸν [g] θώρακα τῆς δικαιοσύνης, 15 καὶ [h] ὑποδη-
σάμενοι τοὺς πόδας [e] ἐν [i] ἑτοιμασίᾳ τοῦ [j] εὐαγγελίου τῆς

b Luke xii 35 Exod xii 11 see 1 Pet i 13
c Paul, here only Luke xii 35, 37 xvii 8 Rev i 13 xv 6 only Ps lxiv 6 Dan x 5
d as above (b) Matt iii 4. Mark i 6 Acts ii 30 Heb vii 5, 10 only Isa xi 5
e Matt xi 8 f L John xix 40 1 Tim ii 9 1 Cor iv 21 1 Chron xv 27 vat
f ch iv 24 reff
g 1 Thess v 8 Rev ix 9, 17 only Isa lix 17
h Mark vi 9 Acts xii 8 only 2 Chron xxviii 15
i here only — Ps ix 37 see Ezra ii 68
j here only see Matt iv 23. Acts xx 24. Rom x 15, from Isa lii 7

14 περιεζωσμενοι D[1]F Naz Chr.

must not be taken in the sense of, '*omnibus debellatis*,' as if **κατεργασάμενοι** = καταπολεμήσαντες [so Chrys. — ἅπαντα —τουτέστι, καὶ πάθη κ. ἐπιθυμίας ἀτόπους κ τὰ ἐνοχλοῦντα ἡμῖν ἅπαντα], nor again, understood of *preparation* only [= παρασκευασάμενοι, 1 Cor. xiv. 8] as Erasm, Beza, Bengel, al. To finish, or accomplish, is the invariable Pauline usage of the word when taken in a good sense) **to stand firm** (at your post as Estius, reporting others,—'ut posteaquam omnia quæ boni militis sunt, perfeceritis, stare et subsistere possitis '—that you may not, after having done your duty well in battle, fall off, but stand your ground to the end The other interpretation, 'stare tanquam triumphatores,' is precluded by what has been said above) **14—20**] *Particulars of the armour, and attitude of the soldier.* **14**] **Stand therefore** (whether 'ready for the fight,' or 'in the fight,' matters very little. all the aoristic participles are in time antecedent to the στῆτε—and the fight ever at hand), **having girt about your loins with** (ἐν, not instrumental, but *local* the girt person is within, surrounded by, the girdle. but this is necessarily expressed in English by '*with*') **truth** (not *truth objective*, which is rather the ῥῆμα θεοῦ below, ver. 17: but '*truthfulness*,' subjective truth to be understood however as based upon the faith and standing of a Christian, necessarily *his* truthfulness *in his place in Christ*. As the girdle [hardly here, however true that may have been, to be regarded as carrying the sword, for that would be confusing the separate images, cf ver 17] kept all together, so that an ungirded soldier would be (see Mey) a contradiction in terms —just so Truth is the band and expediter of the Christian's work in the conflict, without which all his armour would be but encumbrance Gurnall's notion [Christian Armour, vol. i p 378], that 'the girdle is used as an ornament, put on uppermost, to cover the joints of the armour, which would, if seen, cause some uncomeliness' [see also Harl 'sie ist des Christen Schmuck'], is against the context, and against the use of the phrase **ζωνν τ. ὀσφ.** in the N. T), **and having put on the breastplate of righteousness** (see ref. Isa, and Wisd v. 19 As in those passages, righteousness *is* the breastplate—the genitive here being one of apposition. The righteousness spoken of is that of Rom. vi. 13—the purity and uprightness of Christian character which is the result of the work of the Spirit of Christ; the inwrought righteousness of Christ, not merely the imputed righteousness), **and having shod your feet** (as the soldier with his sandals—cf. the frequent description of arming in Homer—ποσσὶ δ' ὑπαὶ λιπαροῖσιν ἐδήσατο καλὰ πέδιλα. The Roman *caliga* may be in the Apostle's mind: see on ver. 11) **with** (local again, not instrumental: see on ver 14) **the** (article omitted after ἐν) **readiness** (the uses of **ἑτοιμασία** ['in classical Greek, ἑτοιμότης, Dem 1268 7.' Mey] in Hellenistic Greek are somewhat curious, and may have a bearing on this passage In Ps ix 17, it has the sense of *inward 'preparedness*,'—τὴν ἑτοιμασίαν τῆς καρδίας [τῶν πενήτων],—of *outward*, in Jos. Antt. x 1. 2, δισχιλίους . . . . ἵππους εἰς ἑτοιμασίαν ὑμῖν παρέχειν ἕτοιμός εἰμι of *preparation*, in an active sense, Wisd. xiii 12, τὰ ἀποβλήματα τῆς ἐργασίας εἰς ἑτοιμασίαν τροφῆς ἀναλώσας ἐνεπλήσθη in Ezra ii 68, it answers to the Heb. מְכוֹן, a foundation, τοῦ στῆσαι αὐτὸν (the temple) ἐπὶ τὴν ἑτοιμασίαν αὐτοῦ, see also Ps lxxxviii. 14, δικαιοσ. κ κρίμα ἑτοιμασία τοῦ θρόνου σου, and Dan xi 7 Theod. From this latter usage [which can hardly be a mistake of the translators, as Mey. supposes] some [Beza, Bengel. al] have believed that as the **ὑποδήματα** are the lowest part of the panoply, the same meaning has place here but no good sense seems to me to be gained for we could not explain it 'pedes militis Christiani *firmantur Evangelio*, ne loco moveatur,' as Beng Nor again can it mean the *preparation* (*active*) of the Gospel, or *preparedness* to preach the Gospel, as Chrys. and most Commentators ['shod as ready messengers of the glad tidings of peace,' Conyb], for the persons addressed were not teachers, but the whole church.

[j] εἰρήνης, 16 [k] ἐπὶ πᾶσιν [l] ἀναλαβόντες τὸν [m] θυρεὸν τῆς
πίστεως, [n] ἐν ᾧ δυνήσεσθε πάντα τὰ [o] βέλη τοῦ [p] πονηροῦ
[τὰ] [q] πεπυρωμένα [r] σβέσαι. 17 καὶ τὴν [s] περικεφαλαίαν
τοῦ [t] σωτηρίου [u] δέξασθε, καὶ τὴν [v] μάχαιραν τοῦ πνεύμα-

k Luke iii 20 xvi 26 2 Cor. vii 4. Col iii 14 1 Thess iii 7, 9 ἐν, = 2 Tim iv 5 Tit ii 9 Heb xiii 28. 1 Pet iv. 11

l ver 13 reff m here only 2 Kings i 21 n simply local, see note o here only. 4 Kings ix 24 p = Matt. (v 37?) xiii 19 (2 Thess iii 3?) 1 John ii 13 v 18 q 1 Cor vii 9 2 Cor xi 29 2 Pet iii 12 Rev i 15 iii 18 only Prov x 20 r Matt xii 20 (from Isa xlii 3) xxv 8 Mark ix 44, &c 1 Thess v 19 Heb xi 34 Job xvi 15 s 1 Thess v 8 only Isa lix 17 t Luke ii 30 iii 6 Acts xxviii 28 (Paul) only Isa lx 6 (-ιος, Tit ii 11) u = Luke ii 28 xvi 6, 7 xxii 17 only v Heb iv 12 al fr Prov. xii 18

16 ἐν BℵN m 17 latt Method, Naz Cyr-jer Cypr επι ADFKL rel goth Method, Chr Thdrt Damasc, Jer Ambst δυνασθε D¹F: δυνησεσθαι ℵ. om 2nd τα BD¹F · ins AD²KLℵ rel.
17. om δεξασθε D¹F Cypr Tert. (δεξασθαι AD³K a b c e f g h l m o 17.)

The only refuge then is in the genitive subjective, '*the preparedness of*,' i. e. arising from, suggested by, '*the Gospel of peace*,' and so Œc. [2], Calv., Harl., Olsh, De W, Mey., Ellic.. al) **of the Gospel of peace** (the Gospel whose message and spirit is peace · so *ὁ μῦθος ὁ τῆς ἐπιστήμης*, Plat. Theæt. p 147 c · see Bernhardy, p. 161), **besides all** (not as E. V. '*above* all,' as if it were the most important nor as Beng, al '*over all*,' so as to cover all that has been put on before —see especially reff. to Luke. And the *all*, as no *τούτοις* is specified, does not apply only to 'quæcunque indu*istis*' [Beng.], but generally, to all things whatever But it is perhaps doubtful, whether **ἐν πᾶσιν** ought not to be read in which case it will be "*in all things*," i. e. on all occasions) **having taken up** (see on ver 13) **the shield** (*θυρεός*, 'scutum ' *οἷόν τις θύρα φυλάττων τὸ σῶμα* the large oval shield, as distinguished from the small and light buckler, *ἀσπίς*, 'clypeus ' Polybius in his description [vi 23] of the Roman armour, which should by all means be read with this passage, says of the *θυρεός*,—*οὗ τὸ μὲν πλάτος ἐστὶ τῆς κυρτῆς ἐπιφανείας πένθ' ἡμιποδίων τὸ δὲ μῆκος, ποδῶν τεττάρων* Kypke quotes from Plutarch, that Philopœmen persuaded the Achæans, *ἀντὶ μὲν θυρεοῦ καὶ δόρατος ἀσπίδα λαβεῖν καὶ σάρισσαν.* He adduces examples from Josephus of the same distinction,— which Phryn p 366, ed. Lob, states to have been unknown to the ancients, as well as *θυρεός* in this sense at all See Lobeck's note, and Hom Od. ι 240) **of** (genitive of apposition) **faith, in which** (as lighting on it and being quenched in it, or perhaps [as Ellic altern with the above], "as protected by and under cover of which") **you shall be able** (not as Mey, to be referred to the last great future fight—but used as stronger than 'in which ye may,' &c, implying the certainty that the shield of faith will at all times and in all combats quench &c.) **to quench all the fiery darts** (cf. Ps. vii 13, *τὰ βέλη αὐτοῦ τοῖς καιομένοις ἐξειργάσατο* · —Herod viii 52, *ὅκως στυπεῖον περὶ τοὺς ὀιστοὺς περιθέντες ἅψειαν, ἐτόξευον ἐς τὸ φράγμα.* —Thucyd ii 75, *καὶ προκαλύμματα εἶχε δέῤῥεις καὶ διφθέρας, ὥστε τοὺς ἐργαζομένους καὶ τὰ ξύλα μήτε* **πυρφόροις ὀιστοῖς** *βάλλεσθαι, εἰς ἀσφάλειάν τε εἶναι*, and other examples in Wetst Apollodorus, Bibl. ii. 4, uses the very expression, *τὴν ὕδραν* . . *βαλὼν* **βέλεσι πεπυρωμένοις** . . Appian calls them *πυρφόρα τοξεύματα* The Latin name was *malleoli*. Ammianus Marcellin. describes them as cane arrows, with a head in the form of a distaff filled with lighted material. Wetst. ib. The idea of Hammond, Bochart, al., that *poisoned* darts are meant ['*causing fever*'], is evidently ungrammatical. See Smith's Dict of Antiq art Malleolus, and Winer, RWB 'Bogen.' If the art. *τά* be omitted, a different turn must be given to the participle, which then becomes predicative and we must render, '*when inflamed*,' even in their utmost malice and fiery power) **of the wicked one** (see reff and notes on Matt. v. 37, John xvii 15 Here, the conflict being personal, the adversary must be not an abstract principle, but a concrete person).

17] **And take** ('accipite oblatam a Domino.' Beng) **the helmet** (*πρὸς δὲ τούτοις περικεφαλαία χαλκῆ.* Polyb. ubi supra) **of** (genitive of apposition as above) **salvation** (the neuter form, from LXX l c · otherwise confined to St Luke. Beng takes it masculine, '*salutaris*, i e. Christi,'—but this is harsh, and does not correspond to the parallel, 1 Thess v 8, where the helmet is the hope of salvation, clearly shewing its subjective character. Here, it is *salvation appropriated*, by faith), **and the sword of** (furnished, forged, by cf. *τ πανοπλ τ θεοῦ* vv. 11, 13 : not

w ch. v. 26 reff. x Rom. iv. 11. 2 Cor. ii. 4. ix. 12 al. fr. y Phil. iv. 6. 1 Tim. ii. 1. v. 5. 2 Chron. vi. 19 al. z 1 Chron. xxi. 36 only. Ps. xxxiii. 1. a ch. ii. 22 reff.

ABDF KLℵ a b c e f g h k l m n o 17

τος, ὅ ἐστιν ʷ ῥῆμα θεοῦ, 18 ˣ διὰ πάσης ʸ προσευχῆς καὶ
ʸ δεήσεως προσευχόμενοι ᶻ ἐν παντὶ ᶻ καιρῷ ᵃ ἐν πνεύματι,
καὶ ᵇ εἰς αὐτὸ ᶜ ἀγρυπνοῦντες ἐν πάσῃ ᵈ προσκαρτερήσει καὶ
ʸ δεήσει περὶ πάντων τῶν ᵉ ἁγίων 19 καὶ ὑπὲρ ἐμοῦ, ἵνα μοι
δοθῇ ᶠ λόγος ᵍ ἐν ʰ ἀνοίξει τοῦ στόματός μου ⁱ ἐν ⁱ παῤῥησίᾳ

b (w. τοῦτο, Rom. ix. 17. xiii. 6. 2 Cor. v. 5. ver. 22. Col. iv. 8.) εἰς, — 1 Pet. iv. 7. c Mark xiii. 33. Luke xxi. 36. Heb. xiii. 17 only. Cant. v. 2. (-πνία, 2 Cor. v. 5.) d here only †. (-ρεῖν, Col. iv. 2.) e ch. i. 1 reff. f = 1 Cor. xii. 8. g see note. h here only †. (-γειν τ. στ., Matt. v. 2. Acts viii. 35. x. 34 al. Ezek. xvi. 63.) i Phil. i. 20. Col. ii. 15. — Paul only. π., ch. iii. 12 reff.

18. rec aft αυτο ins τουτο (*explanatory expansion of αυτο. αυτον speaks also for the reading of but one word*), with D³KL rel Chr-txt Thdrt Damasc-txt al. om ABℵ 17 copt goth Bas Chr₂ Damasc₁. αυτον D¹F, *in illum* G-lat, *in illo* D-lat, *in ipso* vulg (and F-lat). aft αγρυπνουντες ins παντοτε DF Syr goth Bas. om προσκαρτερησει και D¹F. ins τη bef δεησει D¹. for περι, υπερ D¹F m syr Thdrt.

19. μοι bef δοθη ℵ¹: txt ℵ³. rec (for δοθη) δοθειη (with none of our mss). txt

here the genitive of apposition, for ὅ ἐστιν follows after) **the Spirit, which** (neuter, attracted to ῥῆμα: see ch. iii. 13 and reff. there) **is** (see on ἐστιν, Gal. iv. 24 reff.) **the word of God** (the Gospel: see the obvious parallel, Heb. iv. 12: also Rom. i. 16: and our pattern for the use of this sword of the Spirit, Matt. iv. 4, 7, 10), **with** (see reff.: as the state through which, as an instrument, the action takes place. The clause depends on στῆτε οὖν, the principal imperative of the former sentence—not on δέξασθε, which is merely a subordinate one, and which besides [Mey.] would express only how the weapons should be *taken*, and therefore would not satisfy πάσης and ἐν παντὶ καιρῷ) **all** (kind of) **prayer and supplication** ("it has been doubted whether there is any exact distinction between προσευχή and δέησις. Chrys. and Thdrt. on 1 Tim. ii. 1 explain προσευχή as αἴτησις ἀγαθῶν [see Suicer, Thes. s. v. 1],—δέησις as ὑπὲρ ἀπαλλαγῆς λυπηρῶν ἱκετεία [so Grot. as ἀπὸ τοῦ δέους, but see 2 Cor. i. 11]: compare Orig. de Orat. c. 33 [vol. i. p. 271]. Alii alia. The most natural and obvious distinction is that adopted by nearly all recent Commentators, viz. that προσευχή is a 'vocabulum sacrum' (see Harl.) denoting prayer in general, '*precatio*:' δέησις a 'vocabulum commune,' denoting a special character or form of it, 'petitum,' *rogatio*: see Fritz. Rom. x. 1, vol. ii. p. 372: Huther on Tim. l. c." Ellicott) **praying in every season** (literal: cf. Luke xviii. 1 note, and 1 Thess. v. 17. There seems to be an allusion to our Lord's ἐν παντὶ καιρῷ δεόμενοι, ref. Luke) **in the Spirit** (the Holy Spirit: see especially Jude 20, and Rom. viii. 15, 26; Gal. iv. 6 —not, *heartily*, as Est., Grot., al.), **and thereunto** (with reference to their employment which has been just mentioned. Continual habits of prayer cannot be kept up without watchfulness to that very end. This is better than to understand it, with Chr., &c. of persistence in the prayer itself, which indeed comes in presently) **watching in** (element in which the watching, being employed, in) **all** (kind of) **importunity and supplication** (not a hendiadys: rather the latter substantive is explanatory of the former, without losing its true force as coupled to it: '*importunity and* [accompanied with, i. e. exemplified by] *supplication*') **concerning all saints, and** (καί brings into prominence a particular included in the general: see Hartung, i. 145) **for me** (certainly it seems that some distinction between ὑπέρ and περί should be marked: see Eadie's note, where however he draws it too strongly. Kruger, § 68. 28. 3, regards the two in later writers as synonymous. So Meyer, who quotes Demosth. p. 71. 35, μὴ περὶ τῶν δικαίων μηδ' ὑπὲρ τῶν ἔξω πραγμάτων εἶναι τὴν βουλήν, ἀλλ' ὑπὲρ τῶν ἐν τῇ χώρᾳ; and Xen. Mem. i. 1. 17, ὑπὲρ τούτων περὶ αὐτοῦ παραγνῶναι) **that** (aim of the ὑπὲρ ἐμοῦ) **there may be given me** (I do not see the relevance of a special emphasis on δοθῇ as Mey., Ellic. That it is a *gift*, would be of course, if it were prayed for from God) **speech in the opening of my mouth** (many renderings have been proposed. First of all, the words must be joined with the preceding, not with the following, as in E. V., Grot., Kypke, De W., al., which would [see below] be too tame and prosaic for the solemnity of the passage. Œc. (and similarly Chr.? see Ellic.) regards the words as describing *unpremeditated* speech: ἐν αὐτῷ τῷ ἀνοῖξαι ὁ λόγος προϊῄει. But as Mey., this cer-

[k] γνωρίσαι τὸ [k] μυστήριον τοῦ εὐαγγελίου, 20 ὑπὲρ οὗ
[l] πρεσβεύω ἐν [m] ἁλύσει, ἵνα [n] ἐν αὐτῷ [o] παῤῥησιάσωμαι
[p] ὡς δεῖ με λαλῆσαι.
21 [r] Ἵνα δὲ εἰδῆτε καὶ ὑμεῖς [q] τὰ κατ᾽ ἐμέ, [r] τί πράσσω,

k ch i 9 (reff). l 2 Cor v 20 only + (-εια, Luke xiv 32.) m Mark v 3, &c ‖ L. Acts xii 6, 7 xxi 33. xxviii 20. 2 Tim i 16 Rev xx 1 only † Wisd xvii 17 only. Exod xxviii 22 Aq Symm Theod n see note o Acts ix 27 al (6) 1 Thess ii 2 only L.P. Prov xx 9 al p Col iv 4 q Col iv 7 reff [illegible] = ch i 15 r = here only

ABDFKLℵ rel. om του ευαγγελιου BF (Tert) Ambrst.
20. παρρησιασωμαι bef εν αυτω ℵ for εν αυτω, αυτο B
21 και υμεις bef ειδητε ADFℵ latt Thdrt. om και υμεις 17 txt BKL rel syrr basm

tainly would have been expressed by *ἐν αὐτῇ τῇ ἀν* or the like. Calv., 'os apertum cupit, quod erumpat in liquidam et firmam confessionem: ore enim semiclauso proferuntur ambigua et perplexa responsa,' and similarly Rück., al., and De W. But this again is laying too much on the phrase: see below. The same objection applies to Beza and Piscator's rendering, 'ut aperiam os meum:' and to taking the phrase of an opening of his mouth *by God*, as [Chrys. *ἡ ἅλυσις ἐπίκειται τὴν παῤῥησίαν ἐπιστομίζουσα, ἀλλ᾽ ἡ εὐχὴ ἡ ὑμετέρα ἀνοίγει μου τὸ στόμα, ἵνα πάντα ἃ ἐπέμφθην εἰπεῖν, εἴπω*] Corn.-a-lap., Grot., Harl., and Olsh. from Ps. l. 17 and Ezek. xxix. 21. The best rendering is that of Est. ['dum os meum aperio'], Meyer, Eadie, Ellic., al., '*in* [at] *the opening of my mouth*,' i. e. 'when I undertake to speak:' thus we keep the meaning of *ἀνοίγειν τὸ στόμα* [reff. and Job iii. 1, Dan. x. 16], which always carries some solemnity of subject or occasion with it), **in boldness** ([subjective] freedom of speech, not as Grot. ['ut ab hac custodia militari liber per omnem urbem perferre possem sermonem evangelicum,' &c.], Koppe [objective], *liberty of speech*) **to make known** (the purpose of the gift of *λόγος ἐν ἀνοίξει τοῦ στόματος*) **the mystery of the gospel** (contained in the gospel: subjective genitive. 'The genitive is somewhat different to *τὸ μυστήρ. τοῦ θελήματος*, ch. i. 9: there it was the mystery in the matter of, concerning the *θέλημα*, gen. objecti,' Ellic.), **on behalf of which** (viz. *τοῦ μυστ. τοῦ εὐαγγ.*—for as Meyer remarks, this is the object of **γνωρίσαι**, and **γνωρίσαι** is pragmatically bound to **πρεσβεύω**) **I am an ambassador** (*of Christ* [ref.], *to whom*, is understood: we need not supply as Michaelis, to the court of Rome) **in chains** (the singular is not to be pressed, as has been done by Paley, Wieseler, al., to signify the chain by which he was bound to 'the soldier that kept him' [Acts xxviii. 20]: for such singulars are often used collectively: see Bernhardy, Syntax, p. 58 f., Polyb. xxi. 3. 3, *παρὰ μικρὸν εἰς τὴν ἅλυσιν ἐνέπεσον*. Wetst. remarks, 'alias legati, jure gentium sancti et inviolabiles, in vinculis haberi non poterant.' His being thus a captive ambassador, was all the more reason why they should pray earnestly that he might have boldness, &c.), **that** (co-ordinate purpose with **ἵνα δοθῇ**, not subordinate to **πρεσβεύω**. See examples of such a co-ordinate **ἵνα** in Rom. vii. 13, Gal. iii. 14, 2 Cor. ix. 3. But no tautology [as Harl.] is involved: see below) **in** (the matter of, in dealing with: cf. *λήθη ἐν τοῖς μαθήμασι*, Plat. Phileb. p. 252 B., and see Bernhardy, p. 212: not as in 1 Thess. ii. 2, *ἐπαῤῥησιασάμεθα ἐν τῷ θεῷ ἡμῶν*, where *ἐν* denotes the source or ground of the confidence) **it I may speak freely, as I ought to speak** (no comma at *με*, as Koppe—'*that I may have confidence, as I ought, to speak*,' but the idea of speaking being already half understood in *παῤῥησίᾳ*, *λαλῆσαι* merely refers back to it. This last clause is a further qualification of the *παῤῥησία*—that it is a courage and free-spokenness *ὡς δεῖ* and therefore involves no tautology).

21—24.] CONCLUSION OF THE EPISTLE.

21.] **But** (transition to another subject: the contrast being between his more solemn occupations just spoken of, and his personal welfare) **that ye also** (the *καί* may have two meanings: 1) as *I* have been going at length into the matters concerning *you*, so if *you also* on your part, wish to know my matters, &c.: 2) it may relate to some others whom the same messenger was to inform, and to whom he had previously written. If so, it would be an argument for the priority of the Epistle to the Colossians [so Harl. p. lx, Mey., Wieseler, and Wiggers's Stud. u. Krit. 1841, p. 432]: for that was sent by Tychicus, and a similar sentiment occurs there, iv. 7. But I prefer the former meaning) **may know the matters concerning me, how I fare** (not, '*what I am doing*,' as Wolf: Meyer answers well, that he was always doing *one thing*: but as in Ælian, V. H. ii. 35, where

s Col. iv. 7, 9. James i. 16, 19. ii. 5. 2 Pet. iii. 15. see ch. v. 1 reff. 1 Cor. xv. 58.
t Col. i. 7. iv. 7.
u Eph. iii. 7 reff.
v ch. ii. 21. iv. 1. Rom. xvi. 11, 12 al. P.
w see ver. 18 reff.
x = 2 Cor. i. 4 (3ce) al. fr. Isa. lxvi. 13.
y 2 Cor. xiii. 13. 1 Thess. iii. 6. Jude 2.
z Gal. i. 1 reff.
a absol., Col. iv. 18 reff.

πάντα ὑμῖν [k] γνωρίσει Τύχικος ὁ [s] ἀγαπητὸς [s] ἀδελφὸς ABDF KLℵ a b c e f g h k l m n o 17
καὶ [t] πιστὸς [tu] διάκονος [v] ἐν κυρίῳ, 22 ὃν ἔπεμψα πρὸς ὑμᾶς
[w] εἰς αὐτὸ τοῦτο, ἵνα γνῶτε τὰ περὶ ἡμῶν καὶ [x] παρακαλέσῃ τὰς καρδίας ὑμῶν.
23 Εἰρήνη τοῖς ἀδελφοῖς καὶ [y] ἀγάπη μετὰ πίστεως ἀπὸ
[z] θεοῦ [z] πατρὸς καὶ κυρίου Ἰησοῦ χριστοῦ. 24 ἡ [a] χάρις
μετὰ πάντων τῶν ἀγαπώντων τὸν κύριον ἡμῶν Ἰησοῦν
χριστὸν ἐν [b] ἀφθαρσίᾳ.

ΠΡΟΣ ΕΦΕΣΙΟΥΣ.

b Rom. ii. 7. 1 Cor. xv. 42, 50, 53, 54. 2 Tim. i. 10 (Tit. ii. 7 v. r.) only. P.+ Wisd. ii. 23. vi. 18, 19 only.

Chr Damasc Jer Ambrst. om *παντα* D[1]F Syr. *γνωρισει* bef *υμιν* (*see Col* iv. 7) BDF m 17 fuld goth Ambrst: txt AKL(ℵ) rel vulg syr Chr Thdrt Damasc Jer. —ℵ[1] wrote *υ* bef *γνωρ.* but marked it for erasure: ℵ[3] added *μιν* but obliterated it. om *διακονος* ℵ[1]: ins ℵ-corr[1].

23. for *αγαπη*, *ελεος* A.

24. rec at end ins *αμην*, with DKLℵ[3] rel vss gr-lat-ff: om ABFℵ[1] 17. 67[2] æth Jer[1] Ambrst.

SUBSCRIPTION. rec adds *απο ρωμης δια τυχικου*, with KL rel D[2]-lat syrr copt Chr Thdrt Euthal; *εγραφη απο ρωμης* B[2]: no subscr in l: txt AB[1]D 17, also F(prefixing *ετελεσθη*), and ℵ(adding *στιχων τιβ'*).

Gorgias being sick is asked *τί πράττοι*; or as in Plut. inst. Lac. p. 241 [Kypke], where when a Spartan mother asks her son *τί πράσσει πατρίς*; he answers, 'all have perished') **Tychicus** (Acts xx. 4. Col. iv. 7. 2 Tim. iv. 12. Tit. iii. 12. He appears in the first-cited place amongst Paul's companions to Asia from Corinth, classed with **Τρόφιμος** as **Ἀσιανοί**. Nothing more is known of him) **shall make known all to you, the beloved brother** (reff.) **and faithful** (trustworthy) **servant** ('*minister*' is ambiguous, and might lead to the idea of Estius, who says on '*in Domino*,'—'non male hinc colligitur Tychicum sacra ordinatione diaconum fuisse:' see Col. iv. 7, where he is *πιστὸς διάκονος καὶ σύνδουλος*, and note there) **in the Lord** (belongs to **διάκονος**, not to both **ἀδ.** and **διάκ.** He *διηκόνει ἐν κυρίῳ*, Christ's work being the field on which his labour was bestowed); **whom I sent to you for this very purpose** (not '*for the same purpose*,' as E. V.) **that ye may know the matters respecting us** (see Col. iv. 8, where this verse occurs word for word, but with *ἵνα γνῷ τὰ περὶ ὑμῶν* for these words. Does not this variation bear the mark of genuineness with it? The *ἡμῶν* are those mentioned Col. iv. 10) **and that he may comfort** (we need not assign a reason why they wanted comfort:—there would probably be many in those times of peril) **your hearts.** **23, 24.**] *Double* APOSTOLIC BLESSING; addressed (23) to the brethren, and (24) to all real lovers of the Lord Jesus Christ. **23.**] **Peace** (need not be further specified, as is done by some:—the Epistle has no special conciliatory view. It is sufficiently described by being *peace from God*) **to the brethren** (of the Church or Churches addressed: see Prolegg. to this Epistle, § ii.: not as Wieseler, **ἀδελφοῖς** to the Jews, and **πάντων** below to the Gentiles: for least of all in this Epistle would such a distinction be found) **and love with faith** (faith is perhaps presupposed as being theirs: and he prays that love may always accompany it, see Gal. v. 6: or both are invoked on them, see 1 Tim. i. 14) **from God the Father and the Lord Jesus Christ** (see note on Rom. i. 7). **24.**] General benediction on all who love Christ: corresponding, as Mey. suggests, with the malediction on all who love Him not, 1 Cor. xvi. 22. **May the grace** (viz. of God, which comes by Christ) **be with all who love our Lord Jesus Christ in incorruptibility** (i. e. whose love is incorruptible. The method of exegesis of this difficult expression will be, to endeavour to find some clue to the idea in the Apostle's mind. He speaks, in Col. ii. 22, of worldly things which are *εἰς φθορὰν τῇ ἀποχρήσει*—*ἄφθαρτος* is with him an epithet of God [Rom. i. 23. 1 Tim. i. 17]: the dead are raised **ἄφθαρτοι** [1 Cor. xv. 52]: the Christian's crown is **ἄφθαρτος**

[1 Cor ix. 25]. **ἀφθαρσία** is always elsewhere in N. T. [reff.] the *incorruptibility* of future immortality. If we seek elsewhere in the Epistles for an illustration of the term as applied to inward qualities, we find a close parallel in 1 Pet. iii. 4; where the ornament of women is to be *ὁ κρυπτὸς τῆς καρδίας ἄνθρωπος ἐν τῷ* **ἀφθάρτῳ** *τοῦ πρᾳέος κ. ἡσυχίου πνεύματος*—the contrast being between the *φθαρτά, ἀργύριον καὶ χρυσίον*, and the *incorruptible* graces of the renewed spiritual man. I believe we are thus led to the meaning here,—that the love spoken of is *ἐν ἀφθαρσίᾳ*,—in, as its sphere and element and condition, *incorruptibility*—not a fleeting earthly love, but a spiritual and eternal one. And thus only is the word worthy to stand as the crown and climax of this glorious Epistle: whereas in the ordinary [E. V.] rendering, '*sincerity*,'—besides that [as Mey.] this would not be *ἀφθαρσία* but *ἀφθορία* [Tit. ii. 7] or *ἀδιαφθορία* [see Wetst. on Tit. l. c.], the Epistle ends with an anti-climax, by lowering the high standard which it has lifted up throughout to an apparent indifferentism, and admitting to the apostolic blessing all those, however otherwise wrong, who are only not hypocrites in their love of Christ. As to the many interpretations,—that *ἐν* is for *ὑπέρ* [Chr. 2nd alt.], *διά* [Thl.], *μετά* [Thdrt.], *εἰς* [Beza], *σύν* [Piscator]—that **ἐν ἀφθαρσίᾳ** is to be taken with *χάρις* [Harl., Bengel, Stier], that **ἐν ἀφθ.** means 'in immortality,' as the sphere of the *ἀγάπη*, cf. *ἐν τοῖς ἐπουρανίοις*, ch. i. 3,—that it is to be joined with **Ἰησοῦ χριστοῦ** ['Christum immortalem et gloriosum, non humilem,' Wetst.], that it is short for *ἵνα ζωὴν ἔχωσιν ἐν ἀφθαρσίᾳ* [Olsh.], &c. &c. [see more in Mey.], none of them seem so satisfactory as that assigned above).

ΠΡΟΣ ΦΙΛΙΠΠΗΣΙΟΥΣ.

a Gal. i. 10 reff. b Eph. i 1 reff. c Rom. xvi. 8. 1 Cor. iv. 15. Gal. iii. 28 al. d = Acts xxiii. 15. 1 Cor. i. 2. 2 Cor. i. 1.

I. 1 Παῦλος καὶ Τιμόθεος, [a] δοῦλοι χριστοῦ Ἰησοῦ, ABDF
πᾶσιν τοῖς [b] ἁγίοις [c] ἐν χριστῷ Ἰησοῦ τοῖς οὖσιν ἐν Φιλ- KLℵ a b c e f g
ίπποις [d] σὺν [e] ἐπισκόποις καὶ [f] διακόνοις. 2 χάρις ὑμῖν h k l m n o 17

e Acts xx. 28. 1 Tim. iii. 2. Tit. i. 7. 1 Pet. ii. 25 only. 2 Chron. xxxiv. 12. f = Rom. xvi. 1. 1 Tim. iii. 8, 12.

Title. Steph η προς τους φιλιππησιους επιστολη: elz παυλου του αποστολου η προς φιλιππησιους επιστολη, with rel: πρ. φ. επιστ. h k: επ. πρ. φ. l: του αγιου αποστολου παυλου επιστολη προς φιλιππησιους L: ταυτ' αγορευει παυλος φιλιππησιοισιν f: αρχεται πρ. φ. DF: txt ABKℵ m n o 17.

Chap. I. 1. rec ιησ. bef χρ., with FKL rel syrr Chr Thdrt: txt BDℵ coptt. (A uncert.) for σὺν ἐπισκ,, συνεπισκόποις B²D³K 17 Chr Thl Cassiod.

Chap. I. 1, 2.] Address and greeting. 1.] Timotheus seems to be named as being well known to the Philippians (Acts xvi. 3, 10 ff.), and present with St. Paul at this time. The mention is merely formal, as the Apostle proceeds (ver. 3) in the first person singular. Certainly no *official* character is intended to be given by it, as Huther, al., have thought: for of all the Epistles, this is the least official: and those to the Romans and Galatians, where no such mention occurs, the most so. Observe, there is no ἀπόστολος subjoined to Παῦλος (as in Col. i. 1), probably because the Philippians needed no such reminiscence of his authority. Cf. also 1 and 2 Thess. On **δοῦλοι χρ. Ἰησ.**, see Ellicott. **πᾶσιν**] both here and in vv. 4, 7, 8, 25; ch. ii. 17, 26, is best accounted for from the warm affection which breathes through this whole Epistle (see on ver. 3), not from any formal reason, as that the Apostle wishes to put those Philippians who had not sent to his support, on a level in his affection with those who had (Van Hengel),—that he wishes to set himself above all their party divisions (ch. ii. 3: so De W.), &c. **σὺν ἐπισκ.**] This is read by Chrys. **συνεπισκόποις**, and he remarks: *τί τοῦτο; μιᾶς πόλεως πολλοὶ ἐπίσκοποι ἦσαν; οὐδαμῶς· ἀλλὰ τοὺς πρεσβυτέρους οὕτως ἐκάλεσε. ὅτε γὰρ τέως ἐκοινώνουν τοῖς ὀνόμασι, κ. διάκονος ὁ ἐπίσκοπος ἐλέγετο* (see also var. readd.). But thus the construction would be imperfect, the **σύν** having no reference. Theodoret remarks, *ἐπισκόπους τοὺς πρεσβυτέρους καλεῖ· ἀμφότερα γὰρ εἶχον κατ' ἐκεῖνον τὸν καιρὸν ὀνόματα*,—and alleges Acts xx. 28, Tit. i. 5, 7, as shewing the same. See on the whole subject, my note on Acts xx. 17, and the article Bischof, by Jacobson, in Herzog's Realencyclopädie für protestantische Theologie u. Kirche. **κ. διακόνοις**] See on Rom. xii. 7; xvi. 1. Chrys. enquires why he writes *here* to the *κλῆρος* as well as to the *ἅγιοι*, and not in the Epistles to the Romans, or Corinthians, or Ephesians. And he answers it, *ὅτι αὐτοὶ καὶ ἀπέστειλαν, κ. ἐκαρποφόρησαν, κ. αὐτοὶ ἔπεμψαν πρὸς αὐτὸν τὸν Ἐπαφρόδιτον.* But the true reason seems to be, the late date of our Epistle. The ecclesiastical offices were now more plainly distinguished than at

καὶ εἰρήνη ἀπὸ θεοῦ πατρὸς ἡμῶν καὶ Κυρίου Ἰησοῦ
χριστοῦ.
3 [g] Εὐχαριστῶ τῷ θεῷ μου [h] ἐπὶ πάσῃ τῇ [i] μνείᾳ ὑμῶν,
4 πάντοτε ἐν πάσῃ δεήσει μου ὑπὲρ πάντων ὑμῶν [k] μετὰ
χαρᾶς τὴν [l] δέησιν [l] ποιούμενος, 5 [m] ἐπὶ τῇ [n] κοινωνίᾳ ὑμῶν
[n] εἰς τὸ εὐαγγέλιον ἀπὸ τῆς πρώτης ἡμέρας [o] ἄχρι τοῦ νῦν,

g Eph. i. 16 reff. h dat., 2 Cor. iii. 14. vii. 4. Heb. ix. 15, 26. i Eph. i. 16 reff. k Matt. xiii. 20 ‖. Heb. x. 34 al. 1 Chron. xxix. 22. l Luke v. 33. 1 Tim. ii. 1. m = 1 Cor. i. 4 al. n 2 Cor. ix. 13. o Rom. viii. 22. 1 Cor. iv. 11. 2 Cor. iii. 14 al.

3. εγω μεν ευχαριστω τω κυριω ημων επι κ τ λ. D[1]F Ambrst Cassiod.
4. aft πασῃ ins τῃ ℵ[1](ℵ[3] disapproving) c m 80. aft χαρας ins και F harl[2] Thdrt-ms.
5. rec om της, with DFKL rel Chr Thdrt Damasc. ins ABℵ k m.

the time when the two former of those Epistles were written. That to the Ephesians rests on grounds of its own. The simple juxtaposition of the officers with the members of the Church, and indeed *their* being placed *after* those members, shews, as it still seems to me, against Ellicott in loc., the absence of hierarchical views such as those in the Epistles of the apostolic fathers. **2**] See on Rom. i. 7.

3—11] Thanksgiving for their fellowship regarding the Gospel (3—5), confidence that God will continue and perfect the same (6—8), and prayer for their increase in holiness unto the day of Christ (9—11). **3**] See the similar expressions, Rom. i. 9; 1 Cor. i. 4, Eph. i. 16, Col. i. 3, 1 Thess. i. 2, Philem. 4. ἐπί here with a dative is hardly distinguishable in English from the same preposition with a genitive in Rom. i. 10, Eph. i. 16;—**at**, or **in**: the primitive idea of such construction being *addition* by close adherence: 'my whole remembrance of you is *accompanied with* thanks to God.' πάσῃ τῇ μνείᾳ must not be rendered as in E. V. (so even Conyb.) '*every remembrance*,' but **my whole remembrance.** The expression *comprehends in one* all such remembrances: but the article forbids the above rendering: cf. πᾶσα ἡ πόλις, Matt. xxi. 10, also ib. vi. 29, Mark iv. 1; Luke iii. 3. Winer, § 18. 4. Some (Maldon., Bretschn., al.) take ἐπί as assigning the reason for εὐχαριστῶ (as 1 Cor. i. 4), and μνείᾳ ὑμῶν as meaning, '*your remembrance of me*,' viz. in sending me sustenance. But this is evidently wrong: for the ground of εὐχαριστῶ follows, ver. 5. μνεία here, **remembrance**, not '*mention*,' which meaning it only gets by ποιεῖσθαι being joined to it, 'to make an *act of* remembrance,' i. e. to *mention*, Rom. i. 9, Eph. i. 16, 1 Thess. i. 2, Philem. 4. **4**] πάντοτε—πάσῃ—πάντων—here we have the overflowings of a full heart. Render—**always in every prayer of mine making my prayer for you all with joy**: not, as in E. V., '*in every prayer of mine for you all making request with joy*.' For the second δέησις, having the article, is thereby defined to be the *particular* request, ὑπὲρ π. ὑμ.—τὸ μετὰ χαρᾶς μεμνῆσθαι σημεῖον τῆς ἐκείνων ἀρετῆς, Thl., so that the sense is, that every time he prayed, he joyfully offered up that portion of his prayers which was an intercession for them. See Ellic., who defends the other connexion, but has misunderstood my note. **5**] **for** (*ground* of the εὐχ., πάντοτε to ποιούμενος having been *epexegetical* of it) **your fellowship** (with one another: entire accord, unanimous action: not your fellowship *with me*, ὅτι κοινωνοί μου γίνεσθε κ. συμμερισταὶ τῶν ἐπὶ τῷ εὐαγγελίῳ πόνων, Thl.: this must have been further specified, by μετ' ἐμοῦ [1 John i. 3] or the like. Still less must we with Estius, Wetst., al. [and nearly so Chrys.], render ἐπὶ τῇ κοινωνίᾳ, *pro liberalitate vestra erga me*) **as regards the Gospel** (not '*in the Gospel*,' as E. V. and Thdrt., κοινωνίαν δὲ τοῦ εὐαγγελίου τὴν πίστιν ἐκάλεσε: but thus it would be the genitive, and εἰς τὸ εὐ. can hardly be taken as equivalent to it: cf. κοινωνεῖν εἰς, ch. iv. 15. Their mutual accord was *for the purposes of the Gospel*—i. e. the perfecting, of which he proceeds to treat. "The article τῇ is not repeated after ὑμῶν, because κοινωνία εἰς τὸ εὐ. is conceived as one idea, together." Meyer. Ellic. would understand κοιν. as absolute and abstract, 'fellowship,' not 'contribution:' including, without expressly mentioning, 'that particular manifestation of it which so especially marked the liberal and warm-hearted Christians of Philippi:' and it may well be so, even holding my former interpretation: this was the exhibition of their κοινωνία εἰς τὸ εὐαγγ.) **from the first day** (of your receiving it) **until now**. This

6 [p] πεποιθὼς [q] αὐτὸ [q] τοῦτο, [r] ὅτι ὁ [s] ἐναρξάμενος ἐν ὑμῖν
[t] ἔργον [t] ἀγαθὸν [u] ἐπιτελέσει ἄχρι [v] ἡμέρας χριστοῦ Ἰησοῦ,
7 [w] καθώς ἐστιν [x] δίκαιον ἐμοὶ τοῦτο [y] φρονεῖν [z] ὑπὲρ πάν-

ABDF KLℵ a b c e f g h k l m n o 17

p constr., ver. 25. q Acts xxiv. 15, 20. 2 Cor. vii. 11. Gal. ii. 10 al. r aft. τοῦτο, Acts xxiv. 14. Rom. vi. 6 al. fr. Winer, § 23. 5. b. s Gal. iii. 3 only. Deut. ii. 24, 25, 31. t Eph. ii. 10 reff. ἔργ.. = Rom. xiv. 20. u Rom. xv. 28. 2 Cor. vii. 1. viii. 6 al. 1 Kings iii. 12. v 1 Cor. i. 8. 2 Cor. i. 14. ver. 10. ch. ii. 16 al. w = 2 Thess. i. 3. x = 2 Pet. i. 13. y = Gal. v. 10 reff. z = 2 Cor. i. 6 b.

6. rec αχρις, with DFKL rel: αχρι ης A: txt Bℵ a[1]. rec ιησ. bef χρ., with AFKℵ rel am[1](with demid): txt BD c e k n Ambrst Aug.

last clause is by Lachm. and Meyer attached to *πεποιθώς*, but they are surely in error. The reason assigned is, that, if it had belonged to *κοινωνίᾳ*, &c., the article *τῇ* would have been repeated. But the same account which I have quoted from Meyer himself above of its omission after *ὑμῶν* will also apply to its omission here—that the whole *κοινωνία* from the first is taken as one idea, and therefore this feature of it, that it was *ἀπὸ τῆς πρ. ἡμ. ἄχρι τ. νῦν*, need not be specially particularized by the definite article. It is St. Paul's constant habit to place *πέποιθα* first in the sentence (cf. Rom. ii. 19; 2 Cor. ii. 3; Gal. v. 10; ch. ii. 24; 2 Thess. iii. 4; Philem. 26: also Matt. xxvii. 43), pregnant as it is with emphasis, and including the matter of confidence which follows: and we may certainly say that had this clause referred to *πεποιθώς*, it would have followed, not preceded it. Besides which, the emphatic *αὐτὸ τοῦτο* would be rendered altogether vapid, by so long an emphatic clause preceding the verb. Œcum., Beza, and Bengel connect the words with the distantly preceding verb *εὐχαριστῶ*, which (hardly however, as Ellic., on account of the pres. tense and *πάντοτε*) is still more improbable. **πεποιθώς**] parallel with *ποιούμενος*—**being** (i. e. seeing I am) **confident of** . . . **αὐτὸ τοῦτο**] **this very thing** (it points out sharply and emphatically, implying, as here, that the very matter of confidence is one which will ensure the success of the *δέησις*. Conyb. renders it '*accordingly*,' which is far too weak. As regards the construction, *αὐτὸ τοῦτο* is only a secondary accusative, of reference, not governed directly by *πεποιθώς*. It is immediately resolved into *ὅτι ὁ ἐν. κ.τ.λ.*). **6. ὁ ἐναρξ.**] **He who has begun in you a good work,** viz. God: cf. ch. ii. 13. Wakefield, perversely enough, renders, '*he among you who has begun* &c.' By '*a good work*,' he refers his confidence to the *general* character of God as the doer and finisher of good: the one good work in his mind being, their *κοινωνία* &c. *ἐν* is **in**, not '*among*:' but the preposition in **ἐναρξάμενος** seems not to be connected with it, cf. reff., where the verb has an absolute meaning, irrespective of any *immanent* working. The **ἄχρι ἡμέρας χρ. Ἰησοῦ** assumes the nearness of the coming of the Lord (*μέχρι τῆς τοῦ σωτῆρος ἡμῶν ἐπιφανείας*, Thdrt.). Here, as elsewhere, Commentators (even Ellic. recently) have endeavoured to escape from this inference. Thus Thl., Œc., refer the saying not only to the then existing generation of Philippians, but *καὶ τοῖς ἐξ ὑμῶν*: Estius, in the case of each man, '*usque ad mortem suam;*' Calov., understanding not the continuance till the day of Christ, but '*terminus et complementum perfectionis, quod habituri isto die erimus:*' and so nearly Calvin, but saying very beautifully,—'Tametsi enim qui ex corpore mortali sunt liberati, non amplius militent cum carnis concupiscentiis, sintque extra teli jactum ut aiunt: tamen nihil erit absurdi, si dicentur esse in profectu, quia nondum pertigerunt quo aspirant: nondum potiuntur felicitate et gloria quam sperarunt: denique nondum illuxit dies, qui revelet absconditos in spe thesauros. Atque adeo quum de spe agitur, semper ad beatam resurrectionem, tanquam ad scopum, referendi sunt oculi.' Doubtless, this is *our* lesson, and must be our application of such passages: but this surely was not the sense in which the Apostle wrote them. **7.**] *Justification of the above-expressed confidence:*—it was fair and right for him to entertain it. **καθώς**] a word of later Greek, never used by the elder Attic writers; = *καθό* [Thuc.], *καθά, καθάπερ* (see Phryn. Lobeck, p. 425, and note). It takes up, and justifies by analogy, the confidence of the last verse. **ἐστιν δίκ. ἐμοί**] The usual classical constructions are, *ἐμὲ δίκαιόν ἐστι φράζειν*, Herod. i. 39: *ἐμὲ δίκαιον . . . . προσλαμβάνειν*, Plat. Legg. x. 897; *οὗτος δίκαιός ἐστι φέρεσθαι*, ib. i. 32. But Ellic. remarks, that there is nothing unclassical in the present usage; and compares Plat. Rep. i. 334, *δίκαιον τότε τούτοις τοὺς πονηροὺς ὠφελεῖν*. **τοῦτο φρονεῖν**] viz. the confidence of ver. 6. **ὑπέρ**]

των ὑμῶν, διὰ τὸ [a] ἔχειν με ἐν τῇ [a] καρδίᾳ ὑμᾶς ἔν τε τοῖς
[b] δεσμοῖς μου καὶ ἐν τῇ [c] ἀπολογίᾳ καὶ [d] βεβαιώσει τοῦ
εὐαγγελίου, [e] συγκοινωνούς [f] μου τῆς [g] χάριτος πάντας
ὑμᾶς ὄντας. 8 [h] μάρτυς γάρ μου ὁ θεός, [h] ὡς [i] ἐπιποθῶ
πάντας ὑμᾶς ἐν [j] σπλάγχνοις χριστοῦ Ἰησοῦ. 9 καὶ

a 2 Cor vii 3
b ver 13 (see reff there), &c Col iv 18 2 Tim ii 9 Philem 10, 13 Heb xi 36 Nah i 13
c Acts xxii 1 xxv 16 1 Cor. ix 3 2 Cor vii 11 ver 16. 2 Tim iv 16. 1 Pet iii 15 only † Wisd vi 10 only
d Heb vi 16 only Levit xxv 23 Wisd vi 18 only
e Rom xi 17 1 Cor ix 23 Rev i 9 only † (-νεῖν, ch iv 14)
f double gen, ver 25 ch ii 30.
g — Eph ii 8 Col i 6
h Rom i 9 (1 Thess ii 10)
i & constr, 2 Cor ix. 14 ch ii 26 1 Pet ii 2 Ps cxviii 131 w inf, Rom i 11. 2 Cor v 2 (ch ii 26 v r) 1 Thess iii 6 2 Tim i 4 w πρὸς, James iv 5 only
j = 2 Cor vi 12 Col iii 12 Philem 7, 12, 20 Prov xii 10

7. rec om (3rd) εν, with AD[1]F Thl · ins BD[2·3]KLℵ rel latt Syr Chr Thdrt Œc Ambrst Pelag. της χαριτος bef μου DF latt. for μου, μοι k l.

8 for μου, μοι DF(ℵ-corr ?) latt Syr arm Chr Ambrst Pelag rec aft μου ins εστιν (*possibly from Rom* i. 9: *no doubt, as Ellic contends, the Ap. may have twice used the same formula but this is not the question*), with ADKLℵ[3] rel syrr copt om BFℵ[1] 17. 67[2] latt æth Thdor-mops Chr-ms rec ιησ bef χρ, with FKL rel syr copt om ιησ D[3] basm æth. txt ABD[1]Gℵ m 17 am(with demid) sah Chr-ms Damasc-comm Ambrst.

because it is an opinion involving their good see ref Calov. and Wolf understand **φρον. ὑπέρ**, '*to care for*,' and **τοῦτο** to refer to the prayer, ver. 4. but unnaturally. **διὰ τό**] reason why he was justified, &c. as above. **με** is the subject, **ὑμᾶς** the object, as the context (ver 8) clearly shews: not the converse, as Rosenm, al. **ἔν τε . .**] Chrys. finely says, *καὶ τί θαυμαστόν, εἰ ἐν τῷ δεσμωτηρίῳ εἶχεν αὐτούς, οὐδὲ γὰρ κατ' ἐκεῖνον τὸν καιρόν, φησι, καθ' ὃν εἰσῄειν εἰς τὸ δικαστήριον ἀπολογησόμενος, ἐξεπέσατέ μου τῆς μνήμης. οὕτω γάρ ἐστι τυραννικὸν ὁ ἔρως ὁ πνευματικός, ὡς μηδενὶ παραχωρεῖν καιρῷ, ἀλλ' ἀεὶ τῆς ψυχῆς ἔχεσθαι τοῦ φιλοῦντος, καὶ μηδεμίαν θλῖψιν καὶ ὀδύνην συγχωρεῖν περιγενέσθαι τῆς ψυχῆς* His **bonds** were his situation his **defence and confirmation of the Gospel** his *employment* in that situation,—whether he refers to a *public* defence (2 Tim iv 16), or only to that defence of the Gospel, which he was constantly making in private However this may be, the two, **ἀπολογ** and **βεβαίωσις**, are most naturally understood as referring to one and the same course of action otherwise the **τῇ** would be repeated before *βεβ*. One such *ἀπολ* and *βεβ* we have recorded in Acts xxviii. 23 ff These words, **ἔν τε . . . εὐαγγελίου**, are most naturally taken with the foregoing (Chrys, al, Meyer, De W), as punctuated in the text, not with the following (Calv., al) **συγκοιν. κ τ λ**, which render a reason for the whole, **διὰ τό** to **εὐαγγελίου**

συγκ] See above **ὑμᾶς** is thus characterized. 'Ye are fellow-partakers of my grace.' the grace vouchsafed to me by God in Christ, see reff not the grace of *suffering in Him*, as ver 29 (Meyer), still less the grace of *apostleship*, Rom i 5, which the Philippians had furthered by their subsidies (Rosenm, al) ver 8 decides the **χάρις** to be spiritual in its meaning. The rendering *gaudii* in the Vulg. must have arisen from reading *χαρᾶς* The repetition of **ὑμᾶς**, referring to a *ὑμᾶς* gone before, is usual in rhetorical sentences of a similar kind. So Demosth p 1225,—*ὧν ἀκούοντά με, καὶ παρὰ τῶν ἀφικνουμένων . . ,—τίνα με οἴεσθε ψυχὴν ἔχειν*, But Bernhardy, Synt p. 275, remarks that the most accurate writers in verse and prose do not thus repeat the personal pronoun No such pleonasm is found in Homer or Plato.

8.] Confirmation of ver. 7. *οὐχ ὡς ἀπιστούμενος μάρτυρα καλεῖ τὸν θεόν, ἀλλὰ τὴν πολλὴν διάθεσιν οὐκ ἔχων παραστῆσαι διὰ λόγου*, Thl. after Chrys. On **ἐπιποθῶ**, see reff. The preposition indicates the direction of the desire, not its intensification. On **ἐν σπλάγχνοις χριστοῦ Ἰησοῦ**, Bengel remarks, "in Paulo non Paulus vivit, sed Jesus Christus quare Paulus non in Pauli sed in Jesu Christi movetur visceribus." All real spiritual love is but a portion of the great love wherewith He hath loved us, which lives and yearns in all who are vitally united to Him

9—11.] *The substance of his prayer* (already, ver 4, alluded to) *for them*. **καί** refers back to the *δέησις* of ver 4 'and this is the purport of my prayer.' At the same time this purport follows most naturally, after the expression of desire for them in the last verse There is an ellipsis in the sense between

k Matt. xxiv. 20 | Mk. Mark xiv. 35. 1 Cor. xiv. 13. Col. i. 9. iv. 3. 2 Thess. i. 11. iii. 1. (ὅπως, Acts viii. 15.)
l gen. subj., 1 Cor. xvi. 24. Col. i. 8. Philem. 5, 7. Rev. ii. 4, 19.
m here only.

τοῦτο [k] προσεύχομαι, [k] ἵνα ἡ [l] ἀγάπη [l] ὑμῶν ἔτι [m] μᾶλλον ABDF KLℵ a b c e f g h k l m n o 17
καὶ [m] μᾶλλον [n] περισσεύῃ ἐν [o] ἐπιγνώσει καὶ πάσῃ [p] αἰσθή-
σει, 10 [q] εἰς τὸ [r] δοκιμάζειν ὑμᾶς τὰ [s] διαφέροντα, ἵνα ἦτε
[t] εἰλικρινεῖς καὶ [u] ἀπρόσκοποι εἰς [v] ἡμέραν χριστοῦ, 11 [w] πεπληρωμένοι [xy] καρπὸν [y] δικαιοσύνης τὸν διὰ Ἰησοῦ χριστοῦ, εἰς δόξαν καὶ ἔπαινον θεοῦ.

n constr. (see note), Rom. xv. 13. Col. ii. 7. Sir. xix. 24. o Eph. i. 17 reff. p here only. Exod. xxviii. 3. Prov. i. 4. q Eph. i. 12 reff. r = Luke xii. 56. Rom. ii. 18. Job xxxiv. 3. s Rom. ii. 18. Gal. ii. 6. Dan. vii. 3. t 2 Pet. iii. 1 only †. Wisd. vii. 25 only. (-εια, 2 Cor. i. 12. ii. 17.) u Acts xxiv. 16. 1 Cor. x. 32 only †. P. Sir. xxxv. (xxxii.) 21 only. v ver. 6 reff. w = & constr., Col. i. 9. x = John iv. 36. Rom. i. 13. vi. 21, 22. ch. iv. 17. James iii. 18. acc., Col. i. 9. Rev. xvii. 3, 4. Ps. xv. 11 A. (not F.) y Heb. xii. 11. James iii. 18. Prov. xi. 30.

9. περισσευσῃ (*substn of aor: see e. g. vv* 24, 26) BD k m: περισσευοι F: txt AKLℵ rel Clem Chr Thdrt Damasc.
10. om υμας ℵ[1] m: ins ℵ[3]. αλικρινεις (but corrd) ℵ[1].
11. rec καρπων δικ. των, with rel syrr copt Chr: txt A(B)DFKLℵ f m n 17 latt sah æth arm Thdrt-comm Damasc Œc Ambrst Pelag. om τον B 116. 122. for θεου, χριστου D[1]: μοι F(not F-lat): *ejus* harl[1].

τοῦτο and **ἵνα**,—*τοῦτο* introducing the *substance* of the prayer, **ἵνα** its *aim*. See, on **ἵνα** with **προσεύχομαι**, note, 1 Cor. xiv. 13: and Ellic. here. **ἡ ἀγάπη ὑμ.**] not, '*towards me*,' as Chrys. (ὅρα πῶς φιλούμενος ἔτι μᾶλλον ἐβούλετο φιλεῖσθαι), Thl., Grot., all.,—nor *towards God and Christ* (Calov., al.), but either perfectly general, as Ellic., or, 'towards one another:' virtually identical with the **κοινωνία** of ver. 5. In **ἡ ἀγάπη ὑμῶν** its existence is recognized; in *μᾶλλον καὶ μᾶλλον περισσ.*, its deficiency is hinted at. ἐν is not to be taken as if *ἐπίγνωσις* and *αἴσθησις* were departments of Love, *in which it* was to increase: but they are rather elements, in whose increase in their characters Love is also, and as a separate thing, to increase: q. d. 'that your love may increase, but not without an increase in *ἐπίγνωσις* and *αἴσθησις*.' For by these Love is guarded from being ill-judged and misplaced, which, separate from them, it would be: and accordingly, on the increase of these is all the subsequent stress laid. **ἐπίγνωσις** is accurate knowledge of moral and practical truth: **αἴσθησις**, *perceptivity* of the same, the power of apprehending it: "the contrary of that dulness and inactivity of the *αἰσθητήρια τῆς καρδίας* (Jer. iv. 19), which brings about moral want of judgment, and indifference" (Meyer). De W. renders it well, **moral tact**. **10.**] Purpose of the increase in knowledge and perceptiveness: **with a view to your distinguishing things that are different**, and so choosing the good, and refusing the evil. Meyer's objection to this rendering—that the purpose is, not such *distinction*, but the approval of the good, is, after all, mere trifling: for the former is stated as implying the latter. He would render with Vulg., E. V., Chr. (*τὰ διαφέροντα, τουτέστι, τὰ συμφέροντα*), Thl., Erasm., Grot., Est., Beng., al., '*approving* (or, as Ellic., with Syr., æth., '*proving*,' '*bringing to the test*') *things that are excellent*,' which certainly is allowable, such sense of **διαφέρω** being justified by Matt. x. 31, and *τὰ διαφέροντα* for *præstantiora* occurring Xen. Hier. i. 3; Dio Cassius xliv. 25. But the simpler and more usual meaning of both verbs is preferable, and has been adopted by Thdrt. (*διακρίσεως, ὥστε εἰδέναι τίνα μὲν καλά, τίνα δὲ κρείττονα, τίνα δὲ παντάπασι τὰ διαφορὰν πρὸς ἄλληλα ἔχοντα*), Beza, Wolf, all., Wies., De Wette, al. **εἰλικρινεῖς**] **pure**:—a double derivation is given for the word: (1) *εἵλη, κρίνω*: that which is proved in the sunlight,—in which case it would be better written as it is often in our MSS., *εἱλ.*: and (2) *εἶλος* (*εἰλεῖν, ἴλλειν*), *κρίνω*: that which is proved by rapid shaking, as in sifting. This latter is defended by Stallbaum on Plato, Phæd. p. 66 A, where the word occurs in an ethical sense as here (*εἰλικρινεῖ τῇ διανοίᾳ χρώμενος αὐτὸ καθ' αὑτὸ εἰλικρινὲς ἕκαστον ἐπιχειροίη θηρεύειν τῶν ὄντων*): see also ib., p. 81 C: and cf. Ellic.'s note here. **ἀπρόσκοποι**] here as in ref. Acts, used intransitively, **void of offence,—without stumbling**; so Beza, Calv., De W., Wies., al. The transitive meaning, '*giving no offence*' (see ref. 1 Cor.), is adopted by Chr. (*μηδένα σκανδαλίσαντες*), Thdrt. (?), al., Meyer, al.: but it has here no place in the context, where *other men* are not in question. **εἰς ἡμέραν χριστοῦ**] See above on ver. 6: but *εἰς* is not exactly = *ἄχρι*; it has more the meaning of '*for*,'—'so that when that day comes, ye may be found.' Our tem-

12 [z] Γινώσκειν δὲ ὑμᾶς [z] βούλομαι, ἀδελφοί, ὅτι [a] τὰ κατ'
ἐμὲ [b] μᾶλλον [c] εἰς [d] προκοπὴν τοῦ εὐαγγελίου [c] ἐλήλυθεν,
13 ὥστε τοὺς [e] δεσμούς μου [f] φανεροὺς ἐν χριστῷ [f] γενέσθαι
ἐν ὅλῳ τῷ [g] πραιτωρίῳ καὶ τοῖς λοιποῖς πᾶσιν, 14 καὶ

z Rom i 13 x 25 al a Acts xxiv 22 xxv 14 Eph vi 21 Col iv 7 al b comparat — Acts xxi 10 xxvii 13 2 Cor vii 7 viii 17 2 Tim i 18 al Winer, edn 6, § 35 4 c = Wisd xv 5 (not Mark v 26 Acts xix 27) d ver 25 1 Tim iv 15 only † Sir li 17 2 Macc viii 8 only μεγάλην προκ ποιεῖν τῆς ἐπιβολῆς, Polyb ii 13 7 al e ver 7 reff plur masc here only Judg xv 14 neut., Luke viii 29 Acts xvi 26 xx 23 f = Mark xi 14 Acts vii 13 1 Cor iii 13 Gen xlii 16 g John xviii 28 (bis) || Mt Mk, 33 xix 9 Acts xxiii 35 only

13. *γενεσθαι* bef *εν χριστω* DF vulg Chr-comm Thl om *εν χρ.* a[1] ins *τω* bef *χριστω* ℵ[1](ℵ[3] disapproving) 80. for *γενεσθαι, γεγονεναι* ℵ[1] txt ℵ corr[1](?)[3].

poral use of '**against**' exactly gives it. 11 **πεπληρωμένοι καρπὸν δικαιοσ**] **filled with** (the accusative of reference or secondary government, reff) **the fruit of righteousness** (that result of work for God's glory which is the product of a holy life **δικαιοσ** being here, the whole purified moral habit of the regenerate and justified man Cf *καρπ τοῦ πνεύματος*, Gal. v. 22,—*τ. φωτός*, Eph v 9,—*δικαιοσύνης*, James iii 18) **which is** (specifies the *καρπός*—that it is not of nor by man, but) **through Jesus Christ** (by the working of the Spirit which He sends from the Father · "Silvestres sumus oleastri et inutiles, donec in Christum sumus insiti, qui viva sua radice frugiferas arbores nos reddit" Calvin) **unto the glory and praise of God** (belongs to **πεπληρωμένοι**).

12—26] DESCRIPTION OF HIS CONDITION AT ROME: HIS FEELINGS AND HOPES. And first he explains, **12—18**] *how his imprisonment had given occasion to many to preach Christ: how some indeed had done this from unworthy motives, but still to his joy that, any-how, Christ was preached* **12.**] According to Meyer, the connexion is with **ἐπιγνώσει** above, whence *γινώσκειν* is placed first.—q d, 'and as part of this knowledge, I would have you, &c.' [Ellic cites this view as mine also, but erroneously.] **τὰ κατ' ἐμέ**] **my affairs** (reff). **μᾶλλον**] **rather** (than the contrary) not, '*more now than before*,' as Hoelemann, which would be expressed by *μᾶλλον ἤδη* or *νῦν μᾶλλον* **προκοπήν**] **advance** (reff.) The word is common in Polyb. and later authors, but is condemned by Phrynichus, ed Lobeck, p 85, as unknown to the Attic writers. **ἐλήλυθεν**] '*evaserunt*,' **have turned out**: so Herod. i 120, κ τά γε τῶν ὀνειράτων ἐχόμενα, τέλεως ἐς ἀσθενὲς ἔρχεται **13.**] **so that** (effect of this *εἰς προκ. ἐληλυθέναι*) **my bonds** (the fact of my imprisonment) **have become manifest in Christ** (**φανερ. ἐν χριστῷ** is to be taken together They became known, not as a matter simply of notoriety, but of notoriety *in Christ*, i e in connexion with Christ's cause,—as endured for Christ's sake;—and thus the Gospel was furthered) **in the whole prætorium** (i e the *barrack of the prætorian guards* attached to the palatium of Nero [Dio liii 16, *καλεῖται δὲ τὰ βασίλεια παλάτιον . . ὅτι ἔν τε τῷ Παλατίῳ* (monte Palatino) *ὁ Καῖσαρ ᾤκει, καὶ ἐκεῖ τὸ στρατήγιον εἶχε* See Wieseler's note, ii. 403 f]: not the *camp* of the same outside the city ['castra prætorianorum,' Tac. Hist i 31 Suet Tiber. 37]. That this was so, is shewn by the greeting sent ch. iv 22 from *οἱ ἐκ τῆς Καίσαρος οἰκίας*, who would hardly have been mentioned in the other case. The word '*prætorium*' is also used of castles or palaces belonging to Cæsar [Suet. Aug 72, Tiber 39, Calig 37, Tit 8], or to foreign princes [Acts xxiii 35, Juv x. 161], or even to private persons [Juv i 75] it cannot be shewn ever to have signified the palatium at Rome, but the above meanings approach so nearly to this, that it seems to me no serious objection can be taken to it The fact here mentioned *may* be traced to St. Paul being guarded by a prætorian soldier, and having full liberty of preaching the Gospel [Acts xxviii 30 f.]. but more probably his situation had been changed since then,—see Prolegg. to this Epistle, § iii 6 I should now say that the *ὅλῳ*, and the *τοῖς λοιποῖς πᾶσιν*, make it more probable that the prætorium is to be taken in the larger acceptation,—the quadrangular camp now forming part of Aurelian's city walls,—including also the smaller camp on the Palatine) **and to all the rest** (a popular hyperbole:—i e, to others, besides those in the prætorium not to be taken [Chr, Thdrt., E V] as governed by **ἐν** and signifying, '*in all other places*' The matter of fact interpretation would be, that the soldiers, and those who visited him, carried the fame of his being bound for Christ over all Rome),

14] **and** (so that) **most of** (not '*many of*,' as E. V., al) **the brethren in the Lord** (this is the most natural connexion · see on *πέποιθα, -ώς*, standing first

[h] τοὺς πλείονας τῶν [i] ἀδελφῶν [i] ἐν κυρίῳ [k] πεποιθότας
τοῖς [e] δεσμοῖς μου [l] περισσοτέρως [m] τολμᾷν [n] ἀφόβως τὸν
λόγον τοῦ θεοῦ [m] λαλεῖν. 15 τινὲς μὲν καὶ [o] διὰ [pq] φθό-
νον καὶ [lr] ἔριν, τινὲς δὲ καὶ δι' [s] εὐδοκίαν τὸν [t] χριστὸν
[t] κηρύσσουσιν. 16 οἱ μὲν [u] ἐξ ἀγάπης, εἰδότες ὅτι [v] εἰς
[w] ἀπολογίαν τοῦ εὐαγγελίου [v] κεῖμαι, 17 οἱ δὲ [u] ἐξ [x] ἐριθείας
[τὸν] χριστὸν [y] καταγγέλλουσιν οὐχ [z] ἁγνῶς, [a] οἰόμενοι

ABDF KLℵ a b c e f g h k l m n o 17

h Acts xix. 32. xxvii. 12. 1 Cor. ix. 19. x. 5, 6 al. i Eph. vi. 21. Col. iv. 7. k constr., 2 Cor. x. 7. Philem. 21. Prov. xiv. 16. xxviii. 26. l Gal. i. 14 reff. m Rom. xv. 18. see 2 Macc. iv. 2. n Luke i. 74. 1 Cor. xvi. 10. Jude 12 only. Prov. i. 33. Wisd. xvii. 4 only. (-βος, Prov. iii. 24.) o = Matt. xxvii. 18. John vii. 43. x. 19 al. Winer, § 49. c. p Rom. i. 29. Gal. v. 21. 1 Tim. vi. 4. q as above (p). Matt. xxvii. 18 ‖ Mk. Tit. iii. 3. James iv. 5. 1 Pet. ii. 1 only†. Wisd. vi. 23 (25). 1 Macc. viii. 16 only. r as above (p). Rom. xiii. 13. 1 Cor. i. 11. iii. 3. 2 Cor. xii. 20. Tit. iii. 9 only. P.† Sir. xxviii. 11. xl. 5, 9 only. s Matt. xi. 26 ‖. Luke ii. 14. Rom. x. 1. Eph. i. 5, 9. ch. ii. 13. 2 Thess. i. 11 only. Ps. i. 19. t Acts viii. 5. 1 Cor. i. 23 al. u = 2 Cor. ii. 17. ix. 7. 1 Thess. ii. 3. 2 Tim. ii. 22. v Luke ii. 34. 1 Thess. iii. 3. Josh. iv. 6. w ver. 7 reff. x Gal. v. 20 reff. y = Acts iv. 2 al. L.P.† w. person, Acts xvii. 3, 23. Col. i. 28 only. z here only†. (-νόs, ch. iv. 8. -νοτης, 2 Cor. vi. 6.) a = & constr., here only. 1 Macc. v. 61. 2 Macc. v. 21. οἰόμεναι βλάπτειν, Plat. Apol. Socr. p. 41. (John xxi. 25. James i. 7 only. Job xi. 2. 2 Macc. vii. 24 only.)

14. rec om *του θεου*, with D³K syr Chr$_{\kappa.\iota.}$ Thdrt Damasc Thl Œc Tert: ins ABℵ k m 17 vulg(and F-lat) Syr copt goth Clem Chr$_1$(and 2 mss$_{\kappa.\iota.}$) Ambrst Pelag; *κυριου* F; ins bef *τον λογ.* f. (om from *περισσ.* to *κηρυσσουσιν* in next ver L.)

15. om 1st *και* ℵ³. *κηρυσσειν* ℵ¹: txt ℵ-corr¹(appy).

16, 17. rec transp vv 16 and 17, also the *μεν* and *δε* (*to suit order in ver* 15), with D²K rel syr gr-ff: om ver 17 L: txt ABD¹Fℵ k m 17 latt Syr coptt goth æth arm Bas

in the sentence, above, ver. 5. And so De W., al. Meyer, Ellic., Winer, § 20. 2, al., take **ἐν κυρ.** with **πεποιθότας**, as the element in which their confidence was exercised, as *ἐν χριστῷ*, ver. 13. To this *sense* there is no objection: but the other arrangement still seems to me, in spite of Ellic.'s note, more natural. No article is required before **ἐν**: see reff.) **encouraged by** (having confidence in) **my bonds** (*εἰ γὰρ μὴ θεῖον ἦν, φησί, τὸ κήρυγμα, οὐκ ἂν ὁ Παῦλος ἠνείχετο ὑπὲρ αὐτοῦ δεδέσθαι,* Œc.) **are venturing more abundantly** (than before) **to speak the word of God** (it would certainly seem here, from the variations, as if the shorter reading were the original text) **fearlessly.** 15.] The two classes mentioned here are not subdivisions of the *ἀδελφοὶ ἐν κυρίῳ* above, who would more naturally be *οἱ μέν* and *οἱ δέ*, but the first (**καί**) are a new class, over and beyond those *ἀδελφοί*, and the second (in which clause the *καί* refers to the *first*) are identical with the *ἀδελφοί* above. The first were the anti-pauline Christians, of whom we hear so often in the Epistles (see Rom. xiv.; 1 Cor. iii. 10 ff.; iv. 15; ix. 1 ff.; 2 Cor. x. 1 ff.; xi. 1 ff. &c.). **καί**, besides those mentioned ver. 14. But this does not imply that the *καί* is to be referred to *τινες*, as Ellic. represents me;—it introduces a new *motive*, *διὰ κ.τ.λ.*, and consequently, in my view, a new class of persons. **διά**, not strictly '*for the sake of*,' so that they set envy (of me) and strife before them as their *object*—but '*in pursuance of*,'—so **on account of**,—to forward and carry out: see reff. **καί** (2nd)—besides the hostile ones: introducing (see above) another motive again, differing from that last mentioned. **δι' εὐδοκίαν**—**on account of**, in pursuance of, **good will** (towards me). 16, 17.] The two classes of **οἱ μέν, οἱ δέ**, answering to *hi* and *illi*, take up again those of the preceding verse, the last being treated first. **These last indeed** (preach Christ: omitted, as having just occurred: see below) **out of** (induced by, reff.) **love** (this arrangement is better than with Mey., De W., and Ellic. to take **οἱ ἐξ ἀγάπης** and **οἱ ἐξ ἐριθ.** as generic descriptions, as in Rom. ii. 8, of the two classes: for in that case the words *τὸν χρ. καταγγέλλουσιν* would hardly be expressed in ver. 17, whereas in our rendering they come in naturally, *ἐξ ἐριθείας* being emphatically prefixed), **knowing** (motive of their conduct) **that I am set** (not '*lie in prison*:' see reff.:—'am appointed by God') **for the defence** (as in ver. 7: hardly as Chrys., *τουτέστι, τὰς εὐθύνας μοι ὑποτέμνοντες τὰς πρὸς τὸν θεόν*,—helping me in the solemn matter of my account of my ministry to God) **of the Gospel:** 17.] **but the former out of self-seeking** (or 'intrigue' [Conyb.]: not '*contention*,' as E. V., which has arisen from a mistake as to the derivation of the word, see note, Rom. ii. 8) **proclaim Christ insincerely** (so Cic. pro leg. Manil. 1, 'in privatorum periculis caste integreque versatus,'—*μεγάλων ἀέθλων ἁγνὰν κρίσιν*, Pind. Ol. iii. 37), **thinking** (explains *οὐχ ἁγνῶς*;—'in that they think.'

[b] θλίψιν [c] ἐγείρειν τοῖς [d] δεσμοῖς μου. 18 [e] τί γάρ; [f] πλὴν
ὅτι [g] παντὶ [g] τρόπῳ, εἴτε [h] προφάσει εἴτε ἀληθείᾳ, χριστὸς
[y] καταγγέλλεται, καὶ [i] ἐν τούτῳ [i] χαίρω, [k] ἀλλὰ καὶ
χαρήσομαι· 19 οἶδα γὰρ ὅτι τοῦτό μοι [l] ἀποβήσεται εἰς
[l] σωτηρίαν διὰ τῆς ὑμῶν δεήσεως καὶ [m] ἐπιχορηγίας τοῦ

b Eph iii 13 reff. c = here only Prov xvii 11. d ver 7 reff. e Rom iii 3. f Eph v 33 reff w ὅτι, Acts xx 23. 2 Kings xii. 14.

g dat, here only 1 Macc xiv 35 w ἐν, 2 Thess iii 16 acc w κατά, Rom iii 2. h Mark xii 40 ‖ L. John xv 22 Acts xxvii 30 1 Thess ii 5 only Hos x 4 (προφ. ἀληθ. ex in Wetst) dat of manner, 1 Cor xi 5. i Col i 24. k = ch iii 8 Eur Phœn 627, μῆτερ, ἀλλὰ μοι σὺ χαῖρε. l Job xiii 16 ἀποβ = Luke xxi 13 (v 2 John xxi 9) only. m Eph iv 16 only† (γεῖν, Col ii 19)

Tert Ambrst Pelag Aug om τον BF Chr-ms: ins ADKℵ(marks for erasure have been placed but removed) rel Chr Thdrt Damasc. rec (for εγειρειν) επιφερειν, with B[3]K rel syrr txt ABD[1]Fℵ 17 latt coptt goth æth arm Antch Damasc(not txt$_{A,I}$) lat-ff.

18. rec om οτι, with DKL rel copt Chr Thdrt Damasc: om πλην B Ath-ms txt AFℵ c 17 sah Ath Cyr Thl-marg (dum vulg D-lat goth lat-ff, dum tamen Ambrst, verum tamen Cypr) ins εν bef αληθεια D[3] m 80. 116: ℵ[1] has written ε, but marked it for erasure.

In the οἰόμενοι is involved, 'they do not succeed in their purpose,' cf. ref. 1 Macc.) **to raise up tribulation for** (me in) **my bonds** (i. e. endeavouring to take opportunity, by my being laid aside, to depreciate me and my preaching, and so to cause me trouble of spirit. The meaning given by Chrys., al., 'to excite the hatred of his persecutors and so render his condition worse, whether by the complaints of the Jews or otherwise,'—seems to me quite beside the purpose. It surely could not, from any circumstances to us unknown [Calvin's excuse, adopted by Ellic., for the *objective* view of θλίψις], make his imprisonment more severe, that some were preaching Christ from wrong motives) **18**] **What then** (i. e. 'what is my feeling thereupon?' see Ellic.'s note)? **Nevertheless** (i. e. notwithstanding this opposition to myself. see reff.: St. Paul uses πλήν in this sense only. Reading ὅτι after the πλήν, the expression is elliptical, as in ref. Acts. What then? '[nothing,] except that') **in every way** (of preaching,—from whatever motive undertaken and however carried out), **in pretext** (with a by-motive, as in ver 17), **or in verity** ('truth and sincerity of spirit.' the datives are those of the manner and form,—see Winer, § 31. 7. On προφάσει and ἀληθείᾳ, cf. Æschin. cont. Timarch. p. 6, προφάσει μὲν τῆς τέχνης μαθητής, τῇ δὲ ἀληθείᾳ πωλεῖν αὑτὸν προῃρημένος, and other examples in Wetst) **Christ IS PROCLAIMED** (then these adversaries of the Apostle can hardly have been those against whom he speaks so decisively in Galatians, and indeed in our ch. iii 2. These men *preached Christ*, and thus forwarded pro tanto the work of the Gospel, however mixed their motives may have been, or however imperfect their work) **and in this** (ἐν ἀρεταῖς γέγαθε, Pind. Nem. iii. 56: οὐ γὰρ ἂν γνοίης ἐν οἷς | χαίρειν προθυμῇ κἀν- ὅτοις ἀλγεῖς μάτην, Soph. Trach. 1118) **I rejoice, yea and** (on **ἀλλὰ καί**, see Ellic. It does not seem to me necessary, with him, to place a colon at χαίρω) **I shall** (hereafter) **rejoice**: **19**] **for I know that this** (viz the greater spread of the preaching of Christ, last mentioned, ver. 18: not as Thl, Calv, Est., De W., the θλίψιν ἐγείρ κ.τ.λ., in which case ver. 18 would be [Mey.] arbitrarily passed over) **shall turn out to my salvation** (σωτηρία is variously interpreted by Chrys. and Thdrt., of *deliverance* from present custody; by Œc., of *sustenance in life*: by Michaelis, of *victory* over foes: by Grot., of the *salvation of others*. But from the context it must refer to *his own spiritual good*—his own truitfulness for Christ and glorification of Him, whether by his life or death;—and so eventually his own *salvation*, in *degree* of blessedness, not in relation to the absolute fact itself), **through your prayer** (his affection leads him to make this addition—q. d. if you continue to pray for me,—not without the help of your prayers: see similar expressions, 2 Cor i. 11, Rom xv. 30, 31, Philem 22) **and** (your) **supply** (to me, by that prayer and its answer) **of the spirit of Jesus Christ** (the construction obliges us to take **ἐπιχορηγίας** as parallel with **δεήσεως**, and as the article is wanting, as also included under the ὑμῶν. Were the sense as E. V., and ordinarily, '*through your prayer and the supply of the Spirit of Jesus Christ*,' διά or διὰ τῆς would have been repeated, or at least the article τῆς expressed. This I still hold, notwithstanding Ellic.'s note. How such

πνεύματος Ἰησοῦ χριστοῦ
20 κατὰ τὴν [n] ἀποκαραδοκίαν
καὶ [o] ἐλπίδα μου, ὅτι [p] ἐν οὐδενὶ [q] αἰσχυνθήσομαι, ἀλλ' ἐν
[r] πάσῃ [s] παρρησίᾳ ὡς πάντοτε καὶ νῦν [t] μεγαλυνθήσεται
χριστὸς ἐν τῷ σώματί μου, εἴτε διὰ [u] ζωῆς εἴτε διὰ θανάτου.
21 ἐμοὶ γὰρ [v] τὸ ζῆν χριστὸς καὶ [v] τὸ ἀποθανεῖν

ABDF KLℵ a b c e f g h k l m n o 17

n Rom. viii. 19 only. (κεῖν. Ps. xxxv. 7 Aq. Jos. B. J. iii. 7. 26. Polyb. xvi. 2. 8.)
o gen. pers., Acts xxviii. 20. 2 Cor. i. 6. Ps. cxlv. 5.
p = ver. 28.
q Luke xvi. 3. 2 Cor. x. 8. 1 Pet. iv. 16. 1 John ii. 28 only. Ps. xxxiv. 4, 26. lxix. 2.
r = Matt. xxiii. 27. Acts iv. 29. xx. 19. Rom. i. 18. 2 Cor. viii. 7 al. fr.
s Eph. iii. 12 reff.
t = Luke i. 46. Acts v. 13. x. 46. 2 Kings vii. 26. (L.P., exc. Matt. xxiii. 5.)
u = 1 Cor. iii. 22. xv. 19. James iv. 14. 1 Pet. iii. 10 (from Ps. xxxiii. 12).
v constr., 1 Cor. xi. 6.

19. for γαρ, δε B m o sah. χρ. bef ιησ. DF goth.
20. for αποκαραδ., καραδοκιαν F h 18. 44. 123 Ath-3-mss. aft ουδενι ins υμων F. παρρ. bef παση G[1] coptt.
21. aft χριστος ins εστιν F latt.

a meaning can *be dogmatically* objectionable, I am wholly unable to see. Surely, that intercessory prayer should *attain its object*, and the supply take place *in consequence of the prayer*, is only in accord with the simplest idea of any reality in such prayer at all. Then again, is **τοῦ πνεύματος** a subjective genitive, '*supply which the Spirit gives*,'—so Thdrt. [τοῦ θείου μοι πν. χορηγοῦντος τὴν χάριν], Calv., De W., Meyer, all.:—or objective, the Spirit being *that which is supplied* [so Chrys., Thl., Œc., Grot., Beng., al.]? Decidedly, I think, the latter, on account [1] of St. Paul's own usage of ἐπιχορηγεῖν with this very word πνεῦμα in Gal. iii. 5, which is quite in point here, and [2] perhaps also, but see Ellic., of the arrangement of the words, which in the case of a subjective genitive would have been κ. τοῦ πν. Ἰ. χ. ἐπιχορηγίας, as in Eph. iv. 16, διὰ πάσης ἁφῆς τῆς ἐπιχορηγίας.—By a delicate touch at the same time of personal humility and loving appreciation of their spiritual eminence and value to him, he rests the advancement of his own salvation, on the supply of the Holy Spirit won for him by their prayers). **20.**] **according to** (for it is '*our confidence*, which hath great recompense of reward,' Heb. x. 35 f.) **my expectation** (not, '*earnest* expectation,' which never seems to be the sense of **ἀπό** in composition: still less is ἀπό superfluous: but **καραδοκεῖν** signifies to '*attend*,' '*look out*'—[παρὰ τὴν κάραν ὅλην δοκεῖν ('*observare*'), Thl. ad loc.]; and **ἀπό** adds the signification of '*from a particular position*,' or better still that of *exhaustion*, '*look out until it be fulfilled*,'—as in '*exspectare*,' ἀπεκδέχομαι, ἀπέχω, &c. See the word thoroughly discussed in the Fritzschiorum Opuscula, p. 150 ff.) **and hope that** (Est., al., take ὅτι argumentatively, *because*: but thus the expectation and hope will have no explanation, and the flow of the sentence will be broken) **in nothing** (in no point, no particular, see *ref.* It should be kept quite indefinite, not specified as Chrys. [κἂν ὁτιοῦν γένηται]. '*In none*' [of those to whom the Gospel is preached], as Hoelemann, is beside the purpose—no *persons* are adduced, but only the most general considerations) **I shall be ashamed** (general: have reason to take shame for my work for God, or His work in me), **but** (on the contrary: but perhaps after the ἐν οὐδενί this need not be pressed) **in all** (as contrasted with ἐν οὐδενί above) **boldness** (contrast to *shame*:—boldness *on my part*, seeing that life or death are both alike glorious for me—and thus I, my body, the passive instrument in which Christ is glorified, shall any-how be bold and of good cheer in this His glorification of Himself in me) **as always, now also** (that I am in the situation described above, ver. 17) **Christ shall be magnified** (δειχθήσεται ὅς ἐστι, Thdrt.: by His Kingdom being spread among men. So Ellicott, saying rightly that it is more than '*praised*,' as in my earlier editions) **in my body** (*my body* being the *subject* of *life* or *death*,—in the occurrence of either of which he would not be ashamed, the one bringing active service for Christ, the other union with Him in heaven, ver. 21 ff.), **either by** (means of) **life or by** (means of) **death.**

21.] **For** (justification of the preceding expectation and hope, in either event) **to me** (emphatic) **to live** (continue in life, present), (is) **Christ** (see especially Gal. ii. 20. All my life, all my energy, all my time, is His—I *live Christ*. That this is the meaning, is clear, from the corresponding clause and the context. But many have taken **χριστός** for the subject, and **τὸ ζῆν** for the predicate, and others [as Chrys.] have understood **τὸ ζῆν** in the sense of higher spiritual life. Others again, as Calvin, Beza, &c., have rendered,

[w] κέρδος· 22 εἰ δὲ [v] τὸ ζῆν [x] ἐν σαρκί, [y] τοῦτό μοι [z] καρπὸς
[a] ἔργου, [b] καὶ [c] τί [d] αἱρήσομαι οὐ [e] γνωρίζω· 23 [f] συνέχομαι
δὲ ἐκ τῶν δύο, τὴν [g] ἐπιθυμίαν ἔχων [h] εἰς τὸ [i] ἀναλῦσαι

και τι

BCDF KLℵ a b c e f g h k l m n o 17

w ch iii 7. Tit i 11 only † Gen xxxvii 26 Symm
x 1 Tim iii 16 reff
y Matt xv 11 al so ἐκεῖνα, Mark vii 15
z = Rom i 13 ver 11 reff
a = Acts xiii 2 xv. 38. ch ii 30 1 Thess v 13
b see note, and 1 Cor x 2 2 Cor ii 2
c = Matt xxi 31 xxiii 17, 19 Luke vii 42 Xen Cyr i 3 17
d 2 Thess ii 13 Heb xi 25 only Jer viii 3
e intr, here only (Eph i 9 reff) Luke vii 41 al
f Luke iv 38 Acts vii 57 2 Cor v 14 al L P, exc Matt iv 24 Job xxxi 23
g in good sense, Luke xxii 15 1 Thess ii 17 Prov x 24 ἐπιθ πρὸς τὸ ζῆν, Polyb iii 63 6
h 1 Thess iii 10 2 Thess i 5 ii 2 iii 9.
i = here (Luke xii 36) only † to depart, Judith xiii 1 2 Macc xii 7 3 Macc ii 24 (-λυσις, 2 Tim iv 6 Philo in Flacc § 21, vol ii p 544, τὴν ἐκ τοῦ βίου τελευταίαν ἀνάλυσιν.)

22 aft εργου ins εστιν F latt. αιρησωμαι B(ita cod).
23 rec (for δε) γαρ, with (none of our mss) demid(and hal) Syr Thdrt om copt basm txt ABCDFKLℵ rel latt syr sah goth gr-lat-ff om εις DF (latt)

'mihi enim vivendo Christus est et moriendo lucrum,' understanding before τὸ ζ. and τὸ ἀπ., κατά or the like), and to die ('to have died,' aorist, the act of living is to him Christ, but it is the state after death, not the act of dying, which is gain to him [the explanation of the two infinitives given here does not at all affect their purely substantival character, which Ellic defends as against me: τὸ ζῆν is life and τὸ ἀποθανεῖν is death but we must not any the more for that lose sight of the tenses and their meaning τὸ ἀποθνήσκειν would be equally substantival, but would mean a totally different thing]) (is) gain This last word has surprised some Commentators, expecting a repetition of χριστός, or something at all events higher than mere κέρδος But it is to be explained by the foregoing context. 'Even if my death should be the result of my enemies' machinations, it will be no αἰσχύνη to me, but gain, and my παῤῥησία is secured even for that event'

22] But if (the syllogistic, not the hypothetical 'if' assuming that it is so) the continuing to live in the flesh (epexegesis of τὸ ζῆν above), this very thing (τοῦτο directs attention to the antecedent as the principal or only subject of that which is to be asserted · this very ζῆν which I am undervaluing is) is to me the fruit of my work (i e. that in which the fruit of my apostolic ministry will be involved,—the condition of that fruit being brought forth), then (this use of καί to introduce an apodosis is abundantly justified. cf Simonides, fragm. Danae, εἰ δέ τοι δεινὸν τόγε δεινὸν ἦν, καί κεν ἐμῶν ῥημάτων λεπτὸν ὑπεῖχες οὖας Hom Il. ε 897, εἰ δέ τευ ἐξ ἄλλου γε θεῶν γένευ ὧδ' ἀΐδηλος, καί κεν δὴ πάλαι ἦσθα ἐνέρτερος οὐρανιώνων Od. ξ. 112, αὐτὰρ ἐπεὶ δείπνησε κ. ἤραρε θυμὸν ἐδωδῇ, καί οἱ πλησάμενος δῶκε σκύφον, ᾧπερ ἔπινεν. And the construction is imitated by Virg. Georg i. 200, 'si brachia forte remisit, Atque illum præceps prono rapit alveus amni' See Hartung, Partikell i 130, where more examples are given The primary sense is 'also,' introducing a new feature—for whereas he had before said that death was gain to him, he now says, but, if life in the flesh is to be the fruit of my ministry, then [I must add,—this besides arises—], &c) what (i e which of the two) I shall choose (for myself) I know not The above rendering is in the main that of Chr, Thdrt, Œc, Thl, Erasm, Luth, Calv., all, Meyer, De Wette,—and as it appears to me, the only one which will suit the construction and sense. Beza's 'an vero vivere in carne mihi operæ pretium sit et quid eligam ignoro,' adopted [except in his omission of the τοῦτο and his rendering of καρπὸς ἔργου by 'operæ pretium'] by Conyb, is open to several objections (1) the harshness of attaching to οὐ γνωρίζω the two clauses εἰ . , and τί . . . . . (2) the doubtfulness of such a construction at all as οὐ γνωρίζω, εἰ . . (3) the extreme clumsiness of the sentence when constructed, "*whether this life in the flesh shall be the fruit of my labour, and what I shall choose, I know not*" (Conyb) (4) in this last rendering, the lameness of the apodosis in the clause εἰ δὲ [τὸ ζῆν ἐν σαρκὶ τοῦτό] μοι καρπὸς ἔργου, which would certainly, were τοῦτο to be taken with τὸ ζῆν, have been καρπός μοι ἔργου or καρπὸς ἔργου μοι.

23] But (the contrast is to the decision involved in γνωρίζω) I am perplexed (reff and Acts xviii 5 note. held in, kept back from decision, which would be a setting at liberty) by (*from the direction of*,—kept in on both sides) the two (which have been mentioned, viz τὸ ζῆν and τὸ ἀποθανεῖν not, which *follow* this is evident by the insignificant position of ἐκ τῶν δύο behind the emphatic verb συνέχομαι, whereas, had the two been the *new* particulars about to be mentioned, τὸ ἀναλῦσαι and τὸ ἐπιμένειν,

καὶ σὺν χριστῷ εἶναι, πολλῷ γὰρ [j] μᾶλλον [k] κρεῖσ-
σον· 24 τὸ δὲ [l] ἐπιμένειν ἐν τῇ σαρκὶ [m] ἀναγκαιότερον
δι' ὑμᾶς. 25 καὶ τοῦτο [n] πεποιθὼς οἶδα ὅτι [o] μενῶ
καὶ [p] παραμενῶ πᾶσιν ὑμῖν εἰς τὴν ὑμῶν [q] προκοπὴν
καὶ [r] χαρὰν τῆς [r] πίστεως, 26 ἵνα τὸ [s] καύχημα ὑμῶν
[t] περισσεύῃ ἐν χριστῷ Ἰησοῦ [u] ἐν ἐμοὶ διὰ τῆς ἐμῆς

d μεινε ABCΓKLℵ c d e f h k l n o 17

j double compar, Mark vii 36. 2 Cor vii 13. Winer, edn 6, § 35. 1. k = 1 Cor vii 9, 38. 1 Pet iii 17. 2 Pet ii 21. Prov iii 14. (1 Cor xi 17. xii 31. Heb i 4 al12.) l Gal i 18 reff. m = Acts xiii 46. ch ii 25. 1 Cor xii 12. 2 Cor ix 5. Heb viii 3. Tit iii 14 (Acts x 24) only†. 2 Macc ix 21. n constr, ver 6. o = John xx 22, 23. 1 Cor xv 6. p 1 Cor xvi 6. Heb. vii 23. James i 25 only. Gen xliv 33. q ver 12 reff. r see Rom xv 13. 1 Pet i 8. s Paul (Rom iv 2 al8) only, exc Heb iii 6. Deut x 21. t Rom iii 7. 2 Cor i 5 al. Tobit iv 16. u = Rom. xv 17. ii 17 al.

for πολλω, ποσω D[1]F Victorin. Steph om γαρ, with DFKLℵ[1] rel latt basm goth Orig$_1$ Bas Chr Thdrt Thl Œc Aug$_{aliq}$. ins ABCℵ-corr[1] obl f 17 67[2] copt Clem Orig$_2$ Aug$_{sæpe\ et\ expr}$ Ambrst Ambr$_1$.

24. επιμειναι B Petr-alex. om εν ACℵ c k o Clem Orig$_3$ Petr-alex Chr Cyr. ins BDFKL rel Thdrt Damasc Thl Œc.

25. rec συμπαραμενω (*corrn on account of the unusual dative follg*), with D[3]KL rel Chr$_{expr}$ Thdrt Damasc Thl Œc. *permanebo* latt: txt ABCD[1]Fℵ 17. 67[2]. at end add υμων ℵ[1](ℵ[3] disapproving)

it would have been *ἐκ δὲ τῶν δύο συνέχομαι*), **having my desire towards** (εἰς belongs to ἔχων, not to ἐπιθυμίαν. The E. V., '*having a desire to*,' would be ἐπιθυμίαν ἔχων τοῦ, and entirely misses the delicate sense) **departing** (from this world—used on account of σὺν χρ. εἶναι following. The *intransitive* sense of ἀναλύω is not properly such, but as in the Latin *solvere*, elliptical, to *loose* [anchor or the like: see reff.] *for departure*, *for return*, &c.) **and being with Christ** ("valet hic locus ad refellendum eorum deliramentum, qui animas a corporibus divisas dormire somniant: nam Paulus aperte testatur, nos frui Christi præsentia quum dissolvimur." Calv., and similarly Est. Thus much is true: but not perhaps that which some have inferred from our verse, that it shews a change of view respecting the nearness of the Lord's advent—for it is only said *in case of* his death: he immediately takes it up [ver. 25] by an assurance that he should continue with them: and cf. ver 6, ch iii 20, 21, which shew that the advent was still regarded as imminent), **for it is by far better** (ref. Mark, and examples in Wetst., Plato, Hip. Maj. § 56, οἴει σοι κρεῖττον εἶναι ζῆν μᾶλλον ἢ τεθνάναι. Isocr. Helen 213 c, οὕτως ἠγανάκτησεν ὥσθ' ἡγήσατο κρεῖττον εἶναι τεθνάναι μᾶλλον. ib. Archidam. 134 c, πολὺ γὰρ κρεῖττον ἐν ταῖς δόξαις αἷς ἔχομεν τελευτῆσαι τὸν βίον μᾶλλον ἢ ζῆν ἐν ταῖς ἀτιμίαις) **but to continue** (the preposition gives the sense of *still*, cf. Rom vi 1) **in my flesh** (the article makes a slight distinction from ἐν σαρκί, abstract, ver 22) **is more needful** (this comparison contains in itself a mixed construction, between ἀναγκαῖον and αἱρετώτερον or the like) **on account of you** (and others—but the expressions of his love are now directed solely to them. Meyer quotes from Seneca, Epist. 98: 'vitæ suæ adjici nihil desiderat sua causa, sed eorum, quibus utilis est.' Cf. also a remarkable passage from id. Epist. 104 in Wetst.). 25.] **And having this confidence** (Thl., al., take τοῦτο with οἶδα, and render πεποιθώς adverbially, '*confidently*,'—which last can hardly be, besides that οἶδα will thus lose its reference, τοῦτο . . . ὅτι being unmeaning in the context), **I know that I shall remain and continue alive** (so Herod. i. 30, σφι εἶδε ἅπασι τεκνα ἐκγενόμενα, καὶ πάντα παραμείναντα. συμπαραμένω [see var. readd.] occurs in Ps lxxi. 5, and in Thuc. vi 89) **with you all** (the dative may either be after the compound verb, or better perhaps a '*dativus commodi*') **for your advancement and joy in your faith** (both προκ. and χαρ. govern τῆς πίσ. which is the subjective genitive; it is their faith which is to advance, by the continuance of his teaching, and to rejoice, as explained below, on account of his presence among them), 26.] **that your matter of boasting** (not, as Chr., '*mine in you*,' nor, as commonly rendered, '*your boasting*' [καύχησις]. Their Christian matter of boasting in him was, the possession of the Gospel, which they had received from him, which would abound, be assured and increased, by his presence among them) **may abound in Christ Jesus** (its field, element of increase, it being a Christian matter of glorying) **in me** (its field, element, of *abounding in Christ Jesus*, I being the worker of that which

v παρουσίας πάλιν w πρὸς ὑμᾶς. 27 x Μόνον y ἀξίως τοῦ
εὐαγγελίου τοῦ χριστοῦ z πολιτεύεσθε, ἵνα εἴτε ἐλθὼν
καὶ ἰδὼν ὑμᾶς εἴτε a ἀπὼν *ἀκούσω b τὰ περὶ ὑμῶν, ὅτι
c στήκετε ἐν ἑνὶ πνεύματι, d μιᾷ d ψυχῇ e συναθλοῦντες τῇ
πίστει τοῦ f εὐαγγελίου, 28 καὶ μὴ g πτυρόμενοι h ἐν μηδενὶ

v = 1 Cor xvi 17 2 Cor vii 6, 7 ch ii 12 al † 2 Macc viii 12 xv 21 only w Gal iv 18 reff x Gal ii 10 v 13 y Eph iv 1 reff z Acts xxiii 1 only † 2 Macc vi 1 xi 25 only (ευμα, ch iii 20) a mostly w παρων, 1 Cor v 3 2 Cor x 1, 11 xiii 2, 10 Wisd xi 11 xiv 17 alone, Col ii 5 only Job vi 13 Wisd ix 6 only b Luke xxiv 19, 27 Acts xxiv 10. ch ii 19, 20 al Col iv 8 w acc, ch ii 23 al c Gal v 1 reff d Acts iv 32 only 1 Chron xii 38 e ch iv 3 only † f gen obj., see Col ii 12 reff g here only † ἵπποι πτυρόμενοι, Diod. Sic xvii 34 h ver 20

27. om του χριστου ℵ[1] am-ed. ins ℵ-corr[1] om ειτε απων ℵ[1]: ins ℵ-corr[1] obl.
*ἀκούω BD[1]ℵ basm ακουσω ACD[3]FKLℵ-corr[1] obl rel (*audiam* latt).

furnishes this material) **by means of my presence again with you**

27—II. 18] EXHORTATIONS TO UNITED FIRMNESS, TO MUTUAL CONCORD, TO HUMILITY, AND IN GENERAL TO EARNESTNESS IN RELIGION. **27.] μόνον,**—i. e. I have but this to ask of you, in the prospect of my return —see reff. **πολιτεύεσθε]** The *πολίτευμα* being the heavenly state, of which you are citizens, ch iii 20 The expression is found in Jos (Antt iii 5 8) and in Philo, and is very common in the fathers: e g Ps-Ignat Trall 9, p 789, *ὁ λόγος σὰρξ ἐγένετο, κ. ἐπολιτεύσατο ἄνευ ἁμαρτίας,*—Cyr Jer. Catech. Illum. iv. 1, p. 51, *ἰσάγγελον βίον πολιτεύεσθαι* See Suicer in voc. The emphasis is on *ἀξίως τ. εὐ. τοῦ χρ.* **ἵνα εἴτε κ τ λ]** This clause is loosely constructed,—the verb **ἀκούσω** belonging properly only to the second alternative, *εἴτε ἀπών*, but here following on both. Meyer tries to meet this by understanding *ἀκούσω* in the former case, '*hear from your own mouth*.' but obviously, *ἰδών* is the real correlative to *ἀκούσω*, only constructed in a loose manner the full construction would be something of this kind, *ἵνα, εἴτε ἐλθὼν κ. ἰδὼν ὑμᾶς εἴτε ἀπὼν κ. ἀκούσας τὰ περὶ ὑμῶν, γνῶ ὅτι στήκετε.* Then **τὰ περὶ ὑμῶν, ὅτι στήκετε** is another irregular construction—the article generalizing that which the *ὅτι* particularizes, as in *οἶδά σε, τίς εἶ*, and the like.

ἐν ἑνὶ πνεύματι] refers to the unity of spirit in which the various members of the church would be fused and blended in the case of *perfect unity:* but when Meyer and De W deny that the Holy Spirit is meant, they forget that this one spirit of Christians united for their common faith would of necessity be the Spirit of God which penetrates and inspires them cf Eph iv. 3, 4 Then, as this Spirit is the highest principle in us,—he includes also the lower portion, the animal soul, **μιᾷ ψυχῇ συναθλοῦντες]** These words must be taken together, not **ψυχῇ** taken with **στήκετε** as in apposition with **πνεύματι** (Chr., Thl, all), which would leave **συναθλ** without any modal qualification The **ψυχή**, receiving on the one hand influence from the spirit, on the other impressions from the outer world, is the sphere of the affections and moral energies, and thus is that in and by which the exertion here spoken of would take place. **συναθλοῦντες,** either *with one another* (so Chr, Thdrt, Thl., Œc., all., De W, al.), or *with me* (so Erasm, Luth, Beza, Bengel, al, Meyer). The former is I think preferable, both on account of the **ἑνὶ πν.** and **μιᾷ ψυχῇ,** which naturally prepare the mind for an *united* effort, and because *his own* share in the contest which comes in as a new element in ver 30, and which Meyer adduces as a reason for his view, seems to me, on that view, superfluous, *ἐμοί* after *συναθλοῦντες* (cf ch. iv. 3) would have expressed the whole. I would render then as E V, **striving together.** **τῇ πίστει** is a 'dativus commodi'—**for the faith,** cf. Jude 3—not, as Erasm Paraphr., '*with the faith,*' 'adjuvantes decertantem adversus impios evangelii fidem.' for such a personification of *πίστις* would be without example nor is it a dative of the *instrument* (Beza, Calv., Grot, al.), which we have already had in *ψυχῇ*, and which could hardly be with *τοῦ εὐαγ.* added. **28] πτύρω,** akin to *πτοέω, πτώσσω, πτήσσω,* **to frighten,** especially said of animals (ref.), but often also used figuratively, e g. by Plato, Axioch. p 370 A, *οὐκ ἄν ποτε πτυρείης τὸν θάνατον* Ps-Clem Hom. ii. 39, p. 71, *πτύραντες τοὺς ἀμαθεῖς ὄχλους.*

ἐν μηδενί] **in nothing,** see on ver. 20.

The **ἀντικείμενοι,** from the comparison which follows with his own conflict, and the *ὑπὲρ αὐτοῦ πάσχειν*, must be the *adversaries of the faith,* whether Jews or

ὑπὸ τῶν [i] ἀντικειμένων ([j] ἥτις ἐστὶν αὐτοῖς [k] ἔνδειξις
[l] ἀπωλείας, ὑμῶν δὲ σωτηρίας, [m] καὶ τοῦτο ἀπὸ θεοῦ,
29 ὅτι ὑμῖν [n] ἐχαρίσθη τὸ ὑπὲρ χριστοῦ οὐ μόνον τὸ
[o] εἰς αὐτὸν [o] πιστεύειν, ἀλλὰ καὶ τὸ ὑπὲρ αὐτοῦ [p] πάσχειν)
30 τὸν αὐτὸν [qr] ἀγῶνα [qs] ἔχοντες οἷον εἴδετε ἐν ἐμοὶ καὶ νῦν
ἀκούετε ἐν ἐμοί. II. 1 εἴ τις οὖν [t] παράκλησις ἐν χριστῷ,

ABCDF KLℵab cdefg hklm no17

i Gal v 17 reff. j = Col ii 23 attr, Mark xvi 16 1 Tim iii 15 al. k Rom iii 25, 26 2 Cor viii 24 only†. l Matt vii 13 John xvii 12 1 Tim vi 9 reff Jer xxvi (xlvi) 21. m Rom xiii 11 1 Cor vi 6, 8 Eph ii 8 3 John 5. n = Acts iii 14 1 Cor ii 12. o Gal ii 16 reff. p Gal iii 4 reff. q Col ii 1. r as above (q) 1 Thess ii 2 1 Tim vi 12 2 Tim iv 7 Heb. xii 1 only. Isa vii 13. s constr of part., Acts xxvi 3 Col iii 16 al. t = Acts xiii 15 xv 31 Rom xii 8 Heb xii 5 al L P H 1 Macc x 24

28 rec (for *εστιν αυτοις*) *αυτοις μεν εστιν*, with KL rel Thdrt *εστιν αυτοις μεν* D³ syr Chr Thl *αυτοις* (alone) o txt ABCD¹Fℵ 17 am(with fuld tol) syr coptt goth Ambrst Pelag rec *υμιν* (*corrn to suit αυτοις*), with D³FKL rel vulg syr coptt goth Chr₁ Thdrt Ambrst *ημιν* C¹D¹ Damasc txt ABC²ℵ 17 D-lat Chr-ms Aug.
29 *ημιν* A 35. om 1st *το* F 3 68² 73 120 Œc-comm
30. aft *οιον* ins *και* D¹F latt Ambrst Pelag aft *ειδετε*, C¹ rec *ιδετε*, with B²D³FKL d m n Thl Œc: txt AB¹CD¹ℵ rel 67² Clem Chr Thdrt Damasc¹

Gentiles, cf 1 Cor. xvi 9 **ἥτις**, viz *τὸ ὑμᾶς μὴ πτύρεσθαι*, fem, on account of *ἔνδειξις*, following see a similar *ἥτις*, Eph iii 13 **ἐνδ ἀπωλ**, because it will shew that all their arts are of no avail against your union and firmness and hopefulness and thus their own ruin (*spiritual*, as the whole matter is spiritual), in hopelessly contending against you, is pointed out, not perhaps to themselves *as perceiving it*, but to themselves it they *choose* to perceive it **ὑμῶν δὲ σω**] **but** (is a sign) **of your** (see var readd) **salvation** (*spiritual* again not merely, *rescue and safety from them*), **and this** (viz the *sign*, to them of perdition, to you of your salvation not to be referred to *σωτηρίας*, nor merely to *ὑμῶν δὲ σωτ.* [Calv, al], nor to both *ἀπωλ* and *σωτ*, nor to the following sentence [Clem Alex (Strom iv 13, vol i. p 614 P), Chrys, Thdrt., al], but simply to *ἔνδειξις* the sign is one from God) **from God,—because** (proof that the sign is from God, in that He has granted to *you* the double proof of His favour, not only, &c) **to you** (first emphasis) **it was granted** (second emphasis—'gratiæ munus, signum salutis (?) est' Beng The aorist refers to the fact in the dealings of God regarded as a historical whole), **on behalf of Christ** (the Apostle seems to have intended immediately to add *πάσχειν*, but, the *οὐ μόνον κ τ λ.* coming between, he drops *τὸ ὑπὲρ χριστοῦ* for the present, and takes it up again by and by with *ὑπὲρ αὐτοῦ* The rendering of *τὸ ὑπ χ*, *absolute*, '*to you it is given in the behalf of Christ*' (E V), 'quod attinet ad Christi causam,' is manifestly wrong), **not only to believe on Him, but also on his behalf to suffer,**

30] **having** (the nominative instead of the dative, the subjective *ὑμεῖς* being before the Apostle's mind so Eph. iv. 2,—Thuc. iii. 36, *ἔδοξεν αὐτοῖς . . . . ἐπικαλοῦντες* ib vi. 24, *καὶ ἔρως ἐνέπεσε πᾶσιν . . εὐέλπιδες ὄντες* Sallust, Jug 112, '*populo Romano melius visum . . . rati*' see other examples in Kuhner, ii p 377. This is far better than with Lachm., al, to parenthesize *ἥτις . . . . πάσχειν*, which unnecessarily breaks the flow of the sentence) **the same conflict** (one in its nature and object) **as ye saw** (viz. when I was with you, Acts xvi. 16 ff) **in me** (in my case as its example), **and now hear of in me** (*ἐν ἐμοί*, as before not '*de me*' He means, by report of others, and by this Epistle) II 1—11.] *Exhortation to unity and humility* (1—4), *after the example of Christ* (5—11). 1] He introduces in the fervour of his affection (*ὅρα πῶς λιπαρῶς, πῶς σφοδρῶς, πῶς μετὰ συμπαθείας πολλῆς*, Chr) four great points of the Christian life and ministry, and by them enforces his exhortation Mey observes, that the four fall into *two pairs*, in each of which we have first the objective principle of Christian life (*ἐν χριστῷ* and *πνεύματος*), and next the subjective principle (*ἀγάπης* and *σπλάγχ. κ οἰκτιρμοί*) And thus the awakening of motives by these four points is at the same time (so Chrys above) powerful and touching **παράκλησις**] here, **exhortation**, not '*comfort*,' which follows in **παραμύθιον ἐν χριστῷ** specifies the *element* of the exhortation **παραμύθ**] better **comfort**, than '*persuasion*' it corresponds (see above) to *σπλ κ οἰκτιρ* in the other pair see also reff *παραμυθία*, the ear-

εἴ τι [u] παραμύθιον ἀγάπης, εἴ τις [v] κοινωνία πνεύματος, εἴ
[w] τις [x] σπλάγχνα καὶ [y] οἰκτιρμοί, 2 [z] πληρώσατέ μου τὴν
[z] χαράν, [a] ἵνα [b] τὸ αὐτὸ [b] φρονῆτε, τὴν αὐτὴν ἀγάπην
ἔχοντες, [c] σύμψυχοι τὸ ἓν [b] φρονοῦντες, 3 μηδὲν [d] κατ'
[e] ἐριθείαν μηδὲ κατὰ [f] κενοδοξίαν, ἀλλὰ τῇ [g] ταπεινοφροσύνῃ
ἀλλήλους [h] ἡγούμενοι [i] ὑπερέχοντας ἑαυτῶν, 4 μὴ τὰ

u here only† Wisd iii 18 only Thucyd v. 103 Soph Electr 129
v = 1 Cor i 9 2 Cor xiii 13 (Acts ii 42 al Lev vi 2 Wisd viii 18 only)
w see note
x ch i 8 reff
y Rom xii 1 2 Cor i 3 Col iii 12 Heb x 28 only Isa. lxiii 15
z = John iii 29 xv 11 xvi 24 xvii 13 1 John i 4 2 John 12
a = Matt xviii 6 John viii 56
b Rom xii 16 xv 5 2 Cor xiii 11 ch iv 2 τὸ ἓν φρ. here only φρ = Rom viii 5 ch iii 15 al 1 Macc x 20
c here only†
d = Matt xix 3. Acts iii 17 Eph i 11 ch iv 11
e Gal v 20 reff
f here only† Wisd xiv 14 only Polyb iii 81 9 al) (ξος, Gal v 26)
g Eph iv 2 reff
h = Acts xxvi 2 2 Cor ix 5 al Job xlii 6
i Rom xiii 1 ch iii 8 iv 7 1 Pet ii 13 only Exod xxvi 18

CHAP II 1. for τι, τις D¹ ¹L. rec (for last τις) τινα, with 57(ed Alter) al(e sil "si in ullis, in perpaucis certe codicibus græcis" Reiche p 213. Cf also ib. p 211 note 7) τι b e h m o 4. 18 37. 46. 72-4. 116-32-9. 219¹ Clem Chr-ed-montf τε 109 Thdrt ms. txt ABCDFKLℵ rel al₆₅(in Reiche) Bas Chr-mss Damasc Thl Œc
2. for το ἐν, το αυτο ACℵ¹ 17. id ipsum vulg Pelag txt ℵ³ &c
3 rec (for κατ') κατα, with AD¹ rel: txt BCD¹FL l m n 17. rec (for μηδὲ κατὰ) ἤ, with DFKL rel Chr Thdrt: txt ABCℵ(but ℵ³ disapproves κατα) m 17 vulg D-lat copt Victorin Ambrst Aug προηγουμενοι D¹ ²K 80. ins τους bef υπερ. B. υπερεχοντες DF.

her form, occurs in the same sense 1 Cor. xiv. 3, Wisd xix 12 ἀγάπης is the subjective genitive,—'consolation furnished by love' κοιν. πν.] communion,—fellowship, of the *Holy Spirit*, cf. ref. 2 Cor. not, '*spiritual communion*' (De W., al) The MSS. evidence in favour of the reading εἴ τις is overwhelming; and in Tischendorf's language, "nobis servandum erit τις, nisi malumus grammatici quam editoris partes agere" It is in its favour, that almost all the great MSS have εἴ τι before παραμύθιον. For if εἴ τις had been a mere mechanical repetition of the preceding, why not in one place as well as in the other? And if this were once so, and the former τις got altered back to its proper form, why not this also? The construction may be justified perhaps as analogous to ὄχλου . ἐχόντων, Mark viii. 1, see also Luke ii 17, vii. 49 though, it must be confessed, it is the harshest example of its kind **σπλάγχνα**, of *affectionate emotion* in general **οἰκτιρμοί** of the *compassionate* emotions in particular. So Tittm. p. 68 a —**tenderness and compassion**, Conyb — 'herzliche Liebe und Barmherzigkeit,' Luth

I may remark, that the exhortation being addressed to the Philippians, the εἴ τις and εἴ τι are to be taken subjectively— If there be with you any &c. 2] **πληρώσατε** has the emphasis—'he already had joy in them, but it was not *complete*, because they did not walk in perfect unity' cf. ch i 9 **ἵνα**, of the *purpose*, as always—but here as frequently, of a correlative result, *contemplated as* the purpose: never, however, without reason: e g., here the unanimity of the Philippians is the far greater and more important result, to which the πληροῦν μου τὴν χ is but accessory **τὸ αὐτὸ φρονῆτε**] This expression (**be of the same mind**) is more general than τὸ ἓν φρονοῦντες ('*being of one mind*') below And this is all that can be reasonably said of the difference between them In the more fervid portions of such an Epistle as this, we must be prepared for something very nearly approaching to tautology βαβαί, says Chrys, ποσάκις τὸ αὐτὸ λέγει ἀπὸ διαθέσεως πολλῆς. **τ αὐτὴν ἀγάπ. ἔχοντες**] τουτέστιν, ὁμοίως καὶ φιλεῖν κ. φιλεῖσθαι, Chrys **σύμψ τ ἓν φρ**] to be taken together as one designation only σύμψ having the emphasis, and defining the τὸ ἓν φρ, **with union of soul, unanimous** (minding one thing) So that the Apostle does not, as Œc, διπλασιάζει τὸ ὁμοφρονεῖν. 3] **μηδὲν— φρονοῦντες**, scil. from the last verse — **entertaining no thought in a spirit of** (according to, after the manner of) **self-seeking** (see note, Rom ii 8, on the common mistaken rendering of this word), **nor in a spirit of vainglory** (κενοδοξία, ματαία τις περὶ ἑαυτοῦ οἴησις, Suidas), **but by means of humility of mind** (article either generic or possessive: in the latter case assuming **ταπεινοφροσύνη** as a Christian grace which you possess The dative is either modal [ch i 18 Rom iv 20], or instrumental, or more properly perhaps,

k = 2 Cor iv 18 (Gal vi 1 reff) in Mark xvi 12 only Isa xliv 13 1 Cor xi 7 Gal i 14 reff particip., 1 Cor ix 19 Philem 8. 2 Pet iii 15 (ver 3 reff) Job xli 19 o here only † (see note) p = James i 2

ἑαυτῶν ἕκαστοι [k] σκοποῦντες, ἀλλὰ καὶ τὰ ἑτέρων ἕκαστοι. ABCDF
5 τοῦτο [b] φρονεῖτε ἐν ὑμῖν ὃ καὶ ἐν χριστῷ Ἰησοῦ, 6 ὃς KLℵ a b c d e f g
ἐν [m] μορφῇ θεοῦ [n] ὑπάρχων οὐχ [o] ἁρπαγμὸν [p] ἡγήσατο τὸ h k l m n o 17

4 for ἑαυτων, ἑαυτου C² Thl₁. ἑτερον Thl₁. rec (for 1st ἑκαστοι) ἑκαστος, with CDKLℵ rel vss gr-ff. txt ABF 17 vulg spec lat-ff rec σκοπειτε, with L rel copt Chr Thdrt σκοπειτω K k 73 syrr Thl: txt ABCDFℵ c 17 latt goth arm Ath lat-ff. om και D¹FK o latt arm Bas lat-ff(not Aug). for 2nd τα, το D³K a h l n 67² Œc. ins των bef ἑτερων D¹F b¹ c k o rec (for 2nd ἑκαστοι) ἑκαστος, with KL rel D-lat syrr goth Chr Cyr Thdrt om F vulg lat-ff: txt ABDℵ 17 copt Bas. (C defective.) ACℵ Cyr₂ join 2nd ἑκαστ to follg

5. rec aft τουτο ins γαρ, with DFKLℵ³ rel latt syr goth Chr Thdrt Damasc Victorin Hil Ambrst: om ABCℵ¹ k m 17 arm Orig Ath &c. rec (for φρονειτε) φρονεισθω, with C³KL rel copt goth arm Orig Eus Ath Cyr₁ Chr Thdrt₂ Damasc φρονειτω ἑκαστος Cyr_{aliq} Thdot-ancyr txt ABC¹DFℵ 17. 67² latt $Cyr_{sæpe}$ Ambrst Pelag Ruf Hil.

6. om το F 109 Eus₂ Did.

causal see Ellicott's note) **esteeming one another superior to yourselves** (i e each man his neighbour better than himself); **each** (the plural is only found here in the N T, and unusual elsewhere it occurs in Thuc i 2, *ῥᾳδίως ἕκαστοι τὴν ἑαυτῶν ἀπολείποντες*,—Hom. Od. ι 164, *πολλὸν γὰρ ἐν ἀμφιφορεῦσιν ἕκαστοι ἠφύσαμεν*) **regarding** (cf. both for expressions and sense, Herod i 8, *πάλαι τὰ καλὰ ἀνθρώποισι ἐξεύρηται . . ἐν τοῖσιν ἓν τόδε ἐστί, σκοπέειν τινὰ τὰ ἑωυτοῦ* Thuc vi 12, *τὸ ἑαυτοῦ μόνον σκοπῶν*) **not their own matters, but each also the matters of others** ("this second clause [Mey] is a feebler contrast than might have been expected after the absolute negation in the first" The *καί* shews that that first is to be taken with some allowance, for by our very nature, each man must *σκοπεῖν τὰ ἑαυτοῦ* in some measure) On the nature of the strife in the Philippian church, as shewn by the exhortations here, see Prolegg § ii. 7. 5—11] *The exhortation enforced, by the example of the self-denial of Christ Jesus* The monographs on this important passage, which are very numerous, may be seen enumerated in Meyer. **For** (reason for the exhortation of the preceding verse) **think this in** (not '*among*,' on account of the ἐν χρ 'I following On the reading, see various readings, and Fritzschiorum Opuscula, p. 19 note) **yourselves, which was** (*ἐφρονεῖτο*) **also in Christ Jesus** (as regards the dispute, whether the *λόγος ἄσαρκος* or the *λόγος ἔνσαρκος* be here spoken of, see below I assume now, and will presently endeavour to prove, that the Apostle's reference is first to the *taking on Him* of our humanity, and then to his *further humiliation in* that humanity) **who subsisting** (originally see on *ὑπάρχω* and *εἰμί*, Acts xvi. 20 Less cannot be implied in this word than eternal præ-existence. The participle is hardly equivalent to "although he subsisted," as Ellic., still less "inasmuch as he subsisted," but simply states its fact as a link in the logical chain, "subsisting as He did," without fixing the character of that link as causal or concessive) **in the form of God** (not merely the *nature* of God, which however is *implied* but, as in Heb i 3, the *ἀπαύγασμα τ δόξης κ χαρακτὴρ τ. ὑποστάσεως αὐτοῦ*—cf. John v. 37, *οὔτε εἶδος αὐτοῦ ἑωράκατε*, with ib. xvii. 5, *τῇ δόξῃ ᾗ εἶχον πρὸ τοῦ τὸν κόσμον εἶναι παρὰ σοί* "Ipsa natura divina decorum habebat infinitum in se, etiam sine ulla creatura illam gloriam intuente" Beng See also Col. i. 15, 2 Cor iv. 4 That the divine *nature* of Christ is not here meant, is clear. for He did not with reference to *this* ἐκένωσεν ἑαυτόν, ver 7) **deemed not his equality** (notice *ἴσα*, not *ἴσον*, bringing out equality in nature and essence, rather than in Person) **with God a matter for grasping** The expression is one very difficult to render We may observe, (1) that **ἁρπαγμόν** holds the emphatic place in the sentence (2) that this fact casts *τὸ εἶναι ἴσα θεῷ* into the shade, as secondary in the sentence, and as referring to the state indicated by *ἐν μορφῇ θεοῦ ὑπάρχων* above (3) that *ἁρπαγμός* strictly means, as here given, the *act* of seizing or snatching [so in the only place in profane writers where it occurs, viz Plut. de Puerorum educ p. 120 A, *καὶ τοὺς μὲν Θήβησι κ τοὺς Ἤλιδι φευκτέον ἔρωτας, κ τὸν ἐκ Κρήτης καλούμενον* **ἁρπαγμόν** One thing must also be remembered,—that in the word, the leading idea is not 'snatching *from another*,' but 'snatching, grasping, *for one's self*'—it

εἶναι [q] ἴσα [q] θεῷ, 7 ἀλλὰ ἑαυτὸν [r] ἐκένωσεν [m] μορφὴν δούλου

q John v. 18 τιμῷν ἴσα θεοῖς, Diod Sic i. 80 ἴσα τῷ θεῷ σέβειν, Paus Corinth 2 τιμὴν δε λελόγχασ' ἴσα θεοῖσι, Hom Odyss λ 304, see 2 Macc ix 12 ἴσα, Luke vi 34 Rev xxi 16 only Wisd vii 4 only -ος, Matt xx 12 Mark xiv 56, 59 John as above Acts xi 17 only Ezek xl 5 r = here only Jos Antt viii 10 3, τους θησαυρους ἐξεκενωσε (Rom iv 14 1 Cor i 17 ix 15 2 Cor ix 3 only Jer xiv 2 xv 9 only)

7. [αλλα, so BFℵ]

answers to τὰ ἑαυτῶν σκοποῦντες above], not [ἅρπαγμα] the *thing so seized* or snatched. but that here, τὸ εἶναι ἴσα θεῷ, i e a *state*, being in apposition with it, the difference between the *act* [subjective] and the *thing* [objective] would logically be very small: (4) that τὸ εἶναι ἴσα θεῷ is no *new* thing, which He thought it not robbery to *be*, i. e. to *take upon Him*,—but His state already existing, *respecting which* He οὐχ ἡγήσατο &c.. (5) that this clause, being opposed by ἀλλά to His great act of self denial, cannot be a mere secondary one, conveying an additional detail of His Majesty in His præ-existent state, but must carry the whole weight of the negation of selfishness on His part (6) that this last view is confirmed by the ἡγήσατο, taking up and corresponding to ἡγούμενοι above, ver. 3. (7) Other renderings have been — (α) of those who hold τὸ εἶναι ἴσα θεῷ, as above to be virtually identical with ἐν μορφῇ θεοῦ ὑπάρχειν before,—Chrys. says, ὁ τοῦ θεοῦ υἱὸς οὐκ ἐφοβήθη καταβῆναι ἀπὸ τοῦ ἀξιώματος οὐ γὰρ ἁρπαγμὸν ἡγήσατο τὴν θεότητα, οὐκ ἐδεδοίκει μή τις αὐτὸν ἀφέληται τὴν φύσιν ἢ τὸ ἀξίωμα. διὸ καὶ ἀπέθετο αὐτό, θαῤῥῶν ὅτι αὐτὸ ἀναλήψεται καὶ ἔκρυψεν, ἡγούμενος οὐδὲν ἐλαττοῦσθαι ἀπὸ τούτου διὰ τοῦτο οὐκ εἶπεν οὐχ ἥρπασεν, ἀλλὰ οὐχ ἁρπαγμὸν ἡγήσατο, ὅτι οὐχ ἁρπάσας εἶχε τὴν ἀρχήν, ἀλλὰ φυσικήν, οὐ δεδομένην, ἀλλὰ μόνιμον κ. ἀσφαλῆ. And so in the main, Œc, Thl., Aug..—Beza, "*non ignoravit, se in ea re (quod Deo patri coequalis esset) nullam injuriam cuiquam facere, sed suo jure uti nihilominus tamen quasi jure suo cessit*"—and so Calvin, but wrongly maintaining for ἡγήσατο a subjunctive sense: '*non fuisset arbitratus*.' Thdrt, θεὸς γὰρ ὤν, κ φύσει θεός, κ. τὴν πρὸς τὸν πατέρα ἰσότητα ἔχων, οὐ μέγα τοῦτο ὑπέλαβε τοῦτο γὰρ ἴδιον τῶν παρ' ἀξίαν τιμῆς τινος τετυχηκότων. ἀλλὰ τὴν ἀξίαν κατακρύψας, τὴν ἄκραν ταπεινοφροσύνην εἵλετο, κ τὴν ἀνθρωπείαν ὑπέδυ μορφήν and so, nearly, Ambr, Castal, all,—Luther, Erasm, Grot, Calov., all,—'*He did not as a victor his spoils, make an exhibition of &c, but*'. . . (β) of those who distinguish τὸ εἶναι ἴσα θεῷ from ἐν μορφῇ θεοῦ ὑπάρχειν Bengel,—'*Christus, quum posset esse pariter Deo, non arripuit, non duxit rapinam, non subito usus est illa facultate*' De Wette, '*Christ had, when He began His Messianic course, the glory of the godhead potentially in Himself, and might have devoted Himself to manifesting it forth in His life. but seeing that it lay not in the purpose of the work of Redemption that He should at the commencement of it have taken to Himself divine honour, had He done so, the assumption of it would have been an act of robbery*'—Lunemann [in Meyer]: '*Christus, etsi ab æterno inde dignitate creatoris et domini rerum omnium frueretur, ideoque divina indutus magnificentia coram patre consideret, nihilo tamen minus haud arripiendum sibi esse autumabat existendi modum cum Deo æqualem, sed ultro se exinanivit.*' And in fact Arius [and his party] had led the way in this explanation ὅτι θεὸς ὢν ἐλάττων οὐχ ἥρπασε τὸ εἶναι ἴσα τῷ θεῷ τῷ μεγάλῳ καὶ μείζονι See this triumphantly answered in Chrys Hom. vi. in loc. Indeed the whole of this method of interpretation is rightly charged with absurdity by Chrys, seeing that in ἐν μορφῇ θεοῦ ὑπάρχων we have already equality with God expressed: εἰ ἦν θεός, πῶς εἶχεν ἁρπάσαι; κ. πῶς οὐκ ἀπερινόητον τοῦτο, τίς γὰρ ἂν εἴποι, ὅτι ὁ δεῖνα, ἄνθρωπος ὤν, οὐχ ἥρπασε τὸ εἶναι ἄνθρωπος, πῶς γὰρ ἄν τις ὅπερ ἐστίν, ἁρπάσειεν, (8) We have now to enquire, whether the opening of the passage will bear to be understood of our Lord *already incarnate*. De Wette, al, have maintained that the name χριστὸς Ἰησοῦς cannot apply to the λόγος ἄσαρκος But the answer to this is easy, viz that that name applies to the *entire historical Person* of our Lord, of whom the whole passage is said, and not merely to Him in his præ-existent state That one and the same Person of the Son of God, ἐν μορφῇ θεοῦ ὑπάρχων, afterwards ἐν ὁμοιώματι ἀνθρώπων ἐγένετο, gathering to itself the humanity, in virtue of which He is now designated in the concrete, Christ Jesus. So that the dispute virtually resolves itself into the question between the two lines of interpretation given above,—on which I have already pronounced. But it seems to me to be satisfactorily settled by the contrast between ἐν μορφῇ θεοῦ ὑπάρχων

[s] λαβών, ἐν [t] ὁμοιώματι ἀνθρώπων [u] γενόμενος,
8 καὶ [v] σχήματι [w] εὑρεθεὶς ὡς ἄνθρωπος [x] ἐταπείνωσεν ἑαυτόν,
γενόμενος [y] ὑπήκοος [z] μέχρι θανάτου, θανάτου [a] δὲ σταυ-

ABCDF KLℵ a b c d e f g h k l m n o 17

s = here only. t Rom. i. 23. v. 14. vi. 5. viii. 3. Rev. ix. 7 only. Ps. cv. 20. u Rom. i. 3. Acts xix. 23. Gal. iv. 4. v 1 Cor. vii. 31 only. Isa. iii. 17 only. w = Matt. i. 18. Luke xvii. 18. 2 Cor. v. 3. 1 Kings xiii. 15. x Matt. xviii. 4. xxiii. 12 al. Prov. xiii. 7. y Acts vii. 39. 2 Cor. ii. 9 only. Prov. iv. 3. xiii. 1. z = 2 Tim. ii. 9. Heb. xii. 4. 2 Macc. xiii. 14. 3 Macc. vii. 16. a = Rom. iii. 22.

8. ins του bef σταυρου ℵ.

and *μορφὴν δούλου λαβών.* These two cannot belong to Christ in the same incarnate state. Therefore the former of them must refer to his *præ-incarnate* state.

7.] **but emptied Himself** (ἑαυτόν emphatic,—not ἐκένωσεν ἑαυτόν. **ἐκένωσεν**, contrast to **ἁρπαγμὸν ἡγήσ.**—he not only did not *enrich* himself, but he *emptied* himself:—He used His equality with God as an opportunity, not for self-exaltation, but for self-abasement. And the word simply and literally means, '*exinanivit*' [vulg.], as above. He emptied Himself of the *μορφὴ θεοῦ* [not His *essential* glory, but its manifested possession: see on the words above: the glory which He had with the Father before the world began, John xvii. 5, and which He resumed at His glorification]—He ceased while in this state of exinanition, to reflect the glory which He had with the Father. Those who understand **ὅς** above of the *incarnate* Saviour, are obliged to explain away this powerful word: thus Calv., '*inanitio hæc eadem est cum humiliatione de qua postea videbimus:*' Calov., '*veluti deposuit:*' Le Clerc, '*non magis ea usus est, quam si ea destitutus fuisset:*' De W., 'the manner and form of the *κένωσις* is given by the three following participles' [*λαβών, γενόμενος, εὑρεθείς*]: alii aliter) **by taking the form of a servant** (specification of the *method in which* He emptied Himself: not co-ordinate with [as De W., al.] but *subordinate to* **ἐκένωσεν ἑαυτόν.**

The participle **λαβών** does not point to that which has preceded *ἑαυτ. ἐκέν.*, but to a simultaneous act,=as in *εὖ γ' ἐποίησας ἀναμνήσας με* [Plat. Phæd. p. 60 D], see Bernhardy, Synt. p. 383, and Harless on Eph. i. 13. And so of *γενόμενος* below. The **δοῦλος** is contrasted with 'equality with God'—and imports '*a servant* of *God,*'—not *a servant generally*, nor a servant of man and God. And this state, of a *servant of God*, is further defined by what follows), **being made** (by birth into the world,—'*becoming:*' but we must not render the general, **γενόμενος**, by the particular, '*being born*') **in the likeness of men** (cf. *ἐν ὁμοιώματι σαρκὸς ἁμαρτίας*, Rom. viii. 3. He was not a *man, purus putus homo* [Mey.], but the Son of God manifest in the flesh and nature of men. On the interpretation impugned above, which makes all these clauses refer to acts of Christ, in our *nature*, this word *ὁμοιώματι* loses all meaning. But on the right interpretation, it becomes forcible in giving another subordinate specification to *μορφὴν δούλου λαβών*—viz. that He was made in *like form* to *men*, who are *θεοῦ δοῦλοι*).

8.] My interpretation has hitherto come very near to that of Meyer. But here I am compelled to differ from him. He would join **καὶ σχ. εὑρ. ὡς ἄνθρ.** to the foregoing, put a period at **ἄνθρ.**, and begin the next sentence by **ἐταπείνωσεν** without a copula. The main objection to this with me, is, the word **εὑρεθείς**. It seems to denote the taking up afresh of the subject, and introducing a new portion of the history. Hitherto of the act of laying aside the form of God, specified to have consisted in *μορφὴν δούλου λαβεῖν*, and *ἐν ὁμ. ἀνθρώπων γενέσθαι*. But now we take Him up again, this having past; we *find* Him in his human appearance—and what then? we have further acts of self-humiliation to relate. So Van Hengel: "duo enim, ut puto, diversa hic tradit Paulus, et quamnam vivendi rationem Christus inierit, ... et quomodo hanc vivendi rationem ad mortem usque persecutus sit." **And when He was** (having been) **found in having** (guise, outward semblance; e.g. of look, and dress, and speech. **σχήματι** is a more specific repetition of **ὁμοιώμ.** above: and is here *emphatic*: 'being found in *habit*, &c. He did not stop with this outward semblance, but . . . .') **as a man** (for He was not *a man*, but God [in Person], with the humanity taken on Him: *ὡς ἄνθρωπος—ἡ γὰρ ἀναληφθεῖσα φύσις τοῦτο ἦν· αὐτὸς δὲ τοῦτο οὐκ ἦν, τοῦτο δὲ περιέκειτο*, Thdrt.) **He humbled himself** (in His humanity: a further act of self-denial. This time, *ἑαυτόν* does not precede, because, as Meyer well says,—in ver. 7 the pragmatic weight rested on the *reflexive reference* of the act, but here on the *reflexive act* itself) **by becoming** (see on the aorist participle above. It specifies, *wherein the ταπείνωσις consisted*) **obedient** (to God; as before in the *δούλου*: not '*capientibus se, dam-*

ρου. 9 [b] διὸ [b] καὶ ὁ θεὸς αὐτὸν [c] ὑπερύψωσεν καὶ [d] ἐχαρίσατο αὐτῷ [τὸ] [e] ὄνομα τὸ ὑπὲρ πᾶν [e] ὄνομα, 10 ἵνα [f] ἐν
τῷ [e] ὀνόματι Ἰησοῦ πᾶν [g] γόνυ [g] κάμψῃ [h] ἐπουρανίων καὶ

b = [Rom i 24 iv 22] 1 Cor v 9
c here only Ps xxxvi 35 xcvi 9 Song of 3 children, passim Dan iv 34, 37 Theod
d Luke vii 21 Rom viii 32 Gal iii 18 ch i 29 † 2 Macc iii 33
e = Eph i 21 reff
f = John xiv 13 Eph v 20 al
g Eph iii 14 reff κ intr, Rom xiv 11, from Isa xlv 24
h = John iii 12 1 Cor xv 40 al (Eph i 3 reff) Dan ii 23 (26) Theod -edd (οὐρ, F vat)

9. rec om 1st το, with DFKL rel Orig$_2$ Eus$_3$ Ath$_3$ Epiph Chr Cyr$_3$ Thdrt$_2$ Procl Damasc: ins ABCℵ 17 Dion-alex Eus$_2$ Cyr$_{aliq}$ Procop$_3$.—ins εις bef το υπερ F, *ut sit super* Cypr. att ιησ. ins χριστου ℵ[1]: om ℵ[3].

nantibus et interficientibus,' as Grot. See Rom. v 19, Heb. v. 8 f, and ver 9,—διὸ καὶ ὁ θεός,—referring to the τῷ θεῷ here understood) **even unto** (as far as) **death** (the climax of His obedience. **μέχρι θανάτου** must not be taken with ἐταπείνωσεν, as Beng, al, which breaks the sentence awkwardly), **and that the death of the cross** (on this sense of **δέ**, see ref, and note there —τουτέστι, τοῦ ἐπικαταράτου, τοῦ τοῖς ἀνόμοις ἀφωρισμένου, Thl).

9—11.] *Exaltation of Jesus, consequent on this His humiliation*—brought forward as an encouragement to follow His example. "Quod autem beati sint quicunque sponte humiliantur cum Christo, probat ejus exemplo: nam a despectissima sorte evectus fuit in summam altitudinem. Quicunque ergo se humiliat, similiter exaltabitur Quis nunc submissionem recuset, qua in gloriam regni cœlestis conscenditur?" Calvin. **Wherefore** (i. e. on account of this His self-humiliation and obedience see Heb ii 9, note not as Calv, '*quo facto*,' trying to evade the meritorious obedience of Christ thus, 'quod dictio illativa hic magis consequentiam sonet quam causam, hinc patet, quod alioqui sequetur, hominem divinos honores posse mereri et ipsum Dei thronum acquirere, quod non modo absurdum sed dictu etiam horrendum est' strangely forgetting that herein Christ was not *a man*, nor an example what we can do, but the eternal Son of God, lowering Himself to take the nature of men, and in it rendering voluntary and perfect obedience) **also** (introduces the result, reff and Luke i. 35; Acts x. 29) **God** (on His part: reference to the τῷ θεῷ understood after ὑπήκοος above) **highly exalted Him** (not only ὕψωσεν, but ὑπερύψωσεν; His exaltation being a super-eminent one, cf. ὑπερνικᾶν, Rom viii 37, also 2 Cor xii. 7; 2 Thess. i. 3. Not, '*hath* highly exalted' the reference is to a historical fact, viz that of His Ascension), **and gave to Him** (the Father being greater than the incarnate Son, John xiv 28, and having by His exaltation of Jesus to His throne, freely bestowed on him the kingly office, which is the completion of His Mediatorship, Rom xiv 9) **the name which is above every name** (ὄνομα must be kept, against most Commentators, to its plain sense of NAME,—and not rendered '*glory*,' or understood of His office. The name is, the very name which He bore in His humiliation, but which now is the highest and most glorious of all names, **τὸ ὄνομα ἸΗΣΟΥ**. Compare His own answer in glory, Acts ix. 5, ἐγώ εἰμι Ἰησοῦς, ὃν σὺ διώκεις As to the construction in the rec, without the τό before ὄνομα, the *indefinite* ὄνομα is afterwards *defined* to be *that* name, which we all know and reverence, by τὸ ὑπὲρ κ τ λ. The τό before ὄνομα may have been inserted to assimilate the expression to the more usual one), 10.] **that** (intent of this exaltation) **in the name of Jesus** (emphatic, as the ground and element of the act which follows) **every knee should bend** (i e all prayer should be made [not, as E V, '*at* the name of Jesus every knee should bow,'—which surely the words will not bear] But *what* prayer? *to* JESUS, or *to* GOD THROUGH HIM? The only way to answer this question is to regard the general aim of the passage. This undoubtedly is, the *exaltation of Jesus*. The εἰς δόξαν θεοῦ πατρός below is no deduction from this, but rather an additional reason why we should carry on the exaltation of Jesus *until this new particular is introduced* This would lead us to infer that the universal prayer is to be *to* JESUS. And this view is confirmed by the next clause, where every tongue is to confess that Jesus Christ is κύριος, when we remember the common expression, ἐπικαλεῖσθαι τὸ ὄνομα κυρίου, for prayer Rom x 12 f; 1 Cor i 2 [2 Tim. ii 22], Acts [vii 59] ix 14, 21; xxii 16), **of those in heaven** (angels Eph i 20, 21. Heb i. 6) **and those on earth** (men) **and those under the earth** (the dead so Hom. Il. ι 457, Ζεὺς καταχθόνιος, Pluto; so

i John ii 12 1 Cor xv 40 bis 2 Cor v 1 ch iii 19 James iii 15 only † k here only † l Rom xiv 11 xv 9 Matt xi 25 Isa xlv 23 (ὀμεῖται, vat) m = 1 Cor v 8 xi 33 xiv 39 ch iv 1 al

[i] ἐπιγείων καὶ [k] καταχθονίων, 11 καὶ πᾶσα γλῶσσα [l] ἐξ- ABCDF
ομολογήσεται ὅτι κύριος Ἰησοῦς χριστὸς εἰς δόξαν θεοῦ KLℵ a b
πατρός. 12 [m] ὥστε, [n] ἀγαπητοί μου, καθὼς πάντοτε ὑπ- c d e f g
ηκούσατε, μὴ ὡς ἐν τῇ [o] παρουσίᾳ μου μόνον, ἀλλὰ νῦν h k l m
πολλῷ μᾶλλον ἐν τῇ [p] ἀπουσίᾳ μου [q] μετὰ [q] φόβου καὶ n o 17
[q] τρόμου τὴν [r] ἑαυτῶν σωτηρίαν [s] κατεργάζεσθε, 13 θεὸς

only Ps cxxvi 2 n w gen, Matt xii 18 Acts xv 25 Rom i 7 xvi 5, &c 1 Cor x 14 o = ch i 20 reff p here only † q Eph vi 5 reff r 2nd pers, Rom vi 11, 13, 16 1 Cor vi 19 2 Cor vii 11 al s = Rom iv 15 v 3. 2 Cor vii 10 al

11 rec εξομολογησηται, with Bℵ rel Eus Cyr txt ACDFKL a(in lect at end of ms) d e k m Orig Ath-mss[3]. om χριστος F Eus (not F-lat.)
12 for αγαπητοι, αδελφοι A, some lectionaries, demid æth om ως B 3 17. 48. 72 178 Syr copt arm Chr, lat-ff. om 1st εν Fℵ[3] fuld D-lat G-lat Ambrst πολ μαλ. bef νυν DF latt arm Ambrst Pelag om νυν f k 4. 33. 115 Chr-comm Thl. om εν τη απουσ μου F

Thdrt: ἐπουρανίους καλεῖ τοὺς ἀοράτους δυνάμεις, ἐπιγείους δὲ τοὺς ἔτι ζῶντας ἀνθρώπους, καὶ καταχθονίους τοὺς τεθνεῶτας Various erroneous interpretations have been given—e. g. Chr., Thl, Œc, Erasm. understand by καταχθ, the *devils*—and Chr, Thl. give metaphorical meanings, οἱ δίκαιοι κ οἱ ἁμαρτωλοί), 11] **and every tongue** (of all the classes just named) **shall confess** (result of the πᾶν γόνυ κάμψαι) **that Jesus Christ is Lord** (see the predicate κύριος similarly prefixed in 1 Cor. xii. 3) **to the glory** (so as for such confession to issue in the glory) **of God the Father** (which is the great end of all Christ's mediation and mediatorial kingdom, cf. 1 Cor. xv 24—28. 'Ut Dei majestas in Christo reluceat, et Pater glorificetur in Filio. Vide Johan. v. et xvii., et habebis hujus loci expositionem' Calv.) 12—16] *After this glorious example, he exhorts them to earnestness after Christian perfection.* 12 ὥστε] **wherefore**—i. e. as a consequence on this pattern set you by Christ The **ὑπηκούσατε** answers **to** γενόμενος ὑπήκοος ver 8, and **σωτηρία** to the exaltation of Christ. It is therefore better, with Meyer, to refer **ὥστε** to that which has just preceded, than with De Wette, Wiesinger, al, to all the foregoing exhortations, ch. i 27 ff. **ὑπηκούσατε**] i e *to God*, as Christ above not as ordinarily, **'to** *me*' or '*my Gospel*' This last De W grounds on the presence and absence of the Apostle mentioned below those clauses however do not belong to ὑπηκούσατε, but to κατεργάζεσθε. This is evident by μὴ ὡς and νῦν In fact it would be hardly possible logically to connect them with ὑπηκούσατε. As it is, they connect admirably with κατεργάζεσθε, see below **ὡς** is by no means superfluous, but gives the sense **not as if** (it were a matter to be done) **in my presence only,—but now** (as things are at present) **much more** (with more earnestness) **in my absence** (because spiritual help from me is withdrawn from you) **carry out** (bring to an accomplishment) **your own** (emphasis on ἑαυτῶν, perhaps as directing attention to the example of Christ which has preceded,—as He obeyed and won His exaltation, so do *you* obey and carry out *your own* salvation) **salvation** (which is *begun* with justification by faith, but must be carried out, brought to an issue, by sanctification of the Spirit—a life of holy obedience and advance to Christian perfection. For this reason, the E V, '*work out* your own salvation,' is bad, because ambiguous, giving the idea that the salvation is a thing to be gotten, brought in and brought about, by ourselves) **with fear and trembling** (lest you should fail of its accomplishment at the last The expression indicates a state of anxiety and self distrust. see reff.—δεῖ γὰρ φοβεῖσθαι κ. τρέμειν ἐν τῷ ἐργάζεσθαι τὴν ἰδίαν σωτηρίαν ἕκαστον, μήποτε ὑποσκελισθεὶς ἐκπέσῃ ταύτης Œc in Meyer. And the stress of the exhortation is on these words —considering the immense sacrifice which Christ made for you, and the lofty eminence to which God hath now raised Him, be ye more than ever earnest that you miss not your own share in such salvation. The thought before the Apostle's mind is much the same as that in Heb ii. 3, πῶς ἡμεῖς ἐκφευξόμεθα τηλικαύτης ἀμελήσαντες σωτηρίας.) 13] encouragement to fulfil the last exhortation—for you are not left to yourselves, but have the almighty Spirit dwelling in you to aid you "Intelligo," says Calvin, "gratiam supernaturalem,

γάρ ἐστιν ὁ [t] ἐνεργῶν ἐν ὑμῖν καὶ τὸ θέλειν καὶ τὸ [t] ἐνεργεῖν [u] ὑπὲρ τῆς [v] εὐδοκίας. 14 [w] πάντα ποιεῖτε χωρὶς
[x] γογγυσμῶν καὶ [y] διαλογισμῶν, 15 ἵνα γένησθε [z] ἄμεμπτοι

t Paul (1 Cor xii 6 al15) only, exc Matt xiv 2 (James v 16. Isa xli 4 u = Rom xv 8 v = Eph i 4 reff w = 1 Cor x 31 x John vii 12 Acts vi 1 1 Pet iv 9 only Exod xvi 7, 9. y = Luke xxiv 38. 1 Tim ii 8 z Luke i. 6. ch iii 6 1 Thess iii 13 Heb. viii 7 only Gen xvii 1 (-τως, 1 Thess ii 10)

13 rec ins ὁ bef θεος, with D[2] [3]L rel · om ABCD[1]FKℵ 17 Damasc aft ενεργων ins δυναμεις A. aft ευδοκιας ins αυτου C.

15. for γενησθε, ητε AD[1]F latt txt BCD[3]KLℵ rel Chr Thdrt Philo-carp Damasc.

quæ provenit ex Spiritu regenerationis. Nam quatenus sumus homines, jam in Deo sumus, et vivimus, et movemur, verum hic de alio motu disputat, quam illo universali." This working must not be explained away with Pelagius (in Mey.), 'velle operatur *suadendo* et *præmia promittendo*:' it is an efficacious working which is here spoken of: God not only *brings about* the will, but *creates* the will —we owe both the will to do good, and the power, to His indwelling Spirit.

ἐν ὑμ. not *among you*, but **in you**, as in ref. 1 Cor, and 2 Cor. iv. 12, Eph ii 2, Col i. 29. The θέλειν and ἐνεργεῖν are well explained by Calvin "Fatemur, nos a natura habere voluntatem. sed quoniam peccati corruptione mala est, tunc bona esse incipit, quum reformata est a Deo. Nec dicimus hominem quicquam boni facere, nisi volentem. sed tunc, quum voluntas regitur a Spiritu Dei. Ergo quod ad hanc partem spectat, videmus Deo integram laudem asseri, ac frivolum esse quod sophistæ docent, offerri nobis gratiam et quasi in medio poni, ut eam amplectemur si libeat. Nisi enim efficaciter ageret Deus in nobis, non diceretur efficere bonam voluntatem. De secunda parte idem sentiendum Deus, inquit, est [ὁ] ἐνεργῶν ἐνεργεῖν. Perducit igitur ad finem usque pios affectus, quos nobis inspiravit, ne sint irriti sicut per Ezechielem (xi. 20) promittit Faciam ut in præceptis meis ambulent Unde colligimus, perseverantiam quoque merum esse ejus donum" **ὑπὲρ τῆς εὐδοκίας**] **for the sake of His good pleasure,**—i e in order to carry out that good counsel of His will which He hath purposed towards you. εὐδοκίαν δὲ τὸ ἀγαθὸν τοῦ θεοῦ προσηγόρευσε θέλημα· θέλει δὲ πάντας ἀνθρώπους σωθῆναι, κ εἰς ἐπίγνωσιν ἀληθείας ἐλθεῖν, Thdrt Conyb would join **ὑπὲρ τῆς εὐδ** with the following verse, —'do all things for the sake of good will'—and remarks, 'It is strange that so clear and simple a construction, involving no alteration in the text, should not have been before suggested' But surely St Paul could not have written thus. The sense of **εὐδοκία** indeed, would be the same as in ch i. 15 —but that very passage should have prevented this conjecture. It must have been in that case here as there, δι' εὐδοκίαν, or at all events, ὑπὲρ εὐδοκίας the insertion of the article where it is generally omitted from abstract nouns after a preposition, as here, necessarily brings in a reflexive sense,—to be referred to the subject of the sentence and thus we should get a meaning very different from that given by Conyb, viz.: 'Do all things for the sake of (to carry out) *your own* good pleasure.' It has been proposed (I know not by whom, but it was communicated to me by letter · I see it also noticed in Ellic's note, and Van Hengel's refutation of it referred to) to take **ἑαυτῶν** [ver 12] as = ἀλλήλων, and render "with fear and trembling labour heartily for one another's salvation;" thus connecting the ὥστε with ver 4 The suggestion is ingenious, and as far as the *mere question* of the *sense* of ἑαυτῶν goes, perhaps allowable; but see Eph. iv 32, Col. iii. 13, 16; 1 Pet. iv 8, 10. there are, however, weighty and I conceive fatal objections to it 1) the emphatic position of ἑαυτῶν, which restricts it to its *proper* meaning. 2) the occurrence of ἑαυτῶν, in the very verse [4] with which it is sought to connect our passage, *in its proper meaning*—μὴ τὰ ἑαυτῶν ἕκαστοι σκοπεῖτε, ἀλλὰ καὶ τὰ ἑτέρων ἕκαστοι: 3) the context, and inference drawn by ὥστε, which this rendering altogether mistakes see it explained above **14 ff**] *More detailed exhortations*, as to the manner of their Christian energizing. **γογγυσμός**, in every other place in the N T. (reff.), as also in ref. Exod., signifies murmuring against men, not against God (as Mey). And the context here makes it best to keep the same sense such murmurings arising from selfishness, which is especially discommended to us by the example of Christ. Thus I still maintain as against Ellic. his rejection of John vii 12 and 1 Pet. iv 9, as not applicable, not seeming to me to be justified. **διαλογισμῶν**] by the same rule, we should rather understand dis-

a Matt x 16 Rom xvi 19 only †
b = John i 12 xi 52 Rom viii 16, 21 ix 8 1 John iii 1, &c ✓ 2 only

καὶ [a] ἀκέραιοι, [b] τέκνα θεοῦ [c] ἄμωμα [d] μέσον [ef] γενεᾶς
[cg] σκολιᾶς καὶ [h] διεστραμμένης, ἐν [i] οἷς φαίνεσθε ὡς [k] φωστῆρες ἐν κόσμῳ, 16 [l] λόγον [l] ζωῆς [m] ἐπέχοντες, εἰς [n] καύ-

ABCDF KLℵ a b c d e f g h k l m n o 17

c Eph i 4 reff (-μητοι, 2 Pet. iii 14 only) see Deut xxxii 5 d adv, Num xxxv 5 Hom Il μ 167 Od ξ 300 e Acts ii 40 Deut xxxii 5 f Matt xvii 17 || g as above (e) Luke iii 5, from Isa xl 4 Acts ii 40 1 Pet ii 18 only h as above (f) Luke xxiii 2 Acts xiii 8, 10 xx 30 only Prov. vi 14 i constr, Matt i 21 xiv 14 John xv 6 Josh xv 1 Winer, edn 6, § 21 3 k Rev xxi 11 only Gen i 14, 16 l 1 John i 1 only see Acts v 20 xiii 26 m = here only Hom Il. χ 83, μαζον 494, κοτυλην Od π 444, οινον (1 Tim iv 16 reff) n Gal vi 4 reff constr, 1 Cor ix 16

rec (for αμωμα) αμωμητα, with DFKL rel Chr Thdrt Philo-carp Damasc txt ABCℵ 17 (Clem) Cyr rec (for μεσον) εν μεσω (explanatory corrn), with D[2] [3]KL rel txt ABCD[1]Fℵ 17 67[2] Clem. εν τω κοσμω τουτω in hoc mundo F D lat spec Chrom Leo.

16. εχοντες ℵ[1] · txt ℵ corr[1]

putings with men, than doubts respecting God or duty (Mey). It is objected that the N T meaning of διαλογισμός is generally the latter. But this may be doubted (see on 1 Tim ii 8), and at all events the verb διαλογίζω, and its cognate διαλέγομαι, must be taken for 'to dispute' in Mark ix 33, 34 I cannot understand how either word can apply to matters merely internal, seeing that the primary object is stated below to be blamelessness, and good example to others cf μέσον γενεᾶς, κ τ λ 15] ἄμεμπτοι, without blame, ἀκέραιοι, "pure, simplices, vulg æth. sinceres [i], Clarom ὁ μὴ κεκραμένος κακοῖς, ἀλλ' ἁπλοῦς καὶ ἀποίκιλος, Etym Mag . For the distinction between ἀκέραιος, ἁπλοῦς, and ἄκακος, see Tittm Synon i p 27" Ellicott On τέκνα θεοῦ, see especially Rom viii. 14, 15 ἄμωμα, blameless · unblamed, and unblameable · Herod uses it, ii 177, of a law τῷ ἐκεῖνοι ἐς αἰεὶ χρέωνται, ἐόντι ἀμώμῳ νόμῳ The whole clause is a reminiscence of ref Deut, where we have τέκνα μωμητά, γενεὰ σκολιὰ κ διεστραμμένη. For the figurative meaning of σκολιός, cf. reff Acts and 1 Pet, and Plat Legg. xii. p 945 B, ἄν τίς τι εἴπῃ σκολιὸν αὐτῶν ἢ πράξῃ,—Gorg p 525 A, πάντα σκολιὰ ὑπὸ ψεύδους κ. ἀλαζονείας, κ οὐδὲν εὐθὺ διὰ τὸ ἄνευ ἀληθείας τεθράφθαι —and on διεστραμμένη,— διεστρέφετο ὑπὸ κόλακος, Polyb viii 24 3. ἐν οἷς, the masculine referring to those included in γενεά: so Thuc i 136, φεύγει—ἐς Κέρκυραν, ὢν αὐτῶν εὐεργέτης See more examples in Kuhner, ii p. 43. φαίνεσθε, not imperative, as most of the Fathers, Erasm, Calvin, Grot., al, —but indicative, for this is the position of Christians in the world · see Matt v. 14; Eph v. 8. So De W., Meyer, Wiesinger, &c. &c. It has been said (Mey, Wies, al) that we must not render φαίνεσθε 'shine,' which would be φαίνετε but surely there is but very little difference between 'appear' and 'shine' here, and only St John and St. Peter use φαίνω for 'to shine,' John i 5, v. 35, 1 John ii 8, Rev. i. 16; 2 Pet. i. 19,—not St. Paul, for whom in such a matter their usage is no rule. Ellic 1) objects that this must not be alleged against the simple meaning of the word, and 2) wishes to give the middle a special use in connexion with the appearance or rising of the heavenly bodies. But we may answer 1) by such examples as δεινοὶ δέ οἱ ὄσσε φάανθεν, where Rost and Palm translate the passive 'leuchteten' and 2) by urging that such a reference seems here to lay too much pregnancy of meaning on the word. φωστῆρες, not 'lights' merely, but luminaries, 'heavenly bodies' see ref Gen : and Sir xliii. 7, Wisd xiii. 2. ἐπέχοντες] probably as E V. holding forth (hardly, as Ellic, "seeing ye hold forth," but "in that ye hold forth ·" the participle being rather explicative than causal) to them, applying to them, which is the one of the commonest meanings of ἐπέχειν,—see reff Various senses have been given,—e g 'holding fast,' Luther, Estius, Bengel, De Wette, al 'in vertice tenentes,' Erasm. 'sustinentes,' Calv 'possessing,' Meyer, who quotes for this meaning Herod i 104, οἱ δὲ Σκύθαι τὴν Ἀσίαν πᾶσαν ἐπέσχον, and Thuc ii 101, ὁ δὲ τήν τε Χαλκιδικὴν κ Βοττικὴν κ Μακεδονίαν ἅμα ἐπέχων ἔφθειρε,—neither of which justify it for in both these places it is 'to occupy,' not 'to possess ' as also in Polyb iii 112 8, εὐχαὶ κ θυσίαι κ.τ λ . ἐπεῖχον τὴν πόλιν And this sense would manifestly be inapplicable His objection to the ordinary rendering, that the subjects of the sentence themselves shine by means of the λόγος τῆς ζωῆς, surely is irrelevant for may not the stars be said 'præbere,' 'prætendere,' their light, notwithstanding that that light is in them? Chrys., Œc, Thl, interpret it, μέλλοντες ζῆσεσθαι, τῶν σω-

χημα ἐμοὶ [o] εἰς [p] ἡμέραν χριστοῦ, ὅτι οὐκ [q] εἰς [q] κενὸν
[r] ἔδραμον οὐδὲ [q] εἰς [q] κενὸν [s] ἐκοπίασα. 17 ἀλλὰ [t] εἰ [t] καὶ
[u] σπένδομαι [v] ἐπὶ τῇ θυσίᾳ καὶ [w] λειτουργίᾳ τῆς πίστεως
ὑμῶν, χαίρω καὶ [x] συγχαίρω πᾶσιν ὑμῖν· 18 [y] τὸ δ' αὐτὸ
καὶ ὑμεῖς χαίρετε καὶ [x] συγχαίρετέ μοι.

o Eph iv 30. 2 Tim i 12. p ch i 6 reff. q Gal ii 2 reff. κ. 1 Thess iii 1 reff. r = Gal ii 2 reff. s = Rom xvi 6. Gal iv 11. Job xxxix 16. t 2 Cor iv 3, 16. u 2 Tim iv 6 only. Num xxviii 7 al. v see note. w Luke i 23. 2 Cor ix 12. Heb viii 6. ix 21 only. 1 Chron xxiv 3. x Luke i 58. xv 6, 9. 1 Cor xii 26. xiii 6 only. Gen xxi 6 only. ver 30. 1 P H. y = Matt xxvii 44.

καυχησιν D. ουδ' B.
17. [αλλα, so BD[1]F] (A def). και bef ει (et si) F. om και συγχαιρω (homœot) ℵ[1]: ins ℵ-corr[1].
18. δε ℵ 109.

ζομένων ὄντες· and Chrys continues οἱ φωστῆρές, φησι, λόγον φωτὸς ἐπέχουσιν· ὑμεῖς λόγον ζωῆς. τί ἐστι, λόγον ζωῆς σπέρμα ζωῆς ἔχοντες, τουτέστιν, ἐνέχυρα ζωῆς ἔχοντες, αὐτὴν κατέχοντες τὴν ζωήν, τουτέστι σπέρμα ζωῆς ἐν ὑμῖν ἔχοντες.— Thdrt, ἀντὶ τοῦ τῷ λόγῳ προσέχοντες τῆς ζωῆς, ungrammatically, for this would be λόγῳ ζωῆς ἐπέχοντες,—as ὁ δὲ ἐπεῖχεν αὐτοῖς, Acts iii 5: cf. also ref. 1 Tim. **εἰς καύχ. ἐμοί**] for (result of your thus walking, *as concerns myself*) **a matter of boasting for me against** (temporal: reserved for) **the day of Christ, that** (ὅτι οὐ μάτην τὴν ὑπὲρ ὑμῶν ἀνεδεξάμην σπουδήν, Thdrt) **I did not run** (the past tense is from the point of view of that day. On ἔδραμον, see reff) **for nothing, nor labour for nothing** (cf. ref. Job).

17, 18] These verses are closely connected with the preceding; not, as De W., al., with ch. i. 26, which is most unnatural, and never would occur to any reader. The connexion is this: in ver 16 he had tacitly assumed (**εἰς ἡμ. χ.**) that he should live to witness their blameless conduct even till the day of Christ. *Now*, he puts the other alternative—that the dangers which surrounded him would result in his death—and in that case equally he rejoiced, &c. **εἰ καί** implies more probability than καὶ εἰ: in the former the case is presupposed, in the latter merely hypothesized. Klotz in Devar p. 519 f., gives two examples from Xen.'s Anabasis: (1) ὁδοποιήσειέ γ' ἂν αὐτοῖς, καὶ εἰ σὺν τεθρίπποις βούλοιντο ἀπιέναι (iii. 2. 24), a supposition evidently thought improbable: (2) ἐγώ, ὦ Κλέανδρε, εἰ καὶ οἴει με ἀδικοῦντά τι ἄγεσθαι (vi. 4. 27), where as evidently the speaker believes that Cleander does entertain the thought. The difference is explained by the common rules of emphasis. In εἰ καί, the stress is on εἰ, which is simply '*posito*,' and the '*even*' belongs to *that which is assumed*: in καὶ εἰ, the stress is on καί, *even*, and the strangeness belongs not to the thing simply assumed, but to the making of the assumption. In the present case then, the Apostle seems rather to believe the supposition which he makes. **σπένδομαι**] not future, but *present*, **If I am even being poured out**, because the danger was besetting him *now*, and waxing onward to its accomplishment. He uses the word literally, with reference to the shedding of his blood. "He represents his whole apostolic work for the faith of the Philippians, as a *sacrifice*: if he is put to death in the course of it, he will be, by the shedding of his blood, poured out as a libation upon this sacrifice: as among the Jews (Num xxviii 7; xv. 4 ff. Jos Antt. iii 9. 4. Winer, RWB., s. v. Trankopfer) and heathens, in their sacrifices, libations of wine were usual, which were poured over the offerings (Hom Il. λ. 775, σπένδων αἴθοπα οἶνον ἐπ' αἰθομένοις ἱεροῖσιν· cf. also Herod ii 39)." Meyer. Wetst., al., would render it '*affundor*' (καρασπένδομαι), and understand it of the pouring of wine over a live victim destined for sacrifice—but wrongly. The **θυσία** is the *sacrifice*, i. e. the *deed* of sacrifice, not the victim, the thing sacrificed. **λειτουργία**, **priest's ministration**, without another article, signifying therefore the same course of action as that indicated by θυσία, viz. his apostolic labours: see below. **τῆς πίστεως ὑμ.**, gen. objective; your faith *is the sacrifice*, which I, as a priest, offer to God. The image is precisely as in Rom. xv. 16, where he is the priest, offering up the Gentiles to God. And the case which he puts is, that he, the priest, should have his own blood poured out at, upon (i. e. in accession to: not *locally* "upon" for it was not so among the Jews, see Ellic here), his sacrificing and presentation to God of their faith. **χαίρω**: not to be joined with ἐπί, as Chrys., but absolute, **I rejoice for myself** (οὐχ ὡς ἀποθανούμενος λυποῦμαι ἀλλὰ χαίρω, ὅτι σπονδὴ γίνομαι, Thl) **and congratulate you** (so the Vulg rightly, and all: not, '*rejoice with*

19 Ἐλπίζω δὲ ᶻ ἐν κυρίῳ Ἰησοῦ Τιμόθεον ταχέως ABC KLℵ
πέμψαι ᵃ ὑμῖν, ἵνα κἀγὼ ᵇ εὐψυχῶ γνοὺς ᶜ τὰ περὶ ὑμῶν. c d e
20 οὐδένα γὰρ ἔχω ᵈ ἰσόψυχον, ᵉ ὅστις ᶠ γνησίως ᶜ τὰ περὶ h k l
ὑμῶν ᵍ μεριμνήσει· 21 ʰ οἱ πάντες γὰρ ⁱ τὰ ἑαυτῶν ⁱ ζητοῦ- n o
σιν, οὐ τὰ Ἰησοῦ χριστοῦ. 22 τὴν δὲ ᵏ δοκιμὴν αὐτοῦ
γινώσκετε, ὅτι ὡς ˡ πατρὶ τέκνον ˡ σὺν ἐμοὶ ᵐ ἐδούλευσεν
ⁿ εἰς τὸ εὐαγγέλιον. 23 τοῦτον ᵒ μὲν οὖν ἐλπίζω πέμψαι,

z = ver 24. (not 1 Cor xv 19.) a dat, Acts xi 29 1 Cor iv 17 ch ii 16 b here only + Jos Antt xi 6 9 (-χος, Prov xxx 31.) c ch i 27 reff d here only Ps liv 13 only e = Acts x 41, 47 xiii 31, 43 al fr f here only + 2 Macc xiv 8 (-ος, ch iv 3 1 Tim i 2.) g constr, 1 Cor vii 32, 33, 34 ch iv 6 (Matt vi 34 v r) only Exod v 9 (a) h Rom xi 32 Eph iv 13 reff i 1 Cor x 24 xiii 5 k Rom v 4 bis 2 Cor ii 9 viii 2 ix 13 xiii 3 only + Ps lxvii 31 Symm l change of constr, Eph v 27, 33 1 John ii 2 al m = Luke xv 29 n = Rom x 1 ch i 5 al o 1 Cor vi 4, 7 ix 25 al

19. for κυριω, χριστω CD¹F copt. txt ABD³KLℵ rel vulg(and F-lat) vss gr-lat ff. for υμιν, προς υμας D¹ latt. εκψυχω A.

21. rec χρ. bef ιησ., with BL rel fuld(and demid) syr copt gr-ff Ambrst-ms om ιησ. K Cypr txt ACDFℵ 17 vss Clem lat-ff.—rec pref του, with b d f g h n om ABCDFKLℵ rel.

22. for εις το ευαγ, εν τοις δεσμοις του ευαγγελιου C

you,' as most Commentators [even Ellic] Meyer well observes that the following verse is decisive against this. for if *they rejoiced* already, what need of **καὶ ὑμεῖς χαίρετε**?—congratulate you, viz. on the fact that I have been thus poured out for your faith, which would be an honour and a boast for you. De W's objection, after Van Hengel, that to *congratulate* would be *συγχαίρομαι* is futile cf Æschin. p. 34, *τὴν Ἑστίαν ἐπώμοσε τὴν βουλαίαν συγχαίρειν τῇ πόλει ὅτι τοιούτους ἄνδρας ἐπὶ τὴν πρεσβείαν ἐξέπεμψεν*—Demosth p 194,—*Ῥοδίοις . συγχαίρω τῶν γεγενημένων*). 18] and (*'but'* would be too strong the contrast is only in the reciprocity) **on the same account** (accusative of reference, governed by *χαίρ*) **do ye** (imperative, not indicative, as Erasm, al) **rejoice** (answer to *συγχαίρω* above,—for this your honour) **and congratulate me** (answer to *χαίρω* above,—on this my joy)

19—30] ADDITIONAL NOTICES RESPECTING THE APOSTLE'S STATE IN HIS IMPRISONMENT HIS INTENDED MISSION OF TIMOTHEUS AND ACTUAL MISSION OF EPAPHRODITUS The connexion with the foregoing seems to be,—'and yet this *σπένδεσθαι* is by no means certain, for I hope to hear news of you soon, nay, to see you myself.' 19 **ἐν κυρίῳ**] 'my hope is not an idle one, as a worldly man's might be, but one founded on faith in Christ.' 1 Cor xv 19, to which Meyer refers, is wholly different see there. **ταχέως**, see ver 23. **ὑμῖν**] The dative after verbs of sending, &c. need not be regarded (as De W, al., here) as the dativus commodi, but is similar to that case after verbs of giving—indicating the position of the *recipient*. I stated in some former editions, that it is in no case equivalent to the more *local πρὸς ὑμᾶς* But Ellic has reminded me, that this is too widely stated, later writers undeniably using it in this sense See note on Acts xxi 16, and cf. such examples as *πότερον ἠγόμην Ἀβροκόμῃ*, Xen. Eph. iii. 6, and *ἤγαγεν αὐτὸν Ἀθανασίῳ τῷ πάππᾳ*, Epiph. vit. p. 310 d See the discussion in Winer, § 31 5 **κἀγώ**] 'as well as you, by your reception of news concerning me.' **εὐψ.**] **may be of good courage** The *verb* is unknown to the classics the imperative *εὐψύχει* is found in inscriptions on tombs, in the sense of the Latin *'have pia anima'*

20] Reason why he would send Timotheus above all others **for I have none else like-minded** (with myself, not with Timotheus, as Beza, Calv, al) **who** (of that kind, who) **will really** (emphatic:—with no secondary regards for himself, as in ver 21) **care for your affairs** (have real anxiety about your matters, to order them for the best): 21] **for all** (**my present companions**) (who these were, we know not they are characterized, ch iv 21, merely as *οἱ σὺν ἐμοὶ ἀδελφοί*—certainly not Luke—whether Demas, in transition between Philem 24 and 2 Tim. iv 10, we cannot say) **seek their own matters, not those of Jesus Christ** (no weakening of the assertion must be thought of, as that of rendering *οἱ πάντες*, *many*, or *most*,—or understanding the assertion, *care more about &c than &c*,—as many Commentators nor must it be restricted to the *love of ease*, &c, *unwillingness to undertake so long a journey*, as Chr., Œc., Thl: both *οἱ πάντες* and the assertion are absolute). 23] **But the approved worth** (reff) **of him ye know** (viz by trial, when we were at Philippi together, Acts

[p] ὡς ἂν [q] ἀφίδω [r] τὰ περὶ ἐμέ, [s] ἐξ αὐτῆς· 24 πέποιθα δὲ [t] ἐν
κυρίῳ ὅτι καὶ αὐτὸς ταχέως ἐλεύσομαι. 25 [uv] ἀναγκαῖον
δὲ [uw] ἡγησάμην Ἐπαφρόδιτον τὸν ἀδελφὸν καὶ [x] συνεργὸν
καὶ [y] συνστρατιώτην μου, ὑμῶν δὲ [z] ἀπόστολον καὶ [a] λειτουργὸν τῆς [b] χρείας μου, πέμψαι πρὸς ὑμᾶς, 26 [c] ἐπειδὴ
[d] ἐπιποθῶν ἦν πάντας ὑμᾶς, καὶ [e] ἀδημονῶν, διότι ἠκού-

p Rom xv 24 1 Cor xi 34
q here only = Jonah iv 5 (Thucyd vii 71)
r ch i 27 reff
s Mark vi 25 Acts x 33 xi 11 xxi 32 xxiii 30
t = ver 19
u 2 Cor ix 5 2 Macc ix 21
v ch i 24 reff
w Acts xxvi 2 ver 3 al Job xlii 6 Paul only, exc 3 John 3 † 2 Macc viii 7 xiv 5 only
x Rom xvi 3, 9, 21 ch iv 3 Col iv 11 Philem 1, 24
y Philem 2 only † Xen Anab i 2 26
z = John xiii 16 2 Cor viii 23 3 Kings xiv 6 F &c (not vat) only
a Rom xiii 6 xv 16 Heb i 7 (from Ps ciii 4) viii 2 only
b = Acts xx 34 xxviii 10 Rom xii 13 ch iv 16, 19 Tit. iii 14 2 Chron ii 16
c Luke xi 6 Acts xiii 46 1 Cor i 21, 22 al L P (exc Matt xxi 46 v r) Jer xxxi [xlviii] 7
d & constr, ch i 8 reff
e Matt xxvi 37 ‖ Mk only † Job xviii 20 Aq

23 rec απιδω, with B² C(-ει-) D³ K(e sil) L rel txt AB¹D¹Fℵ 17.
24 aft αυτος ins εγω ℵ-corr¹ at end ins προς υμας ACℵ¹(ℵ³ disapproving) vulg Syr copt Chr Thl Ambrst Pelag Facund
26 υμας bef παντας B copt. aft υμας ins ιδειν (*supplement. Meyer defends it, seeing no reason why it should have been supplied here, and not in ch* i 8: *but how could it be insd there, seeing that* εν σπλαγχνοις χρ ιησου *follows?*) ACDℵ¹ a b² f l m n 17 syr copt æth arm Damasc Thl Cassiod om BFKLℵ³ rel Chr Thdrt Victorin Ambrst.

xvi 1, 3,—xvii 14),—viz that as a son (serves) a father, he served with me for (reff.) the Gospel The construction is this the Apostle would have written, 'as a son a father, so he *served* me,'—but changes it to 'so he served *with* me,' from modesty and reverence, seeing that we are not servants one of another, but all of God, in the matter of the Gospel. We must not supply σύν before πατρί —when, in case of several nouns governed by the same preposition, that preposition is omitted before any, it is not before the *first*, cf Plat Rep iii p 414, δεῖ ὡς περὶ μητρὸς κ. τροφοῦ τῆς χώρας ἐν ᾗ εἰσι βουλεύεσθαι· and see Bernhardy, Syntax, p. 205. The examples cited by Ellicott to disprove this, do not seem to me to apply: viz. Æsch. Suppl. 313 [311], Eur Hel. 872 [863] both are instances of local terms coupled by καί, and both occur in poetry, where the exigencies of metre come into play. Winer takes the construction as above, edn 6, § 63, ii. 1 "as a son *with* a father" being, in the English translation [p. 599], a *misrendering* of the German, 'wie dem Vater ein Kind,' and of a kind which considerably diminishes one's confidence in the accuracy of the English edition μέν answers to δέ ver 24: οὖν reassumes ver. 19. ὡς ἂν ἀφίδω] as soon as I shall have ascertained On the force of the preposition, see Heb xii. 2, note. ὡς ἄν, of time, implying uncertainty as to the event indicated see reff. and Cebes, tab. p. 168, προστάττει δὲ τοῖς εἰσπορευομένοις, τί δεῖ αὐτοὺς ποιεῖν, ὡς ἂν εἰσέλθωσιν εἰς τὸν βίον. See also Klotz, Devar. pp. 759. 63 The form ἀφίδω is supposed by Meyer to be owing to the pronunciation of ἴδω with the digamma The word signifies here, see clearly, as in Herod viii 37, ἐπεὶ δὲ ἀγχοῦ τε ἔσαν οἱ βάρβαροι ἐπιόντες καὶ ἀπώρεον τὸ ἱρὸν ..· following the analogy of ἀπέχω and similar words the preposition being not intensive (as Ellic. wrongly reports my view), but exhaustive τὰ περὶ ἐμέ, my matters 24 ἐν κυρίῳ] See above, ver 19 καί, as well as Timothy. 25—30] *Of Epaphroditus his mission: and recommendation of him* Epaphroditus is not elsewhere mentioned. The name was a common one see Wetst h. l, and Tacit. Ann. xv. 55, Suet Domit. 14. There is perhaps no reason for supposing him identical with Epaphras (Col i. 7, iv 12. Philem 23), who was a minister of the Colossian church. We must not attempt to give a strict official meaning to each of the words predicated of Epaphroditus. The accumulation of them serves to give him greater recommendation in the eyes of the Philippians. 25.] συνστρατ. applies to the combat with the powers of darkness, in which the ministers of Christ are the leaders. see besides ref, 2 Tim ii 3 ὑμ. δέ] the contrast is to μου above. ἀπόστολον, not in the ordinary sense of Apostle, so that ὑμῶν should be as ἐθνῶν (ἀπόστολος) in Rom. xi. 13,—but as in ref. 2 Cor. (where see note), almost = ὁ ἀποσταλεὶς ὑφ' ὑμῶν λειτουρ.] minister (in supply) of my want Cf λειτουργία below, ver 30. and on χρείας, reff., especially Acts xx 34 λειτουργὸν δὲ αὐτὸν εἴρηκε τῆς χρείας, ὡς τὰ παρ' αὐτῶν

f here only †. Thucyd. vii. 19. (-ως, Heb. ii. 14.) g Matt. ix. 27. Rom. ix. 15 (from Exod. xxxiii. 19) al. h constr., Ps. lxviii. 27. Ezek. vii. 26. i John xvi. 21, 22. 2 Cor. ii. 3 only. j Luke vii. 4. Tit. ii. 13 only †. Wisd. ii. 6 only. (-ως, 2 Tim. i. 17.) k here only †. l = Rom. xvi. 2. m = ch. i. 8 al. 1 Chron. xxix. 22. n = ch. i. 20 reff. o 1 Cor. xvi. 16, 18 al. p Luke vii. 2. xiv. 8. 1 Pet. ii. 4, 6 (from Isa. xxviii. 16) only. 1 Kings xxvi. 21. q = Matt. xiv. 5 xxi. 26, 46. Philem. 17. r ch. i. 22 reff.

σατε ὅτι ἠσθένησεν. 27 καὶ γὰρ ἠσθένησεν [f] παραπλήσιον ABCDF KLℵ a b c d e f g h k l m n o 17
θανάτῳ· ἀλλὰ ὁ θεὸς [g] ἠλέησεν αὐτόν, οὐκ αὐτὸν δὲ
μόνον, ἀλλὰ καὶ ἐμέ, ἵνα μὴ [hi] λύπην ἐπὶ [h] λύπην [i] σχῶ.
28 [j] σπουδαιοτέρως οὖν ἔπεμψα αὐτόν, ἵνα ἰδόντες αὐτὸν
πάλιν χαρῆτε, κἀγὼ [k] ἀλυπότερος ὦ. 29 [l] προςδέχεσθε
οὖν αὐτὸν [l] ἐν κυρίῳ [m] μετὰ [n] πάσης [m] χαρᾶς, καὶ [o] τοὺς
τοιούτους [p] ἐντίμους [q] ἔχετε, 30 ὅτι διὰ τὸ [r] ἔργον μέχρι

for *οτι ησθ.*, *αυτον ησθενηκεναι* D^{1}F latt goth lat-ff.
27. *θανατου* Bℵ^3 1 Chr Thl-ms. [*αλλα*, so ABDℵ c e n 17.] rec *αυτον* bef *ηλεησεν*, with KL rel vss gr-ff: txt ABC^{2}DFℵ m^1 17 latt Phot lat-ff. rec (for 2nd *λυπην*) *λυπη* (*corrn to more usual constr*), with K rel Thdrt Phot: txt ABCDFLℵ a b c k l^2 o 17 Chr-mss Damasc Thl-ms Œc. for *σχω*, *εχω* D^{1}F.
28. *σπουδαιοτερον* D^{1}F. for *ουν*, *δε* F 17 Thl. (not F-lat.)
29. *προσδεξασθε* A^{2}ℵ 67^2. 73. 80.
30. rec aft *εργον* ins *του χριστου*, with DKL rel, *χριστου* BF 73. 80; *κυριου* Aℵ 17,

ἀποσταλέντα κομίσαντα χρήματα, Thdrt. **πέμψαι**] it was actually a sending *back*, though not so expressed here: see ch. iv. 18. **26.**] reason for the necessity. The imperfect is, as usual, from the position of the receivers of the letter. **ἀδημ.**] See note on ref. Matt. Whether there was any special reason, more than affection, which made Epaphroditus anxious to return on account of this, we cannot say. **27.**] **καὶ γάρ** recognizes and re-asserts that which has before been put as from another, as "*ἔλεγες τοίνυν δή, ὅτι κ.τ.λ.*" "*καὶ γὰρ ἔλεγον, ἔν γε ὄχλῳ.*" Plat. Gorg. 459: see Hartung, Partikell. i. 137,—**for he really was sick.** **παραπλήσιον** does not involve any ellipsis (De W.) as of *ἀφίκετο* or the like, but (as Mey.) it stands adverbially as *παραπλησίως*; so in Polyb. iii. 33. 10, *εἰ πεποιήκαμεν παραπλήσιον τοῖς ἀξιοπίστως ψευδομένοις τῶν συγγραφέων*: and **θανάτῳ** is the dative of *congruence* after it,—sometimes a genitive, as Plat. Soph. p. 217, *λόγων ἐπελάβου παραπλησίων ὧν . . . . διερωτῶντες ἐτυγχάνομεν.* **λύπην ἐπὶ λύπην**] for construction, see reff. The dative after *ἐπί* is more usual: so *φόνος ἐπὶ φόνῳ*, Eur. Iph. Taur. 197 (189): the accus. giving the sense of accession,—"sorrow coming upon sorrow,"—not, sorrow superimposed upon sorrow. The second *λύπην* refers to his own distress in his imprisonment, so often implied in this Epistle: see Prolegg. § iii. 4, 5: 'si ad vincula accessisset jactura amici,' Grot. This is better, than with Chrys., al., to refer it to Epaphroditus's sickness,—*τὴν ἀπὸ τῆς τελευτῆς ἐπὶ τῇ διὰ τὴν ἀῤῥωστίαν*,—which does not agree with *ἀλυπότερος*, ver. 28, implying that *λύπη* would remain even after the departure of Epaphroditus. **28.**] **πάλιν** most naturally, considering St. Paul's habit of prefixing it to verbs, belongs to *χαρῆτε*: and there is here no reason to depart from his usage and attach it to **ἰδόντες**, as Beza, Grot., De W., all., have done. The **κἀγὼ ἀλυπότερος ὦ** is one of the Apostle's delicate touches of affection. If *they rejoiced* in seeing Epaphroditus, *his own* trouble would be thereby lessened.

29.] **οὖν**, as accomplishing the purpose just expressed. The stress is on **προςδέχεσθε**, see ref. There certainly seems to be something behind respecting him, of which we are not informed. If extreme affection had been the sole ground of his *ἀδημονεῖν*, no such exhortation as this would have been needed. **τοὺς τοιούτους**] *ἵνα μὴ δόξῃ αὐτῷ μόνῳ χαρίζεσθαι, . . .* Thl. Then there is an inaccuracy in expression, in reverting back to the [concrete] conduct of Epaphroditus as a reason why *οἱ τοιοῦτοι* [abstract] should be held in honour. **30.**] **διὰ τὸ ἔργον**, viz. of the Gospel, or of Christ (see the glosses in var. readd.);—part of which it was, to sustain the minister of the Gospel. **μέχρι θ. ἤγγ.**] he incurred so serious and nearly fatal a sickness:—not to be understood of danger incurred by the hostility of the authorities, as Chrys., al., also Thdrt.: *καθειργόμενον γὰρ πάντως μαθών, καὶ ὑπὸ πλείστων φυλαττόμενον, εἰσελθὼν ἐθεάσατο, τοῦ κινδύνου καταφρονήσας.* **παραβολευσάμενος**] There is, and must ever remain, some

[s] θανάτου [s] ἤγγισεν [t] παραβολευσάμενος τῇ [u] ψυχῇ, ἵνα
[v] ἀναπληρώσῃ τὸ [w] ὑμῶν [x] ὑστέρημα [w] τῆς πρός με [y] λειτ-
ουργίας.
III. 1 [z] Τὸ λοιπόν, ἀδελφοί μου, [a] χαίρετε [a] ἐν κυρίῳ.
τὰ αὐτὰ γράφειν ὑμῖν ἐμοὶ μὲν οὐκ [b] ὀκνηρόν, ὑμῖν δὲ

s with μέχρι, here only al. Exod xxi 23 dat., see note
w εἰς, Job xxxiii 22
w ἕως, Ps cvi 18
μεχ θαν, ver 8 reff
t here only † (see notes)
u = Acts xv 26 xx 24
v Gal vi 2 reff Gen ii 21
w double gen., ch i 7, 25 Acts v 32
x 1 Cor xvi 17 2 Cor viii 13, 14 ix 12 xi 9. Col i 24 1 Thess iii 10 P only, exc Luke xxi 4 Judg xviii 10
y = ver 17 reff.
z Eph vi 10 reff
a ch iv 4, 10
b Matt. xxv 26 Rom xii. 11 only Prov vi 6, 9

του κυριου 57; του θεου al copt æth Chr-comm: om C. for μεχρι, εως DF. rec παραβουλευσαμενος, with CKL rel Chr Thdrt Damasc Thl Œc txt ADFℵ, παρακολ. B (ita in cod. see table at end of prolegg).—*parabolatus* [see notes] D lat G-lat: *tradens* vulg[and F-lat] æth latt-ff[pref *in interitum* Ambrst] *spernens* syrr: *postponens* copt *obliviscens* goth αναπληρωσει ℵ d εμε ℵ[1] b c o.

Chap. III 1 for τα αυτα, ταυτα F-gr ℵ[1] txt ℵ[3].

doubt whether to read παραβουλ- or παραβολευσάμενος Both words are unknown to Greek writers. The first verb would signify '*male consulere* vitæ,' and is found not unfrequently in the fathers, especially Chrys, which makes it all the more likely to have been introduced here for the other This latter would be formed from παράβολος, '*venturesome*,' as περπερεύομαι from πέρπερος (1 Cor xiii 4), ἀλογεύομαι from ἄλογος (Cic. ad Att vi. 4): similarly ἀσωτεύομαι, φιλανθρωπεύομαι, πονηρεύομαι, &c See Lobeck on Phryn. pp. 67, 591. Thus παραβολεύεσθαι would be used exactly as παραβάλλεσθαι in Polyb. ii. 26 6, ἔφη δεῖν μὴ κινδυνεύειν ἔτι, μηδὲ παραβάλλεσθαι τοῖς ὅλοις, and iii. 94 4, and παραβάλλεσθαι ταῖς ψυχαῖς in Diod. Sic. iii. 16. Phryn (p. 238, ed Lob) says, παραβόλιον· ἀδόκιμον τοῦτο. τῷ μὲν οὖν ὀνόματι οὐ χρῶνται οἱ παλαιοί, τῷ δὲ ῥήματι. φασὶ γὰρ οὕτω, παραβάλλομαι τῇ ἐμαυτοῦ κεφαλῇ. ἐχρῆν οὖν κἀπὶ τούτων λέγειν, παραβάλλομαι ἀργυρίῳ. Hence also nurses of the sick were called *parabolani*. See various patristic interpretations, and illustrations, in Tischendorf and Wetstein. **ἵνα κ.τ.λ**] **that he might fill up** (1 Cor. xvi. 17) **your deficiency** (viz on account of your absence) **in the ministration to me** (the λειτουργία was the contribution of money, which had been sent by Epaphroditus The only ὑστερημα in this kind service was, their inability through absence, to minister it to the Apostle themselves: and this Epaphroditus filled up, and in so doing risked his life in the way above hinted at, i e probably by too constant and watchful attendance on the Apostle. So that there is no blame conveyed by **τὸ ὑμ ὑστέρημα**, as Chr, ὅπερ ἐχρῆν πάντας ποιῆσαι, τοῦτο ἔπραξεν αὐτός,—but the whole is a delicate way of enhancing Epaphroditus's services—'that which you would have done if you could, he did for you—therefore receive him with all joy')

Ch. III 1—IV 1] Warning against certain Judaizers,—enforced by his own example (1—16): also against immoral persons (17—iv. 1).

1] He appears to have been closing his Epistle (τὸ λοιπόν, and reff), but to have again gone off, on the vehement mention of the Judaizers, into an explanation of his strong term **κατατομή** Chrys, al, find a connexion with the foregoing, but it is far-fetched (ἔχετε 'Επαφρ, δι' ὃν ἠλγεῖτε, ἔχετε Τιμόθ, ἔρχομαι κἀγώ τὸ εὐαγγέλιον ἐπιδίδωσι τί ὑμῖν λείπει λοιπόν,) the sense is evidently closed with ch. iii. 30. **τὰ αὐτά**] It seems to me that Wiesinger has rightly apprehended the reference of this somewhat difficult sentence The **χαίρετε ἐν κυρίῳ**, taken up again by the **οὕτως στήκετε ἐν κυρίῳ**, ch. iv. 1, is evidently put here emphatically, with direct reference to the warning which follows—**let your joy (your boast) be in the Lord.** And this same exhortation, **χαίρειν**, is in fact the ground-tone of the whole Epistle. See ch i 18, 25, ii. 17, iv. 4, where the **πάλιν ἐρῶ** seems to refer back again to this saying. So that there is no difficulty in imagining that the Apostle may mean χαίρετε by the **τὰ αὐτά** The word **ἀσφαλές** is no objection to this. because the χαίρ. ἐν κυρ. is in fact an introduction to the warning which follows a provision, by upholding the antagonist duty, against their falling into deceit. And thus all the speculation, whether **τὰ αὐτά** refer to a lost Epistle, or to words uttered (γράφειν ?) when he was with them, falls to the ground And the inference from Polycarp's words in his Epistle to these Philippians, § 3, p. 1008,

ἀσφαλές. 2 c βλέπετε τοὺς d κύνας, c βλέπετε τοὺς κακοὺς ABDF
e ἐργάτας, c βλέπετε τὴν f κατατομήν. 3 ἡμεῖς γάρ ἐσμεν KLℵ a b c d e f g
ἡ g περιτομή, οἱ h πνεύματι θεοῦ i λατρεύοντες καὶ k καυ- h k l m n o 17
χώμενοι ἐν χριστῷ Ἰησοῦ, καὶ οὐκ ἐν l σαρκὶ m πεποι-
θότες, 4 n καίπερ ἐγὼ ἔχων o πεποίθησιν καὶ ἐν σαρκί.
εἴ τις p δοκεῖ ἄλλος m πεποιθέναι ἐν σαρκί, ἐγὼ μᾶλλον,

c 1 Cor i 26 (& note) x 18 Col iv 17. d = Matt vii 6 Rev xxii 15 Ps xxi 16. e Luke x 2 al † Wisd xvii 17 — 2 Cor xi 13. f here only † (-τεμνειν, Levit xxi 5.) g see Rom iii 30 Gal ii 7. h dat, 1 Cor xiv 2, 15. i absol, Luke ii 37 Acts xxvi 7 Heb ix 9 x 2. k w ἐν, Rom ii 17 v 3. 2 Cor x 15 al Jer ix 23, 24. l = Rom ii 28 Gal iii 3 vi 13. m constr, here only Jer xxxi [xlviii] 7 see ch ii 24. n Paul, here only Heb v 8 vii 5 xii 17 2 Pet i 12 only. o Eph iii 12 reff. p = 1 Cor iii 18 viii 2 xiv 37 Gal vi 3 James i 26 Winer, § 65 7 c.

ins το bef ασφαλες d h k m n 80 113—116 120—123 Procop Damasc (A defective)
3 rec for θεου, θεω (*perhaps corrn after such passages as Rom* i 9 2 *Tim* i. 3), with D[1](and lat) ℵ[1] vulg(with F-lat &c, agst ms_1) Syr goth $Thdrt_1$ lat-ff θειω 115 txt ABCD[3]FKLℵ[1] rel al_{60}(Tischdf) gr mss-mentd-by-Aug ("*omnes aut pæne omnes*") lat-mss-in-Aug("*exempl nonnulla*" have θεω) syr-marg copt Eus Ath Orig-int Aug_{expr}.
4 om και D[1]F a n o Aug_1. αλλος bef δοκει D a latt δε αλλως δοκει F: om αλλος al_2 Syr Chr-comm Lucif Ambrst.—αλλως m. for εγω ℵ[1] has πε txt ℵ-corr[1]

ὃς καὶ ἀπὼν ὑμῖν ἔγραψεν ἐπιστολάς, may be a true one, but does not belong here. **ὀκνηρόν**] **troublesome**: Mey. quotes from Plato, Ep. iii 310 D, τἀληθῆ λέγειν οὔτε ὀκνήσω οὔτε αἰσχυνοῦμαι. **2**] **βλέπετε**, not, '*beware of*,' as E. V. (βλ. ἀπό, Mark viii. 15 reff.), but as in reff., **observe**, with a view to avoid cf σκοπεῖν, Rom. xvi. 17 **τοὺς κύνας**] profane, impure persons. The appellation occurs in various references, but in the Jewish usage of it, uncleanness was the prominent idea: see, besides reff, Deut. xxiii 18, Isa. lvi. 10, 11, Matt. xv. 26, 27. The remark of Chrys is worth noting in connexion with what follows· οὐκέτι τέκνα Ἰουδαῖοι· ποτὲ οἱ ἐθνικοὶ τοῦτο ἐκαλοῦντο, νῦν δὲ ἐκεῖνοι. But I would not confine it entirely to them, as the next clause certainly generalizes further **τοὺς κακοὺς ἐργάτας**] cf δόλιοι ἐργάται, 2 Cor xi 13,—ἐργάτην ἀνεπαίσχυντον, 2 Tim. ii. 15,—ἐργάζονται μὲν γάρ, φησιν, ἀλλ' ἐπὶ κακῷ By **ἐργάτας**, he seems to point out persons who actually *wrought*, and professedly for the Gospel, but who were 'evil workmen,' not mere '*evil-doers*' **τ κατατομήν**] 'gloriosam appellationem **περιτομῆς**, *circumcisionis, vindicat Christianis*.' Beng. **Observe the** (I will not say, circumcision, but mere) **CONCISION** ('*amputation*' who have no true circumcision of heart, but merely the cutting off of the flesh Mey. quotes from Diog Laert vi 24, of Diogenes the Cynic, τὴν Εὐκλείδου σχολὴν ἔλεγε χολήν, τὴν δὲ Πλάτωνος διατριβὴν κατατριβήν Cf Gal. v. 12 note. On the thrice repeated article, Erasmus says, 'indicat, eum de certis quibusdam loqui, quos illi noverint') **3**] **for WE are the** **περιτομή**, **the** *real* **CIRCUMcision** (whether bodily circumcised, or not — there would be among them some of both sorts· see Rom. ii 25, 29; Col ii 11), **who serve** (pay religious service and obedience) **by the Spirit of God** (cf. John iv. 23, 24 The dative is instrumental, Rom viii. 13,—expressing the agent, whereby our service is rendered. see Rom. v. 5; viii. 14; xii. 1, Heb. ix. 14. The emphasis is on it· for *both* profess a λατρεία. The **θεοῦ** is expressed for solemnity), **and glory in** (stress on **καυχώμενοι**,—are not ashamed of Him and seek our boast in circumcision, or the law, but make our *boast* in Him) **Christ Jesus, and trust not in the flesh** (stress on **ἐν σαρκί** —'but, in the Spirit in our union with Christ'). **4.**] **Although** (see Hartung, Partik. i 340 πίθου γυναιξί, καίπερ οὐ στέργων, ὅμως, Æsch. Theb. 709· προσεκύνησαν, καίπερ εἰδότες, ὅτι ἐπὶ θανάτῳ ἄγοιτο, Xen. Anab i. 6. 10) **I** (emphatic. There is no ellipsis, but the construction is regular, **καίπερ**, as in the above examples, having a participle after it: had it been **καίπερ ἔχοντες**, this would have been universally seen· now, *only one* of the **οὐ πεποιθότες**, viz **ἐγώ**, is made the exception, but the construction is the same) **have** (not, '*might have*,' as E V. I *have* it, but do not choose to make use of it. I *have it*, in the flesh, but I am still of the number of the **οὐ πεποιθότες**, in spirit) **confidence** (not, '*ground of confidence*,' as Beza, Calv., Grot, &c.: there is no need to soften the assertion, see above·

5 q περιτομῇ r ὀκταήμερος, ἐκ s γένους Ἰσραήλ, φυλῆς
Βενιαμίν, t Ἑβραῖος ἐξ Ἑβραίων, uv κατὰ u νόμον Φαρισαῖος, 6 v κατὰ w ζῆλος x διώκων τὴν y ἐκκλησίαν, v κατὰ
δικαιοσύνην τὴν z ἐν νόμῳ γενόμενος a ἄμεμπτος. 7 [ἀλλὰ]
ἅτινα ἦν b μοι c κέρδη, ταῦτα d ἥγημαι διὰ τὸν χριστὸν

βενια

ABDF LNab defg iklm no17

q constr, 1 Cor xiv 20 ch ii 8 al. r here only + usually of persons ο Λαζαρον μεν τεταρταιον, σὲ δὲ τετραετῆ ζωοποιῶν, Greg Naz Orat xxi vol i p 405 s = Acts xviii 2 al Esth ii 10 t Acts vi 1 2 Cor xi 22 only Gen (xiv 13 Heb) xxxix 14 al u Acts xxii 12 xxiv 5 Heb viii 4 al v = ch ii 3 iv 11 al w 2 Cor vii 11 ix 2 al Ps lxviii 9 neut, here only x = Gal i 13 reff particip., ib i 23 y absol, Eph i 22 reff z Rom ii 12 iii 19 a ch ii 15 reff b dat, Rom xiv 14 1 Cor iv 3 c ch i 21 Tit i 11 only † Gen xxxvii 26 Symm d = Acts xxvi 2 2 Cor ix. 5 al Job xlii 6

5. περιτομή a c g h k l m n o: περιτομῆ f ins τον bef νομον F.

6. rec ζηλον, with D[2] [3]KLℵ[3] rel txt ABD[1]Fℵ[1]. aft εκκλησιαν ins θεον F (122) vulg arm(not ed-1805) Ambrst

7. om αλλα [so BD[1]] AGℵ[1] 17 D lat Cyr Lucif Ambr Aug —αλλι τινα F (sic). μοι bef ην B b c o 238 latt Thdrt Lucif txt ADFKLℵ rel syr copt goth Chr Victorin

nor, with Van Hengel, to understand it of the unconverted state of the Apostle) **also (over and above) in the flesh. If any other man thinks** (δοκεῖ is certainly, as De W, Wiesinger, al, and reff, of *his own judgment of himself*, not of other men's judgment of him, as Meyer, al.. for how can other men's judging of the *fact* of his having confidence be in place here? But it is his own judgment of the existence of the πεποίθησιν ἔχειν which is here in comparison) **he has confidence in the flesh, I more: 5**] "predicates of the ἐγώ, justifying the ἐγὼ μᾶλλον," Meyer. He compares himself with them in three particulars. 1. pure Jewish extraction 2 legal exactitude and position 3. legal zeal. **In circumcision** (i. e. 'as regards circumcision' reff. Many [Erasm., Beng, all] have taken περιτ. as nominative, and understood it concrete, '*circumcisus*,' but wrongly, for the usage applies only collectively, see Winer, edn. 3 [not in edn 6], § 31 3), **of eight days** (Gen xvii. 12 as distinguished from those who, as proselytes, were circumcised in after life. For usage, see reff), **of the race of Israel** (cf Rom. xi. 1; 2 Cor. xi. 22, οὔτε μὴν ἐκ προσηλύτων γεγέννημαι, ἀλλὰ τὸν Ἰσραὴλ αὐχῶ πρόγονον Thdrt.), **of the tribe of Benjamin** (ὥστε τοῦ δοκιμωτέρου μέρους, Chrys or perhaps as Calv., merely 'ut moris erat, singulos ex sua tribu censeri'), **an Hebrew, of Hebrews** (i e from Hebrew parents and ancestry [which the word *parents* was of course meant to imply in my earlier editions not, as Ellic., to limit the assertion to St. Paul's father and mother] on both sides ἐντεῦθεν δείκνυσιν ὅτι οὐχὶ προσήλυτος, ἀλλ' ἄνωθεν τῶν εὐδοκίμων Ἰουδαίων ἐνῆν μὲν γὰρ εἶναι τοῦ Ἰσραήλ, ἀλλ' οὐχ Ἑβραῖον ἐξ Ἑβραίων πολλοὶ γὰρ καὶ διέφθειρον ἤδη τὸ πρᾶγμα, καὶ τῆς γλώσσης ἦσαν ἀμύητοι, ἑτέροις μεμιγμένοι ἔθνεσιν. Chrys. see also Trench, Synonyms, § xxxix. p. 153 ff So Demosth. p 427, δούλους ἐκ δούλων καλῶν ἑαυτοῦ βελτίους κ ἐκ βελτιόνων see other examples in Kypke and Wetst.), **as regards the law** (with reference to relative legal position and observance), **a Pharisee** (cf. Acts xxiii. 6; xxvi 5), **as regards zeal** (for the law), **a persecutor of the church** (of Christ. on the participle, see ref.: Ellic. holds the pres part to have an adjectival force, being predicate to a suppressed verb subst.), **as regards righteousness which is in** (as its element consists in the keeping of) **the law, become blameless** (i. e having carried this righteousness so far as to have become perfect in it, in the sight of men Calvin well distinguishes between the real and apparent righteousness in the law —the former before God, never possessed by any man the latter before men, here spoken of by Paul —'erat ergo hominum judicio sanctus, et immunis ab omni reprehensione. Rara sane laus, et prope singularis videamus tamen quanti eam fecerit').

7] **But whatsoever things** (emphatic [cf ταῦτα below] and general. these above mentioned, and all others. The *law itself* is not included among them, but only his κέρδη from this and other sources) **were to me gains** (different kinds of gain cf Herod. iii. 71, περιβαλλόμενος ἑωυτῷ κέρδεα), **these** (emphatic) **I have esteemed, for Christ's sake** (see it explained below, vv. 8, 9), **as loss** ("this *one* LOSS he saw in all of which he speaks hence no longer the plural, as before κέρδη" Meyer. Ellicott remarks that the singular is regularly used in this formula, referring to

e Acts xxvii. 10, 21 only. Ezra vii. 26.
f = Luke xi. 28. see Rom. ix. 20. x. 18.
g ch. ii. 3 reff. constr., Rom. viii. 3.
h = 2 Pet. iii. 18.
i acc., Matt. xvi. 26 || Mk. Prov. xix. 19.
k Mt. Mk. as above || L. 1 Cor. iii. 15. 2 Cor. vii. 9 only.

[e]ζημίαν. 8 ἀλλὰ [f]μὲν οὖν καὶ [d]ἡγοῦμαι πάντα [c]ζημίαν
εἶναι διὰ τὸ [g]ὑπερέχον τῆς [h]γνώσεως [h]χριστοῦ Ἰησοῦ τοῦ
κυρίου μου, δι' ὃν [i]τὰ πάντα [k]ἐζημιώθην καὶ [d]ἡγοῦμαι
[l]σκύβαλα εἶναι, ἵνα χριστὸν [m]κερδήσω 9 καὶ [n]εὑρεθῶ ἐν
αὐτῷ, [o]μὴ ἔχων [p]ἐμὴν [p]δικαιοσύνην τὴν [q]ἐκ νόμου, ἀλλὰ
τὴν [r]διὰ πίστεως [s]χριστοῦ, τὴν ἐκ θεοῦ [t]δικαιοσύνην
[u]ἐπὶ τῇ πίστει, 10 [v]τοῦ γνῶναι αὐτὸν καὶ τὴν [w]δύναμιν

ABDF KLℵ a b c d e f g h k l m n o 17

l here only †. Sir. xxvii. 4 only. (-βαλίζειν, ib. xxvi. 28.) m Matt. xxv. 17, 22 al.† n = 2 Cor. v. 3. 2 Pet. iii. 14 al. o so ἐλπ. μὴ ἔχ., Eph. ii. 12. p see Rom. x. 3. q Rom. x. 5. see Gal. iii. 21. r Eph. ii. 8 reff. s Eph. iii. 12 reff. t see 2 Cor. v. 21. u = Luke v. 5. Acts iii. 16. Job xxix. 22. v Acts xiv. 9. 1 Cor. ix. 10. w = Acts viii. 10. Rom. i. 16.

8. rec aft *μενουν* ins *γε*, with Aℵ b k m o 17 Did Cyr_3 Thl: om BDFKL rel Bas Chr Cyr Thdrt Damasc Œc Hesych. om 1st *και* B(Blc) ℵ[1] 80: ins ℵ[3]. ins *του* bef *χρ.* B Thdrt. *ιησ.* bef *χρ.* AK b f o vulg(and F-lat) gr-lat-ff. for *μου*, *ημων* A demid(and harl[1]) syr copt æth Bas Cyr Did Thdrt Lucif Aug. om 2nd *ειναι* (*as superfluous, cf ch* ii. 6) BD[1]Fℵ[1] 17 latt arm Lucif Ambr Hil Pelag Ambrst Fulg: ins AD[3]KLℵ[3] rel goth Cyr_3 Aug.
9. *δικαιοσ.* bef *εμην* ℵ[1]: txt ℵ[3]. for *επι τη π.*, *εν πιστει* D[1], *in fide* latt: om Syr: in L 23. 46 syr gr-lat-ff it is joined with the follg.

Kypke and Elsner in loc. But the reason of this usage is analogous to that given above, and not surely lest ζημίαι should be mistaken to mean "punishments." Thus, in the instance from Xen. in Kypke, ἐπὶ μὲν τοῖς οἰκέταις ἀχθομένους καὶ ζημίαν ἡγουμένους, the separate deaths of the servants are all massed together, and the loss thought of as *one*).

8.] **But moreover** (not only have I once for all passed this judgment, but I *continue to count*, &c. The contrast is of the present **ἡγοῦμαι** to **ἥγημαι** above) **I also continue to esteem them all** (not, *all things*, which would require **πάντα** or **τὰ πάντα** [see below] *before* ἡγοῦμαι, emphatic) **to be loss on account of the supereminence** (above them all: τοῦ γὰρ ἡλίου φανέντος, προσκαθῆσθαι τῷ λύχνῳ ζημία. Chrys. On the neuter adjective [or participle] construction, see ref. and 2 Cor. iv. 17) **of the knowledge of Christ Jesus my Lord** ('quod Dominum suum vocat, id ad exprimendam affectus vehementiam facit.' Calv.), **on whose account** (explained by **ἵνα** .... below) **I suffered the loss of** ALL THINGS (now, emphatic and universal. Or, it may be, "them all," as Ellic.: but this almost involves a tautology; and, besides, τὰ πάντα stands too far from ἅτινα for the τά to be reflexive), **and esteem them to be refuse, that I may** (by so disesteeming them: ἵνα gives the aim of what went before) **gain Christ** (not, as the rationalizing Grot., 'Christi favorem:' no indeed, it is Christ Himself,—His perfect image, His glorious perfection, which he wishes to win. He has Him now, but not in full: this can only be when his course is finished, and to this time the next words allude) **and be found** (now, and especially at His coming,—'evadam:' —not as Calv., 'Paulum renuntiasse omnibus . . . *ut recuperaret* [ungrammatical] in Christo.' Cf. ref. 2 Cor.) **in Him** (living and being, and included, in Him as my element), **not having** (specification of **εὑρ. ἐν αὐτῷ**,—but not to be joined, as Lachm., al., with **ἐν αὐτῷ**, which would make this latter superfluous) **my own righteousness** (see on ver. 6) **which is of** (arising from) **the law, but that which is through** (as its medium) **the faith of** (in) **Christ** (a construction of this sentence has been suggested to me, which is perhaps possible, and at all events deserves mention. It consists in making ἐμὴν δικαιοσύνην predicative; "not having as my righteousness that righteousness which is of the law, but that which is through faith in Christ"), **the righteousness which is of** (answering to **ἐκ νόμου**,—as its source, see Eph. ii. 8) **God on my faith** (built on, grounded on, granted on condition of, my faith. It is more natural to take **ἐπὶ τῇ πίστει** with δικαιοσύνην, which it immediately follows, than with Meyer to understand another ἔχων to attach it to. The omission of the article is no objection, but is very frequent, where the whole expression is joined as one idea. Chrys., al., join **ἐπὶ τῇ πίστει** with **τοῦ γνῶναι**, as if it were τοῦ ἐπὶ τ. π. γνῶναι, which of course is unallowable: Calv., Grot., Bengel, make the infinitive **τοῦ γνῶναι** dependent on **πίστει** ["describit

τῆς [x] ἀναστάσεως αὐτοῦ, καὶ [τὴν] [y] κοινωνίαν τῶν [z] παθη- x = Acts i 22 Rom vi 5 ‡
μάτων αὐτοῦ, [a] συμμορφιζόμενος τῷ θανάτῳ αὐτοῦ, 11 [b] εἴ y ch ii 1 reff 1 Cor i 9
πως [c] καταντήσω [c] εἰς τὴν [d] ἐξανάστασιν τὴν ἐκ νεκρῶν. x 16 al z 2 Cor i 5 Heb ii 10
12 [e] οὐχ ὅτι ἤδη ἔλαβον ἢ ἤδη [f] τετελείωμαι, [g] διώκω 1 Pet i 11 iv 13 v 1† a here only †

(φος. ver 21) b = & constr, Rom i 10 xi 14 (w opt., Acts xxvii 12) only c Eph iv 13 reff d here only † = Polyb iii 55 4 e = ch iv 11 reff f = Heb ii 10 v 9 vii 28 Wisd iv 13 g absol., Luke xvii 23 Hagg i 9

10 for αναστ, γνωσεως ℵ[1], πιστεως 108 txt ℵ-corr[1 obl]. om 1st αυτου D[1]. om 2nd την ABℵ[1]. ins DFKLℵ[3] rel. om των ℵ[1] ins ℵ[3]. rec συμμορφουμενος (*more usual form*), with D[3]KLℵ[3] rel Chr Thdrt συνφορτιζομενος *cooneratus* F D-lat goth Iren-int Lucif txt ABD[1]ℵ[1] 17 (67[2]) Orig-ms, Bas Maced

11 rec (for την εκ) των (*see note*), with KL rel copt Thdrt των εκ F: txt ABDℵ 17 latt syr Bas Chr Damasc Iren-int Tert Lucif Ambrst.

12 aft ελαβον add η ηδη δεδικαιωμαι D[1]F Iren-int Sing-cler Ambrst (not Tert Hil

vim et naturam fidei, quod scilicet sit Christi cognitio" Calv], which is also inadmissible, for πίστις, as Mey observes, is never joined with a genitive article and infinitive and when with a genitive, not the nature but the object of faith is described by it), **10**] (aim and employment of this righteousness,—taking up again the ὑπερέχον τῆς γνώσεως, ver. 8. De W., al., treat **τοῦ γν.** as parallel with ἵνα κερδήσω, κ τ λ. But as Mey. remarks, it is no real parallel, for there is more in ἵνα χρ. κερδήσω &c than in τοῦ γνῶναι αὐτόν &c. Besides, thus the process of thought is disturbed,—in which, from **ἵνα** to **ἐπὶ τῇ πίστει** answers to **διὰ τὸν χριστόν** above, and from **τοῦ γν.** to **νεκρῶν** answers to **διὰ τὸ ὑπερέχον τ. γνώσεως αὐτοῦ** See a similar construction, Rom vi. 6), **in order to know Him** (know, in that fulness of experimental knowledge, which is only wrought by being like Him), **and** (not = '*that is to say*.' but additional His Person, and . . . and . . . .) **the power of His resurrection** (i. e. not '*the power by which He was raised*,' but the power which His resurrection *exercises* on believers—in assuring them of their justification, Rom iv. 25, 1 Cor. xv. 17,—mostly however here, from the context which goes on to speak of conformity with His sufferings and death,—in *raising them with Him*,—cf. Rom vi 4, Col ii. 12),—**and the participation of His sufferings** (which is the necessitating condition of being brought under the power of His resurrection, see as above, and 2 Tim ii. 11), **being conformed** (the nominative is an anacoluthon, belonging to **τοῦ γνῶναι**, and referring, as often, to the *logical* subject) **to His Death** (it does not appear to me that St Paul is here speaking, as Mey, al, of his imminent risk of a death of martyrdom, but that his meaning is general, applying to his whole course of suffering and self-denial, as indeed throughout the sentence. This conformity with Christ's death was to take place by means of that perfect self-abjuration which he here asserts of himself—see Rom viii 29, 2 Cor. ii 14, iv 10 ff, 1 Cor xv. 31, and especially Gal ii 20), **if by any means** (so Thucyd ii 77, πᾶσαν γὰρ ἰδέαν ἐπενόουν, εἴ πως σφίσιν ἄνευ δαπάνης κ πολιορκίας προσαχθείη· Herod vi 52, βουλομένην, εἴ κως ἀμφότεροι γενοίατο βασιλῆες. It is used when an end is proposed, but failure is presumed to be possible: see Hartung, ii. 206; Kuhner, ii 581 ὅμως μετὰ ταῦτα πάντα οὔπω θαῤῥῶ· ὅπερ ἀλλαχοῦ λέγει· ὁ δοκῶν ἑστάναι βλεπέτω μὴ πέσῃ. κ. πάλιν, φοβοῦμαι μή πως ἄλλοις κηρύξας, αὐτὸς ἀδόκιμος γένωμαι. Chrys) **I may attain** (not future, but subjunctive aorist. On the sense, see Acts xxvi 7; from which alone, it is evident that it does not signify '*live until*,' as Van Hengel) **unto the resurrection from the dead** (viz the blessed resurrection of the dead in Christ, in which οἱ τοῦ χριστοῦ shall rise ἐν τῇ παρουσίᾳ αὐτοῦ, 1 Cor. xv 23, see also 1 Thess. iv. 16. But the **ἐξ-** in **ἐξανάστ** does not distinctively point out this first resurrection, but merely indicates rising *up*, out of the dust, cf. the verb Mark xii. 19 ‖ L, Acts xv. 5, and the word itself in ref. Polyb.). **12—14.**] This seems to be inserted to prevent the misapprehension, that he conceived himself already to possess this knowledge, and to have grasped Christ in all His fulness. **12**] **not that** (I do not mean, that . . . . , see reff) **I have already acquired** (this χριστὸν κερδῆσαι not the βραβεῖον below [Mey], which is an image subsequently introduced, whereas the reference here must be to something foregoing, nor τὴν ἀνάστασιν, which has just been *stated* as an object of his wishes for the future but as Calv, "nempe ut in solidum communicet Christi passionibus, ut perfectum habeat gustum potentiæ resurrectionis, ut ipsum

δὲ εἰ καὶ ʰ καταλάβω ⁱ ἐφ' ᾧ καὶ ʰ κατελήμφθην ὑπὸ χρισ- ABDF KLℵ a b
τοῦ. 13 ἀδελφοί, ἐγὼ ἐμαυτὸν οὐ ᵏ λογίζομαι ʰ κατειλη- c d e f g
φέναι· 14 ˡ ἓν δέ, ᵐ τὰ μὲν ᵐ ὀπίσω ⁿ ἐπιλανθανόμενος, ᵒ τοῖς h k l m
δὲ ᵒ ἔμπροσθεν ᵖ ἐπεκτεινόμενος, ᵍ κατὰ ʳ σκοπὸν ˢ διώκω n o 17

h = Rom. ix. 30. 1 Cor. ix. 24. Exod. xv. 9. Deut. xxviii. 45. i = Gal. v. 13. 1 Thess. iv. 7. ellips., Mark x. 40. Luke v. 25. k = Rom. iii. 28. xiv. 14 al. Wisd. xv. 12. l ellips., Rom. xiii. 7. 2 Cor. viii. 15. Winer, § 66. 1. b. m = Mark xiii. 16 al. Gen. xix. 17. n w. acc. (and Paul), here only. Deut. iv. 9 al. pass., Luke xii. 6. w. gen., Heb. vi. 10. xiii. 2, 16. elsw., Matt. xvi. 5 ‖ Mk. James i. 24 only. o here only. Isa. xli. 26. σκοπείτω τὰ ἔμπρ., ὡς μηδὲν ἡμᾶς λάθῃ, Xen. Anab. vi. 3. 14. p here only †. q = Acts viii. 26. r here only. Job xvi. 13.

Ambr Aug Jer Pelag). om 1st και DFℵ¹ vulg goth Tert Ambrst Hil Ambr Jer: txt ℵ¹ &c. om 2nd και DF l¹ 67² Tert: for και, ει ℵ¹: txt ℵ-corr¹ &c. rec (for χρ.) του χρ. ιησ., with KL rel: χρ. ιησ. Aℵ c f Chr₁ Thl-ms: ιησ. χρ. a 112: του χρ. D³ Damasc: txt BD¹F 17 goth æth Clem Mac Tert Sing-cler Hil Jer.

13. om εγω D¹. for ου, ουπω AD¹ℵ b² c g h 17 copt æth syr-w-ast Clem Bas Chr-comm₁ Thdrt Damasc Chron Thl Œc Jer$_{aliq}$ Ambrst. κατιληφοτα F.

14. for τοις δε, εις δε τα D¹F. απεκτειραμενος F.

plane cognoscat") **or am already completed** (in spiritual perfection. Philo de Alleg. iii. 23, vol. i. p. 101, πότε οὖν, ὦ ψυχή, μάλιστα νεκροφορεῖν σαυτὴν ὑπολήψῃ; ἆρά γε οὐχ ὅταν τελειωθῇς καὶ βραβείων κ. στεφάνων ἀξιωθῇς;), **but I pursue** (the image of a runner in a course is already before him. So διώκω absolute in Æsch. Theb. 89, ὄρνυται λαὸς . . . ἐπὶ πόλιν διώκων. This is simpler than to suppose that an object, the βραβεῖον, is in his mind, though not expressed. See Ellic.'s note) **if** (nearly = εἴ πως above) **I may also** (besides διώκειν—not as Mey., nicht bloß greife [ἔλαβον], sondern auch ergreife: nor does it answer to the καί following, as De W.) **lay hold of** (Herod. ix. 58, διωκτέοι εἰσί, ἐς ὃ καταλαμφθέντες . . . . δώσουσι δίκας: Lucian, Hermotim. 77, διώκοντες οὐ κατέλαβον) **that for which** (this seems the simplest rendering, and has been the usual one. Meyer's rendering of **ἐφ' ᾧ** '*because*,' after Chrys., Thdrt., Thl., requires καταλάβω to be *absolute*, and would more naturally be expressed ἐφ' ᾧ κἀγὼ κατελήμφθην, the emphatic first person hardly admitting of being supplied from the preceding clause: whereas on our rendering the whole forms but one clause, the first person recurring throughout it. Grot.'s, 'quo ut pervenire possem,' Beza's, &c., 'for which reason,'—all keeping **καταλάβω** absolute, are not open to the above objection) **I was also laid hold of** (the **καί** belongs to the verb, not to ἐγώ understood, nor to the ἐφ' ᾧ, as if there might be other ends for which he was apprehended [Ellic.]: see above—and brings out, that in my case there was another instance of the καταλαβεῖν. For the sense, cf. 1 Cor. xiii. 12, ἐπιγνώσομαι καθὼς καὶ ἐπεγνώσθην: and Plat. Tim. p. 39, τῇ δὴ ταὐτοῦ φορᾷ τὰ τάχιστα περιιόντα ὑπὸ τῶν βραδυτέρων ἰόντων ἐφαίνετο καταλαμβάνοντα καταλαμβάνεσθαι. The time referred to by the aorist was his *conversion*: but we need not, as Chrys., al., press the image of the race, and regard him as *flying*, and *overtaken*) **by Christ.**

13.] Emphatic and affectionate re-statement of the same, but not merely so;—he evidently alludes to some whom he wishes to warn by his example. **Brethren, I** (emphatic: cf. John v. 30; vii. 17; viii. 33; Acts xxvi. 9) **do not reckon myself** (emphatic) **to have laid hold: but one thing** (I do: not λογίζομαι, nor διώκω, nor φροντίζω, none of which correspond to the epexegesis following: nor can we say that nothing requires to be supplied [Grot., al.], for even in **τοῦτο δέ** this would not be so—the sense must have a logical supplement: nor will it do to join ἕν to διώκω [Aug., al.], or to supply ἐστι [Beza]): **forgetting the things behind** (me, as a runner in the course; by which image, now fully before him, the expressions in this verse must be explained: καὶ γὰρ ὁ δρομεὺς οὐχ ὅσους ἤνυσεν ἀναλογίζεται διαύλους, ἀλλ' ὅσους λείπεται . . . . τί γὰρ ἡμᾶς ὠφελεῖ τὸ ἀνυσθέν, ὅταν τὸ λειπόμενον μὴ προστεθῇ; Chr. Thdrt. explains it περὶ τῶν τοῦ κηρύγματος πόνων: but this seems insufficient), **but ever reaching out towards** (as the runner whose body is bent forwards in his course; the **ἐπί** giving the continual addition of exertion in this direction [Mey.] or perhaps merely the direction itself. ὁ γὰρ ἐπεκτεινόμενος, τοῦτ' ἔστιν, ὁ τοὺς πόδας καίτοι τρέχοντας τῷ λοιπῷ σώματι προλαβεῖν σπουδάζων, ἐπεκτείνων ἑαυτὸν εἰς τὸ ἔμπροσθεν, κ. τὰς χεῖρας ἐκτείνων, ἵνα κ. τοῦ δρόμου πλέον τι ἐργάσηται. Chr.) **the things before** (i. e. the perfection not yet reached), **I pursue** (on **διώκω** absolute, see note, ver. 12) **towards the goal** (the contrary of ἀπὸ σκοποῦ, beside the mark, Plat. Tim. p. 25 al.) **for** (to reach, with a view to; or perhaps simply in the

[s] εἰς τὸ [t] βραβεῖον τῆς [u] ἄνω [v] κλήσεως τοῦ θεοῦ ἐν
χριστῷ Ἰησοῦ. 15 ὅσοι οὖν [w] τέλειοι, τοῦτο [x] φρονῶ-
μεν. καὶ εἴ τι [y] ἑτέρως [x] φρονεῖτε, καὶ τοῦτο ὁ θεὸς ὑμῖν
[z] ἀποκαλύψει. 16 [a] πλὴν [b] εἰς ὃ [b] ἐφθάσαμεν, [c] τῷ αὐτῷ
[d] στοιχεῖν.

s εις — 2 Thess i 11, or 1 Cor xi 17 Heb vi 8 — επι, — Luke xv 4.
t 1 Cor ix 24 only † (ενειν, Col iii 14)
u Gal iv 26 Col iii 1

v = (1 Cor i 26) 2 Thess i 11. Heb iii 1 w — 1 Cor ii 6 xiv 20 Heb. v 14
x = 1 Cor xiii 11 Gal v 10 reff y here only † z — Matt xvi 17 (-ψις, Eph i 7)
a Eph v 33 reff b Rom ix 31 Dan iv 10 xii 12 Theod ἐπι, 1 Thess ii 16 Dan iv 25 Theod προς, Eccl viii 14 c dat., Gal vi 16 d (—) Acts xxi 24 Rom iv 12 Gal v 25 vi 16 only. (Eccles xi 6 only)

rec (for εις) επι, with DFKL rel Chr Thdrt txt ABℵ 17 Clem Ath Chron. om του θεου F vulg-ms Clem Novat Sing-cler Haymo for χρ ιησ, κυριω ιησ. χρ. D[1]F.

15 aft τελειοι ins εν χρ ιησου F(not F-lat). aft 1st τουτο ins ουν ℵ[1](ℵ[1] disapproving). φρονουμεν Lℵ n mss-in-Jer Clem om ο D[1].

16. for στοιχειν, συνστ F. rec aft στοιχειν ins κανονι το αυτο φρονειν (*κανονι prob to supply* τω αυτω, *and* το αυτο φρονειν *as a gloss explaing* τω αυτ. στ. *cf Gal* vi. 16; *ch* ii. 2), with D[3]KLℵ[3] rel: aft εφθασαμεν ins το αυτο φρονειν D[1]F m Victorin Ambrst, D[1]F omg κανονι, m insg it aft αυτω om ABℵ[1] 17. 67[2] coptt æth Thdot-ancyr Hil Aug$_{sæpe}$ Facund (Sedul).

direction of: see reff. for both) **the prize** (see 1 Cor. ix 24, 2 Tim iv 8, Rev. ii. 10) **of my heavenly** (reff and κλῆσις ἐπουράνιος Heb iii 1, Ἱερουσ ἐπουράνιος Heb xii 22 Not, '*from above,*' = ἄνωθεν but the allusion is to his appointment having been made directly in heaven, not by delegation on earth) **calling** (not as we familiarly use the word,—'calling in life,' &c.—but to be kept to the *act of his being called* as an Apostle: q d. 'the prize consequent on the faithful carrying out of that summons which I received from God in heaven') **of God** (who was the caller but we must not think of Him, as Grot, al.,—as the arbiter sitting above and summoning to the course,—for in these last words the figure is dropt, and ἡ ἄνω κλῆσις represents real matter of fact) **in Christ Jesus** (to what are these last words to be referred? Chrys, al, join them with διώκω:—ἐν χ. Ἰ τοῦτο ποιῶ, φησιν. οὐ γὰρ ἔνι χωρὶς τῆς ἐκείνου ῥοπῆς τοσοῦτον διελθεῖν διάστημα πολλῆς δεῖ τῆς βοηθείας, πολλῆς τῆς συμμαχίας. But I own the arrangement of the sentence thus seems to me very unnatural—and the constant practice of St Paul to join θεός and things said of θεός with ἐν χριστῷ weighs strongly for the other connexion, viz that with τ κλήσεως τοῦ θεοῦ The objection that then τῆς or τοῦ would be required before ἐν, is not valid, the unity of the idea of the κλῆσις ἐν κυρίῳ, 1 Cor vii 22, would dispense with it) **15, 16**] *Exhortation to them to be unanimous in following this his example.* In order to understand this somewhat difficult passage, we must remember (1) that the description of his own views and feelings which he holds up for their imitation (συμμιμηταί μου γίν) began with having no confidence in the flesh, ver 4, and has continued to ver. 14. Also (2) that the description commencing with **ὅσοι οὖν τέλειοι**, is taken up again from ver 3, ἡμεῖς γάρ ἐσμεν ἡ περιτομή, οἱ πνεύματι θεοῦ λατρεύοντες, κ καυχώμενοι ἐν χ. Ἰησοῦ, κ οὐκ ἐν σαρκὶ πεποιθότες. These two considerations will keep us from narrowing too much the **τοῦτο φρονῶμεν**, and from misunderstanding the **ὅσοι οὖν τέλειοι**. **As many of us then** (refers to ver 3 see above) **as are perfect** (mature in Christian life, = those described above, ver. 3), **let us be of this mind** (viz. that described as entertained by himself, vv. 7—14): **and if in any thing** (accusative of reference: see Kuhner, Gramm. ii. 220 ff) **ye be differently minded** (for **ἑτέρως**, cf. Od. α 232 ff, μέλλεν μέν ποτε οἶκος ὅδ' ἀφνειὸς κ. ἀμύμων | ἔμμεναι, ὄφρ' ἔτι κεῖνος ἀνὴρ ἐπιδήμιος ἦεν· | νῦν δ' **ἑτέρως** ἐβάλοντο θεοί, κακὰ μητιόωντες Demosth. p 298 22, εἰ μέν τι τῶν δεόντων ἐπράχθη, τὸν καιρόν, οὐκ ἐμέ φησιν αἴτιον γεγενῆσθαι, τῶν δ' ὡς **ἑτέρως** συμβάντων ἁπάντων ἐμὲ καὶ τὴν ἐμὴν τύχην αἰτίαν εἶναι Hence it gives the meaning of diversity in a bad sense. The difference referred to seems to be that of too much self-esteem as to Christian perfection see below), **this also** (as well as the rest which He has revealed) **will God reveal to you** (i e. in the progress of the Christian life, you will find the true knowledge of your own imperfection and of Christ's all-sufficiency revealed to you by God's Spirit, Eph. i 17 ff. ὅρα

17 [e] Συμμιμηταί μου γίνεσθε, ἀδελφοί, καὶ [f] σκοπεῖτε
τοὺς οὕτως [g] περιπατοῦντας καθὼς ἔχετε [h] τύπον [i] ἡμᾶς.
18 πολλοὶ γὰρ [g] περιπατοῦσιν, [k] οὓς πολλάκις [h] ἔλεγον

ABDF KLℵ a b c d e f g h k l m n o 17

e here only †. f (but not —) Rom xvi 17 Gal vi 1 reff g Rom vi 4 Eph iv 1 reff h — 1 Thess i 7 2 Thess iii 9 1 Tim. iv 12 Tit. ii 7 1 Pet v 3 i — 2 Thess iii 7–9 k constr, John viii 27 Rom iv 6.

πῶς συνεσταλμένως τοῦτό φησιν. ὁ θεὸς ὑμᾶς διδάξει, τουτέστιν, ὑμᾶς πείσει, οὐχὶ διδάξει ἁπλῶς. ἐδίδασκε μὲν γὰρ ὁ Παῦλος, ἀλλ' ὁ θεὸς ἐνῆγε καὶ οὐκ εἶπεν, ἐνάξει, ἀλλ' ἀποκαλύψει, ἵνα δόξῃ μᾶλλον ἀγνοίας εἶναι τὸ πρᾶγμα οὐ περὶ δογμάτων ταῦτ' εἴρηται, ἀλλὰ περὶ βίου τελειότητος, κ τοῦ μὴ νομίζειν ἑαυτοὺς τελείους εἶναι· ὡς ὅγε νομίζων τὸ πᾶν εἰληφέναι, οὐδὲν ἔχει. Chrys. **τοῦτο** must not be taken as Œc, Grot, &c. as representing *the fact, that ye* **ἑτέρως φρονεῖτε**, but is *the thing, respecting which* ye *ἑτ φρ*).

16] Let not however this diversity, respecting which some of you yet await deeper revelations from God's Spirit, produce any dissension in your Christian unity. **Nevertheless** (notwithstanding that some of you, &c as above. On *πλήν*, see Devarius, and Klotz's note, i. 188; ii 725) **as far as we have attained** (towards Christian perfection **ὃ** *κατωρθώσαμεν*, Thl · including both knowledge and practice, of both which he spoke above in his own case On the construction, see reff), **walk by the same (path)** (reff Polyb. xxviii 5 6, *βουλόμενοι στοιχεῖν τῇ τῆς συγκλήτου προθέσει* · see Fritz ad Rom iii p 142. On the elliptic usage of the infinitive for the imperative see Kuhner, ii p 342, where many examples are given It appears from these that the usage occurs in the *2nd person only:* which determines this to be not '*let us walk*,' but 'walk ye') The exhortation refers to the onward advance of the Christian life—let us go on together, each one in his place and degree of advance, but all in the same path. 17—IV 1] *Exhortation to follow his example* (17) *warning against the enemies of the cross of Christ* (18, 19) · *declaration of the high privileges and hopes of Christians* (20, 21), *and affectionate entreaty to stedfastness* (iv 1) **Be imitators together** (i e with one another: so, and not imitators together with those mentioned below [Mey, Wies], must the word here be rendered The latter would be allowable as far as the word is concerned, but the form of the sentence determines for the other **συμμιμηταί μου γίνεσθε** forms a complete clause, in which **συμμιμηταί** has the place of emphasis, and in *συμμιμηταί* the preposition · it is therefore unallowable to pass on the sense of the *συμ.* to another clause from which it is separated by **καί** and another verb. So that instead of **καὶ σκοπεῖτε** *κ τ λ* being a reason for this meaning, it is in fact a reason against it) of me, **and observe** (for imitation *τοὺς εὐτέλειαν μᾶλλον ἢ πολυχρηματίαν σκοποῦντας*, Xen Symp iv. 42) **those who walk in such manner as ye have an example in us.** The construction is much controverted. Meyer and Wiesinger would separate *οὕτως* and *καθώς*—*observe those who thus walk* (i. e. as implied above); *as ye have* (emphatic—ye are not in want of) *an example in us* (viz Paul and those who thus walk) My objection to this is, that if **οὕτως** and **καθώς** are to be independent—the three verbs **γίνεσθε, σκοπεῖτε, ἔχετε,** being thus thrown into three independent clauses, will be all correlative, and the **ἔχετε τύπον** will not apply to **οὕτως περιπατοῦντας**, but to the foregoing verbs, thus stultifying the sentence. "*Be &c, and observe &c., as ye have an example* (viz of being *συμμιμηταί μου* and of *σκοπεῖν τοὺς οὕτως περιπατοῦντας*) *in us*" Besides which, the **οὕτως περιπατοῦντας** would be (1) very vague as referring back to what *went before*, seeing that no *περιπατεῖν* has been specified, whereas (2) it is directly related to what *follows*, by the **πολλοὶ περιπατοῦσιν** of ver 18 I therefore retain the usual rendering Meyer's objections to it are, (1) that it is **ἔχετε**, not **ἔχουσιν** —but this does not affect the matter · for, the example including in its reference the *τοὺς οὕτως περιπατοῦντας* and the Philippians, the 2nd person would be more naturally used, the 3rd making a separation which would not be desirable: —(2) that it is *ἡμᾶς*, not *ἐμέ*:— but granting that this does not apply to Paul alone, it certainly cannot, as Mey, be meant to include the *τοὺς οὕτ. περ* with him, which would be a way of speaking unprecedented in his writings,—but must apply to himself and his fellow-workers, Timotheus, Epaphroditus, &c Of course the **τύπον** is no objection (as De W) to the proper plural sense of *ἡμᾶς*, for it is used of that wherein they were all united in one category, as in *ἡδεῖς τὴν ὄψιν* (Plat.), *κακοὶ τὴν ψυχήν* (Æsch) · see Kuhner, ii. 27 18] For (reason for *σκοπεῖτε κ τ.λ* in the form of warning against others who walk differently) **many walk**

ὑμῖν, νῦν δὲ καὶ κλαίων λέγω, τοὺς [l] ἐχθροὺς τοῦ [m] σταυροῦ τοῦ χριστοῦ, 19 ὧν τὸ [n] τέλος [o] ἀπώλεια, ὧν ὁ θεὸς
ἡ [p] κοιλία, καὶ ἡ [q] δόξα ἐν τῇ [r] αἰσχύνῃ αὐτῶν, οἱ τὰ
[s] ἐπίγεια [t] φρονοῦντες. 20 ἡμῶν γὰρ τὸ [u] πολίτευμα ἐν
οὐρανοῖς [v] ὑπάρχει, ἐξ [w] οὗ καὶ σωτῆρα [x] ἀπεκδεχόμεθα

l accus attr, 1 John ii 25 Plato, Rep iii 12, p 402, οὔτε αὐτοί, οὔτε οὕς φαμεν ἡμῖν παιδευτέον εἶναι, τοὺς φύλακας Winer, § 59 7

m Gal v 11 reff n = Rom vi. 21 2 Cor xi 15. Heb vi 8 1 Pet iv 17 Wisd iii 19. o = Matt vii 13 ch i 28 Jer xxvi (xlvi) 21 p = Rom xvi 18. Prov xxiv 15 q = Eph iii 13 1 Thess ii 20 r = 2 Cor iv 2 Jude 13 (Luke xiv 9 Heb. xii 2 Rev iii 18 only Obad 10) s ch ii 10 reff. t = ch ii 2 al u here only (see note) 2 Macc xii 7 only (-ευειν, ch i 27) v Gal i 14 reff w so Col. ii 19 (see note) x Gal v 5 reff.

18 ελεγομεν D¹. om και D¹ 55 Syr
20. for γαρ, δε 80 latt goth Syr syr-marg Clem Orig₂ Eus₂ Chr-comm Thl-ed Iren-int lat-ff.

(no need to supply any thing, as κακῶς [Œc], or '*longe aliter*' [Grot.], nor to understand the word '*circulantur*,' as 1 Pet v 8 [Storr, al, but inconsistently with ver. 17],—still less with Calv '*ambulant terrena cogitantes*' [ungrammatical οἱ τὰ ἐπίγ φρ.]· or to consider the sentence as broken off by the relative clause [De W., al], for περιπατοῦσιν is a 'verbum indifferens,' as in ver. 17, τοὺς οὕτως περιπ) **whom I many times** (answers to πολλοί) **mentioned to you** (viz. when I was with you) **but now mention even weeping** (διὰ τί, ὅτι ἐπέτεινε τὸ κακόν, ὅτι δακρύων ἄξιοι οἱ τοιοῦτοι . . . κλαίει τοίνυν ὁ Παῦλος ἐφ' οἷς ἕτεροι γελῶσι καὶ σπαταλῶσιν οὕτως ἐστὶ συμπαθητικός, οὕτω φροντίζει πάντων ἀνθρώπων Chrys), **the enemies** (the article designates the particular class intended) **of the cross of Christ** (not, as Thdrt, Luth, Erasm, all, of the *doctrine* of the Cross —nor is there any reason to identify these with those spoken of ver. 2. Not Judaistic but Epicurean error, not obliquity of creed but of practice, is here stigmatized And so Chrys,—ἐπειδή τινες ἦσαν ὑποκρινόμενοι μὲν τὸν χριστιανισμόν, ἐν ἀνέσει δὲ ζῶντες κ τρυφῇ· τοῦτο δὲ ἐναντίον τῷ σταυρῷ),—**of whom perdition** (everlasting, at the coming of the Lord see ch. i. 28) **is the** (fixed, certain) **end; of whom their belly is the god** (cf the boast of the Cyclops, in Eurip Cycl 334 ff,—ἁ 'γὼ οὔ τινι θύω, πλὴν ἐμοί, θεοῖσι δ' οὔ, | καὶ τῇ μεγίστῃ γαστρὶ τῇδε δαιμόνων | ὡς τοὐμπιεῖν γε καὶ φαγεῖν τοὐφ' ἡμέραν, | Ζεὺς οὗτος ἀνθρώποισι τοῖσι σώφροσιν. Seneca de benef vii 26, 'alius abdomini servit') **and their glory in their shame** ("ἡ δόξα is subjective,—in the judgment of these men,—and τῇ αἰσχύνῃ objective,—according to the reality of morals Cf. Polyb xv. 23. 5, ἐφ' οἷς ἐχρῆν αἰσχύνεσθαι καθ' ὑπερβολήν, ἐπὶ τούτοις ὡς καλοῖς σεμνύνεσθαι καὶ μεγαλαυχεῖν. On εἶναι ἐν, '*versari*,' to be found in, or contained in, any thing, cf Plat Gorg 470 E, ἐν τούτῳ ἡ πᾶσα εὐδαιμονία ἐστίν, —Eur Phœn 1310,—οὐκ ἐν αἰσχύνῃ τὰ σά" Meyer Ambr, Hil, Pel, Aug., Beng, al., refer the expression to circumcision, taking another meaning for αἰσχύνη ['venter et pudor sunt affinia.' Beng], but without reason; and Chrys., al., disown the meaning), **who regard** (it is not easy to give φρονεῖν, φρόνημα, in this sense, by one word in English They betoken the whole aspect, the *set* of the thoughts and desires τὰ ἐπίγεια, are the substratum of all their feelings) **the things on earth** (in opposition to the things above, cf Col. iii 1 ff The construction is that of logical reference to the subject of the sentence, setting aside the strictness of grammatical connexion· so Thuc iii 36,—ἔδοξεν αὐτοῖς . . . ἐπικαλοῦντες . . , and iv. 108; vi. 24; vii. 42 see more examples in Kuhner, ii 377

The οἱ serves as τούς above, to indicate and individualize the class) 20] **For** (I may well direct you to avoid τοὺς τὰ ἐπίγεια φρονοῦντας·—*for*—*our* state and feelings are wholly alien from theirs) **our** (emphatic) **country** (the *state*, to which we belong, of which we by faith are citizens,—ἡ πατρίς, Thl; meaning the Kingdom of God, the heavenly Jerusalem [Gal. iv. 26 Col iii. 1 ff] This objective meaning of the word is better than the subjective one, '*our citizenship*' [πολιτεία, Acts xxii 28 but they seem sometimes to be used indifferently, see Palm and Rost's Lex, and Aristot. Pol iii 4, κύριον μὲν γὰρ τὸ πολίτευμα τῆς πόλεως· πολίτευμα δ' ἐστὶν ἡ πολιτεία, cf however, on the other side, Ellicott and his note throughout], or, '*our conversation*,' as vulg E. V, which rendering seems to want precedent. Conyb renders it '*life*' but this is insufficient, even supposing it justifiable, as

y 1 Cor iv 6. 2 Cor xi 13, 14, 15 only† 1 Kings xxviii 8 Symm Jos Antt vii 10 5
z constr, Rom vii 24

κύριον Ἰησοῦν χριστόν,
21 ὃς [y] μετασχηματίσει τὸ [z] σῶμα
τῆς [a] ταπεινώσεως ἡμῶν [b] σύμμορφον τῷ [z] σώματι τῆς
δόξης αὐτοῦ, κατὰ τὴν [c] ἐνέργειαν [d] τοῦ δύνασθαι αὐτὸν
καὶ [e] ὑποτάξαι αὐτῷ τὰ πάντα.
IV. 1 [f] ὥςτε, ἀδελφοί

ABDF KLℵ a b c d e f g h k l m n o 17

a Luke i 48. Acts viii 33 (from Isa liii 8). James i 10 only. b Rom viii 29 only†. constr, Matt. xii 13. 1 Thess iii 13. Winer, § 66. 3. g. c Eph i 19 reff iii 7. d constr, Luke xxii 6. Acts xiv 9. 2 Cor viii 11. e Eph i 22 refl. f = ch ii 12 reff.

21 rec ins εις το γενεσθαι αυτο bef συμμορφον, with D[3] [3]KL rel syrr Orig Cæs Epiph Chron Victorin Jer. om ABD[1]Fℵ latt (copt) goth æth Eus Ath Cyr[1] Antch Iren-int Orig-int Tert Cypr. rec (for αυτω) εαυτω, with D[3]KLℵ[3] rel 67[2] Thdrt, sibi vulg (and F lat) Hil Ambr. txt ABD[1]Fℵ[1] b[1] f k o 17 Eus Epiph Chr[1]-mss Cyr Thl-mss.

giving the English reader the idea of ζωή, and so misleading him. I may remark, in passing, on the unfortunate misconception of St. Paul's use of the plural, which has marred so many portions of Mr. Conybeare's version of the Epistles, and none more sadly than this,—where he gives the Apostle's noble description of the state and hopes of us Christians, as contrasted with the τὰ ἐπίγ φρονοῦντες,—all in the singular—'*For my life, &c.,—from whence also I look, &c.*') **subsists** (the word is more solemn, as indicating priority and fixedness, than ἐστιν would be: see notes, ch ii. 6, and Acts xvi 20) **in the heavens, from whence** (οὗ does not refer to πολίτευμα, as Beng, al —nor = ὧν, nor to be rendered '*ex quo tempore,*' as Erasm, but ἐξ οὗ is adverbial, '*unde,*' see Winer, § 21. 3, and cf Xen Anab. i 2. 20, ἡμέρας τρεῖς, ἐν ᾧ) **also** (additional particular, following on heaven being our country) **we wait for** (expect, till the event arrives: see note on Rom viii 19, and a dissertation in the Fritzschiorum Opuscula, p 150 ff) **a Saviour** (emphatic: therefore *we* cannot τὰ ἐπίγ. φρονεῖν, because we are waiting for one to deliver us from them. Or, as Saviour [Ellic]: but perhaps the other is preferable, as being simpler), (**viz**) **the Lord Jesus Christ,** [21] (describes *the method, in which* this Saviour shall save us—a way utterly precluding *our* making a God of our body) **who shall transform** (see 1 Cor. xv 51 ff. The words assume, as St Paul always does when speaking incidentally, the ἡμεῖς surviving to witness the coming of the Lord. The change from the dust of death in the resurrection, however we may *accommodate* the expression to it, was not originally contemplated by it, witness the **ἀπεκδεχόμεθα**, and the σῶμα τῆς ταπεινώσεως ἡμῶν. It is quite in vain to attempt to escape from this inference, as Ellicott does, by saying that "every moment of a true Christian's life involves such an ἀπεκδοχήν." This is most true, but in no way accounts for the peculiar expressions used here) **the body of our humiliation** (beware of the hendiadys, by which most Commentators, and even Conyb here enervate the Apostle's fine and deep meaning. The *body* is that object, that material, in which our *humiliation* has place and is shewn, by its suffering and being degraded—πολλὰ πάσχει νῦν τὸ σῶμα, δεσμεῖται, μαστίζεται, μυρία πάσχει δεινά, Chrys. He once had such a ταπείνωσις, and has passed through it to His glory—and He shall change us so as to be like Him.—Whereas the rendering '*our vile body*' sinks all this, and makes the epithet merely refer to that which is common to all humanity by nature. It is besides, perhaps, hardly allowable: for ταπείνωσις cannot—unless the exigency of context require it, as in ref. Luke [not in Prov xvi 19],—signify mere '*vileness,*' ταπεινότης, but must imply the act whereby the body ταπεινοῦται) (**so as to be**) **conformed to** (on this common idiom, εὔφημον, ὦ τάλαινα, κοίμησον στόμα, Æsch Ag 1258, al. freq.,—cf Kühner, ii 121) **the body of His glory** (in which, as its object or material, His glory has place and is displayed: see above), **according to** (after the analogy of) **the working of His power also** (besides the μετασχήμ &c spoken of) **to subject to Him all things** (*the universe*: see the exception, 1 Cor. xv 25—27). ταῦτα δὲ ποιήσει, says Thdrt, ἅτε δὴ δύναμιν ἄῤῥητον ἔχων, κ ῥᾳδίως κ τὴν φθορὰν κ. τὸν θάνατον καταπαύων, κ εἰς ἀθανασίαν τὰ ἡμέτερα σώματα μεταβάλλων, κ παρασκευάζων ἅπαντας εἰς αὐτὸν ἀποβλέπειν. And Chrys —ἔδειξε μείζονα ἔργα τῆς δυνάμεως αὐτοῦ, ἵνα κ τούτοις πιστεύσῃς. **αὐτῷ**, used of the αὐτός of the whole sentence, from the position of the writer, not of the agent in the clause itself. IV. 1.] *Concluding exhortation,* referring to what has passed since ch iii 17,—not further back, for there first he turns directly to them in the second

μου ἀγαπητοὶ καὶ [g] ἐπιπόθητοι, [h] χαρὰ καὶ [h] στέφανός
μου, οὕτως [k] στήκετε ἐν κυρίῳ, [l] ἀγαπητοί.
2 Εὐοδίαν [m] παρακαλῶ καὶ Συντύχην [m] παρακαλῶ τὸ
αὐτὸ [n] φρονεῖν ἐν κυρίῳ. 3 [o] ναὶ [p] ἐρωτῶ καὶ σέ, [q] γνήσιε
[r] σύνζυγε, [s] συνλαμβάνου αὐταῖς, [t] αἵτινες [u] ἐν τῷ εὐαγγε-

g here only † h 1 Thess ii 19 i Prov xvi 31 Ezek xvi 12 k Gal v 1 reff l (alone) Paul, Rom xii 19 2 Cor xii 19 only Heb vi 9 1 Pet ii 11 al5 1 John ii 7 al5 3 John 2, 5, 11 Jude 3, 17, 20. m Eph iv 1 reff n ch ii 2 reff o Philem 20 p = Matt xv 23 1 Thess iv 1 reff q 2 Cor viii 8 1 Tim i 2 Tit i 4 only † Sir vii 18 only (ως, ch ii 20) r here only † Aristoph Plut 945 s = Luke v 7 only Gen xxx 8 F t = Acts x 41, 47 xiii 31, 43 al u = Rom i 9 2 Cor viii 18 x 14 al

Chap. IV. 1 χαρις F(and G, but *gaudium* G-lat) ins και bef ουτως F. om 2nd αγαπητοι D[1] 108 aft 2nd αγαπητοι ins μου B 17.
2 [ευοδιαν, so ABDFKLℵ, &c]
3. rec for ναι, και (error), with h(e sil): txt ABDFKLℵ rel vss gr-lat-ff rec συζυγε bef γνησιε, with KL rel syr Chr Thdrt. εγνησιε γερμανε συνζ F txt ABDℵ

person, with ἀδελφοί, as here,—there also οὕτως occurs, answering to the οὕτως here,—and there, in the Christian's hopes, vv 20, 21, lies the ground of the ὥστε here. **ὥστε**] 'quæ cum ita sint'—since we have such a home, and look for such a Saviour, and expect such a change '—ὥστε κἂν ὁρᾶτε τούτους χαίροντας, κἂν ὁρᾶτε δεδοξασμένους, στήκετε, Chrys Cf. 1 Cor xv. 58. **ἐπιπόθ.**] **longed for** The word occurs in Appian, vi. 43, ὅρκους τε ὤμοσεν αὐτοῖς κ ἔλαβεν, ἐπιποθήτους ἐν τοῖς ὕστερον πολέμοις πολλάκις γενομένους. For the verb, see ch i 8 reff: for the substantive, -πσις, 2 Cor vii 7, 11. **στέφανος**] from ref. 1 Thess., both χαρά and στέφανος apply to the future great day in the Apostle's mind And indeed even without such reference to his usus loquendi, it would be difficult to dissociate the "*crown*" from such thoughts as that in 2 Tim. iv 8. **οὕτως**] see above 'as I have been describing:' not ὡς ἐστήκατε ἀκλινῶς, as Chrys, Thl., Œc, Calv, Beng., '*ita, ut statis, state,*' which would be inconsistent with ch. iii. 17. **ἐν κυρίῳ**] as the element wherein your stedfastness consists **ἀγαπητοί**] an affectionate repetition: μετ' εὐφημίας πολλῆς ἡ παραίνεσις, Thdrt. "Doctrinam suo more vehementioribus exhortationibus claudit, quo eam hominum animis tenacius infigat. Et blandis appellationibus in eorum affectus se insinuat: quæ tamen non sunt adulationis, sed sinceri amoris." Calv 2—9] *Concluding exhortations to individuals* (2, 3), *and to all* (4—9). 2] Euodia and Syntyche (both *women*, cf. αὐταῖς and αἵτινες below) appear to have needed this exhortation on account of some disagreement, both however being faithful, and fellow-workers (perhaps deaconesses, Rom. xvi 1) with himself in the Gospel. θαυμάζει μὲν τὰς γυναῖκας· αἰνίττεται δὲ ὡς ἔριν τινὰ πρὸς ἀλλήλας ἐχούσας, Thdrt The repetition of the verb παρακαλῶ not merely signifies 'vehementiam affectus' (Erasm), but hints at the present separation between them **τὸ αὐτὸ φρονεῖν**] see ch. ii 2, note. He adds **ἐν κυρίῳ**, both to shew them wherein their unanimity must consist, and perhaps to point out to them that their present alienation was *not ἐν κυρίῳ*.

3] **ναί** assumes the granting of the request just made, and carries on further the same matter, see Philem. 20 and note; but does not *conjure*, as Grot, al **γνήσιε σύνζυγε**] **true** ('*genuine*'—true, as distinguished from counterfeit: lit. of legitimate worth [γενήσιος]) **yoke-fellow.** Who is intended, it is quite impossible to say. Various opinions have been, (1) that St. Paul addresses *his own wife* So Clem Alex Strom iii. 6 (53), p 535 P, καὶ ὅ γε Παῦλος οὐκ ὀκνεῖ ἔν τινι ἐπιστολῇ τὴν αὐτοῦ προσαγορεύειν σύνζυγον, ἣν οὐ περιεκόμιζε διὰ τὸ τῆς ὑπηρεσίας εὐσταλές,—Eus. H E iii 30, al. But this is evidently an error, and Thdrt says rightly,—τὸν δὲ σύνζ τινες ἀνοήτως ὑπέλαβον γυναῖκα εἶναι τοῦ ἀποστόλου, οὐ προσεσχηκότες τοῖς ἐν τῇ πρὸς Κορινθίους γεγραμμένοις (1 Cor vii. 8), ὅτι τοῖς ἀγάμοις συνέταξεν ἑαυτόν. Besides which, the adjective in this case would be feminine,—cf. Eur Alcest 326, ποίας τυχοῦσα συνζύγου,—and 354, τοιᾶσδ' ἁμαρτάνοντι συνζύγου perhaps even if it were of two terminations [as adjectives in -ιος frequently in the N T, e g οὐράνιος, Luke ii 13, Acts xxvi. 19 ὁσίους χεῖρας, 1 Tim ii 8, &c. See Winer, § 11. 1], in which case Ellic remarks, it would revert to three terminations; but authority for this statement seems wanting (2) that he was the husband, or brother, of Euodia or Syntyche, so Chrys doubtfully, and Thl., al. But then the epithet would hardly be wanted—nor would the ex-

λίῳ [v] συνήθλησάν μοι, μετὰ καὶ Κλήμεντος καὶ τῶν λοι-
πῶν [w] συνεργῶν μου, ὧν τὰ ὀνόματα ἐν [x] βίβλῳ [x] ζωῆς.
4 [y] Χαίρετε ἐν κυρίῳ πάντοτε· πάλιν ἐρῶ, χαίρετε.
5 τὸ [z] ἐπιεικὲς ὑμῶν [a] γνωσθήτω πᾶσιν ἀνθρώποις. ὁ

ABDF KLℵab cdefg hklm no17

v ch i 27 only †. w ch ii 25 reff. x Rev iii 5 xiii 8 xvii 8 xx 15 xxi 27 (Exod xxxii 32 Ps lxviii 28 Dan xii 1) y ver 10 ch iii 1 z = 1 Tim iii. 3 reff. a constr, Acts ix 24 Lev iv 14.

c o 17 latt copt Thl. om και bef κλημεντος D[1]F a latt arm (Orig) Ambrst Pelag om λοιπων, adding και των λοιπων aft μου, ℵ[1]: txt ℵ[3].
5 ins τοις bef ανθρ. A

pression be at all natural. (3) that he was some fellow labourer of the Apostle. So Thdrt,—**σύνζυγον καλεῖ, ὡς τὸν αὐτὸν ἕλκοντα τῆς εὐσεβείας ζυγόν**, Pelag., all., and De W.,—and of these some (Grot., Calov., al.) have understood *Epaphroditus*,—Estius, *Timotheus*,—Bengel (but afterwards he preferred *Epaphroditus*), *Silas*,—Luther the *chief bishop* at Philippi. (4) Others have regarded **Σύνζυγε** as a proper name: so τινές in Chrys. and Œc., and so Meyer. In this case the γνήσιε would mean, 'who art veritably, as thy name is,' a yoke-fellow. And this might be said by the Apostle, who elsewhere compares the Christian minister to the βοῦς ἀλοῶν. It seems to me that we must choose between the two last hypotheses. The objections to each are about of equal weight: the Apostle nowhere else calls his fellow-labourers σύνζυγοι,—and the proper name Σύνζυγος is nowhere else found. But these are no reasons, respectively, against either hypothesis. We may safely say with Chrys., εἴτε τοῦτο, εἴτε ἐκεῖνο, οὐ σφόδρα ἀκριβολογεῖσθαι δεῖ. **συνλαμβάνου αὐταῖς**] help them (Euodia and Syntyche): but not, as Grot., 'ut habeant, unde se suosque honeste sustentent:' it is *the work of their reconciliation* which he clearly has in view, and in which they would need help. **αἵτινες**] '*utpote quæ*'—seeing that they .... The E.V. here is in error, '*help those women which* ...' The Gospel at Philippi was first received by *women*, Acts xvi. 13 ff., and these two must have been among those who, having believed, laboured among their own sex for its spread. **ἐν τ. εὐαγ.**] see reff. **μετὰ καὶ Κλήμεντος**] These words belong to **συνήθλησαν**, not to συνλαμβάνου, and are rather an additional reminiscence, than a part of the exhortation '*as did Clemens also* &c.' q. d. 'not that I mean, by naming those women with distinction, to imply forgetfulness of those others &c., and especially of Clemens.' The insertion of καί between the preposition and substantive is said to be a habit principally of Pindar,—e. g. ἐν καὶ θαλάσσα, Ol. ii. 28; ἐν καὶ τελευτᾷ, Ol. vii. 26: ἐπὶ καὶ θανάτῳ, Pyth. iv. 330. See Hartung, i. 143. It is not necessary to regard the καί—καί as bound together, so that these examples are in point (against Ellic.). Clemens must have been a fellow-worker with the Apostle *at Philippi*, from the context here, and, from the non-occurrence of any such name among Paul's fellow-travellers, and the fact that οἱ λοιποὶ συνεργοί must have been Philippians,—himself a native of Philippi. It is perhaps arbitrary, seeing that the name is so common, to assume his identity with Clemens afterwards Bishop of Rome, and author of the Epistles to the Corinthians. So Eus. H. E. iii. 4, ὁ Κλήμης, τῆς Ῥωμαίων κ. αὐτὸς ἐκκλησίας τρίτος ἐπίσκοπος καταστάς, Παύλου συνεργὸς κ. συναθλητὴς γεγονέναι πρὸς αὐτοῦ μαρτυρεῖται. see also H. E. v. 6: so Origen, Com. in Joan. t. vi. 36, vol. iv. p. 153: and Jer. Script. Eccl., 15, vol. ii. p. 854. Chrys. does not notice any such idea. See on the whole, Ellicott's note. **ὧν τὰ ὀν. ἐν βίβλῳ ζωῆς**] belongs to the λοιποί, whom *he does not name*: whose names are (not a wish, εἴη, as Bengel, nor are they to be regarded as *dead* when this was written) in the book of life (reff., and Luke x. 20).

4—9.] *Exhortation* to ALL.

4. **πάλιν ἐρῶ**] AGAIN I will say it: referring to ch. iii. 1, where see note. It is the groundtone of the Epistle.

5.] **τὸ ἐπιεικές**, your forbearance, from ἐπί, implying direction, and εἰκός, ἔοικα [not εἴκω, to yield, as Trench, N. T. Syn. 171: see Palm and Rost's Lex., under the word, as also under ΕΙ'ΚΩ and ἔοικα], *reasonableness of dealing*, wherein not strictness of legal right, but consideration for one another, is the rule of practice. Aristot., Eth. Nic. v. 6, defines it to be that which fills up the necessary deficiencies of *law*, which is *general*, by dealing with particular cases as the law-giver would have dealt with them if he had been by. διό, he adds, δίκαιον μέν ἐστι, καὶ βέλτιόν τινος δικαίου· ... καὶ ἔστιν αὕτη ἡ φύσις ἡ τοῦ ἐπιεικοῦς, ἐπανόρθωμα νόμου, ᾗ ἐλλείπει διὰ τὸ καθ-

κύριος [b] ἐγγύς. 6 μηδὲν [c] μεριμνᾶτε, ἀλλ' [d] ἐν παντὶ τῇ
[e] προσευχῇ καὶ τῇ [e] δεήσει μετὰ [f] εὐχαριστίας τὰ [g] αἰτή-
ματα ὑμῶν [h] γνωριζέσθω πρὸς τὸν θεόν. 7 καὶ ἡ εἰρήνη
τοῦ θεοῦ ἡ [i] ὑπερέχουσα πάντα [k] νοῦν [l] φρουρήσει τὰς
καρδίας ὑμῶν καὶ τὰ [m] νοήματα ὑμῶν ἐν χριστῷ Ἰησοῦ.

b = Matt xxvi. 18 Rev i. 3 xxii 10 Joel i 15
c constr, ch ii. 20 reff
d = Eph v 24 1 Thess v 18.
e Eph vi 18 reff
f Eph v 4 reff
g Luke xxiii 24 1 John v 15 only Ps xix 5 al Ezek xliv 23
h = Luke ii 15 Acts ii 28 Eph i 9 al
i ch ii 3 reff
k = Luke xxiv 45 Rev xiii 18 Job xxxiii 16.
l Gal iii 23 reff
m 2 Cor ii 11 iii 14 iv 4 x 5 xi 3 only P† Baruch ii 8 only

6. μετ' Bℵ.

7. for θεου, χριστου A syr-marg Cyr Procop Ambr, Pelag-comm. for νοηματα, σωματα F D-lat spec tol Chrom Oros.

ὅλου. And he describes the ἐπιεικής as ὁ μὴ ἀκριβοδίκαιος ἐπὶ τὸ χεῖρον See Trench, New Test Syn, as above By the γνωσθήτω πᾶσιν ἀνθρ., the Apostle rather intends, 'let no man know of you any inconsistency with ἐπιείκεια' The universality of it justifies its application even to those described above, ch iii 18 f, —that though warned against them, they were to shew all moderation and clemency towards them so Chrys Meyer observes well, that the succession of these precepts seems to explain itself psychologically by the disposition of spiritual joy in the Lord exalting us both above rigorism, and above anxiety of mind (ver 6). ὁ κύριος ἐγγύς] These words may apply either to the foregoing—'the Lord will soon come, He is the avenger, it is yours to be moderate and clement' (so De Wette, all) or to the following—'the Lord is near, be not anxious·' so Chrys, Thdrt, all Perhaps we may best regard it as the transition from the one to the other: Christ's coming is at hand—this is the best enforcer of clemency and forbearance · it also leads on to the duty of banishing anxiety. ὁ κύριος is *Christ*, and the ἐγγύς refers to the παρουσία, see on ch iii 20 6] μηδέν has the emphasis It is the accusative of the object, as τὰ πολλὰ μεριμνᾷν, Xen Cyr viii. 7. 12. ἐν παντί] in every thing: see ref. 1 Thess and note. Meyer remarks that the literally correct rendering of the Vulg. '*in omni* (neut.) *oratione*' led Ambrose wrong, who gives it '*per omnem orationem*.' τῇ προσευχῇ καὶ τῇ δεήσει] by your prayer and your supplication: or better, by the prayer and the supplication appropriate to each thing On the difference between προσευχή and δέησις, see on Eph vi 18, 1 Tim ii 1. Not μετὰ τῆς εὐχαριστίας, because the matters themselves may not be recognized as grounds of εὐχαριστία, but *it* should *accompany* every request Ellic, who doubts this explanation, thinks it "more simple to say that εὐχαριστία, 'thanksgiving for past blessings,' is in its nature more general and comprehensive, προσ and δεησ almost necessarily more limited and specific Hence, though εὐχαρ occurs 12 times in St Paul's Epistles, it is only twice used with the article, 1 Cor xiv. 26, 2 Cor iv. 15" But I much prefer the other view τὰ αἰτήματα] = ἃ ἂν αἰτώμεθα, 1 John v. 15 Plato, Rep viii. p 566, speaks of τὸ τυραννικὸν αἴτημα . . . αἰτεῖν τὸν δῆμον φύλακάς τινας τοῦ σώματος πρὸς τὸν θεόν] unto, 'before,' '*coram*' see Acts viii. 24. 7] *Consequence* of this laying every thing before God in prayer with thanksgiving—*peace unspeakable* καί, and then. ἡ εἰρ. τοῦ θεοῦ, that peace which rests in God and is wrought by Him in the soul, the counterpoise of all troubles and anxieties—see John xvi 33— . . ἵνα ἐν ἐμοὶ εἰρήνην ἔχητε· ἐν τῷ κόσμῳ θλίψιν ἔχετε. Meyer denies that εἰρήνη ever has this meaning but he is certainly wrong The above verse, and John xiv 27, Col iii. 15, cannot be fully interpreted on *his* meaning, mere *mutual concord*. It is of course true, that mutual concord, and τὸ ἐπιεικές, are necessary elements of this peace · but it goes far beyond them See the alternatives thoroughly discussed, as usual, in Ellic.'s note ἡ ὑπερέχουσα πάντα νοῦν] not as Chrys, ὅταν λέγῃ πρὸς τοὺς ἐχθροὺς εἰρηνεύειν . . . πῶς οὐχ ὑπὲρ νοῦν ἐστιν ἀνθρώπινον τοῦτο; nor as Estius, "quia omnem expectationem humanam excedit, quod Deus pro inimicis sibi reconciliandis filium suum dederit in mortem ." nor as Calvin, "quia nihil humano ingenio magis adversum, quam in summa desperatione nihilominus sperare" but as Erasm, all, "res felicior quam ut humana mens queat percipere" νοῦς is the *intelligent faculty*, the perceptive and appreciative power reff On the sentiment itself, cf Eph. iii. 19 φρουρήσει must not with Chrys, Thdrt, Thl, Luth, all and Vulg, be made *optative*

n Eph vi 10 reff ch iii 1
o 1 Tim iii 8, 11 Tit ii 2 only Prov xv 26. (σεμνότης, 1 Tim ii. 2)
p = 2 Cor vii. 11 xi 2 James iii 17 Ps. xviii 9

8 n Τὸ λοιπόν, ἀδελφοί, ὅσα ἐστὶν ἀληθῆ, ὅσα o σεμνά,
ὅσα δίκαια, ὅσα p ἁγνά, ὅσα q προσφιλῆ, ὅσα r εὔφημα,
s εἴ τις t ἀρετὴ καὶ s εἴ τις ἔπαινος, ταῦτα u λογίζεσθε. 9 ἃ
καὶ ἐμάθετε καὶ v παρελάβετε καὶ ἠκούσατε καὶ εἴδετε

ABDF KLℵ a b c d e f g h k l m n o 17

q here only† Sir iv 7 xx 13 only. r here only† Ps lxii 6 Symm (-μία, 2 Cor vi 8) s = Eph iv 29 t Paul, here only = 2 Pet. i (3) 5 bis (1 Pet ii. 9) only Wisd viii 7. u 1 Cor xiii 5 Ps cxxxix 2 Zech. viii 17 v = Gal i. 9, 12 reff

8 aft επαινος ins επιστημης *disciplinæ* D[1]F vulg(not am[1] tol) Sing-cler Ambrst Pelag (not Aug Fulg Sedul).

in sense: it is not a wish, but a declaration—following upon the performance of the injunction above. **τὰς καρδίας ὑμῶν κ. τὰ νοήματα ὑμῶν**] The **heart** is the fountain of the **thoughts**, i e. designs, plans (not *minds*, as E. V.): so that this expression is equivalent to, '*your hearts themselves, and their fruits.*' **ἐν χριστῷ Ἰησοῦ** is not the predicate after *φρουρήσει*—*shall keep &c in Christ*, i. e. keep them from falling from Christ (*ὥστε μένειν κ. μὴ ἐκπεσεῖν αὐτοῦ τῆς πίστεως*, Chrys) but, as usual, denotes the sphere or element of the *φρουρά* thus bestowed—that it shall be a Christian security:—the verb *φρουρήσει* being *absolute.*

8, 9] *Summary exhortation to Christian virtues not yet specified* 8] **τὸ λοιπόν** resumes again his intention of closing the Epistle with which he had begun ch iii, but from which he had been diverted by incidental subjects It is unnatural to attribute to the Apostle so formal a design as De W. does, of now speaking of man's part, as he had hitherto of God's part:—Chrys has it rightly,—*τί ἐστι τὸ λοιπόν; ἀντὶ τοῦ, πάντα ἡμῖν εἴρηται ἐπειγομένου τὸ ῥῆμά ἐστι, καὶ οὐδὲν κοινὸν ἔχοντος πρὸς τὰ παρόντα.*

This beautiful sentence, full of the Apostle's fervour and eloquence, derives much force from the frequent repetition of *ὅσα*, and then of *εἴ τις* **ἀληθῆ**] subjective, **truthful**: not, *true* in matter of fact The whole regards ethical qualities. *ταῦτα γὰρ ὄντως ἀληθῆ, ἡ ἀρετή, ψεῦδος δὲ ἡ κακία. κ. γὰρ ἡ ἡδονὴ αὐτῆς ψεῦδος, κ ἡ δόξα αὐτῆς ψεῦδος, κ. πάντα τὰ τοῦ κόσμου ψεῦδος.* Chrys.
σεμνά] *τὸ σεμνὸν ὄνομα, τὸ καλόν τε κἀγαθόν*, Xen Œc. vi. 14. It is difficult to give it in any one English word '*honest*' and '*honourable*' are too weak: '*reverend*' and '*venerable*,' '*grave*,' are seldom applied to *things*. Nor do I know any other more eligible **δίκαια**] not '*just*,' in respect of others, merely—but **right**, in that wider sense in which *δικαιοσύνη* is used—before God and man: see this sense Acts x. 22; Rom. v 7.

ἁγνά] not merely '*chaste*' in the ordinary confined acceptation but **pure generally**: "castimoniam denotat in omnibus vitæ partibus" Calv. **προσφιλῆ**] **lovely**, in the most general sense no subjects need be supplied, as *τοῖς πιστοῖς*, or *τῷ θεῷ* (Chrys.) for the exhortation is markedly and designedly as *general* as possible.
εὔφημα] again, general, and with reference to general fame—**of good report**, as E.V. The meaning '*sermones qui bene aliis precantur*,' adopted by Storr and Flatt, though philologically justified, is evidently not general enough for our context. **εἴ τις ἀρετὴ ...**] sums up all which have gone before and generalizes still further The E V. '*if there be any virtue*,' &c. is objectionable, not for the reason alleged by Scholefield, Hints, &c. p 85, as 'expressing a doubt of the existence of the thing in the abstract,' which it does not,—but as carrying the appearance of an *adjuration*, '*by the existence of*,' &c which conveys a wrong impression of the sense—**whatever virtue there is** (not 'there *be*,' as Scholef) &c
ἀρετή] **virtue**, in the most general ethical sense **ἔπαινος**, **praise**, not '*pro eo quod est laudabile*,' as Calv, al, but as Erasm, 'laus, virtutis comes.' The *disciplinæ*, which follows 'laus' in the Vulg &c, is a pure interpolation, and beside the meaning see various readings
ταῦτα—viz, all the foregoing—the *ἀληθῆ* &c,—the *ἀρετή*, and the *ἔπαινος*—**these things meditate**: let them be your *νοήματα.* 9] These general abstract things he now particularizes in the concrete as having been exemplified and taught by himself when among them The first **καί** is not '*both*,' as E. V., but **also,—moreover**: which, besides what I have said recommending them above, were also recommended to you by my own example. **ἐμάθετε**] again, not as E. V. '*have learned*,' &c—but all aorists,—referring to the time when he was among them **Those things which** (not '*whatsoever* things:' we are on generals no longer nor would he recommend to

ἐν ἐμοί, ταῦτα πράσσετε, καὶ ὁ ^{w} θεὸς τῆς ^{w} εἰρήνης ^{x} ἔσται
μεθ' ὑμῶν.
10 ^{y} Ἐχάρην δὲ ἐν κυρίῳ ^{z} μεγάλως, ὅτι ^{a} ἤδη ^{a} ποτὲ
^{b} ἀνεθάλετε ^{c} τὸ ὑπὲρ ἐμοῦ ^{d} φρονεῖν· ^{e} ἐφ' ᾧ καὶ ^{d} ἐφρονεῖτε, ^{f} ἠκαιρεῖσθε δέ. 11 ^{g} οὐχ ὅτι ^{h} καθ' ^{i} ὑστέρησιν

w Rom xv 33. xvi 20 1 Cor xiv 33 2 Cor xiii 11 1 Thess v 23 Heb. xiii 20 (2 Thess iii 16)
x Acts vii 9 xviii 10 Isa lviii 11
y ver 4 ch iii 1
z here only 1 Chron xxix 9 Neh xii 43
a Rom i 10 only
b here only trans, Ezek xvii 24 Sir i 18 xi 22 intr, Ps xxvii 7
c 1 Thess iii 8 reff
d see ch i 7
e constr, here only ἐφ' ᾧ, Rom v 12 2 Cor v 4 ch iii 12.
f here only † (-ρῶς, 2 Tim iv 2)
g = John vi 46 2 Cor i 24 iii 5 ch iii 12 ver 17 2 Thess iii 9 only
h = ch ii 3. Matt xix 3. Acts iii 17
i Mark xii 44 only † (-ημα, ch ii 30)

9 ιδετε D²FKL d h m n Clem Thdrt Thl-ms.
10. εθαλατε D¹. for το, του F.

them *all* his own sayings and doings; but the *καί* expressly provides for their being of the kinds specified above) **ye moreover learned, and received** (reff.: here of receiving not by *word of mouth*, but by knowledge of his character the whole is not doctrinal, but ethical) **and heard** (again not of preaching, but of his tried and acknowledged Christian character, which was in men's mouths and thus heard) **and saw** (each for himself) **in me** (*ἐν ἐμοί* will not properly belong to the two first verbs, *ἐμάθ* and *παρελ*, but must be associated by zeugma with them —he himself being clearly the example throughout), **these things** (*ταῦτα*, *ἅ*) **practise** (correlative with, not opposed to, *λογίζεσθε* above —*that λογισμός* being eminently practical, and issuing, in the concrete, in the *ταῦτα πράσσειν*, after Paul's example) **καί**] **and then**: see ver. 7. On **εἰρήνη**, see there.

10—20] *He thanks them for the supply received from Philippi* **10**] **δέ** is transitional, the contrast being between the personal matters which are now introduced, and those more solemn ones which he has just been treating. **ἐν κυρίῳ**] See above, ch iii. 1, ver. 4, "Every occurrence, in his view, has reference to Christ,—takes from Him its character and form." Wiesinger. **ἤδη ποτέ**] **now at length**, as E V 'tandem aliquando:' *χρόνον δηλοῦντός ἐστι μακρόν*, Chrys The **ποτέ** takes up and makes indefinite the **ἤδη** as in *δή ποτέ*, *δή που*, &c. See Klotz ad Devar. p. 607, 8 But no *reproof* is conveyed by the expression, as Chrys. thinks see below **ἀνεθάλετε**] lit. **ye came into leaf**; "metaphora sumta ab arboribus, quarum vis hyeme contracta latet, vere florere incipit," Calv But it is fanciful to conclude with Bengel, that it *was Spring*, when the gift came. see on a similar fancy in 1 Cor v. 7. The word is taken transitively (see reff.) by Grot, all.,— '*ye caused to spring again your care for me*' (see below) but the intransitive only will suit the sense here—**ye budded forth again in caring for my interest** (see below) Your care for *me* was, so to speak, the *life* of the tree; it existed just as much in winter when there was no vegetation, when ye *ἠκαιρεῖσθε*, as when the buds were put forth in spring This is evident by what follows We must thank Meyer, to whom we owe so much in accuracy of grammatical interpretation, for having followed out the right track here, first indicated by Bengel, and rendered *τὸ ὑπὲρ ἐμοῦ* as the accusative governed by *φρονεῖν* The ordinary way (so Wiesinger and Ellicott recently) has been to regard the words as = *τὸ φρονεῖν ὑπὲρ ἐμοῦ*, thus depriving the relative *ἐφ' ᾧ* of any thing to refer to, and producing the logical absurdity [Mey.], *ἐφρονεῖτε ἐπὶ τῷ ὑπὲρ ἐμοῦ φρονεῖν*, or forcing *ἐφ' ᾧ* to some unjustified meaning ('*although*,' as Luth., al,—'*sicut*,' as vulg,—&c.), or understanding it '*for whom*,' as Calv., al., —contrary to the Apostle's usage, in which [reff] *ἐφ' ᾧ* is always neuter. But if we take *τὸ ὑπὲρ ἐμοῦ* together,—'*my interest*,'—and govern it by *φρονεῖν*, all will be simple and clear: **I rejoiced, &c that at last ye flourished in anxiety for my interest: for which purpose** (cf Plat Gorg. p. 502 B, *ἐφ' ᾧ ἐσπούδακε*:—the purpose, namely, *of* flourishing, putting forth the supply which you have now sent. Wiesinger prefers the other, and vindicates it from Meyer's imputation but to me not convincingly as neither Ellicott) **ye also** *were* **anxious** (all that long time, imperfect), **but had no opportunity** (**ἀκαιρέω** is a word of later Greek **εὐκαιρέω**, its opposite, is used by Lucian, Plutarch, Polyb, &c, as also its compounds *ἐνευκαιρέω*, *προσευκαιρέω*, &c See Phryn. ed Lobeck, p 125 Wiesinger well remarks that we must not press this *ἠκαιρεῖσθε* into a definite hypothesis, such as that their financial state was not adequate—that they

k = Heb v 8
l ει θέλει με ἐν τοιούτοις εἶναι ἐν οἷς εἰμι, Arrian, Epict i 22 ellips., 1 Pet ii 12 iii 14 al Ezek xiv 4
m here only — Sir xl 18 (-κεῖν, Deut xxxii 10 -κεια, 1 Tim vi 6)

λέγω· ἐγὼ γὰρ [k] ἔμαθον [l] ἐν οἷς εἰμὶ [m] αὐτάρκης εἶναι. ABDF KLℵ a b c d e f g h k l m n o 17
12 [n] οἶδα καὶ [o] ταπεινοῦσθαι, [n] οἶδα καὶ [p] περισσεύειν. [q] ἐν
παντὶ καὶ [q] ἐν πᾶσιν [r] μεμύημαι καὶ [s] χορτάζεσθαι καὶ
[t] πεινᾶν καὶ [p] περισσεύειν καὶ [u] ὑστερεῖσθαι. 13 πάντα
[v] ἰσχύω [w] ἐν τῷ [x] ἐνδυναμοῦντί με. 14 [y] πλὴν [z] καλῶς

n = 1 Thess ii 4 James iv 17 Job xxxiv 19
o = 2 Cor xi 7 Prov xiii 7 p = ver 18 q see 2 Cor xi 6 r here only † 3 Macc ii 30
s Paul, here only Matt xiv 20 James ii 16 Rev xix 21 Ps xxxvi 19 t Matt iv 2 1 Cor iv 11 xi 21 al Prov xxv 21 u = Luke xv 14. 2 Cor xi 8 Heb xi 37 Sir xiii 4 v = Gal v 6 James v 16 Wisd xvi 20. w = ἐν χριστῷ, &c passim x Eph vi 10 reff y = Eph v 33 reff z Acts x 33 1 Cor vii. 37, 38 James ii 8, 19 2 Pet i 19 3 Kings viii 18

12. rec (for 1st και) δε, with b d e f: txt ABDFKLℵ rel vulg syr goth Clem lat-ff. om και bef περισσευειν A Syr.

13 rec aft με ins χριστω (*gloss: or as in Orig below, filled up from* 1 *Tim* i. 12), with D³KLℵ³ rel syrr goth (Orig₁) Ath(elsw ιησ χρ) Nyssen Chr Thdrt Damasc χρῡ F χω̄ ιῡ Orig₃(elsw adds ιησου τω κυρ ημων)· om ABD¹ℵ 17 vulg(and F-lat) copt æth arm Clem Ambrst Aug Ambr Pelag.

had no means of conveyance, &c—it is perfectly general, and all such fillings up are mere conjecture) **11**] inserted to prevent misunderstanding of the last verse. οὐχ ὅτι] See ch. iii 12 **my meaning is not, that** . καθ', **according to, i.e in consequence of**—see reff., and Od γ 106, πλαζόμενοι κατὰ λήϊδ' Herod ii. 152, κατὰ λήϊην ἐκπλώσαντας· Thuc vi 31, κατὰ θέαν ἥκειν not, as Van Hengel, '*ut more receptum est penuriæ*,' which would be κατὰ τοὺς ὑστεροῦντας (see Rom iii. 5 al) **For I** (emphatic · **for my part**, whatever others may feel) **learned** (in my experience, my training for this apostolic work not '*have learned*.' the aorist is much simpler and more humble—'I was taught ·' the present result of this teaching comes below, *οἶδα*, but not in this word), **in the state in which I am** (not '*in whatsoever state I am*' [E V : which would be ἐν οἷς ἂν εἰμί,—cf. ὅπου ἂν εἰσεπορεύετο, Mark vi 56, ὅσοι ἂν ἥπτοντο αὐτοῦ, ib. Winer, § 42. 3. *a*], nor as Luther, bei welchen ich bin [οἷς masculine], which is against the context. But **ἐν οἷς εἰμί** does not apply only to the Apostle's *present circumstances*, but to any *possible* present ones · '*in which I am at any time*.' see next verse) **to find competence** (we have no word for αὐτάρκης '*Self-sufficing*' will express its meaning of independence of external help [τελειότης κτήσεως ἀγαθῶν, Plat. Def. p. 412], but is liable to be misunderstood. '*competent*' is not in use in this sense, though the abstract noun **competence** is the German genügsam gives it well).

12] See above. **I know** (by this teaching) **also** (the first *καί* expresses that, besides the general finding of competence in all circumstances, he specially has been taught to suffer humiliation and to bear abundance. See Ellic.'s note) **how to be brought low** (generally. but here especially by *need*, in humiliation of circumstances Meyer remarks that 2 Cor. iv. 8, vi. 9, 10, are a commentary on this), **I know also** (*καί* as before, or as an addition to **οἶδα καὶ ταπεινοῦσθαι**) **how to abound** (ὑψοῦσθαι, as Wies. remarks, would be the *proper* general opposite but he chooses the special one, which fits the matter of which he is treating) **in every thing** (not as vulg, E V, all, '*every where*,' nor '*at every time*,' as Chrys, Grot,—nor both, as Thl, &c :—but as usually in St. Paul see ref and note) **and in all things** (not, as Luth, Beng, '*respectu omnium hominum*.' ἐν παντὶ πράγματί, φησι, κ ἐν πᾶσι τοῖς παρεμπίπτουσι, Œc. the expression conveys *universality*, as '*in each and all*,' with us) **I have been taught the lesson** ('*initiated* ·' but no stress to be laid, as by Beng, 'disciplina arcana imbutus sum, ignota mundo ' see the last example below. Beware [against Wiesinger] of joining **μεμύημαι** with **ἐν παντὶ κ. ἐν πᾶσιν**, *initiated in, &c.*, the verb is [against Ellicott] not constructed with *ἐν*, but with an accusative of the person and the thing [μυεῖν τινά τι], which last accusative remains with the passive. so μ' ἀνὴρ ἐμύησ' Ἑλικωνίδα, Anthol. ix 162,—οἱ τὰς τελετὰς μεμυημένοι, Plat Symp. p. 209 The present construction, with an infinitive, occurs, Alciphr ii. 1, κυβερνᾷν μυηθήσομαι) **both to be satiated and to hunger** (the forms πεινᾷν, διχᾷν, for -ῆν, seem to have come in with Macedonian influence. being found first in Aristotle; see Lobeck in Phryn. p 61), **both to abound and to be in need.**

13.] 'After these special notices, he de-

ἐποιήσατε [a] συγκοινωνήσαντές μου τῇ [b] θλίψει. 15 οἴδατε
δὲ καὶ ὑμεῖς, Φιλιππήσιοι, ὅτι ἐν [c] ἀρχῇ τοῦ [c] εὐαγγελίου,
ὅτε [d] ἐξῆλθον ἀπὸ Μακεδονίας, οὐδεμία μοι ἐκκλησία [e] ἐκοι-
νώνησεν εἰς [f] λόγον [gh] δόσεως καὶ [hi] λήμψεως, εἰ μὴ ὑμεῖς
μόνοι, 16 ὅτι καὶ ἐν Θεσσαλονίκῃ καὶ [j] ἅπαξ καὶ [j] δὶς [k] εἰς

a Eph v 11 Rev xviii 4 only+ (-νος, ch i 7) b Eph iii 13 reff c Mark i 1 d Mark xi 12 Luke xvii 20 Gen xxviii 10 e Gal vi 6 reff f 1 Macc x 40 Polyb xv 34 2 g Sir xli 19 xlii 7 h James i 17 only Prov xxi 14 i here only Prov xv 27 Sir as above (g) only j 1 Thess ii 18 Neh xiii 20 k Acts xi 29

14 τη θλιψει bef μου DF latt.
15 om δε D[1] f m 72 115 syr æth-pl Chr Thdrt Thl-mss. ins οτι bef ουδεμια (retaining former οτι) D[1]F om μονοι A[1].
16 om εις AD[1] Syr goth Ps-Ath Œc-txt Victorin: usibus meis Ambrst Aug.

clares his *universal* power,—how triumphantly, yet how humbly!' Meyer I can do (reff., so μηδὲν ἰσχύειν, Plat. Crit. p 50 B) all things (not '*all these things*,' τὰ πάντα, as Van Hengel 'the Apostle rises above mere relations of prosperous and adverse circumstance, to the *general*,' De W.) in (in union with,—by means of my spiritual life, which is not mine, but Christ living in me, Gal ii. 20 the E V '*through*' does not give this union sufficiently) him who strengthens me (i e *Christ*, as the gloss rightly supplies cf 1 Tim i 12) 14] 'Cavet, ne fortiter loquendo contempsisse ipsorum beneficium videatur' Calv μὴ γὰρ ἐπειδή, φησιν, ἐν χρείᾳ οὐ καθέστηκα, νομίσητε μὴ δεῖσθαί με τοῦ πράγματος δέομαι δι' ὑμᾶς Chrys. συγκοινωνήσαντές μου τῇ θλίψει] ὅρα σοφίαν, πῶς ἐπαίρει τὸ πρᾶγμα, Thl · in that ye made yourselves partakers with my present tribulation (not *poverty* by their *sympathy* for him they suffered with him; and their gift was a *proof* of this sympathy) 15–17] *Honourable recollection of their former kindness to him* 15] δέ contrasts this former service with their present one καὶ ὑμεῖς] 'as well as I myself' He addresses them *by name* (as 2 Cor vi 11) to mark them particularly as those who did what follows. but not to the absolute exclusion of others, as Bengel ('antitheton ad ecclesias aliorum oppidorum')· others *may* have done it too, for aught that this appellative implies· that they did not, is by and by expressly asserted ἐν ἀρχῇ τοῦ εὐαγγελίου, *penes vos*, Beng he places himself in their situation, dates from (so to speak) *their* Christian era. This he specifies by ὅτε ἐξῆλθον ἀπὸ Μακεδονίας See Acts xvii 14. By this is not meant, as commonly understood, the supply which he received at Corinth (2 Cor xi 9), in order to which De W, Wies, al, understand ἐξῆλθον as a pluperfect,—but that mentioned below see there ἐξῆλθον being the aorist marking the simple date when I left Macedonia οὐδεμία μοι ἐκκλησία] no church communicated with me as to (in) an account of giving and receiving (i e., every receipt being part of *the department of giving and receiving*, being *one side* of such a reckoning, ye alone opened such an account with me. It is true the Philippians had all the giving, the Apostle all the receiving · the debtor side was vacant in *their* account, the creditor side in *his* but this did not make it any the less an account of "giving-and-receiving," categorically so called This explanation, which is Meyer's, is in my view far the most simple [against Ellic, who apparently has misunderstood it], and preferable to the almost universal one, that his creditor and their debtor side was that which he *spiritually* imparted to them for the introduction of spiritual gifts does not belong to the context, and therefore disturbs it Similar usages of λῆψις κ. δόσις occur e g Artemid i 44, οἱ διὰ δόσεως κ λήψεως ποριζόμενοι Arrian, Epict ii 9, τὸν φιλάργυρον (ἐπαύξουσιν) αἱ ἀκατάλληλοι λήψεις κ δόσεις Cicero, Lælio 16, 'ratio acceptorum et datorum' See Wetst) but you only 16] for even in Thessalonica (which was an early stage of my ἐξελθεῖν ἀπὸ Μακ, before the departure was consummated. The ὅτι gives a reason for and proof of the former assertion—ye were the only ones, &c,—and ye began as early as ἐν Θεσσ, i e. when I was at Thessalonica. In such brachylogical constructions the preposition of rest, as belonging to the act accomplished, overbears the preposition of motion, as belonging to it only in its imperfect state; so οἱ ἐν τῷ Ἡραίῳ καταπεφευγότες, Xen Hell iv. 5 5,—ταῖς λοιπαῖς ἐν τῇ γῇ καταπεφευγυίαις ἐνέβαλλον, Thuc iv 14,—ἀποστελοῦντες . . ἐν τῇ Σικελίᾳ, ib vii. 17, where ἐς τὴν Σ

τὴν [l] χρείαν μοι [k] ἐπέμψατε. 17 [m] οὐχ ὅτι [n] ἐπιζητῶ τὸ
[o] δόμα, ἀλλὰ [n] ἐπιζητῶ τὸν [p] καρπὸν τὸν [q] πλεονάζοντα εἰς
[f] λόγον ὑμῶν. 18 [r] ἀπέχω δὲ πάντα καὶ [s] περισσεύω,
[t] πεπλήρωμαι δεξάμενος παρὰ Ἐπαφροδίτου [u] τὰ παρ' ὑμῶν,
[v] ὀσμὴν [v] εὐωδίας, θυσίαν [w] δεκτὴν [x] εὐάρεστον τῷ θεῷ.
19 ὁ δὲ θεός μου [y] πληρώσει πᾶσαν [z] χρείαν ὑμῶν κατὰ
τὸ [a] πλοῦτος αὐτοῦ [b] ἐν δόξῃ ἐν χριστῷ Ἰησοῦ. 20 τῷ

ABDF KLℵ a b c d e f g h k l m n o 17

l ch ii 25 reff m ver 11 reff n = Matt vi 32 al 1 Macc vii 13 o Matt vii 4 Luke xi 13 Eph iv 8 (from Ps lxvii 18) only Gen xxv 6 p ch i 11 reff q = Rom v 20 vi 1 al P only, exc 2 Pet i 8 2 Chron xxiv 11 r = Matt vi 2 Philem 15 Gen xliii 23 s ver 12 t = Acts ii 28 xiii 52 Rom xv 13, 14 2 Cor. vii 4 ch i 11 u Luke x 7 v Eph v 2 (reff) only w Luke iv 19, 24 Acts x 35. 2 Cor vi 2 only Isa lvi 7 Sir xxxii (xxxv) 7 x Eph v 12 reff y see Luke iii. 5 z = ver 16 Sir xxxix 33 a Eph i 7 reff b 1 Tim iii 16 reff

for μοι, μου DL Chr[1] Procop Thdrt Thl Œc Ambrst Aug.
17. [αλλα, so AB] ins τον bef λογον F 121
18. om παρα επαφροδιτου A · for παρα, απο ℵ corr[1] for τα, το D[1] aft υμ ins πενφθεν D[1], πεμφθεντα F latt Syr Iren-int Cypr Victorin
19 πληρωσαι D[1]F b c g m o 17 67[2] latt Chr[1] Thdrt Thl lat-ff · txt ABD[3]KLℵ rel copt Chr[2] Thdrt-ms. rec τον πλουτον, with D[3]KLℵ[3] rel Cyr τον πλουτος m[1] : txt ABD[1]Fℵ[1] 17. 67[2]. for αυτου, υμων D[1] om 1st εν ℵ[1] : ins ℵ-corr[1] obl.

in Bekker's text is a correction) **ye sent both once and twice** (the account of the expression being, that when the first arrived, they had sent *once* when the second, not only once, but twice So in ref. · and Herod ii 121, *αὐτῷ κ δὶς κ. τρὶς ἀνοίξαντι* iii. 148, *τοῦτο κ δὶς κ. τρὶς εἴπαντος Μαιανδρίου*. The opposite expression, *οὐχ ἅπαξ οὐδὲ δίς*, is found in Plat. Clitoph § 7) **ye sent** (absolute as in ref.) to (for the supply of, ref) **my necessity** 17] Again he removes any chance of misunderstanding, as above in ver. 11 It was not for his own sake but for theirs that he rejoiced at their liberality, because it multiplied the fruits of their faith. **Not that** (see above, ver 11) **I seek** (present, 'it is my character to seek' The preposition in composition denotes, as so often, the direction; not *studiose*, nor *insuper*) **the gift** (**τό**—in the case in question), **but I do seek** (the repetition of the verb is solemn and emphatic) **the fruit which** (thereby, in the case before us) **abounds to your account** (this **εἰς λόγον** refers to the same expression, ver 15—fruit, *μισθόν* in the day of the Lord, the result of your labour for me in the Lord De W, after Van Hengel, doubts whether **πλεονάζοντα** can be constructed with **εἰς**, and would therefore separate them by a comma But surely little would be thus gained, for the **εἰς** would belong to the whole clause, the connecting link being **καρπὸν πλεονάζοντα**, so that even thus the idea of *πλεονάζοντα* must be carried on to *εἰς* and perhaps in 2 Thess. i 3 it is so: see note there). 18] **But** (notwithstanding that the gift is not that which I *desire*, I have received it, and been sufficiently supplied by it) **I have** (emphatic, and exactly as in *ἀπέχειν τὸν μισθόν*—'I have no more to ask from you, but have enough'—not as Erasm, Beza, Grot, &c. 'I have duly received all you sent') **all** (I **want**), **and abound** (over and above) **I am filled** (repetition and intensification of *περισσεύω*), **having received at the hands of Epaphroditus the remittance from you, a savour of fragrance** (a clause in apposition, expressing a judgment,—so frequently in poetry, especially in tragedians,—Il ω. 735, *ἤ τις Ἀχαιῶν ῥίψει, χειρὸς ἑλών, ἀπὸ πύργου, λυγρὸν ὄλεθρον* Eur. Orest. 950, *τιθεῖσα λευκὸν ὄνυχα διὰ παρηΐδων, αἱματηρὸν ἄταν*. See Kuhner, ii. 146. On **ὀσμὴ εὐωδίας** see Eph v 2, note), **a sacrifice acceptable, well pleasing to God** (see Heb xiii 16; 1 Pet ii 5). 19] an assurance taken up from *τῷ θεῷ* above, **μου** because he (Paul) was the receiver · this was his return to them: 'qui quod servo ejus datur remunerabitur.' Beng. **πληρώσει** . . . . all refers to vv 16, 18;—as ye *πεπληρώκατέ μου τὴν χρείαν*. It is an *assurance*, not a *wish* (-σαι), **πᾶσαν**,—not only in the department alluded to, but in **all** Meyer refers to the beatitudes in Matt v. and especially St Luke's *χορτασθήσεσθε* and *γελάσετε*, Luke vi. 21, as illustrative **ἐν δόξῃ**] to be connected with **πληρώσει**, not with **τὸ πλοῦτος αὐτοῦ** · not, *gloriously*, as many Commentators, which is weak and flat in the extreme. but **δόξα** is the instrument and element by and in which 'all your need' will be supplied **in glory**, cf Ps xxi 15 LXX: but not only at the

δὲ [c] θεῷ καὶ [c] πατρὶ ἡμῶν ἡ [d] δόξα [d] εἰς τοὺς αἰῶνας τῶν c Gal i 4 reff d Gal. i 5 reff
αἰώνων, ἀμήν.
21 Ἀσπάσασθε πάντα [e] ἅγιον ἐν χριστῷ Ἰησοῦ. ἀσπά- e = Acts ix 13 Rom i 7 & passim
ζονται ὑμᾶς οἱ σὺν ἐμοὶ ἀδελφοί. 22 ἀσπάζονται
ὑμᾶς πάντες οἱ [e] ἅγιοι, μάλιστα δὲ οἱ ἐκ τῆς Καίσαρος
[f] οἰκίας. f = 1 Cor xvi 15 Gen l 8 (but see note)
23 Ἡ χάρις τοῦ κυρίου Ἰησοῦ χριστοῦ μετὰ τοῦ [g] πνεύ- g Gal vi 18 2 Tim iv 22 Philem 25
ματος ὑμῶν[, ἀμήν].

ΠΡΟΣ ΦΙΛΙΠΠΗΣΙΟΥΣ.

20 aft ημων ins ω ℵ[1]: om ℵ[3]. om των αιωνων KL 80.
22. om υμας F. om δε L 17 Chr-mss Thdrt Thl Ambrst(και μαλ. æth). for εκ, απο B.
23 rec aft κυριου ins ημων, with D a d f k l fuld(with F-lat al) Syr syr-w-ast copt gr-lat-ff om ABFKLℵ rel am D-lat(and G-lat) arm Damasc Thl-mss Œc. rec (for του πνευματος) παντων (cf 2 Cor xiii. 13 *De W. supposes txt to have come from Gal* vi 18), with KLℵ[3] rel syrr Chr Thdrt txt ABDFℵ[1] 17. 67[2] latt coptt æth arm Damasc lat-ff. om αμην BF 67[2] sah Chr Œc Ambrst: ins ADKLℵ rel vss.

SUBSCRIPTION. rec adds εγραφη απο ρωμης, with B[2]KL rel syrr copt Chr Thdrt Euthal, rec adds further δι' επαφροδιτου, with KL rel syrr Thdrt · δια τιμοθεου κ επαφρ. copt . no subscr in 1 εγραφη κ.τ λ., omg πρ φιλ , h k m o txt AB b 17, and D(addg επληρωθη) Γ(prefg ετελεσθη) ℵ(adding στιχοι σ).

coming of Christ [as Meyer, according to his wont], but in the whole glorious imparting to you of the unsearchable riches of Christ, begun and carried on here, and completed at that day. **ἐν χριστῷ Ἰησοῦ**] and this filling (or, 'this glory,' but then *perhaps* τῇ would have been expressed) is, consists, and finds its sphere and element, **in Christ Jesus.** 20] The contemplation both of the Christian reward, of which he has been speaking, and of the glorious completion of all God's dealings at the great day,—and the close of his Epistle,—suggests this ascription of praise. **δέ**] But—however rich you may be in good works, however strong I may be by Christ to bear all things,—not to us, but to our God and Father be the glory On **εἰς τοὺς αἰῶνας τῶν αἰώνων**, see note, Eph. iii 21.

21—23.] GREETING AND FINAL BENEDICTION 21] **πάντα ἅγιον**, every individual saint The singular has love and affection, and should not be lost as in Conyb, 'Salute all *God's people*' **ἐν χριστῷ Ἰησοῦ**] belongs more probably to ἀσπάσασθε,—see Rom xvi 22; 1 Cor xvi 19,—than to ἅγιον, as in ch i. 1, where, as Meyer observes, the expression has a diplomatic formality, whereas here there is no reason for so formal an adjunct.

οἱ σὺν ἐμοὶ ἀδελφοί] These must, on account of the next verse, have been his closer friends, perhaps his colleagues in the ministry, such as Aristarchus, Epaphras, Demas, Timotheus. But there has arisen a question, how to reconcile this with ch. ii. 20? And it may be answered, that the lack of ἰσοψυχία there predicated of his companions, did not exclude them from the title ἀδελφοί, nor from sending greeting to the Philippians. see also ch. i. 14 22] **πάντες οἱ ἅγιοι**, all the Christians here. **οἱ ἐκ τῆς Καίσαρος οἰκίας**] These perhaps were slaves belonging to the familia of Nero, who had been converted by intercourse with St. Paul, probably at this time a prisoner in the prætorian barracks (see ch i 13 note) attached to the palace. This is much more likely, than that any of the actual *family* of Nero should have embraced Christianity The hint which Chrys, al, find here, εἰ γὰρ οἱ ἐν τοῖς βασιλείοις πάντων κατεφρόνησαν διὰ τὸν βασιλέα τῶν οὐρανῶν, πολλῷ μᾶλλον αὐτοὺς χρὴ τοῦτο ποιεῖν, is alien from the simplicity of the close of an Epistle The reason of these being specified is not plain · the connexion perhaps between a *colonia*, and some of the imperial household, might account for it. 23.] See Gal. vi 18.

ΠΡΟΣ ΚΟΛΑΣΣΑΕΙΣ.

a Rom. xv. 32. 1 Cor. i. 1. 2 Cor. i. 1. viii. 5. Eph. i. 1. 2 Tim. i. 1 only. P.
b = (subst.) Eph. i. 1 reff. (adj.) Heb. iii. 1 (1 Thess. v. 27 v. r.) only.
c Eph. i. 1. Phil. i. 1.

I. 1 Παῦλος ἀπόστολος χριστοῦ Ἰησοῦ [a] διὰ θελήματος
θεοῦ, καὶ Τιμόθεος ὁ ἀδελφός, 2 τοῖς ἐν Κολοσσαῖς
[b] ἁγίοις καὶ [c] πιστοῖς ἀδελφοῖς [c] ἐν χριστῷ. χάρις ὑμῖν
καὶ εἰρήνη ἀπὸ θεοῦ πατρὸς ἡμῶν.
3 [d] Εὐχαριστοῦμεν τῷ [e] θεῷ πατρὶ τοῦ [e] κυρίου ἡμῶν

C χαρις ... ABCDF KLℵ a b c d e f g h k l m n o 17

d Eph. v. 20 reff. e Rom. xv. 6. 2 Cor. i. 3. xi. 31. Eph. i. 3. iii. 14. Paul only, exc. 1 Pet. i. 3. Rev. i. 6. see 1 Cor. xv. 24. Gal. i. 4.

TITLE. elz *παυλου του αποστολου η προς κολ. επιστολη*, with rel: Steph *η πρ. κολ. επ. παυλ.*: *του αγιου απ. παυλ. επ. πρ. κολ.* L: *η πρ. κολ. επ. ταυτα διδασκαλιη κολασσαευσι παρα παυλου* f: *πρ. κολ. επ. τ. αγ. απ. παυλ.* h: *επ. πρ. κολ.* k l: *αρχεται πρ. κολ.* F: txt ABDKℵ b m n o 17 syr-marg-gr copt. [In D this ep follows Eph. Usually in D the subscr of one ep and the title of the next are written in 3 lines *προς* . . . | *επληρωθη αρχεται* | *προς* . . ., here however the middle line is omitted.]

CHAP. I. 1. rec *ιησ.* bef *χρ.*, with DK rel vulg-ed(with demid tol) Syr æth Chr Thdrt: txt ABFLℵ 17 am(with fuld) D-lat syr copt Synops Damasc Ambrst Jer Cassiod.

2. Steph *κολασσ.* (*see prolegomena*), with AK rel syrr copt Orig Synops Nyssen Chr-ms Thdrt Enthal Damasc-ms Thl-ms Suid (so also Polyænus Hierocles Herodot-mss Xenoph-mss): txt B^1(see table)DFLℵ e f n (g 17, in title) latt Clem Chr Thdrt-ms Thl lat-ff (so also Herodot Xenoph Strabo al, and coins in Eckhel). aft *χριστω* ins *ιησου* AD^{1}F 17 latt Syr syr-w-ast lat-ff: om BD^{3}KLℵ rel syr æth Chr Thdrt Damasc. rec aft *ημων* ins *και κυριου ιησου χριστου*, with ACFℵ rel vulg-ed(with demid tol) syr-w-ast: om BDKL d k 17 am(with fuld harl mar) sah Syr syr æth-rom Chr(expr., *καίτοι ἐν ταύτῃ τὸ τοῦ χριστοῦ οὐ τίθησιν ὄνομα*) Thl$_{expr}$ Orig-int$_{expr}$.

3. rec ins *και* bef *πατρι* (*from Eph* i. 3), with AC^{2}D^{3}KLℵ rel vulg(and F-lat); *τω*

CHAP. I. 1, 2.] ADDRESS AND GREETING. **1. διὰ θελήματος θεοῦ**] see on reff. **καὶ Τιμόθεος**] as in 2 Cor. i. 1 (see also Phil. i. 1; Philem. 1, and 2 Thess. i. 1). **ὁ ἀδελφός**] see on 2 Cor. i. 1. On his presence with the Apostle at the time of writing this Epistle, see Prolegg. to Past. Epp. § i. 5. Chrys. (and similarly Thl.) says on **ὁ ἀδελφός,** *οὐκοῦν καὶ αὐτὸς ἀπόστολος*: but there seems no reason for this. **2.**] On COLOSSÆ, or COLASSÆ, see Prolegg. § ii. 1.

ἁγίοις should be taken (Mey.) as a substantive, not (De W.) with **ἀδελφοῖς**, in which case **πιστοῖς**, being already (as Mey.) presupposed in *ἁγίοις*, would be tame and superfluous:—and **καὶ πιστοῖς ἀδελφοῖς ἐν χριστῷ** seems to be a specifying clause, 'viz.—to the &c.:' or perhaps added merely on account of the natural diplomatic character of an opening address. **ἐν χρ.** belongs closely to **πιστοῖς ἀδελφοῖς** or perhaps rather to **ἀδελφοῖς** alone, as Phil. i. 14: no article before *ἐν χριστῷ*

Ἰησοῦ χριστοῦ πάντοτε * περὶ ὑμῶν [f] προσευχόμενοι
4 [g] ἀκούσαντες τὴν [h] πίστιν ὑμῶν [h] ἐν χριστῷ Ἰησοῦ καὶ
τὴν [h] ἀγάπην ἣν [h] ἔχετε εἰς πάντας τοὺς ἁγίους 5 διὰ τὴν
[i] ἐλπίδα τὴν [j] ἀποκειμένην ὑμῖν ἐν τοῖς [k] οὐρανοῖς, ἣν
[l] προηκούσατε ἐν τῷ [m] λόγῳ τῆς [m] ἀληθείας τοῦ [n] εὐ-

f w. περί, ch iv 8 Acts viii 15 Heb xiii 18 al Ps lxxi 15 w ὑπέρ, ver 9 reff
g constr, Matt xi 2 Acts xxiii 16 Eph i 15 al.

h Eph i 15 reff. i = Gal v 5 Tit ii 13 Heb vi 18 j Luke xix 20 2 Tim iv 8 Heb ix 27 only Gen xlix 10 Job xxxviii 23 2 Macc xii 45 only ἐν τῷ καλῶς ἀποθανεῖν . . . τῆς ὅλης αὐτοῖς δόξης ἀποκειμένης, Jos Antt. vi 14 7 ἐν μόνῳ τῷ δικαίῳ . τὴν βεβαιοτάτην ἐλπίδα ἀποκεῖσθαι, ib viii 11 2 k Matt v 12 vi 20 xix 21 Phil iii 20 1 Pet i 4 l here only† Xen Mem ii 4.7 Polyb x 5 5 = Jos Antt viii 12 3, προηκηκοως τα μελλοντα see Gal v 21 m Eph i. 13 reff n Gal ii 5, 14

D[1]F Chr: om B C[1](appy) harl[2] syr copt æth Ambrst Aug Cassiod. om χριστου B. * ὑπὲρ (see ver 9, where none vary) BD[1]F m 17 Thl περι ACD[3]KLℵ rel gr-ff.
4 for χριστω, κυριω Aℵ[1]. txt ℵ[3]. rec (for ην εχετε) την (aft Eph i. 15), with D[3]KL rel Syr gr-ff om B. txt ACD[1]Fℵ a m o 17 latt syr copt arm lat-ff

being wanted, because no distinction between these and any other kind of brethren is needed—the idea ἀδελφὸς-ἐν-χριστῷ being familiar. χάρις κ.τ.λ.] see Rom i. 7 3—29.] INTRODUCTION, but unusually expanded, so as to anticipate the great subjects of the Epistle. And herein, 3—8] *Thanksgiving for the faith, hope, and love of the Colossians, announced to him by Epaphras*

3] **We** (I and Timotheus In this Epistle, the plural and singular are too plainly distinguished to allow us to confuse them in translating the plural pervading ch. i., the singular ch. ii., and the two occurring together in ch. iv 3, 4, and the singular thenceforward. The change, as Mey. remarks, is never made without a pragmatic reason) **give thanks to God the Father** πατήρ, like ἥλιος, γῆ, &c. is anarthrous, as indeed often in our own language, from its well-known universal import as a predicate necessarily single of its kind see Eph. i. 2, 3) **of our Lord Jesus Christ, always** (I prefer, against De W, Mey., B-Crus, Eadie, to join πάντοτε to περ. ὑμ προσευχ, rather than to εὐχαριστ. For 1] it would come rather awkwardly after so long an interruption as τῷ θ. πατ. τ. κυρ ἡμ. Ἰησ χρ [see however 1 Cor. xv 58]· and 2] I doubt whether the next clause would begin with **περὶ ὑμῶν**, so naturally as with **πάντοτε περὶ ὑμῶν**, which are found together so usually, cf 1 Cor i 4, 1 Thess i 3 [2 Thess. i. 2]) **praying for you** (Meyer's and Eadie's objection to joining **πάντοτε** with **προσευχόμενος** is, that it is much more natural to say 'we always give thanks when we pray,' than 'we give thanks, always praying' But we must remember that 'prayer with thanksgiving' was the Apostle's recommendation [Phil iv 6], and doubtless his practice, and that the wider term προσευχόμενος included both) **since we heard of** (not, *because* we heard see Eph i 15 The facts which he heard, not the fact of his hearing, were the ground of his thanksgiving) **your faith in** (not τὴν ἐν the immediate element of their faith, not its distinctive character, is the point brought out) **Christ Jesus, and the love which ye have** (these words, dwelling on the fact as reported to him, carry more affectionate commendation than would merely the article τήν of the rec) **towards all the saints,** 5] **on account of** (not to be joined with εὐχαριστ. as Beng, Eadie, al for, as Mey, the ground of such thanksgiving is ever in the spiritual state of the person addressed, see Rom i. 8, 1 Cor i 4 ff; Eph i. 15 &c, and this can hardly [against Eadie] be said to be of such a kind but with ἣν ἔχετε—so Chr.· τοῦτο πρὸς τοὺς πειρασμούς, ὥστε μὴ ἐνταῦθα ζητεῖν τὴν ἄνεσιν. ἵνα γὰρ μή τις εἴπῃ· καὶ τί τὸ κέρδος τῆς ἀγάπης τῆς εἰς τοὺς ἁγίους κοπτομένων αὐτῶν, χαίρωμεν, φησίν, ὅτι μεγάλα ἑαυτοῖς προξενεῖτε ἐν τοῖς οὐρανοῖς So also Calvin, who combats the argument of Est., al, deriving support for the idea of meritorious works from this verse It is obvious that we must not include τὴν πίστιν ὑμῶν in the reference, as Grot, Olsh., De W, al, have done for **πίστις ἐν χ. Ἰ** cannot be referred to any such motive besides, see ver. 8, where he returns again to τὴν ἀγάπην) **the hope** (on the objective sense of **ἐλπίς**, see reff) **which is laid up** (Kypke quotes Plut. Cæs. p 715—κοινὰ ἆθλα τῆς ἀνδραγαθίας παρ' αὐτῷ φυλασσόμενα **ἀποκεῖσθαι**, and Jos. B J ii 8 11,—ταῖς μὲν ἀγαθαῖς [ψυχαῖς] τὴν ὑπὲρ ὠκεανὸν δίαιταν **ἀποκεῖσθαι**) **for you in the heavens**

αγγελίου 6 τοῦ [o] παρόντος εἰς ὑμᾶς, καθὼς καὶ ἐν παντὶ
τῷ κόσμῳ ἐστὶν [p] καρποφορούμενον καὶ [q] αὐξανόμενον
καθὼς καὶ ἐν ὑμῖν, ἀφ' ἧς ἡμέρας ἠκούσατε καὶ [r] ἐπέγνωτε
τὴν [s] χάριν τοῦ θεοῦ [t] ἐν ἀληθείᾳ· 7 καθὼς ἐμάθετε ἀπὸ

ABCDF KLℵ a b c d e f g h k l m n o 17

o = 2 Pet i 12 w εἰς, here only w πρός, Acts xii 20 2 Cor xi 8 Gal iv 18, 20
p Mark iv 20 1, 28 Rom vii 4, 5 ver 10 only. Hab iii 17 Wisd x 7 only mid, here only
q transit, 1 Cor iii 6, 7 2 Cor ix 10 Gen xvii 6. pass, 2 Cor x 15. ver 10. 1 Pet ii 2 Exod i 7
r = 1 Tim iv 3 2 Pet ii 21 Job xxxiv 27
s = John i 14, &c. Acts xi 23 1 Cor i 4 2 Cor ix 8
t Matt xxii 16 1 John iii 18 al 2 Chron xix 9

6 rec ins και bef εστιν (*to preserve the balance of the sentence, that καθ κ εν π. τ. κ. might answer to καθ κ εν υμ*), with D[3]FKL rel latt syr Chr Thdrt Damasc Ambrst om ABCD[1]ℵ k 17 coptt Aug Sedul. rec om και αυξανομενον (*homœotel*), with D[3]K rel Damasc-txt: ins ABCD[1]FLℵ a h m o 17 vss gr-lat-ff.

7. rec aft καθως ins και (*to corresp with καθ. και above*), with D[3]KL rel syr gr-ff: om ABCD[1]Fℵ 17 latt Syr copt æth arm Ambrst Pelag. εμαθατε ℵ.

(reff), **of which ye heard** (aorist, referring to the time when it was preached among them) **before** (not, *before this letter was written*, as Beng, and usually· nor, as Mey, *before ye had the hope*. nor, as De Wette, al., *before the hope is fulfilled:* nor exactly as Eadie, '*have* [see above] *already heard:*' but 'before,' in the absolute indefinite sense which is often given to the idea of priority, —'ere this'—*olim, aliquando*) **in** (as part of) **the word of the truth** (no hendiadys) **of the Gospel** (the word or preaching whose substance was that truth of which the Gospel is the depository and vehicle),

6] **which is present** (emphatic· is now, as it was then. therefore not to be rendered as an imperfect, which stultifies the argument, cf. ἐστὶν καρποφ . . . ἀφ' ἧς ἡμ. below οὐ παρεγένετο, φησίν, κ ἀπέστη· ἀλλ' ἔμεινε, κ. ἐστὶν ἐκεῖ, Chrys) **with you** (pregnant construction,—'came to and remains with' see reff., and Herod vi 24, παρῆν ἐς 'Ασίην, and al. frequently) **as it is also in all the world** (ἐπεὶ δὴ μάλιστα οἱ πολλοὶ ἐκ τοῦ κοινωνοὺς ἔχειν πολλοὺς τῶν δογμάτων στηρίζονται, διὰ τοῦτο ἐπήγαγεν 'καθ κ. ἐν π τ. κόσ.' πανταχοῦ κρατεῖ πανταχοῦ ἕστηκεν. Chrys The expression **παντὶ τ κόσμ.** is no hyperbole, but the pragmatic repetition of the Lord's parting command. Though not yet announced to all nations, it is παρὼν ἐν παντὶ τῷ κόσμῳ—the whole world being the area in which it is proclaimed and working) **bearing fruit and increasing** (the paragraph is broken and unbalanced. The filling up would be, to insert καί after κόσμῳ as in rec Then it would be, '*which is present with you, as also in all the world, and* καρπ and αὐξ [in all the world], *as also among you*' But neglecting this, the Apostle goes forward, more logically indeed [for the reference in the rec of κ ἐστὶν καρπ to the second member of the foregoing comparison, is harsh], but not so perspicuously, enlarging the παρόντος of his first member into ἐστὶν καρπ κ αὐξ. in the second, and then in these words, for fear he should be supposed to have predicated more of the whole world than of the Colossians, returning to καθ κ ἐν ὑμ. Again on **καρπ κ αὐξ**, cf. Thdrt · καρποφορίαν τοῦ εὐαγγελίου κέκληκε τὴν ἐπαινουμένην πολιτείαν. αὔξησιν δὲ τῶν πιστευόντων τὸ πλῆθος As Mey observes, the figure is taken from a *tree*, whose καρποφορία does not exclude its growth: with *corn*, it is otherwise) **as also** (it is καρπ. κ αὐξ) **among you, from the day when ye heard** (it) (the Gospel· better thus, than with De W, to go on to **τὴν χάριν τοῦ θεοῦ** for the object of both verbs ἐπεγν. being not simultaneous with ἠκούσ., and ἐν ἀληθ not being thus satisfied. see below) **and knew** (ἐπ-, intensitive, but too delicately so to be expressed by a stronger word in our language) **the grace of God in truth** (not adverbial, 'truly,' as Beza, Olsh, Mey, De W., al, which would make ἐν ἀλ. a mere qualification to ἐπέγνωτε: still less, as Storr, al., τὴν χάριν ἀληθῆ, or as Grot, ἐν τῷ λόγῳ τῆς ἀλ: but generally said, 'truth' being the whole element, in which the χάρις was proclaimed and received: 'ye knew it in truth,'—in its truth, and with true knowledge, which surely differs very appreciably from the adverbial sense [against Ellicott]. οὐκ ἐν λόγῳ, φησίν, οὐδὲ ἐν ἀπάτῃ, ἀλλ' ἐν αὐτοῖς τοῖς ἔργοις),

7] **as** (scil. ἐν ἀληθείᾳ—'in which truth') **ye learnt from Epaphras** (mentioned again ch. iv. 12 as of Colossæ, and Philem 23, as then a fellow-prisoner with the Apostle. The name *may be* [hardly as Conyb, *is*] identical with Epaphroditus A person of this latter name is mentioned, Phil ii 25, as sent by St. Paul to the church at Philippi, and ib. iv. 18, as having previously brought to him offerings from that church There is no positive reason disproving their iden-

Ἐπαφρᾶ τοῦ ἀγαπητοῦ [u] συνδούλου ἡμῶν, ὅς ἐστιν πιστὸς
ὑπὲρ ἡμῶν [vw] διάκονος τοῦ [w] χριστοῦ, 8 ὁ καὶ [x] δηλώσας
ἡμῖν τὴν [y] ὑμῶν [yz] ἀγάπην [za] ἐν πνεύματι. 9 διὰ τοῦτο
καὶ ἡμεῖς ἀφ᾽ ἧς ἡμέρας ἠκούσαμεν οὐ παυόμεθα [b] ὑπὲρ
ὑμῶν [bc] προσευχόμενοι, καὶ [cd] αἰτούμενοι [e] ἵνα [f] πληρωθῆτε
τὴν [g] ἐπίγνωσιν τοῦ [h] θελήματος αὐτοῦ [i] ἐν [k] πάσῃ [l] σοφίᾳ
καὶ [m] συνέσει [n] πνευματικῇ, 10 [o] περιπατῆσαι [o] ἀξίως τοῦ

u Paul, ch iv 7 only Matt xviii 28, 29, 31, 33 xxiv 49 Rev vi 11 xix 10 xxii 9 only Ezra iv 7, 9
v — vv 23, 25 2 Cor iii 6 Eph iii 7
w 2 Cor xi 23 1 Tim iv 6
x 1 Cor i 11 iii 13 Heb ix 8 xii 27 1 Pet i 11 2 Pet i 14 only Exod vi 3
y Phil i 9 reff
z see Rom xv 30
a Eph ii 22 reff
b Matt v 44 Luke vi 28 (ver 3 James v 16 v r) 1 Kings xii 19
c Mark xi 24
d Eph iii 13 reff
e Phil i 9 reff
f — & constr, Phil i 11
g Eph i 17 reff acc., Phil i 11 Rev xvii 3, 4 Ps xv 11 A (not F)
h — Eph v 17
i Eph v 18
k Phil i 20 reff
l Eph i 8, 17 al
m Eph iii 4 reff
n Rom i 11. 1 Cor ii 13 iii 1 al †
o Eph iv 1 (reff.) 1 Thess ii 12 only

rec (for 2nd ημων) υμων, with CD³FKLℵ³ rel Chr Thdrt Damasc. txt ABD¹ℵ¹ a¹ Ambrst-comm(‘*vice apostoli*’).

9. om και αιτουμενοι (*homœotel*) BK Ps-Ath Arnob. ins ACDFLℵ rel vss gr-lat-ff
τη επιγνωσει D² m o 80.

10. rec aft περιπατησαι ins υμας (*filling up the construction*), with D³KLℵ¹ rel Chr Thdrt Damasc al txt ABCD¹Fℵ¹ m 17 Clem.

tity but probability is against it) **our** (not ‘*my*’) **beloved fellow-servant** (of Christ, Phil i. 1 not necessarily ‘*fellow-bondsman*, as Conyb : συναιχμάλωτος, Philem. 23), **who is a minister of Christ faithful on our behalf** (the stress of the predicatory sentence is on πιστὸς ὑπὲρ ἡμῶν, which ought therefore in the translation not to be sundered He was one acting faithfully “vice Apostoli” [Ambrst], and therefore not lightly to be set aside in favour of the new and erroneous teachers), **who also made known to us your love in the Spirit** (viz. the ἀγάπη of which he described himself in ver 4 as having heard; their love εἰς πάντας τοὺς ἁγίους. This love is emphatically a gift, and in its full reference the chief gift of the Spirit, [Gal. v 22; Rom. xv. 30], and is thus in the elemental region of the Spirit,—as distinct from those unspiritual states of mind which are ἐν σαρκί. This love of the Colossians he lays stress on, as a ground for thankfulness, a fruit of the hope laid up for them,—as being that side of their Christian character where he had no fault [or least fault, see ch iii. 12—14] to find with them. He now proceeds, gently and delicately at first, to touch on matters needing correction).

9—12] *Prayer for their confirmation and completion in the spiritual life.*

9] **For this reason** (on account of your love and faith, &c which Epaphras announced to us) **we also** (καί, on our side—the Colossians having been the subject before; used too on account of the close correspondence of the words following with those used of the Colossians above) **from the day when we heard (it)** (viz. as in ver. 4) **do not cease praying for you** (‘precum mentionem generatim fecit ver 3. nunc exprimit, quid precetur,’ Beng) **and** (brings into prominence a special after a general, cf Eph vi 18, 19) **beseeching that** (on ἵνα after verbs of praying, see note, 1 Cor xiv. 13) **ye may be filled with** (accusative, as in reff) **the thorough knowledge** (ἐπίγν stronger than γνῶσις see 1 Cor xiii 12) **of His** (God's, understood as the object of our prayer) **will** (respecting your walk and conduct, as the context shews · not so much His purpose in Christ, as Chrys [διὰ τοῦ υἱοῦ προσάγεσθαι ἡμᾶς αὐτῷ, οὐκέτι δι᾽ ἀγγέλων], Œc, Thl, al cf. Eph i 9 but of course not excluding the great source of that special will respecting you, His general will to be glorified in His Son) **in all wisdom** (seeing that ἐν πάσῃ σοφίᾳ, in the similar clauses, Eph i 8, ver. 28, ch iii 16, is absolute, I prefer taking it so here, and not, as Ellic, with πνευματικῇ) **and spiritual understanding** (the instrument by which we are to be thus filled,—the working of the Holy Spirit, πνευματικῇ, On σοφία and σύνεσις, the general and particular, see note Eph i 8 · so Bengel here,—“σοφία est quiddam generalius : σύνεσις est solertia quædam, ut quoi is tempore aliquid succurrat, quod hic et nunc aptum est. σύνεσις est in intellectu σοφία est in toto complexu facultatum animæ”) **to walk** (aim of the foregoing imparting of wisdom: ‘so that ye may walk.’ ἐνταῦθα περὶ βίου κ τῶν ἔργων φησίν ἀεὶ γὰρ τῇ πίστει συζεύγνυσι τὴν πολιτείαν Chrys) **worthily of the Lord** (Christ, see reff and cf. ἀξίως τοῦ θεοῦ, 3 John 6) **unto** (‘*with*

p = Acts xi. 18. Rom. vi. 22. x. 1 al. fr.
q here only. Prov. xxxi. 30 only.
r Eph. ii. 10 reff.
s ver. 6.
t Eph. iii. 16 (dat.).
u here only. Ps. lxvii. 28. Eccl. x. 10 only. Dan. ix. 27 Theod.

κυρίου [p] εἰς [k] πᾶσαν [q] ἀρέσκειαν, ἐν παντὶ [r] ἔργῳ [r] ἀγαθῷ
[s] καρποφοροῦντες καὶ [s] αὐξανόμενοι τῇ [g] ἐπιγνώσει τοῦ
θεοῦ, 11 ἐν [k] πάσῃ [t] δυνάμει [u] δυναμούμενοι [v] κατὰ τὸ [w] κράτος τῆς [w] δόξης αὐτοῦ [p] εἰς [k] πᾶσαν [x] ὑπομονὴν καὶ [y] μακροθυμίαν [z] μετὰ χαρᾶς, 12 [a] εὐχαριστοῦντες τῷ [b] πατρὶ τῷ

ABCDF KLℵ a b c d e f g h k l m n o 17

v = ver. 29. Eph. iii. 16. 2 Thess. ii. 9. w see Eph. i. 19. vi. 10. 2 Thess. i. 9. x = Luke xxi. 19. Rom. ii. 7. v. 3, 4. Heb. xii. 1 al. Ps. ix. 18. y = 2 Tim. iii. 10. iv. 2. Heb. vi. 12. James v. 10. Isa. lvii. 15. z = Mark iii. 5. Eph. vi. 7 al. 1 Chron. xxix. 22. a Eph. v. 20 reff. b abs., Acts i. 4, 7. ii. 33. 1 Cor viii. 6. Eph. ii. 18. 1 John passim.

rec εις την επιγνωσιν, with D³KL rel Thdrt Damasc Thl Œc: εν τη επιγνωσει ℵ³ 6. 10. 34. 47 Chr, *in scientia* vulg Syr Hil Pelag: txt ABCD¹Fℵ¹ 17 am(with tol) Clem Cyr Max. (*The constr* [see note] *being found difficult, was emended either by inserting* εν, *or substituting the more usual* εις [see Eph. ii. 21, iv. 15], *which had the additional recommendation of already ending the adjacent participial clauses. Tischdf and Meyer retain rec.*)

12. ins αμα bef τω πατρι B. om 1st τω F. ins θεω και bef πατρι C³F b

a view to,' subjective: or, '*so as to effect,*' objective: the latter is preferable) **all** (all manner of, all that your case admits) **well-pleasing** (the word occurs in Theophr. Character. 5, which is on ἀρέσκεια as a subjective quality. Mey. quotes from Polyb. xxxi. 26. 5, πᾶν γένος ἀρεσκείας προσφερόμενος. The meaning is, 'so that [see above] in every way ye may be well pleasing to God'): **in** (exemplifying element of the καρπ.; see below) **every good work** (not to be joined with the former clause, as Œc., Thl., Erasm., al., to the destruction of the parallelism) **bearing fruit** (the good works being the fruits: the περιπατῆσαι is now further specified, being subdivided into four departments, noted by the four participles καρποφοροῦντες, αὐξανόμενοι, δυναμούμενοι, and εὐχαριστοῦντες. On the construction, see Eph. iii. 18 note) **and increasing** (see on ver. 6 above) **by the knowledge of God** (the instrument of the increase. This is by far the most difficult of the three readings [see var. readd.], the meaning of ἐν and εἰς, being very obvious—the former pointing out the element, the latter the proposed measure, of the increase. And hence, probably, the variations. It is the knowledge of God which is the real instrument of *enlargement*, in soul and in life, of the believer—not a γνῶσις which φυσιοῖ, but an ἐπίγνωσις which αὐξάνει). **11.**] (corresponding to ἐν παντὶ κ.τ.λ. above) **in** (not instrumental [Mey.], but betokening the *element*: all these, ἐν πάσῃ, ἐν παντὶ .... are subjective, not objective. The instrument of this strength comes in below) **all** (departments of every kind of) **strength being strengthened according to** (in pursuance of, as might be expected from, reff.) **the power of His glory** (beware of the hendiadys, 'his glorious power,' into which E. V. has fallen here: the attribute of His glorious majesty here brought out is its **κράτος** [see Eph. i. 19, note], the *power* which it has thus to strengthen. In the very similar expression Eph. iii. 16, it was the πλοῦτος τῆς δόξης αὐτοῦ, the *exuberant abundance* of the same, from which as an inexhaustible treasure our strength is to come) **to** (so as to produce in you, so that ye may attain to) **all patient endurance** (not only in tribulations, but generally in the life of the Spirit. Endurance is the result of the union of outward and inward strength) **and long-suffering** (not only towards your enemies or persecutors, but also in the conflict with error, which is more in question in this Epistle. Chrys.'s distinction, μακροθυμεῖ τις πρὸς ἐκείνους οὓς δυνατὸν καὶ ἀμύνασθαι· ὑπομένει δὲ οὓς οὐ δύναται ἀμύνασθαι, though in the main correct, must not be closely pressed: see [Mey.] Heb. xii. 2, 3) **with joy** (Mey. argues that these words must be joined, as Chr., Œc., Thl., Est., al., with εὐχαριστ., because in the other clauses the participles were preceded by these prepositional qualifications. But this can hardly be pressed, in the frequent disregard of such close parallelism by our Apostle, and seeing that εὐχαριστ. does in fact *take up again* μετὰ χαρᾶς, which if attached to it is flat and unmeaning: and as De Wette says, by joining μετ. χαρ. to εὐχ., we lose the essential idea of joyful endurance,—and the beautiful train of thought, that joyfulness in suffering expresses itself in thankfulness to God. And so Luth., B.-Crus., Olsh., Eadie, al.), **giving thanks to the Father** (the connexion is not, as Chr., Thl., Calov., Calv., al., with οὐ παυόμεθα, the subject being *we*, Paul and Timothy,—but with the last words [see above], and the subjects are '*you*,'—**τῷ πατρί**, viz. of our Lord

[c] ἱκανώσαντι ἡμᾶς [d] εἰς τὴν [e] μερίδα τοῦ [f] κλήρου τῶν
[g] ἁγίων ἐν τῷ [h] φωτί, 13 ὃς [i] ἐῤῥύσατο ἡμᾶς ἐκ τῆς
[k] ἐξουσίας τοῦ [k] σκότους καὶ [l] μετέστησεν εἰς τὴν βασιλείαν τοῦ [m] υἱοῦ τῆς [m] ἀγάπης αὐτοῦ, 14 ἐν ᾧ ἔχομεν τὴν
[n] ἀπολύτρωσιν, τὴν [o] ἄφεσιν τῶν ἁμαρτιῶν, 15 ὅς ἐστιν

c 2 Cor iii. 6 only †
d see πρός, 2 Cor ii 16
e Luke x 42 Acts viii 21 xvi 12
2 Cor vi 15 only L P
Deut xii 12
f = Acts (i 17) viii 31 xxvi 18 Josh xii 7
g Eph i 1 reff
h 1 John ii 9
i = & constr, Luke i 74 Rom vii 24 2 Cor i 10. 2 Tim iii 11 iv 17 2 Pet ii 9 Gen xlviii 16 see 1 Thess i 10 reff
k Luke xxii 53 see Acts xxvi 18
l Luke xvi 4 Acts xiii 22 xix 26 1 Cor xiii 2 only 3 Kings xv 13 μετεστησεν εις την ἑαυτοῦ βασιλειαν, Jos Antt ix 11 1
m so Gen xxxv. 18
n Eph i 7 reff
o Mark i 4 Luke i 77 Acts x 43 al ‡

g k o vss gr-lat-ff; ins only θεω ℵ m. for ικανωσαντι, καλεσαντι D[1]F 17 goth æth arm Did Ambrst Vig-taps · καλεσαντι και ικανωσ B. υμας Bℵ e 17 am(with tol) spec syr-marg æth arm Did Thl Ambrst om εν C[1]

14. εσχομεν B, accepimus copt (A defective.) rec aft απολυτρωσιν ins δια του αιματος αυτου (from Eph i. 7), with rel vulg-ed(with demid) syr Thdrt Œc Iren-int: om ABCDFKLℵ d e l m n o 17 am(with[besides F-lat] fuld) Syr coptt goth Ath Bas Nyssen Chr Cyr_2 spec lat-ff om την αφεσιν D[1]. (om την απολ D-lat.)

Jesus Christ see reff) **who made** (historical—by His gift of the Spirit through His Son) **us** (Christians) **capable** (not, '*worthy*,' as E.t. after the Vulg) **for the share** (participation) **of the inheritance of the saints in the light** (it is much disputed with what ἐν τῷ φωτί is to be joined. Mey , after Chr., Œc., Thl , &c , regards it as instrumental—as the means of the ἱκανῶσαι which has been mentioned. But this seems unnatural, both in sense, and in the position of the words, in which it stands too far from ἱκ to be its qualifying clause. It connects much more naturally with κλήρου, or perhaps better still with the whole, τὴν μερίδα τ. κλήρου τῶν ἁγ , giving τὸ φῶς as the region in which the inheritance of the saints, and consequently our share in it, is situated. This seems supported by the usage of κλῆρος in Acts viii. 21, οὐκ ἔστι σοι μερὶς οὐδὲ κλῆρος ἐν τῷ λόγῳ τούτῳ —cf. also κλῆρον ἐν τοῖς ἡγιασμένοις, ib xxvi 18 And so Thdrt , al , De W., Eadie, al.—Grot., al , would take ἐν τ φωτί with ἁγίων against this the omission of the article is not decisive · but it does not seem so natural, as giving too great prominence to οἱ ἅγιοι ἐν τῷ φωτί as the ἐπώνυμοι of the inheritance, and not enough to the inheritance itself The question as to whether he is speaking of a present inheritance, or the future glory of heaven, seems best answered by Chrys., δοκεῖ δέ μοι κ. περὶ τῶν παρόντων κ. περὶ τῶν μελλόντων ὁμοῦ λέγειν. The inheritance is begun here, and the meetness conferred, in gradual sanctification: but completed hereafter. We are ἐν τῷ φωτί here cf Rom. xiii 12, 13; 1 Thess. v 5, Eph v. 8, 1 Pet. ii 9 al.) ·

13] *Transition, in the form of a laying out into its negative and positive sides, of the ἱκάνωσεν above, to the doctrine concerning Christ, which the Apostle has it in his mind to lay down.* **Who rescued us out of the power** (i. e region where the power extends—as in the territorial use of the words 'kingdom,' 'county,' &c) **of darkness** (as contrasted with light above not to be understood of a person, Satan, but of the whole character and rule of the region of unconverted human nature where they dwelt), **and translated** (add to reff Plat Legg vi p 762 b, πιστεύοντες τῷ μεθίστασθαι κατὰ μῆνας εἰς ἕτερον ἀεὶ τόπον φεύγοντες, and a very striking parallel noticed by Mey , Plat Rep. vii p 518 a, ἔκ τε φωτὸς εἰς σκότος μεθισταμένων κ ἐκ σκότους εἰς φῶς. The word is strictly local in its meaning) **into the kingdom** (not to be referred, as Mey always so pertinaciously maintains, exclusively to the *future* kingdom, nor is μετέστησεν proleptic, but a historical fact, realized at our conversion) **of the Son of His Love** (genitive subjective. the Son upon whom His Love rests the strongest possible contrast to that darkness, the very opposite of God's Light and Love, in which we were The Commentators compare *Benoni*, 'the son of my sorrow,' Gen xxxv 18 Beware of the hendiadys, adopted in the text of the E V On the whole, see Ellicott's note)

14—20.] *Description, introduced by the foregoing, of the pre-eminence and majesty of the Son of God, our Redeemer.*

14] **In whom** (as its conditional element as in the frequent expressions, ἐν χριστῷ, ἐν κυρίῳ, &c. see the parallel, Eph i 7) **we have** (see note, ibid.) **Redemption** (this is perhaps better, taking the art as the idiomatic way of expressing the

p 2 Cor. iv. 4. Rom. viii. 29. 1 Cor. xi. 7 al. Gen. i. 26, 27.

p εἰκὼν τοῦ θεοῦ τοῦ q ἀοράτου, r πρωτότοκος s πάσης — ABCDF KLℵ a b c d e f g h k l m n o 17

q Rom. i. 20. 1 Tim. i. 17. Heb. xi. 27 only. Gen. i. 2. Isa. xlv. 3. 2 Macc. ix. 5 only.
r Luke ii. 7. Rom. viii. 29. Heb. i. 6. xi. 28. xii. 23. Rev. i. 5 only. Exod. iv. 22, constr., see note. s (Mark xiii. 19. xvi. 15.) Rom. viii. 22. ver. 23 (1 Pet. ii. 13) only. Judith xvi. 14.

15. for ος, ο F. ins της bef κτισεως f l n 67[2].

abstract subst., than our Redemption as in my earlier editions. See Ellic.), **the remission** ("on the distinction between ἄφεσις and πάρεσις, see Trench, Synon. § xxxiii." Ellic.) **of our sins** (note, Eph., ut supra. παραπτωμάτων, the more special word, is here replaced by ἁμαρτιῶν the more general: the meaning being the same): **15.**] (The last verse has been a sort of introduction, through our own part in Him, to the Person of the Redeemer, which is now directly treated of, as against the teachers of error at Colossæ. He is described, *in His relation* 1) *to God and His Creation* [vv. 15—17]: 2) *to the Church* [18—20]. This arrangement, which is Meyer's, is far more exact than the triple division of Bähr,—'Source of creation [15, 16]: upholder of creation [17]: relation to the new moral creation [18—20]'), **who is** (*now*—in His glorified state—essentially and permanently: therefore not to be understood, as De W. after Erasm., Calv., Beza, Grot., Beng., al., of the *historical* Christ, God manifested in our flesh on earth: nor again with Olsh., Bleek on Heb. i. al., of the eternal Word: but of Christ's present glorified state, in which He is exalted in our humanity, but exalted to that glory which He had with the Father before the world was. So that the following description applies to Christ's whole Person in its essential glory,—now however, by His assumption of humanity, necessarily otherwise conditioned than before that assumption. See for the whole, notes on Phil. ii. 6, and Heb. i. 2 f.; and Usteri, Paulinisches Lehrbegriff, ii. § 4, p. 286 ff.) **image** (= *the* image) **of the invisible God** (the adjunct **τοῦ ἀοράτου** is of the utmost weight to the understanding of the expression. The same fact being the foundation of the whole as in Phil. ii. 6 ff., that the Son ἐν μορφῇ θεοῦ ὑπῆρχεν, that side of the fact is brought out *here*, which points to His being the visible manifestation of that in God which is invisible: the λόγος of the eternal silence, the ἀπαύγασμα of the δόξα which no creature can bear, the χαρακτήρ of that ὑπόστασις which is incommunicably God's: in one word the ἐξηγητής of the Father whom none hath seen. So that while **ἀόρατος** includes in it not only the *invisibility*, but the incommunicability of God, **εἰκών** also must not be restricted to Christ corporeally visible in the Incarnation, but understood of Him as the manifestation of God in His whole Person and work—præ-existent and incarnate. It is obvious, that in this expression, the Apostle approaches very near to the Alexandrian doctrine of the **λόγος**: how near, may be seen from the extracts from Philo in Usteri: e. g. de somniis, 41, vol. i. p. 656, καθάπερ τὴν ἀνθήλιον αὐγὴν ὡς ἥλιον οἱ μὴ δυνάμενοι τὸν ἥλιον αὐτὸν ἰδεῖν ὁρῶσι, κ. τὰς περὶ τὴν σελήνην ἀλλοιώσεις ὡς αὐτὴν ἐκείνην· οὕτως καὶ **τὴν τοῦ θεοῦ εἰκόνα, τὸν ἄγγελον αὐτοῦ λόγον, ὡς αὐτὸν κατανοοῦσι**: and de Monarch. ii. 5, vol. ii. p. 225, λόγος δέ ἐστιν εἰκὼν θεοῦ, δι' οὗ σύμπας ὁ κόσμος ἐδημιουργεῖτο. See other passages in Bleek on Heb. i. 2. He is, in fact, as St. John afterwards did, adopting the language of that lore as far as it represented divine truth, and rescuing it from being used in the service of error. [This last sentence might have prevented the misunderstanding of this part of my note by Ellic. in loc.: shewing, as it does, that the inspiration of St. Paul and the non-inspiration of Philo, are as fully recognized by me as by himself]), **the first-born of all creation** (such, and not '*every creature*,' is the meaning [so I still hold against Ellic. But see his whole note on this passage, as well worth study]: nor can the strict usage of the article be alleged as an objection: cf. below, ver. 23, and Eph. ii. 21 note: the solution being, that **κτίσις**, as our word 'creation,' may be used anarthrous, in its collective sense.

Christ is ὁ πρωτότοκος, THE FIRST-BORN, Heb. i. 6. The idea was well known in the Alexandrian terminology: τοῦτον μὲν γάρ,—viz. τὸν ἀσώματον ἐκεῖνον, θείας ἀδιαφοροῦντα εἰκόνος—πρεσβύτατον υἱὸν ὁ τῶν ὄντων ἀνέτειλε πατήρ, ὃν ἑτέρωθι πρωτόγονον ὠνόμασε, καὶ ὁ γεννηθεὶς μέντοι μιμούμενος τὰς τοῦ πατρὸς ὁδούς, πρὸς παραδείγματα ἀρχέτυπα ἐκείνου βλέπων, ἐμόρφου εἴδη. Philo, de Confus. Ling. 14, vol. i. p. 414. That the word is used as one whose meaning and reference was already known to the readers, is shewn by its being predicated of Christ as compared with two classes so different, the *creatures*, and the *dead* (ver. 18). The first and simplest meaning is that of *priority of birth*. But this, if insisted on, in

[s] κτίσεως, 16 ὅτι [t] ἐν αὐτῷ [u] ἐκτίσθη [v] τὰ πάντα τὰ ἐν τοῖς
οὐρανοῖς καὶ τὰ ἐπὶ τῆς γῆς, τὰ [w] ὁρατὰ καὶ τὰ [q] ἀόρατα,

t = 1 Cor xv 22. 2 Cor v 19. Gal ii 17. Eph i 4. iii 11.
u Mark xiii 19. Rom i 25 al. Deut iv 32. v = Rom viii. 32. xi 36 al. Job viii 3. w here only. 2 Kings xxiii 21. 1 Chron. xi 23. Job xxxiv 26. xxxvii. 21 only.

16. om 1st τα K 73. 117. 118. om 2nd τα BD[1]FN[1] m 17 $Orig_3$. ins ACD[3]KLN[3] rel $Orig_1$ Eus_4 Cyr-jer Chr Cyr Thdrt Damasc. add τε C Marcell-in-Eus Eus_2 Ath. om 3rd τα BN[1] $Orig_3$. ($Orig_{alw}$ Eus $Thdrt_{alic}$ quote ειτε ορ. ειτε αορ.)

its limited temporal sense, must apply to our Lord's birth from his *human mother*, and could have reference only to those brothers and sisters who were born of her afterwards; a reference clearly excluded here. But a secondary and derived meaning of πρωτότοκος, as a designation of *dignity and precedence, implied by priority*, cannot be denied. Cf. Ps. lxxxviii. 27, κἀγὼ πρωτότοκον θήσομαι αὐτόν, ὑψηλὸν παρὰ τοῖς βασιλεῦσι τῆς γῆς:—Exod. iv. 22, υἱὸς πρωτότοκός μου Ἰσραήλ.—Rom viii 29, and Heb. xii. 23, ἐκκλησίᾳ προτοτόκων ἀπογεγραμμένων ἐν οὐρανοῖς, where see Bleek's note. Similarly πρωτόγονος is used in Soph. Phil 180, οὗτος πρωτογόνων ἴσως οἴκων οὐδενὸς ὕστερος. It would be obviously wrong here to limit the sense entirely to this reference, as the very expression below, αὐτὸς ἐστὶν πρὸ πάντων, shews, in which his priority is distinctly predicated. The safe method of interpretation therefore will be, to take into account the two ideas manifestly included in the word, and here distinctly referred to—priority, and dignity, and to regard the technical term πρωτότοκος as used rather with reference to both these, than in strict construction where it stands. "First-born of every creature" will then imply, that Christ was not only first-born of His mother in the world, but first-begotten of His Father, before the worlds,—and that He holds the rank, as compared with every created thing, of first-born in dignity. FOR, &c., ver. 16, where this assertion is justified. Cf. below on ver. 18.
It may be well to notice other interpretations. 1) Meyer, after Tert., Chr., Thdrt., al., Bengel, al., would restrict the term to its temporal sense. 'primogenitus, ut ante omnia genitus:' on this, see above. 2) The Arians maintained that Christ is thus Himself declared to be a κτίσις of God. It might have been enough to guard them from this, that as Chr. remarks, not πρωτόκτιστος, but πρωτότοκος is advisedly used by the Apostle. 3) The Socinians [also Grot., Wetst., Schleierm., al., after Theod. Mops.] holding the mistaken view of the necessity of the strict interpretation of πρωτότοκος—maintain, that Christ must be *one of* those among whom He is πρωτότοκος—and that consequently κτίσις must be the new spiritual creation—which it certainly cannot mean without a qualifying adjective to indicate such meaning—and least of all here, where the physical κτίσις is so specifically broken up into its parts in the next verse. 4) Worst of all is the rendering proposed by Isidore of Pelusium and adopted by Erasm. and Er.-Schmidt, *'first bringer forth'* [πρωτοτόκος, but used only of a *mother*]. See on the whole, De W.: and a long note in Bleek on the Hebrews, vol. i. pp. 43—48):

16] because (explanatory of the πρωτ. πάσ. κτίσ.—it must be so, seeing that nothing can so completely refute the idea that Christ himself is included in creation, as this verse) in **Him** (as the conditional element, præ-existent and all-including: not *'by Him,'* as E. V. after Chr. [τὸ ἐν αὐτῷ, δι' αὐτοῦ ἐστιν]—this is expressed afterwards, and is a different fact from the present one, though implied in it. The idea of the schoolmen, that in Christ was the 'idea omnium rerum,' adopted in the main by Schl., Neander, and Olsh. ["the Son of God is the intelligible world, the κόσμος νοητός, i. e. creation in its primitive idea, Himself; He bears in Himself their reality," Olsh.], is, as Meyer rightly observes, entirely unsupported by any views or expressions of our Apostle elsewhere: and is besides abundantly refuted by ἐκτίσθη, the historic aorist, indicating the physical *act* of Creation) **was created** (in the act of creation: cf. on ἔκτισται below) **the universe** (thus only can we give the force of the Greek singular with the collective neuter plural, which it is important here to preserve, as 'all things' may be thought of individually, not collectively)—(viz.) **things in the heavens and things on the earth** (Wetst. urges this as shewing that the physical creation is not meant: 'non dicit ὁ οὐρανὸς κ. ἡ γῆ ἐκτίσθη, sed τὰ ἐν &c., quo habitatores significantur qui reconciliantur' [cf. the Socinian view of ver. 15 above]: the right answer to which is—not with De W. to say that the Apostle is speaking of *living* created things only, for manifestly the whole universe is here

x Rom. xii. 6. 1 Cor. iii. 22. y = here only. (see Dan. vii. 9.) Test. xii. Patr. p. 532. z Eph. i. 21 reff. a John i. 3. Heb. i. 2.

[x] εἴτε [y] θρόνοι [x] εἴτε [z] κυριότητες [x] εἴτε [z] ἀρχαὶ [x] εἴτε [z] ἐξ- ABCDF
ουσίαι· [v] τὰ πάντα [ab] δι᾽ αὐτοῦ καὶ [b] εἰς αὐτὸν [u] ἔκτισται, KLℵ a b c d e f g
17 καὶ [c] αὐτὸς [d] ἐστὶν [e] πρὸ πάντων, καὶ [v] τὰ πάντα [t] ἐν h k l m n o 17
αὐτῷ [f] συνέστηκεν, 18 καὶ [c] αὐτός ἐστιν ἡ [g] κεφαλὴ τοῦ

b Rom. xi. 36. 1 Cor. viii. 6. see Heb ii. 10. c = Luke i. 17. d = John viii. 58. Ps. lxxxix. 2. e = John v. 7. Rom. xvi. 7. Gal. i. 17. f here only. (2 Pet. iii. 5.) ἐκ γῆς…κ.…ὕδατος κ. ἀέρος κ. πυρὸς . . συνέστη ὅδε ὁ κόσμος. Phil. de Plant. Noë 2, vol. i. p. 330. ἐκ τοῦ θεοῦ τὰ πάντα, κ. διὰ θεοῦ ἡμῖν συνέστηκεν, Aristot. de Mundo, vi. p. 471. see Plat. Rep. p. 530 a; Tim. p. 29 a. g Eph. i. 22 reff.

κεκτισται F: εκτισαι C. [Tert testifies to this ver agst Mcion: aft κυρ. some of the Gnostics (Thdot Val) insd θεοτητες, see Iren Clem Thdrt.]
17. om τα DF 17[1] Chr-txt.

treated of, there being no reason why *living* things should be in such a declaration distinguished from other things,—but with Mey. to treat τὰ ἐν τ. οὐρρ. κ. τὰ ἐπ. τ. γῆς as an inexact designation of heaven and earth, and all that in them is, Rev. x. 6. In 1 Chron. xxix. 11, the meaning is obviously this, σὺ πάντων τῶν ἐν τῷ οὐρ. κ. ἐπὶ τ. γῆς δεσπόζεις), **things visible and things invisible** (which divide between them the universe: Mey. quotes from Plato, Phæd. p. 79 A, θῶμεν οὖν, εἰ βούλει, ἔφη, δύο εἴδη τῶν ὄντων, τὸ μὲν ὁρατόν, τὸ δὲ ἀειδές. The ἀόρατα are the spirit-world [not, οἷον ψυχή, Chr.: this, being incorporated, would fall under the ὁρατά, for the present purpose], which he now breaks up by εἴτε . . . εἴτε . . . εἴτε), **whether** (these latter be) **thrones, whether lordships, whether governments, whether authorities** (on εἴτε, . . . often repeated, see reff.: and Plat. Rep. p. 493 D, 612 A, Soph. El. 595 f [Mey.]. These distinctive classes of the heavenly powers occur in a more general sense in Eph. i. 21, where see note. For δυνάμεις there, we have θρόνοι here. It would be vain to attempt to assign to each of these their places in the celestial world. Perhaps, as De W., the Apostle chose the expressions as terms common to the doctrine of the Colossian false teachers and his own: but the occurrence of so very similar a catalogue in Eph. i. 21, where no such object could be in view, hardly looks as if such a design were before him. Mey. well remarks, "For Christian faith it remains fixed, and it is sufficient, that there is testimony borne to the existence of different degrees and categories in the world of spirits above; but all attempts more precisely to fix these degrees, beyond what is written in the N. T., belong to the fanciful domain of theosophy." All sorts of such interpretations, by Teller and others, not worth recording, may be seen refuted in De W.): **the whole universe** (see above on τὰ πάντα, ver. 16) **has been created** (not now of the mere act, but of the resulting endurance of creation—leading on to the συνέστηκεν below) **by Him** (instrumental: He is the agent in creation—the act was His, and the upholding is His: see John i. 3, note) **and for Him** (with a view to Him: He is the *end* of creation, containing the reason in Himself why creation is at all, and why it is as it is. See my Sermons on Divine Love, Serm. I. II. The fancies and caprices of those who interpret *creation* here *ethically*, are recounted and refuted by Meyer): **and He Himself** (emphatic, His own Person) **is** (as in John viii. 58, of essential existence: ἦν might have been used, as in John i. 1: but as Mey. well observes, the Apostle keeps the past tenses for the explanatory clauses referring to past facts, vv. 16, 19) **before all things** (in *time*; bringing out one side of the πρωτότοκος above: not in *rank*, as the Socinians: of which latter James v. 12, 1 Pet. iv. 8, are no justifications, for if πρὸ-πάντων be taken as there, we must render, 'and He, above all, exists,' 'He especially exists,' προπάντων being adverbial, and not to be resolved. For the temporal sense, see reff.) **all things** (not '*omnes*,' as Vulg.) **and in Him** (as its conditional element of existence, see above on ἐν αὐτῷ ver. 16) **the universe subsists** ('*keeps together*,' '*is held together in its present state*:' οὐ μόνον αὐτὸς αὐτὰ ἐκ τοῦ μὴ ὄντος εἰς τὸ εἶναι παρήγαγεν, ἀλλὰ καὶ αὐτὸς αὐτὰ συγκρατεῖ νῦν, Chr. On the word, see reff.: and add Philo, quis rer. div. hæres. 12, vol. i. p. 481, ὁ ἔναιμος ὄγκος, ἐξ ἑαυτοῦ διαλυτὸς ὢν κ. νεκρός, **συνέστηκε** κ. ζωπυρεῖται προνοίᾳ θεοῦ).

18—20.] *Relation of Christ to the Church* (see above on ver. 15): **And He** (emphatic: not any angels nor created beings: the whole following passage has a controversial bearing on the errors of the Colossian teachers) **is the Head of the body the church** (not 'the body *of* the church:' the genitive is much more naturally taken as one of apposition, inasmuch

[h] σώματος, τῆς [i] ἐκκλησίας, ὅς ἐστιν [k] ἀρχή, [lm] πρωτότοκος ἐκ [m] τῶν νεκρῶν, ἵνα γένηται [n] ἐν πᾶσιν αὐτὸς [o] πρω-
τεύων· 19 ὅτι [p] ἐν αὐτῷ [q] εὐδόκησεν πᾶν τὸ [r] πλήρωμα

h = ver 24 1 Cor x 17 xii. 12, 27 al i abs, Eph i 22 reff gen apposition, see Rom iv 11 ch iii 24

k = Rev iii 14 Gen xlix 3 Deut xxi 17 l ver 15 m see Rev i 5 n = Phil iv 12 1 Tim iii 11 al. fr o here only Esth v 11 vat 2 Macc vi 18 xiii 15 only p ver 16. q Rom xv 26. 1 Cor i 21 Gal i 15 al Ps lxvii 16 r = John i 16 Rom xv 29 Eph i 23 s ch ii 9

18. for *os*, *o* F m *qui aut quod* G-lat. ins *η* bef *αρχη* B b 67[2] *απαρχη* 17. 118 Chr Damasc, Œc *εν αρχη* Cyr. (17 omits *η* bef *κεφ*) om *εκ* ℵ[1].
19. *ηυδοκ.* AD o Chr Damasc.

as in St. Paul, it is the church which *is*, not which possesses, the body, see reff): **who** (q d 'in that He is' the relative has an argumentative force. see Matthiæ, Gr. § 477 · in which case it is more commonly found with a particle, *ὃς μέν*, or *ὅς γε*) **is the beginning** (of the Church of the First-born, being Himself *πρωτότ. ἐκ τ. νεκρ* : cf. *ἀπαρχὴ χριστός*, 1 Cor. xv. 23, and reff, especially the last But the word evidently has, standing as it does here alone, a wider and more glorious reference than that of mere temporal precedence · cf ref Rev. and note He is the Beginning, in that in Him is begun and conditioned the Church, vv 19, 20), **the First-born from (among) the dead** (i e. the first who *arose* from among the dead but the term *πρωτότοκος* [see above] being predicated of Christ in both references, he uses it here, regarding the resurrection as a kind of birth. On that which is implied in *πρωτότ*, see above on ver. 15), **that** HE (emphatic, again see above) **may become** (not, as Est, 'ex quibus efficitur, Christum .... tenere' but the *aim* and *purpose* of this his priority over creation and in resurrection) **in all things** (reff. Beza, [and so Kypke] argues that because the Apostle is speaking of the Church, **πᾶσιν** must be masculine, allowing however that the neuter has some support from the **τὰ πάντα** which follows In fact this decides the question: the **τὰ πάντα** there are a resumption of the **πᾶσιν** here. The *ἐν* then is not 'inter,' but of the reference :— 'in all matters.' **πανταχοῦ**, as Chrys because the **πάντα** which follows applies not only to things concrete, but also to their combinations and attributes) **pre-eminent** (*first in rank*. the word is a transitional one, from priority in time to priority in dignity, and shews incontestably that the two ideas have been before the Apostle's mind throughout. Add to reff, from Wetst., *πρωτεύειν ἐν ἅπασι κράτιστον*, Demosth. 1416 25: and Plut de puer. educ. p 9 B, *τοὺς παῖδας ἐν πᾶσι τάχιον πρωτεῦσαι*).

19] "Confirmatory of the abovesaid *γίνεσθαι ἐν πᾶσιν αὐτ. πρωτεύοντα*—'of which there can be no doubt, since it pleased &c'" Meyer—**for in Him God was pleased** (on the use of *εὐδοκέω* for *δοκέω* by the later Greeks, see Fritzsche's note, on Rom vol ii pp. 369—72. The subject here is naturally understood to be God, as expressed in 1 Cor i 21; Gal i. 15 clearly not Christ, as Conyb, thereby inducing a manifest error in the subsequent clause, 'by Himself He willed to reconcile all things to Himself,' for it was not to Christ but to the Father that all things were reconciled by Him, cf. 2 Cor. v. 19. See a full discussion on the construction, and the subject to *εὐδόκησεν*, in Ellic's note. His conclusion, that *πλήρωμα* is that subject, I cannot accept) **that the whole fulness** (of God, see ch ii. 9, Eph. iii. 19, and on *πλήρωμα*, note, Eph i. 10, 23 We must bear in mind here, with Mey, that the meaning is not active, 'id quod rem implet,' but passive, 'id quo res impletur' all that fulness of grace which is the complement of the divine character, and which dwells permanently in Christ. 'cumulatissima omnium divinarum rerum copia,' Beza,—as in John i. 16. The various other interpretations have been,—"the essential fulness of the Godhead," so Œc., al; which is manifestly not in question here,—but is not to be set aside, as Eadie, by saying that 'the divine essence dwelt in Christ unchangeably and not by the Father's consent or purpose · it is His in His own right, and not by paternal pleasure' for all that is His own right, is His Father's pleasure, and is ever referred to that pleasure by Himself,—"the fulness of the whole universe," so Conyb, and Castellio in Beza This latter answers well "Quorsum mentio universitatis rerum? Nam res ipsa clamat Apostolum de sola ecclesia hic agere, ut etiam 1 Cor. xv 18 (?), Eph i 10, iv 6, 20 (?)"—'the Church itself,' as Severianus in Cramer's Catena, *τουτέστιν τὴν ἐκκλησίαν τὴν πεπληρωμένην αὐτοῦ ἐν τῷ χριστῷ*,—and Thdrt, *πλήρ τὴν ἐκκλησίαν ἐν τῇ πρὸς Ἐφεσίους ἐκάλεσεν, ὡς τῶν θείων χαρισμάτων πεπληρωμένην*,

t ver 21. Eph ii 16 only †
u ver 16
v here only. Prov x 10 only. see Matt v 9. Eph ii 15
w so Rom iii 25
x ver 16.

ˢ κατοικῆσαι, 20 καὶ δι' αὐτοῦ ᵗ ἀποκαταλλάξαι ᵘ τὰ πάντα
εἰς αὐτόν, ᵛ εἰρηνοποιήσας διὰ τοῦ ʷ αἵματος τοῦ σταυροῦ
αὐτοῦ, δι' αὐτοῦ, ˣ εἴτε τὰ ἐπὶ τῆς γῆς ˣ εἴτε τὰ ἐν τοῖς

ABCDF KLℵ a b c d e f g h k l m n o 17

20. om 2nd δι' αυτου BD¹FL f latt sah arm (Orig₃) Chr-txt Cyr₂ Thl lat-ff: ins ACD³Kℵ rel syrr copt goth Eus Chr$_{aliq}$ Thdrt Damasc Œc. om της bef γης B. for εν, επι L d g h l n 91¹ 113-4 121-2-3 Chr Thdrt Damasc.

ταύτην ἔφη εὐδοκῆσαι τὸν θεὸν ἐν τῷ χριστῷ κατοικῆσαι, τουτέστιν αὐτῷ συνῆφθαι,—and similarly B.-Crus., al., and Schleierm., understanding the fulness of the Gentiles and the whole of Israel, as Rom. xi 12, 25, 26. But this has no support, either in the absolute usage of πλήρωμα, or in the context here. See others in De W.) should dwell, and ('hæc inhabitatio est fundamentum reconciliationis,' Beng.) by Him (as the instrument, in Redemption as in Creation, see above ver. 16 end) to reconcile again (see note on Eph. ii. 16) all things (= the universe: not to be limited to '*all intelligent beings*,' or '*all men*,' or '*the whole Church*:' these πάντα are broken up below into terms which will admit of no such limitation. On the fact, see below) to Him (viz. to God, Eph. ii. 16: not αὑτόν; the writer has in his mind two Persons, both expressed by αὐτός, and to be understood from the context. The aspirate should never be placed over αυτ-, unless where there is a manifest necessity for such emphasis. But we are not [as Conyb.,—also Est., Grot., Olsh., De W.] to understand Christ to be meant: see above), having made peace (the subject is not Christ [as in Eph. ii 15; so Chrys. (διὰ τοῦ ἰδίου σταυροῦ), Thdrt., Œc., Luth., al.], but the Father: He is the subject in the whole sentence since εὐδόκησεν) by means of the blood of (genitive possessive, belonging to, figuratively, as being shed on: 'ideo pignus et pretium nostræ cum Deo pacificationis fuit sanguis Christi, quia in cruce fusus,' Calv.) His Cross,—through Him (emphatic repetition, to bring αὐτός, the Person of Christ, into its place of prominence again, after the interruption occasioned by εἰρην.. αὐτοῦ: not meaning, as Castal. [in Mey.], 'per sanguinem ejus, hoc est, per eum:' for the former and not the latter is explicative of the other),—whether (τὰ πάντα consist of) the things on the earth, or the things in the heavens. It has been a question, in what sense this reconciliation is predicated of the whole universe. Short of this meaning we cannot stop: we cannot hold with Erasm., al., that it is a reconciliation of the *various portions of creation to one another*: 'ut abolitis peccatis, quæ dirimebant concordiam et pacem cœlestium ac terrestrium, jam amicitia jungerentur omnia:' for this is entirely precluded by the εἴτε . . . εἴτε: nor, for the same reason, with Schleierm., understand that the elements to be reconciled are the *Jews* and *Gentiles*, who were at variance about earthly and heavenly things, and were to be set at one in reference to God (εἰς αὐτόν). The Apostle's meaning clearly is, that by the blood of Christ's Cross, reconciliation with God has passed on *all creation as a whole*, including angelic as well as human beings, unreasoning and lifeless things, as well as organized and intelligent. Now this may be understood in the following ways: 1) creation may be strictly regarded in its entirety, and man's offence viewed as having, by inducing impurity upon one portion of it, alienated the whole from God: and thus τὰ πάντα may be involved in our fall. Some support may seem to be derived for this by the undeniable fact, that *the whole of man's world* is included in these consequences (see Rom. viii 19 f.). But on the other side, we never find the *angelic beings* thus involved: nay, we are taught to regard them as our model in hallowing God's name, realizing His kingdom, and doing His will (Matt. vi 9, 10). And again the εἴτε . . εἴτε would not suffer this: reconciliation is thus predicated of each portion *separately*. We are thus driven, there being no question about τὰ ἐπὶ τῆς γῆς, to enquire, how τὰ ἐν τοῖς οὐρρ. can be said to be reconciled by the blood of the Cross. And here again, 2) we may say that angelic, celestial creation was alienated from God because a portion of it fell from its purity: and, though there is no idea of the reconciliation extending *to that portion*, yet the whole, as a whole, may need thus reconciling, by the final driving into punishment of the fallen, and thus setting the faithful in perfect and undoubted unity with God. But to this I answer, *a*) that such reconciliation (?) though it might be a result of the coming of the Lord Jesus, yet could not in any way be effected by the *blood of His Cross*: *b*) that we have no reason to think

οὐρανοῖς. 21 καὶ ὑμᾶς ποτὲ ὄντας [y] ἀπηλλοτριωμένους
καὶ [z] ἐχθροὺς τῇ [a] διανοίᾳ ἐν τοῖς [b] ἔργοις τοῖς [b] πονηροῖς,

y Eph ii. 12 iv 18 only Ps lxviii 8
z Rom v 10 Heb i 13 al, from Ps cix 1
a & dat., Eph iv 18.
b John iii 19 vii 7 2 Tim iv 18 1 John iii 12 2 John 11 only

21. *της διανοιας* *sensus* D[1]F fuld —add *ejus* D-lat spec, *vestri* G-lat —*sensu vestro*

that the fall of some angels involved the rest in its consequences, or that angelic being is evolved from any root, as ours is from Adam nay, in both these particulars, the very contrary is revealed We must then seek our solution in some meaning which will apply to angelic beings in their essential nature, not as regards the sin of some among them. And as thus applied, no reconciliation must be thought of which shall resemble *ours* in its process—for Christ took not upon Him the seed of angels, nor paid any propitiatory penalty in the root of their nature, as including it in Himself But, forasmuch as He is their Head as well as ours,—forasmuch as in Him they, as well as ourselves, live and move and have their being, it cannot be but that the great event in which He was glorified through suffering, should also bring them nearer to God, who subsist in Him in common with all creation. And at some such increase of blessedness does our Apostle seem to hint in Eph. iii 10. That such increase might be described as a *reconciliation*, is manifest we know from Job xv 15, that "the heavens are not clean in His sight," and ib. iv. 18, "His angels He charged with folly" In fact, every such nearer approach to Him may without violence to words be so described, in comparison with that previous greater distance which now seems like alienation, —and in this case even more properly, as one of the consequences of that great propitiation whose first and plainest effect was to reconcile to God, in the literal sense, the things upon earth, polluted and hostile in consequence of man's sin So that our interpretation may be thus summed up: all creation subsists in Christ · all creation therefore is affected by His act of propitiation: sinful creation is, in the strictest sense, *reconciled*, from being at enmity: sinless creation, ever at a distance from his unapproachable purity, is lifted into nearer participation and higher glorification of Him, and is thus *reconciled*, though not in the strictest, yet in a very intelligible and allowable sense. Meyer's note, taking a different view, that the reconciliation is the great *κρίσις* at the *παρουσία*, is well worth reading: Eadie's, agreeing in the main with the above result, is unfortunately, as so usual with him, over-loaded with flowers of rhetoric, never more out of place than in treating lofty subjects of this kind A good summary of ancient and modern opinions is given in De W.

21—23] *Inclusion of the Colossians in this reconciliation and its consequences, if they remained firm in the faith.*

21, 22] **And you, who were once alienated** (subjective or objective?—'*estranged*' [in mind], or '*banished*' [in fact]? In Eph. ii 12, it is decidedly objective, for such is the cast of the whole sentence there so also in ref. Ps. in Eph iv 18 it describes the objective result, with regard to the life of God, of the subjective 'being darkened in the understanding' It is better then here to follow usage, and interpret objectively—'alienated'—made aliens) (**from God**,—not *ἀπὸ τῆς πολιτείας τοῦ Ἰσρ.*, nor *ἀπὸ τῆς ζωῆς τ. θεοῦ* for 'God' is the subject of the sentence), **and at enmity** (active or passive? '*hating God*,' or 'hated by God?' Mey takes the latter, as necessary in Rom v. 10 [see note there]. But here, where the *διάνοια* and *ἔργα τὰ πονηρά* are mentioned, there exists no such necessity: the objective state of enmity is grounded in its subjective causes;—and the intelligent responsible being is contemplated in the whole sentence cf *εἴ γε ἐπιμένετε κ.τ λ* below. I take *ἐχθ.* therefore actively, 'hostile to Him') **in** (dative of reference, not, as Mey is obliged to take it on account of his passive *ἐχθ.* of the cause, 'on account of,' &c.: this is not the fact our passive *ἔχθρα* subsists not on account of any subjective actuality in us, but on account of the pollution of our parent stock in Adam) **your understanding** (intellectual part: see on Eph ii 3, iv 18 Erasm.'s rendering, in his Par., 'enemies to reason,' 'etenim qui carni servit, repugnat rationi,' is clearly wrong **διάνοια** is a '*vox media*,' and cannot signify 'reason·' besides, there is nothing here about 'carni inservire·' that of Tert., Ambr., and Jer, 'enemies to God's will,' rests on the reading *αὐτοῦ* after *διαν*,—see var readd · that of Beza, Mich, Storr, and Bahr,—'*mente operibus malis intenta*,' is allowable constructionally the verb is followed by *ἐν*, cf Ps lxxii 8, *διενοήθησαν ἐν πονηρίᾳ*, Sir. vi. 37, xxxix 1, and consequently the article before *ἐν* would not be needed: but is im-

c ver 20 Eph ii 16 only † d & constr, Eph ii 15 e — ver 28. Eph v 27 reff f Eph i 4 reff g Jude 24 h 1 Cor i 8 1 Tim iii 10 Tit i 6, 7 only P † 3 Macc v 31 i Eph i 4 reff k Eph iii. 2 reff l Rom vi 1 xi 22, 23 1 Tim iv 16 L P [exc John viii 7.] Exod xii. 39 vat m Eph iii 18 reff n 1 Cor vii 37 xv 58 only Ps lvi 8 Symm

νυνὶ δὲ [c] ἀποκατήλλαξεν 22 [d] ἐν τῷ σώματι τῆς [d] σαρκὸς ABCDF KLℵ a b
αὐτοῦ διὰ τοῦ θανάτου, [e] παραστῆσαι ὑμᾶς ἁγίους καὶ c d e f g
[fg] ἀμώμους καὶ [h] ἀνεγκλήτους [gi] κατενώπιον αὐτοῦ, 23 [k] εἴ h k l m n o 17
γε [l] ἐπιμένετε τῇ πίστει [m] τεθεμελιωμένοι καὶ [n] ἑδραῖοι, καὶ

F-lat for νυνι, νυν D¹F. for αποκατηλλαξεν, αποκατηλλαγητε B, αποκατηλλακηται(sic) 17 αποκαταλλαγεντες D¹F spec Iren-int Hil Ambrst Sedul txt ACD³KLℵ rel vulg(and F-lat) syrr copt Chr Thdrt Damasc.

22. om 1st αυτου F. aft θανατου ins αυτου Aℵ a b² c h k spec Syr syr-w-ast Chr-comm Iren-int

pugned by the τοῖς ἔρ. τοῖς πονηροῖς,—not only wicked works, but *the wicked works which ye did*) **in your wicked works** (sphere and element in which you lived, applying to both ἀπηλλ. and ἐχθ. τῇ διαν.), **now however** (contrast to the preceding description,—the participles forming a kind of *πρότασις* so *δέον αὐτοὺς τὴν φρόνησιν ἀσκεῖν μᾶλλον τῶν ἄλλων, οἱ δὲ χεῖρον πεπαίδευνται τῶν ἰδιωτῶν*, Isocr ἀντιδ c 26 *χρεὼν γάρ μιν μὴ λέγειν τὸ ἐόν, λέγει δ' ὦν*, Herod v 50 Eur Alcest 487 (476) See more examples in Hartung, i. p 186. It is probably this δέ which has given rise to the variety of readings and if so, the rec is most likely to have been original, at least accounting for it) **hath He** (i. e. God, as before the apparent difficulty of this may have likewise been an element in altering the reading) **reconciled in** (of the *situation* or *element* of the reconciliation, cf. ver 21, *ἐν τῇ σαρκί μου*, and 1 Pet. ii. 24) **the body of his** (Christ's) **flesh** (why so particularized? 'distinguitur ab ecclesia, quæ corpus Christi dicitur,' Beng,—but this is irrelevant here no one could have imagined that to be the meaning —'corpus humanum quod nobiscum habet commune Filius Dei,' Calv. [and so Grot, Calov],—of which the same may be said —as against the Docetæ, who maintained the unreality of the incarnation so Beza, al ; but St. Paul nowhere in this Epistle maintains, as against any adversaries, the doctrine of its reality I am persuaded that Mey. is right: 'He found occasion enough to write of the reconciliation as he does here and ver 20, in the angel-following of his readers, in which they ascribed reconciling mediatorship with God partly to higher spiritual beings, who were without a *σῶμα τῆς σαρκός*') **by means of His Death** (that being the instrumental cause, without which the reconciliation would not have been effected) **to** (aim and end, expressed without *εἰς τό*. as in Eph i. 4, al. fr) **present you** (see Eph. v. 27 and note · not, as a sacrifice) **holy and unblameable and irreproachable** ('erga Deum . . . . . respectu vestri . . . respectu proximi,' Beng. But is this quite correct? do not **ἀμώμ.** and **ἀνεγκλ.** both refer to blame from without? rather with Meyer, **ἁγίους** represents the positive, **ἀμώμ.** and **ἀνεγκλ.** the negative side of holiness The question whether *sanctitas inhærens* or *sanctitas imputata* is here meant, is best answered by remembering the whole analogy of St. Paul's teaching, in which it is clear that progressive sanctification is ever the end, as regards the Christian, of his justification by faith Irrespective even of the strong testimony of the next verse, I should uphold here the reference to inherent holiness, the work of the Spirit, consequent indeed on entering into the righteousness of Christ by faith · 'locus est observatione dignus, non conferri nobis gratuitam justitiam in Christo, quin Spiritu etiam regeneremur in obedientiam justitiæ quemadmodum alibi [1 Cor i. 30] docet, Christum nobis factum esse justitiam et sanctificationem' Calvin) **before His** (own, but the aspirate is not required: see above on ver. 20. not, that of Christ, as Mey , reading *ἀποκατηλλάγητε*. in Eph. i. 4, a different matter is spoken of) **presence** (at the day of Christ's appearing): 23] (condition of this presentation being realized · put in the form of an assumption of their firmness in the hope and faith of the Gospel)—**if, that is** (i e 'assuming that,' see note on 2 Cor v 3), **ye persist** (more locally pointed than *μένετε*,—usually implying some terminus ad quem, or if not, perseverance to and rest in the end) **in the faith** (ref also Xen Hell. iii. 4 6, *Ἀγησίλαος δὲ . . ἐπέμεινε* [al *ἐνέμ.*] *ταῖς σπονδαῖς*. more frequently with *ἐπί*, see Rost u. Palm sub voce) **grounded** (see Eph. iii 18, note and on the sense, Luke vi. 18, 19) **and stedfast** (1 Cor. xv 58,

μὴ [o] μετακινούμενοι ἀπὸ τῆς [p] ἐλπίδος τοῦ [q] εὐαγγελίου
[q] οὗ ἠκούσατε, τοῦ κηρυχθέντος ἐν [r] πάσῃ [r] κτίσει τῇ
[s] ὑπὸ τὸν οὐρανόν, οὗ ἐγενόμην [t] ἐγὼ [t] Παῦλος [u] διάκονος.
24 νῦν [v] χαίρω [v] ἐν τοῖς [w] παθήμασιν ὑπὲρ ὑμῶν, καὶ
[x] ἀνταναπληρῶ τὰ [y] ὑστερήματα τῶν [z] θλίψεων τοῦ χρισ-

o here only Deut xix 14. xxxii 30 Ezra ix 11 Isa liv 10 only. p constr, Acts xvi 19 Gal v 5 Eph i. 18 iv 4 q attr, Matt xviii 19 Acts i 1 Zeph iii 11 r ver 15 s Acts ii 5 iv 12 Deut xxv 19 t Gal v 2 reff u ver 7 reff v Phil i 18 w — Rom viii 18 2 Cor i 6 2 Tim iii 11 al † x here only † (ἀναπλ., Gal vi 2 reff) ἀνταναπληροῦντες πρὸς τὸν εὐπορώτατον ἀεὶ τοὺς ἀπορωτάτους, Demosth. 182 23 y Phil ii 30 reff z = here only (see note & Rev i 9).

23 rec aft πασῃ ins τῃ, with D³KLℵ³ rel. om ABCD¹Fℵ¹ m o 17 Chr. υπ ουρ., omg τον, F a ins κηρυξ και αποστολος και bef διακονος (see 1 Tim ii. 7) A syr-marg, κηρυξ και æth-rom. for διακ, κηρ κ απ ℵ¹ txt ℵ³.

24 at beg ins ος (*from preceding termination?*) DF latt Ambrst Pelag. rec aft παθημασιν ins μου, with ℵ³ b d g h k o syr Chr om ABCDFKLℵ¹ rel latt syr copt Thdrt Damasc Phot lat-ff ℵ¹ also om υπερ, ins ℵ-corr¹ αναπληρω F k 108 (Orig ?).

where the thought also of μὴ μετακιν. occurs), **and not** (the second of two correlative clauses, it setting forth and conditioned by the first, assumes a kind of subjective character, and therefore if expressed by a negative particle, regularly takes μή, not οὐ So Soph. Electr 380, *μέλλουσι γάρ σε . . ἐνταῦθα πέμψαι, ἔνθα μήποθ' ἡλίου φέγγος προσόψει.* See more examples in Hartung, ii 113 f.) **being moved away** (better passive than middle cf. Xen rep. Lac xv 1, *τὰς δὲ ἄλλας πολιτείας εὕροι ἄν τις μετακεκινημένας κ ἔτι νῦν μετακινουμένας* it is rather their *being* stirred [objective] by the false teachers, than their suffering themselves [subjective] to be stirred, that is here in question) **from the hope** (subjective, but grounded on the objective, see note on Eph i 18) **of** (belonging to, see Eph. as above the sense *'wrought by'* [Mey, De W, Ellic] is true in fact, but hardly expresses the construction) **the Gospel, which ye heard** ("three considerations enforcing the μὴ **μετακινεῖσθαι**: the μετακινεῖσθαι would be for the Colossians themselves inexcusable [*οὗ ἠκούσ*], inconsistent with the universality of the Gospel [*τοῦ κηρυχθ* &c.], and contrary to the personal relation of the Apostle to the Gospel" Mey. This view is questioned by De W, but it certainly seems best to suit the context. and cf Chrys. *πάλιν αὐτοὺς φέρει μάρτυρας, εἶτα τὴν οἰκουμένην ἅπασαν*, and see below),—**which was preached** (*οὐ λέγει τοῦ κηρυττομένου, ἀλλ' ἤδη πιστευθέντος κ κηρυχθέντος*, Chr) **in the whole creation** (see Mark xvi. 15 On the omission of the article before *κτίσει* see above, ver 15, note) **which is under the heaven,—of which I Paul became a minister** (*κ. τοῦτο εἰς τὸ ἀξιόπιστον συντελεῖ. μέγα γὰρ αὐτοῦ ἦν τὸ ἀξίωμα λοιπὸν πανταχοῦ ᾀδομένου, κ. τῆς οἰκουμένης ὄντος διδασκάλου*, Chrys)

24] Transition from the mention of himself to *his joy in his sufferings for the Church, and* (25—29) *for the great object of his ministry* —all with a view to enhance the glory, and establish the paramount claim of Christ. **I now** (refers to **ἐγενόμην**—extending what he is about to say down to the present time—emphatic, of *time*, not transitional merely) **rejoice in** (as the state *in which* I am when I rejoice, and the element of my joy itself. Our own idiom recognizes the same compound reference) **my sufferings** (no *τοῖς* follows **τοῖς παθήμασιν** = *οἷς πάσχω*) **on your behalf** (= **ὑπὲρ** *τ σώμ* below; so that the preposition cannot here imply substitution, as most of the Roman Catholic Commentators [not Est, *'propter vestram gentium salutem'* nor Corn-a-Lap, *'pro evangelio inter vos divulgando'*], nor *'because of you,'* but strictly 'in commodum vestri,' that you may be confirmed in the faith by [not my example merely, as Grot, Wolf, al] the glorification of Christ in my sufferings), **and am filling up** (the **ἀντί** implies, not *'vicissim,'* as Le Clerc, Beza, Bengel, al; nor that **ἀναπλ.** is said of one who '*ὑστέρημα a se* relictum *ipse* explet,' and **ἀνταναπλ** of one who '*alterius ὑστ de suo* explet,' as Winer [cited by Mey.], but the *compensation*, brought about by the filling up being *proportionate to the defect* so in ref: in Dio Cass. xliv 18, *ὅσον . . ἐνέδει, τοῦτο ἐκ τῆς παρὰ τῶν ἄλλων συντελείας ἀνταναπληρωθῇ* in Diog. Laert x 48, *καὶ γὰρ ῥεῦσις ἀπὸ τῆς τῶν σωμάτων ἐπιπολῆς συνεχὴς συμβαίνει, οὐκ ἐπίδηλος αἰσθήσει διὰ τὴν ἀνταναπλήρωσιν*, 'on account of the correspondent supply') **the deficiencies**

a = ver. 18. b = 1 Cor. ix. 17. (Eph. i. 10 reff.)

τοῦ ἐν τῇ σαρκί μου ὑπὲρ τοῦ [a] σώματος αὐτοῦ, ὅ ἐστιν
ἡ [a] ἐκκλησία, 25 ἧς ἐγενόμην ἐγὼ [u] διάκονος κατὰ τὴν [b] οἰ-

ABCDF KLℵ a b c d e f g h k l m n o 17

om τη F. om αυτου D[1]. for ο, ος CD[1] o: om m: txt ABD[2.3]FKLℵ rel 67[2]. om η D[1] d 109.

25. aft εγω ins παυλος Aℵ[1] 17. 31. 71. 120 arm.

(plural, because the θλίψεις are thought of individually, not as a mass: those sufferings which are wanting) **of the tribulations of Christ in my flesh** (belongs to ἀνταναπλ., not [as Aug. on Ps. lxxxvi. c. 3, vol. iv. p. 1104, Storr, al.] to τῶν θλίψ. τοῦ χρ., not only because there is no article [τῶν ἐν τῇ σαρκί μου], which would not be absolutely needed, but on account of the context: for if it were so, the clause τῶν θλίψ. τ. χρ. ἐν τῇ σ. μ. would contain in itself that which the whole clause asserts, and thus make it flat and tautological) **on behalf of** (see on ὑπέρ above) **His body, which is the Church** (the meaning being this: all the tribulations of Christ's body are Christ's tribulations. Whatever the whole Church has to suffer, even to the end, she suffers for her perfection in holiness and her completion in Him: and the tribulations of Christ will not be complete till the last pang shall have passed, and the last tear have been shed. Every suffering saint of God in every age and position is in fact filling up, in his place and degree, the θλίψεις τοῦ χριστοῦ, in his flesh, and on behalf of His body. Not a pang, not a tear is in vain. The Apostle, as standing out prominent among this suffering body, predicates this of himself κατ' ἐξοχήν; the ἀναπλήρωσις to which we all contribute, was on his part so considerable, as to deserve the name of ἀνταναπλήρωσις itself—I am contributing θλίψεις which one after another fill up the ὑστερήματα. Notice that of the **παθήματα** τοῦ χριστοῦ not a word is said [see however 2 Cor. i. 5]: the context does not concern, nor does θλίψεις express, those meritorious sufferings which He bore in His person once for all, the measure of which was for ever filled by the one sufficient sacrifice, oblation, and satisfaction, on the cross: He is here regarded as suffering with His suffering people, bearing them in Himself, and being as in Isa. lxiii. 9, "afflicted in all their affliction." The above interpretation is in the main that of Chrys., Thl., Aug., Anselm, Calv., Beza, Luth., Melancth., Est., Corn.-a-Lap., Grot., Calov., Olsh., De W., Ellic., Conyb. The latter refers to Acts ix. 4, and thinks St. Paul remembered those words when he wrote this: and Vitringa (cit. in Wolf) says well, 'Hæ sunt passiones Christi, quia Ecclesia ipsius est corpus, in quo ipse est, habitat, vivit, ergo et patitur.' The other interpretations are 1) that the sufferings are such as Christ would have endured, had he remained longer on earth. So Phot. (in Eadie): ὅσα . . . . ἔπαθεν ἂν κ. ὑπέστη, καθ' ὃν τρόπον κ. πρὶν κηρύσσων κ. εὐαγγελιζόμενος τὴν βασιλείαν τῶν οὐρανῶν. 2) That the sufferings are not properly Christ's, but only *of the same nature* with His. Thus Thdrt., after stating Christ's sufferings in behalf of the Church, says, καὶ ὁ θεῖος ἀπόστολος **ὡσαύτως** ὑπὲρ αὐτῆς ὑπέστη τὰ ποικίλα παθήματα: and so Mey., Schl., Huther, and Winer. But evidently this does not exhaust the phrase here. To resemble, is not to fill up. 3) Storr, al., would render, '*afflictions for Christ's sake*,'—which the words will not bear. 4) Some of the Roman Catholic expositors (Bellarmine, Cajetan, al.) maintain hence the doctrine of indulgences: so Corn.-a-Lap. in addition: 'Hinc sequitur non male Bellarminum, Salmeroneum, Franc. Suarez, et alios Doctores Catholicos, cum tractant de Indulgentiis, hæc generalia Apostoli verba extendere ad thesaurum Ecclesiæ, ex quo ipsa dare solet indulgentias: hunc enim thesaurum voluit Deus constare meritis et satisfactionibus non tantum Christi, sed et Apostolorum omniumque Christi Sanctorum: uti definivit Clemens VI. extravagante [on this word, I find in Ducange, glossarium in voce, '*extravagantes* in jure canonico dicuntur pontificum Romanorum constitutiones quæ *extra* corpus canonicum Gratiani, sive *extra* Decretorum libros *vagantur*'] *unigenitus*.' But Estius, although he holds the doctrine to be catholic and apostolic, and 'aliunde satis probata,' yet confesses, 'ex hoc Apostoli loco non videtur admodum solide statui posse. Non enim sermo iste, quo dicit Apostolus se pati pro ecclesia, necessario sic accipiendus est, quod pro redimendis peccatorum pœnis quas fideles debent, patiatur, *quod forte nonnihil haberet arrogantiæ*: sed percommode sic accipitur, quomodo proxime dixerat "gaudeo in passionibus meis pro vobis," ut nimirum utraque parte significet afflictiones et persecutiones pro salute fidelium, ipsiusque ecclesiæ promovenda toleratas.' The words in italics are at least an ingenuous confession. Con-

κονομίαν τοῦ θεοῦ τὴν [c] δοθεῖσάν μοι [d] εἰς ὑμᾶς [e] πληρῶσαι
τὸν λόγον τοῦ θεοῦ, 26 τὸ [f] μυστήριον τὸ [g] ἀποκεκρυμμένον [g] ἀπὸ τῶν [g] αἰώνων καὶ ἀπὸ τῶν [h] γενεῶν, νῦν δὲ
[i] ἐφανερώθη τοῖς [k] ἁγίοις αὐτοῦ, 27 οἷς ἠθέλησεν ὁ θεὸς

c = Rom xii 3 xv 15 2 Cor i 4 al freq
d = Rom xv 16.
e = Rom xv 19 see Acts xii 25
f Eph i 9 reff
g Eph iii 9 reff
h = Luke i 48, 50 Acts xiv 16 xv 21 Eph iii 5, 21 Isa xli 4 Jer xl (xxxiii) 6 only
i Rom xvi 26 2 Tim i 10 Tit i 3 al
k = Eph i 1 reff

26. rec νυνι, with ADKL rel Eus Cyr txt BCF א 17 Did. (for ν. δε, ο νυν k m 20-marg 23 49 57 80. 177. 213 syr arm Clem.) φανερωθεν D[1]. (but *manifestatum fuit* D-lat.) for αγιοις, αποστολοις F.

sult on the whole matter, Meyer's and Eadie's notes): **of which** (parallel with οὗ above in service of which, on behoof of which) **I** (emphatic, resuming ἐγὼ Παῦλος above) **became a minister, according to** (so that my ministry is conducted in pursuance of, after the requirements and conditions of) **the stewardship** (see on 1 Cor. ix 17, iv. 1, al also Eph. i 10, iii 2 not, '*dispensation*,' as Chrys., Beza, Calv, Est, al the simpler meaning here seems best, especially when taken with δοθεῖσαν. 'In domo Dei quæ est ecclesia, sum œconomus, ut dispensans toti familiæ, i e singulis fidelibus, bona et dona Dei domini mei,' Corn.-a-lap) **of God** (of which God is the source and chief) **which was given** (entrusted to) **me towards** (with a view to; ref) **you** (among other Gentiles, but as so often, the particular reference of the occasion is brought out, and the general kept back), **to** (object and aim of the stewardship depends on τ οἰκ τ δοθ. μοι) **fulfil the word of God** (exactly as in Rom xv. 19, to fulfil the duty of the stewardship εἰς ὑμᾶς, in doing all that this preaching of the word requires, viz 'ad omnes perducere,' as Beng, see also below· a pregnant expression The interpretations have been very various 'sermonem Dei vocat promissiones . quas Deus præstitit misso ad gentes Apostolo qui Christum eis patefaceret,' Beza 'finem adscribit sui ministerii, ut efficax sit Dei sermo, quod fit dum obedienter accipitur,' Calv.: 'ut compleam prædicationem evang. quam cœpit Christus,' Corn -a-lap 'ut plene ac perfecte annuntiem verbum Dei. vel, secundum alios [Vatabl. al.] ut ministerio meo impleam æternum Dei verbum, i e. propositum et decretum de vocatione gentium ad fidem · vel denique, quod probabilius est, ut omnia loca impleam verbo Dei,' Est.: 'valet, supplere doctrinam divinam, nempe institutione quam Epaphras inchoavit, profliganda et conficienda,' Fritzsche ad Rom, vol iii. p 275, where see much more on the passage. and other interpretations in Eadie, Meyer, and De W. All the above fail in not sufficiently taking into account the οἰκον εἰς ὑμᾶς Chrys. better, εἰς ὑμᾶς, φησί, πληρῶσαι τ λόγ. τ θεοῦ [but this connexion can hardly stand] περὶ τῶν ἐθνῶν λέγει He goes on however to understand πληρῶσαι of perfecting *their faith*, which misses the reference to fulfilling his own office) **26.**] (namely) **the mystery** (see on Eph. i 9) **which has been hidden from** (the time of; **ἀπό** is temporal, not 'from' in the sense of 'hidden from') **the ages and the generations** (before us, or of the world as many Commentators have remarked, not **πρὸ** τ. αἰ., which would be 'from eternity,' but the expression is historical, and within the limits of our world), **but now** (in those times) **was manifested** (historical · at the glorification of Christ and the bestowal of the Spirit. This change of a participial into a direct construction is made when the contrasted clause introduced by it is to be brought into greater prominence than the former one. So Thuc iv. 100, ἄλλῳ τε τρόπῳ πειράσαντες, καὶ μηχανὴν προσήγαγον, ἥπερ εἷλεν αὐτό, τοιάνδε Herod. ix 104, ἄλλας τε κατηγεόμεναί σφι ὁδοὺς—καὶ τέλος αὐτοί σφι ἐγένοντο κτείνοντες πολεμιώτατοι. See Bernhardy, p 473) **to His saints** (all believers, not merely as in Eph. iii. 5, where the reference is different, the Apostles and prophets [see there, and cf. various readings here], as some of the Commentators have explained it [not Thdrt., who expressly says, οἷς ἠβουλήθη ἁγίοις, τουτέστι τοῖς ἀποστόλοις, κ τοῖς διὰ τούτων πεπιστευκόσι], e g Est, Steiger, al, and Olsh, but regarding the Apostles only as the representatives of all believers) **27.**] **to whom** ('quippe quibus,' as Mey. this verse setting forth, not the contents of the mystery before mentioned, but a separate particular, that these ἅγιοι are persons to whom God, &c) **God willed** (it is hardly justifiable to find in this word so much as Chrys and others have done— τὸ δὲ θέλειν αὐτοῦ, οὐκ ἄλογον. τοῦτο δὲ εἶπε χάριτος αὐτοὺς μᾶλλον ὑπευθύνους

l = 1 Cor xii 3 xv 1 2 Cor viii 1. Eph i 9 1 Kings xxviii 15
m (neut) Eph i 7

[l] γνωρίσαι τί τὸ [mn] πλοῦτος τῆς [no] δόξης τοῦ [f] μυστηρίου
τούτου ἐν τοῖς ἔθνεσιν, ὅ ἐστιν χριστὸς ἐν ὑμῖν, ἡ [p] ἐλπὶς
τῆς δόξης, 28 ὃν ἡμεῖς [q] καταγγέλλομεν [r] νουθετοῦντες

ABCDF KLℵ a b c d e f g h k l m n o 17

n Eph i 18 reff o Eph i 6 reff p 1 Tim i 1 so ζωή, ch iii 4 q Phil i 18 reff
r Acts xx 31 (Paul) Rom xv 16 1 Thess v 12, 14 2 Thess iii 15 only P Job iv 3. Wisd xii 2 al

27. rec (for τι το) τις ο, with Cℵ b f h k o Chr Thdrt · txt ABD[2,3]KL rel Clem Eus Thl-comm Œc (τον πλουτον D[1].) for τουτου, του θεου D F Hil Ambrst του ℵ[1] Clem, Chr-txt(with ms) αυτου arm Cyr. rec (for ὁ) ος, with CDKLℵ rel Chr Cyr Thdrt Damasc, *qui* syrr. txt ABF 17. 67[2]; *quod* latt goth.

ποιῶν, ἢ ἀφιεὶς αὐτοὺς ἐπὶ κατορθώματι μεγα φρονεῖν—and similarly Calv, Beza, and De W Such an *inference* from the expression is quite legitimate but not such an *exposition.* No prominence is given to the doctrine, but it is merely asserted in passing) **to make known** (**γνωρίσαι** is not an interpretation of **ἐφανερώθη**, nor an addition to it, nor result of it, as has been supposed see on the reference of the verse above) **what** (how full, how inexhaustible this meaning of **τί**, necessarily follows from its being joined with a noun of quantity like **πλοῦτος**) **is the richness of the glory of this mystery among the Gentiles** (σεμνῶς εἶπε κ ὄγκον ἐπέθηκεν ἀπὸ πολλῆς διαθέσεως, ἐπιτάσεις ζητῶν ἐπιτάσεων. Chrys. Beware therefore of all attempts to weaken down the sense by resolving the substantives into adjectives by hendiadys. This the E. V. has here avoided why not always? Next, as to the meaning of these substantives. All turns on **τῆς δόξης.** Is this the [subjective] glory of the elevated human character, brought in by the Gospel [so Chrys.. Thdrt. (Calv ?)], or is it the glory of God, manifested [objective] by His grace in this mystery, revealing His Person to the Gentiles? Neither of these seems to satisfy the conditions of the sentence, in which **τῆς δόξης** reappears below with **ἡ ἐλπίς** prefixed. On this account, we must understand it of the glory *of which the Gentiles are to become partakers* by the revelation of this mystery: i. e. the glory which is begun here, and completed at the Lord's coming, see Rom. viii 17, 18 And it is the glory of, belonging to, this mystery, because the mystery contains and reveals it as a portion of its contents. The richness of this glory is unfolded and made known by God's Spirit as the Gospel is received ἐν τ ἔθν, as the most wonderful display of it · the Gentiles having been sunk so low in moral and spiritual degradation See Chr. and Calv. in Mey), **which** (mystery this is more in analogy with St Paul's own method of speaking than to understand **ὅ** of **τὸ πλοῦτος**. cf. τὸ ἀνεξιχνίαστον πλοῦτος τοῦ χριστοῦ, Eph iii. 8,—and τὸ τῆς εὐσεβείας μυστήριον, ὃς ἐφανερώθη ἐν σαρκὶ κ τ λ 1 Tim. iii 16. Besides which [τοῦ μυστηρ τούτου] [ἐν τοῖς ἔθνεσιν] is strictly parallel with, being explained by, [χριστὸς] [ἐν ὑμῖν]) **is** (consists in) **Christ** (Himself. not to be weakened away into ἡ τοῦ χρ γνῶσις [Thl],—'doctrina Christi' [Grot]: cf Gal ii. 20, Eph iii 17, 1 Tim. iii 16, al.) **among you** (not to be confined to the rendering, 'in you,' individually, though this is the *way in which* Christ is among you · ἐν ὑμῖν here is parallel with ἐν τοῖς ἔθνεσιν above before the Gospel came they were χωρὶς χριστοῦ, Eph. ii. 12), **the** HOPE (emphatic; explains how Christ among them was to acquaint them τί τὸ πλοῦτος &c., viz by being Himself the HOPE of that glory) **of the glory** (not abstract, 'of glory' τῆς δόξης is, the glory which has just been mentioned). **28**] **Whom** (Christ) **we** (myself and Timothy but generally, of all who were associated with him in this true preaching not, as Conyb , 'I,' which here quite destroys the force: the emphasis is on ἡμεῖς WE preach Christ—not circumcision, not angel worship, not asceticism, as the source of this hope) **proclaim** (as being this ἐλπὶς τῆς δόξης), **warning** (see on Eph vi. 4, and below) **every man, and teaching every man** (I am inclined with Mey to take **νουθετοῦντες** and **διδάσκοντες** as corresponding in the main to the two great subjects of Christian preaching, repentance and faith · but not too closely or exclusively we may in fact *include* Thl's view,—**νουθ** μὲν ἐπὶ τῆς πράξεως, **διδ δὲ** ἐπὶ δογμάτων,—Steiger's, that the former belongs more to early, the latter to more advanced instruction, and Huther's, that the former affects the heart, while the latter informs the intellect [see Eadie's note] for all these belong, the one class to repentance, the other to faith, in the widest sense) **in all wisdom** (method of this teaching. not as Est [giving the other but preferring this], 'in perfecta

πάντα ἄνθρωπον καὶ διδάσκοντες πάντα ἄνθρωπον [s] ἐν
πάσῃ σοφίᾳ, ἵνα [t] παραστήσωμεν πάντα ἄνθρωπον [u] τέλειον
ἐν χριστῷ· 29 [v] εἰς ὃ [v] καὶ [w] κοπιῶ [x] ἀγωνιζόμενος [y] κατὰ
τὴν [y] ἐνέργειαν αὐτοῦ τὴν [z] ἐνεργουμένην ἐν ἐμοὶ [a] ἐν
δυνάμει.

II. 1 [b] Θέλω γὰρ ὑμᾶς εἰδέναι, [c] ἡλίκον [d] ἀγῶνα [d] ἔχω

s ver 9 ch iii 10 t = ver 22 Eph v 27 reff u = 1 Cor ii 6 xiv 20 Heb v 14 al see Eph iv 13 v = 2 Thess i 11 w Matt vi 28 Acts x 35 Rom xvi 6, 12 bis 1 Tim iv 10 al Ps cxxvi 1 x Luke xiii 24 John xviii 36 ch iv 12 1 Tim vi 10 vi 12 2 Tim iv 7† Sir iv 28 al Dan vi 14 Theod y Eph i 19 reff z Paul, Rom vii 5 al[15] Matt xiv 2 || James v 16 only Isa xli 4 a Mark ix 1 Rom i 4 1 Cor iv 20 xv 43 al b 1 Cor xi 3 c James iii 5 bis only† d Phil i 30 (reff) 1 Thess ii 2

28 om και διδασκοντες παντα ανθρωπων (*homœotel*) L 67². 73 109 Clem₁ Œc-comm: om παντα ανθρ D¹F(and lat) f 17 æth Clem₁ lat-ff. (om 1st π. ανθρ Syr. om 3rd 11. 48. 72: om εν παση to 3rd ανθρ [*homœotel*] a d) aft σοφια ins πνευματικη F(and lat) D-lat. rec aft χριστ. ins ιησου, with D² ³KLℵ³ rel vulg(and F-lat) syr copt goth Chr$_{aliq}$ Thdrt lat-ff: om ABCD¹Fℵ¹ h 17 Clem₂ Chr-comm₂ Ambrst Primas.

cognitione Dei et mysteriorum fidei, quæ est vera sapientia,' and so Aug, Anselm, al.-latt this is usually in the accusative but the Greek Commentators, *τουτέστι, μετὰ πάσης σοφίας κ συνέσεως*), **that we may present** (see above ver. 22) **every man** (notice the emphatic triple repetition of **πάντα ἄνθρ**, shewing that the Apostle was jealous of every the least invasion, on the part of the false teachers, of those souls with whom he was put in charge At the same time it carries a solemn individual appeal to those thus warned and taught as Chrys,—*τί λέγεις; πάντα ἄνθρωπον; ναί, φησι, τοῦτο σπουδάζομεν τί γάρ, εἰ καὶ μὴ γένηται τοῦτο, ἔσπευδεν ὁ μακ. Π τέλειον ποιῆσαι* There is hardly perhaps, as Mey, Bisp, Ellic, al, suppose, an allusion to the Judaizers, those who would restrict the Gospel) **perfect in Christ** (element of this perfection, in union with and life in Him,—comprehending both knowledge and practice The presentation spoken of is clearly that at the great day of Christ's appearing): 29] His own personal part in this general work **for which end** (viz. the *παραστῆσαι*, &c) **I also** (**καί** implies the addition of a new particular over and above the **καταγγέλλειν**, carrying it onwards even to this) **toil in conflict** (of spirit, in the earnestness with which he strove for this end, see ch. ii. 1—3. not, with adversaries. this was so, but is not relevant here. See Phil i 30 1 Thess. ii 2), **according to** (after the proportion of, as is to be expected from) **His** (Christ's—see Phil. iv 13 not God's, as Chrys, Grot, Calv., al) **working which worketh** (not passive, as Est See on Gal. v 6, Eph. iii. 20, and Fritzsche on Rom. vii 5) **in me in power** (reff. there is no allusion to miraculous gifts, as Ambrst, Mich, al).

CHAP II FIRST PART OF THE EPISTLE. His earnestness in entering into and forwarding the Christian life among them, so amply set forth in ch. i., is now more pointedly directed to warning them against false teachers. This he does by 1) *connecting his conflict just spoken of, with the confirmation in spiritual knowledge of themselves and others whom he had not seen* (vv 1—3) 2) *warning them against false wisdom which might lead them away from Christ* (vv. 4—23) and that a) *generally and in hints* (vv. 4—15),—b) *specifically and plain-spokenly* (vv 16—23) 1] **For** (follows on, and justifies, while it exemplifies, **ἀγωνιζόμενος**, ch i. 29) **I would have you know how great** (emphatic, not only that I have an *ἀγών*, but how great it is The word is unusual, see reff) **a conflict** (of anxiety and prayer, cf. ch. iv 12 his present imprisoned state necessitates this reference here · he could not be in conflict with the false teachers) **I have on behalf of you and those in Laodicea** (who probably were in the same danger of being led astray, see ch iv 16: on Laodicea, see Prolegg to Apocalypse, § iii 13), **and** (it would not appear on merely grammatical grounds, whether this *καί* generalizes from the two specific instances, you and those in Laodicea, to the genus, including those two in the *ὅσοι* [see the two first reff., where however *ἄλλοι* is added]—or adds another category to the two which have preceded, as in the third ref, *Μακεδόνες καὶ . καὶ καὶ ὅσοι τῆς Θρῄκης τὴν παραλίην νέμονται*. This must be decided on other grounds, viz those furnished by the context. see below) **(for) as**

ὑπὲρ ὑμῶν καὶ τῶν ἐν Λαοδικείᾳ [e] καὶ ὅσοι οὐχ [f] ἑώρακαν
τὸ [f] πρόσωπόν μου [g] ἐν σαρκί, 2 ἵνα [h] παρακληθῶσιν αἱ
[i] καρδίαι αὐτῶν, [k] συμβιβασθέντες ἐν ἀγάπῃ καὶ [l] εἰς
πᾶν [m] πλοῦτος τῆς [n] πληροφορίας τῆς [o] συνέσεως, [l] εἰς

...και οσοι F (and G also).

ABCD KLℵ a b c d e f g h k l m n o 17

e Acts iv. 6. Herod. i. 57. vii. 185. f here only. (Acts xx. 25. Rev. xxii. 4. Gen. xliii. 3.) ἰδεῖν, 1 Thess. ii. 17. iii. 10. g 1 Tim. iii. 16 reff. h = 1 Thess. iii. 2. 2 Thess. ii. 17. Deut. iii. 28. Job iv. 3. i ch. iv. 8. Eph. vi. 22. k Eph. iv. 16 only. Isa. xl. 14. constr. partic., Acts xxvi. 2. 2 Cor. ix. 11. ch. iii. 16. Jude 16. Winer, edn. 6, § 63. 2. l ch. i. 29. m neut., Eph. i. 7 reff. n 1 Thess. i. 5. Heb. vi. 11. xx. 22 only †. (-ρεῖσθαι, ch. iv. 12.) o Eph. iii. 4 reff.

Chap. II. 1. rec (for υπερ) περι, with D[1.3]FKL rel Chr Thdrt Damasc: txt ABCD[3]ℵ 17. rec εωρακασι (*more usual*), with D[3]KLℵ[3] rel Cyr: txt ABCD[1]ℵ[1] Thdrt-ms.—εορ. CD[3](and E) ℵ d e n. om εν σαρκι ℵ: ins ℵ-corr[1].

2. rec συμβιβασθεντων (*grammatical correction*), with D[3]KL rel: txt ABCD[1]ℵ 17. 67[2] latt syr Clem Cyr Œc-schol lat-ff. om και D[1] Hil Ambrst Vig. rec παντα πλουτον, with KLℵ[3] rel: παντα τον πλουτον D Chr: παν το πλουτος AC 17 (*παν το rendered the substitution of the commoner masculine form still more obvious*): txt Bℵ[1]

many as have not seen ("the form ἑώρακαν is decidedly Alexandrian . . . . The 'ſonſtige Gebrauch Pauli' urged against it by Mey. is imaginary, as the third person plural does not elsewhere occur in St. Paul's Epistles." Ellicott) **my face in the flesh** (my corporal presence: **ἐν σαρκί** must not be joined with the verb, as Chrys. seems to have done, who adds, δείκνυσιν ἐνταῦθα, ὅτι ἑώρων συνεχῶς ἐν πνεύματι; for in ver. 5 the σαρκί is attached to the Apostle. But it is not necessary nor natural, with Estius, to see any 'ταπείνωσις, ut intelligant pluris faciendam esse præsentiam spiritus quam carnis.' Rather is the tendency of this verse the other way—to exalt the importance of the Apostle's bodily presence with a church, if its defect caused him such anxiety), **that** (object of the ἀγών) **their hearts** (these are the words on which the interpretation of the former καὶ ὅσοι must turn. If αὐτῶν apply to a separate class of persons, who had not seen him, whereas the Colossians and Laodiceans *had*, how are we to bring them into the ἀγών? In ver. 4 the third person αὐτῶν becomes ὑμᾶς. Where is the link, on this hypothesis, that binds them together? The sentence will stand thus: "I am anxious for you who have seen me, and for others who have not: for these last, that &c. &c. This I say that no man may deceive *you*." What logical deduction can there be, from the circumstances of *others*, to *theirs*, unless they are included in the fact predicated of those others? in a word, unless the ὅσοι above include the Colossians and Laodiceans? Thus the αὐτῶν extends to the whole category of those who had never seen him, and the ὑμᾶς of ver. 4 singles them specially out from among this category for special exhortation and warning. This seeming to be the only logical interpretation of the αὐτῶν and ὑμᾶς, the καί above must be ruled accordingly, to be not copulative but generalizing: see there) **may be confirmed** (see reff. It can hardly be doubted here, where he is treating, not of troubles and persecutions, but of being shaken from the faith, that the word, so manifold in its bearings, and so difficult to express in English, carries with it the meaning of strengthening, not of comforting merely. If we could preserve in 'comfort' the trace of its derivation from 'confortari,' it might answer here: but in our present usage, it does not convey any idea of strengthening. This I still hold against Ellicott), **they being knit together** (so E. V. well: not '*instructi*,' as vulg. On the construction, see reff. and Eph. iii. 18; iv. 2) **in love** (the bond of perfectness as of union: disruption being necessarily consequent on false doctrine, their being knit together in love would be a safeguard against it. Love is thus the *element* of the συμβιβασθῆναι) **and** (besides the elementary unity) **unto** (as the *object* of the συμβ.) **all** (the) **richness of the full assurance** (reff. see also Luke i. 1) **of the** (Christian) **understanding** (the accumulated substantives shew us generally the Apostle's anxious desire for a special reason to impress the importance of the matter on them. οἶδα, φησιν, ὅτι πιστεύετε, ἀλλὰ πληροφορηθῆναι ὑμᾶς βούλομαι, οὐκ εἰς τὸν πλοῦτον μόνον, ἀλλ' εἰς πάντα τὸν πλοῦτον, ἵνα καὶ ἐν πᾶσι καὶ ἐπιτεταμένως πεπληροφορημένοι ἦτε, Chrys.), **unto** (parallel with the former, and explaining πᾶν τὸ πλ. τ. πληρ. τῆς συν. by ἐπίγν. τοῦ μ. τ. θεοῦ) **the thorough-knowledge** (on ἐπίγνωσις and γνῶσις, here clearly distinguished, see on ch. i. 9) **of the mystery of God** (the additions here found in the rec. and elsewhere seem to be owing to the common practice of an-

[p] ἐπίγνωσιν τοῦ [q] μυστηρίου τοῦ θεοῦ,* 3 ἐν ᾧ εἰσὶν πάντες
οἱ [rs] θησαυροὶ τῆς [t] σοφίας καὶ [t] γνώσεως [su] ἀπόκρυφοι.

p ch. i. 9. q Eph. i. 9 reff. r Epp., 2 Cor. iv. 7. Heb. xi. 26 only. Gospp., Matt. ii. 11 al[8]. Mark x. 21. Luke vi. 45 (bis) al[3]. Josh. vi. 19. s Isa. xlv. 3. 1 Macc. i. 23. t 1 Cor. xii. 8. u Mark iv. 22. Luke viii. 17 only. Ps. ix. 8, 9 (29, 30). Dan. xi. 43 Theod.

67[2] Clem. * rec aft *του θεου* has καὶ πατρὸς καὶ τοῦ χριστοῦ, with D[3]KL rel syr(2nd *και* w. ast.) Thdrt Damasc; *εν χριστω* $Clem_2$ Ambrst; *του εν χ.* 17; ὅ ἐστιν χριστός D[1] Aug; *quod de christo* æth; χριστοῦ B Hil(addg, *deus christus sacramentum est*); *και χριστου* Cyr; πατρὸς καὶ τοῦ χριστοῦ 47. 73 Syr copt Chr Pelag; *patris et domini nostri christi* demid; *κ. πατρος τ. χριστου* ℵ[3] 115; πατρὸς τοῦ χριστοῦ AC b[1] o am(with fuld hal) sah: πατρὸς χριστοῦ ℵ[1]: om m 67[2]. 71. 80[1]. 116 arm(ed-1805).

3. rec ins *της* bef *γνωσεως*, with AD[3]KLℵ[3] rel $Clem_1$ $Orig_3$ Eus_1 Chr Thdrt Damasc: om BCD[1]ℵ[1] 17 $Clem_1$ $Orig_2$ Eus_1 Cyr Did Thl-ms.

notating on the divine name to specify to which Person it belongs. Thus **τοῦ θεοῦ** having been original, *πατρός* was placed against it by some, *χριστοῦ* or *τοῦ χριστοῦ* by others: and then these found their way into the text in various combinations, some of which from their difficulty gave rise again to alterations, as may be seen in various readings. The reading in text, as accounting for all the rest, has been adopted by Griesb., Scholz, Tischdf. [edn. 2], Olsh., De Wette, al.: *τοῦ θεοῦ χριστοῦ* by Mey. and Steiger. This latter is also edited, in pursuance of his plan, by Lachm. The shorter reading was by that plan excluded from his present text, as not coming before his notice. In the present digest, the principal differing readings are printed in the same type as that in the text, because I have been utterly unable to fix the reading on any *external* authority, and am compelled to take refuge in that which appears to have been the origin of the rest. One thing is clear, that *τοῦ θεοῦ χριστοῦ*, which Ellicott adopts 'with some confidence,' is simply one among many glosses, of which it is impossible to say that any has overwhelming authority. Such expressions were not corrected ordinarily by *omission* of any words, but constantly by supplementing them in various ways): **in which** (mystery, as Grot., Beng., Mey., De W., al. [Bisping well remarks, that the two in fact run into one, as Christ is Himself the *μυστήριον τοῦ θεοῦ*. He might have referred to ch. i. 27 and 1 Tim. iii. 16]—not '*in whom*,' as E. V. [but 'wherein' in marg.], and so, understanding 'whom' of *Christ*, Chrys., Thdrt., al.: for it is unnatural to turn aside from the main subject of the sentence,—the *μυστήριον*, and make this relative clause epexegetic of the dependent genitive merely. To this view the term *ἀπόκρυφοι* also testifies: see below) **are all the secret** (the ordinary rendering is, to make *ἀπόκρυφοι* the predicate after *εἰσίν*: '*in which are all, &c. hidden*.' The objection to this is, that it is contrary to fact: the treasures are not hidden, but revealed. The meaning given by Bähr, B.-Crus., and Robinson [Lex.], 'laid up,' lying concealed, *ἀποκείμενα*, does not belong to the word, nor is either of the places in the canonical LXX [reff.] an example of it. The rendering which I have adopted is that of Meyer, and I am persuaded on consideration that it is not only the only logical but the only grammatical one also. The ordinary one would require *ἀποκεκρυμμένοι*, or with *ἀπόκρυφοι*, a different arrangement of the words *ἐν ᾧ ἀπόκρυφοί εἰσιν*, or *ἐν ᾧ εἰσὶν ἀπόκρυφοι*. The objection, that for our rendering *οἱ ἀπόκρυφοι* would be required [Bähr], shews ignorance of the logic of such usage. Where the whole subject is covered by the extent of the predicate, the latter, even though separated by an intervening clause from the former, does not *require* the specification by the article. It *may* have it, but need not. Thus if all the men in a fortress were Athenians, I *might* say 1) *οἱ ἄνδρες ἐν τούτῳ ἐν τῷ τείχει οἱ Ἀθηναῖοι*: but I might also say 2) *οἱ ἄνδρες ἐν τούτῳ ἐν τῷ τείχει Ἀθηναῖοι*. If however, part of the men were Platæans, I *must* use 1), and could not use 2). Here, it is not asserted that 'all the treasures, &c. which are secret, are contained in the mystery,' others being implied which are not secret,—but the implication is the other way: 'the treasure[illegible] are all secret, and all contained in [illegible]stery.' Ellicott's rendering of *ἀπόκ*[illegible] as an adverbial predicate, 'hiddenly,' [illegible]s quite admissible, and tallies better w[illegible]h the

4 τοῦτο [δὲ] λέγω ἵνα μηδεὶς ὑμᾶς [v] παραλογίζηται ἐν ABCD
[w] πιθανολογίᾳ. 5 εἰ γὰρ καὶ τῇ σαρκὶ [x] ἄπειμι, [y] ἀλλὰ KLℵ a b c d e f g
τῷ [z] πνεύματι [a] σὺν ὑμῖν [a] εἰμί, [b] χαίρων καὶ [b] βλέπων h k l m n o 17
ὑμῶν τὴν [c] τάξιν καὶ τὸ [d] στερέωμα τῆς [e] εἰς χριστὸν [e] πίσ-

v James i. 22 only. Gen. xxix. 25. Josh. ix. 22. Judg. xvi. 10 F. w here only †. πιθανολογεῖν πειρᾶται, Diod. Sic. i. 39. x Phil. i. 27 reff. y = 1 Cor. viii. 6. z = 1 Cor. v. 3. a = Luke viii. 38. xxii. 56. Phil. i. 23. 1 Thess. iv. 17. 2 Pet. i. 18 al. b cf. Jos. B. J. iii. 10. 2, προθυμιας . . . . ὑμᾶς . . . . εὖ ἔχοντας χαίρω καὶ βλέπων. c Luke i. 8. 1 Cor. xiv. 40. Heb. v. 6, 11, & vi. 20 (from Ps. cix. 4). vii. 11, &c. only L.P.H. Job xxxviii. 12. d here only. Ezek. xiii. 5. Gen. i. 6, &c. Ps. xvii. 2. (-ρεοῦν, Acts xvi. 5.) e Acts xx. 21. xxiv. 24. xxvi. 18. Philem. 5. Paul (or *of* Paul) only.

4. om δε A[1](appy) Bℵ[1] Ambrst Aug. rec (for μηδεις) μη τις, with KLℵ[3] rel Clem$_1$: txt ABCDℵ[1] m 17 Clem$_1$. ημας C. παραλογιζητε C[3] 17. πειθανολ. D[2]L.

5. aft αλλα ins γε D[1]. for στερεωμα, *id quod deest* (i. e. υστερημα) D-lat tol Aug Ambrst.

classification and nomenclature of predicates, which he has adopted from Donaldson: but I question whether the rendering given above be not both more simple and more grammatical) **treasures** (see Plat. Phileb. p. 15 e, ὥς τινα σοφίας εὑρηκὼς θησαυρόν: Xen. Mem. iv. 2. 9, ἄγαμαί σου διότι οὐκ ἀργυρίου κ. χρυσίου προείλου θησαυροὺς κεκτῆσθαι μᾶλλον ἢ σοφίας: also ib. i. 7. 14) **of wisdom and knowledge** (σοφ., the general, γνῶσις, the particular; see note on Eph. i. 8).

4.] See summary at the beginning of the chapter. [**But** (the contrast is between the assertion above, and the reason of it, now to be introduced)] **this** (viz. vv. 1–3, not ver. 3 only, as Thl., Calv., al.: for ver. 1 is alluded to in ver. 5,—and vv. 1—3 form a logically connected whole) **I say, in order that** (aim and design of it) **no one may deceive you** (the word is found in this sense in Æsch. p. 16, 33, ἀπάτῃ τινὶ παραλογισάμενος ὑμᾶς,—ib. in Ctesiph. [Wetst.], ἢ τοὺς ἀκούοντας ἐπιλήσμονας ὑπολαμβάνεις ἢ σαυτὸν παραλογίζῃ—also in Diod. Sic., &c., in Wetst. See also Palm u. Rost sub voce) **in** (element in which the deceit works) **persuasive discourse** (add to the ref. Plat. Theæt. p. 162 e, σκοπεῖτε οὖν . . . εἰ ἀποδέξεσθε πιθανολογίᾳ τε κ. εἰκόσι περὶ τηλικούτων λεγομένους λόγους, and see 1 Cor. ii. 4): **5.**] personal ground, why they should not be deceived: **for though I am also** (in **εἰ καί** the force of the καί does not extend over the whole clause introduced by the εἰ, as it does in **καὶ εἰ**, but only belongs to the word immediately following it, which it couples, as a notable fact, to the circumstance brought [illegible] in the apodosis: so πόλιν μέν, εἰ [illegible] ῃ βλέπεις, φρονεῖς δ' ὅμως, οἵᾳ νόσ[illegible]ύνεστι, Soph. Œd. Tyr. 302. See Ha[illegible]ung, i. 139) **absent** (there is no ground whatever from this expression for inferring that he had been at Colossæ, as Wiggers supposed, Stud. u. Krit. 1838, p. 181: nor would the mere expression in 1 Cor. v. 3 authorize any such inference were it not otherwise known to be so) **in the flesh** (ver. 1 reff.), **yet** (ἀλλά introduces the apodosis when it is a contrast to a hypothetically expressed protasis: so Hom. Il. α. 81 f., εἴπερ γάρ τε χόλον γε κ. αὐτῆμαρ καταπέψῃ, ἀλλά τε καὶ μετόπισθεν ἔχει κότον, ὄφρα τελέσσῃ. See Hartung, ii. 40) **in my spirit** (contrast to τῇ σαρκί: not meaning as Ambrst. and Grot., 'Deus Paulo revelat quæ Colossis fierent') **I am with you** (reff.) **rejoicing** (in my earlier editions, I referred χαίρων to the fact of rejoicing at being able thus to be with you in spirit: but I see, as pointed out by Ellic., that this introduces a somewhat alien thought. I would now therefore explain it, not exactly as he does, by continuing the σὺν ὑμῖν, but as referring to their general state: rejoicing as such presence would naturally suggest: the further explanation, καὶ βλέπων &c., following) **and** (strictly copulative: there is no logical transposition, as De W., al.: nor is καί explicative, '*rejoicing, in that I see*'—as Calv., Est., al.: nor, which is nearly allied, is there any hendiadys, '*I rejoice, seeing,*' as Grot., Wolf, al.: nor need ἐφ' ὑμῖν be supplied after χαίρων, as Winer and Fritzsche: but as above. The passage of Jos. in ref. is rather a coincidence of terms than an illustration of construction) **seeing your order** (ἡ συμπᾶσα σχέσις κ. τάξις τῆς οἰκουμένης, Polyb. i. 4. 6: see also 36. 6; Plat. Gorg. p. 504 a. It is often used of the organization of a state, e. g. Demosth. p. 200. 4, ταύτην τὴν τάξιν αἱρεῖσθαι τῆς πολιτείας. Here it imports the orderly arrangement of a harmonized and undivided church. Mey.) **and** (as τάξις was the outward manifestation, so this is the inward fact

τεως ὑμῶν. 6 ὡς οὖν [f] παρελάβετε τὸν χριστὸν Ἰησοῦν
τὸν κύριον, [g] ἐν αὐτῷ [g] περιπατεῖτε, 7 [h] ἐρριζωμένοι καὶ
[i] ἐποικοδομούμενοι ἐν αὐτῷ καὶ [k] βεβαιούμενοι [ἐν] τῇ
πίστει [l] καθὼς ἐδιδάχθητε, [m] περισσεύοντες [ἐν αὐτῇ] [m] ἐν
[n] εὐχαριστίᾳ. 8 [o] βλέπετε μή τις ὑμᾶς [p] ἔσται [q] ὁ [r] συλ-

f 1 Cor xi 23 xv 1 Gal i 9, 12 al of *Christ*, John i 11 only
g constr, Rom. vi 4 2 Cor. iv 2 x 3 Eph v 2 al Prov viii 20 w αὐτῷ here only
h Eph iii 18 only Isa xl 24 Ald only
i 1 Cor iii 10, &c Eph ii 20 Jude 20 only Num xxxii 28 only Ps xl 12. cxviii 23 only
k Mark xvi 20 Rom xv 8 1 Cor i 6, 8 2 Cor i 21 Heb ii 3. xiii 9
l ch i 7
m constr, Phil i 9 reff
n Eph v 4 reff
o Gal v 15 reff
p indic, Gal iv 10. 1 Thess iii 5 Heb iii 12
q constr, Gal i 7 reff
r here only † see 1 Cor ix 27.

6 *τον κυριον ιησ. χρ* D *τον κυριον ιησ.*, omg *χρ*, 17.
7. om *εν αυτω* ℵ[1] 71. ins ℵ-corr[1]. rec aft *βεβαιουμενοι* ins *εν*, with ACD[3]KLℵ rel demid(and hal) syrr copt gr-ff: om BD[1] k 17 vulg(and F-lat) Thl Archel Ambrst. om *τη* bef *πιστει* AC aft *καθως* ins *και* D[1] latt om *εν αυτη* (*passing on to εν ευχ*) ACℵ[1] m 17 am(with fuld tol) copt Archel ins BD[3]KL rel 67[2] syrr copt gr-ff, *εν αυτω* D[1]ℵ[3] vulg-ed(with demid) syr-marg Pelag.
8. *εσται* bef *υμας* ACDℵ txt BKL rel. *συλαγων* ℵ[1].

on which it rested) **the solid basis** (ὅτε πολλὰ συναγαγὼν συγκολλήσεις πυκνῶς κ ἀδιασπάστως, τότε στερέωμα γίνεται. Chrys It does not mean '*firmness*' [Conyb], nor '*stedfastness*' [E V.], nor indeed any abstract quality at all. but, as all nouns in -*μα*, the concrete product of the abstract quality) **of your faith on Christ** 6] **As then** (he has described his conflict and his joy on their behalf—he now exhorts them to justify such anxiety and approval by consistency with their first faith) **ye received** (from Epaphras and your first teachers) **Jesus the Christ the Lord** (it is necessary, in order to express the full sense of τὸν χρ. Ἰησ. τὸν κύρ., to give something of a predicative force both to τὸν χρ and to τὸν κύρ : see 1 Cor xii. 3 [but hardly so strong as "for your Lord," as rendered in my earlier editions. see Ellicott here].

The expression ὁ χρ Ἰησ. ὁ κύρ. occurs only here. the nearest approach to it is in 2 Cor iv 5, . . . κηρύσσομεν . . . χριστὸν Ἰησ κύριον where also κύρ is a predicate: but this is even more emphatic and solemn Cf. also Phil. iii 8, τὸ ὑπερέχον τῆς γνώσεως χρ. Ἰησοῦ τοῦ κυρ μου. On the sense, Bisping says well: "Notice that Paul here says, παρελάβετε τὸν χριστόν, and not παρελ τὸν λόγον τοῦ χρ True faith is a spiritual communion for in faith we receive not only the doctrine of Christ, but Himself, into us in faith He Himself dwells in us we cannot separate Christ, as Eternal Truth, and His doctrine"), **in Him walk** (carry on your life of faith and practice), **rooted** (see Eph. iii 18) **and being continually built up in Him** (as both the soil and the foundation—in both cases the conditional element It is to be noticed 1) how the fervid style of St Paul, disdaining the nice proprieties of rhetoric, sets forth the point in hand by inconsistent similitudes: the walking implying motion, the rooting and building, rest, 2) that the rooting, answering to the first elementary grounding in Him, is in the past the being built up, answering to the continual increase in Him, is present See Eph. ii 20, where this latter is set forth as a fact in the past) **and confirmed in the** (or, **your**) **faith** (dat of reference it seems hardly natural with Mey to take it instrumental, as there is no question of instrumental means in this passage), **as ye were taught, abounding in it** (reff) **in thanksgiving** (the field of operation, or element, in which that abundance is manifested. "Non solum volo vos esse confirmatos in fide, verum etiam in ea proficere et proficiendo abundare per pleniorem mysteriorum Christi cognitionem idque cum gratiarum actione erga Deum, ut auctorem hujus totius boni" Est).

8—15] See summary, on ver 1—*general warning against being seduced by a wisdom which was after men's tradition, and not after Christ,—of whose perfect work, and their perfection in Him, he reminds them* 8.] **Take heed lest there shall be** (the future indicative expresses strong fear lest that which is feared should really be the case; so Aristoph Eccles 487, περισκοπουμένη κἀκεῖσε καὶ τἀκ δεξιᾶς, μὴ ξυμφορὰ γενήσεται τὸ πρᾶγμα. Hartung, ii. 138 see reff. and Winer, § 56 2 b α) **any one who** (cf τινές οἱ ταράσσοντες, ref. Gal and note [illegible] points at some known person) **leads you away as his prey** (Mey. connects the word in imagery with the foregoing περιπατεῖτε —but this perhaps is hardly necessary after

αγωγῶν διὰ τῆς [s] φιλοσοφίας καὶ [t] κενῆς [u] ἀπάτης κατὰ τὴν
[v] παράδοσιν τῶν [v] ἀνθρώπων, κατὰ τὰ [w] στοιχεῖα τοῦ
[w] κόσμου καὶ οὐ κατὰ χριστόν, 9 ὅτι ἐν αὐτῷ [x] κατοικεῖ
πᾶν τὸ [x] πλήρωμα τῆς [y] θεότητος [z] σωματικῶς 10 καὶ ἐστε

s here only. t = Acts iv. 25, from Ps. ii. 1. Eph. v. 6 al. u Eph. iv. 22 reff. v Mark vii. 8. παρ., Gal. i. 14 reff. w Gal. iv. 3 reff. x ch. i. 19 (reff.). y here only †. (see note.) z here only †. (-κός, 1 Tim. iv. 8.)

F (and also G) κοσμου ...

ABCDF KLℵ a b c d e f g h k l m n o 17

the disregard to continuity of metaphor shewn in vv. 6, 7. The meaning 'to rob' [so with τὸν οἶκον, Aristæn. ii. 22], adopted here by Thdrt. [τοὺς ἀποσυλᾶν τ. πίστιν ἐπιχειροῦντας], 'to *undermine*,' Chrys. [ὥσπερ ἄν τις χῶμα κάτωθεν διορύττων μὴ παρέχῃ αἴσθησιν, τὸ δ' ὑπονοστεῖ], hardly appears suitable on account of the κατὰ . . . . κατά, which seem to imply motion. We have [see Rost and Palm's Lex.] συλαγωγεῖν παρθένον in Heliod. and Nicet., which idea of *abduction* is very near that here) **by means of his** (or the article may signify, as Ellic., the current, popular, philosophy of the day: but I prefer the possessive meaning: see below) **philosophy and empty deceit** (the absence of the article before κενῆς shews the καί to be epexegetical, and the same thing to be meant by the two. This being so, it may be better to give the τῆς the possessive sense, the better to mark that it is not all philosophy which the Apostle is here blaming: for Thdrt. is certainly wrong in saying ἣν ἄνω πιθανολογίαν, ἐνταῦθα φιλοσοφίαν ἐκάλεσε,—the former being, as Mey. observes, the form of imparting,—this, the thing itself. The φιλοσοφ. is not necessarily *Greek*, as Tert. de præscr. 7, vol. ii. p. 20 ['fuerat Athenis']—Clem. Strom. i. 11, 50, vol. i. p. 346, P. [οὐ πᾶσαν, ἀλλὰ τὴν Ἐπικούρειον], Grot. al. As De W. observes, Josephus calls the doctrine of the Jewish sects philosophy: Antt. xviii. 2. 1,—Ἰουδαίοις φιλοσοφίαι τρεῖς ἦσαν, ἥ τε τῶν Ἐσσηνῶν κ. ἡ τῶν Σαδδουκαίων, τρίτην δὲ ἐφιλοσόφουν οἱ Φαρισαῖοι. The character of the philosophy here meant, as gathered from the descriptions which follow, was that mixture of Jewish and Oriental, which afterwards expanded into gnosticism), **according to the tradition of men** (this tradition, derived from men, human and not divine in its character, set the rule to this his philosophy, and according to this he ἐσυλαγώγει: such is the *grammatical* construction; but seeing that his philosophy was the instrument by which, the charge given belongs in fact to his philosophy), **according to the elements** (see on Gal. iv. 3: the rudimentary lessons: i. e. the ritualistic observances ['nam continuo post exempli loco speciem unam adducit, circumcisionem scilicet,' Calv.] in which they were becoming entangled) **of the world** (all these belonged to the earthly side—were the carnal and imperfect phase of knowledge—now the perfect was come, the imperfect was done away), **and not** (negative characteristic, as the former were the affirmative characteristics, of this philosophy) **according to Christ** ("who alone is," as Bisp. observes, "the true rule of all genuine philosophy, the only measure as for all life acceptable to God, so for all truth in thought likewise: every true philosophy must therefore be κατὰ χριστόν, must begin and end with Him"): 9.] (supply, 'as all true philosophy ought to be') **because in Him** (emphatic: in Him *alone*) **dwelleth** (now, in His exaltation) **all the fulness** (cf. on ch. i. 19, and see below) **of the Godhead** (Deity: the essential being of God: 'das Gott sein,' as Meyer. **θεότης**, the abstract of θεός, must not be confounded with θειότης the abstract of θεῖος, divine, which occurs in Rom. i. 20, where see Fritzsche's note. θεότης does not occur in the classics, but is found in Lucian, Icaromenippus, c. 9: τὸν μέν τινα πρῶτον θεὸν ἐπεκάλουν, τοῖς δὲ τὰ δεύτερα κ. τὰ τρίτα ἔνεμον τῆς θεότητος. 'The fulness of the Godhead' here spoken of must be taken, as indeed the context shews, metaphysically, and not as 'all fulness' in ch. i. 19, where the historical Christ, as manifested in redemption, was in question; see this well set forth in Mey.'s note. There, the lower side, so to speak, of that fulness, was set forth—the side which is presented to us here, is the higher side. Some strangely take πλήρωμα here to mean the Church—so Heinr. in Mey.: "Ab eo collecta est omnis ex omnibus sine discrimine gentibus ecclesia, eo tanquam οἴκῳ, tanquam σώματι, continetur gubernaturque." Others again hold *Christ* here to *mean* the Church, in whom [or which] the πλήρωμα dwells: so τινές in Thdrt. and Chrys.) **bodily** (i. e., manifested corporeally, in His present glorified Body—cf. on οἰκεῖ above, and Phil. iii. 21. Before His incarnation, it dwelt in Him, as the λόγος ἄσαρκος, but not σωματικῶς, as now that He is the λόγος ἔνσαρκος. This is the obvious, and

ἐν αὐτῷ [a] πεπληρωμένοι, * ὅς ἐστιν ἡ [b] κεφαλὴ πάσης
[c] ἀρχῆς καὶ [c] ἐξουσίας, 11 ἐν ᾧ καὶ [d] περιετμήθητε [e] περιτομῇ [f] ἀχειροποιήτῳ ἐν τῇ [g] ἀπεκδύσει τοῦ σώματος [h] τῆς

a = Eph iii 19 reff. b Eph i 22 reff. c Eph i 21 reff. d Gal ii 3 reff. e Eph ii 11 reff. dat., 1 Cor ix 7. f 2 Cor v 1. Mark xiv 58 only†. g here only† (-δύσασθαι, ver. 15.) h gen., Rom vi 6. vii 23, 24.

10. * ὅ BDF os ACKLℵ rel Cyr jer Chr Thdrt Damasc. om η D[1]F. ins της bef αρχης ℵ. for αρχ. κ. εξουσ., εκκλησιας D[1]: αρχης εκκλησιας ℵ[1].

11. rec aft του σωματος ins των αμαρτιων (explanatory, cf Rom vi 6), with D[2] [3]KLℵ[3] rel syrr goth Epiph Chr Thdrt Aug(altern) om ABCD[1]Fℵ[1] f 17 latt copt æth arm Clem Ath Bas Cyr Thdrt Damasc Thl Orig-int Hil Ambrst Aug(altern) Fulg Jer Pelag.

I am persuaded only tenable interpretation And so Calov., Est., De W., Mey., Eadie, al. Others have been 1) '*really*,' as distinguished from τυπικῶς so,—resting for the most part on ver. 17, where the reference is quite different,—Aug., Corn.-a-Lap., Grot., Schottg., Wolf, Nösselt, al 2) '*essentially*,' οὐσιωδῶς, as contrasted with the energic dwelling of God in the prophets: the objection to which is that the word cannot have this meaning. so Cyr., Thl., Calv., Beza, Usteri, p 324, Olsh., al), **and ye are** (already—there is an emphasis in the prefixing of ἐστε) **in Him** (in your union with Him,—'Christo cum sitis semel insiti,' Erasm in Mey) **filled up** (with all divine gifts—so that you need not any supplementary sources of grace such as your teachers are directing you to,—reff τῆς γὰρ ἀπ' αὐτοῦ χάριτος ἀπελαύσατε, as Thdrt. cf. John i 16, ἐκ τοῦ πληρώματος αὐτοῦ ἡμεῖς πάντες ἐλάβομεν not, as Chrys., Thl., De W., 'with the fulness of the Godhead,' which is *not true*, and would require ἧς ἐστε καὶ ὑμεῖς ἐν αὐτ. πεπλ. Nor must ἐστε be taken as imperative, against the whole context, which is assertive, no less than usage—'verbum ἐστέ nunquam in N. T. sensu imperandi adhibitum invenio, v. c. ἐστὲ οἰκτίρμονες, sed potius γίνεσθε, cf. 1 Cor x. 32; xi. 1; xv 58 et Eph iv. 32; v. 1, 7, 17, &c. Itaque si Paulus imperare hoc loco quicquam voluisset, scripturus potius erat κ. γίνεσθε ἐν αὐτῷ πεπληρ.' Wolf. What follows, shews them that He their perfection, is not to be mixed up with other dignities, as objects of adoration, for He is the Head of all such)—**who** (or, **which**: but the neuter seems to have been written to agree with πλήρωμα) **is the Head of every government and power**: 11.] (nor do you need the rite of circumcision to make you complete, for you have already received in Him the spiritual *substance*, of which that rite is but the shadow) **in whom ye also were circumcised** (not as E. V. '*are* circumcised,'—the reference being to the historical fact of their baptism) **with a circumcision not wrought by hands** (see Eph. ii. 11, and Rom. ii. 29. The same reference to spiritual [ethical] circumcision is found in Deut. x 16; xxx. 6: Ezek. xliv 7 Acts vii. 51), **in** (consisting in—which found its realization in) **your putting off** (= when you threw off ἀπεκδ., the putting off and laying aside, as a garment. an allusion to actual circumcision,—see below) **of the body of the flesh** (i.e as ch. i. 22, the body of which the material was flesh but more here so also its designating attribute, its leading principle, was fleshliness—the domination of the flesh which is a σὰρξ ἁμαρτίας, Rom viii 3. This body is put off in baptism, the sign and seal of the new life. "When ethically circumcised, i.e. translated by μετάνοια out of the state of sin into that of the Christian life of faith, we have no more the σῶμα τῆς σαρκός for the body, which we bear, is disarrayed of its sinful σάρξ *as such*, quoad its sinful quality we are no more ἐν τῇ σαρκί as before, when lust ἐνηργεῖτο ἐν τοῖς μέλεσιν [Rom. vii. 5, cf ib ver. 23] we are no more σάρκινοι, πεπραμένοι ὑπὸ τὴν ἁμαρτίαν [Rom. vii 14], and walk no more κατὰ σάρκα, but ἐν καινότητι πνεύματος [Rom vii 6], so that our members are ὅπλα δικαιοσύνης τῷ θεῷ [Rom vi. 13] This Christian transformation is set forth in its *ideal* conception, irrespective of its imperfect realization in our experience" Meyer. To understand τὸ σῶμα to signify '*the mass*,' as Calv. ['corpus appellat massam ex omnibus vitiis conflatam, eleganti metaphora'], Grot. ['omne quod ex multis componitur solet hoc vocabulo appellari'], al,—besides that it is bound up very much with the reading τῶν ἁμαρτιῶν, is out of keeping with N. T. usage, and with the context, which is full of images connected with *the body*),—**in** (parallel to ἐν before—then the circumcision without hands was *explained*, now it is again adduced with another epithet bringing it nearer home to them) **the circumcision of Christ** (belonging to,

i Rom vi 4 only † j Mark vii 4 [8] Heb vi 2 ix 10 only † sing, here only k Eph ii 6 reff

σαρκὸς ἐν τῇ d περιτομῇ τοῦ χριστοῦ, 12 i συνταφέντες αὐτῷ ABCDF KLℵ a b c d e f g h k l m n o 17
ἐν τῷ j βαπτισμῷ, ἐν ᾧ καὶ k συνηγέρθητε διὰ τῆς πίστεως

12 rec βαπτισματι (*usual word*), with ACD3KLℵ1 rel, *baptismate* Tert Hil: txt BD1Fℵ3 672 Chr1, *baptismo* latt Ambrst συνηγερθημεν C.

brought about by union with, Christ. nearly =, but expresses more than '*Christian circumcision*,' inasmuch as it shews that the root and cause of this circumcision without hands is in Christ, the union with whom is immediately set forth. Two other interpretations are given 1) that in which Christ is regarded as the *circumciser* ὁ χρ περιτέμνει ἐν τῷ βαπτίσματι, ἀπεκδύων ἡμᾶς τοῦ παλαιοῦ βίου, Thl, but not exactly so Chrys, who says, οὐκέτι φησὶν ἐν μαχαίρᾳ ἡ περιτ., ἀλλ' ἐν αὐτῷ τῷ χρ οὐ γὰρ χεὶρ ἐπάγει, καθὼς ἐκεῖ, τ. περιτομὴν ταύτην, ἀλλὰ τὸ πνεῦμα Beza combines both—'Christus ipse nos intus suo spiritu circumcidit' 2) that in which Christ is the *circumcised*—so Schottg., "per circumcisionem Christi nos omnes circumcisi sumus. Hoc est: circumcisio Christi qui se nostri causa sponte legi subjecit, tam efficax fuit in omnes homines, ut nulla amplius circumcisione carnis opus sit, præcipue quum in locum illius baptismus a Christo surrogatus sit" [i. p. 816] The objection to both is, that they introduce irrelevant elements into the context. *The circumcision which Christ works*, would not naturally be followed by **συνταφέντες αὐτῷ**, *union with* Him *that which was wrought on Him* might be thus followed, but would not come in naturally in a passage which describes, not the universal efficacy of the rite once for all performed on Him, but the actual undergoing of it in a spiritual sense, by each one of us), 12] (goes on to connect this still more closely with the person of Christ—q d, in the circumcision of Christ, to whom you were united, &c)—**buried together** (i e 'when you were buried:' the aorist participle, as so often, is contemporary with the preceding past verb) **with Him in your baptism** (the new life being begun at baptism,—an image familiar alike to Jews and Christians,—the process itself of baptism is regarded as the burial of the former life originally, perhaps, owing to the practice of immersion, which would most naturally give rise to the idea · but to maintain from such a circumstance that immersion is *necessary* in baptism, is surely the merest trifling, and a resuscitation of the very ceremonial spirit which the Apostle here is arguing against. As reasonably might it be argued, from the ἀπέκδυσις here, that nakedness was an essential in that sacrament. The things represented by both figures belong to the essentials of the Christian life the minor details of the sacrament which corresponded to them, may in different ages or climates be varied; but the spiritual figures remain. At the same time, if circumstances concurred,—e g a climate where the former practice was always safe, and a part of the world, or time of life, where the latter would be no shock to decency,—there can be no question that the external proprieties of baptism ought to be complied with. And on this principle the baptismal services of the Church of England are constructed); **in which** (i e. baptism· not, as Mey. [and so most expositors], '*in whom*,' i.e. Christ For, although it is tempting enough to regard the ἐν ᾧ καί as parallel with the ἐν ᾧ καί above, we should be thus introducing a second and separate leading idea into the argument, manifestly occupied with one leading idea, viz the completeness of your Christian circumcision,—cf ἀκροβυστίᾳ again below,—as realized in your baptism whereas on this hypothesis we should be breaking off from baptism altogether,—for there would be no link to connect the present sentence with the former, but we must take up again from ἐξουσίας This indeed is freely confessed by Mey, who holds that all allusion to baptism *is* at an end here, and that the following is a benefit conferred by *faith* as separate from baptism. But see below. His objection, that if ἐν ᾧ applied to baptism, it would not correspond to the *rising again*, which should be ἐξ οὗ, or at all events the unlocal δι' οὗ, arises from the too precise materialization of the image As ἐν before did not necessarily apply to the mere going under the water, but to the process of the sacrament, so ἐν now does not necessarily apply to the coming up out of the water, but also to the process of the sacrament *In it*, we both die and rise again,—both unclothe and are clothed) **ye were also raised again with Him** (not your material, but your spiritual resurrection is in the foreground it is bound on, it is true, to *His* material resurrection, and brings with it in the background, *yours* ·

[l] τῆς [m] ἐνεργείας τοῦ θεοῦ τοῦ [n] ἐγείραντος αὐτὸν ἐκ [τῶν]
νεκρῶν. 13 καὶ ὑμᾶς [o] νεκροὺς ὄντας ἐν τοῖς [op] παραπτώμασιν καὶ τῇ [q] ἀκροβυστίᾳ τῆς σαρκὸς ὑμῶν, [r] συνεζωοποίησεν ὑμᾶς σὺν αὐτῷ [s] χαρισάμενος ἡμῖν πάντα τὰ

l gen (see note), Mark xi 22 Acts iii 16 Rom. iii 22 Gal ii 16, 20 al
m Eph i 19 reff
n Gal i 1 reff
o Eph ii 1, 5
p Gal vi 1 reff
q Rom ii 30 al Paul only, exc Acts xi 3 Gen xvii 11
r Eph ii 5 only † (2 Macc iii 33 al)
s = Luke vii 41, 42 2 Cor ii 7, 10 xii 13 Eph iv 32 (bis) ch iii 13 (bis) L P †

om των ACKLℵ a d f k l m Chr Thl · ins BDF rel 67² Thdrt Damasc

13. om εν (as Eph ii. 1) BLℵ¹ f g h k m 17 goth gr-ff$_m$ Tert-ms Ambr · ins ACDFK ℵ-corr¹ rel ins εν bef τη ακροβυστια D¹F. for συνεζ, εζωοποιησεν D¹F Tert rec om 2nd υμας, with DFℵ³ b c latt copt goth Chr · ins ACKLℵ¹ rel tol syr Thdrt-ms Damasc Œc, ημας B a e g l² m 17 rec (for ημιν) υμιν, with Lℵ³ (a¹?) c d e m 17 vulg æth Thdrt lat-ff txt ABCDFKℵ¹ rel vss gr-lat-ff. at end add ημων D, and Syr arm.

but in the spiritual, the material is included and taken for granted, as usual in Scripture) by (means of the mediate, not the efficient cause, the hand which held on, not the plank that saved. I am quite unable to see why this illustration is, as Ellic. states, "in more than one respect, not dogmatically satisfactory." Surely it is dogmatically exact to say that Faith is the hand by which we lay hold on Christ the Ark of our refuge) **your faith in** (so Chrys., Thdrt, Œc, Thl, Erasm, Beza, Calv, Grot., Est., Corn.-a-lap, Mey., al, Beng ['fides est (opus) operationis divinæ'], al, and Luther. De W. understands faith wrought by God ['durch den Glauben den Gott wirket,' Luth 'mittelst des Glaubens Kraft der Wirksamkeit Gottes,' De W]. But both usage and the context are against this The genitive after πίστις is ever [against Ellic. here] of the *object* of faith, see reff, and on Eph i 19) **the operation of God** (in Christ—that mighty power by which the Father raised Him, cf. Rom viii 11; ἣν ἐνήργηκεν ἐν χριστῷ, Eph i 20) **who raised Him from the dead** (πιστεύοντες γὰρ τῇ τοῦ θεοῦ δυνάμει προσμένομεν τὴν ἀνάστασιν, ἐνέχυρον ἔχοντες τοῦ δεσπότου χριστοῦ τὴν ἀνάστασιν Thdrt But there is very much more asserted than the mere προσμένειν τὴν ἀνάστασιν—the power of God in raising the dead to life is one and the same in our Lord and in us—the physical power exerted in Him is not only a pledge of the same physical power to be exerted in us, but a condition and assurance of a spiritual power already exerted in us, whereby we are in spirit risen with Christ, the physical resurrection being included and taken for granted in that other and greater one):

12—15] *Application, first to the (Gentile) Colossians, then to all believers, of the whole blessedness of this participation in Christ's resurrection, and assertion of the antiquation of the law, and subjection of all secondary powers to Christ* **And you, who were** (or perhaps more strictly, **when you were**) **dead** (allusion to ἐκ [τῶν] νεκρῶν immediately preceding) **in your trespasses** (see Eph. ii 1, notes) **and (in) the uncircumcision of** (i. e. which consisted in. this is better than, with Ellic, to regard the gen. as simply possessive) **your flesh** (i e. having on you still your fleshly sinful nature, the carnal præputium which now, as spiritual, you have put away. So that, as Mey. very properly urges, it is not in ἀκροβυστία, but in τῆς σαρκός, that the ethical significance lies—ἀκροβυστία being their state still, but now indifferent), **He** (God—who, not Christ, is the subject of the whole sentence, vv 13—15. See the other side ingeniously, but to me not convincingly defended in Ellic's note here. He has to resort to the somewhat lame expedient of altering αὐτῷ into αὑτῷ: and even then the sentence would labour under the theological indecorum of making our Lord not the Resumer of His own Life merely, but the very Worker of acts which are by Himself and His Apostles always predicated of the Father It will be seen by the whole translation and exegesis which follows, that I cannot for a moment accept the view which makes Christ the subject of these clauses) **quickened you** (this repetition of the personal pronoun is by no means unexampled, cf Aristoph. Acharn. 391,—νῦν οὖν με πρῶτον πρὶν λέγειν ἐάσατε | ἐνσκευάσασθαί μ' οἷον ἀθλιώτατον see also Soph Œd Col. 1407 Demosth p 1225. 16—19. Bernhardy, p 275 f) **together with Him** (Christ brought you up,—objectively at His Resurrection, and subjectively when you were received among His people,—out of this death The question as to the reference, whether to spiritual or physical resurrection, is answered by remembering that the former includes the latter), **having**

t Acts iii 19 Rev iii 5 vii 17 xxi 4 only Ps l 10
u = Matt xii 30 Rom viii 31 Gal iii 21 v 23

ABCDF KLℵ a b c d e f g h k l m n o 17

p παραπτώματα, 14 t ἐξαλείψας τὸ u καθ' ἡμῶν v χειρόγραφον τοῖς w δόγμασιν ὃ ἦν x ὑπεναντίον ἡμῖν, καὶ αὐτὸ
y ἦρκεν z ἐκ τοῦ z μέσου a προςηλώσας αὐτὸ τῷ σταυρῷ,

v here only † Tobit v 3 ix 5 only w Eph ii 15 reff dat., Gal ii 11 x Heb x 27 only Gen xxii 17 Exod xxiii 27 Job xiii 24 y = Eph iv 31 reff z Matt xiii 49 Acts xvii 34 xxiii 10 1 Cor v 2 2 Cor vi 17, from Isa lii 11 2 Thess ii 7 only. Isa lvii 2 a here only † 3 Macc iv 9 σταυρῷ προςηλῶσαι, Jos B J ii 14 9

14. for ημιν, ημων ℵ[1] 114 · txt ℵ-corr[1]. for ηρκεν, ηρεν D[1]F a b c f g h k Orig Thdrt Thl. om του A 67[2].

forgiven (the aorist participle [which aor. '*having forgiven*' is in English, we having but one past active participle] is here not contemporaneous with συνεζωοπ but antecedent this forgiveness was an act of God wrought once for all in Christ, cf ἡμῖν below, and 2 Cor. v 19, Eph iv. 32) us (he here passes from the particular to the general—from the Colossian Gentiles to all believers) **all our transgressions** (ἃ τὴν νεκρότητα ἐποίει, Chrys · but this, though true, makes the χαρισάμ. apply to the συνεζ, which it does not), **having wiped out** (contemporary with χαρισάμενος—in fact the same act explained in its conditions and details. On the word, see reff., and Plat Rep vi p. 501, τὸ μὲν ἄν, οἶμαι, ἐξαλείφοιεν, τὸ δὲ πάλιν ἐγγράφοιεν. Dem 468 1, εἴθ' ὑμεῖς ἔτι σκοπεῖτε εἰ χρὴ τοῦτον [τὸν νόμον] ἐξαλεῖψαι, καὶ οὐ πάλαι βεβούλευσθε,) **the handwriting in decrees** (cf the similar expression τὸν νόμον τῶν ἐντολῶν ἐν δόγμασιν, Eph ii. 15, and notes Here, the force of -γραφον passes on to the dative, as if it were τὸ γεγραμμένον τοῖς δόγμασιν—cf Plato, Ep vii p 343 a, κ. ταῦτα εἰς ἀμετακίνητον, ὃ δὴ πάσχει τὰ γεγραμμένα τύποις. This explanation of the construction is negatived by Ellicott, on the ground of χειρόγραφος being "a synthetic compound, and apparently incapable of such a decomposition " referring to Donaldson, Gram § 369 [it is § 377] But there it is laid down that in synthetic compounds of this kind, the accent makes the difference between transitive and intransitive, without any assertion that the verbal element may not pass on in the construction. If χειρόγραφον means written by hands, then surely the element in which the writing consists may follow. Meyer would make the dative instrumental. but it can be so only in a very modified sense, the contents taken as the instrument whereby the sense is conveyed The **χειρόγρ** represents the *whole law*, the obligatory bond which was against us [see below], and is apparently used because the Decalogue, representing that law, was written on tables of stone with the finger of God. The most various interpretations of it have been given Calv., Beza, al., understand it of the mere *ritual law:* Calov., of the *moral*, against **πάντα τὰ** παραπτ. above: Luther, Zwingl, al., of the *law of conscience*. Thdrt.'s view is very curious he interprets τὸ χειρόγρ. to mean our human body,—ὁ τοίνυν θεὸς λόγος, τὴν ἡμετέραν φύσιν ἀναλαβών, πάσης αὐτὴν ἁμαρτίας ἐλευθέραν ἐφύλαξε, κ ἐξήλειψε τὰ κακῶς ὑφ' ἡμῶν ἐν αὐτῇ γενόμενα τῶν ὀφλημάτων γράμματα He urges as an objection to the usual interpretation, that the law was for Jews, not Gentiles, whereas the Apostle says καθ' ἡμῶν But this is answered by remembering, that the law was just as much against the Gentiles as against the Jews · it stood in their way of approach to God, see Rom iii 19. through it they would be compelled to come to Him, and by it, whether written on stone or on fleshy tablets, they were condemned before Him. Chrys., Œc., Thl, al., would understand τὸ χειρόγραφον ὃ ἐποίησε πρὸς Ἀδὰμ ὁ θεὸς εἰπὼν ᾗ ἂν ἡμέρᾳ φάγῃς ἀπὸ τοῦ ξύλου, ἀποθάνῃ—but this is against the whole anti-judaistic turn of the sentence) **which was hostile to us** (the repetition of the sentiment already contained in **καθ'** ἡμῶν seems to be made by way of stronger emphasis, as against the false teachers, reasserting and invigorating the fact that the law was no help, but a hindrance to us. There does not appear to be any force of '*sub*contrarius' in ὑπεναντίος, Mey refers, besides reff, to Herod iii 80, τὸ δ' ὑπεναντίον τούτου εἰς τοὺς πολιήτας πέφυκε — to ὑπεναντιότης, Diog Laert x 77 · ὑπεναντίωμα, Aristot poet xxvi 22 ὑπεναντίωσις, Demosth. 1405 18), **and** (not only so, but) **has taken it** (the handwriting *itself*, thus obliterated) **away** (i e 'from out of the way,' cf reff · Dem de corona, p 331, τὸ καταψεύδεσθαι κ. δι' ἔχθραν τι λέγειν ἀνελόντας ἐκ μέσου · other places in Kypke, ii. 323 and the contrary expression, Dem. 682 1,—οὐδὲν ἂν ἦν ἐν μέσῳ πολεμεῖν ἡμᾶς πρὸς Καρδιανοὺς ἤδη), **by nailing** (contemporary with the beginning of ἦρκεν) **it to the cross** ("since by the death of Christ on

15 [b] ἀπεκδυσάμενος τὰς [c] ἀρχὰς καὶ τὰς [c] ἐξουσίας [d] ἐδει-
γμάτισεν ἐν [e] παῤῥησίᾳ, [f] θριαμβεύσας αὐτοὺς ἐν αὐτῷ.

b ch iii 9 only † (-δυσις, ver 11) c = Eph i 21 reff d Matt i 19 only † (παραδειγ, Heb vi 6 Num xxv 4) e Eph iii 12 reff f 2 Cor ii 14 only †

15. aft απεκδυσαμενος ins την σαρκα, omg τας αρχας και, F Hil$_1$ Pac, so, but retaining τ. αρχ κ, Syr goth Hil$_{sæpe}$ Aug ins και bef εδειγματισεν B. εν εαυτω G, *in semetipso* latt lat-ff· (rec has ἐν αὐτῷ) · εν τω ξυλω (*interpretation of* αὐτῷ) Orig$_8$ Ath Chr Thdrt Macar Epiph Œc. [*licet in aliis exemplaribus habeatur in semetipso sed apud Græcos habetur in ligno* Orig in Josh. Hom. viii. 3, vol. ii. p. 416.]

the cross the condemnatory law lost its hold on us, inasmuch as Christ by this death bore the curse of the law for mankind [Gal iii 13],—in the fact of *Christ* being nailed to the Cross *the Law* was nailed thereon, in so far as, by Christ's crucifixion, it lost its obligatory power and ceased to be ἐν μέσῳ" Meyer. Chrys finely says, οὐδαμοῦ οὕτως μεγαλοφώνως ἐφθέγξατο. ὁρᾷς σπουδὴν τοῦ ἀφανισθῆναι τὸ χειρ. ὅσην ἐποιήσατο, οἷον πάντες ἦμεν ὑφ' ἁμαρτίαν κ. κόλασιν, αὐτὸς κολασθεὶς ἔλυσε κ. τὴν ἁμαρτίαν κ. τὴν κόλασιν ἐκολάσθη δὲ ἐν τῷ σταυρῷ)

15] The utmost care must be taken to interpret this verse according to the requirements of grammar and of the context. The *first* seems to me to necessitate the rendering of **ἀπεκδυσάμενος**, not, as the great majority of Commentators, '*having spoiled*' (ἀπεκδύσας), a meaning unexampled for the middle, and precluded by the plain usage, by the Apostle himself, a few verses below, ch. iii. 9, of the same word ἀπεκδυσάμενοι,—but '*having put off*,' 'divested himself of' Then the *second* must guide us to the meaning of **τὰς ἀρχὰς καὶ τὰς ἐξουσίας**. Most Commentators have at once assumed these to be the *infernal powers*, or *evil angels* relying on Eph. vi. 12, where undoubtedly such is the specific reference of these general terms. But the terms *being general*, such specific reference must be determined by the context of each passage,—or, indeed, there may be no such specific reference at all, but they may be used in their fullest general sense. Now the words have occurred before in this very passage, ver 10, where Christ is exalted as the κεφαλὴ πάσης ἀρχῆς κ ἐξουσίας and it is hardly possible to avoid connecting our present expression with that, seeing that in τὰς ἀρχὰς κ τὰς ἐξουσίας the articles seem to contain a manifest reference to it. Now, what is the context? Is it in any way relevant to the fact of the law being antiquated by God in the great Sacrifice of the atonement, to say that He, in that act (or, according to others, Christ in that act), spoiled and triumphed over the *infernal potentates*? Or would the following οὖν deduce any legitimate inference from such a fact? But, suppose the matter to stand in this way The law was διαταγεὶς δι' ἀγγέλων (Gal iii. 19 cf. Acts vii 53), ὁ δι' ἀγγέλων λαληθεὶς λόγος (Heb. ii 2) cf also Jos Antt xv 5 3, ἡμῶν τὰ κάλλιστα τῶν δογμάτων, κ. τὰ ὁσιώτατα τῶν ἐν τοῖς νόμοις δι' ἀγγέλων παρὰ τ. θεοῦ μαθόντων;—*they* were the promulgators of the χειρόγραφον τοῖς δόγμασιν In that promulgation of theirs, God was pleased to reveal Himself of old. That writing, that investiture, so to speak, of God, was first wiped out, soiled and rendered worthless, and then nailed to the Cross—abrogated and suspended there. Thus God ἀπεξεδύσατο τὰς ἀρχὰς κ. τὰς ἐξουσίας—divested Himself of, put off from Himself, that ἀγγέλων διαταγή, manifesting Himself henceforward without a veil in the exalted Person of Jesus And the act of triumph, by which God has for ever subjected all principality and power to Christ, and made Him to be the only Head of His people, in whom they are complete, was that sacrifice, whereby all the law was accomplished In that, the ἀρχαὶ κ. ἐξουσίαι were all subjected to Christ, all plainly declared to be powerless as regards His work and His people, and triumphed over by Him, see Phil ii 8, 9 · Eph i 20, 21 No difficulty need be created, on this explanation, by the objection, that thus more prominence would be given to angelic agency in the law than was really the fact the answer is, that the prominence which is given, is owing to the errors of the false teachers, who had evidently *associated the Jewish observances* in some way *with the worship of angels* St. Paul's argument will go only to this, that whatever part the angelic powers may have *had*, or be supposed to have had, in the previous dispensation, all such interposition was now entirely at an end, that dispensation itself being once for all antiquated and put away. Render then,—**putting off** (by the absence of a copula, the vigour of the sentence is increased The participle is con-

16 Μὴ οὖν τις ὑμᾶς [g]κρινέτω [h]ἐν [i]βρώσει * καὶ ἐν [k]πόσει ἢ ἐν [l]μέρει [mn]ἑορτῆς ἢ [no]νουμηνίας ἢ [np]σαββάτων,
17 * ὅ ἐστιν [qrs]σκιὰ τῶν [r]μελλόντων, τὸ δὲ [s]σῶμα τοῦ

ABCDF KLℵ a b c d e f g h k l m n o 17

g = Matt vii 1. John vii 24. Rom xiv 3. James iv 11. h so Rom ii 1. xiv 22. 1 Pet ii 12. i = Rom xiv 17. 1 Cor viii 4. 2 Cor ix 10. Heb xii 16 (John iv 32. vi 27 bis, 55. Matt vi 19, 20) only. Gen ii 9 al. k John vi 55. Rom xiv 17 only. Dan i 10 only. l = 2 Cor iii 10. ix 3 (1 Pet iv 16 v. r.) only. Demosth 688. 5, 698. 21. m Paul, here only. Matt. xxvi 5 al fr in Gospp. Acts xviii 21. n 1 Chron xxiii 31. 2 Chron ii 4. xxxi 3. o here only. p plur., Matt xii 1, &c. Luke iv 16 a). q = Heb viii 5. x 1 (Matt. iv 16. Mark ii 32. Luke i 79. Acts v 15) only †. (Job xiv 2.) r Heb x 1. s so Jos B J ii 2. 5, σκιὰν αἰτησόμενος βασιλείας, ἧς ἥρπασεν ἑαυτῷ τὸ σῶμα. Philo de conf ling 37, vol i p 434, τὰ μὲν ῥητὰ τῶν χρησμῶν σκιάς τινας ὡσανεὶ σωμάτων εἶναι.

16. * rec ἤ (*to suit the rest of the sentence*), with ACDFKLℵ rel vulg syr goth Orig$_2$ Eus$_2$ Mcion-c$_2$ Aug$_{aliq}$ Ambr: txt B (Syr) copt Orig$_1$ Jer Aug$_1$ Tich.—και νουμ. και σαβ Syr: *et* (4 times) Mcion-t. νουμηνια η σαββατω D[1]F Mcion-e.—νεομηνιας BF l.

17. * rec ἅ, with ACDKLℵ rel vulg(and F-lat) syrr Orig Eus$_2$ Aug$_1$: txt BF spec copt goth Epiph Ambrst Aug. om του DFKLℵ[3] rel Chr Thdrt Damasc Thl: ins ABCℵ[1] m Œc, ο χριστος Syr.

temporary with ἦρκεν above, and thus must not be rendered '*having* put off') **the governments and powers** (before spoken of, ver. 10, and ch. i. 16: see above) **He** (God, who is the subject throughout: see also ch. iii. 3 —not *Christ*, which would awkwardly introduce two subjects into the sentence) **exhibited them** (as completely subjected to Christ,—not only put them away from Himself, but shewed them as placed under Christ. There seems no reason to attach the sense of putting to shame [παραδειγματίσαι] to the simple verb. That this sense is involved in Matt. i. 19, is owing to the circumstances of the context) **in** (element of the δειγματίσαι) **openness** (of speech, declaring and revealing by the Cross that there is none other but Christ the Head πάσης ἀρχῆς κ. ἐξουσίας), **triumphing over them** (as in 2 Cor. ii. 14, *we* are said [see note there] to be led captive in Christ's triumph, our real victory being our defeat by Him,—so here the principalities and powers, which are next above us in those ranks of being which are all subjected to and summed up in Him) **in Him** (Christ: not '*in it*,' viz. *the cross*, which gives a very feeble meaning after the ἐγείραντος αὐτόν, and συνεζωοπ. σὺν αὐτῷ above). The ordinary interpretation of this verse has been attempted by some to be engrafted into the context, by understanding the χειρόγρ. of a *guilty conscience*, the ἀρχ. κ. ἐξ. as the *infernal powers, the accusers of man*, and the scope of the exhortation as being to dissuade the Colossians from fear or worship of *them*. So Neander, in a paraphrase (Denkwürdigkeiten, p. 12) quoted by Conyb. and Howson, edn. 2, vol. ii. p. 178 note. But manifestly this is against the whole spirit of the passage. It was θρησκεία τῶν ἀγγέλων to which they were tempted—and οἱ ἄγγελοι can bear no meaning but the angels of God.

16—23.] *More specific warning against false teachers* (see summary on ver. 1), *and that first* (vv. 16, 17) *with reference to legal observances and abstinence.*

16.] **Let no one therefore** (because this is so—that ye are complete in Christ, and that God in Him hath put away and dispensed with all that is secondary and intermediate) **judge you** (pronounce judgment of right or wrong over you, sit in judgment on you) **in** (reff.) **eating** (not, in St. Paul's usage, *meat* [βρῶμα], see reff., in John iv. 32, vi. 27, 55, it seems to have this signification. Mey. quotes Il. τ. 210, Od. α. 191, Plat. Legg. vi. p. 783 c, to shew that in classical Greek the meanings are sometimes interchanged. The same is true of πόσις and πόμα) **and** (or *or*) **in drinking** (i. e. in the matter of the whole cycle of legal ordinances and prohibitions which regarded eating and drinking: these two words being perhaps taken not separately and literally,—for there does not appear to have been in the law any special prohibition against *drinks*,—but as forming together a category in ordinary parlance. If however it is desired to press each word, the reference of πόσις must be to the Nazarite vow, Num. vi. 3), **or in respect** (reff.: Chrys. and Thdrt. give it the extraordinary meaning of 'in part,'—ἐν μέρει ἑορτῆς· οὐ γὰρ δὴ πάντα κατεῖχον τὰ πρότερα. Mey. explains it, 'in the category of'—which is much the same as the explanation in the text) **of a feast or new-moon or sabbaths** (i. e. yearly, monthly, or weekly celebrations, see reff.).

17.] **which** (if the sing. be read, the relative may refer either to the aggregate of the observances mentioned, or to the *last* mentioned, i. e.

χριστοῦ. 18 μηδεὶς ὑμᾶς [t] καταβραβευέτω [u] θέλων ἐν

t here only † ἐπιστάμεθα Στράτωνα ὑπὸ Μειδίου καταβραβευθέντα, Demosth Mid p 544 ult (βραβ, ch iii 15)
u = (see note) (1) 2 Pet iii 5 (2) 1 Kings xviii 22 2 Kings xv 26 3 Kings x 9 2 Chron ix 8 Ps cxlvi 10

the Sabbath. Or it may be singular by attraction, and refer to all, just as if it were plural, see Matt xii. 4) is (or as in rec *are* not, '*was*,' or *were* he speaks of them in their nature, abstractedly) **a shadow** (not, a *sketch*, σκιαγραφία or -φημα, which meaning is precluded by the term opposed being σῶμα, not the finished picture,—but literally the *shadow* see below) **of things to come** (the blessings of the Christian covenant these are the substance, and the Jewish ordinances the mere type or resemblance, as the shadow is of the living man. But we must not, as Mey, press the figure so far as to imagine the shadow to be cast back by the τὰ μέλλοντα going before [cf also Thdrt, somewhat differently, προλαμβάνει δὲ ἡ σκιὰ τὸ σῶμα ἀνίσχοντος τοῦ φωτός· ὡς εἶναι σκιὰν μὲν τὸν νόμον, σῶμα δὲ τὴν χάριν, φῶς δὲ τὸν δεσπότην χριστόν]: nor with the same Commentator, interpret τῶν μελλ. of the *yet future* blessings of the state following the παρουσία,—for which ἐστιν [see above] gives no ground. Nor again must we imagine that the *obscurity* [Suicer, al] of the Jewish dispensation is alluded to, there being no subjective comparison instituted between the two,—only their objective relation stated); **but the body** (the substance, of which the other is the shadow) **belongs to Christ** (i e. the substantial blessings, which those legal observances typified, are attached to, brought in by, found in union with, Christ see on the whole figure Heb. viii. 5; x. 1). We may observe, that if the ordinance of the Sabbath had been, *in any form*, of lasting obligation on the Christian church, it would have been quite impossible for the Apostle to have spoken thus The fact of an obligatory rest of one day, whether the seventh or the first, would have been directly in the teeth of his assertion here: the holding of such would have been still to retain the shadow, while we possess the substance And no answer can be given to this by the transparent special-pleading, that he is speaking only of that which was *Jewish* in such observances, the whole argument being general, and the axiom of ver 17 universally applicable.

I cannot see that Ellicott in loc. has at all invalidated this. To hold, as he does, that the sabbath was a σκιά of *the Lord's day*, is surely to fall into the same error as we find in the title of 1 Cor. x in our authorized bibles,—'The Jewish Sacraments were types of ours.' The antitype is not to be found in another and a higher type, but in the eternal verity which both shadow forth An extraordinary punctuation of this verse was proposed by some mentioned by Chrys. οἱ μὲν οὖν τοῦτο στίζουσι, τὸ δὲ σῶμα, χριστοῦ. ἡ δὲ ἀλήθεια ἐπὶ χριστοῦ γέγονεν· οἱ δὲ, τὸ δὲ σῶμα χριστοῦ μηδεὶς ὑμᾶς καταβραβευέτω· and Aug. ep. 149 [59] 27, vol. ii. p 841 f., has 'corpus autem Christi nemo vos convincat Turpe est, inquit . . ut cum sitis corpus Christi, seducamini umbris.' No wonder that the same father should confess of the passage, 'nec ego sine caligine intelligo.'

18—23] See above—*warning*, 2ndly, *with reference to angel-worship and asceticism.* 18] **Let no one of purpose** (such is by far the best rendering of θέλων,—to take it with καταβραβ. and understand it precisely as in ref 2 Pet. And thus apparently Thl.. θέλουσιν ὑμᾶς καταβραβεύειν διὰ ταπεινοφροσ Mey. pronounces this meaning 'ganz unpaßend,' and controverts the passages brought to defend it; *omitting however* ref 2 Pet. So also does Ellicott, believing it to "impute to the false teachers a frightful and indeed suicidal malice, which is neither justified by the context, nor in any way credible." But his own "*desiring to do it*" is hardly distinguishable from that other nor does it at all escape the imputation of motive which he finds so improbable But surely it is altogether relevant, imputing to the false teachers not only error, but insidious designs also. Others take θέλων with ἐν ταπ., keeping however its reference as above, and understanding, as Phot in Œc, τοῦτο ποιεῖν after it. So Thdrt, τοῦτο τοίνυν συνεβούλευον ἐκεῖνοι γίνεσθαι ταπεινοφροσύνῃ δῆθεν κεχρημένοι,—Calv, 'volens id facere,'—Mey, Eadie, al. This latter, after Bengel, assigns as his reason for adopting this view, that the participles θέλων, ἐμβατεύων, φυσιούμενος, κρατῶν, form a series. This however is not strictly true —for θέλων would stand in a position of emphasis which does not belong to the next two rather should we thus expect ἐν ταπ. θέλων κ θρ τῶν ἀγγ. I cannot help thinking this rendering flat and spiritless. Others again suppose a harsh Hebraism, common in the LXX [reff., especially Ps. cxlvi. 10], but not found in the N T., by which θέλειν ἐν is put for חָפֵץ בְּ, 'to have pleasure in' So

v Eph. iv. 2 reff.
w Acts xxvi. 5. James i. 26, 27 only †. Wisd. xiv. 18, 27 only. (-σκός, James i. 26. -σκεύειν, Wisd. xiv. 16.)

ᵛ ταπεινοφροσύνῃ καὶ ʷ θρησκείᾳ τῶν ἀγγέλων, ἃ ἑόρακεν

ABCDF KLℵ a b c d e f g h k l m n o 17

18. om εν ℵ[1] : ins ℵ-corr[1]. θρησκια CDF 17. ℵ[1] has written μελλοντων before αγγελων : marked for erasure by ℵ-corr[1]. rec aft ᾶ ins μη (*see note*), with CD[2,3]KLℵ[3] rel vulg syrr goth Orig Chr Thdrt Damasc Lucif Orig-int Aug; ουκ F: om ABD[1]ℵ[1] 17. 67[2] mss-in-Aug spec copt Orig-edd Tert Lucif Ambrst. [εορακεν, so B[1]CDℵ.] for αυτου, αυτων ℵ[1] : txt ℵ-corr[1,3].

Aug., Est., Olsh., al. The principal objection to this rendering here is, that it would be irrelevant. Not the delight which the false teacher takes in his ταπ. &c., but the fact of it as operative on the Colossians, and its fleshly sources, are adduced) **defraud you of your prize** (see reff. Demosth. Mey. points out the difference between **καταβρ.**, a *fraudulent adjudication with hostile intent* against the person wronged, and **παραβραβεύειν**, which is merely, as Thdrt. explains this, ἀδίκως βραβεύειν. So Polyb. xxiv. 1. 12, τινὲς δ' ἐγκαλοῦντες τοῖς κρίμασιν, ὡς παραβεβραβευμένοις, διαφθείραντος τοῦ Φιλίππου τοὺς δικαστάς. Supplying this, which Chrys. has not marked, we may take his explanation: καταβραβευθῆναι γάρ ἐστιν ὅταν παρ' ἑτέρων μὲν ἡ νίκη, παρ' ἑτέρων δὲ τὸ βραβεῖον. Zonaras gives it better, in Suicer ii. 49: **καταβρ.** ἐστι, τὸ μὴ τὸν νικήσαντα ἀξιοῦν τοῦ βραβείου, ἀλλ' ἑτέρῳ διδόναι αὐτό, ἀδικουμένου τοῦ νικήσαντος. This deprivation of their prize, and this wrong, they would suffer at the hands of those who would draw them away from Christ the giver of the prize [2 Tim. iv. 8. James i. 12. 1 Pet. v. 4], and lower them to the worship of intermediate spiritual beings. The various meanings, —'ne quis brabentæ potestatem usurpans atque adeo abutens, vos currentes moderetur, perperamque præscribat quid sequi quid fugere debeatis præmium accepturi' [Beng.],—'nemo adversum vos rectoris partes sibi ultro sumat' [Beza and similarly Corn.-a-Lap.],—'præmium, id est libertatem a Christo indultam, exigere' [Grot.],—are all more or less departures from the meaning of the word) **in** (as the element and sphere of his καταβραβ.) **humility** (αἵρεσις ἦν παλαιὰ λεγόντων τινῶν ὅτι οὐ δεῖ τὸν χριστὸν ἐπικαλεῖσθαι εἰς βοήθειαν, ἢ εἰς προσαγωγὴν τὴν πρὸς τὸν θεόν, ἀλλὰ τοὺς ἀγγέλους ὡς τάχα τοῦ τὸν χριστὸν ἐπικαλεῖσθαι πρὸς τὰ εἰρημένα μείζονος ὄντος τῆς ἡμετέρας ἀξίας. τοῦτο δὲ τάχα ταπεινούμενοι ἔλεγον. Zonaras in canon 35 of the Council of Laodicea, in Suicer i. p. 45. Similarly Thdrt., λέγοντες ὡς ἀόρατος ὁ τῶν ὅλων θεός, ἀνέφικτός τε κ. ἀκατάληπτος, κ. προσήκει διὰ τῶν ἀγγέλων τὴν θείαν εὐμένειαν πραγματεύεσθαι. Aug. Conf. x. 42, vol. i. p. 807, says: "Quem invenirem, qui me reconciliaret tibi? abeundum mihi fuit ad angelos? . . . . multi conantes ad te redire, neque per se ipsos valentes, sicut audio, tentaverunt hæc, et inciderunt in desiderium curiosarum visionum, et digni habiti sunt illusionibus." So that no ironical sense need be supposed) **and** (explicative, or appending a specific form of the general ταπεινοφρ.) **worship of the angels** (genitive objective, '*worship paid to the holy angels*:' not subjective, as Schöttg., Luther, Rosenm., al.: cf. Jos. Antt. viii. 8. 4, τοῦ ναοῦ κ. τῆς θρησκείας τῆς ἐν αὐτῷ τοῦ θεοῦ; Justin M. cohort. ad Græc. § 38, p. 35,—ἐπὶ τὴν τῶν μὴ θεῶν ἐτράπησαν θρησκείαν. With reference to the fact of the existence of such teaching at Colossæ, Thdrt. gives an interesting notice: οἱ τῷ νόμῳ συνηγοροῦντες καὶ τοὺς ἀγγέλους σέβειν αὐτοῖς εἰσηγοῦντο, διὰ τούτων λέγοντες δεδόσθαι τὸν νόμον. ἔμεινε δὲ τοῦτο τὸ πάθος ἐν τῇ Φρυγίᾳ κ. Πισιδίᾳ μέχρι πολλοῦ. οὗ δὴ χάριν κ. συνελθοῦσα σύνοδος ἐν Λαοδικείᾳ τῆς Φρυγίας νόμῳ κεκώλυκε τὸ τοῖς ἀγγέλοις προσεύχεσθαι· κ. μέχρι δὲ τοῦ νῦν εὐκτήρια τοῦ ἁγίου Μιχαὴλ παρ' ἐκείνοις κ. τοῖς ὁμόροις ἐκείνων ἔστιν ἰδεῖν. The canon of the council of Laodicea [A.D. 360] runs thus: οὐ δεῖ χριστιανοὺς ἐγκαταλείπειν τὴν ἐκκλησίαν τοῦ θεοῦ, κ. ἀπιέναι, κ. ἀγγέλους ὀνομάζειν, κ. συνάξεις ποιεῖν, ἅπερ ἀπηγόρευται. εἴ τις οὖν εὑρεθῇ ταύτῃ τῇ κεκρυμμένῃ εἰδωλολατρείᾳ σχολάζων, ἔστω ἀνάθεμα, ὅτι ἐγκατέλιπε τὸν κύρ. ἡμ. Ἰ. χρ. τ. υἱ. τοῦ θεοῦ, κ. εἰδωλολατρείᾳ προσῆλθε. See, for an account of subsequent legends and visions of the neighbourhood, Conyb. and Hows., ii. p. 480, note, edn. 2),—**standing on the things which he hath seen** (an inhabitant of, *insistens* on, the realm of sight, not of faith: as Aug. above, 'incidens in desiderium curiosarum visionum.' First a word respecting the reading. The μή of the rec. and οὐκ of others, seem to me to have been unfortunate insertions from misunderstanding the sense of ἐμβατεύων. That it *may* mean 'prying into,' would be evident from the simplest metaphorical

[x] ἐμβατεύων, [y] εἰκῆ [z] φυσιούμενος ὑπὸ τοῦ [a] νοὸς τῆς σαρκὸς αὐτοῦ, 19 καὶ οὐ [b] κρατῶν τὴν [c] κεφαλήν, ἐξ [d] οὗ πᾶν
τὸ σῶμα διὰ τῶν [e] ἁφῶν καὶ [f] συνδέσμων [g] ἐπιχορηγούμενον

x here only Josh xix 49 1 Macc xii 25 al3 only. τολμηρον ἐμβατευειν την απερινοητον φύσιν, Xen Conviv p 898 Raphel y Gal iii 4 reff z 1 Cor iv 6, &c v 2 viii 1 xiii 4 only † a = Rom i 28, xii 2 b = Acts iii 11 Cant iii 4 c Eph i 22 reff d Phil iii 20 constr gender, 1 Tim iii 16 e Eph iv 16 only ‡ (Lev xiii 2 al fr) f Acts viii 23 Eph iv 3 ch iii 14 only Isa lviii 6 g Gal iii 5 reff

19 aft κεφαλην ins χριστον D[1] syr arm Novat

application of its primary meaning of treading or entering on: but whether it *does* so mean here, must be determined by the context. And it surely would be a strange and incongruous expression for one who was advocating a religion of *faith*,—whose very charter is μακάριοι οἱ μὴ ἰδόντες κ. πεπιστευκότες,—to blame a man or a teacher for ἃ μὴ ἑόρακεν ἐμβατεύειν, placing the *defect of sight* in the very emphatic forefront of the charge against him. Far rather should we expect that one who διὰ πίστεως περιεπάτει, οὐ διὰ εἴδους, would state of such teacher as one of his especial faults, that he ἃ ἑόρακεν ἐνεβάτευεν, found his status, his standing-point, in the realm of sight And to this what follows corresponds This insisting on his own visual experience is the result of fleshly pride as contrasted with the spiritual mind. Of the other meanings of ἐμβατεύειν, that of 'coming into possession of property,' 'inheriting,' might be suitable, but in this sense it is usually constructed with εἰς, cf. Demosth. 1085 24, 1086. 19 The ordinary meaning is far the best here see reff., and cf. Æsch. Pers 448—νῆσος . . . ἣν ὁ φιλόχορος Πὰν ἐμβατεύει, Eur Electr. 595—κασίγνητον ἐμβατεῦσαι πόλιν [this view I still maintain as against Ellicott]), vainly (groundlessly. εἰκῇ must not be joined with ἐμβατ, as De W, Conyb, al.,—for thus the emphasis of that clause is destroyed see above) puffed up (no inconsistency with the ταπεινοφρ above: for as Thdrt says, τὴν μὲν ἐσκήπτοντο, τοῦ δὲ τύφου τὸ πάθος ἀκριβῶς περιέκειντο) by (as the working principle in him) the mind (intent, bent of thought and apprehension) of his own flesh (ὑπὸ σαρκικῆς διανοίας, οὐ πνευματικῆς, Chrys. But as usual, this adjectival rendering misses the point of the expression,—the διάνοια is not only σαρκική, but is τῆς σαρκός—the σάρξ, the ordinary sensuous principle, is the fons of the νοῦς—which therefore dwells in the region of visions of the man's own seeing, and does not in true humility hold the Head and in faith receive grace as one of His members. I have marked αὐτοῦ rather more strongly than by '*his*' only its expression conveys certainly some idea of self-will. On the psychological propriety of the expression, see Ellicott's note), **19**] and not (objective negative source of his error) holding fast (see ref Cant The want of firm holding of Christ has set him loose to ἐμβατεύειν ἃ ἑόρακεν) the Head (Christ see on Eph i 22. Each must hold fast the Head for himself, not merely be attached to the other members, however high or eminent in the Body), from whom (better than with Mey., '*from which*,' viz the Head,—Christ, according to him, being referred to 'nicht persönlich, sondern sächlich:' but if so, why not ἐξ ἧς—what reason would there be for any change of gender? The only cause for such change must be sought in *personal* reference to Christ, as in ref 1 Tim, and this view is confirmed by the τ αὔξησιν τ. θεοῦ below, shewing that the figure and reality are mingled in the sentence. Beng gives as his first alternative, 'ex quo, sc tenendo caput:' but this would be δι' οὗ, not ἐξ οὗ. The Head itself is the *Source* of increase the holding it, the *means*) all the body (in its every part not exactly = '*the whole body*,' in its entirety, which would, it accurately expressed, be τὸ πᾶν σῶμα, cf. τὸν πάντα χρόνον, Acts xx 18,—ὁ πᾶς νόμος, Gal v 14 On the whole passage see Eph iv 16, an almost exact parallel) by means of the joints (see against Meyer's meaning, '*nerves*,' on Eph l c) and bands (sinews and nerves which bind together, and communicate between, limb and limb) being supplied (the passive of the simple verb is found in 3 Macc vi 40, Polyb iv. 77. 2, πολλαῖς ἀφορμαῖς ἐκ φύσεως κεχορηγημένος πρὸς πραγμάτων κατάκτησιν ib. iii. 75 3, vi. 15 4, al The ἐπι, denoting continual accession, suits the αὔξει below) and compounded (see on Eph Notice, as there, the present participles, denoting that the process is now going on *Wherewith* the body is supplied and compounded, is here left to be inferred, and need not be, as by some Commentators, minutely pursued into detail. It is, as Thl., τὸ ζῆν κ. αὔξειν πνευ-

καὶ ʰ συνβιβαζόμενον ⁱ αὔξει τὴν ᵏ αὔξησιν τοῦ θεοῦ.
20 εἰ ˡ ἀπεθάνετε σὺν χριστῷ ᵐ ἀπὸ τῶν ⁿ στοιχείων τοῦ
κόσμου, τί ὡς ζῶντες ἐν κόσμῳ ᵒ δογματίζεσθε 21 Μὴ

ABCDF KLℵ a b c d e f g h k l m n o 17

h Eph. iv. 16 reff. i (-ξειν) Eph. ii. 21 only. Isa. lxi. 11. k Eph. iv. 16 only †. 2 Macc. v. 16 only. constr., as John vii. 24. l = Gal. ii. 19. m = Rom. vii. 2, ix. 3. 2 Cor. xi. 3. 2 Thess. i. 9. n Gal. iv. 3 reff. o here only. Esth. iii. 9. Esdr. vi. 34. 2 Macc. x. 8. xv. 36 only.

αυξη ℵ[1] m 44. 108-9-10. 219: txt ℵ-corr[1].

20. rec aft ει ins *ουν*, with ℵ[3] rel syr Thdrt Ambr Ambrst, *autem* demid, *enim* Syr: aft *αποθανετε(sic)* ℵ[1]: om ABCDFKLℵ-corr[1](appy) d k 17. 67[2] am(with fuld tol) copt goth arm Cyr Tert Cypr. rec ins τω bef *χριστω*, with k: om ABCDFKLℵ rel 67[2] Chr Thdrt Damasc. ins δια bef τι D[1]. aft τι ins παλιν D[1]F; ετι vulg arm. ins τω bef κοσμω F; *in hoc mundo* D-lat fuld Ambrst.

ματικῶς,—as Chrys.,—understanding it however after πᾶν τὸ σῶμα,—ἔχει τὸ εἶναι, κ. τὸ καλῶς εἶναι. The supply is as the sap to the vine—as the πᾶσα αἴσθησις κ. πᾶσα κίνησις [Thl.] to the body) **increaseth with** (accusative of the cognate substantive, see Ellic. and Winer, § 32. 2) **the increase of God** (i. e. 'the increase wrought by God,'—God being the first cause of life to the whole, and carrying on this growth in subordination to and union with the Head, Jesus Christ: not as Chrys., merely = κατὰ θεόν, τὴν ἀπὸ τῆς πολιτείας τῆς ἀρίστης,—nor to be tamed down with Calv., al., to "significat, non probari Deo quodvis augmentum, sed quod ad caput dirigitur." Still less must we adopt the adjectival rendering, 'godly growth,' Conyb., making that an *attribute* of the growth, which is in reality its *condition of existence*). The Roman Catholic Commentators, Corn.-a-Lap., Estius, Bisping, endeavour by all kinds of evasions to escape the strong bearing of this passage on their following (and outdoing) of the heretical practices of the Judaizing teachers in this matter of the θρησκεία τῶν ἀγγέλων. The latter (Bisp.) remarks,—"It is plain from this passage, as indeed from the nature of things, that the Apostle is not blaming every honouring of the angels, but only such honouring as put them in the place of Christ. The true honouring of the angels and saints is after all in every case an honouring of Christ their Head." On this I may remark 1) that the word *'honouring'* (Verehrung) is simply disingenuous, there being no question of honouring, but of *worship* in the strict sense (θρησκεία). 2) That whatever a Commentator may say in his study, and Romanists may assert when convenient to them, the honour and worship actually and practically paid by them to angels and saints does by very far exceed that paid to Christ their Head. Throughout Papal Europe, the worship of Christ among the body of the middle and lower orders is fast becoming obliterated, and supplanted by that of His Mother.

20.] *Warning against asceticism.* **If ye died** (in your baptism, as detailed above, vv. 11 ff.) **with Christ from** (a pregnant construction: 'died, and so were set free from:' not found elsewhere in N. T.: cf. Rom. vi. 2; Gal. ii. 19, where we have the dative) **the elements** (cf. ver. 8: the rudimentary lessons, i. e. ritualistic observances) **of the world** (see on ver. 8: Christ Himself was set free from these, when, being made under the law, He at His Death bore the curse of the law, and thus it was antiquated in Him), **why, as** *living* (emphatic, as though you had *not died*, see Gal. vi. 14) **in the world, are ye being prescribed to** (the active use of the verb, '*to decree*,' is common in the later classics, and occurs in the LXX, and Apocrypha. The *person to whom* the thing is decreed or prescribed is put in the *dative* [2 Macc. x. 8], so that, according to usage, such person may become the *subject* of the *passive* verb: cf. Thuc. i. 82, ἡμεῖς ὑπ' Ἀθηναίων ἐπιβουλευόμεθα [ἐπιβουλεύειν τινί],—Herod. vii. 144, αἱ δὲ νῆες . . . . οὐκ ἐχρήσθησαν [χρῆσθαί τινι], and see Kühner, Gram. ii. p. 35. Some, as Bernhardy, p. 346, and Ellicott, prefer considering this form as *middle*, and give it the sense of "doceri vos sinitis." It seems to be of very little consequence which we call it; the meaning in either case is almost identical: "why is the fact so?" or, "why do you allow it?" To my mind, the passive here carries more keen, because more hidden, rebuke. The ἀδικεῖσθε and ἀποστερεῖσθε of 1 Cor. vi. 7 rest on somewhat different ground. There, the voluntary element comes into emphasis, and the *middle* sense is preferable. See note there. I cannot see, with Meyer, why we should be so anxious to divest the sentence of all appearance of blaming the Colossians, and cast all its blame on the false teachers. The passive [see above] would demand a reason for the fact being so—'Cur ita siti estis, ut . . . ,' which is just as much a reproach as the middle

[p]ἅψῃ μηδὲ [q]γεύσῃ μηδὲ [r]θίγῃς—22 ἅ [s]ἐστιν πάντα [s]εἰς
[t]φθορὰν [u]τῇ [v]ἀποχρήσει—κατὰ τὰ [wx]ἐντάλματα καὶ [wy]δι-
δασκαλίας τῶν ἀνθρώπων, 23 [z]ἅτινά ἐστιν [a]λόγον [b]μὲν

p 1 Cor vii 1 2 Cor vi 17, from Isa lii 11 Levit xi 8 q Acts x 10 xx 11 xxiii 14 2 Macc vi 20 r Heb xi 28 xii 20 only Exod xix 12 only s Matt xix 5 Eph i 12 al fr t = Gal vi 8 reff u dat, Rom xi 20, 30 v here only † w Matt xv 9 ||, from Isa xxix 13 x Matt as above || Mk only Job xxiii 11, 12 vat Isa as above only y Eph iv 14 1 Tim i 10 reff z = ch iii 5 Rom ix 4 al change of gender, Phil i 28 a here only b so μεν (see note) Acts i 1 iii 13 Rom vii 12 Gal iv 24 Winer, § 63 ii 2 e

'Cui, sinitis, ut . .' The *active* renderings, '*decreta facitis*,' Melancth. [in Eadie], '*decernitis*,' Ambrst. [ib.], are wrong both in grammar and in fact. The reference to δόγμασιν ver. 14 is plain. They were being again put under that χειρόγρ. which was wiped out and taken away) **"Handle not, neither taste, nor even touch"** (it will be understood that these words follow immediately upon δογματίζεσθε without a stop, as τὰ δογματιζόμενα;—just as the inf. in 2 Macc. x. 8. Then as to the meaning,—I agree with Calv, Beza, Beng, and Meyer in referring all the three to *meats*,—on account mainly of vv. 22, 23 [see below], but also of γεύσῃ coming as a defining term between the two less precise ones ἅψῃ and θίγῃς. Others have referred the three to different objects ἅψῃ and θίγῃς variously to meats, or unclean objects, or women γεύσῃ universally to meats Mey. remarks of the negatives, the relation of the three prohibitions is, that the first μηδέ is '*nec*,' the second '*ne . . quidem*' This would not be necessary from the form of the sentence, but seems supported by the word θίγῃς introducing a climax Wetst and the Commentators illustrate ἅψῃ and θίγῃς as applied to meats, by Xen Cyr. i. 3 5, ὅταν μὲν τοῦ ἄρτου ἅψῃ, [ὁρῶ] εἰς οὐδὲν τὴν χεῖρα ἀποψώμενον, ὅταν δὲ τούτων τινὸς θίγῃς, εὐθὺς ἀποκαθαίρῃ τὴν χεῖρα εἰς τὰ χειρόμακτρα)—**which things** (viz. the things forbidden) **are set** (ἐστιν emphatic, 'whose very nature is . . .') **all of them for destruction** (by corruption, see reff.) **in their consumption** (i e are appointed by the Creator to be decomposed and obliterated with their consumption by us So Thdrt —πῶς . . νομίζετέ τινα μὲν τῶν ἐδεσμάτων ἔννομα, τινὰ δὲ παράνομα, κ. οὐ σκοπεῖτε ὡς μόνιμον τούτων οὐδέν; εἰς κόπρον γὰρ ἅπαντα μεταβάλλεται· and similarly Œc.—φθορᾷ γάρ, φησιν, ὑπόκειται ἐν τῷ ἀφεδρῶνι—Thl., Erasm, Luth., Beza, Calv., Grot, Wolf, Olsh, Mey., al. The argument in fact is similar to that in Matt xv. 17, and 1 Cor. vi 13

Two other lines of interpretation have been followed · 1) that which carries the sense on from the three verbs, "*Handle not &c. things which tend to* [*moral*] *corruption in their use*" De W, Baum-Crus, al But this suits neither the collocation of the words, nor ἀποχρήσει, the '*using up*,' '*consumption*,' which should thus rather be χρήσει. 2) that which makes ἅ refer to δόγματα, and renders '*which δόγματα all tend to* [*everlasting*] *destruction in their observance*,' but this is just as much against the sense of ἀπόχρησις, and would rather require τήρησις, if indeed τῇ ἀποχρήσει be not superfluous altogether. See these same objections urged at greater length in Meyer's note)—**according to** (connects with δογματίζεσθε Μὴ . . θίγῃς. the subsequent clause being a parenthetical remark; thus defining the general term δόγματα to consist in human, not divine commands) **the commands and systems** (διδασκαλία is the wider term comprising many ἐντάλματα In reff., the wider term is prefixed: here, where examples of separate ἐντάλματα have been given, we rise from them to the system of doctrine of which they are a part) **of men** (not merely ἀνθρώπων, bringing out the individual authors of them, but τῶν ἀν describing them generically as *human*, not divine This I would press as against Ellic, who views the τῶν as the art of correlation, rendered necessary by τὰ ἐντάλματα But even if this usage were to be strictly pressed with such a word as ἀνθρώπων, the substantive nearest to it, διδασκαλίας, has no article), **such as** (ἅτινα brings us from the general objective, human doctrines and systems, to the specific subjective, the particular sort of doctrines and systems which they were following q. d, 'and that, such sort of ἐντ κ διδασκ as . ') **are possessed of** (ἐστὶν ἔχοντα does not exactly = ἔχει, but betokens more the abiding attribute of these δόγματα—'enjoy,' as we say) **a reputation** (λόγον ἔχειν occurs in various meanings. Absolutely, it may signify '*avoir raison*,' as Demosth p. 204, ἔστι δὲ τοῦτο οὑτωσὶ μὲν ἀκοῦσαι λόγον τινὰ ἔχον, which meaning is obviously out of place here:—as is also '*to take account of*,' Herod i 62, Ἀθηναῖοι δὲ οἱ ἐκ τοῦ ἄστεος, ἕως . . λόγον οὐδένα εἶχον But the meaning '*to have the repute of*,' —found Herod v 66, Κλεισθένης . . ὅσπερ δὴ λόγον ἔχει τὴν Πυθίην ἀναπεῖσαι ['is said to have influenced the

[a] ἔχοντα σοφίας ἐν [c] ἐθελοθρησκείᾳ καὶ [d] ταπεινοφροσύνῃ καὶ [e] ἀφειδίᾳ σώματος, οὐκ [f] ἐν τιμῇ τινι,—πρὸς [g] πλησμονὴν τῆς σαρκός;

ABCDF KLℵ a b c d e f g h k l m n o 17

c here only †. (see note.) d ver. 18. e here only †. (-δῶς, Prov. xxi. 26.) f 1 Thess. iv. 4. (τὰ καινὰ τῶν ὑποδημάτων ἐν τιμῇ τινι . . . . ἐστιν, Lucian de merced. cond. 17. Wetst.) g here only. Exod. xvi. 8 al.

23. εθελοθρησκια (for -κεια) CD¹ℵ e g l 17: A uncert: θρησκια F. aft ταπεινοφροσυνη ins του νοος F(and F-lat) D-lat goth lat-ff. om 2nd και B spec Hil. αφειδεια B: txt CDFKLℵ rel. (A defective.)

Pythia'],—and Plat. Epinomis, p. 987 b, *ὁ μὲν γὰρ ἑωσφόρος ἕσπερός τε ὢν αὐτὸς Ἀφροδίτης εἶναι σχεδὸν ἔχει λόγον* ['Veneris esse dicitur,' as Ficinus],—manifestly fits the context here, and is adopted by most Commentators) **indeed** (the *μέν* solitarium leaves the *δέ* to be supplied by the reader, or gathered from what follows. It is implied by it, not by the mere phrase *λόγον ἔχειν* [see the examples above], that they had the repute only without the reality) **of wisdom in** (element of its repute) **voluntary worship** (words of this form are not uncommon: so we have *ἐθελοπρόξενος*, a volunteer or self-constituted proxenus, in Thuc. iii. 70,—*ἐθελοκωφέω*, to pretend to be deaf, Strab. i. p. 36,—*ἐθελοδουλεία*, voluntary slavery, Plat. Symp., p. 184 c, &c. &c.; see Lexx., and Aug., Ep. 149 [59, cited above on ver. 17], says 'sic et vulgo dicitur qui divitem affectat thelodives, et qui sapientem thelosapiens, et cætera hujusmodi.' Mey. cites Epiphan. Hær. xvi. p. 34, explaining the name Pharisees, *διὰ τὸ ἀφωρισμένους εἶναι αὐτοὺς ἀπὸ τῶν ἄλλων διὰ τὴν ἐθελοπερισσοθρησκείαν παρ' αὐτῶν νενομισμένην.* See many more examples in Wetst. The *θρ.* was mainly that of *angels*, see above, ver. 18: but the generality of the expression here may take in other voluntary extravagancies of worship also) **and humility** (see ver. 18) **and unsparingness of the body** (Plato defines *ἐλευθερία, ἀφειδία ἐν χρήσει κ. ἐν κτήσει οὐσίας*, Def. p. 412 D: Thuc. ii. 43 has *ἀφειδεῖν βίου*: Diod. Sic. xiii. 60, *ἀφειδῶς ἐχρῶντο τοῖς ἰδίοις σώμασιν εἰς τὴν κοινὴν σωτηρίαν*, &c. &c., see Wetst.), **not in any honour of it** (on the interpretations, see below. **τιμή** is used by St. Paul of honour or respect bestowed on the body, in 1 Cor. xii. 23, 24: of honourable conduct in matters relating to the body, 1 Thess. iv. 4 [see note there: cf. also Rom. i. 24]: and such is the meaning I would assign to it here—these *δόγματα* have the repute of wisdom for (in) &c., and for (in) unsparingness of the body, not in any real honour done to it—its true honour being, dedication to the Lord, 1 Cor. vi. 13),—**to the satiating of the flesh?** I connect these words not with the preceding clause, but with *δογματίζεσθε* above—'*why are ye suffering yourselves* [see on the passive above] *to be thus dogmatized* [in the strain *μὴ ἅψῃ* &c. according to &c., which are &c.], *and all for the satisfaction of the flesh*'—for the following out of a *διδασκαλία*, the ground of which is the *φυσιοῦσθαι ὑπὸ τοῦ νοὸς τῆς σαρκός*, ver. 18? Then after this follow most naturally the exhortations of the next chapter; they are not to seek the *πλησμονὴ τῆς σαρκός*—not *τὰ ἐπὶ τῆς γῆς φρονεῖν*, but *νεκρῶσαι τὰ μέλη τὰ ἐπὶ τῆς γῆς*. The ordinary interpretation of this difficult passage has been, as E. V. '*not in any honour to the satisfying of the flesh,*' meaning thereby, that such commands do not provide for the honour which we owe to the body in the supply of the proper refreshment to the flesh. But two great objections lie against this, and are in my judgment fatal to the interpretation in every shape: 1) that *ἡ σάρξ* cannot be used in this indifferent sense as equivalent to *τὸ σῶμα*, in a sentence where it occurs together with *τὸ σῶμα*, and where it has before occurred in an ethical sense: 2) that *πλησμονή* will not bear this meaning of mere ordinary supplying, 'satisfying the wants of:' but must imply satiety, 'satisfying to repletion.' The children of Israel were to eat the quails *εἰς πλησμονήν*, Ex. xvi. 8: cf. also Deut. xxxiii. 23: Lam. v. 6; Hab. ii. 16: also *διὰ τὰς ἀλόγους οἰνοφλυγίας κ. πλησμονάς*, Polyb. ii. 19. 4. Meyer renders—'*these commands have a repute for wisdom, &c.,—not for any thing which is really honourable* (i.e. which may prove that repute to be grounded in truth), *but in order thereby to the satiation of men's sensual nature:*' and so, nearly, Ellicott. The objections to this are, 1) the strained meaning of *τιμή τις*,—2) the insertion of '*but*' before *πρός*, or as in Ellic. '*only*' after it, both which are wholly gratuitous. This same latter objection applies to the rendering of Beza, al., 'nec tamen ullius sunt pretii, *quum* ad ea spectant quibus farcitur caro,'—besides that this latter paraphrase is unwarranted. See other renderings still

III. [1] Εἰ οὖν [h] συνηγέρθητε τῷ χριστῷ, [i] τὰ ἄνω [h] Eph ii 6 reff ch ii 12
[k] ζητεῖτε, οὗ ὁ χριστός ἐστιν [l] ἐν δεξιᾷ τοῦ θεοῦ καθήμενος· [i] Gal iv 26. Phil iii 14
2 [i] τὰ ἄνω [m] φρονεῖτε, μὴ τὰ [n] ἐπὶ τῆς γῆς. [3] ἀπεθάνετε [k] = Matt vi 33 1 Pet iii 11, from Ps xxxiii 14. 1 Macc ii 20
γάρ, καὶ ἡ ζωὴ ὑμῶν [o] κέκρυπται σὺν τῷ χριστῷ [p] ἐν

l = Eph i 20 reff m = Phil ii 2 reff n see Phil iii 19. o = Rev ii 17 Ps xxvi 5
p = Luke iv 26, 27 Acts ii 29 Num xxiii 21

CHAP III 1. for τω, εν ℵ[1] txt ℵ corr[1] for ου, που F.
2 for 1st τα, ἃ F. om της a 67[2].
3. om 1st τω D. for $\overline{\chi s}$, $\overline{\theta s}$ (but corrd) ℵ[1]. om εστιν ℵ[1] 120. txt ℵ corr[1] εστιν bef ο χρ. 116. om 2nd τω KL d e l n o 67[2].

further off the point in Mey and De W Among these I fear must be reckoned that of Conyb., 'are of no value to check (?) the indulgence of fleshly passions,' and that of Bähr and Eadie, regarding λόγον—τινι as participial, and joining ἐστιν with πρός—a harshness of construction wholly unexampled and improbable. The interpretation above given seems to me, after long consideration, the simplest, and most in accord with the context It is no objection to it that the antithesis presented by οὐκ ἐν τιμῇ τινι is thus not to ἐν ἐθελοθρ. κ τ λ., but merely to ἀφειδίᾳ σώματος for if the Apostle wished to bring out a negative antithesis to these last words only, he hardly could do so without repeating the preposition, the sense of which is carried on to ἀφειδίᾳ

CHAP. III 1—IV. 6] SECOND PART OF THE EPISTLE *Direct exhortations to the duties of the Christian life—founded on their union with their risen Saviour*

1—4] *Transition to the new subject, and grounding of the coming exhortations.* 1] **If then** (as above asserted, ch. ii. 12, 20 the εἰ implies no doubt of the fact, but lays it down as ground for an inference, see ch. ii. 20, and cf. Xen. Mem i 5 1) **ye were raised up together with Christ** (not as E. V. '*are risen*' the allusion, as above, ch ii. 12—13, is to a definite time, your baptism. And it is important to keep this in view, that we may not make the mistake so commonly made, of interpreting συνηγέρθητε in an *ethical* sense, and thereby stultifying the sentence—for if the participation were an ethical one, what need to exhort them to its ethical realization? The participation is an objective one, brought about by that faith which was the condition of their baptismal admission into Him This faith the Apostle exhorts them to energize in the ethical realization of this resurrection state), **seek the things above** (heavenly, spiritual things cf Matt. vi. 33, Gal. iv. 26, Phil. iii 20) **where Christ is** ('se trouve,' not merely the copula. If you are united to Him, you will be tending to Him, and He is in heaven),—**seated on the right hand of God** (see Eph i. 20. Here, as every where, when the present state of Christ is spoken of, the Ascension is taken for granted) **care for the things above** (φρονεῖτε, wider than ζητεῖτε, extending to the whole region of their thought and desire), **not the things on the earth** (cf. οἱ τὰ ἐπίγεια φρονοῦντες, Phil iii. 19 i e. matters belonging to this present mortal state—earthly pleasure, pelf, and pride. There is no reason, with Thl., Calv., Schrad., Huther, to suppose him still aiming at the false teachers, and meaning by τὰ ἐπὶ τῆς γῆς, τὰ περὶ βρωμάτων κ ἡμερῶν [Thl.] in this part of the Epistle he has dropped the controversial and taken the purely ethical tone). **For ye died** (ch. ii 12. '*are dead*,' though allowable, is not so good, as merely asserting a state, whereas the other recalls the fact of that state having been entered on. That being made partakers with Christ's death, cut you loose from the τὰ ἐπὶ τῆς γῆς: see Rom. vi 4—7), **and your life** (that resurrection life [which is "your real and true life" as Ellic., objecting to this explanation. The only real life of the Christian is his resurrection life in and with Christ. The fact is, Ellic. has mistaken my meaning in this term see my remarks on it below], which you now have only in its first fruits, in possession indeed, but not in *full* possession, see below, and cf Rom viii. 19—23) **is hidden** (οὔπω ἐφανερώθη, 1 John iii 2· is laid up, to be manifested hereafter that such is the sense, the next verse seems plainly to shew) **with Christ** (who is also Himself hidden at present from us, who wait for His ἀποκάλυψις [1 Cor. i 7 2 Thess i. 7 1 Pet i 7, 13; iv 13], which shall be also ours, see ver 4, and Rom. viii 19) **in God** (with Christ who is εἰς τὸν κόλπον τοῦ Πατρός —it is in Him, as in a great depth, that all things concealed are hidden, and He

τῷ θεῷ. 4 ὅταν ὁ χριστὸς [q] φανερωθῇ, ἡ [r] ζωὴ ἡμῶν,
τότε καὶ ὑμεῖς σὺν αὐτῷ [q] φανερωθήσεσθε [s] ἐν δόξῃ.
5 [t] Νεκρώσατε οὖν τὰ [u] μέλη τὰ [n] ἐπὶ τῆς γῆς, [v] πορ-
νείαν, [wx] ἀκαθαρσίαν, [y] πάθος, [z] ἐπιθυμίαν κακήν, καὶ τὴν

ABCDF KLℵ a b c d e f g h k l m n o 17

q = 1 John ii 28 iii 2 (ch i 26 reff) r so ἐλπίς, ch i 27 s = 1 Tim iii 16 reff t Rom iv 19 Heb xi 12 only † u Rom vi 13 vii 5 al Exod xxix 17 v Matt v 32 al fr Gen xxxviii 24 w Rom i 24 Gal v 19 al Prov vi 16 x Eph iv 19 y Rom i 26 1 Thess iv 5 only † Job xxi 4 Symm — Xen Mem iii 10 8 z Rom i 24 2 Pet ii 18 al. ἐπ κακ, Prov xxi 26.

4. for ημων, υμων (*see note*) CD[1]Fℵ k 17 latt goth gr-lat-ff: txt BD[2] [3]KL rel syrr copt Orig Dial Œc Hil[1] Ambr. (A uncert.) om συν αυτω A 57 Nyssen. ins aft φανερ 73 118 vulg

5 rec aft τα μελη ins υμων, with AC[3]DFKLℵ[3] rel latt syrr copt goth Clem[1] Damasc[1] Iren-int Cypr Hil om BC[1]ℵ[1] 17. 67[2] Clem[1] Orig[5] Eus Damasc-comm(appy) Sing-cler aft πορνειαν ins και D sah, αποθεμενοι syr arm Jer.

brings them out as seems good to Him Notice the solemnity of the repetition of the articles · and so all through these verses) **When Christ shall be manifested** (shall emerge from his present state of hiddenness, and be personally revealed), **who is our** (no emphasis—ἡμῶν applies to Christians generally—see on ὑμ. below) **life** (not as Eadie, 'shall appear in the character of our life' [ὅτ χρ ἡ ζωὴ ἡμ φανερωθῇ] Christ IS personally Himself that life, and we possess it only by union with Him and His resurrection see John xiv. 19), **then shall ye also** (καί takes out the special from the general—ye, as well as, and among, other Christians with the reading ἡ ζ ὑμῶν, the καί would mean, 'as well as Christ') **with Him be manifested in glory** (see on the whole, the parallel 1 John iii. 2. Though the *completed life of the resurrection* seems so plainly pointed out by this last verse as the sense to be given to ἡ ζωή, this has not been seen by many Commentators, who hold it to be *ethical*, hidden, inasmuch as inward and spiritual —ἐν τῷ κρυπτῷ, Rom. ii 29 [De W], and ideal or, inasmuch as it is unseen by the world [Beng, similarly Storr, Flatt, Bisping, al]. The root of the mistake has been the want of a sufficiently comprehensive view of that resurrection life of ours which is now hidden with Christ It includes in itself both spiritual, ethical, and corporeal. and the realization of it as far as possible, here, is the sum of the Christian's most earnest endeavours but the life itself, in its full manifestation, is that perfection of body, soul, and spirit, in which we shall be manifested with Him at His appearing. Cf. Thdrt. ἐκείνου γὰρ ἀναστάντος πάντες ἠγέρθημεν· ἀλλ' οὐδέπω ὁρῶμεν τῶν πραγμάτων τὴν ἔκβασιν. κέκρυπται δὲ ἐν αὐτῷ τῆς ἡμετέρας ἀναστάσεως τὸ μυστήριον)

5—17.] *General exhortations* and herein (5—11)—*to laying aside of the vices of the old man*,—(12—17) *to realizing the new life in its practical details* **Put to death therefore** (the οὖν connects with the ἀπεθάνετε of ver. 3 follow out, realize this state of death to things on earth—νεκρώσατε—notice the aorist implying a definite act —cf. ἐσταύρωσαν Gal. v. 24, θανατοῦτε Rom viii 13, in the same reference) **your members which are on the earth** (literally, as to τὰ μέλη · your feet, hands, &c reduce these to a state of death as regards their actions and desires below specified—as regards, in other words, their denizenship of this earth With this you have no concern—they are members of Christ, partakers of His resurrection, renewed after His image. The metaphorical sense of μέλη, regarding πορν &c, as 'membra quibus vetus homo, i e. ratio ac voluntas hominis depravata perinde utitur ac corpus membris' Beza, —'naturam nostram quasi massam ex diversis vitiis conflatam imaginatur.' Calv, —seems unnecessary. And the understanding of φρονοῦντα with τὰ ἐπὶ τῆς γῆς, as Grot., after Thdrt. [τουτέστι τὴν ἐπὶ τὰ χεῖρω τοῦ φρονήματος ῥοπήν], is certainly a mistake. cf. τὰ ἐπὶ τῆς γῆς above, ver. 2),—**fornication** (these which follow, are the carnal functions of the earthly members It is one instance of that form of the double accusative, where the first denotes the whole, the second a part of it, as τὸν δ' ἄορι πλῆξ' αὐχένα, λῦσε δὲ γυῖα, Il. λ 240,—ποῖόν σε ἔπος φύγεν ἕρκος ὀδόντων; Od. α. 64. See Kuhner, ii p 230), **impurity** (reff.), **lustfulness** (see Rom. i. 26, whence it would appear that the *absolute* word need not be understood of *unnatural* lust, the specifying genitive ἀτιμίας giving it there that meaning. We may understand it generally as in Plat Phædr. p. 265 b, τὸ ἐρωτικὸν πάθος, — 'morbum libidinis,' Beng), **shameful desire** (more general than πάθος as Mey remarks, π. is

[xa] πλεονεξίαν. [b] ἥτις ἐστὶν [c] εἰδωλολατρεία, 6 δι' ὃ ἔρχεται
ἡ [d] ὀργὴ τοῦ [d] θεοῦ. 7 [e] ἐν οἷς καὶ ὑμεῖς [e] περιεπατήσατέ
ποτε, ὅτε [f] ἐζῆτε [f] ἐν τούτοις· 8 νυνὶ δὲ [g] ἀπόθεσθε καὶ
ὑμεῖς τὰ πάντα, [hi] ὀργὴν [hi] θυμὸν [hk] κακίαν, [hl] βλασφημίαν
[m] αἰσχρολογίαν ἐκ τοῦ στόματος ὑμῶν, 9 μὴ [n] ψεύδεσθε

a Mark vii 22 Luke xii 15 Paul, Rom i 29 al⁴ 2 Pet ii 3, 14 only Ps cxviii 36 Ezek xxii 27
b = ch ii 23 reff
c 1 Cor x 14 Gal v 20 1 Pet iv 3 only† (-τρης, Eph v 5)
d John iii 36 Rom i 18 Eph v 6 Rev xix 15 Ps lxxvii 36
e = Rom vi 4 2 Cor iv 2 Eph ii. 2, 10 v 2 ch iv 5 al freq Eccl xi 9
f = Rom vi 2 ch ii 20 (of *things*)
g Eph iv 22 reff
h Eph iv 31
i Eph as above (h). Rom ii 8
k Eph as above Rom i 29 Tit iii 3
l Matt xii 31 1 Tim vi 4 al Ezek xxxv 12
m here only†
n w εις, here only Susan 55 only w dat, Acts v 4

6 rec for ὅ, ἅ (*see Eph* v 6), with ABC²D²·³KLℵ rel vulg(with F-lat) syrr coptt goth Clem₂ Iren-int Cypr *quod aut quæ* G-lat · txt C¹(appy) D¹F æth om ἡ C¹F. rec aft θεου ins επι τους υιους της απειθειας (*from Eph* v 6, *where* none *omit it*), with AC(D)FKLℵ rel Clem₁(mss vary) : om B (D has it written, contrary to its custom, at the end of the line which should finish with θεου) sah æth Clem₁ or ₂ Iren-int Ambrst-txt

7. rec (for τουτοις) αυτοις, with D³FKL rel syrr Chr Thdrt *illis* latt txt ABCD¹ℵ 17 coptt goth.

8. om και υμεις ℵ¹ : ins ℵ-corr¹ for τα π, κατα παντα F · *universum aut secundum omnia* G-lat : *omnem* spec Jer Vig · om æth (Clem). at end ins μη εκπορευεσθω F sah æth Vig Ambrst

always ἐπιθ, but not vice versa. The relation is the same as between πορνεία and ἀκαθαρσία), **and covetousness** (τὴν πλ as Beng.—'articulus facit ad epitasin, et totum genus vitii a genere enumeratarum modo specierum diversum complectitur' On **πλεονεξία**, see on Eph. iv 19, and Trench, N. T. Synonyms, § xxiv), **for it is** ('quippe quæ sit') **idolatry** (the πλεονέκτης has set up self in his heart —and to serve self, whether by accumulation of goods or by satiety in pleasure, is his object in life. He is therefore an idolater, in the deepest and worst, namely in the practical significance. τὸ μαμωνᾶ, κύριον ὁ Σωτὴρ προσηγόρευσε, διδάσκων ὡς ὁ τῷ πάθει τῆς πλεονεξίας δουλεύων, ὡς θεὸν τὸν πλοῦτον τιμᾷ, Thdrt.), **on which account** (on account of the πλεονεξία, which amounts to idolatry, the all-comprehending and crowning sin, which is a negation of God and brings down His especial anger) **cometh** (down on earth, in present and visible examples) **the wrath of God. in which** (vices. Mey's remark that the reading δι' ὅ makes this ἐν οἷς necessarily refer to the ἐπὶ τοὺς υἱοῖς τ ἀπειθ which he reads after θεοῦ, does not apply if δι' ὅ be interpreted as above to refer to πλεονεξία. There does not seem to occur in St Paul any instance of ἐν, after περιπατεῖν absolute, referring to persons Cf 2 Thess iii 11 [περιπ ἀτάκτως], John xi. 54, Eph. ii. 3, which last, if the clause ἐπ. τ. υἱ. τ. ἀπ were inserted here, would certainly go far to decide the matter) **ye also walked once, when ye lived** (before your death with Christ to the world) **in these things** (the assertion is not tautological. cf. Gal. v 25, εἰ ζῶμεν πνεύματι, πνεύματι καὶ στοιχῶμεν. When ye were alive to these things, ye regulated your course by them, walked in them "Vivere et ambulare inter se differunt, quemadmodum potentia et actus vivere præcedit, ambulare sequitur" Calv) 8.] **but now** (that ye are no longer *living* in them · opposed to ποτὲ ὅτε above) **do ye also** (as well as other believers) **put away the whole** (τὰ πάντα seems to have a backward and a forward reference—'the whole,—both those things which I have enumerated, and those which are to follow' The mistake of rendering ἀπόθεσθε, '*have put off*,' which one would hardly look for in a Commentator, occurs in Eadie here—cf. Eph iv. 22),—**anger, wrath** (see on Eph iv 31), **malice** (ib), **evil speaking** (ib), **abusive conversation** (the context makes this more probable here, than '*filthy conversation*' [so E. V ; Clem. Alex, περὶ αἰσχρολογίας, Pæd ii 6, p. 198 P., he however himself uses αἰσχρολογεῖν for to abuse in words, Pæd iii. 11, p 296 P : Chrys, who calls it ὄχημα πορνείας], for these four regard want of charity, of kindness in thought and word, rather than sins of uncleanness, which were before enumerated. And the occasional usage of the word itself bears this out, cf Plat. Rep iii. p 395 end, κακηγοροῦντάς τε καὶ κωμῳδοῦντας ἀλλήλους κ αἰσχρολογοῦντας Polyb viii 13. 8, ἡ κατὰ τῶν φίλων αἰσχρολογία) **out of your mouth** (these words most naturally belong to the two last specified sins, and must be constructed either with ἀπόθεσθε, which seems best,

εἰς ἀλλήλους, ᵒ ἀπεκδυσάμενοι τὸν ᵖ παλαιὸν ᵖ ἄνθρωπον
σὺν ταῖς ᑫ πράξεσιν αὐτοῦ, 10 καὶ ʳ ἐνδυσάμενοι τὸν ˢ νέον
τὸν ᵗ ἀνακαινούμενον εἰς ᵘ ἐπίγνωσιν ᵛ κατ' ʷ εἰκόνα τοῦ
ˣ κτίσαντος αὐτόν, 11 ὅπου οὐκ ʸ ἔνι Ἕλλην καὶ Ἰουδαῖος,
ᶻ περιτομὴ καὶ ᶻ ἀκροβυστία, ᵃ Βάρβαρος, Σκύθης, ᵇ δοῦλος, ᵇ ἐλεύθερος, ἀλλὰ τὰ ᶜ πάντα καὶ ᶜ ἐν πᾶσιν χριστός.

ABCDF KLℵ a b c d e f g h k l m n o 17

o ch ii 15 only † (-δυσις, ch ii 11) p Rom vi 6 Eph iv 22 q = Matt xvi 27 Luke xxiii 51 Rom viii 13 2 Chron xii 15 r = Eph iv 24 reff s = 1 Cor v 7 t 2 Cor iv 16 only † (-νωσις, Tit iii 5 -νίζειν, Ps cii 5) u = Eph i 17 reff v Gal iv 28 reff w ch i 15 reff x Eph ii 10 reff y Gal iii 28 reff z Gal v 6 reff a Acts xxviii 2, 4 Rom i 14 1 Cor xiv 11 bis only Ezek xxi 31 b Eph vi 8 al c = 1 Cor (xii 6) xv 28 see Herod iii 157 Polyb v 26 5

10 επενδυσαμενοι ℵ[1].

11. aft ενι add αρσεν και θηλυ (*see Gal* iii 28) D[1]F vulg-sixt(with hal F-lat) lat-ff aft βαρβαρος ins και D[1]F latt Syr æth Petr-alex Jer lat-ff aft δουλος ins και AD[1]F latt lat-ff om BCD[3]KLℵ rel syr Clem. om τα ACℵ[1] 17 Clem Petr-alex Naz Cyr Œc-txt: ins BDFKLℵ[3] rel Chr Thdrt Damasc.

or with 'proceeding,' implied in *αἰσχρολογίαν*),—**lie not towards** (*εἰς* the indifferent general preposition of direction: so *κατά* with *ψεύδομαι* in a hostile sense, James iii. 14. Plat Euthyd p 284 a, *οὐδὲν κατά σου ψεύδεται*. We have *πρὸς ἐκεῖνον ψευσάμενον*, Xen Anab i. 3. 5) **one another,—having put off** (the participles contain the motive for all the preceding, from *ἀπόθεσθε*—so Thdrt [*τοῦτον ἀπεκδύσασθε ἐν τῷ βαπτίσματι*], Calv. [*postquam exuistis*], Mey., al. Vulg. [*exuentes*], Luth., Calov., Beng., Olsh., De W., Conyb., al., understand them as contemporary with *ἀπόθεσθε*, — *putting off*, -οι, *and put off*. But surely this is very flat, and besides would, if it is to answer to the foregoing, contain a superfluous member, the *ἐνδυσάμ. κ τ λ.* there being no exhortation to graces in the former sentence, only dehortation from vices. Besides, as Mey remarks, the objective description in ver. 11 belongs to an assignment of motive, not to a hortative sentence: and the hortative figure begins ver 12) **the old man** (i e as Mey, 'die vorchristliche Individualität;' the nature which they had before their conversion: see on reff.) **with his deeds** (habits, ways of acting: see reff., and cf Demosth 126. 21, *ἔπραττον ὅπως ἡ πόλις ληφθήσεται, καὶ κατεσκευάζοντο τὴν πρᾶξιν*), **and having put on the new** (the other was the negative ground: this is the positive. See on Eph iv 23, and ii. 15), **who** (the two are personal: not 'which,'—except in its old personal sense) **is continually being renewed** (notice the present participle. "The new man is not any thing ready at once and complete, but ever in a state of development [by the Holy Spirit, Tit iii 5], by which a *new* state and nature is brought about in it, specifically different from that of the old man." Mey.) **towards perfect knowledge** (which excludes all falsehood, and indeed all the vices mentioned above) **according to the image of Him that created him** (the new creation of the spirit unto fulness of knowledge and truth, the highest form of which would be the perfect knowledge of God, is regarded by the Apostle as analogous to man's first creation. As he was then made in the image of God, so now: but it was then his naturally, now spiritually in *ἐπίγνωσις*. Some join **κατ' εἰκ** with *ἀνακαιν.*, some with *ἐπίγνωσ.* The sense will be the same, but grammatically it is far better to join it with *ἀνακαιν.* Thus the norm and method of the renewal is, *κατ' εἰκ. τ. κτίσαντος αὐτόν* [the new man],—i e God, who is ever the Creator, not as Chrys, al., Christ. To understand the whole passage as referring to a restoration of the image of God in the first creation, as Calov, Est, and De W, is to fall far short of the glorious truth. It is not to restore the old, but to create the new, that redemption has been brought about. Whatever may have been God's image in which the first Adam was created, it is certain that the image of God, in which Christ's Spirit re-creates us, will be as much more glorious than that, as the second man is more glorious than the first) **where** (viz in the realm or sphere of the new man) **there is not** (on *ἔνι* see Gal iii 28) **Greek and Jew** (difference of nation, with special allusion also to the antiquation of the Abrahamic privilege as regarded his natural seed), **circumcision and uncircumcision** (difference of legal ceremonial standing),—**barbarian** (having as yet specified by pairs, he now brings forward a few single categories, which in the new man were non-existent as marks of distinction, see below. The proper *contrast* to **Βάρβαρος** would

12 [c] Ἐνδύσασθε οὖν, ὡς [d] ἐκλεκτοὶ τοῦ [d] θεοῦ ἅγιοι καὶ d Rom viii 33 Tit i 1 gen, Rom i 6, 7
ἠγαπημένοι, [e] σπλάγχνα [f] οἰκτιρμοῦ, [g] χρηστότητα, [h] τα- e = Phil i 8 reff
πεινοφροσύνην, [gh] πραΰτητα, [gh] μακροθυμίαν, 13 [i] ἀνεχόμενοι f Phil ii 1 reff g Gal v 22, 23 reff
ἀλλήλων καὶ [kl] χαριζόμενοι [m] ἑαυτοῖς ἐάν τις [n] πρός τινα h Eph iv 2 reff
ἔχῃ [o] μομφήν· καθὼς καὶ ὁ κύριος [k] ἐχαρίσατο ὑμῖν, i = Luke ix 41 2 Cor xi 1, &c
οὕτως καὶ ὑμεῖς· 14 [p] ἐπὶ πᾶσιν δὲ τούτοις τὴν ἀγάπην, Eph iv 2. Isa xlvi 4

k = ch ii 13 reff l Eph iv 32 m = 1 Cor vi 7 ver 16 al n = Acts xxiv 19 xxv 19 1 Cor vi 1 o here only † p Luke iii 20. xvi 26. 2 Chron xxix 10

12 ωσει D¹F om του bef θεου AD¹F c ins BCD³KLℵ rel. om και B 17 lect-17 sah Did. ins ACDFKLℵ rel rec οικτιρμων, with K b c Orig-ms Thdrt: και οικτιρμον D¹ txt ABCD² ³FLℵ rel Clem Orig Bas Chr Damasc. rec πραοτητα, with DFKL rel · txt ABCℵ 17 Antch Max.

13 εχει FL c f k 17 Thl for μομφην, μεμψιν D¹ οργην F. rec (for κυριος) χριστος (*the practice of interpreting the indefinite* κυριος *was so common, that* χριστος *was far more probably substd, esp as it occurs in Eph* iv. 32), with CD² ³KLℵ-corr¹(?)³ rel syr coptt goth Clem₂ Chr Thdrt Damasc Ambrst θεος ℵ¹ 17, simly arm Aug₁ txt ABD¹F latt Aug₁ Pelag. ημιν D¹K a k n 17 Clem Thdrt (so ℵ¹, but corrd). at end ins ποιειτε D¹F sah æth Ambrst.

have been Ἕλλην, which has been already expressed), **Scythian** (the citations in Wetst sufficiently shew, that the Σκύθαι were esteemed, as Beng, 'barbaris barbariores' It is remarkable that in one of those citations, from Polyb, they are classed with the *Galatians*, εἰρήνης οὔσης παρεσπόνδησαν, Σκυθῶν ἔργον κ Γαλατῶν ἐπιτελοῦντες), **bond, free** (he perhaps does not say '*bond and free*,' because these relations actually subsisted but the persons in them were not thus regarded in Christ—no man is, *quoad a Christian*, δοῦλος, nor [see also Gal. iii 28] ἐλεύθερος) **but** CHRIST (emphatically closes the sentence) **is all** (every distinctive category of humanity is done away as to worth or privilege, and all have been absorbed into and centre in this one, χριστοῦ εἶναι, yea χριστὸς εἶναι—His members, in vital union with Him) **and in all** (equally sprinkled on, living in, working through and by every class of mankind) 12] **Put on therefore** (as a consequence of having put on the new man, to whom these belong) **as the elect of God** (see reff and 1 Thess i 1), **holy and beloved** (it seems best to take, as Mey, ἐκλεκτοί for the subject, and ἅγ. and ἠγ for predicates,—1) because ἐκλεκτοί is a word which must find its ground independently of us, in the absolute will of God, and therefore cannot be an adjunctive attribute of ἅγιοι [καὶ] ἠγαπ —and 2) because ἐκλεκτοὶ θεοῦ is used in reff. and ἐκλεκτοί in several other places, as a substantive), **bowels of compassion** (see reff, and Luke i 78 The expression is a Hebraism and the account of it to be found in the literal use of σπλάγχνα as the seat of the sympathetic feelings · cf. Gen xliii. 30), **kindness** (see on Gal v. 22), **lowliness** (towards one another—see on Eph. iv 2), **meekness** (Eph. ib. but here it is primarily *towards one another*, not however excluding but rather implying meekness towards God as its ground), **long-suffering** (ib), **forbearing one another** (see ib) **and forgiving each other** (ἑαυτοῖς is not = ἀλλήλοις, as De W., al.. but the mutual forgiveness of the Christian body is put in marked correspondence to that great act of forgiveness which has passed upon the whole body, in Christ 'Forgiving yourselves,' did it not convey to our ears a wrong idea, would be the best rendering doing as a body for yourselves, that which God did once for you all), **if any have cause of blame** (the phrase is a classical one—cf. Eur Orest. 1068, ἓν μὲν πρῶτά σοι μομφὴν ἔχω—Phœn. 781; Soph Aj 180, and other examples in Wetst.) **as also** (καί, besides, and more eminent than, the examples which I am exhorting you to shew of this grace) **the Lord** (Christ in Eph. iv 32, the forgiveness is traced to its source, ὁ θεὸς ἐν χριστῷ Mey. compares the expression ἡ χάρις τοῦ κυρίου ἡμῶν) **forgave** (see on Eph. iv. 32) **you, so also ye** (scil. χαριζόμενοι—do not supply an imperative, by which the construction is unnecessarily broken Chrys carries this χαρίζεσθαι to an exaggerated extent, when he says that it extends not only to τὴν ψυχὴν ὑπὲρ αὐτῶν θεῖναι—τὸ γὰρ 'καθὼς' ταῦτα ἀπαιτεῖ—καὶ οὐδὲ μέχρι θανάτου μόνον στῆναι δεῖ, ἀλλ' εἰ δυνατὸν καὶ μετὰ ταῦτα, thinking perhaps on Rom ix 3)

14] **but** (the contrast lies between

q constr., Mark xii 42 xv 42 Eph v 5
r ch ii 19 reff
s Heb vi 1 only Judg ix 16, 19

ᵠὅ ἐστιν ʳσύνδεσμος τῆς ˢτελειότητος· 15 καὶ ἡ ᵗεἰρήνη ABCDF KLℵ a b
τοῦ χριστοῦ ᵘβραβευέτω ἐν ταῖς καρδίαις ὑμῶν, εἰς ἣν c d e f g h k l m
καὶ ᵛἐκλήθητε ʷἐν ἑνὶ σώματι· καὶ ˣεὐχάριστοι γίνεσθε. n o 17

t = John xiv 27 Phil iv 7 u here only Wisd x 12 = Polyb ii 25 3 al. fr (-εῖον, Phil iii 14) v = Gal i 6 reff w = 1 Cor vii 15. Eph ii 16 x here only Prov xi 16 only = Xen Cyr viii 3. 49

14. rec (for ὅ) ητις (*grammatical emendation*), with D³KLℵ³ rel txt ABCF 17(*sic*) latt Clem₂ Ambrst, ος D¹ℵ¹ for τελει., ενοτητος D¹F Ambrst.

15 om ἡ F rec (for χριστου) θεου (*cf Phil* iv. 7), with C²D³KLℵ³ rel goth Chr Ambrst. txt ABC¹D¹Fℵ¹ m 17 latt syrr coptt æth arm Clem₂ Damasc Aug Pelag om ενι B 67² sah (om εν ενι σ. 33-5). γενεσθε D¹

ταῦτα πάντα, which have been individually mentioned, and ἐπὶ πᾶσι τούτοις, that which must over-lie them as a whole) over (carrying on the image ἐνδύσασθε—see below Calvin's '*propter* omnia hæc' is every way wrong:—'in addition to,' as Eadie, al, falls short of the fitness and beauty of the passage, weakening what is really the literal sense into a metaphorical one. The E V, '*above all these things*,' looks ambiguous, but by repeating '*put on*,' it seems as if our translators meant '*above*' to be taken locally and literally) **all these things** (put on) **love** (the article gives a fine and delicate sense here, which we cannot express—ἡ ἀγάπη is not merely love, but 'the [well-known] love which becomes Christians:' the nearest rendering would perhaps be '*Christian love*,' but it expresses too much), **which thing** (reff. · there is a slight causal force,—'for it is') **is the bond of perfectness** (the idea of an upper garment, or perhaps of a girdle, as Calov. supposed, seems to have been before the Apostle's mind This completes and keeps together all the rest, which, without it, are but the scattered elements of completeness: πάντα ἐκεῖνά, φησιν, αὕτη συσφίγγει παροῦσα· ἀπούσης δὲ διαλύονται κ. ἐλέγχονται ὑπόκρισις ὄντα κ. οὐδέν, Thl. Wetst cites from Simplic. in Epictet, p 208, καλῶς οἱ Πυθαγόρειοι περισσῶς τῶν ἄλλων ἀρετῶν τὴν φιλίαν ἐτίμων, κ. σύνδεσμον αὐτὴν πασῶν τῶν ἀρετῶν ἔλεγον The genitive after σύνδεσμος is not the genitive of apposition, as in Eph. iv 3, but of that which is held together by the σύνδεσμος, as in Plat. Rep x. p. 616 c, εἶναι γὰρ τοῦτο τὸ φῶς ξύνδεσμον τοῦ οὐρανοῦ, οἷον τὰ ὑποζώματα τῶν τριήρων, οὕτω πᾶσαν ξυνέχον τὴν περιφοράν. Those who, as some of the Roman Catholic expositors (not Bisping), find here justification by works, must be very hard put to discover support for that doctrine The whole passage proceeds upon the ground of previous justification by faith see ch. ii. 12, and our ver 12, ὡς ἐκλ. τ. θ. Some render σύνδεσμος 'the sum total,' or inclusive idea, 'Inbegriff' so Bengel, Usteri, De W, Olsh, al · and it appears to bear this sense in Herodian iv. 12 11, πάντα τὸν σύνδεσμον τῶν ἐπιστολῶν,—but not in the N T.; and besides, the sense would be logically inconsistent with ἐπὶ πᾶσιν τούτοις, implying that Love does not include, but covers and supplements all the former. Still worse is the wretched adjectival rendering of τῆς τελ as = τέλειος, 'the perfect band,' as Grot., Erasm-par, Est, al): **and** (simply an additional exhortation, not an inference, 'and so,' as Beng.; compare Eph. iv. 3, where peace *is* the σύνδεσμος. It is exceedingly interesting to observe the same word occurring in the same trains of thought in the two Epistles, but frequently with different application See the Prolegg. to this Epistle, § iv 7) **let Christ's peace** (the peace which He brings about, which He left as his legacy to us [ref. John], which is emphatically and solely His This peace, though its immediate and lower reference here is to mutual concord, yet must not on account of the context be limited to that lower side Its reference is evidently wider, as βραβευέτω shews. see below. It is the whole of Christ's Peace in all its blessed character and effects) **rule** (sit umpire—be enthroned as decider of every thing. Cf. Demosth. 3. 6, 7, ἐξὸν ἡμῖν κ. τὰ ἡμέτερ' αὐτῶν ἀσφαλῶς ἔχειν κ. τὰ τῶν ἄλλων δίκαια βραβεύειν. ib. 1231. 19, τοῦτον τὸν τρόπον ὑμῶν ταῦτα βραβευόντων and in the later sense of simply to *rule*, Polyb. ii. 25. 3, ἅπαν τὸ γιγνόμενον ὑπὸ τῶν Γαλατῶν θυμῷ μᾶλλον ἢ λογισμῷ βραβεύεται, al, in Schweigh. Lex. Polyb, also in Jos and Philo It is forcing the passage, to introduce the idea of a combat and a prize, as Chrys, &c.. and philologically wrong to render, as Calv., '*palmam ferat*,' explaining it '*superior sit omnibus carnis affectibus*' As much beside the purpose is Grot.'s 'dijudicet, nempe si quid est inter nos controversum.' similarly Kypke and

16 ὁ [y] λόγος τοῦ χριστοῦ [z] ἐνοικείτω ἐν ὑμῖν [a] πλουσίως,
[b] ἐν πάσῃ σοφίᾳ [c] διδάσκοντες καὶ [d] νουθετοῦντες [e] ἑαυτοὺς

y — 1 Cor i 5. z Rom viii 11. 2 Cor vi 16. 2 Tim i 5, 14 only. Lev xxvi 12. a 1 Tim vi. 17. Tit iii 6. 2 Pet i 11 only † b Eph i 8. ch i 9, 28. c constr, ch ii 2 reff. d ch i 28 reff. P. e — ver 13.

16. for χριστου, θεου AC[1] k o 17 sah Thdrt Thl-marg · κυριου (*from above*) ℵ[1] copt

Hammond ['componat omnia vestra cum aliis dissidia'] against this is ἐν ταῖς καρδίαις ὑμῶν, which makes the office of the *peace* spoken of not *adjudicare*, but *prævenire lites*) **in your hearts,—to which** (with a view to which, as your blessed state of Christian perfection in God—see Isa xxvi 3, lvii. 19: Eph ii. 14—17) **ye were also** (the καί marks the introduction of an additional motive—'to which, besides my exhortation, ye have this motive: that,' &c) **called** (reff.) **in one body** (as members of one body—oneness of body being the sphere and element in which that peace of Christ was to be carried on and realized. This reminiscence refers to the whole context from ver 8, in which the exhortations had been to mutual Christian graces διὰ τί γὰρ ἄλλο ἐσμὲν ἓν σῶμα, ἢ ἵνα ὡς μέλη ὄντες ἀλλήλων ταύτην τηρῶμεν, κ μὴ διϊστώμεθα: Thl.). **and be thankful** (to God, who called you: so the context before and after certainly demands: not 'one to another,' as Conyb., which though an allowable sense of εὐχάριστος, breaks the connexion here, which is as Chrys. on ver. 16—παραινέσας εὐχαρίστους εἶναι, καὶ τὴν ὁδὸν δείκνυσι The ἐκλήθητε was the word which introduced the exhortation—all conduct inconsistent with the '*calling in one body*' being in fact unthankfulness to God, who called us Jer, Erasm.-not., Calv., al, render it '*amiable*,' '*friendly*,' against which the same objection lies. See Eph. v. 4; and ib. 19, 20 where the same class of exhortations occurs) **16.**] See the connexion in Chrys above This thankfulness to God will shew itself in the rich indwelling in you and outflowing from you of the word of Christ, be it in mutual edifying converse, or in actual songs of praise **Let Christ's word** (the Gospel. genitive subjective, the word which is His—He spoke it, inspired it, and gives it power) **dwell in you** (not 'among you,' as Luther, De W., al which does not suit ἐνοικ. As Ellic. observes, St. Paul's usage [reff, remembering that ref. 2 Cor is a quotation] seems to require that the indwelling should be individual and personal Still we may say with Mey that the ὑμεῖς need not be *restricted* to individual Christians it may well mean the whole community—you, as a church The word dwelling in them richly, many would arise to speak it to edification, and many would be moved to the utterance of praise. And to this collective sense of ὑμῖν, ἑαυτούς below seems to correspond, see above on ver 13) **richly** (i e in abundance and fulness, so as to lead to the following results), **in all wisdom** (these words seem to be better taken with the following than with the foregoing. For 1) ch. i. 28 already gives us νουθ. . . κ. διδ. . ἐν πάσῃ σοφίᾳ 2) ἐνοικείτω has already its qualifying adverb πλουσίως emphatically placed at the end of the sentence 3) The two following clauses will thus correspond—ἐν πάσῃ σοφίᾳ διδάσκοντες . . . ἐν τῇ χάριτι ᾄδοντες. And so Beng., Olsh, De W, Mey, al. the usual arrangement has been with E V., all [not Chrys], to join them with the preceding) **teaching and warning** (see on ch i 28) **each other** (see on ver. 13) **in psalms, hymns, spiritual songs** (on the meaning of the words, see notes, Eph. v. 19 The arrangement here adopted may be thus vindicated ψ ὕμν. ᾠδ. πν. must be joined with the preceding, not with the following, because 1) the instrumental dative is much more naturally taken after διδ κ νουθ ἑαυτ, from the analogy of Eph v 19, λαλοῦντες ἑαυτοῖς ψ. κ. ὕμν. κ. ᾠδ [πν], ᾄδοντες κ τ.λ. 2) ᾄδοντες here has already two qualifying clauses, one before and one after, ἐν τῇ χάριτι and ἐν ταῖς καρδίαις ὑμῶν · Meyer's note here is important "Notice moreover that Paul here also [see on Eph. ut supra] is not speaking of 'divine service' properly so called, for this teaching and admonishing is required of his *readers generally* and mutually, and as a proof of their *rich* possession of the word of Christ:—but of the communication of the religious life among one another (e g at meals, at the Agapæ, and other meetings, in their family circles, &c.), wherein spiritual influence caused the mouth to overflow with the fulness of the heart, and gave utterance to brotherly instruction and reproof in the higher form of psalms, &c, perhaps in songs already known,—or extemporized, according to the peculiarity and productivity of each man's spiritual gift perhaps sung by individuals alone [which would especially be the case when they

[f] ψαλμοῖς [f] ὕμνοις [f] ᾠδαῖς [g] πνευματικαῖς, [h] ἐν τῇ [h] χάριτι
[f] ᾄδοντες ἐν ταῖς [f] καρδίαις ὑμῶν τῷ θεῷ. 17 καὶ [i] πᾶν [i] ὅ
τι ἂν ποιῆτε ἐν [k] λόγῳ ἢ ἐν [k] ἔργῳ, πάντα [l] ἐν ὀνόματι
κυρίου Ἰησοῦ [m] εὐχαριστοῦντες τῷ [nn] θεῷ [n] πατρὶ δι'
αὐτοῦ.

ABCDF KLℵ a b c d e f g h k l m n o 17

f Eph. v. 19 reff. g Rom. i. 11 [Eph., as above] al[10]. Paul only, exc. 1 Pet. ii. 5 bis †. h ch. iv. 6. ἡ χάρ., absol., = Acts xviii. 27. 2 Cor. iv. 15. Gal. v. 4. Eph. iv. 7. ch. iv. 18 (reff.). i Matt. vii. 24. x. 32. Acts iii. 23. k Rom. xv. 18. 2 Cor. x. 11. 1 John iii. 18. l = John xiv. 13.—ellips., 2 Cor. viii. 15, from Exod. xvi. 18. Winer, § 64. 4. m Rom. i. 8. xiv. 6 bis. Eph. v. 20 al. fr. (Judith viii. 25.) n Gal. i. 3. Eph. vi. 23.

Clem: txt BC[2]DFKLℵ[3] rel latt syr goth gr-lat-ff. rec, aft ψαλμοις ins και (*cf Eph* v. 19), with C[2]D[2.3]KL rel demid Syr coptt: om ABC[1]D[1]Fℵ lat syr goth Clem Chr$_2$ Pelag. rec aft υμνοις ins και (*cf Eph* v. 19), with AC[3]D[2.3]KL rel vulg-ed(with fuld-vict) Syr copt Chr: om BC[1]D[1]Fℵ 17 am(with demid tol) syr goth Clem. rec om τη bef χαριτι, with A(C)D[3]KLℵ[1] Chr Damasc: ins BD[1]Fℵ[3] 67[2] Clem Chr-comm$_2$ Thdrt. (In C τι of χαριτι is left out and εν χαρι marked as wrong.) rec (for ταις καρδιαις) τη καρδια (*from Eph* v. 19), with D[3]KL rel Clem Thdrt Damasc Thl Œc: txt ABCD[1]Fℵ b[1] m 67[2] vss Chr lat-ff. rec (for θεω) κυριω (*from Eph* v. 19), with D[3]KL rel demid Thdrt Ambrst-ms Pelag: χω or κω C[2]: txt ABC[1]D[1]Fℵ 17. 67[2] Clem Chr$_{\text{aliq}}$ Œc Ambrst-ed Paulin.

17. om και D[1]F latt goth lat-ff. εαν BFL o: om sah: txt ACDKℵ rel. ποιειτε K[2]L sah. for κυρ. ιησ., ιησ. χριστου ACD[1]F: κυριου L: κυρ. ιησ. χρ. ℵ[1]: του κυρ. ι. χρ. ℵ[3]: txt BD[3]K rel am syr goth Thdrt Damasc Ambrst. (*In the probability of the alteration of our whole passage from Eph* v. 19, 20 [*where there are hardly any varns*], *txt is most likely to have been original.*) rec ins και bef πατρι (*Eph* v. 20), with DFKL rel latt syr (Clem): txt ABCℵ Syr coptt goth æth Ambr Paulin.

were extemporized], or in chorus, or in the form of antiphonal song [Plin. Ep. x. 97]." How common religious singing was in the ancient church, independently of 'divine service' properly so called, see in Suicer, Thes. ii. p. 1568 f. Euseb., H. E. ii. 17, v. 28, testifies to the existence of a collection of rhythmical songs which were composed ἀπαρχῆς by Christians [ψαλμοὶ δὲ ὅσοι κ. ᾠδαί, ἀδελφῶν ἀπαρχῆς ὑπὸ πιστῶν γραφεῖσαι, τὸν λόγον τοῦ θεοῦ τὸν χριστὸν ὑμνοῦσι θεολογοῦντες, v. 28]. On singing at the Agapæ, see Tert. Apol. 39, vol. i. p. 477: "post aquam manualem et lumina, ut quisque de scripturis sanctis vel proprio ingenio potest, provocatur in medium Deo canere"); **in grace** (*the* grace—of Christ [see reff. for the absolute use of ἡ χάρις]—ἀπὸ τῆς χάριτος τοῦ πνεύματός φησιν ᾄδοντες, Chrys.: so Œc., διὰ τῆς παρὰ τοῦ ἁγίου πνεύματος δοθείσης χάριτος: not as Erasm., Luth., Melancth., Calv. ['pro dexteritate quæ grata sit'], and indeed Chrys. [altern.: ταῖς ἐν χάριτι ᾠδαῖς], Beza, Corn.-a-lap., al., '*gracefully*,'—which would be irrelevant as applied to the singing of the heart: see below—nor as Anselm, and De W., Conyb., al., '*thankfully*,' which would be a flat and unmeaning anticipation of εὐχαριστοῦντες below. The article marks 'the grace,' which is yours by God's indwelling Spirit) **singing in your hearts to God** (this clause has generally been understood as qualifying the former. But such a view is manifestly wrong. That former spoke of their teaching and warning one another in effusions of the spirit which took the form of psalms, &c.: in other words, dealt with their intercourse *with one another*; this on the other hand deals with their own private intercourse *with God*. The second participle is coordinate with the former, not subordinate to it. The mistake has partly arisen from imagining that the former clause related to public worship, in its external form: and then this one was understood to enforce the genuine heartfelt expression of the same. But this not being so, that which is founded on it falls with it. The singing **τῷ θεῷ** is an analogous expression to that in 1 Cor. xiv. 28,—ἐὰν δὲ μὴ ᾖ διερμηνευτής, . . . ἑαυτῷ . . . λαλείτω κ. τῷ θεῷ. So the ἐν ταῖς καρδ. ὑμ. describes the method of uttering this praise, viz. by the thoughts only: τῷ θεῷ designates to whom it is to be addressed,—not, as before, to one another, but to God):

17.] *general exhortation*, comprehending all the preceding spiritual ones. **And every thing whatsoever ye do in word or work** (so far is a 'nominativus pendens'), **all things** (do) **in the name of the Lord Jesus** (not as Chrys., Œc., Thl., &c., τουτέστιν αὐτὸν καλῶν βοηθόν, nor as Thdrt., who treats it as a dehortation from the worship of angels, which they were to exclude by their always τὰ ἔργα κοσμῆσαι τῇ μνήμῃ τοῦ δεσπότου χρισ-

18 Αἱ γυναῖκες, [o]ὑποτάσσεσθε τοῖς ἀνδράσιν, ὡς [p]ἀνῆκεν
[q]ἐν κυρίῳ. 19 οἱ ἄνδρες, ἀγαπᾶτε τὰς γυναῖκας καὶ μὴ
[r]πικραίνεσθε πρὸς αὐτάς. 20 τὰ τέκνα, [s]ὑπακούετε τοῖς
γονεῦσιν κατὰ πάντα· τοῦτο γὰρ [t]εὐάρεστόν ἐστιν [q]ἐν
κυρίῳ. 21 οἱ πατέρες, μὴ [u]ἐρεθίζετε τὰ τέκνα ὑμῶν, ἵνα

o Eph v 22 reff. p Eph v 4 Philem 8 only † 1 Macc xi 35 al. q Eph iv 17 1 Thess iv 1 al fr Paul only. r Rev viii 11 x 9, 10 only — Exod xvi 20 Job xxvii 2 vat. s Matt viii 27 Eph vi 1 al. t Eph v 10 reff. u 2 Cor ix 2 only Deut xxi 20. Prov xix 7

18. om αι F rec ins ιδιοις bef ανδρασιν (*from Eph* v. 22), with D²L rel Thdrt om ABCD¹ ³FKℵ c d¹ e k 17 vulg arm Clem Thl Ambrst Pelag. aft ανδρ ins υμων D¹F syr-w-ast Thl Pelag ins τω bef κυριω F.

19 aft γυναικας ins υμων C²D¹F latt Syr syr-w-ob copt æth arm lat-ff pref εαυτων ℵ³: om ABC¹D³KLℵ¹ rel Clem. παραπικραιν C²K 113-4 Thl-marg

20 rec εστιν bef ευαρεστον (*after Eph* vi 1), with FKL rel Chr Thdrt Damasc txt ABCDℵ m 17 latt rec (for εν) τω, with rel spec syr copt Clem. txt ABCDFKLℵ b e f g l m n 17 67² latt goth Chr Thdrt Damasc.

21. for ερεθιζετε, παροργιζετε (*from Eph* vi. 4) ACD¹FLℵ m 17 Thdrt-ms Thl: txt BD²·³K rel Clem

τοῦ:—but much as the common ἐν χριστῷ—so that the name of Christ is the element in which all is done—which furnishes a motive and gives a character to the whole) **giving thanks to God the Father** (where ἡμῶν is not expressed, the words **θεὸς πατήρ** must be taken as approximating in sense to that more technical meaning which they now bear, without exclusive reference to either our Lord or ourselves,—and should be rendered '*God the Father*') **through Him** (as the one channel of all communication between God and ourselves, whether of grace coming to us, or of thanks coming from us Cf His own saying οὐδεὶς ἔρχεται πρὸς τὸν πατέρα εἰ μὴ δι' ἐμοῦ).

18—IV 1.] SPECIAL EXHORTATIONS TO RELATIVE SOCIAL DUTIES. 18, 19, *to the married* 20, 21, *to children and parents*. 22—IV 1, *to slaves and masters*. Seeing that such exhortations occur in Ephesians also in terms so very similar, we are not justified, with Chrys, al, in assuming that there was any thing in the peculiar circumstances of the Colossian church, which required more than common exhortation of this kind It has been said, that it is only in Epistles addressed to the Asiatic churches, that such exhortations are found but in this remark the entirely general character of the Epistle to the Ephesians is forgotten Besides, the exhortations of the Epistle to Titus cannot be so completely severed from these as to be set down in another category, as Eadie has endeavoured to do. See throughout the section, for such matters as are not remarked on, the notes to Eph. v 22—vi 9 **18 ὡς ἀνῆκεν**] The verb is in the imperfect—as ἔδει and χρῆν, conveying always in its form a slight degree of blame, as implying the non-realization of the duty pointed out—just as when we say, 'It was your duty to,' &c See Winer, § 41 3, end. The words **ἐν κυρίῳ** belong to ἀνῆκεν, not to ὑποτάσσεσθε, as is shewn by the parallel expression in ver. 20 was fitting, in that element of life designated by ἐν κυρίῳ. **19**] See the glorious expansion of this in Eph v 25—33 **πικραίνεσθαι** occurs in the same sense in Demosth 1464 18 also in Plat. Legg p 731 d, —τὸν θυμὸν πραΰνειν κ μὴ ἀκραχολοῦντα, γυναικείως πικραινόμενον, διατελεῖν. Kypke illustrates the word from Plutarch, de ira cohibenda, p 457, 'ubi dicit, animi prodere imbecillitatem quum viri πρὸς γύναια διαπικραίνονται:' and from Eurip. Helen. 303. ἀλλ' ὅταν πόσις πικρὸς | ξυνῇ γυναικί, κ τὸ δῶμ' ἐστι (lege σώζεσθαι) πικρόν, θανεῖν κράτιστον **20**] See Eph vi. 1. **κατὰ πάντα**, the exceptions not being taken into account· St Paul's usual way of stating a general rule It is best to take **εὐάρεστον**, as Mey. absolutely, as προσφιλῆ, Phil. iv. 8. the Christian qualification being given by the ἐν κυρίῳ· De W, al., understand τῷ θεῷ, which would render that qualification meaningless. **21**] See on Eph vi 1, for **πατέρες**. **μὴ ἐρεθ.**] do not irritate them—τοῦτό ἐστι, μὴ φιλονεικοτέρους αὐτοὺς ποιεῖτε ἔστιν ὅπου καὶ συγχωρεῖν ὀφείλετε, Chrys In ἵνα μὴ ἀθ., it is assumed that the result of such irritation will be to cause repeated punishment, and so eventual desperation, on the part of the child It would be well if all who have to educate children took to heart Bengel's remark

μὴ [v] ἀθυμῶσιν. 22 οἱ δοῦλοι, [s] ὑπακούετε κατὰ πάντα
τοῖς [w] κατὰ σάρκα κυρίοις, μὴ ἐν [x] ὀφθαλμοδουλείαις ὡς
[y] ἀνθρωπάρεσκοι, ἀλλ᾽ ἐν [z] ἁπλότητι καρδίας φοβούμενοι
τὸν κύριον. 23 ὃ ἐὰν ποιῆτε, [a] ἐκ ψυχῆς [b] ἐργάζεσθε
ὡς τῷ [c] κυρίῳ καὶ οὐκ [c] ἀνθρώποις, 24 εἰδότες ὅτι ἀπὸ
κυρίου [d] ἀπολήμψεσθε τὴν [e] ἀνταπόδοσιν τῆς [f] κληρονομίας.
τῷ κυρίῳ χριστῷ [g] δουλεύετε. 25 ὁ γὰρ [h] ἀδικῶν [i] κομιεῖται

ABCDF KLℵ a b c d e f g h k l m n o 17

v here only. 1 Kings xv. 11. 2 Kings vi. 8.
w κατ., = Rom. ix. 11. xi. 21. κ. σ., Eph. vi. 5 reff.
x Eph. vi. 6 only †.
y Eph. vi. 6 only. Ps. lii. 5 only.
z Eph. vi. 5 al[6]. P. 1 Chron. xxix. 17.
a Eph. vi. 7 (reff.) only. b 1 Cor. xvi. 10. Gal. vi. 10 al. Exod. xxxv. 9. c dat., Rom. vi. 10 al.
d = Gal. iv. 5 reff. e here only. Isa. xxxiv. 8. (-δομα, Rom. xi. 9.) f = Eph. i. 14 reff. gen. appos., Rom. iv. 11. ch. i. 18. g = Matt. vi. 24 ‖ L. Acts xx. 19. 1 Thess. i. 9. Ps. ii. 11. h = Rev. xxii. 11. Ps. cv. 6. i = 2 Cor. v. 10. Eph. vi. 8 al. Ps. xxxix. 15.

22. ins ως bef 1st εν C[1]. οφθαλμοδουλειᾳ (*the sing occurs in the similar passage Eph* vi. 5) ABDF Damasc Thl: -λειαι k: κατ᾽ -ειαν (*as Eph* vi. 5) Chr(txt and comm$_1$): txt CKLℵ rel Clem Chr-comm$_1$ Thdrt Œc.—for -λει, -λι- CDF b[2] c e f l n 17. αλλα B. rec (for κυριον) θεον, with D[3]Kℵ[3] rel D-lat copt goth Thdrt: txt ABCD[1]FLℵ[1] 17 am(with [besides F-lat] harl) syrr arm Clem Ambrst.

23. rec (for ο εαν) και παν ο τι εαν (*from ver* 17), with D[2·3]KL rel (αν a d[1] f m) Syr gr-lat-ff; παν οτι εαν 67[1]: παν ο αν 67[2]: παν ο εαν ℵ[3]: txt ABCD[1]Fℵ[1] 17 latt copt goth Thl-ms lat-ff. aft κυριω ins δουλευοντες A o 8-pe (copt) Clem. om και B.

24. for απολ., ληψεσθε AC[?]Lℵ[3] a b[1] c f g h k m (n ?) Chr Thdrt.—(λημψ. A c ?) aft κληρονομιας ins υμων C[2] m 80. 116 arm Chr-comm Thdrt. rec aft τω ins γαρ, with D[3]KL rel syrr goth Clem: om ABCD[1]ℵ 17 vulg copt Pelag Bede.—του κυριου ημων ιησου χριστου ω δουλευετε F, and, omg ημ. ιησ., D-lat Ambrst.

here; 'ἀθυμία, *fractus animus*, pestis juventutis.' Wetst. quotes from Æneas Tacticus, ὀργῇ δὲ μηθένα μετιέναι τῶν τυχόντων ἀνθρώπων· ἀθυμότεροι γὰρ εἶεν ἄν. **22.**] See on Eph. vi. 5 ff. The **ὀφθαλμοδουλεῖαι** here are the concrete acts of the -εία of Eph. vi. 6, the abstract spirit. **τὸν κύριον,** Him who is absolutely, and not merely κατὰ σάρκα, your master. τοῦτό ἐστι φοβεῖσθαι τὸν θεόν, ὅταν, μηδενὸς ὁρῶντος, μηδὲν πράττωμεν πονηρόν. ἂν δὲ πράττωμεν, οὐχὶ τὸν θεόν, ἀλλὰ τοὺς ἀνθρώπους φοβούμεθα, Chrys. **23.**] **ἐκ ψυχῆς,** as Chrys., μετ᾽ εὐνοίας, μὴ μετὰ δουλικῆς ἀνάγκης, ἀλλὰ μετ᾽ ἐλευθερίας κ. προαιρέσεως. The datives may be taken as of reference, or *commodi*. In Eph. vi. 7 the construction is filled up by δουλεύοντες. Mey. observes against De W., that **οὐκ** is an absolute not a mere relative negative: 'doing things unto men' is to be laid aside altogether, not merely less practised than the other: "as workers to the Lord and non-workers to men," Ellic.
24.] = Eph. vi. 8, but more specific as to the *Christian* reward. **εἰδότες, knowing as ye do . . .** The **ἀπὸ κυρίου** is emphatically prefixed—'that it is from the Lord that you shall . . . . .' **ἀπό,** as Winer, § 47. b, is distinguished from παρά, as indicating not immediate bestowal, but that the Lord is the ultimate source and conferrer of the inheritance—**from the Lord**—not '*at the hands of the Lord*.' You must look to Him, not to men, as the source of all Christian reward. [Eadie, p. 265, has represented Winer as saying the contrary of that which he does say.] **ἀνταπόδοσις** occurs in Thuc. iv. 81, in the sense of a mutual exchange of places taken in war: in Polyb. vi. 5. 3, in that of a compensation, τοῦτο ἱκανὸν ἀνταπόδοσιν ποιήσει ἐκείνου,—and xx. 7. 2, ὥσπερ ἐπιτηδὲς ἀνταπόδοσιν ποιουμένη ἡ τύχη: and hence in that of 'an opposite turn,' xxvii. 2. 4, ἀνταπόδοσιν λαμβάνει τὰ πράγματα,—iv. 43. 5, ἀνταπόδοσιν ποιεῖται ὁ ῥοῦς πρός, &c. Here the sense would appear to be, with a marked reference to their present state of slavery, **the compensation.** **κληρ.,** genitive of apposition (reff.). The very word **κληρονομία** should have kept the Roman Catholic expositors from introducing the merit of good works here.
The last clause, without the γάρ, is best taken imperatively, as a general comprehension of the course of action prescribed in the former part of the verse: **serve ye the Lord Christ.** So Vulg. '*domino Christo servite*.' **25.**] This verse seems best to be taken as addressed to the slaves by way of encouragement to regard Christ as their Master and serve Him—seeing that all their wrongs in this world, if they leave them in His hands, will be in due time righted by Him, the just judge,

ʲ ὃ ἠδίκησεν, καὶ οὐκ ἔστιν ᵏ προσωποληψία. IV. 1 οἱ
κύριοι, τὸ δίκαιον καὶ τὴν ˡ ἰσότητα τοῖς δούλοις ᵐ παρ-
έχεσθε, εἰδότες ὅτι καὶ ὑμεῖς ἔχετε κύριον ἐν οὐρανῷ.
2 Τῇ ⁿᵒ προσευχῇ ᵒᵖ προσκαρτερεῖτε ᑫ γρηγοροῦντες ἐν

j constr, Gal ii 12 al
k Eph vi 9 Rom ii 11 James ii 1 only † see Acts x 34
l 2 Cor viii 13, 14 only Job xxxvi 29 Zech iv 7 only
m mid, Luke vii 4 Acts xix 24
n absol, Matt xxi 22 Luke xxii 45 1 Cor vii 5 Ps iv 1
o Acts i 14. ii 42 vi 4 Rom xii 12
p as above (o) Mark iii 9 Acts ii 46 viii 13 x 7 Rom xiii 6 only Numb xiii 21 only Susan 6 Theod
q Mark xiii 37 1 Cor xvi 13 1 Thess v 6 Jer i 2 1 Macc xii 27

25 rec (for γαρ) δε (*conseq of former*), with D^3KL rel syrr gr-ff txt ABCD^1Fℵ 17 latt copt goth Clem lat-ff κομισεται BD^3KLℵ^3 d m Clem Chr-comm Thdrt Thl, κομισηται k · κομιζεται F. txt ACD^1ℵ rel Damasc (*see on Eph* vi 8). at end add παρα τω θεω F vulg(not am) arm Chr lat-ff.

Chap IV 1 παρεχετε C b^1 f 72 114 Clem Chr_2 Thl-ms rec ουρανοις (*from Eph* vi. 9), with DFKLℵ^3 rel Chr Thdrt txt ABC^2ℵ^1 m 17 Clem Orig Damasc (C^1 illegible)

with whom there is no respect of persons For he that doeth wrong shall receive (see, as on the whole, Eph. vi 8) that which he did wrongfully (the tense is changed because in ἀδικῶν he is speaking of present practice—in ἠδίκησεν, he has transferred the scene to the day of the Lord, and the wrong is one of past time), and there is not respect of persons (= εἴτε δοῦλος εἴτε ἐλεύθερος, Eph. vi 8). At His tribunal, every one, without regard to rank or wealth, shall receive the deeds done in the body. So that in your Christian uprightness and conscientiousness you need not fear that you shall be in the end overborne by the superior power of your masters there is A judge who will defend and right you ἐστὶ δικαιοκρίτης ὃς οὐκ οἶδε δούλου κ δεσπότου διαφοράν, ἀλλὰ δικαίαν εἰσφέρει τὴν ψῆφον, Thdrt. Some, as Thl, Beng, al, suppose the verse spoken *with reference to* the slaves, but οὐκ ἔστιν προσωποληψία is against this, unless we accept Bengel's far-fetched explanation of it: "tenues sæpe putant, sibi propter tenuitatem ipsorum esse parcendum"

Ch IV. 1.] Meyer contends for the strict meaning of '*equality*' for ἰσότητα, and that it never has the signification of '*fairness*' But (see examples in Wetst) the common conjunction of ἴσον κ δίκαιον would naturally lead to assigning to ἴσον the same transferred meaning which 'æquus' has in Latin, and to ἰσότης the same which 'æquitas' has I would render then, equity,—fairness: understanding by that, an extension of τὸ δίκαιον to matters not admitting of the application of strict rules—a large and liberal interpretation of justice in ordinary matters In every place cited by Meyer where the word is used ethically and not materially, this rendering is better than his In Polyb ii 38 8 the case is different it there imports absolute political equality. Erasm, Corn.-a-lap, al., understand *impartiality*, not preferring one above another but this does not seem to be in question here Calv. says 'Non dubito quin Paulus ἰσότητα hic posuerit pro jure analogo aut distributivo. quemadmodum ad Ephesios τὰ αὐτά. Neque enim sic habent domini obnoxios sibi servos, quin vicissim aliquid ipsis debeant quemadmodum jus analogum valere debet inter omnes ordines' Thdrt. ἰσότητα οὐ τὴν ἰσοτιμίαν ἐκάλεσεν, ἀλλὰ τὴν προσήκουσαν ἐπιμέλειαν, ἧς παρὰ τῶν δεσποτῶν ἀπολαύειν χρὴ τοὺς οἰκέτας Chrys.: τί δέ ἐστιν ἰσότης, πάντων ἐν ἀφθονίᾳ καθιστᾶν, κ. μὴ ἐᾶν ἑτέρων δεῖσθαι, ἀλλ' ἀμείβεσθαι αὐτοὺς τῶν πόνων Cf Philem 16 παρέχεσθε] '*supply on your side*' see Kruger, Griechische Sprachlehre, § 52 8, who gives several examples of the dynamic middle in this very verb Ellic well insists on and explains its force, as referring rather to the powers put forth by the subject, whereas the active simply and objectively states the action. εἰδότες] See ch. iii 24. καὶ ὑμεῖς] as well as they as you are masters to them, so the Lord to you.

2—6] Special concluding exhortations and 2—4] *to prayer*; see Rom xii 12 1 Thess v 17

2] γρηγ watching in it, i e not remiss and indolent in your occupation of prayer (τῇ πρ.), but active and watchful, cheerful also, as ἐν εὐχαριστίᾳ, which defines and characterizes the watchfulness ἐπειδὴ γὰρ τὸ καρτερεῖν ἐν ταῖς εὐχαῖς ῥᾳθυμεῖν πολλάκις ποιεῖ, διὰ τοῦτό φησι γρηγοροῦντες, τουτέστι νήφοντες, μὴ ῥεμβόμενοι οἶδε γάρ, οἶδεν ὁ διάβολος ὅσον ἀγαθὸν εὐχή διὸ βαρὺς ἔγκειται οἶδε δὲ καὶ Παῦλος πῶς ἀκηδιῶσι πολλοὶ εὐχόμενοι. διό φησι γρ ἐν αὐτ ἐν εὐχαρ — τοῦτο γάρ φησιν ἔργον ὑμῶν ἔστω, ἐν ταῖς εὐχαῖς

r ch. ii. 7. εὐχ., Eph. v. 4 reff. s ch. i. 3. t Phil. i. 9 reff. u Acts xiv. 27. 1 Cor. xvi. 9. 2 Cor. ii. 12. Isa. xlv. 1. v inf. of object, ch. i. 22. w Eph. i. 9 reff. x = 2 Cor. xi. 6. ch. i. 26. y Eph. vi. 20. z = Acts vi. 3.

αὐτῇ [r] ἐν [r] εὐχαριστίᾳ, 3 [st] προσευχόμενοι ἅμα καὶ [s] περὶ
ἡμῶν, [t] ἵνα ὁ θεὸς [u] ἀνοίξῃ ἡμῖν [u] θύραν τοῦ λόγου [v] λαλῆσαι τὸ [w] μυστήριον τοῦ χριστοῦ, δι᾽ ὃ καὶ δέδεμαι, 4 ἵνα
[x] φανερώσω αὐτὸ [y] ὡς δεῖ με λαλῆσαι. 5 Ἐν [z] σοφίᾳ
[a] περιπατεῖτε πρὸς [b] τοὺς ἔξω, τὸν καιρὸν [c] ἐξαγοραζόμενοι. 6 ὁ [d] λόγος ὑμῶν πάντοτε [de] ἐν [e] χάριτι [f] ἅλατι

ABCDF KLℵ a b c d e f g h k l m n o 17

a ch. iii. 7 reff. b (Acts xxvi. 11.) = 1 Cor. v. 12. 1 Thess. iv. 12. Mark iv. 11. (Sir. prol.) c Gal. iii. 13. iv. 5. Eph. v. 16 only. Dan. ii. 8 only. d 1 Cor. ii. 4. e ch. iii. 16. f Matt. v. 13 bis. Mark ix. 50 bis (ἅλς, ib. 49, 50). Luke xiv. 34 bis only. Lev. ii. 13.

2. om εν αυτη ℵ[1] : ins ℵ-corr[1]. om εν ευχαριστια D[1] Cypr Ambrst.
3. for αμα, ινα ℵ[1](but corrd) : αρα m. om του bef λογου D[1]F. aft λογου ins εν παρρησια A. for χριστου, θεου B[1] 4. 41. 238 æth. for ὅ, ὅν BF : txt ACDKLℵ rel vulg(and F-lat) Clem Cyr.
4. aft ινα ins και D[1].

εὐχαριστεῖν, κ. ὑπὲρ τῶν φανερῶν κ. ὑπ. τῶν ἀφανῶν, κ. ὑπὲρ ὧν ἑκόντας, κ. ὑπὲρ ὧν ἄκοντας ἐποίησεν εὖ, κ. ὑπὲρ βασιλείας, κ. ὑπὲρ γεέννης, κ. ὑπὲρ θλίψεως, κ. ὑπὲρ ἀνέσεως. οὕτω γὰρ ἔθος τοῖς ἁγίοις εὔχεσθαι, κ. ὑπὲρ τῶν κοινῶν εὐεργεσιῶν εὐχαριστεῖν. Chrys. **3.] ἡμῶν,** not '*me*,'—see ch. i. 1, 3. This is plainly shewn here by the singular following after. **ἵνα]** see on 1 Cor. xiv. 13. Here, the idea of final result is prominent: but the purport is also included. **θύραν τ. λόγου]** Not as Calv., al., *oris apertionem*, Eph. vi. 19; but as in reff., objective, an opening of opportunity for the extension of the Gospel by the word. This would, seeing that the Apostle was a prisoner, naturally be given first and most chiefly, as far as he was concerned, by his liberation: cf. Philem. 22. **λαλῆσαι]** inf. of purpose—**so that we may speak. δι᾽ ὃ κ. δ.]** **for** (on account of) **which** (mystery) **I am** (not only a minister but) **also bound.**

4.] The second **ἵνα** gives the purpose of the previous verse, not the purpose of δέδεμαι, as Chrys. [τὰ δεσμὰ φανεροῖ αὐτόν, οὐ συσκιάζει], Bengel ['vinctus sum ut patefaciam: paradoxon'],—nor to be joined with προσευχόμενοι, as Beza, De W., al. If that might be so, the door opened, &c.,—then he would make it known as he ought to do—then he would be fulfilling the requirements of that apostolic calling, from which now in his imprisonment he was laid aside. Certainly this is the meaning,—and not, as ordinarily understood, cf. Chrys., al., that he might boldly declare the Gospel *in his imprisonment*. **5, 6.]** *Exhortations as to their behaviour in the world.*

5. ἐν σοφίᾳ] in (as an element) **wisdom** (the practical wisdom of Christian prudence and sound sense). **πρός,** as in οὐδὲν πρὸς Διόνυσον,—εἴ του δέοιτο πρὸς Τιμόθεον πρᾶξαι, Demosth. p. 1185, signifying simply **in relation to,** in the intercourse of life. Ellic. refers to a good discussion of this preposition in Rost and Palm's Lex. vol. ii. p. 1157. On **οἱ ἔξω,** see reff. They are those outside the Christian brotherhood. πρὸς τὰ μέλη τὰ οἰκεῖα οὐ τοσαύτης ἡμῖν δεῖ ἀσφαλείας, ὅσης πρὸς τοὺς ἔξω· ἔνθα γὰρ ἀδελφοί, εἰσὶ κ. συγγνῶμαι πολλαὶ κ. ἀγάπαι. Chrys. **τ. καιρ. ἐξαγορ.]** see on Eph. v. 16. The opportunity *for what*, will be understood in each case from the circumstances, and our acknowledged Christian position as watching for the cause of the Lord. The thought in Eph., ὅτι αἱ ἡμέραι πονηραί εἰσι, lies in the background of the word ἐξαγοραζόμενοι.

6.] Let your speech (πρὸς τοὺς ἔξω still) **be always in** (as its characteristic element) **grace** (i. e. gracious, and winning favour: cf. Luke iv. 22), **seasoned with salt** (not insipid and void of point, which can do no man any good: we must not forget that both these words have their spiritual meaning: χάρις, so common an one as to have almost passed out of its ordinary acceptation into that other,—the grace which is conferred on us from above, and which our words and actions should reflect:—and ἅλας, as used by our Saviour in reff. [see note on Mark], as symbolizing the unction, freshness, and vital briskness which characterizes the Spirit's presence and work in a man. So that we must beware here of supposing that mere Attic 'sales' are meant, or any vivacity of outward expression only, and keep in mind the *Christian* import. Of the Commentators, Thdrt. comes the nearest,—πνευματικῇ συνέσει κοσμεῖσθε. There seems to be no allusion here to the conservative power of salt: the matter in hand at present is not avoiding corrupt conversation. Still less does the meaning of *wit* belong to this place. A

[g] ἠρτυμένος, [h] εἰδέναι πῶς δεῖ ὑμᾶς [i] ἑνὶ [i] ἑκάστῳ ἀποκρίνεσθαι.
7 [k] Τὰ κατ' ἐμὲ πάντα [l] γνωρίσει ὑμῖν Τύχικος ὁ
[m] ἀγαπητὸς [m] ἀδελφὸς καὶ [m] πιστὸς [mn] διάκονος καὶ [o] σύνδουλος [np] ἐν κυρίῳ, 8 ὃν ἔπεμψα πρὸς ὑμᾶς εἰς [q] αὐτὸ
τοῦτο, ἵνα γνῷ [r] τὰ περὶ ὑμῶν καὶ [s] παρακαλέσῃ τὰς [s] καρδίας ὑμῶν, 9 σὺν Ὀνησίμῳ τῷ πιστῷ καὶ [m] ἀγαπητῷ
[m] ἀδελφῷ, ὅς ἐστιν [t] ἐξ ὑμῶν· πάντα ὑμῖν [l] γνωριοῦσιν τὰ
[u] ὧδε. 10 Ἀσπάζεται ὑμᾶς Ἀρίσταρχος ὁ [v] συναιχμά-

g Mark ix 50 Luke xiv 34 only Cant viii 2 Symm
h inf Mark vii 4 Acts xi 10 Heb v 5 Rev xvi 9
i Acts xx 31 Eph iv 16 reff
k Acts xxiv 22 xxv 14 Eph vi 21. Phil i 12
l 1 Cor xii 3 xv 1 2 Cor viii 1 Eph i 9 al. 1 Kings xxviii 15
m Eph vi. 21 (reff)
n = ch i 7, 23
o ch i 7 reff.
p Phil i 14
q Acts xxii 15, 20 xxv 25 2 Cor ii 3 vii 11
r Phil i 27 reff
s ch ii 2 (reff)
t ver 12
u Paul, 1 Cor iv 2 only
v Rom xvi 7 Philem 23 only †

6. ημων D[1] υμας bef πως δει B d 108.
7. aft τα ins δε א[1] (א[3] disapproving) om και συνδουλος א[1].
8. for γνω and 1st υμων, γνωτε and ημων (*as in Eph* vi. 22) ABD[1]F m 17 æth Thdrt-txt Jer, txt CD[2,3]KL(א) rel vulg(and F-lat) syrr copt goth Chr Thdrt-comm lat-ff —aft γνω ins τε א[1] om א[3] who also altered υμων to ημων but corrected it again both here and in ver 9. παρακαλεσαι D[1]· -σει L f: παρακαλεση τε 17.
9 αγαπητω και πιστω DF latt goth Chr lat-ff. γνωρισουσιν BFא[3] Damasc, -σωσιν D[1]· γνωριζουσι m txt ACD[3]KLא[1] rel Chr. at end add πραττομενα F latt Jer Pelag Bede.

local allusion is *just possible* Herod vii. 30 says of Xerxes, Ἀναυα δὲ καλεομένην Φρυγῶν πόλιν παραμειβόμενος, καὶ λίμνην ἐκ τῆς ἅλες γίνονται, ἀπίκετο ἐς Κολοσσάς, πόλιν μεγάλην Φρυγίης) **εἰδέναι**] to know—i e so that you may know · see ref., "loosely appended infin, expressive of consequence," as Ellicott. See Winer, edn 6, § 44. 1 Cf. 1 Pet. iii. 15, which however is but one side of that readiness which is here recommended. **7—18**] Close of the Epistle. **7—9**] *Of the bearers of the Epistle, Tychicus and Onesimus.* **7.**] On Tychicus, see Eph. vi 21. **ὁ ἀγ ἀδελφός**, as dear to his heart **πιστ διάκ**, as his tried companion in the ministry,—**σύνδ ἐν κυρίῳ**, as one with him in the motives and objects of his active work ὥστε, as Chrys., αὐτῷ πάντοθεν τὸ ἀξιόπιστον ξυνήγαγεν There is a delicate touch of affection in ἵνα γνῷ τὰ περὶ ὑμ, which can hardly, in the doubtfulness of the reading, be the work of a corrector It implies that there were painful circumstances of trial, to which the subsequent **παρακαλέσῃ** also has reference. δείκνυσιν αὐτοὺς ἐν τοῖς πειρασμοῖς ὄντας, Chrys The objection (Eadie), that thus the **εἰς αὐτὸ τοῦτο** will announce another purpose from that enounced above in τὰ κατ' ἐμὲ π γνωρ, will apply just as much to the other reading;—for any how the αὐτὸ τοῦτο must include the καὶ παρακαλέσῃ κ τ λ But the fact is, that αὐτὸ τοῦτο may apply exclusively to the *following*, without any reference to what has *preceded* see Rom ix 17, the parallel place, Eph. vi 22, Phil. i. 6. **9 σὺν Ὀνησ**] There can hardly be a doubt [compare ver. 17 with Philem 2, 10 ff] that this is the Onesimus of the Epistle to Philemon. When Calv wrote "vix est credibile hunc esse servum illum Philemonis, quia furis et fugitivi nomen dedecori subjectum fuisset," he forgot that this very term, ἀδελφὸς ἀγαπητός, is applied to him, Philem. 16 **ἐξ ὑμῶν**] most probably, a native of your town **πάντ ὑμ. γν τ ὧδε**] A formal restatement of τὰ κατ' ἐμὲ π γν above Is it likely, with this restatement, that the same should be again stated in the middle of the sentence, as would be the case with the reading ἵνα γνῶτε τὰ περὶ ἡμῶν? **10—14.**] *Various greetings from brethren.* **10.**] Aristarchus was a Thessalonian (Acts xx. 4), first mentioned Acts xix. 29, as dragged into the theatre at Ephesus during the tumult, together with Gaius, both being συνέκδημοι Παύλου. He accompanied Paul to Asia (ib xx. 4), and was with him in the voyage to Rome (xxvii. 2) In Philem 24, he sends greeting, with Marcus, Demas, and Lucas, as here. On **συναιχμάλωτος**, Meyer (after Fritzsche, Rom. vol i prolegg p xvi) suggests an idea, which may without any straining of probability be adopted, and which would explain why Aristarchus is here συναιχμ, and in Philem 24, συνεργός, whereas Epaphras is here, ch i. 7, merely a σύνδουλος, and in Philem 23 a συναιχμάλωτος. His view is, that the

λωτός μου, καὶ Μάρκος ὁ [w] ἀνεψιὸς Βαρνάβα, περὶ οὗ
[x] ἐλάβετε [x] ἐντολάς (ἐὰν ἔλθῃ πρὸς ὑμᾶς, [y] δέξασθε αὐτόν),
11 καὶ Ἰησοῦς ὁ λεγόμενος Ἰοῦστος· οἱ ὄντες [z] ἐκ [z] περιτομῆς οὗτοι μόνοι [a] συνεργοὶ [b] εἰς τὴν [c] βασιλείαν τοῦ [c] θεοῦ,
[d] οἵτινες ἐγενήθησάν μοι [e] παρηγορία. 12 ἀσπάζεταί ὑμᾶς

ABCDF KLℵ a b c d e f g h k l m n o 17

w here only. Num. xxxvi. 11. Tobit vii. 2 only. x John x. 18. Acts xvii. 15. 2 John 4 only. y = 2 Cor. vii. 15 al. z Acts x. 45. xi. 2. Rom. iv. 12. Gal. ii. 12. Tit. i. 10 only. a Phil. ii. 25 reff. b = Phil. ii. 22. c Rom. xiv. 17. 1 Cor. iv. 20 al. d = Acts x. 41, 47. xiii. 31, 43 al. e here only †. (-ρεῖν, Job xvi. 2 Symm.)

10. δεξασθαι D[1]F 17 syrr Thl(but mentions txt) Ambrst.
11. aft *συνεργοι* ins *μου εισιν* D[1]F latt arm (Dial$_8$) Ambrst.

Apostle's friends may have voluntarily shared his imprisonment by turns: and that Aristarchus may have been his fellow-prisoner when he wrote this Epistle, Epaphras when he wrote that to Philemon. *συναιχμάλωτος* belongs to the same image of *warfare* as *συνστρατιώτης*, Phil. ii. 25; Philem. 2. **Μάρκος**] can hardly be other than John Mark, cf. Acts xii. 12, 25, who accompanied Paul and Barnabas in part of their first missionary journey, and because he turned back from them at Perga (ib. xiii. 13; xv. 38), was the subject of dispute between them on their second journey. That he was also the Evangelist, is matter of pure tradition, but not therefore to be rejected. **ἀνεψιός**] not '*sister's son:*' this rendering has arisen from mistaking the definition given by Hesych., *ἀνεψιοί, ἀδελφῶν υἱοί*,—meaning that *ἀνεψιοί* are *sons of brothers*, i. e. *cousins*. (Ellic. in notes on his translation of the Epistle, suggests that '*sister's-son*' may after all be no mistake, but an archaism to express, as the German Geschwisterkind, a *cousin*.) "Pollux dicit, filios filiasque fratrum et sororum, dici *ἀνεψιούς*, ex his prognatos *ἀνεψιαδοῦς, ἀνεψιαδᾶς*, — tertio gradu *ἐξανεψιούς, ἐξανεψιάς* a Menandro dici." Lobeck on Phrynichus, p. 306. This is decisively shewn in Herod. vii. 5, **Μαρδόνιος** . . . *ὃς ἦν Ξέρξῃ μὲν ἀνεψιός*, **Δαρείου** *δὲ ἀδελφεῆς παῖς*. It is also used in a wider sense (see Hom. Il. *α*. 464): but there is no need to depart here from the strict meaning. **περὶ οὗ . . .**] What these commands were, must be left in entire uncertainty. They had been sent previous to the writing of our Epistle (*ἐλάβετε*): but from, or by whom, we know not. They concerned Marcus, not Barnabas (as Thl., al.): and one can hardly help connecting them, associated as they are with *ἐὰν ἔλθῃ, δέξασθε αὐτόν*, with the dispute of Acts xv. 38. It is very possible, that in consequence of the rejection of John Mark on that occasion by St. Paul, the Pauline portion of the churches may have looked upon him with suspicion.

11. Ἰησοῦς . . . Ἰοῦστος] Entirely unknown to us. A Justus is mentioned Acts xviii. 7, as an inhabitant of Corinth, and a proselyte: but there is no further reason to identify the two. The surname Justus (צדיק) was common among the Jews: cf. Acts i. 23, and Jos. Vit. 9, 65, 76. **These alone who are of the circumcision** (the construction is of the nature of an anacoluthon, *οἱ ὄντες ἐκ π.* being equivalent to 'of those of the circumcision.' We have a similar construction frequently in the classics: e. g. *ἄμφω δ' ἑζομένω γεραρώτερος ἦεν Ὀδυσσεύς*, Il. *γ*. 211: *ὅρκια πιστὰ ταμόντες ὁ μὲν βασιλευέτω αἰεί*, Od. *ω*. 483. See many more examples in Kühner, ii. § 678. 2. This seems far better, with Meyer and Lachmann, than with rec. Ellic. al. to place the stop at *περιτομῆς* and attach the clause to the three preceding names. For thus we lose [in spite of the assertion by Ellic. that the *μόνοι* naturally refers the thought to the category last mentioned] the fact that there were other *συνεργοί* not of the circumcision who had been a comfort to him. The judaistic teachers were for the most part in opposition to St. Paul: cf. his complaint, Phil. i. 15, 17) **are my fellow-workers towards the kingdom of God** (the rest would not be called by this name—so that De W.'s objection to the construction does not apply, that the opponents would not be called *συνεργοί*; for they *are not* so called), **men that proved** (the passive meaning of *ἐγενήθησαν* is not safely to be pressed: see notes on Eph. iii. 7; 1 Thess. i. 5, 6; 1 Pet. i. 15. The aor. alludes to some event recently passed: to what precisely, we cannot say) **a comfort to me** (they are my *συνεργοί* 'quippe qui . . . .' Hierocles, de nuptiis, apud Stob. [Kypke], has the same phrase: *ἡ γυνὴ δὲ παροῦσα μεγάλη γίνεται κ. πρὸς ταῦτα παρηγορία*: so Plutarch, de auditione, p. 43 [id.], *νόσημα παρηγορίας . . . δεόμενον*). **12.**] On Epaphras, see ch. i. 7 note. The sentence

Ἐπαφρᾶς ὁ [f] ἐξ ὑμῶν [g] δοῦλος [g] χριστοῦ Ἰησοῦ, πάντοτε
[h] ἀγωνιζόμενος ὑπὲρ ὑμῶν ἐν ταῖς προσευχαῖς, ἵνα [ik] στῆτε
τέλειοι καὶ [lm] πεπληροφορημένοι [k] ἐν [n] παντὶ [n] θελήματι τοῦ
θεοῦ. 13 [o] μαρτυρῶ γὰρ αὐτῷ ὅτι ἔχει πολὺν [p] πόνον
ὑπὲρ ὑμῶν καὶ τῶν ἐν Λαοδικείᾳ καὶ τῶν ἐν Ἱεραπόλει.
14 ἀσπάζεται ὑμᾶς Λουκᾶς ὁ [q] ἰατρὸς ὁ ἀγαπητὸς καὶ

f ver 9. g Gal i 10 reff. h ch i 29 reff. i Eph vi 13, 14. k John viii 44. Rom v 2. see 1 Cor xv 1. l Rom xii 2. ch i 28. James i 4. m Luke i 1. Rom iv 21. xiv 5. 2 Tim iv 5, 17 only. Eccles viii 11 only. n see Acts xiii 22. o Acts xxii 5. Rom x 2. Gal iv 15. Gen xxxi 48. p Rev xvi 10, 11. xxi 4 only. Isa lxv 14. q Mark ii 17 || v 26 || Luke iv 23 only. Jer viii 22.

12. rec om ιησου, with DFK syrr goth Chr Thdrt Ambrst: ins ABCLℵ m 17 vulg(not F-lat) copt arm Aug Pelag. for υπερ, περι D¹F. ημων ℵ¹. σταθητε Bℵ¹: ητε c g l² 91 116. 122² Ambrst. rec πεπληρωμενοι (more usual), with D³KL rel: txt ABCD¹Γℵ 17 67². om του bef θεου k 67². for θεου, χριστου D¹ l.

13. rec (for πολυν πονον) ζηλον πολυν (gloss, see note), with KL rel syr, πολυν ζηλον D³ 17. πολυν αγωνα 6 67²: txt ABCℵ copt, πολυν κοπον D¹F, *multum laborem* latt lat-ff.

is better without a comma at **ὑμῶν**, both as giving more spirit to the *δοῦλος χ. Ἰ.*, and setting the *ἐξ ὑμ.* in antithesis to the *ὑπὲρ ὑμῶν* below. On **ἀγων.** besides reff., see Rom. xv 30. By mentioning Epaphras's anxious prayers for them, he works further on their affections, giving them an additional motive for stedfastness, in that one of themselves was thus striving in prayer for them. **ἵνα** here gives the direct aim of **ἀγωνιζ.** See above on ver 3—**that ye may stand,—perfect and fully persuaded** (see reff.),—**in** (be firmly settled in, without danger of vacillating or falling) **all the** (lit. 'in every' but we cannot thus express it in English) **will of God.** This connexion, of **στῆτε** with *ἐν*, as Mey., seems better than, as ordinarily (so also De W. and Ellic.), to join *ἐν* with the participles. Eadie characterizes it as needless refinement in Mey. to assert that thus not only a modal-bestimmung but a local-bestimmung is attached to *στῆτε*: but the use of *στῆναι ἐν* in the reff seems to justify it.

13.] **πόνος,**—an unusual word in the N. T., hence the var. readd.,—is usual in the toil of conflict in war, thus answering to **ἀγωνιζόμ.** above: so Herod. vi 114, *ἐν τούτῳ τῷ πόνῳ ὁ πολέμαρχος Καλλίμαχος διαφθείρεται*: similarly viii 89. Plat. Phædr. 247 b, *ἔνθα δὴ πόνος τε κ. ἀγὼν ἔσχατος ψυχῇ πρόκειται*. Demosth. 687. 18, *εἰ δ' ἐκεῖνος ἀσθενέστερος ἦν τὸν ὑπὲρ τῆς νίκης ἐνεγκεῖν πόνον*. On account of this mention of Laodicea and Hierapolis, some have thought that Epaphras was the founder of the three churches. See Prolegg. § ii 2, 7.

Λαοδικείᾳ] LAODICEA was a city of Phrygia Magna (Strabo xii 8, Plin. v 29: according to the subscription [rec.] of 1 Tim., the chief city of Phrygia Pacatiana), large (*ἡ τῆς χώρας ἀρετὴ κ. τῶν πολιτῶν τινες εὐτυχήσαντες, μεγάλην ἐποιήσαντο αὐτήν*, Strab.) and rich (Rev iii 17, and Prolegg to Rev § iii 13. Tac. Ann. xiv. 27. 'Laodicea, tremore terræ prolapsa, nullo a nobis remedio, propriis opibus revaluit.' *δυνατωτέρα τῶν ἐπὶ θαλάττῃ*, Philostr. Soph. i 25), on the river Lycus (hence called Λ. *ἡ ἐπὶ Λύκῳ* or *πρὸς τῷ Λύκῳ*, see Strabo, ib.), formerly called Diospolis, and afterwards Rhoas, its subsequent name was from Laodice, queen of Antiochus II (Steph. Byz.). In A.D. 62, Laodicea, with Hierapolis and Colossæ, was destroyed by an earthquake (Tacit. l. c.), to which visitations the neighbourhood was very subject (*εἰ γάρ τις ἄλλη κ. ἡ Λαοδίκεια εὔσειστος, κ. τῆς πλησιοχώρου πλέον*, Plin. ib.). There is now on the spot a desolate village called Eski-hissar, with some ancient ruins (Arundel, Seven Churches). Winer, RWB.

Ἱεραπόλει] Six Roman miles north from Laodicea: famed for many mineral springs (Strabo, xiii. 4, describes them at length, also the caverns which exhale noxious vapour. See also Plin. ii 95), which are still flowing (Schubert, i 283). Winer, RWB.

14.] This **Λουκᾶς** has ever been taken for the Evangelist: see Iren. iii 14. 1, p. 201, and Prolegg. to St. Luke, § i. In **ὁ ἰατρὸς ὁ ἀγαπητός** there may be a trace of what has been supposed, that it was in a professional capacity that he first became attached to St. Paul, who evidently laboured under grievous sickness during the earlier part of the journey where Luke first appears in his company. Compare Gal. iv 13 note, with Acts xvi 6, 10. But this is too uncertain to be more than an interesting conjecture.

r Acts ii. 46. v. 42. viii. 3. xx. 20.
s Rom. xvi. 5. 1 Cor. xvi 19. Philem. 2.
t Acts viii. 28. xv. 21. 2 Cor. iii. 15. Exod. xxiv. 7.
u 1 Thess. v. 27.
v = 1 Cor. xvi. 2. Rev. ii. 13.
w = Rom. xvi. 22. 1 Thess. v. 27. 2 Thess. iii. 14. see 1 Cor. v. 9.
x John xi. 37. Rev. xiii. 12, 15, 16. Eccl. iii. 14.
y transposn. w. ἵνα, Gal. ii. 10 reff.

Δημᾶς. 15 ἀσπάσασθε τοὺς ἐν Λαοδικείᾳ ἀδελφοὺς καὶ ABCDF
Νυμφᾶν καὶ τὴν [rs] κατ' οἶκον αὐτῶν [s] ἐκκλησίαν. 16 καὶ KLℵab
ὅταν [tu] ἀναγνωσθῇ [v] παρ' ὑμῖν [uw] ἡ ἐπιστολή, [x] ποιήσατε cdefg
[x] ἵνα καὶ ἐν τῇ Λαοδικέων ἐκκλησίᾳ [t] ἀναγνωσθῇ, καὶ [y] τὴν hklm
ἐκ Λαοδικείας ἵνα καὶ ὑμεῖς [t] ἀναγνῶτε. 17 καὶ εἴπατε no17
Ἀρχίππῳ [z] Βλέπε τὴν [ab] διακονίαν ἣν [c] παρέλαβες [d] ἐν
κυρίῳ, ἵνα αὐτὴν [be] πληροῖς. 18 Ὁ [fg] ἀσπασμὸς [fh] τῇ ἐμῇ
[fh] χειρὶ [f] Παύλου. [i] μνημονεύετέ μου τῶν [k] δεσμῶν. ἡ
[l] χάρις [l] μεθ' ὑμῶν.

ΠΡΟΣ ΚΟΛΑΣΣΑΕΙΣ.

z = w. ἵνα. 1 Cor. xvi. 10. 2 John 8. w. πῶς, 1 Cor. i. 26. Eph. v. 15. a Eph. iv. 12 reff. b Acts xii. 25. see 2 Tim. iv. 5. τὴν διακονίαν ἐκπλήσοντες, Philo in Flacc. § 19, vol. ii. p. 540. c 1 Cor. xi. 23. xv. 1, 3. Gal. i. 9, 12 al. d ch. iii. 18 reff. e = Matt. iii. 15. Acts xiv. 26 al. Ps. xix. 4. f 1 Cor. xvi. 21. 2 Thess. iii. 17. g as above (f). Luke i. 29, 41, 44. xi. 43 ∥. xx. 46 only +. h as above (f). Gal. vi. 11. Philem. 19. i = Gal. ii. 10. k Phil. i. 7 reff. l absol. in valedictions, Eph. vi. 24. 1 Tim. vi. 22. 2 Tim. iv. 22. Tit. iii. 15. Heb. xiii. 25 only. elsw. with τοῦ κυρ., &c. Rom. xvi. 20 [24]. 1 Cor. xvi. 23. 2 Cor. xiii. 13. 1 Thess. v. 28. 2 Thess. iii. 18 al.

15. rec **αὐτοῦ** (*see note*), with DFKL rel Chr Thdrt Damasc: *αυτης* (*reading* Νύμφαν, *as* B² *accentuates, as a woman*) B 67²: txt ACℵ 17.
16. om *η επιστολη* B. om last *και* D¹ o Ambrst: *και* bef *ινα* F.
18. rec at end ins *αμην*, with DKLℵ³ rel vss ff: om ABCFℵ¹ 17. 67² æth-rom Ambrst.

SUBSCRIPTION. rec adds *εγραφη απο ρωμης δια τυχικου και ονησιμου*, with KL rel (of which, b h k m o om *πρ. κολ.*: aft *τυχ.* ins *και τιμοθεου* m): om l: A adds *απο ρωμη*(*sic*): B² adds *εγραφη απο ρωμης*: *η προς κολ.* a: txt B¹C 17 æth, and D(addg *επληρωθη*) F(prefixing *ετελεσθη*) ℵ(adding *στιχων τ*).

Δημᾶς] one of Paul's *συνεργοί*, Philem. 24, who however afterwards deserted him, from love to the world, 2 Tim. iv. 10. The absence of any honourable or endearing mention here may be owing to the commencement of this apostasy, or some unfavourable indication in his character.

15—17.] *Salutations to friends.*
15.] **καί,** before Νυμφᾶν, as so often, selects one out of a number previously mentioned: Nymphas was one of these Laodicean brethren. The var. readings, *αὐτοῦ, αὐτῆς*, appear to have arisen from the construction (see below) not being understood, and the alteration thus having been made to the singular, but in various genders. *αὐτῶν* refers to *τῶν περὶ Νυμφᾶν*: cf. Xen. Mem. i. 2. 62, *ἐάν τις φανερὸς γένηται κλέπτων—τούτοις θάνατός ἐστιν ἡ ζημία*: and see Bernhardy, p. 288; Kühner ii. § 419 b. On the *ἐκκλησία* spoken of, see note, Rom. xvi. 5.

16.] **ἡ ἐπιστ.**, the present letter, reff. **ποιήσ. ἵνα**] as *ποίει, ὅκως* . . . Herod. i. 8. 209,—*ὡς σαφέστατά γᾶν εἰδείην . . . ἐποίουν*, Xen. Cyr. vi. 3. 18. **τὴν ἐκ Λαοδ.**] On this Epistle, see Prolegg. to Eph. § ii. 17, 19; and Philem. § iii. 2, 3. I will only indicate here the right rendering of the words. They cannot well be taken, as *τινές* in Chrys., to mean *οὐχὶ τὴν Π. πρὸς αὐτοὺς ἀπεσταλμένην, ἀλλὰ τὴν παρ' αὐτῶν Παύλῳ* (so also Syr., Thdrt., Phot. in Œc., Erasm., Beza, Calv., Wolf, Est., Corn.-a-Lap., al.), both on account of the awkwardness of the sense commanding them to read an Epistle sent from Laodicea, and not found there, and on account of the phrase **τὴν ἐκ** so commonly having the pregnant meaning of 'which is there and must be sought from there;' cf. Kühner, ii. § 623 a. Herod. iii. 6. Thucyd. ii. 34; iii. 22; vi. 32; vii. 70, and other examples there. We may safely say that a letter not from, but *to* the Laodiceans is meant. For the construction of this latter sentence, *ποιήσατε* again is of course to be supplied.

17.] Archippus is mentioned Philem. 2, and called the Apostle's *συνστρατιώτης*. I have treated on the inference to be drawn from this passage as to his abode, in the Prolegg. to Philemon, § iii. 1. He was evidently some officer of the church, but *what*, in the wideness of *διακονία*, we cannot say: and conjectures are profitless (see such in Est. and Corn.-a-Lap.). Meyer well remarks, that the authority hereby implied on the part of the congregation to exercise reproof and discipline over their teachers is remarkable: and that the hierarchical turn given to the passage by Thl and Œc (*ἵνα ὅταν ἐπιτιμᾷ Ἀρχ. αὐτοῖς, μὴ ἔχωσιν ἐγκαλεῖν ἐκείνῳ ὡς πικρῷ, . . . ἐπεὶ ἄλλως ἄτοπον τοῖς μαθηταῖς περὶ τοῦ διδασκάλου διαλέγεσθαι*, Thl) belongs to a later age. As to the words themselves,—**Take heed to the ministry which thou receivedst in the Lord** (the sphere of the *reception* of the ministry, in which the recipient lived and moved and promised at his ordination not, of the ministry itself [*τὴν ἐν κυρ*],—nor is **ἐν** to be diverted from its simple local meaning), **that** (aim and end of the *βλέπε*,—in order that) **thou fulfil it** (reff)

18.] AUTOGRAPH SALUTATION **ὁ . . . . Παύλου**] See ref 1 Cor, where the same words occur. **μνημ . . . δεσμ.**] These words extend further than to mere pecuniary support, or even mere prayers they were ever to keep before them the fact that one who so deeply cared for them, and loved them, and to whom their perils of false doctrine occasioned such anxiety, was a prisoner in chains and that remembrance was to work and produce its various fruits—of prayer for him, of affectionate remembrance of his wants, of deep regard for his words When we read of 'his chains,' we should not forget that they moved over the paper as he wrote. His *right* hand was chained to the soldier that kept him. See Smith's Dict of Antiq under 'Catena' **ἡ χάρις**—cf reff. and ch. iii. 16 'The grace' in which we stand (Rom. v 2): it seems (reff) to be a form of valediction belonging to the later period of the Epistles of St. Paul.

ΠΡΟΣ ΘΕΣΣΑΛΟΝΙΚΕΙΣ Α.

I. 1 Παῦλος καὶ Σιλουανὸς καὶ Τιμόθεος τῇ ἐκκλησίᾳ Θεσσαλονικέων [a]ἐν [b]θεῷ [ab]πατρὶ καὶ κυρίῳ Ἰησοῦ χριστῷ. [c]χάρις ὑμῖν καὶ [c]εἰρήνη.

a here (2 Thess. i. 1) only.
b Gal. i. 1 reff.
c Rom. i. 7 al.

ABDF KLℵ a b c d e f g h k l m n o 17

TITLE. rec παυλου του αποστολου η προς θεσσ. επιστολη πρωτη: Steph η του αγιου παυλου πρ. θεσσ. πρωτη επ.: του αγ. απ. π. επ. πρ. θ. πρωτη L: αρχεται πρ. θεσσαλονικαιους F: επ. παυλου πρ. θεσσ. πρωτη o: θετταλικοις πολιταις ταδε κηρυξ ουρανοφοιτης f: επιστολη πρ. τ. θεσσ. α' l: πρ. θεσσ. επ. α' h k: txt ABKℵ m[1] n 17, and (prefixing αρχεται) D.

CHAP. I. 1. ins και bef πατρι K syr: add ημων A m 116. 8-pe vulg-sixt basm æth arm-marg Did Ambrst Pelag. και κυριου ιησου χριστου A (d) 17 (copt). rec aft ειρηνη ins απο θεου πατρος ημων και κυριου ιησου χριστου (*from later epistles, e.g.* 1 *Cor* i. 3, 2 *Cor* i. 2, &c), with ADKLℵ rel fuld(with tol) syr-w-ast (copt): om BF vulg fri Syr basm æth-rom arm Chr-comm Thl Orig-int$_{expr}$("... *pax. Et nihil ultra*") Ambrst Pelag. (C defective.)

CHAP. I. 1.] ADDRESS AND GREETING. The Apostle names Silvanus and Timotheus with himself, as having with him founded the church at Thessalonica, see Acts xvi. 1: xvii. 14. Silvanus is placed before Timotheus, then a youth (Acts xvi. 1 f., see further in Prolegg. to 1 Tim. § i. 3, 4), as being one ἡγούμενος ἐν τοῖς ἀδελφοῖς (Acts xv. 22. 32; xviii. 5), and a προφήτης (ib. xv. 32, see also 2 Cor. i. 19; 1 Pet. v. 12). He does not name himself *an Apostle*, probably for (an amplification of) the reason given by De Wette,—because his Apostleship needed not any substantiation to the Thessalonians. For the same reason he omits the designation in the Epistle to the Philippians. This last fact precludes the reasons given,—by Pelt, al., '*id ei tum non jam moris fuisse*,' by Chrys.,—διὰ τὸ νεοκατηχήτους εἶναι τοὺς ἄνδρας, κ. μηδέπω αὐτοῦ πεῖραν εἰληφέναι,—by Estius, Pelt (altern.), and Zwingl., *out of modesty*, not to distinguish himself from Silvanus and Timotheus,—by Jowett, "probably the name 'Apostle,' which in its general sense was used of many, was gradually, and at no definite period, applied to him with the same special meaning as to the Apostles at Jerusalem." **τῇ ἐκκλησίᾳ**] So in 2 Thess., Gal., Corr., in the other Epistles, viz. Rom., Eph., Col., Phil., more generally, e. g.,—πᾶσιν τοῖς οὖσιν ἐν Ῥώμῃ ἀγαπητοῖς θεοῦ, κλητοῖς ἁγίοις. This is most probably accounted for by the circumstances of the various Epistles. We may notice that the gen. plur. of the persons constituting the church occurs only in the addresses of these two Epistles. We may render 'of Thessalonians,' or 'of the Thessalonians:' better the former. **ἐν θεῷ πατρί**] The construction need not be filled up by τῇ or τῇ οὔσῃ, as Chr., al.: nor with Schott, by understanding χαίρειν λέγουσιν, which would be unnecessary, seeing that the apostolic greeting follows. The words form a ("*tertiary*," Ellic.) predication respecting τῇ ἐκκλησίᾳ, or Θεσσαλονικέων, which requires no supplementing. See Winer, edn. 6,

C ευχαριστ ABCDF KLℵ a b c d e f g h k l m n o 17

2 ᵈ Εὐχαριστοῦμεν τῷ ᵈ θεῷ πάντοτε περὶ πάντων ὑμῶν
ᵉ μνείαν [ὑμῶν] ᵉ ποιούμενοι ᵉ ἐπὶ τῶν προσευχῶν ἡμῶν
ᶠ ἀδιαλείπτως, 3 ᵍ μνημονεύοντες ὑμῶν τοῦ ʰ ἔργου τῆς
πίστεως καὶ τοῦ ᵏ κόπου τῆς ˡ ἀγάπης καὶ τῆς ˡ ὑπομονῆς

d Rom i 8. 1 Cor i 4. Col i 3. Phil i 3. Philem 4 (Judith viii 25. 2 Macc i 11). e Eph i 16 reff.
f Rom i 9. ch ii 13. v. 17 only†. 1 Macc xii 11 al. g w. gen, Luke xvii 32. John xvi 4, 21. Acts xx 35 al. 1 Chron xvi 15. h Rom xiii 12. Gal v 19. Eph iv 12. i Heb vi 10. k 1 Cor iii 8. xv 58. Gen xxxi 42. l so Rom ii 7.

2. om 1st υμων C fri: περι π. υμων bef παντοτε a 17. 74. 120. om 2nd υμων (*because* υμων *preceded? See Eph* i. 16 *var readd*) ABℵ[1] 17 67[2] am(with harl[2]). ins CDFKLℵ[3] rel latt coptt syrr gr-lat-ff. (om from μνειαν to end of ver m.) ποιουμενος C[1] d 17, *faciens* D-lat (corrd by C[1], appy) for ημων, υμων A. (so also ch ii 18 for ημας, υμας A[1].)

3. του εργ. της πιστ. bef υμων (*transposn from misunderstandg*) DF latt Syr æth Ambrst (το εργον F, των εργων Syr.) τον κοπον and την υπομονην D[1]F.

§ 20 2. **ἐν θεῷ πατρί** marks them as not being heathens,—**κ. κυρίῳ Ἰησοῦ χριστῷ**, as not being Jews. So De W. after Chrys but perhaps the **πατρί** already marks them as Christians The ἐν, as usual, denotes *communion* and *participation in*, as the element of spiritual life. **χάρις ὑμῖν κ. εἰρήνη**] "Gratia et pax a Deo sit vobis, ut, qui humana gratia et sæculari pace privati estis, apud Deum gratiam et pacem habeatis" Anselm (in Pelt) The words which follow in the rec are not yet added in this his first Epistle Afterwards they became a common formula with him

2—III 13.] First portion of the Epistle, *in which he pours out his heart to the Thessalonians respecting all the circumstances of their reception of and adhesion to the faith* 2—10] Jowett remarks, that few passages are more characteristic of the style of St. Paul than this one. both as being the overflowing of his love in thankfulness for his converts, about whom he can never say too much · and as to the very form and structure of the sentences, which seem to grow under his hand, gaining force in each successive clause by the repetition and expansion of the preceding See this exemplified in detail in his note. 2.] **εὐχαριστοῦμεν**, coming so immediately after the mention of Paul, Silvanus, and Timotheus, can hardly be here understood of the Apostle alone, as Pelt, Conyb and Hows, Jowett, al. For undoubted as it is that he often, e g. ch iii. 1, 2, where see note, uses the plural of himself alone, yet it is as undoubted that he uses it also of himself and his fellow-labourers—e g., 2 Cor i 18, 19. And so De W, Lunemann, al., take it here. **πάντοτε περὶ πάντων**] We have the same alliteration Eph v 20 These words belong to εὐχαριστ, not to μνείαν ποι On these latter words see Rom. i 9 f. **ἀδιαλείπτως** seems by the nearly parallel place, Rom. i. 9, to belong to μνείαν ὑμ. ποι, not to μνημονεύοντες, as Lun, Pelt, al. Such a formula would naturally repeat itself, as far as specifications of this kind are concerned. Still it must be borne in mind, that the order there is slightly different 3] μνημον is not intransitive, as Erasm.-Schmid, al but as in reff '*commemorantes*,' Beza. ὑμῶν is by Œcum, Calv, al, regarded as the genitive after μνημον standing alone, and ἕνεκα supplied before the other genitives But such a construction may be doubted, and at all events it is much simpler here to regard ὑμ. as the genitive governed by τοῦ ἔργου, . . τοῦ κόπου, and τῆς ὑπομονῆς, and prefixed, as belonging to all three. **πίστις, ἀγάπη, ἐλπίς**, are the three great Christian graces of 1 Cor. xiii See also ch v 8, Col. i 4, 5. and Usteri, paulinisch. Lehrbegriff, p 236 ff **τοῦ ἔργου τῆς πίστεως**] Simple as these words are, all sorts of strange meanings have been given to them. Koppe and Rosenmuller hold τ ἔργου to be pleonastic · Calv, Calov, al, render (ungrammatical) '*your faith wrought by God*,' Krebs, '*the reality* (ἔργ as contrasted with λόγος) *of your faith*,' Chrys, Thl, Thdrt, Œc, al, '*the endurance of your faith in suffering*' &c Comparing the words with the following genitives, they seem to mean, 'that work (energetic activity) which faith brings forth' (as Chrys ἡ πίστις διὰ τῶν ἔργων δείκνυται the gen, as also those following, being thus a *possessive* one. see Ellicott here) q d. 'the activity of your faith' see 2 Thess. i 11: or perhaps, as Jowett (but not so well), "'your work of faith,' i e the Christian life, which springs from faith." thus making the gen one of *origin* **τοῦ κόπου**] probably *towards the sick and needy strangers*, cf Acts xx 35;

τῆς [m] ἐλπίδος τοῦ κυρίου ἡμῶν Ἰησοῦ χριστοῦ [n] ἔμπροσθεν
τοῦ [o] θεοῦ καὶ [o] πατρὸς ἡμῶν, 4 εἰδότες, ἀδελφοὶ [p] ἠγαπημένοι ὑπὸ θεοῦ, τὴν [q] ἐκλογὴν ὑμῶν· 5 ὅτι τὸ [r] εὐαγγέλιον [r] ἡμῶν οὐκ [s] ἐγενήθη εἰς ὑμᾶς ἐν [t] λόγῳ μόνον,

ABCDF KLℵ a b c d e f g h k l m n o 17

m accumulation of genitives, 2 Cor iv 4. Eph i 6. iv 13 al fr n = Matt x 32 ch ii 19 iii 9, 13 o Gal i 4 reff p 2 Thess ii 13 Deut xxxiii 12 q Acts ix 15 Rom ix 11 xi 5, 7, 28 2 Pet i 10 only † r 2 Thess ii 14 reff s form, Acts iv 4 Col iv 11 al γιγν. εἰς, Acts xxviii 6 Gal iii 14 see πρός, 1 Cor ii 3 ἐπί, Luke iii 2 t 1 Cor iv 19, 20 see Col iii 17 reff

om της ελπιδος A Ambrst-txt for ελπ., αγαπης 17· pref και k 19 tol Chr-comm, Ambrst-comm

4 ins του bef θεου ACKℵ b k m o sah Thl-marg(and comm)· om BDFL rel gr-lat-ff

5. aft ευαγ ins του θεου ℵ for εις, προς (*see 1 Cor* ii. 3) AC²DF Chr Thl· εφ' 46 txt BKLℵ rel Chr-ms Thdrt Damasc. (C¹ illegible) μονω (*mechanical*

Rom xvi 6, 12—not *in the word and ministry* (De W), cf ch v. 12 which is irrelevant here τῆς ἀγάπ. not as *springing from*, but as *belonging to*, love,—*characterizing* it (Lun) see above **τ ὑπομ τῆς ἐλπίδος] your endurance of hope**—i e endurance (in trials) which belongs to (see above), characterizes, your hope, and also nourishes it, in turn cf Rom xv. 4, ἵνα διὰ τῆς ὑπομονῆς, κ. διὰ τῆς παρακλήσεως τῶν γραφῶν τὴν ἐλπίδα ἔχωμεν **τοῦ κυρ. ἡμ Ἰ χ.]** specifies the hope—that it is a hope of the coming of the Lord Jesus Christ (cf ver. 10). Olsh. refers the words to all three preceding substantives—but this seems alien from St Paul's style. On all three Jowett says well, 'your faith, hope, and love, a faith that had its outward effect on your lives· a love that spent itself in the service of others a hope that was no mere transient feeling, but was content to wait for the things unseen when Christ should be revealed' **ἔμπρ. τ θ κ. πατρ. ἡμ]** belongs most naturally to μνημονεύοντες—**making mention . . . . before God**: not to the genitives preceding (see Rom. iv 17; xiv. 22), as Thdrt, al

4] **εἰδότες** refers back to μνημονεύοντες, **in that we know**—or **for we know.** Thdrt, Erasm, Grot., al., take it for οἴδατε γάρ, or εἰδότες ἐστέ, wrongly referring it to the Thessalonians Pelt joins it with μνείαν ποιούμενοι: but the construction as above seems the best **ὑπὸ θεοῦ** belongs to ἠγαπημένοι, as in 2 Thess ii 13, see also Rom i 7 not to εἰδότες, as Est thinks possible (ὑπό for παρά?), nor to ἐκλογήν—either as E. V, '*your election of God*,' which is ungrammatical (requiring τὴν ὑπ θ ἐκ), or as Œc, Thl, all, ὑπὸ θ. τὴν ἐκλ. ὑμ. (εἶναι), which would introduce an irrelevant emphasis on ὑπὸ θεοῦ. **ἐκλογή** must not be softened down: it is the **election** unto life of individual believers by God, so commonly adduced by St. Paul (reff.· and 1 Cor i. 27; 2 Thess. ii. 13). **ὑμῶν**, objective genitive after ἐκλογήν—knowing that God ἐξελέξατο ὑμᾶς

5] **ὅτι** has been taken to mean '*videlicet, ut*,' and the verse to be an epexegesis of ἐκλογήν but as Lun remarks, evidently verses 5, 6 ff are meant not to explain *wherein* their election *consisted*, but to give reasons in matter of fact for concluding (εἰδότες) the existence of that election ὅτι must then be because, and a colon be placed at ὑμῶν These reasons are (1) the power and confidence with which he and Silvanus and Timotheus preached among them (ver 5), and (2) the earnest and joyful manner in which the Thessalonians received it (vv. 6 ff) Both these were signs of God's grace to them—tokens of their election vouchsafed by Him **τὸ εὐαγγ. ἡμ, the gospel which we preached ἐγενήθη εἰς]** See reff, especially Gal came to you is perhaps the nearest. **εἰς** betokens the direction. πρός, with ἐγέν, would give nearly the same sense, or perhaps that of *apud*, see ref. 1 Cor &c. We must not take ἐγενήθη εἰς ὑμ for a constr. prægnans (ἦλθ. εἰς καὶ ἐγ. ἐν), which with ἦν it might be for ἐγενήθη εἰς carries motion in itself without any thing supplied. On 'the passive form ἐγενήθη, alien to the Attic, and originally Doric, but common in the κοινή' (Lun), see note on Eph iii 7; Lobeck on Phryn. p. 108 ff., Kuhner, i 193; Winer, § 15. It was attempted in my earlier editions to press the *passive sense* in the frequent occurrences of this form in this Epistle But wider acquaintance with the usage has since convinced me that this is not possible, and that we must regard it as equivalent in meaning to the more usual ἐγένετο The prepositions ἐν following indicate the form and manner in which the *preaching was carried on*, not (as Pelt, al) that in which the Thessalonians received it, which is not treated till ver 6. **δυνάμει** is not '*miracles*,' as Thdrt, Œc, all, nor *efficacia et*

ἀλλὰ καὶ ἐν [t] δυνάμει καὶ [u] ἐν πνεύματι ἁγίῳ καὶ ἐν
[v] πληροφορίᾳ πολλῇ, καθὼς οἴδατε οἷοι [w] ἐγενήθημεν ἐν
ὑμῖν δι' ὑμᾶς. 6 καὶ ὑμεῖς [x] μιμηταὶ ἡμῶν ἐγενήθητε
καὶ τοῦ κυρίου, [y] δεξάμενοι τὸν λόγον ἐν θλίψει πολλῇ
[z] μετὰ [a] χαρᾶς πνεύματος ἁγίου, 7 [b] ὥςτε γενέσθαι ὑμᾶς
[c] τύπον πᾶσιν τοῖς πιστεύουσιν ἐν τῇ Μακεδονίᾳ καὶ ἐν τῇ

u 1 Cor ii 4. 2 Cor vi 6
v Col ii 2 Heb vi 11 x 22 only † (-ρεῖσθαι, Col iv 12)
w = 1 Cor i 30 2 Cor vii 14 al
x 1 Cor iv 16 xi 1 Eph v 1 ch ii 14 Heb vi 12 only †
y = Luke viii 13 Acts viii 14 xi 1 xvii 11 1 Cor ii 14 ch ii 13 James i 21 Prov iv 10
z = Phil i 4 ii 29 1 Chron xxix 22
a Rom xiv 17
b = Phil i 13 al
c = 1 Tim iv 12 reff

repetition) DK c d k om 3rd εν c e l n o 17 67² D-lat tol copt Thdrt-ms. om 4th εν Bℵ 17 tol coptt om 5th εν ACℵ f 17 67² am

6. for θεου, κυριου A aft χαρας ins και B

7. rec τυπους (alteration to suit υμας), with ACFKLℵ rel syr gr-ff τυπος D³ 49 (by mistake? or perhaps [Mill] a neuter form as πλουτος?) txt BD¹ 17. 67² latt Syr coptt Ambrst Pelag. rec om 2nd εν, with KL rel (c g h m o Chr om τη also) ins ABCDFℵ k 17 latt syr Thdrt Ambrst Pelag.

vis agens in cordibus fidelium (Bullinger) (see above), but **power**, viz of utterance and of energy. **πν ἁγίῳ**] beware again of the supposed figure of ἓν διὰ δυοῖν, by which all character of style and all logical exactness is lost Even Conyb here has fallen into this error, and rendered "*power of the Holy Ghost*" It is a predicate advancing *beyond ἐν δυνάμει*—not only in force and energy, but **in the Holy Ghost**—in a manner which could only be ascribed **to** the operation of the Holy Spirit **πληροφορίᾳ πολλῇ**] **much confidence** (of faith), see reff Many irrelevant meanings have been given *fulness of spiritual gifts*, which the Thessalonians had received (Lomb, Corn-a-lap, Turretin) *certainty of the truth*, felt by them (Macknight, Benson, al): '*fulfilment of the apostolic office*' (Estius). The confidence (see above) was that in which *Paul and Silvanus and Timotheus preached to them.* **καθὼς κ τ.λ**] Appeal to their knowledge that the fact was so These words restrict the foregoing to the *preachers*, as explained above *καὶ τί, φησι, μακρηγορῶ; αὐτοὶ ὑμεῖς μάρτυρές ἐστε, οἷοι ἐγενήθημεν πρὸς ὑμᾶς.* Œc. This interpretation is fixed by *καθώς*, referring back to the whole previous description. The sense has been variously given · Conyb, '*And you, likewise know*'—but '*likewise*' surely confounds the connexion Pelt, even further from the mark, ... 'ita accipimus, ut Apostolum exemplum suum Thessalonicensibus imitandum statuamus.' **οἷοι ἐγενήθ**] **what manner of men we proved,** as Ellic. . not 'quales facti sumus,' see above on this note nor as vulg, '*quales fuerimus*,' the point of the fact appealed to is, the proof given, what manner of men they were, by the manner of their preaching "The *ποιότης* was evinced in the power and confidence with which they delivered their message." Ellic.. *the proof given by the manner of their preaching* **ἐν ὑμῖν**] local merely **among you.** **δι' ὑμᾶς**] **for your sakes**—conveying the purpose of the Apostle and his colleagues, and in the background also *the purpose of* GOD—'you know what God enabled us to be,—how mighty in preaching the word,—for your sakes—thereby proving that he loved you, and had chosen you for His own' **6**] Further proof of the same, that ye are *ἐκλεκτοί*, by the method in which *you received* the Gospel thus preached by us. **καὶ ὑμεῖς** corresponds with **τὸ εὐ. ἡμῶν** above It is somewhat difficult here to fix exactly the point of comparison, in which they imitated their ministers and Christ Certainly it is not merely, in *receiving the word*—for to omit other objections, this would not apply at all to Him.—and therefore, not in any qualifying detail of their *method* of reception of the word—not in *δύναμις*, nor in *πν. ἁγ.*, nor in *πληρ. πολλ.* So far being clear, we have but one particular left, and that respects the circumstances under which, and the spirit with which and here we find a point of comparison even with Christ Himself viz joyful endurance in spirit under sufferings. This it was in which they imitated the Apostles, and their divine Master, and which made them patterns to other churches (see below). For this *θλῖψις* in which they *ἐδέξαντο τὸν λόγον*, see Acts xvii 5—10, ch ii. 14, iii 2, 3, 5. **δεξάμενοι**] **in that ye received** **χαρὰ πνεύματος ἁγίου** (ref), **joy wrought by the Holy Spirit** On the gen of origin, see Ellic.'s note here **7.**] *Further specification of the eminence of the Thessalo-*

Ἀχαΐᾳ. 8 [d]ἀφ᾽ ὑμῶν γὰρ [e]ἐξήχηται ὁ [f]λόγος τοῦ [f]κυρίου
οὐ μόνον ἐν τῇ Μακεδονίᾳ καὶ Ἀχαΐᾳ, ἀλλ᾽ ἐν παντὶ
τόπῳ ἡ [g]πίστις ὑμῶν ἡ [g]πρὸς τὸν θεὸν [h]ἐξελήλυθεν,
ὥςτε μὴ [i]χρείαν [i]ἔχειν ἡμᾶς λαλεῖν τι. 9 [k]αὐτοὶ γὰρ
περὶ ἡμῶν [l]ἀπαγγέλλουσιν [m]ὁποίαν [n]εἴςοδον ἔσχομεν

ABCDF KLℵ a b c d e f g h k l m n o 17

d = 1 Cor xiv 36. e here only. Joel iii 14. Sir xl 13 only. f = Acts viii 25 xiii 48, 49 xv 36 xix 10, 20 2 Thess iii 1. g here (Philem 5 v. r.) only. h = Matt ix 26 & Acts, passim Heb xi 12 1 John i 2 only. Gen xiv 13. i w. inf., ch iv 9 reff. k = Gal ii 2 reff. l Paul, 1 Cor xiv 25 only. Gospp Gal ii 6 James i 24 only †. m Acts xxvi 29 1 Cor iii 13 Gal ii 6. n Acts xiii 24 ch ii 1 Heb. x 19 2 Pet. i 11 only. 1 Kings xvi 4.

8 om γαρ ℵ[1] k. ins ℵ corr[1] for κυρ., θεου ℵ[1]. ins εν τη bef αχαια (*repeated from former ver, as* "necessary to mark Ach. as a distinct province." *For this very reason Meyer retains it*) CDFKLℵ rel latt syrr Cyr Damasc Œc Ambrst Pelag. ins τη f k o: om AB c m 17 Chr Thdrt Thl rec (for αλλ' εν) αλλα και εν (και *insd as being usual after* ου μονον), with D[3]KL rel æth Chr Cyr Thdrt txt ABCD[1]F m 17 am(with fuld demid) syrr coptt, ℵ[1] has αλλα¯, of which ℵ corr[1 or 3] has made αλλα εν. rec ημας bef εχειν (*for emphasis to contrast with* αυτοι *follg*), with KL rel Chr Damasc. txt ABCDFℵ (e) m 17 Thdrt for λαλειν, παλιν C.
9 for ημων, υμων B a h k n o 120-1-2-3 D-lat coptt Chr[1]-ms[1] Thdrt Damasc Œc rec (for εσχ.) εχομεν (with 17 ?) txt ABCDFKLℵ rel latt Chr Thdrt Thl-marg lat-ff

nians' Christian character **τύπον,** of the whole church as one: see Bernhardy, p. 60. **πᾶσιν τοῖς πιστεύουσιν**] **to the whole of the believers**: **οἱ πιστεύοντες,** like ὁ πειράζων, designates the *kind*. Chrys. understands this participle as if it were πιστεύσασιν.—καὶ μὴν ἐν ὑστέρῳ ἦλθε πρὸς αὐτούς· ἀλλ' οὕτως ἐλάμψατε, φησίν, ὡς τῶν προλαβόντων γενέσθαι διδασκάλους. οὐ γὰρ εἶπεν, ὥστε τύπους γενέσθαι πρὸς τὸ πιστεῦσαι, ἀλλὰ τοῖς ἤδη πιστεύουσι τύπος ἐγένεσθε. But it was not so: for the only church in Europe which was in Christ before the Thessalonian, was the Philippian (Acts xvi 12—xvii 1, see ch. ii. 2). **Μακ. κ. Ἀχ.**] Cf. Rom. xv 26, Acts xix. 21: the two Roman provinces, comprehending Northern and Southern Greece. There is no reference, as Thdrt., to the Greeks being ἔθνη μέγιστα κ. ἐπὶ σοφίᾳ θαυμαζόμενα, and so their praise being the greater: these are mentioned simply because the Apostle had been, since their conversion, in Macedonia, and had left Silvanus and Timotheus there,—and was now in Achaia. **8.**] *Proof of the praise in ver. 7*. **ἀφ' ὑμῶν** is merely local, **from you**, as in ref., not '*by you*' (as preachers) (ὑφ' ὑμῶν), as Rückert, "locorum Paulinorum 1 Thess i 8 et 1 Thess iii 1—3 explanatio." nor '*by your means*,' viz. in saving Silas and myself from danger of our lives and so enabling us to preach (δι' ὑμῶν), as Storr, and Flatt. **ἐξήχηται**] δηλῶν ὅτι ὥσπερ σάλπιγγος λαμπρὸν ἠχούσης ὁ πλησίον ἅπας πληροῦται τόπος, οὕτω τῆς ὑμετέρας ἀνδρείας ἡ φήμη καθάπερ ἐκείνη σαλπίζουσα ἱκανὴ τὴν οἰκουμένην ἐμπλῆσαι Chrys. **ὁ λόγ. τ. κυρίου,** cannot be as De W. '*the fame of the reception of the Gospel by you*:' the sense seems to be that your ready reception and faith as it were sounded forth the λόγον τοῦ κυρίου, the word of the Lord, the Gospel message, loudly and clearly, through all parts. The logical construction of this verse is somewhat difficult. After the οὐ μόνον ἐν τ. Μακ. κ. Ἀχ., we expect merely ἀλλ' ἐν παντὶ τόπῳ: but these words appear, followed by a new subject and a new predicate. Either then we must regard this new subject and predicate as merely an epexegesis of the former, ἐξήχηται ὁ λόγ. τοῦ κυρ., or, with Lünemann, we must place a colon at κυρίου, and begin a new sentence with οὐ μόνον. This last is very objectionable: for it leaves ἀφ' ὑμ. . . κυρίου standing alone in the most vapid and spiritless manner, with the strong rhetorical word ἐξήχηται unaccounted for and unemphatic. The other way then must be our refuge, and I cannot see those objections to it which Lün. has found. It is quite according to the versatile style of St. Paul, half to lose sight of the οὐ μόνον ἀλλ', and to go on after ἐν παντὶ τόπῳ with a new sentence, and especially as that new sentence explains the somewhat startling one preceding. **πρός, towards,** directed towards God as its object (and here, as contrasted with idols, see next verse)—not = the more usual εἰς, *to* and *into*, as Ellic. correcting my previous *on* (ἐπί). De Wette, al., suppose with some probability that the report of the Thessalonians' faith may have been spread by Christian travelling merchants, such as Aquila and Priscilla. **ὥςτε μὴ . . . .**]

πρὸς ὑμᾶς, καὶ πῶς [o] ἐπεστρέψατε πρὸς τὸν θεὸν ἀπὸ
τῶν [p] εἰδώλων, [q] δουλεύειν θεῷ [r] ζῶντι καὶ [s] ἀληθινῷ,
10 καὶ [t] ἀναμένειν τὸν υἱὸν αὐτοῦ ἐκ τῶν οὐρανῶν, ὃν
[u] ἤγειρεν [u] ἐκ τῶν νεκρῶν, Ἰησοῦν τὸν [v] ῥυόμενον ἡμᾶς
ἀπὸ τῆς [w] ὀργῆς τῆς ἐρχομένης.

II. 1 Αὐτοὶ γὰρ οἴδατε, ἀδελφοί, τὴν [x] εἴσοδον ἡμῶν
τὴν πρὸς ὑμᾶς, ὅτι οὐ [y] κενὴ γέγονεν, 2 ἀλλὰ [z] προπα-

o = Acts xiv 15. 2 Cor iii 16. Amos iv 6. p = Acts xv 20. Rom ii 22. 1 John v 21 al Num xxv 2. q = Acts xx 19. Gal iv 8. Ps ii 11. r Acts xiv 15. 1 Kings xvii 36 f. s John xvii 3. 1 John v 20 (see) al Isa lxv 16. t here only. Job vii 2. Isa lix 11. u Gal i 1 reff. v w. ἀπὸ, Matt vi 13. Rom xv 31. 2 Thess iii 2. 2 Tim iv 18 only. Ps cxxxix 1. w ἐκ, Col i 13. w = Matt iii 7 || L. Rom ii 5. ch ii 16. Zeph ii 2. x ch i 9 reff. y Acts iv 25. 1 Cor. xv 10, 14, 58. Deut xxxii 47. z here only †. παρῃτιωμησαν οὐ προπαθόντες, Thuc iii 67. cf also iii 82.

10. rec om 2nd των, with ACK Œc: ins BDFLℵ rel Chr Damasc Thdrt Thl. for απο, εκ Bℵ 17. 73.

Chap. II. 2. rec aft αλλα ins και, with (none of our mss) D lat: om ABCDFKLℵ rel vulg syr coptt Syr lat-ff.

The report being already rife, we found no occasion to speak of your faith, or in your praise. 9.] αὐτοί, the people ἐν τ. Μακ. κ. Ἀχ., κ. ἐν παντὶ τόπῳ: see reff., and Bernhardy, p. 288. περὶ ἡμῶν] concerning us, Paul and Silvanus and Timotheus; not as Lün., '*us both*,' including the Thessalonians. This he does, to square the following clauses, which otherwise are not correspondent: but there are two objections to his view: (1) the emphatic position of περὶ ἡμῶν, which seems to necessitate its keeping its strict meaning: (2) that it would in this case have been much more naturally ὑμῶν than ἡμῶν, as the second person has prevailed throughout, and our εἴσοδος to you was quite as much a matter happening to you as to us. That καὶ περὶ ὑμῶν, πῶς should be abbreviated as we find it, will surely not surprise any one familiar with the irregularities, in point of symmetry, of St. Paul's style. The ἀπαγγελλόμενα here correspond to the two members of the above proof, verses 5 and 6. ὁποίαν has no reference to *danger*, as Chrys., al. εἴσοδος, merely access, in the way of *coming to them*: see ch. ii. 1: not of itself *facilis aditus*, as Pelt. πῶς, merely how that, introducing matter of fact,—not '*how*,' 'in what manner,' how joyfully and energetically, as Lünem.: if so, the long specification (πρὸς . . . ἐρχομένης), which follows the (thus) unemphatic verb, drags wearily: whereas, regarded as indicating matter of fact only, the πῶς is unemphatic, and the matter of fact itself, carrying the emphasis, justifies the full statement which is made of it. ζῶντι κ. ἀληθινῷ] ζῶντα μὲν αὐτὸν ὠνόμασεν, ὡς ἐκείνων οὐ ζώντων· ἀληθινὸν δέ, ὡς ἐκείνων ψευδῶς θεῶν καλουμένων. Thdrt. 10.] The especial aspect of the faith of the Thessalonians was *hope*: hope of the return of the Son of God from heaven: a hope, indeed, common to them with all Christians in all ages, but evidently entertained by them as pointing to an event more immediate than the church has subsequently believed it to be. Certainly these words would give them an idea of the *nearness* of the coming of Christ: and perhaps the misunderstanding of them may have contributed to the notion which the Apostle corrects 2 Thess. ii. 1 ff.: see note there. By ὃν ἤγ. ἐκ τῶν νεκρῶν, that whereby (Rom. i. 4) Jesus was declared to be the Son of God with power, is emphatically prefixed to His name. τὸν ῥυόμενον] who delivereth: not = τ. ῥυσόμενον,—still less as E. V., *past*, '*who delivered*,' but descriptive of His office, = 'our Deliverer,' as ὁ πειράζων, &c. τῆς ἐρχ.—which is coming: cf. Eph. v. 6, Col. iii. 6. Ch. II. 1–16.] *He reminds the Thessalonians of his manner of preaching among them* (1—12, answering to ch. i. 9 a): *praises them for their reception of the Gospel, and firmness in persecution* (13—16, answering to ch. i. 9 b). 1.] γάρ refers back to ὁποίαν, ch. i. 9: 'not only do strangers report it, but you know it to be true.' He makes use now of that knowledge to carry out the description of his preaching among them, with a view, by recapitulating these details, to confirm them, who were as yet but novices, in the faith. κενή] It is evident from vv. 2 ff., that this does not here apply to the *fruits* but to the *character* of his preaching: the *result* does not appear till ver. 13. And within this limitation, we may observe that the verb is γέγονεν, not

a Matt xxii 6 Luke xi 45 xviii 32 Acts xiv 5 only 2 Kings xix 43
b Acts ix 27, 28 xiii 46 xiv 3 al³ Eph vi 20 only 1 P Prov xx 9 al
c so Acts ix 27, 28 Eph vi 20

θόντες καὶ [a] ὑβρισθέντες, καθὼς οἴδατε, ἐν Φιλίπποις,
[b] ἐπαῤῥησιασάμεθα [c] ἐν τῷ θεῷ ἡμῶν λαλῆσαι πρὸς ὑμᾶς
τὸ [d] εὐαγγέλιον τοῦ [d] θεοῦ ἐν πολλῷ [e] ἀγῶνι. 3 ἡ γὰρ
[f] παράκλησις ἡμῶν οὐκ ἐκ [g] πλάνης οὐδὲ ἐξ [h] ἀκαθαρσίας,
οὐδὲ ἐν [i] δόλῳ, 4 ἀλλὰ καθὼς [j] δεδοκιμάσμεθα ὑπὸ τοῦ
θεοῦ [k] πιστευθῆναι τὸ εὐαγγέλιον, οὕτως λαλοῦμεν, οὐχ

ABCDF KLℵ a b c d e f g h k l m n o 17

= ἐπί, Acts xiv 3 d Rom i 1 xv 16 2 Cor xi 7 vv 8 9 1 Pet iv 17 only (see Mark i 14 Acts xx 24 1 Tim i 11) e — Paul i 30 (reff) f — Phil ii 1 reff g — Matt xxvii 64 Eph iv 14 al Prov xiv 8 h Paul (Rom vi 19 ch iv 7 al) only, exc Matt xxiii 27 Hos ii 10 i John i 48 2 Cor xii 16 1 Pet ii 1 al Job xiii 7 j — Rom xiv 22 1 Cor xvi. 3 (see below [m]) k Rom iii 2 1 Cor ix 17 constr, Acts xxi 3 Gal ii 7

3 rec (for 2nd ουδε) ουτε, with D³KL rel Chr_{aliq} Thdrt(ουτε twice) Damasc Thl Œc · txt ABCD¹Fℵ 17 67², ουδ' m

ἐγένετο, to be understood therefore not of any mere intent of the Apostle at the time of his coming among them, but of some abiding character of his preaching. It cannot then be understood as Koppe, —'*veni ad vos eo consilio . . . ut vobis prodessem, non ut otiose inter vos viverem*' and nearly so Rosenm It probably expresses, that his εἴσοδος was and continued '*no empty scheme*' ('*no light matter*,' as we say, οὐχ ἡ τυχοῦσα, Chrys.), but an earnest, bold, self denying endeavour for their good. This he proceeds to prove. 2] **προπαθόντες, having previously suffered**. reff On the fact, see Acts xvi. **ἐπαῤῥησιασ**] Lunemann seems to be right (against De W.) in rendering it **we were confident**, not '*we were free of speech*.' See however, on the other side, Ellic's note **ἡμῶν**, because all true confidence is in God as *our God* This word reproduces the feeling with which Paul and Silas opened their ministry among them. διὰ τὸν ἐνδυναμοῦντα θεὸν τοῦτο ποιῆσαι τεθαῤῥήκαμεν Œcum **λαλῆσαι** is infinitive of the object after ἐπαῤῥησ— **we had the confidence to speak**· as E V, **were bold to speak** This seems more probable than with De W, Mey on Eph vi 20, and Ellic, to regard it as the epexegetical inf. "defining still more clearly the *oral* nature of the boldness" Chrys. can hardly be quoted on that side, as Ellic doubtfully. **τοῦ θεοῦ**, for solemnity, to add to the weight of their εἴσοδος. **ἐν πολλῷ ἀγῶνι**] in (amidst) **much conflict**, viz under outward circumstances conflicting much with our work· and therefore that work could be no κενόν, which was thus maintained

3, 4] *Reasons why* he ἐπαῤῥησιάσατο λαλῆσαι . . . ἐν πολλῷ ἀγῶνι·—viz the true and single-minded character of his ministry, and his duty to God as the steward of the Gospel. 3 **παράκλησις**] **exhortation** to you, viz. our whole course of preaching Supply is, not '*was*,' cf λαλοῦμεν below. "The two senses of παράκλησις, exhortation and consolation, so easily passing into one another (compare ver 11), are suggestive of the external state of the early church, sorrowing amid the evils of the world, and needing as its first lesson to be comforted; and not less suggestive of the first lesson of the Gospel to the individual soul, of peace in believing" Jowett **ἐκ**] **having its source in** **πλάνης**] here probably **error**. "The word is used transitively and intransitively In the former case, it is '*imposture*' (Matt xxvii. 64) or '*seduction*' (Eph. iv. 14)· in the latter and more usual, **error**." Lunem. **ἀκαθαρσίας**] hardly, as Chrys, ὑπὲρ μυσαρῶν πραγμάτων οἷον γοήτων κ μάγων,—though such a reference is certainly possible, considering the vile degradation of that class at the period,—but here apparently of the impure desire of gain, cf. ver. 5, where ἐν προφάσει πλεονεξίας seems to correspond with ἐξ ἀκαθαρσίας Still such a meaning seems to want example If it be correct, this represents (Lun) the subjective side, the *motive*, as ἐκ πλάνης the objective side, the *ground* **ἐν δόλῳ**] this of the *manner*, or perhaps, as Ellic., the *ethical sphere, in which* 'nor did we make use of deceit to win our way with our παράκλησις' See 2 Cor ii 17 4] **καθώς**, **according as, in proportion as** **δεδοκιμ**] see reff,—**we have been approved,—thought fit**. cf πιστόν ἡγήσατο, 1 Tim i 12. Lunem cites Plut Thes. 12 ἐλθὼν οὖν ὁ Θησεὺς ἐπὶ τὸ ἄριστον, οὐκ ἐδοκίμαζε φράζειν αὐτὸν ὅστις εἴη. We must not introduce any ascertained fitness of them in themselves into the idea (οὐκ ἂν ἐξελέξατο, εἰ μὴ ἀξίους ἐγίνωσκε Thl · so Chr, Œc, Olsh). it is only the free choice of God which is spoken of On **πιστευθ τὸ εὐαγγ** see reff, and Winer, edn 6, § 32 5. **οὕτως**

ὡς ἀνθρώποις [l] ἀρέσκοντες, ἀλλὰ θεῷ τῷ [m] δοκιμάζοντι
τὰς καρδίας ἡμῶν. 5 οὔτε γάρ ποτε [n] ἐν [o] λόγῳ [p] κολακείας [n] ἐγενήθημεν, καθὼς οἴδατε, οὔτε ἐν [q] προφάσει
[r] πλεονεξίας, [s] θεὸς [s] μάρτυς, 6 οὔτε [t] ζητοῦντες ἐξ ἀνθρώπων [t] δόξαν, οὔτε ἀφ᾽ ὑμῶν οὔτε ἀπ᾽ ἄλλων, δυνάμενοι
ἐν [u] βάρει εἶναι ὡς [v] χριστοῦ [v] ἀπόστολοι, 7 ἀλλ᾽ ἐγενή-

l Gal i 10 reff m = Luke xvi 19 1 Cor iii 13 2 Cor viii, 8 ch v 21 al Prov xvii 3 n see 1 Tim iv. 15 o compare Eph i 13 reff. p here only + q Mark xii 40 ‖ (Mt v r) L John xv 22 Acts xxvii 30 Phil i 18 only Hos x 4 r Col iii 5 reff 2 Pet ii 3 s Rom i 9 2 Cor i 23 Phil i 8 ver 10 t John v 44 (vii 18) u = here (Gal vi 2 reff) only (see note) v 1 Cor i 1 2 Cor i 1 xi 13. Eph i 1 Jude 17 al

4. δεδοκειμασμενοι F. rec ins τω bef θεω (*as more usual with art follg*), with AD³FKLℵ³ rel · om BCD¹ℵ¹ 67² Clem bas Œc.
5. om 2nd εν Bℵ³ a 17 ins ο bef θεος F
6 for υμων, ημων A for απ᾽, απο DFL rel txt ABCℵ (k o m 17, e sil).

answers not to the following **ὡς**, but to the preceding **καθώς**, and is emphatic—'*even so.*' **ἀρέσκοντες**, in the strict sense of the *present tense*,—**going about to please,—striving to please** **ὡς** belongs to the whole sentence, not merely to ἀνθρ. ἀρέσκ. (as Lun.) for in that case the second member would involve almost too harsh an ellipsis. **ἡμῶν, of us,**—not said generally, of all men. but of us, Paul and Silvanus and Timotheus As Lunem justly observes against De W., τὰς καρδίας here and τὰς ἑαυτ. ψυχάς below, are conclusive against imagining that St. Paul in this place is speaking of *himself alone*. Yet Conyb. renders it, '*my heart*,' and τὰς ἑ. ψ., '*my own life*.'

5 ff] *Proofs again of the assertions of vv.* 3, 4 **For neither did we become conversant** (see reff γενέσθαι ἔν τινι, *in re quadam versari*, so οἱ μὲν ἐν τούτοις τοῖς λόγοις ἦσαν, Xen. Cyr. iv. 3 23. On the impracticability of maintaining a passive sense in the form ἐγενήθημεν, see above, on ch. i. 5) **in speech of** (consisting of) **flattery** (not '*incurring repute of flattery*,' as Hamm, Le Clerc, Michael., al. [similarly as to meaning, Pelt], which would be irrelevant, as he is not speaking of what *others thought* of their ministry, but of their own behaviour in it On κολακ. Lun. quotes Theophrastus, Char 2,—τὴν δὲ κολακείαν ὑπολάβοι ἄν τις ὁμιλίαν αἰσχρὰν εἶναι, συμφέρουσαν δὲ τῷ κολακεύοντι,—and Ellic remarks, "It seems more specifically to illustrate the ἐν δόλῳ of ver 3, and forms a natural transition to the next words, the essence of κολακεία being self-interest ὁ δὲ ὅπως ὠφέλειά τις αὐτῷ γίγνηται εἰς χρήματα καὶ ὅσα διὰ χρημάτων, κόλαξ Aristot. Eth. Nic iv 12 ad fin") **as ye know, nor** (ἐγενήθημεν) **in pretext** (employed in that which was meant to be a pretext, not '*in occasione avaritiæ*,' as vulg and Le Clerc, nor is πρόφασις '*species*,' as Wolf) **of** (serving to conceal) **avarice; God is witness** (τῆς μὲν κολακείας αὐτοὺς ἐκάλεσε μάρτυρας, δῆλα γὰρ τοῖς ἀκούουσι τῶν κολάκων τὰ ῥήματα· τῆς δὲ πλεονεξίας οὐκέτι αὐτούς, ἀλλὰ τὸν τῶν ὅλων ἐπόπτην Thdrt., and similarly Chrys But perhaps it is simpler, seeing that no ὑμεῖς is expressed with οἴδατε, to refer θεὸς μάρ. to the whole).

6] **ζητοῦντες** belongs to ἐγενήθημεν above **ἐξ ἀνθρώπων**, emphatic · τὴν γὰρ ἐκ θεοῦ καὶ ἐζήτουν κ ἐλάμβανον. Œc The real distinction here between **ἐκ** and **ἀπό** seems to be, that ἐκ belongs more to the *abstract ground* of the δόξα, ἀπό to the *concrete object* from which it was in each case to accrue This is strictly correct, not, as Ellic., who has misunderstood my distinction, 'artificial and precarious' nor is it ever safe to assume identity of meaning, in St Paul's style, of different prepositions, except where the form of the sentence absolutely requires it The glory which they sought was not at all to come out of human sources, whether actually from the Thessalonians or from any others.

δυνάμενοι] **though we had the power.** **ἐν βάρει εἶναι**] Thdrt., Est, Grot, Calov, all, refer this to πλεονεξ. mentioned above, and understand it of using the power of living by the gospel, which St. Paul, &c might have done, but did not · so ἐπιβαρεῖν, ver. 9 2 Thess. iii. 8, καταβαρεῖν, 2 Cor. xii. 16, ἀβαρῆ ἐμαυτὸν ἐτήρησα, ib xi. 9. But the words are separated from the πλεονεξία by the new idea beginning at ζητοῦντες, to which, and not to the former clause, this is subordinated I therefore take them with Chrys (Œc, Thl, undecided), Ambrst, Erasm, Calv, &c., Olsh, De W., Lun.,—as equivalent to ἐν τιμῇ εἶναι—εἰκὸς γὰρ τοὺς παρὰ θεοῦ πρὸς ἀνθρώπους ἀποσταλέντας, ὡσανεὶ ἀπὸ τοῦ οὐρανοῦ νῦν

θημεν * ʷ ἤπιοι ˣ ἐν ˣ μέσῳ ὑμῶν, ὡς ἐὰν ʸ τροφὸς ᶻ θάλπῃ
τὰ ἑαυτῆς τέκνα, 8 οὕτως ᵃ ὁμειρόμενοι ὑμῶν ᵇ εὐδοκοῦμεν

ABCDF KLℵ a b c d e f g h k l m n o 17

w 2 Tim ii 24 only † see note. x Matt x 16 xviii 20 Luke ii 46. Heb ii 12 (from Ps xxi 22) al. y here only Gen xxxv 8 4 Kings xi 2 ‖ Chron Isa xlix 23 only. z Eph v 29 only Deut xxii 6. a here only Job iii 21 (ABIC ℵ) ἱμ., Ps lxii 1 Symm. b Gal i 15 reff.

7. αλλα Bℵ. * νήπιοι (*prob from attaching the* ν *of the precedg word to* ηπιοι. *In such a case, where it is almost as likely that the* ν *of* νηπ *may have dropped out, and the evidence is so divided, the* sense *may fairly be taken as our guide see note*) BC^1D^1Fℵ[1] a m latt copt æth Clem(from context) Orig[1] expr Cyr mss-in-Thl Orig-int Ambrst Pelag Aug ηπιοι AC^2D^3KLℵ[3] rel syrr sah Clem₁ Orig₁ Chr-comm Œc-comm Thdrt-comm Damasc Thl-comm(alt,—ἢ καὶ νήπιοι) εμμεσω AC 17 rec αν, with AD^3 K(e sil) Lℵ[1] rel Orig₂ Thdrt. txt BCDFℵ[3]. θαλπει KL d f k m.

8. rec ιμειρομενοι, with rel Cyr txt ABCDFKLℵ d e (f k) m n Chr aliq Damasc-ms Thl expr(ὁμειρ τινὲς δὲ ἱμειρόμενοι ἀνέγνωσαν· οὐκ ἔστι δέ). (17 def) ηυδοκουμεν B ευδοκησαμεν 17, *volebamus* vulg(and F-lat) syrr coptt Pelag. *cupimus* old-lat

ἥκοντας πρέσβεις, πολλῆς ἀπολαῦσαι τιμῆς Chr **βάρος** is used of importance, dignity,—'*weight*,' as we say e. g. Diod Sic iv 61, ἀπὸ τούτων τῶν χρόνων Ἀθηναῖοι, διὰ τὸ βάρος τῆς πόλεως, φρονήματος ἐνεπίμπλαντο, κ τῆς τῶν Ἑλλήνων ἡγεμονίας ὠρέχθησαν, and in this sense St Paul's Epistles were called βαρεῖαι, 2 Cor. x. 10. Cf. also βάρος δόξης, where however βάρος is used *sensu proprio*, as opposed to ἐλαφρόν, 2 Cor. iv. 17 Render therefore, **when we might have stood on our dignity** Heins, Pisc, Hamm, understand the words of ecclesiastical censures—'quum severitatem exercere apostolicam posset,'—and oppose them to ἐγεν. ἤπιοι below: but see there. **ὡς χρ ἀπ**] not '*as the other Apostles*' (Grot, Pelt, referring to 1 Cor. ix 5, but ungrammatical), but **as** (being) **Apostles of Christ** It is simpler to take ἀπόστολοι here in its wider sense, than to limit the sentence to St. Paul alone

7.] **ἀλλά** contrasts, not with the mere subordinate clause of the last verse (δυνάμ. κ τ λ), but with its whole sense, and introduces the positive side of their behaviour—q d 'so far from being any of the aforesaid, we were ...' **ἐγενήθ**, as before, with a reference to God enabling us **ἤπιοι, mild**: so Od β 47, πατὴρ δ' ὡς ἤπιος ἦεν Herodian iv. 1, ἤπιον ἄρχοντα κ πατέρα Pausan. Eliac. ii. 18, βασιλέα γὰρ οὐ τὰ πάντα ἤπιον, ἀλλὰ καὶ τὰ μάλιστα θυμῷ χρώμενον Ἀλέξανδρον τοῦ Φιλίππου (Wetst.) see also Herod iii 89 and Ellic's note here Surely the reading νήπιοι, being (1) by far the *commoner word*, (2) so *easily introduced* by the final ν of the preceding word, can hardly, in the teeth of the sense, come under consideration seeing too that the primary authorities are not unanimous **ἐν μέσ ὑμ**] i e 'in our converse with you;' but with an allusion to our not lifting ourselves above you,—ὡς εἷς ἐξ ὑμῶν, Œc It is best to retain the comma after ὑμῶν, not as Lün, to place a colon: for though there is a break in the construction, it is one occasioned by the peculiar style of the Apostle, which should not be amended by punctuation. The emphasis on **ἑαυτῆς** should not be lost sight of—**as when a nurse** (a *suckling mother*) **cherishes** (reff.) **her own children.** See Gal iv 19, for the same figure **8**] **οὕτως** belongs to εὐδοκοῦμεν, and is the apodosis to ὡς above **ὁμειρόμενοι**] ὁμείρεσθαι is found in reff only (and in both, the MSS differ), except in the glossaries Hesych, Phavor., and Phot. explain it by ἐπιθυμεῖν. Thl says, τουτέστι, προσδεδεμένοι ὑμῖν, κ. ἐχόμενοι ὑμῶν, παρὰ τὸ ὁμοῦ κ τὸ εἴρω, τὸ συμπλέκω. and Phot. gives ὁμοῦ ἡρμόσθαι as its meaning. But as Lünem. observes after Winer, edn. 6, § 16 B), "This is suspicious, 1) because the verb here governs a genitive and not a dative, 2) because there is no instance of a similar verb compounded with ὁμοῦ or ὁμός. Now as in Nicander (Theriaca, ver. 402) the simple form μείρεσθαι occurs in the sense of ἱμείρεσθαι, it can hardly be doubted that μείρεσθαι is the original root, to which ἱμείρεσθαι and ὁμείρεσθαι (having the same meaning) are related, having a syllable prefixed for euphony. Cf. the analogous forms κέλλω and ὀκέλλω,—δύρομαι and ὀδύρομαι,—φλέω and ὀφλέω,—αὔω and ἰαύω, &c., and see Kuhner, i. p. 27" It will thus perhaps be best rendered by **loving you, earnestly desiring you.** **εὐδοκ**] not present, but imperfect, without an augment, as is also generally the aorist εὐδόκησα in N T see Winer, § 12 3 a **we delighted**, 'it was my joy to . . '

[c] μεταδοῦναι ὑμῖν οὐ μόνον τὸ [d] εὐαγγέλιον τοῦ [d] θεοῦ,
ἀλλὰ καὶ τὰς [e] ἑαυτῶν [f] ψυχάς, διότι ἀγαπητοὶ ἡμῖν
ἐγενήθητε. 9 [g] μνημονεύετε γάρ, ἀδελφοί, τὸν [h] κόπον
ἡμῶν καὶ τὸν [i] μόχθον· [j] νυκτὸς καὶ [j] ἡμέρας [k] ἐργαζόμενοι, [l] πρὸς τὸ μὴ [m] ἐπιβαρῆσαί τινα ὑμῶν, ἐκηρύξαμεν
[n] εἰς ὑμᾶς τὸ [d] εὐαγγέλιον τοῦ [d] θεοῦ. 10 ὑμεῖς [o] μάρτυρες καὶ [o] θεός, ὡς [p] ὁσίως καὶ [q] δικαίως καὶ [r] ἀμέμπτως
ὑμῖν τοῖς πιστεύουσιν [s] ἐγενήθημεν, 11 [t] καθάπερ οἴδατε,

εγενηητε C ABDF LℵN a b d e f g h k l m n o 17

c constr, Rom i 11 2 Macc viii 12 Xen Anab iv. 5 5 μεταδ. Eph iv 28 reff
d ver 2 reff
e 1st pers., Rom viii 23 1 Cor xi 31 al
f = Matt ii 20 Acts xv 26 xx 24 al Exod xxi 23
g w acc, Matt xvi 9 2 Tim ii 8 only 1 Chron xvi 12
h see below (l) Matt xxvi 10 ‖ 2 Cor vi 5 al Deut i 12
i (in N T always w κοπος) 2 Cor xi 27 2 Thess iii 8 only Num xxiii 21
j Mark v 5 ch iii 10 2 Tim i 3 Isa xxxiv 10
k = Matt xxi 28 1 Cor iv 12 ch iv 11 Exod. v 18
l = 2 Cor iii 13
m 2 Cor ii 5 2 Thess iii 8 only†
n Mark xiii 10 Luke xxiv 47
o ver 5 reff
p here only† Wisd vi 10 only
q Luke xxiii 41 1 Cor xv 34 Tit ii 12 1 Pet ii 23 only Prov xxviii 18
r ch v 23 only† (-τος, Phil ii 15)
s constr (see ch i 5), appy here only
t Paul (Rom iv 6 xii 4 al[8]) only, exc Heb iv 2 Lev xxvii 8 see Heb v 4. Jer

rec (for εγενηθητε) γεγενησθε (*corrn in error, from imagining ευδοκουμεν to be present*), with K rel Chr$_1$ Thdrt txt ABCDFLℵ a m 17 Bas Chr$_1$.

9 rec aft νυκτος add γαρ, with D[3]KL rel syr-marg Chr-txt Thdrt · om ABD[1]Fℵ d k 17 latt syrr coptt Chr$_2$ Thl Ambrst Aug. for εις υμας, υμιν ℵ[1]. txt ℵ-corr[1]: om εις c

10 aft μαρτ. ins εστε D[1]F vss lat-ff. for ως οσιως, προς αγιος (sic) F (not G).

Conyb **τὰς ἑαυτ ψυχάς**, as remarked above, shews beyond doubt that he is including here Silas and Timotheus with himself **μεταδοῦναι** will not strictly apply to *τὰς ἑαυ. ψυχ*, but we must borrow from the compound verb the idea of giving, or offering The comparison is exceedingly tender and beautiful · as the nursing-mother, cherishing her children, joys to give not only her milk, but her life, for them,—so we, bringing up you as spiritual children, delighted in giving, not only the milk of the word, but even (and here it was matter of fact) our own lives, for your nourishment in Christ And that, **because ye became** (the passive form *ἐγενήθητε* must not be pressed to a passive meaning, as in my earlier editions see on ch. i. 5) **very dear to us** 9] *Proof of the dearness of the Thessalonians to Paul and his companions* not of *ἐγενήθ. ἤπιοι*, to which it would be irrelevant,—nor of their readiness to give their lives, &c (as Ellic), for this verse does not refer to dangers undergone, but to *labour, in order not to trouble any* It is no objection to this (Ellic) that *διότι κ τ λ.* is a subordinate causal member of the preceding sentence, seeing that it is precisely St. Paul's habit to break the tenor of his style by inserting confirmations of such clauses. **μνημ.** is indic (*γάρ*) **τ κόπον κ τ. μόχθον**] a repetition (reff) to intensify —as we should say **labour and pains**: no distinction can be established **νυκτός** first, not merely because the Jews and Athenians ('Athenienses inter duos occasus,' Plin N H ii 77) so reckoned it, but *for emphasis*, being the most noteworthy, and the *day* following as matter of course. See besides reff Acts xx 31. **ἐργαζόμενοι** (reff) in its strict meaning of manual labour—viz., at tent-cloth making, Acts xviii. 3 **πρ τὸ μὴ ἐπιβ**] **in order not to burden any of you**, viz by accepting from you the means of sustenance One can hardly say with Chrys., *ἐνταῦθα δείκνυσιν ἐν πενίᾳ ὄντας τοὺς ἄνδρας* for we know St. Paul's strong feeling on this point, 2 Cor. xi 9, 10. **εἰς ὑμᾶς**, to **you**—not quite = *ὑμῖν* the latter represents the preaching more as a thing *imparted*. this as a thing *diffused*. On the supposed inconsistency of the statement here with the narrative in Acts xvii, see Prolegomena, § ii. 3, and note

10–12] *General summary of their behaviour and teaching among the Thessalonians* 10] **ὑμεῖς μάρτ.**, of the outward appearance. **ὁ θεός**, of the heart **ὁσίως κ δικ**] Cf. Plat. Gorg. p 507 A, B,—*καὶ μὴν περὶ μὲν ἀνθρώπους τὰ προσήκοντα πράττων δίκαι' ἂν πράττοι, περὶ δὲ θεοὺς ὅσια*,—and Polyb xxiii 10 8, *παραβῆναι κ τὰ πρὸς τοὺς ἀνθρώπους δίκαια κ τὰ πρὸς τ θεοὺς ὅσια* This distinction, perhaps "precarious" (Ellic.) where the words occur separately, or seem to require no very precise application, is requisite here where both divine and human testimony is appealed to. **ὑμῖν τ πιστ**] not the dat. commodi (Ellic), nor '*towards* you believers,' nor is it governed by *ἀμέμπτως*, but as Œc , Thl , Lünem , dat of the *judgment*, as in 2 Pet iii. 14,

u ὡς v ἕνα v ἕκαστον ὑμῶν ὡς πατὴρ τέκνα ἑαυτοῦ w παρα- ABDF KLℵ a b c d e f g h k l m n o 17
καλοῦντες ὑμᾶς καὶ x παραμυθούμενοι, 12 καὶ y μαρτυρό-
μενοι z εἰς τὸ a περιπατεῖν ὑμᾶς ab ἀξίως τοῦ b θεοῦ τοῦ
c καλοῦντος ὑμᾶς εἰς τὴν ἑαυτοῦ βασιλείαν καὶ d δόξαν.
13 καὶ διὰ τοῦτο καὶ ἡμεῖς e εὐχαριστοῦμεν τῷ θεῷ f ἀδιαλείπτως, ὅτι g παραλαβόντες h λόγον hi ἀκοῆς παρ᾽ ἡμῶν

u = Luke xx 37 (1 Mk. v r) Jude 7. v w gen part., Luke iv 40 xvi 5 Acts ii 3 xvii 27. xxi 26 al. w = Eph iv 1 reff. x = (see note) ch v 14 (John xi 19, 31) only † 2 Macc xv 9 Thucyd viii 72 (-θια, 1 Cor xiv 3 -θιον, Phil ii 1) y Gal v 3 reff Thucyd vi 80 viii 53. z Acts iii 19 vii 19 Rom i 11, 20. 1 Cor x 6 a = Eph iv 1 (reff) Col i 10 only b 3 John 6 only c = Gal i 6 reff d = Rom v 2 viii 18 al e ch i 2 reff f Rom i 9. ch i 2 v 17 only † 2 Macc. iii 26 al g 1 Cor xi 23 xv 1 Gal. i 9, 12 al h = Heb iv 2 see Jer x 22 i = Rom x 16

11 for 1st ως, πως F (qualiter latt, but in ver 10 quam) εις ο. om υμας ℵ.
12 rec μαρτυρουμενοι, with D¹F a h l¹ m Thdrt Thl. txt BD³KLℵ rel Chr Damasc Œc—om και μαρτ A 114 Ambrst-ed. rec περιπατησαι (aor more usual), with D³KL rel txt ABD¹Fℵ k m 17. καλεσαντος Aℵ 73 vulg coptt æth Chr-txt Thdrt Ambrst-ed Vig Pelag
13 rec om 1st και, with DFKL rel latt Chr Aug. ins ABℵ syr copt Thdrt-ms Ambrst

σπουδάσατε ἄσπιλοι κ. ἀμώμητοι αὐτῷ εὑρεθῆναι For otherwise we lose the force of the slight emphasis on ὑμ τοῖς πιστ., q. d 'whatever we may have seemed to the unbelieving' "tametsi aliis non ita videremur," Bengel. See Bernhardy, p. 337 f. The charge of *want of point*, brought by Jowett against the words τοῖς πιστεύουσιν, hence appears to be unfounded. The former verse having referred to external occupation, in which he must have consorted with unbelievers, he here narrows the circle, to speak of his behaviour among the brethren themselves

11, 12.] *Appeal to the detailed judgment of each one, that this was so.* This ὁσίως κ. δικαίως κ ἀμέμπτως in their judgment is substantiated by the fact, that οἱ περὶ τὸν Παῦλον busied themselves in establishing every one of them in the faith.

11] **καθάπερ** refers what follows to what has gone before, as co-ordinate with it **ὡς ἕνα ἕκαστ ὑμᾶς**] The construction is that of nouns in apposition, in cases where the one designates the individuals of whom the other is the aggregate In this case the noun of larger designation generally comes first The simplest instance that can be given is ταῦτα πάντα, where ταῦτα is the aggregate, πάντα the individualizing noun (whereas in πάντα ταῦτα, ταῦτα is the individuals, and πάντα merely the adjective designation of their completeness) so here ἕνα ἕκαστον ὑμῶν . . ὑμᾶς differs very little from πάντας ὑμᾶς. As regards the participles, the simplest way of constructing them is to supply ἐγενήθημεν, which has just preceded Ellicott would rather regard them as an instance of St. Paul's common participial anacolutha, which may also be but here the construction is simple without such a supposition. Both **παρακλ.** and **παραμυθ** seem here best taken, with Lunem, as applying to *exhortation*, but in a sense nearly allied to consolation. see note on ver 3 The subject of the exhortation follows, **εἰς τὸ** κ.τ λ.. and this would be closely connected with their bearing up under trouble and persecution cf. vv. 14 ff

12 μαρτυρόμ] see reff. it strengthens the two former participles; conjuring. This is the sense of the verb not only in later but in earlier writers also. see reff **εἰς τὸ** . . belongs to all three participles preceding the εἰς implying the direction, and of course, in a subjective sentence, consequently the *purpose* of their action **καλοῦντος**, pres because the action is extended on to the future by the following words. **βασιλείαν** and **δόξαν** must not be incorporated by the silly ἓν διὰ δυοῖν· God calls us to His *kingdom*, the kingdom of our Lord Jesus, which He shall establish at His coming: and He calls us to His *glory*,—to partake of that glory in His presence, which our Lord Jesus had with Him before the world began; John xvii. 5, 24 See Rom v. 2

13.] **διὰ τοῦτο** is best and most simply referred, with Lunem., to the fact announced in the preceding words—viz. that God καλεῖ ὑμᾶς εἰς, &c Seeing that He is thus calling you, your thorough reception of His word is to us a cause of thanksgiving to Him. That διὰ τοῦτο is made thus 'to refer to a mere appended clause' (Ellic) is no objection: see above on ver. 9. It is surely not possible with Jowett, to refer διὰ τοῦτο 'to the verses both before and after.' **καὶ ἡμεῖς**] We also, i. e. as well as πάντες οἱ πιστεύοντες ἐν τ. Μακεδ. κ. ἐν τ 'Αχ, ch. i. 7 **παραλαβόντες . . ἐδέξασθε**] The former verb denotes only the *hearing*, as

τοῦ [j] θεοῦ [k] ἐδέξασθε οὐ λόγον ἀνθρώπων ἀλλὰ [l] καθώς
[l] ἐστιν ἀληθῶς λόγον θεοῦ, ὃς καὶ [m] ἐνεργεῖται [m] ἐν ὑμῖν
τοῖς πιστεύουσιν. 14 ὑμεῖς γὰρ [n] μιμηταὶ ἐγενήθητε, ἀδελφοί, τῶν [o] ἐκκλησιῶν τοῦ [o] θεοῦ τῶν οὐσῶν ἐν τῇ Ἰουδαίᾳ
ἐν χριστῷ Ἰησοῦ, ὅτι τὰ αὐτὰ ἐπάθετε καὶ ὑμεῖς ὑπὸ τῶν
[p] ἰδίων [q] συμφυλετῶν, καθὼς καὶ αὐτοὶ ὑπὸ τῶν Ἰουδαίων,

j arrangt of words, see Gal ii 9. 2 Pet iii 2. k = ch i 6 reff. l see Matt i 18. 1 Pet ii 15. m Col i 29 reff. n ch i 6 reff. o Acts xx 28. 1 Cor i 2. xi 16. 2 Thess i 4 al. p 2nd pers, Luke vi 41. 1 Pet iii 1. q here only † (Λοσ, Zech xiii 7 Aq.)

the words from θεου (ver 13) to θεου (ver 14) are written twice by ℵ[1]: the second copy is marked for erasure by ℵ-corr[1]. αληθως bef εστιν B 17: om αληθως (twice) ℵ[1]: ins (1st time) bef εστιν ℵ-corr[1]. for υμιν, ημιν ℵ.

14. rec (for τα αυτα) ταὐτά, with A: txt BDFKLℵ rel Orig. om και υμεις D[1]. for 1st υπο, απο D[1]F Orig-ed: for 2nd υπο, απο F.

objective matter of fact: the latter, the *receiving into their minds* as subjective matter of belief: see reff. **ἀκοῆς παρ' ἡμῶν** is perhaps to be taken together—**of hearing** (genitive of apposition) **from us**—i. e. 'which you heard from us.' So Est, Pelt, Olsh, Lunem, all. Or **παραλ παρ' ἡμῶν** may be taken together, as De W., strongly objecting to the construction ἀκοῆς παρ' ἡμῶν, and understanding by λόγος ἀκοῆς the preached word (Wort der Kunde). Lunem answers,—that the construction ἀκοῆς παρ' ἡμῶν is unobjectionable, as ἀκούειν παρά τινος occurs John i 41, al, and substantives and adjectives often retain in construction the force of the verbs from which they are derived (Kuhner, ii 217, cites from Plat Alcib ii p 141, οἶμαι δὲ οὐκ ἀνήκοον εἶναι ἔνιά γε χθιζά τε καὶ πρώιζα γεγενημένα).—that De W.'s rendering is objectionable, because thus no reason is given for separating παρ' ἡμῶν from παραλ, and because ἀκοῆς is superfluous and vapid if the same is already expressed by παραλαβ παρ' ἡμῶν. On the other rendering which is adopted and defended also by Ellicott, there is a significant contrast, St Paul distinguishing himself and his companions, as mere publishers, from God, the great Source of the Gospel. **τ. θεοῦ**] **of** (i e 'belonging to,' 'coming from,' not '*speaking of*,' as Grot, al, see below) **God** (i e. which is God's. But we must not supply '*as*,' with Jowett: no subjective view of theirs being implied in these words, but simply the objective fact of their reception of the word from Paul, Silvanus, and Timotheus). **ἐδέξ.**] See above on παραλ. **Ye received it** (being) **not** (no 'as' must be inserted: he is not speaking of the *Thessalonians' estimate* of the word, but [see above] of the fact of their receiving it as it really was) **the word of men** (having man for its author), **but as it is in reality, the word of God,** which (Bengel, al, take ὅς as referring to θεός: but the Apostle uses always the active ἐνεργεῖν of God, cf. 1 Cor. xii 6. Gal ii. 8, iii 5. Eph i. 11. Phil ii 13 al.,—and [reff.] the middle [not passive] of things) **is also** (besides being merely heard) **active in you that believe.**

14.] Proof of this ἐνεργεῖται,—that they had imitated in endurance the Judæan churches. **ὑμεῖς γάρ** resumes ὑμῖν above. **μιμηταί**] not in intention, but in fact. (On ἐγενήθητε, see on ch i. 5.) Calvin suggests the following reason for his here introducing the conflict of the Judæan churches with the Jews: 'Poterat illis hoc venire in mentem: Si hæc vera est religio, cur eam tam infestis animis oppugnant Judæi, qui sunt sacer Dei populus? Ut hoc offendiculum tollat, primum admonet, hoc eos commune habere cum primis Ecclesiis, quæ in Judæa erant: postea Judæos dicit obstinatos esse Dei et omnis sacræ doctrinæ hostes.' But manifestly this is very far-fetched, and does not naturally lie in the context: as neither does Olsh.'s view, that he wishes to mark out the judaizing Christians, as persons likely to cause mischief in the Thessalonian church. The reason for introducing this character of the Jews here was because (Acts xvii 5 ff) *they* had been the stirrers up of the persecution against himself and Silas at Thessalonica, to which circumstance he refers below. By the mention of them as the adversaries of the Gospel in Judæa he is carried on to say that there, as well as at Thessalonica, they had ever been its chief enemies. And this is a remarkable coincidence with the history in the Acts, where we find him at this time, in Corinth, in more than usual conflict with the Jews (Acts xviii. 5, 6, 12). On **ἐν χριστῷ Ἰησοῦ** Œc remarks, εὐφυῶς διεῖλεν· ἐπειδὴ γὰρ καὶ αἱ συναγωγαὶ τῶν Ἰουδαίων ἐν θεῷ εἶναι δοκοῦσι, τὰς τῶν πιστῶν ἐκκλησίας καὶ ἐν τῷ θεῷ καὶ ἐν τῷ υἱῷ αὐτοῦ λέγει

15 τῶν καὶ τὸν κύριον ἀποκτεινάντων Ἰησοῦν καὶ τοὺς
προφήτας, καὶ ἡμᾶς ʳ ἐκδιωξάντων, καὶ ˢ θεῷ μὴ ˢ ἀρεσ-

r here [and Luke xi 49] only Ps cxviii 157 Joel ii 20
s Rom viii 8 (1 Cor vii 32) ch iv 1 ἀρ, Gal i 10 reff

ABDF KLℵ a b c d e f g h k l m n o 17

15. rec ins ιδιους bef προφητας, with D² ³KL rel syr goth Chr Thdrt Mcion-t om ABD¹Fℵ 17 67² latt coptt æth Orig₂ Dial Tert$_{expr}$ —[for ημας Steph & Mill (not rec) have υμας, appy by mistake.] αρεσαντων F.

εἶναι. συμφυλέτης, ὁμοεθνής, Hesych Herodian says, πολίτης, δημότης, φυλέτης, ἄνευ τῆς σύν, συνέφηβος δὲ καὶ συνθιασώτης κ συμπότης μετὰ τῆς σύν ὅτι καὶ πρόσκαιρος αὐτῶν ἡ κοινωνία, ἐπὶ δὲ τῶν προτέρων οὐχ ὁμοίως And this criticism seems just · the Latins also using *civis meus* not *concivis*, of the enduring relation of fellow-citizen,—but *commilito meus*, not *miles meus*, of the temporary relation of fellow-soldier. See Scaliger, in Lobeck on Phrynichus, p 471 (also p. 172). Ellicott would regard these words merely as supererogatory compounds belonging to later Greek These **συμφυλέται** were not Jews wholly nor in part, but Gentiles only For they are set in distinct contrast here to *οἱ Ἰουδαῖοι*. **τὰ αὐτὰ . . καθώς**] The proper apodosis to *τὰ αὐτά* would be *ἅ*, or *ἅπερ*. But such inaccuracies are found in the classics. Kuhner (ii. 571) cites from Plat. Phæd p 86 A, *εἴ τις διισχυρίζοιτο τῷ αὐτῷ λόγῳ ὥσπερ σύ* so also Legg. p 671 C, Xen. An i 10 10 **αὐτοί**, not '*we ourselves*,' as Erasm, al but the members of the Judæan churches mentioned above. The same construction occurs in Gal i. 22, 23 15, 16] *Characterization of the Jews as enemies of the Gospel and of mankind* Jowett's note is worth quoting "Wherever the Apostle had gone on his second journey, he had been persecuted by the Jews and the longer he travelled about among Gentile cities, the more he must have been sensible of the feeling with which his countrymen were regarded. Isolated as they were from the rest of the world in every city, a people within a people, it was impossible that they should not be united for their own self-defence, and regarded with suspicion by the rest of mankind. But their inner nature was not less repugnant to the nobler as well as the baser feelings of Greece and Rome Their fierce nationality had outlived itself though worshippers of the true God, they knew Him not to be the God of all the nations of the earth. hated and despised by others, they could but cherish in return an impotent contempt and hatred of other men What wonder that, for an instant (? on all this see below), the Apostle should have felt that this Gentile feeling was not wholly groundless? or that he should use words which recall the expression of Tacitus 'Adversus omnes alios hostile odium?' Hist v 5" 15 **τῶν καί**] The repeated *καί* serves for enumeration **τὸν κύρ ἀποκτ Ἰησ** is thus arranged to give prominence to **τὸν κύρ**, and thus enhance the enormity of the deed it should be rendered **who killed Jesus the Lord**, **τὸν κύρ** being in a position of emphasis **κ τοὺς προφήτας**] belongs to *ἀποκτεινάντων* (see Matt xxiii 31—37, Acts vii 52), not to *ἐκδιωξ* as De W His objection, that all the prophets were not killed, is irrelevant neither were they all persecuted The *ἰδίους* of rec appears to have been an early insertion Tert ascribes it to Marcion. **ἐκδιωξ**] **drove out by persecution**, viz. from among you, Acts xvii 5 ff.,—not for the simple verb *διωξ*. (De W.), nor does the preposition merely strengthen the verb (Lunem.),—but it retains its proper meaning (*ὁ δῆμος αὐτῶν ἐξεδίωξε τοὺς δυνατούς, οἱ δὲ ἀπελθόντες . . .* Thuc. i. 24), and the aorist refers it to a definite event, as in the case of *ἀποκτεινάντων* when their *habit* is spoken of, the participles are *present*, e g *ἀρεσκόντων* and *κωλυόντων* below. **ἡμᾶς** refers to Paul and Silas **θεῷ μὴ ἀρεσκ**] The **μή** gives a subjective sense not exactly that of Bengel, al, '*Deo placere non quærentium*' For in strictness, as Ellicott, the shade of subjectivity is only to be found in the aspect in which the subject and the participle is presented to the reader and therefore can hardly be reproduced in English. Compare on the usage, Winer, edn 6, § 55 5, g β, and Ellicott's note here. In **πᾶσιν ἀνθρώποις ἐναντίων**, most Commentators, and recently Jowett (see above), have seen the *odium humani generis* ascribed to the Jews by Tacitus (Hist v. 5), and by several other classic authors (Juv Sat. xiv. 103 ff. Diod. Sic xxxiv. p. 524, &c.). But it is hardly possible that St Paul, himself a Jew, should have blamed an exclusiveness which arose from the strict monotheism and legal purity of the Jew and besides this, the construction having been hitherto carried on by copulæ, but now dropping them, most naturally goes on from *ἐναντίων* to *κωλυόντων*, **in that they prevent**, and thus *κωλ.* specifies

κόντων καὶ πᾶσιν ἀνθρώποις [t] ἐναντίων, 16 [u] κωλυόντων
ἡμᾶς τοῖς ἔθνεσιν λαλῆσαι ἵνα σωθῶσιν, [v] εἰς τὸ [w] ἀνα-
πληρῶσαι αὐτῶν τὰς ἁμαρτίας πάντοτε. [x] ἔφθασεν δὲ
[y] ἐπ' αὐτοὺς ἡ [y] ὀργὴ [z] εἰς τέλος.
17 Ἡμεῖς δέ, ἀδελφοί, [a] ἀπορφανισθέντες ἀφ' ὑμῶν
[b] πρὸς καιρὸν ὥρας [c] προσώπῳ οὐ [c] καρδίᾳ, [d] περισσο-

t = Acts xxvi 9 xxviii 17 1 Thess ii 8 (Mark vi 48. Matt xv 30 Acts xxvii 4) only Prov. xiv 7
u = Matt xix 14 Acts viii 36 xvi 6 1 Kings xxv 26
v ver 12
w Gal vi 2 reff Gen xv 16
x Matt xii 28 ‖ L. Eccl viii 14 etc, Phil iii 16 reff (ch iv 15 2 Cor x 14)
y ch i 10 reff Luke xxi 23
z Matt x 22 xxiv 13 Luke xviii 5 John xiii 1 Amos ix 8
a here only †
b here only, see John v 35 1 Cor vii 5 2 Cor vii 8 Gal ii 5
c 2 Cor v 12
d Gal i 14 reff

16 σωθησονται F. om τας αμαρτιας B εφθακεν BD[1]: txt ACD[2,3]FKLℵ rel Orig$_2$ Eus$_4$ Chr Thdrt Damasc η οργη bef επ' αυτους B vulg(and F-lat) Orig$_1$. aft η οργη ins του θεου DF latt goth lat-ff

wherein the ἐναντιότης consists, viz. in opposing the salvation of mankind by the Gospel. So that the other seems to be irrelevant (so nearly Lünem.).

16. εἰς τό] not of the result merely, '*so that*,'—but of the *intention*, not of the Jews themselves, but of their course of conduct, viewed as having an intent in the divine purposes as so often in St. Paul **ἀναπλ.]** to bring up the measure of their sins to the prescribed point **πάντοτε]** ταῦτα δὲ καὶ πάλαι ἐπὶ τῶν προφητῶν κ. νῦν ἐπὶ τοῦ χριστοῦ κ. ἐφ' ἡμῶν ἔπραξαν, ἵνα πάντοτε ἀναπληρωθῶσιν αἱ ἁμαρτίαι αὐτῶν, Œcum The idea is, not of a new measure having to be filled πάντοτε, but of their being πάντοτε employed in filling up *the measure*. **But** (this their opposition to God and men shall not avail them for) **the** (predestined, or predicted, or merited) **wrath** (of God) **came upon them** (he looks *back* on the fact in the divine counsels as a thing in past time, q. d 'was appointed to come' not 'has come.' No sense of *anticipation* need be sought in ἔφθασεν in later Greek, except when it governs an accusative of the person, as ch iv. 15, see reff) **to the utmost** (to the end of it, i e the wrath so that it shall exhaust all its force on them not 'at last' Wahl, al nor to be taken with ἡ ὀργή, the wrath which shall endure to the end [ἡ εἰς τ. P], as Thl, Œc, al nor to be referred to the Jews, 'so as to make an end of them,' De W)

17—III. 13.] *He relates to them how he desired to return after his separation from them and when that was impracticable, how he sent Timotheus at whose good intelligence of them he was cheered, thanks God for them, and prays for their continuance in love and confirmation in the faith.* **17.]** ἡμεῖς δέ resumes the subject broken off at ver 13 the δέ introducing a contrast to the description of the Jews in vv. 15, 16. **ἀπορφανισθέντες]** ὀρφανός is properly used, as with us, of children who have lost their parents But it is found in a wider sense, e g. John xiv 8,—Pind, Isthm. vii. 16, ὀρφανὸν μυρίων ἑτάρων,—Olymp. ix 92, ὀρφανοὶ γενεᾶς (ὀρφ τέκνων, Dion. Hal Antt i. p. 69, Kypke) Hesych ὀρφανός, ὁ γονέων ἐστερημένος καὶ τέκνων (compare the similitude, ver. 7) The word ἀπορφανίζω occurs Æsch. Choeph 247, of the eagles' brood deprived of their parents. Here it is used in deep affection, the preposition giving the sense of *local* severance, which is further specified by ἀφ' ὑμῶν following. There is no occasion to press the metaphor, as Chrys, al **πρὸς καιρὸν ὥρας] for the space of an hour,** i e. for a very short time it is a combination of the expressions πρὸς καιρὸν and πρὸς ὥραν, see reff. It refers, not to his present impression that the time of separation would still be short (as Flatt and De W.), for thus the past participle ἀπορφανισθέντες forbids, but to the time alluded to in that past participle—**when we had been separated from you for the space of an hour** **προσώπ. οὐ κ.]** datives of the manner in which (i e as Ellic 'marking, with the true limiting power of the case, the metaphorical place,' which in the interpretation of the metaphor would be manner or form, 'to which the sense is restricted') no separation in heart took place **περισσοτ. ἐσπ.] the more abundantly** (because our separation was so short. Lünem. says well "Universal experience testifies, that the pain of separation from friends and the desire of return to them are more vivid, the more freshly the remembrance of the parting works in the spirit, i. e. the less time has elapsed since the parting" Therefore the explanation of Œc. and Thl, after Chrys, is unpsychological περισσοτέρως ἐσπουδάσαμεν, ἢ ὡς εἰκὸς ἦν τοὺς πρὸς ὥραν ἀπολειφθέν-

e Eph. iv. 3 reff. f ch. iii. 10. Gen. xliv. 23. see Col. ii. 1. Rev. xxii. 4. g in good sense, Phil. i. 23 reff. h Gal. v. 2 reff. i (μέν, solitarium), Col. ii. 23 reff. k Phil. iv. 16 reff. l Acts xxiv. 4. Rom. xv. 22. Gal. v. 7.

ABDF KLℵ a b c d e f g h k l m n o 17

τέρως [e] ἐσπουδάσαμεν τὸ [f] πρόσωπον ὑμῶν [f] ἰδεῖν ἐν
πολλῇ [g] ἐπιθυμίᾳ. 18 διότι ἠθελήσαμεν ἐλθεῖν πρὸς ὑμᾶς,
[h] ἐγὼ [i] μὲν [h] Παῦλος, καὶ [k] ἅπαξ καὶ [k] δίς, καὶ [l] ἐνέκοψεν
ἡμᾶς ὁ σατανᾶς. 19 τίς γὰρ ἡμῶν [m] ἐλπὶς ἢ [n] χαρὰ ἢ
[no] στέφανος [op] καυχήσεως,—[q] ἢ οὐχὶ καὶ ὑμεῖς,— ἔμπροσθεν
τοῦ κυρίου ἡμῶν Ἰησοῦ [s] ἐν τῇ αὐτοῦ [s] παρουσίᾳ; 20 ὑμεῖς
γάρ ἐστε ἡ [t] δόξα ἡμῶν καὶ ἡ [n] χαρά. III. 1 διὸ μηκέτι

1 Pet. iii. 7 only. Dan. ix. 26 Theod.-Ald. only. m so of Christ, 1 Tim. i. 1. n Phil. iv. 1. o Ezek. xvi. 12. xxiii. 42. Prov. xvi. 31. p Rom. iii. 27. 1 Cor. xv. 31 al. P. only, exc. James iv. 16. q — Rom. ii. 4. r ch. i. 3 reff. s 1 Cor. xv. 23. ch. iii. 13. v. 23. 1 John ii. 28. παρ. — also Matt. xxiv. 3, &c. ch. iv. 15. 2 Thess. ii. 1, 8. James v. 7, 8 al. (Phil. i. 26 reff.) t — Eph. iii. 13 reff.

18. rec διο, with D[3]KL rel Chr Thdrt Damasc: txt ABD[1]Fℵ m 17. 67[2]. ανεκοψεν F 121.

19. for καυχ., αγαλλιασεως A; *exultationis* Tert. om 3rd ἤ ℵ[1]. rec aft ιησου ins χριστου, with FL rel vulg-ed(with fuld[1] &c) coptt goth Chr Thl Tert al: om ABDKℵ d e h l 17. 67[2] am(and fuld[2]) syrr Thdrt Damasc Œc Ambrst-ed.

20. om 2nd ἡ ℵ[1] 109.

τας. Luth., Bretschn., De W., and Ellic. understand it 'the more,' i. e. than if I *had* been separated from you in heart: but the above seems both simpler and more delicate in feeling) **endeavoured** (implies actual setting on foot of measures to effect it) **in much desire** (i. e. very earnestly) **to see your face.** **18.**] **Wherefore** (as following up this earnest endeavour) **we would have come** (had a plan to come: "not ἐβουλόμεθα, which would indicate merely the disposition: see Philem. 13, 14" [Lün.]) **to you, even I Paul** (the introduction of these words here, where he is about to speak of himself alone, is a strong confirmation of the view upheld above [on ch. i. 9] that he has hitherto been speaking of himself and his companions. The μέν answers to a suppressed δε, q. d. περὶ δὲ τῶν ἄλλων οὐ νῦν ὁ λόγος, or the like. Grot., al., think the suppressed δέ refers to the rest having intended it once only, but the Apostle more times, taking κ. ἅπ. κ. δίς with ἐγ. μ. Παῦ.), **not once only but twice** (literally, 'both once and twice:' not used widely [ἅπ. κ. δίς], but meaning that on *two special occasions* he had such a plan: see ref. The words refer to ἐσπουδάσ., not to ἐγὼ μ. Π.,—see above), **and** (not '*but*:' the simple copula, as in Rom. i. 13, gives the matter of fact, without raising the contrast between the intention and the hindrance) **Satan** (i. e. the devil: not any human adversary or set of adversaries, as De W., al.; whether Satan acted by the Thessalonian Jews or not, is unknown to us, but by whomsoever acting, the agency was *his*) **hindered us** (reff.). **19.**] *accounts for this his earnest desire to see them, by the esteem in which he held them.* The words **ἔμπρ. τ. κυρ. ἡμ. Ἰησ. κ.τ.λ.** must not be transposed in the rendering ("construi haec sic debent, τίς γ. ἡμ. ἐλπ. . . . . ἔμπρ. τ. κυρ. . . . . ἢ οὐχὶ κ. ὑμ." Grot.): for the Apostle, after having asked and answered the question τίς γὰρ κ.τ.λ., breaks off, and specifies that wherein this hope and joy mainly consisted, viz. the glorious prospect of their being found in the Lord at His appearing. But he does not look forward to this as anticipating a reward for the conversion of the Thessalonians (Est., al.), or that their conversion will compensate for his having persecuted the Church before, but from generous desire to be found at that day with the fruits of his labour, and that they might be his boast and he theirs before the Lord: see 2 Cor. i. 14; Phil. ii. 16. On **στέφ. καυχ.**, see reff. and Soph. Aj. 460. **ἢ οὐχὶ καὶ ὑμεῖς**] The ἤ, as Ellic., 'introduces a second and negative interrogation, explanatory and confirmatory of what is implied in the first:' see Winer, edn. 6, § 57. 1. b. **καί**, 'as well as others my converts.' **ἐν τῇ αὐτ. παρ.** further specifies the *ἔμπρ. τοῦ κυρίου*. **20.**] **γάρ** sometimes serves to render a reason for a foregoing assertion, by asserting it even more strongly, q. d. 'it must be so, for the fact is certain.' So Soph. Philoct. 746, "δεινόν γε τοὐπίσαγμα τοῦ νοσήματος." "δεινὸν γάρ, οὐδὲ ῥητόν:" see Hartung, Partikell. i. p. 474. I should be inclined to ascribe to ver. 20, on this very account, a wider range than ver. 19 embraces: q. d. **you will be our joy in the day of the Lord: for ye are** (at all times, ye *are*, abstractedly) **our glory and joy.** This seems to me far better than,

[u] στέγοντες [v] εὐδοκήσαμεν [w] καταλειφθῆναι ἐν Ἀθήναις
μόνοι, 2 καὶ ἐπέμψαμεν Τιμόθεον τὸν ἀδελφὸν ἡμῶν καὶ
[xy] συνεργὸν τοῦ [y] θεοῦ ἐν τῷ εὐαγγελίῳ τοῦ χριστοῦ, [z] εἰς
τὸ [a] στηρίξαι ὑμᾶς καὶ [b] παρακαλέσαι ὑπὲρ τῆς πίστεως
ὑμῶν 3 [c] τὸ μηδένα [d] σαίνεσθαι ἐν ταῖς θλίψεσιν ταύταις·

u 1 Cor ix 12 xiii 7 ver 5 only + Sir viii 17 only. v Gal i 15 reff. w = (John viii 9) Acts xviii 19 al Ruth ii 11. x Phil ii 25 reff. y 1 Cor iii 9. z ch ii 12 reff.

a Acts xviii 23 Rom i. 11 xvi 25 Ps l 12 (14) b = Col ii 2 2 Thess ii 17 Deut iii 28 Job iv 3 c so inf, w το, Rom iv 13 Phil iv 10. see note d here only † οἱ δέ, σαινομεναι ταῖς λεγομενοις, ἐδακρυον τε κ φμωζον, Diog Laert viii 41 (Kypke)

Chap. III. 1 διοτι B δio και a ηυδοκησαμεν BN.

2. rec (for συνεργον του θεου) διακονον του θεου και συνεργον ημων, with D[3]KL rel Syr syr(altern) Chr Thdrt Damasc; διακονον τ. θ. AN 67[2] 73 vulg syr(altern) copt basm æth Bas Pelag-txt, διακονον και συν. του θεου F; συνεργον, omg του θεου, B (harl[1] διακ for συνεργ) arm Pelag-comm: txt (*from objections to which expression the variations probably arose*) D[1] 17 Ambrst rec aft παρακαλεσαι ins υμας, with D[3]KL rel Syr: om ABD[1]FN m 17 latt copt arm Chr Thdrt[1] Damasc Ambrst Pelag. rec (for υπερ) περι, with D[3]L rel Thdrt[1]: txt ABD[1]FKN 17 Bas Chr Thdrt[1]

3 rec for το, τω (*see note*), with a c. τον b[1] ινα F 73 του l 67: txt ABDKLN rel Damasc.

with Ellic, to regard the γάρ as only 'confirmatory and explicative'

III. 1] **διό,** because of our affection for you just expressed; 'hac narratione quæ sequitur, desiderii illius sui fidem facit,' Calvin. **μηκ στέγοντες]** **no longer being able to** (**μηκέτι** gives the subjective feeling as distinguished from οὐκέτι, which would describe the mere objective matter of fact) **bear** (reff) (our continued absence from you), **we** (I Paul, from above, ch. ii 18) **determined** (**εὐδοκήσαμεν** does not carry with it any expression of *pleasure* ['promptam animi inclinationem designat,' Calv], except in so far as we say 'it was our pleasure,'—referring merely to the resolution of the will) **to be left behind** (see Acts xvii 15, 16) **in Athens alone,** 2] **and sent Timotheus our brother and fellow-worker with God** (ref and Ellic's note here) **in** (the field of his working) **the Gospel of Christ** (there does not appear to be any special reason for this honourable mention of Timotheus [as Chrys, τοῦτο οὐ τὸν Τιμόθεον ἐπαίρων φησίν, ἀλλ' αὐτοὺς τιμῶν], further than the disposition to speak thus highly of him on the part of the Apostle. Such is the more natural view, when we take into account the fervid and affectionate heart of the writer. See, however, note on 1 Tim v 23; with which timid character of Timotheus such designations as this may be connected), **in order to confirm you, and exhort on behalf of** (in order for the furtherance of) **your faith,** 3] **that no one might be disquieted** (ref. Soph. Antig 1211, παιδός με σαίνει φθόγγος Eur Rhes 53, σαίνει μ' ἔννυχος φρυκτώρια, &c. In these places **σαίνω** is a *vox media*, conveying the meaning of agitation, disquieting, which the context must interpret for better or worse) **in** (in the midst of) **these tribulations** (which are happening to us both) The construction of **τὸ μηδένα σαίνεσθαι** is doubted. Lunem enters into the matter, as usual, at length and thoroughly He first deals with the rec **τῷ μηδ σ.**, and exposes as ungrammatical the view which would regard it as a *dativus commodi*, as = εἰς τὸ . . , rejecting also Ruckert's more grammatical view, that it indicates "*unde nasciluram* τὴν παράκλησιν *speraverat, quum Timotheum misit, apostolus*" Then as to **τὸ μ. σ.**,—we may take it either 1) with Matthæi, supplying a second εἰς from the former εἰς τὸ στηρ. But then why is not the second εἰς expressed, as in Rom iv 11? Or, 2) with Schott, as a pendent accusative, in the sense '*quod attinet, ad.*' But this is a very rare construction, which has been often assumed without reason (see Bernhardy, pp. 132 ff), and therefore should only be resorted to when no other supposition will help the construction 3) Winer, edn 3 (not in edn 6), § 15. 3 anm, whom De W and Ellicott follow, makes it dependent on παρακαλέσαι, and treats it as a further explanation of ὑπὲρ τῆς πίστεως — viz. '*to exhort, that none should become unstable.*' But if τὸ μηδ. σαίν. depended on παρακαλέσαι, then παρακαλεῖν, in the sense of '*to exhort,*' would be followed by a simple accusative of the thing, which though perhaps possible, see 1 Tim vi 2, is very harsh. [Consult however Ellicott's note, as to the mere mediate dependence of such clauses on the governing verb in comparison with the immediate dependence of substantives] Besides, if τὸ μ σ.

αὐτοὶ γὰρ οἴδατε ὅτι [e] εἰς τοῦτο [e] κείμεθα· 4 καὶ γὰρ ὅτε
[f] πρὸς ὑμᾶς [f] ἦμεν, [g] προελέγομεν ὑμῖν ὅτι [h] μέλλομεν
[i] θλίβεσθαι, καθὼς καὶ ἐγένετο καὶ οἴδατε. 5 διὰ τοῦτο
[k] κἀγὼ μηκέτι [l] στέγων ἔπεμψα [m] εἰς τὸ γνῶναι τὴν πίστιν
ὑμῶν, μή πως [n] ἐπείρασεν ὑμᾶς ὁ [o] πειράζων καὶ [p] εἰς
κενὸν γένηται ὁ [q] κόπος ἡμῶν. 6 ἄρτι δὲ ἐλθόντος Τιμο-
θέου πρὸς ἡμᾶς ἀφ' ὑμῶν καὶ [r] εὐαγγελισαμένου ἡμῖν τὴν
πίστιν καὶ τὴν ἀγάπην ὑμῶν, καὶ ὅτι [s] ἔχετε [st] μνείαν ἡμῶν

ABDF KLℵ a b c d e f g h k l m n o 17

e Luke ii. 34. Phil. i. 17. f Matt. xiii. 56. Mark xiv. 49. John i. 1 al. g 2 Cor. xiii. 2. Gal. v. 21 only. Isa. xli. 26 only. h pres., Gal. ii. 14 reff. but see note. i = 2 Cor. i. 6. iv. 8. vii. 5. 2 Thess. i. 6, 7. 1 Tim. v. 10. Heb. xi. 37 (Matt. vii. 14. Mark iii. 9) only. Ps. cl. 2. k = (see note) John i. 31. Rom. xi. 3. 2 Cor. xi. 17. l ver. 1 reff. m ch. ii. 12 reff. n indic., Gal. iv. 11. Col. ii. 8. Winer, edn. 6, § 56. 2. b, β. o Matt. iv. 3. p 2 Cor. vi. 1. Gal. ii. 2. Phil. ii. 16 bis. Isa. lxv. 23. q 1 Cor. iii. 8. xv. 58. Gen. xxxi. 42. r = Luke i. 19. ii. 10. Rom. x. 15, from Isa. lii. 7. s 2 Tim. i. 3. elsw. as Eph. i. 16 reff. w. ποιεῖσθαι. t here only. see 2 Macc. vii. 20.

4. *προςελεγομεν* D[1] : *ελεγομεν* F. aft *καθως* om *και* F D-lat.
5. *υμων* bef *πιστιν* B m 73.
6. ins *υμων* bef *πιστιν* ℵ. *μνειαν* bef *εχετε* DF : *ημων* bef *εχετε* 17, *mem. nostr. hab.* D-lat vulg(and F-lat).

were a further specification of *ὑπὲρ τῆς πίστεως ὑμῶν*, it would not be accusative but genitive. 4) It only remains that we should take **τὸ μ. σ.** as in apposition with the whole foregoing sentence, *εἰς τὸ στ. ὑ. κ. παρ. ὑπ. τ. πίστ. ὑμ.*—so that *τὸ μηδ. σαίν.* serves only to repeat the same thought, which was before positively expressed, in a negative but better defined form: **τό** being nearly = *τουτέστι*. So that the sense is: **to confirm you and exhort you on behalf of your faith, that is, that no one may be shaken in these troubles: τὸ μηδ.** being dependent, not on a second *εἰς* understood, as in (1), but on the first *εἰς*, which is expressed. With this view I entirely agree, only adding, that instead of making *τό* = *τουτέστι*, I would rather say that *τουτέστι* might have been *inserted before τὸ μηδένα.* **αὐτοὶ γὰρ . . .**] *Reason why no one should be shaken.* Griesb., al., parenthesize *αὐτοὶ—οἴδατε* ver. 4: but wrongly, for *διὰ τοῦτο* ver. 5, connects with this sentence immediately. **οἴδατε**; probably not for Theodoret's reason: *ἄνωθεν ἡμῖν ταῦτα προηγόρευσεν ὁ δεσπότης χριστός*,—but for that given in ver. 4. **εἰς τοῦτο**, viz. to *θλίβεσθαι*, contained in *θλίψεις* above: the subject to *κείμεθα* being 'we Christians.' **4.**] reason for *οἴδατε*. **πρὸς ὑμ.**, see reff. **μέλλομεν** may be taken either as the recit. present, or better as representing the counsel of God, as in *ὁ ἐρχόμενος* and the like. The subject to *μέλλ.*, as above, being 'we Christians.' **οἴδατε**, viz. by experience. **5.**] **διὰ τοῦτο**, because tribulation had verily begun among you (*καθὼς καὶ ἐγένετο*). **κἀγώ** seems to convey a delicate hint that Timotheus also was anxious respecting them: or it may have the same reference as *καὶ ἡμεῖς*, ch. ii. 13,—viz. to the other Christians who had heard of their tribulation. De W. would render, not, '*therefore I also &c.*'—but '*therefore also, I &c.*' But this would require (as Lün.) *διὰ καὶ τοῦτο*—or *καὶ διὰ τ.* **εἰς τὸ γν.**] **that I** (not '*he*') **might know** (be informed about): belongs to the subject of the verb *ἔπεμψα*. **μή πως κ.τ.λ.**] **lest perchance the tempter** (ref.) **have tempted** (not, as Whitby, al., '*seduced*') **you** (indicative betokening the fact absolute), **and our labour might be** (subjunctive, betokening the fact conditional) **to no purpose** (reff.). Fritz. and De W. rather harshly take *μή πως* in two different meanings,—with the first clause as '*an forte*,' and with the second as '*ne forte*.' **6—8.**] *Of the good news brought by Timotheus.* **6.**] **ἄρτι δέ** is by Lünem. (and De W. hesitatingly) separated by a comma from *ἐλθόντος*, and joined to *παρεκλήθημεν* ver. 7. But the direct connexion of **ἄρτι** with an aorist verb is harsher than with an aorist participle, and **παρεκλ.** has already its **διὰ τοῦτο**, which refers back to the whole preceding clause as contained in the *τοῦτο*. I would therefore join *ἄρτι* with *ἐλθόντος*. **But Timotheus having just now come** &c. **εὐαγγ.**] **having brought good news of**: see reff. *οὐκ εἶπεν ἀπαγγείλαντος, ἀλλὰ εὐαγγελισαμένου· τοσοῦτον ἀγαθὸν ἡγεῖτο τὴν ἐκείνων βεβαίωσιν κ. τὴν ἀγάπην.* Chrys. First their Christian state comforted him,—then, their constant remembrance of himself. Thdrt. remarks: *τρία τέθεικεν ἀξιέραστα, τὴν πίστιν, κ. τ. ἀγάπην, κ. τοῦ διδασκάλου τὴν μνήμην. δηλοῖ ἡ μὲν πίστις τῆς εὐσεβείας τὸ βέβαιον ἡ δὲ*

[t] ἀγαθὴν πάντοτε, [u] ἐπιποθοῦντες ἡμᾶς ἰδεῖν [v] καθάπερ
καὶ ἡμεῖς ὑμᾶς, 7 διὰ τοῦτο [w] παρεκλήθημεν, ἀδελφοί,
[x] ἐφ' ὑμῖν [y] ἐπὶ πάσῃ τῇ [z] ἀνάγκῃ καὶ θλίψει ἡμῶν διὰ τῆς
ὑμῶν πίστεως· 8 ὅτι νῦν [a] ζῶμεν ἐὰν ὑμεῖς [b] στήκετε ἐν
κυρίῳ. 9 τίνα γὰρ [c] εὐχαριστίαν δυνάμεθα τῷ θεῷ [d] ἀνταποδοῦναι περὶ ὑμῶν [y] ἐπὶ πάσῃ τῇ χαρᾷ [e] ᾗ [f] χαίρομεν δι'

u w inf, Rom i 11 2 Cor ix 2 2 Tim i 4 (Ps cxviii 28, but w τοῦ) see Phil i 8 reff
v ch ii 11 reff
w = 2 Cor i 4 & passim Isa lxvi 13.
x 2 Cor vii 7 Judg xxi 15 vat
y = 2 Cor i 4. iii 14 vii 4 al
z = 1 Cor vii 26 2 Cor vi 4 al 1 Kings xxii 2
a = 2 Cor xiii 4 see Rom vii 9, or x 5
b Gal v 1 reff
c Eph v 4 reff
d Luke xiv 14 bis Rom xi 35 xii 19 2 Thess i 6 Heb x. 30 only L P H Ps cxv 12 (3)
e attr, Eph i 6 reff
f so Matt ii 10 (John iii 29) see Judg xi 33

7 παρακεκλημεθα A 3 23. 57. for επι, εν F 109 vulg goth Pelag. rec θλιψ και αναγκ, with KL rel Chr Thdrt Damasc. txt ABDFℵ m 17 latt syrr copt arm Ambrst Pelag for ημων, υμων AB². ins και bef δια A. πιστεως bef υμων A fuld.
8 rec στηκητε, with Dℵ¹ (b² c e h 17, e sil): txt A B(ita cod.) FKLℵ³ rel Chr-ms
9 for θεω, κυριω D¹Fℵ¹ copt. for υμων, ημων B¹. η εχαιρομεν D¹.

ἀγάπη τὴν πρακτικὴν ἀρετήν· ἡ δὲ τοῦ διδασκάλου μνήμη, κ ὁ περὶ αὐτὸν πόθος, μαρτυρεῖ τῇ περὶ τὴν διδασκαλίαν στοργῇ. **πάντοτε** belongs more naturally to the foregoing see 1 Cor. i. 4, xv 58, Gal iv 18; Eph. v 20 "ἐπιποθεῖν τι (huc etiam redire structuram ἐπιποθεῖν sq. infinitivo nemo nescit) idem valet quod πόθον ἔχειν ἐπί τι, desiderium ferre in aliquid versum, cf LXX Ps xlii. (xli) 1, ὃν τρόπον ἐπιποθεῖ ἡ ἔλαφος ἐπὶ τὰς πηγὰς τῶν ὑδάτων" Fritz in Rom i 11 So that *direction*, not intensity (which as Fritz also remarks, after the analogy of περιπόθητος, should be expressed by **περι-**, not ἐπιποθεῖν) is the force of the preposition. **ἡμεῖς ὑμᾶς**] scil. ἰδεῖν ἐπιποθοῦμεν. 7] **διὰ τοῦτο**, viz on account of what has just been mentioned, from ἄρτι . . . . ,—**τοῦτο** combining the whole of the good news in one. **ἐφ' ὑμῖν, with reference to you**· as we say, **over you** *You* were the object of our consolation: the faith which you shewed was the means whereby that object was applied to our minds **ἐπὶ πάσ τῇ ἀνάγ κ θλ ἡμ**] **in** (reff, i e '*in the midst of*,'—'*in spite of*') **all our necessity and tribulation**: *what* necessity and tribulation does not appear;—but clearly some external trouble, not, as De W, *care and anxiety for you*, for this would be removed by the message of Timotheus We may well imagine such external trouble, from Acts xviii 5—10 8] **for now** (not so much an adverb of *time*, here, as implying the fulfilment of the condition [ἐάν] which follows so Eur Iph in Aul 644 "συνετὰ λέγουσα μᾶλλον εἰς οἶκτόν μ' ἄγεις" "ἀσύνετα νῦν ἐροῦμεν, εἰ σέ γ' εὐφρανῶ" See more examples in Hartung, Partikell ii p 25, Kuhner. ii p 185) **we live** (the ἀνάγκη and θλῖψις being conceived as a *death* but not to be referred to *everlasting* life, as Chrys. [ζωὴν λέγων τὴν μέλλουσαν], nor weakened to 'vivit qui felix est' [Pelt], but with direct reference to the infringement of the powers of life by **ἀνάγκ** and θλ, as Lunem, "we are in full strength and freshness of life, we do not feel the sorrows and tribulations with which the outer world surrounds us") **if ye stand fast in the Lord** The conditional form of this last sentence, with **ἐάν**, not ἐπεί, carries it forward as an exhortation for the future also, while the solœcistic indicative gives the Apostle's confident expectation that such would be the case. The reading must not be dismissed, as Ellic, by taking refuge in Scrivener's assertion that permutations of similar vowels are occasionally found even in the best MSS I have examined the Vatican Codex through the greater part of the N T, and can safely say that these permutations are found only in such cases as H, I, and EI, and O and Ω in doubtful inflexions, as ἑωρακ. and ἑορακ.; not in cases like the present, nor in any ordinary occurrences of long and short vowels See remarks on Rom. v 1; and prolegg. to Vol I ch vi § i 36, 37. There were (ver 10) ὑστερήματα in their faith, requiring καταρτισις 9] And this vigour of life shews itself in the earnest desire of abundant thanksgiving so the **γάρ** accounts for, and specifies the action of, the ζωή just mentioned. **τινα, what**— i. e what sufficient —? **ἀνταπ**] reff · *thanks* is itself a *return* for God's favours see especially ref. Ps ἐπί, may be taken as above (ref. y), or as **for,—in return for** the two meanings in fact run up into one. **πάσ τῇ χαρᾷ**, **all the joy** i e. not the joy from so many different

ὑμᾶς [g] ἔμπροσθεν τοῦ θεοῦ ἡμῶν; 10 [h] νυκτὸς καὶ [h] ἡμέρας
[i] ὑπερεκπερισσοῦ δεόμενοι [k] εἰς τὸ [l] ἰδεῖν ὑμῶν τὸ [l] πρόσωπον καὶ [m] καταρτίσαι τὰ [n] ὑστερήματα τῆς πίστεως ὑμῶν.
11 [o] αὐτὸς δὲ ὁ [p] θεὸς καὶ [p] πατὴρ ἡμῶν καὶ ὁ κύριος ἡμῶν
Ἰησοῦς [q] κατευθύναι τὴν ὁδὸν ἡμῶν πρὸς ὑμᾶς. 12 ὑμᾶς
δὲ ὁ κύριος [r] πλεονάσαι καὶ [s] περισσεύσαι τῇ ἀγάπῃ εἰς
ἀλλήλους καὶ εἰς πάντας, [t] καθάπερ καὶ ἡμεῖς εἰς ὑμᾶς,

ABDF KLℵ a b c d e f g h k l m n o 17

g — ch i 8 reff. h ch ii 9 reff. i Eph iii 20 reff. Dan. iii 22 Theod-ald-compl (-σσῶς, ch v 13.) k constr., Phil i 23 reff. l ch ii 17 reff. m — Matt iv 21 (Luke vi 40) Gal vi 1 Ezra iv 12, 13, 16. n Phil ii 30 reff. o ch iv 16. v 23 2 Thess ii 16 iii 16. p Gal i 4 reff. q Luke i 79 2 Thess iii 5 only Ps v 8. r trans., here only Num xxvi 54 Ps lxx 21 (intr., Rom v 20 al.) Paul only, exc 2 Pet i 8. s trans., 2 Cor iv 15 ix 8 Eph i 8 only‡. t ver 6.

11 for θεου, κυριου ℵ[1]. om ιησ. D[1]. rec aft ιησους ins χριστος, with D[3b]FKL rel vulg syrr copt goth Ath: om ABD[1a]ℵ 17 am(with demid harl[1] tol) D-lat æth-rom Ambr Vocat. for 3rd ημων, υμων ℵ[1]
12 for κυριος, θεος A 73: κυρ ιησους D[1]F(not F-lat). om am[1] Syr. της αγαπης F.

sources, but the joy in its largeness and depth: q. d. τῇ χαρᾷ τῇ μεγάλῃ. ᾗ attr. for ἥν,—see Matt. ii. 10: not as John iii. 29,—see note there. **ἔμπρ. τ. θεοῦ ἡμ.** shews the joy to be of the very highest and best,—no joy of this world, or of personal pride, but one which will bear, and does bear, the searching eye of God, and is *His* joy (John xv. 11). **10.] νυκτ. κ. ἡμ.** see on ch. ii 9. **ὑπερεκπ.** see reff., and cf. Mark vi 51. **δεόμενοι** belongs to the question of ver. 9—q. d., 'what thanks can we render, &c., proportioned to the earnestness of our prayers, &c.?' So that δεόμενοι would best be rendered **praying as we do**. **εἰς τό**—direction, or aim, of the prayers. **καταρτίσαι τὰ ὑστ.]** τὰ ἐλλείποντα πληρῶσαι, Thdrt: cf. 2 Cor ix. 12. These **ὑστερήματα** were consequences of their being as yet novices in the faith: partly theoretical, e. g. their want of stability respecting the παρουσία, and of fixed ideas respecting those who had fallen asleep in Christ,—partly practical, ch iv 1. One can hardly conceive a greater perverseness than that of Baur, who takes this passage for a proof that the Thessalonian church had been long in the faith.

11—13.] *Good wishes, with respect to this his earnest desire, and to their continued progress in love and holiness.* **11. αὐτός]** Not as De W. in contrast with the δεόμενοι just spoken of,—but as Chrys., αὐτὸς δὲ ὁ θεὸς ἐκκόψαι τοὺς πειρασμοὺς τοὺς πανταχοῦ περιέλκοντας ἡμᾶς, ὥστε ὀρθὴν ἐλθεῖν πρὸς ὑμᾶς,—i. e. it exalts the absolute power of God and the Lord Jesus,—if He expedites the way, it will be accomplished. **αὐτός** then is in contrast with *ourselves*, who have once and again tried to come to you, but have been hindered by Satan. Lünem. remarks that ὁ θεός is best taken absolute, and ἡμῶν referred to πατήρ only. More majesty is thus given to the αὐτὸς ὁ θεός, although αὐτός refers to the whole. Cf. 2 Thess ii 16, 17. **κατευθύναι]** not infinitive, but third person singular optative aorist. It certainly cannot be passed without remark, that the two nominatives should thus be followed, here and in 2 Thess. ii 16, 17, by a singular verb. It would be hardly possible that this should be so, unless some reason existed in the subjects of the verb. Mere *unity of will* between the Father and the Son (Lünem.) would not be enough, unless absolute unity were also in the writer's mind. Athanasius therefore seems to be right in drawing from this construction an argument for the unity of the Father and the Son. **πρὸς ὑμᾶς** more naturally belongs to κατευθύναι than to τὴν ὁδὸν ἡμῶν, in which case it should be τὴν ὁδ. ἡμ. τὴν πρὸς ὑμ. **12.] ὑμᾶς δέ**—emphatic—'sive nos veniemus sive minus,' Bengel. **ὁ κύριος** may refer either to the Father, or to Christ. It is no objection to the former, that τ. θεοῦ κ. πατρ. ἡμ. is repeated below, any more than it is to the latter that τ. κυρ. ἡμ. Ἰ. is so repeated. I should rather understand [still, notwithstanding Ellic.'s note] it of the Father: see 2 Cor ix 8. **πλεονάσαι]** transitive, see reff: **enlarge you**—not merely in *numbers*, as Thdrt., but in *yourselves*, in richness of gifts and largeness of faith and knowledge—fill up your ὑστερήματα, ver. 10. **περισσεύσαι** (reff.), **make you to abound**. **εἰς πάντας]** **toward all men**, not, as Thdrt., πάντας τοὺς ὁμοπίστους, but as Est., '*etiam infideles et vestræ salutis inimicos*.' **καθ. κ. ἡμεῖς**, viz. περισσεύομεν τῇ ἀγάπῃ:—ἔχετε γὰρ μέτρον κ.

13 [u] εἰς τὸ [v] στηρίξαι ὑμῶν τὰς καρδίας [w] ἀμέμπτους ἐν
[x] ἁγιωσύνῃ [y] ἔμπροσθεν τοῦ [p] θεοῦ καὶ [p] πατρὸς ἡμῶν [z] ἐν
τῇ [z] παρουσίᾳ τοῦ κυρίου ἡμῶν Ἰησοῦ μετὰ πάντων τῶν
[a] ἁγίων αὐτοῦ.

IV. 1 [b] Λοιπὸν οὖν, ἀδελφοί, [c] ἐρωτῶμεν ὑμᾶς καὶ
[d] παρακαλοῦμεν [e] ἐν κυρίῳ Ἰησοῦ, ἵνα καθὼς [f] παρελάβετε
παρ᾽ ἡμῶν [g] τὸ πῶς δεῖ ὑμᾶς [h] περιπατεῖν καὶ [i] ἀρέσκειν
[i] θεῷ, καθὼς καὶ [h] περιπατεῖτε, ἵνα [k] περισσεύητε μᾶλλον.

u Eph i 12 reff. v Rom i 11 xvi 25 ver 2 Ps i 12. (14) w Phil ii 15 reff constr, Phil iii 21 reff x Rom i 4. 2 Cor vii 1 only Ps xcvi 12 y — ch i 3 reff z ch ii 19 reff a see Ps lxxxviii 7 Dan iv 10 Theod Jude 14. b 1 Cor i 16 iv 2 2 Cor xiii 11 (2 Thess iii 1) c = Phil iv 3 ch v 12 2 Thess ii 1 al d = Eph iv 1 reff e = 2 Cor ii 17 Eph iv 17 al f = 1 Cor xi 23 xv 1 Gal i 9, 12 al. g art., Mark ix 23 Luke i 62 Rom viii 26 h = Rom vi 4 al fr i ch ii 15 reff k Rom iii 7 Phil i 26 ver 10 al fr Eccl iii 19

13. *τας καρδιας* bef *υμων* DF latt. *αμεμπτως* BL Ps-Ath. *αγιοσυνη* B[1]DF: *δικαιοσυνη* A 23. 57. rec aft *ιησου* ins *χριστου*, with FL rel vulg syrr copt goth æth-pl Ps-Ath[4]. om ABDKℵ d l m n am æth Damasc Ambr—om *ιησ* also m at end ins *αμην* (*an ecclesiastical lection ending here*) AD[1]ℵ[1] m vulg copt æth arm Pelag Bede om BD[2]FKLℵ[3] rel fuld[1] syrr goth Tert Ambrst Vocat.

Chap. IV 1. rec ins *το* bef *λοιπον*, with B[2] a c g h k Chr Thdrt: om AB[1]DFKℵ rel Chr-ms Damasc. om *ουν* B[1] d[1] k m 17 Syr copt Chr Thl: *autem* D-lat. ins *τω* bef *κυριω* ℵ. rec om 1st *ινα*, with AD[3]KLℵ rel syr Chr Thdrt Damasc. ins BD[1]F m 17 latt Syr arm Chr-ms Ambrst Pelag. rec om *καθως και περιπατειτε* (*see notes*), with D[3]KL rel Syr Chr Thdrt Damasc Thl Œc: ins ABD[1]Fℵ m 17 vulg copt goth æth arm Ambrst *περισσευσητε* B.

παράδειγμα τῆς ἀγάπης ἡμᾶς, Thl

13.] εἰς τὸ στηρίξαι—the further and higher aim of *πλεον κ περισσ*—**in order to confirm** (i. e *εἰς τὸ τὸν κύριον στηρίξαι*—'in order that He may confirm') **your hearts** (not merely *ὑμᾶς*. *ἐκ γὰρ τῆς καρδίας ἐξέρχονται διαλογισμοὶ πονηροί*, Chrys) **unblameable** (i. e. so as to be unblameable cf reff and *εἰσόκε θερμὰ λοῦτρα θερμήνῃ*, Il ξ 6,—*εὔφημον, ὦ τάλαινα, κοίμησον στόμα*, Æsch. Ag 1258,—*τῶν σῶν ἀδέρκτων ὀμμάτων τητώμενος*, Soph Œd. Col 1200) **in holiness** (belongs to *ἀμέμπτ*,—the sphere in which the blamelessness is to be shewn—not to *στηρίξαι*) **before** (Him who is) **God and our Father** (or **our God and Father** This ensures the genuineness of this absence of blame in holiness that it should be not only before men, but also before God), **at** (in) **the coming**, &c. **ἁγίων**—we need not enter into any question whether these are angels, or saints properly so called the expression is an O. T one,—Zach xiv. 5, LXX,—and was probably meant by St. Paul to include both. Certainly (2 Thess. i 7. Matt. xxv. 31, al) He will be accompanied with the *angels* but also with the spirits of the just, cf ch. iv 14.

Chap. IV 1—V. 24] Second portion of the Epistle *consisting of exhortations and instructions* 1—12] *Exhortations* and 1—8] *to a holy life.* 1] **λοιπόν** has no reference to time, *ἀεὶ κ. εἰς τὸ διηνεκές*, Chr, Thl., but introduces this second portion, thus dividing it from the first, and implying the *close* of the Epistle. St. Paul uses it towards the end of his Epistles see in addition to reff., Eph. vi. 10, Phil. iv. 8. **οὖν**, in furtherance of the wish of ch iii. 12, 13: *τούτῳ κεκρημένοι τῷ σκόπῳ προσφέρομεν ὑμῖν τὴν παραίνεσιν* **ἐρωτῶμεν**] in the classics, only used of *asking a question* but in N. T. (as the Heb שָׁאַל, Lün, which however, in the sense of *requesting*, is rendered in the LXX by *αἰτεῖν*) it has both meanings of our verb '*to ask*' (reff). **παρακ. ἐν κυρ Ἰησ.] we exhort you in** (as our element of exhortation, in whom we do all things pertaining to the ministry [see Rom ix 1] Eph iv 17—not '*by*,' as a 'formula jurandi,' which is contrary to N T usage, see Fritzsche on Rom ix 1) **the Lord Jesus, that as ye received** (see on ch. ii 13) **from us how** (*τό* is not superfluous: it collects and specifies what follows, q d—'the manner of your,' &c) **ye ought to walk and to please God** (i e, to please God in your walk and conduct—to walk, and thereby to please God), **as also ye are walking** (this addition, says Lün, is required as well [see var readd] by internal considerations. For **ἵνα περισσ** requires the assumption of a prior commencement [see ver 10] and such a commencement would not be implied in the preceding text, without **καθὼς καὶ**

l Acts v. 28 xvi 24 1 Tim i 5, 18 only +
m = 2 Cor i 5
n John vi 40 see 1 Pet ii 15
o Rom vi 19, 22 1 Cor i 30 2 Thess ii 13 1 Tim ii 15 Paul only, exc Heb xii 14 1 Pet i 2 2 Macc xiv 36
p w ἀπο, Acts xv 20 ch v 22 Job i 1, 8 gen without ἀπο, Acts xv 29 1 Tim iv 3. 1 Pet. ii 11
q Matt v 32 al fr Gen xxxviii 24
r = Phil iv 12 Job xxxiv 19
s = see note

2 οἴδατε γὰρ τίνας [l] παραγγελίας ἐδώκαμεν ὑμῖν [m] διὰ τοῦ
κυρίου Ἰησοῦ. 3 [n] τοῦτο γάρ ἐστιν [n] θέλημα τοῦ θεοῦ, ὁ
[o] ἁγιασμὸς ὑμῶν, [p] ἀπέχεσθαι ὑμᾶς ἀπὸ τῆς [q] πορνείας,
4 [r] εἰδέναι ἕκαστον ὑμῶν τὸ ἑαυτοῦ [s] σκεῦος [s] κτᾶσθαι ἐν

ABDF KLℵ a b c d e f g h k l m n o 17

2 παρεδωκαμεν D¹F δεδωκ ℵ m 73 80. aft κυριου ins ημων D¹F 45 Syr æth Chr Thl Hil. om ιησ (and not δια τ κυρ) 17 aft ιησ. ins χριστου F a 19 27 45 syrr Chr Hil
3 ins το bef θελημα AF e Clem Antch Damasc: om BDKL rel Chr Thdrt. om του D¹F l. for της, πασης ℵ³ 73 115 Syr Chr Thdrt Thl πασι(sic) της F.
4. ins ενα bef εκαστον B²(see table) D³ᵃ 73 (vss) Chr εκαστος AF. κτασθαι

περιπατεῖτε Evidently the Apostle would originally have written ἵνα, καθ παρ παρ' ἡμ τὸ πῶς κ τ λ . . ., οὕτως καὶ περιπατῆτε· but while writing, altered this his intended expression, that he might not say too little, wishing to notice the good beginning already made by the Thessalonians. The repetition of ἵνα after so long an intervening clause is too natural to have given rise [as De W thinks] to the insertion) **that ye abound yet more**, viz: ἐν τῷ οὕτως περιπατεῖν· not, as Chrys, ἵνα ἐκ πλείονος περιουσίας μὴ μέχρι τῶν ἐντολῶν ἵστασθε, ἀλλ' ἵνα καὶ ὑπερβαίνητε. 2] takes up the **καθὼς παρελάβετε** of the former verse, and appeals to their memory in its confirmation See similar appeals in Gal iv. 13, 1 Cor. xv 1 **παραγγ**] **commands**, see reff. The stress is on **τίνας**, to which τοῦτο answers, ver 3. **διὰ τ. κ. Ἰησ.] by**, i e **coming from**, παραγγελθείσας διά. So τὰς διὰ τῶν ὀλίγων πολιτείας, Demosth. p 189· δι' ἑαυτοῦ, of himself, Xen. Cyr. viii. 1 43: see Bernhardy, p 236 3.] *further specification* (γάρ) *of the* παραγγελίαι see above. **τοῦτο** is the subject, not the predicate (as De W) see Rom. ix 8 Gal. iii 7 not superfluous, as Pelt, but emphatically prefixed (so Lunem). **θέλημα τ. θεοῦ** serves to take up again the διὰ τ κυρ Ἰησοῦ. The article *may be* omitted, because the predicate θέλημα τ. θ. is not distributed (?) but in this case, τὸ θέλ. would be equally applicable, there being no danger of τὸ θέλ being mistaken for 'the whole will,' but rather specifying 'that which forms part of the will' This explanation is not to be abandoned, as Ellic, on account of the merely occasional omission of the article after a noun substantive, mentioned by Middleton and Ellic for the reason of that omission is to be sought rather in logic than in idiom. Rather perhaps should we say that there is in Greek a tendency to omit articles before predicates, even where such an omission cannot be logically pressed **ὁ ἁγ ὑμ** is in apposition with θέλ τ. θ. as a 'locus communis,' the will of God respecting us being known to be, our sanctification and then this sanctification being afterwards specified as consisting in ἀπέχεσθαι, &c Therefore **ἁγιασμός** must be taken in the most general sense, and that which is afterwards introduced, ἀπέχεσθαι, &c, as a *part* of our ἁγιασμός. **ὑμῶν** is the objective genitive, **of you** **ἀπέχεσθαι** and **εἰδέναι** are not the negative and positive sides of **ὁ ἁγ ὑμ** as Lunem and Ellic.,—for the negative comes in again in verses 5, 6,—but the latter (εἰδέναι to διεμαρτυράμεθα, ver. 6) further specifies and ensures the former. 4] **εἰδέναι, know how** (reff.). On the meaning of **τὸ σκεῦος**, there has been much difference. Very many Commentators understand it of '*the body*.' (So, among others, Chrys. [see below], Thdrt., Œc, Thl, Tert, Pelag, Calv, Corn.-a-Lap, Beza, Grot., Calov., Ham, Beng, Macknight, Pelt, Olsh, Baumg.-Crus.) But it is fatal to this interpretation, (1) that it must force an untenable meaning on **κτᾶσθαι**, which can only mean '*to acquire*,' not '*to possess*.' Chrys., whose sense of Greek usage led him to feel this, tries to fit the meaning '*to acquire*' into the sense ἡμεῖς αὐτὸ κτώμεθα, ὅταν μένῃ καθαρὸν κ. ἐστιν ἐν ἁγιασμῷ ὅταν δὲ ἀκάθαρτον, ἁμαρτία—(so Olsh also), but this is lame enough, and would not, as De W remarks, answer for the other member of the sentence, μὴ ἐν πάθει ἐπιθυμίας (2) that the mere use of **σκεῦος**, without any explanation, could hardly point at the *body* In all the passages ordinarily quoted to support it, the metaphor is further explained by the context:—e. g, Barnab, ep 7, 11, pp 741, 760, τὸ σκεῦος τοῦ πνεύματος αὐτοῦ,—Philo, quod det pot. insid § 46, vol. i. p 223,

[o] ἁγιασμῷ καὶ τιμῇ, 5 μὴ ἐν [t] πάθει [u] ἐπιθυμίας [v] καθάπερ
καὶ τὰ ἔθνη τὰ μὴ [w] εἰδότα τὸν θεόν, 6 [x] τὸ μὴ [y] ὑπερ-

t Rom i 26 Col iii 5 (reff.) only
u Rom i 24 al fr
v ch iii 6, 12 only Jer v 22
w Gal. iv 8 2 Thess i 8 (Jer iv 22)
x art., ver 1 reff
y here

bef το ε σκευος DF goth. ins εν bef τιμη ℵ[1] d.

τῆς ψυχῆς ἀγγεῖον τὸ σῶμα,—de migr. Abr § 36, vol i p 467, τοῖς ἀγγείοις τῆς ψυχῆς σώματι κ. αἰσθήσει,—Cic. disp. Tusc. i. 22. 'corpus quidem quasi vas est aut aliquod animi receptaculum,'—Lucret iii 441: 'corpus, quod vas quasi constitit ejus (sc animæ).' 2 Cor iv. 7 is evidently no case in point, ὀστρακίνοις being there added, and the body being simply *compared* to an *earthen vessel* (3) that the order of the words is against it In **τὸ ἑαυτοῦ σκεῦος**, the emphasis must lie on **ἑαυτοῦ**—cf. 1 Cor. vii 2, ἕκαστος τὴν ἑαυτοῦ γυναῖκα ἐχέτω Had the body been meant, this would be without import, and it would more naturally have been τὸ σκεῦος ἑαυτοῦ (or αὐτοῦ) (4) But a more fatal objection than any of the former is, that the context is entirely against the meaning The ἁγιασμός has been explained to consist in **ἀπέχεσθαι ἀπὸ τῆς πορνείας.** And now this **πορνεία** comes to be specified, wherein it consists, and how it may be guarded against: viz. in carrying on the divinely-appointed commerce of the sexes in holiness and honour In fact, the thought is exactly as in 1 Cor vii 2, διὰ τὰς πορνείας ἕκαστος τὴν ἑαυτοῦ γυναῖκα ἐχέτω, κ. ἑκάστη τὸν ἴδιον ἄνδρα ἐχέτω. Many have therefore understood σκεῦος in its literal meaning as applied to τὸ πρᾶγμα,—i. e. the *woman* (or indeed the *man*, on the other side, inasmuch as the woman has ἐξουσία over his body, see 1 Cor vii 4. So that thus it would be an exhortation to the woman also so De Wette) Thus the context would be satisfied, and the emphatic position of **ἑαυτοῦ** (as in 1 Cor. vii 2);—and **κτᾶσθαι** would retain its proper meaning **that each of you should know how to acquire his own vessel** (for this purpose) **in sanctification** (κτᾶσθαι ἐν ἁγ. belong together) **and honour.** This sense of **σκεῦος** is found in the Jewish books (Megill. Esth. i. 11: "In convivio dixerunt aliqui mulieres Medicæ sunt pulcriores alii, Persicæ sunt pulcriores Dixit Ahasuerus Vas meum, quo ego utor, nec Persicum est nec Medicum, sed Chaldaicum"). And the expression κτᾶσθαι γυναῖκα is common. cf Xen. Symp. ii 10. ταύτην (Ξανθίππην) κέκτημαι Ruth iv. 10, Sir. xxxvi. 24 And so Thdr. Mops (σκεῦος τὴν ἰδίαν ἑκάστου γαμετὴν ὀνομάζει), some in Thdrt. (τινὲς τὸ ἑαυτοῦ σκεῦος τὴν ὁμόζυγα ἡρμήνευσαν), Aug (contr. Jul iv 10, [56,] vol x p 765,—'ut sciret unusquisque possidere vas suum, hoc est, uxorem:' cf also ib. v 9 [35], p 805 de nupt et conc i 8 [9], p 418,—'non solum igitur conjugatus fidelis vase non utatur alieno, quod faciunt a quibus uxores alienæ appetuntur sed nec ipsum proprium in concupiscentiæ carnalis morbo possidendum sciat.' But he mistakes **κτᾶσθαι** for *possidere*, and so understands the command as given *conjugatis fidelibus*), Thom Aquin, Zwingle, Est., Heins., Wetst, Schottg, Michaelis, Koppe, Schott, De Wette, Lunem., al. (Much of the foregoing note is from De W and Lun) The objection to the above view, that thus only *men* would be addressed (Calv, al.) is easily answered (besides as above, under 4) by observing that in other places also, where **πορνεία** is in question, the male only is exhorted, e. g. 1 Cor vi. 15–18 the female being included by implication, and bound to interpret on her side that which is said of the other 5] **ἐν πάθει ἐπιθ,—πάθει** having the emphasis,—'in the mere *passio* of lust,'—as Thdr. Mops. (Lun), ὡς ἂν τοῦτο ποιοῦντος οὐκέτι ταύτῃ ὡς γυναικὶ συνόντος ἀλλὰ διὰ μίξιν μόνην ἁπλῶς, ὅπερ πάθος ἐπιθυμίας ἐκάλεσεν.

καθ καί] the **καί** so usual after particles of comparison, points to the association in the same category which the particle supposes καὶ ἡμῖν ταὐτὰ δοκεῖ ἅπερ καὶ βασιλεῖ, Xen. Anab ii 1 22 See examples in Hartung, Partikell. ii. 127: and cf ch ii 13; iii 6, 12, &c. **τὰ μὴ εἰδ τ θ] μή**, because the Gentiles are spoken of by the writer from this point of view It is not a mere fact which is stated, but that fact as logically interwoven with the course of the context. and hence the subjective negative See reff 6.] I cannot help regarding it as most unnatural, to interpret this verse of a new subject introduced, viz. the not wronging one another in the business of life. How such Commentators as De Wette and Lunem can have entertained this view, I am at a loss to imagine For (1) the sense is carried on from vv. 4, 5, without even the repetition of ἕκαστον ὑμῶν to mark the change of topic: and (2) when the Apostle sums up the whole

βαίνειν καὶ [z] πλεονεκτεῖν ἐν [a] τῷ πράγματι τὸν ἀδελφὸν
αὐτοῦ, διότι [b] ἔκδικος κύριος περὶ πάντων τούτων, καθὼς
καὶ [c] προείπαμεν ὑμῖν καὶ [d] διεμαρτυράμεθα. 7 οὐ γὰρ
[f h] ἐκάλεσεν ἡμᾶς ὁ θεὸς [g i] ἐπὶ [k] ἀκαθαρσίᾳ, ἀλλ' [h] ἐν
[l] ἁγιασμῷ. 8 [m] τοιγαροῦν ὁ [n] ἀθετῶν οὐκ ἄνθρωπον
[n] ἀθετεῖ, ἀλλὰ τὸν θεὸν τὸν [καὶ] [o p] δόντα τὸ [o] πνεῦμα
αὐτοῦ τὸ ἅγιον [p] εἰς ὑμᾶς.

ABDF KLℵ a b c d e f g h k l m n o 17

z 2 Cor ii 11 vii 2 xii 17, 18 only P Ezek xxii 27 Hab ii 9 only. a (see note) 2 Cor vii 11 b Rom xiii 4 only † Wisd xii 12 Sir xxx 6 only. c Acts i 16. Gal v 21 only † d Luke xvi 28 Acts ii 40 al7 1 Tim v 21 2 Tim ii 14 iv 1 Heb ii 6 only L.P H Ezek xvi 2 f = Rom viii 30 ix 11 1 Cor vii 15 Eph iv 1 2 Thess ii 14 al g Gal v 13. h 1 Cor vii 15. Gal i 6 Eph iv 4 i Eph ii 10 k = Rom i 24 vi 19 Gal v 19 al (see ch. ii 3) l ver 3 reff m Heb xii 1 only Prov i 31 al n = Luke x 16 John xii 48 Isa. xxxiii 1 (see Gal ii 21 reff) o Luke xi 13 John iii 34 Acts v 32 viii 18 xv 8 Rom v 5 al p = Luke xv 22 see 2 Cor. i 22.

6. rec ins ο bef κυριος, with D³FKLℵ³ rel Clem om ABD¹ℵ¹ 17 προειπομεν AKL rel Clem Chr Thdrt txt BDFℵ n o. διεμαρτυρομεθα D³K d e f l¹ m n o
7. αλλα BD³.
8 om 1st τον D¹F om και ABD³ o 17 D-lat Syr goth Ath Did Chr Thdrt-ms Thl Ambr Ambrst Pelag ins D¹FKLℵ vulg syr Clem Thdrt Damasc Œc Bede. for δοντα, διδοντα (corrn to make the gift of the spirit present) BDFℵ¹ Ath Did · txt AKLℵ³ rel 67² vss Clem Chr Thdrt Damasc. αυτο το πν. το αγ εις A. rec ημας (to suit the idea that ανθρ was the Ap himself), with A c vulg-ed(and F-lat) syr-txt Chr txt BDFKLℵ rel am(with fuld harl² tol) Syr syr-marg copt goth arm Clem Did Chr-ms Damasc Œc.

in ver 7, he mentions merely impurity, without the slightest allusion to the other To say that more than one kind of sin must be mentioned because of περὶ πάντων τούτων, is mere trifling the πάντα ταῦτα (not ταῦτα πάντα, which would collect many individuals into a whole) generalizes from the sin mentioned to a wider range. The interpretation which I impugn, is also that of Zwingle, Calv, Grot, Calov, Le Clerc, Wolf, Koppe, Flatt. I understand the verse, with Chrys, Thdrt, Œc, Thl, Jer, Erasm, Est, Corn-a Lap, Heins, Whitby, Wetst, Kypke, Beng, Michaelis, Pelt, Olsh, all, to refer to the *sins of uncleanness*, and continue vv 4, 5—**that he should not** (viz τινά, contained in the αὐτοῦ following so that τὸ μὴ . . is a further specification of ὁ ἁγιασμός, rather than parallel with εἰδέναι) **set at nought** (the order of the sentence requires that ὑπερβ. should not stand *absolutely*, as De W., Lün., al, for '*transgress*' [μὴ νῦν ὑπέρβαιν', ἀλλ' ἐναισίμως φέρε, Eur Alc 1077· ὅτε κέν τις ὑπερβήῃ κ ἁμάρτῃ, Il ι 497], but *transitively* otherwise τινα would have occurred after ὑπερβαίνειν to mark the distinction of construction. and ὑπερβ. with an accusative of person signifies either '*to pass by*' or '*take no notice*,' 'posthabere,' as Herod iii 89, ὑπερβαίνων τοὺς πρυσεχέας. or '*to go beyond*' or '*surpass*,' as Plat Tim 24 D, πάσῃ πάντας ἀνθρώπους ὑπερβεβηκότες ἀρετῇ. Of these, the former seems most applicable here: see below) **or overreach his brother in the matter** (viz of τὸ ἑαυτοῦ σκεῦος κτᾶσθαι—that there should be among you none of those strifes on account of the πάθη ἐπιθυμίας, the 'teterrima belli causa' in the heathen world. As Jowett rightly observes, "It is not necessary to suppose that any idea of unchastity is conveyed by the term πλεονεκτεῖν, any more than in the tenth commandment, 'Thou shalt not covet thy neighbour's wife' The meaning exclusively arises from the connexion and application of the word." How τῷ πράγματι can ever signify τοῖς πράγμασιν, 'business affairs' [De W., alt], I cannot imagine; and it is equally futile [with E. V. arm] to take τῷ for τῳ = τινι in the N T. "It is probable that the obscurity of the passage arises partly from the decency in which the Apostle clothes it" Jowett), **because God is the avenger** ('*righter*,' in such cases of setting at nought and overreaching) **of all these things** (viz. cases of ὑπερβασία and πλεονεξία, and by inference, lustful sins like them) **as also** (see on ver 5) **we before told you and constantly testified** 7.] This verse (see above) is in my view decisive for the above rendering of ver 6. There is no mention here of *avarice* · nor is it possible to understand **ἀκαθαρσία,** when ver 3 has gone before, of any thing but carnal impurity. Chap ii. 3, which is adduced to shew that it may here represent covetousness, is a very doubtful ex-

9 Περὶ δὲ τῆς [q] φιλαδελφίας οὐ [r] χρείαν [r] ἔχετε γράφειν ὑμῖν· αὐτοὶ γὰρ ὑμεῖς [s] θεοδίδακτοί ἐστε [t] εἰς τὸ
[u] ἀγαπᾷν [u] ἀλλήλους· 10 καὶ γὰρ ποιεῖτε αὐτὸ εἰς πάντας
τοὺς ἀδελφοὺς τοὺς ἐν ὅλῃ τῇ Μακεδονίᾳ. [v] παρακαλοῦμεν δὲ ὑμᾶς, ἀδελφοί, [v] περισσεύειν μᾶλλον 11 καὶ

q Rom xii 10 Heb xiii 1 1 Pet i 22 2 Pet i 7 bis, only† (-φος, 1 Pet iii 8)
r Matt iii 14. xiv 6 John xiii 10 ch i 8 v 1 Dan iii 16. constr, see Heb v 12
s here only† see John vi 45, aft Isa liv 13. 1 Cor ii 13
t Phil i 23 ch iii 10 al
u John xiii 34 bis xv 12, 17 Rom xiii 8 1 Pet i 22 1 John iii 11, 23 iv 7, 11, 12 only
v ver 1

9 for εχετε, εχομεν D¹FN³ b 67² latt syr goth Chr Thl lat-ff: ειχαμεν B am(with hal harl²) Pelag (*corrn on acct of the harsh constr for which reason also* c 43 67¹. 73 80 copt *have* γραφεσθαι *as in ch* v 1): txt AD³KLN¹ rel Syr copt Thdrt Damasc.
10. om γαρ F. ins και bef εις B. om 2nd τους AD¹F Chr-ms. for τους, υμων N¹. txt BD² ³KLN³ rel. for αδελφοι, αγαπητοι A.

ample: see there. ἐπί, for the purpose of,—on condition of:—ἐν, in, 'in the element of,' not = εἰς, the *aim*: but **ἁγιασμός** is the whole sphere of our Christian life. 8] Hence, the sin of (rejecting) setting at nought such limitations and rules is a fearful one—no less than that of setting at nought God the giver of the Holy Spirit. In **ἄνθρωπον ἀθετεῖ** there is an obvious allusion to ὑπερβαίνειν κ. πλεονεκτεῖν τ. ἀδελφόν above. There is no need to supply any thing after **ἀθετῶν**—**ὁ ἀθετῶν** simply describes him who commits the act of rejecting, q. d. the rejecter—*what* he rejects, is not to be supplied in the construction, but is clear from the context—viz. τὸν ἀδελφὸν αὐτοῦ. The distinction between ἄνθρωπον (anarthrous) and **τὸν** θεόν, seems to be, that the former is indefinite; not (any) **man**, but (definite) **God**. **τὸν [καὶ] δόντα]** q. d. who also is the AUTHOR of our sanctification. [**καί**—'novum hic additur momentum,' Bengel. It introduces a climax, whereby the sin is intensified.] **δόντα**, as being one great definite act of God by His Son. **τὸ πν. αὐτοῦ τὸ ἅγ.]** This form of expression (q. d. 'His own [αὐτοῦ emphatic] Spirit, the Holy One') is probably chosen, and not τὸ ἅγ. πν. αὐτοῦ, for precision, to bring out τὸ ἅγιον as connected with ἁγιασμός preceding. **εἰς ὑμᾶς** is not = ὑμῖν, but gives the idea of direction: see Gal iv 6; ch. ii. 9. **9—12]** *Exhortations to brotherly love* (9, 10 a), *and to honest diligent lives* (10 b—12). **9.] δέ** is transitional, the implied contrast being to the sin last spoken of. **φιλαδελφία** (reff.) here refers more immediately (cf. ποιεῖτε αὐτό below) to deeds of kindness by way of relief to poor brethren. **οὐ χρείαν ἔχετε]** This is a not unusual touch of delicate rhetoric with St Paul (cf 2 Cor. ix. 1. Philem 19. ch v 1). It conveys tacit but gentle reproof. The knowledge and the practice already exist: but the latter is not quite in proportion to the former. τῷ εἰπεῖν, οὐ χρεία ἐστί, μεῖζον ἐποίησεν ἢ εἰ εἶπεν. Chrys. The construction οὐ χρείαν ἔχετε γράφειν ὑμῖν (defended by De Wette and Winer), has been pronounced inadmissible by Lünemann: such use of the infinitive active being only found where no special personal reference is attached to the verb, as ὑμῖν here: so that this would require ἐμὲ γρ. or γράφεσθαι. He therefore reads ἔχομεν. But with so many corrections (see var. readd.), and with the known irregularities of St. Paul's style in such constructions, it surely is not safe to speak so positively. I should regard the construction, not as analogous with χῶρον οὐχ ἁγνὸν πατεῖν, Soph. Œd. Col 37; ἄξιος θαυμάσαι, Thuc. i. 38, and the like,—but as a mixed one between ἔχομεν γράφειν and ἔχετε γράφεσθαι. **αὐτοὶ ὑμεῖς**, in opposition to ἡμᾶς, the subject to be supplied from γράφειν: but **αὐτοί** is not *sponte*, which would not agree with **θεοδίδακτοι**. The stress of the sentence is on **αὐτοὶ ὑμεῖς**, not on the **θεο-** in θεοδίδακτοι, as Olsh.,—"where *God* teaches, there, the Apostle says, *he* may be silent:" but as Lün. observes, the **θεο-** comes in over and above as it were; διδακτοί would convey the *fact*. θεοδίδακτοι = διδακτοί, κ. ταῦτα παρὰ θεοῦ. And this teaching is practical—its tendency and object being εἰς τὸ ἀγ. ἀλλ.,—to produce mutual love. **10]** follows up the θεοδίδακτοί ἐστε by a matter of fact, shewing the teaching to have been in some measure effectual. **καὶ γάρ]** the **καί** belongs to ποιεῖτε—'besides being taught it, ye *do* it,'—**ποιεῖτε** carrying the emphasis of the sentence. **αὐτό**, scil. τὸ ἀγαπᾷν ἀλ. **περισσεύειν**, viz. in this ἀγάπῃ. (But there does not seem any reason, with Jowett, to ascribe this ἀταξία to their *uneasiness about the state of the dead*: much rather [as he also

w Rom xv 20. 2 Cor v 9 only † x = Luke xxiii 56 (xiv 4 Acts xi 18 xxi 14) only y = here only z ch ii 9 reff a 1 Cor iv 12 Wisd xv 17

ʷ φιλοτιμεῖσθαι ˣ ἡσυχάζειν καὶ πράσσειν ʸ τὰ ἴδια καὶ ABDF KLℵ a b c d e f g h k l m n o 17
ᶻᵃ ἐργάζεσθαι ταῖς ᵃ χερσὶν ὑμῶν, καθὼς ὑμῖν ᵇ παρηγγεί-
λαμεν, 12 ἵνα ᶜ περιπατῆτε ᵈ εὐσχημόνως πρὸς ᵉ τοὺς ἔξω
καὶ μηδενὸς ᶠ χρείαν ᶠ ἔχητε.
13 ᵍ Οὐ θέλομεν δὲ ὑμᾶς ᵍʰ ἀγνοεῖν, ἀδελφοί, περὶ τῶν

b Mark vi 8 2 Thess iii 4, &c 1 Tim i 3 iv 11 v 7 al Josh vi 6 c = Rom vi 4 xiii 13 Eph iv 1 al fr d Rom xiii 13. 1 Cor xiv 40 only † (-μων, 1 Cor. vii 35) e (see Acts xxvi 11) Mark iv 11 1 Cor v 12 Col iv 5 (ἔκτος, Sir prol) f w gen, Matt vi 8 xxvi 65 Luke v. 31 al Prov xviii 2. g Rom i. 13 xi 25 1 Cor x 1 xii 1 2 Cor i 8 h Gal i 22 reff

11 rec ins ιδιαις bef χερσιν (*gloss, to suit τα ιδια precedg*), with AD³KLℵ¹ rel Thdrt Damasc Œc om BD¹Fℵ³ k 67² vss Bas Chr Damasc Thl Ambrst Pelag. παρηγγ bef υμιν ℵ³.

13 rec (for θελομεν) θελω, with d syrr coptt txt ABDFKLℵ rel latt goth arm

states: see below] to their mistaken anticipations of the immediate coming of the Lord) It would seem as if, notwithstanding their liberality to those without, there were some defect of quiet diligence and harmony within, which prompted this exhortation see 2 Thess iii 11, 12. Thdrt assigns another reason for it· *οὐκ ἐναντία τοῖς προῤῥηθεῖσιν ἐπαίνοις ἡ παραίνεσις. συνέβαινε γὰρ τοὺς μὲν φιλοτίμως χορηγεῖν τοῖς δεομένοις τὴν χρείαν, τοὺς δὲ διὰ τὴν τούτων φιλοτιμίαν ἀμελεῖν τῆς ἐργασίας εἰκότως τοίνυν κἀκείνους ἐπῄνεσε, καὶ τούτοις τὰ πρόσφορα συνεβούλευσε.* (So also Est., Benson, Flatt, Schott, and De W) Lunem. objects to this, that thus the Church would be divided into two sections, the one exhorted to persist and abound in their liberality, the other to work diligently to support themselves; whereas there is no trace in the text of such a division He therefore would abandon the idea of a connexion, and treat vv 11, 12 as applying to a totally distinct subject, accounting for its introduction in such close *grammatical* connexion with ver. 10, by St Paul's rapid transitions in the practical parts of his Epistles But we may well answer, that instances are frequent enough of exhortations being addressed to whole churches which in their application would require severing and allotting to distinct classes of persons **11 φιλοτιμεῖσθαι ἡσυχάζειν]** **to make it your ambition to be quiet**—have no other *φιλοτιμία* than that of a quiet industrious holy life Thl (as an alternative) and Calvin would take *φιλοτιμεῖσθαι* alone, and understand it "optima æmulatio, quum singuli benefaciendo se ipsos vincere conantur" but thus the omission of any copula before ἡσυχ would introduce great harshness into the sentence. **πράσσειν τὰ ἴδια**| *τὰ ἴδια πράττω κ τ ἴδια πράττει οἱ πολλοί, λέγουσιν εἰκῇ, δέον, τὰ ἐμαυτοῦ πράττω, κ. τὰ σαυτοῦ πράττεις λέγειν, ὡς οἱ παλαιοί, ἢ τὰ ἴδια ἐμαυτοῦ πράττω κ τὰ ἴδια σαυτοῦ πράττεις.* Phryn ed Lob, p. 441. where see examples in the note From **ἐργ τ. χερσ ὑμ**, it appears that the members of the Thessalonian church were mostly of the class of persons thus labouring Observe the present infinitives, indicative of continued habit

12] *Purpose of ver.* 11. **εὐσχημόνως**] **honourably** *ἀτάκτως*, 2 Thess iii. 6, 11, is the opposite **πρός**, **with regard to**. as in the proverb *οὐδὲν πρὸς Διόνυσον,—πρὸς Τιμόθεον πρᾶξαι*, Demosth, p. 1185 See Bernhardy, p. 265 **τοὺς ἔξω**] the unbelieving world (reff.). **μηδενός** (subjective, as ruled by the *χρείαν ἔχητε*) is much better taken *neuter* than masculine; for as Lun. observes, to stand in need of *no man*, is for man an impossibility

13—Ch V. 11] Instructions and exhortations concerning the time of the end. and herein **13—18**] *instructions respecting the resurrection of the departed at the Lord's coming* We can hardly help suspecting some connexion between what has just preceded, and this section It would certainly seem as if the preaching of the kingdom of Jesus at Thessalonica had been partially misunderstood, and been perverted into a cause why they should not quietly follow active life, and why they should be uneasy about those who fell asleep before that kingdom was brought in, imagining that they would have no part in its glories Cf Acts xvii 7 **13**] **οὐ θέλ κ τ λ**, is with our Apostle (see reff) a common formula of transition to the imparting of weighty information **τ κοιμ**] **those who are sleeping**; so the present is used in the well-known epitaph, *ἱερὸν ὕπνον* | *κοιμᾶται· θνῄσκειν μὴ λέγε τοὺς ἀγαθούς* Or we may understand it, 'those who [from time to time] fall asleep [among you],' as suggested in the Journal of Sacred Lit for April, 1856, p 15· but the other seems simpler It was an ex-

j κοιμωμένων, ἵνα μὴ k λυπῆσθε καθὼς καὶ l οἱ λοιποὶ οἱ
μὴ ἔχοντες ἐλπίδα. 14 εἰ γὰρ m πιστεύομεν m ὅτι Ἰησοῦς
ἀπέθανεν καὶ n ἀνέστη, o οὕτως καὶ ὁ θεὸς τοὺς j κοιμηθέντας διὰ τοῦ Ἰησοῦ p ἄξει σὺν αὐτῷ. 15 τοῦτο γὰρ ὑμῖν

j pres, 1 Cor xi 30 j = Matt xxvii 52 Acts vii 60 xiii 36 1 Cor vii 39 xv 6, &c Isa xiv 8 k = Matt xvi 23 2 Cor vi 10 vii 9 al Neh v. 6 l = Acts v 13 Eph ii 3 ch v 6 m John xiv 10 Acts ix 26 Rom x 9 Job xv 31 n = Mark viii 31 al fr Isa xxvi 19 o = Rev xi 5 p = 2 Tim iv 11

gr-lat-ff. rec κεκοιμημενων, with DFKL rel Orig(mss vary) Hippol Chr Cyr Thdrt Damasc κοιμημενων 17 txt ABℵ e n 67[2] Orig-mss Chr-ms Damasc. λυπεισθε AD[1] [2]FL b[1] c d Cyr for καθως, ως D[1]Fℵ[3] 67[2] Orig Hippol 14 επιστευομεν ℵ[1]. ο θεος bef και B 67[2] syr. κεκοιμημενους F

pression (reff) conveying definite meaning to the Thessalonians as importing *the dead in Christ* (ver 16) No inference must therefore be drawn from the Apostle's use of this word, as to the intermediate state (as De W after Weizel, *for* the sleep of the soul,—and Zwingle, Calvin, al, *against* it) for the word is a mere common term **ἵνα μὴ λ**] object of my not wishing you to be ignorant **μὴ λυπ** is *absolute*, that ye mourn not·—not (as Thdrt, Calvin, al) **μὴ λυπ καθώς . .**, 'that ye may not mourn (so much) as others &c.' He forbids **λυπεῖσθαι** altogether. But we must remember, *what sort* of λυπεῖσθαι it was Surely not absolutely the mourning for *our* loss in their *absence*, but for *theirs* (see above), and *in so far*, for ours also. See Chrysostom's very beautiful appeal in loc. **οἱ λοιποί**] viz. the heathen, and those Jews who did not believe a resurrection. **οἱ μὴ ἔχοντες ἐλπίδα**] viz, in the *resurrection*. Lun. cites,—Theocr Idyll iv 42, ἐλπίδες ἐν ζωοῖσιν, ἀνέλπιστοι δὲ θανόντες: Æsch Eum 638, ἅπαξ θανόντος οὔτις ἔστ' ἀνάστασις Catull. v. 4 ff, 'Soles occidere et redire possunt· | nobis quum semel occidit brevis lux | nox est perpetua una dormienda:' Lucret iii 912 f, 'nec quisquam expergitus exstat | frigida quem semel est vitai pausa secuta.' Jowett adds 'the sad complaints of Cicero and Quintilian over the loss of their children, and the dreary hope of an immortality of fame in Tacitus and Thucydides' [But when he goes on to say that the language of the O. T, though more religious, is in many passages hardly more cheering, and substantiates this by Isa xxxviii. 18, 19, it is surely hardly fair to give the dark side, without balancing it with such passages as Ps. lxxiii 23—26, Prov xiv 32 In the great upward struggle of the ancient church under the dawn of the revelation of life and immortality, we find much indeed of the αἴλινον αἴλινον εἰπέ—but the τὸ δ' εὖ νικάτω has its abundant testimonies also] This shews of *what kind* their λύπη was· viz a grief whose ground was unbelief in a resurrection which regarded the dead as altogether cut off from Christ's heavenly kingdom. 14] *Substantiation* (γάρ) *of that implied in last verse, that further knowledge will remove this their grief*· and that knowledge, grounded on the resurrection of our Lord **εἰ**] not '*seeing that*' but hypothetical '*posito*, that we, &c' **ἀπέθ κ ἀνέστη** go together,—forming the same process through which οἱ κοιμώμενοι are passing "The Apostle here, as always, uses the direct term ἀπέθανε in reference to our Lord, to obviate all possible misconception· in reference to the faithful he appropriately uses the consolatory term κοιμᾶσθαι see Thdrt in loc" Ellicott. **οὕτως**] The two clauses do not accurately correspond We should expect καὶ πιστεύομεν ὅτι οὕτως καὶ οἱ ἐν Ἰησοῦ κοιμηθέντες ἀναστήσονται, or the like. Still the **οὕτως** betokens identity of lot for the two parties concerned, viz, death, and resurrection. In this they resemble· but in the expressed particulars here, they differ. Christ's, was simply ἀνέστη: theirs shall be a resurrection through Him, at His coming. **διὰ τ Ἰησοῦ**] I feel compelled to differ from the majority of modern scholars (not Ellicott), in adhering to the old connexion of these words with τ. κοιμηθέντας. I am quite aware of the grammatical difficulty: but as I hope to shew, it is not insuperable. But if we join **διὰ τ Ἰησ** with **ἄξει**, we obtain a clause which I am persuaded the Apostle could never have written,—flat and dragging in the extreme—**διὰ τοῦ Ἰησοῦ ἄξει σὺν αὐτῷ**—**αὐτῷ** referring to **Ἰησοῦ** already mentioned in the same clause Whereas, on the other connexion, we have **Ἰησοῦς** and **οἱ κοιμηθέντες διὰ τοῦ Ἰησοῦ** set over against one another, the very article, and the unemphatic position of the words, shewing the reference back,—and we have

q 1 Cor ii 7 xiv 6 3 Kings xxi (xx) 35 r 2 Cor iv 13 (v 15) Herodian ii 1

λέγομεν ᵠ ἐν λόγῳ κυρίου, ὅτι ʳ ἡμεῖς οἱ ʳ ζῶντες οἱ ˢ περιλειπόμενοι εἰς τὴν ᵗ παρουσίαν τοῦ κυρίου οὐ μὴ ᵘ φθά-

ABDF KLℵ a b c d e f g h k l m n o 17

s ver 17 only † 2 Macc i 31 viii 14 only μονος τῶν πατρῴων περιλειπομενος φιλων ἔτι, Herodian ii 1. t ch ii 19 reff u = here only (ch ii 16 reff) Wisd vi 13

15. for κυριου, ιησου B χριστου Mcion-t.

αὐτῷ naturally and forcibly referring back to Ἰησοῦς and διὰ τοῦ Ἰησοῦ, in the preceding clauses. In other words, the logical construction of the sentence seems to me so plainly to require the connexion of διὰ τοῦ Ἰησοῦ with κοιμηθέντας, that it must be a grammatical impossibility only, which can break that connexion. But let us see whether there be such an impossibility present οἱ κοιμηθέντες are confessedly the *Christian* dead, and none else. They are distinguished by the Apostle's use of and adhesion to the word, from the merely *θανόντες*. What makes this distinction? Why are they asleep, and not dead? *By whom* have they been thus privileged? Certainly, *διὰ τοῦ Ἰησοῦ* We are said *πιστεύειν δι' αὐτοῦ* (Acts iii 16), — *εὐχαριστεῖν δι' αὐτοῦ* (Rom. i. 8), *εἰρήνην ἔχειν δι' αὐτοῦ* (ib. v 1), *καυχᾶσθαι δι' αὐτοῦ* (ib 11), *παρακαλεῖσθαι δι' αὐτοῦ* (2 Cor. i. 5), &c. &c.: why not also *κοιμᾶσθαι δι' αὐτοῦ*? And when Lunem. objects, that the extent of the idea οἱ κοιμηθέντες is understood from the former part of the sentence, εἰ πιστεύομεν *κ.τ.λ.*,—this very reason seems to me the most natural one for the specification—**If we believe that Jesus died and rose again, then even thus also those, of whom we say that they sleep, just because of Jesus will God, &c** the emphasis being on the διά Jowett keeps this connexion, merely saying however, "nor will the order of the words allow us to connect them with ἄξει;" a reason surely insufficient for it He is certainly in error when he continues, "The only remaining mode is to take *διά* for *ἐν* (?), 'those that are asleep in Christ.'" ἄξει σὺν αὐτῷ] **will bring** (back to us) **with Him** (Jesus) i. e when Jesus shall appear, they also shall appear with Him, being (as below) raised at His coming Of their disembodied souls there is here no mention. nor is the meaning, as often understood, that God will bring them (their disembodied souls, to be joined to their raised bodies) with Him. but the bringing them with Jesus = their being raised when Jesus appears 15] *Confirmation of last verse by direct revelation from the Lord.* τοῦτο—this which follows taken up by ὅτι ἐν λόγῳ κυρ, in (virtue of · an assertion made within the sphere and element of that certainty, which the word of the Lord gives) **the word of the Lord,**—i e. by direct revelation from Him made to me *τουτέστιν, οὐκ ἀφ' ἑαυτῶν, ἀλλὰ παρὰ τοῦ χριστοῦ μαθόντες λέγομεν*, Chr *ἐκ θείας ἡμῖν ἀποκαλύψεως ἡ διδασκαλία γεγένηται*, Thdrt. That St. Paul had many special revelations made to him, we know from 2 Cor xii 1 Cf also Gal i. 12; Eph iii 3; 1 Cor xi 23; xv. 3, and notes ἡμεῖς οἱ ζῶντες] Then beyond question, he himself expected to be alive, together with the majority of those to whom he was writing, at the Lord's coming. For we cannot for a moment accept the evasion of Theodoret (cf also Chrys and the majority of ancient Commentators, down to Bengel, and even some of the best of the moderns, warped by their subjectivities. cf. Ellicott here), —*οὐκ ἐπὶ τοῦ ἑαυτοῦ προσώπου τέθεικεν, ἀλλ' ἐπὶ τῶν κατ' ἐκεῖνον τὸν καιρὸν περιόντων ἀνθρώπων*.—nor the ungrammatical rendering of Turretin and Pelt—'we, if we live and remain' (*ἡμεῖς ζῶντες, περιλειπόμενοι*) —nor the idea of Œc., al, that οἱ ζῶντες are the *souls*, οἱ κοιμηθέντες the *bodies*:—but must take the words in their only plain grammatical meaning, that οἱ ζῶντες οἱ περιλ are a class distinguished from οἱ κοιμηθέντες, by being yet in the flesh when Christ comes, in which class, by prefixing ἡμεῖς, he includes his readers and himself. That this *was* his expectation, we know from other passages, especially from 2 Cor. v. 1—10, where see notes. It does not seem to have been so strong towards the end of his course; see e.g Phil i. 20—26. Nor need it surprise any Christian, that the Apostles should in this matter of detail have found their personal expectations liable to disappointment, respecting a day of which it is so solemnly said, that no man knoweth its appointed time, not the angels in heaven, nor the Son (Mark xiii. 32), but the Father only. At the same time it must be borne in mind, that this inclusion of himself and his hearers among the ζῶντες and περιλειπόμενοι, does not in any way enter into the fact revealed and here announced, which is respecting that class of persons only as they

σωμεν τοὺς [t] κοιμηθέντας, 16 ὅτι [v] αὐτὸς ὁ κύριος [w] ἐν
[x] κελεύσματι, [w] ἐν φωνῇ [y] ἀρχαγγέλου καὶ [w] ἐν [z] σάλπιγγι
[a] θεοῦ [b] καταβήσεται ἀπ' οὐρανοῦ, καὶ οἱ νεκροὶ [c] ἐν χριστῷ
[d] ἀναστήσονται πρῶτον, 17 ἔπειτα [r] ἡμεῖς οἱ [r] ζῶντες οἱ
[e] περιλειπόμενοι [f] ἅμα σὺν αὐτοῖς [g] ἁρπαγησόμεθα ἐν νε-

v = ch iii 11 reff (see note) w = Rom xi. 29 1 Cor iv 21 2 Thess i 8 Ps xciv 2 x here only Prov xxx 27 only Thucyd ii 92 init y Jude 9 only † z Matt xxiv 31 1 Cor xiv 8 xv 52 Rev iv 1 & passim Exod xix 13 al a so 1 Chron xvi 42 Rev xv 2 b John iii 13 Eph iv 9 Prov xxx 4 c = 1 Cor xv 18 d ver 14 e ver 15 f ch v 10 g = 2 Cor xii 2 Rev xii 5 John vi 15. Acts viii 39

16. aft νεκροι ins οι F, *mortui qui in Christo sunt* latt goth om οι νεκροι in Cyr. for πρωτον, πρωτοι D[1]F latt Thdrt[1] Cyr Thl-marg Tert Ambrst lat-ff. txt ABD[3]KLℵ rel syrr copt goth Orig Dial

17. οι ζωντες bef ημεις K n om ημεις 80. om οι περιλειπομενοι F Tert Ambr

are, and must be, *one portion* of the faithful at the Lord's coming, not respecting the question, *who shall*, and *who shall not* be among them in that day **οἱ περιλειπ εἰς . .**] Dr. Burton, doubting whether περιλειπόμενοι εἰς τ. π can mean '*left to the coming*' (but why not? εἰς as defining the terminus temporis is surely common enough, cf. Phil. i. 10; Acts iv 3, εἰς τέλος John xiii 1 al. fr), puts a comma at περιλειπόμενοι, and takes εἰς τὴν π with οὐ μὴ φθάσωμεν, rendering, *those who are alive at the last day will not enter into the presence of the Lord before those who have died.* But 1) ἡ παρουσία τοῦ κυρίου is never used *locally*, of the *presence* of the Lord, but always *temporally*, of His *coming:* and 2) the arrangement of the sentence would in that case be οὐ μὴ φθ. τοὺς κοιμ εἰς τ. π τοῦ κυρ. **οὐ μὴ φθάσωμεν**] **shall not** (emphatic—'there is no reason to fear, that . ') **prevent** (get before, so that they be left behind, and fail of the prize). **16**] A reason of the foregoing assertion, by detailing the method of the resurrection. **Because**—[not '*that*,' so as to be parallel with ὅτι before, as Koch] **the Lord Himself** (not, as De W, '*He, the Lord*'—which would be to the last degree flat and meaningless,—nor as Olsh, 'the Lord *Himself*,' in contrast to any other kind of revelation.—nor as Lunem, as the chief Person and actor in that day, emphatically opposed to His faithful ones as acted on,—but said for solemnity's sake, and to shew that it will not be a mere *gathering to* Him, but HE HIMSELF will descend, and we all shall be summoned before Him) **with** ('*in*,' as the element,—the accompanying circumstance) **a signal-shout** (κέλευσμα is not only '*the shout of battle*,' as Conyb; but is used of any signal given by the voice, whether of a captain to his rowers, Thuc. ii. 92: of a man shouting to another at a distance, Herod. iv. 141 of a huntsman to his dogs, Xen. Cyneg. vi. 20 Here it seems to include in it the two which follow and explain it), viz **with the voice of an archangel** (Christ shall be surrounded with His angels, Matt xxv. 31 al To enquire, *which* archangel, is futile: to understand the word of *Christ Himself* [Ambrst., Olsh], or the Holy Spirit [al], impossible), **and with the trumpet of God** (θεοῦ as in reff., the trumpet especially belonging to and used in the heavenly *state* of God; not *commanded by God* [Pelt, Olsh, al],—nor does θεοῦ import *size* or *loudness* [Bengel, al], although these qualities of course are understood On the trumpet as summoning assemblies, cf Num. x 2, xxxi 6; Joel ii 1:—as accompanying the divine appearances, Ex xix. 16, Ps. xlvii. 5; Isa. xxvii 13; Zech ix 14; Matt xxiv 31, 1 Cor. xv. 52) **shall descend from heaven** (cf. Acts i 11): **and the dead in Christ** (ἐν χρ. must not, as Pelt, Schott, be joined with **ἀναστήσονται** for apart from the question whether this would give *any* admissible meaning, it would bring ἐν χριστῷ into an emphatic position of prominence, which would confuse the whole sentence) **shall first rise** (πρῶτον has no reference whatever to the *first resurrection* [Rev. xx. 5, 6], here, for *only the Lord's people* are here in question but answers to **ἔπειτα** below: *first*, the dead in Christ shall rise: *then*, we, &c): **then we who are living, who remain** (as above) **shall be caught up** (reft. the great change spoken of 1 Cor. xv. 52, having first suddenly taken place) **all together** (see Rom iii. 12, ch v. 10 note: ἅμα does not belong to σὺν αὐτοῖς) **with them** (the raised of ver 16) **in (the) clouds** (ἔδειξε τὸ μέγεθος τῆς τιμῆς ὥσπερ γὰρ αὐτὸς ὁ δεσπότης ἐπὶ νεφελῆς φωτεινῆς ἀνελήφθη, οὕτω καὶ οἱ εἰς αὐτὸν πεπιστευκότες . ἐπὶ νεφελῶν ὀχούμενοι ὑπαντήσουσι τῷ τῶν ὅλων κριτῇ . . . .

φέλαις εἰς [h] ἀπάντησιν τοῦ κυρίου εἰς [i] ἀέρα, καὶ [k] οὕτως
πάντοτε [l] σὺν κυρίῳ [l] ἐσόμεθα. 18 [m] ὥςτε [n] παρακαλεῖτε
ἀλλήλους [o] ἐν τοῖς λόγοις τούτοις.

V. 1 Περὶ δὲ τῶν [p] χρόνων καὶ τῶν [pq] καιρῶν, ἀδελφοί,
οὐ [r] χρείαν ἔχετε ὑμῖν [r] γράφεσθαι· 2 αὐτοὶ γὰρ [s] ἀκριβῶς
οἴδατε, ὅτι [ἡ] [t] ἡμέρα [t] κυρίου ὡς [u] κλέπτης ἐν νυκτὶ

ABDF KLℵ a b c d e f g h k l m n o 17

h always w εἰς, in N T & LXX (not Apocrypha, 2 Macc xii 30 al). Matt xxv (1 v r) 6 Acts xxviii 15 only 1 Kings ix 14
i Eph ii 2 reff
k = Acts vii 8 xvii 33 xxviii 14 1 Cor xi 28 xiv 25 al
l = Phil i 23
m = Phil ii 12 reff
n = 2 Cor i 4 al fr Isa lxvi 13
o = 2 Cor vii 6, 7 Lit i 0
p Acts i 7 Dan ii 21
q = Matt xvi 3 2 Tim iii 1
r constr, see ch iv 9
s = Matt ii 8 Luke i 3 Acts xviii 25, 26 xxiii 15 20 xxiv 22 (Eph v 15) only Deut xix 18 Wisd xix 18 only Dan vii 19 Theod
t κυρ, Acts ii 20, from Joel ii 31 2 Pet iii 10 only. Isa ii 12 τ κυρ, 2 Thess ii 2 see 1 Cor i 8 2 Cor i 14 al
u see Matt xxiv 43 2 Pet iii 10 Rev iii 3 xvi 15 Jer xxix 10 (xlix 9)

Ambrst-ed (not F-lat) περιλειμενοι(sic) B. εις υπαντησιν τω χριστω D[1]F latt Tert Orig-int Jer[1] for παντοτε, παντες D[1]. for συν, εν B.

Chap. V. 1. for χρειαν εχετε, χρια εστιν F D-lat(and G-lat but not F-lat) arm Tert Ambrst γραφεσθαι bef υμιν ℵ[3] 115. του γρ. υμιν ℵ[1].
2. om ἡ bef ημερα BDFℵ 17 67[2] ins AKL rel Eus.

Thdrt) **to meet the Lord** (as He descends so Aug de civit. Dei xx 20 2, vol vii. p 688. 'non sic accipiendum est tanquam in aere nos dixerit semper cum Domino mansuros, quia nec ipse utique ibi manebit, quia veniens transiturus est, venienti quippe itur obviam, non manenti' Christ is *on His way to this earth* and when De W says that there is no plain trace in St Paul of Christ's kingdom on earth,—and Lün, that the words shew that the Apostle did not think of Christ as descending down to the earth, surely they cannot suppose him to have been so ignorant of O T prophecy, as to have allowed this, its plain testimony, to escape him **εἰς ἀπάντησιν** occurs [reff] twice more in the N T, and each time implies meeting one who was *approaching*—not merely 'meeting with' a person) **into the air** (belongs to **ἁρπαγησόμεθα**, not to **εἰς ἀπ τοῦ κυρ** as in E. V.), **and thus we** (i e we and they united, *ἡμεῖς ἅμα, σὺν αὐτοῖς*, who were the subject of the last sentence) **shall be always with the Lord.** That he advances no further in the prophetic description, but breaks off at our union in Christ's presence, is accounted for, by his purpose being accomplished, in having shewn that they who have died in Christ, shall not be thereby deprived of any advantage at His coming The rest of the great events of that time—His advent on this earth, His judgment of it, assisted by His saints (1 Cor vi. 2, 3),—His reign upon earth,—His final glorification with His redeemed in heaven,—are not treated here, but not therefore to be conceived of as alien from the Apostle's teaching. 18] **ὥστε, so then: reff παρακ, comfort:** cf. *ἵνα μὴ λυπῆσθε*, ver 13 **λόγοις,** not *things*, here or any where · but words: **these words,** which I have by inspiration delivered to you It will be manifest to the plain, as well as to the scholar-like reader, that attempts like that of Mr. Jowett, to interpret such a passage as this by the rules of mere figurative language, are entirely beside the purpose The Apostle's declarations here are made in the practical tone of strict matter of fact, and are given as literal details, to console men's minds under an existing difficulty Never was a place where the analogy of symbolical apocalyptic language was less applicable Either these details must be received by us as matter of practical expectation, or we must set aside the Apostle as one divinely empowered to teach the Church. It is a fair opportunity for an experimentum crucis. and such test cannot be evaded by Mr. Jowett's intermediate expedient of figurative language

Ch V 1—11] *Exhortation to watch for the day of the Lord's coming, and to be ready for it* 1—3] *the suddenness and unexpectedness of that day's coming*

1] On **χρόν** and **καιρ**, see Acts i. 7, note. They had no need, for the reason stated below: that St. Paul had already by word of month taught them as much as could be known 2.] **[ἡ] ἡμέρα κυρίου** is not the *destruction of Jerusalem*, as Hammond, Schottg, al,—nor the day of *each man's death*, as Chrys, Œc, Thl, Est, al.,—*but the day of the Lord's coming*, the **παρουσία**, which has been spoken of, in some of its details, above So Thdrt —*ἡ δεσποτικὴ παρουσία*. This is plain, by comparing 2 Thess. ii. 2 1 Cor i 8, v 5 2 Cor. i 14 Phil. i. 6, 10,

οὕτως ἔρχεται. 3 ὅταν λέγωσιν [v] Εἰρήνη καὶ [w] ἀσφά-
λεια, τότε [x] αἰφνίδιος αὐτοῖς [y] ἐφίσταται [z] ὄλεθρος ὥςπερ
ἡ [a] ὠδὶν τῇ [b] ἐν [bc] γαστρὶ [b] ἐχούσῃ, καὶ οὐ μὴ [d] ἐκφύγωσιν.
4 ὑμεῖς δέ, ἀδελφοί, οὐκ ἐστὲ ἐν [e] σκότει, ἵνα [f] ἡ ἡμέρα
ὑμᾶς ὡς [u] κλέπτης [g] καταλάβῃ· 5 πάντες γὰρ ὑμεῖς [h] υἱοὶ
φωτός ἐστε καὶ [h] υἱοὶ [i] ἡμέρας. οὐκ ἐσμὲν [k] νυκτὸς οὐδὲ
[i] σκότους. 6 [l] ἄρα [l] οὖν μὴ [m] καθεύδωμεν ὡς [καὶ] [n] οἱ

v Ezek xiii 10. w = Acts v 23 (Luke i 4) only Deut xii 10 x Luke xxi 34 only † Wisd. xvii 15 2 Macc xiv 17 only (ὡς, 2 Macc v 5 xiv 22) y = Luke xxi 34 2 Tim iv 6 (Luke xx 1 al fr) z (=) 1 Cor v. 5 2 Thess i 9 1 Tim vi 9 only Prov xxi 7 a Matt xxiv 8 || Mk Acts ii 24 only. Exod xv 14 al b Matt i 18, 23 (from Isa vii 14 F) xxiv 19 || Rev xii 2 only. Exod xxi 22 c = as above (b) Luke i 31 (Tit i 12) only d = Luke xxi 36 Rom ii 3 2 Cor xi 33 Judg vi 11 e = John iii 19 Rom xiii 12 al f so 1 Cor iii 13 Heb x 25 g = John xii 35 Numb xxxii 23 h Luke x 6 xvi 8 John xii 36 Eph ii 2 v 6 i = Rom xiii 13 2 Pet i 19 k gen., 1 Cor i 12, iii 22, 23 al l Rom v 18 al10 P m Paul, Eph v 14 ver 10 only Gospp (literally) Matt viii 24 & fr Sir xxii 7 n ch iv 13 reff

3 rec aft οταν ins γαρ, with KL rel vulg arm-marg Damasc; δε BDℵ³ syr copt Eus Chr Thdrt. om AFℵ¹ 17 D-lat Syr goth arm Iren-int Tert Cypr Ambrst λεγουσιν F. επισταται BLℵ φανησεται F D-lat(not F-lat) Hes(in Aug)₂. (A def)—επιστ bef αυτοις B. εκφευξονται D¹F

4 υμας bef η ημερα (*throwing the emphasis on υμας*) ADF latt Eus txt BKLℵ rel goth Epiph Chr Thdrt Damasc.—add εκεινη F latt.—om ἡ c 17. κλεπτας AB copt. καταλαβοι F.

5 rec om γαρ, with K(e sil) rel am · ins ABDFLℵ c m 17 latt syrr copt æth arm Eus Clem Chr Thdrt Thl Ambrst Aug Pelag aft ημερ ins και D¹F fuld Chr-ms. (not D-lat F-lat) for εσμεν, εστε D¹F fuld(with mar hal²) Syr goth Ambrst

6. om 1st και ABℵ¹ b 17 am(and F-lat) syr copt æth Clem₂ Antch ins DFKLℵ³ rel vulg Syr Chr Thdrt Ambrst

ii 16. It is both the suddenness, and the terribleness (surely we cannot with Ellic. omit this element, in the presence of the image in the next verse) of the Day's coming, which is here dwelt on cf next verse. **οὕτως** fills up the comparison—**as a thief in the night** (comes), **so** . **it comes** (not for future, but expressing, as so often by the present, the absolute truth and certainty of that predicated—it is its attribute, to come) **3.**] Following out of the comparison *ὡς κλ ἐν νυκτί*, into detail **λέγωσιν**, viz men in general—the children of the world, as opposed to the people of God. cf. *ὄλεθρος* below The vivid description dispenses with any copula **εἰρ κ ἀσφ**, scil. *ἐστιν*, see ref Ezek **αἰφνίδ** has the emphasis, becoming a kind of predicate. **ἐφίσταται**, generally used of any sudden unexpected appearance see reff, and Acts iv. 1. It is pressing too close the comparison *ὥσπερ ἡ ὠδὶν κ τ λ.*, when De W. says that it "assumes the day to be *near*,—for that such a woman, though she does not know the day and the hour, yet has a definite knowledge of the *period*." for it is not the woman, nor her condition, that is the subject of comparison, but the *unexpected pang* of labour which comes on her. **4, 5**] But the Thessalonians, and Christians in general, are not to be thus overtaken by it **4**] **ἐν σκότει** refers back to *ἐν νυκτί* above—in the ignorance and moral slumber of the world which knows not God *τῷ παραβολικῷ ἐπέμεινε σχήματι, κ. σκότος μὲν καλεῖ τὴν ἄγνοιαν, ἡμέραν δὲ τὴν γνῶσιν*, Thdrt *τὸν σκοτεινὸν κ ἀκάθαρτον βίον φησί*, Chrys. Both combined give the right meaning. **ἵνα**] not '*so that*,' here or any where else · but that,—**in order that** · it gives the *purpose* in the divine arrangement · for with God all results are purposed **ἡ ἡμέρα**] not, '*that* day,' but **the** DAY—the meaning of **ἡμέρα** as distinguished from **σκότος** being brought out, and *ἡ ἡμέρα* being put in the place of emphasis accordingly. This not having been seen, its situation was altered, to throw the *first* stress on *ὑμᾶς*, which properly has the *second*. That this is so, is plain from what follows, ver. 5. **5.**] **You** (a) **and all we Christians** (b) have no reason to fear, and no excuse for being surprised by, the DAY of the Lord; **for we are sons of light and the day** (Hebraisms, see reff. signifying that we *belong to*, having our origin from, the light and the day), **and are not of** (do not supply '*sons*'—the genitives are in regular construction after *ἐσμεν*, signifying *possession*—**we belong not to**) **night nor darkness.** See, on the day of the Lord as connected

λοιποί, ἀλλὰ [op] γρηγορῶμεν καὶ [pq] νήφωμεν. 7 οἱ γὰρ
[m] καθεύδοντες νυκτὸς [m] καθεύδουσιν, καὶ οἱ [r] μεθυσκόμενοι
νυκτὸς [s] μεθύουσιν· 8 ἡμεῖς δὲ [h] ἡμέρας ὄντες [q] νήφωμεν,
[t] ἐνδυσάμενοι [u] θώρακα πίστεως καὶ ἀγάπης, καὶ [v] περικεφαλαίαν [w] ἐλπίδα σωτηρίας, 9 ὅτι οὐκ [x] ἔθετο ἡμᾶς ὁ
θεὸς [x] εἰς [y] ὀργήν, ἀλλὰ εἰς [z] περιποίησιν σωτηρίας διὰ
τοῦ κυρίου ἡμῶν Ἰησοῦ χριστοῦ, 10 τοῦ ἀποθανόντος

ABDF KLℵ a b c d e f g h k l m n o 17

o — Mark xiii 37. 1 Cor xvi 13 al fr (Jer i 12) p 1 Pet v 8 q Paul, 2 Tim iv 5 only 1 Pet i 13 iv 7 v 8 only † r Luke xii 45 Eph v 18 only Prov iv 17 s Matt xxiv 49 John ii 10 Acts ii 15 1 Cor xi 21 Rev xvii 2, 6 only Joel i 5 t Eph iv 24 reff u Eph vi 14 reff v Eph vi 17 only Isa lix 17 w so Rom v 2 x Acts xiii 47 1 Tim i 12 1 Pet ii 8 Jer xxv 12 y Rom xiii 4. z — 2 Thess ii 14. (Eph i 14 reff -ποιεῖσθαι, Acts xx 28)

7. for μεθυσκομενοι, μεθυοντες B. 8 om και αγαπης ℵ[1].
9 ο θεος bef ημας B m [αλλα, so BD[3]ℵ 17.] om χριστου B.

with darkness and light, Amos v 18 ff. There, its aspect to the ungodly is treated of —here, its aspect to Christians.

6—8] *Exhortation to behave as such* i e. to watch and be sober—*ἐπίτασις ἐγρηγόρσεως τὸ νήφειν ἔνι γὰρ καὶ ἐγρηγορέναι καὶ μηδὲν διαφέρειν καθεύδοντος*, (Ec. (after Chrys) 6] **οἱ λοιποί**—i e the careless world 7] Explanation of the assertion regarding *οἱ λοιποί* above from the common practice of men. There is no distinction, as Macknight pretends, between *μεθυσκόμενοι* and *μεθύουσιν* ('the former denoting the *act* of getting drunk, the latter the *state* of being so'), but they are synonymous, answering to *καθεύδοντες* and *καθεύδουσιν* Nor are the expressions to be taken in a spiritual sense, as Chrys , al (*μέθην ἐνταῦθά φησιν, οὐ τὴν ἀπὸ τοῦ οἴνου μόνον, ἀλλὰ καὶ τὴν ἀπὸ πάντων τῶν κακῶν* 'Spiritual sleep and intoxication belong to the state of darkness,' Baum -Crus) the repetition of the same verbs as subjects and predicates (Lun) shews that **νυκτός** is merely a designation of *time*, and to be taken literally 8] Contrast (**δέ**) of our course, who are of the day And this not only in being awake and sober, but in being *armed*—not only watchful, but as sentinels, on our guard, and *guarded* ourselves Notice, that these arms are defensive only, as against a sudden attack—and belong therefore not so much to the Christian's conflict with evil, as (from the context) to his guard against being surprised by the day of the Lord as a thief in the night The best defences against such a surprise are the three great Christian graces, Faith, Hope, Love,—which are accordingly here enumerated · see ch i 3, and 1 Cor xiii 13 In Eph vi 13–17, we have offensive as well as defensive weapons, and the symbolism is somewhat varied, the *θώραξ* being *δικαιοσύνη*, *πίστις* being the *θυρεός*, while the helmet remains the same. See on the figure, Isa lix. 17, Wisd. v 17 ff We must not perhaps press minutely the meaning of each part of the armour, in the presence of such variation in the two passages 9] Epexegesis of **ἐλπίδα σωτηρίας**—'and we *may* with confidence put on such an hope as our helmet'—**for God set us not** ('appointed us not' [reff]; keep the aorist meaning,—referring to the time when He made the appointment) **to** ('*with a view to*'—so as to issue in, become a prey to) **wrath, but to acquisition** (*περιποιέω*, '*to make to remain over and above*,' hence '*to keep safe*.' opp. to *διαφθείρω*, Herod i. 110, vii. 52, &c Thuc iii. 102 [L and S.]. Hence *περιποίησις*, '*a keeping safe*:' Plat Def 415 c, *σωτηρία, περιποίησις ἀβλαβής*. If this last remarkable coincidence be taken as a key to our passage, **σωτηρίας** will be a genitive of apposition, 'a keeping safe, consisting in salvation' But [reff] it seems more according to the construction to understand **περιπ.** simply as acquisition, as it undoubtedly is in ref 2 Thess. Jowett's note, "*περιποιεῖν*, to make any thing over hence *περιποίησις*, possession," if I understand it rightly, alleges a meaning of the verb which has no existence '*To make to remain over*' is as different as possible from 'to make over [to another person]') **of salvation through** (**διὰ** . . refers to *περιπ. σωτ.* not to *ἔθετο*) **our Lord Jesus Christ,**

10] **who died for us, that whether we wake or sleep** (in what sense? surely not in an ethical sense, as above for they who sleep will be overtaken by Him as a thief, and His day will be to them darkness, not light If not in an ethical sense, it must be in that of *living* or *dying*, and the sense as Rom xiv. 8 [For we cannot adopt the trifling sense given by Whitby, al ,—' whether He come in the night, and

* ὑπὲρ ἡμῶν, ἵνα εἴτε [a] γρηγορῶμεν εἴτε [b] καθεύδωμεν [c] ἅμα
σὺν αὐτῷ ζήσωμεν. 11 διὸ [d] παρακαλεῖτε ἀλλήλους, καὶ
[e] οἰκοδομεῖτε [f] εἷς τὸν [f] ἕνα, καθὼς καὶ ποιεῖτε.
12 [g] Ἐρωτῶμεν δὲ ὑμᾶς, ἀδελφοί, [h] εἰδέναι τοὺς [i] κοπιῶντας ἐν ὑμῖν καὶ [k] προϊσταμένους ὑμῶν [l] ἐν κυρίῳ
καὶ [m] νουθετοῦντας ὑμᾶς, 13 καὶ [n] ἡγεῖσθαι αὐτοὺς [o] ὑπερ-

a (ver 6) = here only (Neh viii 3.) b = Matt ix 24 only (ver 6 reff) Dan xii 2 c = ch iv 17 Rom iii 12 d = 2 Cor i 4. 2 Thess ii 17 Isa. lxvi 13 e = 1 Cor viii 1 x 23 xiv 4, 17 f 1 Cor iv 6 g = Phil iv 3 ch iv 1 2 Thess ii 1 al h = here only see 1 Cor xvi 18 Prov xxvii 23 Gen xxxix 6 i Rom xvi 6, 12 1 Cor xv 10. Gal iv 11 Ps cxxvi 1 k 1 Tim iii 4, 5 reff l Rom xvi 2, 8, 12 1 Cor xvi 19 al m Col i 28 reff P n = here only o here only † (-σσου, ch iii 10 reff ὑπερπ., Mark vii 37)

10. *περί Bℵ[1] 17 · υπερ ADFKLℵ[3] rel. καθευδομεν KL b c f g h k l m o Chr Thl (in ver 6 KL have -δομεν) ζησομεν A 48 lect-1 · ζωμεν D[1] 73
12 προιστανομενους Aℵ νουθετουντες A.
13 for και, ωστε F; ut latt. ηγεισθε B b d e f g k l m syr copt goth.

so find us taking our natural rest, or in the day when we are waking'] Thus understood however, it will be at the sacrifice of perspicuity, seeing that **γρηγορεῖν** and **καθεύδειν** have been used ethically throughout the passage If we wish to preserve the uniformity of metaphor, we *may* [though I am not satisfied with this] interpret in this sense that our Lord died for us, that whether we watch [are of the number of the watchful, i e. already Christians] or sleep [are of the number of the sleeping, i e. unconverted] we should live, &c Thus it would = 'who died that all men might be saved' who came, not to call the righteous only, but sinners to life. There is to this interpretation the great objection that it confounds with the λοιποί, the ἡμᾶς who are definitely spoken of as set by God not to wrath but to περιποίησιν σωτηρίας So that the sense live or die, must, I think, be accepted, and the want of perspicuity with it. The construction of a subjunctive with εἴτε . εἴτε is not classical: an optative is found in such cases, e. g Xen. Anab ii. 1. 14, καὶ εἴτε ἄλλο τι θέλοι χρῆσθαι εἴτ' ἐπ' Αἴγυπτον στρατεύειν . . See Winer, edn 6, § 41, p 263, Engl transl 310, note.
ἅμα] **all together** not to be taken with σύν, see reff 11] *Conclusion from the whole*—**διό**, '*quæ cum ita sint*'—since all this is so or perhaps in literal strictness, as Ellic, *quamobrem* which however is exceedingly close to the above meaning **παρακαλεῖτε**, more naturally comfort, as in ch iv 18, than '*exhort.*' For as Lun remarks, the exhortation begun ver 6 has passed into consolation in vv 9, 10 **οἰκ. εἷς τὸν ἕνα**] **edify the one the other**. see ref and cf (Kypke) Theocr. Idyl. xxii 65 εἷς ἑνὶ χεῖρας ἄειρον—Lucian, Asin p 169, ἐγὼ δὲ ἕν' ἐξ ἑνὸς ἐπιτρέχων—Arrian, Epict i. 10, ἓν ἐξ ἑνὸς ἐπισεσώρευκεν. Whitby, Ruckert, al, would read **εἰς τὸν ἕνα**, and render '*edify yourselves into one body*' (Whitb. εἰς ἕν)—or '*so as to shew the One, Christ, as your foundation*, on whom the building should be raised' (Ruckert but this should be ἐπὶ τῷ ἑνί). The only allowable meaning of εἰς τὸν ἕνα would be, '*into the One*,' viz., Christ, as in Eph. iv 13 But the use of τὸν ἕνα for Christ, without any further designation, would be harsh and unprecedented 12—24] *Miscellaneous exhortations, ending with a solemn wish for their perfection in the day of Christ* 12, 13.] *In reference to their duties to the rulers of the church among them* The connexion (**δέ**, a slight contrast with that which has just passed) is perhaps as Chrys., but somewhat too strongly—ἐπειδὴ εἶπεν οἰκοδομεῖτε εἷς τὸν ἕνα, ἵνα μὴ νομίσωσιν ὅτι εἰς τὸ τῶν διδασκάλων ἀξίωμα αὐτοὺς ἀνήγαγε, τοῦτο ἐπήγαγε, μονονουχὶ λέγων, ὅτι κ. ὑμῖν ἐπέτρεψα οἰκοδομεῖν ἀλλήλους· οὐ γὰρ δυνατὸν πάντα τὸν διδάσκαλον εἰπεῖν. Rather, as the duty of comforting and building up one another has just been mentioned, the transition to those whose especial work this is, is easy, and one part of forwarding the work is the recognition and encouragement of them by the church

12] **εἰδέναι** in this sense is perhaps a Hebraism the LXX (in ref Prov) express ידע by ἐπιγινώσκειν. The persons indicated by **κοπιῶντας, προϊσταμένους**, and **νουθετοῦντας**, are the same, viz the πρεσβύτεροι or ἐπίσκοποι· see note on Acts xx. 17, 28 **ἐν ὑμ.** is **among you**, not as Pelt, al '(bestowing labour) *on you*' **ἐν κυρίῳ**, as the element in which, the matter with regard to which, their presidency takes place = 'in divine

κπερισσῶς ἐν ἀγάπῃ διὰ τὸ [p] ἔργον αὐτῶν. [q] εἰρηνεύετε
ἐν [r] ἑαυτοῖς. 14 [s] παρακαλοῦμεν δὲ ὑμᾶς, ἀδελφοί, [m] νουθετεῖτε τοὺς [t] ἀτάκτους, [u] παραμυθεῖσθε τοὺς [v] ὀλιγοψύχους, [w] ἀντέχεσθε τῶν [x] ἀσθενῶν, [y] μακροθυμεῖτε πρὸς
πάντας. 15 [z] ὁρᾶτε [z] μή τις [a] κακὸν [a] ἀντὶ [a] κακοῦ τινὶ
[ab] ἀποδῷ, ἀλλὰ πάντοτε [c] τὸ ἀγαθὸν [d] διώκετε καὶ εἰς
ἀλλήλους καὶ εἰς πάντας. 16 πάντοτε χαίρετε, 17 [f] ἀδια-

ABDF KLℵ a b c d e f g h k l m n o 17

p = Acts xiii 2 xiv 26 xv 38 Phil i 22 al. q Mark ix 50 Rom xii 18 2 Cor xiii 11 only Job v 21 Sir vi 5. r = Col iii 13 reff. s = Eph iv 1 reff. t here only + Deut xxxii 10 Aq (-ως, 2 Thess iii 6, 11 -εῖν, 2 Thess iii 7). u = ch ii 11 (reff). v here only Prov xiv 29 xviii 14 Isa lvii 15 al. w Matt vi 24 Luke xvi 13 Tit i 9 only Prov iii 18. x = 1 Cor viii 7 (-ων [part], Rom xiv 1 1 Cor viii 11). y Matt xviii 26, 29 Luke xviii 7 1 Cor xiii 4 Heb vi 15 James v 7 bis, 8 2 Pet iii 9 only Prov xix 11. z Matt xviii 10 al. a Rom xii 17 1 Pet iii 9 (Prov xvii 13). b = Matt vi 4, 6 Luke xix 8 al. c Gal vi 10 reff. d = Rom ix 30, 31 xii 13 xiv 19 1 Cor xiv 1 Heb xii 14 1 Pet iii 11, from Ps xxxiii 14 Sir xxvii 8. f ch i 2 ii 13 Rom i 9 only + 2 Macc ix 4 al.

rec υπερεκπερισσου (*more usual word, cf ch* iii 10), with AD[3]KLℵ rel: txt BD[1]F ins και bef ειρην ℵ[1](ℵ[3] disapproving) for εαυτ., αυτοις D[1]Fℵ a b[1] d l n o 73 vulg syr Chr Thdrt (Thl· γράφεται καὶ ἐν αὐτοῖς)· txt ABD[3]KL rel copt goth Clem Damasc, *ipsis* D-lat G-lat Ambrst-ms.

14 νουθετειν . . παραμυθεισθαι . αντεχεσθαι F 115 G-lat(altern).

15. αποδοιη D[1] αποδοι D[2](appy) Fℵ[1]. txt ABKLℵ[3] rel. om 1st και ADFℵ[1] in 17. 67[2] Syr copt goth Ambrst-ed Pelag ins BKLℵ[3] rel am(with fuld al) syr Chr Thdrt Damasc Ambrst-ms.

16 aft χαιρετε ins εν τω κυριω F harl[2] Ambrst. (not F-lat.)

things' οὐκ ἐν τοῖς κοσμικοῖς, ἀλλ' ἐν τοῖς κατὰ κύριον Thl. **13**] ἡγεῖσθαι ἐν ἀγάπῃ is an unusual expression for **to esteem in love**, for such seems to be its meaning. Lün compares ἔχειν τινὰ ἐν ὀργῇ (Thuc ii 18). We have περὶ πολλοῦ ἡγεῖσθαι, Herod. ii 115 (Job xxxv 2 does not apply). **ὑπερεκπερισσῶς** is best taken with ἐν ἀγάπῃ: it will not form a suitable qualification for ἡγεῖσθαι, which is merely a verbum medium. And so Chrys, all. **διὰ τὸ ἔργ αὐτ.** may mean, **because of the** *nature* **of their work**, viz that it is the Lord's work, for your souls: or, **on account of their activity in their office**, as a recompense for their work. Both these motives are combined in Heb. xiii. 17. The reading εἰρηνεύετε ἐν αὐτοῖς (see var. readd.) can hardly mean, as Chrys., al,—μὴ ἀντιλέγειν τοῖς παρ' αὐτῶν λεγομένοις (Thdrt.),—but is probably, as De W, a mistaken correction from imagining that this exhortation must refer to the presbyters as well as the preceding: whereas it seems only to be suggested by the foregoing, as enforcing peaceful and loving subordination without party strife: cf ἀτάκτους below. **ἑαυτοῖς** not = ἀλλήλοις (see ref Col. and note there, and cf. Mark ix 50). **14—22**] *General exhortations with regard to Christian duties.* There appears no reason for regarding these verses as addressed to the presbyters, as Conybeare in his translation (after Chrys, Œc, Thl, Est, al). They are for *all*: for each to interpret according to the sphere of his own duties. By the **ἀδελφοί**, he continues the same address as above. The attempt to give a stress to ὑμᾶς ('you, brethren, I exhort,' Conyb) is objectionable: (1) because in that case the order of the words would be different (ὑμᾶς δέ, ἀδ., παρ, or ὑμᾶς δὲ παρ, ἀδ),—(2) because the attention has been drawn off from οἱ προϊστάμενοι by εἰρηνεύετε ἐν ἑαυτοῖς intervening. **14 ἀτάκτους**] This as ch iv. 11, 2 Thess iii 6, 11, certainly implies that there was reason to complain of this ἀταξία in the Thessalonian church. "**ἄτακτος** is especially said of the soldier who does not remain in his rank: so *inordinatus* in Livy." Lün: hence **disorderly**. **ὀλιγοψύχους**] such e. g. as needed the comfort of ch iv 13 ff. **ἀντέχεσθε**] **keep hold of** (reff)—i e **support**. **οἱ ἀσθενεῖς** must be understood of the spiritually weak, not the literally sick: see reff. **πρὸς πάντας**] not, 'all the foregoing' (ἀτάκτους, ὀλιγοψύχους, ἀσθενῶν); but all men: cf next verse. **15.**] **ὁρᾶτε μή** gives a slight warning that the practice might creep on them unawares. It is not addressed to any particular section of the church, but to all; to each for himself, and the church for each. **16**] Chrys. refers this to ver 15: ὅταν γὰρ τοιαύτην ἔχωμεν ψυχὴν ὥστε μηδένα ἀμύνεσθαι, ἀλλὰ πάντας εὐεργετεῖν, πόθεν, εἰπέ μοι, τὸ τῆς λύπης κέντρον παρεισελθεῖν δυνήσεται, ὁ γὰρ οὕτω χαίρων τῷ

λείπτως προςεύχεσθε, 18 g ἐν παντὶ h εὐχαριστεῖτε· i τοῦτο
γὰρ θέλημα θεοῦ ἐν χριστῷ Ἰησοῦ εἰς ὑμᾶς. 19 τὸ
πνεῦμα μὴ k σβέννυτε, 20 l προφητείας μὴ m ἐξουθενεῖτε,
21 πάντα δὲ n δοκιμάζετε· τὸ καλὸν o κατέχετε, 22 ἀπὸ
παντὸς p εἴδους q πονηροῦ r ἀπέχεσθε. 23 s αὐτὸς δὲ ὁ

g 2 Cor vii 16 Eph v 24 Phil iv 6 h absol., Matt xv 36 ‖ al + Wisd xviii 2 i ch iv 3 k Matt xii 20 xxv 8 Mark ix 44 &c., from Isa lxvi 24 Eph vi 16 Heb xi 34 only l = Rom xii 6 1 Cor xii 10 xiii 2 8 al m = Luke xviii 9 Rom xiv 3 al Prov i 7 n = ch ii 4 (2nd) reff o = Luke viii 15 1 Cor xi 2 xv 2 Heb iii 6, 14 x 23 † p Luke iii 22 ix 29 John v 37 2 Cor v 7 only Jer xv 3 πᾶν εἶδος πονηρίας, Jos Antt x 3 1 q so καλοῦ τε κ. κακοῦ, Heb v 14 Deut i 39 r ch iv 3 reff s = ch iii 11 reff (see note)

18. aft γαρ ins εστιν D¹F. ins του bef θεου A(appy) ℵ¹(ℵ³ disapproving). εις υμας bef εν χριστω ιησ. A om ιησ. L 177.

19. ζβεννυτε B¹DF.

21. rec om δε (*perhaps absorbed by δο follg so Meyer*), with Aℵ¹ b¹ c f g k 17 Syr copt Orig Chr_{aliq} Thdrt Œc Tert Ambrst-ms ins BDFKLℵ³ rel 67² latt syr goth $Clem_2$ Bas Chr_1 Damasc Thl Ambrst-ed Pelag. δοκιμαζοντες K a b c f g k l² o syr-txt Bas Chr_1 Cyr $Damasc_1$.

παθεῖν κακῶς, ὡς κ. εὐεργεσίαις ἀμύνεσθαι τὸν πεποιηκότα κακῶς, πόθεν δυνήσεται ἀνιαθῆναι λοιπόν. But perhaps this is somewhat far-fetched. The connexion seems however to be justified as he proceeds: καὶ πῶς οἷόν τε τοῦτό, φησιν, ἂν ἐθέλωμεν, δυνατόν. εἶτα καὶ τὴν ὁδὸν ἔδειξεν. ἀδιαλείπτως προσεύχεσθε κ.τ.λ. And Thl. ὁ γὰρ ἐθισθεὶς ὁμιλεῖν τῷ θεῷ κ. εὐχαριστεῖν αὐτῷ ἐπὶ πᾶσιν ὡς συμφερόντως συμβαίνουσι, πρόδηλον ὅτι χαρὰν ἕξει διηνεκῆ. 17.] See Chrys and Thl above. προσεύχεσθε, not of the mere spirit of prayer, as Jowett: but, as in parallel, Eph. vi. 18, of direct supplications to God. These may be unceasing, in the heart which is full of his presence and evermore communing with Him.

18. ἐν παντί] in every thing,—every circumstance: see reff., and cf. ὑπὲρ πάντων, Eph. v. 20: κατὰ πάντα, Col. iii. 22, 23. Chrys., al., explain it '*on every occasion*' (καιρῷ); but 2 Cor. ix. 8, ἐν παντὶ πάντοτε, precludes this. τοῦτο perhaps refers back to the three—χαίρ., προσεύχ., εὐχαρ., or perhaps, as Ellic. and most modern expositors, to εὐχαρ. alone.

After γάρ, supply ἐστίν, and understand θέλημα, not '*decree*,' but will, in its practical reference to your conduct. ἐν χρ. Ἰησ.] in, as its medium, Christ being the Mediator. 19.] Chrys., Thl., Œc., understand this ethically: σβέννυσι δ' αὐτὸ βίος ἀκάθαρτος. But there can be no doubt that the *supernatural* agency of the Spirit is here alluded to,—the speaking in tongues, &c., as in 1 Cor. xii. 7 ff. It is conceived of as a flame, which may be checked and quenched: hence the ζέων τῷ πνεύματι of Acts xviii. 25, Rom. xii. 11. The word is a common one with the later classics applied to *wind*: e.g. Plut. de Is. and Osir. p. 366 E,—τὰ βόρεια πνεύματα κατασβεννύμενα κομιδῇ τῶν νοτίων ἐπικρατούντων. Galen. de Theriaca i. 17, uses the expression of the spirit of life in children: speaking of poison, he says, τὸ ἔμφυτον πνεῦμα ῥᾳδίως σβέννυσιν. See more examples in Wetst. 20.] On προφητείας, see 1 Cor xii. 10, note. They were liable to be despised in comparison with the more evidently miraculous gift of tongues: and hence in 1 Cor xiv. 5, &c., he takes pains to shew that prophecy was in reality the greater gift. 21.] πάντα δὲ δοκιμάζετε refers back to the foregoing: but try all (such χαρίσματα): see 1 Cor. xii. 10; xiv. 29, 1 John iv. 1.

τὸ καλὸν κατέχετε is best regarded as beginning a new sentence, and opposed to ἀπὸ παντ. εἴδ. κ.τ.λ. which follows: not however as disconnected from the preceding, but suggested by it. In this, and in all things, hold fast the good.

22. ἀπὸ π. εἴδ. πον. ἀπέχ.] These words cannot by any possibility be rendered as in E. V., '*abstain from all appearance of evil*.' For (1) εἶδος never signifies '*appearance*' in this sense. (2) the two members of the sentence would thus not be logically correspondent, but a new idea would be introduced in the second which has no place in the context: for it is not against being deceived by false *appearance*, nor against giving occasion by behaviour which *appears like* evil, that he is cautioning them, but merely to distinguish and hold fast that which is good, and reject that which is evil. εἶδος is the *species*, as subordinated to the *genus*. So Porphyr. (in Lunem.) isagoge de quinque vocibus 2: λέγεται δὲ εἶδος καὶ τὸ ὑπὸ τὸ ἀποδοθὲν γένος· καθ' ὃ εἰώθαμεν λέγειν τὸν μὲν ἄνθρωπον εἶδος τοῦ ζώου, γένους ὄντος τοῦ ζώου· τὸ δὲ λευκὸν τοῦ χρώματος εἶδος· τὸ δὲ τρίγωνον τοῦ σχή-

t Phil iv 9 reff
u Eph v 26 reff
v here only † (-τελῶς, Deut xiii 16 Aq) constr, see note
w James i 4 only Deut xxvii 6 al
x Job vii 15 A (not F) see 1 Cor ii 14 xv 44 Jude 19

[t] θεὸς τῆς [t] εἰρήνης [u] ἁγιάσαι ὑμᾶς [v] ὁλοτελεῖς, καὶ [w] ὁλόκληρον ὑμῶν τὸ [x] πνεῦμα καὶ ἡ [x] ψυχὴ καὶ τὸ [x] σῶμα
[y] ἀμέμπτως [z] ἐν τῇ [z] παρουσίᾳ τοῦ κυρίου ἡμῶν Ἰησοῦ
χριστοῦ [a] τηρηθείη. 24 [b] πιστὸς ὁ [c] καλῶν ὑμᾶς, ὃς καὶ
ποιήσει.
25 Ἀδελφοί, [d] προσεύχεσθε [d] περὶ ἡμῶν 26 ἀσπάσασθε
τοὺς ἀδελφοὺς πάντας [e] ἐν [e] φιλήματι ἁγίῳ. 27 [f] ἐνορκίζω

ABDF KLℵ a b c d e f g h k l m n o 17

y ch ii 10 only † (-τος, Phil ii 15) z ch ii 19 reff a = 1 Cor vii 37 2 Cor xi 9 al Wisd x 5 b 1 Cor i 9 x 13 2 Cor i 18 2 Thess iii 3 2 Tim ii 13 al c & particip, Gal v 8 d Col i 3 reff e Rom xvi 16 1 Cor xvi 20 2 Cor xiii 12 1 Pet v 14 φιλ, Luke vii 45 xxii 48 only Prov xxvii 6 Cant i 2 only f here only † ορκ, & constr, Mark v 7 Acts xix 13 ἐξορκ, Matt xxvi 63 Gen. xxiv 3

23. αγιασει F copt τηρηθειην D[1] om (leaving a space) F-gr G-lat.
24 ins ο bef πιστος F (not G), *fidelis deus* F-lat. ημας A e[1]. ποιησαι F. (not G)
25 aft προσευχεσθε ins και BD[1] m syr goth Damasc. for περι, υπερ F Damasc
27 rec (for ενορκ) ορκιζω, with D[2]·[3]FKLℵ rel txt ABD[1]E 17 Synops Damasc.

ματος εἶδος. And *πονηροῦ* is not an adjective, but a substantive —**from every species** (or **form**) **of evil** The objection which Bengel brings against this, '*species mali* esset *εἶδος τοῦ πονηροῦ*,' is null, as such articles in construction are continually omitted, and especially when the genitive of construction is an abstract noun Lün. quotes *πρὸς διάκρισιν καλοῦ τε κ. κακοῦ*, Heb. v. 14· *πᾶν εἶδος πονηρίας*, Jos Antt x. 3 1. **23, 24.**] **αὐτὸς δέ** —contrast to all these feeble endeavours on your own part. **εἰρήνη** here most probably in its wider sense, as the accomplishment of all these Christian graces, and result of the avoidance of all evil It seems rather far-fetched to refer it back to ver. 13. **ὁλοτελεῖς** seems to refer to the entireness of sanctification, which is presently expressed in detail. Jerome, who treats at length of this passage, ad Hedibiam (ep. cxx.) quæst xii, vol. i p. 1001, explains it, 'per omnia vel in omnibus, sive plenos et perfectos.' and so Pelt, 'ut fiatis integri.' and the reviewer of Mr. Jowett in the Journal of S Lit., April, 1856 'sanctify you [to be] entire.' But I prefer the other interpretation: in which case it = *ὅλους*. **καί** introduces the detailed expression of the same wish from the lower side—in its effects **ὁλόκληρον**] emphatic predicate, as its position before the article shows: **entire**—refers to all three following substantives, though agreeing in gender with *πνεῦμα*, the nearest. Cf. besides reff, Levit. xxiii 15, *ἑπτὰ ἑβδομάδας ὁλοκλήρους*. **τὸ πν. κ ἡ ψυχ κ τ. σῶμα**] *τὸ πνεῦμα* is the SPIRIT, the highest and distinctive part of man, the immortal and responsible *soul*, in our common parlance· **ἡ ψυχή** is the lower or animal soul, containing the passions and desires (*αἰτία κινήσεως ζωικῆς ζώων*, Plato, Deff p 411), which we have in common with the brutes, but which in *us* is ennobled and drawn up by the *πνεῦμα*. That St Paul had these distinctions in mind, is plain (against Jowett) from such places as 1 Cor. ii. 14. The spirit, that part whereby we are receptive of the Holy Spirit of God, is, in the unspiritual man, crushed down and subordinated to the animal soul (*ψυχή*). he therefore is called *ψυχικὸς πνεῦμα μὴ ἔχων*, Jude 19: see also note on 1 Cor as above. **ἀμέμπτως** defines and fixes *ὁλόκληρον τηρηθ* that, as Ellic., regarding quantity, this defining quality. **ἐν**, for it will be *in* that day that the result will be seen,—that the *ὁλόκληρον τηρηθῆναι* will be accomplished **24**] *Assurance from God's faithfulness, that it will be so.* **πιστός** (reff)—true to His word and calling *ἀντὶ τοῦ ἀληθής*, Thdrt **ὁ καλῶν**] not = *ὁ καλέσας*, but bringing out God's office, as the Caller of his people. cf. Gal v. 8 **ποιήσει**, viz. that which was specified in the last verse. **25—28**] CONCLUSION. **25.**] Cf Rom. xv. 30, Eph vi. 19, Col iv. 3, 2 Thess. iii 1. **περί** is not so definite as *ὑπέρ*—**pray concerning us**—make us the subject of your prayers—our person—our circumstances—our apostolic work. Ellic. however remarks, that this distinction is precarious, and hardly appreciable **26.**] From this verse and the following, it would appear that this letter was given into the hands of the *elders* **ἐν**, simply '*in*,'—the kiss being the vehicle of the salutation in our idiom, '*with*' **27.**] The meaning of this conjuration is, that an assembly of all the brethren should be held, and the

ὑμᾶς τὸν κύριον, [gh] ἀναγνωσθῆναι [hi] τὴν ἐπιστολὴν πᾶσιν
τοῖς ἀδελφοῖς.
28 Ἡ [k] χάρις τοῦ κυρίου ἡμῶν Ἰησοῦ χριστοῦ μεθ'
ὑμῶν.

g Acts viii 28 al fr Esdr iii 15
h Col iv 16 1 Macc v 14
i — Rom xvi 22 see 1 Cor v 9
k see Col iv 18 reff

ΠΡΟΣ ΘΕΣΣΑΛΟΝΙΚΕΙΣ Α.

rec ins *αγιοις* bef *αδελφοις* (*gloss from the margin*), with AKLℵ[3] rel vulg syrr copt goth æth-pl Chr Thdrt Damasc: om BDFℵ[1] æth-rom Euthal Ambrst Cassiod

28. rec at end ins *αμην*, with AD[2] [3]KLℵ rel vss Chr Thdrt: om BD[1]F o 17. 67[2] am Ambrst.

Subscription. rec adds *εγραφη απο αθηνων*, with AB[2]KL rel Syr copt: *a Laodicea* D[2]-lat syr 1 o goth have no subscr: *εργ α αθ* b h k m: *πρ. θεσσ.*, omg *α'*, 17 pref *του αγιου απ. παυλου* L: txt B[1]ℵ, and (adding *επληρωθη*) D, (prefixing *ετελεσθη*) F.

Epistle then and there publicly read. The aorist, **ἀναγνωσθῆναι**, referring to a single act, shews this (but consult Ellic.'s note). On the construction *τὸν κύρ* see reff. Jowett offers various solutions for the Apostle's vehemence of language. I should account for it, not by supposing any distrust of the elders, nor by the other hypotheses which he suggests, but by the earnestness of spirit incidental to the solemn conclusion of an Epistle of which he is conscious that it conveys to them the will and special word of the Lord. **πᾶσιν**] i. e. in Thessalonica, assembled together. 28.] See on 2 Cor xiii. 13.

ΠΡΟΣ ΘΕΣΣΑΛΟΝΙΚΕΙΣ Β.

a 1 Thess i 1
b Gal i 1 reff
c = Eph i 10 reff
d Eph v 28 reff
e Phil i 7
f = here only Xen Mem i 5 3 Anab ii 3 25
g here only † αὐξ, Paul elsw transit 1 Cor iii 6 al but see Eph ii 21
h see 1 Thess iii 12 reff
i 1 Thess ii 11 reff
k here only † Ps li 1 xcvi 7 cv 47

ABDF KLℵ a b c d e f g h k l m n o 17

I. 1 Παῦλος καὶ Σιλουανὸς καὶ Τιμόθεος τῇ ἐκκλησίᾳ
Θεσσαλονικέων ^a ἐν ^a θεῷ ^c πατρὶ ἡμῶν καὶ κυρίῳ Ἰησοῦ
χριστῷ. 2 χάρις ὑμῖν καὶ εἰρήνη ἀπὸ ^b θεοῦ ^b πατρὸς
καὶ κυρίου Ἰησοῦ χριστοῦ.
3 ^c Εὐχαριστεῖν ^d ὀφείλομεν τῷ θεῷ πάντοτε περὶ ὑμῶν,
ἀδελφοί, ^e καθὼς ^f ἄξιόν ἐστιν, ὅτι ^g ὑπεραυξάνει ἡ πίστις
ὑμῶν καὶ ^h πλεονάζει ἡ ἀγάπη ^i ἑνὸς ἑκάστου πάντων
ὑμῶν εἰς ἀλλήλους, 4 ὥστε αὐτοὺς ἡμᾶς ἐν ὑμῖν ^k ἐγ-

Title. rec παυλου του αποστολου η πρ. θεσσ. επ. δευτερα. του αγ. αποστ. παυλου πρ. θεσσ. επιστ. β′ L. πρ θεσσ β′ επ. παυλου o. ανδρασι θεσσαλιης ταδε δευτερα ουρανιος φως f. η πρ θεσσ β′ επ k. πρ θεσσ δευτ επ h. πρ θεσσ επ β′ l. txt ABℵ m n 17, and (prefixing αρχεται) DF.

Chap. I. 1. σιλβανος DF 67². ins και bef πατρι ℵ¹(but corrd) 1. 80. om κυριω F (not F-lat). χριστ bef ιησ. DF. (not F-lat.)
2. rec aft πατρος ins ημων (as in other epp), with AFKLℵ rel vulg syrr copt goth Chr Thdrt Ambrst-ven: om BD 17 Thl Ambrst rom Pelag.
3. om last υμων ℵ¹.
4. rec ημας bef αυτους, with ADFKL rel: txt Bℵ m 17. 73. rec (for εγκ.)

Ch. I. 1, 2.] Address and greeting. On ver. 1, see 1 Thess i. 1, note.

2.] πατρός, absol.: see Gal. i. 1, 3; 1 Tim. i. 2; 2 Tim. i. 2; Tit. i. 4.

3—12.] Introduction. *Thanksgiving for their increase in faith and love, and their endurance under persecution* (vv. 3, 4): *promise of a rich recompense at Christ's coming* (vv. 5—10), *and good wishes for their Christian perfection* (vv. 11, 12).

3. **καθὼς ἄξιόν ἐστιν**] as it is right—refers to the whole preceding sentence. **ὅτι**, not '*that*,'—εὐχαριστεῖν ὅτι—which would make καθὼς ἄξ. ἐστ. flat and superfluous,—but because, dependent on the clause preceding, καθὼς ἄξ. ἐστιν, it is right, because &c. "**ὀφείλομεν** expresses the duty of thanksgiving from its *subjective* side as an inward conviction,—**καθὼς ἄξιόν ἐστιν**, on the other hand, from the *objective* side, as something answering to the state of circumstances." Lün. **ὑπεραυξάνει**] 'Frequentavit hujus generis voce Paulus (ὑπερλίαν 2 Cor. xi. 5, ὑπερπλεονάζω 1 Tim. i. 14, ὑπερπερισσεύομαι 2 Cor. vii. 4 [cf. also Rom. v. 20], ὑπερνικάω Rom. viii. 37, ὑπερυψόω Phil. ii. 9), non quod iis delectaretur, sed quia vir vehemens natura duce sua cogitata gravibus verbis enuntiavit.' Fritzsche ad Rom. v. 20. **εἰς ἀλλήλους** goes with ἀγάπη.

4.] **αὐτοὺς ἡμᾶς**—as well as our informants, and others who heard about

καυχᾶσθαι ἐν ταῖς [l] ἐκκλησίαις τοῦ [l] θεοῦ ὑπὲρ τῆς [m] ὑπο- l 1 Thess ii 14 reff
μονῆς ὑμῶν καὶ πίστεως ἐν πᾶσιν τοῖς [n] διωγμοῖς ὑμῶν καὶ m Col i 11 reff
ταῖς θλίψεσιν [o] αἷς [p] ἀνέχεσθε, 5 [q] ἔνδειγμα τῆς [r] δικαίας n Mark iv 17 Mt x 30 Rom viii 35
[r] κρίσεως τοῦ θεοῦ, [s] εἰς τὸ [t] καταξιωθῆναι ὑμᾶς τῆς 2 Cor xii 10 2 Tim iii 11
βασιλείας τοῦ θεοῦ, ὑπὲρ ἧς [u] καὶ πάσχετε, 6 [v] εἴπερ Prov xi 19 Lam iii 19 2 Macc xii
δίκαιον [w] παρὰ θεῷ [x] ἀνταποδοῦναι τοῖς [y] θλίβουσιν ὑμᾶς 23 only o attr, Eph i.
θλῖψιν, 7 καὶ ὑμῖν τοῖς [y] θλιβομένοις [z] ἄνεσιν μεθ᾽ ἡμῶν 6 reff p = Eph iv 2 reff

q here only+ (-ξις, Phil i 28) r John v 30 viii 24. Rev xvi 7 xix 2 Isa lviii 2 2 Macc ix 18 s Phil i 23. 1 Thess iii 10 al t Luke xx 35 xxi 36 Acts v 41 only+ Gen xxxi 28 compl 2 Macc xiii 12 only u = Rom viii 17 v Rom viii 9, 17 al w = Rom ii 13 1 Cor iii 19 al x 1 Thess iii 9 reff y 1 Thess iii 4 reff z Acts xxiv 23 2 Cor ii 12 vii 5 viii 13 only. 2 Chron xxiii 15.

καυχασθαι (*more usual word*), with DKL rel, καυχησασθαι F. txt ABℵ 17 Chr-ms. om 2nd ταις D[1]F. ενεχεσθε B.
6 ins τω bef θεω A Orthod. ins αυτοις bef τοις θλιβουσιν F vulg D-lat
7 for ημων, υμων ℵ[1].

you,—see 1 Thess i 8. There is ample reason (against Jowett) for the emphasis on *αὐτοὺς ἡμᾶς* The fact of an Apostle making honourable mention of them in other churches was one which deserved this marking out, to their credit and encouragement **ἐν ὑμῖν**] as the object of our *ἐγκαυχ* **ἐν ταῖς ἐκκλησίαις τοῦ θεοῦ**] i e at Corinth and in Achaia **ὑπομονῆς καὶ πίστεως**] No *ἓν διὰ δυοῖν* (Grot, Pelt), — nor is there the slightest necessity, with Lunem., to take **πίστις** here in a different sense from that in ver 3 The same faith which was receiving so rich increase, was manifesting itself by its fruit in the midst of persecutions and afflictions. **πᾶσιν** belongs only to **τοῖς διωγμοῖς (ὑμῶν)**, as is shewn by the article before *θλίψεσιν*, and by **αἷς ἀνέχεσθε**, which is parallel with *ὑμῶν*. **αἷς ἀνέχεσθε**] attr for **ὧν ἀνέχεσθε**,—not for **ἃς ἀνέχεσθε**, as De W., al., for *ἀνέχομαι* always governs a genitive in the N T **ἀνέχ**, **ye are enduring**: the persecutions continued at the time of the Epistle being written 5—10] *Comfort under these afflictions, to think that they were only part of God's carrying out his justice towards them and their persecutors.* 5] The sentence, in construction, is in apposition with the preceding *τῆς ὑπομ* to *ἀνέχεσθε*,—but in the nominative · *ὅ(τι) ἐστίν* or the like having to be supplied In Phil i 28 we have the like sentiment, with *ἥτις ἐστίν* supplied There is a similar construction in Rom viii 3 **ἔνδειγμα**] cf *ἔνδειξις* in ref —**a proof** manifested in you being called on and enabled to suffer for Christ, and your adversaries filling up the measure of their opposition to God. The **δικαία κρίσις** is, that just judgment which will be completed at the Lord's coming, but is even now preparing—this being an earnest and token of it **εἰς τὸ** *κ τ λ*] **in order to** (belongs to the implied assertion of the foregoing clause—'which judgment is even now bringing about &c' **εἰς τό** is not merely of the *result*, as Lun. nor is it of the purpose of your endurance, *αἷς ἀνέχεσθε εἰς τὸ κ τ.λ*, as Estius characteristically, to bring in the Romish doctrine of merit —but of the purpose of God's dispensation of *δικαία κρίσις*, by which you will be ripened and fitted for his kingdom [Ellic. denies this, and would take *εἰς τό* of the object to which the *δικαία κρίσις* tended. But surely when we are speaking of the *divine* proceedings, the tendency involves the purpose, and there is no need for a *semi* telic force]) **your being counted worthy of the Kingdom of God, on behalf of which** (for this meaning of *ὑπέρ*, see Acts v 41; ix 16; Rom i. 5, xv 8, 2 Cor xii. 10; xiii. 8, al) **ye also** (**καί**, as in ref., points out the connexion—q. d *'ye accordingly'*) **are suffering**, 6] **if at least** (reff: it refers back to **δικαίας** above, and introduces a substantiation of it by an appeal to our ideas of strict justice) **it is just with** (in the esteem of, reff) **God to requite to those who trouble you, tribulation** (according to the strict *jus talionis*), **and to you who are troubled, rest** (reff literally, **relaxation**: 'the glory of the kingdom of God on its negative side, as liberation from earthly affliction' Lun.) **with us** (viz. the writers, Paul, Silvanus, and Timotheus, who are troubled like yourselves not '*with us [all] Christians*,' as De W, al,—for all Christians were not *θλιβόμενοι*, which is the condition of this *ἄνεσις* in our sentence still less,

ἐν τῇ [a] ἀποκαλύψει τοῦ [b] κυρίου Ἰησοῦ ἀπ' οὐρανοῦ μετ' ABDF
ἀγγέλων δυνάμεως αὐτοῦ 8 [c] ἐν [cd] πυρὶ [de] φλογὸς [fg] διδόν- KLℵ a b c d e f g
τος [gh] ἐκδίκησιν τοῖς [i] μὴ εἰδόσιν θεὸν καὶ τοῖς μὴ [k] ὑπ- h k l m n o 17
ακούουσιν τῷ εὐαγγελίῳ τοῦ κυρίου ἡμῶν Ἰησοῦ, 9 [l] οἵτινες
[m] δίκην [n] τίσουσιν [o] ὄλεθρον αἰώνιον [p] ἀπὸ [q] προςώπου τοῦ
κυρίου καὶ ἀπὸ τῆς [r] δόξης τῆς [r] ἰσχύος αὐτοῦ, 10 ὅταν
ἔλθῃ [s] ἐνδοξασθῆναι ἐν τοῖς [t] ἁγίοις αὐτοῦ καὶ [u] θαυμασθῆ-
ναι ἐν πᾶσιν τοῖς πιστεύσασιν, ὅτι [v] ἐπιστεύθη τὸ [w] μαρτύ-

a = Rom ii 5 1 Cor i 7 al b gen, 1 Cor i 7 1 Pet i 7, 13 (see 2 Cor xii 1) c 1 Cor iii 13 d here (Acts vii 30 v r) only bir viii 10 see Heb i 7 Rev i 14 ii 18. xix 12 e as above (d) & Luke xvi 24 only f = Rev xviii 7 g Ps xvii 47 Ezek xxv 14, 17 (ἀποδιδ, Num xxxi 3) h Luke xviii 7, 8 xxi 22 Acts vii 24 Rom xii 19 2 Cor vii 11 Heb x 30 1 Pet ii 14 only i 1 Thess iv 5 Gal iv 8 (Jer ix 6) k = Acts vi 7 Rom vi 17 l = Acts x 41 47 xiii 31, 43 al fr m Acts (xxv 15 rec) xxviii 4 Jude 7 only Ezek xxv 12 n here only Prov xx 22 xxiv 29 o 1 Thess v 3 reff p = Col ii 20 reff q Acts iii 19 r Isa ii 10, 19, 21 see Eph i 19 vi. 10. s ver 12 only Exod xiv 4 Ezek xxviii 22 Psa lxxxviii 7 t Eph i 1 reff u = here only Wisd viii 11 see Rev xiii 3 Luke vii. 9 v pass, 1 Tim iii 16. w = Acts iv 33 1 Cor i 6 2 Tim i 8

8 for πυρι φλογος, φλογι πυρος (*alteration to sense, see reff*) BDF latt syrr copt æth arm ancient-writers-in-Iren Mac Thdrt-comm(appy) Thl-marg Œc Tert Aug Pelag · txt AKLℵ rel syr-marg Chr Thdrt-txt Damasc Thl Ambrst διδους D[1]F *dare* G-lat Iren-int Tert ins τον bef θεον ℵ[3]L a b f g rec aft ιησου ins χριστου, with AFℵ rel latt Syr goth Chr Iren-int om BDKL b d e k l n o 17 syr copt æth Chr ms Thdrt Damasc Thl Œc

9 ολεθριον A 17 73 Ephr Chr-ms Tert om του DF 67[2] Chr[1] Thl

10 ενθαυμασθηναι D[1]F rec πιστευουσιν (with a f 17, e sil), *credentibus* G-lat copt goth Iren int[1] · txt ABDFKLℵ rel Ephr Chr Thdrt, *qui crediderunt* vulg syr Iren-int[1] Ambrst

'*with us Jews*,' you being Gentiles [Bengel, al]) **at the revelation** (manifestation in His appearing, reff) **of the Lord Jesus from heaven** (cf 1 Thess iv 16) **with the angels of His power** (no hendiadys—not as E V, 'his mighty angels,' which as usual, obscures and stultifies the sense for the *might of the angels* is no element here, but His *might*, of which they *are* the *angels*—serving His power and proclaiming His might) **in (the) fire of flame** (further specification of the ἀποκάλυψις above does not belong to the following. On the analogy, see Exod iii 2; xix. 18, Dan vii 9, 10) **allotting** (distributing as their portion reff) **vengeance to those who know not God** (the Gentiles, see reff), **and to those** (the τοῖς repeated indicates a new class of persons) **who obey not the Gospel of our Lord Jesus** (the unbelieving Jews, see Rom x. 3, 16), **which persons** (οἵτινες, generic and classifying, refers back to their characteristics just mentioned, thus containing in itself the reason for τίσουσιν &c following [against Ellic.]. See ὅστις discussed by Hermann, Præf ad Soph (Ed. Tyr pp vii—xv) **shall pay the penalty of everlasting destruction from** (local, as in Matt. vii 23, ἀποχωρεῖτε ἀπ' ἐμοῦ οἱ ἐργαζόμενοι τὴν ἀνομίαν,—'apart from,' see reff [so Pisc., Beza, Schott, Olsh, Lunem, al] It has been interpreted of *time*,—'*from the time of the appearing* &c' [Chr, Œc., Thl., &c], but ἀπὸ προσώπου will not bear this —also of the *cause*, which would make ver 9 a mere repetition of ἐν τῇ ἀποκ to διδόντος ἐκδ. above [so Grot., Beng, Pelt, De W, Baumg-Crus, al]) **the face of the Lord and from the glory of his Power** (i. e from the manifestation of his power in the glorification of his saints [see ref. Isa.]. De W makes these words, ἀπὸ δόξης κ τ λ, an objection to the *local* sense of ἀπό But it is not so:—the δόξα being the visible localized result of the ἰσχύς; see next verse) **when He shall have come** (follows on δίκην τίσουσιν &c. above On the aor subj with ὅταν, see Winer, edn 6, § 42 5) **to be glorified** (aor: by the great manifestation at His coming) **in** (not '*through*' [τουτέστι, διά, Chrys so Œc, Thl, Pelt, al.], nor '*among*' but *they* will be the *element* of His glorification. He will be glorified *in* them, just as the Sun is reflected in a mirror) **his saints** (not angels, but holy men), **and to be wondered at in** (see above) **all them that believed** (aor participle, looking back from that day on the past),—**because our testimony to you** (ref, not τὸ ἐφ' ὑμ, as ἐφ' belongs immediately to μαρτύριον) **was believed** (parenthesis, serving to include the Thessalonians among the πιστεύσαντες),—**in that day** (of which we all know to be joined with θαυμασθ, &c, not with ὅτι ἐπιστεύθη, &c, as Syr., Ambr, Grot.,

ριον ἡμῶν [x] ἐφ' ὑμᾶς, ἐν τῇ [y] ἡμέρᾳ [y] ἐκείνῃ. 11 [z] εἰς ὃ
[z] καὶ [a] προσευχόμεθα πάντοτε περὶ ὑμῶν, [a] ἵνα ὑμᾶς
[b] ἀξιώσῃ τῆς [c] κλήσεως ὁ θεὸς ἡμῶν καὶ [d] πληρώσῃ πᾶσαν
[e] εὐδοκίαν [f] ἀγαθωσύνης καὶ [g] ἔργον [g] πίστεως [h] ἐν δυνάμει,
12 ὅπως [i] ἐνδοξασθῇ τὸ ὄνομα τοῦ κυρίου ἡμῶν Ἰησοῦ
ἐν ὑμῖν καὶ ὑμεῖς ἐν αὐτῷ κατὰ τὴν χάριν τοῦ θεοῦ ἡμῶν
καὶ κυρίου Ἰησοῦ χριστοῦ.

x Luke ix 5. y 2 Tim i 12, 18 iv 8. z = Col i 29. a Phil i 9 reff. b = 1 Tim v 17. Heb iii. 3 x 20 only (see Luke vii 7. Acts xv 38) t. c = Phil iii 14. Heb iii 1 (1 Cor i 26). d = John iii 29. 2 Cor x 6 al fr. e = (see note) here only (Eph i. 5 reff.). f Gal v 22 reff. g 1 Thess i 3. h Col i 29 reff. i ver 10.

11 om ημων D[1] am syr Vig. υμων D[3]KL e m n. ins υμων bef ο θε. ημων F arm: ins sua vulg(and F-lat). πληρωσει AK o. αγαθοσυνης DFL Damasc.

12 rec aft 1st ιησου ins χριστου, with AF b c f h 17 vulg syrr æth-pl Chr Ambrst: om BDKLℵ rel coptt æth-rom Thdrt-ms Damasc Œc. ημεις A.

al., who also take ἐπιστ. as a future, 'for in that day our testimony with regard to you will be substantiated.' Most unwarrantable—requiring also ἐπιστώθη instead of -εύθη. Calvin says, 'repetit in die illa . . . . ideo autem repetit, ut fidelium vota cohibeat, ne ultra modum festinent.' I should rather say, to give more fixity and definiteness to the foregoing.) We may observe, as against Jowett's view of the arguments here being merely "they suffer now; therefore their enemies will suffer hereafter:—their enemies will suffer hereafter; therefore they will be comforted hereafter,"—that the arguments are nothing of the kind, resting entirely on the word δίκαιον, bringing in as it does all the relations of the Christian covenant, of them to God, and God to them,—and by contrast, of God to their enemies and persecutors. 11.] **With a view to which** (consummation, the ἐνδοξασθῆναι, &c., above, in *your case*, as is shewn below: not '*wherefore*,' as E. V., Grot., Pelt, &c.) **we pray also** (as well as wish. Had the καί imported [as Lün.] that the *prayer of the Apostle* was added on behalf of the Thessalonians to the fact (?) of the ἐνδοξασθῆναι, it would have been καὶ ἡμεῖς προς.) **always concerning you, that** (see note on 1 Cor. xiv 13) **our God may count you** (emphatic) **worthy** (not—'*make you worthy*,' as Luth., Grot., Olsh., al., which the word cannot mean. The verb has the secondary emphasis: see below) **of your calling** (just as we are exhorted to *walk* ἀξίως τῆς κλήσεως ἧς ἐκλήθημεν, Eph iv. 1—the calling being taken not merely as the first act of God, but as the enduring state produced by that act [see especially 1 Cor vii 20], the normal termination of which is, *glory*. So that κλῆσις is not 'the good thing to which we are called,' as Lün. which besides would require τῆς κλήσεως ἀξιώσῃ· now that τῆς κλήσεως is sheltered behind the verb, it is taken as a matter of course, 'your calling,' an acknowledged fact), **and may fulfil** (complete,—bring to its fulness in you) **all** (possible) **right purpose of goodness** (it is quite impossible, with many ancient Commentators, E. V., &c., to refer **εὐδοκίαν** to *God*—'*His good pleasure*' In that case we must at least have τὴν εὐδοκίαν—and **ἀγαθωσ** will not refer with any propriety either to God, of whom the word is never used [occurring Rom xv 14; Gal. v. 22, Eph. v 9 only, and always of MAN], or to the Thessalonians [π. ἀγαθωσύνην εὐδοκίας]. It [εὐδοκία] must then apply to the Thessalonians, as it does to human agents in Phil. i 15. And then ἀγαθωσύνης may be either a gen. *objecti*, 'approval of that which is good,'—or a gen. *appositionis*, a εὐδοκία *consisting* in ἀγαθωσύνη. The latter I own seems to me [agst Ellic.] far the best: as ἀγαθωσύνη is in all the above citations a subjective quality, and the *approval* of that which is good would introduce an element here which seems irrelevant) **and** (all) **work of faith** (activity of faith: see ref 1 Thess. note. The genitive is again one of apposition), **in power** (belongs to πληρώσῃ, q. d. *mightily*),—**that** &c. On **ὄνομα**, cf. Phil ii. 9 ff. Lunemann refers ἐν αὐτῷ to ὄνομα, 'and ye in *it*.' but surely the expression is one too appropriated in sacred diction, for it to refer to any but our Lord Himself: cf 1 Cor. i 5, 2 Cor xiii. 4; Eph. i. 4; iv. 21, Col. ii 10, al.

k = 1 Thess. iv. 1 reff. l = John i. 30. 2 Cor. i. 8. viii. 23. 1 Thess. iii. 2. m = 1 Thess. ii. 19 reff. n Heb. x. 25 only †. 2 Macc. ii. 7 only (-άγειν, Matt. xxiv. 31).

II. 1 [k] Ἐρωτῶμεν δὲ ὑμᾶς, ἀδελφοί, [l] ὑπὲρ τῆς [m] παρουσίας τοῦ κυρίου ἡμῶν Ἰησοῦ χριστοῦ καὶ ἡμῶν [n] ἐπισυν-
αγωγῆς ἐπ᾽ αὐτόν, 2 [o] εἰς τὸ μὴ [p] ταχέως [q] σαλευθῆναι
ὑμᾶς [r] ἀπὸ τοῦ [s] νοὸς μηδὲ [t] θροεῖσθαι, μήτε [u] διὰ [u] πνεύματος μήτε [v] διὰ [v] λόγου μήτε δι᾽ ἐπιστολῆς ὡς δι᾽ ἡμῶν,
[w] ὡς ὅτι [x] ἐνέστηκεν ἡ [y] ἡμέρα τοῦ [y] κυρίου. 3 μή τις

ABDF KLℵ a b c d e f g h k l m n o 17

o constr., Phil. i. 23. 1 Thess. iii. 10. p = 1 Tim. v. 22. q = Luke vi. 48. Acts ii. 25 (from Ps. xv. 8). iv. 31. see Heb. xii. 26, 27. r constr. prægn., Rom. vi. 7. vii. 2. ix. 3. 2 Tim. ii. 26. s = Rom. vii. 23, 25. 1 Cor. xiv. 14. t Matt. xxiv. 6 ‖ Mk. only. Cant v. 4 only. u = Acts i. 2. xi 28. xxi. 4. Rom. v. 5. Eph. iii. 16 al. L.P. (Heb. ix. 14. 1 Pet. i. 22.) v ver. 15. Acts xv. 27, 32. w 2 Cor. v. 19. xi. 21 only. Winer, edn. 6, § 65. 9. x (=) Rom. viii. 38. 1 Cor. iii. 22. vii. 26. Gal. i. 4. 2 Tim. iii. 1. Heb. ix. 9 only. 1 Macc. xii. 44. y see 1 Thess. v. 2 reff.

CHAP. II. 1. om 1st ημων B syr.

2. aft νοος ins υμων D vulg Syr syr-w-ast sah æth Ambrst Jer Pelag. rec for μηδε, μητε (*to suit μητε thrice follg: but the sense is difft*), with D³KL rel: μηποτε 17: txt ABD¹Fℵ Orig.—μηδε δια λογ. D¹: μηδε 4 times F, but μητε δια λογ. F¹. om ἡ D¹. om last του F Damasc Thl. rec (for κυριου) χριστου, with D³K rel goth: txt ABD¹FLℵ m 67² latt syrr coptt æth arm Orig Hippol Chr Thdrt Damasc Thl Œc Tert Jer Aug Ambrst Pelag, κυριου ιησου 17.

CH. II. 1—12.] DOGMATICAL PORTION OF THE EPISTLE. *Information* (by way of correction) *concerning the approach of the day of the Lord: its prevenient and accompanying circumstances.* This passage has given rise to many separate treatises: the principal of which I have enumerated in the Prolegomena, § v. **1.] But** (passing from those things which he prays *for* them, to those which he prays *of* them) **we entreat** (reff.) **you, brethren** (to win their affectionate attention), **in regard of** (the Vulg., E. V., and many ancient Commentators, render ὑπέρ, '*per*,' '*by*,' and understand it as introducing a *formula jurandi*, as in Il. ω. 466, καί μιν ὑπὲρ πατρὸς . . . λίσσεο. But this construction is not found in the N. T.; and it is most unnatural that the Apostle should thus conjure them by that, concerning which he was about to teach them. It is best therefore to take **ὑπέρ**, as so often, *not quite* = περί, but very nearly so, the meaning '*on behalf of*' being slightly hinted—for the subject had been misrepresented, and justice is done to it by the Apostle; and so Chrys. [περὶ τῆς παρουσίας τ. χριστοῦ ἐνταῦθα διαλέγεται κ. περὶ τῆς ἐπισυναγ. ἡμῶν] al.: see reff.) **the coming of our Lord Jesus Christ, and our gathering together** (i. e. the gathering together of us, announced in 1 Thess. iv. 17) **to Him** (Lün. condemns *to*, and would render '*up to*' as 1 Thess. iv. 17: but so much does not seem to lie in the preposition). **2.] in order that** (aim of ἐρωτῶμεν) **ye should not be lightly** (soon and with small reason) **shaken** (properly of the waves agitated by a storm) **from** (see reff.) **your mind** (**νοῦς** here in its general sense—your mental apprehension of the subject:—not 'your former more correct sentiment,' as Est., Corn.-a-lap., Grot., al.) **nor yet troubled** (reff.), **neither** (on **μηδέ**, which is disjunctive [δέ], and separates negative from negative,—and **μήτε**, which is adjunctive [τε], and connects the separate parts of the same negation, see Winer, Gr. edn. 6, § 55. 6; and cf. Luke ix. 3) **by spirit** (by means of spiritual gift of prophecy or the like, assumed to substantiate such a view) **nor by word** (*of mouth*: belongs closely to μήτε δι᾽ ἐπιστ. following, as is shewn by ver. 15, where they again appear together) **nor by epistle as by** (agency of) **us** (pretending to be from us. Let no pretended saying, no pretended epistle of mine, shake you in this matter. That there were such, is shewn by this parallel position of the clauses with διὰ πνεύματος, which last agency certainly was among them. Sayings, and an epistle, to this effect, were ascribed to the Apostle. So Chrys.: ἐνταῦθα δοκεῖ μοι αἰνίττεσθαι περιϊέναι τινὰς ἐπιστολὴν πλάσαντας δῆθεν ἀπὸ τοῦ Παύλου, κ. ταύτην ἐπιδεικνυμένους λέγειν ὡς ἄρα ἐφέστηκεν ἡ ἡμέρα τοῦ κυρίου, ἵνα πολλοὺς ἐντεῦθεν πλανήσωσιν. However improbable this may seem, our expression would seem hardly to bear legitimately any other meaning. Cf. also ch. iii. 17, and note. It is impossible to understand the ἐπιστολὴ ὡς δι᾽ ἡμῶν of the first Epistle, *wrongly understood*, which certainly would have been more plainly expressed, and the Epistle not as here disowned, but explained. Jowett says, "The most probable hypothesis is, that the Apos-

ὑμᾶς [z] ἐξαπατήσῃ [a] κατὰ μηδένα [a] τρόπον· ὅτι ἐὰν μὴ
ἔλθῃ ἡ [b] ἀποστασία πρῶτον καὶ [c] ἀποκαλυφθῇ ὁ [d] ἄνθρωπος τῆς [d] ἁμαρτίας, ὁ [e] υἱὸς τῆς [e] ἀπωλείας, 4 ὁ
[f] ἀντικείμενος καὶ [g] ὑπεραιρόμενος [h] ἐπὶ πάντα λεγόμενον

z Rom vii 11 xvi 18 1 Cor iii 18 2 Cor xi 3 1 Tim ii 14 only Exod viii 29 vat Susan 56 Theod only
a Acts xv 11 xxvii 25 Rom iii 2 2 Macc xi 31
b Acts xxi 21 only 3 Kings xx (xxi) 13 Ald 2 Chron xxix 19 Jer ii 19 (xxxvi [xxix] 32 compl) 1 Macc ii 15 only
c vv 6, 8 see ch i 7
d here only
e John xvii 12 see Isa lvii 4. ἀπ, 1 Tim vi 9 reff
f Gal v 17 reff
g 2 Cor xii 7 only Ps lxxi 16
h — John xiii 18, from Ps xl 9

3 for αμαρτιας, ανομιας (*see vv* 7, 8) BN coptt Orig$_2$ Cyr-jer Damasc Niceph Tert (once *delinquentiæ*, once *delicti*) Ambrst-ed(*iniquitatis*) Ambr txt ADFKL rel vulg Orig$_3$ Hippol Cyr-jer-ms Chr Thdrt$_4$ Iren-int.
4 for υπεραιρομ, επαιρομενος F Hippol Orig$_1$ Procop$_1$(in Niceph) om και υπερ N^1

tle is not referring definitely to any particular speech or epistle, but to the possibility only of some one or other being used against him" But this seems hardly definite enough) **to the effect that** (*'as if,'* or *'as that.'* Lunem is quite wrong in saying that ὡς shews that the matter indicated by ὅτι is groundless,—see 2 Cor. v. 19, and note) **the day of the Lord is present** (not, *'is at hand.'* ἐνίστημι occurs six times besides [reff.] in the N. T, and always in the sense of *being present* in two of those places, Rom viii 38, 1 Cor. iii. 22, τὰ ἐνεστῶτα are distinguished expressly from τὰ μέλλοντα. Besides which, St Paul could not have so written, nor could the Spirit have so spoken by him. The teaching of the Apostles was, and of the Holy Spirit in all ages has been, that the day of the Lord *is at hand*. But those Thessalonians imagined it to be already come, and accordingly were deserting their pursuits in life, and falling into other irregularities, as if the day of grace were closed So Chrys,—ὁ διάβολος . . . . ἐπειδὴ οὐκ ἴσχυσε πεῖσαι ὅτι ψευδῆ τὰ μέλλοντα, ἑτέραν ἦλθεν ὁδόν, καὶ καταθεὶς ἀνθρώπους τινὰς λυμεῶνας, ἐπεχείρει τοὺς πειθομένους ἀπατᾷν, ὅτι τὰ μεγάλα ἐκεῖνα καὶ λαμπρὰ τελος εἴληφε. τότε μὲν οὖν ἔλεγον ἐκεῖνοι τὴν ἀνάστασιν ἤδη γεγονέναι νῦν δὲ ἔλεγον ὅτι ἐνέστηκεν ἡ κρίσις καὶ ἡ παρουσία τοῦ χριστοῦ, ἵνα τὸν χριστὸν αὐτὸν ψεύδει ὑποβάλωσι, καὶ πείσαντες ὡς οὐκ ἔστι λοιπὸν ἀντίδοσις οὐδὲ δικαστήριον καὶ κόλασις καὶ τιμωρία τοῖς κακῶς πεποιηκόσιν, ἐκείνους τε θρασυτέρους ἐργάσωνται, καὶ τούτους ταπεινοτέρους καὶ τὸ δὴ πάντων χαλεπώτερον, ἐπεχείρουν οἱ μὲν ἁπλῶς ῥήματα ἀπαγγέλλειν ὡς παρὰ τοῦ Παύλου ταῦτα λεγόμενα, οἱ δὲ καὶ ἐπιστολὰς πράττειν ὡς παρ' ἐκείνου γραφείσας. Hom. in 2 Thess i. 1, vol xi. p 469).

3] **Let no man deceive you in any manner** (not only in either of the foregoing, but in any whatever) **for (that day shall not come)** (so E. V. supplies, rightly. There does not seem to have been any intention on the part of the Apostle to fill up the ellipsis it supplies itself in the reader's mind. Knatchbull connects ὅτι with ἐξαπατήσῃ, and supplies ἐνέστηκεν after it but this is very harsh) **unless there have come the apostasy first** (of which he had told them when present, see ver 5 and probably with a further reference still to our Lord's prophecy in Matt xxiv. 10—12. There is no need, with Chrys., Thdrt, Thl, Aug, to suppose **ἀποστασία** to mean *Antichrist himself* [τί ἐστιν ἡ ἀποστασία; αὐτὸν καλεῖ τὸν ἀντίχριστον ἀποστασίαν, Chr], nor to regard him as its only cause rather is he the chief fruit and topstone of the apostasy), **and there have been revealed** (ref ch i. As Christ in his time, so Antichrist in his time, is *'revealed'*—brought out into light he too is a μυστήριον, to be unfolded and displayed· see vv 8, 9) **the man of sin** (in whom sin is as it were personified, as righteousness in Christ. The gen. is called by Ellicott that of the *predominating quality*), **the son of perdition** (see ref John, where our Lord uses the expression of Judas. It seems merely to refer to Antichrist himself, whose essence and inheritance is ἀπώλεια,—not to his influence over others, as Thdrt [both: ὡς κ αὐτὸν ἀπολλύμενον, κ ἑτέροις πρόξενον τούτου γενόμενον], Œc, Pelt, al), **he that withstands** (the construction is not to be carried on by zeugma, as if ἐπὶ πάντα κ τ λ belonged to ἀντικείμενος as well as to ὑπεραιρόμενος [the omission of the second article is no proof of this, as Pelt supposes, but only that both predicates belong to one and the same subject], but ἀντικείμενος is absolute, *'he that withstands* CHRIST,' the ἀντίχριστος, 1 John ii 18), **and exalts himself above** (in a hostile sense, reff) **every one that is called God** (cf λεγόμενοι θεοί, 1 Cor viii 5 "The expression includes the *true* God, as well as the false ones of the heathen—but λεγόμενον is a natural addition from Christian caution, as πάντα θεόν would have

θεὸν ἢ [i] σέβασμα, ὥςτε αὐτὸν [k] εἰς τὸν [l] ναὸν τοῦ θεοῦ ABDF
[m] καθίσαι [n] ἀποδεικνύντα ἑαυτὸν ὅτι ἐστὶν θεός. 5 οὐ KLℵ a b c d e f g
[o] μνημονεύετε ὅτι ἔτι [p] ὢν [pq] πρὸς ὑμᾶς ταῦτα ἔλεγον ὑμῖν; h k l m n o 17
6 καὶ νῦν τὸ [r] κατέχον οἴδατε, [s] εἰς τὸ [t] ἀποκαλυφθῆναι
αὐτὸν ἐν τῷ ἑαυτοῦ [u] καιρῷ. 7 τὸ γὰρ [v] μυστήριον ἤδη

i Acts xvii. 23 only†. Wisd. xiv. 20. xv. 17 only. Bel & Dr. 27 Theod. k constr., Matt. ii. 23. l 1 Cor. iii. 16, &c. 2 Cor. vi. 16 al. Jer. vii. 4. m intr., Matt. v. 1. Heb. i. 3 al. fr. Paul. 1 Cor. x. 7 only. 1 Chron. xxix. 23. n = Acts ii. 22. xxv. 7. 1 Cor. iv. 9 only†. 1 Macc. x. 34. Xen. Hell. iv. 4. 8. o w. ὅτι, Acts xx. 31. Eph. ii. 11 only. P. w. ὡς, 2 Macc. x. 6. p Matt. xiii. 56. Mark vi. 3. ix. 19. Luke ix. 41. q = 1 Cor. xvi. 6, 7. Gal. i. 18. iv. 18 al. r = Rom. i. 13. s ver. 2. t ver. 3. u = Matt. xxvi. 18. Luke i. 20. 1 Tim. vi. 15 al. v see 1 Tim. iii. 16. Jos. B. J. i. 24. 1. τοῦ Ἀντιπάτρου βίον οὐκ ἂν ἁμάρτοι τις εἰπὼν κακίας μυστήριον (but see note).

ins ℵ-corr[1] obl. rec ins ως θεον bef καθισαι, with D[3]FKL rel Syr syr-w-ast Chr Thdrt$_2$: om ABD[1]ℵ 17 vulg coptt æth arm Orig$_3$ Hippol Cyr-jer Chr-ms Thdrt$_{sag}$ Damasc Iren-int Tert Cypr Aug Ambrst Ruf. αποδεικνυοντα AF m Orig$_1$ Cyr-jer Cyr Thdrt$_3$ Damasc$_1$: txt BDKLℵ rel Orig$_2$ Hippol Thdrt$_1$.

5. for ων, εμου οντος D[1] Ambrst.

6. for εαυτ., αυτου AKℵ[1] o k m 17 Orig$_2$ Cyr-jer Damasc.

7. aft ηδη ins γαρ ℵ[1](ℵ[1] disapproving).

been a senseless and indeed blasphemous expression for a Christian." Lünem.) **or an object of adoration** (= *numen*, and is a generalization of θεόν. Cf. the close parallel in Dan. xi. 36, 37 [Theod. and similarly LXX]: κ. ὁ βασιλεὺς ὑψωθήσεται κ. μεγαλυνθήσεται ἐπὶ πάντα θεόν, κ.τ.λ.), **so that he sits** (not αὐτὸν . . . . . . καθίσαι, as Grot., Pelt, al., but καθίσαι, intransitive, as in reff.) in (*constr. prægnans*—'enters into and sits in.' The aor. usually denotes that one definite act and not a series of acts is spoken of: but here, from the peculiar nature of the verb, that one act is the *setting himself down*, and the *session* remains after it: cf. Matt. v. 1; xix. 28, &c.) **the temple of God** (this, say De W. and Lünemann after Irenæus, Hær. v. 30. 4, p. 330 [cited in Prolegg. § v. 3 note],—cannot be any other than *the temple at Jerusalem:* on account of the definiteness of the expression, **ὁ ναὸς τοῦ θεοῦ**, and on account of **καθίσαι.** But there is no force in this. ὁ ναὸς τοῦ θεοῦ is used metaphorically by St. Paul in 1 Cor. iii. 17 bis: and why not here? see also 1 Cor. vi. 16; Eph. ii. 21. From these passages it is plain that such figurative sense was familiar to the Apostle. And if so, καθίσαι makes no difficulty. Its figurative sense, as holding a place of power, sitting as judge or ruler, is more frequent still: see in St. Paul, 1 Cor. vi. 4: and Matt. xxiii. 2: Rev. xx. 4: to which indeed we might add the many places where our Lord is said καθίσαι on the right hand of God, e.g. Heb. i. 3; viii. 1; x. 12; xii. 2; Rev. iii. 21. Respecting the *interpretation*, see Prolegomena, § v.) **shewing himself** (πειρώμενον ἀποδεικνύναι, Chrys. Hardly that, but the sense of the *present*, as in ὁ πειράζων—it is his *habit* and *office* to exhibit himself as God) **that he is God** (not '*a* god,' nor is it equivalent to ὁ θεός—but designates the divine dignity which he predicates of himself. The construction is an attraction, for ἀποδ. ὅτι αὐτὸς . . .; and the emphasis is on **ἐστιν**, 'that he IS God'). **5.**] conveys a reproach—they would not have been so lightly moved, if they had remembered this. **6.**] **And now** (not *temporal*, but as νυνὶ δέ in 1 Cor. xiii. 13, 'rebus sic stantibus'—'now' in our argument. We must not for a moment think of the ungrammatical rendering of Whitby, Masker., Heydenr., Schrader, Olsh., B.-Crus., and Wieseler, '*that which at present hinders*,' which must be τὸ νῦν κατέχον: and for which ver. 7, Rom. xii. 3, 1 Cor. vii. 17, are no precedent whatever, not presenting any case of inversion of an adverb from its emphatic place between an article and a participle. νῦν is a mere adverb of passage, and the stress is on τὸ κατέχον) **ye know that which hinders** (viz. '*him*'—the man of sin: not, *the Apostle from speaking freely*, as Heinsius,—nor the *coming of Christ*) **in order that** (the aim of κατέχον [in God's purposes]—q. d. 'that which keeps him back, that he may not be revealed before his,' &c.) **he may be revealed** (see on ver. 3) **in his own time** (the time appointed him by God: reff.). **7.**] **For** (explanation of last verse) **the** MYSTERY (as opposed to the ἀποκάλυψις of the man of sin) ALREADY (as opposed to ἐν τῷ ἑαυτοῦ καιρῷ above) **is working** (not '*is being wrought*,' passive, as Est., Grot., all. I retain the inversion of the words, to mark better the primary and secondary emphasis: see below) **of lawlessness** (i. e. ungodliness—refusal to

[w] ἐνεργεῖται τῆς [x] ἀνομίας, [y] μόνον ὁ [r] κατέχων ἄρτι ἕως
[z] ἐκ μέσου γένηται, 8 καὶ τότε [t] ἀποκαλυφθήσεται ὁ
[a] ἄνομος, ὃν ὁ κύριος Ἰησοῦς * [b] ἀνελεῖ τῷ [c] πνεύματι
τοῦ [c] στόματος αὐτοῦ καὶ [d] καταργήσει τῇ [e] ἐπιφανείᾳ τῆς
[f] παρουσίας αὐτοῦ, 9 οὗ ἐστιν ἡ [f] παρουσία [g] κατ' [gh] ἐνέργειαν τοῦ σατανᾶ [i] ἐν πάσῃ [i] δυνάμει καὶ [j] σημείοις καὶ

w absol, Gal v. 6 (reff.) x Matt vii 23 xiii 41 Rom iv 7 al Exod. xxxiv 9 y so Gal ii 10 (also arrangt of words) z Col ii 14 reff a Luke xxii 37 al L P, exc 2 Pet ii 8 Ezek xxi 3 al fr b Paul, Acts xiii 28 xxii 20 xxvi 10 only Luke xxii 2 al Isa xi 4 αναλισκειν, Luke ix 54 Gal v 15 only Joel ii 3 c Ps xxxii 6 Isa i c d Gal iii 17 reff — 1 Cor xv 24 2 Tim i 10. Heb ii 14 e 1 Tim vi 14 2 Tim i 10 iv 1, 8 Tit ii 13 only P 2 Kings vii 23 f ver 1 g — Col i 29 Eph iii 7 iv 16 h Eph i 19 reff i Col i 29 reff j Matt. xxiv 24 ‖ Mk John iv 18 Acts vii 36 al[8] Rom xv 19 2 Cor xii. 12 Heb ii 4 only Exod xi 10

8. rec om ιησους, with BD[3]KL[1] rel Orig[1] Mac Cyr-jer Thdrt[1] Damasc[h.l.] Œc Vig. ins AD[1]FL[2]ℵ 17 latt syrr coptt arm Orig[1] Hippol Constt Ath Bas Cyr-jer-ms Ephr Chr Thdrt[sæpe] Damasc Thl Iren[1] Tert Jer Fulg Hil Ambr Aug Ruf Ambrst Primas Pelag. *rec ἀναλώσει, with D[3]KL rel Orig[1] Mac Cyr-jer Thdrt[1] Damasc[1] Œc Vig: αναλοι ℵ[1]: ανελοι D[1](appy) Fℵ[3] 17 67[2] (Orig[2]). ανελει AB Orig[1] Hippol Mac Cyr-jer Ath. την επιφανειαν D[1] f Cyr-jer-edd.

recognize God's law—see reff The genitive is one of apposition: the **ἀνομία** is that wherein the *μυστήριον* consists:—not a genitive of the working cause, as Thdrt [*ὡς κεκρυμμένην ἔχοντας τῆς ἀνομίας τὴν πάγην*],—nor must we understand by the words, Antichrist himself, as Olsh., comparing *τὸ τῆς εὐσεβείας μυστήριον*, 1 Tim iii 16,—nor *the unexampled depths of ungodliness*, as Krebs, al., from Joseph B. J in reff As to the order of the words, cf. Arrian, exp. Alex. i. 17. 6, *κ. εὑρέσθαι συγγνώμην τῷ πλήθει τῶν Θηβαίων τῆς ἀποστάσεως*, Lün) **only until he that now hinders** (*ὁ κατέχων* is placed before *ἕως* for emphasis, as in ref Gal, *μόνον τῶν πτωχῶν ἵνα μνημονεύωμεν*) **be removed** (the phrase is used of any person or thing which is taken out of the way, whether by death or other removal. So in reff. and Plut. Timol. p. 238 3 [Wetst.] *ἔγνω ζῆν καθ' ἑαυτὸν ἐκ μέσου γενόμενος*,—Ter. Phorm v. 9 40, 'ea mortem obiit, e medio abiit.' See also Herod viii 22. and for the opposite, *ἐν μέσῳ εἶναι*, Xen. Cyr. v. 2 26 Various erroneous arrangements and renderings of this sentence have been current of which the principal have arisen from fancying that the participle **κατέχων** requires some verb to be supplied after it. So Vulg ['tantum ut qui tenet nunc, teneat, donec de medio fiat.' so Syr, Erasm., Est, all], and E. V. ['only he who now letteth, will let,' so Beza, Whitby, al.],—*κατέχει* [so Bengel, Pelt, al] —*ἐστίν* [so Knatchb, Burton, al]). 8.] **and then** (when he that hinders shall have been removed, the emphasis is on **τότε**) **shall be revealed the lawless one** (the same as the *αὐτόν* of ver. 6 viz. the *ἄνθρωπος τῆς ἁμαρτίας*), whom (by this relative clause is introduced his ultimate fate at the coming of the Lord. To this the Apostle is carried on by the fervency of his spirit, and has to return again below to describe the working of Antichrist previously) **the Lord Jesus will destroy by the breath of His mouth** (from Isa. xi 4,—*πατάξει γῆν τῷ λόγῳ τοῦ στόματος αὐτοῦ, κ. ἐν πνεύματι διὰ χειλέων ἀνελεῖ ἀσεβῆ*. It is better to keep the expression in its simple majesty, than to interpret it, as Thdrt.,—*φθέγξεται μόνον, κ. πανωλεθρίᾳ παραδώσει τὸν ἀλιτήριον* — Thdr-mops, — *μόνον ἐπιβοήσας*. Chrys. on this is fine: *καθάπερ γὰρ πῦρ ἐπελθὸν ἁπλῶς τὰ μικρὰ ζωΰφια καὶ πρὸ τῆς παρουσίας αὐτῆς πόῤῥωθεν ὄντα ναρκᾶν ποιεῖ κ. ἀναλίσκει οὕτω καὶ ὁ χριστὸς τῷ ἐπιτάγματι μόνον* (but see above) *κ. τῇ παρουσίᾳ τὸν ἀντίχριστον ἀναλώσει. ἀρκεῖ παρεῖναι αὐτόν, καὶ ταῦτα πάντα ἀπόλωλε*) **and annihilate** (not, as Olsh, '*deprive of his influence*,' nor can Rev xix. 19 be brought to bear here) **by the appearance of His coming** (not 'the *brightness* of his coming,' as very many Commentators, and E. V, but as Beng 'apparitio adventus ipso adventu prior est, vel certe prima ipsius adventus emicatio, uti *ἐπιφάνεια τῆς ἡμέρας*' the mere outburst of His presence shall bring the adversary to nought Cf. the sublime expression of Milton,—'far off His coming shone') 9, 10] **whose** (refers back to the *ὅν* above—going back in time, to describe the character of his agency) **coming is** (the present is not used for the future, nor is the Apostle setting himself at the time prophesied of,—but it describes the essential attribute, as so often) **according to** (such as might be expected from,—

ʲ τέρασιν ᵏ ψεύδους 10 καὶ ἐν πάσῃ ˡ ἀπάτῃ ᵏ ἀδικίας τοῖς
ᵐ ἀπολλυμένοις, ᵒ ἀνθ' ᵒ ὧν τὴν ἀγάπην τῆς ἀληθείας οὐκ
ᵖ ἐδέξαντο ᑫ εἰς τὸ σωθῆναι αὐτούς. 11 καὶ διὰ τοῦτο
πέμπει αὐτοῖς ὁ θεὸς ʰ ἐνέργειαν ʳ πλάνης, ᑫ εἰς τὸ πιστεῦσαι αὐτοὺς ˢ τῷ ψεύδει, 12 ἵνα ᵗ κριθῶσιν ἅπαντες οἱ μὴ
πιστεύσαντες ᵘ τῇ ἀληθείᾳ, ἀλλ' ᵛ εὐδοκήσαντες [ἐν] τῇ
ἀδικίᾳ.
13 Ἡμεῖς δὲ ʷ ὀφείλομεν ʷ εὐχαριστεῖν τῷ θεῷ πάντοτε
περὶ ὑμῶν, ἀδελφοὶ ˣ ἠγαπημένοι ὑπὸ κυρίου, ὅτι ʸ εἵλατο

ABDF KLℵ a b c d e f g h k l m n o 17

k constr, see Luke xviii 8 9. Rom xi 6 xii 24 al Ps cxlii 8, 11 ψ, ver 11 l Eph iv 22 reff m = Matt xviii 14 Rom ii 12 1 Cor i 18. 2 Cor ii 15. iv 3 Lev xxiii 30 o Luke i 20 xii 3 xix 44 Acts xii 23 only Gen xxii 18 p = 1 Cor ii 14 James i 21 Jer v 3 q ver 2 r Matt xxvii 64 1 Thess ii 3 1 John iv 6 Prov xiv 8 s Rom i 25. t = Matt vii 1 John iii 17, 18 James v 9 al fr u = Rom ii 18 1 Cor xiii 6 Col ii 5 2 Tim iii 8. v w. ἐν, Matt iii 17 ‖ Mk L 1 Cor x 5 2 Cor xii 10 1 Chron xxix 3 dat without ἐν, 1 Macc i 43 w ch i 3 x 1 Thess i 4 Deut xxxiii 12 y = Phil i 22 Heb xi 25 only Deut xxvi 18 (see Deut vii 6, 7 x 15)

10 rec ins της bef αδικ, with DKLℵ³ rel Hippol Chr Thdrt om ABFℵ¹ 17 $Orig_6$ Cyr-jer (*prob the τη of απατη gave occasion for the insn*) rec ins εν bef τοις απολλυμενοις, with D¹KLℵ³ rel syrr $Orig_1$ om ABD¹Fℵ¹ 17 latt coptt æth $Orig_4$ Cyr-jer $Damasc_1$ Iren-int Tert Aug Ambrst. aft αληθειας ins χριστου D¹ εξεδεξαντο F. (εδεξ to σωθηναι, exc 1st ε and ηναι, rewritten by a recent hand in A.)

11. om και D¹ 67² vulg Syr copt æth Chr Cyr-ms Œc Pelag rec πεμψει (*see notes*), with D³KLℵ³ rel D-lat(and G-lat) vulg-ed(and F-lat) syr copt Hippol ($Orig_1$?) Thdor-mops Cyr_2 Iren-int Cypr txt ABD¹Fℵ¹ 67² am(with fuld) $Orig_2$ Bas Cyr-jer $Damasc_1$ Iren-int-mss. om αυτους F.

12 [απαντες, so AFℵ 17 $Orig_2$ Cyr] αλλα ℵ. om εν (*prob to balance the two members of the sentence*) BD¹Fℵ³ d h m 17 latt sah $Orig_2$ Hippol Cyr Cyr-jer $Iren\text{-}int_{aliq}$ Tert ins AD¹KLℵ¹ rel syrr copt $Orig_2$ Chr $Thdrt_1$ $Damasc_1$ Cypr Jer

13 for κυριου, θεου D¹ vulg lat-ff_5: ins του bef κυριου Aℵ απο κω F.

correspondent to) **the working of Satan** (Satan being the agent who works in the ἄνομος) **in** (manifested in, consisting in) **all** (kinds of) **power and signs and wonders of falsehood** (**πάσῃ** and **ψεύδους** both belong to all three substantives: the varieties of his manifested power, and signs and wonders, all have falsehood for their base, and essence, and aim Cf. ref John), **and in all** (manner of) **deceit** (not, as E V. '*deceivableness*,' for it is the *agency* of the man of sin—active deceit, of which the word is used) **of unrighteousness** (belonging to, consisting in, leading to, ἀδικία) **for** (the dativus incommodi) **those who are perishing** (on their way to perdition), (WHY? not by God's absolute decree, but) **because** (in requital for this, that) **they did not** (when it was offered to them) **receive the love of the truth** (the opposite of the ψεῦδος which characterizes all the working of the man of sin see as before, John viii 44) **in order to their being saved** 11] **And on this account** (because they did not receive, &c) **God is sending to them** (not, as E V, following rec, '*shall send*' the verb is *present*, because the mystery of iniquity is already working. πέμπει must not for a moment be understood of *permissiveness* only on God's part —He is the judicial sender and doer—it is He who hardens the heart which has chosen the evil way All such distinctions are the merest folly · whatever God *permits*, He *ordains*) **the working of error** (is causing these seducing influences to work among them The E V. has weakened, indeed almost stultified the sentence, by rendering ἐνέργ πλάνης '*a strong delusion*,' i e the passive state resulting, instead of the active cause), **in order that they should believe the falsehood** (which the mystery of sin is working among them It is better here to take τῷ definite, referring to what has gone before, than abstract),—**that** (the higher or ultimate purpose of God) **all might be judged** (i e here '*condemned*,' by the context) **who did not** (looking back over their time of probation) **believe the truth, but found pleasure in iniquity** I have above given the *rendering* of this important passage For the history and criticism of its interpretation, see the Prolegomena, § v

13—III 15] HORTATORY PORTION OF THE EPISTLE. 13—17] *Exhortation, grounded on thankfulness to God for their election by Him, to stand fast in the faith, and prayer that God would enable them to do so.* 13] **δέ** contrasts Paul, Silvanus,

ὑμᾶς ὁ θεὸς ᶻ ἀπ᾿ ἀρχῆς εἰς σωτηρίαν ᵃ ἐν ᵃᵇ ἁγιασμῷ
ᵃ πνεύματος καὶ πίστει ἀληθείας, 14 εἰς ὃ ᶜ ἐκάλεσεν ὑμᾶς
διὰ τοῦ ᵈ εὐαγγελίου ἡμῶν, εἰς ᵉ περιποίησιν ᶠ δόξης τοῦ
κυρίου ἡμῶν Ἰησοῦ χριστοῦ. 15 ᵍ ἄρα ᵍ οὖν, ἀδελφοί,
ʰ στήκετε, καὶ ⁱᵏ κρατεῖτε τὰς ˡ παραδόσεις ᵐ ἃς ἐδιδάχθητε
εἴτε ⁿ διὰ λόγου εἴτε ⁿ δι᾿ ἐπιστολῆς ἡμῶν. 16 ᵒ αὐτὸς δὲ

z = 1 John i 1, ii 13 iii 8. a 1 Pet i 2. b 1 Thess iv 3, 4, 7 reff. c = Rom viii 30. Gal i 6. d 2 Cor iv 3. 1 Thess i 5. see Rom ii 16. xv 25. 2 Tim ii 8. e = 1 Thess v 9 (Eph i 14 reff). f = John xvii 22. Rom v 2. g Rom v 18. vii 3, 25 al[8]. Paul only. h Gal v 1 reff. i Mark vii 3, 8. k = Col ii 19. Rev ii 13, 14, 15, 25 ‡. l = Gal i 14 reff. m constr, Mark x 38. Luke xii 47. Rev xvi 9. Winer, edn 6, § 32. 5. n ver 2. o = 1 Thess iii 11 reff.

[ειλατο, so ABDFLℵ (in ?) 17 Thdrt-ms.] ημας D¹ℵ¹ l am(with fuld hal F-lat). for απ αρχης, απαρχην BF vulg syr Cyr Damasc-comm Did Ambr Pelag: txt ADKLℵ rel gr-lat-ff.

14. aft εις ο ins και Fℵ m vulg syr arm Ambrst. for υμας, ημας ABD¹ Vig. for ημων, υμων ℵ¹: txt ℵ-corr¹ ³.

15. aft παραδοσεις ins ημων D¹ Ambrst.

and Timotheus, with those of whom he has been recently speaking. **ὀφείλομεν**] q. d. **find it our duty**: subjective: **are bound**, as E. V. **ἠγ. ὑπὸ κυρ.**] Lunemann remarks, that as τῷ θεῷ has preceded, and ὁ θεός follows, **κύριος** here must be the Lord Jesus: cf. Rom. viii 37. Gal. ii. 20. Eph. v. 2, 25. Otherwise, the expression is perhaps more normally used of the Father, ver. 16: Eph. ii. 4. Col. iii. 12. John iii. 16, al. freq. **ὅτι**] may enounce either (as Ellicott) the *matter and grounds* of the thanksgiving, *that* God . . ., or the *reason* of it, *because* God . . . St. Paul does not elsewhere use **αἱρέομαι** of divine election, but ἐκλέγομαι (1 Cor. i. 27, 28. Eph. i. 4) or προορίζω (Rom. viii. 29. Eph. i. 11). It is a LXX expression: see reff. **ἀπ᾿ ἀρχῆς** must be taken in the general sense, as in reff.: not in the special, 'from the beginning of the gospel,' as Phil. iv. 15. It answers to πρὸ τῶν αἰώνων 1 Cor. ii. 7, πρὸ καταβολῆς κόσμου Eph. i. 4, πρὸ χρόνων αἰωνίων 2 Tim. i. 9, all of which are spoken of the decrees of God. **εἰς σωτηρίαν**] in contrast to the ἀπώλεια lately spoken of. **ἐν ἁγ. πν. κ. π. ἀλ.**] the elements in which the εἵλατο εἰς σωτ. takes place: not, as De W., the aim (ἐν for εἰς) of the εἵλατο. **πνεύματος** is the Holy Spirit—**the sanctification of** (wrought by) **the Spirit**: not, 'sanctification of (your) spirit.' This is the divine side of the element: the human side follows, the πίστις ἀληθείας, 'your own reception, by faith, of the truth.' **14. εἰς ὅ**] **to which** (i. e. the being saved in sanctification of the Spirit and belief of the truth) **He** (God) **called you through our Gospel** (our preaching of the Gospel to you), **in order to** (your) **acquisition** (see on 1 Thess. v. 9) **of the glory of our Lord Jesus Christ** (i. e. your sharing in the glory which He *has*, see ref. John. Rom. viii. 17, 29: not the glory of which He is the bestower or source, as Pelt, al. Equally wrong is the interpretation of Œc., Thl., Corn.-a-Lap., al.—ἵνα δόξαν περιποιήσῃ τῷ υἱῷ αὐτοῦ of Luther, al., "zum herrlichen Eigenthum,"—'ut essetis gloriosa possessio domini nostri J. C.:' for, not to mention other objections, the whole context has for its purpose *the lot of the Thessalonians* as contrasted with that of those spoken of, vv. 10—12;—and the sense of περιποίησις is indicated by the parallel 1 Thess. v. 9). **15.**] **Therefore**—seeing that such is God's intent respecting you. Mr. Jowett here describes the Apostle as being "unconscious of the logical inconsistency" of appealing to them to do any thing, after he has just stated their election of God. Rather we should say, that he was deeply conscious, as ever, of the logical necessity of the only practical inference which man can draw from God's gracious purposes to him. No human reasoning powers can connect the two,—God's sovereignty and man's free-will: all we know of them is, that the one is as certain a truth as the other. In proportion then as we assert the one strongly, we must ever implicate the other as strongly: a course which the great Apostle never fails to pursue: cf. Phil. ii. 12, 13, al. freq. **στήκ.** is a contrast to σαλευθῆναι, ver. 2. On the sense of παραδόσεις, as relating to matters of *doctrine*, see Ellic.'s note, and the reff. given by him. **ἅς** is the accusative of second reference. **ἐπιστ. ἡμῶν**, as contrasted with the ἐπιστ. ὡς δι᾿ ἡμῶν of ver. 2, refers to 1 Thess. **16, 17.**] **αὐτός**, as a majestic introduction, in contrast with ἡμῶν, see 1 Thess. iii. 11, and

ὁ κύριος ἡμῶν Ἰησοῦς χριστὸς καὶ ὁ [p] θεὸς ὁ [p] πατὴρ
ἡμῶν, ὁ [q] ἀγαπήσας ἡμᾶς καὶ δοὺς [r] παράκλησιν αἰωνίαν
καὶ ἐλπίδα ἀγαθὴν [s] ἐν χάριτι, 17 [t] παρακαλέσαι ὑμῶν τὰς
καρδίας καὶ [u] στηρίξαι ἐν παντὶ [v] ἔργῳ καὶ λόγῳ [v] ἀγαθῷ.
III. 1 [w] Τὸ λοιπὸν [x] προσεύχεσθε, ἀδελφοί, [y] περὶ ἡμῶν,
[x] ἵνα ὁ [z] λόγος τοῦ [z] κυρίου [a] τρέχῃ καὶ [b] δοξάζηται καθὼς
καὶ [c] πρὸς ὑμᾶς, 2 καὶ ἵνα [d] ῥυσθῶμεν ἀπὸ τῶν [e] ἀτόπων

ABDF KLℵ a b c d e f g h k l m n o 17

p Gal i. 4 reff. q Eph ii. 4. 1 John iv. 10, 11 elsw. of Christ, see Rom viii. 37. Gal ii. 20. r = Luke ii. 25. Rom xv. 4, 5. 2 Cor i. 3 &c. (Heb vi. 18) al. L. P. H. Ps. xciii. 19. s = Gal i. 6. t = Col ii. 2 reff. u = Luke xxii. 32. Rom i. 11. xvi. 25 al. Ps. i. 12 (14). v Eph ii. 10 reff. w Eph vi. 10 reff. x 1 Cor xiv. 13. Phil i. 9. Col i. 9. iv. 3. ch. i. 11. y ch. i. 3 al. fr. z 1 Thess i. 8 reff. a = here only. (Gal ii. 2 reff.) see Ps. cxlvii. 15 (4). b Rom xi. 13. see ch. i. 12. Acts xiii. 48. c see 1 Thess iii. 4 reff. d 1 Thess i. 10 reff. e Luke xxiii. 41. Acts xxv. 5. xxviii. 6 only. Job iv. 8.

16. χρ ιησ. B: ιησ ο χρ. A. the 1st και is written above the line by ℵ[1](appy). om ο bef θεος BD[1]K 17. rec (for ο, bef πατηρ) και, with AD[3](and lat) KL rel vulg(with am &c) syr goth Chr Thdrt Ambr Ambrst: om ο ℵ[3]: txt BD[1]Fℵ[1] 17 Syr Ambrst Vig. om ο αγαπ ημας ℵ[1]: ins ℵ-corr[1]. αιωνιον F.

17. τας καρδιας bef υμων Aℵ vss. rec aft στηριξαι ins υμας, with D[3]KL rel copt Thdrt: om ABD[1]Fℵ m 17 latt syrr arm Chr Œc Ambrst gr-lat-ff. rec λογω και εργω, with FK rel, om και λογω 17: om εργω και d: txt ABDLℵ e m latt copt æth Chr Thl Thdrt Œc Ambrst Vig.

Chap. III. 1. om το F. αδελφοι bef προσευχεσθε F f o: π ημ bef αδελφ. D 73 goth. for κυριου, θεου F k 17.

as *ensuring* the efficacy of the wish—q. d. 'and then you are safe.' Our Lord Jesus Christ is placed first, not merely because He is the mediator between men and God (Lün.), but because the sentence is a climax. ὁ ἀγ. ἡμ. κ.τ.λ. probably refers to ὁ θεὸς κ. ὁ πατ. ἡμ. alone: and yet when we consider how impossible it would have been for the Apostle to have written *οἱ ἀγαπήσαντες*, and that the singular verb following undoubtedly refers to both, I would not too hastily pronounce this. See note on 1 Thess. iii. 11. **ἀγαπήσας—who loved us**—refers to a single fact—the love of the Father in sending His Son—or the love of the Father and Son in our accomplished Redemption. **κ. δούς—and gave**—by that act of Love. **παράκλ. αἰων.**] **consolation**, under all trials, and that **eternal**,—not transitory, as this world's consolations: sufficient in life, and in death, and for ever: cf. Rom viii. 38 f. This for all time present: and then **ἐλπ. ἀγ.** for the future. **ἐν χάριτι** belongs, not to **ἐλπ. ἀγ.**, but to **δούς**, and is the medium through, or element in which, the gift is made. Better thus than to refer it to both the participles **ἀγαπ. κ. δούς**, for **ὁ ἀγαπήσας** as applied to God (or the Lord Jesus) usually stands absolute, cf. Rom. viii. 37, Gal. ii. 20; Eph. v. 2. **παρακαλέσαι**] as in 1 Thess iii. 11, 3 pers. sing. opt. aor. **comfort**, with reference to your disquiet respecting the *παρουσία*. After *στηρ.* understand *ὑμᾶς*, which has been supplied—see var. readd.,—better than *τὰς καρδ. ὑμῶν*, which are not the agents in *ἔργον* and *λόγος*. This latter is not *'doctrine,'* as Chrys., Calv. ('tam in piæ et sanctæ vitæ cursu, quam in sana doctrina'),—for *ἔργον* (**work**) and *λόγος* (**word**), seeing that *παντί* applies to both, must be correlative, and both apply to matters in which the man is an agent. Still less must we understand *ἐν* as = *διά* (Chrys., Thl. 2, Beng., al.): the sphere, and not the instruments, of the consolation and confirmation, is spoken of.

Ch. III. 1—5.] *Exhortation to pray for him and his colleagues* (1, 2). *His confidence that the Lord will keep them* (3)—*and that they will obey his commands* (4). *Prayer for them* (5). 1.] On **τὸ λ.** (= *λοιπόν*), see 1 Thess iv. 1. **ἵνα**] On the use of telic conjunctions with verbs like *προσεύχομαι*, see note on 1 Cor xiv. 13. **ὁ λ. τ. κυρ.**] **the Lord's word** —i. e. the Gospel: see reff. **τρέχῃ**] Contrast to *'being bound.'* see 2 Tim. ii. 9—**may spread rapidly**. **δοξ.**] See reff. The word of the Lord is then glorified, when it becomes the power of God to salvation to the believer—see Rom. i. 16. **καθὼς καὶ πρὸς ὑμᾶς**] for they had thus received it: 1 Thess. i. 6. **πρὸς ὑμᾶς**] **among you** (reff.). 2.] And in order for that to be the case,—that we may be free to preach it. On **ἄτοπος**, Lünem. says, "it is properly used of that which is not in its right place. When of *persons*, it designates one who

καὶ πονηρῶν ἀνθρώπων. οὐ γὰρ [f]πάντων ἡ πίστις.
3 [g]πιστὸς δέ ἐστιν ὁ κύριος, ὃς [h]στηρίξει ὑμᾶς καὶ [i]φυ-
λάξει ἀπὸ τοῦ πονηροῦ. 4 [k]πεποίθαμεν δὲ ἐν κυρίῳ [k]ἐφ'
ὑμᾶς, ὅτι ἃ [l]παραγγέλλομεν καὶ ποιεῖτε καὶ ποιήσετε.
5 ὁ δὲ κύριος [m]κατευθύναι ὑμῶν τὰς καρδίας εἰς τὴν
[n]ἀγάπην τοῦ [n]θεοῦ καὶ εἰς τὴν [o]ὑπομονὴν [p]τοῦ χριστοῦ.

f gen, Acts i 7 see Matt xx 23 g = 1 Thess. v 24 reff h = ch ii 17 reff i w ἀπό, Luke xii 15 1 John v 21 only Ezek xxxiii 8. Sir xii 11 k = 2 Cor ii 3 (Matt xvii 43) see Gal v 10 l 1 Thess iv 11 reff m Luke i 79 1 Thess iii 11 only Prov xxi. 2 n Luke xi 42 John v 42 1 John ii 5, 15 iii 17 iv 12 v 3 o Rom ii 7 Rev i 9 iii 10 al fr. p gen, as 2 Cor i 5 Col i 24. Heb xi 26

3 om εστιν F, but insd bef η πιστις ver 2 in F vulg D-lat. for κυριος, θεος (*corrn, see* 1 *Cor* i 9, 10, 13 2 *Cor* i. 18) AD[1]F latt(not am demid) arm-marg Ambrst txt BD[3]KLℵ rel syr Cyr Jer.—ο κυριος bef εστιν ℵ[1]. aft ος ins και A 37 syr-w-ast Vocat · pref in στηρισει B τηρησει F.

4 rec aft παραγγελλομεν ins υμιν (*corrn, see ver* 6), with AD[3]FKL rel demid om BD[1]ℵ 17. 67[2] vulg(with am fuld) Chr_2-comm Ambrst Pelag Bede. aft παραγγ. ins και εποιησατε BF. om και bef ποιειτε AD[1]ℵ[1] for ποιησετε, ποιησατε D[1]: ποιησητε 17 · om και ποιησετε F

5 τας καρδιας bef υμων D vss. rec om 2nd την (with none of our mss). ins ABDFKLℵ rel.

does or says that which is inappropriate under the circumstances. Thus it answers to *ineptus* in Latin (Cic de Orat. ii. 4). From 'aptitude,' it passes to its wider ethical meaning, and is used of men who act contrary to divine or human laws Thus it gets the general signification of bad or ungodly. See examples in Kypke, Obss ii. p 145,—in Losner and Wetst." Who are these men? It is obvious that the key to the answer will be found in Acts xviii. They were the Jews at Corinth, who were at that time the especial adversaries of the Apostle and his preaching. And this is confirmed by the clause which he has added to account for their ἀτοπία and πονηρία **οὐ γὰρ πάντων ἡ πίστις—for to all men the** (Christian) **faith does not belong**—all men do not receive it—have no receptivity for it—obviously pointing at Jews by this description It is more natural to understand the article here as definite, the faith, than as abstract for faith, as such, would not bear much meaning here.

3.] Calvin says, "Ceterum de aliis magis quam de se anxium fuisse Paulum, ostendunt hæc ipsa verba In eum maligni homines improbitatis suæ aculeos dirigebant, in eum totus impetus irruebat curam interea suam ad Thessalonicenses convertit, nequid hæc illis tentatio noceat." **πιστός** seems to be chosen in allusion to πίστις which has just preceded; but the allusion cannot be more than that of sound, as the things spoken of are wholly different. **ὁ κύριος** is our Lord see ch. ii. 16, and ver 5 **δέ**, in contrast with the men just mentioned **στηρίξει**] in reference to his wish, ch ii. 17. **τοῦ πονηροῦ** may mean 'the evil one,' as in Matt. xiii 19: Eph. vi. 16, al.: and so Ellic. But here the assurance seems, as before said, to correspond to the wish ch ii 17. and thus στηρίξαι ἐν παντὶ ἔργῳ κ. λόγῳ ἀγαθῷ = στηρίξει κ. φυλάξει ἀπὸ τοῦ πονηροῦ. in which case τ. πον. is *neuter*. We may observe that the words are nearly a citation from the Lord's prayer.

4.] forms a transition to the exhortations which are to follow, vv 6 ff. **ἐν κυρίῳ**, as the element in which his confidence is exercised, shews it to be one assuming that they will act consistently with their Christian profession and so gives the expectation the force of an exhortation, but at the same time of a hopeful exhortation **ἐφ' ὑμᾶς** (reff), **with reference to you**—the *direction* of his confidence. **καὶ ποιεῖτε κ. ποιήσετε** is all the apodosis—not **ὅτι ἃ παραγγ. κ ποιεῖτε, καὶ ποιήσετε**, as Erasm.

5.] There does not appear to be any distrust of the Thessalonians implied by this repeated wish for them, as De W supposes Rather is it an *enlargement*, taken up by the δέ (not only so, but) *of the* ἃ παραγγέλλομεν κ ποιεῖτε κ ποιήσετε. **ὁ κύρ.** is our Lord, as before. **ἡ ἀγάπη τ θεοῦ** here, from the fact of his wishing that their hearts may be *directed into it*, must be subjective, *the love of man to God* The objective meaning, *God's love*, is out of the question. The other subjective meanings, *the love which God works* (Pelt), ... *which God commands* (Le Clerc), are far-fetched. ἡ ὑπομονὴ τ. χριστοῦ has very generally been understood as in E. V., '*the patient waiting for*

6 [1] Παραγγέλλομεν δὲ ὑμῖν, ἀδελφοί, [q] ἐν ὀνόματι τοῦ ABDF
κυρίου Ἰησοῦ χριστοῦ, [r] στέλλεσθαι ὑμᾶς ἀπὸ παντὸς KLℵ a b c d e f g h k l m n o 17
ἀδελφοῦ [s] ἀτάκτως [t] περιπατοῦντος καὶ μὴ κατὰ τὴν
[u] παράδοσιν ἣν [v] παρελάβοσαν παρ' ἡμῶν. 7 αὐτοὶ γὰρ
οἴδατε πῶς δεῖ [w] μιμεῖσθαι ἡμᾶς, ὅτι οὐκ [x] ἠτακτήσαμεν ἐν
ὑμῖν, 8 οὐδὲ [y] δωρεὰν [z] ἄρτον [z] ἐφάγομεν [a] παρά τινος,
ἀλλ' ἐν [b] κόπῳ καὶ [b] μόχθῳ [c] νύκτα καὶ [c] ἡμέραν [d] ἐργαζόμενοι, [d] πρὸς τὸ μὴ [d] ἐπιβαρῆσαί τινα ὑμῶν· 9 [e] οὐχ

q Acts iii 6. 1 Cor v 4. vi 11. r 2 Cor viii 20 only. Mal ii 5 (ὑποστ., Gal ii 12. Heb x 38). s ver 11 only †. (ος 1 Thess v 14.) t w. adv., 1 Thess ii 12 al fr. u ch ii 15 reff. v 1 Cor xi 23. xv 1, 3. Gal i 9, 12 al. w (ver 9.) Heb xiii 7. 3 John 11 only †. Wisd iv 2 vat. xv 9 only. x here only †. Xen Cyr vii 2. 6. see above (s). y = Matt x 8. Rom iii 24 al. Isa lii 3. z = ver 12. Mark iii 20. Luke vii 33. xiv 1, 15 al. Gen iii 19. a = Acts xxvi 12 al fr. b 1 Thess ii 9 reff. c Acts xx 31. xxvi 7. Paul only, exc Mark iv 27. Esth iv 16. elsw. gen., as Mark v 5. so Paul, ch ii 9. d absol., 1 Thess ii 9 reff. e = John vi 46. 2 Cor i 24. iii 5. Phil iii 12. iv 11, 17 only.

6. rec aft *κυριου* ins *ημων*, with AD[3]FKLℵ rel om BD[1] Cypr[1](elsw$_1$ om *κυρ*.) rec *παρελαβε* (*corrn of plur. The less usual form in txt is the preferable one*), with (none of our mss) Syr *παρελαβετε* BF syr goth Anton Thdrt$_1$ Ambrst Sing-cler *παρελαβον* D[3]KLℵ[3] rel gr-ff (most vss and lat-ff have the plur, but which form, is of course uncert). txt Aℵ[1] 17 Bas, *ελαβοσαν* D[1]. for *παρ'*, *αφ'* B.

8 *ουτε* F. *αλλα* ℵ *νυκτος κ. ημερας* BFℵ 17 Chr-ms Damasc$_1$ txt ADKL rel.

Christ.' So Œc, Ambr, Erasm, Corn-a-lap, Beza, all. But **ὑπομονή** will not bear this meaning. It occurs thirty-four times in the N. T., and always in the sense of **endurance,—patience**. Nor again can the expression mean '*endurance for Christ's sake*,' which the simple genitive will not convey: but it must be, as Chrys (1) *ἵνα ὑπομένωμεν, ὡς ἐκεῖνος ὑπέμεινεν*, *the patience* **of Christ** (gen. possess.),—**which Christ shewed**. 6—15.] *Dehortation from disorderly, idle habits of life.* He had given a hint in this direction before, in the first Epistle (v. 11, 15): he now speaks more plainly, doubtless because their restlessness and excitement concerning the *παρουσία* had been accompanied by an increase of such habits. His dissuading them from associating with such persons, seems to shew that the core of the Church (as Lün.) was as yet sound in this respect. 6.] **παραγγέλλομεν δέ** takes up the assurance of ver. 4, and tests its general form by a special command. **ἐν ὀνόμ. κ.τ.λ.** strengthens the *παραγγ.*, and does not belong to the following. **στέλλεσθαι**] lit. 'to take in, or shorten sail:' *ἱστία μὲν στείλαντο, θέσαν δ' ἐν νηῒ μελαίνῃ*, Il. α. 433: hence, to draw in or shorten, generally: *πότερά σοι παῤῥησίᾳ | φράσω τὰ κεῖθεν, ἢ λόγον στειλώμεθα*, Eur. Bacch. 625,—to conceal: *ἐβουλεύετο μὲν στέλλεσθαι, οὐ μὴν ἠδύνατό γε κρύπτειν τὸ γεγονός*, Polyb. Frag. hist. 39 (from Suidas, voc. *στείλασθαι*),—*οὐ δυναμένων τὴν ἐκ τῆς συνηθείας καταξίωσιν στέλλεσθαι* ('cohibere consuetam reverentiam'), ib. viii. 22. 4. So here, 'cohibere vos'—**to keep yourselves from**: see reff.: obviously without allusion as yet to any formal excommunication, but implying merely avoidance in intercourse and fellowship. The accusative is repeated before the infinitive, probably because the clause *ἐν ὀνόμ.*, &c., intervenes. The **παράδοσις** refers to the oral instruction which the Apostle had given them when he was present, and subsequently confirmed by writing (1 Thess. iv. 11, 12). **παρελάβοσαν**] plural, as belonging to the *πάντες* implied in *παντός*, so in *ἔβαν οἰκόνδε ἕκαστος*. On the form **-οσαν**, which is said to have been originally Macedonian, and thence is found in the Alexandrian (*ἐσχάζοσαν*, Lycophr. 21), Lobeck remarks (Phryn. p. 349), "ex modorum et temporum metaplasmis, quos conjunctim tractare solent dialectorum scriptores, nullus diutius viguit eo quo tertiæ aoristi secundi personæ plurales ad similitudinem verborum in *μι* traducuntur,—*εἴδοσαν* Niceph., *ἐφεύροσαν* Anna Comnena, *μετήλθοσαν* Nicet. (and *παρήλθοσαν*)." We have *ἤλθοσαν ἔθνη*, Ps. lxxviii. 1, see other examples from LXX in Winer, edn. 6, § 13. 2. f. 7.] **πῶς δεῖ μιμ. ἡμ.** is a concise way of expressing 'how ye ought to walk in imitation of us.' **ἀτακτέω** also occurs in Lysias *κατὰ* '**Αλκιβ. α.** p. 141. 18, in this sense, of 'leading a disorderly life.' 8.] **ἄρτον ἐφάγομεν**, a Hebraistic expression for 'got our sustenance.' **παρά τινος**, 'at any one's expense,' **from any one** as a gift: there seems to be an allusion in the construction to the original sense of *δωρεάν*. **ἐργαζόμ.** belongs to *ἄρτον ἐφ.* as a contrast to *δωρεάν*: **but by working, &c.**

e ὅτι οὐκ f ἔχομεν f ἐξουσίαν, ἀλλ' ἵνα g ἑαυτοὺς h τύπον
δῶμεν ὑμῖν i εἰς τὸ w μιμεῖσθαι ἡμᾶς. 10 καὶ γὰρ ὅτε
h ἦμεν k πρὸς ὑμᾶς, τοῦτο l παρηγγέλλομεν ὑμῖν, ὅτι εἴ
τις οὐ θέλει d ἐργάζεσθαι, μηδὲ ἐσθιέτω. 11 m ἀκούομεν
γάρ τινας n περιπατοῦντες o ἐν ὑμῖν p ἀτάκτως, μηδὲν
q ἐργαζομένους, ἀλλὰ r περιεργαζομένους· 12 s τοῖς δὲ
s τοιούτοις l παραγγέλλομεν καὶ t παρακαλοῦμεν t ἐν κυρίῳ
Ἰησοῦ χριστῷ, ἵνα u μετὰ v ἡσυχίας d ἐργαζόμενοι τὸν
ἑαυτῶν w ἄρτον w ἐσθίωσιν. 13 ὑμεῖς δέ, ἀδελφοί, μὴ x ἐγ-
κακήσητε y καλοποιοῦντες. 14 εἰ δέ τις οὐχ ὑπακούει τῷ
λόγῳ ἡμῶν z διὰ a τῆς ἐπιστολῆς, τοῦτον b σημειοῦσθε

f Matt vii 29 John xix 10, 11 1 Cor ix 6 Sir ix 13 g 1st person, Rom viii 23 1 Cor xi. 31 1 Thess ii 8 al h = Phil iii 17 reff i Phil i 23 reff k 1 Thess iii 4 reff l ver 4 m = Matt xi 2 Acts xxiii 16. Eph i 15 al. n ver 6 o = John xi 54 Eph ii 3 p ver 6 (reff) only+ q Matt vii 23 Gal vi 10 Ps xiv 2 r here only+ Sir iii 23 only Polyb xviii 34 2 see 1 Tim v 13 reff s Rom xvi 18 2 Cor xi 13 al t 1 Thess iv 1 u Mark iii 5 al 1 Chron xxix 22 v Acts xxii 2 1 Tim ii 11, 12 only Sir xxviii 16 (-ιος, 1 Tim ii 2) w ver 8. x Eph iii 13 reff y here only Levit v 4 Ald (καλῶς π F vat) only see Mark iii 4 al z = 1 Cor xvi 3 2 Cor x 9, 11 ch ii 2, 15 (see note) a = Rom xvi 22 Col iv 16 1 Thess v 27 see 1 Cor. v 9 b here only Ps iv 6 only ἐσημειώσαντο τον τοπον, Polyb xxii 11 12

10. om τουτο א[1]. for ου, μη D[1]

11 εν υμιν bef περιπατουντας D syr copt. om ατακτως 67[3]

12 rec δια του κυρ ημ ιησου χρ, with D[3]KLא[3] syrr Chr Thdrt Damasc[1] Thl Œc txt AB(D[1])Fא[1] 17 latt copt goth Damasc[1] lat-ff (*said by De Wette to be a corrn from 1 Thess iv. 1. but is not rec rather a corrn to the more usual form?*).

13. rec εκκακ txt ABא m, ενκακειτε D[1] καλον ποιουντες F: το καλον ποι. h 73. 113-marg 114-21-2[2] 219[2] Chr$_{aliq}$

14 υμων B b[1] m æth Chr-in-Thl$_{expr}$ Thl δι' επιστολης F. rec (aft σημ.) ins και, with D[1]FKL rel vulg syrr Bas Ambrst Aug$_{sæpe}$· om A(appy) BD[3]א 17 copt

The sentence may also be taken as De W. and Ellic, regarding **ἐν κόπῳ κ. μόχ** as the contrast to **δωρεάν**, and **ἐργαζ νύκτ. κ ἡμ** as a parallel clause to **ἐν κόπ. κ. μόχ.** 9] See 1 Cor. ix. 4 ff., where he treats of his abstinence from this his apostolic power **οὐχ ὅτι, my meaning is not, that . . . .** See reff. and Hartung, Part ii 153. **ἑαυτούς** is used in the plural for *ἡμᾶς αὐτούς* and *ὑμᾶς αὐτούς* for shortness, but never in the singular for *ἐμαυτόν* or *σεαυτόν*, where no such reason exists: see Bernhardy, Syntax, p 272 **10.] καὶ γάρ,—and** we carried this further: we not only set you an example, but inculcated the duty of diligence by special precept. The **γάρ** is co-ordinate with that in ver. 7. The *καί* does not bring out *ὅτε ἦμεν πρ ὑμᾶς* as a new feature, as Thdrt, for of this period the last three verses have treated—but it brings out **τοῦτο**, on which the stress lies, as an additional element in the reminiscence. This seems to me clearly to be the force here, and not the merely conjunctive, as Ellic maintains **τοῦτο**, viz. what follows. **εἴ τις κ τ λ.]** Schottgen and Wetst quote this saying from several places in the rabbinical books. **11.]** *Ground for reminding them of this his saying.* **περιεργαζομένους] being busybodies**; or, **being active about trifles**, 'busy only with what is not their own business' (Jowett who refers to Quintilian's 'non agere sed satagere'): see reff. So in the charge against Socrates, Plat Apol § 3, **Σωκράτης** *ἀδικεῖ κ.* **περιεργάζεται** *ζητῶν τά τε ὑπὸ γῆς κ τὰ ἐπουράνια, κ τὸν ἥττω λόγον κρείττω ποιῶν, κ ἄλλους ταὐτὰ ταῦτα διδάσκων.* **12] παρακαλοῦμεν**, scil *αὐτούς*. **ἐν κυρ** see on ver 6. **μετὰ ἡσυχ.** may be taken either subjectively, —**with a quiet mind**,—or objectively, **with quietness**, i e. in outward peace. The former is most probable, as addressed to the offenders themselves **ἑαυτῶν**, emphatic—that which they themselves have earned. **13] δέ**—ye who are free from this fault. On *ἐγκ* and *ἐκκ* see notes on 2 Cor iv 1 and Gal vi 9 **καλοποιοῦντες**, from the context, cannot mean '*doing good*' (*to others*), but doing well, living diligently and uprightly: see also Gal. vi. 9, where the same general sentiment occurs. Chrys's meaning is surely far-fetched *στέλλεσθε μέν, φησιν, ἀπ' αὐτῶν κ. ἐπιτιμᾶτε αὐτοῖς, μὴ μὴν περιΐδητε λιμῷ διαφθαρέντας.* **14]** Many Commentators (Luth., Calv, Grot,

μὴ ᶜ συναναμίγνυσθαι αὐτῷ, ἵνα ᵈ ἐντραπῇ· 15 καὶ μὴ ὡς
ἐχθρὸν ᵉ ἡγεῖσθε, ἀλλὰ ᶠ νουθετεῖτε ὡς ἀδελφόν. 16 ᵍ αὐτὸς
δὲ ὁ ʰ κύριος τῆς ʰ εἰρήνης δῴη ὑμῖν τὴν εἰρήνην ⁱ διὰ
παντὸς ἐν ᵏ παντὶ ᵏ τρόπῳ. ὁ ˡ κύριος ˡ μετὰ πάντων
ὑμῶν.
17 Ὁ ᵐ ἀσπασμὸς ⁿ τῇ ἐμῇ ⁿ χειρὶ Παύλου, ὅ ἐστιν

ABDF KLℵ a b c d e f g h k l m n o 17

c 1 Cor v. 9 only. Hos vii. 8 F (συμμιγν., vat.) only. d = 1 Cor iv. 14. Tit ii. 8 only. Ps xxxiv. 26 al. (Matt xxi. 37 ‖ Mk al.) e Acts xxvi. 2. 2 Cor ix. 5. Phil ii. 3 al. Job xix. 11. f Col i. 28 reff. P. g = 1 Thess iii. 11 reff. (see note.) h Phil iv. 9 reff. i Matt xviii. 10. Acts ii. 25. x. 2. Rom xi. 10 (from Ps lxviii. 24) al. k Phil i. 18 reff. l here only. Ruth ii. 4. m = 1 Cor xvi. 21. Col iv. 18 only. (Matt xxiii. 7 ‖ al. †) n 1 Cor. Col. as above. Gal vi. 11. Philem 19.

goth Chr Tert. [συναναμιγνυσθαι, so AB(D¹F)ℵ D-lat copt goth Tert.]
15. om και D¹ Tert.
16. for κυρ., θεος F d f g vulg-sixt Thl Ambrst Pelag. om την A 67². for τροπω, τοπω (*more usual expression, see* 1 *Cor* i. 2 &c) A¹D¹F 17 latt goth Chr-montf Ambrst Pelag: txt A²BD³KLℵ rel syr copt Thdrt Damasc.

Calov., Le Clerc, Beng., Pelt, Winer, al.) have joined **διὰ τῆς ἐπιστολῆς** with what follows, and explained it (usually, see below),—'*note that man by an Epistle* (*to me*).' But **τῆς** is decidedly against this rendering,—unless we suppose that it signifies 'your' answer to this. [Bengel and Pelt, taking τῆς ἐπ. for this Epistle, would render, 'notate nota censoria, hanc Epist., ejus admonendi causa, adhibentes eique inculcantes' (Beng.),—'Eum hac epistola fretì severius tractate' (Pelt): but both these require σημειοῦσθε to be diverted from its simple meaning.] The great objection to the above connexion is that St. Paul has already pointed out the manner of treating such an one, ver. 6, and is not likely to enjoin a further reference to himself on the subject. It is far better therefore, with Chrys. (there seems no reason for qualifying this by *apparently*, as Ellic.), Est., Corn.-a-Lap., Beza, Hamm., Whitby, Schott, Olsh., De W., Baum.-Crus., Lün., Ellic., all., to join διὰ τῆς ἐπ. with the preceding τῷ λόγ. ἡμ., and render it **our word by this Epistle**, as ἡ ἐπιστολή is undoubtedly used in reff., and the *word* is that in ver. 12. **σημειοῦσθε**] **mark**, see ref. Polyb.: the ordinary meaning of the word: put a σημεῖον on him, by noticing him for the sake of avoidance. On what is called the dynamic middle, see Krüger, Sprachlehre, § 52. 8. 4. **15.**] **καί** is more delicate than ἀλλά or δέ would be: q. d. 'and I know that it will follow as a consequence of your being Christians, that ye will, &c.' **ὡς** in the first clause seems superfluous: it is perhaps inserted to correspond with the other clause, or still further to soften the ἐχθρὸν ἡγεῖσθε. So ὥσπερ, Job xix. 11, xxxiii. 10. **16.**] *Concluding wish.* On **αὐτὸς δέ**, see on ch. ii. 16. **ὁ κύριος τῆς εἰρήνης**] As the Apostle constantly uses ὁ θεὸς τῆς εἰρ. for the God of Peace (see Rom xv. 33, xvi. 20. 2 Cor. xiii. 11, al.), we here must understand our Lord Jesus Christ. **ἡ εἰρήνη** must not be understood only of *peace with one another*: for there has been no special mention of mutual disagreement in this Epistle: but of *peace in general,* outward and inward, here and hereafter, as in Rom xiv. 17. See Fritz. on Romans, vol. i. p. 22. The stress is on ὑμῖν—**May the Lord of Peace give** *you* **(that) Peace always in every way** (whether it be outward or inward, for time or for eternity). **μετὰ πάντων ὑ.**] therefore with the ἀτάκτως περιπατοῦντες also (Lün.): not as Jowett, pleonastic. The man who was to be admonished as an **ἀδελφός**, would hardly be excluded from the Apostle's parting blessing. **17, 18.**] Conclusion. **17.**] *Autographic salutation.* The Epistle, as it follows from this, was not written with the Apostle's own hand, but dictated. So with other Epistles, see Rom xvi. 22. 1 Cor. xvi. 21. Col. iv. 18. **ὅ**] **which circumstance**: not attraction for ὅς. The whole of vv. 17, 18, not merely the benediction, are included. By the words **οὕτως γράφω**, we must not conceive that any thing was *added*, such as his signature,—or as Œc., οἷον τὸ ἀσπάζομαι ὑμᾶς, ἢ τὸ ἔῤῥωσθε, ἤ τι τοιοῦτον: they are said of that which he is writing at the time. His reason for this caution evidently was, the **ἐπιστολὴ ὡς δι' ἡμῶν**, spoken of ch. ii. 2. And the words **ἐν πάσῃ ἐπιστολῇ** must not, with Lün., be limited to any future Epistles which he might send to the Thessalonians, but understood of a caution which he intended to practise in future with all his Epistles: or at least with such as required, from circumstances, this identification. Thus we have (1 Thess. being manifestly an exception, as written before the rule was established) Gal written with his own hand (see note on Gal

° σημεῖον ἐν πάσῃ ἐπιστολῇ. οὕτως γράφω. 18 ἡ ᵖ χάρις
τοῦ κυρίου ἡμῶν Ἰησοῦ χριστοῦ μετὰ πάντων ὑμῶν.

o = Luke ii 12. 2 Cor xii 12. 4 Kings xix 29.
p see Col iv 18 reff.

ΠΡΟΣ ΘΕΣΣΑΛΟΝΙΚΕΙΣ Β.

18. om ημων F om τ. κυρ. ημ Syr rec at end ins αμην, with ADFKLℵ³ rel om Bℵ¹ 17 67² fuld(with harl tol) Ambrst.

Subscription rec adds απο αθηνων, with AB²KL rel: απο ρωμης f g h: απο ρω η απο αθ. b no subscr in l o προς θεσσ β' επληρωθη αρχεται προς τειμοθεον α' D ετελεσθη προς θ. β' αρχεται προς τιμ α' F txt B¹(ℵ) 17 goth æth.—(om β' ℵ, but adds στιχων ρπ) [After this in ABKℵ 5 9 16. 137. 189. 196 the Ep to Heb follows: so also, apparently, in C, see Tischdf. Cod. Eph. proleg. p. 15.]

vi. 11), 1 Cor authenticated (xvi 21); 2 Cor sent by Titus and therefore perhaps not needing it (but it may have existed in xiii 12, 13 without being specified), Rom not requiring it as not insisting on his personal authority (but here again the concluding doxology may have been autographic) Col authenticated (iv 18): Eph apparently without it (but possibly vi 24 may have been autographic): Phil from its character and its bearer Epaphroditus not requiring it (but here again iv 23 may be autographic) and the Epistles to individuals would not require such authentication, not to mention that they are probably all autographic—that to Philemon certainly is, see ver 19 there. (So for the most part De Wette.)

ΠΡΟΣ ΤΙΜΟΘΕΟΝ Α.

a Rom xvi 26 1 Cor vii 6 (25) 2 Cor. viii 8. Tit i 3 (ii 15) only † Esdr i 18 (16)
b Luke i 47 epp., ch ii 3 Tit. i 3 ii 10 iii 4 Jude 25 only Ps lxiv 5 see ch iv 10
c = Col i 27
d 2 Cor viii 8 Phil iv 3 Tit i 4 only † Sir vii 18 only (-ως, Phil ii 20)
e = 1 Cor iv 14, 17 2 Cor vi 13 Phil ii 22 ver 18 2 Tim i 2 ii 1 Tit i 4 Philem 10 3 John 4
f Gal ii 20 ver 4 ch (ii 7, 15) iii 13 (iv 12) 2 Tim i 13 Tit iii 15 James ii 5 elsw., ἐν τῇ π

I. 1 Παῦλος ἀπόστολος χριστοῦ Ἰησοῦ, a κατ' a ἐπι- ADFK LℵAab
ταγὴν b θεοῦ b σωτῆρος ἡμῶν, καὶ χριστοῦ Ἰησοῦ τῆς cdefg hklm
c ἐλπίδος ἡμῶν, 2 Τιμοθέῳ d γνησίῳ e τέκνῳ f ἐν f πίστει· no17

TITLE elz παυλου του αποστ η πρ τιμ επιστολη πρωτη Steph η πρ τιμ. επ πρω: πρ τιμ. πρωτης επιστολης(sic) παυλου L. txt Aℵ h m n o 17, and (prefg αρχεται) DF.

CHAP. I. 1. rec ιησ bef χριστου, with AKL rel txt DFℵ 17 syr copt goth Damasc Ambrst. for επιταγην, επαγγελιαν ℵ ins του bef σωτηρος D[1] 13 —του σωτ ημ. θῦ in 80. 116. 213 rec και κυριου ιησ χρ, with D[3]KLℵ rel Thdrt Damasc: txt AD[1]F 17 latt syrr sah Chr-comm Ambrst Ambr Cass (Cursives vary in the similar phrase in ver 2)

CHAP I. 1, 2] ADDRESS AND GREETING. 1. κατ' ἐπιτ] See reff, especially Tit. a usual expression of St. Paul, and remarkably enough occurring in the doxology at the end of the Epistle to the Romans, which there is every reason to think was written long after the Epistle itself. It is a more direct predication of divine command than διὰ θελήματος θεοῦ in the earlier Epistles θεοῦ σωτῆρος ἡμ] Apparently an expression belonging to the later apostolic period,—one characteristic of which seems to have been the gradual dropping of the article from certain well-known theological terms, and treating them almost as proper names (see, however, Ellicott's note). Thus in Luke i. 17 it is ἐπὶ τῷ θεῷ τῷ σωτῆρί μου and indeed in almost every place in the pastoral Epistles except this, σωτήρ has the article. In ref Jude, the expression is the same as here καὶ χρ Ἰησ] See a similar repetition after δοῦλος χρ. Ἰησοῦ in Rom. i 4 & 6 The Apostle loves them in his more solemn and formal passages—and the whole style of these Epistles partakes more of this character, as was natural in the decline of life. τῆς ἐλπίδος ἡμῶν] It is not easy to point out the exact reference of this word here, any further than we may say that it gives utterance to the fulness of an old man's heart in the near prospect of that on which it naturally was ever dwelling It is the ripening and familiarization of χριστὸς ἐν ὑμῖν ἡ ἐλπὶς τῆς δόξης of ref Col See also Tit. i. 2. I am persuaded that in many such expressions in these Epistles, we are to seek rather a psychological than a pragmatical explanation Theodoret notices the similar occurrence of words in Ps. lxiv. (lxv) 6, ἐπάκουσον ἡμῶν ὁ θεὸς ὁ σωτὴρ ἡμῶν, ἡ ἐλπὶς πάντων τῶν περάτων τῆς γῆς—which is interesting, as it might have suggested the expression here, familiar as the Apostle was with O. T. diction Ellic. refers, for the same expression, to Ignat. Trall § 2, p 676
γνησίῳ τ] Cf. Acts xvi. 1: 1 Cor iv 14–17, and Prolegg. to this Epistle, § i 1 ff γνησίῳ, true, genuine—cf. Plat. Politic p. 293, οὐ γνησίας οὐδ' ὄντως οὔσας

[g] χάρις, [g] ἔλεος, [g] εἰρήνη ἀπὸ θεοῦ πατρὸς καὶ χριστοῦ
Ἰησοῦ τοῦ κυρίου ἡμῶν. 3 [h] Καθὼς [i] παρεκάλεσά σε
[k] προσμεῖναι ἐν Ἐφέσῳ, πορευόμενος εἰς Μακεδονίαν, ἵνα
[l] παραγγείλῃς [m] τισὶν μὴ [n] ἑτεροδιδασκαλεῖν, 4 μηδὲ [o] [p] προσ-

g 2 Tim i 2 (Tit i 4 rec) 2 John 3 only see Jude 2
h anacol., Gal ii 4, 5 ib 6 Rom v 12 al Winer, edn 6 § 63 i 1
i = (under like circumst) 2 Cor viii 6 ix 5 xii 18
k = Acts xviii 18 (of Paul) only (Matt xv 32 ‖ Mk Acts xi 23 xiii 43 ch v 5 only Judg iii 25 Wisd iii 9 only)
l Luke ix 21 Acts i 4 iv 18 xv 5 Paul, 1 Cor vii 10 & passim 1 Kings xviii 8
m = 1 Cor iv 18 2 Cor iii 1 x 2 Gal i 7 ii 12 iv 6, 19 ch iv 1 v 15 vi 10, 21 2 Tim ii 18
n ch vi 3 only † Ignat ad Polyc c 3, p 721
o = & constr., Paul, ch iii 8 iv 1, 13 Tit i 14 only Acts viii 6, 10, 11 xvi 14 Heb ii 1 2 Pet i 19
p Tit i 14

2 rec aft *πατρος* ins *ημων*, with D[3]KLℵ[3] rel syr sah om AD[1]Fℵ[1] 17 latt copt goth Orig-int Ambrst-ed Pelag

. . . . ἀλλὰ μεμιμημένας ταύτην.
ἐν πίστει] When Conyb. says, "'*in faith*,' not '*in the faith*,' which would require τῇ" (so Ellic., without the protest),—he forgets (1) the constant usage by which the article is omitted after prepositions in cases where it is beyond doubt in the mind of the writer and must be expressed in translation (2) the almost uniform anarthrousness of these Epistles. He himself translates the parallel expression in Tit. i. 4, '*mine own son according to our common faith*,' which is in fact supplying the article Render therefore **in the faith**: joining it with *γνησίῳ τέκνῳ* and compare reff. **ἔλεος** and **εἰρήνη** are found joined in Gal. vi. 16, in which Epistle are so many similarities to these (see Prolegg to these Epistles, § i. 32, note). The expression **θεὸς πατήρ**, absolute, is found in St. Paul, in Gal. i. 1, 3: Eph. vi 23 Phil ii 11 Col. iii. 17 (*τῷ θ. π.*) 1 Thess i 1: 2 Thess. i. 1 2 Tim i 2 Tit i 4 So that it belongs to all periods of his writing, but chiefly to the later.

3—20] *From specifying the object for which Timotheus was left at Ephesus* (vv 3, 4), *and characterizing the false teachers* (5—7), *he digresses to the true use of the law which they pretended to teach* (8—10), *and its agreement with the gospel with which he was entrusted* (11) *thence to his own conversion, for the mercies of which he expresses his thankfulness in glowing terms* (12—17) *Thence he returns to his exhortations to Timotheus* (18—20) On these repeated digressions, and the inferences from them, see Prolegg ch vii § i 36 f. **3**] The sentence begins **As I exhorted thee**, &c, but in his negligence of writing, the Apostle does not finish the construction: neither verse 5, nor 12, nor 18, will form the apodosis without unnatural forcing.

παρεκάλεσα] Chr. lays stress on the word, as implying great mildness—ἄκουε τὸ προσηνές, πῶς οὐ διδασκάλου κέχρηται ῥωμῇ, ἀλλ' οἰκέτου σχεδόν· οὐ γὰρ εἶπεν ἐπέταξα οὐδὲ ἐκέλευσα, οὐδὲ παρῄνεσα, ἀλλὰ τί; παρεκάλεσά σε This has been met (Huther, al.), by remarking that he says *διεταξάμην* to Titus, Tit. i. 5. The present word however was the usual one to his fellow-helpers, see reff. and *διεταξάμην* there refers rather to a matter of detail—'as I prescribed to thee.' The sense of **προσμεῖναι, to tarry**, or **stay** at a place, is sufficiently clear from ref. Acts. The **προς-** implies a fixity when the word is absolutely used, which altogether forbids the joining *προσμεῖναι* with *πορευόμενος* understood of Timotheus, as some have attempted to do. The aorist *προσμεῖναι* refers to the *act of remaining behind* when the Apostle departed, the *present* would have marked an *endurance of stay*. Various endeavours have been made to escape from the difficulties of the fact implied Schneckenburger would read *προσμείνας*. others would take *προσμεῖναι* as imperative, most unnaturally. No one can doubt, that the straightforward rendering is, **As I besought thee to tarry in Ephesus, when I was going to Macedonia** . . . . And on this straightforward rendering we must build our chronological considerations See the whole subject discussed in the Prolegomena, ch. vii § ii . and cf. Ellicott's note here.
πορευόμενος, present, **when I was on my way. ἵνα**, &c. object of his tarrying. **παραγγείλῃς**, see reff.
τισίν] so constantly (reff) in these Epistles sometimes *οἱ ἀντιλέγοντες* Tit i 9, *οἱ πολλοί* ib 10 Huther infers from *τισί*, that the number at this time was not considerable but this is hardly safe. "The indefinite pronoun is more probably *slightly* contemptuous 'le mot *τινες* a quelque chose de méprisant,' see Arnaud, on Jude 4, compare Gal. ii 12" Ellicott. **ἑτεροδιδασκαλεῖν**] There seems to be in *ἑτερο-*, as in *ἑτεροζυγοῦντες*

ἔχειν [q] μύθοις καὶ [rs] γενεαλογίαις [t] ἀπεράντοις, [u] αἵτινες ADFK Lℵ a b c d e f g h k l m n o 17

q ch. iv. 7. 2 Tim. iv. 4. Tit. i. 14. 2 Pet. i. 16 only†. Sir. xx. 19 only. r Tit. iii. 9. s Tit. as above only. 1 Chron. v. 5, 7, & ix. 22 Ald. only. (-γεῖν, Heb. vii. 6.) t here only. Job xxxvi. 26 only. u — Acts x. 41, 47. Paul, passim.

2 Cor. xi. 14, the idea of *strange*, or *incongruous*, not merely of different: cf. also ἑτερόγλωσσος, 1 Cor. xiv. 21. And the compound -διδασκαλεῖν, not -διδάσκειν, brings in the sense of '*acting as a teacher*:' not to be teachers of strange things. Eusebius has the substantive, H. E. iii. 32 —διὰ τῆς τῶν ἑτεροδιδασκάλων ἀπάτης,— in the sense of heretical teachers—which however is too fixed and developed a meaning to give here. We have καλοδιδάσκαλος, Tit. ii. 3. The meanings of 'other teaching' and 'false teaching,' when we remember that the faith which St. Paul preached was incapable (Gal. i. 8, 9) of any the least compromise with the errors subsequently described, lie very close to one another. **προσέχειν**, to give attention to: see reff.: "as it were, a mean term between ἀκούειν and πιστεύειν, compare Polyb. iv. 84. 6, διακούσαντες οὐδὲν προσέσχον, Jos. B. J. vii. 5. 3, οὔτε προσεῖχον οὔτε ἐπίστευον." Ellicott. **μύθοις**] We can only judge from the other passages in these Epistles where the word occurs, what kind of fables are alluded to. In Tit. i. 14, we have μὴ προσέχοντες Ἰουδαϊκοῖς μύθοις. In our ch. iv. 7, they are designated as βέβηλοι καὶ γραώδεις. In 2 Tim. iv. 4, they are spoken of absolutely, as here. If we are justified in identifying the 'fables' in Tit. with these, they had a Jewish origin: but merely to take them, as Thdrt., for the Jewish traditional comments on the law (μύθους δὲ οὐ τὴν τοῦ νόμου διδασκαλίαν ἐκάλεσεν, ἀλλὰ τὴν ἰουδαϊκὴν ἑρμηνείαν τὴν ὑπ' αὐτῶν καλουμένην δευτέρωσιν [מִשְׁנָה, mischna]), does not seem to satisfy the βέβηλοι καὶ γραώδεις. And consequently others have interpreted them of the gnostic mythology of the Æons. So Tert. adv. Valentinianos, ch. 3, vol. ii. p. 515: 'qui ex alia conscientia venerit fidei, si statim inveniat tot nomina æonum, tot conjugia, tot genimina, tot exitus, tot eventus, felicitates, infelicitates dispersæ atque concisæ divinitatis, dubitabitne ibidem pronuntiare, has esse fabulas et genealogias indeterminatas, quas apostoli spiritus his jam tunc pullulantibus seminibus haereticis damnare prævenit?' And Iren., in his præf., p. 1, assumes these words in the very outset, almost as his motto—ἐπεὶ τὴν ἀλήθειαν παραπεμπόμενοί τινες ἐπεισάγουσι λόγους ψευδεῖς κ. γενεαλογίας ματαίας αἵτινες ζητήσεις μᾶλλον παρέχουσι, καθὼς ὁ ἀπόστολός φησιν, ἢ οἰκοδομὴν θεοῦ τὴν ἐν πίστει .. Others again (as Suidas's definition, μῦθος, λόγος ψευδής, εἰκονίζων τὴν ἀλήθειαν) would give an entirely general meaning to the word,—'false teaching' of any kind. But this is manifestly too lax: for the descriptions here (ver. 7, e. g.) point at a Jewish origin, and a development in the direction of γενεαλογίαι ἀπέραντοι. It does not seem easy to define any further these μῦθοι, but it is plain that any transitional state from Judaism to gnosticism will satisfy the conditions here propounded, without inferring that the full-blown gnosticism of the second century must be meant, and thus calling in question the genuineness of the Epistle. On the whole subject, see Prolegg. ch. vii. § i. 8 ff. **γενεαλ. ἀπερ.**] De W. in his note on Tit. i. 14, marks out well the references which have been assigned to this expression: "γενεαλογίαι cannot be 1) *properly genealogical registers*,—either for a pure genealogico-historical end (Chr., Ec., Thl., Ambr., Est., Calov., Schöttg., Wolf); or for a dogmatico-historical one, to foster the religious national pride of Jews against Gentiles, cf. Phil. iii. 4 f. (Storr, Flatt, Wegsch., Leo), or to ascertain the descent of the Messiah (Thdrt., Jer., Wegsch.: according to Nicol. Lyr., to shew that Jesus was not the Messiah), least of all genealogies of Timotheus himself (Wetst.),—for all this does not touch, or too little touches religious interests: nor are they 2) *gentile theogonies* (Chr. gives this as well as the former interpretation: also Ec., Thl., Elsn.), nor again 3) *pedigrees of the cabalistic sephiroth* (Vitring. Obss. 1, v. 13: see Wolf), which will hardly suit γενεαλ., nor 4) *Essenian genealogies of angels* (Mich., Heim., al.), of the existence of which we have no proof, nor 5) *allegorizing genealogies*, applications of psychological and historical considerations to the genealogies contained in the books of Moses; as in Philo (Dahne, Stud. u. Krit. 1833, 1008),—a practice too peculiar to Philo and his view: but most probably 6) *lists of gnostic emanations* (Tert. contr. Val. 3,—præscr. 33, Iren. præf. [see above], Grot., Hamm., Chr., Mosh., Mack, Baur, al.), &c." But again, inasmuch as γενεαλογίαι are coupled in Tit. iii. 9 with μάχαι νομικαί, it seems as if we must hardly understand the ripened fruits of gnosticism, but rather

[sv] ζητήσεις [w] παρέχουσιν [x] μᾶλλον ἢ [y] οἰκονομίαν θεοῦ τὴν [z] ἐν πίστει·
5 τὸ δὲ [a] τέλος τῆς [b] παραγγελίας ἐστὶν

v John iii 25 Acts xv 2 xxv 20 Paul, ch vi 4 2 Tim ii 23 Tit iii 9 only+ w Paul, Gal vi 17 Col iv 1 ch vi 17 only = Matt xxvi 10 al Isa vii 13 x John iii 19 Acts xxvii 11 2 Tim iii 4 y Eph i 10 reff z ver 2 reff. a = Rom x 4 1 Pet i 9 only (Phil iii 19 reff) b ver 18 1 Thess iv 2 reff

4. εκζητησεις AN 17. elz *οικοδομιαν*, with D[1]: *οικοδομην* D[1] Iren(in Epiph): *ædificationem* latt goth Syr syr-marg Iren-int lat-ff. txt AFKLN rel syr copt æth Chr Thdrt [Dr Bloomfield's statement, ed 9, that A has *οἰκοδομίαν*, and that Chr and Thdrt seem not to have been aware of any other reading, is contrary to fact A reads *οἰκονομίαν*, and so do Chr and Thdrt: see both cited in the notes] om *την* F.

the first beginnings of those genealogies in the abuse of Judaism. See Prolegg. "It is curious that Polybius uses both terms in similarly close connexion, Hist. ix 2. 1" Ellicott. **ἀπεράντοις** may be used merely in popular hyperbole to signify the tedious length of such genealogies The meaning '*profitless*' (Chr., *ἤτοι πέρας μηδὲν ἔχουσαι, ἢ οὐδὲν χρήσιμον, ἢ δυσκατάληπτον ἡμῖν*, and so Thdrt; see below) would be a natural deduction from the other, and is therefore hardly to be so summarily set aside as it has been by De W, al **αἵτινες**, of the kind which. **ζητήσεις**] objective, questions. not subjective, '*questionings*' see reff in these Epistles, in which *ζητήσεις* are not themselves, but lead to, *ἔρεις, μάχαι*, &c. **παρέχουσιν**] minister, as E. V, is the best rendering '*afford*,' '*give rise to*,' '*furnish*' see below **μᾶλλον ἤ** is a mild way of saying *καὶ οὐ* see reff. **οἰκονομίαν θεοῦ . . .**] This has been taken two ways: 1) objectively *the dispensation* (reff) *of God* (towards man) *which is* (consists) *in* (the) *faith* in which case *παρέχουσιν* must bear something of a transferred meaning,—zeugmatic, as the grammarians call it,—as applied to *οἰκονομίαν*, implying, "rather than they *set forth*," &c. And to this there can be no objection, as the instances of it are so common. This meaning also suits that of *οἰκονομία* in the reff, even 1 Cor ix 17, where the *οἰκονομία* is the objective matter wherewith the Apostle was entrusted, not his own subjective fulfilment of it 2) subjectively —'*the exercising of the stewardship of God in faith*:' so Conyb or as paraphrased by Storr (in Huther) *ζητοῦντας αὐτοὺς ποιοῦσι, μᾶλλον ἢ οἰκονόμους θεοῦ πιστούς* But to this there is the serious objection, that *οἰκονομία* in this subjective sense, '*the fulfilment of the duty of an οἰκονόμος*,' wants example: and even could this be substantiated, *οἰκονομίαν παρέχειν*, in the sense required, would seem again questionable. I would therefore agree with Huther and Wiesinger (and Ellicott) in the objective sense —**the dispensation of God**. Then **τὴν ἐν πίστει** has also been variously taken. Chrys says, *καλῶς εἶπεν, οἰκονομίαν θεοῦ· μεγάλα γὰρ ἡμῖν δοῦναι ἠθέλησεν ὁ θεός, ἀλλ' οὐ δέχεται ὁ λογισμὸς τὸ μέγεθος αὐτοῦ τῶν οἰκονομιῶν διὰ πίστεως οὖν τοῦτο γίνεσθαι δεῖ.* And Thdrt. *αἱ μὲν περιτταὶ ζητήσεις ἀνόνητοι, ἡ δὲ πίστις φωτίζει τὸν νοῦν, καὶ ἐπιδείκνυσι τὰς θείας οἰκονομίας* But the words will hardly bear either of these The only legitimate meaning seems to be—**which is in faith**, i. e. finds its sphere, and element, and development among men, in faith. Thus **ἐν πίστει** stands in contrast to *ζητήσεις*, in which the *οἰκονομία θεοῦ does not* consist; and the way for the next sentence is prepared, which speaks of *πίστις ἀνυπόκριτος* as one of the means to the great end of the gospel. 5] **But** (contrast to the practice of these pretended teachers of the law) **the end** (purpose, aim Chrys quotes *τέλος ἰατρικῆς ὑγιεία*) **of the commandment** (viz. of the law of God in [ver. 11] the gospel not, although in the word there may be a slight allusion to it,—of that which Timothy was *παραγγέλλειν*, ver 3 This commandment is understood from the *οἰκονομία* just mentioned, of which it forms a part) **is Love** (as Rom. xiii. 10. We recognize, in the restating of former axiomatic positions, without immediate reference to the subject in hand, the characteristic of a later style of the Apostle) **out of** (arising, springing from, as its place of birth—the heart being the central point of life. see especially ver. 1 Pet) **a pure heart** (pure from all selfish views and leanings: see Acts xv. 9 on the psychology, see Ellicott's note and Delitzsch, Biblische Psychologie, iv. 12, p 201) **and good conscience** (is this *συνείδησις ἀγαθή*, 1) a conscience good by being freed from guilt by the application of Christ's blood,—or is it 2) a conscience pure in motive, antecedent to the act of

ἀγάπη [c] ἐκ [d] καθαρᾶς [c] καρδίας καὶ [ef] συνειδήσεως [e] ἀγαθῆς ADFK LℵA b
καὶ πίστεως [g] ἀνυποκρίτου· [6] ὧν [h] τινὲς [i] ἀστοχήσαντες c d e f g
[k] ἐξετράπησαν εἰς [l] ματαιολογίαν, [7] θέλοντες εἶναι [m] νομο- h k l m
διδάσκαλοι, μὴ [n] νοοῦντες μήτε ἃ λέγουσιν, μήτε περὶ n o 17

c Mark x 30, & Luke x 27 from Deut vi 5 Rom vi 17 2 Tim ii 22 1 Pet i 22 d Matt v 8 e Acts xxiii 1 (Paul) ver 19 1 Pet iii 16, 21 f = Acts xxiv 16 Heb xiii 18 al (Eccles x 20.) Wisd xvii 11 only g Rom xii 9 2 Cor vi 6 2 Tim i 5. James iii 17 1 Pet i 22 only † Wisd v 18 xviii 16 only h = ver 3 reff i ch vi 21 2 Tim ii 18 only † constr, here only ἀστοχοῦσι τοῦ μετρίου κ πρέποντος, Plut de Def Orac p 414, Wetst k ch v 15 vi 20 2 Tim iv 4 Heb. xii 13 only Amos v 8 only l here only † (-γος, Tit i 10) m Luke v 17 Acts v 34 only † n = Matt xv 17 Eph iii 4, 20 al Prov i 2, 6

5 om αγαθης F.

love? This must be decided by the usage of this and similar expressions in these Epistles, where they occur several times [reff and 1 Tim iii 9 2 Tim i 3 1 Tim iv. 2 Tit i 15] From those examples it would appear, as De W, that in the language of the pastoral Epistles *a good conscience* is joined with *soundness in the faith*, a *bad conscience* with *unsoundness* So that we can hardly help introducing the element of *freedom from guilt by the effect of that faith on the conscience*. And the earlier usage of St Paul in Acts xxiii 1, compared with the very similar one in 2 Tim i 3, goes to substantiate this) and faith unfeigned (this connects with τὴν ἐν πίστει above, it is faith, not the pretence of faith, the mere 'Scheinglaube' of the hypocrite, which, as in Acts xv 9, καθαρίζει τὰς καρδίας, and as in Gal v 6, δι' ἀγάπης ἐνεργεῖται Wiesinger well remarks that we see from this, that the general character of these false teachers, as of those against whom Titus is warned, was not so much error in doctrine, as leading men away from the earnestness of the loving Christian life, to useless and vain questionings, ministering only *strife*): 6] (the connexion is—it was by declining from these qualities that these men entered on their paths of error) of which (the καθαρὰ καρδία,—συνείδησις ἀγαθή, and πίστις ἀνυπόκριτος—the sources of ἀγάπη, which last they have therefore missed by losing them) some having failed (reff.: 'missed their mark' but this seems hardly precise enough it is not so much to miss a thing at which a man is aiming, as to leave unregarded one at which he ought to be aiming as Schweigh. Lex Polyb, 'rationem alicujus rei non habere, et respectu ejus sibi male consulere' Thus Polyb i 33 10, τῆς μὲν πρὸς τὰ θηρία μάχης δεόντως ἦσαν ἐστοχασμένοι, τῆς δὲ πρὸς τοὺς ἱππεῖς, πολλαπλασίους ὄντας τῶν παρ' αὐτοῖς, ὁλοσχερῶς ἠστόχησαν v 107 2, πρὸς μὲν τὸ παρὸν ἐνδεχομένως ἐβουλεύσατο, τοῦ δὲ μέλλοντος ἠστόχησε see also vii. 11. 3) turned aside to (ἐξ. away from the path leading to the τέλος, ver 5, in which they should have been walking the idiom is often found in the examples cited by Wetst: e g. Plat Phædr, δεῦρ' ἐκτραπόμενος κατὰ τὸν Ἴλισσον ἴωμεν,—Thuc v. 65, τὸ ὕδωρ ἐξέτρεπε κατὰ τὴν Μαντινικήν,—and in Polyb, ἐκτρέπεσθαι εἰς ὀλιγαρχίαν, vi 4 9,—εἰς τὴν συμφυῆ κακίαν, ib 10 2 and 7 and in Hippocr de temp morbi, even nearer to our present phrase,—εἰς μακρολογίαν ἐξετράποντο) foolish speaking (of what kind, is explained ver 7, and Tit iii 9, which place connects this expression with our ver 4 It is the vain questions arising out of the law which he thus characterizes Herod [ii 118] uses μάταιος λόγος of an *idle tale*, an *empty fable* — εἰρομένου δέ μευ τοὺς ἱρέας, εἰ μάταιον λόγον λέγουσι οἱ Ἕλληνες τὰ περὶ Ἴλιον γενέσθαι), wishing to be (giving themselves out as, without really being so Paus. i 4 6, αὐτοὶ δὲ Ἀρκάδες ἐθέλουσιν εἶναι τῶν ὁμοῦ Τηλέφῳ διαβάντων ἐς τὴν Ἀσίαν Cf Palm and Rost's Lex sub voce) teachers of the law (of what law? and in what sense? To the former question, but one answer can be given The law is that of Moses; *the law*, always so known The usage of νομοδιδάσκαλος (reff) forbids our giving the word, as coming from a Jew, any other meaning That this is so, is also borne out by Tit. i 11 Then as to the sense in which these men professed themselves teachers of the law. (1) Clearly not, as Baur, by their very antinomianism,—teachers of the law by setting it aside: this would at best be an unnatural sense to extract from the word, and it is not in any way countenanced by vv 8 ff as Baur thinks. see below (2) Hardly, in the usual position of those Judaizing antagonists of St Paul against whom he directs his arguments in Rom, Gal, and Col Of these he would hardly have predicated ματαιολογία, nor would he have said μὴ νοοῦντες κ τ.λ. *Their* offence was not either of these things, promulgating of idle fables, or ignorance

τίνων ^{o} διαβεβαιοῦνται· 8 ^{p} οἴδαμεν δὲ ὅτι ^{q} καλὸς ὁ
^{q} νόμος, ἐάν τις αὐτῷ ^{r} νομίμως ^{s} χρῆται, 9 ^{p} εἰδὼς τοῦτο,

o Tit iii 8 only † p Paul, Rom ii 2 iii 19 vii 14 (w ὁ νόμος) viii 22, 28 1 Cor viii 1, 4 2 Cor v 1 (Heb x 30 1 John iii 2, 14 v 15, 18, 19, 20) οἴδατε, & εἰδότες, & εἰδώς, Paul, passim q Rom vii 16 καλός, Paul16 in other epp in pastoral Epp, 24 times r 2 Tim ii 5 only † s = Acts xxvii 17 1 Cor vii 21, 31 ix 12, 15 ch v 23 Prov x 26

8 for χρῆται, χρησηται A 73 Clem.

of their subject, but one not even touched on here—an offence against the liberty of the Gospel, and its very existence, by re-introducing the law and its requirements. (3) We may see clearly by the data furnished in these pastoral Epistles, that it was with a different class of adversaries that the Apostle had in them to deal: with men who corrupted the material enactments of the moral law, and founded on Judaism not assertions of its obligation, but idle fables and allegories, letting in latitude of morals, and unholiness of life. It is against this *abuse of the law* that his arguments are directed: no formal question arises of the *obligation* of the law these men struck, by their interpretation, at the root of all divine law itself, and therefore at that root itself does he meet and grapple with them. [See more in Prolegg.] Hence the following description), **understanding neither** (notice **μήτε . . μήτε**, making the two branches of the negation parallel, not progressively exclusive, as would be the case with *μηδέ*: they understand as little about the one as about the other) **the things which they say** (the actual diatribes which they themselves put forth, they do not understand: they are not honest men, speaking from conviction, and therefore lucidly: but men depraved in conscience [Tit i. 14, 15], and putting forth things obscure to themselves, for other and selfish purposes), **nor concerning what things they make their affirmations** (nor those objective truths which properly belong to and underlie the matters with which they are thus tampering. This explanation of the sentence is called in question by De W., on the ground of the parallel expression in Tit iii. 8, **περὶ τούτων βούλομαί σε διαβεβαιοῦσθαι**, in which he maintains that in **διαβεβαιοῦσθαι περί τινος, περί τινος** represents the mere *thing asserted*, not the objective matter *concerning which* the assertion is made,—and he therefore holds our sentence to be a mere tautology,—**ἃ λέγουσιν** answering exactly to **περὶ τίνων διαβεβαιοῦνται**. But in reply we may say, that there is not the slightest necessity for such a construction in the passage of Titus: see note there. And so Huth., Wies. Cf. Arrian Epict ii 21, *τί δ᾽ ἐροῦσι καὶ περὶ τίνων ἢ πρὸς τίνας, καὶ τί ἔσται αὐτοῖς ἐκ τῶν λόγων τούτων, οὐδὲ καταβραχὲς πεφροντίκασι*)

8 ff.] On the other hand the law has its right use:—not that to which they put it, but to testify against sins in practice the catalogue of which seems to be here introduced, on account of the lax moral practice of these very men who were, or were in danger of, falling into them not, as Baur imagines, because they were antinomians and set aside the (moral) law They did not set it aside, but perverted it, and practised the very sins against which it was directed **Now** (slight contrast to last verse, taking up the matter on general grounds) **we know** (see ref especially Rom. vii 14 a thoroughly pauline expression) **that the law is good** (Rom. vii. 16: not only, as Thdrt., **ὠφέλιμον**, but in a far higher sense, as in Rom vii 12, 14: good abstractedly,—in accordance with the divine holiness and justice and truth; see ver 18, ch. iv. 4) **if a man** (undoubtedly, in the *first place*, and mainly, a *teacher*: but not [as Bengel, De W., and Ellic.] to be confined to that meaning all that is here said might apply just as well to a private Christian's thoughts and use of the law, as to the use of it by teachers themselves) **use it lawfully** (i. e. not, as most expositors, *according to its intention as law* [*ἐάν τις ἀκολουθῇ αὐτοῦ τῷ σκόπῳ*, Thdrt.], and as directed against the following sins *in Christians*: but clearly, from what follows, as De W. insists [see also Ellic.], and as Chrys. obscurely notices amongst other interpretations, **νομίμως** *in the Gospel sense* i. e. as *not binding on*, nor *relevant to Christian believers*, but only *a means of awakening repentance in the ungodly and profane* Chr.'s words are: **τίς δὲ αὐτῷ νομίμως χρήσεται, ὁ εἰδὼς ὅτι οὐ δεῖται αὐτοῦ.** His further references of *νομίμως*, 'as leading us to Christ,'—as 'inducing to piety not by its injunctions but by purer motives,' &c., are not in place here), **being aware of this** (belongs to **τις**, the teacher, or former of a judgment on the matter. **εἰδώς** implies both the possession and the application of the knowledge 'heeding,' or 'being aware of'), **that for a just man** (in what sense? in the mere sense of '*virtuous*,' '*righteous*,' in the world's acceptation of the term?

t = Luke ii. 34. Phil. i. 17. 1 Thess. iii. 3.
u = Luke xxii. 37 ‖. 2 Thess. ii. 8 (1 Cor. ix. 21).
v Tit. i. 6, 10. Heb. ii. 8 only †. 1 Kings ii. 12 Symm.

ὅτι δικαίῳ νόμος οὐ [t] κεῖται, [u] ἀνόμοις δὲ καὶ [v] ἀνυποτάκ-
τοις, [wx] ἀσεβέσιν καὶ [xy] ἁμαρτωλοῖς, [z] ἀνοσίοις καὶ [a] βεβή-
λοις, [b] πατρολῴαις καὶ [b] μητρολῴαις, [c] ἀνδροφόνοις,

ADFK Lℵ a b c d e f g h k l m n o 17

w Rom iv. 5. v. 6. 1 Pet. iv. 18. 2 Pet. ii. 5. iii. 7. Jude 4, 15 bis only. Prov. xxi. 28. (-βεῖν, 2 Pet. ii. 6. -βεια, 2 Tim. ii. 16.) x 1 Pet. iv. 18. Prov. xi. 31. (Jude 15.) y Rom. iii. 7 al. fr. Ps. xlix. 16. z 2 Tim. iii. 2 only. Ezek. xxii. 9. Wisd. xii. 4. 2 Macc. vii. 34. viii. 32 only. a ch. iv. 7. vi. 20. 2 Tim. ii. 16. Heb. xii. 16 only. Levit. x. 10 al. (-λοῦν, Matt. xii. 5.) b here only †. c here only †. 2 Macc. ix. 28 only.

9. for ανομοις δε, αλλ' ανομοις F. ins και bef ασεβεσιν D[1] syr goth Lucif. ins και bef ανοσιοις F. rec πατραλ. and μητραλ., with rel Thl: πατραλ. but μητρολ. K g n: txt ADFLℵ d f h k l m 17 Thdrt-ms Œc, πατριλ. μητραλ. o.

in Chrys.'s third alternative, δίκαιον ἐνταῦθα καλεῖ τὸν κατωρθωκότα τὴν ἀρετήν? or as Thl., ὃς δι' αὐτὸ τὸ καλὸν τήν τε πονηρίαν μισεῖ καὶ τὴν ἀρετὴν περιπτύσσεται? All such meanings are clearly excluded by ver. 11, which sets the whole sentence in the full light of Gospel doctrine, and necessitates a corresponding interpretation for every term used in it. **δίκαιος** therefore can only mean, righteous in the *Christian sense*, viz. by *justifying faith and sanctification of the Spirit*,—'*justitia per sanctificationem*,' as De Wette from Croc.,—one who is included in the actual righteousness of Christ by having put Him on, and so not *forensically amenable to the law*,—partaker of the inherent righteousness of Christ, inwrought by the Spirit, which unites him to Him, and so not *morally needing it*) **the law** (as before: not, '*a law*' in general, as will be plain from the preceding remarks: nor does the omission of the article furnish any ground for such a rendering, in the presence of numerous instances where νόμος, anarthrous, is undeniably 'the Law' of Moses. Cf. Rom. ii. 25 bis; ib. 27; iii. 28, 31 bis; v. 20; vii. 1; x. 4: Gal. ii. 19; vi. 13,—to say nothing of the very many examples after prepositions. And of all parts of the N. T. anarthrousness need least surprise us in these Epistles, where many theological terms, having from constant use become technical words, have lost their articles. No such compromise as that of Bishop Middleton's, that the Mosaic law is *comprehended* in νόμος, will answer the requirements of the passage, which strictly deals with the Mosaic law and with nothing else: cf. on the catalogue of sins below. As De Wette remarks, this assertion = that in Rom. vi. 14, οὐ γὰρ ἐστὲ ὑπὸ νόμον, ἀλλὰ ὑπὸ χάριν,—Gal. v. 18, εἰ πνεύματι ἄγεσθε, οὐκ ἐστὲ ὑπὸ νόμον) **is not enacted** (see very numerous instances of νόμος κεῖται in Wetst. The following are some: Eur. Ion 1046, 7, ὅταν δὲ πολεμίους δρᾶσαι κακῶς | θέλῃ τις, οὐδεὶς ἐμποδὼν κεῖται νόμος: Thucyd. ii. 37, νόμων . . . ὅσοι τε ἐπ' ὠφελείᾳ τῶν ἀδικουμένων κεῖνται: Galen. a. Julian. (Wetst.), νόμος οὐδεὶς κεῖται κατὰ τῶν ψευδῶς ἐγκαλούντων), **but for lawless** (reff.: not as in 1 Cor. ix. 21) **and insubordinate** (reff. Tit.: it very nearly = ἀπειθής, see Tit. i. 16; iii. 3,—this latter being more subjective, whereas ἀνυποτάκτ. points to the objective fact. This first pair of adjectives expresses opposition to *the law*, and so stands foremost as designating those for whom it is enacted), **for impious and sinful** (see especially ref. 1 Pet. This second pair expresses opposition to *God*, whose law it is—**ἀσεβής** being the man who does not reverence Him, **ἁμαρτωλός** the man who lives in defiance of Him), **for unholy and profane** (this last pair betokens separation and alienation from God and His law alike—those who have no share in His holiness, no relation to things sacred. "The ἀσεβής is unholy through his lack of *reverence*: the ἀνόσιος, through his lack of *inner purity*." Ellic.), **for father-slayers and mother-slayers** (or it may be taken in the wider sense, as Ellic., 'smiters of fathers:' so Hesych.: ὁ τὸν πατέρα ἀτιμάζων, τύπτων ἢ κτείνων. In Demosth. κατὰ Τιμοκράτους, p. 732. 14, the word is used of ἡ τῶν γονέων κάκωσις: cf. the law cited immediately after. And Plato, Phæd. 114 a, apparently uses it in the same wide sense, as he distinguishes πατράλοιαι and μητράλοιαι from ἀνδροφόνοι.

Hitherto the classes have been general, and [see above] arranged according to their opposition to the law, or to God, or to both: now he *takes the second table of the decalogue and goes through its commandments*, to the ninth inclusive, *in order*. πατρολῴαις καὶ μητρολῴαις are the transgressors of the *fifth*), **for manslayers** (the *sixth*), **for fornicators, for sodomites** (sins of abomination against both sexes: the *seventh*), **for slave-dealers** (εἴρηται ἀνδραποδιστὴς παρὰ τὸ ἄνδρα ἀποδίδοσθαι, τουτέστι πωλεῖν, Schol.

10 [d] πόρνοις, [e] ἀρσενοκοίταις, [f] ἀνδραποδισταῖς, [g] ψεύσταις, [d] Eph v 5 reff [e] 1 Cor vi 9 only † see Levit xviii. 22
[h] ἐπιόρκοις, καὶ [i] εἴ τι [k] ἕτερον τῇ [lm] ὑγιαινούσῃ [ln] διδασ- [f] here only † [g] Paul, Rom iii 4 Tit i 12 only otherwise,
καλίᾳ [o] ἀντίκειται, 11 κατὰ τὸ [p] εὐαγγέλιον τῆς [p] δόξης
τοῦ [q] μακαρίου θεοῦ, ὃ [r] ἐπιστεύθην ἐγώ. 12 [s] χάριν [s] ἔχω

John (viii 44 al) only Prov xix 22 h here only † (-κεῖν, Matt v 33 κιa, Wisd xiv 25) i & constr, 2 Cor v 17 Eph iv 29 Phil ii 1 k = Rom viii 39 xiii 9 l 2 Tim iv 3 Tit i 9 ii 1 see ch vi 3 m = as above (l) 2 Tim i 13 Tit i 13 ii 2 (Luke v 31 al) only ὑγ περὶ θεῶν δόξαι, Plut de audiend Poetis, p 20 F, Wetst τους ὑγ λογους, Philo de Abr 38, vol ii p 32 n = as above (l) Matt xv 9 (, from Isa xxix 13 Eph iv 14 Col ii 22 ch iv 1, 6 (13), 16 (v 17) vi 1 2 Tim iii 10 (16) Tit ii 7, 10 only o Luke xiii 17 xxi 15 1 Cor xvi 9 Gal v 17 Phil i 28 2 Thess ii 4 ch v 14 only Zech iii 1 p 2 Cor iv 4 only see 1 Thess ii 2 reff q Paul, Rom iv 7, 8 (from Ps xxxi 1 2) xiv 22 1 Cor vii 40 Tit ii 13 but of God, ch vi 15 only r = & constr, Rom iii 2 1 Cor ix 17 Gal ii 7 1 Thess. ii 4 Tit i 3. s Luke xvii 9 2 Tim i 3 (Philem 7 v r) Heb xii 28 only 2 Macc iii 33

10 εφιορκοις D[1]. om αντικειται A at end add τη D[1] vulg arm Bas lat-ff

12. rec at beg ins και, with DKL rel syrr goth Damasc Œc-txt Lucif Ambrst · om

Aristoph. Plut. ver 521. The etymology is wrong, but the meaning as he states cf Xen Mem. i. 2. 6, τοὺς λαμβάνοντας τῆς ὁμιλίας μισθὸν ἀνδραποδιστὰς ἑαυτῶν ἀπεκάλει · and Pollux, Onomast iii 78, ἀνδραποδιστής, ὁ τὸν ἐλεύθερον καταδουλούμενος ἢ τὸν ἀλλότριον οἰκέτην ὑπαγόμενος [Ellic] The Apostle puts the ἀνδραποδιστής as the most flagrant of all breakers of the *eighth* commandment. No theft of a man's goods can be compared with that most atrocious act, which steals *the man himself*, and robs him of that free will which is the first gift of his Creator And of this crime all are guilty, who, whether directly or indirectly, are engaged in, or uphold from whatever pretence, the making or keeping of slaves), **for liars, for perjurers** (breakers of the *ninth* commandment It is remarkable that he does not refer to that very commandment by which the law wrought on himself when he was alive without the law and sin was dead in him, viz the *tenth*. Possibly this may be on account of its more spiritual nature, as he here wishes to bring out the grosser kinds of sin against which the moral law is pointedly enacted The subsequent clause however seems as if he had it in his mind, and on that account added **a** concluding general and inclusive description), **and if any thing else** (he passes to sins themselves from the committers of sins) **is opposed** (reff) **to the healthy teaching** (i. e that moral teaching which is spiritually sound : = ἡ κατ' εὐσέβειαν διδασκαλία, ch vi. 3, where it is parallel with ὑγιαίνοντες λόγοι οἱ τοῦ κυρ. ἡμ Ἰησ. χριστοῦ. "The formula . . . . stands in clear and suggestive contrast to the sickly [ch vi 4] and morbid [2 Tim. ii. 17] teaching of Jewish gnosis." Ellic)—**according to** (belongs, not to ἀντίκειται, which would make the following words a mere flat repetition of τῇ ὑγιαιν. διδασκ. [see ch. vi 1, 3]—nor to διδασκαλίᾳ, as Thl.,—τῇ ὑγ. διδ τῇ οὔσῃ κατὰ τὸ εὐαγγ ,—all. (see D[1] in digest),—for certainly in this case the specifying article must have been inserted,—and thus also the above repetition would occur; —but to the whole preceding sentence,—the entire exposition which he has been giving of the freedom of Christians from the moral law of the decalogue) **the gospel of the glory** (not, '*the glorious gospel,*' see ref 2 Cor. all propriety and beauty of expression is here, as always, destroyed by this adjectival rendering. The gospel is 'the glad tidings of the glory of God,' as of Christ in l c , inasmuch as it reveals to us God in all His glory, which glory would be here that of justifying the sinner without the law by His marvellous provision of redemption in Christ) **of the blessed God** (μακάριος, used of God, is called unpaulinisch by De Wette, occurring only in 1 Tim. [ref] in other words, one of those expressions which are peculiar to this later date and manner of the Apostle. On such, see Prolegomena), **with which I** (emphatic) **was** (aorist, indicating simply the past, pointing to the time during which this his commission had been growing into its fulness and importance) **entrusted** (not these τινές ὃ ἐπιστεύθην is a construction only and characteristically pauline · see reff. The connexion with the following appears to be this his mind is full of thankfulness at the thought of the commission which was thus entrusted to him he does not regret the charge, but overflows with gratitude at the remembrance of Christ's grace to him, especially when he recollects also what he once was; how nearly approaching [for I would not exclude even that thought as having contributed to produce these strong expressions] some of those whom he has just mentioned. So that he now goes off

t Eph. vi. 10 reff. u = Acts xxvi. 2. 2 Cor. ix. 5. ch. vi. 1. Job xiii. 6. v = 1 Thess. v. 9 reff. w = Eph. iv. 12 reff. x John vi. 62. ix. 8. Gal. iv. 13 only. Judg. xviii. 29.

τῷ [t] ἐνδυναμώσαντί με χριστῷ Ἰησοῦ τῷ κυρίῳ ἡμῶν,
ὅτι πιστόν με [u] ἡγήσατο, [v] θέμενος [v] εἰς [w] διακονίαν,
13 [x] τὸ πρότερον ὄντα [y] βλάσφημον καὶ [z] διώκτην καὶ
[a] ὑβριστήν· ἀλλὰ [b] ἠλεήθην, ὅτι [c] ἀγνοῶν ἐποίησα ἐν
[d] ἀπιστίᾳ. 14 [e] ὑπερεπλεόνασεν δὲ ἡ χάρις τοῦ κυρίου

ADFK LℵA a b c d e f g h k l m n o 17

y Acts vi. 11. 2 Tim. iii. 2. 2 Pet. ii. 11. Rev. xiii. 5 only. Isa. lxvi. 3 only. Wisd. i. 6 al. z here only †. Hos. vi. 8 Symm. a Rom. i. 30 only. Prov. vi. 17 al. b pass., ver. 16. Rom. xi. 30, 31. 1 Cor. vii. 25. 2 Cor. iv. 1. 1 Pet. ii. 10. Prov. xxi. 10. c = Acts xvii. 23 (Paul). Rom. ii. 4. x. 3. Sir. v. 15. d Rom. iii. 3. iv. 20. xi. 20, 23. Heb. iii. 19†. Wisd. xiv. 25 only. e here only †.

AFℵ 17. 67[2]. 73. 80 vulg copt æth arm Chr Thdrt Pelag Vig Bede. ενδυναμουντι ℵ[1] 17. 72.—om με ℵ[1].

13. rec for το, τον, with D[3]KL rel: txt AD[1]Fℵ 17. 67[2] Dial Chr-ms. aft οντα ins με A 73. [αλλα, so ADFLℵ rel.]—D[1] adds δια τουτο. for εν, τη D[1].

from the immediate subject, even more completely and suddenly than is his wont in his other writings, as again and again in these pastoral Epistles: shewing thereby, I believe, the tokens of advancing age, and of that faster hold of individual habits of thought and mannerisms, which characterizes the decline of life): **(12 ff.]** See summary, on ver. 3.) **I give thanks** (**χάριν ἔχειν** [reff.] is only used by the Apostle here and in 2 Tim. ref.) **to Him who enabled me** (viz. for His work: not only as Chr., in one of his finest passages,—*φορτίον ὑπῆλθε μέγα, καὶ πολλῆς ἐδεῖτο τῆς ἄνωθεν ῥοπῆς. ἐννόησον γὰρ ὅσον ἦν πρὸς καθημερινὰς ὕβρεις, λοιδορίας, ἐπιβουλάς, κινδύνους, σκώμματα, ὀνείδη, θανάτους ἵστασθαι, καὶ μὴ ἀποκάμνειν, μηδὲ ὀλισθαίνειν, μηδὲ περιτρέπεσθαι, ἀλλὰ πάντοθεν βαλλόμενον μυρίοις καθ' ἑκάστην ἡμέραν τοῖς βέλεσιν, ἀτενὲς ἔχοντα τὸ ὄμμα ἑστάναι καὶ ἀκατάπληκτον*,—see also Phil. iv. 13,—for he evidently is here treating of the divine enlightening and strengthening which he received for the ministry: cf. Acts ix. 22, where the same word occurs—a coincidence not to be overlooked. So Thdrt.: *οὐ γὰρ οἰκείᾳ δυνάμει χρώμενος ταύτην τοῖς ἀνθρώποις προσφέρω τὴν διδασκαλίαν, ἀλλ' ὑπὸ τοῦ σεσωκότος ῥωννύμενός τε καὶ νευρούμενος*), **Christ Jesus our Lord** (not to be taken as the dativus commodi after *ἐνδυναμώσαντι*, but in apposition with *τῷ ἐνδυν.*), **that** (not, '*because*:' it is the main ground of the *χάριν ἔχω*: the specification of *τῷ ἐνδυναμώσαντι* introducing a subordinate ground) **He accounted me faithful** (cf. the strikingly similar expression, 1 Cor. vii. 25, *γνώμην δίδωμι ὡς ἠλεημένος ὑπὸ κυρίου πιστὸς εἶναι*:—He knew me to be such an one, in His foresight, as would prove faithful to the great trust), **appointing me** (cf. ref. 1 Thess. The expression is there used of that appointment of God in His sovereignty, by which our course is marked for a certain aim or end: and so it is best taken here,—not for the act of '*putting me into*' the ministry, as E. V. But the present sense must be kept: not '*having appointed*,' **θέμενος** constituting the *external proof* of *πιστόν με ἡγήσ.*) **to the ministry** (what sort of **διακονία**, is declared, Acts xx. 24, *ἡ διακονία ἣν ἔλαβον παρὰ τοῦ κυρίου Ἰησοῦ, διαμαρτύρασθαι τὸ εὐαγγέλιον τῆς χάριτος τοῦ θεοῦ*),

13.] (and all the more is he thankful, seeing that he was once a direct opponent of the Gospel) **being before** (the participle is slightly concessive: as Ellic. from Justiniani, 'cum tamen essem;' almost equivalent to 'though I was') **a blasphemer** (see Acts xxvi. 9, 11) **and persecutor and insulter** (one who added insult to persecution. See on **ὑβριστής**, Trench, N. T. Synonyms, p. 112 f. The facts which justified the use of such a term were known to St. Paul's conscience: we might well infer them, from his own confessions in Acts xxii. 4, 19, and xxvi. 9—12. He describes himself as *περισσῶς ἐμμαινόμενος αὐτοῖς*): **howbeit** ("**ἀλλά** has here its full and proper seclusive ['aliud jam hoc esse, de quo sumus dicturi,' Klotz., Devar. ii. p. 2], and thence often antithetical force. God's mercy and St. Paul's want of it are put in sharp contrast." Ellic.) **I had mercy shewn me** (reff.), **because I did it ignorantly** (so Rom. x. 2, of the Jews, *ζῆλον θεοῦ ἔχουσιν, ἀλλ' οὐ κατ' ἐπίγνωσιν*. Cf. also as a most important parallel, our Lord's prayer for His murderers, Luke xxiii. 34) **in unbelief** (**ἀπιστία** was his *state*, of which his ignorance of what he did was a *consequence*. The clause is a very weighty one as applying to others under similar circumstances; and should lead us to form our judgments in all charity respecting even persecutors—and if of them, then surely even with a wider extension of charity to those generally, who lie in the ignorance of

ἡμῶν μετὰ [f] πίστεως καὶ ἀγάπης τῆς [f] ἐν χριστῷ Ἰησοῦ.
15 [gh] πιστὸς ὁ [h] λόγος καὶ [i] πάσης [k] ἀποδοχῆς ἄξιος, ὅτι
χριστὸς Ἰησοῦς [lr] ἦλθεν εἰς τὸν [l] κόσμον [m] ἁμαρτωλοὺς
[m] σῶσαι, ὧν [n] πρῶτός εἰμι ἐγώ· 16 ἀλλὰ διὰ τοῦτο [o] ἠλεήθην, ἵνα [p] ἐν ἐμοὶ [n] πρώτῳ [q] ἐνδείξηται χριστὸς Ἰησοῦς

f Eph. i 15 Col i 4 2 Tim i 13. iii 15 P g = Acts xiii 34 (from Isa lv 3) al h ch iii 1 iv 9 2 Tim ii 11 Tit i 9 iii 8 Rev xxi 5 xxii 6 only i Phil i 20 reff k ch iv 9 only † ἀποδοχῆς ἀξιοῦται παρ' ἐνίοις (of a *writer*), Polyb ii 56 1 ὁ λόγος ἀποδοχῆς τυγχάνει id i 5 5 (see Wetst) l John i 9 xii 46 xvi 28 m here only see Matt xviii 11 ‖ L n = Mark xii 28, 29 o ver 13 p = Matt xvii 12 1 Cor ix 15 q Eph ii 7 reff

15 om τον ℵ.

16. for πρωτω, πρωτον L a[1] c m o coptt Thdrt: om D[1] æth Aug$_1$. rec ιησ bef χρ, with KLℵ rel syrr copt: om F 1 Serap: txt AD k 17 vulg goth Thdrt$_1$ lat-ff.

unbelief, whatever be its cause, or its effects), **14**] **but** (contrast still to his former state, and epexegetical of ἠλεήθην;—not to ἠλεήθ.,—'not only so, but,' as Chr, De W, al) **the grace of our Lord** (His mercy shewn to me—but not in strengthening me for His work, endowing me with spiritual gifts, &c., as Chr., al. for the ἠλεήθην is the ruling idea through the whole, and he recurs to it again ver. 16, never having risen above it to that of his higher gifts) **superabounded** (to be taken not comparatively, but superlatively, see Rom. v. 20, note) **with** (accompanied by) **faith and love** (see the same pauline expression, Eph. vi 23, and note there) **which are** (τῆς probably improperly used by attraction for τῶν: there is no reason why πίστις as well as ἀγάπη should not be designated as ἐν χριστῷ Ἰησοῦ) **in** (as their element, and, as it were, *home*) **Christ Jesus** (all these three abounded—grace, the objective side of God's ἔλεος to him — Christian faith and love—the contrast to his former hatred and unbelief,—God's gifts, the subjective side. This is much better than to regard μετὰ πίστεως καὶ ἀγάπης as giving that wherein the χάρις ὑπερεπλεόνασεν) **15**] **faithful** (worthy of credit. ἀντὶ τοῦ, ἀψευδὴς καὶ ἀληθής, Thdrt. Cf. Rev. xxi. 5, οὗτοι οἱ λόγοι ἀληθινοὶ καὶ πιστοί εἰσιν similarly xxii 6. The formula πιστὸς ὁ λόγος is peculiar to the pastoral Epistles, and characteristic I believe of their later age, when certain sayings had taken their place as Christian axioms, and were thus designated) **is the saying, and worthy of all** (all possible, i e. universal) **reception** (see reff. Polyb., and Wetst and Kypke, h. l. A word which, with its adjective ἀποδεκτός [ch. ii. 3· v. 4], is confined to these Epistles. We have the verb, οἱ μὲν οὖν ἀποδεξάμενοι τὸν λόγον αὐτοῦ ἐβαπτίσθησαν, Acts ii 41), **that Christ Jesus came into the world** (an expression otherwise found only in St John But in the two reff. in Matt. and Luke, we have the ἦλθεν) **to save sinners** (to be taken in the most general sense, not limited in any way), **of whom** (sinners, not, as Wegscheider, σωζομένων or σεσωσμένων. the aim and extent of the Lord's mercy intensifies the feeling of his own especial unworthiness) **I am** (not, '*was*') **chief** (not, 'one of the chief,' as Flatt,—nor does πρῶτος refer to *time*, which would not be the fact [see below] the expression is one of the deepest humility: αὐτὸν ὑπερβαίνει τῆς ταπεινοφροσύνης ὅρον, says Thdrt : and indeed it is so, cf Phil. iii 6, 1 Cor xv. 9; Acts xxiii 1; xxiv. 16; but deep humility ever does so· it is but another form of ἐμοὶ τῷ ἁμαρτωλῷ, Luke xviii 13: other men's crimes seem to sink into nothing in comparison, and a man's own to be the chief and only ones in his sight)· **16**] **howbeit** (as E V. "not resumptive, but as in ver. 13, seclusive and antithetical, marking the contrast between the Apostle's own judgment on himself, and the mercy which God was pleased to shew him." Ellic) **for this purpose I had mercy shewn me, that in me** (as an example, "in my case" see reff. and cf. εἰς ὑποτύπωσιν below) **first** (it can hardly be denied that in πρώτῳ here the senses of '*chief*' and '*first*' are combined This latter seems to be necessitated by μελλόντων below. Though he was not in time 'the first of sinners,' yet he was the first as well as the most notable example of such marked long-suffering, held up for the encouragement of the church) **Christ Jesus might shew forth** (dynamic middle see note on ref Eph, and Ellicott there) **the whole of His** (not merely '*all*' [all possible, πᾶσαν] nor 'all His' [Conyb, Ellic · πᾶσαν τὴν . . . .], but '*the whole*,' 'the whole mass of μακροθυμία, of which I was an example,' ὁ ἅπας seems to be found here only If the rec. reading be in question, in all other cases where ὁ πᾶς occurs with a substantive in the N. T., it is one which admits of partition, and may therefore be rendered by 'all the' or 'the

r see 1 Cor xiii. 2 | s Paul, Gal iii 28. Eph vi 13 only | t Rom ii. 4. 1 Pet. iii 20. 2 Pet iii 15 al Prov. xxv 15

[r]τὴν [s]ἅπασαν [t]μακροθυμίαν, [u]πρὸς [v]ὑποτύπωσιν [w]τῶν ADFK
μελλόντων [x]πιστεύειν [x]ἐπ' αὐτῷ [y]εἰς [z]ζωὴν αἰώνιον. LN a b c d e f g
17 τῷ [z]δὲ [a]βασιλεῖ τῶν [ab]αἰώνων, [c]ἀφθάρτῳ, [d]ἀοράτῳ, h k l m n o 17
[e]μόνῳ [e]θεῷ, [f]τιμὴ καὶ [f]δόξα εἰς [g]τοὺς αἰῶνας τῶν αἰώνων,

u = Acts iii 10. 2 Cor viii. 10. x 4 al. v 2 Tim i 13 only † w constr (w τύπος), 1 Cor x 6. x w. dat (Matt xxvii 42 v. r.) Luke xxiv 25 only in N. T., exc Rom ix 33. x 11. 1 Pet. ii 6, all from Isa xxviii 16. y = Acts xi 18. Rom vii 10. z Rom. xvi 25. a here only. Tobit xiii. 6, 10. see Sir xxxvi. 17. b = Heb i 2. xi 3. c Rom i. 23. 1 Cor ix 25. xv 52. 1 Pet i 4, 23. iii 4 only † Wisd. xii. 1. xviii 4 only. d Col i. 15, 16 reff. e John v 44 (xvii 3. Rom xvi. 27) Jude 25 only. f of God, Paul here only (δόξα, Gal. i 5.) 2 Pet i 17. Rev iv 9, 11. v. 12. g Gal i. 5 reff.

rec for απασαν, πασαν, with DKL rel txt AFN d m 17 Serap Chr$_1$. aft μακροθ. ins αυτου D Syr coptt æth Thdrt$_1$ Aug$_1$. aft μελλοντων ins αγαθων (but marked for erasure)N[1].

17. for αφθαρτ., αθανατω D[1] vulg syr-marg lat-ff: aft αορ add αθανατω F. rec aft μονω ins σοφω (see Rom xvi. 27), with D[2 3]KLN[1] rel syr Nyssen Naz Thl-comm: om AD[1]FN[1] (m?) 17 latt Syr coptt æth arm Eus Cyr Thdrt$_2$ (from comm, he plainly did not read σοφ.) Chr-comm Œc-comm.

whole:' e g Acts xx. 18, πῶς μεθ' ὑμῶν τὸν πάντα χρόνον ἐγενόμην: see also ref. Wetst. has two examples from Polyb in which ὁ πᾶς has the meaning of '*the utmost*:' τῆς πάσης ἀλογιστίας ἐστὶ σημεῖον,—and τῆς ἁπάσης (as here) ἀτοπίας εἶναι σημεῖον) **long-suffering** (not, *generosity, magnanimity*: nor is the idea of *long*-suffering here irrelevant, as some have said. Christ's mercy gave him all that time for repentance, during which he was persecuting and opposing Him,—and therefore it was his *long*-suffering which was so wonderful), **for an example** (cf. 2 Pet. ii. 6, ὑπόδειγμα μελλόντων ἀσεβεῖν τεθεικώς. Wetst has shewn by very copious extracts, that ὑποτύπωσις is used by later writers, beginning with Aristotle, for a *sketch*, an *outline*, afterwards to be filled up. This indeed the recorded history of Paul would be,—the filling up taking place in each man's own case: see ref. 2 Tim., note. Or the meaning 'sample,' 'ensample,' as in 2 Tim. i. 13, will suit equally well) **of** (to, see Ellicott's note, and Donaldson, Gr. Gr. § 450) **those who should** (the time of μελλόντων is not the time of writing the Epistles, but that of the mercy being shewn: so that we must not say "who *shall*," but "who *should*") **believe on Him** (the unusual ἐπ' αὐτῷ is easily accounted for, from its occurrence in so very common a quotation as πᾶς ὁ πιστεύων ἐπ' αὐτῷ οὐ καταισχυνθήσεται, see reff. The propriety of the expression here is, that it gives more emphatically the ground of the πιστεύειν—brings out more the *reliance* implied in it—almost q. d., 'to rely on Him for eternal life.' Ellicott has, in his note here, given a full and good classification of the constructions of πιστεύω in the N. T.) **to** (belongs to πιστεύειν [see above] as its aim and end [cf. Heb. x. 39] not to ὑποτύπωσιν, as Bengel suggests) **life eternal**: 17.] **but** (δέ takes the thought entirely off from himself and every thing else, and makes the following sentence exclusive as applied to God. 'Ex sensu gratiæ fluit doxologia.' Bengel. Compare by all means the very similar doxology, Rom. xvi. 25 ff.: and see, on their similarity, the inferences in the Prolegomena, ch. vii. § i. 33, and note) **to the King** (this name, as applied to God, is found, in N. T., only in Matt. v. 35 [not xxv. 34 ff.] and our ch. vi. 15. See below) **of the ages** (i. e. of eternity: cf. the reff. Tobit, where the same expression occurs, and Sir.—θεὸς τῶν αἰώνων: also Ps. cxliv. 13, ἡ βασιλεία σου βασιλεία πάντων τῶν αἰώνων,—מַלְכוּת כָּל־עֹלָמִים. Comparing these with the well-known εἰς τοὺς αἰῶνας τῶν αἰώνων, εἰς τοὺς αἰῶνας, and the like, it is far more likely that οἱ αἰῶνες here should mean eternity, than the ages of this world, as many have understood it. The doxology is to the Father, not to the Trinity [Thdrt.], nor to the Son [Calov., al.]: cf. ἀοράτῳ), **incorruptible** (in ref. Rom only, used of God), **invisible** (reff. see also ch. vi. 16: John i. 18. Beware of taking ἀφθάρτῳ, ἀοράτῳ with θεῷ, as recommended by Bishop Middleton, on the ground of the articles being wanting before these adjectives. It is obvious that no such consideration is of any weight in a passage like the present. The abstract adjectives of attribute are used almost as substantives, and stand by themselves, referring not to βασιλεῖ immediately, but to Him of whom βασιλεύς is a title, as well as they: q. d. 'to Him who is the King of the ages, the Incorruptible, the Invisible, . . .'), **the only God** (σοφῷ has apparently come from the doxology at the end of Romans, where it is most appro-

ἀμήν. 18 ταύτην τὴν [h] παραγγελίαν [i] παρατίθεμαί σοι,
[k] τέκνον Τιμόθεε, κατὰ τὰς [l] προαγούσας ἐπὶ σὲ [m] προφητείας, ἵνα [n] στρατεύῃ [o] ἐν αὐταῖς τὴν [p] καλὴν [q] στρατείαν,
19 [r] ἔχων [r] πίστιν καὶ [s] ἀγαθὴν [s] συνείδησιν, ἣν [t] τινὲς
[u] ἀπωσάμενοι [v] περὶ τὴν πίστιν [w] ἐναυάγησαν· 20 [x] [v] ὧν

h ver 5 1 Thess iv 2 reff
i = (Matt xiii 24 al) 2 Tim ii 2 only
k ver 2 reff
l = Heb vii 18 lit, Matt xxi 9 ch v. 24 al fr
m Rom xii 6 1 Cor xii 10, &c 1 Thess v 20 ch iv 14
n Luke iii 14 1 Cor ix 7 2 Cor x 3 James iv 1 1 Pet ii 11 only Judg xix 8 vat Isa xxix 7
o = 1 Thess iv 16
p = ch vi 12 2 Tim iv 7 see John x 11 1 Pet iv 10
q 2 Cor x 4 only †
r Matt xxi 21 Mark xi 22 Acts xiv 9 Rom xiv 22 1 Cor xiii 2 Philem 5 James ii 1, 14, 18
s ver 5 reff
t ver 3 reff
u Acts vii 27, 39 xiii 46 Rom xi. 1, 2 only L P Ezek xliii 9
v so ch vi 21 2 Tim ii 18 Tit ii 7
w 2 Cor. xi 25 only †
x 2 Tim i 15 ii 17

18 απαγγελιαν F στρατευση D¹א¹ Clem
19 εναυγαγησαν A.

priate), be honour and glory to the ages of the ages (the periods which are made up of αἰῶνες, as these last are of years,—as years are of days see note, Eph iii. 21: and Ellic. on Gal i 5), Amen

18 ff] He now returns to the matter which he dropped in ver. 3, not indeed formally, so as to supply the apodosis there neglected, but virtually. the παραγγελία not being the one there hinted at, for that was one not given *to* Timotheus, but *to be given by* him. Nor is it that in ver. 5, for that is introduced as regarding a matter quite different from the present—viz. the aberrations of the false teachers, who do not here appear till the exhortation to Timotheus is over. What this command is, is plain from the following This command I commit (as a deposit, to be faithfully guarded and kept: see ref. 2 Tim. and ch. vi. 20: Herod. vi. 86, beginning) to thee, son Timotheus (see on ver. 2), according to (in pursuance of these words belong to παρατίθεμαί σοι, not as Œc, Flatt, al, to ἵνα στρατεύῃ below) the former prophecies concerning thee (the directions, or, prophecies properly so called, of the Holy Spirit, which were spoken concerning Timotheus at his first conversion, or at his admission [cf ch iv. 11] into the ministry, by the προφῆται in the church We have instances of such prophetic intimations in Acts xiii 1, 2,—[xi 28,] —xxi 10, 11. By such intimations, spoken perhaps by Silas, who was with him, and who was a προφήτης [Acts xv 32], may St. Paul have been first induced to take Timotheus to him as a companion, Acts xvi. 3 All other meanings, which it has been attempted to give to προφητείας, are unwarranted, and beside the purpose here as e. g '*the good hopes conceived of thee,*' Heinrichs The ἐπὶ σέ belongs to προφητείας, the preposition of motion being easily accounted for by the *reference to a subject* implied in the word), that thou mayest (purpose, and at the same time purport, of the παραγγελία cf. note, 1 Cor xiv 13, and Ellicott on Eph i 16) war (στρατεύεσθαι, of the whole business of the employed soldier; not merely of fighting, properly so called) in them (not as De W. '*by virtue of them,*' but as Mack, Matth, and Wies, '*in,*' as clad with them, as if they were his defence and confirmation This is not zu kämpfen, as Huther, seeing that the whole expression is figurative) the good warfare (not, as Conyb, 'fight the good fight,'—by which same words he renders the very different expression in 2 Tim. iv 7, τὸν ἀγῶνα τὸν καλὸν ἠγώνισμαι It is the *whole campaign,* not the fight alone, which is here spoken of), holding fast (more than '*having*,' but we must hardly, as Matth, carry on the metaphor and think of the shield of faith Eph vi 16, such continuation being rendered unlikely by the unmetaphorical character of τὴν ἀγαθὴν συνείδησιν) faith (subjective: cf περὶ τὴν πίστιν below) and good conscience (cf. ver. 5),—which (latter, viz. *good conscience*—not, both) some having thrust from them (there is something in the word implying the violence of the act required, and the importunity of conscience, reluctant to be so extruded. So Bengel · 'recedit invita: semper dicit, noli me lædere') made shipwreck (the similitude is so common a one, that it is hardly necessary to extend the figure of a shipwreck beyond the word itself, nor to find in ἀπωσάμενοι allusions to a rudder, anchor, &c. See examples in Wetst) concerning (see reff, and cf. Acts xix 25, οἱ περὶ τὰ τοιαῦτα ἐργάται, also Luke x. 40 The same is elsewhere expressed by ἐν,—so Diog Laert v. 2 14, ἐν τοῖς ἰδίοις μάλα νεναυαγηκώς,—Plut. Symp i 4, ἐν οἷς τὰ πλεῖστα ναυαγεῖ συμπόσια See other examples in Kypke: Winer, edn 6, § 49 i · and Ellicott's note here) the faith (objective) · of whom (genitive partitive. among whom) is Hymenæus (there is a Hymenæus mentioned 2 Tim. ii 17, in conjunction

ἐστιν Ὑμέναιος καὶ Ἀλέξανδρος, οὓς [y] παρέδωκα τῷ Σατανᾷ, ἵνα [z] παιδευθῶσι μὴ [a] βλασφημεῖν.

II. 1 [b] Παρακαλῶ οὖν [c] πρῶτον πάντων [d] ποιεῖσθαι

ADFK LℵN a b c d e f g h k l m n o 17

y = 1 Cor v 5 Luke xxiii 25 1 Chron xii 27 z 1 Cor xi 32 2 Cor vi 9 2 Tim ii 25 Heb xii 6, 7, 10 Rev iii 19 Prov xix 18 a absol, Acts xxvi 11 (Paul) Matt ix 3 al 2 Macc x 34 b ch i 3 reff c Rom i 8 1 Cor xi 18 d Phil i 4

CHAP II 1. παρακαλει D[1]F sah lat-ff$_5$. om 1st παντων F Orig$_1$.

with Philetus, as an heretical teacher There is no reason to distinguish him from this one. nor any difficulty occasioned [De W] by the fact of his being here παραδοθεὶς τῷ σατανᾷ, and there mentioned as overthrowing the faith of many He would probably go on with his evil teaching in spite of the Apostle's sentence, which could carry weight with those only who were sound in the faith) **and Alexander** (in all probability identical with Ἀλέξανδρος ὁ χαλκεύς, 2 Tim iv. 14. There is nothing against it in what is there said of him [against De Wette]. He appears there to have been an adversary of the Apostle, who had withstood and injured him at his late visit to Ephesus but there is no reason why he should not have been still under this sentence at that time) **whom I delivered over to Satan** (there does not seem to be, as almost always taken for granted, any necessary assertion of excommunication properly so called The delivering to Satan, as in 1 Cor. v. 5, seems to have been an apostolic act, for the purpose of active punishment, in order to correction. It might or might not be accompanied by extrusion from the church it appears to have been thus accompanied in 1 Cor v. 5 —but the two must not be supposed identical The upholders of such identity allege the fact of Satan's empire being conceived as including all outside the church [Acts xxvi. 18 al.]. but such expressions are too vague to be adduced as applying to a direct assertion like this Satan, the adversary, is evidently regarded as the buffeter and tormentor, cf. 2 Cor. xii 7—ever ready, unless his hand were held, to distress and afflict God's people,—and ready therefore, when thus let loose by one having power over him, to execute punishment with all his malignity.

Observe that the verb is not perfect but aorist. He did this when he was last at Ephesus. On the ecclesiastical questions here involved, Ellic. has, as usual, some very useful references) **that they may be disciplined** (the subj. after the aorist indicates that the effect of what was done still abides, the sentence was not yet taken off, nor the παίδευσις at an end

παιδεύω, as in reff, *to instruct by punishment, to discipline*) **not to blaspheme** (God, or Christ, whose holy name was brought to shame by these men associating it with unholy and unclean doctrines).

CH. II. 1—15] *General regulations respecting public intercessory prayers for all men* (1—4)· *from which he digresses into a proof of the universality of the gospel* (4—7)—*then returns to the part to be taken by the male sex in public prayer* (8): *which leads him to treat of the proper place and subjection of women* (9—15) **I exhort then** ('οὖν is without any logical connexion,' says De W Certainly,—with what immediately precedes; but the account to be given of it is, that it takes up the general subject of the Epistle, q d, 'what I have then to say to thee by way of command and regulation, is this·' see 2 Tim ii 1. "The particle οὖν has its proper collective force ['ad ea, quæ antea posita sunt, lectorem revocat' Klotz.]: 'continuation and retrospect,' Donaldson, Gr § 601" Ellic), **first of all** (to be joined with **παρακαλῶ**, not, as Chr. [τί δ' ἐστὶ τὸ πρῶτον πάντων; τουτέστιν, ἐν τῇ λατρείᾳ τῇ καθημερινῇ], Thl, Calv., Est, Bengel, Conyb., E. V., and Luther, with **ποιεῖσθαι**, in which case, besides other objections, the verb would certainly have followed all the substantives, and probably would have taken πρῶτον πάντων with it It is, in order and importance, his first exhortation) **to make** (cf. ref. Phil It has been usual to take **ποιεῖσθαι** *passive*. and most Commentators pass over the word without remark. In such a case, the appeal must be to our sense of the propriety of the middle or passive meaning, according to the arrangement of the words, and spirit of the sentence. And thus I think we shall decide for the middle In the prominent position of ποιεῖσθαι, if it were passive, and consequently objective in meaning, 'that prayer, &c be made,' it can hardly be passed over without an emphasis, which here it manifestly cannot have. If on the other hand it is middle, it is subjective, belonging to the person or persons who are implied in παρακαλῶ and thus serves only as a word of passage to the more important substantives which follow And in this

[d,e,f] δεήσεις, [e,f] προσευχάς, [g] ἐντεύξεις, [e,h] εὐχαριστίας, ὑπὲρ
πάντων ἀνθρώπων, 2 ὑπὲρ βασιλέων καὶ πάντων τῶν
ἐν [i] ὑπεροχῇ ὄντων, ἵνα [k] ἤρεμον καὶ [l] ἡσύχιον βίον

e Phil iv 6. f Phil as above (e). ch v 5. 2 Chron vi. 19. g ch iv 5 only †. 2 Macc iv 8 only. ἐντεύξεις ἐποιεῖτο πρὸς τὸν βασιλέα, Polyb v 35 4. see Rom viii 26, 34. xi 2. h = Eph v 4 reff. i 1 Cor ii 1 only. 1 Kings ii 3 F. 2 Macc xiii 6. (-χειν, Rom xiii 1.) k here only † (-ια, Job iv 16 Symm.). l 1 Pet iii iv only. Isa lxvi 2 only. (-ια, vv 11, 12.)

2 om 1st εν F k 109[2] lect-7. ηρεμιον F.

way the Greek fathers themselves took it: e. g. Chrys.—πῶς ὑπὲρ παντὸς τοῦ κόσμου, καὶ βασιλέων, κ.τ.λ. ποιούμεθα τὴν δέησιν) supplications, prayers, intercessions (the two former words, δεήσεις and προσευχαί, are perhaps best distinguished as in Eph. vi. 18, by taking προσευχή for *prayer* in general, δέησις for *supplication* or *petition*, the special content of any particular prayer. See Ellicott's note cited there, and cf. ref. Phil. ἐντεύξεις, judging from the cognate verbs ἐντυγχάνω, and ὑπερεντυγχάνω (reff. Rom.), should be marked with a reference to 'request concerning *others*,' i. e. *intercessory* prayer. [Ellic. denies this primary reference, supporting his view by ch. iv. 5, where, he says, such a meaning would be inappropriate. But is not the meaning in that very place most appropriate? It is not their intercession for a *person*: but it is by ἔντευξις, prayer on its behalf and over it, that πᾶν κτίσμα is hallowed. The meaning in Polybius, copiously illustrated by Raphel, an *interview* or appointed meeting, *compellatio aliqua de re*, would in the N. T., where the word and its cognates are always used in reference to prayer, for persons or things, necessarily shade off into that of pleading or intercession.] Very various and minute distinctions between the three have been imagined:—e. g. Theodoret.—δέησις μέν ἐστιν ὑπὲρ ἀπαλλαγῆς τινῶν λυπηρῶν ἱκετεία προσφερομένη· προσευχὴ δέ, αἴτησις ἀγαθῶν· ἔντευξις δέ, κατηγορία τῶν ἀδικούντων.—Origen, περὶ εὐχῆς, § 14 [not 44, as in Wetst. and Huther], vol. i. p. 220,—ἡγοῦμαι τοίνυν, δέησιν μὲν εἶναι τὴν ἐλλείποντός τινι μεθ' ἱκετείας περὶ τοῦ ἐκείνου τυχεῖν ἀναπεμπομένην εὐχήν· τὴν δὲ προσευχήν, τὴν μετὰ δοξολογίας περὶ μειζόνων μεγαλοφυέστερον ἀναπεμπομένην ὑπό του· ἔντευξιν δέ, τὴν ὑπὸ παῤῥησίαν τινὰ πλείονα ἔχοντος περί τινων ἀξίωσιν πρὸς θεόν κ. τ. λ. The most extraordinary of all is Aug.'s view, that the four words refer to the liturgical form of administration of the Holy Communion—δεήσεις being "*precationes* . . . quas facimus in celebratione sacramentorum antequam illud quod est in Domini mensa incipiat benedici.—*orationes* [προσευχαί], cum benedicitur et sanctificatur . . . *interpellationes* vel . . *postulationes* [ἐντεύξεις], fiunt cum populus benedicitur: . . . quibus peractis, et participato tanto sacramento, εὐχαριστία, *gratiarum actio*, cuncta concludit." Ep. cxlix. [lix.] 16, vol. ii. p. 636 f), thanksgivings, for all men (this gives the intercessory character to all that have preceded. On the wideness of Christian benevolence here inculcated, see the argument below, and Tit. iii. 2); for (i. e. 'especially for'—this one particular class being mentioned and no other) kings (see Tit. iii. 1, Rom. xiii. 1 ff.; 1 Pet. ii. 13. It was especially important that the Christians should include earthly powers in their formal public prayers, both on account of the object to be gained by such prayer [see next clause], and as an effectual answer to those adversaries who accused them of rebellious tendencies. Jos. [B. J. ii. 10. 4] gives the Jews' answer to Petronius, Ἰουδαῖοι περὶ μὲν Καίσαρος καὶ τοῦ δήμου τῶν Ῥωμαίων δὶς τῆς ἡμέρας θύειν ἔφασαν, and afterwards [ib. 17. 2], he ascribes the origin of the war to their refusing, at the instigation of Eleazar, to continue the sacrifices offered on behalf of their Gentile rulers. See Wetst., who gives other examples: and compare the ancient liturgies—e. g. the bidding prayers, Bingham, book xv. 1. 2: the consecration prayer, ib. 3. 1, and on the general practice, ib. 3. 14. '*Kings*' must be taken generally, as it is indeed generalized in the following words: not understood to mean '*Cæsar and his assessors in the supreme power*,' as Baur, who deduces thence an argument that the Epistle was written under the Antonines, when such an association was usual) and all that are in eminence (not absolutely in *authority*, though the context, no less than common sense, shews that it would be so. Cf. Polyb. v. 41. 3,—τοῖς ἐν ὑπεροχαῖς οὖσι περὶ τὴν αὐλήν. He, as well as Josephus [e. g. Antt. vi. 4. 3], uses ὑπεροχαί absolutely for authorities: see Schweigh. Lex. Polyb. Thdrt. gives a curious reason for the addition of these words: μάλα σοφῶς τὸ κοινὸν τῶν ἀνθρώπων προστέθεικεν, ἵνα μή τις κολα-

m διάγωμεν ἐν n πάσῃ o εὐσεβείᾳ καὶ p σεμνότητι. 3 τοῦτο
γὰρ q καλὸν καὶ r ἀποδεκτὸν s ἐνώπιον τοῦ t σωτῆρος
ἡμῶν t θεοῦ, 4 ὃς πάντας ἀνθρώπους θέλει σωθῆναι καὶ

ADFK Lℵ a b c d e f g h k l m n o 17

m Tit iii 3 only ‡ 2 Macc xii 38 n = Phil i 20 reff o Paul, ch iii 16 iv 7, 8 vi 3 5, 6, 11 2 Tim iii 5 Tit i 1 only Acts iii 12 2 Pet i 3, 6, 7 iii 11 only Isa xi 2 (-βεῖν, ch v 4 -βής, Acts x 2 -βῶς, 2 Tim iii 12) p ch iii 4 Tit ii 7 only † 2 Macc iii 12 only (-νος, ch iii 8) q = Rom xiv 21 2 Cor viii 21 Isa v 20 r ch v 4 only † (δοχή, ch i 15 -δέχεσθαι Acts ii 41) s = Luke xvi 15 Acts iv 19 ch v 4 1 John iii 22 3 Kings iii 10 t ch i 1 reff

om πασῃ D1
3 om γαρ Aℵ1 17 672 coptt Cyr2

κείαν νομίσῃ τὴν ὑπὲρ τῶν βασιλέων εὐχήν. The succeeding clause furnishes reason enough the security of Christians would often be more dependent on inferior officers than even on kings themselves), **that** (aim of the prayer—not, as Heydenreich and Matthies,—subjective, that by such prayer Christian men's minds may be tranquillized and disposed to obey,—but objective, that we may obtain the blessing mentioned, by God's influencing the hearts of our rulers or as Chrys, that we may be in security by their being preserved in safety) **we may pass** (more than '*lead*' [ἄγειν] it includes the whole of the period spoken of —thus Aristoph Vesp. 1006 [see also Eccles. 240], ὥσθ' ἡδέως διάγειν σε τὸν λοιπὸν χρόνον,—Soph Œd Col 1615, τὸ λοιπὸν ἤδη τὸν βίον διάξετον see numerous other examples in Wetst) **a quiet** (the adjective ἤρεμος is a late word, formed on the classical adverb ἠρέμα, the proper adjective of which is ἠρεμαῖος, used by Plat Rep p 307 a, Legg 734 a &c Cf Palm and Rost's Lex. sub voce) **and tranquil life** (ἐκείνων γὰρ πρυτανευόντων εἰρήνην, μεταλαγχάνομεν καὶ ὑμεῖς τῆς γαλήνης, καὶ ἐν ἡσυχίᾳ τῆς εὐσεβείας ἐκπληροῦμεν τοὺς νόμους, Thdrt On the distinction between ἤρεμος, tranquil from trouble *without*, and ἡσύχιος, from trouble *within*, see Ellicott's note) **in all** ('possible,' 'requisite') **piety** (I prefer this rendering to '*godliness*,' as more literal, and because I would reserve that word as the proper one for θεοσέβεια see ver 10 below εὐσέβεια is one of the terms peculiar in this meaning to the pastoral Epistles, the second Epistle of Peter [reff], and Peter's speech in Acts iii 12 See Prolegg, and note on Acts iii 12) **and gravity** (so Conyb and it seems best to express the meaning For as Chrys.,—εἰ γὰρ μὴ ἐσώζοντο, μηδὲ εὐδοκίμουν ἐν τοῖς πολέμοις, ἀνάγκη καὶ τὰ ἡμέτερα ἐν ταραχαῖς εἶναι καὶ θορύβοις. ἢ γὰρ καὶ αὐτοὺς ἡμᾶς στρατεύεσθαι ἔδει, κατακοπέντων ἐκείνων· ἢ φεύγειν πανταχοῦ καὶ πλανᾶσθαι and thus the gravity and decorum of the Christian life would be broken up).

3, 4] **For this** (viz. ποιεῖσθαι δεήσεις κ.τ.λ. ὑπὲρ πάντων ἀνθρώπων, &c. ver. 1· what has followed since being merely the continuation of this) **is good and acceptable** (both adjectives are to be taken with ἐνώπιον, &c, not as De W and Ellic. '**καλόν**, *good in and of itself*' compare ref 2 Cor, καλὰ οὐ μόνον ἐνώπιον κυρίου, ἀλλὰ καὶ ἐνώπιον ἀνθρώπων. I still hold, against Ellicott, to this connexion, shrinking from the crude and ill-balanced form of the sentence which the other would bring in. **ἀποδεκτόν**, peculiar [cf. ἀποδοχή, ch i 15] to these Epistles See 2 Cor vi 2) **in the sight of our Saviour** (a title manifestly chosen as belonging to the matter in hand, cf next verse On it, see ch i 1) **God who** (i e. seeing that He) **willeth all men to be saved** (see ch iv. 10: Tit. ii 11. πάντας ἀνθρώπους is repeated from verse 1 Chrys's comment is very noble μιμοῦ τὸν θεόν. εἰ πάντας ἀνθρώπους θέλει σωθῆναι, εἰκότως ὑπὲρ ἁπάντων δεῖ εὔχεσθαι εἰ πάντας αὐτὸς ἠθέλε σωθῆναι, θέλε καὶ σύ εἰ δὲ θέλεις, εὔχου τῶν γὰρ τοιούτων ἐστὶ τὸ εὔχεσθαι Huther rightly remarks, that Mosheim's view, "nisi pax in orbe terrarum vigeat, fieri nullo modo posse ut voluntati divinæ quæ omnium hominum salutem cupit, satisfiat," destroys the true context and train of thought see more below Wiesinger remarks σωθῆναι,—not σῶσαι, as in Tit iii 5, as adapted to the mediatorial effect of prayer, not direct divine agency: but we may go yet further, and say that by θέλει πάντας ἀνθρ σωθῆναι is expressed human acceptance of offered salvation, on which even God's predestination is contingent. θέλει σῶσαι πάντας could not have been said: if so, He *would* have saved all, in matter of fact. See the remarks, and references to English and other divines, in Ellicott's note Calvin most unworthily shuffles out of the decisive testimony borne by this passage to universal redemption. "Apostolus simpliciter intelligit nullum mundi vel populum vel ordinem salute excludi, quia omnibus sine

εἰς [u] ἐπίγνωσιν [v] ἀληθείας ἐλθεῖν. 5 εἷς γὰρ θεός, εἷς καὶ
[w] μεσίτης θεοῦ καὶ ἀνθρώπων, ἄνθρωπος χριστὸς Ἰησοῦς,
6 ὁ [x] δοὺς [x] ἑαυτὸν [y] ἀντίλυτρον ὑπὲρ πάντων, τὸ [z] μαρτύ-

u = Rom iii 20. Eph i 17 reff. 2 Macc ix. 11. v 2 Tim ii 25. iii 7. Tit i 1. Heb x 26. w Gal iii 19, 20 reff. x = Gal i 4. Tit ii 14. 1 Macc vi 44. y here only† (λυτρ., Matt xx 28). z = 1 Cor i 6. ii 1. 2 Tim i 8.

5 ιησ bef χρ K b f 114 115 Syr Chr Thdrt-ms Thl.
6 om υπερ L. for το, και ℵ[1] om το μαρτυριον A pref οὗ D[1]F 80 115 vulg-

exceptione evangelium proponi Deus velit. De hominum generibus, non singulis personis sermo est, nihil enim aliud intendit, quam principes et extraneos populos in hoc numero includere." As if kings and all in eminence were not in each case individual men), and **to come to (the) certain knowledge** (on ἐπίγνωσις, fuller and more assured than γνῶσις, see 1 Cor. xiii 12: Col i. 11, ii 2) **of (the) truth** (the expression is a favourite one in these Epistles, see reff. This realization of the truth is in fact identical with σωτηρία, not only [Huther] as that σωτηρία is a *rescue* from life in untruth, but in its deepest and widest sense of *salvation*, here and hereafter cf. John xvii 3, αὕτη ἐστὶν ἡ αἰώνιος ζωή, ἵνα γινώσκωσίν σε τὸν μόνον ἀληθινὸν θεόν . . . . . and ib. 17, ἁγίασον αὐτοὺς ἐν τῇ ἀληθείᾳ).

5.] **For** (further grounding of the acceptableness of prayer for *all* men,—in the UNITY of God But this verse is joined by the γάρ directly to the preceding, not to ver. 1. Chrys. gives it rightly—δεικνὺς ὅτι σωθῆναι θέλει πάντας) **there is** ONE **God** (He is ONE in essence and one in purpose—not of different minds to different nations or individuals, but of one mind towards all Similarly Rom. iii. 30, and, which is important for the understanding of that difficult passage, Gal. iii 20 The double reference, to the unity in essence and unity of purpose, for which I have contended there, is plain and unmistakeable here), ONE **Mediator** (see reff. It occurs, besides the places in the Gal, only in the Epistle to the Heb., viii 6, ix 15; xii. 24 There is no necessity that the idea should, as De W and Schleierm, be connected with that of a mutual covenant, and so be here far-fetched as regards the context [borrowed from the places in the Heb., according to De W] the word is used as standing alone, and representing the fact of Christ Jesus being the only *go-between*, in whatever sense) **also** (the εἷς prefixed to the καί for emphasis) **of** (between) **God and men** (if one only goes between, then that One must be for *all*), **(the) man Christ Jesus** (why ἄνθρωπος? Thdrt answers, ἄνθρωπον δὲ τὸν χριστὸν ὠνόμασεν, ἐπειδὴ μεσίτην ἐκάλεσεν· ἐνανθρωπήσας γὰρ ἐμεσίτευσεν· and so most Commentators. But it is not here the Apostle's object, to set forth the nature of Christ's mediation as regards its being brought about,—only as regards its unity and universality for mankind. And for this latter reason he calls him here by this name MAN,—that He gathered up all our human nature into Himself, becoming its second Head. So that the ἄνθρωπος in fact carries with it the very strongest proof of that which he is maintaining. Notice it is not ὁ ἄνθρωπος, though we are obliged inaccurately thus to express it in personality, our Lord was not *a man*, but in nature He was man. It might be rendered, "Christ Jesus, Himself man."

I should object, as against Ellicott, to introduce *at all* the indefinite article not *individual* but *generic* humanity is predicated: and "a man" unavoidably conveys the idea of human individuality. It is singularly unfortunate that Ellic. should have referred to Augustine, Serm xxvi. as cited by Wordsw., in corroboration of the rendering "a man" the Latin *homo* being of course as incapable of deciding this as the Greek ἄνθρωπος, and "*a man*" being only Dr. Wordsworth's translation of it. Nay, the whole tenor of the passage of Augustine (ed Migne, vol v. p 174) precludes such a rendering The stupidity of such writers as Baur and the Socinians, who regard such an expression as against the deity of Christ, is beyond all power of mine to characterize. In the face of εἷς θεός, εἷς μεσίτης θεοῦ καὶ ἀνθρώπων, to maintain gravely such a position, shews utter blindness from party bias even to the plainest thoughts expressed in the plainest words), **who gave himself** (reff, especially Tit) **a ransom** (ἀντί-, as in ἀντιμισθία, Rom i 27, 2 Cor vi 13· ἀντάλλαγμα, Matt xvi 26, expresses more distinctly the reciprocity which is already implied in the simple word in each case That the main fact alluded to here is the *death* of Christ, we know but it is not brought into prominence, being included in, and superseded by the far greater and more comprehensive

ριον [a] καιροῖς [a] ἰδίοις, 7 [b] εἰς ὃ [c] ἐτέθην ἐγὼ [cd] κήρυξ καὶ
[c] ἀπόστολος ([e] ἀλήθειαν λέγω, οὐ [ef] ψεύδομαι), [c] διδάσκαλος
[c] ἐθνῶν [g] ἐν πίστει καὶ ἀληθείᾳ. 8 [h] Βούλομαι οὖν προς-

ADΓK LℵA b c d e f g h k l m n o 17

a Gal vi 9. ch vi 15. Tit i 3 only. χρωμενοι τοις ιδιοις καιροις, Polyb i 30. 10. b ch i 12 reff. c 2 Tim i 11. d 2 Tim as above. 2 Pet ii 5 only. Gen xli 43. Dan iii 4. Sir xx 14 only. e Rom ix 1. f Gal i 20 reff. g ch i 2 reff. h = ch. v 14. Tit iii 8.

sixt(with harl¹, not F-lat) Ambrst. aft ιδιοις ins εδοθη D¹F harl¹ Ambrst.
7 for εις ὁ, εν ω F latt. for ετεθην, επιστευθην A. rec aft λεγω ins εν χριστω (*from Rom* ix. 1), with D³KLℵ¹ rel goth Thdrt om AD¹Fℵ³ c n 67² latt syrr coptt æth Chr Damasc Thl Œc Ambrst Pelag. for πιστει, πνευματι A: γνωσι ℵ.

fact, that He gave HIMSELF, in all that He undertook for our redemption: see Phil ii. 5–8) **on behalf of all** (not of a portion of mankind, but of *all men*, the point of ver 1, ὑπὲρ πάντων ἀνθρώπων), —**the testimony** ('that which was [to be] testified:' so St John frequently uses μαρτυρία, 1 John v. 9–11 "an accusative in apposition with the preceding sentence," Ellicott. This oneness of the Mediator, involving in itself the universality of Redemption, was the great subject of Christian testimony: see below) **in its own seasons** (reff; in the times which God had appointed for it. On the *temporal dative*, see Ellicott's note), **for** (towards) **which** (the μαρτύριον) **I was placed as a herald** (pastoral Epistles and 2 Pet. only but see 1 Cor i. 21, 23, ix 27, xv 14) **and apostle** (the proclaiming this universality of the Gospel was the one object towards which my appointment as an apostle and preacher was directed. Those who hold the spuriousness of our Epistle regard this returning to himself and his own case on the part of the writer as an evidence of his being one who was acting the part of Paul. So Schleierm and De W. They have so far truth on their side, that we must recognize here a characteristic increase of the frequency of these personal vindications on the part of the Apostle, as we so often have occasion to remark during these Epistles —the disposition of one who had been long opposed and worried by adversaries to recur continually to his own claims, the assertion of which had now become with him almost, so to speak, a matter of stock-phrases. Still, the propriety of the assertion here is evident: it is only in the manner of it that the above habit is discernible. See more on this in the Prolegomena. The same phrase occurs verbatim in ref 2 Tim),—**I speak the truth, I lie not**—(in spite of all that Huther and Wiesinger say of the evident appropriateness of this solemn asseveration here, I own I am unable to regard it as any more than a strong and interesting proof of the growth of a habit in the Apostle's mind, which we already trace in 2 Cor. xi. 31, Rom. ix. 1, till he came to use the phrase with less force and relevance than he had once done. Nothing can be more natural than that one whose life was spent in strong conflict and assertion of his Apostleship, should repeat the fervour of his usual asseveration, even when the occasion of that fervour had passed away. Nor can I consent to abandon such a view because it is designated "questionable and precarious" by Ellic., who is too apt in cases of difficulty, to evade the real conflict of decision by strong terms of this kind)—**a teacher of the Gentiles** (it was especially in this latter fact that the ὑπὲρ πάντων ἀνθρώπων found its justification. The historical proof of his constitution as a teacher of the Gentiles is to be found in Acts ix 15, xxii 21, xxvi 17; but especially in Gal ii. 9) **in (the) faith and (the) truth** (do these words refer subjectively to his own conduct in teaching the Gentiles, or objectively to that in which he was to instruct them? The former view is taken by Thdrt. and most Commentators: μετὰ τῆς προσηκούσης πίστεως καὶ ἀληθείας τοῦτο πᾶσι προσφέρω: the latter by Heydenreich, al. Huther [also Ellic.] takes the words as signifying the *sphere in which* he was appointed to fulfil his office of διδ ἐθνῶν,—πίστις being *faith*, the subjective relation, and ἀλήθεια *the truth*, the objective good which is appropriated by faith. Wiesinger, as meaning that he is, in the right faith and in the truth, the διδ. ἐθν. Bengel regards them merely as another asseveration belonging to the assertion that he is διδ ἐθν.,—'in faith and truth I say it.' This latter at once discommends itself, from its exceeding flatness though Chrys. also seems to have held it—ἐν πίστει πάλιν· ἀλλὰ μὴ νομίσῃς ἐπειδὴ ἐν πίστει ἤκουσας, ὅτι ἀπάτη τὸ πρᾶγμά ἐστι. καὶ γὰρ ἐν ἀληθείᾳ φησίν. εἰ δὲ ἀλήθεια, οὐκ ἔστι ψεῦδος. In judging between these, we must take

εύχεσθαι τοὺς ἄνδρας ἐν παντὶ τόπῳ, ˡ ἐπαίροντας ᵏ ὁσίους
ˡ χεῖρας ˡ χωρὶς ὀργῆς καὶ ˡᵐ διαλογισμοῦ. 9 ⁿ ὡςαύτως
καὶ γυναῖκας ᵒ ἐν ᵖ καταστολῇ ᑫ κοσμίῳ ʳ μετὰ ˢ αἰδοῦς

l Luke xxiv 50 Ps lxii 4 (5) k Acts ii 27 xiii 34, 35 Tit i 8 Heb vii 26 Rev xv 4 xvi 5 only Prov xxii 11 θεοῖς ὁσίας δεξιὰς κ ἀριστερὰς ανίσχοντες, Demosth Meid 302 l Phil ii 14 m = Phil as above Luke xxiv 38 n = ch iii 8, 11 Tit ii 3, 6 Prov xxvii 15 o = Matt vi 29 Tit i 6 p here only Isa lxi 3 only see note q ch iii 2 only Eccl xii 9 only r Mark iii 5, &c. 1 Chron xxix 22 s here (Heb. xii 28 v r) only †

8 διαλογισμων FℵB3 a c 17. 67[2] syr copt Orig$_4$ Eus Mac Bas Thdrt$_2$ Damasc-comm Jer: txt ADKLℵ[1] rel vulg spec goth Orig$_3$ Chr. (*The plur is every where used in the N. T. except here and Luke ix. 46, 47. hence appy the alteration*)

9 om 1st και Aℵ[1] 17 Clem. rec ins τας bef γυναικας (*to suit τους ανδρας above*), with KL rel Chr Thdrt. om AD[1]Fℵ 17 67[2] Clem Orig$_2$. κοσμιως D[1]Fℵ[3] 17

into account the usage of ἀλήθεια above, ver 4, in a very similar reference, when it was to be matter of teaching to all men There it undoubtedly is, though anarthrous, *the truth* of God. I would therefore take it similarly here, as Wiesinger, —the sphere in which both his teaching and their learning was to be employed—*the truth of the Gospel* Then, if so, it is surely harsh to make ἐν πίστει subjective, especially as the ἐν is not repeated before ἀληθείᾳ It too will most properly be objective,—and likewise regard that in which, as an element or sphere, he was to teach and they to learn *the faith*. This ἐν π κ ἀλ will be, not the object of διδάσκαλ, but the sphere or element in which he is the διδάσκαλος) 8.] See summary at beginning of chapter **I will then** ("in βούλομαι the active wish is implied · it is no mere willingness or acquiescence," Ellic. On the distinction between βούλομαι and θέλω, see Donaldson, Cratyl. § 463, p. 650 f ed. 2 and Ellic. on ch. v 14) **that the men** (the E. V by omitting the article, has entirely obscured this passage for its English readers, not one in a hundred of whom ever dream of a distinction of the sexes being here intended But again the position of τοὺς ἄνδρας forbids us from supposing that such distinction was the Apostle's main object in this verse. Had it been so, we should have read τοὺς ἄνδρας προσεύχεσθαι As it now stands, the stress is on προσεύχεσθαι, and τοὺς ἄνδρας is taken for granted Thus the main subject of ver 1 is carried on, the duty of PRAYER, in general—not [as Schleierm objects] one portion merely of it, the allotting it to its proper offerers) **pray in every place** (these words ἐν παντὶ τόπῳ regard the general duty of praying, not the particular detail implied in τοὺς ἄνδρας · still less are we to join τοὺς ἄνδρας [τοὺς] ἐν παντὶ τόπῳ. It is a *local* command respecting prayer, answering to the temporal command ἀδιαλείπτως προσεύχεσθε, 1 Thess. v. 17 It is far-fetched and irrelevant to the context to find in the words, as Chr, Thdrt, al., Pcl., Erasm., Calv., Beza, Grot., al, the Christian's freedom from prescription of place for prayer—πρὸς τὴν νομικὴν διαγόρευσιν τέθεικεν· οὐ γὰρ [vulgo ὃς γὰρ] τοῖς Ἱεροσολύμοις περιέγραψε τὴν λατρείαν, Thdrt: and Chrys, ὅπερ τοῖς Ἰουδαίοις θέμις οὐκ ἦν), **lifting up holy hands** (see LXX, ref. Ps. also Ps xxvii. 2, xliii 20, Clem Rom Ep 1 to Corinthians, ch 29, p 269 · προσέλθωμεν αὐτῷ ἐν ὁσιότητι ψυχῆς, ἁγνὰς καὶ ἀμιάντους χεῖρας αἴροντες πρὸς αὐτόν. These two passages, as Huther observes, testify to the practice in the Christian church The form ὁσίους with a feminine is unusual but we must not, as Winer suggests [edn 6, § 11. 1], join it to ἐπαίροντας His own instances, στρατιὰ οὐράνιος, Luke ii 13,—ἶρις ὅμοιος λίθῳ, Rev iv 3, furnish some precedent and the fact that the ending -ιος is common to all three establishes an analogy "Those hands are holy, which have not surrendered themselves as instruments of evil desire: the contrary are βέβηλοι χεῖρες, 2 Macc. v 16 compare, for the expression, Job xvii 9, Ps xxiii. 4, and in the N T, especially James iv 8, καθαρίσατε χεῖρας καὶ ἁγνίσατε καρδίας" Huther. See classical passages in Wetst) **without** (separate from, "putting away," as Conyb) **wrath and disputation** (i. e in tranquillity and mutual peace, so literally, *sine disceptatione*, as vulg., see note on ref. Phil Ellic's objection, that we should thus import from the context a meaning unconfirmed by good lexical authority, is fully met by the unquestionable usage of the verb διαλογίζω in the N T. for to *dispute*. At the same time, seeing that the matter treated of is *prayer*, where *disputing* hardly seems in place, perhaps *doubting* is the better sense, which, after all, is a disputation within one's self). 9.] **So also** (ὡςαύτως, by the parallel passage, Tit ii 3, seems to be little more than a copula, not

καὶ [t] σωφροσύνης [u] κοσμεῖν ἑαυτάς, μὴ [v] ἐν [v] πλέγμασιν
καὶ [w] χρυσῷ ἢ [x] μαργαρίταις ἢ [y] ἱματισμῷ [z] πολυτελεῖ,
10 ἀλλ' ὃ [a] πρέπει γυναιξὶν [b] ἐπαγγελλομέναις [c] θεοσέβειαν,

ADFK LℵA b c d e f g h k l m n o 17

t Acts xxvi. 25 (Paul). ver. 15 only †. 2 Macc. iv. 37 only. u Matt. xii. 44 || L. xxiii. 29. xxv. 7. Luke xxi. 5. Tit. ii. 10. 1 Pet. iii. 5. Rev. xxi. 2, 19 only. Ezek. xvi. 11, 13. v here only. Isa. xxviii. 5 Aq. Theod. w Paul, Acts xvii. 29. 1 Cor. iii. 12 only. Matt. ii. 11 al. Sir. xlv. 10. x Matt. vii. 6. xiii 45, 46. Rev. xvii. 4. xviii. 12, 16. xxi. 21 bis only †. y Luke vii. 25. ix. 29. John xix. 24, from Ps. xxi. 18. Acts xx. 33 only. Ps. xliv. 9. z Mark xiv. 3. 1 Pet. iii. 4 only. Prov. i. 13. a Eph. v. 3 reff. b = ch. vi. 21 (Tit. i. 2 reff.) only ‡. c here only. Job xxviii. 28. Gen. xx. 11. (-βής, John ix. 31.)

Orig-ms$_1$: -ιων K. καταπλεγμασιν A. rec (for 3rd και) η, with D²KL rel G-lat(altern) syr goth Clem: om 17: txt AD¹Fℵ Syr (copt) Orig. χρυσιω (*from* 1 *Pet* iii. 3) AF 17 Chr-ms Thl-ms: txt DKLℵ rel Clem Orig.

necessarily to refer to the matter which has been last under treatment) **I will that women** (without the article, the reference to *τοὺς ἄνδρας* above is not so pointed: i. e. we need not imagine that the reference is necessarily to the same matter of detail, but may regard the verse [see below] as being to the general duties and behaviour of women, as not belonging to the category of *οἱ προσευχόμενοι ἐν παντὶ τόπῳ*) **adorn themselves** (there is no need, as Chrys. and most Commentators, to supply *προσεύχεσθαι* to complete the sense: indeed if I have apprehended the passage rightly, it would be altogether irrelevant. The *ὡσαύτως* serving merely as a copula [see above], the *προσεύχεσθαι* belonging solely and emphatically to *τοὺς ἄνδρας*,—the question, 'what then are women to do?' is answered by insisting on modesty of appearance and the ornament of good works, as contrasted [ver. 12] with the man's part. The public assemblies are doubtless, in ver. 12, still before the Apostle's mind, but in a very slight degree. It is the general duties of women, rather than any single point in reference to their conduct in public worship, to which he is calling attention: though the subject of public worship led to his thus speaking, and has not altogether disappeared from his thoughts. According to this view, the construction proceeds direct with the infinitive *κοσμεῖν*, without any supposition of an anacoluthon, as there must be on the other hypothesis) **in orderly** (ref.) **apparel** (cf. Tit. ii. 3, note: "in seemly guise," Ellic. **καταστολή**, originally '*arrangement*,' '*putting in order*,' followed in its usage that of its verb **καταστέλλω**. We have in Eur. Bacch. 891, *αὐτὸν* [*τὸν πλόκαμον*] *πάλιν* **καταστελοῦμεν**,—'*we will re-arrange the dishevelled lock*:' then Aristoph. Thesm. 256, *ἴθι νῦν* **κατάστειλόν** *με τὰ περὶ τὼ σκέλη*—*clothe, dress me*. Thus in Plut. Pericl. 5, we read of Anaxagoras, that his **καταστολὴ** *περιβολῆς*, '*arrangement of dress*,' was *πρὸς οὐδὲν ἐκταραττομένη πάθος ἐν τῷ λέγειν*. Then in Jos. B. J. ii. 8. 4, of the Essenes, that their *καταστολὴ καὶ σχῆμα σώματος* was *ὅμοιον τοῖς μετὰ φόβου παιδαγωγουμένοις παισίν*, which he proceeds to explain by saying *οὔτε δὲ ἐσθῆτας, οὔτε ὑποδήματα ἀμείβουσι, πρὶν ἢ διαῤῥαγῆναι, κ.τ.λ.* So that we must take it as meaning 'the apparel,' the whole investiture of the person. This he proceeds presently to break up into detail, forbidding *πλέγματα, χρυσόν, μαργαρίτας, ἱματισμὸν πολυτελῆ*, all which are parts of the *καταστολή*. This view of the meaning of the word requires *ἐν καταστολῇ κοσμίῳ* to belong to *κοσμεῖν*, and then to be taken up by the *ἐν* following, an arrangement, as it seems to me, also required by the natural construction of the sentence itself) **with shamefastness** (not, as modern reprints of the E. V., 'shame*faced*ness,' which is a mere unmeaning corruption by the printers of a very expressive and beautiful word: see Trench, N. T. Synonyms, § xx.) **and self-restraint** (I adopt Conybeare's word as, though not wholly satisfactory, bringing out the leading idea of **σωφροσύνη** better than any other. Its fault is, that it is a word too indicative of *effort*, as if the unchaste desires were continually breaking bounds, and as continually held in check: whereas in the *σώφρων*, the safe-and-sound-minded, no such continual struggle has place, but the better nature is established in its rule. Trench [ubi supra] has dealt with the two words, setting aside the insufficient distinction of Xenophon, Cyr. viii. 1. 31,—where he says of Cyrus, *διῄρει δὲ αἰδῶ καὶ σωφροσύνην τῇδε, ὡς τοὺς μὲν αἰδουμένους τὰ ἐν τῷ φανερῷ αἰσχρὰ φεύγοντας, τοὺς δὲ σώφρονας καὶ τὰ ἐν τῷ ἀφανεῖ*. "If," Trench concludes, "**αἰδώς** is the 'shamefastness,' or tendency which shrinks from overpassing the limits of womanly reserve and modesty, as well as from the dishonour which would justly attach thereto, σω-

δι' [d] ἔργων [d] ἀγαθῶν. 11 γυνὴ ἐν [e] ἡσυχίᾳ [f] μανθανέτω d = Acts ix 36 Rom xiii 3 2 Cor ix 8
ἐν [g] πάσῃ [h] ὑποταγῇ. 12 διδάσκειν δὲ γυναικὶ οὐκ [i] ἐπι- ch v 10 al
τρέπω, οὐδὲ [k] αὐθεντεῖν ἀνδρός, ἀλλ' εἶναι ἐν [e] ἡσυχίᾳ. e 2 Thess iii. 12 reff f absol, 1 Cor xiv 31
13 Ἀδὰμ γὰρ πρῶτος [l] ἐπλάσθη, εἶτα Εὕα. 14 καὶ g Phil i 20 reff

h 2 Cor ix 13 Gal ii 5. ch iii 4 only† (-τασσειν, Tit ii 5) i Luke viii 32 ǁ Mt ix 50, 61 Acts xxvi 1 al Job xxxii 14. k here only† (-της, Wisd xii 6) l Rom ix. 20 only Gen ii 7, 8

12. rec *γυναικι δε διδασκειν*, with KL rel syr Thdr-mops Chr Thdrt Damasc Ambr, and, om *δε*, k Did. txt ADFℵ m 17 latt goth arm Cypr Ambrst Jer.

φροσύνη is that habitual inner self-government, with its constant rein on all the passions and desires, which would hinder the temptation to this from arising, or at all events from arising in such strength as should overbear the checks and hindrances which *αἰδώς* opposed to it." Ellic gives for it, "sober-mindedness," and explains it, "*the well-balanced state of mind, arising from habitual self-restraint*" See his notes, here, and in his translation), **not in plaits** (of hair cf 1 Pet iii. 3, *ἐμπλοκὴ τριχῶν*, and see Ellicott's note) **and gold** (*καὶ περιθέσεως χρυσίων*, 1 Pet l c, perhaps, from the *καί*, the gold is supposed to be twined among, or worn with, the plaited hair. See Rev xvii 4), **or pearls, or costly raiment** (= *ἐνδύσεως ἱματίων*, 1 Pet l c),—**but, which is becoming for women professing** (*ἐπαγγέλλεσθαι* is ordinarily in N T. 'to promise,' see reff But the meaning 'to profess,' 'præ se ferre,' is found in the classics, e. g. Xen. Mem i. 2 7, *ἐθαύμαζε δέ, εἴ τις ἀρετὴν ἐπαγγελλόμενος ἀργύριον πράττοιτο* cf. Palm and Rost's Lex, and the numerous examples in Wetst) **godliness** (*θεοσέβεια* is found in Xen. An. ii. 6. 26, and Plato, Epinomis, pp. 985 d, 989 e The adjective *θεοσεβής* is common enough),—**by means of good works** (not *ἐν* again, because the adornment lies in a different sphere and cannot be so expressed. The adorning which results from good works is brought about by [*διά*] their practice, not displayed by appearing to be invested with them [*ἐν*]. Huther's construction, after Thdrt., Œc, Luth., Calv., and Mack and Matthies,—*ἐπαγγελλ θεοσέβειαν δι' ἔργων ἀγαθῶν*,—is on all grounds objectionable —1) the understanding *ὅ* as *ἐν τούτῳ ὅ* or *καθ' ὅ*, which of itself might pass, introduces great harshness into the sentence —2) the junction of *ἐπαγγελλομέναις δι'* is worse than that of *κοσμεῖν δι'*, to which he objects —3) the arrangement of the words is against it, which would thus rather be *γυναιξὶν δι' ἔργων ἀγαθῶν θεοσέβειαν ἐπαγγελλομέναις* —4) he does not see that his objection, that the adornment of women has been already specified by *ἐν καταστολῇ κ τ λ*, and therefore need not be again specified by *δι' ἔργων ἀγ*, applies just as much to his own rendering, taking *ὅ* for *καθ' ὅ* or *ἐν τούτῳ ὅ*)

11.] **Let a woman learn** (in the congregation, and every where: see below) **in silence in all** (possible) **subjection** (the thought of the public assemblies has evidently given rise to this precept [see 1 Cor xiv 31], but he carries it further than can be applied to them in the next verse)· **but** (the contrast is to a suppressed hypothesis of a claim to do that which is forbidden· cf a similar *δέ*, 1 Cor. xi. 16) **to a woman I permit not to teach** (in the church [primarily], or, as the context shews, any where else), **nor to lord it over** (*αὐθέντης μηδέποτε χρήσῃ ἐπὶ τοῦ δεσπότου, ὡς οἱ περὶ τὰ δικαστήρια ῥήτορες, ἀλλ' ἐπὶ τοῦ αὐτόχειρος φονέως*, Phryn. But Euripides thus uses it, Suppl. 442 *καὶ μὴν ὅπου γε δῆμος αὐθέντης χθονός, ὑποῦσιν ἀστοῖς ἥδεται νεανίαις*. The fact is that the word itself is originally a 'vox media,' signifying merely 'one who with his own hand' . . . and the context fills up the rest, *αυθέντης φόνου*, or the like. And in course of time, the meaning of 'autocrat' prevailing, the word itself and its derivatives henceforth took this course, and *αὐθεντέω, -ία, -ημα*, all of later growth, bore this reference only Later still we have *αὐθεντικός, from first authority* ['id enim *αὐθεντικῶς*, nuntiabatur,' Cic. ad Att. x 9] It seems quite a mistake to suppose that *αὐθέντης* arrived at its meaning of a despot by passing through that of a murderer) **the man, but** (supply ["*βούλομαι*, not *κελεύω*, which St Paul does not use" Ellic] '*I command her*' the construction in 1 Cor xiv. 34 is the same) **to be in silence** 13] *Reason of this precept, in the original order of creation.* **For Adam was first** (not of all men, which is not here under consideration, and would stultify the subsequent clause —but first in comparison

Ἀδὰμ οὐκ [m] ἠπατήθη, ἡ δὲ γυνὴ [n] ἐξαπατηθεῖσα [o] ἐν
[p] παραβάσει [o] γέγονεν, 15 [q] σωθήσεται δὲ [r] διὰ τῆς [s] τεκνο-
γονίας, ἐὰν μείνωσιν [t] ἐν πίστει καὶ ἀγάπῃ καὶ [u] ἁγιασμῷ
μετὰ [v] σωφροσύνης.

ADFK LℵA a b c d e f g h k l m n o 17

m Eph. v. 6. James i. 26 only. Job xxxi. 27. n 2 Thess. ii. 3 reff. o Luke xxii. 44. Acts xxii. 17. p Gal. iii. 19 reff. q = ch. iv. 16. see Phil. i. 19. r = 1 Cor. iii. 15. see note. s here only†. (-νεῖν, ch. v. 14.) t ch. i. 2 reff. u = 1 Thess. iv 4, 7 (reff.). Heb. xii. 14. v ver. 9.

14. rec απατηθεισα (*on this reading, critical considerations are somewhat uncertain. On the one hand,* **ἐξαπ.** *may have come from Rom* vii. 11. 2 *Cor* xi. 3 : *on the other,* **ἀπ.** *may be a corrn to suit* **ἠπατήθη** *above. And this latter, as lying so much nearer the corrector's eye, seems the more prob : especially as in Gen* iii. 13 *it stands* ὁ ὄφις ἠπάτησέν με), with D³KLℵ³ rel 67² : txt AD¹Fℵ¹ c 17 Bas Chr₁.

15. for δε, γαρ D¹ : om a¹.

with Eve) **made** (see ref. Gen., from which the word ἐπλάσθη seems to be taken : cf. 1 Cor. xi. 8, 9, and indeed that whole passage, which throws light on this), **then Eve.** 14.] *Second reason*—as the woman was *last in being*, so she was *first in sin*—indeed *the only victim* of the Tempter's deceit. **And Adam was not deceived** (not to be weakened, as Thdrt.: τὸ οὐκ ἠπατήθη, ἀντὶ τοῦ, οὐ πρῶτος, εἴρηκεν : nor, as Matthies, must we supply ὑπὸ τοῦ ὄφεως : nor, with De W., Wiesinger, al., must we press the fact that the woman only was *misled* by the senses. Bengel and Huther seem to me [but cf. Ellicott] to have apprehended the right reference : 'serpens mulierem decepit, mulier virum non decepit, sed ei persuasit.' As Huther observes, the ἠπάτησεν, in the original narrative, is used of the woman only. We read of no communication between the serpent and the *man*. The "subtlest beast of all the field" knew his course better : *she* listened to the lower solicitation of sense and expediency : he to the higher one of conjugal love) : **but the woman** (not now *Eve*, but generic, as the next clause shews : for Eve could not be the subject to σωθήσεται) **having been seduced** BY DECEIT (stronger than ἀπατηθεῖσα, as *exoro* than *oro* : implying the full success of the ἀπάτη) **has become involved** (the thought is—the present state of transgression in which the woman [and the man too : but that is not treated here] by sin is constituted, arose [which was not so in the man] from her originally having been *seduced by deceit*) **in transgression** (here as always, breach of a positive command : cf. Rom. iv. 15).

15.] **But** (contrast to this her great and original defect) **she** (general) **shall be saved through** (brought safely through, but in the higher, which is with St. Paul the only sense of σώζω, see below) **her child-bearing** (in order to understand the fulness of the meaning of σωθήσεται here, we must bear in mind the history itself, to which is the constant allusion. The curse on the woman for her **παράβασις** was, ἐν λύπαις τέξῃ τέκνα [Gen. iii. 16]. Her **τεκνογονία** is that in which the curse finds its operation. What then is here promised her? Not only exemption from that curse in its worst and heaviest effects : not merely that she shall safely bear children : but the Apostle uses the word **σωθήσεται** purposely for its higher meaning, and the construction of the sentence is precisely as ref. 1 Cor.—*αὐτὸς δὲ σωθήσεται, οὕτως δὲ ὡς διὰ πυρός.* Just as that man should be saved through, as passing through, fire which is his trial, his hindrance in his way, in spite of which he escapes,—so she shall be saved, through, as passing through, her child-bearing, which is her trial, her curse, her [not means of salvation, but] hindrance in the way of it. The other renderings which have been given seem to me both irrelevant and ungrammatical. Chrys., Thl., al., for instance, would press **τεκνογονία** to mean the Christian education of children : Heinrichs, strangely enough, holds that her τεκνογ. is the *punishment* of her sin, and that being undergone, she shall be saved **διὰ** τῆς τ., i.e. by having paid it. Conyb. gives it '*women will be saved by the bearing of children*,' i.e., as he explains it in his note, "are to be kept in the path of safety (?) by the performance of the peculiar functions which God has assigned to their sex." Some, in their anxiety to give διά the instrumental meaning, would understand **διὰ τῆς τεκνογ.** 'by means of *the Child-bearing*,' i.e. 'the Incarnation :' a rendering which needs no refutation. I see that Ellicott maintains this latter interpretation : still I find no reason to qualify what I have above written. 1 Cor. iii. 15 seems to me so complete a key of Pauline usage of σώζεσθαι διά, that I cannot abandon the path opened by it, till far stronger reason has

III. 1 [w] Πιστὸς ὁ λόγος· εἴ τις [x] ἐπισκοπῆς [y] ὀρέγεται,
[z] καλοῦ [z] ἔργου [a] ἐπιθυμεῖ. 2 δεῖ οὖν τὸν [b] ἐπίσκοπον

w ch i 15 reff. x = Acts i 20, from Ps cviii 8 (Luke xix 44 1 Pet ii 12 [v 6 v r] only) y ch vi 10 Heb xi 16 only + (act, Job viii 20 Symm) z Matt v 16 xxvi 10 || Mk John x 32, 33 Epp., ch v 10, 25 vi 18 Tit ii 7, 14 iii 8, 14 Heb x 24. 1 Pet ii 12 only a constr., Acts xx 33 only (Paul) Prov xxiii 3, 6 b Acts xx 28. Phil i 1 Tit i 7 1 Pet ii 25 only 4 Kings xi 18 Job xx 29 Isa lx 17

CHAP III 1 for πιστος, ανθρωπινος (*probably introduced from the* humanus *of some of the latin mss* · see Ellic here, and cf var readd, ch i 15) D · G-lat has both

been shewn than he here alleges In his second edition he has not in any way strengthened his argument, nor has he taken any notice of the Pauline usage which I allege. After all, it is mainly a question of exegetical tact · and I own I am surprised that any scholar can believe it possible that St. Paul can have expressed the Incarnation by the bare word ἡ τεκνογονία He himself in this same Epistle, v 14, uses the cognate verb, of the ordinary bearing of children: and these are the only places where the compound occurs in the N. T), **if they** (generic plural as before singular) **have remained** (shall be found in that day to have remained—a further proof of the higher meaning of **σωθήσεται**) **in faith and love and holiness** (see reff, where the word is used in the same reference, of holy chastity) **with self-restraint** (see above on ver. 9).

CH. III. 1—13] *Precepts respecting overseers* (presbyters) [1—7], *and deacons* [8—13] 1] **Faithful is the saying** (see on ch. i. 15, from the analogy of which it appears that the words are to be referred to what follows, not, as Chrys., Thl, Erasm, al., to what has preceded) **if any man seeks** (it does not seem that he uses ὀρέγεται with any reference to an ambitious seeking, as De W. thinks in Heb xi 16 the word is a 'vox media,' and even in ch vi 10, the blame rests, not on ὀρεγόμενοι, but on the thing sought: and in Polyb ix. 20 3, the word is used as one merely of passage, in giving directions respecting the office sought κελεύοντες ἀστρολογεῖν κ. γεωμετρεῖν τοὺς ὀρεγομένους αὐτῆς [τῆς στρατηγίας]. So that De W.'s inference respecting ambition for the episcopate betraying the late age of the Epistle, falls to the ground) **(the) overseership** (or, bishopric; office of an ἐπίσκοπος; but the ἐπίσκοποι of the N. T. have officially nothing in common with our *Bishops* See notes on Acts xx 17, 28. The identity of the ἐπίσκοπος and πρεσβύτερος in apostolic times is evident from Tit. i 5—7. see also note on Phil. i 1, the article Bischof in Herzog's Real-Encyclopadie, and Ellic's note here), **he desires a good work** (not 'a good *thing*' but a good *employment* · see 1 Thess v 13 2 Tim iv 5 · one of the καλὰ ἔργα so often spoken of [reff]) **It behoves then** (οὖν is best regarded as taking up καλὸν ἔργον, and substantiating that assertion "bonum negotium bonis committendum," Bengel) **an** (τόν generic, singular of τοὺς ἐπισκόπους) **overseer to be blameless** (Thucyd v. 17, Πλειστοάναξ δὲ . . νομίζων . . . κἂν αὐτὸς τοῖς ἐχθροῖς ἀνεπίληπτος εἶναι . . . . , where the Schol has, μὴ ἂν αὐτὸς παρέξων κατηγορίας ἀφορμήν. Thdrt. draws an important distinction μηδεμίαν πρόφασιν μέμψεως παρέχειν δικαίαν· τὸ γὰρ ἀνεπίληπτον, οὐ τὸ ἀσυκοφάντητον λέγει· ἐπεὶ καὶ αὐτὸς ἀπόστολος παντοδαπὰς συκοφαντίας ὑπέμεινεν), **husband of one wife** (two great varieties of interpretation of these words have prevailed, among those who agree to take them as *restrictive*, not *injunctive*, which the spirit of the passage and the insertion of μιᾶς surely alike forbid They have been supposed to prohibit either 1) *simultaneous polygamy*, or 2) *successive polygamy*. 1) has somewhat to be said for it. The custom of polygamy was then prevalent among the Jews [see Just Mart Tryph 134, p 226, —διδασκάλοις ὑμῶν οἵτινες καὶ μέχρι νῦν καὶ τέσσαρας κ. πέντε ἔχειν ὑμᾶς γυναῖκας ἕκαστον συγχωροῦσι · and Jos. Antt. vii 2 (so cited in Suicer and Huther, but the reference is wrong), πάτριον ἐν ταὐτῷ πλείοσιν ἡμῖν συνοικεῖν], and might easily find its way into the Christian community. And such, it is argued, was the Apostle's reference, not to second marriages, which he himself commands ch v 14, and allows in several other places, e g Rom. vii. 2, 3 · 1 Cor. vii. 39 But the objection to taking this meaning is, that the Apostle would hardly have specified that as a requisite for the episcopate or presbyterate, which we know to have been fulfilled by all Christians whatever · no instance being adduced of polygamy being practised in the Christian church, and no exhortations to abstain from it. As to St Paul's command and permissions, see below Still, we must not lose sight of the circumstance that the earlier Commentators were unanimous for

[c] ἀνεπίλημπτον εἶναι, [d] μιᾶς γυναικὸς [d] ἄνδρα, [e] νηφάλιον,
[f] σώφρονα, [g] κόσμιον, [h] φιλόξενον, [i] διδακτικόν·
3 μὴ

ADFK
I ℵ a b
c d e f g
h k l m
n o 17

c ch v 7 vi 14 only†
d Tit i 6
e ver 11 Tit ii 2 only† (-φεῖν, 1 Thess v 6)
f Tit i 8 ii 2, 5 only† (-φρόνως, Tit ii 12)
g ch ii 9 only Eccles xii 9 only
h Tit i 8. 1 Pet iv 9 only† (-νία, Rom xii 13)
i 2 Tim ii 24 only†

2. rec νηφαλεον, with D[3]K a c f n Damasc. -λαιον FLℵ[3] d o txt AD[1]ℵ[1] rel Orig$_{\text{sæpe}}$ Naz

this view. Chrys is the only one who proposes an alternative.—τὴν ἀμετρίαν κωλύει, ἐπειδὴ ἐπὶ τῶν Ἰουδαίων ἐξῆν καὶ δευτέροις ὁμιλεῖν γάμοις, κ. δύο ἔχειν κατὰ ταὐτὸν γυναῖκας Thdrt: τὸ δὲ μιᾶς γυναικὸς ἄνδρα, εὖ μοι δοκοῦσιν εἰρηκέναι τινές. πάλαι γὰρ εἰώθεισαν καὶ Ἕλληνες κ. Ἰουδαῖοι κ. δύο κ. τρισὶ κ πλείοσι γυναιξὶ νόμῳ γάμου κατὰ ταὐτὸν συνοικεῖν. τινὲς δὲ καὶ νῦν, καίτοι τῶν βασιλικῶν νόμων δύο κατὰ ταὐτὸν ἄγεσθαι κωλυόντων γυναῖκας, καὶ παλλακῖσι μίγνυνται κ. ἑταίραις. ἔφασαν τοίνυν τὸν θεῖον ἀπόστολον εἰρηκέναι, τὸν μιᾷ μόνῃ γυναικὶ συνοικοῦντα σωφρόνως, τῆς ἐπισκοπικῆς ἄξιον εἶναι χειροτονίας οὐ γὰρ τὸν δεύτερον, φασίν, ἐξέβαλε γάμον, ὅ γε πολλάκις τοῦτο γενέσθαι κελεύσας. And similarly Thl., Œc, and Jer. 2) For the view that *second marriages* are prohibited to aspirants after the episcopate,—is, the most probable meaning [see there] of ἑνὸς ἀνδρὸς γυνή in ch. v. 9,—as also the wide prevalence in the early Church of the idea that, although second marriages were not forbidden to Christians, abstinence from them was better than indulgence in them. So Hermas Pastor, ii. 1. 4, p 921 f, 'Domine, si vir vel mulier alicujus discesserit, et nupserit aliquis eorum, numquid peccat?' 'Qui nubit, non peccat. sed si per se manserit, magnum sibi conquirit honorem apud Dominum' and Clem Alex Strom. iii 12 [81], p 548 P, ὁ ἀπόστολος [1 Cor vii 39, 40] δι' ἀκρασίαν κ πύρωσιν κατὰ συγγνώμην δευτέρου μεταδίδωσι γάμου, ἐπεὶ κ. οὗτος οὐχ ἁμαρτάνει μὲν κατὰ διαθήκην, οὐ γὰρ κεκώλυται πρὸς τοῦ νόμου, οὐ πληροῖ δὲ τῆς κατὰ τὸ εὐαγγέλιον πολιτείας τὴν κατ' ἐπίτασιν τελειότητα And so in Suicer, i p 892 f, Chrys, Greg. Naz [τὸ πρῶτον (συνοικέσιον) νόμος, τὸ δεύτερον συγχωρησις, τὸ τρίτον παρανομία τὸ δὲ ὑπὲρ τουτο, χοιρώδης Orat xxxvii 8, p 650],—Epiphanius [δευτερόγαμον οὐκ ἔξεστι δέχεσθαι ἐν αὐτῇ (τῇ ἐκκλησίᾳ) εἰς ἱερωσύνην. Doct. compend de fide, p. 1104], Orig,—the Apostolical Canon xvii [ὁ δυσὶ γάμοις συμπλακεὶς μετὰ τὸ βάπτισμα, ἢ παλλακὴν κτησάμενος, οὐ δύναται εἶναι ἐπίσκοπος, ἢ πρεσβύτερος, ἢ διάκονος, ἢ ὅλως τοῦ καταλόγου τοῦ ἱερατικοῦ], &c Huther cites from Athenagoras the expression εὐπρεπὴς μοιχεία applied to second marriage With regard to the Apostle's own command and permissions of this state [see above], they do not come into account here, because they are confessedly (and expressly so in ch v. 14) for those whom it was not contemplated to admit into ecclesiastical office 3) There have been some divergent lines of interpretation, but they have not found many advocates Some [e g Wegscheider] deny altogether the formal reference to 1) or 2), and understand the expression only of a chaste life of fidelity to the marriage vow "that neither polygamy, nor concubinage, nor any offensive deuterogamy, should be able to be alleged against such a person." But surely this is very vague, for the precise words μιᾶς γυναικὸς ἀνήρ. Bretschneider maintains that μιᾶς is here the indefinite article, and that the Apostle means, an ἐπίσκοπος should be the husband of a wife This hardly needs serious refutation Winer however has treated it, edn. 6, § 18. 9 note, shewing that by no possibility can the indefinite εἷς stand where it would as here cause ambiguity, only where unity is taken for granted Worse still is the Romanist evasion, which understands the μία γυνή of the Church The view then which must I think be adopted, especially in presence of ch v 9 [where see note] is, that to candidates for the episcopate [presbytery] St Paul forbids second marriage He requires of them pre-eminent chastity, and abstinence from a licence which is allowed to other Christians How far such a prohibition is to be considered binding on us, now that the Christian life has entered into another and totally different phase, is of course an open question for the present Christian church at any time to deal with It must be as matter of course understood that regulations, in all *lawful* things, depend, even when made by an Apostle, on circumstances and the superstitious observance of the letter in such cases is often pregnant with mischief to the people and cause of Christ), sober (probably in the more extended sense of the word ['vigilantem animo,' Beng: διεγηγερμένον, καὶ προσκοπεῖν τὸ πρακτέον δυνάμενον, Thdrt. τουτέστι

[k] πάροινον, μὴ [l] πλήκτην, ἀλλ' [m] ἐπιεικῆ, [n] ἄμαχον,
[o] ἀφιλάργυρον, 4 τοῦ ἰδίου οἴκου καλῶς [p] προϊστάμενον,

k Tit i 7 only†
l Tit i 7 only† Ps xxxiv 15 Symm
m Phil iv 5 Tit iii 2 James iii. 17 1 Pet ii 18 only Ps lxxxv 5 only
n Tit iii 2 only†
o Heb xiii 5 only†
p here bis ver 12 ch v 17 Rom xii 8 1 Thess v 12 Tit iii 8, 14 only Γ Prov xxvi 17

3 rec aft πληκτ ins μη αισχροκερδη (from Tit i 7), with rel om ADFKI ℵ m 17. 67[2] latt syrr coptt goth gr-lat-ff. αλλα Aℵ
4. προισταvομενον ℵ

διορατικόν, μυρίους ἔχοντα πάντοθεν ὀφθαλμούς, ὀξὺ βλέποντα, καὶ μὴ ἀμβλύνοντα τὸ τῆς διανοίας ὄμμα, κ τ λ Chrys], as in 1 Thess. v 6, 8,—a pattern of active sobriety and watchfulness. for all these adjectives, as far as διδακτικόν, are descriptive of *positive* qualities · μὴ πάροινον giving the negative and more restricted opposite), **self-restrained** (or, **discreet**; see above on ch. ii 9), **orderly** ('quod σώφρων est intus, id κόσμιος est extra,' Beng thus expanded by Theodoret καὶ φθέγματι καὶ σχήματι καὶ βλέμματι καὶ βαδίσματι ὥστε καὶ διὰ τοῦ σώματος φαίνεσθαι τὴν τῆς ψυχῆς σωφροσύνην), **hospitable** (loving, and entertaining strangers see reff. and Heb. xiii. 2. This duty in the early days of the Christian church was one of great importance Brethren in their travels could not resort to the houses of the heathen, and would be subject to insult in the public deversoria), **apt in teaching** (τὰ θεῖα πεπαιδευμένον, καὶ παραινεῖν δυνάμενον τὰ προσήκοντα, Thdrt : so we have τοὺς ἱππικοὺς βουλομένους γενέσθαι, Xen Sympos ii 10 not merely *given to* teaching, but able and skilled in it All *might teach*, to whom the Spirit imparted the gift · but *skill* in teaching was the especial office of the minister, on whom would fall the ordinary duty of instruction of believers and refutation of gainsayers) 3—7] (His *negative qualities* are now specified, the positive ones which occur henceforth arising out of and explaining those negative ones) ·

3] **not a brawler** (properly, '*one in his cups*,' 'a man rendered petulant by much wine ·' τὸ τοίνυν παρ' οἶνον λυπεῖν τοὺς παρόντας, τοῦτ' ἐγὼ κρίνω παροινίαν, Xen Sympos. vi. 1. And perhaps the literal meaning should not be lost sight of At the same time the word and its cognates were often used without reference to wine see παροινέω, -ία, -ιος, in Palm and Rost's Lex. As πλήκτης answers to πάροινος, it will be best to extend the meaning to signify rather the character, than the mere fact, of παροινία), **not a striker** (this word also may have a literal and narrower, or a metaphorical and wider sense. In this latter it is taken by Thdrt οὐ τὸ ἐπιτιμᾶν εἰς καιρὸν κωλύει ἀλλὰ τὸ μὴ δεόντως τοῦτο ποιεῖν But perhaps the coarser literal sense is better, as setting forth more broadly the opposite to the character of a Christian ἐπίσκοπος), **but** (this contrast springs out of the two last, and is set off by them) **forbearing** (reasonable and gentle: φέρειν εἰδότα τὰ πρὸς αὐτὸν πλημμελήματα, Thdrt. See note on Phil iv 5, and Trench, N. T. Syn. § xliii., but correct his derivation, as in that note), **not quarrelsome** (cf. 2 Tim ii. 24 Conyb's '*peaceable*' is objectionable, as losing the negative character), **not a lover of money** ('*liberal*,' Conyb : but this is still more objectionable it is not the positive virtue of liberality but the negative one of abstinence from love of money, which, though it may lead to the other in men who *have* money, is yet a totally distinct thing Thdrt.'s explanation, while true, is yet characteristic of an ἐπίσκοπος of later days οὐκ εἶπεν ἀκτήμονα· σύμμετρα γὰρ νομοθετεῖ ἀλλὰ μὴ ἐρῶντα χρημάτων. δυνατὸν γὰρ κεκτῆσθαι μέν, οἰκονομεῖν δὲ ταῦτα δεόντως, καὶ μὴ δουλεύειν τούτοις, ἀλλὰ τούτων δεσπόζειν)

4.] (This positive requisite again seems to spring out of the negative ones which have preceded, and especially out of ἀφιλάργυρον The negatives are again resumed below with μὴ νεόφυτον) **presiding well over his own house** (**ἰδίου**, as contrasted with the church of God below, **οἴκου**, in its wide acceptation, '*household*,' including all its members), **having children** (not '*keeping* [or *having*] *his children*' [ἔχοντα τὰ τέκνα], as E V and Conyb. The emphatic position of τέκνα, besides its anarthrousness, should have prevented this mistake: cf also Tit i 6,—μιᾶς γυναικὸς ἀνήρ, τέκνα ἔχων πιστά, κ τ λ) **in subjection** (i e. who are in subjection) **with all gravity** ('*reverent modesty*,' see ch ii 2 These words are best applied to the *children*, not to the head of the house, which acceptance of them rather belongs to the rendering impugned above It is the σεμνότης of the children, the result of his προστῆναι, which is to prove that he *knows how* to preside over his own house,—not his own σεμνότης in governing them the matter of fact, that he has children who are in subjection to him in all gravity,—not

τέκνα ἔχοντα ἐν [q] ὑποταγῇ [r] μετὰ [s] πάσης [t] σεμνότητος.
5 εἰ δέ τις τοῦ ἰδίου οἴκου [p] προστῆναι οὐκ οἶδεν, πῶς [u] ἐκκλησίας [u] θεοῦ [v] ἐπιμελήσεται; 6 μὴ [w] νεόφυτον, ἵνα μὴ
[x] τυφωθεὶς εἰς [y] κρίμα [z] ἐμπέσῃ τοῦ [a] διαβόλου. 7 δεῖ δὲ

H δει δε .... ADFH KLℵ a b c d e f g h k l m n o 17

q ch. ii. 11 reff. r Mark iii. 5 al. fr. 1 Chron. xxix. 22. s Phil. i. 20 reff. t ch. ii. 2. Tit. ii. 7 only †. 2 Macc. iii. 12 only. u 1 Cor. i. 2. x 32. xi. 16, 22. xv. 9. Gal. i. 13. 1 Thess. ii. 14. 2 Thess. i. 4. ver. 15. P. v Luke x. 34, 35 only. Gen. xliv. 21. (-λεια, Acts xxvii. 3. -λῶς, Luke xv. 8.) w here only. Job xiv. 9. Ps. cxxvii. 3. cxliii. 12. Isa. v. 7 only. x ch. vi. 4. 2 Tim. iii. 4 only †. y = Mark xii. 40 || L. Rom. iii. 8 al. fr. z Matt. xii. 11. Luke x. 36. xiv. 5. ch. vi. 9. Heb. x. 31 only. Prov. xxviii. 10. a = Paul, Eph. iv. 27. vi. 11. 2 Tim. ii. 26 only. Matt. iv. 1. Heb. ii. 14 al. fr. Job i. 6, &c. (adj., ver. 11.)

7. rec aft δει δε ins αυτον, with DKL rel: om AFHℵ 17 copt.—εχειν bef καλην DF latt.

his own keeping or endeavouring to keep them so. Want of *success* in ruling at home, not want of will to rule, would disqualify him for ruling the church. So that the distinction is an important one): **but** (contrast, as in ch. ii. 12, to the suppressed but imagined opposite case) **if any man knows not** (the use of εἰ οὐ here is perfectly regular: see Ellicott's note) **how to preside over his own house** (shews, by his children being insubordinate, that he has no skill in domestic government), **how shall he** (this future includes '*how can he*,' but goes beyond it—appealing, not to the man's power, which conditions his success, but to the resulting matter of fact, which will be sure to substantiate his failure) **take charge of** (so Plat. Gorg. p. 520 a: *οἱ φάσκοντες προεστάναι τῆς πόλεως καὶ ἐπιμελεῖσθαι*) **the church of God** (*ὁ τὰ σμικρὰ οἰκονομεῖν οὐκ εἰδώς, πῶς δύναται τῶν κρειττόνων καὶ θείων πιστευθῆναι τὴν ἐπιμέλειαν;* Thdrt. See the idea followed out popularly in Chrys.)?

6.] (the negative characteristics are resumed) **not a novice** (*νεόφυτον τὸν εὐθὺς πεπιστευκότα καλεῖ· ἐγὼ γάρ, φησίν, ἐφύτευσα. οὐ γάρ, οὕς τινες ὑπέλαβον, τὸν νέον τῆς ἡλικίας ἐκβάλλει,* Thdrt. So Chr. [*νεοκατήχητος*], Thl. [*νεοβάπτιστος*.] An objection has been raised to this precept by Schleierm., that it could hardly find place in the apostolic church, where all were *νεόφυτοι*. Matthies answers, that in Crete this might be so, and therefore such a precept would be out of place in the Epistle to Titus, but the Ephesian church had been many years established. But De W. rejoins to this, that the precepts are perfectly *general*, *not of particular application*. The real reply is to be found, partly by narrowing the range of *νεόφυτος*, partly in assigning a later date to these Epistles than is commonly held. The case here contemplated is that of one very recently converted. To ordain such a person to the ministry would, for the reason here assigned, be most unadvisable. But we cannot imagine that such period need be extended at the most to more than three or four years, in cases of men of full age who became Christians; and surely such a condition might be fulfilled in any of the Pauline churches, supposing this Epistle to bear any thing like the date which I have assigned to it in the Prolegg. ch. vii. § ii.), **lest being besotted with pride** (from **τῦφος**, smoke, steam, and hence metaphorically, the pother which a man's pride raises about him so that he cannot see himself or others as they are. So *τὰ τῆς ψυχῆς, ὄνειρος καὶ τῦφος*, Marc. Antonin. ii. 17: *τὸν τῦφον ὥσπερ τινὰ καπνὸν φιλοσοφίας εἰς τοὺς σοφιστὰς ἀπεσκέδασε*, Plut. Mor. [p. 580 e. Palm. Lex.] Hence **τυφοῦσθαι**, which is used only in this metaphorical sense, to be thus blinded or bewildered with pride or self-conceit. So *τετυφωμένος ταῖς εὐτυχίαις*, Strabo xv. p. 686,—*ἐπὶ πλούτοις τε καὶ ἀρχαῖς*, Lucian, Necyom. 12. See numerous other examples in Palm and Rost's Lex., from whence the above are taken) **he fall into the judgment of the devil** (these last words are ambiguous. Is *τοῦ διαβόλου* [1] the genitive objective [as Rom. iii. 8], '*the judgment into which the devil fell*,'—or [2] the genitive subjective, '*the judgment which is wrought by the devil*?' [1] is held by Chrys. [*εἰς τὴν καταδίκην τὴν αὐτήν, ἣν ἐκεῖνος ἀπὸ τῆς ἀπονοίας ὑπέμεινε*], Thdrt. [*τῇ τοῦ διαβόλου τιμωρίᾳ περιπεσεῖται*], Thl., Œc., Pel., Calv. ['in eandem cum diabolo condemnationem ruat.' See below under (2)], Beza, Est., Grot. ['id est, pœna qualis diabolo evenit, qui de cœlo dejectus est, 2 Pet. ii. 4, nempe ob superbiam, Sir. x. 13'], Beng., Wolf ['repræsentato diaboli exemplo'], Heinr., Heydenreich, Mack, De W., Wiesinger, al.: and by Ellicott. [2] by Ambr. [apparently: 'Satanas præcipitat eum'], Heumann, Matthies ["if a Christian church-overseer allowed himself to be involved in a charge of pride, the adversary (*in concreto* living men, his un-

καὶ [b] μαρτυρίαν καλὴν ἔχειν ἀπὸ [c] τῶν [c] ἔξωθεν, ἵνα μὴ εἰς [d] ὀνειδισμὸν [ae] ἐμπέσῃ καὶ [ef] παγίδα τοῦ [a] διαβόλου.

b = Paul, Acts xxii 18 1 Tit i 13 only John i 7, 19 al

c Matt. xxiii 25 Luke xi 39, 40 (Paul usually, οἱ ἔξω, Col iv 5 reff) 1 Pet iii 3 Rev xi 2 only Ezek xli 17 (ἔξωθεν, Paul, 2 Cor vii 5 only) d Rom xv 3, from Ps lxviii 9 Heb x 33 xi 26 xiii 13 only e ch vi 9 Prov xii 13 f Luke xxi 35 Rom xi 9, from Ps lxviii 22 ch vi 9 2 Tim ii 26 only

struments) might by it have reason as well for the accusation of the individual as for inculpation of the congregation, cf ch v 14, Eph iv 27," cited by Huther], Calv. [as an alternative. "activam significationem non rejicio, fore ut diabolo causam sui accusandi præbeat." He adds, "sed verior Chrysostomi opinio"], Beza [altern], Huther. It is hardly worth while recounting under this head, the views of those who take **τοῦ διαβόλου** for *a slanderer*, inasmuch as **ὁ διάβολος** never occurs in this sense in the N T [on *διάβολος*, adjective, in this sense, see below, ver. 11]. This is done in both verses 6 and 7, by Luther [Lästerer], Rosenm, Michaelis, Wegsch, Flatt. in verse 6 and not in verse 7, by Erasm., Mosheim, al In deciding between the above, one question must first be answered · are we obliged to preserve the same character of the genitive in verses 6 and 7? because, if so, we must manifestly take [2] for [*ὀνειδισμὸν κ.*] *παγίδα τοῦ διαβόλου* [see below] cannot bear any other meaning than '*the* [reproach and] *snare which the devil lays*' This question must be answered, not by any mere consideration of uniformity, but by careful enquiry into the import of the substantive *κρῖμα* I conceive we cannot understand it here otherwise than as a *condemnatory sentence* The word is a *vox media*, *οὐκ εὔκριτον τὸ κρῖμα*, Æsch Suppl 392 but the dread here expressed of *falling into it* necessarily confines it to its adverse sense. This being so, Bengel's remark is noticeable —"diabolus potest *opprobrium* inferre, *judicium* non potest non enim judicat, sed judicatur.' To this Huther answers, that we must not consider the *κρῖμα* of the devil as necessarily parallel with God's *κρῖμα*, any more than with man's on his neighbour. "To understand," he continues, "the *κρῖμα τοῦ διαβόλου*, we must compare Eph. ii. 2, where the devil is called *τὸ πνεῦμα τὸ νῦν ἐνεργοῦν ἐν τοῖς υἱοῖς τῆς ἀπειθείας* so that whatever the world does to the reproach [zur Schmach] of Christ's Church, is the doing of the spirit that works in the world, viz. of the devil." But surely this reply is quite inadequate to justify the use of the decisive *κρῖμα*: and Huther himself has, by suggesting '*reproach*,' evaded the real question, and taken refuge in the unquestioned meaning of the next verse. He goes on to say, that only by understanding this of a *deed* of the Prince of the antichristian world, can we clearly establish a connexion with the following verse, pointed out as it is by *δέ*. But this is still more objectionable *δὲ καί* disjoins the two particulars, and introduces the latter as a separate and additional matter From the use of the decisive word *κρῖμα*, I infer that it cannot be an act of the adversary which is here spoken of, but an act in which *ὁ ἄρχων τοῦ κόσμου τούτου κέκριται* Then as to uniformity with ver. 7, I should not be disposed to make much account of it. For one who so loved similarity of external phrase, even where different meanings were to be conveyed, as St Paul, to use the genitives in *κρῖμα τοῦ διαβόλου* and *παγὶς τοῦ διαβόλου* in these different meanings, is surely nothing which need cause surprise. *τοῦ διαβόλου* is common to both. the devil's condemnation, and the devil's snare, are both alike alien from the Christian, in whom, as in his divine Master, the adversary should find nothing, and with whom he should have nothing in common. The *κρῖμα τοῦ διαβόλου* is in fact but the consummation of that state into which the *παγὶς τοῦ διαβόλου* is the introduction. I therefore unhesitatingly adopt [1]—*the condemnation into which Satan fell through the same blinding effect of pride*).

7] **Moreover** (*δέ*, bringing in the contrast of addition; '*more than this*,' .... *καί*, the addition itself of a new particular) **he must have a good testimony** (reff.) **from those without** (lit. '*those from without*' the unusual -*θεν* [reff] being added as harmonizing with the *ἀπό*, the testimony coming 'from without'), **lest he fall into** (a question arises which must be answered before we can render the following words Does *ὀνειδισμόν* [1] stand alone, '*into reproach, and the snare of the devil*,' or is it [2] to be joined with *παγίδα* as belonging to *διαβόλου*? For [1], which is the view of Thl, Est, Wolf, Heyden, Huther, Wiesinger, al [and Ellic doubtfully], it is alleged, that *ὀνειδισμόν* is separated from *καὶ παγίδα* by *ἐμπέσῃ*. But this alone cannot decide the matter The Apostle

8 [g] Διακόνους [h] ὡσαύτως [i] σεμνούς, μὴ [j] διλόγους, μὴ
οἴνῳ πολλῷ [k] προσέχοντας, μὴ [l] αἰσχροκερδεῖς, 9 [m] ἔχον-

g Rom xvi 1. Phil i 1. h ch ii 9 reff. i Phil iv 8. ver 11. Tit ii 2 only. Prov iii 6. j here only †. k ch i 4 reff. l Tit i 7 (reff) only †. m = ch i 19.

ADFH KLℵ a b c d e f g h k l m n o 17

8. om σεμνους ℵ[1] 109. 219[*].

may have intended to write merely *εἰς ὀνειδισμὸν ἐμπέσῃ τοῦ διαβόλου* Then in adding *καὶ παγίδα*, we may well conceive that he would keep *εἰς ὀν. ἐμπ.* for uniformity with the preceding verse, and also not to throw *κ παγίδα* into an unnatural prominence, as would be done by placing it before *ἐμπέσῃ*. We must then decide on other grounds Wiesinger, seeing that the *ὀνειδισμὸς τοῦ διαβόλου*, if these are to be taken together, must come immediately from *οἱ ἔξωθεν*, objects, that he doubts whether any where the devil is said *facere per se* that which he *facit per alterum* But surely 1 John iii 8 is a case in point: *ὁ ποιῶν τὴν ἁμαρτίαν ἐκ τοῦ διαβόλου ἐστίν, ὅτι ἀπ' ἀρχῆς ὁ διάβολος ἁμαρτάνει εἰς τοῦτο ἐφανερώθη ὁ υἱὸς τοῦ θεοῦ, ἵνα λύσῃ* **τὰ ἔργα τοῦ διαβόλου**, —and indeed Eph ii 2, *τὸ πνεῦμα τὸ νῦν ἐνεργοῦν ἐν τοῖς υἱοῖς τῆς ἀπειθείας* Huther supports this view by ch v 14· but I am unable to see how that verse touches the question· for whether the *ὀνειδισμός* belong to *τοῦ διαβ.* or not, it clearly must come in either case from *οἱ ἔξωθεν*. One consideration in favour of this view has not been alleged —that *ἡ παγὶς τοῦ διαβόλου* seems, from 2 Tim ii. 26, to be a familiar phrase with the Apostle, and therefore less likely to be joined with another governing substantive.

For [2], we have Thdrt. [*τῶν ἔξωθεν τῶν ἀπίστων λέγει ὁ γὰρ καὶ παρ' ἐκείνοις πλείστην ἔχων πρὸ τῆς χειροτονίας διαβολήν, ἐπονείδιστος ἔσται, καὶ πολλοῖς ὀνείδεσι περιβαλεῖ τὸ κοινόν, καὶ εἰς τὴν προτέραν ὅτι τάχιστα παλινδρομήσει παρανομίαν, τοῦ διαβόλου πάντα πρὸς τοῦτο μηχανωμένου*], al, — Bengel ["diabolus potest antistiti malis testimoniis laboranti plurimum excitare molestiæ, per se et per homines calumniatores"], De W, al. The chief grounds for this view are, [a] grammatical—that the *εἰς* is not repeated before *παγίδα*. I am not sure, whether we are right in applying such strict rules to these Pastoral Epistles but the consideration cannot but have some weight. [b] contextual—that the Apostle would hardly have alleged the mere *ἐμπεσεῖν εἰς ὀνειδισμόν* as a matter of sufficient importance to be parallel with *ἐμπ εἰς παγίδα τοῦ διαβόλου* This latter, I own, inclines me to adopt [2], but I would not by any means speak strongly in repudiation of the other) **the reproach and the snare of the devil** (reff. This latter is usually taken as meaning, the danger of relapse [cf Thdrt cited above] so Calv.. "ne infamiæ expositus, perfrictæ frontis esse incipiat, tantoque majore licentia se prostituat ad omnem nequitiam. quod est diaboli plagis se irretire. Quid enim spei restat ubi nullus est peccati pudor?" Grot gives it a different turn. 'ne contumeliis notatus quærat se ulcisci.' These, and many other references, may well be contained in the expression, and we need not, I think, be at the pains precisely to specify any one direction which the evil would take Such an one's steps would be shackled—his freedom hampered—his temper irritated—his character lost—and the natural result would be a fall from his place, to the detriment not of himself only, but of the Church of Christ)

8—13] *Precepts regarding deacons and deaconesses* (see below on ver. 11).

8] The construction continues from the preceding—the *δεῖ εἶναι* being in the Apostle's mind as governing the accusatives **In like manner** (the *ὡσαύτως* seems introduced by the similarity of character,—not merely to mark an additional particular) **the deacons** (mentioned as a class, besides here, only Phil. i. 1, where, as here, they follow the *ἐπίσκοποι*. Phœbe, Rom. xvi. 1, is a *διάκονος* of the church at Cenchrea The term or its cognates occur in a vaguer sense, but still indicating a special office, in Rom. xii 7. 1 Pet. iv 11 The connexion of the ecclesiastical deacons with the seven appointed in Acts vi. is very doubtful. see Chrysostom's and Œc's testimony, distinguishing them, in note there But that the ecclesiastical order sprung out of similar necessities, and had for its field of work similar objects, can hardly be doubted. See Suicer, *διάκονος* Winer, RWB.. Neander, Pfl. u Leit i p 54 note) **(must be) grave, not of double speech** (= *δίγλωσσος*, Prov xi. 13 [Ellic. adds *διχόμυθος*, Eurip Orest 890], not quite as Thl, *ἄλλα φρονοῦντας κ. ἄλλα λέγοντας*, but rather as Thdrt. [and Thl, additional], *ἕτερα τούτῳ, ἕτερα δὲ ἐκείνῳ λέγοντας*), **not addicted** (applying themselves, reff.) **to much wine** (= *μὴ οἴνῳ πολλῷ δεδουλωμένας*, Tit ii 3), not

C ριον της ACDFH KLℵ a b c d e f g h k l m n o 17

τας τὸ ⁿ μυστήριον τῆς πίστεως ἐν ᵒ καθαρᾷ ᵒ συνειδήσει.
10 ᵖ καὶ οὗτοι ᵖ δὲ ᵠ δοκιμαζέσθωσαν πρῶτον, εἶτα ʳ δια-
κονείτωσαν, ˢ ἀνέγκλητοι ὄντες. 11 γυναῖκας ᵗ ὡσαύτως

n = 1 Cor ii 7 see ver 16 Rom xi 25 and note. o 2 Tim i 3 only. κ. c. Heb ix 14 συν ch i 5 reff. p Paul, Rom xi 3. 2 Tim iii 12 only. Matt x 18. xvi 18 al. q = Luke xiv 19. 1 Cor ii 13. 2 Cor viii 8. 1 Thess v 21. Prov xvii 3. r = ver 13. 1 Pet iv 11 only. s 1 Cor i 8. Col i 22. Tit i 6, 7 only. P.†. 3 Macc v 31. t ver 8.

9 for εν καθ συνειδ, και καθαρας συνειδησεως ℵ[1].
10 for ουτοι, αυτοι H 73. for ειτα, και ουτω D[1] vulg goth Jer Ambrst.

greedy of gain (hardly, as E. V., to be *doubly rendered,—'greedy of filthy* lucre,'—so also Thdrt., ὁ ἐκ πραγμάτων αἰσχρῶν κ. λίαν ἀτόπων κέρδη συλλεγειν ἀνεχόμενος. It would appear from Tit. i. 11, διδάσκοντες ἃ μὴ δεῖ αἰσχροῦ κέρδους χάριν, that all κέρδος is αἰσχρόν which is set before a man as a by-end in his work for God: so likewise in 1 Pet. v. 2,—ἐπισκοποῦντες μὴ . . . . μηδὲ αἰσχροκερδῶς . . . . 'nor with a view to gain,' such gain being necessarily base when thus sought. This particular of the deacons' character assumes special importance, if we connect it with the collecting and distributing alms. Cyprian, Ep. 54 [12 ad Corn. Pap. § 1, Migne, Patr. Gr. vol. iii. p. 797], stigmatizes the deacon Felicissimus as 'pecuniæ commissæ sibi fraudator'), **holding the mystery of the (or their) faith** (that great objective truth which man of himself knows not, but which the Spirit of God reveals to the faithful: cf. Rom. xvi. 25 f. 1 Cor. ii. 7—10: and even Him who in fact *is* that mystery, the great object of all faith: see note on ver. 16, τὸ τῆς εὐσεβείας μυστήριον. That expression makes it probable that τῆς πίστεως is here to be taken subjectively: *the*, or *their, faith*: the apprehension which appropriates to them the contents of God's revelation of Christ. That revelation of the Person of Christ, their faith's μυστήριον, they are to hold. See Ellic.'s note) **in pure conscience** (see reff. and ch. i. 19. From those passages it appears, that we must not give the words a special application to their official life as deacons, but understand them of earnestness and singleness of Christian character,—being in heart persuaded of the truth of that divine mystery which they profess to have apprehended by faith). 10.] **And moreover** (the δέ introduces a caution—the slight contrast of a necessary addition to their mere present character. On this force of καὶ . . . δέ, see Hartung, i. 182. Ellic., here. There is no connexion in καὶ . . . δέ with the former requirements regarding ἐπίσκοποι) **let these** (who answer, in their candidateship for the diaconate, to the above character) **be put to the proof first** (viz. with regard to their blamelessness of life, cf. ἀνέγκλ. ὄντες below: e. g. by testimonials, and publication of their intention to offer themselves: but no formal way is specified, only the reality insisted on), **then let them act as deacons** (or, *minister*: but more probably here in the narrower technical sense, as in reff.(?) Not '*be made* deacons,' as Conyb.: the word is of *their* act in the office, not of their reception of it, which is of course understood in the background), **if they are** (found by the δοκιμή to be) **irreproachable.** 11.] **(The) women in like manner** (who are these? Are they (1) women who were to serve as deacons,—deaconesses?—or (2) wives of the deacons?—or (3) wives of the deacons and overseers?—or (4) women in general? I conceive we may dismiss (4) at once, for Chrys.'s reason: τί γὰρ ἐβούλετο μεταξὺ τῶν εἰρημένων παρεμβαλεῖν τι περὶ γυναικῶν,—(3) upheld by Calv., Est., Calov., and Mack, may for the same reason, seeing that he returns to διάκονοι again in ver. 12, be characterized as extremely improbable,—(2) has found many supporters among modern Commentators: Luth., Beza, Beng. [who strangely adds, 'pendet ab *habentes* ver. 9'], Rosenm., Heinr., Huther, Conyb., al., and E. V. But it has against it (*a*) the omission of all expressed reference to the deacons, such as might be given by αὐτῶν, or by τάς. (*b*) the expression of ὡσαύτως, by which the διάκονοι themselves were introduced, and which seems to mark a new ecclesiastical class. (*c*) the introduction of the injunction respecting the deacons, ἔστωσαν μιᾶς γυναικὸς ἄνδρες, as a new particular, which would hardly be if their wives had been mentioned before. (*d*) the circumstance, connected with the mention of Phœbe as διάκονος of the church at Cenchrea in Rom. xvi. 1, that unless those are deaconesses, there would be among these injunctions no mention of an important class of persons employed as officers of the church. We come thus to consider (1), that these γυναῖκες are *deaconesses,—ministræ*, as Pliny calls them in his letter to Trajan [see note on Rom. xvi. 1]. In this view the ancients are, as

u = 2 Tim iii 3 Tit ii 3 only Esth vii 4 (vi 6, 7 reff) v ver 2 w 2 Tim iv 5 reff x ver 4, 5

ᵗ σεμνάς, μὴ ᵘ διαβόλους, ᵛ νηφαλίους, πιστὰς ʷ ἐν πᾶσιν. ACDFH KLℵ a b c d e f g h k l m n o 17
12 ˡ διάκονοι ἔστωσαν ˡ μιᾶς γυναικὸς ˡ ἄνδρες, τέκνων
καλῶς ˣ προϊστάμενοι καὶ τῶν ἰδίων οἴκων. 13 οἱ γὰρ

11 σεμνους A rec νηφαλεους, with D³K e l¹ m n o Damasc. -λαιους FL d f 39 72 93 123 txt ACD¹Hℵ rel.
12 aft διακ ins δε F καλων F

far as I know, unanimous. Of the moderns, it is held by Grot, Mosh, Mich, De W, Wiesinger, Ellicott It is alleged against it—(a) that thus the return to the διάκονοι, verse 12, would be harsh, or, as Conyb "on that view, the verse is most unnaturally interpolated in the midst of the discussion concerning the deacons" But the ready answer to this is found in Chrys's view of verse 12, that under διάκονοι, and their household duties, he comprehends in fact both sexes under one: ταῦτα καὶ περὶ γυναικῶν διακόνων ἁρμόττει εἰρῆσθαι· (b) that the existence of deaconesses as an order in the ministry is after all not so clear To this it might be answered, that even were they nowhere else mentioned, the present passage stands on its own grounds, and if it seemed from the context that such persons were indicated here, we should reason from this to the fact of their existence, not from the absence of other mention to their non-indication here. I decide then for (1) that these women are *deaconesses*) **(must be) grave, not slanderers** (corresponds to μὴ διλόγους in the males, being the vice to which the female sex is more addicted. Cf Eurip. Phœn. 298 ff, φιλόψογον δὲ χρῆμα θηλειῶν ἔφυ, | σμικράς τ' ἀφορμὰς ἢν λάβωσι τῶν λόγων, | πλείους ἐπεισφέρουσιν ἡδονὴ δέ τις | γυναιξί, μηδὲν ὑγιὲς ἀλλήλαις λεγειν **διάβολος** in this sense [reff] is peculiar in N. T. to these Epistles), **sober** (see on ver 2, corresponding to μὴ οἴνῳ πολλῷ προσέχοντας), **faithful in all things** (corresponds to μὴ αἰσχροκερδεῖς trusty in the distribution of the alms committed to them, and in all other ministrations).

12.] General directions respecting those in the diaconate (of both sexes, the female being included in the male, see Chrys cited above), with regard to their domestic condition and duties, as above (verses 4, 5) respecting the episcopate **Let the deacons be husbands of one wife** (see on this above, ver 2), **ruling well over children** (the emphatic position of the anarthrous τέκνα, as above ver. 4, makes it probable that the *having children to rule* is to be considered as a qualification see Tit i 6, note Chrys gives a curious and characteristic reason for the precept· πανταχοῦ τίθησι τὴν τῶν τέκνων προστασίαν, ἵνα μὴ ἀπὸ τούτου οἱ λοιποὶ σκανδαλίζωνται) **and their own houses** 13.] *The importance of true and faithful service in the diaconate* **For those who served well the office of deacon** (the aor participle, not the perf, because the standing-point of the sentence is at first the great day, when their διακονία has passed by In fact this aor participle decides between the interpretations see below) **are acquiring** (the Apostle having begun by placing himself at the great day of retribution, and consequently used the aor. participle, now shifts, so to speak, the scene, and deals with their present conduct. q. d, 'Those who shall then be found to have served well, &c. . . . . . *are now*, &c.' On περιποιέω and περιποίησις, see notes, Eph i 14 1 Thess v. 9) **for themselves** (emphatic—besides the service they are rendering to the church) **a good standing-place** (viz at the great day · cf ch. vi. 19, ἀποθησαυρίζοντας ἑαυτοῖς θεμέλιον καλὸν εἰς τὸ μέλλον, ἵνα ἐπιλάβωνται τῆς ὄντως ζωῆς.—and Dan xii 3 [Heb and E V], where however the metaphor is different. The interpretations of **βαθμόν**, *a step*, or place to stand on [in LXX, the *threshold*, or step, before a door see reff], have been very various (1) Ambr, Jer, Pel., Thl., Erasm., Bull, Beza, Corn-a Lap., Est, Grot, Lightf, Beng., Wolf, Mosh, Schottg, Wordsw, al, understand it of a *degree of ecclesiastical preferment*, scil from the office of deacon to that of presbyter, and take καλόν for a comparative Against this is (a) the forcing of καλόν, (b) the improbability that such a rise upwards through the ecclesiastical offices was known in the Apostle's time (c) the still greater unlikelihood, even if it were known, that he would propose as a motive to a deacon to fulfil his office well, the ambitious desire to rise out of it. (2) Mack, Matth, Olsh, Huther, al, following Calv. and Luther, understand by it a high place of honour in the esteem of the church [see on παῤῥησία below]: "qui probe

καλῶς ʸ διακονήσαντες ᶻ βαθμὸν ἑαυτοῖς καλὸν ᵃ περιποιοῦνται, καὶ ᵇ πολλὴν ᵇ παῤῥησίαν ἐν ᵈ πίστει τῇ ᵈ ἐν
χριστῷ Ἰησοῦ. 14 Ταῦτά σοι γράφω, ἐλπίζων ἐλθεῖν

y ver 10. z here only. 1 Kings v 5. 4 Kings xx 9 10 11 vat. Sir vi 20 only. a Luke xvii 33. Acts xx 28 only. Gen xxxi 18. Isa xxxi 5. (ποιησις, Eph i 14.) b Philem 8. c Eph iii 12 reff. — 1 John iii 21. Heb iv 16. d Gal iii 26. Eph i 15. Col i 4. 2 Tim iii 15.

. ιησου H ACD FKLℵ a b c d e f g h k l m n o 17

13 for τη εν, την εν F.
14 ελπιζω F h¹ m om προς σε F 67² arm

functi fuerint hoc ministerio, non parvo honore dignos esse." Calv. Against this is (a) that there is not a more distinct reference made to the estimation of the church; indeed that the emphatic ἑαυτοῖς [see above] is altogether against such reference: (b) that thus again an unworthy motive would be set before the deacons: (c) that again [see below] παῤῥησία will not on this interpretation, bear any legitimate rendering. (d) the aor. part. διακονήσαντες, as before (3) Mosc., al., take it *spiritually*, as meaning *progress in the faith*. Chrys. is claimed for this view, but this is somewhat doubtful His words are, τουτέστι, προκοπὴν καὶ παῤῥησίαν πολλὴν τὴν ἐν πίστει χρ. Ἰησοῦ ὡσεὶ ἔλεγεν, οἱ ἐν τοῖς κάτω δείξαντες ἑαυτοὺς διεγηγερμένους, ταχέως καὶ πρὸς ἐκεῖνα ἀνελεύσονται· where, notwithstanding that προκοπήν would seem to mean subjective progress, Thl.'s explanation of ἐκεῖνα,—τὰ ἀνώτερα, the higher office, seems best to fit the sentence and thus προκοπή must be objective,—*preferment* But (a) the whole [especially βαθμὸν περιποιοῦνται] is of too objective a character thus to be interpreted of a merely subjective process—besides that (b) thus also the *present* περιποιοῦνται would require a present participle διακονοῦντες (4) Thdrt [below], Croc., Flatt, Heinrichs [modified. see below], De W., Wiesinger, understand it nearly as above—of the station or standing-place which the faithful deacon acquires before God, with reference to his own salvation. The opinions of these Commentators are, however, somewhat various as to the exact time to which the standing on this βαθμός is to be referred Thdrt says εἰ καὶ ἐλάττονα, φησί, τιμὴν ἔχουσι κατὰ τόνδε τὸν βίον, ἀλλ' οὖν εἰδέναι προσήκει, ὡς τὴν ἐγχειρισθεῖσαν πεπληρωκότες διακονίαν, τὸν τιμιώτατον βαθμὸν ἐν τῷ μέλλοντι λήψονται βίῳ, καὶ τῆς πρὸς τὸν δεσπότην χριστὸν ἀπολαύσονται παῤῥησίας. Heinrichs, with whom De W. and Wiesinger are disposed to agree, understands that they procure to themselves a good *expectation of salvation* a βαθμός i. e. in *this life, with reference to* the future one. I believe, from the form of the sentence, that the truth will be found by combining the two views. The διακονήσαντες, as above stated, is used with reference to their finished course at that day. The περιποιοῦνται transfers the scene to the present time. The βαθμός is that which they are now securing for themselves, and will be found standing on at that day belonging therefore in part to both periods, and not necessarily involving the idea of different degrees of blessedness, though that idea [cf. 1 Cor iii 15] is familiar to St Paul,—but merely predicating the soundness of the ground on which these διάκονοι will themselves stand) **and much confidence** (this also is variously understood, according as βαθμός is interpreted Those who think of *ecclesiastical preferment*, render παῤῥησία 'freedom of speech as regards the faith [obj.],' i. e. in teaching ['*majore fiducia aliis Evangelium prædicabunt*,' Grot.], or in resisting error,—or, 'libertas ingenue agendi,' as Est.: or 'a wide field for spiritual action,' as Matthies. To these there might be no objection, but for the adjunct to παῤῥησία, ἐν πίστει τῇ ἐν χριστῷ Ἰησοῦ Thus defined, παῤῥησία must necessarily have a subjective reference,—i. e. to the confidence towards God possessed by those who have made good advance in faith in Christ, as in reff And so Thdrt [above], Ambr., Croc., Cocc. Flatt, Calv., Beza [these two understand it more generally, of the confidence wrought by a good conscience], Bengel, Wies., De W., Ellic., al.) **in [the] faith** (subjective, from what follows) **which is in** (see reff ἐν denotes more the repose of faith *in*, εἰς the reliance of faith *on*, Christ) **Christ Jesus**

14—16.] Close of the above directions *by a solemn statement of their object and its glorious import* **These things** (the foregoing precepts, most naturally hardly, as Bengel, 'totam epistolam') **I write** (expressed in the epistolary aorist, Philem 19, 21 but in the present, 1 Cor xiv 37 2 Cor i 13, xiii 10 Gal. i. 20 [1 John i. 4. ii 1, &c.]) **to thee, hoping** ('though I hope' "part ἐλπίζων per καίπερ seu similem particulam esse resolvendum, nexus orationis docet" Leo, cited by Huther) **to come to thee sooner**

e John xiii 27 xx 4 Heb xiii 19, 23 only Wisd xiii 9 1 Macc ii 40 1 Pet ii 5 28 reff
f 2 Pet iii 9 only Deut vii 10
h = Eph ii 3 reff
k ver 5 reff Paul only
i = (Matt xii 45) Heb. x 21 1 Pet iv 17 see Acts x 41, 47 xiii 31, 43 al Paul, passim attr., Phil 1

πρός σε [e]τάχιον· 15 ἐὰν δὲ [f]βραδύνω, ἵνα εἰδῇς πῶς δεῖ
ἐν [g]οἴκῳ [g]θεοῦ [h]ἀναστρέφεσθαι, [i]ἥτις ἐστὶν [k]ἐκκλησία

ACDF KLℵ a b c d e f g h k l m n o 17

for ταχιον, εν ταχει ACD[1] 17 ταχειον o. txt D[3]FKLℵ rel Chr Thdrt Damasc.
15. ιδης A(appy) D[1]F aft δει ins σε D[1] vulg arm Orig lat-ff. ειτις (itacism) C.

(than may seem) (on the comparative,—which must not be broken down into a positive, as it is by almost all the Commentators,—see John xiii. 27 note, and Winer, edn. 6, § 35 4. Also Acts xvii 21; xxv 10; xxvii. 13: Heb xiii. 19, 23, which last is exactly parallel with this Some supply it,—before this Epistle come to thee or, before thou shalt have need to put these precepts into practice but the above seems simpler, and suits better the usage elsewhere): **but if I should delay (coming)** (from ἐλπίζων to βραδύνω may be regarded as parenthetical, the ἵνα belonging immediately to γράφω), **that thou mayest know how thou oughtest to conduct thyself** (reff. Huther would take πῶς δεῖ ἀναστρέφεσθαι generally,—'*how men ought to behave themselves*,' alleging, that in the preceding, there is no direct prescription how Timotheus is himself to act, and that if we supply σε [as D[1] in digest], we confine the reference of οἶκος θεοῦ to the Ephesian church The latter objection need not detain us long If the church in general is the house of God, then any portion of it may clearly partake of the title and the dignity. To the former, we may reply, that in fact, the whole of what has preceded does regard Timotheus's own behaviour He was to see to all these things—to take care that all these precepts were observed) **in the house of God** (see reff. also Heb. iii 2, 5, 6, and notes 1 Cor iii 16 2 Cor vi 16 Eph. ii 22 —that congregation among whom God dwells, by His Spirit);—**for such** (the house of God the ἥτις brings out into prominence the appository explanation, and specially applies it to the antecedent) **is the congregation** (ἐκκλησίας οὐ τοὺς οἴκους λέγει τοὺς εὐκτηρίους, κατὰ τὴν τῶν πολλῶν συνήθειαν, ἀλλὰ τῶν πιστῶν τὸν σύλλογον. Theod -mops.) **of the living God** (thus designated for solemnity, and to shew His personal and active presence among them), **the pillar** (see below) **and basement** (= θεμέλιος, 2 Tim. ii. 19 'firmamentum.' It is a climax, not as Bengel, "instar unius vocabuli solidissimum quiddam exprimentis" the στύλος is the intermediate, the ἑδραίωμα the final support of the building: as Wahl,—"omne id, cui ut primario et præ ceteris insigni innititur aliquid") **of the truth** (these latter words are variously referred: being (1) by Camero, Er-Schmid., Limborch, Le Clerc, Schottg, Beng, Mosh, Rosenm, Heinr, Wegsch, Heydeur, Flatt, al. [see in Wolf. Not Chillingworth, as stated in Bloomf · see below], joined with the following sentence, putting a period at ζῶντος, and proceeding στύλος καὶ ἑδραίωμα τῆς ἀληθείας καὶ ὁμολογουμένως μέγα ἐστὶν τὸ μυστ κ.τ λ. To this I can only say, that if any one imagines St Paul, or any other person capable of writing this Epistle, able to have indited such a sentence, I fear there is but little chance in arguing with him on the point in question To say nothing of its abruptness and harshness, beyond all example even in these Epistles, how palpably does it betray the botching of modern conjectural arrangement in the wretched anti-climax—στύλος καὶ ἑδραίωμα [rising in solemnity] τῆς ἀληθείας, καὶ [what grander idea, after the basement of the whole building, does the reader suppose about to follow?] ὁμολογουμένως μέγα! These two last words, which have [see below] their appropriate majesty and grandeur in their literal use at the emphatic opening of such a sentence as the next, are thus robbed of it all, and sink into the very lowest bathos; the metaphor being dropped, and the lofty imagery ending with a vague generality. If a sentence like this occurred in the Epistle, I should feel it a weightier argument against its genuineness than any which its opponents have yet adduced. (2) by Gregory of Nyssa [de vita Mosis vol i p 385, οὐ μόνον Πέτρος καὶ Ἰάκωβος καὶ Ἰωάννης στύλοι τῆς ἐκκλησίας εἰσὶ . . ὁ θεῖος ἀπόστολος . . . καὶ τὸν Τιμόθεον στύλον καλὸν ἐτεκτήνατο, ποιήσας αὐτόν, καθὼς φησὶ τῇ ἰδίᾳ φωνῇ, στύλον καὶ ἑδραίωμα τῆς ἀληθείας], Chillingworth [Religion of Protestants, &c., ch iii 76 but he allows as possible, the reference to the Church: "if you will needs have St. Paul refer this not to Timothy, but to the Church, I will not contend about it any further, than to say, Possibly it may be otherwise"],—by others

[k] [l] Θεοῦ [l] ζῶντος, [m] στῦλος καὶ [n] ἑδραίωμα τῆς ἀληθείας.

l Acts xiv 15 (Paul) 2 Cor iii 3 vi 16 ch iv 10 Heb iii 12 ix 14 x 31 xii 22 Rev vii 2 xv 7 Hos i 10 m Gal ii 9 Rev iii 12 x 1 only 3 Kings vii 41 n here only † (-os, Col i 23.)

mentioned in Wolf, and in our own days by Conybeare, it is taken as referring to TIMOTHEUS —"*that thou mayest know how to conduct thyself in the house of God, which is &c. as a pillar and basement of the truth.*" In the very elaborate discussion of this passage by Suicer [s v. *στύλος*], he cites those fathers who seem more or less to have favoured this idea Of these we must manifestly not claim for it those who have merely used the word *στύλος* or *columna* of an Apostle or teacher, or individual Christian,—as that is justified, independently of our passage, by Gal ii 9 Rev iii 12 —but Greg Naz applies the very words to Eusebius of Samosata [Ep xliv. 1, vol. iii. (Migne) p. 39], and to Basil [Orat xviii. 1, vol i. p 330]: and Basil in the Catena says, *εἰσὶ καὶ στύλοι τῆς Ἱερουσαλὴμ οἱ ἀπόστολοι, κατὰ τὸ εἰρημένον, στύλος καὶ ἑδραίωμα τῆς ἀληθείας*: and in the Epistle of the churches of Lyons and Vienne, Euseb v 1, it is said of Attalus, *στύλον καὶ ἑδραίωμα τῶν ἐνταῦθα ἀεὶ γεγονότα.* Other cognate expressions, such as *τὸ στερέωμα τῆς πίστεως* [Chrys, of St Peter, Hom xxxii vol v. p 199, and Basil, of Eusebius, as above], *πίστεως ἔρεισμα* [Greg Naz, of Basil, Or. xviii as above], *τὸ τῆς ἐκκλησίας στήριγμα* [Thl. on Luke xxii, of St Peter], *θρησκείας στηρίγματα* [of Pastors, Nicephorus Hist vii 2], are adduced by Suicer The principal modern reasons for adopting this view have been (a) polemical—as against Roman Catholic infallibility of the Church, or (b) for uniformity of symbolism, seeing that in Gal ii 9, Rev iii 12, *men* are compared to pillars [see this very copiously illustrated in Suicer] On both of these I shall treat expressly below. To the *grammatical* construction of the sentence thus understood, there is no objection The nominative *στύλος* after *δεῖ* would be not only allowable, but necessary, if it expressed, not a previous predicate of the understood *σε*, but the character which by the *ἀναστρέφεσθαι* he was to become or shew forth cf Plat and Demost in Kuhner, § 646, 2 anm, who however has not apprehended the right reason of the idiom But to the sentence itself thus arranged and understood, there are weighty, and I conceive fatal objections · to wit, (c) if *στύλος κ τ λ* had been meant to apply to Timotheus, it would hardly have been possible that *σε* should be omitted He would thus be the prominent object in the whole passage, not as now the least prominent, lurking behind *ἀναστρέφεσθαι* to make way for greater things (d) I can hardly think, that, in this case, *στύλος* would have been anarthrous Though 'a pillar' might be the virtual meaning, *σε, τὸν στύλον*, or *σε ἀναστρέφεσθαι, . . ὁ στύλος*, would certainly be the Greek expression (e) In this case also, the *καὶ ὁμολογουμένως* which follows would most naturally refer, not to the great deposit of faith in Christ which is entrusted to the church to keep,—but to the very strong and unusual expression which had just been used of a young minister in the church,—'and confessedly great is the dignity of the least of the ministers of Christ for,' &c (3) The reference to THE CHURCH is upheld by Chrys [*οὐχ ὡς ἐκεῖνος ὁ ἰουδαικὸς οἶκος θεοῦ τοῦτο γάρ ἐστι τὸ συνέχον τὴν πίστιν καὶ τὸ κήρυγμα ἡ γὰρ ἀλήθειά ἐστι τῆς ἐκκλησίας καὶ στύλος καὶ ἑδραίωμα* This inversion of the sentence may have arisen from taking *τῆς ἀληθείας* as a genitive of apposition], Thdrt [*οἶκον θεοῦ καὶ ἐκκλησίαν τῶν πεπιστευκότων τὸν σύλλογον προσηγόρευσε τούτους ἔφη στύλον καὶ ἑδραίωμα τῆς ἀληθείας. ἐπὶ γὰρ τῆς πέτρας ἐρηρεισμένοι καὶ ἀκλόνητοι διαμένουσι, καὶ διὰ τῶν πραγμάτων κηρύττοντες τὴν τῶν δογμάτων ἀλήθειαν*], Theodor-mops [as cited above, on *ἐκκλησία*, as far as *σύλλογον*, then he proceeds, *ὅθεν καὶ στύλον αὐτὴν καὶ ἑδραίωμα τῆς ἀληθείας ἐκάλεσεν, ὡς ἂν ἐν αὐτῇ τῆς ἀληθείας τὴν σύστασιν ἐχούσης*], Thl, Œc, Ambr, Pel, the Roman Commentators, Luth, Calv. ["nonne Ecclesia mater est piorum omnium, quæ ipsos regenerat Dei verbo, quæ educat alitque tota vita, quæ confirmat, quæ ad solidam perfectionem usque perducit? eadem quoque ratione columna veritatis prædicatur quia doctrinæ administrandæ munus, quod Deus penes eam deposuit, unicum est instrumentum retinendæ veritatis, ne ex hominum memoria pereat"], Beza, Grot ["veritatem sustentat atque attollit ecclesia, efficit ne labatur ex animis, efficit ut longe lateque conspiciatur"], Calov, Wolf, &c De Wette, Huther, Wiesinger, al. And this interpretation agrees with 2 Tim ii. 19 see note there But there is brought against it the objection, that there is thus introduced confusion of metaphor The *ἐκκλησία*, which was the *οἶκος* above, now becomes *στύλος*, a part of the *οἶκος*. This is not difficult to answer. The

16 καὶ [o] ὁμολογουμένως [p] μέγα ἐστὶν τὸ τῆς [q] εὐσεβείας
[r] μυστήριον, ὃς [s] ἐφανερώθη [t] ἐν σαρκί, [u] ἐδικαιώθη ἐν

ACDF KLℵ a b c d e f g h k l m n o 17

o here only. Hos xiv 5 compd only. Jos Antt ii 9 6 init al in Wetst. p Eph v 32 Rom xvi 26 Col i 26 (reff) q ch iii 2 reff r see 1 Thess ii 7 see 1 John i 2 2 Tim i 10 s w μυστ, Col ii 1 Philem 16 t 2 Cor x 3 Gal ii 20. Phil i 22, 24 u — Matt xi 19? see note

16 On the famous disputed reading in this verse, I give an analysis of the present state of the evidence —I rec θεος, i e. $\overline{\Theta C}$, with the follg (not A, nor C see below) D³K (F has $\overline{OC}$ without any apparent stroke in the O) L ℵ³ has written ΘЄ above the OC of the codex [cent xii.] rel. The testimonies of the fathers for θεος are very doubtful. Few make a *direct citation of* the passage as thus read those which seem to do so being naturally explained on the supposition of their supplying *θεός* as the subject of *ὅς* The readg θεος is *directly supported* by Chrysostom, Theodoret, Euthalius, Macedonius (who has been charged by some of the Latins with introducing the reading), Damascenus, Theophylact, Œcumenius Those *supposed to favour* the reading are Ignatius (ad Eph 19, p 660,—*θεοῦ* [but the Syriac has *υἱοῦ*] *ἀνθρωπίνως φανερουμενου*. al *ὡς ἀνθρώπου φαινομένου*), the Apostolic Constitutions(*θεὸς κύριε ὁ ἐπιφανεὶς ἡμῖν ἐν σαρκί*) Hippolytus(agst Noetus *θεὸς ἐν σώματι ἐφανερώθη*) Gregory Thaumaturgus or rather Apollinaris(in Phot *θεὸς ἐν σαρκὶ φανερωθείς*) The testimonies of Athanasius, Nyssen, Cyr, usually adduced in favour of *θεός*, are either uncertain from various readings, or inapplicable (see below). II. ος, i e OC, is found in the follg A(this is now *matter of certainty* The black line at present visible in the O, is a modern retouching of an older but not original fainter one, due apparently to the darkening of the stroke of an Є seen through from the other side. I have examined the page, and find that a portion of the virgula of the Є, seen through, and now corroded through, extends nearly through the Θ, not however quite in, but somewhat above, its centre, as Sir Frederick Madden has observed to me It was to complete this that Junius made a dot See also Ellicott's note, Past Epp edn 2, p 103 Besides which, the mark of abbreviation above the line is modern, not corresponding with those in the MS Sir Frederick Madden now informs me that a very powerful microscope has been applied by Professor Maskelyne, at his request, to the passage in the MS, and the result has been that *no trace of either virgula in the* O *or mark of contraction over it, can be discovered* It is to be hoped therefore, that A will never again be cited on the side of rec) C(see Tischendorf, prolegg to his edn of the Codex Ephremi, p 30)Fℵ¹ 17 73 181 mss mentd by Liberatus (Cent VI) Victor Tununensis (Cent VI)

house contains in itself both *στύλος* and *ἑδραίωμα*—the pillar and the basement both belong to the house Why may not the *στύλος* be taken collectively? the very word *ἐκκλησία*, occurring since, has pluralized the idea—the building consists of the *κλητοί*, who are so many *στύλοι*—why should it not in the aggregate be described as the *στύλος*? This seems to me far better than, with some in Suicer, to suppose a monumental pillar, or base of an image, to be meant The way in which the congregation of the faithful is the pillar and basement of the truth is admirably given by Thdrt and Calvin above viz. in that it is the element in which and medium by which the truth is conserved and upheld) 16] **And** (follows on the preceding it is indeed worth all thy care to conduct thyself worthily in this house of God—for that truth which is there conserved and upheld is great and glorious above all others, being [see below] none other in fact than THE LORD HIMSELF, in all His gracious manifestation and glorious triumph) **confessedly** ('as is acknowledged on all hands:' so Thucyd. vi 90, Ἴβηρας καὶ ἄλλους τῶν ἐκεῖ ὁμολογουμένως νῦν βαρβάρων μαχιμωτάτους: Xen. Anab. ii 6 1, Κλέαρχος ὁμολογουμένως ἐκ πάντων τῶν ἐμπείρως αὐτοῦ ἐχόντων δόξας γενέσθαι ἀνὴρ καὶ πολεμικός, κ τ.λ see other examples in Palm and Rost, Lex., and in Wetst In this word there is a reference to the *ἐκκλησία* as the upholder of the truth *confessedly among the κλητοί* But we must not therefore take the word in a formal sense, 'as we confess,' and then *in consequence* regard the following words as a portion of a confession or song of praise [see below]. The adverb is of too general signification for this special reference) **great is the mystery** (see ver 9 that which was hidden from man until God revealed it, historically, in Redemption) **of piety** (see ch. ii 2, note 'of the religious life' In order to comprehend fully what follows, we must endeavour to realize the train of thought in the Apostle's mind at the time. This '*mystery*' of the life of God in man, is in fact the unfolding of Christ to and in him the key-text to our passage being Col i 27, οἷς ἠθέλησεν ὁ θεὸς γνωρίσαι τί

v πνεύματι, w ὤφθη ἀγγέλοις, x ἐκηρύχθη ἐν ἔθνεσιν, y ἐπι- v see 1 Pet iii 18

w = & constr, Matt xvii 3 | Luke i 11 xxii 43 xxiv 34 1 Cor xv 5, &c Exod iii 2 x passive 1 Cor xv 12 2 Cor i 19 (Col i 23) y = passive, Rom x 10 2 Thess i 10 only

& Hincmar (Cent IX), who charge Macedonius with introducing θεός.—goth syr (or syr marg) coptt,—Cyr(de recta fide ad Theodosium, τὸ μέγα τῆς εὐσεβείας μυστήριον, τουτέστι χριστός, ὃς ἐφανερώθη . . . οἶμαι οὐχ ἕτερον τὸ τῆς εὐσεβείας μυστήριον ἢ αὐτὸς ἡμῶν ὁ ἐκ τοῦ θεοῦ πατρὸς λόγος, ὃς ἐφανερώθη &c That Cyril read ὃς as in the mss, and not θεος as in the present edd, is testified by Œc and Photius h l and by the scholia of several mss of the N T) Thdor-mops(Acts of the Council of Constantinop, Mansi ix 221) Epiph$_2$ Pseud-Chrys(but ὃ quod al) Gelasius of Cyzicum (or rather Macarius of Jerusalem [Cent IV] cited by Gelas. in the Acts of the Nicene Council) Jerome(on Isa liii. 11)—ὃς or ὃ is read in Syr III. ὃ (correction to agree with μυστηριον) D[1](accg to Wetstein and Griesbach and recently Tischendorf) latt lat-ff exc Jerome.—The reading ὃς seems to be supported by the follg. Barnabas(epist 12, p 764, 'Ιησοῦς οὐχ ὁ υἱὸς ἀνθρώπου ἀλλ' ὁ υἱὸς τοῦ θεοῦ τύπῳ καὶ ἐν σαρκὶ φανερωθείς) Theodotus(ὁ σωτὴρ ὤφθη κατιὼν τοῖς ἀγγέλοις) Justin ? to Diognetus(ἀπέστειλε λόγον ἵνα κόσμῳ φανῇ, ὃς . . . διὰ ἀποστόλων κηρυχθεὶς ὑπὸ ἐθνῶν ἐπιστεύθη) Clem alex in Œcum(ὢ μυστήριον· μεθ' ἡμῶν εἶδον οἱ ἄγγελοι τὸν χριστόν) Orig('Ιησοῦς ἐν δόξῃ ἀναλαμβάνεσθαι λέγεται) Orig-int(Is qui verbum caro factus apparuit positus (or positus) in carne, sicut Apostolus dicit quia (perhaps qui ?) manifestus est in carne, justificatus &c) Greg-Nyss(τὸ μυστήριον ἐν σαρκὶ ἐφανερώθη. καλῶς τοῦτο λέγων, οὗτος ὁ ἡμέτερος λόγος) Basil(τοῦ μεγάλου μυστηρίου ὅτι ὁ κύριος ἐφανερώθη ἐν σαρκί) Nestorius in Arnob-jun(τὸ ἐν τῇ Μαρίᾳ γεννηθὲν . . . ἐφανερώθη γάρ, φησίν, ἐν σαρκί, ἐδικαιώθη &c) Didymus(secundum quod dictum est manifestatur in carne, on 1 John iv).—Now that it may be fairly said, that merely external considerations have settled this question, we are not driven to combine internal considerations Still the grounds which have confirmed me in deciding for ὃς, may be seen detailed in the note.

τὸ πλοῦτος τῆς δόξης τοῦ μυστηρίου τούτου ἐν τοῖς ἔθνεσιν, **ὅ ἐστιν χριστὸς ἐν ὑμῖν, ἡ ἐλπὶς τῆς δόξης** This was the thought in St. Paul's mind; that the great revelation of the religious life is, CHRIST And in accordance with his practice in these Epistles, written as I believe, far on in his course, and after the figures and results of deep spiritual thoughts had been long familiar to him, he at once without explanation, or apology as beforetime in Col. i 27, or expression of the χριστός justifying the change of gender in the relative, joins the deep and latent thought with the superficial and obvious one, and without saying that the mystery *is in fact* Christ, passes from the mystery to the Person of Christ as being one and the same. Then, thus passing, he is naturally led to a summary of those particulars wherein Christ has been revealed as a ground for the εὐσέβεια of His Church And, the idea of μυστήριον being prominent before him, he selects especially those events in and by which Christ was *manifested forth*—came forth from that secrecy in which he had beforetime been hidden in the counsels of God, and shone out to men and angels as the Lord of life and glory Let me say in passing, that it should be noticed, in a question which now happily no longer depends on internal considerations, how completely the whole glorious sentence is marred and disjointed by the substitution of θεός. It is not the objective fact of *God being manifested*, of which the Apostle is speaking, but the life of God lived in the church,—the truth, of which the congregation of believers is the pillar and basement,—as identical [John xiv 6] with Him who is its centre and heart and stock—as unfolded once for all in the unfolding of Him The intimate and blessed link, furnished by the **ὅς**, assuring the Church that it is not they that live, but Christ that liveth in them, is lost if we understand μυστήριον merely as a fact, however important, historically revealed. There is hardly a passage in the N. T, in which I feel more deep personal thankfulness for the restoration of the true and wonderful connexion of the original text)—who (thus, and not 'which,' nor 'He who,' should we render, preserving the same transition, from the mystery, to Him of whom now all that follows is spoken. ὅς is, as stated in Ellicott, and of course implied here, "a relative to an omitted though easily recognized antecedent, viz. Christ") **was manifested in the flesh** (it has been often maintained of late, e g. by Mack, Winer, Huther, Wiesinger, Conyb, al, that these sentences, from their parallelism and concinnity, are taken from some hymn or confession of the ancient church. We cannot absolutely say that it may not have been so. but I should on all grounds regard it as very

y Rom x. 13. 1 Cor vii. 14. xiv. 10 — στεύθη z ἐν κόσμῳ, a ἀνελήμφθη b ἐν δόξῃ. IV. 1 c Τὸ δὲ — ACDF KLℵ a b c d e f g h k l m n o 17

z Phil ii 15. Col ii 20. 1 Pet v 9. 2 Pet i 4. ἐν τῷ κ., Gospp & 1 John, but Paul, 2 Cor i 12. Eph ii 12 only.
a = Mark xvi 19. Acts i 2, &c. x 16 only. 4 Kings ii 9, 10, 11. b = Luke ix 31. 1 Cor xv 43. 2 Cor iii 7, &c. Phil iv 19. Col iii 4 only. L.P. c see Acts xvi 7.

doubtful. I can see no reason why the same person who wrote the rhetorical passages, Rom viii 38, 39; xi 33—36; 1 Cor. viii 4—7, and numerous others, might not, difference of time and modified mental characteristics being allowed for, have written this also. Once written, it would be sure to gain a place among the choice and treasured sayings of the Church, and might easily find its way into liturgical use. but I should be most inclined to think that we have here its first expression. The reason which some of the above Commentators adduce for their belief,—the abrupt insulation of the clauses disjoined from the thought in the context, has no weight with me: I on the other hand feel that so beautiful and majestic a sequence of thoughts springing directly from the context itself, can hardly be a fragment pieced in, but must present the free expansion of the mind of the writer in the treatment of his subject. On the sense of this clause, cf John i. 14, ὁ λόγος σὰρξ ἐγένετο,—and 2 Tim i 10. This is put first in the rank, as being the preliminary to all the rest. It is followed by the next clause, because the assertion and assurance of Christ's perfect unsinning righteousness was the aim of his manifestation in our flesh all those thirty years which preceded His public ministry (see below), **was justified** (i. e. approved to be righteous,—according to the uniform Pauline usage: not as De W., al., 'proved to be what he was.' The Apostle is following the *historical order of events during the manifestation of our Lord on earth*. That this is so, is manifest by the final clause being, ἀνελήμφθη ἐν δόξῃ. I take these events then in their order, and refer this to our Lord's baptism and temptation, in which His righteousness was approved and proved) **in the Spirit** (He was dwelt on by the Spirit in His baptism—led up by the Spirit to His great trial, and ἐν πνεύματι, the Spirit of God being His Spirit [but cf. Ellicott's note], that of which he said τὸ πνεῦμα μὲν πρόθυμον, ἡ δὲ σὰρξ ἀσθενής, He was proved to be righteous and spotless and separate from evil and its agent. See Rom. i. 3, 4, where another proof of this His spiritual perfection is given, viz the great and crowning one of the Resurrection from the dead. Some have thought of that proof here also. others, of the continued course of His miracles, *especially* the Resurrection. Bengel of the Resurrection and Ascension, by which He entered into His glory: alii aliter. But I prefer keeping the historical order, though I would by no means limit the δικαίωσις to that time only. *then* it was chiefly and prominently manifested), **was seen by angels** (viz by means of His Incarnation, and specifically, when they came and ministered to Him after His temptation. This seems to be regarded as the first, or at all events is the first recorded occasion on which they ministered to Him. And thus Chrys. and Thdrt.'s remark may apply: τὴν γὰρ ἀόρατον τῆς θεότητος φύσιν οὐδὲ ἐκεῖνοι ἑώρων, σαρκωθέντα δὲ ἐθεάσαντο, Thdrt. —μεθ' ἡμῶν, as Chrys. This, one of the particulars of the glory and manifestation of the incarnate Saviour, is, though not immediately concerning the mystery of piety as upheld in the Church, cited as belonging to the *unfolding* of that mystery in Christ), **was preached among the nations** (that preaching commencing with the sending out of the Apostles, and though not then, in the strict technical sense, carried on ἐν ἔθνεσιν, yet being the beginning of that which waxed onward till it embraced all nations. See and compare Rom. xvi. 26 [Eph iii 8]. So that we are still proceeding with our Lord's ministry, taking ἔθνεσιν in that wider sense in which the Jews themselves are numbered among them [so also Chrys., Huther], and the fact itself as the great commencement of the proclamation of Christ to men), **was believed on in the world** (including all that winning of faith first from His disciples [John ii. 11], then from the Jews [ib. 23, viii 30], and Samaritans [iv. 41, 42] see also id x. 42. Our clause bears with it a reminiscence of his own great saying, John iii. 16 ff.,—οὕτως γὰρ ἠγάπησεν ὁ θεὸς τὸν κόσμον ὥστε τὸν υἱὸν αὐτοῦ τὸν μονογενῆ ἔδωκεν, ἵνα πᾶς ὁ πιστεύων εἰς αὐτὸν μὴ ἀπόληται ἀλλ' ἔχῃ ζωὴν αἰώνιον. οὐ γὰρ ἀπέστειλεν ὁ θεὸς τὸν υἱὸν αὐτοῦ εἰς τὸν κόσμον ἵνα κρίνῃ τὸν κόσμον, ἀλλ' ἵνα σωθῇ ὁ κόσμος δι' αὐτοῦ. ὁ πιστεύων εἰς αὐτὸν οὐ κρίνεται. ὁ δὲ μὴ πιστεύων ἤδη κέκριται κ τ λ), **was received up in glory** (at His Ascension [against De Wette, who understands it of *celestial precedence* (von einem himmlischen Vorgange). but qu. his meaning?] cf ref. ἐν δόξῃ is

[cd] πνεῦμα [e] ῥητῶς [d] λέγει, ὅτι ἐν [fg] ὑστέροις [f] καιροῖς [h] ἀπο-
στήσονταί [i] τινες τῆς πίστεως, [k] προσέχοντες [l] πνεύμασιν

προσ-έχοντες

ACDF KLℵ a d e f g i k l m n o 17

d Acts xxi 11 Rev ii 7, &c xiv 13 xxii 17
e here only † later Gr writers freq see Wetst
f here only see 1 Pet i 5
g adj here (Matt xxi 31 v r) only 1 Chron xxix 29 only (as adv, Matt iv 2)
h = Luke viii 13 Heb iii 12 1 Macc i 15
i = ch i 3 reff
k ch i 4 reff
l = 1 Cor xii 10 xiv 32 1 John iv 1 3 Kings xxii 21

best taken as a pregnant construction—was taken up into, and reigns in, glory.
It is this distinct reference to the fact of our Lord's personal Ascension, which in my mind rules the whole sentence and makes it, whatever further reference each clause may have, a chain of links of the divine manifestation of the Person of Christ, following in chronological order from His incarnation to His assumption into glory The order and connexion of the clauses has been very variously understood, as may be seen in Wolf, and in De Wette The triple antithesis, so characteristic of St Paul, can hardly escape any reader *ἐν σαρκί, ἐν πνεύματι,—ἀγγέλοις, ἔθνεσιν,—ἐν κόσμῳ, ἐν δόξῃ*· but further it is hardly worth while to reproduce the distinctions which some have drawn, or motives for arrangement which they have supposed).

Ch IV 1—16] *Of future false teachers* (1—6); *directions to Timotheus in reference to them* (7—11); *general exhortations to him* (12—16) 1] **But** (contrast to the glorious mystery of piety which has been just dwelt on) **the Spirit** (viz the Holy Spirit of prophecy, speaking in the Apostle himself, or in others,—or, which is most probable, in both—in the general prophetic testimony which He bore throughout the church · cf *γίνωσκε*, spoken from the same point of prophetic foresight, 2 Tim iii 1. Some [even Wiesinger] have supposed the Apostle to refer to some prophetic passage of the O T, or to the general testimony of the O T prophecies [Dan vii 25, viii 23; xi 30], or those of our Lord [Matt. xxiv. 4 ff, 11], or of the Apostles [2 Thess ii 3 ff 1 John ii. 18. 2 Pet iii. 3. Jude 18], or all these combined. But in the two former cases, we should hardly have had **τὸ πνεῦμα λέγει**, but *ἡ γραφή*, or *ὁ κύριος*, or the like; **τὸ πνεῦμα** implying rather the present agency of the Spirit and the latter is only a less clear way of putting the explanation given above. for why should writings be referred to, when the living men were yet testifying in the power of the Spirit among them? Besides, see the way in which such written prophecies *are* referred to, in Jude 17) **expressly** ('plainly,' 'in so many words.' **ῥητῶς** is a post-classical word, found once in Polyb. [iii 23 5 given by Schweigh, Lex, and Palm and Rost, wrongly, ii 23 5; and by Liddell and Scott, in conseq, *Polyb* without a reference], **ὑπὲρ δὲ Σικελίας τἀναντία διαστέλλονται ῥητῶς**, and often in later writers—cf examples in Wetst, especially Sext Empir,—*ὁ Ξενοφῶν ἐν τοῖς ἀπομνημονεύμασι ῥητῶς φησιν, ἀπαρνεῖσθαι αὐτὸν* [*τὸν Σωκράτην*] *τὸ φυσικόν*, see also Plut Brut 29), **saith, that in after times** (not as E. V. 'in *the latter times*,' which though not quite so strong as 'in the *last times*,' yet gives the idea of close connexion with them whereas here the Apostle speaks only of times subsequent to those in which he was writing · see the difference in 2 Tim. iii 1 and compare Acts xx 29) **certain men** (not the false teachers rather, those who will be the result of their false teaching) **shall depart** (or decline: not by formal apostasy, or the danger would not be that which it is here represented but subjectively, declining in their own minds and lives from holding Christ in simplicity) **from the faith** (objective—the doctrine which faith embraces, as so often), **giving heed to** (see reff the participle contains the reason and process of their declension) **seducing spirits** (**πνεύμασιν**, as Huther remarks, is in contrast with **τὸ πνεῦμα**, ver 1,—it is to be understood as in 1 John iv 1 and 6, in which last verse we have the cognate expression **τὸ πνεῦμα τῆς πλάνης** Wolf's 'spiritualibus seductoribus,' or 'doctoribus seducentibus' is quite inadmissible The spirits are none other than the spirits of evil, tempting, energizing in, seducing, those who are described, just as *the Spirit* directs and dwells in those who abide in the faith), **and teachings of dæmons** (doctrines taught by, suggested by, evil spirits gen. subjective cf *σοφία δαιμονιώδης*, James iii 15, and Tert de præscr hær c 7, vol ii p 19, "Hæ sunt doctrinæ hominum et dæmoniorum, prurientibus auribus natæ" see Col ii 22 So Thdrt [Chrys is vague], and the fathers generally · (Grot, vaguely,) Wolf, Bengel, Olsh, De W, Huther, Wiesinger, Conyb, Ellic Two wrong interpretations have been given (1) understanding the genitive as objective, '*teachings concerning dæmons*,' so Mede, Works, p 626 ff, supporting his view by **διδαχαὶ βαπτισμῶν**, Heb vi 2, &c, and Heydenreich ['a characteristic designation of the essene-gnostic

m Matt xxvii 64. 2 Cor vi 8. 2 John 7 (bis) only Job xix 4 Jer xxiii 32 only
m πλάνοις καὶ n διδασκαλίαις o δαιμονίων,
2 ἐν p ὑποκρίσει q ψευδολόγων, r κεκαυτηριασμένων τὴν ἰδίαν s συνείδησιν,

ACDF KLℵ a c d e f g h k l m n o 17

n ch i 10 reff. o Paul, 1 Cor x 20 (bis), 21 (bis) only Gospp, passim Acts xvii 18 James ii 19 Rev ix 20 xvi 14 only Ps xcv 5. p Paul, Gal ii 13 only (see reff there) q r here only † s ch i 5 reff Tit i 15.

Chap. IV 1 om και D[1] lat-ff. διδασκαλειας ℵ[1] m.
2. κεκαυστηριασμενων ALℵ d m o Orig-ed Cyr Thdrt[1] txt CDFK rel Clem Orig.

false teachers, who had so much to say of the higher spirit-world, of the æons, &c.' in Huther]—but against the context, in which there is no vestige of allusion to idolatry [notwithstanding all that is alleged by Mede], but only to a false and hypocritical asceticism. (2) applying δαιμονίων to the false teachers, who would seduce the persons under description [so Mosheim, Mack, al., and even Calvin—'quod perinde est ac si dixisset, attendentes pseudo-prophetis et diabolicis eorum dogmatibus'], but this is without example harsh and improbable. The student may refer, as a curiosity, to the very learned disquisition of Mede on these δαιμόνια—not merely for the really valuable information which it contains, but also as a lesson, to assure the ground well, before he begins to build with such pains) in the (following in the . . , ἐν giving the element, in which see below) hypocrisy of those who speak lies (the whole clause belongs to τινὲς ἀποστήσονται, the previous one, προσέχοντες . . . δαιμονίων, being complete in itself. Bengel gives the construction well: 'construe cum deficient. Hypocrisis ea quæ est falsiloquorum, illos auferet. τινές, aliqui, illi sunt seducti; falsiloqui, seductores. falsiloquorum, genitivus, unice pendet ab hypocrisi. τὸ falsiloquorum dicit relationem ad alios: ergo antitheton est in ἰδίαν, sua.' This is much better than to join the gen. ψευδολόγων with δαιμονίων [so Wegscheider and Conyb., but understanding that which is said of the dæmons as meant of those who follow them], or with διδασκαλίαις [Estius,—'doctrinis, inquam, hominum in hypocrisi loquentium mendacium'],—as making the sentence which follows apply to the false teachers [cf. κωλυόντων], whom the τινές follow. And so De W., Huther, Wiesinger, and Mede himself, book iii ch 2, p 677), of men branded (with the foul marks of moral crime: so Cic., Catil. i 6, 'quæ nota domesticæ turpitudinis non inusta vitæ tuæ est?' Livy, iii 51, 'ne Claudiæ genti eam inustam maculam vellent.' Plato, Gorg. 524 E, ὁ Ῥαδάμανθυς . . . πολλάκις τοῦ μεγάλου βασιλέως ἐπιλαβόμενος ἢ ἄλλου ὁτουοῦν βασιλέως ἢ δυνάστου κατεῖδεν οὐδὲν ὑγιὲς ὂν τῆς ψυχῆς, ἀλλὰ διαμεμαστιγωμένην καὶ οὐλῶν μεστὴν ὑπὸ ἐπιορκιῶν καὶ ἀδικίας. See more examples in Wetst. and Kypke. καυτηριάζω is properly to burn in a mark with a καυτήρ, a branding-instrument of hot iron. Thl. explains: ἐπεὶ συνίσασιν ἑαυτοῖς ἀκαθαρσίαν πολλήν, διὰ τοῦτο τὸ συνειδὸς αὐτῶν ἀνεξαλείπτους ἔχει τοὺς καυτῆρας τοῦ ῥυπαροῦ βίου. Thdrt. gives an explanation more ingenious than correct: κεκ. δὲ τὴν ἰδ. συν. αὐτοὺς κέκληκε, τὴν ἐσχάτην αὐτῶν ἀπαλγησίαν διδάσκων. ὁ γὰρ τοῦ καυτῆρος τόπος νεκρωθεὶς τὴν προτέραν αἴσθησιν ἀποβάλλει. The idea rather seems to be as Bengel, "qui ipsi in sua sibi conscientia, injustitiæ et perfidiæ maculis, infames sunt:" cf. Tit i 15, iii 11, where αὐτοκατάκριτος seems to express much the same. Or, as Ellic., 'they knew the brand they bore, and yet, with a show of outward sanctity [compare ὑποκρίσει], they strove to beguile and seduce others, and make them as bad as themselves.' The genitive still depends on ὑποκρίσει, as does κωλυόντων also) on their own conscience (τὴν ἰδίαν, as Beng. above—these false teachers are not only the organs of foul spirits, but are themselves hypocritical liars, with their own consciences seared by crime. The accusative is one of reference: cf. ch. vi. 5), hindering from marrying (this description has been thought by some to fit the Jewish sects of Essenes and Therapeutæ, who abstained from marriage, Jos. B. J. ii. 8. 2. Philo de vit. contempl. 4, 8, vol. ii pp. 476, 482: cf. Col. ii 18 ff. But as De W. remarks, the abstinence by and by mentioned seems too general to suit the idea that they were Jews [see below]: besides that the Epistle does not describe them as present—but as to come in after times), (commanding) (see a like ellipsis [zeugma], in which a second but logically necessary verb is omitted, and must be supplied from the context,—in ch. ii 12, 1 Cor. xiv 34. Bengel quotes a similar construction from Chrys., ταῦτα λέγω, οὐ κηδεύειν κωλύων, ἀλλὰ μετὰ συμμετρίας τοῦτο ποιεῖν) to abstain from meats (compare Col. ii 16. It does not appear here from what sort of food this abstinence would be enjoined: but probably the eating of flesh is alluded to.

3 ᵗκωλυόντων γαμεῖν, ᵘἀπέχεσθαι ᵛβρωμάτων, ἃ ὁ θεὸς
ʷἔκτισεν εἰς ˣμετάλημψιν ʸμετὰ ʸᶻεὐχαριστίας τοῖς πιστοῖς
καὶ ᵃἐπεγνωκόσιν τὴν ᵃἀλήθειαν. 4 ὅτι πᾶν ᵇκτίσμα θεοῦ
ᶜκαλόν, καὶ οὐδὲν ᵈἀπόβλητον, ʸμετὰ ʸᶻεὐχαριστίας λαμ-
βανόμενον· 5 ᵉἁγιάζεται γὰρ ᶠδιὰ ᶠλόγου θεοῦ καὶ ᵍἐν-

t = Luke xxiii 2 Acts viii 36 1 Cor xiv 39 1 Thess ii 16 1 Kings xxv 26 u w. gen., Acts xv 20 1 Pet ii 11 Jer vii. 10 compl w ἀπὸ Acts xv 20 1 Thess iv 3 v 22 constr., ch ii 12 1 Cor xiv 34 v plur., Matt xiv 15 ‖ L Mark vii 19 Luke iii 11 1 Cor vi 13 bis Heb ix 10 xiii 9 only Mal i 12 al w 1 Cor xi 9 Eph iii 9 Col i 16 al Deut iv 32 x here only † (μεταλαβεῖν τροφῆς Acts xxvii 33) y Phil iv 6 z Eph v 4 reff a Col i 6 (reff) 2 John 1 al b James i 18 Rev v 13 viii 9 only † Wisd ix 2 al c Gen i 31 d here only † Levit xix 7 Aqu e = 1 Cor vii 14 Exod xxix 37 f see 3 Kings xvii 1 Sir xlviii 3 g ch ii 1 reff

Euseb. H E iv. 29, quotes from Irenæus [i 28. 1, p 107], ἀπὸ Σατυρνίνου καὶ Μαρκίωνος οἱ καλούμενοι Ἐγκρατεῖς ἀγαμίαν ἐκήρυξαν, ἀθετοῦντες τὴν ἀρχαίαν πλάσιν τοῦ θεοῦ, καὶ ἠρέμα κατηγοροῦντες τοῦ ἄῤῥεν καὶ θῆλυ εἰς γένεσιν ἀνθρώπων πεποιηκότος· καὶ τῶν λεγομένων παρ' αὐτοῖς ἐμψύχων ἀποχὴν εἰσηγήσαντο, ἀχαριστοῦντες τῷ πάντα πεποιηκότι θεῷ These seem to be the persons here pointed at and though the announcement of their success in after time is prophetic, we may fairly suppose that the seeds of their teaching were being sown as the Apostle wrote The existence of gnosticism in its earlier form is certainly implied in ch. vi 20 and in 2 Tim ii 17, 18, we find that denial of the resurrection which characterized all the varieties of subsequent gnosticism. See the whole subject discussed in the Prolegg ch vii § i 12 ff), **which God made for participation with thanksgiving for (dat commodi) those who believe, and have received the (full) knowledge of the truth** This last description of the worthy partakers of God's bounties is well illustrated by Calvin 'Quid ergo? annon solem suum quotidie oriri facit Deus super bonos et malos (Matt v 45)? annon ejus jussu terra impiis panem producit? annon ejus benedictione etiam pessimi aluntur? est enim universale illud beneficium quod David Psal civ. 14 decantat. Respondeo, Paulum de usu licito hic agere, cujus ratio coram Deo nobis constat Hujus minime compotes sunt impii, propter impuram conscientiam quæ omnia contaminat, quemadmodum habetur ad Titum, i 15. Et sane, proprie loquendo, solis filiis suis Deus totum mundum et quicquid in mundo est destinavit, qua ratione etiam vocantur mundi hæredes. Nam hac conditione constitutus initio fuerat Adam omnium dominus, ut sub Dei obedientia maneret Proinde rebellio adversus Deum jure quod illi collatum fuerat, ipsi una cum posteris spoliavit. Quoniam autem subjecta sunt Christo omnia, ejus beneficio in integrum restituimur, idque per fidem . . . Posteriore membro definit quos vocat fideles, nempe qui notitiam habent sanæ doctrinæ' On μετὰ εὐχαριστίας, see 1 Cor x 30. and below on ver 4 4, 5] *Reason for the above assertion* Because (ὅτι is more the objective,—γάρ, which follows, the subjective causal particle· ὅτι introduces that which rests on a patent fact, as here on a Scripture quotation,—γάρ, that which is in the writer's mind, and forms part of his own reasoning) **every thing which God has made is good** (in allusion to ref Gen. See also Rom xiv. 14, 20); **and nothing** (which God has made) **is to be rejected** (Wetst. cites Hom. Il γ 65, οὔτοι ἀποβλητ' ἐστὶ θεῶν ἐρικυδέα δῶρα—on which the Schol,—ἀπόβλητα, ἀποβολῆς ἄξια τὰ ὑπὸ θεῶν, φησί, δεδομένα δῶρα οὐκ ἔστι μὲν ἀρνήσασθαι) **if received with thanksgiving** ("properly, even without this condition, all things are pure: but he did not rise to this abstraction, because he was regarding meats not *per se*, but *in their use*, and this latter may become impure by an ungodly frame of mind." De Wette) **for** (see on ὅτι and γάρ above) **it** (this *subject* is gathered out of the preceding clause by implication, and = 'every κτίσμα which is partaken of with thanksgiving') **is hallowed** (more than '*declared pure*,' or even than '*rendered pure*' the latter it does not want, the former falls far short of the work of the assigned agents. The emphasis is on **ἁγιάζεται**, and a new particular is introduced by it—not purity merely, but *holiness*,—fitness for the godly usage of Christian men To this, which is more than mere making or declaring pure, it is set apart by the εὐχαριστία; so that the minus is proved by the majus. There is certainly a slight trace of reference to the higher consecration in the Lord's Supper. The same word εὐχαριστία is common to both Ordinary meals are set apart for ordinary Christian use by asking a blessing on them: *that meal*, for more than ordinary use, by asking on it its own peculiar blessing) **by means of the word of**

τεύξεως 6 Ταῦτα [h] ὑποτιθέμενος τοῖς ἀδελφοῖς, καλὸς
ἔσῃ [ik] διάκονος [k] χριστοῦ Ἰησοῦ, [l] ἐντρεφόμενος τοῖς λόγοις τῆς πίστεως, καὶ τῆς καλῆς [m] διδασκαλίας ᾗ [n] παρηκολούθηκας. 7 τοὺς δὲ [o] βεβήλους καὶ [p] γραώδεις [q] μύ-

ACDF KLℵ a c d e f g h k l m n o 17

h = here (Rom xvi 4) only Jer xliii (xxxvi) 25 i = 1 Cor iii 5 Eph iii 7 Col i 23 al k 2 Cor xi 23 Col i 7 l here only † τοῖς λογοις ἐνετραφη, Galen ap Wetst Luke i 3 2 Tim iii 10 only † 2 Macc viii 11 ix 27 only γραωδη μυθολογιαν, Strabo, i p 32 A Wetst m ch i 10 reff n Mark xvi 17 o ch i 9 reff p here only. q ch i 4 reff

6. rec ιησ. bef χριστου, with D[3] rel am Syr Chr Thdrt-ms Aug · txt ACD[1]FKLℵ e g m latt syr copt arm Ambrst Pelag for η, ης A 80 8-pe

God and intercession (*what* 'word of God?' how to be understood? treating the plainer word first, the **ἔντευξις** is evidently intercession [see on ch. ii. 1] *on behalf of the κτίσμα partaken of*—that it may be 'sanctified to our use.' This, bound on as **λόγου θεοῦ** is to ἐντεύξεως by the non-repetition of the preposition, may serve to guide us to its meaning. And first, negatively. It cannot mean any thing which does not form part of the εὐχαριστία such as God's word in the Scripture just cited [Mack], or in any other place [Grot., al.]. or God's word in the foundation truths of Christianity. Then, positively it must mean in some sense the εὐχαριστία, or something in it But not, as Wahl and Leo, the 'word addressed to God,' 'oratio ad Deum facta,' which would be an unprecedented meaning for λόγος θεοῦ. the only way open for us is, that the εὐχαριστία itself, or some part of it, is in some sense *the word of God*. This may be (1) by its consisting in whole or in part of Scripture words, or (2) by the effusion of a Christian man, speaking in the power of God's Spirit, being known as λόγος θεοῦ This latter is perhaps justified by the reff. · but still it seems to me hardly probable, and I should prefer the former. [So Ellic. also] It would generally be the case, that any form of Christian thanksgiving before meat would contain words of Scripture, or at all events thoughts in exact accordance with them · and such utterance of God's revealed will, bringing as it would the assembled family and their meal into harmony with Him, might well be said ἁγιάζειν the βρώματα on the table for their use. Many of the Commentators quote from the Constt. Ap. vii 49, p. 1057, Migne, the following grace before meat, used in the primitive times. εὐλογητὸς εἶ κύριε ὁ τρέφων με ἐκ νεότητός μου, ὁ διδοὺς τροφὴν πάσῃ σαρκί· πλήρωσον χαρᾶς καὶ εὐφροσύνης τὰς καρδίας ἡμῶν, ἵνα πάντοτε πᾶσαν αὐτάρκειαν ἔχοντες, περισσεύωμεν εἰς πᾶν ἔργον ἀγαθὸν ἐν χριστῷ Ἰησοῦ τῷ κυρίῳ ἡμῶν, δι' οὗ σοὶ δόξα τιμὴ καὶ κράτος εἰς τοὺς αἰῶνας, ἀμήν Here almost every clause is taken from some expression of Scripture). **6—11**] *Recommendatory application to Timotheus of what has been just said, as to form part of his teaching, to the avoidance by him of false and vain doctrine, and to the practice of godliness.* **These things** (hardly, as Rosenm., Heinr, Heyd, ch. iii. 16 f, nor as Chrys, ποῖα, ἅπερ εἶπεν ὅτι τὸ μυστήριον μεγα ἐστίν, ὅτι τὸ τούτων ἀπέχεσθαι δαιμόνιόν ἐστιν, ὅτι διὰ λόγου καὶ ἐντεύξεως θεοῦ ἁγιάζεται—but simply the matter treated since the beginning of the chapter,—the coming apostasy after these ascetic teachers and the true grounds of avoiding it This best suits the following context and the ὑποτιθέμενος, which certainly would not be used of the μέγα μυστήριον) **suggesting** (or counselling, cf. Il. θ 36, βουλὴν δ' Ἀργείοις ὑποθησόμεθ', ἥτις ὀνήσει: Herod i 156, Κροῖσος μὲν δὴ ταῦτά τε οἱ ὑπετίθετο · Palm and Rost's Lex sub voce, 2, c, and Ellic.'s note here) **to the brethren, thou wilt be a good servant of Christ Jesus, ever training thyself in** (the idea of ἐντρέφομαι is not '*nourish oneself with*,' but to grow up amongst, or to be trained in cf. Eur. Phœn. 368, γυμνάσιά θ', οἷσιν ἐνετράφην so ἐντρέφεσθαι νόμοις, ἔθεσιν, ὅπλοις, μουσικῇ, λόγοις, τρυφῇ, Plat, Plutarch, al see Palm and Rost's Lex. The present, as Chrys., denotes *continuance* in this training, τὸ διηνεκὲς τῆς εἰς τὰ τοιαῦτα προσοχῆς δηλῶν, and again, μηρυκώμενος [*ruminans*], συνεχῶς τὰ αὐτὰ στρέφων, ἀεὶ τὰ αὐτὰ μελετῶν. Cf 2 Tim. iii. 14) **the words of the faith** (the fundamental doctrines of the Gospel), **and of the good instruction** (not '*words of the faith and good doctrine*,' as Conyb. The repetition of the article forbids this, severs the ᾗ παρηκολούθηκας from τοῖς λόγοις τῆς πίστεως, and attaches it to καὶ τῆς καλῆς διδασκαλίας only) **the course of which thou hast followed** (I have thus endeavoured to give **παρηκολούθηκας** —'hast followed along, by tracing its course and accompanying it ' see reff., and Ellic 's

θους ʳ παραιτοῦ· ˢ γύμναζε δὲ σεαυτὸν ᵗ πρὸς ᵘ εὐσέβειαν·
8 ἡ γὰρ ᵛ σωματικὴ ʷ γυμνασία ˣ πρὸς ὀλίγον ἐστὶν ʸ ὠφέ-
λιμος· ἡ δὲ ᵘ εὐσέβεια ˣ πρὸς πάντα ʸ ὠφέλιμός ἐστιν,
ᶻ ἐπαγγελίαν ἔχουσα ᶻᵃ ζωῆς ᵃ τῆς ᵃ νῦν καὶ τῆς ᵇ μελλού-

r = & constr, Acts xxv 11 (Paul) ch v 11 2 Tim ii 23 Tit iii 10 2 Macc ii 31 s Heb v 14 xii 11 2 Pet ii 14 only † 2 Macc x 15 only (see below [w]) t = Rom iii 20 al see note u ch ii 2 reff v Luke iii 22 only † 4 Macc i 32 (-κῶς, Col ii 9) w here only † (see above [s]) x = (see note) here only (James iv 14 Heb xii 10) y past epp only 2 Tim iii 16 Tit iii 8 † z 2 Tim i 1 a here only see ch vi 17 2 Tim iv 10 Tit ii 12 also Rom iii 26 viii 25 xi 5 2 Cor viii 14 2 Pet iii 7 b = Rom viii 38. Heb vi 5

7 for μυθους, θυμους C. om (2nd) δε D¹ 113 7 am(with fuld) *exercens* Ambrst.
8. om 1st προς ℵ¹. επαγγελιας K d e g h l m o syr goth Euthal Œc₂.

note). 7] **But profane and anile** (Baur understands this epithet to refer to the gnostic idea of an *old universal mother*, the σοφία or ἀχαμώθ [see Irenæus, i 4 1 ff pp 18 f.]. but Wiesinger well replies that this will not suit the word γραώδης [from γραῦς, εἶδος, as θεοειδής], which must be subjective,—nor βέβηλος, which on this supposition would not be appropriate) **fables** (see notes on ch i. 4 and 7, and Prolegg) **decline** (lit. 'excuse thyself from,' see reff, Luke xiv. 18, 19, and Palm and Rost's Lex.) **but exercise thyself for piety** (τουτέστι, πρὸς πίστιν καθαρὰν καὶ βίον ὀρθόν τοῦτο γὰρ εὐσέβεια· γυμνασίας ἄρα χρεία καὶ πόνων διηνεκῶν ὁ γὰρ γυμναζόμενος καὶ ἀγῶνος μὴ ὄντος ἀγωνίζεται ἱδρῶτος ἄχρι Thl [not Thdrt, as Huther]. **πρός**, with a view to, as an athlete with a view to the games. cf Soph El 456, πρὸς εὐσέβειαν ἡ κόρη λέγει,—and the common expressions πρὸς ἡδονὴν λέγειν, δρᾶν, δημηγορεῖν, &c Soph Antig 1170, τἄλλ' ἐγὼ καπνοῦ σκιᾶς οὐκ ἂν πριαίμην ἀνδρὶ πρὸς τὴν ἡδονήν)
8] **for the exercise** (gymnastic training: see below) **of the body is to small extent** (*'for but little,'*—in reference only to a small department of a man's being: not as in ref. James, *'for a short time,'* as the contrast **πρὸς πάντα** below shews) **profitable** (to what sort of exercise does he allude? Ambr, Thom-Aq, Lyra, Calv., Grot., Heydenr, Leo, Matthies, al, take it as alluding to corporal austerities for religion's sake: 'hoc nomine appellat quæcunque religionis causa suscipiuntur externæ actiones, ut sunt vigiliæ, longa inedia, humi cubatio, et similia,' Calv. But against this are two considerations 1) that these are not now in question, but the immediate subject is the excellence of being trained and thoroughly exercised in piety · 2) that if they were, it would hardly be consistent with his previous severe characterization of these austerities, ver 3, to introduce them thus with even so much creditable mention.

Wiesinger has taken up this meaning again and contended very strongly for it, maintaining that the πρὸς ὀλίγον ὠφέλιμος must be *moral*, not corporeal. But it may fairly be answered, if it be moral, then it cannot be said to be πρὸς ὀλίγον, for it would contribute to εὐσέβεια And indeed he may be refuted on his own ground he says that the σωματ γυμνασία *must belong to* εὐσέβεια for that if it meant bodily exercise merely, πνευματικὴ γυμνασία, not εὐσέβεια, would be the proper contrast to it. But surely we may say, if σωματικὴ γυμν. does *belong to* εὐσέβεια, how can it form a contrast to it? On *his* hypothesis, not on the other, we should require πνευματικὴ γυμνασία as the contrast A part cannot be thus contrasted with the whole It is therefore far better to understand the words, as Chrys, Thl, Thdrt [οἱ τῆς τοῦ σώματος, φησίν, εὐεξίας ἐπιμελούμενοι πρὸς ὀλίγον ταύτης ἀπολαύουσιν], Pel, Corn-a-Lap, Estius, Wolf, al, Bengel, Mack, De W, Huther, of mere gymnastic bodily exercise, of which the Apostle says, that it has indeed its uses, but those uses partial only. Bengel adds, perhaps more ingeniously than conclusively, "Videtur Timotheus juvenis interdum usus fuisse aliqua exercitatione corporis [ch v. 23] quam Paulus non tam prohibet quam non laudat" Two curious interpretations of the expression have been given, one by Chrys., as a sort of afterthought · ὃ δὲ λέγει, τοιοῦτόν ἐστι μηδὲ εἰς γυμνασίαν ποτε καταθῇς σεαυτὸν διαλεγόμενος πρὸς ἐκείνους, ἀλλὰ ταῦτα τοῖς αὐτοῦ παραίνει οὐ γάρ ἐστι πρὸς τοὺς διεστραμμένους μαχόμενον ὀνῆσαί τί ποτε,—the other by Braun [Selecta sacra i 10 156, cited by Huther], who understands by it the ceremonial law) **but piety** (the first member of the antithesis contained the *means*, ἡ σωματικὴ γυμνασία: this, the end, εὐσέβεια,—that which is sought by γυμνασία πρὸς εὐσέβειαν) **is profitable for all things** (not one portion only of a man's being, but every portion of it, bodily and spiritual, temporal and eternal), **having** (seeing that

σης. 9 ᶜ πιστὸς ὁ λόγος καὶ ᶜ πάσης ᶜ ἀποδοχῆς ᶜ ἄξιος·
10 ᵈ εἰς τοῦτο γὰρ [καὶ] ᵉ κοπιῶμεν καὶ *ᶠ ὀνειδιζόμεθα, ὅτι
ᵍ ἠλπίκαμεν ἐπὶ ʰⁱ θεῷ ʰ ζῶντι, ὅς ἐστιν ⁱ σωτὴρ πάντων

ACDF KLℵ a c d e f g h k l m n o 17

c ch i 15 reff d Rom xiv 9 2 Cor ii 9 al e Rom xvi 6 1 Cor iv 12 Eph iv 28. Col i 29 Ps cxxvi 1 f Matt v 11 | L Rom xv 3 from Ps lxviii 9 1 Pet iv 14 al g w. ἐπί and dat, Rom xv 12, from Isa xi 10 ch vi 17 (bis, v r) only acc, ch v 5 1 Pet i 13 (iii 5 v r) ἐν, 1 Cor xv 19 ch vi 17 only dat only, Matt xii 21 εἰς, John v 45. 2 Cor i 10 1 Pet iii 5. h ch iii 15, reff i see ch i 1 reff

9 om πασης ℵ¹.

10 rec bef κοπ ins και (*possibly conformation to Col* i 29), with FKL rel Chr₁ Thdrt Thl Œc om ACDℵ 17. 67² vulg Syr copt arm Chr Ambrst Pelag

*ἀγωνιζόμεθα (*possibly a substitution, as agreeing better with κοπιωμεν· see Col* i. 29) ACFKℵ¹ c 17 Chr₁ Cyr · ονειδιζομεθα DLℵ³ rel Chr₃-edd Thdrt Damasc lat-ff ηλπισαμεν D¹ 17 επι θεον ζωντα D¹.

it has) **promise of the life** (we may, as far as the construction is concerned, take ζωῆς, as Ellic, abstract, *of life*, and then divide it off into τῆς νῦν and τῆς μελλούσης But see below), **which is now and which is to come** (how is the genitive ζωῆς to be taken? is it the objective genitive, giving the substance of the promise, LIFE, in its highest sense? in this case it would be ἐν τῷ νῦν αἰῶνι καὶ ἐν τῷ μέλλοντι And seeing it is not that, but τῆς νῦν κ. τῆς μελλούσης, we should have to understand ζωή in two different meanings,—long and happy life here, and eternal life hereafter—it bears a promise of this life and of the life to come. This to say the least is harsh. It would be better therefore to take ἐπαγγελία as '*the promise*,' in the sense of 'the chief blessedness promised by God,' the blessed contents of His promise, whatever they be, and ζωῆς as the possessive genitive the best promise belonging to this life and to that which is to come It may be said, this also is harsh, and to some extent I acknowledge it,—it is not however a harshness in *thought*, as the other, but only in construction, such as need not surprise us in these Epistles The concrete ἐπαγγελία instead of the abstract is already familiar to us, Luke xxiv 49 Acts i. 1, xiii 32, al. and the possessive genitive after ἐπαγγ is justified by Rom xv 8, ἐπαγγ τῶν πατέρων, and by the arrangement of the sentence) **9] Faithful is the saying, and worthy of all acceptation** (see on ch i. 15 The words refer to what *follows*, not as Heinr to ch iii 16, nor as De W, Huther, Wies, al, to what went immediately before see on γάρ below. The connexion is with καὶ τῆς μελλούσης Piety has the promise of that life attached to it, according to the well known Christian saying which follows. Otherwise verse 10 comes in disjointedly and unaccountably) · **for** (γάρ is introduced from a mixture of two constructions, rendering a reason for καὶ τῆς μελλούσης, as if πιστὸς ὁ λόγος had not been inserted. We have the same construction in 2 Tim. ii 11, where Huther, though he regards the γάρ as decisive against it here, refers the πιστὸς ὁ λόγος to what follows) **to this end** (viz. the σωτηρία implied in that which follows, introduced by ὅτι,—as in reff · thus alone can the saying as a πιστὸς λόγος cohere together · and so Thdrt., Thl, Beza, Grot., Beng., Mosh, Wegsch, Leo, Wahl —not, as De W, Huther, Ellic., al., for the obtaining of the promise mentioned above [De W. claims Thdrt. and Bengel for this meaning, but wrongly the former says, τί δήποτε, &c εἰ μή τίς ἐστι τῶν πόνων ἀντίδοσις; ἀλλὰ γάρ ἐστιν ἀντίδοσις ἀΐδιος γὰρ θεὸς ἀγωνοθετεῖ τοῖς ἀθλοῦσι, καὶ πάντων ἐστὶν ἀνθρώπων σωτὴρ κτλ, and the latter, 'hoc nomine, hoc fine, hac spe,' referring to ἠλπίκαμεν]) **we** (Christians in general) **[both] toil** (more than labour [ἐργαζόμεθα] it gives the idea of 'toil and moil' see reff) **and suffer reproach** (climax we might toil and be had in honour, but as it is, we have both fatigue and shame to bear. The reading ἀγωνιζόμεθα is very strongly supported, but appears to have been introduced from Col i 29), **because we have fixed our hope** (the same perfect occurs John v 45. 2 Cor i 10 · ch v 5, vi 17 it refers to the time when the strong resolve and waiting began, and to its endurance since that time) **on** (for construction see reff, and Ellicott's note here. Thus in Polyb i 12. 6, τὰς . . . ἀγορὰς . . . ἐφ' οἷς εἶχον τὰς μεγίστας ἐλπίδας) **the living** (inserted for emphasis and solemnity, to bring out the fact that the God in whom we trust is a veritable personal agent, not a creature of the imagination) **God, who is the Saviour of all men** (cf ch. ii 4; Tit. ii 11: His will is that all men should be saved, and He has made full and sufficient provision for the salvation of all. so that, as far as salvation stands in Him, He is the Saviour of all men. And it is in virtue of

ἀνθρώπων, [k] μάλιστα πιστῶν. 11 [l] Παράγγελλε ταῦτα
καὶ δίδασκε. 12 μηδείς σου τῆς [m] νεότητος [n] καταφρονείτω,
ἀλλὰ [o] τύπος γίνου τῶν πιστῶν, ἐν λόγῳ, ἐν [p] ἀνα-
στροφῇ, ἐν ἀγάπῃ, ἐν πίστει, ἐν [q] ἁγνείᾳ. 13 ἕως ἔρχομαι,

k Acts xx 38 xxv 26 xxvi 3 Gal vi 10 Phil iv 22 ch v 8, 17 2 Tim iv 13 Tit i 10 Philem 16. 2 Pet ii 10 only l 1 Thess iv 11 reff constr, 2 Thess iii 4 m Mark x 20 ‖ (Mt. v r) L Acts xxvi 4 (Paul) only Gen viii 21 n Matt vi 24 xviii 10 Luke xvi 13 Rom ii 4 1 Cor xi 22 ch vi 2 Heb xii 2 2 Pet ii 10 only Wisd xiv 30 o = Phil iii 17 1 Thess i 7 2 Thess iii 9 Tit ii 7 1 Pet v 3 p Gal i 13 Eph iv 22 Heb xiii 7 James iii 13 1 Pet i 15 al[5] 2 Pet ii 7 iii 11 only † Tobit iv 14 2 Macc v 8 only q ch v 2 only 2 Chron xxx 19

12. rec aft *εν αγαπη* ins *εν πνευματι*, with KL rel Thdrt Damasc om ACDFℵ 17 latt syrr copt æth arm Clem Chr Ambrst Jer Aug

this universality of salvation offered by God, that we have rested our hopes on Him and become *πιστοί*), **especially them that believe** (in these alone does that universal salvation, which God has provided, become actual. He is the same *σωτήρ* towards and of all but these alone appropriate His *σωτηρία*. Bengel rightly observes, 'Latet nervus argumenti a minori ad majus' but he applies the *σωτὴρ πάντων* to *this life*, and *μάλιστα πιστῶν* to the life to come So also Chrys *εἰ δὲ τοὺς ἀπίστους σώζει ἐνταῦθα, πολλῷ μᾶλλον τοὺς πιστοὺς ἐκεῖ?* But this does not seem to suit the context, nor the higher sense to which *σωτήρ* is every where in the N T. confined, and most especially in these Epistles, where it occurs very frequently The true 'argumentum a minori ad majus' lies in this—" if God be thus willing for all to be saved, how much more shall he save them that put their trust in Him " For the expression, see reff, and especially Gal vi. 10) **11**] **Command** (see ch i. 3) **these things** (viz those insisted on since ver 7) **and teach them** **12—16**] *General exhortations to Timotheus* **Let no one despise thy youth** (as to the construction, Chrys [*μηδεὶς διὰ τὴν νεότητα καταφρονήσῃ σου*], Leo, Mack, Matthies, take *σοῦ* as immediately governed by *καταφρονήσῃ*, and *τῆς νεότητος* as a second genitive — '*thee for thy youth*' But though I cannot think with Huther that such a construction would be illegitimate [for in what does *καταφρονέω* differ in logical reference from *κατηγορέω*?—cf *εἰ . . . παρανόμων . ἤμελλον αὐτοῦ κατηγορεῖν*, Demosth. Meid. p. 515 26], yet ver. 15 seems to rule in favour of the simpler construction, where we have *σου* preceding its governing substantive with no such ambiguity As to the matter of the *youth* of Timotheus, see Prolegg. ch. vii. § ii. 35, note ; and remember, that his age relative to that of the Apostle himself, whose place he was filling, rather than his absolute age, is evidently that which is here meant. By the *ἕως ἔρχομαι*, we see that this comparison was before the Apostle's mind. The interpretation of Bengel, '"talem te gere quem nemo possit tanquam juvenem contemnere " libenter id faciunt senes inanes,' thus endeavouring to eliminate the *fact*, of Timotheus's youth, is forced, and inconsistent with the *τῆς* It is quite true [cf. what follows—*ἀλλὰ τύπος γίνου*, &c.] that the exhortation is to *him*, not to the Ephesian church . but it is grounded on the *fact of his youth*, in whatever light that fact is to be interpreted),—**but become** (by gaining their respect for the following acts and qualities) **a pattern of the believers** (the comma after *πιστῶν*, in which I have followed Lachmann, gives more force and independence to the clause adversative to *μηδεὶς κ τ λ*, and then leaves the specifications to follow),—**in word** (the whole of thine utterances, in public and private *ἐν λόγῳ* is elsewhere contrasted, as in Col iii 17, with *ἐν ἔργῳ*), **in behaviour** (the other outward sign of the life within *ἐν ἔργῳ*, Col l c, but expressing more—'in quotidiana consuetudine,' as Beng The *ἀναστροφή* may testify, in cases where no actual deed is done), **in love, in faith** (the two great springs of Christian conduct, the one it is true set in motion by the other,—cf Gal. v 6, *πίστις δι' ἀγάπης ἐνεργουμένη*,—but both, leading principles of the whole man), **in purity** (probably, not chastity, in the more restricted sense, though in ch v 2 it certainly has this meaning from the context. but in the wider and higher meaning which the context here requires, all believers being in view, of general holiness and purity. Cf for this,—*ἁγνός*, ch. v 22 : 2 Cor vii. 11 James iii. 17,—*ἁγνίζω*, James iv 8. 1 Pet i 22. From these passages the quality would appear definable as *simplicity of holy motive* followed out in *consistency of holy action*). **13**] **Till I come** (not as De W., as long as thou in my absence presidest over the Ephesian church: for this supposes the Apostle to be the normal president of that Church

r ch. i. 4 reff. s Acts xiii. 15. 2 Cor. iii. 14 only. Neh. viii. 8. t = Phil. ii. 1 reff. u ch. i. 10 reff. v (—) Matt. xxii. 5. Heb. ii. 3. viii. 9 only. Jer. iv. 17. xxxviii. (xxxi.) 32. Wisd. iii. 10. 2 Macc. iv. 14 only. w Paul (Rom. i. 11. 1 Cor. i. 7. vii. 7. xii. 4, &c. 2 Tim. i. 6) only, exc. 1 Pet. iv. 10†. x ch. i. 18 reff. y Acts xiv. 23. z (in N. T. always w. χειρῶν) Acts viii. 18. 2 Tim. i. 6. Heb. vi. 2 only. 2 Chron. xxv. 27. a = here only (Luke xxii. 66. Acts xxii. 5 only†. Susanna 51 Theod.-F.). Ignat. Trall. 7, 13. Philad. 7, pp. 681, 685, 701. b Mark xiii. 11. Acts iv. 25 only. Ps. i. 2. c = here only. see 1 Thess. ii. 5.

ACDF KLℵ a c d e f g h k l m n o 17

[r] πρόσεχε τῇ [s] ἀναγνώσει, τῇ [t] παρακλήσει, τῇ [u] διδασκαλίᾳ. 14 μὴ [v] ἀμέλει τοῦ ἐν σοὶ [w] χαρίσματος, ὃ ἐδόθη
σοι διὰ [x] προφητείας [y] μετὰ [z] ἐπιθέσεως τῶν χειρῶν τοῦ
[a] πρεσβυτερίου. 15 ταῦτα [b] μελέτα, [c] ἐν τούτοις [c] ἴσθι·

14. πρεσβυτερου ℵ[1] m.

and Timotheus his locum-tenens, which was not the case. Timotheus was put there with a special commission from the Apostle: that commission would cease at the Apostle's coming, not because he would resume residence and presidence, but because he would enforce and complete the work of Timotheus, and thus, the necessity for special interference being at an end, the church would revert to the normal rule of its own presbytery), **attend to the** (public, see below) **reading** ("scripturæ sacræ, in ecclesia. Huic adjunguntur duo præcipua genera, *adhortatio*, quæ ad agendum, et *doctrina*, quæ ad cognoscendum pertinet, ch. vi. 2 fin. Rom. xii. 7 ff." Beng. This is certainly the meaning, cf. Luke iv. 16 ff. Acts xiii. 15. 2 Cor. iii. 14,—not that of Chrys. [ἀκούωμεν ἅπαντες, καὶ παιδευώμεθα μὴ ἀμελεῖν τῆς τῶν θείων γραφῶν μελέτης], Grot., Calv. ["certe fons omnis sapientiæ est Scriptura, unde haurire debent pastores quicquid proferunt apud gregem"], al., who understand private reading. Whether the O. T. Scriptures alone, or in addition to them the earlier gospels were at this time included in this public reading, cf. Just. Mart. Apol. i. [ii.] 67, p. 83 [τὰ ἀπομνημονεύματα τῶν ἀποστόλων ἢ τὰ συγγράμματα τῶν προφητῶν ἀναγινώσκεται, μέχρις ἐγχωρεῖ], cannot be determined with any certainty), **to the** (also public) **exhortation, to the** (also public) **teaching** (cf. Bengel above. Chrys. takes παρακλήσει as social, διδασκαλίᾳ as public,—τῇ παρακλήσει τῇ πρὸς ἀλλήλους, τῇ διδασκαλίᾳ τῇ πρὸς πάντας—so Grot., 'in *monendis* aliis privatim, *docendis* publice:' but why so?). **14.] Do not neglect** (= ἀναζωπυρεῖν, 2 Tim. i. 6,—do not suffer to decay and smoulder by carelessness. 'negligunt qui non exercent, nec putant se posse excidere,' Bengel) **the spiritual gift which is in thee** (see more at length in 2 Tim. i. 6. The spiritual gift is that of teaching and ruling the church. Thdrt. says, too narrowly [and so nearly Ellic.], χάρισμα τὴν διδασκαλίαν ἐκάλεσε· it was not teaching only, but the whole grace of God given him for the office to which he was set apart by special ordination), **which was given thee** (by God, 1 Cor. xii. 4, 6) **by means of prophecy** (not as Mack, 'on account of prophecies,' alleging the plural in ch. i. 18. That verse [see note] refers to the same fact as this—viz. that, either at the first conversion of Timotheus, or at his ordination to the ministry [and certainly the latter seems here to be pointed at], the Holy Spirit spoke, by means of a prophet or prophets, His will to invest him with χαρίσματα for the work, and thus the gift was said to be conferred, as to its certainty in the divine counsels, by such prophecy—'ita jubente per os prophetarum Spiritu Sancto,' Beza. All attempts to make διά bear other meanings ['potest tamen sic accipi ut idem valeat quod εἰς προφητείαν, i. e. ad prophetandum, vel ἐν προφητείᾳ ita ut quod sit hoc donum exprimat apostolus,' Beza] are illegitimate and needless: see Acts xiii. 1, 2, 3, which is a case precisely analogous: the gift was in Paul and Barnabas διὰ προφητείας, μετὰ ἐπιθέσεως χειρῶν. Bengel strangely joins προφητείας with πρεσβυτερίου, parenthesizing μετὰ ἐπιθ. τ. χειρῶν, alleging that '*impositio manus* proprie fit per unam personam et quidem digniorem: *prophetia* vero fiebat etiam per æquales,' &c. But this certainly was not so: see below), **with laying on of the hands** (see on Acts vi. 6. Neander, Pfl. u. Leit. i. 267. There is no real difference, as De W. thinks, between this and 2 Tim. i. 6. There was a special reason there for putting Timotheus in mind of the fact that the Apostle's own hands *were* laid on him: but that fact does not exclude this. See references on the χειροθεσία in Ellicott's note) **of the presbytery** (reff. of the body of elders who belonged to the congregation in which he was ordained. Where this was, we know not: hardly in Lystra, where he was first converted: might it not be in Ephesus itself, for this particular office?). **15.] These things** (viz. the things enjoined vv. 12–14) **do thou care for, in these things be** [employed] (Wetst. cites Plut. Pomp. p. 656 b, ἐν

ἵνα σοῦ ἡ [d] προκοπὴ φανερὰ ᾖ πᾶσιν. 16 [e] ἔπεχε σεαυτῷ
καὶ τῇ [f] διδασκαλίᾳ. [g] ἐπίμενε αὐτοῖς· τοῦτο γὰρ ποιῶν,
καὶ σεαυτὸν [h] σώσεις καὶ τοὺς [i] ἀκούοντάς σου.

V. 1 Πρεσβυτέρῳ μὴ [k] ἐπιπλήξῃς, ἀλλὰ [l] παρακάλει
ὡς πατέρα· νεωτέρους, ὡς ἀδελφούς· 2 [m] πρεσβυτέρας,
ὡς μητέρας· νεωτέρας, ὡς ἀδελφάς, ἐν [n] πάσῃ [o] ἁγνείᾳ.

d Phil i 12, 25 only † Sir li 17 2 Macc viii 8 only
e = Luke xiv 7 Acts iii 5 (& constr) only Sir xxxi (xxxiv) 2 (Acts xix 22 Phil ii 16 only)
f ch i 10 reff
g Rom. vi 1 xi 22, 23 Col i 23 Exod xii 39 vat
h = ch ii 15
i 2 Tim ii 14
k here only † Jos Antt xii 4 2 Polyb i 12 7 al (-πληξις, 2 Macc vii 33)
l = ch ii 1 al fr
m fem, here only Zech viii 4
n = Phil i 20 reff
o ch iv 13 only 2 Chron xxx 19

15. rec ins εν bef πασιν (*from misunderstanding?*), with D³KL rel æth Chr(explaining μὴ ἐν τῷ βίῳ μόνον ἀλλὰ καὶ ἐν τῷ λόγῳ) Thdrt Damasc: om ACD¹F℞ 17 latt syr copt goth arm Clem Cyr lat-ff

16 ins εν bef αυτοις D¹ vulg(not tol) goth lat-ff om σου ℵ¹.

Chap V. 1. om ως πατερα ℵ¹.

τούτοις ὁ Καῖσαρ . . . . ἦν. Lucret. iii. 1093, 'versamur ibidem, atque insumus usque ' Hor Ep. i. 1. 11, 'quod verum atque decens curo et rogo et omnis in hoc sum.' To which I may add a more striking parallel, Hor. Sat. i. 9. 2, 'Nescio quid meditans nugarum, et totus in illis'), **that thy progress** (ref προκοπή is branded as a "vox non immerito a grammaticis contemta" by Lobeck, Phryn p 85 towards perfection; certainly in the Christian life, as Heydenr., De W this is *implied*, but the more direct meaning is, 'with reference to the duties of thine office' and especially as respects the caution given ver 12, that no man despise thy youth) **may be manifest to all** 16] **Give heed to thyself** (summary of ver 12. On ἔπεχε, see Ellicott's note) **and to thy teaching** (summary of ver 13 "Duo sunt curanda bono pastori ut docendo invigilet, ac se ipsum purum custodiat. Neque enim satis est, si vitam suam componat ad omnem honestatem, sibique caveat ne quod edat malum exemplum, nisi assiduum quoque docendi studium adjungat sanctæ vitæ: et parum valebit doctrina, si non respondeat vitæ honestas et sanctitas" Calv). **Continue** (reff) **in them** (most naturally, the ταῦτα of ver 15· but the words are ambiguous and puzzling. Grot. gives a curious interpretation. '*mane apud Ephesios*,' which is certainly wrong. Bengel, as an alternative, refers it to τοὺς ἀκούοντας below, which is no better. I have punctuated it so as to connect this clause with what follows, and thus to render it not quite so harsh, seeing that it then will assume the form of a recapitulatory conclusion), **for doing this** ('*in* doing this,' as E V, better than '*by* doing this,' which asserts too much) **thou shalt save** (in the day of the Lord · the highest meaning, and no other, is to be thought of in both cases) **both thyself and those that hear thee** (thyself, in the faithful discharge of the ministry which thou hast received of the Lord thy hearers, in the power of thine influence over them, by God's word and ordinances)

Ch. V. 1—25] General directions to him for governing the church

1, 2] *Injunctions respecting his behaviour to the elder and younger of either sex.* **πρεσβυτέρῳ**] The reference to an *office* was called in question as early as Chrys ἆρα τὸ ἀξίωμα νῦν φησιν, οὐκ ἔγωγε οἶμαι, ἀλλὰ περὶ παντὸς γεγηρακότος. This indeed is evident from the quadruple specification in these verses So even Mack, though he maintains that the νεώτεροι of Acts v. 6 were official Leo, as cited by Wiesinger, gives well the connexion with the last chapter · "quum supra scripsisset, nemini licere ex juventute Timothei ejus despiciendi occasionem sumere, nunc jam ipsum hortatur Timotheum, ut semper memor suæ νεότητος ita se gerat erga seniores uti revera deceat virum juniorem" But this connexion must not be too closely pressed. Some important general instructions have intervened since the μηδείς σου τῆς νεότητος καταφρονείτω. **ἐπιπλήξῃς**] Thus Il. μ. 211, Ἕκτορ, ἀεὶ μέν πώς μοι ἐπιπλήσσεις ἀγορῇσιν | ἐσθλὰ φραζομένῳ **ἀλλὰ παρακάλει**] ὡσανεὶ πρὸς πατέρα, φησί, προσενεχθείης ἁμαρτάνοντα, οὕτω πρὸς ἐκεῖνον διαλέγου, Chrys. **νεωτέρους**] understand παρακάλει Thus the prohibition, μὴ ἐπιπλήξῃς, applies to all, all being included in the παρακάλει which is the other and adopted alternative **ὡς ἀδελφούς**] as on an equality with them, not lording it over them. **ὡς ἀδελφάς**] 'Hic respectus egregie adjuvat castitatem,' Bengel μηδὲ ὑποψίαν, φησί, δῷς ἐπειδὴ γὰρ αἱ πρὸς τὰς νεωτέρας γενόμεναι ὁμιλίαι δυσκό-

3 Χήρας [p] τίμα τὰς [q] ὄντως χήρας. 4 εἰ δέ τις χήρα
τέκνα ἢ [r] ἔκγονα ἔχει, [s] μανθανέτωσαν πρῶτον τὸν ἴδιον
οἶκον [t] εὐσεβεῖν, καὶ [u] ἀμοιβὰς [v] ἀποδιδόναι τοῖς [w] προ-

ACDF KLℵ a c d e f g h k l m n o 17

p Paul, here only, exc Eph vi 2, from Exod xx 12. Epp., 1 Pet ii 17 bis only. q Mark xi 32 Paul, 1 Cor xiv 25 Gal iii 21 vv 5, 16 ch vi 19 only Num xxii 37 only r here only Deut vii 13 al freq in LXX s = & constr., Phil iv 11 Tit iii 14 see ver 13 t Acts xvii 23 only † (see ch ii 2 reff) u here only † Isa i 23 Symm οἱ . ἀπεδωκ' ἀμοιβὰς οὐ καλας Eurip Orest 468 (see Wetst) v Rom xii 17 1 Thess v 15 al w 2 Tim i 3 only † Sir viii 4 2 Macc viii 19 xi 25 only

4 εγγονα D[1] 44 109 μαθετωσαν D[1]. των ιδιων οικων D[1].

λως διαφεύγουσιν ὑποψίαν, δεῖ δὲ γίνεσθαι παρὰ τοῦ ἐπισκόπου καὶ ταῦτο, διὰ τοῦτο "ἐν πάσῃ ἁγνείᾳ" προστίθησι Chrys. See similar sentiments from profane writers in Wetst. The Commentators cite the apologist Athenagoras (legat pro christ. 32, p. 310). καθ' ἡλικίαν τοὺς μὲν υἱοὺς κ θυγατέρας νοοῦμεν, τοὺς δὲ ἀδελφοὺς ἔχομεν καὶ ἀδελφάς καὶ τοῖς προβεβηκόσι τὴν τῶν πατέρων καὶ μητέρων τιμὴν ἀπονέμομεν "The rule of Jerome (Ep. 52 [2]. 5, vol. i p. 259) is simple 'omnes puellas et virgines Christi aut æqualiter ignora aut æqualiter dilige'" Ellic. 3—16] *Directions concerning widows* This whole passage is somewhat difficult, and has been very variously understood. The differences will be seen below. 3 τίμα] Is this to be interpreted generally, '*honour*' merely, or with reference to the context? The best guide to an answer will be what follows. If the command be merely to hold them in honour, why should the destitute be held in more honour than those who had families? The command χήρας τίμα would surely apply to all alike. But seeing that it *does not* apply to all alike, we must necessarily limit its general meaning to that particular in which the one would be honoured, and the other not. Thus without giving or seeking for an unusual meaning to τίμα, we may fairly interpret it of this particular kind of honour, viz. being inscribed on the Church's κατάλογος (ver 9) as a fit object of charitable sustenance. That such a roll existed in the very earliest days of the church, we know from Acts vi 1 Cf also Ignat ad Polyc. c. 4, p. 721 f Justin M. Apol i 67, p. 84: Euseb. H. E. vi. 43. Thus Huther and De W, and Ellic., after Grot, Calv, all. τὰς ὄντως χήρας] cf ver 16 below,—those who are really in a widowed (destitute) state, as contrasted with those described ver 4 But then the enquiry has been made, Is this ὄντως χήρα to be defined by mere external circumstances, or not rather by the religious character, described below, ver 5? Or are we to bind [as Chrys, al] the two together? In a certain sense, I believe we must thus unite them The Apostle commands, 'Honour [by placing on the list] those who are widows indeed' for it is these especially, they who are destitute of earthly friends, who are most likely to carry out the true religious duties of a widow. Thus, without the two qualifications being actually united, the former is insisted on as ordinarily ensuring the latter. 4.] The case of the χήρα who is not ὄντως χήρα, having earthly relations answerable for her support. ἔκγονα] τέκνα τέκνων, Hesych , grandchildren: not as E V '*nephews*,' at least, not in its present sense μανθανέτωσαν] What is the subject? (1) The ancient Commentators mostly understand αἱ χῆραι, implied in τὶς χήρα so vulg. (*discat*. also D-lat, 2 cursives have μανθανέτω), Chr (see below), Thdrt, Œc, Jer, Pel, Ambr, Luth, Calv, Grot, Calov, Huther, al (2) But some of the ancients took τὰ τέκνα ἢ ἔκγονα as the subject: e. g Œc. 2, Thl, and so Beza, Wolf, Mosh, Wegscheid, Heydenr, Flatt, Mack, De W, Wiesinger, Ellicott There is much to be said for both views, and as we advance, we shall give the interpretations on both hypotheses, (1) and (2). πρῶτον] Either, '*first of all duties*,' which seems supported by ver 8 below, or *first*, before applying to the church for sustenance. These meanings will apply to both the above alternatives. whether we understand the subject to be the *widows*, or the *children and grandchildren*. τὸν ἴδιον οἶκον εὐσεβεῖν] On hypothesis (1),—*to behave piously towards*, i e *to rule religiously* (Luth., so vulg.), their own household This seems somewhat to force εὐσεβεῖν, see below; while the sense of τὸν ἴδιον οἶκον is thus the simple and usual one, as the widow in question would be the head of the household. On hypothesis (2), *to behave piously towards*, i. e. *to honour with the honour which God commands*, their own family, i e. the widowed mother or grandmother who is one of their own family. This sense of εὐσεβής, εὐσέβεια, and εὐσεβέω, is common enough (see especially Palm and Rost's Lex) the reference being generally (not always, it is true) to superiors,—those who demand σέβας,—those who stand in the place of God This sense of τὸν ἴδιον οἶκον is not so usual,

γόνοις· τοῦτο γάρ ἐστιν [xy] ἀποδεκτὸν [x] ἐνώπιον τοῦ θεοῦ.
5 ἡ δὲ [z] ὄντως χήρα καὶ [a] μεμονωμένη [b] ἤλπικεν [b] ἐπὶ τὸν
θεόν, καὶ [c] προσμένει ταῖς [d] δεήσεσιν καὶ ταῖς [d] προσευχαῖς [e] νυκτὸς καὶ [e] ἡμέρας· 6 ἡ δὲ [f] σπαταλῶσα [g] ζῶσα
[g] τέθνηκεν. 7 καὶ ταῦτα [h] παράγγελλε, [i] ἵνα [j] ἀνεπίλημπτοι ὦσιν. 8 εἰ δέ τις [k] τῶν [k] ἰδίων καὶ [l] μάλιστα [τῶν]

x ch ii 3
y as above (x) only †
(ἀποχη, ch i 15
-δέχεσθαι, Acts ii 41)
z ver 3 reff
a here only †
(Ezek xlv 6 Aqu
b see ch iv 10 reff
c = Acts xiii 43 (of Paul) see Acts xi 23
d ch ii 1 reff
e Paul, 1 Thess ii 9 iii 10 2 Tim i 3 Mark v 5 Rev iv 8 al Isa xxxiv 10
f James v 5 only Ezek xvi. 49 Sir xxi 15 only (-λη, Sir xxvii 13 κατασπαταλαω, Prov xxix 21 Amos vi 4 [cf Wetst])
g see Rev iii 1 πενης αποθανων, φροντιδων απηλλαγη, ζων γαρ τεθνηκε, Stob 238 Wetst
h ch iv 11 Josh vi 6
i Mark vi 8 2 Thess iii 12
j ch iii 2 vi 14 only †
k John i 11 xiii 1 Acts iv 23 xxiv 23 only 2 Macc xii 22
l ch iv 10 reff

rec ins *καλον και* (*from ch* ii 3) bef *αποδεκτον*, with (d, e sil) m o copt goth · om ACDF KLℵ rel vulg syrr gr-lat-ff. (17 def)
5 om *τον* ℵ[1].—for *θεον*, *κυριον* D[1]ℵ[1] Aug Fulg
7 om *και* ℵ[3].
8 om (2nd) *των* AD[1]Fℵ · ins CD[2,3]KL rel Chr Thdrt Damasc.

but not therefore to be rejected To dishonour their widowed mother or grandmother, would be to dishonour their own family, in that one of its members who most required respect. **καὶ ἀμοιβὰς ἀποδιδόναι τοῖς προγόνοις**] On hypothesis (1), as Chrys., *ἀπῆλθον ἐκεῖνοι· οὐκ ἠδυνήθης αὐτοῖς ἀποδοῦναι τὴν ἀμοιβήν· οὐ γὰρ δὴ καὶ αὐτὴ ἐγέννησας ἐκείνους, οὐδὲ ἀνέθρεψας ἐν τοῖς ἐκγόνοις αὐτοῦ ἀμείβου ἀποδίδου τὸ ὀφείλημα διὰ τῶν παιδῶν.* But surely it is a very strange way of requiting one's progenitors for their care of us, to be kind towards our own children · and besides, what would this have to do with the question, whether or not the widow was to be put on the charity roll of the church? But on hypothesis (2), this sentence certainly becomes more clear and natural Let them, the children or grandchildren, learn first to be piously grateful to (these members of) their own families, and to give back returns (a return in each case) to their progenitors (so called, although living, because, the *mother and grandmother* having been both mentioned, *πρόγονοι* was the only word which would include them in one category) **τοῦτο γὰρ . .**] see ch ii. 3 **5**] see above on ver. 3 **ἡ ὄντως χήρα**, as opposed to the widow just described, **κ μεμονωμένη**, as contrasting her condition with that of her who has children or grandchildren. Thus what follows is said more for moral eulogy of such a widow, than as commending her to the charity of the church but at the same time, as pointing out that one who thus places her hopes and spends her time, is best deserving of the Church's help **ἤλπικεν**, ch iv 10, **has set and continues to set her hope** **ἐπὶ τὸν θεόν**, on God as its portion and ultimate aim,—as distinguished from *ἐπὶ τῷ θεῷ*, ch. iv 10, on God as its present stay. **προσμένει**] compare reff, and the similar use of *προσκαρτερεῖν*, Rom xii 12, Col. iv 2. **ταῖς δεήσ κ ταῖς προσευχ**] see on ch. ii 1 The articles may refer to the public prayers of the Church, or may be possessive—'to her supplications and her prayers:' or may serve merely to designate the two great divisions of prayer. **νύκτ κ ἡμ**] so St. Luke of Anna the prophetess, ii. 37,—*νηστείαις κ δεήσεσιν λατρεύουσα νύκτα καὶ ἡμέραν.* **6**] Contrast (**δέ**) to the character just described and that certainly with a view to point out that this kind of widow is no object for the charity of the Church, as not being at all a partaker of the life unto God. **σπαταλῶσα**] Wetst from the glossaries, gives *σπαταλᾷ, λίαν τρυφᾷ, ἀσώτως ζῇ*. In the Anthol., iv 28 14, we have coupled *πᾶν τὸ βρότων σπατάλημα κ. ἡ πολύολβος ἐδωδή.* It appears to be allied to *σπαθάω* (*σπάω*),—see Aristoph., Nub. 53, and Schol (in Wetst), and Ellic, here **ζῶσα τέθνηκεν**] while alive in the flesh, has no real life in the Spirit · see ref —and Matt viii 22 Eph v. 14 Wetst. quotes many such expressions from profane writers · one, as compared with this passage, remarkably illustrative of the moral difference between Christianity and heathenism · Soph Antig. 1183,—*τὰς γὰρ ἡδονὰς ὅταν | προδῶσιν ἄνδρες, οὐ τίθημ' ἐγὼ | ζῆν τοῦτον, ἀλλ' ἔμψυχον ἡγοῦμαι νεκρόν* The very expression is found in Stobæus, see reff I cannot help regarding the idea as in the background,—'and, if devoid of spiritual life, then not to be taken into account by the Church' **7.**] **ταῦτα** most naturally applies to the characters just given of widows, not more generally ·

m Gal vi 10 Eph ii 19 only Isa iii 6
n Rom xii 17, from Prov iii 4 2 Cor viii 21 only P 2 Macc xiv 9
o Rev ii 13
p = Paul, 2 Tim ii 12, 13 iii 5 Tit i 16 ii 12 only Matt x 33 bis Luke xii 9 Acts iii 13, 14 vii 35 2 Pet ii 1 1 John ii 22, 23 Jude 4 Rev iii 8 t (Gen xviii 15)
q = 1 Cor vi 6 vii 12 &c x 27. xiv 22, &c 2 Cor vi 14, 15 Tit i 15
r Paul, 2 Tim iii 13 only Heb x 29 al + Wisd xv 18 only
s here only Deut xiv 18 2 Macc vii 30 only Xen Hell iii 4 15
t adv here only (σαων, John ii 10 Rom ix 12, from Gen xxv 23 Heb vii 7 only)

m οἰκείων οὐ n προνοεῖ, τὴν o πίστιν op ἤρνηται, καὶ ἔστιν
q ἀπίστου r χείρων. 9 χήρα s καταλεγέσθω μὴ t ἔλαττον

b νοει την ACDF KLℵ a b c d e f g h k l m n o 17

προνοειται (*corrn, the active occurring only here in N. T*) D[1]FKℵ[1].

and in that case ἵνα ἀνεπίλημπτοι (see reff) ὦσιν must refer to the widows also, not to the τέκνα and ἔκγονα, or to these and the widows together, as Heydenr , or more widely still, as Grot , al. This narrower reference is confirmed by the next verse, which takes up the duty of the relations, being connected not by γάρ, but by δέ. 8] τίς, not only of the τέκνα ἢ ἔκγονα above, or any persons connected with widows,—but the saying is perfectly general, grounding their duties on an axiomatic truth. Agreeably with their former interpretation, Chrys , &c regard τίς as meaning 'a widow ' Calv and Thdrt. unite both, widows and children οἱ ἴδιοι seem to be generally any connexions,—οἱ οἰκεῖοι, those more immediately included in one's own family as dwelling in the same οἶκος — see reff. Mack is certainly wrong in regarding οἰκείοι (without τῆς πίστεως) as meaning those connected by the faith The omission of the article (see var readd) would make the two belong to one and the same class. οὐ προνοεῖ, viz. in the way noted above,—of support and sustenance. Notice εἰ οὐ, in its regular usage, the negation being closely connected with the verb· "neglects to provide." On the construction of προνοεῖν, see Ellic 's note. τὴν πίστιν ἤρνηται] 'fides enim non tollit officia naturalia, sed perficit et firmat' Bengel The Roman-Catholic Commentator Mack has some good remarks here, on the faith of which the Apostle speaks "Faith, in the sense of the Apostle, cannot exist, without including love. for the subject-matter of faith is not mere opinion, but the grace and truth of God, to which he that believes gives up his spirit, as he that loves gives up his heart the subject-matter of faith is also the object of love Where therefore Love is not, nor works, there is not, nor works, Faith either so that he who fulfils not the offices of love towards his relatives, is virtually an unbeliever " ἀπίστου χείρων] For even among heathens the common duties of family piety are recognized if therefore a Christian repudiates them, he lowers himself beneath the heathen Cf Matt v 46, 17. Also, as Calv. suggests in addition, the Christian who lives in the light of the Gospel, has less excuse for breaking those laws of nature which even without the Gospel are recognized by men According to hypothesis (1) or (2) above, this general statement applies to the widows or to their children and grandchildren not, as Matthies, to their *mutual* relations, about which the context contains no hint But surely it would be very harsh to understand it of the widows and this forms an additional argument for hypothesis (2)

9—16.] *Further regulations respecting widows* 9] Is χήρα subject or predicate? 'let a widow καταλεγέσθω,' or 'let a woman καταλεγέσθω χήρα?' I own, from the arrangement of the words, I am inclined to believe the latter to be the case. The verb καταλεγέσθω introduces the new particular Had χήρα then been the subject, the verb, having the emphasis, must have preceded. As it is, χήρα has the emphasis, as it would have, were it the predicate, spoken of those of whom the κατάλογος consisted I render therefore,—**Let a woman be inserted in the catalogue as a widow.** But now, for what purpose? καταλέγειν is to enrol on a list or roll so Aristoph. Acharn. 1029. ὅταν στρατιώτας καταλέγωσι . . .,—Lysistr, ὁ δὲ Δημόστρατος | ἔλεγεν ὁπλίτας καταλέγειν Ζακυνθίων Xen Rep Lac. iv 3, τούτων δ' ἕκαστος ἄνδρας ἑκατὸν καταλέγει. Lysias, p 172. 37, οὐ τοίνυν οὐδ' εἰς τὸν κατάλογον 'Αθηναίων καταλέξας οὐδένα φανήσομαι see other examples in Palm and Rost's Lex , and in Wetst But *what catalogue* are we to understand? [In replying to this question I agree in the main with De Wette, from whose note the substance of the following remarks is adopted] Hardly, (1) that of those who are to receive relief from the Church (so Chrys h. 1, Thdrt , Œc , Thl , Jer., Erasm , Calv , Est, Wolf, Neand , al) for thus the rule, that she is to be *sixty years of age*, would seem a harsh one, as many widows might be destitute at a far earlier age as also the rule that she must not have been *twice married*, especially as the Apostle himself below commands second

ἐτῶν ἑξήκοντα γεγονυῖα, [u] ἑνὸς ἀνδρὸς γυνή, 10 ἐν [v] ἔργοις
[v] καλοῖς [w] μαρτυρουμένη, εἰ [x] ἐτεκνοτρόφησεν, εἰ [y] ἐξενοδό-

u see ch iii 2, 12. v ch iii 1 reff. w = Acts vi 3 x 22. xxii 12 Heb xi 2, 39. x here only† Arrian, Epict i. 23, διατί ἀποσυμβουλεύεις τῷ σοφῷ τεκνοτροφεῖν; y here only† Herod vi 127.

marriage for the younger widows. Again, the duties enjoined in ver. 10 presuppose some degree of competence, and thus, on this hypothesis, the widows of the poorer classes would be excluded from sustenance by charity,—who most of all others would require it. Also, for the reason alleged in ver. 11, *sustenance* can hardly be in question—for then the re-marrying would simply take them off the roll, and thus be rather a benefit, than a detriment to the Church. Nor again (2) can we understand the roll to be that of the *deaconesses*, as Pelag., Beza, Schleierm., Mack, al.: although the Theodosian code, founded on this interpretation, ordained "nulla nisi emensis LX annis secundum præceptum Apostoli ad Diaconissarum consortium transferatur," xvi. 2. 27 (De W.). For a) the age mentioned is unfit for the work of the deaconesses' office, and in the council of Chalcedon the age of the deaconesses was fixed at 40. b) not only widows but virgins were elected deaconesses (Balsamon, ad Can. xix. conc. Niceni, παρθένοι . . . . τεσσαρακονταετοῦς ἡλικίας γενόμεναι, ἠξιοῦντο καὶ χειροτονίας διακονισσῶν εὑρισκόμεναι πάντως ἄξιαι. Suicer, i. 865). (3) it is implied in ver. 12, that these widows were bound not to marry again, which was not the case with the deaconesses. It seems therefore better to understand here *some especial band of widows*, sustained perhaps at the expense of the church, but not the only ones who were thus supported,—set apart for ecclesiastical duties, and bound to the service of God. Such are understood here by Chrys. himself in his homily on the passage [311 in div. N. T. loc 3, vol iii. p. 523, Migne],—καθάπερ εἰσὶ παρθένων χοροί, οὕτω καὶ χηρῶν τὸ παλαιὸν ἦσαν χοροί, καὶ οὐκ ἐξῆν αὐταῖς ἁπλῶς εἰς τὰς χήρας ἐγγράφεσθαι. οὐ περὶ ἐκείνης οὖν λέγει τῆς ἐν πενίᾳ ζώσης καὶ δεομένης βοηθείας, ἀλλὰ περὶ ταύτης τῆς ἑλομένης χηρείαν. They are also mentioned as τάγμα χηρῶν, τὸ χηρικόν, πρεσβύτιδες, προκαθήμεναι: i. e. such widows as corresponded in office for their own sex in some measure to the presbyters,—sat unveiled in the assemblies in a separate place, by the presbyters, and had a kind of supervision over their own sex, especially over the widows and orphans: were vowed to perpetual widowhood, clad with a 'vestis vidualis,' and ordained by laying on of hands. This institution of the early church, which was abolished by the eleventh canon of the council of Laodicea (in the translation of Dionys. Exiguus,—'mulieres quæ apud Græcos presbyteræ appellantur, apud nos autem viduæ seniores, univiræ, et matriculariæ nominantur, in ecclesia tanquam ordinatas constitui non debere'), is sufficiently affirmed by Chrys. l. c. Epiphan. hær. lxxix. 4, vol ii. [Migne], p. 1060 f., and long before by Tert. de veland. virg. 9, vol ii. p. 902: 'ad quam sedem [viduarum] præter annos LX non tantum univiræ, i. e. nuptæ aliquando, eliguntur, sed et matres et quidem educatrices filiorum.' De W. imagines he finds also a trace of it in Herm. Pastor, i. vision 2. 4, p. 900: 'καὶ Γραπτὴ μὲν ('Grapte diaconissa fuisse videtur.' Hefele, not.) νουθετήσει τὰς χήρας καὶ τοὺς ὀρφανούς:' and in Lucian de morte peregrini, Opp. iii. 335 Reig.,—ἕωθεν μὲν εὐθὺς ἦν ὁρᾷν παρὰ τῷ δεσμωτηρίῳ περιμένοντα γραΐδια, χήρας τινὰς καὶ παιδία ὀρφανά. He also refers to the dissertation of Mosheim on this place, in which he has thoroughly gone into all the bearings of the subject and maintained the above view. So also Grot., Fritzsch., and Michaelis: so Wiesinger,—and in a somewhat modified shape, Huther, repudiating the idea of formal ordination and setting apart of widows so early as the apostolic age. In this he is probably right. De W. makes the allusion to this 'institute of widows' one proof of the post-apostolic date of the Epistle: but on this see Prolegg. ch. vii. § i. 27. **Let a woman be enrolled a widow, who is not less than sixty years old** (γεγονυῖα is joined by the vulg. ['quæ fuerit unius viri uxor'], Jer., Luth., Calv., Beza, Grot., Mack, al., to the next clause: but against this is usage [ὅτε ἐγένετο ἐτῶν δώδεκα, Luke ii. 42: cf. also Plat. Legg. vi. p. 765, ἐτῶν μὲν γεγονὼς μὴ ἔλαττον ἢ πεντήκοντα: and see other examples in Wetst.], and the fact that μιᾶς γυναικὸς ἄνδρα stands alone in ch. iii. 2. Besides, if it belonged to the next clause, it would have in it any place but the *first*), **the wife of one husband** (cf. ch. iii. 2. Here, as contemporaneous polygamy is out of the question, and thus one element of difficulty in the other case is eliminated, we can hardly understand any thing other than that the πρεσβύτις should have been the wife of only one husband: i. e., not

χησεν, εἰ [z] ἁγίων [a] πόδας [ab] ἔνιψεν, εἰ [c] θλιβομένοις [d] ἐπήρ-
κεσεν, εἰ παντὶ [e] ἔργῳ [e] ἀγαθῷ [f] ἐπηκολούθησεν. 11 νεωτέρας δὲ χήρας [g] παραιτοῦ· ὅταν γὰρ [h] καταστρηνιάσουσιν

ACDΓ KLℵ a b c d e f g h k l m n o 17

z Eph i 1 reff. a John xiii 5, &c. only Gen xviii 4. b as above (a). Matt vi 17 xv 2 Mark vii 3 John ix 7, &c only. c 1 Thess iii 4 = Paul only, exc Heb xi 37 d ver 16 bis only † 1 Macc viii 26 e = Eph ii 10 ch ii 10 reff f = here (Mark xvi 20 ver 24 1 Pet ii 21) only Isa lv 3 g ch iv 7 reff h here only † constr, James ii 13 στρηνιάω, Rev xviii 7, 9 στρῆνος, Rev xviii 3

11 rec καταστρηνιασωσι (*corrn to suit* οταν. *The txt could hardly arise from the transcriber's eye having glanced on to* θελ-ουσιν, *as Ellic*), with CDKLℵ rel txt AF Chr-ms

married a second time: so Tertull. ad uxor. i. 7, vol. i p. 1286. "digamos non sinit præsidere, . . . viduam allegi in ordinem nisi univiram non concedit." So that the parallel expressions here and in ch. iii 2 will be consistently interpreted. See the mistaken views of Thdrt [τὸ σωφρόνως ἐν γάμῳ βιοῦν νομοθετεῖ], &c., treated of under ch iii 2), **having a good character** (testimony from without, cf reff. and ch iii 7) in (the element or region in which that μαρτυρία is versed) **good works** (reff), if ('the conditions have as yet been expressed by participles in agreement with the noun: the construction is now changed for the hypothetical.' De W: but εἰ does not depend immediately on καταλεγέσθω: the intervening clauses must be taken for granted. So that it may more properly be said to be dependent on μὴ . . μαρτυρουμένη:—such an one, if in addition she, &c.) **she** (at any time—keep the aor.) **brought up children** (her own? or those of others? If [1], the barren might seem hardly dealt with: if [2], the word must be somewhat forced aside from its ordinary meaning [see τεκνοτροφία in Palm and Rost's Lex., where in the examples cited, die Kinderzeugung mitinbegriffen ist]. Still this latter, considering that ἐξενοδόχησεν is the next good work specified, seems most probable: and so, but for the most part combining it with the other, Beng, De W., Huther, Wiesinger, al. Grot. understands it, 'si nec abortum sibi fecerit, nec ob paupertatem exposuerit liberos . . . , sed omnes sibi natos educaverit, et quidem honeste ac pie.' Calv.,—'non sterilitatem hic damnari a Paulo, sed matrum delicias, quæ sobolis alendæ tædia devorare recusant'), **if she** (at any time) **received strangers** (practised hospitality. This clearly points out a person above the rank of the poor and indigent: though Chrys pithily replies, κἂν πένης ᾖ, οἰκίαν ἔχει· οὐ γὰρ δὴ αἴθριος μένει. One is glad to hear that all the Christian widows at Constantinople were so well off. But it can hardly have been so in the apostolic age. Cf. ch. iii 2. Tit i 8. Rom xii 13. Heb xiii 2), **if she** (at any time) **washed the feet of the saints** ('synecdoche partis, pro omni genere officiorum humilitatis,' Beng. εἰ τὰς ἐσχάτας ὑπηρεσίας τοῖς ἁγίοις ἀνεπαισχύντως ἐξετέλεσε, Thl. Still, we must not dismiss from our consideration the external act itself: as Thdrt. ἐποίουν γὰρ τοῦτο πάλαι. see John xiii 14, and note, in which, though a formal ceremony in obedience to our Saviour's words is repudiated, the principle of humbly serving one another, which would lead to such an act on occasion presented, is maintained), **if she** (at any time) **relieved** (cf. Herod. i. 91, καιομένῳ αὐτῷ ἐπήρκεσε:—Eur. Hec. 963, τί χρὴ τὸν εὖ πράσσοντα μὴ πράσσουσιν εὖ | φίλοις ἐπαρκεῖν;—and examples in Wetst. It is more rarely found with an accus. see Palm and Rost's Lex.) **the distressed** (not merely the *poor*, as Beng., but those afflicted in any way; cf. example from Herod. above), **if she followed every good work** (Chrys. in his fine homily on this passage, cited above, § 15, says τί ἐστιν ἐν παντὶ ἔργ. ἀγ. ἐπηκολούθ. ὥστε καὶ εἰς δεσμωτήριον εἰσιέναι καὶ τοὺς δεδεμένους ἐπισκέπτεσθαι, καὶ ἀῤῥωστοῦντας ἐπισκοπεῖν. καὶ θλιβομένους παραμυθεῖσθαι, καὶ ὀδυνωμένους παρακαλεῖν, καὶ πάντα τρόπον τὰ κατὰ δύναμιν εἰσφέρειν ἅπαντα, καὶ μηδὲν ὅλως παραιτεῖσθαι τῶν εἰς σωτηρίαν καὶ ἀνάπαυσιν τῶν ἀδελφῶν γινομένων τῶν ἡμετέρων. Bengel's idea, 'Antistitum et virorum est, *bonis operibus præire*, Tit iii 8, 14: mulierum, *subsequi*, adjuvando pro sua parte,' is ingenious, but wrong. cf. Plat. Rep. p. 370 c,—ἀλλ' ἀνάγκη τὸν πράττοντα τῷ πραττομένῳ ἐπακολουθεῖν μὴ ἐν παρέργου μέρει).

11.] **But younger widows decline** (to place on the κατάλογος, see above on verse 9. not 'avoid,' *for fear of scandal*, as Chrys. in the homily above cited: nor both of these combined, as Huther: nor 'decline as objects for the alms of the church,' as some above. Baur's idea [Paulus u. s. w. p. 497], that χήρας is the predicate,—'*the younger women decline as widows*,' refuse to put on the list of widows, is not justified by the construction, nor does it derive any support from the rendering given above of χήρα καταλεγέσθω, verse

τοῦ Χριστοῦ, ˡ γαμεῖν θέλουσιν, 12 ᵏ ἔχουσαι ˡ κρίμα, ὅτι
τὴν πρώτην ᵐ πίστιν ᵐⁿ ἠθέτησαν· 13 ἅμα δὲ καὶ ᵒ ἀργαὶ
ᵖ μανθάνουσιν ᑫ περιερχόμεναι τὰς οἰκίας· οὐ μόνον δὲ

l of the woman, ver 14. 1 Cor vii 28 (36) only† (2 Macc xiv 25 bis only) k = ver 20 John ix 41 xv. 22, 24 l = Rom ii 2 Gal v 10 reff m = Polyb viii 2 5 al fr n Mark vii 9 Gal ii 21 iii 15 Heb x 28 al Ps lxxxviii 34 o Gospp, Matt (xii 36 xx 3, 6) only Epp, Tit i 12 James ii 20 2 Pet i 8 only Wisd xv 15 p constr, here only see ver 4 reff q Acts xix 13 xxviii 13 Heb xi 37 only Job i 7

9) **for when they shall wax wanton** (a very full account of the usage of ἐάν and ὅταν with the indic is given in Klotz, Devar. ii. pp. 468 ff. Ellicott sums it up by saying that in such cases the whole conditional force is restricted to the particle, and there is no necessary internal connexion between the verb in the protasis and that in the apodosis He does not hold this to be applicable here, and therefore prefers the rec. reading) **against** (στρηνιάω, and στρῆνος, see reff —from στρηνής [strenuus], '*strong*,' — 'to be strong,' whence **κατα στρ**, *to be strong against*,—to rebel against [see Ellic here] and in the particular matter here treated, 'to become wanton against') **Christ** (their proper bridegroom Jerome's expression, ep 123 [11] ad Ageruchiam [Gerontiam] 3, vol i p. 901, which the Commentators blame as too strong, in fact gives the sense well,—"quæ fornicatæ sunt [-cantur ?] in injuriam viri sui Christi" Thl. similarly, but too vaguely, — ὅταν καθυπερηφανεύσονται τοῦ χριστοῦ, μὴ ἀποδεχόμεναι αὐτὸν νυμφίον), **they desire to marry** (again),—**having** (bearing on themselves, as a burden see reff. and Gal. v. 10) **judgment** (from God and as the context necessarily implies, *condemnation* but we must not so express it in a version that which is left to be fixed by the context in the original, should be also left in a translation The meaning 'bringing on themselves the imputation of having,' &c , given by De W. and upheld by Huther, al , appears to me to be ungrammatical), **because they set at nought their first faith** (i. e. broke, made void, their former promise. So Chrys , interpreting it, τὰς πρὸς τὸν χριστὸν καταπατῆσαι συνθήκας, Hom xv. ut supra and again, πίστιν τὴν συνθήκην λέγει, Hom in loc Thdrt. τῷ χριστῷ συνταξάμεναι σωφρόνως ζῆν ἐν χηρείᾳ, δευτέροις ὁμιλοῦσι γάμοις Thl ἐψεύσαντο τὴν συμφωνίαν τὴν πρὸς χριστόν. Tert. de monogam 13, vol. ii. p 918,—"quod primam fidem resciderunt, illam videlicet a qua in viduitate inventæ et professæ eam non perseverant" Aug in Ps. lxxv. 12, § 16, vol. iv p. 968 "Quid est 'primam fidem irritam fecerunt'? voverunt et non reddiderunt." Having devoted themselves to widowhood as their state of life, and to the duties of the order of πρεσβύτιδες as their occupation, they will thus be guilty of a dereliction of their deliberate promise. Of the later vows of celibacy, and ascetic views with regard to second marriages, there is no trace . see below Calv. [al] interprets τὴν πρώτην πίστιν ἠθέτησαν of *falling away from the faith*,—'quia a fide baptismi et Christianismo prorsus deficiant,' and defends this view against that given above, calling it 'nimis frigidum ' but as it seems to me quite unsuccessfully He expresses well, however, the difference between this addiction to single life and the later compulsory vows: 'non ideo cœlibes se fore promittebant olim viduæ, ut sanctius agerent vitam quam in conjugio sed quod non poterant marito et ecclesiæ simul esse addictæ.'—see the rest of his note) **13.] Moreover they also learn to be idle** (so Syr , Chr , Thl , Beza, Huther, Winer, Ellic ["It is needless to say that Winer does not conceive 'an ellipsis of οὖσαι for εἶναι' Bloomf.,—a mistake of which such a scholar could not be capable." Ellic. edn 1], al ,—a harsh construction, but, it is said, not without example however, the only one cited is from Plat. Euthyd. p 276 b: οἱ ἀμαθεῖς ἄρα σοφοὶ μανθάνουσι, where the word σοφοί does not occur in Bekker's text, and seems on critical grounds very suspicious Still I conceive that the present sentence will admit of no other construction, on account of the emphatic position of ἀργαί, which is further heightened by οὐ μόνον δὲ ἀργαί below. De W. objects to it, that idleness is the cause, not the effect, of going about, &c but it may well be answered, that not only does a spirit of idleness give rise to such going about, but such going about confirms the habit of idleness Bengel would lay the stress on μανθάνουσιν—'reprehenditur *discendi* genus sequiturque species, —*discunt, quæ domos obeundo discuntur*, i e statum familiarum curiose explorant.' But μανθ does not seem to bear this meaning The usual interpretation has been to take περιερχ. as an infin , '*learn to go about*' so vulg , Luth., &c . but the objection to this is, that μανθάνω with a participle always means *to be aware of, take notice of*, the act implied in the verb e. g διαβεβλημένος ὑπὸ 'Αμάσιος οὐ μανθάνεις, Herod. iii. 1) **going about**

ᵒ ἀργαί, ἀλλὰ καὶ ʳ φλύαροι καὶ ˢ περίεργοι, λαλοῦσαι ACDF
ᵗ τὰ μὴ δέοντα. 14 ᵘ βούλομαι οὖν νεωτέρας ᵛ γαμεῖν, KLℵ a b c d e f g
ʷ τεκνογονεῖν, ˣ οἰκοδεσποτεῖν, μηδεμίαν ʸᶻ ἀφορμὴν ᶻ διδόναι h k l m n o 17
τῷ ᵃ ἀντικειμένῳ ᵇ λοιδορίας ᶜ χάριν 15 ἤδη γάρ ᵈ τινες
ᵉ ἐξετράπησαν ᶠ ὀπίσω τοῦ Σατανᾶ. 16 εἴ τις [ᵍ πιστὸς ἢ]

r here only † (-ρεῖν, 3 John 10) s Acts xix 19 only (-γεω, Sir xli 22 γαζεσθαι, 2 Thess iii 11 Σωκράτης περιεργάζεται, Plat Apol Socr 19 b) t so Tit i 11 u = ch ii 8 Tit iii 8 v ver 11 w here only † (-νια, ch ii 15) x here only † (-της Matt xx 25) y Gal v 13 reff z 1 Cor x 12 a absol., 1 Cor xvi 9 Phil i 28 2 Thess ii 4 (ch i 12 Luke xiii 17 xxi 15) L P Isa lxvi 6 b 1 Pet iii 9 only Prov x 18 (-ρος 1 Cor v 11 -ρεῖν, John ix 28) c Paul, Gal iii 19 Eph iii 1, 14 Tit. i 5, 11 Gospp., Luke vii 47 only 1 John iii 12 Jude 16 only d = ch i 1, 3 reff e ch i 6 reff f Acts v 37 xx 30 Rev xiii 3 Judg ii 19 g = Eph i 1 reff

14 ins *τας* bef *νεωτερας* D[1] m 73. 80.

15. om ver 67[2]. *εξετραπησαν* bef *τινες* AF txt CDKLℵ rel vulg syrr copt gr-lat-ff

16. om *πιστος η* (*passing from πιστ. to πιστ.?*) ACFℵ 17 am(with harl[1]) copt arm (Ath) ins DKL rel fuld(with tol harl[2]) syrr Chr Thdrt Damasc Ambrst. (om *η πιστη* vulg-ed F-lat Ambr Aug Pelag$_3$—demid G-lat æth have *si quis fideles*[-*em* æth] *habet*

from house to house (lit "the houses," viz of the faithful For the construction compare Matt ix. 35, *περιῆγεν ὁ Ἰησοῦς τὰς πόλεις*) **but not only** (to be) idle, **but also gossips** (*περιοδεύουσαι τὰς οἰκίας, οὐδὲν ἀλλ' ἢ τὰ ταύτης εἰς ἐκείνην φέρουσι, καὶ τὰ ἐκείνης εἰς ταύτην* Thl. 'Ex otio nascebatur curiositas, quæ ipsa garrulitatis est mater.' Calv) **and busybodies** (reff), **speaking** (not merely '*saying*:' the subject-matter, as well as the form, is involved in *λαλοῦσαι*) **things which are not fitting** (his fear is, that these younger widows will not only do the Church's work idly, but make mischief by bearing about tales and scandal) **I will** (consult Ellic's note on *βούλομαι*. We may generally state that *θέλω* is the resting inclination of the will, *βούλομαι* its active exertion) **then** ("*οὖν* has here its proper collective force, 'in consequence of these things being so, I desire'" Ellic) **that younger widows** (such, and not the younger *women*, is evidently the Apostle's meaning [*χήρας* is supplied in several cursives, Chr, Thdrt., Jer.] The whole passage has concerned *widows*—and to them he returns again, ver 16) **marry** (not as Chrys., *ἐπειδὴ αὐταὶ βούλονται βούλομαι κἀγώ . . . . ἔδει μὲν οὖν τὰ τοῦ θεοῦ μεριμνᾶν, ἔδει τὴν πίστιν φυλάττειν. ἐπειδὴ δὲ ἐκεῖνα οὐ γίνεται, βέλτιον ταῦτα γενέσθαι* [so also, characteristically, the R-Cath. Mack] for it is not younger widows *who have been taken into the catalogue* of *πρεσβύτιδες* of whom he is speaking, but *younger widows in general* Chrys.'s interpretation would make the Apostle contradict himself The *οὖν* on which Mack lays stress as favouring this meaning, simply infers from the temptations of young widows just described There is no inconsistency here with the view expressed in 1 Cor vii 39, 40 the time and circumstances were different), **bear children, govern households** (i. e in their place, and with their share of the duties: *οἰκουρεῖν*, as Chrys Both these verbs belong to later Greek · cf Lobeck on Phryn, p 373), **give no occasion** (starting-point, in their behaviour or language) **to the adversary** (who is meant? Chrys. and the ancients for the most part understand, *the devil* [*μὴ βουλόμενος τὸν διάβολον ἀφορμὴν λαμβάνειν*] and so, lately, Huther, defending it by his interpretation of *λοιδορίας χάριν* [see below]. But St. Paul's own usage of *ἀντικείμενος* [reff, see also Tit ii. 8] is our best guide. Ordinarily using it of human adversaries, he surely would here have mentioned *ὁ διάβολος*, had he intended him And the understanding him to be here meant brings in the next verse very awkwardly, as he there has an entirely new part assigned him. Understand therefore, any adversary, Jew or Gentile, who may be on the watch to get occasion, by the lax conduct of the believers, to slander the Church) **for the sake of reproach** (to be joined with *ἀφορμήν* the *ἀφορμή*, when taken advantage of by the adversary, would be used *λοιδορίας χάριν*, for the sake and purpose of reproaching the people of God Mack would join *λ. χ.* with *βούλομαι*,—most unnaturally 'I will, on account of the reproach which might otherwise come on the Church, *νεωτέρας γαμεῖν* &c .'—Leo,—with *τῷ ἀντικειμένῳ*,—which would more naturally be *τῷ λοιδορίας χάριν ἀντικειμένῳ* **λοιδορία** must be kept to its true sense, *reproach* brought on the Gospel, not forced, as Huther, for the sake of his view of *ὁ ἀντικείμενος*, to that of

[g] πιστὴ ἔχει χήρας, [h] ἐπαρκείτω αὐταῖς, καὶ μὴ [i] βαρείσθω
ἡ ἐκκλησία, ἵνα ταῖς [k] ὄντως χήραις [h] ἐπαρκέσῃ.
17 Οἱ καλῶς [l] προεστῶτες πρεσβύτεροι [m] διπλῆς [n] τιμῆς
[o] ἀξιούσθωσαν, [p] μάλιστα οἱ [q] κοπιῶντες ἐν λόγῳ καὶ [r] διδασκαλίᾳ. 18 [s] λέγει γὰρ ἡ [s] γραφὴ Βοῦν [t] ἀλοῶντα οὐ

h here (bis) and ver 10 only † 1 Macc viii 26. i Matt xxvi 43 (1 Mk v r) Luke ix 32 xxi 34 2 Cor i 8 v 4 only † Isa i 4 Aqu., Symm., &c k ver 3 l ch iii 4, 5 reff m Matt xxiii 15 Rev xviii 6 (bis) only Isa xl 2 n = Acts xxviii 10? Sir xxxviii 1 o = 2 Thess i 11 Heb iii 3 x 29 only (see Luke vii 7 Acts xv 38) † p ch iv 10 reff q Rom xvi 6 1 Cor iv 12 (o) i 29 ch iv 10 Ps cxxvi 1 r ch i 10 reff s Paul, Rom iv 3 al[4] Mark xv 8 James iv 5 al t Deut xxv 4 1 Cor ix 9 (from l. c.), 10 only

viduas[am æth]) επαρκεισθω AFℵ 17 (επαρικ. F)
17. om εν F.
18. ου φιμ bef β. αλ. AC m 17 vulg copt arm Chr Thdrt Ambrst · txt DFKLℵ rel

disgrace brought on the church by the fall of the widows);—for already ('particula provocat ad experientiam,' Beng) some (widows) have been (we are obliged here to give a *perfect* rendering in English. Our language will not, as the habit of mixed constructions in the Greek permits, bear the placing an indefinite past event in a definite portion of time such as ἤδη expresses) turned away (out of the right path, ref) after (so as to follow) Satan ('eoque occasionem dedere calumniæ,' Beng When De W. doubts whether St. Paul's experience could have been long enough to bear out such an assertion—and thus impugns the genuineness of the Epistle,—this is very much a matter of dates. and even taking the earliest commonly assigned, the assertion might be strictly true, applying as it does not only to Ephesus, but to the far wider range of his apostolic ministry). 16] Not a repetition of vv 4, 8, but an extension of the same duty to more distant relatives than those there spoken of If any believing [man or] woman has widows (in [his or] her family—dependent in any degree, however distant—e g as sister, or sister in-law, aunt, niece, cousin, &c), let such person relieve them (see above, ver 10), and let the church not be burdened (with their support "later and less correct form for βαρύνειν," see Ellic), that it may relieve those who are widows in reality (really χῆραι — destitute of help)

17—25] *Directions respecting* (17—19) *presbyters*, (20—25) *church discipline and certain matters regarding his own official and personal life.*

17] Let the presbyters who well preside (not, as in some former editions, *have well presided*. the perf of ἵστημι has the *present* signification throughout. I owe the correction of this inadvertence to Bishop Ellicott. Preside, viz over their portion of the Church's work. Chrys. has well expressed the meaning, but not all the meaning; for wisdom and ability must be taken also into account —τί δέ ἐστι, καλῶς προεστῶτας; ἀκούσωμεν τοῦ χριστοῦ λέγοντος ὁ ποιμὴν ὁ καλὸς τὴν ψυχὴν αὐτοῦ τίθησιν ὑπὲρ τῶν προβάτων ἄρα τοῦτό ἐστι καλῶς προεστάναι, μηδενὸς φείδεσθαι τῆς ἐκείνων κηδεμονίας ἕνεκα), be held worthy of double (not, as compared with the *widows*, as Chr,—[alt 1. διπλῆς τῆς πρὸς τὰς χήρας, ἢ τῆς πρὸς τοὺς διακόνους, ἢ ἁπλῶς διπλῆς τιμῆς, πολλῆς λέγει], Thl [1], Constt -ap [ii 28, p 674, Migne], Erasm, Calv, al,—the *deacons*, as Chr [2, see above], Thl. [2],—the *poor*, as Flatt, &c —but as compared with those who have not distinguished themselves by καλῶς προεστάναι, and evidently, as Chrys 3, it is not to be taken in the mere literal sense of *double*, but implies increase generally—see reff, and below) honour (so Plat. Legg v p. 378 D, τίμιος μὲν δὴ καὶ ὁ μηδὲν ἀδικῶν ὁ δὲ μηδ' ἐπιτρέπων τοῖς ἀδικοῦσιν ἀδικεῖν πλέον ἢ διπλασίας τιμῆς ἄξιος ἐκείνου and see other examples in Wetstein From the general tenor of those, as well as from the context here, it is evident that not merely honour, but *recompense* is here in question but the word need not be *confined* to that meaning honour, and honour's fruit, may be both included in it Grot conceives an allusion to the double portion of the firstborn [Deut xxi. 17] Elsner, to the double share of provision which used to be set before the presbyters in the Agapæ [Heydr, Baur cf. Constt.-apost as above] But as De W remarks, that practice was much more probably owing to a misunderstanding of this passage) · especially those that labour in (the) word and teaching (therefore the preaching of the word, and teaching, was *not the office of all* the πρεσβύτεροι Conyb rightly remarks, that this is a proof of the early date of the Epistle Of these two expressions, λόγος

u Matt xxii 12, 34 Mark i 25 | L iv 39 1 Pet ii 15 only Deut i c only
v Matt x 10 Luke x 7 James v 4 al † Wisd xvii 17 al only † Gen xliii 18 Schol only Exod xxiii 1 28) Deut xix 15
w [Luke vi 7, v r] John [viii 4] xviii 29 Tit i 6
x Mark iv 20 Acts xvi 21 xxii 18 Heb xii 6 (from Prov iii 12)
y 1 Cor xiv 5 xv 2
z = Matt xviii 16 2 Cor xiii 1 (Heb x

[u] φιμώσεις· [u] καὶ ἄξιος ὁ [v] ἐργάτης τοῦ μισθοῦ αὐτοῦ.
19 κατὰ πρεσβυτέρου [w] κατηγορίαν μὴ [x] παραδέχου, [y] ἐκτὸς
[y] εἰ μὴ [z] ἐπὶ δύο ἢ τριῶν μαρτύρων. 20 τοὺς [δὲ] ἁμαρ-

μαρτυρων C. ADF KLℵ a b c d e f g h k l m n o 17

syrr goth Damasc Tert —κημωσεις D for τ. μισθου, της τροφης(appy) ℵ[1]
20 rec om δε, with D[3]KLℵ rel vulg syrr copt gr-lat-ff ins AD[1] demid(with F-lat) G-lat goth Thl aft αμαρτ, F

would more properly express *preaching;* διδασκαλία, the work of *instruction,* by catechetical or other means). 18] *Ground for the above injunction.* See the first citation ('*an* [or 'the,' an anarthrous emphatic word] *ox while treading,*' &c, not, '*the ox that treadeth,*' &c, as E V) treated by the Apostle at more length, 1 Cor ix. 9 It is doubted whether the words ἄξιος ὁ ἐργάτ κ τ.λ are a citation at all Some have referred them to Levit. xix. 13 Deut. xxiv 14, which passages however say nothing of the kind, being special directions about paying a labourer's wages before night Thdrt and Thl suppose it to be quoted from the New Testament, i. e from our Lord's saying, reff Matt., Luke. But it is very unlikely that the Apostle should cite these under the title of ἡ γραφή and Calvin's view seems most probable, that he adduces the sentiment, as our Lord Himself does, as a popular and well-known saying (so Wolf and Huther) This verse it is which makes it extremely probable, that τιμή above refers to the honorarium of pecuniary recompense 19] See the summary above **Against a presbyter** (Chrys, Thl, are certainly wrong in supposing that age, not office is again here indicated the whole passage is of presbyters by office—cf ver 22 below) **entertain not an accusation, except** (reff pleonastic expressions such as ἐκτὸς εἰ μή, χωρὶς εἰ or εἰ μή, are found in later writers, such as Plutarch, Dio Cassius, &c we have πλὴν εἰ μή in Demosth 141 21, 719 1 Aristot de Anim. i 5. 9, al. See Lobeck on Phrynichus, p 459) **before** (lit. *in presence of,* and perhaps we ought to press the meaning but from the occurrence of ἐπὶ στόματος δύο μαρτ κ τ λ. in ref Deut., it is more likely figurative, 'in the presence of,' signifying merely 'vorhandenseyn,' their presence in the case) **two or three witnesses** (De W. asks, —but were not these required in every case, not only in that of a presbyter? Three answers are given one by Chrys. τὸ δε ἐπὶ ἄλλων, φησί, μάλιστα δὲ κατὰ πρεσβυτέρου], Thdrt [συμβαίνει γὰρ ἐκκλησίας αὐτὸν προστασίαν πεπιστευμένον καὶ λυπῆσαι τῶν ἁμαρτανόντων τινάς, εἶτα ἐντεῦθεν ἐκείνους δεομένως διατεθέντας συκοφαντίαν ὑφῆναι. δεῖ τοίνυν ἀπαντῆσαι τῶν μαρτύρων τὸν ἀριθμόν], and so Calvin at more length: the other by Huther, that Timotheus was not constituted judge in private men's matters, only over the officers of the church in faults with which they might be charged as regarded the execution of their duty a third by Bengel,—'privatus poterat, lege Mosis, citari uno teste, non condemnari presbyterum ne citari quidem Paulus jubet, &c.' But this is manifestly a distinction without point—the κατηγορίαν παραδέχεσθαι being used not of mere citation, but of entertaining the charge as a valid one in other words, as including citation and conviction as well So nearly Grotius, but bringing out a different distinction, which is manifestly here not in question—'poterat ad unius testis dictum vir plebeius capi aut contra eum inquisitio incipi non ita autem contra Senatorem, cui æquiparatur Presbyter' The first reason seems the more probable that he is only recalling the attention of Timotheus to a known and prescribed precaution, which was in this case especially to be always observed. Somewhat otherwise Ellicott see his note) 20] **[But] those who are doing wrong** (if δέ is read, these are the sinning presbyters, and cannot well be any others Without the particle, the application may be doubted De W, Wiesinger, and Ellic, following a few others [Aret, Heinr, Matthies, al], maintain the *general* reference So appears Chrys to have done, understanding πρεσβ merely of age, and going on without any further remark, and so [apparently] Thdrt But, even thus, the other view is the more likely, from the strong language used in ver 21, and the return again to the subject in ver. 22, and so most Commentators. The pres part. is no argument against it (against De W. and Wiesinger). 'those who are

τάνοντας [a] ἐνώπιον [a] πάντων [b] ἔλεγχε, ἵνα καὶ οἱ λοιποὶ
φόβον [c] ἔχωσιν. 21 [d] διαμαρτύρομαι [e] ἐνώπιον τοῦ θεοῦ
καὶ χριστοῦ Ἰησοῦ καὶ τῶν [fg] ἐκλεκτῶν [f] ἀγγέλων, ἵνα
ταῦτα [h] φυλάξῃς χωρὶς [i] προκρίματος, μηδὲν ποιῶν κατὰ
[k] πρόσκλισιν. 22 [l] χεῖρας [m] ταχέως μηδενὶ [l] ἐπιτίθει,

a see Gal ii 14 b Matt xviii 15 1 Cor xiv 24 Eph v 11 2 Tim iv 2 Tit i 9, 13 ii 15 Prov ix 7 c 2 Cor 12 reff d Luke xvi 28 Acts ii 40 al7 1 Thess iv 6 2 Tim ii 14 iv 1 Exod xix 21 see note, Heb ii 6 e = Gal i 20 ch vi 13. 2 Tim ii 14 iv 1 f here only g Rom viii 33 xvi 13 Col iii 12 2 Tim ii 10 Tit i 1 al Prov xvii 3 h = Rom ii 26 Gal vi 13 2 Tim i 12, 14 i here only † (κρίνειν, Wisd vii 8) k here only † Clem ad Cor i § 47, 50 pp 318, 312 l = Acts vi 6 viii 17, 19 xiii 3 Num xxvii 18. m = 2 Thess ii 2

21 rec (for χρ ιησ) κυριου ιησ. χρ, with D³KL rel Syr goth Chr txt AD¹FℵN 17 latt copt æth arm Clem Ath Bas Thdrt Hil Ambr προσκλησιν (*prob from confusion of ι & η so freq in MSS. cf Luke* xiv. 13) ADL rel Ath Chr(ἵνα σε μηδεὶς προκαταλάβῃ μηδὲ προοικειώσηται) txt FKℵ c h latt(*in alteram partem declinando*) syr goth Clem Bas Thdrt Damasc Thl(τουτέστιν κατὰ προσπάθειαν προσκλινόμενος τῷ ἑτέρῳ μέρει)
22 επιτιθου D¹

[detected in] sinning,' who are proved to be living in sin, may well be intended by it the fact of their being ἁμαρτάνοντες is not ascertained till they have been charged with fault, and the evidence of the witnesses taken) **reprove in the presence of all** (not all *the presbyters*, the 'consessus presbyterorum' see on καὶ οἱ λοιποί below but the whole congregation Had it not been for ecclesiastical considerations, we should never have heard of such a limited meaning for ἐνώπιον πάντων), **that the rest also** (not, the other presbyters, which would have certainly been pointed out if intended,—but in its usual sense of 'the rest,' generally the καί seems to make this even plainer that the warning may not be confined to a few, but may also spread over the whole church) **may have fear** (see Deut xiii 11 fear, on seeing the public disgrace consequent on sin ἔχωσιν, as above, ver 12)

21.] **I adjure thee** (see reff, especially 2 Tim iv. 1) **in the presence of God, and of Christ Jesus** (on the supposed reference to one Person only, see Ellic's note), **and of the elect angels** (the holy angels, who are the chosen attendants and ministers of God Thus ἐκλεκτῶν is an epithet distributed over the whole extent of ἀγγέλων, not one designating any one class of angels above the rest, as De W. Bengel says rightly, ἐκλεκτῶν, "epitheton, Timothei reverentiam acuens —the angels, God's chosen ministers" Various meanings have been proposed *good angels as distinguished from bad* (so Thl, Ambr, Grot, Est, Wolf, al),—but οἱ ἄγγελοι without any such designation, are ever good angels —*the guardian angels* of Timotheus and the Ephesian church (Mosheim) 'those especially selected by God as His messengers to the human race, as Gabriel' (Conyb.), —which, if we suppose these to be any particular class of angels, would be the best, but I doubt ἐκλεκτός, absolute, ever bearing this meaning, and much prefer that upheld above. Calvin says "electos vocat angelos non tantum ut a reprobis discernat, sed excellentiæ causa, ut plus reverentiæ habeat eorum testimonium" There is a parallel form of adjuration in Jos. B. J. ii. 16. 4, where Agrippa is endeavouring to persuade the Jews to remain in the Roman allegiance μαρτύρομαι δ' ἐγὼ ὑμῶν τὰ ἅγια καὶ τοὺς ἱεροὺς ἀγγέλους τοῦ θεοῦ, καὶ πατρίδα τὴν κοινήν Schleiermacher thinks this mention of one class of angels as '*elect*,' inconsistent with the Apostle's warning against genealogies and idle questions but with the above interpretation such objection falls to the ground Baur would explain the expression by the gnostic notion of angels more immediately connected with our Lord, alluded to by Irenæus, i 4 5, p 21, οἱ ἡλικιῶται αὐτοῦ ἄγγελοι see ib 7 1, p 32 But Irenæus' text is μετὰ τῶν ἡλικιωτῶν αὐτοῦ τῶν ἀγγέλων, which hardly justifies the interpretation and if it did, the whole lies too far off the matter in our text, to be brought to bear upon it), **that thou keep these things** (viz. the injunctions, vv 19, 20. De W., taking ver 20 generally, is obliged, although he confesses that the connexion with ver 19 would be best if only vv 19, 21 came together, to explain ταῦτα of ver. 20 only, see below) **without prejudice** ('præjudicium'—previous condemnation before hearing a man's case a word only found here), **doing nothing according to partiality** (bias towards, as the other was bias against, an accused presbyter. Diod

n Gal vi 6 reff & constr, 2 John 11 Isa ix 11 Ald compl. o Acts vii 6 Paul, Rom xiv 4 xv 20 2 Cor x 15, 16 Ps cviii 11 p Paul, 2 Cor. vii 11 xi 2 Phil iv 8 Tit ii 5 Prov xv 26 q = 1 Cor vii 37 2 Cor xi 9 1 Thess v 23 James i 27 Wisd x 5 r here only + Herod i 71 s ch i 8 t here only + u Luke v 33 Acts xxiv 26 only ‡ Ezek xxxi 34 2 Macc viii 8 only v = Matt viii 17 Gal iv 13 al fr 2 Macc ix 21, 22.

μηδὲ ⁿ κοινώνει ἁμαρτίαις ° ἀλλοτρίαις. σεαυτὸν ᵖ ἁγνὸν ADFK
ᵠ τήρει· 23 μηκέτι ʳ ὑδροπότει, ἀλλὰ οἴνῳ ὀλίγῳ ˢ χρῶ, LℵabcdefG
διὰ τὸν ᵗ στόμαχον καὶ τὰς ᵘ πυκνάς σου ᵛ ἀσθενείας. hklmno17

23 [αλλα, so AD¹Fℵ 17.] rec (aft στομ) ins σου, with D³FKL rel vss Ath Chr Thdrt Damasc Ambrst-ms al om AD¹ℵ 17 (arm) Ambrst-ed Gaud ins δια bef τας πυκν F

Sic., iii 27, uses the word in its literal sense: τὸ δένδρον διὰ τὴν γινομένην πρὸς αὐτὸ πλεονάκις πρόσκλισιν τοῦ ζώου, τετριμμένον ἐστί.—Diog Laert, procem 20, in its metaphorical: εἰ δὲ αἵρεσιν νοοῦμεν πρόσκλισιν ἐν δόγμασιν. Thdrt. says well, δύο παρακελεύεται· μήτε τῇ τῶν κατηγόρων ἀξιοπιστίᾳ πιστεύσαντα κατακρίνειν, ἢ φιλαπεχθημόνως διακείμενον τοῦτο ποιεῖν πρὸ τῆς ἀκριβοῦς ἐξετάσεως· μήτε τῶν ἐλέγχων προφανῶς γενομένων ἀναβάλλεσθαι τὴν ψῆφον τῇ πρὸς τὸν κρινόμενον χάριτι τὸ δίκαιον διαφθείροντα.) 22 f.] The same subject is continued, and direction given whereby the scandal just dealt with may be prevented: viz. by *caution in ordaining* at first. The reference is primarily to presbyters of course extending also in its spirit to all other church offices. This reference, which is maintained by Chrys., Thdrt., Thl., Grot., Est., Flatt, Mack, al., is denied by De W., Wiesinger, and Huther: the two former (as also Hammond, Ellic.) understanding the command of receiving back into the church excommunicated persons, or heretics, which from later testimonies (Cypr., the Nicene council, &c.) they shew to have been the practice. Huther, rightly rejecting this idea, yet interprets it of laying on of hands as merely conveying ecclesiastical blessing on many various occasions. But surely this is too vague and unimportant for the solemn language here used. Regarding the whole, to v. 25, as connected, and belonging to one subject, I cannot accept any interpretation but the obvious and ordinary one: see especially ch. iv. 14: 2 Tim. i. 6. **Lay hands hastily on no one, nor be partaker in other men's sins** (as he would do by being the means of negligently admitting into the ministry unfit and ungodly persons, being properly held responsible for the consequence of those bad habits of theirs which more care might have ascertained. ἁμαρτίας points to the former ἁμαρτάνοντας) —**keep THYSELF** (highly emphatic: not merely others over whom thou art called to preside and pronounce judgment in admitting them to the ministry. And the emphasis is peculiarly in place here, as applying to that which has just preceded. If he were to admit improper candidates to the ministry from bias or from negligence, his own character, by his becoming a partaker in their sins, would suffer: whatever thou doest therefore, be sure to maintain, by watchful care and caution, *thyself* above all stain of blame) **pure** (not here to be referred to personal purity and chastity, though that of course would be the most important of all elements in carrying out the precept: but as above. On the *word*, see Ellic.). **No longer** (habitually) **drink water, but use a little wine, on account of thy stomach, and thy frequent illnesses** (the question, why this injunction is here inserted, has never been satisfactorily answered. Est., Grot., al., De W., Ellic., al., take it as a modification of σεαυτὸν ἁγνὸν τήρει, so as to prevent it from being misunderstood as enjoining asceticism. But on our explanation of the words, and I may add on any worthy view of the context, such a connexion will at once be repudiated. Chrys. has caught the right clue, when he says δοκεῖ δέ μοι καὶ ἄλλως ἐπίνοσος εἶναι. καὶ τοῦτο δεικνυσι λέγων, διὰ τὰς πυκνάς σου ἀσθενείας, ἀπό τε τοῦ στομάχου, ἀπό τε τῶν ἄλλων μερῶν· but he has not followed it up. Timotheus was certainly of a feeble bodily frame, and this feebleness appears, from other hints which we have respecting him, to have affected his character. See especially 1 Cor. xvi. 10, 11, and note there. Is it not very possible, that such feebleness, and perhaps timidity, may have influenced him as an overseer of the church, and prevented that keen-sighted judgment and vigorous action which a bishop should ever shew in estimating the characters of those who are candidates for the ministry? If this was so, then it is quite natural that in advising him on this point, St. Paul should throw in a hint, in fatherly kindness, that he must not allow these maladies to interfere with the efficient discharge of his high office, but take all reasonable means of raising his bodily

24 τινῶν ἀνθρώπων αἱ ἁμαρτίαι [w] πρόδηλοί εἰσιν, [x] προ-
άγουσαι εἰς [y] κρίσιν· τισὶν δὲ καὶ [z] ἐπακολουθοῦσιν.
25 [a] ὡσαύτως καὶ τὰ [b] ἔργα τὰ [b] καλὰ [w] πρόδηλα· καὶ τὰ
[c] ἄλλως ἔχοντα κρυβῆναι οὐ δύνανται.

w Heb vii 14 only †. Judith viii 29. 2 Macc. iii 17. xiv 39 only. x ch i 18 reff. y Paul, 2 Thess i 5 only. Matt v 21 al fr. z ver 10 reff. a ch ii 9 al. b ch iii 1 reff. c here only. Esth i 19 ix 27. Job xi 12.

25. aft ωσαυτως ins δε AF goth om DKLℵ rel vulg syr coptt gr-lat-ff. rec (for τα ε τα κ) τα καλα εργα, with KL rel Chr Thdrt txt ADFℵ m 17 latt syr copt goth Thl Aug Ambr Pelag. rec aft προδηλα ins εστι, with KL rel εισιν DF c k o 17. 67[1] om Aℵ 67[2] rec δυναται (gramml corrn), with FKLℵ rel Chr txt AD e g k m 17 Thdrt

condition above them. I feel compelled to adopt this view, from the close connexion of the next verse with the whole preceding passage, and the exceedingly unnatural isolation of this, unless it bears such a reference. It is impossible to avoid remarking, that the characteristic, but unnecessary anxiety of Ellicott to rescue the apostolic Timotheus from any imputation of feebleness of character, has blinded him to the delicate connexion of thoughts here, as frequently in the second Epistle). 24] *The same subject continued*: τὸν περὶ τῆς χειροτονίας ἀναλαμβάνει λόγον Thdrt. If my view of the last verse is correct, the connexion will be found in the fact, that the conservation of himself in health and vigour would ensure his being able to deal ably and firmly with the cases which should come before him for decision. To guide him still further in this, the Apostle subjoins this remark, indicating two classes of characters with which he would have to deal in judging, whether favourably or unfavourably. **Of some men the sins** (connects with ἁμαρτίαις ἀλλοτρίαις, ver 22) **are evident** (there does not seem to be any relation of *time* in πρόδηλοι, '*manifest beforehand*,'—for thus the meaning would be,—as in πρόδηλος πότμος, κίνδυνος, &c., that the sins were manifest *before they were committed*, which would reduce this case to the other [see below]: but the προ- seems rather of place than of time,—πρὸ τῶν ὀφθαλμῶν,—openly manifest,—notorious by common report), **going before them** (so that the man's bad report comes to the person appointed to judge, *before* the *man himself*: not transitive, as Heinrichs,—'peccata in judicium eos vocant') **to judgment** (i. e. so that when they come before thee to be judged of as candidates, their sins have arrived before them): **but some men again they** (their sins) **follow** (i. e. after-proof brings out the correctness or otherwise of the judgment. Their characters come before thee unanticipated by adverse rumour: but thou mayest by examination discover those flaws in their conduct which had been skilfully concealed — the sins which, so to speak, follow at their heels. Therefore be watchful, and do not let the mere non-existence of previous adverse rumour lead thee always to presume fitness for the sacred office). 25] **So also** (in like manner on the other side of men's conduct) **the good works** (of some) **are openly manifest. and those which are otherwise situated** (which are not πρόδηλα) **cannot be hidden** (will come out, just as the sins in ver 24, on examination. The tendency of this verse is to warn him against hasty condemnation, as the former had done against hasty approval. Sometimes thou wilt find a man's good character go before him, and at once approve him to thee: but where this is not so, do not therefore be rash to condemn—thou mayest on examination soon discover, if there really be any good deeds accompanying him: for they are things which cannot be hidden—the good tree like the bad will be known by his fruits, and that speedily, on enquiry). I have abstained from detailing all the varieties of interpretation of these verses, following as they do those already specified on verses 20—22. They may be seen shortly enumerated in De W. and Ellicott, and commented on at somewhat tedious length in Wiesinger. Chrys., al., confuse the context by understanding κρίσις of eternal judgment, and the sentiment as equivalent to ἐκεῖ πάντα γυμνά ἐστιν. And so even Ellicott, who in objecting to the above interpretation (which is also Dr. Wordsworth's) charges it somewhat naively with *failure in explaining the context*. That *it* only does explain it satisfactorily, is, in my view, the decisive consideration in its favour.

VI. 1 [d]Ὅσοι εἰσὶν ὑπὸ [d]ζυγὸν δοῦλοι, τοὺς [e]ἰδίους [e]δε- ADFK
σπότας πάσης [f]τιμῆς ἀξίους [g]ἡγείσθωσαν, ἵνα μὴ τὸ L ℵ a b c d e f g
[h]ὄνομα τοῦ θεοῦ καὶ ἡ [i]διδασκαλία [hk]βλασφημῆται. 2 οἱ h k l m n o 17
δὲ [l]πιστοὺς ἔχοντες δεσπότας, μὴ [m]καταφρονείτωσαν, ὅτι
ἀδελφοί εἰσιν· ἀλλὰ μᾶλλον [n]δουλευέτωσαν, ὅτι [l]πιστοί

d Matt xi 29, 30 Acts xv 10 Gal v 1 Rev vi 5 only Levit xxvi 13 Isa ix 4
e Tit ii 9 Prov xxii 7
f Rom xiii 7
g ch i 12 reff
h Rom ii 24, from Isa lii 5 James ii 7 Rev xiii 6 Tit ii 5
i ch i 10 reff
k — as above (h) Rom iii 8 Tit iii 2
l — Tit i 6 reff
m ch iv 12 reff
n = Eph vi 7

CHAP VI 1 for δουλοι, δουλου F -ειας b[1] k 73 sah aft δουλ π is written by ℵ[1], but marked and erased. for θεου, κυριου D[1] 17 vulg goth Pelag Ambrst Gelas. βλασφημειται K L 17.

CH. VI] *The Apostle's exhortations are continued, and pass from ecclesiastical to civil relations* and first to the duties of *Christian slaves* This chapter has been charged (Schleierm , al) with want of coherence But to a careful observer the thread of connexion is very plain I have endeavoured to indicate it as we pass on. Such a thread being detected, the idea of Schleierm (partly approved by De W) of its being a clumsy compilation out of the Epistles to Titus and 2 Tim hardly requires refutation 1] **Let as many as are slaves under the yoke** (I have adopted the rendering of De W. and Huther, attaching δοῦλοι to the predicate, as the simpler construction The other, '*as many slaves as are under the yoke*,' making ὑπὸ ζυγόν emphatic as distinguishing either 1) those *treated hardly*, or 2) those who were *under unbelieving masters*, has undoubtedly something to be said for it, but does not seem to me so likely, from the arrangement of the words Had ὑπὸ ζυγόν been intended to bring out any distinction, it would have more naturally preceded εἰσίν I take then ὑπὸ ζυγὸν δοῦλοι as the predicate · 'bondsmen under yoke') **hold their own** (ἰδίους, as in Eph v 22, al , to bring out and emphasize the relation; see note there) **masters worthy of all** (fitting) **honour, that the name of God and his doctrine** (cf. Tit ii 10, where, writing on the same subject, he admonishes slaves ἵνα τὴν διδασκαλίαν τὴν τοῦ σωτῆρος ἡμῶν θεοῦ κοσμῶσιν ἐν πᾶσιν. Hence it would appear that the article here is possessive, and ἡ διδασκ corresponding to τὸ ὄνομα) **be not spoken evil of** (Chrys gives the sense well ὁ ἄπιστος ἂν μὲν ἴδῃ τοὺς δούλους διὰ τὴν πίστιν αὐθάδως προφερομένους, βλασφημήσει πολλάκις ὡς στάσιν ἐμποιοῦν τὸ δόγμα ὅταν δὲ ἴδῃ πειθομένους, μᾶλλον πεισθήσεται, μᾶλλον προσέξει τοῖς λεγομένοις This verse obviously applies only to those slaves who had unbelieving masters. This is brought out by the reason given, and by the contrast in the next verse, not by any formal opposition in terms. The account to be given of the absence of such opposition is, that this verse contains the general exhortation, the case of Christian slaves under *unbelieving* masters being by far the most common The *exception* is treated in the next verse).

2] **But** (see above) **let those who have believing masters not despise them because** (belongs to καταφρονείτωσαν only, containing the ground of their contempt,—not to the exhortation μὴ καταφρονείτωσαν) **they** (the masters, not the slaves) **are brethren, but all the more serve them** (μᾶλλον has the emphatic position: cf Eph v 11, where it merely signifies 'rather,' and the verb has the emphasis, μᾶλλον δὲ καὶ ἐλέγχετε. Cf also Hom Od. ο 369, φίλει δέ με κηρόθι μᾶλλον and in the same sense ἐπὶ μᾶλλον, Herod i. 94,—ἐπεί τε δὲ οὐκ ἀνιέναι τὸ κακόν, ἀλλ' ἐπὶ μᾶλλον ἔτι βιάζεσθαι, iii 104, iv 181 "The slaves who were under heathen masters were *positively* to regard their masters as deserving of honour, —the slaves under Christian masters were, *negatively*, not to evince any want of respect The former were not to regard their masters as their inferiors, and to be insubordinate; the latter were not to think them their equals, and to be disrespectful" Ellicott), **because those who receive** (mutually receive · the interchange of service between them in the Christian life being taken for granted, and this word purposely used to express it So Eur. Andr 712 ff, κἂν τολυιπὸν ᾖ | σώφρων καθ' ἡμᾶς, σώφρον' ἀντιλήψεται | θυμούμενος δέ, τεύξεται θυμουμένων, ἔργοισι δ' ἔργα διάδοχ' ἀντιλήψεται This sense, in the active, also occurs Theogn. 110, οὔτε κακοὺς εὖ δρῶν, εὖ πάλιν ἀντιλάβοις. And Plut Pericl circa init. has it with the middle and the genitive construction,—τῇ μὲν γὰρ αἰσθήσει, κατὰ πάθος τῆς πληγῆς ἀντιλαμβανομένῃ τῶν προστυγχανόντων . . ; and so Porphyr de abstinentia, i 16, μήτε

εἰσιν καὶ ἀγαπητοὶ οἱ τῆς [o] εὐεργεσίας [p] ἀντιλαμβανόμενοι.
[q] ταῦτα [q] δίδασκε καὶ [r] παρακάλει. 3 Εἴ τις [s] ἑτεροδιδα-
σκαλεῖ, καὶ μὴ [t] προσέρχεται [u] ὑγιαίνουσιν [u] λόγοις τοῖς
τοῦ [v] κυρίου ἡμῶν Ἰησοῦ χριστοῦ καὶ τῇ κατ᾽ [w] εὐσέβειαν
[u] διδασκαλίᾳ, 4 [x] τετύφωται, μηδὲν ἐπιστάμενος, ἀλλὰ

o Acts iv 9 only Ps lxxvii 11
p — here (Luke i 54, from Isa xli 9 Acts xx 35) only L P see note
q ch iv 11 see ch v 7
r Tit ii 15
s ch i 3 only† Ignat ad Polyc c 3, p 721
t — and Paul, here only γνώμῃ προσέρχεσθαι, Philo de Gigant 9, vol i p 267
u ch i 10 reff
v Acts xx 35
w ch ii 2 reff
x ch iii 6 2 Tim iii 4 only†

2 εχοντας AD¹F k m. om οτι αδελφοι εισιν ℵ¹ c om οτι to δουλευετωσαν n
for ευεργεσιας, ευσεβειας F 46
3 προσεχετε ℵ¹
4. for γινεται, γεννωνται D¹ Lucif. φθονοι D¹ latt copt goth Pelag Ambrst-ed

ἐσθίων πλειόνων ἡδονῶν ἀμτιλήψεται On other senses, see below) the benefit (of their μᾶλλον δουλεύειν. There is an apt and interesting passage in Seneca, de beneficiis, iii 18: 'Quæritur a quibusdam, an beneficium dare servus domino possit?' This question he answers in the affirmative 'servos qui negat dare aliquando domino beneficium, ignarus est juris humani. refert enim, cujus animi sit qui præstat, non cujus status' and at some length explains when, and how, such benefits can be said to be bestowed The passage is remarkable, as constituting perhaps one of those curious indications of community of thought between the Apostle and the philosopher which could hardly have been altogether fortuitous. For instance, when Seneca proceeds thus, "Quidquid est quod servilis officii formulam excedit, quod non ex imperio sed ex voluntate præstatur, beneficium est," we can hardly forbear connecting the unusual sense here of εὐεργεσία after the μᾶλλον δουλευέτωσαν, with the moralist's discussion) are faithful and beloved Very various meanings and references have been assigned to these last words Chrys., Thl, Grot, Kypke, al., interpret εὐεργεσίας of the kindness of the master to the slave ("*quia fideles sunt et dilecti qui beneficii participes sunt* [vulg]. primum, quia fide in Deum sunt præditi deinde diligendi eo nomine quod curam gerant, ut vobis benefaciant. id est ut vos vestiant, pascant, ab injuriis protegant.' Grot.) On the other hand, Ambr. (?), Lomb., Th.-Aq, Calv, Beza, Bengel, al., understand it of God's grace in redemption But thus, if we make οἱ τῆς εὐεργ ἀντιλ. the subject, as by the article it must be, the sentence will express nothing but a truism · if we escape from this by turning those words into the predicate (as E V, "because they are faithful and beloved, partakers of the benefit"), we are violating the simplest rules of grammar. These things (viz. those immediately preceding, relating to slaves) teach and exhort 3—5] *Designation of those who oppose such wholesome teaching*—fervid indeed, and going further (see Prolegg) than strict adherence to the limits of the context would require, but still suggested by, and returning to the context. cf ver. 5 fin and note If any man is a teacher of other ways (see on ch i 3 sets up as an adviser of different conduct from that which I have above recommended), and does not accede to (so a convert to the true faith was called προσήλυτος. and we have in Origen, ii 233 [Wolf], προσιόντας τῷ λόγῳ in the sense of just converted, and in ib 393, προσερχομένους τῷ θείῳ λόγῳ So also Irenæus, in two places cited by Wolf see also Philo in reff There was therefore no need for Bentley's conjecture, προσέχεται [see itacism in ℵ, var read.] or προσέχει, or προσίσχεται, though the use of these is commoner see ch i. 4 reff Cf. also Ellic's note) wholesome words (reff), (namely) those of our Lord Jesus Christ (either, precepts given by Him respecting this duty of subjection, such as that Matt xxii 21,—which however seems rather far-fetched or words agreeing with His teaching and expressing His will, which is more probable), and to the doctrine which is according to (after the rules of) piety,—he is (the apodosis begins here, not as Mack, al., with the spurious ἀφίστασο, ver. 5) besotted with pride (see ch iii 6, note), knowing (being one who knows not '*although* he knows') nothing (not οὐδέν, which would be used to express the bare fact of absolute ignorance or idiotcy), but mad after (so Plat Phædr. p 228, ἀπαντήσας δὲ τῷ νοσοῦντι περὶ λόγων ἀκοήν, ἰδὼν μὲν ἰδὼν ἥσθη ὅτι ἕξοι τὸν συγκορυβαντιῶντα Bengel and Wetst. quote from Plut de laud propr. p 546 f, νοσεῖν περὶ δόξαν,—de ira cohib p 460 d, ν περὶ σφραγίδια πολυτελῆ, *insanire amore gloriæ, vel sigillorum pretiosorum* See more examples in Kypke "περὶ

[y] νοσῶν περὶ [z] ζητήσεις καὶ [a] λογομαχίας, ἐξ ὧν γίνεται ADFK
[b] φθόνος, [b] ἔρις, [c] βλασφημίαι, [d] ὑπόνοιαι [d] πονηραί, 5 [f] δια- Lℵ a b c d e f g
παρατριβαὶ [gh] διεφθαρμένων ἀνθρώπων τὸν [h] νοῦν καὶ h k l m n o 17
[i] ἀπεστερημένων [j] τῆς [j] ἀληθείας, νομιζόντων [k] πορισμὸν
εἶναι τὴν [l] εὐσέβειαν. 6 Ἔστιν δὲ [k] πορισμὸς μέγας ἡ
[l] εὐσέβεια μετὰ [m] αὐταρκείας. 7 οὐδὲν γὰρ [n] εἰσηνέγκαμεν

y here only †. Wisd. xvii. 18 bis only. see note. z ch. i. 4 reff. a here only †. (-χεῖν, 2 Tim. ii. 14.) b Phil. i. 15 reff. c = Eph. iv. 31. Col. iii. 8 al. d Sir. iii. 24. e here only †. Sir. as above, only. (-νοεῖν, Acts xiii. 25.) f here only †. g Luke xii. 33. 2 Cor. iv. 16. Rev. viii. 9. xi. 18 only. Ps. xiii. 1. διεφθαρμένου τοὺς ὀφθαλμούς, Demosth. 1268. 6. h see 2 Tim. iii. 8. i = here only †. (Mark x. 19. 1 Cor. vi. 7, 8. vii. 5. James v. 4 only. Mal. iii. 5 al.) j 2 Tim. iii. 8. iv. 4. Tit. i. 14. k here bis only †. Wisd. xiii. 19. xiv. 2 only. δυοὶ κεχρῆσθαι μόνοις πορισμοῖς, γεωργίᾳ καὶ φειδοῖ, Plut. Cat. Maj. § 25. (-ίζειν, Wisd. xv. 12.) l ch. ii. 2 reff. m 2 Cor. ix. 8 only †. (-κης, Phil. iv. 11.) n = Luke v. 18, 19. Heb. xiii. 11 only. Numb. xxxi. 54.

ερεις DFL latt syr copt Damasc Luc Ambr Ambrst Pelag.

5. rec (for διαπαρατρ.) παραδιατριβαι, with b Thl: διατριβαι K d l: txt ADFLℵ rel Clem Bas Chr Thdrt Hesych Suid Damasc Œc. απεστραμμενων απο της D[1]: *destitutorum a* D-lat G-lat Lucif. rec at end ins αφισταco απο των τοιουτων, with KL rel tol[2] spec syrr æth-pl gr-ff Ambrst: om AD[1]Fℵ 17. 67[2] latt coptt goth æth-rom Lucif Ambr Bede.

6. aft ευσεβεια ins θεου F.

with a *genitive* serves to mark an object as the central point, as it were, of the activity [e. g. 1 Cor. xii. 1, the πνευμ. δῶρα formed as it were the centre of the ἄγνοια]: the further idea of any *action* or *motion* round it is supplied by περί with the accusative. Cf. Winer, edn. 6, § 47. e: Donalds. Gr. § 482." Ellicott) **questionings** (reff.) **and disputes about words** (see ref. The word is found only in ecclesiastical writers: see Wetst. Calv. explains it well, "contensiosas disputationes de verbis magis quam de rebus, vel, ut vulgo loquuntur, sine materia, aut subjecto"), **from which cometh envy, strife, evil speakings** (the context of such passages as Col. iii. 8, shews that it is not *blasphemy*, properly so called [ἐκ δὲ τῆς ἔριδος ἡ κατὰ τοῦ θεοῦ βλασφημία τολμᾶται, Thdrt.], but mutual slander and reproach which is here meant), **wicked suspicions** (not *concerning God* [περὶ θεοῦ ἃ μὴ δεῖ ὑποπτεύομεν, Chrys.], but of one another: not "'*opiniones malæ*,' quales Diagoræ, non esse Deum," as Grot.), **incessant quarrels** (δια—gives the sense of continuance; παρατριβή, primarily '*friction*,' is found in later writers in the sense of irritating provocation, or hostile collision: so Polyb. ii. 36. 5, τὰ μὲν οὖν κατὰ Καρχηδονίους καὶ Ῥωμαίους ἀπὸ τούτων ἤδη τῶν καιρῶν ἐν ὑποψίαις ἦν πρὸς ἀλλήλους καὶ παρατριβαῖς:—xxiii. 10. 4, διὰ τὴν πρὸς τὸν Φιλοποίμενα παρατριβήν: see also iv. 21. 5; xxi. 13. 5; xxiv. 8. 4. According to the other reading, παρά would give the sense of useless, vain, perverse, and διατριβή would be disputation, thus giving the sense 'perverse disputings,' as E. V. Chrys., Œc., Thdrt., explain our word ἀπὸ μεταφορᾶς τῶν ψωραλέων προβάτων [Œc.]: and Chrys. says, καθάπερ τὰ ψωραλέα τῶν προβάτων παρατριβόμενα νόσου καὶ τὰ ὑγιαίνοντα ἐμπίπλησιν, οὕτω καὶ οὗτοι οἱ πονηροὶ ἄνδρες) **of men depraved in mind** (reff.; and see Ellic. on the pyschology and construction) **and destitute of the truth, who suppose that godliness is gain** (lit., 'a gainful trade,' as Conyb.: see reff.:—and therefore do not teach contentment and acquiescence in God's providence, as in ver. 6: but strive to make men discontented, and persuade them to use religion as a means of worldly bettering themselves).

6.] He then goes off, on the mention of this erroneous view, to shew how it really stands with the Christian as to the desire of riches: its danger, and the mischief it has occasioned. **But** (although they are in error in thus thinking, there *is* a sense in which such an idea is true ['eleganter et non sine ironica correctione in contrarium sensum eadem verba retorquet.' Calv.], for) **godliness accompanied with contentment** [see above, and Phil. iv. 11] **is great gain** (alluding, not to the Christian's reward in the next world, as Thdrt., τὴν γὰρ αἰώνιον ἡμῖν πορίζει ζωήν, Erasm., Calv., al.,—but as Chrys., Thl., Ambr., al.,—the πορισμός is in the very fact of possessing piety joined with contentment, and thus being able to dispense with those things which we cannot carry away with us).

7.] Reason why this is so. **For we brought nothing into the world, because neither can we carry any thing out** (the insertion of δῆλον or ἀληθές, or substitution of ἀλλά or καί for ὅτι, betray themselves as having

εἰς τὸν κόσμον, ὅτι οὐδὲ [o] ἐξενεγκεῖν τι δυνάμεθα· 8 ἔχοντες
δὲ [p] διατροφὰς καὶ [q] σκεπάσματα, τούτοις [r] ἀρκεσθησόμεθα.
9 Οἱ δὲ [s] βουλόμενοι πλουτεῖν [t] ἐμπίπτουσιν εἰς [u] πειρασμὸν καὶ [t] παγίδα καὶ [v] ἐπιθυμίας πολλὰς [w] ἀνοήτους καὶ
[x] βλαβεράς, [y] αἵτινες [z] βυθίζουσιν τοὺς ἀνθρώπους εἰς
[a] ὄλεθρον καὶ [b] ἀπώλειαν. 10 [c] ῥίζα γὰρ πάντων τῶν

o = Luke xv 22 Acts v 6, &c (Mark viii 23 Heb vi 8) only Exod xii 39
p here only † 1 Macc vi 49 only
q here only †
r = Luke iii 14 Heb xiii 5 3 John 10, but w ἐπί (2 Cor xii 9 al) ‡ 2 Macc v 15
s = James iv 4
t ch iii (6) 7 reff Prov xii 1
u Matt vi 13 xxvi 41 al fr Paul, 1 Cor x 13 Gal iv 14 only
v Rom i 24 al fr
w Rom i 14 Gal iii 1, 3 Tit iii 3 only L P Prov xvii 28
x here only Prov x 26 (only ?)
y — Acts x 41, 47 al fr
z Luke v 7 only † 2 Macc xii 4 only (-θος, 2 Cor xi 25)
a 1 Cor v 5 1 Thess v 3 2 Thess i 9 only P Prov xxi 7
b Paul, Rom ix 22 Phil i 28 iii 19 2 Thess ii 3 2 Pet ii 1 al[5] Rev xvii 8, 11 Isa xiv 23.
c = Heb xii 15, from Deut xxix 18 Sir i 20

7 rec ins δηλον bef οτι (*see note*), with D[3]KLℵ[3] rel syrr Bas Mac Chr Thdrt Damasc. αληθες D[1] syr-marg, *verum quoniam* D-lat Ambrst, *haud dubium quod* vulg, *in veritate quod* goth αλλ' Polyc(ἀλλ' οὐδὲ ἐξ τι ἔχομεν) Cypr Aug Paulin και copt æth arm: txt AFℵ 17

8 διατροφην DFK *victum* D-lat G-lat lat-ff αρκεσθησωμεθα K d n Chr-ms Damasc.

9 aft παγιδα ins του διαβολου D[1]F latt Chr Antch Thdrt-txt Ambr Chrom Cæs-arel.

all sprung from the difficulty of the shorter and original construction The meaning appears to be,—we were appointed by God to come naked into the world, to teach us to remember that we must go naked out of it But this sense of ὅτι is not without difficulty. De W. cites Il π 35, γλαυκὴ δέ σε τίκτε θάλασσα, πέτραι τ' ἠλίβατοι, ὅτι τοι νόος ἐστὶν ἀπηνής,—and Od χ 36, ὦ κύνες, οὔ μ' ἔτ' ἐφάσκεθ' ὑπότροπον οἴκαδ' ἱκέσθαι | δήμου ἄπο Τρώων, ὅτι μοι κατεκείρετε οἶκον, in both which it has nearly the sense required, of '*seeing that*' The sentiment is found in Job i 21, Eccl v. 14 and in words remarkably similar, in Seneca, Ep 102 24, 'non licet plus efferre, quam intuleris' See other examples in Wetst) · **8**] **but** (contrast to the avaricious, who forget this, or knowing it do not act on it not as De W, = οὖν, which would be a direct inference from the preceding verse) **having** (if we have) **food** (the δια- gives the sense of 'sufficient for our continually recurring wants,'—'the needful supply of nourishment.' the plur corresponds to the plur ἔχοντες, and implies 'in each case') **and covering** (some take it of both clothing and dwelling perhaps rightly, but not on account of the plural · see above — Chrys., al., of clothing only,—τοιαῦτα ἀμφιέννυσθαι, ἃ σκεπάσαι μόνον ἡμᾶς ὀφείλει καὶ περιστεῖλαι τὴν γύμνωσιν These words occur together [Huther] in Sextus Empiricus ix 1), **with these** (so ἀγαπάω, στέργω χαίρω, &c. take a dative of the cause or object of the feeling See ref Luke, and Matthiæ, § 403) **we shall be sufficiently provided** (the fut has an authoritative sense so in Matt v 48, and Xen. Hell ii 3 34, cited by Huther, ὑμεῖς οὖν, ἐὰν σωφρονῆτε, οὐ τούτου, ἀλλ' ὑμῶν φείσεσθε —but is not therefore equivalent to an imperative, 'let us be content' for its sense is not properly subjective but objective—'to be sufficed,' or 'sufficiently provided' and it is passive, not middle). **9**] **But** (contrast to the last verse) **they who wish to be rich** (not simply, 'they who *are rich*' cf. Chrys: οὐχ ἁπλῶς εἶπεν, οἱ πλουτοῦντες, ἀλλ', οἱ βουλόμενοι ἐστὶ γάρ τινα καὶ χρήματα ἔχοντα καλῶς οἰκονομεῖν καταφρονοῦντα αὐτῶν), **fall** (reff) **into temptation** (not merely '*are tempted*,' but are involved in, cast into and among temptations; "in ἐμπίπτειν is implied the power which the πειρασμός exercises over them" Huther) **and a snare** (being entangled by the temptation of getting rich as by a net), **and many foolish and hurtful lusts** (foolish, because no reasonable account can be given of them [see Ellic on Gal iii 1] hurtful, as inflicting injury on all a man's best interests), **such as sink men** (mankind, generic) **into destruction and perdition** (temporal and eternal, but especially the latter: see the usage in reff of both words by St. Paul not mere moral degradation, as De W.). **10**.] **For the love of money is the** (not '*a*,' as Huther, Conyb, and Ellicott, after Middleton A word like ῥίζα, a recognized part of a plant, does not require an article when placed as here in an emphatic position we might have ἡ γὰρ ῥίζα, or ῥίζα γάρ: cf. 1 Cor xi 3 [which, notwithstanding what Ellic has alleged against it, still appears to me to be strictly in

d here only. Jer viii 10 complut only (-γος, 2 Tim iii 2) e ch i 3 reff f ch iii 1 Heb xi 16 only † (ait., Job viii 20 Symm) g Mark xiii 22 only. Prov vii 21

κακῶν ἐστιν ἡ [d] φιλαργυρία, ἧς [e] τινὲς [f] ὀρεγόμενοι
[g] ἀπεπλανήθησαν ἀπὸ τῆς πίστεως καὶ ἑαυτοὺς [h] περι-
έπειραν [i] ὀδύναις πολλαῖς. 11 Σὺ δέ, ὦ [j] ἄνθρωπε [τοῦ]
[j] θεοῦ, ταῦτα [k] φεῦγε· [lm] δίωκε δὲ [m] δικαιοσύνην, [n] εὐσέβειαν,
[o] πίστιν, [o] ἀγάπην, [op] ὑπομονήν, [q] πραυπάθειαν. 12 [rs] ἀγω-
νίζου τὸν [rt] καλὸν [ru] ἀγῶνα τῆς πίστεως, [v] ἐπιλαβοῦ τῆς

ADFK LℵA b c d e f g h k l m n o 17

h here only † Jos B J iv 7 4 end i Rom ix 2 only Jer viii 18 j 2 Tim iii 17 only Josh xiv 6 4 Kings iv 7 al k = (Paul only) 1 Cor vi 18 x 14 2 Tim ii 22 Sir xxi 2 l = 1 Thess v 15 reff Xen Cyr viii 1 30 Thuc ii 63 m Rom ix 30 2 Tim ii 22 n iv 3, 5, 6 o 2 Tim iii 10 Tit ii 2 2 Pet i 6, 7 p Col i 11 reff q here only † Philo de Abr 37, vol ii p 31, εἴκουσι διὰ τὴν τοῦ δεσπότου πραυπάθειαν r 2 Tim iv 7 Eur Alc 648 s Col i 29 reff t ch i 18 reff u Phil i 30 reff v Paul, ver 19 only Luke ix 47 Heb ii 16 viii 9 al Prov iv 13

10 for πολλαις, ποικιλαις ℵ[1].

11. om του Aℵ[1] 17 ins DFKLℵ[3] rel gr-ff om ευσεβειαν ℵ[1] rec (for πραυπαθειαν) πραοτητα, with DKLℵ[3] (πραυτ. D[1]ℵ[3]) rel Chr Thdrt: txt AFℵ[1] Petr Ephr Hesych (perhaps alluded to in Ign Trall 8, p 681, τὴν πραυπάθειαν ἀναλαβόντες)

point to shew that for which it is here adduced], παντὸς ἀνδρὸς ἡ κεφαλὴ ὁ χριστός ἐστιν, κεφαλὴ δὲ γυναικὸς ὁ ἀνήρ, κεφαλὴ δὲ τοῦ χριστοῦ ὁ θεός. Here in the first clause it is requisite to throw παντὸς ἀνδρός into emphasis but had the arrangement been the same as that of the others, we should have read κεφαλή (not ἡ κεφ.) παντὸς ἀνδρὸς ὁ χριστός but no one would therefore have thought of rendering '*a* head') root of all evils (not, is the only root whence all evils spring but is the root whence all [manner of] evils may and as matter of fact do arise. So that De W.'s objections to the sentiment have no force for neither does it follow [1] that the covetous man cannot possibly retain any virtuous disposition,—nor [2] that there may not be other roots of evil besides covetousness: neither of these matters being in the Apostle's view. So Diogenes Laert. vit. Diogen. [vi. 50], τὴν φιλαργυρίαν εἶπε μητρόπολιν πάντων τῶν κακῶν and Philo de judice 3, vol ii p. 346, calls it ὁρμητήριον τῶν μεγίστων παρανομημάτων See other examples in Wetst) after which (φιλαργυρία, see below) some lusting (the method of expression, if strictly judged, is somewhat incorrect for φιλαργυρία is of itself a desire or ὄρεξις, and men cannot be properly said ὀρέγεσθαι after it, but after its object ἀργύριον Such inaccuracies are, however, often found in language and we have examples of them in St. Paul elsewhere: e g ἐλπὶς βλεπομένη, Rom viii. 24,—ἐλπίδα . . . . ἣν καὶ αὐτοὶ οὗτοι προσδέχονται, Acts xxiv. 15) wandered away from the faith (ch i 19, iv. 1), and pierced themselves through (not 'all round' or 'all over,' as Beza, Elsner, al. the περί refers to the thing pierced *surrounding the instrument piercing* so περιπ. τὴν κεφαλὴν περὶ λόγχην, Plut. Galb 27 see Palm and Rost, and Suicer, sub voce) with many pains (the ὀδύναι being regarded as the weapons ἄκανθαί εἰσιν αἱ ἐπιθυμίαι—καὶ καθάπερ ἐν ἀκάνθαις, ὅθεν ἂν τις ἅψηται αὐτῶν, ᾕμαξε τὰς χεῖρας καὶ τραύματα ἐργάζεται οὕτω καὶ ἀπὸ τῶν ἐπιθυμιῶν τὸ αὐτὸ πείσεται ὁ ταύταις ἐμπεσών, κ. τὴν ψυχὴν ἀλγηδόσι περιβαλεῖ Chrys)

11—16.] *Exhortation and conjuration to Timotheus, arising out of these considerations.*

11.] But (contrast to τινές above) thou (emphatic), O man of God (the designation of prophets in the O T cf LXX, 1 Kings ix 6, 7, 8, 10, al, and hence perhaps used of Timotheus as dedicated to God's service in the ministry but also not without a solemn reference to that which it expresses, that God, and not riches [see the contrast again ver 17] is *his* object of desire), flee these things (φιλαργυρία and its accompanying evils) but (the contrast is to the following these things, underlying the mention of them) follow after (ref 2 Tim, where both words occur again) righteousness (see Ellic.'s note and references), piety (so δικαίως, εὐσεβῶς, Tit. ii 12), faith (not mere rectitude in keeping trust, for all these words regard the Christian life), love, patience (under afflictions stedfast endurance: better than '*stedfastness*' [Conyb.], which may be an *active* endurance), meek-spiritedness (ref.. we have πραυπαθέω in Philo de profugis, 1, vol. i 547, —πραυπαθής in Basil M. These two last qualities have reference to his behaviour towards the opponents of the Gospel)

12.] Strive the good strife (see ref and ch. i 18 1 Cor ix 24 ff Phil iii 12 ff.) of the faith (not 'of faith,' abstract and subjective but that noble conflict which the faith,—the profession of the soldier of Christ, entails on him), lay hold

[v] αἰωνίου [w] ζωῆς, [x] εἰς ἣν [x] ἐκλήθης, καὶ [y] ὡμολόγησας
τὴν [t] καλὴν [z] ὁμολογίαν [a] ἐνώπιον πολλῶν μαρτύρων.
13 [b] Παραγγέλλω σοι [c] ἐνώπιον τοῦ θεοῦ τοῦ [d] ζωογο-
νοῦντος τὰ πάντα, καὶ χριστοῦ Ἰησοῦ τοῦ [e] μαρτυρήσαντος
[f] ἐπὶ Ποντίου Πιλάτου τὴν [t] καλὴν [z] ὁμολογίαν, 14 [g] τη-

w Acts xiii 46 (Paul) Tit i 2 iii 7 al
x 1 Cor i 9 Col iii 15 2 Thess ii 14 1 Pet ii 9, 21 v 10
y = John xii 42 Acts xxiii 8 Rom x 10
z (—) 2 Cor ix 13 Heb iii 1 iv 14 x 23 only P H t (Levit xxii 18 al)
a = Rom xii 17 2 Cor viii 21 ch v 20 3 John 6.
b Acts x 42 xvi 18 al fr Josh vi 6
c ch v 21 reff.
d Luke xvii 33. Acts vii. 19 only Exod i 17, 18, 22
e — (but see note) here only see Acts xxiii 11 constr, Rev i 2 xxii 16, 20
f — (see note) Mark xiii 9 Acts xxiii 30 xxiv 19, 20 xxv 9, 10, 26 xxvi 2 1 Cor vi 1 6 μαρτυρήσας ἐπὶ τῶν ἡγεμόνων Clem Rom ad Cor i 5, p 220
g — Matt xix 17 John xiv 15 Paul, here only see 1 Cor vii 19

12 rec aft εις ην ins και, with o (d h l m, e sil) syr-w-ast Thl Œc Ambrst-ms. om ADFKLℵ rel latt Syr copt æth arm Petr-alex Ephr Chr Thdrt Damasc Pelag

13 παραγγελλων, omg (as also ℵ[1] 17) σοι, F. om 1st του ℵ: om του θεου 109 rec (for ζωογονουντος) ζωοποιουντος, with KLℵ rel Cyr-jer txt ADF 17 Ath Cyr Thdrt$_{aliq}$ Œc-comm ιησ bef χρ Fℵ Syr Did Thl Tert.

upon (as the aim and object of the life-long struggle, the prize to be gained: so that the second imperative is, as Winer well observes, edn 6, § 42, not the mere result of the first, as in 'divide et impera,' but correlative with it and contemporaneous 'strive , and while doing so, endeavour to attain') **everlasting life, to which thou wast called** (here apparently the image is dropped, and the realities of the Christian life spoken of. Some have supposed an allusion to the athletes being summoned by a herald: but it seems far-fetched—and indeed inaccurate: for it was to the *contest*, not to the *prize*, that they were thus summoned), **and didst confess** (we must not supply εἰς ἣν again before ὡμολόγησας, with Mack, al,—'*in reference to which*,'—a most unnatural construction: but regard it, with De W, as simply coupled to ἐκλήθης) **the good confession** (of faith in Christ: *the* confession, which every servant of Christ must make, on taking upon himself His service, or professing it when called upon so to do. From the same expression in the next verse, it would seem, that the article rather represents the notoriousness of the confession, 'bonam illam confessionem,' than its definite general character. There is some uncertainty, to what occasion the Apostle here refers; whether to the baptism of Timotheus,—so Chrys. [?], Œc, Thl. [alt], Ambr., Grot, Beng, &c.: to his ordination as a minister,—so Wolf, al.: to his appointment over the church at Ephesus,—so Mack: to some confession made by him under persecution,—so, justifying it by what follows, respecting our Lord, Huther, al. Of these the first appears to me most probable, as giving the most general sense to ἡ καλὴ ὁμολογία, and applying best to the immediate consideration of αἰώνιος ζωή, which is the common object of all Christians. The reference supposed by Thdrt [πάντας παρ' αὐτοῦ δεξαμένους τὸ κήρυγμα μάρτυρας εἶχε τῆς καλῆς ὁμολογίας], Calv, al, to Timotheus's *preaching*, is clearly inadmissible) **before many witnesses.**

13] I charge thee (ch i. 3) **in the presence of God who endues all things with life** (for the sense, see ref.: most probably a reference to αἰώνιος ζωή above: hardly, as De W, al., after Chrys, to the *resurrection*, reminding him that death for Christ's sake was not to be feared: for there is here no immediate allusion to *danger*, but only to the duty of personal firmness in the faith in his own religious life), **and of Christ Jesus, who testified** ('*testari confessionem* erat Domini, *confiteri confessionem* erat Timothei,' Bengel. See Ellicott's note) **before Pontius Pilate** (De W, al [and Ellicott: see below on ὁμολογ] would render it, as in the Apostles' creed, '*under Pontius Pilate*:' but the immediate reference here being to His *confession*, it seems more natural to take the meaning, 'coram:' and so Chrys, who as a Greek, and familiar with the Creed, is a fair witness)—**the good confession** (viz. that whole testimony to the verity of his own Person and to the Truth, which we find in John xviii, and which doubtless formed part of the oral apostolic teaching. Those who render ἐπί, 'under,' understand this *confession* of our Lord's *sufferings and death*—which at least is far-fetched. There is no necessity, with Huther, to require a strict parallel between the circumstances of the confession of our Lord and that of Timotheus, nor to infer in consequence of this verse that his confession must have been one

ρῆσαί σε τὴν [g] ἐντολὴν [h] ἄσπιλον, [i] ἀνεπίλημπτον, [k] μέχρι
τῆς [l] ἐπιφανείας τοῦ κυρίου ἡμῶν Ἰησοῦ χριστοῦ, 15 ἣν
[m] καιροῖς [m] ἰδίοις [n] δείξει ὁ [o] μακάριος καὶ [p] μόνος [q] δυνάστης,
ὁ [r] βασιλεὺς τῶν βασιλευόντων καὶ [s] κύριος τῶν [t] κυριευ-
όντων, 16 ὁ μόνος ἔχων [u] ἀθανασίαν, φῶς [v] οἰκῶν [w] ἀπρόσ-

ADFK Lℵ a b c d e f g h k l m n o 17

h James i 27 1 Pet i 19 2 Pet iii 14 only † Job xv 15 Symm i ch iii 2 v 7 only † k of time, Matt xi 23 Acts x 30 xx 7 al Job viii 2 l 2 Thess ii 8 2 Tim i. 10 iv 1, 8 Tit ii 13 only 2 Kings vii 23 m Gal vi 9 ch ii 6 Tit i 3 only n John ii 18 xiv 8 o ch i 11 reff of God, there only p ch i 17 q Luke i 52 Acts viii 27 only Levit xix 15 2 Macc xii 15 r of the Father, Matt v 35 ch i 17. s Rev xvii 14 xix 16 see Deut x 17 Ps cxxxv 3 t Luke xxii 25 Rom vi 9, 14 vii 1 xiv 9 2 Cor i 24 only L P Gen iii 16 u 1 Cor xv 53, 54 only † Wisd viii 13 al[4] v Paul only, but elsw w prep. Rom vii 17, 18, 20 viii 9, 11 1 Cor iii 16 vii 12, 13 constr, Prov x 31 w here only †

14 om *σε* D[1] 43 Did *χρ.* bef *ιησ* ℵ
16 ins *και* bef *φως* D[1] vulg Did, Ambrst Pelag Aug. for *απροσ.*, *αορατον* 67[2].

before a heathen magistrate: it is the *fact* of a confession having been made in both cases that is put in the foreground—and that our Lord's was made in the midst of danger and with death before him, is a powerful argument to firmness for his servant in his own confession Another rendering of this verse is given by Mack, al it makes τὴν καλὴν ὁμολογίαν governed by παραγγέλλω, and understands by it the same confession as in verse 12 'I enjoin on thee,—in the presence . . . . and of Christ Jesus who bore testimony before Pontius Pilate—the good confession' But this is quite inadmissible. For it is opposed both to the sense of παραγγέλλω, and to the following context, in which ἡ ἐντολή, not ἡ καλὴ ὁμολογία, is the thing to be observed), **that thou keep** (preserve cf. ἄσπιλον below, and ch v 22) **the commandment** (used not to designate any special command just given, but as a general compendium of the rule of the Gospel, after which our lives and thoughts must be regulated cf παραγγελία in the same sense, ch i 5) **without spot and without reproach** (both epithets belong to τὴν ἐντολήν, not to σε, as most Commentators, some, as Est, maintaining that ἀνεπίληπτος can be used of persons only. But this De W has shewn not to be the case: we have ἡ ἀνεπίληπτος τέχνη in Philo de opif 22, vol i p 15 ἀνεπιληπτότερον τὸ λεγόμενον in Plato, Phileb p 43 c Besides, the ordinary construction with τηρεῖν is that the qualifying adjective should belong to its object. cf ch. v. 22. James i. 27 2 Cor. xi 9 The commandment, entrusted to thee as a deposit [cf ver 20], must be kept by thee unstained and unreproached Consult Ellic.'s note) **until the appearance** (reff.) **of our Lord Jesus Christ** (τουτέστι, says Chrys, μέχρι τῆς σῆς τελευτῆς, μέχρι τῆς ἐξόδου But surely both the usage of the word ἐπιφάνεια and the next verse should have kept him from this mistake. Far better Bengel "fideles in praxi sua proponebant sibi diem Christi ut appropinquantem nos solemus nobis horam mortis proponere" We may fairly say that whatever impression is betrayed by the words that the coming of the Lord would be in Timotheus's lifetime, is chastened and corrected by the καιροῖς ἰδίοις of the next verse. *That*, the certainty of the coming in God's own time, was a fixed truth respecting which the Apostle speaks with the authority of the Spirit: but the day and hour was hidden from him as from us and from such passages as this we see that the apostolic age maintained that which ought to be the attitude of all ages, constant expectation of the Lord's return)

15, 16.] **which in His own times** (reff. τουτέστι τοῖς προσήκουσι, τοῖς ὀφειλομένοις, Chrys "Numerus pluralis observandus, brevitatem temporum non valde coarctans," Bengel) **He shall manifest** (make visible, cause to appear, "display," Ellic) **(who is) the blessed** (ἡ αὐτομακαριότης, Chrys) **and only Potentate** (Baur, al, believe the polytheism or dualism of the Gnostics to be hinted at in μόνος but this is very unlikely The passage is not polemical and cf the same μόνος in John xvii 3), **the King of kings and Lord of lords** (this seems the place,—on account of this same designation occurring in reff. Rev applied to our Lord,—to enquire whether these verses 15, 16 are said of the Father or of the Son. Chrys. holds very strongly the latter view but surely the καιροῖς ἰδίοις, compared with καιρούς, οὓς ὁ πατὴρ ἔθετο ἐν τῇ ἰδίᾳ ἐξουσίᾳ, Acts i 7, determines for the former so also does ὃν εἶδεν οὐδεὶς κ.τ λ. verse 16, which Chrys leaves untouched), **who only has immortality** (Huther quotes [Ps-]Justin M., quæst. ad Orthod. 61, p 164 μόνος ἔχων τὴν ἀθανασίαν λέγεται ὁ θεός, ὅτι οὐκ ἐκ θελήματος ἄλλου ταύτην ἔχει, καθάπερ οἱ λοιποὶ πάντες ἀθάνατοι, ἀλλ' ἐκ τῆς

ιτου, ὃν εἶδεν οὐδεὶς ἀνθρώπων οὐδὲ ἰδεῖν δύναται, ᾧ ˣ τιμὴ
καὶ ʸ κράτος αἰώνιον, ἀμήν.
17 Τοῖς πλουσίοις ἐν ᶻ τῷ νῦν ᶻ αἰῶνι ᵃ παράγγελλε μὴ
ᵇ ὑψηλοφρονεῖν, μηδὲ ᶜ ἠλπικέναι ἐπὶ πλούτου ᵈ ἀδηλότητι,
ἀλλ' *ἐν τῷ θεῷ τῷ ᵉ παρέχοντι ἡμῖν πάντα ᶠ πλουσίως

x in doxol, Paul, ch i 17 only Rev iv 9 v 13 al
y in doxol, 1 Pet iv 11 v 11 Jude 25 Rev i 6, v 13
z 2 Tim iv 10 Tit ii 12 only see ch iv 8
a ch i 3 reff
b Rom xi 20 only † see Rom xii 16
c ch iv 10 reff
d here only † (-λος, 1 Cor xiv 8 -λως, 1 Cor ix 26) ἡ ἀδ τῶν προσδοκωμένων, Polyb xxxvi 4 2
e = Acts xxviii 2 (Col iv 1 mid) 1 Col iii 16 Tit. iii 6 2 Pet i 11 only †

ιδεν A Did ανθρωπων bef ουδεις F goth. ins το bef κρατος ℵ om και F n 72 93 116 122.

17. for αιωνι, καιρω ℵ[1]. του νυν αιωνος D vulg Syr coptt Bas Jer Ambrst Pelag. υψηλα φρονειν ℵ for ηλπικεναι, ελπιζειν F Damasc. πλουτω D[1] 73.
*ἐπί (as above) AD[1]Fℵ 17. 67[2] Orig-mss Chr Thl εν D[3]KL rel Orig Thdrt Damasc. om τω bef θεω D[1]Fℵ Orig-mss Thl: ins AD[3]KL rel Orig. rec aft θεω add τω ζωντι (see ch iv 10), with (D)KL rel latt(inclg vulg-ed fuld-vict) syrr Orig Chr$_1$ Thdrt lat-ff$_5$ (om τω D[1]). om AFℵ 17 67[2] am(with fuld[1] demid tol harl) coptt æth arm Orig mss Bas Jer$_2$. ins τα bef παντα A m 17 Bas Chr. rec πλουσιως bef παντα, with rel om παντα F. txt ADKLℵ m 17 latt syrr coptt Orig Bas Antch Chr Thdrt Thl Damasc Œc Pelag.

οἰκείας οὐσίας. Bengel remarks 'Adjectivum *immortalis* non exstat in N T. sed ἄφθαρτος, *incorruptibilis*: neque ἀθάνατος aut ἀθανασία habent LXX. Utrumque habet Sapientiæ liber qui semper Græcus fuit'), **dwelling in light unapproachable** (ἄλλο τὸ φῶς αὐτὸς καὶ ἄλλο ὃ οἰκεῖ, οὐκοῦν καὶ τόπῳ ἐμπεριείληπται; ἄπαγε· οὐχ ἵνα τοῦτο νοήσωμεν, ἀλλ' ἵνα τὸ ἀκατάληπτον τῆς θείας φύσεως παραστήσῃ, φῶς οἰκεῖν αὐτὸν εἶπεν ἀπρόσιτον, οὕτω θεολογήσας ὡς ἦν αὐτῷ δυνατόν. Chrys), **whom no one of men [ever] saw, nor can see** (the Commentators quote Theophilus ad Autol, i. 5, p 341 εἰ τῷ ἡλίῳ ἐλαχίστῳ ὄντι στοιχείῳ οὐ δύναται ἄνθρωπος ἀτενίσαι διὰ τὴν ὑπερβάλλουσαν θέρμην καὶ δύναμιν, πῶς οὐχὶ μᾶλλον τῇ τοῦ θεοῦ δόξῃ ἀνεκφράστῳ οὔσῃ ἄνθρωπος θνητὸς οὐ δύναται ἀντωπῆσαι, These words, as compared with John i. 18, seem to prove decisively that the whole description applies to the Father, not to the Son), **to whom be honour and power everlasting, Amen** (see ch. i 17, where a similar ascription occurs) Some of the Commentators (Mack, Schleierm) think that verses 15, 16 are taken from an ecclesiastical hymn. and Mack has even arranged it metrically. See ch. iii. 16, 2 Tim ii 11 ff, notes

17—19.] *Precepts for the rich.* Not a supplement to the Epistle, as commonly regarded: the occurrence of a doxology is no sufficient ground for supposing that the Apostle intended to close with it: cf ch i 17. Rather, the subject is resumed from verses 6—10 We may perhaps make an inference as to the late date of the Epistle, from the existence of wealthy members in the Ephesian church.

17.] **To those who are rich in this present world** (no τοῖς before ἐν τῷ νῦν αἰ., because πλούσιοι-ἐν-τῷ-νῦν-αἰῶνι is the designation of the persons spoken of. Had there been a distinction such as Chrys brings out,—εἰσὶ γὰρ καὶ ἄλλοι πλούσιοι ἐν τῷ μέλλοντι [τῷ δὲ διορισμῷ ἀναγκαίως ἐχρήσατο εἰσὶ γὰρ πλούσιοι καὶ τοῦ μέλλοντος αἰῶνος, οἱ τὸν μόνιμον πλοῦτον καὶ διαρκῆ κεκτημένοι. Thdrt.], the τοῖς would have been more naturally prefixed Such a distinction would besides have been improbable, as drawing a line between the two characters, which it is the object of the exhortation to keep united in the same persons See the distinction in Luke xii 21) **give in charge not to be high-minded** (ταῦτα παραινεῖ, εἰδὼς ὅτι οὐδὲν οὕτω τίκτει τῦφον, καὶ ἀπόνοιαν, καὶ ἀλαζονείαν, ὡς χρήματα, Chrys), **nor to place their hope** (i e to have hoped, and continue to be hoping: see on ch. iv. 10) **on the uncertainty** (reff) **of riches** (not = τῷ πλούτῳ τῷ ἀδήλῳ, but far more forcible, hyperbolically representing the hope as reposed on the very quality in riches which least justified it. On the sense, Thdrt says, ἄδηλον γὰρ τοῦ πλούτου τὸ κτῆμα· νῦν μὲν γὰρ παρὰ τούτῳ φοιτᾷ, νῦν δὲ πρὸς ἐκεῖνον μεταβαίνει· καὶ πολλοὺς ἔχων κυρίους, οὐδενός ἐστι κτῆμα An uncertain author, in the Anthology, having complained of the fickleness of Fortune, says, μισῶ τὰ πάντα τῆς ἀδηλίας χάριν), **but in** (see var readd: no distinction of meaning need be sought between ἐπί and ἐν

εἰς [g] ἀπόλαυσιν, 18 [h] ἀγαθοεργεῖν, [i] πλουτεῖν [j] ἐν [k] ἔργοις ADFK LℵaЬ
[k] καλοῖς, [l] εὐμεταδότους εἶναι, [m] κοινωνικούς, 19 [n] ἀποθη- cdefg hklm
σαυρίζοντας ἑαυτοῖς [o] θεμέλιον καλὸν [p] εἰς τὸ [p] μέλλον, ἵνα no17
[q] ἐπιλάβωνται τῆς [r] ὄντως ζωῆς. 20 [r] Ὦ Τιμόθεε, τὴν

g Heb xi 25 only† (λαυειν, Prov vii 18 Wisd ii 6) h Acts xiv 17 only† i = Luke xii 21 Rom x 12 j Eph ii 4 ii 41 1 vi 1 k ch iii 1 reff l here only† m here only† Demosth 192 17 — Polyb n here only† Sir iii 4 see Matt vi 19, 20 Tobit iv 9 o see 1 Cor iii 11 Heb p Luke xiii 9 only q ver 12 r ch v 3 reff

18. πλουτιζειν F.
19 αποθησαυριζειν D vulg Ambrst-ed. τον μελλοντα F rec (for οντως) αιωνιου, with D[3]KL rel mar Chr : txt AD[1]Fℵ 17 latt syrr coptt æth arm Constt Clem Orig Bas Nyssen Naz Thdrt Euthal Œc Aug Jer Ambrst Pelag, αιωνιου οντως m.

see Winer, edn. 6, § 50. 2) **God** ('transfertur Ejus officium ad divitias, si spes in iis locatur,' Calv), **who affordeth us all things richly** (πλοῦτος of a nobler and higher kind is included in His bounty that βούλεσθαι πλουτεῖν which is a bane and snare in its worldly sense, will be far better attained in the course of his abundant mercies to them who hope in Him And even those who would be wealthy without Him are in fact only made rich by His bountiful hand 'alias nemo foret πλούσιος,' Beng) **for enjoyment** (for the purpose of enjoying cf ch iv 3, εἰς μετάλημψιν The term **ἀπόλαυσις**, the reaping enjoyment from, and so having done with [cf ἀπέχω &c], forms a contrast to **ἠλπικέναι ἐπί**, in which riches are not the subject of ἀπόλαυσις, but are looked on as a reliance for the future),—**to do good** (ref. 'to practise benevolence,' as Conyb), **to be rich in good works** (honourable deeds · ἀγαθός is good towards another, καλός good in itself, noble, honourable),—**to be free-givers, ready-contributors** (Chrys. takes κοινωνικούς for affable, communicative, —ὁμιλητικούς, φησι, προσηνεῖς so also Thdrt.: τὸ μὲν [εὐμεταδ.] ἐστι τῆς τῶν χρημάτων χορηγίας τὸ δὲ τῆς τῶν ἠθῶν μετριότητος· κοινωνικοὺς γὰρ καλεῖν εἰώθαμεν τοὺς ἄτυφον ἦθος ἔχοντας. But it seems much better to take it of communicating their substance, as the verb in Gal vi. 6, and κοινωνία in Heb. xiii. 16, where it is coupled with εὐποιΐα), (**by this means**) ('therefrom,' implied in the ἀπό) **laying up for themselves as a treasure** (hoarding up, not uncertain treasure for the life here, but a substantial pledge of that real and endless life which shall be hereafter So that there is no difficulty whatever in the conjunction of ἀποθησαυρίζοντας θεμέλιον, and no need for the conjectures κειμήλιον [Le Clerc] or θέμα λίαν καλὸν [' Lamb-Bos]. For the expression, cf. ch. iii. 13) **a good foundation** (reff., and Luke vi 48) **for the future** (belongs to ἀποθησαυρίζοντας), **that** (in order that, as always not the mere *result* of the preceding 'as it were,' says De W, 'setting foot on this foundation,' or firm ground) **they may lay hold of** (ver 12) **that which is really** (reff.) **life** (not merely the goods of this life, but the possession and substance of that other, which, as full of joy and everlasting, is the only true life)

20, 21.] CONCLUDING EXHORTATION TO TIMOTHEUS. **O Timotheus** (this personal address comes with great weight and solemnity. 'appellat familiariter ut filium, cum gravitate et amore,' Beng), **keep the deposit** (entrusted to thee reff. 2 Tim [μὴ μειώσῃς οὐκ ἔστι σά τὰ ἀλλότρια ἐνεπιστεύθης· μηδὲν ἐλαττώσῃς, Chrys I cannot forbear transcribing from Mack and Wiesinger the very beautiful comment of Vincentius Lirinensis in his Commonitorium [A.D 434], § 22 f p 667 f · "O Timothee, inquit, depositum custodi, devitans profanas vocum novitates [reading καινοφωνίας—see var readd]. 'O!' exclamatio ista et præscientiæ est pariter et caritatis. Prævidebat enim futuros, quos etiam prædolebat, errores. Quid est 'depositum custodi?' Custodi, inquit, propter fures, propter inimicos, ne dormientibus hominibus superseminent zizania super illud tritici bonum semen quod seminaverat filius hominis in agro suo. 'Depositum,' inquit, 'custodi.' Quid est 'depositum?' id est quod tibi creditum est, non quod a te inventum quod accepisti, non quod excogitasti: rem non ingenii sed doctrinæ, non usurpationis privatæ sed publicæ traditionis rem ad te perductam, non a te prolatam, in qua non auctor debes esse sed custos, non institutor sed sectator, non ducens sed sequens. 'Depositum,' inquit, 'custodi' catholicæ fidei talentum inviolatum illibatumque conserva Quod tibi creditum est, hoc penes te maneat, hoc a te tradatur Aurum accepisti, aurum redde Nolo mihi pro aliis alia sub-

[s] παραθήκην φύλαξον, [t] ἐκτρεπόμενος τὰς [u] βεβήλους
[v] κενοφωνίας καὶ [w] ἀντιθέσεις τῆς [w] ψευδωνύμου [x] γνώσεως,
21 ἥν [y] τινὲς [z] ἐπαγγελλόμενοι [a] περὶ τὴν πίστιν [b] ἠστόχησαν. 22 Ἡ [c] χάρις μετὰ σοῦ.

ΠΡΟΣ ΤΙΜΟΘΕΟΝ Α.

s 2 Tim i 12, 14 (both times w φυλάττειν) only Levit vi 2, 4 2 Macc iii 10, 15 only. t ch i 6 reff u ch i 9 reff v 2 Tim ii 16 (there also w βεβ.) only † w here only † x see Rom xv 14 1 Cor i 5 al. y = ch i 3 reff z = ch ii. 10 (Tit i 2 reff) only † a so ch i 19 (and constr) 2 Tim ii 18 b ch i 6 2 Tim ii 18 only † c absol, Col iv 18 reff

20 rec *παρακαταθηκην*, with b f g Chr txt ADFKLℵ rel (syr-marg gr coptt) Clem Ign Thdrt Damasc Œc. *καινοφωνιας* (*itacism*) F 73 Epiph Bas Chr, *vocum novitates* latt Iren Tert Ps-Ath

22 for *μετα σου, μεθ' υμων* (*see 2 Tim* iv. 22, *Tit* iii 15, *where there is hardly any variation in mss*) AFℵ 17 g G-lat(altern) copt txt DKL rel vss gr-lat-ff. rec at end ins *αμην*, with D²KLℵ³ rel om AD¹Fℵ¹ 17 fuld¹

SUBSCRIPTION —rec *προς τιμ πρωτη εγραφη απο λαοδικειας, ητις εστι μητροπολις φρυγιας της πακατιανης*, with KL rel syr (*καπατιανης* KL e g k o) om subscr b l m: *απο αθηνων δια τιτου του μαθητου αυτου* copt *απο μακεδονιας* 6 *απο Νικοπολεως* 114· txt A [addg (qu. A² ?) *απο Λαοδικειας*] ℵ [adding *στιχων σν*] 17 D-lat² Syr Euthal, *πρ τιμ. α' επληρωθη* D, *επληρωθη επ πρ τιμ α'* F

jicias, nolo pro auro aut impudenter plumbum, aut fraudulenter æramenta supponas nolo auri speciem, sed naturam plane . . . Sed forsitan dicit aliquis nullusne ergo in ecclesia Christi profectus habebitur religionis? Habeatur plane, et maximus . . . sed ita tamen, ut vere profectus sit ille fidei, non permutatio. Siquidem ad profectionem pertinet, ut in semetipsa unaquæque res amplificetur, — ad permutationem vero, ut aliquid ex alio in aliud transvertatur. Crescat igitur oportet et multum vehementerque proficiat tam singulorum quam omnium, tam unius hominis quam totius ecclesiæ ætatum et seculorum gradibus, intelligentia, scientia, sapientia: sed in suo duntaxat genere, in eodem scilicet dogmate, eodem sensu, eademque sententia. Imitetur animarum religio rationem corporum, quæ licet annorum processu numeros suos evolvant et explicent, eadem tamen quæ erant permanent . . ."], viz, the sound doctrine which thou art to teach in thy ministry in the Lord, cf Col. iv. 17. This is the most probable explanation Some regard it as the ἐντολή above, ver. 14 some as meaning the grace given to him for his office, or for his own spiritual life· but ch. i. 18, compared with 2 Tim. ii. 2, seems to fix the meaning as above. Herodotus has a very similar use of the word, ix. 45, ἄνδρες Ἀθηναῖοι, παραθήκην ὑμῖν τάδε τὰ ἔπεα τίθεμαι. And with this the following agrees for it is against *false doctrine* that the Apostle cautions him), **turning away from** (cf. ἀποτρέπου, 2 Tim iii. 5) **the profane babblings** (empty discourses· so also 2 Tim ii 16) **and oppositions** (apparently, dialectic antitheses and niceties of the false teachers. The interpretations have been very various Chrys. says, ὁρᾷς πῶς πάλιν κελεύει μηδὲ ὁμόσε χωρεῖν πρὸς τοὺς τοιούτους; ἐκτρεπόμενός, φησιν, τὰς ἀντιθέσεις ἄρα εἰσὶν ἀντιθέσεις, πρὸς ἃς οὐδὲ ἀποκρίνεσθαι χρή; — understanding by ἀντιθ., sayings of theirs opposed to this teaching. But this can hardly be Grot, 'nam ipsi inter se pugnabant' but this is as unlikely. Pelag, Luth, al., understand 'disputations' Mosheim, the dualistic oppositions in the heretical systems Mack, the contradictions which the heretics try to establish between the various doctrines of orthodoxy Baur, the oppositions between the Gospel and the law maintained by Marcion On this latter hypothesis, see Prolegomena There would be no objection philologically to understanding 'propositions opposed to thee,' and τοὺς ἀντιδιατιθεμένους, cf. 2 Tim ii 25, would seem to bear out such meaning but seeing that it is coupled with κενοφωνίας, it is much more probably something entirely subjective to the ψευδώνυμος γνῶσις) **of that which is falsely-named** (ὅταν γὰρ πίστις μὴ ᾖ, γνῶσις οὐκ ἔστι Chrys) **knowledge** (the true γνῶσις, being one of the greatest gifts of the Spirit to the Church, was soon counterfeited by various systems of hybrid theology, calling themselves by this honoured name In the Apostle's time, the misnomer was already current but we are not therefore justified in assuming that it had received so definite an application, as afterwards it did to the various forms of Gnostic heresy All that we can hence gather is, that the true spiritual *γνῶσις* of the Christian was already being counterfeited by persons bearing the characteristics noticed in this Epistle. Whether these were the Gnostics themselves, or their precursors, we have examined in the Prolegomena to the Pastoral Epistles),

21] **which** (the *ψευδών. γνῶσις*) **some professing** (ch. ii 10) **erred** (reff. the indefinite past, as marking merely the event, not the abiding of these men still in the Ephesian church) **concerning the faith**

22.] CONCLUDING BENEDICTION. **The grace** (of God,—ἡ χ, the grace for which we Christians look, and in which we stand) **be with thee** On the subscription we may remark, that the notice found in A al, owes its origin probably to the notion that this was the Epistle from Laodicea mentioned Col. iv. 16 So Thl *τίς δὲ ἦν ἡ ἀπὸ Λαοδικείας; ἡ πρὸς Τιμόθεον πρώτη· αὕτη γὰρ ἐκ Λαοδικείας ἐγράφη* The further addition in rec al betrays a date subsequent to the fourth century, when the province of Phrygia Pacatiana was first created See Smith's Dict. of Geography, art. Phrygia, circa finem.

ΠΡΟΣ ΤΙΜΟΘΕΟΝ Β.

DFK ℵ a b c e f g h k l m n o 17

I. 1 Παῦλος ἀπόστολος χριστοῦ Ἰησοῦ [a] διὰ θελήματος θεοῦ [b] κατ' [c] ἐπαγγελίαν [c] ζωῆς τῆς ἐν χριστῷ
Ἰησοῦ, 2 Τιμοθέῳ ἀγαπητῷ [d] τέκνῳ. [d] χάρις, [d] ἔλεος,

a 1 Cor i 1. 2 Cor i 1. viii 5. Eph i 1. Col i 1. Rom xv 32 only P. b = 2 Cor xi 21. 1 Tim i 1 (reff). c 1 Tim iv 8. d 1 Tim i 2 reff.

TITLE elz π τ. αποστ η πρ. τ. επ δευτερα: Steph η πρ τ επ δευτ.· του αγ. απ. π επ β' πρ τιμ. L txt AKℵ h k m n o 17, and (pretg αρχεται) DF.

CHAP. I. 1. rec ιησ bef χρ, with AL rel Syr goth txt DFKℵ d e g n 17 demid syr copt Damasc Ambrst Cassiod. επαγγελιας ℵ o(omg ζωης)

CHAP. I. 1, 2.] ADDRESS AND GREETING. 1. **διὰ θελ θεοῦ**] Cf reff **κατ' ἐπαγγ ζωῆς**] **according to (in pursuance of, with a view to the fulfilment of) the promise** (ref.) **of life, which is in Christ Jesus** (all this is to be taken with *ἀπόστολος*, not with *θελήματος*. Thdrt explains it well, *ὥστε με τὴν ἐπαγγελθεῖσαν αἰώνιον ζωὴν τοῖς ἀνθρώποις κηρύξαι* Chrysostom sees, in this mention of the promise of life in Christ, a consolation to Timotheus under present troubles· *ἀπὸ τῆς ἀρχῆς ποιεῖται τὴν παραμυθίαν — εἰ ἐπαγγελία ἐστί, μὴ ζήτει αὐτὴν ἐνταῦθα· ἐλπὶς γὰρ βλεπομένη οὐκ ἔστιν ἐλπίς.* And this idea seems to be borne out by the strain of the subsequent portion of the Epistle, which is throughout one of confirmation and encouragement. So Bengel, —"nervus ad Timotheum hortandum, ver. 10, cap ii 8"). 2 **ἀγαπητῷ τέκνῳ**] "Can it be accidental," says Mack, "that instead of *γνησίῳ τέκν*, as Timotheus is called in the first Epistle, i. 2, and Titus i. 4,—here we have *ἀγαπητῷ*? Or may a reason for the change be found in this, that it now behoved Timotheus to stir up afresh the faith and the grace in him, before he could again be worthy of the name *γνησίον τέκνον* in its full sense?" This may be too much pressed: but certainly there is throughout this Epistle an altered tone with regard to Timotheus—more of mere love, and less of confidence, than in the former and this would naturally shew itself even in passing words of address When Bengel says, "in Ep i., scripserat, genuino: id compensatur hic versu 5," he certainly misses the delicate sense of ver 5. see below. To find in **ἀγαπητῷ** *more* confidence, as Heyd (and Chrys, maintaining that *οἱ κατὰ πίστιν ὅταν ὦσιν ἀγαπητοί, δι' οὐδὲν ἕτερόν εἰσιν, ἀλλ' ἢ δι' ἀρετήν*), can hardly be correct· the expression of feeling is *different* in kind, not comparable in degree: suiting an Epistle of warm affection and somewhat saddened reminding, rather than one of rising hope and confidence. I regret to be, on this point, at issue throughout this second Epistle, with my friend Bishop Ellicott, who seems to me too anxious to rescue the character of Timotheus from the slightest imputation of weakness thereby marring the delicate texture of many of St. Paul's characteristic periods, in which tender reproof, vigorous reassurance, and fervent affection are exquisitely intermingled See reff. and notes.

[d] εἰρήνη ἀπὸ [e] θεοῦ [e] πατρὸς καὶ χριστοῦ Ἰησοῦ τοῦ κυρίου
ἡμῶν.
3 [f] Χάριν [f] ἔχω τῷ θεῷ, ᾧ [g] λατρεύω ἀπὸ [h] προγόνων ἐν
[i] καθαρᾷ [i] συνειδήσει, ὡς [j] ἀδιάλειπτον ἔχω τὴν περὶ σοῦ
[k] μνείαν ἐν ταῖς [l] δεήσεσίν μου [m] νυκτὸς καὶ ἡμέρας,
4 [n] ἐπιποθῶν σε ἰδεῖν, [o] μεμνημένος σου τῶν δακρύων, ἵνα
χαρᾶς [p] πληρωθῶ, 5 [q] ὑπόμνησιν [r] λαβὼν τῆς ἐν σοὶ

C χαριν
ÄCDF KLℵ a b c d e f g h k l m n o 17

e Gal i 1 reff 1 = Luke xvii 9 1 Tim i 12 Heb xii 28 only L P H 2 Macc iii 33
g Matt iv 10 (from Deut vi 13 x 20) Acts vii 7 Rom i 9 al
h 1 Tim v 4 only † Sir viii 4 2 Macc viii 19 xi 25 only
i 1 Tim iii 9 only see Heb. ix 14 συν-, 1 Tim i 5 reff
j Rom ix 2 only † (ὡς, Rom i 9)
k μ ἔχειν, 1 Thess iii 6 elsw, as Eph i 16 reff, w το εἰσθαι
l Paul, Rom x 1 2 Cor i 11 al9 2 Chron vi 19, &c
m 1 Tim v 5 reff
n 1 Thess iii 6 reff
o = 1 Cor xi 2. Heb xiii 3 Ps cv 7
p = Luke ii 40 Acts ii 28 xiii 52 Paul, Rom xv 13, 14 al freq
q 2 Pet i 13 iii 1 only † Wisd xvi 11 2 Macc vi 17 only (-μιμνησκειν, ch ii 14.)
r = Heb xi 29 2 Pet i 9

2 for χρ ιησ., κυριου ιησ. χρ. (retaining του κυ below) ℵ[1] k m
3 aft θεω ins μου D[1] 17 sah goth Orig Ambrst Pelag Cassiod om ACD[3]FKLℵ rel vulg(with am fuld, agst demid hal) syrr copt Chr Thdrt. λατρευων C[1].
4. επιποθω F copt. (G-lat has both)
5 rec λαμβανων, with DKLℵ[1] rel Chr Thdrt Damasc Thl Œc· txt (*see note*) ACFℵ[1] 17.

3—5] *Thankful declaration of love and anxiety to see him* **I give thanks** (reff) **to God whom I serve from my ancestors** (i. e. as Bengel, "majores, innuit, non Abrahamum &c, quos patres, nunquam *προγόνους* appellat sed progenitores proximos." The reason for the profession may perhaps be found in the following mention of the faith of the mother and grandmother of Timotheus, which was already in the Apostle's mind. We may observe that he does not, as De W charges him, place on the same ground the Jewish and Christian service of God but simply asserts what he had before asserted, Acts xxiii. 1, xxiv 11,—that his own service of God had been at all times conscientious and single-hearted, and that he had received it as such from his forefathers) **in pure conscience, how** (not '*that,*' as Chrys. [*εὐχαριστῶ τῷ θεῷ ὅτι μέμνημαί σου, φησίν, οὕτω σε φιλῶ*], Luth, E. V, al.,—nor '*when,*' as Calv ['quoties tui recordor in precibus meis, id enim facio continenter, simul etiam de te gratias ago'],—nor 'since,' '*seeing that,*' as Heyd, Flatt, al,—nor '*as,*' as De W, Huther, Ellic, al · but as in the parallel, Rom i 9, the construction is a mixed one between *μάρτυς μου ἐστὶν ὁ θεός, ὡς ἀδιάλ ἔχω,* and *εὐχαριστῶ ἀδιάλειπτον ἔχων*· and hence the meaning 'how' must be retained, and with it the involution of construction, which is characteristic of one with whom expressions like these had now become fixed in diction, and liable to be combined without regard to strict logical accuracy) **unceasing I make my mention** (not 'mention' only, on account of the article, which specifies the *μνεία* as a thing constantly happening) **concerning thee** (so Herod. i 36, *παιδὸς μὲν περὶ τοῦ ἐμοῦ μὴ μνήσθητε ἔτι*—Xen Cyr i 6. 12, *οὐδ' ὁτιοῦν περὶ τούτου ἐπεμνήσθη*—Plat Laches, p 181 a, *ὅδ' ἐστὶ Σωκράτης, περὶ οὗ ἑκάστοτε μέμνησθε* and Heb. xi. 22) **in my prayers, night and day** (see Luke ii 37 note · belongs to *ἀδιάλειπτ. ἔχω κ τ λ*, not to *δεήσεσιν*, much less, as Mack, al, to the following, for which 1 Thess ii 9, iii 10 are no precedents, as here such an arrangement would deprive the participle *ἐπιποθῶν* of its place of emphasis); **longing** (*ἐπί*, as the prep in composition so often, seems to mark not intensification, but direction: see Ellic's note) **to see thee, remembering thy tears** (shed at our parting), **that I may be filled with joy** (the expressions in this verse are assurances of the most fervent personal love, strengthened by the proof of such love having been reciprocal. From these he gently and most skilfully passes to a tone of fatherly exhortation and reproof) **having remembrance** (the aor participle may be taken either (1) as dependent on *ἵνα*, and the condition of *πληρωθῶ*,—or, which is more probable, (2) as in apposition with *ἐπιποθῶν* and *μεμνημένος*) **of the unfeigned faith** [which was] (Ellic objects to '*was,*' and would render '*is,*' see note above on ver 2 But I do not see how St Paul could be said *ὑπόμνησιν λαβεῖν* of a thing then present Surely the remembrance is of the time when they parted, and the faith then existing But the sentence does not require any temporal filling up—'the unfeigned faith in thee' is quite enough, and is necessarily thrown into the past by the *ὑπό-*

[s] ἀνυποκρίτου πίστεως, [t] ἥτις [u] ἐνῴκησεν πρῶτον ἐν τῇ
[v] μάμμῃ σου Λωΐδι καὶ τῇ μητρί σου Εὐνίκῃ, [w] πέπεισμαι
δὲ ὅτι καὶ ἐν σοί.
6 [x] δι' ἣν [x] αἰτίαν [y] ἀναμιμνήσκω σε
[z] ἀναζωπυρεῖν τὸ [a] χάρισμα τοῦ θεοῦ, ὅ ἐστιν ἐν σοὶ διὰ

s 1 Tim i 5 reff. t Acts x 41, 47 al fr Paul, passim u Rom viii 11 2 Cor vi 16 Col iii 16 ver 14 only. Lev xxvi 12 v here only † w constr, Rom viii 38 xiv 14 xv 14 ver 12 x Paul, ver 12 Tit i 13 only Luke viii 47 Acts x 21 xxii 24 xxiii 28 Heb ii 11 only L P H y Mark xi 21 xiv 72 1 Cor iv 17 2 Cor vii 15 Heb x 32 only Gen viii 1 vat (μνησις, Luke xxii 19) z here only LXX intr, Gen xlv 27 1 Macc xiii 7 only Clem I ad Cor § 27, p 268 Ign Eph § 1, p 644 a 1 Tim iv 14 (reff)

ενοικησεν D[1] 17

6 for αναμ, υπομιμνησκω D. for χαρ, θελημα ℵ[1]. for θεου, χριστου A.

μνησιν λαβών See more below) in thee (there is perhaps a slight reproach in this ὑπόμνησιν and τῆς ἐν σοί, as if it were a thing once certain as fact, and as matter of memory, but now only, as below, resting on a πέπεισμαι ὅτι· and in presence of such a possible inference, and of ὑπόμνησιν, I have ventured therefore to render τῆς ἐν σοί, 'which was in thee,' viz. at the time of τὰ δάκρυα,—its present existence being only by and by introduced as a confident hope) **such as dwelt first** (before it dwelt in thee) **in thy grandmother** (*μάμμην τὴν τοῦ πατρὸς ἢ μητρὸς μητέρα, οὐ λέγουσιν οἱ ἀρχαῖοι, ἀλλὰ τίτθην* [l. *τήθην*]. Phryn., p 133, where see Lobeck's note. It is thus used, as he shews, by Josephus, Plutarch, Appian, Herodian, &c., and Pollux says [iii. 17], *ἡ δὲ πατρὸς ἢ μητρὸς μήτηρ τήθη καὶ μάμμη καὶ μάμμα.* But he adduces all the stricter philologists as agreeing with Phrynichus) **Lois** (not elsewhere mentioned), **and thy mother Eunice** (*Τιμόθεος, υἱὸς γυναικὸς Ἰουδαίας πιστῆς, πατρὸς δὲ Ἕλληνος*, Acts xvi 1 see also ch. iii. 15 Both these were probably converts on Paul's former visit to Lystra, Acts xiv. 6 ff), but (the **δέ** gives the meaning 'notwithstanding appearances' It is entirely missed by Ellic., and not fairly rendered in the E. V, '*and*,' see note below) **I am persuaded that** (supply *ἐνοικεῖ*, not *ἐνοικήσει*, as Grot., al) **also in thee** (there is undoubtedly a want of entire confidence here expressed; and such a feeling will account for the mention of the faith of his mother and grandmother, to which if he wavered, he was proving untrue. This has been felt by several of the ancient Commentators, e g Thdrt,—*τῇ μετ' εὐφημίας μνήμῃ τῶν προγόνων ὁ θεῖος ἀπόστολος κρατύνει τὴν πίστιν ἐν τῷ μαθητῇ οὐδὲν γὰρ οὕτως ὀνίνησιν ὡς οἰκεῖον παράδειγμα καὶ ἐπειδὴ συμβαίνει τινὰς ἐξ εὐσεβῶν γενομένους μὴ ζηλῶσαι τὴν τῶν προγόνων εὐσέβειαν, ἀναγκαίως ἐπήγαγε "Πέπεισμαι δὲ ὅτι καὶ ἐν σοί" εἶτα τοῦτο αὐτὸ τῆς παραινέσεως ὑποβάθραν ποιεῖται*)

6—14] *Exhortation to Timotheus to be firm in the faith, and not to shrink from suffering enforced* (9—11) *by the glorious character of the Gospel, and free mercy of God in it, and* (11—13) *by his own example* **For which cause** (reff viz. because thou hast inherited, didst once possess, and I trust still dost possess, such unfeigned faith;—*ταῦτα περὶ σου πεπεισμένος*, Thdrt) **I put thee in mind to stir up** (see examples in reff and in Wetst The metaphorical use of the word was so common, that there is hardly need to recur to its literal sense Cf especially, Iambl vit Pythagor c. 16 *ἀπεκάθαιρε τὴν ψυχήν, καὶ ἀνεζωπύρει τὸ θεῖον ἐν αὐτῇ.* At the same time it is well to compare, as Chrys does, 1 Thess v 19, *τὸ πνεῦμα μὴ σβέννυτε* He adds, *ἐν ἡμῖν γάρ ἐστι καὶ σβέσαι καὶ ἀνάψαι τοῦτο. ὑπὸ μὲν γὰρ ἀκηδίας καὶ ῥᾳθυμίας σβέννυται, ὑπὸ δὲ νήψεως καὶ προσοχῆς διεγείρεται*) **the gift of God** (*χάρισμα*, singular, as combining the whole of the gifts necessary for the ministry in one aggregate [*τὴν χάριν τοῦ πνεύματος, ἣν ἔλαβες εἰς προστασίαν τῆς ἐκκλησίας*, Chrys] not 'the gift of the Spirit imparted to all believers:' see 1 Tim iv. 14, note. Of those ministerial gifts, that of *παῤῥησία* would be most required in this case, "videtur Timotheus, Paulo diu carens, nonnihil remisisse: certe nunc ad majora stimulatur." Bengel), **which is in thee by means of the laying on of my hands** (these words, especially when compared with 1 Tim. iv. 14, mark the sense of *χάρισμα* to be as above, and not the general gifts of the Spirit which followed the laying on of hands after baptism Any apparent discrepancy with that passage, from the Apostle here speaking of the laying on of *his own hands alone*, may be removed by regarding the Apostle as chief in the ordination, and the presbytery as his assistants, as is the case with Bishops at the present day As to the *διὰ τῆς ἐπιθ.*, we can only appeal, against

τῆς [a] ἐπιθέσεως τῶν [a] χειρῶν μου. 7 οὐ γὰρ ἔδωκεν ἡμῖν
ὁ θεὸς [b] πνεῦμα [c] δειλίας, ἀλλὰ δυνάμεως καὶ ἀγάπης
καὶ [d] σωφρονισμοῦ. 8 μὴ οὖν [e] ἐπαισχυνθῇς τὸ [f] μαρτύ-

ACDF KLℵ a b c d e f g h k l m n o 17

b = Rom viii 15. 2 Cor iv 13. Eph i 17. c here only. Levit xxvi 36 F. Ps liv 4 (-λος, Matt viii 26 -λιᾶν, John xiv 27 ‖ Mk. Rom i 16 al. Job xxxiv 19 vat. Isa. i 29 F only. d here only † (see note). e vv 12, 16. Luke ix 26 (bis). f = 1 Tim ii 6 reff.

the Roman-Catholic expositors, e g Mack, to the whole spirit of St Paul's teaching, as declaring that by such an expression he does not mean that the inward spiritual grace is operated merely and barely by the outward visible sign,—but is only asserting, in a mode of speech common to us all, that the solemn dedication by him of Timotheus to God's work, of which the laying on of his hands was the sign and seal, did bring with it gifts and grace for that work. In this sense and in this alone, the gift came *διὰ τῆς ἐπιθέσεως*, that laying on being the concentrated and effective sign of the setting apart, and conveying in faith the answer, assumed by faith, to the prayers of the church. That the Apostle had *authority* thus to set apart, was necessary to the validity of the act, and thus to the reception of the grace:—but the authority did not *convey* the grace I may just add that the 'indelibility of orders,' which Mack infers from this passage, is simply and directly refuted by it If the *χάρισμα τὸ ἐν σοί* required *ἀναζωπυρεῖσθαι*, if, as Chrys. above, *ἐν ἡμῖν ἐστι καὶ σβέσαι καὶ ἀνάψαι τοῦτο*,—then plainly it is *not* indelible)

7.] **For** (q d, 'and there is reason for my thus exhorting thee, seeing that thou hast shewn a spirit inconsistent with the character of that *χάρισμα*' The particle is passed over by Ellicott) **God did not give** (when we were admitted to the ministry not '*has not given*' [*δέδωκεν*]) **us the Spirit** (q d, 'the spirit which He gave us was not ' see Rom. viii 15 and note. The usage of **πνεῦμα** without the art in the sense of the spirit of man dwelt in by the Spirit of God, and as the Spirit of God working in the spirit of man, as e g continually in Rom viii [vv. 4 5, 9 bis, 13, 14], in 1 Cor ii 4; cf 1 Cor. xi 17, forbids our rendering **πνεῦμα** '*a spirit*' [subjective], as Conyb al) **of cowardice** (the coincidence in sound with the **πνεῦμα** *δουλείας* of Rom viii 15, is remarkable, and the most decisive of all testimonies against De Wette's unworthy and preposterous idea that this passage is an imitation from that. Rather I should account the circumstance a fine and deep indication of genuineness —the habitual assertion of the one axiom having made even its sound and chime so familiar to the Apostle's ear, that he selects, when enouncing another like it, a word almost reproducing that other. There is also doubtless a touch of severity in this *δειλίας*, putting before Timotheus his timidity in such a light as to shame him. *οὐχ ἵνα δειλιῶμεν τοὺς ὑπὲρ τῆς εὐσεβίας κινδύνους*, Thdrt), **but** (the spirit) **of power** (as opposed to the weakness implied in *δειλία*), **and love** (as opposed to that false compliance with men, which shrinks from bold rebuke·—that lofty self-abandonment of love for others, which will even sacrifice repute, and security, and all that belongs to self, in the noble struggle to do men good), **and correction** (the original meaning of **σωφρονισμός**, '*admonition of others that they may become* **σωφρ**,'—*τὸ σωφρονίζειν τινά*, cf. Tit ii 4,—must be retained, as necessary both on account of that usage of the verb, and on account of the context. It is this bearing bold testimony before others, from which Timotheus appears to have shrunk cf *μὴ οὖν ἐπαισχυνθῇς τὸ μαρτύριον*, ver. 8 It also suits the construction of the other two genitives [against Huther], which both express *that which the Spirit inspires a man with.* For the meaning itself, cf Palm and Rost's Lex. We have examples of it in Hippodamus [Stob. 43. 93, p. 250],—*τοὶ μὲν νέοι δέονται σωφρονισμῶ καὶ καταρτύσιος* Plut. Cat. maj 5,—*ἐπὶ διορθώσει καὶ σωφρονισμῷ τῶν ἄλλων*. Appian de rebus Punicis viii 65,—*εἰσὶ γὰρ οἳ καὶ τόδε νομίζουσιν, αὐτὸν ἐς Ῥωμαίων σωφρονισμὸν ἐθελῆσαι γείτονα καὶ ἀντίπαλον αὐτοῖς φόβον ἐς ἀεὶ καταλιπεῖν*. The word in after times became a common one for *discipline* or *ecclesiastical correction* see examples under *σωφρονίζω* and *-ισμός* in Suicer Some, retaining this proper meaning, understand by it that the Spirit *σωφρονίζει ἡμᾶς* so [ult.] Chrys, Thl. [*ἢ ἵνα σωφρονισμὸν ἔχωμεν τὸ πνεῦμα*]; but this does not suit the construction of the other genitives, in which it is not power over us, or love towards us, that is meant, but power and love *wrought in us* as towards others, and opposed to cowardice and fear of man Thl gives as another alternative the right meaning—*ἢ ἵνα καὶ ἄλλοις ὦμεν σωφρονισταὶ καὶ παιδευταί* The making *σωφρονισμός* = *σωφροσύνη*, as E. V and

ριον τοῦ κυρίου ἡμῶν μηδὲ ἐμὲ τὸν [g] δέσμιον αὐτοῦ, ἀλλὰ
[h] συγκακοπάθησον τῷ [i] εὐαγγελίῳ κατὰ [k] δύναμιν θεοῦ
9 τοῦ [l] σώσαντος ἡμᾶς καὶ [mn] καλέσαντος [no] κλήσει ἁγίᾳ,

g = (Paul) Eph. iii 1. iv 1 Philem 1, 9 h ch ii 3 only † (κακοπαθ., ch ii 9) i dat., Phil i 27 k = 2 Cor viii 3 Eph iii 20 Heb vii 16 l Tit iii 5 see 1 Tim i 1 reff m = Gal i 6 reff n 1 Cor vii 20 Eph iv 1 o Eph i 18 Phil iii 14. Jer xxxviii (xxxi) 6 Judith xii 10 F only

8 om ημων ℵ[1] · ins ℵ-corr[1] ins του bef θεου D[1] 17.

many Commentators, is surely not allowable, though Chrys. puts it doubtfully as an alternative. The only way in which it can come virtually to that, is by supposing the *σωφρονισμός* to be exercised *by ourselves over ourselves*, as Thdrt.: ἵνα σωφρονίσωμεν τῶν ἐν ἡμῖν κινουμένων παθημάτων τὴν ἀταξίαν But this does not seem to me to suit the context so well as the meaning given above) **8.] Be not then** (seeing that God gave us such a Spirit, not the other) **ashamed of** (for construction see reff I cannot see, with Ellic, that the aor subjunc. with μή, 'ne te pudeat unquam,' as Leo, implies in matter of fact that "Timothy had as yet evinced no such feeling" Surely, granting that such is the primary constructional inference from the words, it would be just in keeping with the delicate tact of the Apostle, to use such form of admonition, when in fact the blame had been already partly incurred See note on ver. 1) **the testimony of our Lord** (i e the testimony which thou art to give concerning our Lord, gen objective · not '*the testimony which He bore*,' gen subjective, as Corn -a-lap , al ,—nor, as Chrys. [apparently], '*the martyrdom of our Lord*,' nor must we, with Mack, lay stress on *κυρίου*, and understand the *μαρτύριον* to be especially this, that Jesus *is the Lord* The ἡμῶν is added, hardly for the reason Bengel gives, 'hunc opponit Cæsari, quem sui sic appellabant,' which would hardly have been thus expressed, requiring more prominence to be given to ἡμῶν,—but because, being about to introduce *himself*, he binds by this word Timotheus and himself together), **nor of me His prisoner** (I would hardly say, with De W , Huther, al , that this refers only to the services which the Apostle expected from Timotheus in coming to him at Rome such thought may have been in his mind, and may have mingled with his motive in making the exhortation but I believe the main reference to be to his duty as upholding St. Paul and his teaching in the face of personal danger and persecution. It is impossible to deny that the above personal reference does enter again and again: but I cannot believe it to be more than secondary On the expression, *τὸν δέσμιον αὐτοῦ*, see Eph iii. 1 note: the gen. implies not possession, but the reason for which he was imprisoned, cf. Philem. 13, δεσμοὶ τοῦ εὐαγγελίου), **but suffer hardship with me for the Gospel** (this is the meaning [ref], and not '*suffer hardship together with the Gospel*,' as Thdrt. [τῶν κηρύκων τὸ πάθος τοῦ εὐαγγελίου προσηγόρευσε πάθος], Calv [?], Grot [' προσωποποιεῖ evangelium, eique sensum tribuit, quomodo alibi legi, morti, peccato'] . for St. Paul, speaking of his own bonds, ch ii. 9, says, ὁ λόγος τοῦ θεοῦ οὐ δέδεται. This *συγκακοπάθησον* extends the sphere of his fellow-suffering with the Apostle beyond his mere visiting Rome) **according to the power of God** (*what power?* that which God has manifested in our salvation, as described below [gen. subj], or that which God imparts to us [gen. obj],—*God's power*, or *the power which we get from God?* On all grounds, the former seems to me the juster and worthier sense the former, as implying indeed the latter *à fortiori*—that God, who by His strong hand and mighty arm has done all this for us, will help us through all trouble incurred for Him. Chrys gives this meaning very finely ἐπεὶ φορτικὸν ἦν τὸ εἰπεῖν, κακοπάθησον, πάλιν αὐτὸν παραμυθεῖται λέγων, οὐ κατὰ τὰ ἔργα ἡμῶν· τουτέστι, μὴ τῇ δυνάμει λογίζου τῇ σῇ, ἀλλὰ τῇ τοῦ θεοῦ ταῦτα φέρειν. σὸν μὲν γὰρ τὸ ἑλέσθαι καὶ προθυμηθῆναι, θεοῦ δὲ τὸ κουφίσαι καὶ παῦσαι εἶτα καὶ τῆς δυνάμεως αὐτοῦ δείκνυσι τὰ τεκμήρια πῶς ἐσώθης ἐννόει, πῶς ἐκλήθης ὥσπερ φησὶν ἀλλαχοῦ, κατὰ τὴν ἐνέργειαν αὐτοῦ τὴν ἐνεργουμένην ἐν ἡμῖν. οὕτω τοῦ ποιῆσαι τὸν οὐρανὸν μείζων δύναμις αὕτη ἦν, τὸ πεῖσαι τὴν οἰκουμένην), **who saved us** (all believers: there is no reason for limiting this ἡμᾶς to Paul and Timotheus. It is painful to see such Commentators as De Wette so blinded by a preconceived notion of the spuriousness of the Epistle, as to call this which follows 'eine ganz allgemeine überflüssige Erinnerung an die christlichen Heilsthatsachen.' I need hardly

p Rom xi 6 al fr Ps xxvii 4
q Rom viii 28 Eph i 11 (reff) iii 11
r Gal ii 9 reff
s = 2 Cor xii 2 Tit i 2
John xii 1 Amos i 1 iv 7

οὐ [p] κατὰ τὰ ἔργα ἡμῶν, ἀλλὰ [q] κατὰ ἰδίαν [q] πρόθεσιν
καὶ [r] χάριν τὴν [r] δοθεῖσαν ἡμῖν ἐν χριστῷ Ἰησοῦ [s] πρὸ
[t] χρόνων [t] αἰωνίων, 10 [u] φανερωθεῖσαν δὲ νῦν διὰ τῆς [v] ἐπιφανείας τοῦ σωτῆρος ἡμῶν Ἰησοῦ χριστοῦ, [w] καταρ-
γήσαντος μὲν τὸν θάνατον, [x] φωτίσαντος δὲ ζωὴν καὶ

ACDF KLℵ a b c d e f g h k l m n o 17

t Rom xvi 25 Tit i 2 only see Gen ix 12 14 ch iv 1, 8 Tit ii 13 only P 2 Kings vii 23
u = Col i 26 reff
v 2 Thess ii 8. 1 Tim vi 14
w = 2 Thess ii 9 reff (Gal iii 17 reff)
x = 1 Cor iv 5 only Neh ix 12, 19 Jos Antt viii 5 3 trans, John i 9 Rev xxi 3 intr, Rev xxii 5.

9 [*κατα*, so ACℵ b k 17 · *καθ'* F.] *αιωνιαν* ℵ[1].
10. *φανερωθεντος* K *επιφανιας* CD[1]F. *χρ.* bef *ιησ.* AD[1]ℵ[1] sah · txt CD[3]FKLℵ[3](appy) rel vulg syrr copt goth Orig lat-ff.

say to the reader who has been hitherto following the course and spirit of the passage, that it is in the strictest coherence, as indeed is shewn by Chrys. above 'Be not cowardly nor ashamed of the Gospel, but join me in endurance on its behalf, according to God's power, who has given such proofs of that power and of its exercise towards us, in saving us,—calling us in Christ,—destroying death—&c, of which endurance I am an example [11—13]—which example do thou follow' [13, 14]), **and called us** (this, as indeed the whole context, shews that it is the Father who is spoken of see note on Gal i. 6), **with an holy** (*τουτέστιν, ἁγίους ἐξειργάσατο ἁμαρτωλοὺς ὄντας καὶ ἐχθρούς*, Chrys **κλῆσις** expressing the *state*, rather than merely the summoning into it [as does '*vocation*' also], *ἁγία* is its quality) **calling** (see Eph iv 1, i 18 Rom viii 28—30, and notes), **not according to** (after the measure of, in accordance with) **our works but according to** (after the measure of, in pursuance of) **his own purpose** (*τουτέστιν οὐδενὸς ἀναγκάζοντος, οὐδενὸς συμβουλεύοντος, ἀλλ' ἐξ ἰδίας προθέσεως, οἴκοθεν ἐκ τῆς ἀγαθότητος αὐτοῦ ὁρμώμενος*, Chrys *οὐκ εἰς τὸν ἡμέτερον ἀποβλέψας βίον, ἀλλὰ διὰ μόνην φιλανθρωπίαν*, Thdrt. "Originem tam vocationis nostræ quam totius salutis designat · non enim erant nobis opera quibus Deum prævenniremus sed totum a gratuito ejus proposito et electione pendet" Calv), **and** (according to) **the grace which was given to us** (this expression, which properly belongs only to an *actual imparting*, is used, because, as De W, that which God determines in Eternity, is as good as already accomplished in time. No weakening of *δοθεῖσαν* into *destinatam* must be thought of) **in Christ Jesus** (as its element and condition, see Eph i. 4, iii 11) **before the periods of ages** (see reff ; *τουτέστιν, ἀναρχῶς*, Chrys. It is hardly possible in the presence of Scripture analogy to take the expression *πρὸ χρόνων αἰωνίων* as 'meaning [? Conyb] the Jewish dispensation ·' still less, as Dr Burton, that 'the scheme of redemption was arranged by God immediately after the fall, before any ages or dispensations' Even Calvin's interpretation, 'perpetuam annorum seriem a mundo condito,' fails to reach the full meaning. In the parallel, Rom xvi 25, the mystery of redemption is described as having been *χρόνοις αἰωνίοις σεσιγημένον*,—which obviously includes ages previous to the *καταβολὴ κόσμου* as well as after it,— see Eph. iii 11, compared with i. 4 1 Cor. ii. 7), **but** (contrast to the concealment from eternity in the manifestation in time) **manifested now** (*νυνὶ τοῖς προορισθεῖσι τὸ πέρας ἐπέθηκε*, Thdrt. See Col. i 26; Tit i 3) **by the appearing** (in the flesh · here only used thus, see reff. but not referring to the birth only 'His whole manifestation') **of our Saviour Jesus Christ, who abolished** ('*when He made of none effect*,' Ellic , objecting to my rendering, as confounding an anarthrous participle with one preceded by the article. But, *pace tanti viri*, and recognizing to the full the distinction, I must hold that the slightly ratiocinative force of the anarthrous participle is more accurately represented by "who abolished," than by introducing the temporal element contained in "when He" The bald literal rendering, '*abolishing* [not, '*having abolished*,' the aor participles are synchronous throughout] *as He did*,' is most nearly approached by '*who abolished*' and it is an approximation to the sense, not grammatical purism, which must be our object) [indeed] **death** (cf especially 1 Cor xv 26 By the death of Christ, Death has lost his sting, and is henceforth of no more account consequently the mere act of natural death is evermore treated by the

[y] ἀφθαρσίαν διὰ τοῦ εὐαγγελίου, 11 [z] εἰς ὃ [z] ἐτέθην ἐγὼ
[z] κήρυξ καὶ [z] ἀπόστολος καὶ [z] διδάσκαλος [z] ἐθνῶν. 12 [a] δι'
ἣν [a] αἰτίαν καὶ ταῦτα πάσχω· ἀλλ' οὐκ [b] ἐπαισχύνομαι,
οἶδα γὰρ ᾧ [c] πεπίστευκα, καὶ [d] πέπεισμαι ὅτι [e] δυνατός
ἐστιν τὴν [f] παραθήκην μου φυλάξαι [g] εἰς [h] ἐκείνην τὴν

y Rom ii 7 1 Cor xv 42 &c Eph vi 24 P † Wisd ii 23 vi 18, 19 only z 1 Tim ii 7 (reff) a ver 6 b ver 8 c w dat, Acts xxvii 25 Rom iv 3 (from Gen xv 6). x 16 Tit iii 8 al d ver 5 e Rom xi 23 see Rom xiv 4 2 Cor ix 8 f (in N T always w φυλ) ver 14 1 Tim vi 20 only Levit vi 2, 4 2 Macc iii 10, 15 only g — Eph iv 30 Phil ii 16 b h ver 18 2 Thess i 10 ch iv 8

11 om 2nd και C c d   om εθνων AN[1] 17.

Lord Himself and his Apostles as of no account: cf. John xi 26; Rom. viii 2, 38; 1 Cor. xv 55, Heb. ii 14: and its actual and total abolition foretold, Rev. xxi 4 θάνατον must be kept here to its literal sense, and its spiritual only so far understood as involved in the other. The delivering from the *fear of death* is manifestly not to the purpose, even did διὰ τοῦ εὐαγγ belong to both participles Notice τὸν θάνατον As Bengel says, 'Articulus notanter positus' As if he had said, 'Orcum illum.' ζωὴν and ἀφθαρσίαν below have no articles), but (contrast to the gloom involved in θάνατον) **brought to light** (threw light upon, see ref 1 Cor., and thus made visible what was before hidden · ἀντὶ τοῦ πρυμηνύσαντος, Thdrt) **life** (i. e. the new and glorious life of the Spirit, begun here below and enduring for ever · the only life worthy of being so called) **and incorruptibility** (immortality —of the new life, not merely of the risen body that is not in question here, but is, though a glorious yet only a secondary consequence of this ἀφθαρσία; see Rom. viii. 11) **by means of the** (preaching of the) **Gospel** (which makes these glorious things known to men. These words are better taken as belonging only to φωτ δὲ ζω. κ. ἀφθ., not to καταργ. μὲν τὸν θάν. For this former is an absolute act of Christ, the latter a manifestation to those who see it), **for which** (viz. the εὐαγγέλιον, the publication of this good news to men) **I was appointed a herald, and an apostle, and a teacher of the Gentiles** (see the same expression, and note, in 1 Tim ii. 7. The connexion in which he here introduces himself is noticed above, on ver. 8. It is to bring in his own example and endurance in sufferings, and grounds of trust, for a pattern to Timotheus) **on which account** (viz because I ἐτέθην, as above) **I also** (besides doing the active work of such a mission. Or καί may be taken with ταῦτα, as Ellic,—'even these things') **am suffering these things** (viz the things implied in τὸν δέσμιον αὐτοῦ, ver 8, and further specified by way of explanation and encouragement to Timotheus below, ver. 15) · **but I am not ashamed** (cf. μὴ ἐπαισχυνθῇς, ver. 8), **for I know whom I have trusted** (hardly to be formally expressed so strongly as De W. '*in whom I have put my trust*' [εἰς ὃν πεπ], though the meaning, in the spiritual explanation, is virtually the same. the metaphor here is that of a pledge deposited, and the depositor *trusting* the depositary. and it is best to keep to the figure. The ᾧ refers to God, as Tit. iii. 8 Acts xxvii. 25 ?), **and am persuaded that He is able** (refl. as used of God) **to keep my deposit** (how are the words to be taken,—and what is meant by them? Does μου import, the deposit which *He* has entrusted to *me*, or the deposit which *I* have entrusted to *Him*? Let us consider the latter first. In this case μου is the gen subjective Now what is there which the Apostle can be said to have entrusted to God? Some say, (a) his *eternal reward*, the crown *laid up* for him, ch iv. 8; so Thl, Beza, Calov., Wolf ['hoc est κληρονομία quæ dicitur τετηρημένη ἐν οὐρανοῖς, 1 Pet. i 4: habes hic τὸ φυλάσσειν']: but then we should have this reward represented as a matter not of God's free grace, but of his own, delivered to God to keep (b) his *soul*, as in 1 Pet. iv. 19 Luke xxiii 46 so Grot. ['Deus apud nos deponit verbum suum: nos apud Deum deponimus spiritum nostrum'], Beng ['anima nostra: nos ipsi, et portio nostra cœlestis Paulus, decessui proximus, duo deposita habebat alterum Domino, alterum Timotheo committendum'], Conyb and others [see this treated below] (c) his *salvation*, so Ambr, Calv., Huther, al [see ib.] (d) the believers who had been converted by his means, as Chrys and Thl. [alt.], and as in the Ep ad Heron of the Pseudo-Ignatius, 7, p 916,—φύλαξόν μου τὴν παραθήκην . . . παρατίθημί σοι τὴν ἐκκλησίαν Ἀντιοχέων, which hardly needs refutation, as altogether unsupported by the context Then, under the former head, which would make μου a gen possessive,

i 1 Tim i 10 only † k 1 Tim i 10 iii 9 see note 8 Heb ii 2 1 John ii 7 [h] ἡμέραν. 13 [i] ὑποτύπωσιν [k] ἔχε [lm] ὑγιαινόντων [mn] λόγων, ACDΓ KLℵ a b c d e f g h k l m n o 17

l 1 Tim i 10 reff   m 1 Tim vi 3   n = Acts xviii 15 Tit i. 9 ii

12 om μου D[1] a k

we have the following meanings assigned —(e) the *Holy Spirit*, as Thdrt [ὅσην παρέσχε μοι τοῦ πνεύματος χάριν ἀκήρατον φυλάξει μέχρι τῆς αὐτοῦ παρουσίας] — (f) *the faith, and its proclamation to the world*. So Chrys [τί ἐστι παρακαταθήκη, ἡ πίστις, τὸ κήρυγμα: but only as an alternative, see above], Ellic., not Grot. as De W see above (g) the *apostolic office* [Corn.-a-lap., Heinrichs, De W, al] which the Apostle regarded as a thing entrusted to him, a stewardship, 1 Cor ix 17: (h) the *faithful* who had been converted by him, in the [alternative in Chrys and Thl] view of their having been *committed to him by Christ* (i) *his own soul*, as entrusted to him by God, as Bretschneider, al, after Josephus, B J iii. 8 5, where speaking against suicide, he says, εἰλήφαμεν παρ' αὐτοῦ τὸ εἶναι . . . ψυχὴ ἀθάνατος ἀεί, καὶ θεοῦ μοῖρα τοῖς σώμασιν ἐνοικίζεται εἶτα ἂν μὲν ἀφανίσῃ τις ἀνθρώπου παρακαταθήκην, ἢ διάθηται κακῶς, πονηρὸς εἶναι δοκεῖ καὶ ἄπιστος And even more strikingly Philo, quis rerum div. hæres, 26, vol i p. 491 —τοῦτ' ἔπαινός ἐστι τοῦ σπουδαίου, τὴν ἱερὰν ἣν ἔλαβε παρακαταθήκην, ψυχῆς, αἰσθήσεως, λόγου, θείας σοφίας, ἀνθρωπίνης ἐπιστήμης, καθαρῶς καὶ ἀδόλως, μὴ ἑαυτῷ, μόνῳ δὲ τῷ πεπιστευκότι φυλάξαντος And Hermas Pastor, ii 3, p. 918 "qui ergo mentiuntur, abnegant Dominum, non reddentes Domino depositum, quod acceperunt" On all these, and this view of the παραθήκη generally, I may remark, that we may fairly be guided by the same words παραθήκην φύλαξον in ver. 14 as to their sense here And from this consideration I deduce an inference precisely the contrary to that of De Wette He argues from it, that παραθήκη must necessarily have the same meaning in both places, without reference to the verb with which it is joined. and consequently that because in ver. 14 it signifies a matter entrusted to Timotheus, therefore here it must signify a matter entrusted to St. Paul But this surely is a very lax and careless way of reasoning. The analogy between the two verses, if good for any thing, goes further than this As, in ver 14, παραθήκην φυλάξαι is said of the subject of the sentence, viz Timotheus, keeping a deposit entrusted to him,—so here παραθήκην φυλάξαι must be said of the subject of the sentence, viz. God, keeping a deposit entrusted to Him. Otherwise, while keeping the mere word παραθήκη to the same formal meaning in both places, we shall, most harshly and unnaturally, be requiring the phrase παραθήκην φυλάξαι to bear, in two almost consecutive verses, two totally different meanings. The analogy therefore of ver 14, which De W uses so abundantly for his view, makes, if thoroughly considered, entirely against it, and in fact necessitates the adoption of the first alternative, viz. the objective genitive,—and the *deposit committed by the Apostle to God*. And when we enquire what this deposit was, we have the reply, I conceive, in the previous words, ᾧ πεπίστευκα [see this especially shewn in the quotation from Philo above, where the πεπιστευκώς is *God*, not man] He had entrusted HIMSELF, body, soul, and spirit, to the keeping of his heavenly Father, and lay safe in his hands, confident of His abiding and effectual care A strong confirmation of this view is gained,—notwithstanding what Ellic. says of the moral reference there, and not here: for the parallel is to be sought not between φυλάξαι and ἁγιάσαι, but between φυλάξαι and τηρῆσαι, which is a very close one,—from 1 Thess. v. 23, αὐτὸς δὲ ὁ θεὸς τῆς εἰρήνης ἁγιάσαι ὑμᾶς ὁλοτελεῖς, καὶ ὁλόκληρον ὑμῶν τὸ πνεῦμα καὶ ἡ ψυχὴ καὶ τὸ σῶμα ἀμέμπτως ἐν τῇ παρουσίᾳ τοῦ κυρίου ἡμῶν Ἰησοῦ χριστοῦ τηρηθείη) for (with reference to, as an object,—'against,' as we say, in a temporal sense. not simply '*until*') that day (viz. the day of the παρουσία, see reff, and cf especially ch. iv. 8) 13.] The utmost care is required, in interpreting this verse, to ascertain the probable meaning of the words in reference to the context. On the right appreciation of this depends the question, whether they are to be taken in their strict meaning, and simple grammatical sense, or to be forced to some possible but far-fetched rendering. It has been generally, as far as I know by all the Commentators, assumed that ὑποτύπωσιν ἔχε = ἔχε (= κάτεχε, see reff.) τὴν ὑποτύπωσιν, and that then ὑγιαινόντων λόγων is to be taken as a subject gen. after ὑποτύπ., i e as in E V., '*Hold fast the form of sound words*.' thus making the exhortation perfectly general,—equivalent in fact to the following one in ver. 14 But to this there are several objections. The

[o] ὧν παρ' ἐμοῦ ἤκουσας [p] ἐν πίστει καὶ ἀγάπῃ [q] τῇ ἐν
χριστῷ Ἰησοῦ· 14 τὴν [r] καλὴν [s] παραθήκην [t] φύλαξον
[t] διὰ [t] πνεύματος ἁγίου τοῦ [u] ἐνοικοῦντος ἐν ἡμῖν.

o attr, Eph i 6 reff p 1 Tim i 2 reff q 1 Tim i 14 reff r 1 Tim i 18 reff s ver 12 t Acts i 2 xi 28 xxi 4 Rom v 5 Eph iii 16 2 Thess ii 2 Heb ix 14 1 Pet i 22 u ver 5 reff

14 rec παρακαταθηκην, with b f g. txt ACDFKLℵ rel (in ver 12 b g k al have παρακαταθ)

want of the art. before ὑποτύπωσιν might indeed be got over: a definite word emphatically prefixed to its verb is frequently anarthrous. But (1) this sense of ἔχε can hardly be maintained in its present unemphatic position The sense is found (or something approaching to it, for it would require to be stronger here than in either place) in the reff., but in both, the verb *precedes* the substantive, as indeed always throughout the N T. where any stress whatever is to be laid on it. Cf, for some examples of both arrangements, (a) ἔχω preceding, with more or less reference to its sense of having or holding, as a matter to be taken into account, Matt v 23, viii 9 ||, xi 15 || (always thus), al ,—Mark ix. 50, x. 21, xi. 22, al.,—Luke iii 11, viii. 6, xi. 5, al ,—John iii. 15, 16, 29, 36, al ,—Acts ii 44, 47, ix 14, 31, &c ,—Rom. ii. 20, iv 2, vi. 22 (cf. ver. 21), xii 6, &c . and (b) ἔχω following its substantive, with always the stress on the subst, and not on the verb, Matt. iii. 11, v 16, viii 20, &c.,—Mark iii. 22, 26, viii. 14—18, &c.,—Luke iii. 8, viii 13, &c.,—John ii 3, iv. 17 (instances of *both* arrangements, and each in full significance), &c ,—Rom xiv 22, &c. I cannot therefore assent to the view, which would give ἔχε the chief emphasis in the sentence, but must reserve that emphasis for ὑποτύπωσιν Then (2) there is an objection to taking ὑποτύπωσιν as '*a form*' with a subjective genitive,—a '*form consisting of sound words*.' The word is once only used (ref) elsewhere, and that in these Epistles, as a 'pattern,' 'specimen ' and there can hardly be a doubt that so uncommon a word must be taken, as again used by the same writer, in the same meaning, unless the context manifestly point to another. (3) A third objection, not so important as the other two, but still a valid one, will be that according to the usual rendering, the relative ὧν would much more naturally be ἥν, referring as it ought to do in that case to ὑποτύπωσιν, the object of ἔχε, not to the λόγοι of which that ὑποτύπωσις was composed This being so, we shall have the rendering so far,—**Have (take) an ensample of (the) healthy words which thou heardest of me in faith and love which are in Christ Jesus** Then two questions arise for us. to what (1) does ὑποτύπωσιν ἔχε refer? I answer,—to the saying immediately preceding, οἶδα γὰρ κ τ λ This was one of those πιστοὶ λόγοι or ὑγιαίνοντες λόγοι, of which we hear so often in these Epistles; one which, in his timidity, Timotheus was perhaps in danger of forgetting, and of which therefore the Apostle reminds him, and bids him take it as a specimen or pattern of those sound words which had been committed to him by his father in the faith To what (2) do the words ἐν πίστει κ. ἀγάπῃ τ ἐν χρ Ἰησ. refer? Certainly not, as Thdrt , to παρ' ἐμοῦ, taking ἐν as = περὶ (τὴν παρ' ἐμοῦ περὶ πίστεως κ. ἀγάπης γεγενημένην διδασκαλίαν) not, again, to ἔχε, to which in our understanding of ὑποτύπωσιν ἔχε, such a qualification would be altogether inapplicable. but to ἤκουσας, reminding Timotheus of the readiness of belief, and warmth of affection, with which he had at first received the wholesome words from the mouth of the Apostle, and thus tacitly reproaching him for his present want of growth in that faith and love, q. d Let me in thus speaking, 'I know whom I have believed &c ,' call to thy mind, by one example, those faithful sayings, those words of spiritual health, which thou once heardest with such receptivity and ardour as a Christian believer. [I am bound to add, that Chrys., having too much sense of the import of the Greek arrangement, does not fall into the ordinary mistake of making ἔχε = κάτεχε and emphatic, but, as will be seen, understands it, "From the ὑγιαίνοντες λόγοι which I delivered thee, take thine examples and maxims on every subject." But that would rather require ὑγιαίνοντας λόγους οὓς . . . I subjoin his words, καθάπερ ἐπὶ τῶν ζωγράφων ἐνετυπωσάμην, φησίν, εἰκόνα σοι τῆς ἀρετῆς, καὶ τῶν τῷ θεῷ δοκούντων (εὐδοκούντων?) ἁπάντων, ὥσπερ τινὰ κανόνα κ. ἀρχέτυπον κ ὅρους καταβαλὼν εἰς τὴν σὴν ψυχήν. ταῦτα οὖν ἔχε, κἂν περὶ πίστεως, κἂν περὶ ἀγάπης, κἂν περὶ σωφρονισμοῦ δέῃ τι βουλεύσασθαι, ἐκεῖθεν λάμβανε τὰ παραδείγματα. Ellic.'s note seems not altogether

15 Οἶδας τοῦτο ὅτι ᵛ ἀπεστράφησάν με πάντες οἱ ἐν
τῇ Ἀσίᾳ, ʷ ὧν ἐστιν Φύγελος καὶ Ἑρμογένης. 16 ˣʸ δῴη
ᶻ ἔλεος ὁ κύριος τῷ Ὀνησιφόρου ᶻ οἴκῳ, ὅτι πολλάκις με
ᵃ ἀνέψυξεν καὶ τὴν ᵇ ἅλυσίν μου οὐκ ᶜ ἐπαισχύνθη, 17 ἀλλὰ
γενόμενος ἐν Ῥώμῃ ᵈᵉ σπουδαιότερον ἐζήτησέν με καὶ εὗρεν.

ACD¹ KLℵ a c d e f h k l n o 17

v = Matt v 42. Tit i 14. Heb xii 25. w Wisd xvi 8. w gen, 1 Tim i 20. ch ii 17. x form, Eph i 17 reff. y here only. Isa xlvii 6. z = Acts x 2. xvi 15, 31. 1 Cor i 16. 1 Tim iii 4 al. a here only intr in LXX, Exod xxiii 12. 2 Kings xvi 14 al (-ψυξις, Acts iii 20). b Eph vi 20 reff. c ver 8. d 2 Cor viii 17 bis, 22 only. Ezek xli 25 (-ρως, Luke vii 4. Phil ii 28. Tit iii 13). e compar, Phil i 12 reff.

15 rec φυγελλος, with A rel copt Orig Thdrt: txt CDFKLℵ c e m n 17 latt syr goth arm Bas Chr Damasc Jer Ambrst Pelag.

16 rec επησχυνθη, with Kℵ rel Chr: txt ACDL c d f k¹ m o 17 Bas Œc Thdrt-ed (ℵ¹ altered to txt but erased αι)—καταισχυνθη F.

17. σπουδαιως (*corrn appy, the comparative not appearing appropriate?*) CD¹Fℵ 17. 67² Orig Bas: txt D³KL rel Chr Thdrt Damasc, σπουδαιοτερως A 73. ανεζητησεν C.

perspicuous. He does not enter into the difficulty: and his "not for κάτεχε, though somewhat approaching it in meaning," leaves the student under some doubt as to whether he does or does not agree with the E. V.] Then as following on this single example, the whole glorious deposit is solemnly committed to his care:—being a servant of One who will keep that which *we* have entrusted to HIM, do thou in thy turn keep that which HE, by my means, has entrusted to *thee*. 14] **that goodly deposit keep, through the Holy Spirit who dwelleth in us** (not thee and me merely, but all believers: cf. Acts xiii. 52. Chrys. remarks: *οὐ γάρ ἐστιν ἀνθρωπίνης ψυχῆς οὐδὲ δυνάμεως, τοσαῦτα ἐμπιστευθέντα, ἀρκέσαι πρὸς τὴν φυλακήν. διὰ τί; ὅτι πολλοὶ οἱ λησταί, σκότος βαθύ, ὁ διάβολος ἐφέστηκεν ἤδη κ. ἐφεδρεύει*).

15—18.] *Notices of the defective adherence of certain brethren.* These notices are intimately connected with what has preceded. He has held up to Timotheus, as an example, his own boldness and constancy: and has given him a sample of the faithful sayings which ruled his own conduct, in ver. 12. He proceeds to speak of a few of the discouragements under which in this confidence he was bearing up: and, affectionate gratitude prompting him, and at the same time by way of an example of fidelity to Timotheus, he dilates on the exception to the general dereliction of him, which had been furnished by Onesiphorus. **Thou knowest this, that all who are in Asia** (it does not follow, as Chrys., that *εἰκὸς ἦν, ἐν Ῥώμῃ εἶναι πολλοὺς τότε τῶν ἀπὸ τῶν Ἀσίας μερῶν*: this would rather require *οἱ ἀπὸ τῆς Ἀσίας*: but he uses the expression with reference to him to whom he was writing, who was in Asia) **repudiated me** (not as E. V., '*are* turned away from me' [perf.]: the act referred to took place at a stated time, and from what follows, that time appears to have been on occasion of a visit to Rome. They were ashamed of Paul the prisoner, and did not seek him out, see ch. iv. 16.—*ἔφυγον τοῦ ἀποστόλου τὴν συνουσίαν διὰ τὸ Νέρωνος δέος*, Thdrt.: but perhaps not so much from this motive, as from the one hinted at in the praise of Onesiphorus below. The **πάντες** must of course apply to all of whom the Apostle *had had trial* [and not even those without exception, vv. 16—18]: the E. V. gives the idea, that a *general apostasy* of all in Asia from St. Paul had taken place. On ASIA, i. e. the proconsular Asia, see note, Acts xvi. 6), **of whom is** (*ἐστιν* is hardly to be pressed as indicating that *at the present moment* Phygelus and Hermogenes were in Rome and were shunning him: it merely includes them in the class just mentioned) **Phygelus and Hermogenes** (why their names are specially brought forward, does not appear. Suetonius, Domit. c. 10, mentions a certain Hermogenes of Tarsus, who was put to death by Domitian 'propter quasdam in historia figuras'). 16] **May the Lord give mercy** (an expression not found elsewhere in N. T.) **to the house of Onesiphorus** (from this expression, here and in ch. iv. 19, and from what follows, ver. 18, it has been not improbably supposed, that Onesiphorus himself was no longer living at this time. Some indeed, as Thdrt. [*οὐ μόνον αὐτῷ ἀλλὰ καὶ παντὶ τῷ οἴκῳ τὸν θεῖον ἀντέδωκεν ἔλεον*], Calv. ["ob cum toti familiæ bene precatur. Unde colligimus Dei benedictionem non tantum super caput justi sed super totam domum residere"], al., take it as merely an extension of the gratitude of the Apostle from

18 ^xf^ δῴη αὐτῷ ὁ κύριος ^gh^ εὑρεῖν ^h^ ἔλεος παρὰ κυρίου ἐν
^i^ ἐκείνῃ τῇ ^i^ ἡμέρᾳ. καὶ ὅσα ἐν Ἐφέσῳ ^k^ διηκόνησεν
^e^ βέλτιον σὺ γινώσκεις.
II. 1 Σὺ οὖν, ^l^ τέκνον μου, ^m^ ἐνδυναμοῦ ^n^ ἐν τῇ χάριτι
^o^ τῇ ἐν χριστῷ Ἰησοῦ, 2 καὶ ἃ ἤκουσας παρ' ἐμοῦ ^p^ διὰ
πολλῶν μαρτύρων, ταῦτα ^q^ παράθου πιστοῖς ἀνθρώποις,
οἵτινες ^r^ ἱκανοὶ ἔσονται καὶ ἑτέρους διδάξαι. 3 ^s^ συγ-

f = Rom xi 5 Rev iii 21 vi 1 & passim g = Luke ix 12 Acts vii 11 (Rom iv 1) Gen vi 8 h here only Numb xi 15 i ver 12 k trans, 2 Cor iii 3 viii 19, 20 1 Pet i 12 iv 10 only †

l 1 Tim i 2 reff m Acts ix 22 Rom iv 20 Eph vi 10 al³ Paul, or of Paul, exc Heb xi 34 Ps li 7 n = Eph vi 10 o 1 Tim i 14 reff p = Rom ii 27 iv 11 2 Cor ii 4 al (Winer, edn 6, § 47 i) δια μαρτυρων κλαιειν, Philo, leg ad Cai § 29, vol ii p 573 q = 1 Tim i 18 only (Matt xiii 24 al) r = and constr, 1 Cor xv 9 s ch i 8 only †

18 ελεον (not in ver 16) D³K o n. for κυριου, θεω D¹ κυριω D³ Chr-ms Thdrt₁.

Onesiphorus to his household: but ch iv. 19 is against this Thdrt. indeed [as also Chrys] understands that Onesiphorus was *with him* at this time: but the aorists here [cf γενόμενος] will hardly allow that), **because on many occasions he refreshed me** (from ψύχω, not from ψυχή. Any kind of refreshing, of body or mind, may be implied), **and was not ashamed of** (ver 8) **my chain** (reff) **but when he was in Rome, sought me out with extraordinary diligence** (literally: with more diligence than could have been looked for. Or perhaps, **the more diligently** scil. because I was in chains *They* all ἀπεστράφησάν με *he* not only did not this, but earnestly sought me) **and found me** 18.] **May the Lord grant to him to find mercy from the Lord** (the account to be given of the double κύριος, κυρίου, here is simply this—that δῴη ὁ κύριος had become so completely a formula, that the recurrence was not noticed This, which is Huther's view, is far better than to suppose the second κυρ merely = ἑαυτοῦ, or to enter into theological distinctions between κύριος as the Father, and παρὰ κυρίου as from the Son, the Judge) **in that day** (see on ver. 12) **and how many services he did** (to me: or, to the saints: the general expression will admit of either) **in Ephesus** (being probably an Ephesian, cf. ch. iv. 19), **thou knowest well** (the comparative is not for the positive, here or any where. but the signification is, 'better, than that I need remind thee').

CH II 1—26] *Exhortations to Timotheus, founded on the foregoing examples and warnings.* 1] **Thou therefore** (οὖν follows, primarily on his own example just propounded [cf. συγκακοπάθησον below], and secondarily on that of Onesiphorus, in contrast to those who had been ashamed of and deserted him), **my child, be strengthened** (reff. The *pres* indicates an abiding state, not a mere insulated act, as παράθου below The verb is passive, not middle see reff, and Fritzsche on Rom iv 20) **in the grace which is in Christ Jesus** (τουτέστι διὰ τῆς χάριτος τοῦ χριστοῦ, Chrys But more than that the grace of Christ, the empowering influence in the Christian life, being necessary for its whole course and progress, is regarded as the *element in* which it is lived: cf αὐξάνετε ἐν χάριτι, 2 Pet ult χάρις must not be taken, with Ambr., Calov, Mack, al, for his *ministerial office*), **and the things which thou heardest from me with many witnesses** (i e with the intervention, or [as Conyb] attestation of many witnesses διά [reff] imports the agency of the witnesses as contributing to the whole matter treated of so διὰ πολλῶν δακρύων, and διὰ προφητείας, 1 Tim. iv 14 These witnesses are not, as Chrys, Thdrt, the congregations whom Timotheus had heard the Apostle teaching [ἅπερ ἤκουσάς μου πολλοὺς διδάσκοντος, Thdrt], or as Clem. Alex in Œc, testimonies from the law and prophets: nor as Heydenr, the other Apostles: much less, as he gives in another alternative, the Christian martyrs: but *the presbyters and others present at his ordination*, cf 1 Tim iv 14; vi. 12; and ch i 6 No word such as μαρτυρούμενα or βεβαιούμενα [Heydenr] need be supplied), **these deliver in trust** (cf. παραθήκην above, ch i. 14) **to faithful men** (i. e. not merely 'believers,' but 'trustworthy men,' men who τὴν καλὴν παραθήκην φυλάξονται) **such as shall be** (not merely 'are,' but 'shall be'—give every hope of turning out) **able to teach them to** (so I take ἑτέρους, not as a first, but as a second accusative after διδάξαι, the first being included in ταῦτα above) **others also** (καί carries the mind on to a

κακοπάθησον ὡς [t] καλὸς [u] στρατιώτης χριστοῦ Ἰησοῦ. ACDF
4 οὐδεὶς [v] στρατευόμενος [w] ἐμπλέκεται ταῖς τοῦ βίου [x] πρα- KLℵ a b c d e f g
γματείαις, ἵνα τῷ [y] στρατολογήσαντι [z] ἀρέσῃ. 5 ἐὰν δὲ h k l m n o 17

t = John x 11. 1 Tim iv 6. 1 Pet iv 10.
u Paul, here only (συστρ., Philem 2)
v 1 Tim i 18 reff
w 2 Pet ii 20 only. Prov xxviii 18 only
x here only. 1 Chron xxviii 21 (-τευεσθαι, Luke xix 13)
y here only †. Jos B J v. 9. 4
z Rom viii 8. Gal i 10 reff

Chap II 3 rec (for συγκακοπαθ) συ ουν κακοπαθησον, with C[3]D[2,3]KL rel goth gr-ff (Bloomf.'s assertion that Syr '*must have read*' σὺ οὖν, is contrary to fact, see Ellic: and his express citation of B for that reading, when B *does not contain this Ep. at all*, is, it is to be feared, but a sample of the value of his statements in such matters) txt AC[1]D[1]Fℵ 17 Syr syr-marg-gr copt arm, *labora* latt Aug Ambrst Pelag Gild συνστρατιωτης D[1]. rec ιησ. bef χρ., with D[3]KL rel Syr gr-ff· txt ACD[1]F m 17 latt goth syr copt Aug Ambrst Pelag

4. aft στρατευομενος ins τω θεω F vulg Cypr Ambrst-txt Gild Jer Pelag; *domino* goth. θεου arm-ed-marg

further step of the same process—implying 'in their turn.' These ἕτεροι would be *other trustworthy men* like themselves). The connexion of this verse with the foregoing and the following has been questioned. I believe it to be this 'The true keeping of the deposit entrusted to thee will involve thy handing it on unimpaired to others, who may in their turn hand it on again. But in order to this, thou must be strong in grace—thou must be a fellow-sufferer with me in hardships—thou must strive lawfully—thou must not be entangled with this life's matters' So that ver. 2 serves to prepare him to hear of the necessity of endurance and faithful adhesion to his duty as a Christian soldier, considering that he has his deposit not only to keep, but to deliver down unimpaired. It is obviously a perversion of the sense to regard this verse as referring (as Bengel, 'παράθου, antequam istinc ad me proficiscare') merely to his journey to Rome—that *during that time* he should, &c the ἔσονται, and the very contemplation of a similar step on the part of these men at a future time, are against such a supposition.

Mack constructs a long argument out of this verse to shew that there are *two sources* of Christian instruction in the Church, written teaching and oral, and ends with affirming that those who neglect the latter for the former, have always shewn that they in reality set up their own opinion above all teaching. But he forgets that these two methods of teaching are in fact but one and the same. *Scripture* has been *God's way* of *fixing tradition*, and rendering it trustworthy at any distance of time, of obviating the very danger which in this Epistle we see so imminent, viz. of one of those teachers, who were links in this chain of transmission, becoming inefficient and transmitting it inadequately. This very Epistle is therefore a warning to us not to trust oral tradition, seeing that it was so dependent on men, and to accept no way of conserving it but that which God's providence has pointed out to us in the canonical books of Scripture

3.] **Suffer hardship with me** (Conyb. happily renders it, 'Take thy share in suffering.' The **συγ-** binds it **to** what precedes and follows, referring primarily to the Apostle himself, though doubtless having a wider reference to all who similarly suffer see above, on the connexion of ver 2), **as a good soldier of Jesus Christ** 4.] **No soldier when on service is** (suffers himself to be · the passive sense predominates 'is,' as his normal state Or the verb may be middle, as Ellic, '*entangleth himself*,' and vulg, '*implicat se*') **entangled** (cf.; 'ἐν βιαίοις ἐνπλακέντων πόνοις, Plat Legg vii p 814 e. Grot. quotes from Cicero 'occupationibus implicatus:' and we have in de Off ii 11, 'qui contrahendis negotiis implicantur') **in the businesses of life** (cf Plato, Rep vi p. 500, οὐδὲ γάρ που . . . . σχολὴ τῷ γε ὡς ἀληθῶς πρὸς τοῖς οὖσι τὴν διάνοιαν ἔχοντι κάτω βλέπειν εἰς ἀνθρώπων πραγματείας: Arrian, Epict. iii. 22 [Wetst.], ὡς ἐν παρατάξει, μήποτ' ἀπερίσπαστον εἶναι δεῖ, ὅλον πρὸς τῇ διακονίᾳ τοῦ θεοῦ . . . οὐ προσδεδεμένον καθήκουσιν ἰδιωτικοῖς, οὐδ' ἐμπεπλεγμένον σχέσεσιν: Ambros. de Offic. i 36 [184], vol iii p. 49, 'si is, qui imperatori militat, a susceptionibus litium, actu negotiorum forensium, venditione mercium prohibetur humanis legibus, quanto magis &c' Ps-Athanas. quæst in Epistolas Pauli 117 εἰ γὰρ ἐπιγείῳ βασιλεῖ ὁ μέλλων στρατεύεσθαι οὐκ ἀρέσει, ἐὰν μὴ ἀφήσῃ πάσας τὰς τοῦ βίου φροντίδας, πόσῳ μᾶλλον μέλλων στρατεύεσθαι τῷ ἐπουρανίῳ βασιλεῖ, see other examples in Wetst. "Vox Græca πραγμάτεια (פרקמטיא), pro mercatura,

καὶ [a] ἀθλῇ τις, οὐ [b] στεφανοῦται ἐὰν μὴ [c] νομίμως [a] ἀθλήσῃ. 6 τὸν [d] κοπιῶντα [e] γεωργὸν δεῖ πρῶτον τῶν καρπῶν

a here (bis) only † (Λθλησις, Heb x. 32) b Heb ii 7, 9 (from Ps viii 5) only c 1 Tim i. 8 only † (see note) d Matt vi 28 Acts xx 35 (Paul) Rom xvi 6 al Job xxxix 16 e Paul, here only Matt xxi 33, &c and ‖ John xv 1 James v 7 only Jer. xiv 4

5. om δε A: *nam* vulg 6 πρωτερον (ω marked for erasure) ℵ[1]: txt ℵ[3].

sæpius occurrit in Pandectis Talmudicis" Schöttgen On the whole matter, consult Grotius's note), **that he may please him who called him to be a soldier** (who originally enrolled him as a soldier the word signifies *to levy soldiers*, or *raise a troop*, and ὁ στρατολογήσας designates the commander of such troop So ἀντὶ τῶν ἀπολωλότων ἀνδρῶν στρατολογήσαντες ἐξ ἁπάσης φυλῆς, Dion. Hal xi 24. The same writer uses στρατολογία for a *muster*, a levy of soldiers,—vi. 44; ix 38 The 'cui se probavit' of the vulgate is unintelligible, unless as Grot. suggests, it is an error for '*qui* se probavit.' The taking of these precepts according to the letter, to signify that no minister of Christ may have a secular occupation, is quite beside the purpose: for 1) it is not ministers, but all soldiers of Christ who are spoken of 2) the position of the verb ἐμπλέκεται shews that it is not the fact of the *existence* of such occupation, but the being *entangled* in it, which is before the Apostle's mind. 3) the Apostle's own example sufficiently confutes such an idea Only then does it become unlawful, when such occupation, from its engrossing the man, becomes a hindrance to the work of the ministry,—or from its nature is incompatible with it)

5] The soldier must serve on condition of not dividing his service now we have another instance of the same requirement and in the conflicts of the arena there are certain laws, without the fulfilment of which no man can obtain the victory **But** (the above is not the only example, but) **if any one also** (q. d. to give another instance) **strive in the games** (it is necessary to adopt a periphrasis for ἀθλῇ. That of E V. '*strive for masteries*,' is not definite enough, omitting all mention of the games, and by consequence not even suggesting them to the ordinary reader The vulg. gives it 'certat in agone' and Luth, merely kämpfet so also Ostervald and Diodati Scio,—'lidia en los juegos publicos' The word ἀθλεῖν, in the best Attic writers, means 'to work,' 'to endure,' and ἀθλεύειν, 'to contend in the games' [See however Ellic's note.] This usage belongs to later Greek see Palm and Rost's Lex), **he is not crowned** (even in case of his gaining the victory? or is the word inclusive of all efforts made to get the crown,—'he has no chance of the crown?' rather the former, from ἀθλήσῃ below), **unless he have striven** (this seems to assume the getting of the victory) **lawfully** (according to the prescribed conditions [not merely of the contest, but of the preparation also, see Ellic.]. It is the usual phrase so Galen, comm. in Hippocr i. 15· οἱ γυμνασταὶ καὶ οἱ νομίμως ἀθλοῦντες, ἐπὶ μὲν τοῦ ἀρίστου τὸν ἄρτον μόνον ἐσθίουσιν, ἐπὶ δὲ τοῦ δείπνου τὸ κρέας: Arrian, Epict iii. 10,—εἰ νομίμως ἤθλησας, εἰ ἔφαγες ὅσα δεῖ, εἰ ἐγυμνάσθης, εἰ τοῦ ἀλείπτου ἤκουσας [Wetst., where see more examples]. Compare the parallel place, 1 Cor ix. 24.—τί ἐστιν, ἐὰν μὴ νομίμως, οὐκ, ἐάν τις τὸν ἀγῶνα εἰσέλθῃ, ἀρκεῖ τοῦτο, οὐδὲ ἐὰν ἀλείψηται, οὐδὲ ἐὰν συμπλακῇ, ἀλλὰ ἂν μὴ πάντα τὸν τῆς ἀθλήσεως νόμον φυλάττῃ, καὶ τὸν ἐπὶ σιτίων, καὶ τὸν ἐπὶ σωφροσύνης καὶ σεμνότητος, καὶ τὸν ἐν παλαίστρᾳ, καὶ πάντα ἁπλῶς διέλθοι τὰ τοῖς ἀθληταῖς προσήκοντα, οὐδέποτε στεφανοῦται Chrys).

6] Another comparison shewing the necessity of active labour as an antecedent to reward. **The husbandman who is engaged in labour** (who is actually employed in gathering in the fruit: not κοπιάσαντα) **must first partake of the fruits** (which he is gathering in. the whole result of his ministry, not here further specified The saying is akin to βοῦν ἀλοῶντα μὴ φιμώσεις—the right of first participation in the harvest belongs to him who is labouring in the field do not thou therefore, by relaxing this labour, forfeit that right. By this rendering, keeping strictly to the sense of the *present* part, all difficulty as to the position of πρῶτον is removed. Many Commentators [Calv., E. V. marg, al, Grot, al, take πρῶτον for '*ita demum*'] not observing this have supposed, in the sense, a transposition of πρῶτον, and given it as if it were τὸν γεωργὸν δεῖ, κοπιῶντα πρῶτον, τῶν καρπῶν μεταλ, or as Wahl and Winer [so in older editions of his grammar, e. g edn 3, p 458 but now, edn. 6, § 61. 1, he merely states the two renderings, without giving an opinion],—τὸν

f Acts ii 46 (xxiv 25 w acc) xxvii 33 Heb vi 7 xii 10 only + Sir xviii 9 al (-λημψις, 1 Tim iv 3)

[f]μεταλαμβάνειν. 7 [g]νόει ὃ λέγω· δώσει γάρ σοι ὁ κύριος ACDF
[h]σύνεσιν [i]ἐν πᾶσιν. 8 [k]μνημόνευε Ἰησοῦν χριστὸν [lm]ἐγη- KLℵ a b c d e f g
γερμένον [m]ἐκ νεκρῶν, [n]ἐκ σπέρματος Δαυείδ, κατὰ τὸ h k l m n o 17
[o]εὐαγγέλιόν [o]μου, 9 [p]ἐν ᾧ [q]κακοπαθῶ [r]μέχρι [s]δεσμῶν

g = Matt xxiv 15 Eph iii 4 20. Isa xliv. 7 h Paul (1 Cor i 19 Eph iii 4 Col i 9 ii 2) only, exc Mark xii 23 Luke ii 47 Prov ii 2 i ch iv 5 reff k w. acc, Matt xvi 9 1 Thess ii 9 Rev xviii 5 1 Chron xvi 12 l constr particip, Acts vii 12 xix 35 xxiv 10 m Gal i 1 reff n John vii 42 Rom i 3 o Rom ii 16 xvi 25 only see 2 Cor iv 3 1 Thess i 5 2 Thess ii 14 p Phil iv 3 1 Thess iii 2 q ch iv 5. James v 13 only Jonah iv 10 only. (-θεια, James v 10.) r = Phil ii 8 Heb xii 4. 2 Macc. xiii 14 3 Macc vii 16 s Phil. i 7 reff

7. rec for ὅ, ἅ, with DKLℵ³ rel vulg syr copt txt ACFℵ¹ 17 Syr goth Chr-comm. rec δῴη (*probably change for the sake of softening, and rendering more likely, the exprn. The choice between the readings is difficult, the rec having a claim, as the harder one but the authority for txt is strong*), with KL rel syr Chr Thdrt, δωει C³. txt AC¹DFℵ 17 67² latt copt arm Damasc Ambrst Pelag Hil Vig-taps
8 μνημονευειν χρ ιησ. D¹ 111

γ τὸν θέλοντα τῶν κ μεταλ, δεῖ πρῶτον κοπιᾷν but in both cases κοπιάσαντα would seem to be, if not absolutely required, yet more natural Thdrt. and Œc. understand πρῶτον of the preference which the teacher has over the taught,—πρὸ γὰρ τῶν κεκτημένων οἱ γηπόνοι μεταλαγχάνουσι τῶν καρπῶν Ambr, Pel, Mosh believe the bodily support of ministers to be imported by τῶν κ μεταλ: but Chrys answers this well, οὐκ ἔχει λόγον· πῶς γὰρ οὐχ ἁπλῶς γεωργὸν εἶπεν, ἀλλὰ τὸν κοπιῶντα; but his own idea hardly seems to be contained in the words,—πρὸς τὴν μέλλησιν ἵνα μηδεὶς δυσχεραίνῃ, ἤδη, φησίν, ἀπολαμβάνεις, ἢ ὅτι ἐν αὐτῷ τῷ κόπῳ ἡ ἀντίδοσις and certainly there is no allusion to that of Athanasius [in De W.], that it is the duty of a teacher first to apply to himself that which he teaches to others nor to that of Bengel, 'Paulus Timothei animam excoluit, c. i. 6, ergo fructus ei imprimis ex Timotheo debentur') 7] **Understand** (νοεῖν . "ist die innerlich tiefe, sittlich ernste Verstandesthätigkeit." Beck, Biblische Seelenlehre, p. 56 It is the preparatory step to συνιέναι,—id. ib. note, and p. 59,—which is "ein den Zusammenhang mit seinen Gründen und Folgen begreifendes Erkennen") **what I say** (ἐπεὶ οὖν τὰ παραδείγματα ἔθηκε τὸ τῶν στρατιωτῶν κ ἀθλητῶν κ. γεωργῶν, καὶ πάντα ἁπλῶς αἰνιγματωδῶς . . . ἐπήγαγε, νόει ἃ λέγω, Chrys · so also Thdrt., all not as Calv, who denies the above, "hoc non addidit propter similitudinum obscuritatem, sed ut ipse suggereret Timotheo quanto præstantior sit sub Christi auspiciis militia, et quanto amplior merces" this would not agree with σύνεσιν δώσει): **for the Lord** (Christ) **shall give thee thorough understanding** (on σύνεσις, see citation from Beck above) **in all things** (i e thou art well able to penetrate the meaning and bearing of what I say for thou art not left to thyself, but hast the wisdom which is of Christ to guide thee. There is perhaps a slight intimation that he might apply to this fountain of wisdom more than he did.—'the Lord, if thou seekest it from Him').

8—13] This statement and substantiation of two of the leading facts of the gospel, seems, especially as connected with the exhortations which follow on it vv. 14 ff, to be aimed at the false teachers by whose assumption Timotheus was in danger of being daunted The Incarnation and Resurrection of Christ were two truths especially imperilled, and indeed denied, by their teaching At the same time these very truths, believed and persisted in, furnished him with the best grounds for stedfastness in his testimony to the Gospel, and attachment to the Apostle himself, suffering for his faithfulness to them. and on his adherence to these truths depended his share in that Saviour in whom they were manifested, and in union with whom, in His eternal and unchangeable truth, our share in blessedness depends **Remember, that Jesus Christ has been raised up from the dead** (the accus. after μνημόνευε imports that it is the *fact respecting* Jesus Christ, not so much He Himself, to which attention is directed [see reff] Ellic. takes exactly the other view, citing in its favour Winer, § 15. 4, who however implicitly maintains my rendering, by classing even 1 John iv 2, 2 John 7, with Heb xiii 23, γινώσκετε τὸν ἀδ. Τιμόθεον ἀπολελυμένον, which he renders "ihr wisset, dass . . entlassen ist." Ellic. refers to my note on 1 John iv. 2, as if it were inconsistent with the rendering here · but the verb there is ὁμολογεῖν,

ὡς ᵗ κακοῦργος, ἀλλὰ ὁ λόγος τοῦ θεοῦ οὐ δέδεται. 10 διὰ
τοῦτο ᵘ πάντα ᵘᵛ ὑπομένω διὰ τοὺς ʷ ἐκλεκτούς, ἵνα καὶ

t Luke xxiii 32, 33, 39 only. Prov xxi 15. Sir xi 33. xxx (xxxiii) 26 only. u 1 Cor xiii 7 v constr, Heb x 32. xii 2, 3. James i 12. Wisd xvi 22. w Rom viii 33. xvi 13. Col iii 12. 1 Tim v 21. Tit i 1 al. Prov xvii 3.

9 aft εν ω ins και F [αλλα, so ACD¹ℵ 17.] om ου ℵ¹.

not μνημονεύειν, which I conceive makes all the difference. According to Ellic.'s rendering, unless we refer ἐν ᾧ to Christ, which he does not, the context becomes very involved and awkward. The gen. is more usual in later Greek (see Luke xvii. 32. John xv. 20; xvi. 4, 21: Acts xx 35, &c.)—but the accus. in classical, see Palm and Rost sub voce, and cf Herod. i 36, Æschyl. Pers 769 [783 Dindorf], Soph Ag. 1273, Philoct 121, Eur Androm. 1165 [1141 Matthiæ], &c.), (Jesus Christ, who was) **of the seed of David** (this clause must be taken as = τὸν ἐκ σπέρμ. Δαυίδ, and the unallowable and otherwise unaccountable ellipsis of the article may probably be explained, as De W., by the words being part of a recognized and technical profession of faith. Compare Rom. i. 3, which is closely parallel. Mack's attempt to join ἐκ σπέρμ. Δ. to ἐγηγερμένον ἐκ νεκρ., 'that Jesus Christ was raised from the dead in His flesh, as He sprung from David,' is hardly worth refutation), **according to my Gospel** ('the Gospel entrusted to me to teach,' as in reff. Here the expression may seem to be used with reference to the false teachers,—but as in the other places it has no such reference, I should rather incline to regard it as a solemn way of speaking, identifying these truths with the preaching which had been the source of Timotheus's belief. Baur, in spite of ἐν ᾧ &c. following, understands this εὐαγγ. μου of the *Gospel of St Luke*, as having been written under the authority of St Paul. See Prolegg to St Luke's Gospel in Vol. I. § iii 6, note), **in which** ('cujus annuntiandi munere defungens,' Beza. see reff.) **I suffer hardship** (see ver 3) **even unto** (consult Ellic.'s note and his references on μέχρι) **chains** (see ch i 16) **as a malefactor** ('κακοπαθῶ, κακοῦργος—malum passionis, ut si præcessisset malum actionis,' Bengel), **but the word of God is not bound** (δεσμοῦνται μὲν αἱ χεῖρες, ἀλλ' οὐχ ἡ γλῶττα, Chrys. similarly Thdrt. But we shall better, though this reference to himself is not precluded [cf ch. iv 17. Acts xxviii 31], enlarge the words to that wider acceptation, in which he rejoices, Phil i 18. As regarded himself, the word of God *might* be said to be bound, inasmuch as he was prevented from the free proclamation of it: his person was not free, though his tongue and pen were. This more general reference Chrys. himself seems elsewhere to admit [as cited in Heydenr.]: ὁ διδάσκαλος ἐδέδετο καὶ ὁ λόγος ἐπέτετο· ἐκεῖνος τὸ δεσμωτήριον ᾤκει, καὶ ἡ διδασκαλία πτερωθεῖσα πανταχόσε τῆς οἰκουμένης ἔτρεχε. The purpose of adding this seems to be, to remind Timotheus, that *his* sufferings and imprisonment had in no way weakened the power of the Gospel, or loosened the ties by which he [Timotheus] was bound to the service of it: hardly as Chrys.: εἰ ἡμεῖς δεδεμένοι κηρύττομεν, πολλῷ μᾶλλον ὑμᾶς τοὺς λελυμένους τοῦτο ποιεῖν χρή). **10.] For this reason** (what reason? 'quia me vincto evangelium currit,' says Bengel: and with this agree Huther, De W., al. But neither 1) is this sound logic, nor 2) is it in accordance with the Apostle's usage of διὰ τοῦτο . . ἵνα. 1) The fact, that the word of God is not bound, is clearly not the reason why he suffers these things for the elect: nor can we say with Huther, that the *consciousness* of this fact is that in which he endures all. De W. takes the predominant idea to be, the dispersion and success of God's word, in and by which the Apostle is encouraged to suffer. But this would certainly, as Wolf says, render the connexion 'dilutior et parum cohærens.' 2) In 1 Tim i 16, διὰ τοῦτο ἠλεήθην . . ἵνα, and Philem 15 διὰ τοῦτο ἐχωρίσθη . . ἵνα, the reference of δ. τ. is evidently to what follows: cf also Rom iv. 16, 2 Cor xiii 10. I would therefore refer the words to the following, and consider them, as in the above instances, as a marked way of indicating the reason presently to be given: 'for this purpose, ... that,' so Chrys., Thdrt., Wolf, Wiesinger, al.) **I endure all things** (not merely suffer [obj.], but readiness and persistence [subj.] are implied in the word, and the universal πάντα belongs to this subj. meaning—'I am enduring, ready to bear, all things') **for the sake of the elect** (see reff., especially Tit i 1. The Apostle does not, as De W., refer merely to those elect of God who are not yet converted, but generally to the whole category, both those who are

x = Luke xx 35. Acts xxvi 22 (Paul) Heb xi 35. 2 Macc iv 6. y Rom iii 24. vii 39 1 Tim i 14 iii 13 ver 1 ch i 1, 13. iii 15 z 1 Pet v 10 see 2 Cor iv 17

αὐτοὶ σωτηρίας [x] τύχωσιν [y] τῆς [y] ἐν χριστῷ Ἰησοῦ μετὰ
[z] δόξης [a] αἰωνίου. 11 [a] πιστὸς ὁ [a] λόγος· εἰ γὰρ [bc] συναπ-
εθάνομεν, καὶ [bd] συνζήσομεν· 12 εἰ [e] ὑπομένομεν, καὶ [f] συμβα-
σιλεύσομεν· εἰ [g] ἀρνησόμεθα, κἀκεῖνος [g] ἀρνήσεται ἡμᾶς·
13 εἰ [h] ἀπιστοῦμεν, ἐκεῖνος [i] πιστὸς μένει· [g] ἀρνήσασθαι
γὰρ ἑαυτὸν οὐ δύναται.

ACDF KLℵ a c d e f g h k l m n o 17

a 1 Tim i 15 reff. b 2 Cor vii 3. c Mark xiv 31. 2 Cor as above only †. Sir xix 10 only. d Rom vi 8. 2 Cor as above only †. e Matt x 22. xxiv 13 || Mk. James v 11. 1 Pet ii 20. f 1 Cor iv 8 only †. g = 1 Tim v 8 reff. h Matt xvi 11, 16. Luke xxiv. 11, 41. Acts xxviii 24. Rom. iii 3 only †. Wisd x 7 al. (-τος, 1 Tim v 8.) i = 1 Thess. v 24 reff.

11 συνζησωμεν CL m[1] o

12. συμβασιλευσωμεν ACL. rec αρνουμεθα, with DKLℵ[3] rel syr goth: txt ACℵ[1] 17 vulg(not am demid) Chr Thl Cypr Tert.—om κ. συμβ. to πιστ next ver F.

13 rec om γαρ, with Kℵ[3] rel vulg D-lat syr goth Damasc lat-ff: ins ACDFLℵ[1] e g l m 17 Syr copt Chr Thdrt Ath.

already turned to him, and those who are yet to be turned: cf. the parallel declaration in Col. i. 24, ἀνταναπληρῶ τὰ ὑστερήματα τῶν θλίψεων τοῦ χριστοῦ . . . . ὑπὲρ τοῦ σώματος αὐτοῦ, ὅ ἐστιν ἡ ἐκκλησία), that they also (as well as ourselves, with reference to what is to follow, the certainty that we, who suffer with Him, shall reign with Him.—De W. [see above] says, 'those yet unconverted, as well as those already converted:' and the mere καὶ αὐτοί might seem to favour this view; but it manifestly is not so) may obtain the salvation which is in (as its element and condition of existence) Christ Jesus with eternal glory (salvation here, in its spiritual presence and power—χάριτί ἐστε σεσωσμένοι, Eph. ii. 5: and glory hereafter, the full development and expansion of salvation, Rom. viii. 21). Faithful is the saying (see on reff.: another of those current Christian sayings, probably the utterances originally of the Spirit by those who spoke προφητείας in the Church,—and, as in 1 Tim. iii. 16, bearing with it so much of balance and rhythmical arrangement, as to seem to be a portion of some hymn): for (Chrys., Œc., al., regard this γάρ as rendering a reason why the λόγος is πιστός, understanding πιστ. ὁ λ. of what has gone before, viz. the certainty that ὁ ζωῆς οὐρανίου τυχών, καὶ αἰωνίου τεύξεται. But this is most unnatural. The γάρ is not merely explicative, as Grot., Huther, al., but as in 1 Tim. iv. 9, renders a reason for the πιστός,—in the assertion of the fact in well-known words: for the fact is so, that if &c.) if we died with Christ (on account of the aorist, pointing to some one definite event, the reference must be to that participation in Christ's death which takes place at baptism in all those who are His, and which those who follow Him in sufferings emphatically shew that they then did really take on them: see Rom. vi. 3, 4, 8. Col. ii. 12. Certainly, if the aor. stood alone, it might be taken proleptically, looking back on life from that future day in which the συνζήσομεν will be realized: but coupled as it is with the present ὑπομένομεν and the future ἀρνησόμεθα, we can hardly take it otherwise than literally as to time of an event already past, and if so, strictly as in the parallel Rom. vi. 8, where the reference is clear), we shall also live with Him (hereafter in glory): if we endure (with Him: the συν must be supplied, cf. εἴπερ συνπάσχομεν, Rom. viii. 17), we shall also reign with Him (see Rom. v. 17; viii. 17. In the former pair, death and life are opposed; in this, subjection [ὑπο-μ.] and dominion. See the interesting anecdote of Nestor, quoted from the martyrology by Grotius): if we shall deny (Him), He also will deny us (see Matt. x. 33): if we disbelieve (not, His Resurrection, as Chrys.: εἰ ἀπιστοῦμεν ὅτι ἀνέστη, οὐδὲν ἀπὸ τούτου βλάπτεται ἐκεῖνος: nor His Divinity, as Œc. (2) ὅτι θεὸς ἐστί, but Him, generally. Ellic.'s note [which see] has convinced me that ἀπιστία seems always in the N. T. to imply not 'untrueness,' 'unfaithfulness,' but definitely 'unbelief:' see note on Rom. iii. 3, in Vol. II. edn. 5), He remains faithful (to His own word cited above): for He cannot deny Himself (i. e. if we desert faith in Him, He will not break faith with us; He having declared that whosoever denies Him shall be denied by Him, and we having pledged ourselves to confess Him,—we may become unbelieving, and break our pledge, but He will not break His: as He has said, it shall surely be. See Rom. iii. 3. Chrys. gives

14 Ταῦτα [j] ὑπομίμνησκε [k] διαμαρτυρόμενος [k] ἐνώπιον τοῦ
κυρίου μὴ [l] λογομαχεῖν, ἐπ' οὐδὲν [m] χρήσιμον, [n] ἐπὶ [o] κατα-
στροφῇ τῶν [p] ἀκουόντων. 15 [q] σπούδασον σεαυτὸν [r] δόκιμον [s] παραστῆσαι τῷ θεῷ, [t] ἐργάτην [u] ἀνεπαίσχυντον,

j Luke xxii 61. John xiv 26. Tit. iii. 1. 2 Pet. i. 12. 3 John 10. Jude 5. k ch. iv. 1 reff. l here only †. m constr., Ezek. xv. 4. n = Gal. v. 13. o 2 Pet. ii. 6. p 1 Tim. iv. 16. q ch. iv. 9, 21. r ch. ... s = Luke ii. 22. t = Paul, 2 Cor. xi. 13. Phil. iii. 2. 1 Tim. v. 18. Matt. xx. 1. u here only †.

14. διαμαρτυρουμενος C 238 Thdrt. om του D[1] 112. for κυριου, θεου CFN b e m syr-marg copt arm Chr Thl Ambrst. λογομαχει AC[1] latt æth Orig int lat-ff: txt C[3]DFKL N rel syrr copt goth Clem Chr Thdrt Damasc. rec for επ' ουδ., εις ουδεν, with DKL N[3] rel Chr_{aliq} $Thdrt_2$: επ ουδενι γαρ F lat-ff. txt ACN 17.
15. for θεω, χριστω A Damasc.

a curious explanation ἀληθὴς ἐστι, βεβαιός ἐστιν, ἄν τε εἴπωμεν, ἄν τε μὴ εἴπωμεν .... ἐκεῖνος γὰρ ὁ αὐτὸς μένει καὶ ἀρνουμένων καὶ μὴ ἀρνουμένων. ἀρνήσασθαι γὰρ ἑαυτὸν οὐ δύναται, τουτέστι, μὴ εἶναι. ἡμεῖς λέγομεν ὅτι οὐκ ἔστιν, εἰ καὶ μὴ τὸ πρᾶγμα οὕτως ἔχει. οὐκ ἔχει φύσιν μὴ εἶναι, οὐ δυνατόν· τουτέστιν, εἰς τὸ μὴ εἶναι αὐτὸν χωρῆσαι· ἀεὶ μένει, ἀεὶ ἔστιν αὐτοῦ ἡ ὑπόστασις. μὴ τοίνυν ὡς χαριζόμενοι αὐτῷ, οὕτω διακείμεθα, ἢ ὡς καταβλάπτοντες. But manifestly there is no such motive as this last brought forward, nor is the assertion ἐκεῖνος μένει, but ἐκ πιστὸς μένει. Mack proposes another alternative,—'If we fall from the faith and forfeit our own salvation, He still carries forward His own gracious will, in saving mankind by the Gospel.' But that given above seems best to suit the context).

14—26.] *Application of the above general exhortations to the teaching and conversation of Timotheus, especially with reference to the false teachers.* 14.] **These things** (those which have just preceded vv. 8—13) **call to their minds** (reff.: the minds viz. of those among whom thou art ministering, as the context shews: see a similar ellipsis in Tit. iii. 8), **testifying to them before the Lord not to contend with words** (see 1 Tim. vi. 4. The var. reading λογομάχει changes the whole arrangement, and attaches διαμαρτ. ἐνώπιον τοῦ κυρίου to the preceding. The chief objections to this are 1) that ὑπομίμνησκε διαμαρτυρόμενος ἐνώπ. τοῦ κυρίου is a very lame and inconsistent junction of terms, the strong emphasis of the διαμ. κ.τ.λ. not agreeing with the far weaker word ὑπομίμνησκε: 2) that in the other places where διαμαρτύρομαι occurs in St. Paul, it precedes an exhortation, e.g. 1 Tim. v. 21, ch. iv. 1, and μαρτύρομαι Eph. iv. 17),—**(a thing) useful** (χρήσιμον is in apposition with the preceding sentence, as καθαρίζον in the rec. reading of Mark vii. 19: see Winer, edn. 6, § 59. 9 b) **for no purpose** (the reading ἐπ' οὐδέν, which has been put by,—cf. Ellic. here,—on account of the rec., illustrating St. Paul's love of prepositional variation, does in fact illustrate it quite as much, ἐπί having dat. and accus. in the same sentence, cf. Ps. cxvii. 9 var. &c. χρήσιμος is constructed with εἰς in LXX, e.g., Ezek. xv. 4: Wisd. xiii. 11. Cf. also Wisd. xv. 15), (**but practised**) **to** (on condition of following from it as a necessary consequence as if it had been by covenant attached to it) **the ruin** (the opposite of οἰκοδομή, cf. καθαίρεσις, 2 Cor. xiii. 10) **of them that hear.** 15.] The connexion is close,—by averting them from vain and unprofitable things, approve thine own work, so that it may stand in the day of the Lord. **Strive** (reff.) **to present thyself** (emphatic, as distinguished from those alluded to in the preceding verse) **to God approved** (reff.: tested by trial, and found to have stood the test. Not to be joined with ἐργάτην, as Mack), **a workman** (a general word, of any kind of labourer, used [see reff.] of *teachers*: perhaps from the parable in Matt. xx) **unshamed** (by his work being found unworthy: cf. Phil. i. 20,—ἐν οὐδενὶ αἰσχυνθήσομαι, and 1 Cor. iv. 4: "cui tua ipsius conscientia nullum pudorem incutiat," Beng. Kypke quotes from Jos. Antt. xviii. 9 [but I cannot find the passage], μηδὲ δευτερεύειν ἀνεπαισχυντον ἡγοῦ, 'neque credas id pudore vacare, si secundum teneas locum.' Chrys., al., would take the word actively, '*not being ashamed of his work*,' τουτέστι, μηδὲν ὅλως αἰσχυνόμενον πράττειν τῶν εἰς εὐσέβειαν ἡκόντων, κἂν δουλεῦσαι δέῃ, κἂν ὁτιοῦν παθεῖν. Chrys.: and so Agapetus in Wetst., παρ' ἄλλῳ ἐρεθέντα μηδαμῶς παρορᾷ, ἀλλὰ μανθάνει μὲν ἀνεπαισχύντως: but the above seems more according to the context. The opposite to ἐργ.

v here only. Prov. iii. 6. xi. 5 only. w 2 Cor. vi. 7. Eph. i. 13. James i. 18. (see Gal. ii. 14.)

[v] ὀρθοτομοῦντα τὸν [w] λόγον τῆς ἀληθείας. 16 τὰς δὲ ACDF KLℵ a b c d e f g h k l m n o 17
[x] βεβήλους [y] κενοφωνίας [z] περιΐστασο· [a] ἐπὶ πλεῖον γὰρ
[b] προκόψουσιν [c] ἀσεβείας, 17 καὶ ὁ λόγος αὐτῶν ὡς [d] γάγ-

x 1 Tim. i. 9 reff. y 1 Tim. vi. 20 (there also w. βεβ.) only †. z = Tit. iii. 9 (John xi. 42. Acts xxv. 7) only †. a Acts iv. 17. xx. 9. xxiv. 4 (Paul). ch. iii. 9 only. Jer. ii. 12. b Luke ii. 52. Rom. xiii. 12. Gal. i. 14. ch. iii. 9, 13 only †. Ps. xliv. 4 Allus in Hexapl. προῦκοψαν εἰς τοσοῦτον παρανομίας, Jos. B. J. vi. 2. 2. (-πή, 1 Tim. iv. 15.) c Rom. i. 18. xi. 26. Tit. ii. 12. Jude 15, 18 only. Jer. v. 6. (-βεῖν, 2 Pet. ii. 6. -βής, 1 Tim. i. 9.) d here only †.

16. καινοφωνιας F D-lat Chr Lucif Aug Ambrst. (G-lat has both.) ασεβεις D[1]K; ασεβεια D[3].

ἀνεπαίσχυντος is ἐργάτης δόλιος, 2 Cor. xi. 13), **rightly administering** (the *meaning* of ὀρθοτομέω is very variously derived and explained,—'recte secare' being unquestionably the *rendering*. (1) Melanchthon, Beza, Grot., al., suppose the meaning deduced from the *right division of the victims*, Levit. i. 6 ff.: (2) Vitringa [de Synagog. p. 714, De W.], Calv., al., from the *cutting and distributing of bread* by the steward or father of a household: 'ac si pater alendis filiis panem in frusta secando distribueret.' (3) Priceus, 'a *lapicidis*, quos melius ἐργάτας vocaveris quam victimarios illos. Eurip. de Neptuno Trojam ædificante, λαΐνους πύργους πέριξ ὀρθοῖς ἔτεμνε κανόσιν,'—Apuleius, '*non*, inquit, *e monte meo afferam lapidem directim cæsum*, i.e. ὀρθοτετμημένον. Glossarium, *directum*, κατὰ κανόνα ὀρθωθέν:' (4) Thdrt. [ἐπαινοῦμεν τῶν γεωργῶν τοὺς εὐθείας τὰς αὔλακας ἀνατέμνοντας], Lamb-Bos, al., from *plowers*, who are said τέμνειν τὴν γῆν, σχίζειν and ἐπισχίζειν ἀρούρας: (5) Most Commentators, from the more general form of the last explanation, the *cutting* a *way* or a *road*: as 'καινοτομεῖν, novam viam secare, nova via incedere,' so 'ὀρθοτομεῖν, rectam viam secare,' but here used transitively, the λόγος τῆς ἀληθείας being itself the ὁδός: so in Prov. xi. 5, δικαιοσύνη ἀμώμους ὀρθοτομεῖ ὁδούς, and Eurip. Rhes. 422, εὐθεῖαν λόγων τέμνων κέλευθον: Gal. ii. 14, ὀρθοποδεῖν πρὸς τὴν ἀλήθειαν τοῦ εὐαγγελίου. So De W.: but Huther objects, and I think with reason, that in all these places the idea of a *way* is expressly introduced, and that without such expression we cannot supply the idea in λόγον. (6) Huther's own view, that, the original meaning being 'rightly to divide,' the idea of τέμνειν was gradually lost, as in καινοτομεῖν, so that the word came to signify 'to manage rightly,' 'to treat truthfully without falsifying,' seems to approach the nearest to the requirements of the context: the opposite being, as he observes, καπηλεύειν τὸν λόγον τοῦ θεοῦ, 2 Cor. ii. 17. (7) The meaning given by Chrys. and Œc.—τέμνε τὰ νόθα, καὶ τὰ τοιαῦτα μετὰ πολλῆς τῆς σφοδρότητος ἐφίστασο καὶ ἔκκοπτε, does not seem to belong to the word. (8) It is plain that the patristic usages of it, as e.g. in the Clementine Constt. vii. 33 [Grot.] ὀρθοτομοῦντας ἐν τοῖς κυρίου δόγμασι,—Clem. Alex., Strom. vii. 16 [104], p. 896 P., τὴν ἀποστολικὴν καὶ ἐκκλησιαστικὰν ὀρθοτομίαν τῶν δογμάτων,—Greg.-Naz. apol. fugæ, pp. 23, 28 [Kypke, from Fuller], opposing to ὀρθοτομεῖν, κακῶς ὁδεύειν,—have *sprung from this passage*, and cannot be cited as precedents, only as interpretations) **the word of the** (the art. seems here better expressed: cf. ver. 18 below, and the usage throughout these Epistles, e. g. 1 Tim. iii. 15; iv. 3; vi. 5; ch. iii. 8; iv. 4; Tit. i. 14) **truth.** 16.] **But** (contrast not to the ὀρθοτομεῖν merely, but to the whole course of conduct recommended in the last verse) **profane babblings** (see ref. 1 Tim.) **avoid** (= ἐκτρέπεσθαι, 1 Tim. vi. 20: so Origen has περιΐστασθαι κινδύνους [in Hammond]: Joseph. B. J. ii. 8. 6, of the Essenes, τὸ ὀμνύειν αὐτοῖς περιΐσταται: Lucian, Hermotim. c. 86, οὕτως ἐκτραπήσομαι καὶ περιστήσομαι, ὥσπερ τοὺς λυττῶντας τῶν κυνῶν: Marc. Antonin. iii. 4, χρὴ μὲν οὖν καὶ τὸ εἰκῆ καὶ μάτην ἐν τῷ εἱρμῷ τῶν φαντασιῶν περιΐστασθαι: see other examples in Wetst. The meaning seems to come from a number of persons falling back from an object of fear or loathing, and standing at a distance round it. Beza's sense, 'cohibe, i.e. observa et velut obside, nempe ne in ecclesiam irrepant,' has no countenance from usage): **for they** (the false teachers: not the κενοφωνίαι: cf. ὁ λόγος αὐτῶν below) **will advance** (intransitive, see reff.,—not transitive, governing ἀσεβείας in the accus.: see below) **to a worse pitch of impiety** (cf. ref. Jos., and Diodor. Sic. xiv. 98, ὁ δὲ βασιλεὺς οὐ βουλόμενος τὸν Εὐαγόραν προκόπτειν ἐπὶ πλεῖον . . . .), **and their word will eat**

γραινα [e] νομὴν ἕξει. [f] ὧν ἐστιν Ὑμέναιος καὶ Φίλητος, e (see note) — here (John x 9) only. f gen, 1 Tim i 19 ch i 15
18 [g] οἵτινες [h i] περὶ τὴν ἀλήθειαν [k] ἠστόχησαν, λέγοντες g = Acts x 41 (?) 47 al Paul passim
[τὴν] ἀνάστασιν ἤδη γεγονέναι, καὶ [l] ἀνατρέπουσιν τὴν h so 1 Tim i 19
[m] τινῶν πίστιν. 19 ὁ [n] μέντοι [o] στερεὸς [p] θεμέλιος τοῦ i 1 Tim vi 21
θεοῦ ἕστηκεν, ἔχων τὴν [q] σφραγῖδα ταύτην [r] Ἔγνω κύριος

k 1 Tim i 6 reff. l Tit i 11 only. Prov x 3. m 1 Tim i 3 reff. n John iv 27 al. James ii 8. Jude 8 only. o Heb. v 12, 14. 1 Pet v 9 only. Deut xxxii 18. p 1 Cor iii 11. Heb vi 1 al. Ps lxxxvi 1. q Rom iv 11. 1 Cor ix 2 only, exc Rev (v 1 and al12). Cant viii 6. r Gal iv 9 reff. Num xvi 5.

18. om 2nd την Fℵ 17. την πιστ. την τινων ανατρ D goth · την πιστ. τιν αν. F. αν την πιστιν τιν. ℵ3 17. αν. την π την τιν ℵ1.
19. for θεου, κυριου ℵ1 · χριστου 91. aft κυρ ins παντας ℵ1(ℵ3 disapproving).

(νομή [*pasture*, ref John. Aristot Hist. An 10], *from* νέμεσθαι [τὸ φῦμα ἐκραγὲν ἐνέμετο πρόσω, Herod iii 133], is the medical term for the consuming progress of mortifying disease: cf νομαὶ σαρκὸς θηριώδεις, Plut Mor. p 165 e: τὸ ἕλκος θᾶττον ποιεῖται νομήν, Polyb i 81 6, and Hippocrates and Galen in Wetst. It is also used of the devastating progress of fire, as in Polyb. i 48 5, τὴν μὲν νομὴν τοῦ πυρὸς ἔνεργον συνέβαινε γίγνεσθαι, and xi 5 5, τὸ πῦρ λαμβάνει νομήν) **as a gangrene** (γάγγραινα, from γράω, γραίνω, to eat into, is defined by Hippocrates [in Wetst.] to be the state of a tumour between inflammation and entire mortification—ἕπεται ταῖς μεγάλαις φλεγμοναῖς ἡ καλουμένη γάγγραινα, νέκρωσίς τε οὖσα τοῦ πάσχοντος μορίου, καὶ ἣν μὴ διὰ ταχέων τις αὐτὴν ἰάσηται, νεκροῦται ῥᾳδίως τὸ πάσχον τοῦτο μόριον, ἐπιλαμβάνει τε τὰ συνεχῆ, καὶ ἀποκτείνει τὸν ἄνθρωπον. Sometimes it is identical with καρκῖνος, a cancer): **of whom is** (ref.) **Hymenæus** (see note, 1 Tim i. 20) **and Philetus** (of him nothing further is known), **men who concerning the truth went astray** (cf 1 Tim vi 21), **saying that the resurrection has already taken place** (cf Tert de resurr carnis, c. 19, vol ii p 820,—"resurrectionem quoque mortuorum manifeste adnuntiatam in imaginariam significationem distorquent, adseverantes ipsam etiam mortem spiritaliter intelligendam. Non enim hanc esse in vero quæ sit in medio dissidium carnis atque animæ, sed ignorantiam Dei, per quam homo mortuus Deo non minus in errore jacuerit quam in sepulcro. Itaque et resurrectionem eam vindicandam, qua quis adita veritate sed animatus et revivificatus Deo, ignorantiæ morte discussa, velut de sepulcro veteris hominis eruperit . . . exinde ergo resurrectionem fide consecutos cum domino esse, cum eum in baptismate induerint." So also Irenæus, ii 31 2, p 164, "esse autem resurrectionem a mortuis, agnitionem ejus quæ ab eis dicitur veritatis." [See Ellicott's note.] This error, which belonged to the Gnostics subsequently, may well have been already sown and springing up in the apostolic age. If the form of it was that described by Tertullian, it would be one of those instances of wresting the words of St Paul himself [cf Col ii 12. Rom vi 4, al.] of which St Peter speaks 2 Pet iii 16. See on this Aug Ep. lv [cxix] 4, vol. iii. p 206. Thdrt [so also Pel] gives a curious and certainly mistaken meaning,—τὰς ἐκ παιδοποιΐας διαδοχὰς ἀνάστασιν οἱ δυσώνυμοι προσηγόρευον. [so Aug Hær 59, de Seleucianis, vol viii. p 42,—"Resurrectionem non putant futuram, sed quotidie fieri in generatione filiorum."] Schottg. another, but merely as a conjecture,—that the resurrection of some of the bodies of the saints with Christ [Matt xxvii 52] may have been by them called 'the Resurrection of the dead'), **and are overturning** (ref) **the faith of some.**

19.] *Firm endurance*, notwithstanding this overturning of the faith of some, *of the church of God: its signs and seals.* **Nevertheless** (cf Ellicott) **God's firm foundation standeth** (not as E V ungrammatically, '*the foundation of God standeth sure*.' But what is ὁ στερεὸς θεμ. τ. θεοῦ? Very various interpretations have been given. παρασαλεῦσαι, says Thdrt, οὐ δύνανται τὴν τῆς ἀληθείας κρηπῖδα: ὁ θεὸς γὰρ τοῦτον τέθεικε τὸν θεμέλιον. Coccejus, Michaelis, Ernesti, explain it the *fundamental doctrine of the Resurrection*: Ambr, *the promises of God*: Bengel, Vatabl., *fidem Dei immotam*: Bretschn, al, *Christ*, 1 Cor. iii 11: Heinrichs, Rosenm, *the Christian religion*: Calv, Calov, Wolf, Corn.-a-Lap, al, *Dei electionem*. Rather, as Mosh, Kypke, Heydenr., Mack, De W, Huther, Wiesinger, al, ἐκκλησία τεθεμελιωμένη ὑπὸ θεοῦ—the congregation of the faithful, considered as a foundation of a building placed by God,—the οἰκία spoken of in the next verse. So Estius: "Ipsa ecclesia rectissime firmum ac solidum Dei fundamentum vocatur, quia super

τοὺς ὄντας [s] αὐτοῦ, καί [t] Ἀποστήτω ἀπὸ ἀδικίας πᾶς ὁ
[u] ὀνομάζων τὸ ὄνομα κυρίου. 20 ἐν μεγάλῃ δὲ οἰκίᾳ οὐκ
ἔστιν μόνον [v w] σκεύη χρυσᾶ καὶ ἀργυρᾶ, ἀλλὰ καὶ [x] ξύλινα
καὶ [y] ὀστράκινα, καὶ [w z] ἃ μὲν [w] εἰς τιμήν, [w z] ἃ δὲ [w] εἰς
[a] ἀτιμίαν. 21 ἐὰν οὖν τις [b] ἐκκαθάρῃ ἑαυτὸν ἀπὸ τούτων,
ἔσται [w] σκεῦος [w] εἰς τιμήν, [c] ἡγιασμένον, [d] εὔχρηστον τῷ

ACDF KLℵ a b c d e f g h k l m n o 17

s gen., Rom. xiv. 8. 1 Cor. i. 12. iii. 23. Num. l. c. t = 1 Tim. iv. 1 reff. Num. xvi. 27. Isa. lii. 11. u = Rom. xv. 20 only. (Eph. i. 21 reff.) Isa. xxvi. 13. v Matt. xii. 29. Heb. ix. 21. Rev. ii. 27. xviii. 12 bis, al. Exod. iii. 22. w Rom. ix. 21. x Rev. ix. 20 only. Lev. xi. 32. y 2 Cor. iv. 7 only. Levit. vi. 28 (in both places w. σκ.). z Matt. xiii. 18. xxi. 35. Luke xxiii. 33 al. Polyb. i. 7. 3. a Rom. i. 26. ix. 21. 1 Cor. xi. 14. xv. 43. 2 Cor. vi. 8. xi. 21 only. P. Isa. xxii. 18. b 1 Cor. v. 7 only. Deut. xxvi. 13. Judg. vii. 4 vat. only. c Acts xx. 32. xxvi. 18 (both Paul). Rom. xv. 6 al. Isa. x. 17. d ch. iv. 11. Philem. 11 only. Prov. xi. 10 Ald. xxxi. 13. Wisd. xiii. 13 only.

rec (for κυριου) χριστου, with c e: txt ACDFKLℵ rel vss gr-lat-ff. (17 defective.)
21. εκκαθερη A. om εσται σκευος ℵ[1]: ins ℵ-corr[1]. rec ins και bef ευχρηστον, with C[1]D[2,3]KLℵ[3] rel vulg syr Orig$_3$ Thdrt$_1$: om C[?]D[1]Fℵ[1] f 17 Syr copt goth

petram, i. e. Christum, a Deo firmiter fundata, nullis aut Satanæ machinis aut tentationum fluctibus subverti potest aut labefactari: nam etsi quidam ab ea deficiunt, ipsa tamen in suis electis perseverat usque in finem." He then cites 1 John ii. 19: Matt. xxiv. 24: John x. 28: Rom. viii. 35, 39: and proceeds, "Ex his admodum fit verisimile, firmum Dei fundamentum intelligi fideles electos: sive, quod idem est, ecclesiam in electis." Against the tottering faith of those just mentioned, he sets the στερεὸς θεμ., and the ἕστηκεν. It cannot be moved: Heb. xii. 28), **having** ("'*seeing it hath*,' part. with a very faint causal force, illustrating the previous declaration: cf. Donalds. Gr. § 615." Ellic.) **this seal** (probably in allusion to the practice of engraving inscriptions over doors [Deut. vi. 9; xi. 20] and on pillars and foundation stones [Rev. xxi. 14]. The seal [inscription] would indicate *ownership* and *destination*: both of which are pointed at in the two texts following) (1) **The Lord knoweth** (see 1 Cor. viii. 3, note: 'novit amanter [?], nec nosse desinit,' as Bengel) **them that are His** (the LXX runs: ἐπέσκεπται καὶ ἔγνω ὁ θεὸς τοὺς ὄντας αὐτοῦ καὶ τοὺς ἁγίους, καὶ προσηγάγετο πρὸς ἑαυτόν): **and** (2) **Let every one that nameth the name of the Lord** (viz. *as* his Lord: not exactly equivalent to 'calleth on the name of the Lord') **stand aloof from iniquity** (the passage in Isa. stands, ἀπόστητε, ἀπόστητε, ἐξέλθατε ἐκεῖθεν, καὶ ἀκαθάρτου μὴ ἅψησθε, ... ἀφορίσθητε οἱ φέροντες τὰ σκεύη κυρίου. It is clearly no reason against this passage being here *alluded to*, that [as Conyb.] it is *expressly cited* 2 Cor. vi. 17. Ellic. remarks, that it is possibly in continued allusion to Num. xvi. 26, ἀποσχίσθητε ἀπὸ τῶν σκηνῶν, τῶν ἀνθρώπων τῶν σκληρῶν τούτων). **20.**] Those who are truly the Lord's are known to Him and depart from iniquity: but in the visible church there are many unworthy members. This is illustrated by the following similitude. **But** (contrast to the preceding definition of the Lord's people) **in a great house** (= ἐν τῇ οἰκουμένῃ πάσῃ, Chrys., who strenuously upholds that view; so also Thdrt. and the Greek Commentators, Grot., al.: but far better understood of the church, for the reason given by Calv.: "contextus quidem huc potius nos ducit, ut de ecclesia intelligamus: neque enim de extraneis disputat Paulus, sed de ipsa Dei familia:" so also Cypr., Aug., Ambr., all. The idea then is much the same as that in the parable of the drag-net, Matt. xiii. 47—49: not in the parable of the tares of the field, as De W.: for there it is expressly said, ὁ ἀγρὸς ἐστὶν ὁ κόσμος) **there are not only vessels of gold and silver, but also of wood and earthenware; and some for honour, some for dishonour** (viz. in the use of the vessels themselves: not, as Mack, al., to bring honour or dishonour on the house or its inhabitants. Estius, anxious to avoid the idea of heretics being in the church, would understand the two classes in each sentence as those distinguished by gifts, and those not so distinguished: and so Corn.-a-Lap., al.: but this seems alien from the context: cf. especially the next verse. On the comparison, see Ellic.'s references). **21.**] Here the thing signified is mingled with the similitude: the voluntary act described belonging, not to the vessels, but to the members of the church who are designated by them. **If then** (οὖν deduces a consequence from the similitude: q. d. 'his positis') **any man** (member of the church) **shall have purified himself** (not as Chrys., παντελῶς καθάρῃ: but as Bengel, 'purgando sese exierit de numero horum:' the ἐκ corresponds to the ἀπο be-

δεσπότῃ, [c] εἰς πᾶν [e] ἔργον [e] ἀγαθὸν [f] ἡτοιμασμένον. 22 τὰς
δὲ [g] νεωτερικὰς ἐπιθυμίας [h] φεῦγε, [hik] δίωκε δὲ [hil] δικαιοσύνην,
[h] πίστιν, [h] ἀγάπην, [m] εἰρήνην [ir] μετὰ τῶν [n] ἐπικαλουμένων
τὸν κύριον [o] ἐκ [o] καθαρᾶς [o] καρδίας. 23 τὰς δὲ [pq] μωρὰς

e Paul, 2 Cor ix 8 Col i 10 1 Tim v 10 ch iii 17 Tit i 16 iii 1 al[6] Acts ix 36 Heb xiii 21 f Gospp, Matt iii 3 (from Isa xl 3) al fr Epp, 1 Cor ii 9 Philem 22 Heb xi 16 only Rev viii 6 al g here only † αὐθάδεια νεωτερικη, Jos Antt xvi 11 7 ν ζῆλοι, Polyb x 24 7 h = 1 Tim vi 11 (reff) i Rom ix 30 1 Tim as above k 1 Thess v 15 l so Rom vi 13 al m see note 1 Macc vi 49, 58. x 4 n Acts vii 59 Rom x 12 (&c) mostly w ὄνομα Acts ii 21 (from Joel ii 32) al o 1 Tim i 5 reff p Tit iii 9 q Gospp Matt (only) v 22 al[6] 1 Cor i 25, 27 iii 18 iv 10 Tit iii 9 only Isa xxxii 6

Ephr Chr Thdrt[1] Œc Ambrst Aug[2]. (A uncert) for 2nd εις, προς DF.
22 αγαπην bef πιστιν F for των, παντων F 73. παντων των AC 17 Syr æth Chr-txt Thdrt Isid: txt DKLℵ rel vulg Syr copt goth Chr-comm Damasc Thl Œc Ambrst al. for επικαλ, αγαπωντων A.

low, and I have attempted to give that in the following) from among these (viz. the latter mentioned vessels in each parallel, but more especially the σκεύη εἰς ἀτιμίαν, from what follows), **he shall be a vessel for honour** (Chrys remarks ὁρᾷς ὅτι οὐ φύσεως οὐδὲ ὑλικῆς ἀνάγκης ἐστὶ τὸ εἶναι χρυσοῦν ἢ ὀστράκινον ἀλλὰ τῆς ἡμετέρας προαιρέσεως (?), ἐκεῖ μὲν γὰρ τὸ ὀστράκινον οὐκ ἂν γένηται χρυσοῦν, οὐδὲ τοῦτο εἰς τὴν ἐκείνου καταπεσεῖν εὐτέλειαν δυνήσεται ἐνταῦθα δὲ πολλὴ μεταβολὴ καὶ μετάστασις σκεῦος ὀστράκινον ἦν ὁ Παῦλος, ἀλλ' ἐγένετο χρυσοῦν σκεῦος χρυσοῦν ἦν (?) ὁ Ἰούδας, ἀλλ' ἐγένετο ὀστράκινον), **hallowed** (not to be joined, as Calv. and Lachmann, who expunges the comma after τιμήν, — with εἰς τιμήν, seeing that εἰς τιμήν stands absolutely in the former verse **ἡγιασμένος** [reff] is a favourite word with our Apostle to describe the saints of God), **useful** (see instances of the meaning of this epithet in the two N. T. reff.) **for the master** (of the house), **prepared for every good work** (κἂν μὴ πράττῃ, ἀλλ' ὅμως ἐπιτήδειόν ἐστι, δεκτικόν δεῖ οὖν πρὸς πάντα παρεσκευάσθαι, κἂν πρὸς θάνατον, κἂν πρὸς μαρτύριον κἂν πρὸς παρθενίαν, κἂν πρὸς ταῦτα πάντα Chrys)

22] Exhortations, taken up again from ver 16, on the matter of which the intervening verses have been a digression **But** (contrast to the last-mentioned character, ver. 21, in the introduction of νεωτ ἐπιθ.) **youthful lusts** (not 'cupiditates rerum novarum,' as Salmasius, see against him Suicer, vol. i p 1167,—νεωτερικαὶ οὐχ αὗται εἰσὶν αἱ τῆς πορνείας μόνον, ἀλλὰ πᾶσα ἐπιθυμία ἄτοπος, νεωτερική ἀκουέτωσαν οἱ γεγηρακότες, ὅτι οὐ δεῖ τὰ τῶν νεωτέρων ποιεῖν κἂν ὑβριστὴς ᾖ τις, κἂν δυναστείας ἐρᾷ, κἂν χρημάτων, κἂν σωμάτων, κἂν ὁτουοῦν δήποτε, νεωτερικὴ ἡ ἐπιθυμία, ἀνόητος οὔπω τῆς καρδίας βεβηκυίας οὐδὲ τῶν φρενῶν ἐν βάθει τεθεισῶν, ἀλλ' ᾐωρημένων, ἀνάγκη ταῦτα πάντα γίνεσθαι Chrys, and Thdrt, τουτέστι τρυφήν, γέλωτος ἀμετρίαν, δόξαν κενήν, καὶ τὰ τούτοις προσόμοια See also Basil Cæs in Suicer, as above) **fly from, but** (contrast to the hypothesis of the opposite course to that recommended above) **follow after righteousness** (moral rectitude, as contrasted with ἀδικία, ver 19 not, as Calov, 'the righteousness which is by faith;' far better Calvin 'hoc est, rectam vivendi rationem' See the parallel, 1 Tim vi 11), **faith, love, peace with** (μετά belongs to εἰρήνην, not to δίωκε, cf Heb xii. 14, εἰρήνην διώκετε μετὰ πάντων also Rom xii. 18) **those who call upon the Lord** (Christ, see 1 Cor. i 2) **out of a pure heart** (these last words belong to ἐπικαλουμένων, and serve to designate the earnest and single-minded, as contrasted with the false teachers, who called on Him, but not out of a pure heart: cf. ch. iii. 5, 8, and especially Tit i 15, 16 Chrys. draws as an inference from this, μετὰ δὲ τῶν ἄλλων οὐ χρὴ πρᾶον εἶναι, which is directly against ver 25 Thdrt. far better, drawing the distinction between *love* and *peace* · ἀγαπᾶν μὲν γὰρ ἅπαντας δυνατόν, ἐπειδήπερ τοῦτο καὶ ὁ εὐαγγελικὸς παρακελεύεται νόμος, Ἀγαπᾶτε τοὺς ἐχθροὺς ὑμῶν εἰρηνεύειν δὲ οὐ πρὸς ἅπαντας ἔνεστι, τῆς γὰρ κοινῆς τοῦτο προαιρέσεως δεῖται τοιοῦτοι δὲ πάντες οἱ ἐκ καθαρᾶς καρδίας τὸν δεσπότην ἐπικαλούμενοι See Rom. xii 18)

23] **But** (contrast again to the hypothesis of the contrary of the last exhortation) **foolish** (Tit iii. 9) **and undisciplined** (ἀπαίδευτος can hardly be wrested from its proper sense and made to mean 'unprofitable πρὸς παιδείαν,' but, as in reff., must mean *lacking* παιδεία, shewing want of wholesome discipline. Grot. limits it too narrowly, when he says, "Intelligit hic Paulus quæstiones immodestas: nam et Græci pro ἀκόλαστον dicunt ἀπαίδευτον [sine disciplina] · quia idem est κολάζειν et παιδεύειν") **questionings de-**

καὶ [r] ἀπαιδεύτους [ps] ζητήσεις [t] παραιτοῦ, εἰδὼς ὅτι [u] γεννῶ-
σιν [v] μάχας· 24 [w] δοῦλον δὲ κυρίου οὐ δεῖ [x] μάχεσθαι,
ἀλλὰ [y] ἤπιον εἶναι πρὸς πάντας, [z] διδακτικόν, [a] ἀνεξίκα-
κον, 25 ἐν [b] πραΰτητι [c] παιδεύοντα τοὺς [d] ἀντιδιατιθεμένους,
[e] μήποτε δώῃ αὐτοῖς ὁ θεὸς [f] μετάνοιαν [f] εἰς [gh] ἐπίγνωσιν

ACDF KLℵ a b c d e f g h k l m n o 17

r here only. Prov. viii. 5. xv. 14. s 1 Tim. i. 4 reff. t = 1 Tim. iv. 7 reff. u Paul, Acts xxii. 3, 28. Rom. ix. 11. 1 Cor. iv 15. Gal. iv. 23, 24, 29. Philem. 10 only. Heb. i. 5, from Ps. ii. 7. 1 John ii. 29 al. fr. v 2 Cor. vii. 5. Tit. iii. 9. James iv. 1 only. = Gen. xiii. 7. w = Gal. i. 10 reff. x John vi. 52. Acts vii. 26. James iv. 2 only. Gen. xxvi. 20. y 1 Thess. ii. 7 only †. z 1 Tim. iii. 2 only †. a here only †. (-κία, Wisd. ii. 19.) b Gal. v. 23 reff. c 1 Tim. i. 20 reff. d here only †. e = here only (not Gen. xxiv. 5). see Luke iii. 15. f 2 Cor. vii. 10. g Eph. i. 17 reff. h 1 Tim. ii. 4. ch. iii. 7. Tit. i. 1.

24. [αλλα, so ADFℵ 17.] for ηπιον, νηπιον D[1]F (*see* 1 *Thess* ii. 7).
25. for εν, συν F latt (*cum in modestia* D-lat). rec πραοτητι, with D[3]KL rel: πριχοτητι F: txt ACD[1]ℵ 17. 67[2] Ephr Bas Chr-mss. αντιδιαθεμενους C: αντικειμενους F. rec (for δωη) δω, with D[3]KLℵ[3] rel: txt ACD[1]Fℵ Ephr Chr-ms Isid. om μετανοιαν ℵ[1]. at end ins ελθειν A.

cline (reff.), **being aware that they gender strifes** (reff.): **but** (contrast to the fact of μάχαι) **the** (better than *a*, as De W. The meaning being much the same, and **δοῦλον** in the emphatic place representing τὸν δοῦλον, the definite art., in rendering, gives the emphasis, and points out the individual servant, better than the indefinite) **servant of the Lord** (Jesus; see 1 Cor. vii. 22. It is evident from what follows, that the servant of the Lord here, in the Apostle's view, is not so much every true Christian,—however applicable such a maxim may be to him also,—but the minister of Christ, as Timotheus was: cf. διδακτικόν, &c. below) **must not strive** (the argument is in the form of an enthymeme:—'propositionem ab experientia manifestam relinquit. Assumptio vero tacitam sui probationem includit, eamque hujusmodi: servum oportet imitari Dominum suum.' Estius), **but be gentle** (ref.) **towards all, apt to teach** (ref.:—so E. V. well: for, as Bengel, 'hoc non solum soliditatem et facilitatem in docendo, sed vel maxime patientiam et assiduitatem significat.' In fact these latter must be, on account of the contrast which the Apostle is bringing out, regarded as prominent here), **patient of wrong** (so Conyb., and perhaps we can hardly find a better expression, though 'wrong' does not by any means cover the meaning of the κακόν: 'long-suffering' would be unobjectionable, were it not that we have μακρόθυμος, to which that word is already appropriated. Plutarch, Coriolan. c. 15, says, that he did not repress his temper, οὐδὲ τὴν ἐρημίᾳ ξύνοικον, ὡς Πλάτων ἔλεγεν, αὐθάδειαν εἰδὼς ὅτι δεῖ μάλιστα διαφεύγειν ἐπιχειροῦντα πράγμασι κοινοῖς καὶ ἀνθρώποις ὁμιλεῖν, καὶ γενέσθαι τῆς πολλὰ γελωμένης ὑπ' ἐνίων ἀνεξικακίας ἐραστήν), **in meekness correcting** (not '*instructing*,' see reff., and note on ἀπαιδεύτους, ver. 23) **those who oppose themselves** (better than as Ambrst., 'eos qui diversa sentiunt:' to take the general meaning of διατίθεσθαι, satisfies the context better, than to supply τὸν νοῦν. The Vulg., 'eos qui resistunt veritati,' particularizes too much in another way), **if at any time** (literally, '*lest at any time*:' but **μήποτε** in later Greek sometimes loses this aversative meaning and is almost equivalent to εἴποτε. Cf. Viger, p. 457, where the annotator says of μήποτε, 'vocula tironibus sæpissime crucem figens, cum significat *fortasse*, vel *si quando*,' and he then cites this passage. The account to be given of the usage is that, from μή being commonly used after verbs of fearing, &c.,—then after verbs expressing anxiety of any kind [φροντίζω, μή . . . Xen.: σκοπῶ, μή . . . Plat.: ὑποπτεύειν, μή . . . Xen.: αἰσχύνομαι, μή . . . Plat.], its proper aversative force by degrees became forgotten, and thus it, and words compounded with it, were used in later Greek in sentences where no such force can be intended. De W. refers to Kypke for examples of this usage from Plut. and Athenæus: but Kypke does not notice the word here at all) **God may give them repentance** (because their consciences were impure [see above on ver. 22] and lives evil. Cf. Ellic.'s remarks on μετάν.) **in order to the knowledge of** [**the**] **truth** (see note, 1 Tim. ii. 4), **and they may awake sober** (from their moral and spiritual intoxication: so ἐκνήφ., in ref. 1 Cor., and this same word in Jos.: the θρῆνοι there, as the ensnarement by the devil here, being regarded as a kind of intoxication. There is no one word in English which will express **ἀνανήψαι**: Conyb. has paraphrased it by '*escape, restored to soberness*' ['*return to soberness*,' Ellic.]: perhaps the E. V., '*recover themselves*,' is as near an ap-

h ἀληθείας, 26 καὶ i ἀνανήψωσιν k ἐκ τῆς τοῦ l διαβόλου
l παγίδος m ἐζωγρημένοι ὑπ' n αὐτοῦ εἰς τὸ n ἐκείνου
θέλημα.

i here only † ἐκ θρήνων ἀνανήψειν Jos Antt vi 11 10 (ἐκνήφ, 1 Cor xv 34) k constr prægn, 2 Thess ii 2 Rom vi 7 vii 2 ix 3 l 1 Tim iii 6, 7 reff m Luke v 10 only 2 Chron xxv 12 n see note

26 ανανηψουσιν C · αναλημψωσιν D[1] ανανηψωσιν A-corr n o (A[1] erased)

proach to the meaning as we can get. We have the word used literally by Plutarch, Camillus, c 23. ὁ Κάμιλλος περὶ μέσας τὰς νύκτας προσέμιξε τῷ χάρακι . . . . ἐκταράττων ἀνθρώπους κακῶς ὑπὸ μέθης κ μόλις ἐκ τῶν ὕπνων ἀναφέροντας πρὸς τὸν θόρυβον. ὀλίγοι μὲν οὖν ἀνανήψαντες ἐν τῷ φόβῳ κ διασκευασάμενοι, τοὺς περὶ τὸν Κάμιλλον ὑπέστησαν . . Sir Thomas North renders it, 'There were some notwithstanding did *bustle up* at the sudden noise' See also examples in Wetst) **out of the snare of the devil** (gen subj, 'the snare which the devil laid for them' There is properly no confusion of metaphor, the idea being that these persons have in a state of intoxication been entrapped, and are enabled, at their awaking sober, to escape But the construction is elliptic, ἀνανήψωσιν ἐκ = ἐκφύγωσιν ἀνανήψαντες ἐκ), **having been** (during their spiritual μέθη) **taken captive by him unto** (for the fulfilment of, in pursuance of) **the will of Him** (viz God that Other, indicated by **ἐκείνου** Thus I am now persuaded the words must be rendered: **αὐτοῦ**, referring to the devil, and it being signified that the taking captive of these men by him only takes place as far as God permits; according to His will Rendering it thus, as do Aret., Estius, and Ellicott, I do not hold the other view, which makes αὐτοῦ and ἐκείνου both refer to the devil, to be untenable. I therefore give my note much as it stood before, that the student may have both sides before him. The difficulty is of course to determine whether the pronouns are used of the same person, or of different persons. From the Greek expositors downwards, some have held a very different rendering of the words from either of those here indicated. Thl. e. g.,—ἐν πλάνῃ, φησί, νήψονται, ἀλλὰ ζωγρηθέντες ὑπὸ θεοῦ εἰς τὸ ἐκείνου θέλημα, τουτέστι τοῦ θεοῦ, ἴσως ἀνανήψουσιν ἀπὸ τῶν ὑδάτων τῆς πλάνης This, it is true, does not get rid of the difficulty respecting the pronouns, but it pointed a way towards doing so: and thus Wetst, Bengel, and Mack, understand **αὐτοῦ** to apply to the δοῦλος κυρίου,—**ἐκείνου** to God —'*taken prisoners by God's servant according to His will*' [Bengel however, as Beza, Grot, joins εἰς τὸ ἐκ θέλ with ἀνανήψωσιν, which is unnatural, leaving ἐζωγρ ὑπ' αὐτοῦ standing alone] The great objection to this is, the exceeding confusion which it introduces into the figure, in representing men who are just recovering their sense and liberty, as ἐζωγρημένοι,—and in applying that participle, occurring as it does just after the mention of παγίς, not to that snare, but to another which does not appear at all Aret and Estius proposed the rendering given above,—'taken captive by the devil according to God's will,' i e as Est, 'quamdiu Deus voluerit, cujus voluntati nec diabolus resistere potest' De W. charges this with rendering **εἰς** as if it were κατά, but the charge is not just for the permitting the devil to hold them captive, on this view, would be strictly εἰς, 'in pursuance of,' 'so as to follow,' God's purpose. The real objection perhaps is, that it introduces a new and foreign element, viz the fact that this capture is overruled by God—of which matter there is here no question. There is no real difficulty whatever in the application of αὐτοῦ and ἐκείνου to the same person Kuhner, § 629, anm 3, gives from Plato, Cratyl. p 430, δεῖξαι αὐτῷ ἂν μὲν τύχῃ, ἐκείνου εἰκόνα, ἂν δὲ τύχῃ, γυναικός [where the reason for the use of ἐκείνου, viz to emphasize the pronoun, is precisely as here; see below] from Lysias, c Eratosth p. 429, ἕως ὁ λεγόμενος ὑπ' ἐκείνου καιρὸς ἐπιμελῶς ὑπ' αὐτοῦ ἐτηρήθη [which cases of ἐκεῖνος followed by αὐτός must not be dismissed, as Ellic, as inapplicable they shew at all events that there was no absolute objection to using the two pronouns of the same person See below] But he does not give an account of the idiom, which seems to be this ἐκεῖνος, from its very meaning, always carries somewhat of emphasis with it, it is therefore unfit for mere reflexive or unemphatic use, and accordingly when the subject pointed out by ἐκεῖνος occurs in such unemphatic position, ἐκεῖνος is replaced by αὐτός On the other hand, where emphasis is required, ἐκεῖνος is repeated · e g Soph Aj. 1039, κεῖνος τὰ κείνου στεργέτω, κἀγὼ

o so Acts ii 17 James v 3 1 Pet i 5 1 John ii 18 (Jude 18) Isa ii 2 p Paul (Rom viii 38 1 Cor iii 22 vii 26. Gal i 4

III. [1] Τοῦτο δὲ γίνωσκε, ὅτι ἐν [o] ἐσχάταις ἡμέραις ACDF KLℵ a b
[p] ἐνστήσονται καιροὶ [q] χαλεποί. [2] ἔσονται γὰρ οἱ ἄν- c d e f g
θρωποι [r] φίλαυτοι, [s] φιλάργυροι, [tu] ἀλαζόνες, [tv] ὑπερήφανοι, h k l m n o 17
[w] βλάσφημοι, [t] γονεῦσιν [tx] ἀπειθεῖς, [y] ἀχάριστοι, [z] ἀνόσιοι,

2 Thess ii 2) only, exc Heb ix 9 1 Macc xii 44 q Matt viii 28 only Isa xviii 2 only Wisd iii 19 al r here only (see note) † s Luke xvi 14 only † t Rom i 30 u Rom as above only Job xxviii 8 Prov xxi 24 Hab ii 5 only (-ιεια, James iv 16) v Luke i 51 Rom i 30 James iv 6 1 Pet v 5 (from Prov iii 34) only Ps lxxviii 21, 51 (-ιαι, Mark vii 22) w 1 Tim i 13 reff x Luke i 17 Acts xxvi 19 Rom i 30. Tit i 16 iii 3 only Deut xxi 18 y Luke vi 35 only † Wisd xvi 29 Sir xxix 17, 25 only z 1 Tim i 9 (reff) only.

Chap III. 1 γινωσκετε AF 17 æth-rom Aug txt CDKLℵ rel vulg(and F-lat) syrr copt goth æth-pl gr-latt-ff
2 om οι ℵ 72. 111-5 αλαζοντες F for αχαριστοι, αχριστοι C[1] αχρηστοι K m.

τάδε And this emphatic or unemphatic use is not determined by priority of order, but by logical considerations. So here in ἐζωγρημένοι ὑπ' αὐτοῦ, the αὐτοῦ is the mere reflex of διαβόλου which has just occurred,—whereas in εἰς τὸ ἐκείνου θέλημα, the ἐκείνου would, according to this rendering, bring out and emphasize the danger and degradation of these persons, who had been, in their spiritual μέθη, just taken captive at the pleasure of ἐκεῖνος, their mortal foe Still, it now seems to me it is better to adhere to the common meaning of the two pronouns, even though it should seem to introduce a new idea. The novelty however may be somewhat removed by remembering that God's sovereign power as the giver of repentance was already before the Apostle's mind)

Ch III 1—9] *Warning of bad times to come, in which men shall be ungodly and hypocritical —nay, against such men as already present, and doing mischief*

1.] **But** (the contrast is in the dark prophetic announcement, so different in character from the hope just expressed) **this know, that in the last days** (see 1 Tim. iv 1, where the expression is somewhat different The period referred to here is, from all N T analogy [cf 2 Pet. iii 3: Jude 18], that immediately preceding the coming of the Lord That day and hour being hidden from all men, and even from the Son Himself, Mark xiii 32, —the Spirit of prophecy, which is the Spirit of the Son, did not reveal to the Apostles its place in the ages of time They, like the subsequent generations of the Church, were kept waiting for it, and for the most part wrote and spoke of it as soon to appear; not however without many and sufficient hints furnished by the Spirit, of an interval, and that no short one, first to elapse In this place, these last days are set before Timotheus as being on their way, and indeed their premonitory symptoms already appearing The discovery which the lapse of centuries and the ways of providence have made to us, χρονίζει ὁ κύριός μου ἐλθεῖν, misleads none but unfaithful servants while the only modification in the understanding of the premonitory symptoms, is, that *for us*, He with whom a thousand years are as one day has spread them, without changing their substance or their truth, over many consecutive ages Cf. ref 1 John, —where we have the still plainer assertion, ἐσχάτη ὥρα ἐστίν) **grievous times shall come** (we can hardly express ἐνστήσονται nearer in English · '*instabunt*,' of the Vulg, though blamed by De W, is right, in the sense in which we use 'instant' of the present month or year [Ellic quotes Auct ad Herenn ii 5, 'dividitur (tempus) in tempora tria, præteritum, instans, consequens'], '*aderunt*' of Grot. and Bengel amounts in fact to the same. See note on 2 Thess ii 2) 2] **for** (reason for χαλεποί) **men** (οἱ generic · the men who shall live in those times) **shall be selfish** (οἱ πάντα πρὸς τὴν ἑαυτῶν ὠφέλειαν ποιοῦντες, Theod-Mops. Aristotle, in his chapter περὶ φιλαυτίας, Eth Nicom ix 8, while he maintains that there is a higher sense in which τὸν ἀγαθὸν δεῖ φίλαυτον εἶναι,—allows that οἱ πολλοί use the word of τοὺς ἑαυτοῖς ἀπονέμοντας τὸ πλεῖον ἐν χρήμασι, καὶ τιμαῖς, καὶ ἡδοναῖς ταῖς σωματικαῖς. and adds, δικαίως δὴ τοῖς οὕτω φιλαύτοις ὀνειδίζεται), **covetous** (ref. we have the subst, 1 Tim. vi 10, and the verb, 2 Macc x. 20), **empty boasters** (ἀλαζόνες, καυχώμενοι ἔχειν ἃ μὴ ἔχουσιν, Theod-Mops see ref and definitions from Aristotle in note), **haughty** (μεγάλα φρονοῦντες, ἐπὶ τοῖς οὖσιν, Theod-Mops . ref and note), **evil speakers** (κατηγορίαις χαίροντες, Theod-Mops Not 'blasphemers,' unless, as in ref 1 Tim, the context specifies to what the evil-speaking refers), **disobedient to parents** ('character temporum colligendus maximus etiam ex juventutis moribus.' Bengel), **ungrateful, unholy** (ref ἐπιμέλειαν τοῦ δικαίου μὴ ποιούμενοι, Theod-Mops., and Beza's 'qui-

3 [a] ἄστοργοι, [b] ἄσπονδοι, [c] διάβολοι, [d] ἀκρατεῖς, [e] ἀνήμεροι,
[f] ἀφιλάγαθοι, 4 [g] προδόται, [h] προπετεῖς, [i] τετυφωμένοι,
[j] φιλήδονοι [k] μᾶλλον ἢ [l] φιλόθεοι, 5 ἔχοντες [m] μόρφωσιν
[n] εὐσεβείας τὴν δὲ δύναμιν αὐτῆς [o] ἠρνημένοι. καὶ τούτους
[p] ἀποτρέπου. 6 ἐκ τούτων γάρ εἰσιν οἱ [q] ἐνδύνοντες εἰς
τὰς οἰκίας καὶ [r] αἰχμαλωτίζοντες [s] γυναικάρια [t] σεσωρευ-

a Rom i 31 only + Æschin p 47 29
b here (Rom i 31 rec) only +
c = 1 Tim iii (6, 7 r ff) 11 Tit ii 3 only Esth vii 4
d here only Prov xxvii 20 (only?)
e here only +
f here only + see Tit i 8
g Luke vi 16 Acts vii 52 only + 2 Macc v 15 x 13, 22 only
h Acts xix 36 only Prov x 14 xiii 3 Sir ix 18 only
i 1 Tim. iii 6 vi 4 only +
j here only + Polyb xl 6 10
k 1 Tim i 4 reff
l here only + Arist Rhet ii 17 6
m Rom ii 20 only +
n 1 Tim ii 2 reff
o = 1 Tim v 8 reff
p here only + Sir xx 29 see ch iv 4
q here only +
r Luke xxi 24 Rom vii 23 2 Cor x 5 only 3 Kings viii 46
s here only + ἀνδράρια, Aristoph Acharn 517 ἀνθρωπάρια, id Plut 416
t Rom xii 20 (from Prov xxv 21, 22) only

3. ασπονδοι bef αστοργοι D m 73 Chr lat ff · om αστοργοι ℵ om both 238 Syr.
6 rec αιχμαλωτευοντες, with D[3]KL rel Orig-ed Damasc: txt ACD[1]Γℵ 17 Orig-mss Chr Thdrt Thl Œc. rec ins τα bef γυναικαρια, with a d f o om ACDFKLℵ rel

bus nullum jus est nec fas' are perhaps too wide. it is rather 'irreligious'), **without natural affection** (ref and note), **implacable** (it does not appear that the word ever means 'truce-*breakers*,' *οὐ βέβαιοι περὶ τὰς φιλίας, οὐδὲ ἀληθεῖς περὶ ἃ συντίθενται*, — as Theod-Mops. In all the places where it occurs in a subjective sense, it is, '*that will make*' or '*admit no truce*.' e. g, Æsch Agam 1235, *ἄσπονδόν τ' ἀρὰν φίλοις πνέουσαν*: Eur Alcest. 426, *τῷ κάτωθεν ἀσπόνδῳ θεῷ* Demosth. p 314 16, *ἄσπονδος κ. ακήρυκτος πόλεμος* the same expression, *ἄσπ πόλεμος*, occurs in Polyb. i. 65. 6. For the primary objective sense, 'without *σπονδή*,' see Thucyd. i 37; ii 22, v 32, and Palm and Rost's Lex.), **calumniators** (reff), **incontinent** (we have the subst *ἀκρασία*, 1 Cor vii 5), **inhuman** (*ὠμοί, ἀπάνθρωποι*, Œc.), **no lovers of good** (*ἐχθροὶ παντὸς ἀγαθοῦ*, Thl), **traitors, headlong** (either in action, 'qui præcipites sunt in agendo,' Beng or in passion [temper], which would in fact amount to the same), **besotted by pride** (see note, 1 Tim iii 6), **lovers of pleasure rather than lovers of God** (*τὸν λαὸν . . φιλήδονον κ φιλοπαθῆ μᾶλλον ἢ φιλάρετον κ. φιλόθεον* Philo, de agric. § 19, vol. i. p. 313), **having a** (or **the**?) **form** (outward embodiment the same meaning as in ref, but here confined, by the contrast following, to the mere outward semblance, whereas there, no contrast occurring, the outward embodiment is the real representation "The more correct word would be *μόρφωμα* [Æsch Ag. 873, Eum 112], *μόρφωσις* being properly active, e.g. *σχηματισμὸς κ μόρφωσις τῶν δενδρῶν*, Theophr de caus. plant iii 7 4 there is, however, a tendency in the N T, as in later writers, to replace the verbal nouns in -*μα* by the corresponding nouns in -*σις*. cf *ὑποτύπωσις*, ch. i 13." Ellicott) **of piety, but having repudiated** (not pres, '*denying*,' as E V.,—'*renouncing*,' as Conyb, their condemnation is, that they are living in the semblance of God's fear, but *have repudiated* its reality) **the power of it** (its living and renewing influence over the heart and life). Cf. throughout this description, Rom. i. 30, 31. Huther remarks, "We can hardly trace any formal rule of arrangement through these predicates. Here and there, it is true, a few cognate ideas are grouped together the two first are connected by *φίλος*. then follow three words betokening high-mindedness *γονεῦσιν ἀπειθεῖς* is followed by *ἀχάριστοι* this word opens a long series of words beginning with ἀ privative, but interrupted by *διάβολοι* · the following, *προδόται, προπετεῖς*, seem to be a paronomasia. the latter of these is followed by *τετυφωμένοι* as a cognate idea a few more general predicates close the catalogue. But this very interpenetration serves to depict more vividly the whole manifoldness of the manifestation of evil." **And from these turn away** (ref.: cf *ἐκτρέπεσθαι*, 1 Tim. vi. 20. This command shews that the Apostle treats the symptoms of the last times as not future exclusively, but in some respects present see note above, ver 1)

6] **for** (reason of the foregoing command, seeing that they are already among you) **among the number of these are they who creep** (*εἶδες τὸ ἀναίσχυντον πῶς ἐδήλωσε διὰ τοῦ εἰπεῖν, ἐνδύνοντες τὸ ἄτιμον, τὴν ἀπάτην, τὴν κολακείαν*, Chrys Cf. Aristoph. Vesp. 1020, *εἰς ἀλλοτρίας γαστέρας ἐνδύς*. Bengel interprets it 'irrepentes clanculum') **into** [men's] **houses and take captive** (as it were prisoners, a word admirably describing the influence acquired by **sneaking proselytizers** over

u and constr, Rom viii 13 Gal v 18 v Matt iv 24 ‖ Mk L Tit iii 3 (also w ἐπιθ) Heb xi 1 xiii 9 James i 2 1 Pet i 6 iv 10 only † 1 Chron xxix 2 w 2 Macc ix 11 x Eph i 17 reff y ch ii 25 1 Tim ii 4 Tit i 1 z Paul, here only Matt xxiii 37 ‖ L Acts i 11 vii 28 only Isa. xxxviii 19

μένα ἁμαρτίαις, ᵘ ἀγόμενα ἐπιθυμίαις ᵛ ποικίλαις, 7 ᵛ πάντοτε
μανθάνοντα καὶ μηδέποτε ʷ εἰς ˣʸ ἐπίγνωσιν ʸ ἀληθείας
ʷ ἐλθεῖν δυνάμενα. 8 ᶻ ὃν τρόπον δὲ Ἰαννῆς καὶ Ἰαμβρῆς

ACDF KLℵ a b c d e f g h k l m n o 17

gr-ff. aft επιθυμιαις ins και ηδοναις A syr Chr-txt Thdrt₁
8. ιωαννης C¹: *Jamnes* am(with fuld demid) Cypr Lucif Opt Aug μαμβρης

those presently described: attach to themselves entirely, so that they follow them as if dragged about by them: a late word, said to be of Alexandrian or Macedonian origin, and condemned by the Atticist: see Ellicott) **silly women** (the diminutive denotes contempt) **laden with sins** (De W. alone seems to have given the true reason of the insertion of this particular. The stress is on σεσωρευμένα: they are burdened, their consciences oppressed, with sins, and in this morbid state they lie open to the insidious attacks of these proselytizers who promise them ease of conscience if they will follow them), **led about by lusts of all kinds** (I should rather imagine, from the context, that the reference here is not so much to 'fleshly lusts' properly so called,—though from what we know of such feminine spiritual attachments, ancient [see below] and modern, such must by no means be excluded,—as to the ever-shifting [ποικίλη] passion for change in doctrine and manner of teaching, which is the eminent characteristic of these captives to designing spiritual teachers—the running after fashionable men and fashionable tenets, which draw them [ἄγουσι] in flocks in the most opposite and inconsistent directions), **evermore learning** (always with some new point absorbing them, which seems to them the most important, to the depreciation of what they held and seemed to know before), **and never** (on μηδ., see Ellicott) **able to come to the thorough knowledge** (reff., and notes: the decisive and stable apprehension, in which they might be grounded and settled against further novelties) **of the truth** (this again is referred by Chrys., all., to moral deadening of their apprehension by profligate lives. ἐπειδὴ ἑαυτὰς κατέχωσαν ταῖς ἐπιθυμίαις ἐκείναις καὶ τοῖς ἁμαρτήμασιν, ἐπωρώθη αὐτῶν ἡ διάνοια. It may be so, in the deeper ground of the psychological reason for this their fickle and imperfect condition: but I should rather think that the Apostle here indicates their character as connected with the fact of their captivity to these teachers. With regard to the fact itself, we have abundant testimony that the Gnostic heresy in its progress, as indeed all new and strange systems, laid hold chiefly of the female sex: so Irenæus, i. 13. 3, p. 61, of the Valentinian Marcus, μάλιστα περὶ γυναῖκας ἀσχολεῖται, and in ib. 6, p. 63 f., καὶ μαθηταὶ δὲ αὐτοῦ τινες . . . ἐξαπατῶντες γυναικάρια πολλὰ διέφθειραν: and Epiphanius, Hær. xxvi. 12, vol. i. p. 93, charges the Gnostics with ἐμπαίζειν τοῖς γυναικαρίοις and ἀπατᾷν τὸ αὐτοῖς πειθόμενον γυναικεῖον γένος, then quoting this passage. Jerome, Ep. cxxxiii. ad Ctesiphontem 4, vol. i. p. 1031 f., collects a number of instances of this: "Simon Magus hæresim condidit Helenæ meretricis adjutus auxilio. Nicolaus Antiochenus omnium immunditiarum repertor choros duxit fœmineos. Marcion Romam præmisit mulierem quæ decipiendos sibi animos præpararet. Apelles Philumenem suarum comitem habuit doctrinarum. Montanus . . . Priscam et Maximillam . . . primum auro corrupit, deinde hæresi polluit. . . . Arius ut orbem deciperet, sororem principis ante decepit. Donatus . . . Lucillæ opibus adjutus est. Agape Elpidium . . . cæcum cæca duxit in foveam. Priscilliano juncta fuit Galla."

The general answer to Baur,—who again uses this as a proof of the later origin of these Epistles,—will be found in the Prolegomena, ch. vii. § i. De Wette remarks, "This is an admirable characterization of zealous soul-hunters (who have been principally found, and are still found, among the Roman Catholics) and their victims. We must not however divide the different traits among different classes or individuals: it is their combination only which is characteristic." "Diceres, ex professo Paulum hic vivam monachismi effigiem pingere." Calvin).

8.] **But** (q. d. it is no wonder that there should be now such opponents to the truth, for their prototypes existed also in ancient times) **as Jannes and Jambres withstood Moses** (these are believed to be traditional names of the Egyptian magicians mentioned in Exod. vii. 11, 22. Origen says [in Matt. comment. 117, vol. iii. p. 916], "quod ait, 'sicut Jannes et Mambres [see var. readd.] restiterunt Mosi,' non invenitur in publicis scripturis, sed in libro secreto, qui suprascribitur

[a] ἀντέστησαν Μωυσεῖ, οὕτως καὶ οὗτοι [a] ἀνθίστανται [b] τῇ
ἀληθείᾳ, ἄνθρωποι [cd] κατεφθαρμένοι τὸν [d] νοῦν, [e] ἀδόκιμοι
[f] περὶ τὴν [f] πίστιν. 9 ἀλλ' οὐ [g] προκόψουσιν [g] ἐπὶ πλεῖον·
ἡ γὰρ [h] ἄνοια αὐτῶν [i] ἔκδηλος ἔσται πᾶσιν, ὡς καὶ ἡ
ἐκείνων ἐγένετο. 10 σὺ δὲ [k] παρηκολούθησάς μου τῇ

a Paul, Rom ix 19 xiii 2 bis Gal ii 11 Eph vi 13 ch iv 15 Matt v 39 Luke xxi 15 al Job xli 2 b = 2 Thess ii 12 reff c here (2 Pet ii 12 v r) only Gen vi 12 d see 1 Tim vi 5 reff e Rom i 28 1 Cor ix 27 2 Cor xiii 5, 6, 7 Tit i 16 Heb vi 8 only Prov xxv 4 Isa i 22 only f 1 Tim i 19 vi 21 see ch ii 18 g ch ii 16 reff h Luke vi 11 only Prov xxii 15 i here only † 3 Macc iii 19 k 1 Tim iv 6 reff

F latt goth gr-ff(not Chr Thdrt Damasc) lat-ff(not Aug[1]). ins τω bef μωυσει F 73 80 (μωσει, A c l m) for ουτοι, αυτοι F. αντισταντι D[1], αντεστησαν 17. 238 αντιστησονται Chr-comm

9 for ανοια, διανοια A for εσται, εστιν F. (G-lat has both)

10 rec παρηκολουθηκας, with DKL rel Chr Thdrt Damasc txt ACℵ 17, ηκολου-

Jannes et Mambres liber." But Thdrt's account is more probable [τὰ μέντοι τούτων ὀνόματα οὐκ ἐκ τῆς θείας γραφῆς μεμάθηκεν ὁ θεῖος ἀπόστολος, ἀλλ' ἐκ τῆς ἀγράφου τῶν Ἰουδαίων διδασκαλίας], especially as the names are found in the Targum of Jonathan on Exod. vii. 11, Num. xxii 22. Schottgen has [in loc] a long account of their traditional history. and Wetst. quotes the passages at length They were the sons of Balaam—prophesied to Pharaoh the birth of Moses, in consequence of which he gave the order for the destruction of the Jewish children, —and thenceforward appear as the counsellors of much of the evil,—in Egypt, and in the desert, after the Exodus,—which happened to Israel They were variously reported to have perished in the Red Sea, or to have been killed in the tumult consequent on the making the golden calf, which they had advised. Origen, contra Cels iv 51, vol i. p. 543, mentions the Pythagorean Noumenius as relating the history of Jannes and Jambres. so also Euseb. præp evang. ix 8, vol. iii [Migne], p 112. Pliny, H. Nat xxx 1, says, "Est et alia Magices factio, a Mose et Jamne et Jotape Judæis pendens, sed multis millibus annorum post Zoroastrem" The later Jews, with some ingenuity, distorted the names into Joannes and Ambrosius), **thus these also withstand the truth, being men corrupted** (reff. the Lxx. quote καταφθαρεὶς τὸν βίον from a fragment of Menander) **in mind, worthless** (not abiding the test, 'rejectanei') **concerning the faith** (in respect of the faith. περὶ τὴν πίστιν is not, as Huther, equivalent to περὶ τῆς πίστεως, but expresses more the local meaning of περί. '*circa*,' as the Vulg. here has it In 1 Tim i. 19, περὶ τὴν πίστιν ἐναυάγησαν, we have the local reference brought out more strongly, the faith being, as it were, a rock, on, round which they had been shipwrecked).

9] **Notwithstanding** (Ellic. well remarks that ἀλλά here after an affirmative sentence should have its full adversative force) **they shall not advance further** (in ch ii 16, it is said, ἐπὶ πλεῖον προκόψουσιν ἀσεβείας and it is in vain to deny that there is an apparent and literal inconsistency between the two assertions. But on looking further into them, it is manifest, that while there the Apostle is speaking of an immediate spread of error, here he is looking to its ultimate defeat and extinction as Chrys, κἂν πρότερον ἀνθήσῃ τὰ τῆς πλάνης, εἰς τέλος οὐ διαμενεῖ) **for their folly** (unintelligent and senseless method of proselytizing and upholding their opinions [see ref. Luke], —and indeed folly of those opinions themselves) **shall be thoroughly manifested** (ref πάντ' ἐποίησεν ἔκδηλα, Demosth 21. 10) **to all, as also that of those men was** (Exod viii. 18; ix. 11 but most probably the allusion is to their traditional end).

10—17.] *Contrast, by way of reminding and exhortation, of the education, knowledge, and life of Timotheus with the character just drawn of the opponents* **But thou followedst** (ref not, as Chrys, Thl, Œc, al, τούτων σὺ μάρτυς,—for some of the undermentioned occurred before the conversion of Timotheus, and of many of them this could not be properly said,—but 'followedst as thy pattern' 'it was my example in all these things which was set before thee as thy guide—thou wert a follower of me, as I of Christ' So Calvin ['laudat tanquam suarum virtutum imitatorem, ac si diceret, jam pridem assuefactus es ad mea instituta, perge modo qua cœpisti'], Aret., De W, Huther,

l διδασκαλίᾳ, τῇ m ἀγωγῇ, τῇ n προθέσει, τῇ o πίστει, τῇ
pq μακροθυμίᾳ, τῇ o ἀγάπῃ, τῇ opr ὑπομονῇ, 11 τοῖς s διωγμοῖς, τοῖς t παθήμασιν, οἷά μοι ἐγένετο ἐν Ἀντιοχείᾳ, ἐν
Ἰκονίῳ, ἐν Λύστροις· οἵους s διωγμοὺς u ὑπήνεγκα καὶ
v ἐκ πάντων με v ἐρρύσατο ὁ κύριος· 12 w καὶ πάντες w δὲ

ACDF KLℵ a b c d e f g h k l m n o 17

l 1 Tim i 10 reff. m here only — Esth ii 20 ἀγωγὴ τοῦ βίου, Polyb iv 74 1 & 4. see note. n = Acts xi 23 2 Macc iii 8 o 1 Tim vi 11 Tit ii 2 2 Pet i 6, 7 p Col i 11 q Gal v 22 reff r Luke viii 15. 2 Cor i 6 vi 4 xii 12 al Ps ix 18. s 2 Thess i 4 reff t = Rom viii 18 2 Cor i 5 Col i 24 + u 1 Cor x 13 1 Pet ii 19 only Job ii 10 Prov vi 33 v Col. i 13 reff w 1 Tim iii 10 reff

θησας F μοι D¹ for αγωγη, αγαπη D¹ om τη αγαπη A 179 Thl
11 εγενοντο A 72 lectt 7 18 txt CDFKLℵ rel for ερρυ, ερυσατο AD¹ d for κυριος, θεος D

Wiesinger, all The *aorist* is both less obvious and more appropriate than the *perfect*: this *was* the example set before him, and the reminiscence, joined to the exhortation of ver. 14, bears something of reproach with it, which is quite in accordance with what we have reason to infer from the general tone of the Epistle. Whereas the *perfect* would imply that the example had been really ever before him, and followed up to the present moment: and so would weaken the necessity of the exhortation) **my teaching, conduct** (reff · and add 2 Macc. iv. 16, vi 8, xi 24 τῇ διὰ τῶν ἔργων πολιτείᾳ, Thdrt. All these words are dependent on μου, not to be taken [Mack] as applying to Timotheus, 'Thou followedst my teaching in thy conduct, &c,' which would introduce an unnatural accumulation of encomia on him, and would besides assume that he had been persecuted [cf. τοῖς διωγμοῖς], which there is no reason to suppose), **purpose** (ref τοῦτο περὶ προθυμίας καὶ τοῦ παραστήματος τῆς ψυχῆς, Chrys Ellic remarks, that in all other passages in St. Paul's Epistles, πρόθεσις is used with reference to God), **faith** (ὁποίαν ἔχω περὶ τὸν δεσπότην διάθεσιν, Thdrt), **long-suffering** (ὅπως φέρω τὰ τῶν ἀδελφῶν πλημμελήματα, Thdrt: or perhaps, as Chrys, πῶς οὐδέν με τούτων ἐτάραττε,—his patience in respect of the false teachers and the troubles of the time), **love** (ὅπερ οὐκ εἶχον οὗτοι, Chrys), **endurance** (πῶς φέρω γενναίως τῶν ἐναντίων τὰς προσβολάς, Thdrt), **persecutions** ('to these ὑπομονή furnished the note of transition' Huth), **sufferings** (not only was I persecuted, but the persecution issued in infliction of suffering), **such** (sufferings) **as befell me in Antioch** (of Pisidia), **in Iconium, in Lystra** (why should these be especially enumerated? Thdrt assigns as a reason, τοὺς ἄλλους καταλιπὼν τῶν ἐν τῇ Πισιδίᾳ καὶ τῇ Λυκαονίᾳ συμβεβηκότων αὐτῷ κινδύνων ἀνέμνησε Λυκάων γὰρ ἦν καὶ αὐτὸς πρὸς ὃν ἔγραφε, καὶ ταῦτα τῶν ἄλλων ἦν αὐτῷ γνωριμώτερα And so Chrys, and many both ancient and modern It may be so, doubtless and this reason, though rejected by De W., Huther, Wiesinger, al, seems much better to suit the context and probability, than the other, given by Huther, al, that these persecutions were the first which befell the Apostle in his missionary work among the heathen It is objected to it, that during the former of these persecutions Timotheus was not with St Paul But the answer to that is easy. At the time of his conversion, they were recent, and the talk of the churches in those parts and thus, especially with our rendering, and the aor sense of παρηκολούθησας, would be naturally mentioned, as being those sufferings of the Apostle which first excited the young convert's attention to make them his own pattern of what he too must suffer for the Gospel's sake. Baur and De Wette regard the exact correspondence with the Acts [xiii 50; xiv 5, 19; xvi. 3] as a suspicious circumstance. Wiesinger well asks, would they have regarded a discrepancy from the Acts as a mark of genuineness?), **what persecutions** (there is a zeugmatic construction here—understand, 'thou sawest, in proposing to thyself a pattern thou hadst before thee . . .' [I cannot see how, as Ellic. asserts, this rendering vitiates the construction Doubtless his rendering, '*such persecutions as*,' is legitimate, but it seems to me feeble after the preceding οἷα] Heydem, Mack, al, understand these words as an exclamation: οἵους διωγμ. ὑπήνεγκα! I need hardly observe that such an exclamation would be wholly alien from the character and style of the Apostle) **I underwent, and out of all the Lord delivered me** (ἀμφότερα [both clauses of the sentence] παρακλήσεως· ὅτι καὶ ἐγὼ προθυμίαν παρειχόμην γενναίαν, καὶ [ὅτι] οὐκ ἐγ-

οἱ [x] θέλοντες [y] εὐσεβῶς ζῆν ἐν χριστῷ Ἰησοῦ [z] διωχθήσον-
ται. 13 πονηροὶ δὲ ἄνθρωποι καὶ [a] γόητες [b] προκόψουσιν
[b] ἐπὶ τὸ [c] χεῖρον, [d] πλανῶντες καὶ [e] πλανώμενοι. 14 σὺ δὲ
[f] μένε [f] ἐν [g] οἷς ἔμαθες καὶ [h] ἐπιστώθης, εἰδὼς παρὰ τίνων

x John v 35, 40 Heb xiii 18
y Tit ii 12 only† Xen Mem ii 2 14 (see 1 Tim ii 2 reff)
z = Matt v 10 al fr Ps vii 1 2 Macc v 8
a here only† (-τεια 2 Macc xii 24 λογοι γοητικοι, Prov xxvi 22 Aq) see note
b ver 9
c Paul, 1 Tim v 8 only Mark v 25 Heb x 29 al† Wisd xv 18 only
d Matt xxiv 4, &c 1 John ii 26 Rev ii 20 al Deut xiii 5
e Tit iii 3 reff
f 1 Cor vii 20, 24 1 John ii 28 and passim Eccles vii 16 2 Macc viii 1
g attr, Matt xxiv 50 Luke ii 20 al fr Paul, Rom vi 16 bis 2 Cor ii 10, &c
h here only 3 Kings viii 26

12 ζην bef ευσεβως AN m 17 syr copt Orig$_2$ Ath$_1$ txt CDFKL rel latt Syr goth Ath$_2$ Chr Thdrt Thl.
13 for χειρον, πλειον 67[2] γοηται D[1] γοηταις D[2] [3]F
14 rec τινος (applying it to Paul alone · see ch ii. 2), with C[3]DKL rel vulg(and F-lat) syrr copt goth æth Chr Thdrt Damasc Hil Aug · txt AC[1]FN 17 Ambrst

κατελείφθην. Chrys.). 12] Yea, and (or, and moreover I have explained this καὶ . δὲ on 1 Tim iii 10 'They who will, &c, must make up their minds to this additional circumstance,' viz. persecution) all who are minded (purpose see reff. 'whose will is to,' Ellic hardly so strong as '*who determine*,' Conyb Nor can it be said that θέλοντες is emphatic, as Huth. It requires its meaning of '*purpose*' to be clearly expressed, not slurred over but that meaning is not especially prominent) to live piously (ref) in Christ Jesus ('extra Jesum Christum nulla pietas,' Beng and this peculiar reference of εὐσέβεια [cf 1 Tim. iii. 16] should always be borne in mind in these Epistles) shall be persecuted. 13] But (on the other hand a reason why persecutions must be expected, and even worse and more bitter as time goes on The opposition certainly, as seems to me [see also Wiesinger and Ellicott], is to the clause immediately preceding, not, as De W. and Huther maintain, to ver. 10 f. There would thus be no real contrast whereas on our view, it is forcibly represented that the breach between light and darkness, between εὐσεβεια and πονηρία, would not be healed, but rather widened, as time went on) evil men (in general,—over the world. particularized, as applying to the matter in hand, by the next words) and seducers (lit *magicians*, in allusion probably to the Egyptian magicians mentioned above Jos contra Apion. ii 16, has the word in this sense,—τοιοῦτός τις ἡμῶν ὁ νομοθέτης, οὐ γόης, οὐδ' ἀπατεών Demosth p. 374. 20, puts into the mouth of Æschines, respecting Philip, ἄπιστος, γόης, πονηρός See Wetst, and Suicer in voc, and consult Ellic's note here) shall grow worse and worse ('*advance in the direction of worse*' see above, ver. 9 There the *diffusion* of evil was spoken of. here its *intensity*), deceiving and being deceived (πλανώμενοι is not middle [as Bengel, 'qui se seducendos permittunt'] but passive rather *for contrast's sake*, as the middle would be vapid, than for the reason given by Huther, that if so, it would stand first, because he that deceives others is first himself deceived: for we might say exactly the same of the passive Nor is the active participle to be assigned to the γόητες and the passive to the πονηροί, as Bengel also both equally designate both But his remark is striking and just, 'Qui semel alios decipere cœpit, eo minus ipse ab errore se recipit, et eo facilius alienos errores mutuo amplectitur')

14] But do thou continue in the things which (the object to ἔμαθες, and the remoter object to ἐπιστώθης, must, in the construction, be supplied out of the ἐν οἷς) thou learnedst (= ἤκουσας παρ' ἐμοῦ, ch ii 2) and wert convinced of (so Homer, Od φ 217 f, where Odysseus shews his scar,—εἰ δ' ἄγε δὴ καὶ σῆμα ἀριφραδὲς ἄλλο τι δείξω, | ὄφρα μὲ εὖ γνῶτον, πιστωθῆτόν τ' ἐνὶ θυμῷ, and Soph Œd Col 1040, σὺ δ' ἡμῖν, Οἰδίπους, | ἕκηλος αὐτοῦ μίμνε, πιστωθεὶς ὅτι | ἢν μὴ θάνω 'γὼ πρόσθεν, οὐχὶ παύσομαι. The Vulg. 'credita sunt tibi' followed by Luth, Beza, Calv, besides the Roman-Catholic expositors, would require ἐπιστεύθης, cf 1 Cor. ix 17 al), knowing (as thou dost) from what teachers (viz. thy mother Lois and grandmother Eunice, ch. i 5 cf. ἀπὸ βρέφους below · not Paul and Barnabas, as Grot, nor the πολλοὶ μάρτυρες of ch ii 2 If the singular τίνος, then the Apostle must be meant) thou learnedst them, and (knowing) that (the Vulg. renders ὅτι *quia*, and thus breaks off the connexion with εἰδώς: and so also Luth., 'und weil' . . . . Bengel [adding, 'ætiologia duplex Similis constr. διὰ . . . . καὶ ὅτι, Joh. ii.

ἔμαθες, 15 καὶ ὅτι [j] ἀπὸ [k] βρέφους [τὰ] [l] ἱερὰ [m] γράμματα
οἶδας τὰ δυνάμενά σε [n] σοφίσαι εἰς σωτηρίαν διὰ [o] πίστεως
[p] τῆς [o] ἐν χριστῷ Ἰησοῦ. 16 πᾶσα γραφὴ [q] θεόπνευστος
καὶ [r] ὠφέλιμος [r] πρὸς [s] διδασκαλίαν, πρὸς [t] ἐλεγμόν, πρὸς

ACDF KLN a b c d e f g h k l m n o 17

j here only. k Luke i. 41, 44. ii. 12, 16. xviii. 15. Acts vii. 19. 1 Pet. ii. 2 only†. Sir. xix. 11. 1 Macc. i. 61. 2 Macc. vi. 10 only. l adj., 1 Cor. ix. 13 (bis) only. Josh. vi. 7. 2 Macc. viii. 23. m = John v. 47. vii. 15. Esth. vi. 1. n = here (2 Pet. i. 16) only. Ps. xviii. 7. civ. 22. cxviii. 98. o Eph. i. 15 reff. p ch. ii. 10 reff. q here only †. r 1 Tim. iv. 8 reff. s ver. 10. t here only. Lev. xix. 17. Num. v. 18. 4 Kings xix. 3 al.

15. om 1st τα C^2D^1Fℵ 17 Damasc$_1$. ins AC^1D^3KL rel Clem. οιδες D

16. om και vulg Syr copt Clem (Orig$_2$[?] see note) Thdor-mops(in Facund) Tert Ambrst Pelag Cassiod: ins ACDFKLℵ rel Orig Chr Thdrt Damasc. rec ελεγχον, with DKL rel Orig Chr Thdrt Damasc: txt ACFℵ.

24,—ἐπιγνοὺς . . . καὶ ὅτι, Act. xxii. 29']. But the other construction is much more natural) from a child (ἀπὸ πρώτης ἡλικίας, Chrys. The expression carries the learning back to his extreme infancy see Ellic here) thou hast known the (with or without the art., this will be the rendering) **holy scriptures** (of the O T. This expression for the Scriptures, not elsewhere found in the N T [hardly, as Huther, John vii 15], is common in Josephus. see Wetst cf also reff 2 Macc.) **which are able** (not as Bengel, "'quæ *poterant*' vis præteriti ex *nosti* redundat in participium" for οἶδας is necessarily *present* in signification 'thou hast known . . which were' would be a solœcism) **to make thee wise** (reff So Hes Op. 647,—οὔτε τι ναυτιλίης σεσοφισμένος, οὔτε τι νηῶν Diog Laert. v. 90, in an epigram, ἀλλα διεψεύσθης, σεσοφισμένε) **unto** (towards the attainment of) **salvation, by means of** (the instrument whereby the σοφίσαι is to take place· not to be joined to σωτηρίαν, as Thl., Bengel, al ; not so much for lack of the art. τὴν prefixed, as because the τῆς ἐν χ. Ἰησ would thus become an unnatural expansion of the merely subordinate πίστεως) **faith, namely that which** (σωτηρία διὰ πίστεως being almost a technical phrase, it is best to keep πίστις here abstract, and then to particularize) **is in** (which rests upon, is reposed in) **Christ Jesus** 16.] The immense value to Timotheus of this early instruction is shewn by a declaration of the profit of Scripture in furthering the spiritual life There is considerable doubt about the construction of this clause, **πᾶσα . ὠφέλιμος** Is it to be taken, (1) **πᾶσα γραφὴ** (subject) **θεόπνευστος** (predicate) (ἐστιν), **καὶ ὠφ**, i. e. '*every Scripture* [see below] *is* **θεόπνευστος** *and* **ὠφέλιμος**' or (2) **πᾶσα γραφὴ θεόπνευστος** (subject) **καὶ ὠφέλ** (ἐστιν) (predicate), i e *Every* **γραφὴ θεόπνευστος** *is also* **ὠφέλιμος**? The former is followed by Chrys [πᾶσα οὖν ἡ τοιαύτη θεόπνευστος], Greg -Nyss [διὰ τοῦτο πᾶσα γραφὴ θεόπνευστος λέγεται], Ath, Est ['duo affirmantur omnem scripturam esse divinitus inspiratam, et eandem esse utilem,' &c], all, by Calv., Wolf, al · by De W, Wiesinger, Conyb, &c, and the E V. The latter by Orig [πᾶσα γραφὴ θεόπνευστος οὖσα ὠφέλιμός ἐστι, in Jesu nave Hom xx 3, vol ii p 411 repeated in the Philocal c 12, vol xxv. p 65, ed Lomm], Thdrt [θεόπνευστον δὲ γραφὴν τὴν πνευματικὴν ὠνόμασεν], al by Grot ['bene expressit sensum Syrus : omnis Scriptura quæ a Deo inspirata est, etiam utilis,' &c], Erasm. ['tota Scr quæ nobis non humano ingenio &c., magnam habet utilitatem,' &c], Camerar., Whitby, Hammond, al.· by Rosenm, Heinr, Huther, &c and the Syr [above], Vulg ['omnis Scriptura divinitus inspirata utilis est,' &c.], Luth. [denn alle Schrift von Gott eingegeben ist nütze u. s w.], &c In deciding between these two, the following considerations must be weighed (a) the requirement of the context. The object of the present verse plainly is to set before Timotheus the value of his early instruction as a motive to his remaining faithful to it. It is then very possible, that the Apostle might wish to exalt the dignity of the Scripture by asserting of it that it was θεόπνευστος, and then out of this lofty predicate might unfold καὶ ὠφελ, &c.—its various uses in the spiritual life On the other hand it may be urged, that thus the two epithets do not hang naturally together, the first consisting of the one word θεόπνευστος, and the other being expanded into a whole sentence: especially as in order at all to give symmetry to the whole, the ἵνα ἄρτιος ᾖ κ.τ λ must be understood as the purposed result of the θεοπνευστία as well as the ὠφέλεια of the Scriptures, which is hardly natural (b) the requirements of the grammatical construction of καί, which must on all grounds be retained as genuine.

[u] ἐπανόρθωσιν, πρὸς [v] παιδείαν τὴν ἐν δικαιοσύνῃ· 17 ἵνα

u here only + Esdr viii 52 1 Macc xiv 34 only v Eph vi 4 Heb xii 5, 7, 8, 11 only Prov xv 10

om προς επανορθωσιν F (added on marg of G.)

Can this καί be rendered '*also*,' and attached to ὠφέλιμος? There seems no reason to question its legitimacy, thus taken Such an expression as this, πᾶς ἀνὴρ πλεονέκτης, καὶ εἰδωλολάτρης, though a harsh sentence, would be a legitimate one And constructions more or less approximating to this are found in the N T. e g, Luke i. 36, Ἐλισάβετ ἡ συγγενίς σου καὶ αὐτὴ συνειληφυῖα Acts xxvi 26, πρὸς ὃν καὶ παῤῥησιαζόμενος λαλῶ xxviii 28, αὐτοὶ καὶ ἀκούσονται: Rom. viii 29, οὓς προέγνω καὶ προώρισεν Gal iv. 7, εἰ δὲ υἱὸς καὶ κληρονόμος. In all these, καί introduces the predicatory clause, calling special attention to the fact enounced in it. Cf also such expressions as καὶ τοῦτο μὲν ἧττον καὶ θαυμαστόν, Plato, Symp p 177 b,—σκέψαι τάλαν, ὡς καὶ καταγέλαστον τὸ πρᾶγμα φαίνεται, Aristoph Eccl 125,—ἣ μᾶλλον καὶ ἐπετίθεντο, Thuc iv. 1 I own on the whole the balance seems to me to incline on the side of (2), unobjectionable as it is in construction, and of the two, better suited to the context I therefore follow it, hesitatingly, I confess, but feeling that it is not to be lightly overthrown See on the whole, Ellicott, who takes the same view **Every Scripture** (not 'every writing.' the word, with or without the art, never occurs in the N. T except in the sense of 'Scripture;' and we have it, as we might expect in the later apostolic times, anarthrous in 2 Pet i. 20, πᾶσα προφητεία γραφῆς. Where it occurs anarthrous in the Gospels, it signifies a passage of Scripture, '*a Scripture*,' as we say · e g. John xix 37 It is true, that πᾶσα γραφή *might be* numbered with those other apparent solœcisms, πᾶσα οἰκοδομή, Eph. ii 21, πᾶσα Ἱεροσόλυμα, Matt. ii 3, where the subst being used anarthrous, πᾶς = πᾶς ὁ but, in the presence of such phrases as ἑτέρα γραφὴ λέγει [John 1 c], it is safer to keep to the meaning, unobjectionable both grammatically and contextually, 'every Scripture'—i e. 'every part of [= *in the sense*, 'all'] Scripture') **given by inspiration of God** (as γραφή answers to γράμματα above, so θεόπνευστος to ἱερά De W. has well illustrated the word. "θεόπνευστος '*divinitus inspirata*,' Vulg, is an expression and idea connected with πνεῦμα [properly *breath*], the power of the divine Spirit being conceived of as a breath of life the word thus amounts to 'inspired,' 'breathed through,' 'full of the Spirit' It [the idea] is common to Jews, Greeks, and Romans. Jos. contra Apion. i. 7, τῶν προφητῶν τὰ μὲν ἀνωτάτω καὶ τὰ παλαιότατα κατὰ τὴν ἐπίπνοιαν τὴν ἀπὸ τοῦ θεοῦ μαθόντων. Æschyl. Suppl 18; ἐπίπνοια Διός, and similarly Polyb x 2 12. Plat. republ vi 499 b, legg v. 738 c Phocyl 121, τῆς δὲ θεοπνεύστου σοφίης λόγος ἐστὶν ἄριστος. Plut. mor p 904, τοὺς ὀνείρους τοὺς θεοπνεύστους · Cic pro Arch 8, 'poetam . . . quasi divino quodam spiritu af-[l. in-]flari' de nat. deor. ii. 66, 'nemo vir magnus sine aliquo afflatu divino unquam fuit:' de div i. 18, 'oracula instinctu divino afflatuque funduntur.' First of all, θεόπνευστος is found as a predicate of persons ὁ θεόπνευστος ἀνήρ Wetst. [from Marcus Ægyptius], cf Jos and Cic. in the two passages above,—2 Pet i. 21, ὑπὸ πνεύματος ἁγίου φερόμενοι ἐλάλησαν ἀπὸ θεοῦ ἄνθρωποι: Matt xxii. 43, Δαυεὶδ ἐν πνεύματι καλεῖ αὐτὸν κύριον then it was also applied to things, cf the last passage of Cicero, and Phocyl, Plutarch, above." On the meaning of the word as applied to the Scriptures, see Prolegg to Vol I 'On the inspiration of the Gospels' and compare Ellicott's note here. As applied to the prophets, it would not materially differ, except that we ever regard one speaking *prophecy*, strictly so called, as more immediately and thoroughly the mouthpiece of the Holy Spirit, seeing that the future is wholly hidden from men, and God does not in this case use or inspire *human testimony to facts*, but suggests the *whole substance* of what is said, *direct* from Himself) **is also** (besides this its quality of inspiration on the construction, see above) **profitable for** (towards) **teaching** (ἃ γὰρ ἀγνοοῦμεν ἐκεῖθεν μανθάνομεν, Thdrt This, the *teaching of the person* reading the Scriptures, not the *making him a teacher*, as Estius characteristically, is evidently the meaning It is not Timotheus's ability as a teacher, but his stability as a Christian, which is here in question), **for conviction** (ἐλέγχει γὰρ ἡμῶν τὸν παράνομον βίον, Thdrt The above remark applies here also), **for correction** (παρακαλεῖ γὰρ καὶ τοὺς παρατραπέντας ἐπανελθεῖν εἰς τὴν εὐθεῖαν ὁδόν, Thdrt So Philo, Quod Deus immut. 37,

w here only † x 1 Tim vi 11 only Josh xiv 6 y ch ii 21 (reff) z Acts xxi 5 only † a 1 Tim v 21 reff b 1 Pet iv 5 see Acts x 42 Rom xiv 9

[w] ἄρτιος ᾖ ὁ τοῦ [x] θεοῦ [x] ἄνθρωπος, [y] πρὸς πᾶν [y] ἔργον
[y] ἀγαθὸν [z] ἐξηρτισμένος IV. 1 [a] Διαμαρτύρομαι [a] ἐνώπιον τοῦ θεοῦ καὶ χριστοῦ Ἰησοῦ τοῦ μέλλοντος
[b] κρίνειν [b] ζῶντας καὶ [b] νεκρούς, καὶ τὴν [c] ἐπιφάνειαν αὐτοῦ καὶ τὴν βασιλείαν αὐτοῦ, 2 [d] κήρυξον τὸν [d] λόγον,

ACDF KLℵ a b c d e f g h k l m n o 17

c 2 Thess ii 8 1 Tim vi 14 ch i 10 ver 8. Tit ii 13 only 2 Kings vii 23 constr (see note), Deut iv 26. d here only see Rom x 8 al

17 for αρτιος, τελιος D¹. εξηρτιμενος F εξηρτημ. K e n o.

Chap IV 1 rec aft διαμαρτυρομαι ins ουν εγω, with D³K rel om ACD¹FLℵ 17 67² latt Syr copt æth arm Ath Cyr lat-ff rec aft και ins του κυριου, with D³KL rel Syr syr-w-ast om ACD¹Fℵ am(with fuld demid) copt goth Bas Did Cyr lat-ff (om του θεου και 17) rec ιησ bef χρ, with D³KL rel syrr æth Ath Chr Thdrt txt ACD¹Fℵ am(with fuld demid) copt goth Bas Did Cyr lat-ff for κρινειν, κριναι F b 17 67² 73 Thdrt Thl rec κατα την επιφ, with D³KLℵ³ rel syr goth Thdrt Damasc txt ACD¹Fℵ¹ 17 67² am(with fuld harl tol) copt Cyr (Chr also refers to it κατὰ (?) τὴν ἐπιφ αὐ κ τ βασ αὐτοῦ κρίνειν, πότε; ἐν τῇ ἐπιφανείᾳ αὐτοῦ τῇ μετὰ δόξης, τῇ μετὰ βασιλείας. ἢ τοίνυν τοῦτο λέγει ὅτι οὐχ οὕτως ἥξει ὡς νῦν, ἢ ὅτι διαμαρτύρομαί σοι τὴν ἐπιφάνειαν αὐτ κ τ βασ) Cæs-arel Fulg-Bede.

vol i p 299, ἐπὶ τῇ τοῦ παντὸς ἐπανορθώσει βίου similarly Polyb. p. 50, 26 al freq in Raphel · so Epictetus, ib), **for discipline** (ref. Eph and note) **in** (if the construction is filled out, the παιδείαν is abstract, and the τὴν ἐν particularizes, discipline, viz. that which . . . . .) **righteousness** (which is versed in, as its element and condition, righteousness, and so disciplines a man to be holy, just, and true). **that** (result of the profitableness of Scripture: reasons why God has, having Himself inspired it, endowed it with this profitableness) **the man of God** (ref 1 Tim and note) **may be perfect** (ready at every point · 'aptus in officio,' Beng.), **thoroughly made ready** (see note on ref Acts It is blamed by the etymologists as an ἀδόκιμον. Jos. Antt iii 2 2, has πολεμεῖν πρὸς ἀνθρώπους τοῖς πᾶσι καλῶς ἐξηρτισμένους) **to every good work** (rather to be generally understood than officially: the man of God is not only a teacher, but any spiritual man and the whole of the present passage regards the universal spiritual life. In ch. iv. 1 ff. he returns to the official duties of Timotheus but here he is on that which is the common basis of all duty).

Ch IV. 1—8] *Earnest exhortation to Timotheus to fulfil his office, in the near prospect of defection from the truth, and of the Apostle's own departure from life* **I adjure thee** (ref) **before God, and Christ Jesus, who is about to judge living and dead** (λέγει τοὺς ἤδη ἀπελθόντας καὶ τοὺς τότε καταλειφθησομένους ζῶντας, Thl so also Thdrt, and Chrys., alt 2 not as Chrys, alt 1, ἁμαρτωλοὺς λέγει καὶ δικαίους), **and by** (i e 'and I call to witness,' as in Deut. iv 26, διαμαρτύρομαι ὑμῖν τόν τε οὐρανὸν καὶ τὴν γῆν, the construction being changed from that in the first clause This is better than with Huther, to take the accusatives as merely acc. jurandi, as in 1 Cor. xv. 31; James v. 12 With κατά, it would be, 'at His, &c ·' cf. Matt xxvii 15, Acts xiii. 27, Heb iii 8) **his appearing** (reff) **and his kingdom** (these two, τ. ἐπιφ αὐτοῦ κ. τ. βασ. αὐτοῦ, are not to be taken as a hendiadys, as Bengel,—'ἐπιφάνεια est revelatio et exortus regni'—but each has its place in the adjuration —His *coming*, at which we shall stand before Him;—His *kingdom*, in which we hope to reign with Him), 2] **proclaim** (notice the sudden and unconnected aorists. Ellic. well observes after Schoemann, Isæus, p. 235, that the use of the imper. aor. seems often due, both in the N T and in classical authors, to the "habitus aut affectus loquentis") **the word** (of God The construction after διαμ. is carried on in 1 Tim v. 21 with ἵνα. in our ch ii 14 with infinitives here with simple imperatives, which is more abrupt and forcible), **press on** (ἐπίστηθι is generally referred to the last clause—'be diligent in preaching' μετ' ἐπιμονῆς κ. ἐπιστασίας λάλησον, as Thl. and Thdrt, οὐχ ἁπλῶς καὶ ὡς ἔτυχεν αὐτὸν κηρύττειν παρεγγυᾷ, ἀλλὰ πάντα καιρὸν ἐπιτήδειον πρὸς τοῦτο νομίζειν. De W. doubts this meaning being justified, and would rather keep the verb to its simpler meaning 'accede [ad cœtus Chris-

ᵉἐπίστηθι ᶠεὐκαίρως ᵍἀκαίρως, ʰἔλεγξον, ⁱἐπιτίμησον,
ᵏπαρακάλεσον, ἐν ˡπάσῃ ᵐμακροθυμίᾳ καὶ ⁿδιδαχῇ. 3 ἔσται γὰρ καιρὸς ὅτε τῆς ᵒὑγιαινούσης ᵒδιδασκαλίας οὐκ
ᵖἀνέξονται, ἀλλὰ κατὰ τὰς ἰδίας ἐπιθυμίας ἑαυτοῖς ᵠἐπι-
σωρεύσουσιν ʳδιδασκάλους ˢκνηθόμενοι τὴν ᵗἀκοήν, 4 καὶ

e = here only, see note, also ver 6, and Jer xxvi (xlvi) 14 f Mark xiv 11 only† Sir xviii 22 only (-πος, Heb iv 16 -ρεῖν, Mark vi 31 -ρια, Matt xxvi 16) g here only† Sir xxxv (xxxii) 4 (-ρος, Sir xx 19 -ρεῖσθαι, Phil iv 10) h = Matt xviii 15 1 Cor xiv 24 Eph v 11 Tit i 9, 13 ii 15 Prov x 10 i Paul, here only Gospp (exc John) passim, and Jude 9, from Zech iii 2 k absol, 1 Cor iv 13 Tit i 9 l = Phil i 20 reff m = Col i 11 reff n Paul, Rom vi 17 xvi 17 1 Cor xiv 6 26 Tit i 9 only Matt vii 28 al Ps lix tit only o 1 Tim i 10 reff p Acts xviii 14 2 Cor xi 1, &c Heb xiii 22 Job vi 26 q here only† (Symm, Cant ii 4 Job xiv 17) r Eph iv 11 reff s here only† see note t = 1 Cor xii 17 Heb v 11 2 Pet ii 8 2 Macc xv 39

2 ακαιρ bef ευκαιρ C. παρακαλ bef επιτιμ Fℵ¹ m latt goth Orig Ambrst Pelag Aug Ambr. for πασῃ, μασῃ(sic) ℵ
3 ενεξονται C for κατα, προς D rec τας επιθ τας ιδ, with KL rel copt Chr Damasc Aug: txt ACDFℵ g m 17 latt goth Ephr Thdrt Thl Œc lat-ff επισωρ bef εαυτ. F m 73 vulg arm lat-ff for κνηθομενοι, τερπομενοι 67²

tianos],' as Bretsch and so Huther But there seems no need to confine the sense so narrowly The quotations in De W. himself justify the meaning of 'press on,' 'be urgent,' generally: not perhaps in preaching only, but in the whole work of the ministry. Cf Demosth p 1187 G, ἐπειδὴ . . ἐφειστήκει δ' αὐτῷ Καλλίστρατος καὶ Ἰφικράτης . . . . οὕτω δὲ διέθεσαν ὑμᾶς κατηγοροῦντες αὐτοῦ, — 'pressed upon him,' 'urgebant eum ' id. p 70 16, διὰ ταῦτ' ἐγρήγορεν ἐφέστηκεν, . . .) **in season, out of season** (μὴ καιρὸν ἔχε ὡρισμένον, ἀεὶ σοὶ καιρὸς ἔστω μὴ ἐν εἰρήνῃ, μὴ ἐν ἀδείᾳ, μηδὲ ἐν ἐκκλησίᾳ καθήμενος μόνον· κἂν ἐν τοῖς κινδύνοις, κἂν ἐν δεσμωτηρίῳ ᾖς, κἂν ἅλυσιν περικείμενος, κἂν μέλλῃς ἐξιέναι ἐπὶ θάνατον, καὶ παρ' αὐτὸν τὸν καιρὸν ἔλεγξον, μὴ ὑποσταλῇς ἐπιτιμῆσαι τότε γὰρ καὶ ἡ ἐπιτίμησις ἔχει καιρόν, ὅταν ὁ ἔλεγχος προχωρήσῃ, ὅταν ἀποδειχθῇ τὸ ἔργον, Chrys I cannot forbear also transcribing a very beautiful passage cited by Suicer i 146 from the same father, Hom xxx vol. v p 221 ἂν δ' ἄρα τοῖς αὐτοῖς ἐπιμένωσι καὶ μετὰ τὴν παραίνεσιν, οὐδὲ οὕτως ἡμεῖς ἀποστησόμεθα τῆς πρὸς αὐτοὺς συμβουλῆς καὶ γὰρ καὶ κρῆναι, κἂν μηδεὶς ὑδρεύηται, ῥέουσι καὶ οἱ ποταμοί, κἂν μηδεὶς πίνῃ, τρέχουσι δεῖ τοίνυν καὶ τὸν λέγοντα, κἂν μηδεὶς προσέχῃ, τὰ παρ' ἑαυτοῦ πάντα πληροῦν καὶ γὰρ νόμος ἡμῖν, τοῖς τὴν τοῦ λόγου διακονίαν ἐγκεχειρισμένοις, παρὰ τοῦ φιλανθρώπου κεῖται θεοῦ, μηδέποτε τὰ παρ' ἑαυτοῦ ἐλλιμπάνειν, μηδὲ σιγᾶν, κἂν ἀκούῃ τις, κἂν παρατρέχῃ This latter passage gives the more correct reference,—not so much to *his* opportunities, as the former, but to *theirs* [as Ellic. quotes from Aug on Ps cxxviii, vol iv. p 1689, "sonet verbum Dei volentibus opportune, nolentibus importune"] Bengel, from Priceus, gives examples of similar expressions "Nicetas Choniates, παιδαγωγῷ ἐμβριθεῖ ἐοικώς, **εὐκαίρως ἀκαίρως** ἐπέπληττεν Julian: ἐπορεύετο ἐπὶ τὰς τῶν φίλων οἰκίας **ἄκλητος κεκλημένος** Virgilii: '*digna indigna* pati,' Terentii 'cum milite isto *præsens absens* ut sies.'" So *fanda nefanda, plus minus, nolens volens*, &c), **convict, rebuke** (reff), **exhort, in** (not '*with*,' it is not the *accompaniment* of the actions, but the element, the temper in which they are to be performed) **all** (possible) **long-suffering and teaching** (not subjective, '*perseverance in teaching*,' as Conyb, but '*teaching*' itself it [objective] is to be the element in which these acts take place, as well as μακροθυμία [subjective]. The junction is harsh, but not therefore to be avoided Of course, hendiadys [= ἐν πάσῃ μακροθυμίᾳ διδαχῆς, Grot, Rosenm] is out of the question On διδαχή and διδασκαλία, see Ellicott's note) **3, 4**] *Reason why all these will be wanted* **For there shall be a time when they** (men, i e professing Christians, as the context shews) **will not endure** (not bear—as being offensive to them reff) **the healthy doctrine** (reff. viz of the Gospel), **but according to** (after the course of) **their own desires** (instead of, in subjection to God's providence) **will to themselves** (emphatic) **heap up** (one upon another: τὸ ἀδιάκριτον πλῆθος ἐδήλωσε, Chrys There is no meaning of 'heap upon themselves,' 'to their own cost,' as Luth, 'werden sie ihnen selbst Lehrer aufladen:' so Heydenr also) **teachers, having itching ears** (ζητοῦντές τι ἀκοῦσαι καθ' ἡδονήν, Hesych., 'sermones quærunt vitia sua titillantes,' Grot. This in fact amounts to the same as Chrys.'s, τῆς ἡδονῆς χάριν λέγοντας

ἀπὸ μὲν τῆς ἀληθείας τὴν [t] ἀκοὴν [u] ἀποστρέψουσιν, ἐπὶ
δὲ τοὺς [v] μύθους [w] ἐκτραπήσονται. 5 σὺ δὲ [x] νῆφε [y] ἐν
πᾶσιν, [z] κακοπάθησον, [a] ἔργον ποίησον [b] εὐαγγελιστοῦ,
τὴν [c] διακονίαν σου [d] πληροφόρησον. 6 ἐγὼ γὰρ ἤδη
[e] σπένδομαι καὶ ὁ καιρὸς τῆς ἐμῆς [f] ἀναλύσεως [g] ἐφέστηκεν·

ACDF KLℵ a b c d e f g h k l m n o 17

u Acts iii 26 ch i 15 Tit i 14 al. v 1 Tim i 4 reff. w 1 Tim i 6 reff. x Paul, 1 Thess v 6, 8 only. 1 Pet i 13 iv 7 v 8 only† y Col i 16 Phil iv 12 1 Tim iii 11 ch ii 7 Tit ii 9 Heb xiii 18 z ch ii 9. James v 13 only Jonah iv 10 only (θεια, James v 10) a = Acts xv 38 Phil i 22 al b Acts xxi 8 Eph iv 11 only† c Eph iv 22 reff d = ver 17 (Luke i. 1 Rom iv 21 xiv 5) only‡ (Eccles viii 11 only) e Phil ii 17 only 1 Chron xi 18 f here only την ἐκ τοῦ βιου ἀναλυσιν, Philo in Flacc 21, vol ii p 544 (-λυειν, Phil i 23) g = (Paul) 1 Thess v 3 Luke xxi 34 L P Wisd. vi 5, 8 see Acts xxviii 2 ver 2

5. om κακοπαθησον ℵ[1]. aft κακοπαθησον ins ως καλος στρατιωτης χρ ιησου A
6 for εμης αναλ, αναλ μου ACFℵ m 17 copt arm Eus Ath Ephr Pallad Cypr[1] txt DKL rel am(with demid F-lat) syrr Chr Thdrt Euthal-mss Damasc[1] Thl Œc Cypr[1].

καὶ τέρποντας τὴν ἀκοὴν ἐπιζητοῦντες, though De W. draws a distinction between them. Plut. de superst p 167 b [Wetst], μουσικὴν φησὶν ὁ Πλάτων . . ἀνθρώποις οὐ τρυφῆς ἕνεκα καὶ κνήσεως ὤτων δοθῆναι see more examples in Wetst), and **shall avert their ears from the truth, and be turned aside** (ref and note) **to fables** (the art. seems to imply that they would be at least *like* the fables already believed see 1 Tim i 4, and cf. Ellic. here). 5 ff.] He enforces on Timotheus the duty of worthily fulfilling his office, *in consideration of his own approaching end* For this being introduced, various reasons have been given — (1) he himself would be no longer able to make head against these adverse influences, and therefore must leave Timotheus and others to succeed him so Heydenr, Huther, al (2) "ego quamdiu vixi manum tibi porrexi tibi meæ assiduæ exhortationes non defuerunt, tibi mea consilia fuerunt magno adjumento, et exemplum etiam magnæ confirmationi jam tempus est ut tibi ipse magister sis atque hortator, natareque incipias sine cortice cave ne quid morte mea in te mutatum animadvertatur," Calv similarly Grot (3) "causa quæ Timotheum moveat ad officium Pauli discessus et beatitudo finis coronat opus" Beng, and so Chrys, Hom in loc, in a very beautiful passage, too long for transcription: (4) to stir up Timotheus to imitation of him so Pel, Ambr, Heim, al. [in De W] There seems no reason why any one of these should be chosen to the exclusion of the rest we may well, with Flatt, combine (1) and (4), at the same time bearing (2) and (3) in mind —'I am no longer here to withstand these things be thou a worthy successor of me, no longer depending on, but carrying out for thyself my directions· follow my steps, inherit their result, and the honour of their end'

5.] **But** (as contrasted with the description preceding) **do thou** (emphatic) **be sober** (it is difficult to give the full meaning of **νῆφε** in a version. The reference is especially to the clearness and wakefulness of attention and observance which attends on sobriety, as distinguished from the lack of these qualities in intoxication. 'Keep thy coolness and presence of mind, that thou be not entrapped into forgetfulness, but discern and use every opportunity of speaking and acting for the truth,' Mack. cf also Ellic) **in all things, suffer hardship** (reff), **do the work of an Evangelist** (reff here probably in a wider sense, including all that belongs to a preacher and teacher of the Gospel), **fill up the measure of** (fill up, in every point, leaving nothing undone in Beza's rendering, 'ministerii tui plenam fidem facito, i e. veris argumentis comproba te germanum esse Dei ministrum,'—so Calv 'ministerium tuum probatum redde,'—is justified by usage (reff), but hardly in accordance with ver. 17 see there) **thy ministry.** 6] For the connexion, see above **For I am already being offered** (as a drink-offering i e. the process is begun, which shall shed my blood '*Ready to be offered*' [E V, Conyb, so also Matthies, Est, al.] misses the force of the present Grot would render it 'jam nunc aspergor vino, id est, præparor ad mortem' but such a meaning for σπένδομαι does not seem to be justified see ref Phil. That σπένδομαι is there followed by ἐπὶ τῇ θυσίᾳ κ τ λ, and here stands absolutely, is surely no reason why this usage should not be as significant and as correct as that, against De W), **and the time of my departure** (ἀνάλυσις [ref] is merely this, and not *dissolutio*, as Vulg, Matthies,—nor as Elsner [so also Wolf] imagines, is there any allusion to guests

7 τὸν [hi] ἀγῶνα τὸν [i] καλὸν [ik] ἠγώνισμαι, τὸν [l] δρόμον
[m] τετέλεκα, τὴν πίστιν [n] τετήρηκα· 8 [o] λοιπὸν [p] ἀπόκειταί
μοι ὁ τῆς δικαιοσύνης [q] στέφανος, ὃν [r] ἀποδώσει μοι ὁ
κύριος ἐν [s] ἐκείνῃ τῇ [s] ἡμέρᾳ, ὁ [t] δίκαιος [u] κριτής, οὐ μόνον
δὲ ἐμοί, ἀλλὰ καὶ πᾶσιν τοῖς [v] ἠγαπηκόσιν τὴν [w] ἐπι-

h Phil i 30 reff. i 1 Tim vi 12 Eur Alc 648. k Col i 29 reff. l Acts xiii 25 xx 24 (both Paul) only. Jer viii. 6 m — Paul, here only Matt vii 28 al Sir vii 25 see Gal v 16 n — Paul, Eph iv 3 only see 1 Tim. vi 14 o — Acts xxvii 20 1 Cor i 16 2 Cor xiii 11 al p Col i 5 reff q 1 Cor ix 25 James i 12 1 Pet v 4 Rev ii 10 Prov iv 9 r = Rom ii 6 Rev xxii 12 al Ps l 12 (14) s ch i 12, 18. 2 Thess i 10 t Ps vii 11 2 Macc xii 6 u — Paul, here only Acts x 42 Heb xii 23 James v 9 v — 1 Pet iii 10, from Ps xxxiii 12 Ps xxxix 16 w ver 1

7 for τ αγ. τ κα, τον καλον αγωνα ACFℵ m 17 vulg Ath Chr_1 Cypr Pelag txt DKL rel syr copt goth $Orig_3$ Eus lat-ff.
8. om πασιν D^1 67^2 vulg(and F-lat) Syr Ambrst om τοις ηγαπηκοσιν $ℵ^1$ txt $ACD^3FKLℵ^3$ rel syr copt goth Chr_{expr} Thdrt Ps-Ath Damasc Cypr Archel Jer Aug_{aliq}.

breaking up [ἀναλύοντες] from a banquet and making libations [σπένδοντες] —'allusisse Apostolum ad *σπονδὰς* crediderim *ἀναλυόντων* e convivio, sensumque esse, sese ex hac vita molestiisque exsatiatum abiturum, libato non vino sed sanguine suo' He quotes from Athenæus i 13, *ἔσπενδον ἀπὸ τῶν δείπνων ἀναλύοντες.* But against this we have only to oppose that most sound and useful rule, that an allusion of this kind must never be imagined unless where necessitated by the context: and certainly here there is no trace of the idea of a banquet having been in the mind of the Apostle, various as are the images introduced) **is at hand** (not, is present, 'ist vorhanden,' Luth · which would be *ἐνέστηκεν*, see 2 Thess ii 2 note) 7.] **I have striven the good strife** (it is hardly correct to confine *ἀγών* to the sense of 'fight.' that it *may be*, but its reference is much wider, to *any contest*, see note on ref 1 Tim and here probably to that which is specified in the next clause see especially Heb xii 1), **I have finished my race** (see reff: the image belongs peculiarly to St Paul. In Phil iii 12 ff. he follows it out in detail See also 1 Cor ix 24 ff Heb xii 1, 2 Wetst. quotes Virg Æn iv 653, "Vixi, et quem dederat cursum fortuna, peregi"), **I have kept the faith** (not, as Heydenr, '*my plight to observe the laws of the race*' but as Bengel rightly observes, "res bis per metaphoram expressa nunc tertio loco exprimitur proprie" The constant use of *ἡ πίστις* in these Epistles in the objective technical sense, must rule the expression here This same consideration will preclude the meaning '*have kept my faith*,' '*my fidelity*,' as Raphel, Kypke, al) 8] **henceforth** (perhaps this adverb expresses *λοιπόν* better than any other. It appears to be used in later Greek, from Polybius downwards, in this sense of 'proinde,' 'itaque' cf. Polyb ii. 68 9, iv. 32. 5; x 15. 2) **there is laid up** (reff) **for me the** (not '*a*,' as E. V) **crown** (reff, and cf Phil. iii. 14) **of righteousness** (i e the bestowal of which is conditional on the substantiation and recognition of righteousness—q. d 'a crown among the righteous·' *τὸν τοῖς δικαίοις ηὐτρεπισμένον λέγει*, Thdrt. and so De W after Chrys., *δικαιοσύνην ἐνταῦθα πάλιν τὴν καθόλου φησὶν ἀρετήν.* This is better than with Huther, al, to take the gen. as one *appositionis*, as in James i 12, *ὁ στ. τῆς ζωῆς*· and 1 Pet v. 4, *ὁ τῆς δόξης στ* both these, *ζωή* and *δόξα*, may well constitute the crown, but it is not easy to say how *δικαιοσύνη* can Thdrt's alternative, *τὸν δικαίᾳ ψήφῳ δωρούμενον* [so Heydenr., Matth, al.], is equally objectionable There is, as Calv. has shewn, no sort of inconsistency here with the doctrines of grace "neque enim gratuita justificatio quæ nobis per fidem confertur, cum operum remuneratione pugnat quin potius rite conveniunt ista duo, gratis justificari hominem Christi beneficio, et tamen operum mercedem coram Deo relaturum. Nam simulatque nos in gratiam recipit Deus, opera quoque nostra grata habet, ut præmio quoque [licet indebito] dignetur." See further on this point Estius's note, and Conc. Trident Canones, Sess. vi. c 16, where the remarkable expression is quoted from the Epist. of Pope Cælestinus I. 12, "Dei tanta est erga omnes homines bonitas, ut eorum velit esse merita, quæ sunt ipsius dona"), **which the Lord** (Christ: cf. *ἐπιφάν. αὐτοῦ* below) **shall award** (more than 'give' see reff., and Matt. vi. 4, 6, &c., xvi. 27. the idea of *requital* should be expressed. Compare however Ellicott's note) **me in that day** (reff), **the righteous** (subj, '*just*,' but the word 'righteous' should be kept as answering to 'righteousness' above) **judge** (see Acts x 42 In

x ch ii 18 reff y 1 Cor iv 19 Phil ii 19, 24 al 4 Kings i 11 z Matt xxvii. 46 ‖ Mk Acts ii 27 2 Cor iv 9 ver 16 al Ps xv 10 a 1 John ii 15 b 1 Tim vi 17 Tit ii 12 only see 1 Tim iv 8 e ch ii 21 reff

φάνειαν αὐτοῦ. 9 ˣ Σπούδασον ἐλθεῖν πρός με ʸ ταχέως
10 Δημᾶς γάρ με ᶻ ἐγκατέλιπεν, ᵃ ἀγαπήσας τὸν ᵇ νῦν
ᵇ αἰῶνα, καὶ ἐπορεύθη εἰς Θεσσαλονίκην, Κρήσκης εἰς
Γαλατίαν, Τίτος εἰς Δαλματίαν· 11 Λουκᾶς ἐστιν μόνος
μετ᾽ ἐμοῦ. Μάρκον ᶜ ἀναλαβὼν ᵈ ἄγε μετὰ σεαυτοῦ·
ἔστιν γάρ μοι ᵉ εὔχρηστος εἰς ᶠ διακονίαν. 12 Τυχικὸν

ACDF KLℵ e b c d e f g h k l m n o 17

c = Acts xx 13, 14 xxiii 31, both of Paul Exod iv 20 d = 1 Thess iv 14 f = Eph iv 12 Col iv 17 1 Tim i 12 ver 5† (Esth vi 3 F 1 Macc xi 58 only)

9 πρ. εμε D

10 εγκατελειπεν ACD³FL o 17: κατελ. D¹ for γαλατιαν, γαλλιαν Cℵ 73. 80. 123 am¹ æth-rom Ath Eus Epiph(οὐ γὰρ ἐν τῇ Γαλατίᾳ, ὥς τινες πλανηθέντες νομίζουσιν, ἀλλὰ ἐν τῇ Γαλλίᾳ). δελματιαν C n o 67² δερματιαν A.

11. συν εμοι μονος D¹ latt goth Iren-int Ambrst. αγαγε A d f 31-8. 72. 238 Thdrt Damasc txt CDFKLℵ rel Chr.

this assertion of just judgment, there is nothing, as De W. imagines, to controvert the doctrines of grace see above);—**and** (but) **not only to me** (better than 'not to me only,' E. V., &c. [οὐδὲ ἐμοὶ μόνῳ], which though true, does not correctly represent the sense), **but also to all who have loved** (who shall then be found to have loved and still to be loving, see Winer, edn. 6, § 40. 4 a· *loved*, i. e. [reff] looked forward with earnest joy to) **His appearing** (ver 1).

9—22] *Request to come to Rome. Notices of his own state and that of others. greetings*

9 ff] **Do thine endeavour** (so also Tit. iii 12) **to come to me quickly** (this desire that Timotheus should come to him, appears in ch. i 4, 8: its reason is now specified): **for** (I am almost alone) **Demas** (mentioned Col iv 14 with Luke, as saluting the Colossians, and Philem. 24, also with Luke [and others], as one of the Apostle's συνεργοί) **deserted me, loving** (ἀγαπήσας [used perhaps in contrast to ver 8 above] is contemporary with ἐγκατέλιπεν—'*through love of*' so Ellic. also, who has hardly represented me rightly, when he quotes me as holding the *temporal* sense of the participle) **this present world** (τῆς ἀνέσεως ἐρασθείς, τοῦ ἀκινδύνου καὶ τοῦ ἀσφαλοῦς, μᾶλλον εἵλετο οἴκοι τρυφᾶν, ἢ μετ᾽ ἐμοῦ ταλαιπωρεῖσθαι καὶ συνδιαφέρειν μοι τοὺς παρόντας κινδύνους, Chrys), **and went to Thessalonica** ('his birthplace,' says De W · cf οἴκοι, Chrys, above but how ascertained? He may have gone there for the sake of traffic, which idea the ἀγαπήσας τὸν νῦν αἰῶνα would seem to support), **Crescens** (not named elsewhere He is said traditionally to have preached the Gospel in Galatia [Constt apost. vii. 46, p 1056], and, more recently [in Sophronius], to have founded the church at Vienne in *Gaul* this latter interpretation of **Γαλατίαν** [τὰς Γαλλίας οὕτως ἐκάλεσεν, see var. readd] Thdrt. also adopts All this traditional fabric is probably raised by conjecture on this passage. Winer, RWB) **to Galatia** (see Prolegg. to Gal § ii. 1), **Titus** (Prolegg. to Titus, § i.) **to Dalmatia** (part of the Roman province of Illyricum [Suet. Aug. 21. Tib. 9], on the coast of the Adriatic [Plin. iii 22 Strabo, vii p. 315], south of Liburnia [Plin. iii. 26], Winer, RWB. See the art. Dalmatia in Dr Smith's Dict. of Geography Thdrt says, referring to ἀγαπήσας τὸν νῦν αἰῶνα, οὗτοι [Crescens and Titus] τῆς κατηγορίας ἐκείνης ἐλεύθεροι· ὑπ᾽ αὐτοῦ γὰρ ἀπεστάλησαν τοῦ κηρύγματος ἕνεκα. But this hardly agrees with ἐπορεύθη, which must be understood with both names see also the contrast in ver 12 They had certainly left the Apostle of their own accord. why, does not appear) **Luke** (see Prolegg. to Luke's Gospel, § i) **is alone with me** (De W's question, 'where then was Aristarchus [Acts xxvii. 2 Col iv. 10 Philem 24]?' is one which we have no means of answering but we may venture this remark: a forger, such as De W. supposes the writer of this Epistle to be, would have taken good care to account for him). **Mark** (Col iv 10, note Philem. 24. John Mark, Acts xv. 38) **take up** (on thy way: so ἀναλαμβάνειν implies in the two first reff, and probably also here) **and bring with thee for he is to me useful for the ministry** (for help to me in my apostolic labours · not, as Conyb, '*his services are profitable to me*,' adding in a note below, "διακονίαν, not, '*the* ministry,' as E V" —no such conclusion can be drawn from the omission of the art after a preposi-

.. απεσ- δὲ ἀπέστειλα εἰς Ἔφεσον. 13 τὸν [g] φελόνην ὃν [h] ἀπέλιπον
τειλα d ἐν Τρωάδι παρὰ Κάρπῳ ἐρχόμενος φέρε, καὶ τὰ [i] βιβλία,
ACDF KLℵ a b [j] μάλιστα τὰς [k] μεμβράνας. 14 Ἀλέξανδρος ὁ [l] χαλκεὺς
c e f g h k l m n o 17 πολλά μοι κακὰ [m] ἐνεδείξατο· [n] ἀποδώσει αὐτῷ ὁ κύριος

g here only † h = Paul, ver 20. Tit i. 5 only (Heb iv. 6, 9. x. 26. Jude 6 only.) 2 Macc x. 19. i = Luke iv. 17, 20. Neh viii. 1, &c. j 1 Tim iv. 10 reff. k here only † l here only. Gen iv. 22. m = Tit ii. 10. iii. 2. Heb vi. 10, 11. see Eph. ii. 7 (reff.) n ver. 8 reff.

13. απελειπον ACFL 17. 14. rec (for αποδωσει) αποδωη, with D³KL rel am(with tol) Orthod Thdrt(πρόῤῥησίς ἐστιν, οὐκ ἀρά) Damasc₁(elsw₁ -δώσει, but there περὶ ἀρᾶς ὑπ' ἀποστόλων γενομένης) Thl(ἀντὶ τοῦ ἀποδώσει· μᾶλλον γὰρ προφητεία ἐστὶν ἢ ἀρά) Jer: txt ACD¹Fℵ m 17. 67² vulg Chr Eulog(in Phot) Damasc₁(see above) Œc Aug(*non ait reddat sed reddet*).

tion, and least of all in these Epistles. Cf. *θέμενος εἰς διακονίαν*, ref. 1 Tim.—Grot. suggests, 'forte ob Latini sermonis consuetudinem') but (apparently a slight contrast is intended to those above, who *ἐπορεύθησαν* of their own accord) **Tychicus** (see Eph. vi. 21 note) **I sent to Ephesus** (on the various attempts to give an account of this journey, and its bearing on the question, whether Timotheus was at Ephesus at this time, see Prolegg. to this Epistle, § i. 5). 13.] **The cloak** (*φελόνης* is said to be a corrupted form of *φαινόλης*, lat. *pænula*, a thick outer cloak: but as early as Chrys., there has been a doubt whether this is the meaning here. He says, *φελόνην ἐνταῦθα τὸ ἱμάτιον λέγει, τινὲς δέ φασι τὸ γλωσσόκομον* [bag or case, John xiii. 29] *ἔνθα τὰ βιβλία ἔκειτο*: and so Syr. and all: but it is against this idea, as indeed Bengel remarks, that the books should be *afterwards mentioned*. It would be unnatural, in case a bag of books had been left behind, to ask a friend to bring the bag, *also the books*, and *especially the parchments*: 'the bag of books and parchments which I left' would be its most obvious designation. A long discussion of the meanings of *φελόνης*, and of the question whether it is rightly supposed to be a corruption from *φαινόλης*, may be found in Wolf ad loc.: see also Ellic. The Jews also had the word פליון for a cloak) **which I left** (behind me: *οἱ δι' ἀσθένειαν ἀπολειφθέντες*, Xen. Mem. iv. 1. 32: for what reason, is not clear: but in St. Paul's life of perils, it may well be conceived that he may have been obliged to leave such things behind, against his intention) **in Troas** (respecting his having been at Troas lately, see Prolegg. to Past. Epp. § ii. 16, 30, 31) **with** ('chez') **Karpus when thou art coming** (setting out to come) **bring, and the books** (i. e. papyrus rolls: on these, and on *μεμβράνας*, see Dict. of Antiquities, art. Liber. *τί δὲ αὐτῷ βιβλίων ἔδει μέλλοντι ἀποδημεῖν πρὸς τὸν θεόν, καὶ μάλιστα ἔδει, ὥστε αὐτὰ τοῖς πιστοῖς παραθέσθαι, καὶ ἀντὶ τῆς αὐτοῦ διδασκαλίας ἔχειν αὐτά*. Chrys. This may have been so: but there is nothing inconsistent with his near prospect of death, in a desire to have his cloak and books during the approaching winter), **especially the parchments** (which as more costly, probably contained the more valuable writings: perhaps the sacred books themselves. On a possible allusion to these books, &c., which the Apostle had with him in his imprisonment at Cæsarea, see note, Acts xxvi. 24).

14.] **Alexander the smith** (Eustathius, on Hom. Od. γ. p. 139 [Wetst.], says, *χαλκεὺς δὲ ὁ πρὸ βραχέων χρυσόχοος, κατὰ ὄνομα γενικὸν ἀπὸ πρώτου φανέντος μετάλλου. διὸ καὶ ὁ Ἥφαιστος χαλκεὺς ἐλέγετο, καὶ χαλκεύειν τὸ οἱανοῦν ἐλατὴν ὕλην σφύρᾳ παίειν*. Similarly the Etymol. [ib.],—*ἀπὸ γὰρ τοῦ πρώτου φανέντος μετάλλου πάντας τοὺς δημιουργοὺς ἐκάλουν οὕτως οἱ παλαιοί*. See ref. Gen., and 2 Chron. xxiv. 12. Perhaps the same with the Alexander of 1 Tim. i. 20, where see note. There is nothing here said, inconsistent with his being an Ephesian resident. It has been indeed supposed that he was at Rome, and that the following caution refers to Timotheus's approaching visit: but the aor. *ἐνεδείξατο* seems to suit better the other hypothesis. It must ever remain uncertain, whether the Alexander whom we find put forward by the Jews in the Ephesian tumult, Acts xix. 33, 34, is this same person: nothing in that narrative is against it. The title *ὁ χαλκεύς* may be intended to mark *another* Alexander: but it may also be a mere cursory designation of the same person) **did to me much evil** (such, as in E. V., is the nearest representation in our language of the phrase **κακὰ ἐνδείξασθαι**. Cf. Gen. l. 15, *μή ποτε μνησικακήσῃ ἡμῖν Ἰωσὴφ καὶ ἀνταπόδομα ἀνταποδῷ ἡμῖν*

κατὰ τὰ ἔργα αὐτοῦ. 15 ὃν καὶ σὺ ° φυλάσσου· ᵖ λίαν
γὰρ ᵠ ἀντέστη τοῖς ἡμετέροις λόγοις. 16 ἐν τῇ πρώτῃ
μου ʳ ἀπολογίᾳ οὐδείς μοι ˢ συνπαρεγένετο, ἀλλὰ πάντες
με ᵗ ἐγκατέλιπον· μὴ αὐτοῖς ᵘ λογισθείη· 17 ὁ δὲ κύριός μοι

ACDF KLℵ a b c e f g h k l m n o 17

o w acc., — Acts xxi 25 2 Kings xx 10
p Paul, 2 Cor xi 5 xii 11 only, but ὑπὲρ λ Matt ii 16 al
q ch iii 8 reff
r Phil i 7 reff — Acts xxii 1 xxv 16
s Luke xxiii 48 only Ps lxxxii 8 only
t ver 10.
u — Rom iv 26 iv 4, 8, from Ps xxxi 2 2 Cor v 19 Paul, esp

14 om αυτου ℵ[1].
15 rec (for ανεστη) ανθεστηκεν, with D[3]KLℵ[3] rel αυθηστη F. txt ACD[1]ℵ' 17.
16 for συνπαρ, παρεγενετο ACFℵ[1] k 17 Chr[1] Euthal mss. εγκατελειπον ACD[3]FL 17.

πάντα τὰ κακὰ ἃ ἐνεδειξάμεθα εἰς αὐτόν —and ver. 17, ἄφες αὐτοῖς . . . ὅτι πονηρά σοι ἐνεδείξαντο In both these places ἐνδείξασθαι represents the Hebrew verb גָּמַל, 'affecit ' similarly in the Song of the Three Children, ver. 19, ἐντραπείησαν πάντες οἱ ἐνδεικνύμενοι τοῖς δούλοις σου κακά· and 2 Macc xiii 9, τοῖς δὲ φρονήμασιν ὁ βασιλεὺς βεβαρβαρωμένος ἤρχετο, τὰ χείριστα τῶν ἐπὶ τοῦ πατρὸς αὐτοῦ γεγονότων ἐνδειξόμενος τοῖς Ἰουδαίοις This usage is easily explained From the primary sense of the middle verb '*to manifest*,' applied to a *subjective quality* [reff. Tit, Heb, and εὔνοιαν, Aristoph Plut 785,—γνώμην Herod viii 111 al. in Lexx], we have idiomatically the same sense applied to *objective facts* in Hellenistic Greek · Palm and Rost give from Plutarch, ἐνδείξασθαι φιλανθρωπίας, a phrase intermediate between the two usages. Then in rendering ἐνδείξασθαί τινι κακά, it is for us to enquire, whether we shall be best expressing the mind of the original by changing the subjective ἐνδείξασθαι into an objective verb, or by changing the objective subst. κακά to a subjective quality [κακίαν] —and the answer to this is clear The κακά were facts which we must not disguise. The ἐνδείξασθαι, not the κακά, is used in an improper and secondary meaning, and therefore in rendering the phrase in a language which admits of no such idiom, it is the verb which must be made objective to suit the substantive, not vice versâ. Conyb 's rendering, '*charged me with much evil*,' as also his alternative, '*manifested many evil things* (?) *against me*,' would, it seems to me, require the active verb) **the Lord shall requite him according to his works** (the optative of the rec. makes no real difficulty : it is not personal revenge, but zeal for the cause of the Gospel which the wish would express, cf ver 16 below, where his own personal feelings were concerned) **whom do thou also beware of** (see above on Alexander), **for he exceedingly withstood our** (better than 'my,' seeing that μοι occurs in the same sentence, and immediately follows. The plural may be used because the λόγοι were such as were common to all Christians — arguments for, or declarations of, our common faith) **words**

16] **In my first defence** (open self-defence, before a court of justice, see reff For a discussion of this whole matter, see the Prolegg and Ellic 's note I will only remark here, that any other defence than one made *at Rome*, in the latter years of the Apostle's life, is out of the question) **no one came forward with me** ("verbum συμπαραγίνεσθαι indicat patronos et amicos, qui alios, ad causam dicendam vocatos, nunc præsentia sua, nunc etiam oratione [not in the time of Cicero, who clearly distinguishes, De Orat. ii. 74, between the orator or *patronus*, and the *advocati*. speaking of the former he says, 'orat reus, urgent advocati ut invehamur, ut maledicamus, &c' But in Tacit Annal xi 6, the orators are called *advocati*] adjuvare solebant. Id Cicero, cap 29, pro Sulla, *adesse supplici*, et cap 14, pro Milone, simpliciter *adesse* dicit Græci dicunt nunc παραγίνεσθαι, nunc παρεῖναι, nunc συμπαρεῖναι" Wolf So Demosth, κατὰ Νεαίρας, 1369. 17, συμπαραγενόμενος αὐτῷ δοκιμαζομένῳ), **but all men deserted me· may it not be laid to their charge** (by God reff τὴν πατρικὴν περὶ αὐτῶν ἔδειξεν εὐσπλαγχνίαν. οὐ κακοηθείας ἦν, ἀλλὰ δειλίας ἡ ὑποχώρησις, Thdrt.)· **but the Lord** (Jesus) **stood by me, and strengthened** ('*put strength in*' a word especially used of and by our Apostle, reff) **me, that by my means the proclamation** (of the Gospel) **might be delivered in full measure** (see on ver 5) **and all the Gentiles might hear** (one is tempted, with Thdrt, al, to interpret this of his preservation for further missionary journeys [Thdrt thinks this defence happened *during* his journey to Spain] but the spirit of the whole context seems to forbid this, and to compel us to confine this πληροφορία to the effect of the single

[v]παρέστη καὶ [w]ἐνεδυνάμωσέν με, ἵνα δι' ἐμοῦ τὸ [x]κήρυγμα
[y]πληροφορηθῇ καὶ ἀκούσωσιν πάντα τὰ ἔθνη· καὶ [z]ἐρύ-
σθην ἐκ [a]στόματος [ab]λέοντος.
18 [z]ῥύσεταί με ὁ κύριος
ἀπὸ παντὸς [c]ἔργου [c]πονηροῦ, καὶ σώσει εἰς τὴν βασι-

v = Rom xvi 2 only. Jer xv 11. w ch ii 1 reff. x Matt xii 41 || L. Rom xvi 25. 1 Cor i 21. ii 4. xv 14. Tit i 3 only. 2 Chron xxx 5. Prov ix 3. Jon iii 2. Esdr ix 3 only. y = ver 5 (reff.) z w ἐκ, Col i 13 reff. w ἀπό, 1 Thess i 10 reff. a here only. Psa xxi 21 (see Ps lvi 4.) b Heb xi 33. 1 Pet v 8. Rev iv 7 al[5] only. c Col i 21 reff. see 2 Cor ix 8. 2 Thess ii 17.

17. om μοι A. for πληροφορηθη, πληρωθη F k 73 Œc-comm. rec ακουση (gramml corrn), with KL rel Chr Thdrt: txt ACDFℵ 17 Eus Euthal. rec ερρυσθ., with DFL rel: txt ACℵ m.

18. rec ins και bef ρυσεται, with D[3]FKL rel syr r æth: om ACD[1]ℵ 67[2] vulg copt arm.

occasion referred to,—his acquittal before the 'corona populi,' in whose presence the trials took place so Bengel—"una sæpe occasio maximi est momenti. gentes—quarum Roma caput." And so Huther and Wiesinger, and in the main, De W.) and I was delivered from the mouth of the lion (the Fathers mostly understood this of Nero: so Chrys., Thdrt., Phil., Œc., Euseb., &c. see Suicer, ii. p 233. And Esth [add.] xiv. 13, E. V., is quoted, "where Esther says concerning Artaxerxes, Put a word into my mouth ἐνώπιον τοῦ λέοντος." Whitby —or, seeing that according to the chronology adopted by some, he was not in Rome at the time [see Prolegomena to Past. Epp. § ii. 33], of his *locum tenens, Helius Cæsareanus*: so Pearson, Annales Paulini, p. 24,—or of the *Jewish accuser*, as Wieseler, Chron. ii p. 476. But these are hardly probable: nor again is it, that the Apostle was literally in danger of being thrown to wild beasts, and established his right as a Roman citizen to be exempted from that punishment [Bengel's objection to this, 'ex ore *leonum* diceret, si proprie bestias innueret,' is of no force as the popular cry 'Christianos ad leonem' shews: see also ref. Psalm, of which doubtless the words were a reminiscence]: nor again is the idea [Calv., Ellic., al.], that the expression is figurative for *great danger,—the jaws of death,* or the like: for the Apostle *did not fear* death, but looked forward to it as the end of his course, and certainly would not have spoken of it under this image. The *context* seems to me to demand another and very different interpretation. None stood with him—all forsook him: but the Lord stood by him and strengthened him: *for what?* that he might *witness a good confession,* and that the κήρυγμα might be expanded to the utmost. The result of this strengthening was, that he was delivered ἐκ στόματος λέοντος: he was strengthened, *witnessed a good confession, in spite of desertion and discouragement*. Then let us pass on to his confidence for the future, the expression of which is bound on to this sentence by **ῥύσεται**, indicating the identity of God's deliverance,—and **παντός** indicating the *generalization of the danger of which this was a particular case*. And how is the danger generally described? as **πᾶν ἔργον πονηρόν**: and it is implied that the falling into such danger would preclude him from enduring to Christ's heavenly kingdom. It was then an ἔργον πονηρόν from which he was on this occasion delivered. What ἔργον πονηρόν? The *falling into the power of the tempter*, the giving way, in his own weakness and the desertion of all, and betraying the Gospel for which he was sent as a witness. The *lion* then is the *devil*, ὁ ἀντίδικος ἡμῶν διάβολος ὡς λέων ὠρυόμενος περιπατεῖ ζητῶν τίνα καταπίῃ, 1 Pet. v. 8). **18.] The Lord (Jesus) shall deliver me from every evil work** (see above: from every danger of faint-heartedness, and apostasy: so, even without adopting the above meaning of ἐκ στόματος λέοντος, Chrys., καὶ γὰρ καὶ τοῦτο τὸ δυνηθῆναι μέχρις αἵματος ἀντικαταστῆναι πρὸς τὴν ἁμαρτίαν, καὶ μὴ ἐνδοῦναι, ἑτέρου λέοντός ἐστι ῥύσασθαι, τοῦ διαβόλου. So also Grot., De W., al. The meaning adopted by Huther, Wiesinger, al., that the ἔργα πονηρά are *the works of his adversaries* plotting against him, is totally beside the purpose: he had no such confidence (ver. 6), nor would his conservation to Christ's heavenly kingdom depend in the least upon such deliverance. Besides which, the correspondence of this declaration of confidence to the concluding petition of the Lord's Prayer cannot surely be fortuitous, and then πονηροῦ, here joined to ἔργου as neuter, must be subjective, evil resulting from our *falling* into temptation, not evil happening to us from without. It is

d 1 Cor xv 40, &c Phil ii 10 Heb xi 16 xii 22 al[4] 2 Macc iii 39
e Gal i 5 reff
f ch i 16 reff
g ver 13
h ver 9
i = Matt (xvi 3) xxiv 20 | Mk John x 22 (Acts xxvii 20) only
k Gal vi 18 1 Thil iv 23 Philem 25
l Col iv 18 reff

ACDF KLℵab cefg hklm no17

λείαν αὐτοῦ τὴν [d]ἐπουράνιον· [e]ᾧ ἡ [e]δόξα εἰς τοὺς [e]αἰῶνας
τῶν αἰώνων, ἀμήν.
19 Ἄσπασαι Πρίσκαν καὶ Ἀκύλαν καὶ τὸν Ὀνησιφόρου
[f]οἶκον. 20 Ἔραστος ἔμεινεν ἐν Κορίνθῳ, Τρόφιμον δὲ
[g]ἀπέλιπον ἐν Μιλήτῳ ἀσθενοῦντα. 21 [h]σπούδασον πρὸ
[i]χειμῶνος ἐλθεῖν. ἀσπάζεταί σε Εὔβουλος καὶ Πούδης
καὶ Λῖνος καὶ Κλαυδία καὶ οἱ ἀδελφοὶ πάντες.
22 Ὁ κύριος [Ἰησοῦς χριστὸς] μετὰ τοῦ [k]πνεύματός
σου. ἡ [l]χάρις μεθ' ὑμῶν.

ΠΡΟΣ ΤΙΜΟΘΕΟΝ.

Chr-ms lat-ff. (17 def.) for ᾧ, αυτω A k om ἡ F.
20. απελειπον CL 17. (A uncert) μηλωτω A (C[1]?) μελητω 17
21 ασπαζονται F vulg(not am fuld F-lat) om παντες ℵ[1].
22 om 1st clause 67[2] om ιησ. χρ. F(not F-lat) ℵ[1] 17 8-pe æth: om χριστος A 31 111 ins CDKLℵ[3] rel for η χ. μεθ' υμ, ερρωσο εν ειρηνη D[1] rec at end ins αμην, with DKLℵ[3] rel vulg syrr copt om ACFℵ[1] 17 67[2] æth Ambrst.

Subscription rec προς τ. δευτερα της εφεσιων εκκλησιας πρωτον επισκοπον χειροτονηθεντα εγραφη απο ρωμης οτε εκ δευτερου παρεστη παυλος τω καισαρι νερωνι, similarly KL rel txt C 17, and ℵ(adding στιχων ρπ). πρ. τ. β D(addg επληρωθη) F(pretg ετελεσθη). so also A, addg απο λαοδικειας

hardly necessary to observe, that πονηροῦ here cannot be gen masc., 'of the evil one,'—as Pelagius and Mosheim, in De W), and shall preserve me safe (σώσει in its not uncommon, pregnant sense of 'bring safe' cf σώζειν πόλινδε, Il ε 224, ἐς οἴκους, Soph. Philoct. 311; ἐς τὴν Ἑλλάδα, Xen An vi. 1. 8. 6. 23, al. freq) **unto his kingdom in heaven** (though it may be conceded to De W that this expression is not otherwise found in St. Paul, it is one to which his existing expressions easily lead on. e. g. Phil i 23, compared with iii 20) **to whom be the glory unto the ages of ages, Amen** (it is again objected, that in St Paul we never find doxologies ascribing glory to *Christ*, but always to God. This however is not strictly true cf Rom ix 5 And even if it were, the whole train of thought here leading naturally on to the ascription of such doxology, why should it not occur for the first and only time? It would seem to be an axiom with some critics, that a writer can never use an expression once only. If the expression be entirely out of keeping with his usual thoughts and diction, this may be a sound inference: but this is certainly not the case in the present instance. Besides, the petition of the Lord's Prayer having been transferred to our Lord as its fulfiller [cf. John xiv. 13, 14], the doxology, which seems to have come into liturgical use almost as soon as the prayer itself [see Matt. vi 13 var readd.], would naturally suggest a corresponding doxology here).

19—21] *Salutations and notices* **Salute Prisca and Aquila** (see notes, Acts xviii 2 Rom xvi 3) **and the house of Onesiphorus** (himself probably deceased See on ch i 16) **Erastus** (Acts xix. 22, an Erastus was sent forward into Macedonia by the Apostle from Ephesus,—and Rom xvi. 23, an Erastus sends greeting, who is described as the οἰκονόμος τῆς πόλεως [Corinth] This latter would seem to be the person here mentioned) **abode in Corinth** (on the inferences to be drawn from this, see Prolegg to Past Epp. § ii. 30 f), **but Trophimus** (he accompanied the Apostle from Greece into Asia, Acts xx 4 He was an Ephesian, id. xxi. 29, and was with the Apostle in Jerusalem on his last visit there) **I left** (not '*they* [the Asian brethren who came to Rome] *left*,' as Hug) **in Miletus** (see again this discussed in Prolegg. to this Epistle, § i 5 Various conjectures have been made to escape the difficulty here presented ἐν Μελίτῃ [Baronius, Beza, Grot., Est., &c.]—a Miletus in *Crete* [Michaelis, Schrader]) **sick. Endeavour**

to come before winter (when the voyage would be impossible, and so the visit thrown over to another year. See also on ver 13) **Eubulus** (otherwise unknown) **greets thee, and Pudens** (see excursus at the end of the Prolegg to this Epistle on Pudens and Claudia), **and Linus** (Iren iii. 3 3, p 176, *οἱ ἀπόστολοι . . . . Λίνῳ τὴν τῆς ἐπισκοπῆς* [at Rome] *λειτουργίαν ἐνεχείρισαν. τούτου τοῦ Λίνου Παῦλος ἐν ταῖς πρὸς Τιμόθεον ἐπιστολαῖς μέμνηται.* So also Euseb. H E iii 4), **and Claudia** (see excursus as before), **and all the brethren.**

22.] CONCLUDING BLESSING The **Lord [Jesus Christ] be with thy spirit** (reff) (the) **grace** (of God) **be with you** (the members of the church where Timotheus was. see Prolegg.).

ΠΡΟΣ ΤΙΤΟΝ.

a Paul, here only elsw., δ. Ἰ. χριστοῦ, see Rom. i. 1. Gal. i. 10. Phil. i. 1. Col. ii. 12.
b Col. iii. 12 reff.
c Eph. i. 17 reff.
d 1 Tim. ii. 4. 2 Tim. ii. 25. iii. 7.
e 1 Tim. ii. 2 reff.
f Acts ii. 26 (from Ps. xv. 9). xxvi. 6. Rom. iv. 18. viii. 20. 1 Cor. ix. 10. L.P.
g Acts xiii. 46 (Paul). 1 Tim. vi. 12. ch. iii. 7.

Ib ADFH IbKLℵ a b c e f g h k l m n o 17

I. 1 Παῦλος [a] δοῦλος [a] θεοῦ, ἀπόστολος δὲ Ἰησοῦ
χριστοῦ κατὰ πίστιν [b] ἐκλεκτῶν [b] θεοῦ καὶ [cd] ἐπίγνωσιν
[d] ἀληθείας τῆς κατ' [e] εὐσέβειαν, 2 [f] ἐπ' ἐλπίδι [g] ζωῆς

TITLE rec παυλου του απ η πρ τιτ. επιστολη του αγιου απ. π. επ. πρ τιτ L. txt Aℵ k l m n o 17, and prefg αρχεται DF.

CHAP. I. 1 χρ bef ιησ A 106 108 fuld(with tol) syr copt Ambrst-ed Cassiod om ιησ D[1]: txt D[3]FHKLℵ rel
2 for επ' (εφ' D[1]), εν FH om c m 17

CHAP. I. 1—4.] ADDRESS AND GREETING. 1.] The occurrence of **δοῦλος θεοῦ**, not elsewhere found in the superscriptions of St Paul's Epistles, is a mark of genuineness: a forger would have been sure to suit every expression of this kind to the well-known habits of the Apostle. **ἀπ. δέ**] **δέ** further defines—a servant of God,—this is general:—*but* a more particular designation also belongs to the present matter. **κατὰ πίστιν** has been variously rendered: (1) '*according to the faith of*,' &c., so E. V., Luth., Matthies, al. (2) similarly Calv., Beza, Aret., 'mutuus est inter meum apostolatum et fidem electorum Dei consensus.' (3) '*so as to bring about faith in*,' &c.,—as De W., justifying it by κατὰ τὴν λητ̄ην ἐκπλώσαντες, Herod. ii. 152, κατὰ θεαν ἥκειν, Thuc. vi. 31,—so also Thdrt. [ὥστε πιστεῦσαι τῆς ἐκλογῆς ἀξίους. Œc. 2, Thl. 1, Jer., Grot., al., but see below.] We may at once say that (1) and (2) are inadmissible, as setting up a standard which the Apostle would not have acknowledged for his Apostleship, and as not suiting ἐπίγνωσιν below, which also belongs to the κατά. Nor do the instances given to justify (3) apply here: for as Huther has observed, in them it is the *acquisition* of the noun which is spoken of: so that here it would be to *get*, not to *produce* faith. The best sense seems to be that which he gives,—that of *reference*, '*with regard* to,' i. e. to bring about, cherish, and perfect: nearly in the same sense as εἰς ὑπακοὴν πίστεως, Rom. i. 5. See also 2 Tim. i. 1. I would render then '*for*.' **Paul, a servant of God, but an Apostle of Jesus Christ, for** (on this sense of **κατά**, *destination*, see Ellic.'s note) **the faith of the elect of God** (those whom God has chosen of the world—reff.: and *their* faith is the only true faith—the only faith which the apostolic office would subserve) **and the thorough knowledge** (reff. and notes: subjective, and κατά as before —to promote the knowledge. Thl. gives as an alternative,—διότι ἐπεγνων τὴν ἀλήθειαν, διὰ τοῦτο ἐπιστεύθην κ τ λ.) **of the truth—which is according to** (belongs to, —is conversant in and coincident with: for as Chrys., ἐστὶν ἀλήθεια πραγμάτων ἀλλ' οὐ κατ' εὐσέβειαν, οἷον τὸ εἰδέναι τὰ γεωργικά, τὸ εἰδέναι τέχνας, ἀληθῶς ἐστὶν

g αἰωνίου, ἣν h ἐπηγγείλατο ὁ i ἀψευδὴς θεὸς kl πρὸ χρόνων l αἰωνίων, 3 m ἐφανέρωσεν δὲ n καιροῖς n ἰδίοις τὸν
λόγον αὐτοῦ ἐν o κηρύγματι ὃ p ἐπιστεύθην ἐγὼ q κατ'
q ἐπιταγὴν τοῦ q σωτῆρος ἡμῶν q θεοῦ, 4 Τίτῳ r γνησίῳ
r τέκνῳ κατὰ s κοινὴν πίστιν. χάρις καὶ εἰρήνη ἀπὸ θεοῦ
πατρὸς καὶ χριστοῦ Ἰησοῦ τοῦ t σωτῆρος ἡμῶν.

. του σωτη H ACDFIb KLℵ a b c e f g h k l m n o 17

h — Mark xiv 11 Acts vii 5 Rom iv 21 al (1 Tim. ii 10) Esth iv 7
i here only† Wisd vii. 17 only
k John xii 1 2 Cor xii 2 Amos i 1 iv 7
l Rom xvi 25. 2 Tim i. 9
m Col i 26 reff
n Gal vi 9 1 Tim ii 6 vi 15 only
o 2 Tim iv 17 reff
p and constr, Rom iii 2 1 Cor ix 17 Gal. ii 7 1 Thess ii 4 1 Tim i 11
q 1 Tim i 1 reff
r 1 Tim i 2 reff.
s — Acts ii 44. iv 32 Jude 3 only Wisd vii 3
t add to Ἰησ χρ Paul, pastl epp. (2 Tim i 10 ch ii 13 iii 6) only other epp, 2 Pet (i 1, 11 ii 20 iii 18) only

4. rec (for και) ελεος (*see* 1 *Tim* i. 2, 2 *Tim* i 2), with AC²KL rel syr Thdrt txt C¹DFℵ 17 latt Syr copt æth arm Chr_{expr} $Damasc_{expr}$ $Orig\text{-}int_{expr}$ Ambrst (υμιν και 17).
rec (for χρ ιησ) κυριου ιησ. χρ, with D³FKL rel syr Chr txt ACD¹Ibℵ 17 vulg copt goth arm Thdrt-ms Pelag Jer.

εἰδέναι· ἀλλ' αὕτη κατ' εὐσέβειαν ἡ ἀλήθεια κατά cannot, as De W., import the *aim*, 'which *leads to* εὐσ.' it does not *lead to* it, but rather runs parallel with) piety. 2] in hope (on condition of, in a state of, see note on ἐφ' ᾧ, Rom v 12) of life eternal (to what are the words ἐπ' ἐλπίδι ζ. αἰ. to be referred? Not back to ἀπόστολος, regarding them as a co-ordinate clause with κατὰ πίστιν κ τ λ [not for the reason assigned by Huther, that thus καί would be required, cf the similar sentence, Rom xvi. 25, 26,—but because such a personal reference would not agree with ver 3 below, where his preaching, not his prospects, is in question] —not to κατὰ πίστιν καὶ ἐπίγ. τ. ἀλ. as subordinate to it—nor to εὐσέβειαν, nor to any one *portion* of the preceding sentence for by such reference we develope an inferior member of the former sentence into what evidently is an expansion of the main current of thought, and thus give rise to a disproportion.—but to the whole, from κατὰ πίστιν to εὐσέβ., as subordinate to that whole, and further conditioning or defining it q d, that the elect of God may believe and thoroughly know the truth which is according to piety, in hope of eternal life), which (eternal life not ἀλήθεια, nor ἐλπίς) God who cannot lie (so μαντήιον ἀψευδές, Herod i 49 Eur Orest 364, ἀψευδὴς θεός, ὅς μοι τάδ' εἶπεν ἐμφανῶς παρασταθείς see Wetst and cf Heb vi 18) promised from eternal ages (the very distinct use of πρὸ χρόνων αἰωνίων in 2 Tim i 9, where the meaning '*from ancient times*' is precluded, should have kept Commentators from endeavouring to fix that sense on the words here The solution of the difficulty, that no promise was actually made till the race of man existed, must be found by regarding, as in 2 Tim. l c, the construction as a mixed one,—compounded of the actual promise made in time, and the divine purpose from which that promise sprung, fixed in eternity Thus, as there God is said to have given us grace in Christ from eternal ages, meaning that the gift took place as the result of a divine purpose fixed from eternity, so here He is said to have promised eternal life from eternal ages, meaning that the promise took place as the result of a purpose fixed from eternity So Thdrt ταῦτα γὰρ ἄνωθεν μὲν καὶ πρὸ αἰώνων ἐδέδοκτο τῷ τῶν ὅλων θεῷ· δῆλα δὲ πεποίηκεν, ὅτε ἐδοκίμασε), 3] but (contrast to the eternal and hidden purpose, and to the promise, just mentioned) manifested in its own seasons (not, '*His own seasons*' [Ellic al], cf ref Gal —the times belonging to it, τουτέστι, τοῖς ἁρμόζουσι, τοῖς ὠφελημένοις, Thl,—fixed by Him for the manifestation) His word (we naturally expect the same object as before, viz ζωὴν αἰώνιον but we have instead, τὸν λόγον αὐτοῦ,—not to be taken in apposition with ἥν, as Heinrichs —i e. the Gospel, see Rom. xvi 25) in (as the element or vehicle of its manifestation) the proclamation (see 2 Tim. iv. 17) with which (on the construction, see reff) I was entrusted according to (in pursuance of, reff) the command of our Saviour God 4] to Titus (see Prolegg § i) my true (genuine, see on 1 Tim. i 2) child according to (in respect of, or agreeably to, in conformity with the appointed spread and spiritually generative power of that faith) the common faith (common to us both and to all the people of God hardly as Grot, 'Judæis, qualis Paulus, et Græcis qualis Titus ' for there is no hint of such a distinction being brought out in this Epistle) grace and peace from God the Father (see on 1 Tim. i 2), and Christ Jesus our Saviour (reff).

5 [u] Τούτου χάριν [v] ἀπέλιπόν σε ἐν Κρήτῃ, ἵνα τὰ [w] λεί-
ποντα [x] ἐπιδιορθώσῃ καὶ [y] καταστήσῃς [z] κατὰ πόλιν πρεσβυτέρους ὡς ἐγώ σοι [a] διεταξάμην, 6 [b] εἴ τις ἐστὶν [c] ἀνέγ-
κλητος, [d] μιᾶς γυναικὸς ἀνήρ, τέκνα ἔχων [e] πιστά, μὴ
[f] ἐν [g] κατηγορίᾳ [h] ἀσωτίας ἢ [i] ἀνυπότακτα. 7 δεῖ γὰρ

d κος ανηρ

ACDFIb KLℵ
a b c d e f g h k l m n o 17

u Eph iii 1 reff. v = Paul, 2 Tim iv 13, 20 only (Heb iv 6, 9 x 26 Jude 6 only) 2 Macc x 19 w = Luke xviii 22 ch iii 13 (James i 4, 5 ii 15) only Wisd xix 4 x here only † y = Acts vi 3 Heb v 1 al Gen xli 34 z = Acts xv 21, 36 xx 23 (Paul) a = Acts xx 13 (of Paul) mid., Acts vii 44 xxiv 23 1 Cor vii 17 xi 34 only b = Eph iv 29 Phil iv 8 c 1 Tim. iii 10 reff d 1 Tim iii 2 e = Acts x 45 xvi 1 2 Cor vi 15 al f = 1 Tim ii 9 g 1 Tim v 19 reff h Eph v 18 1 Pet iv 4 only Prov xxviii 7 2 Macc iv 6 only i 1 Tim i 9. ver 10 Heb ii 8 only † 1 Kings ii 12 Symm

5 rec κατελιπον, with D³KLℵ³ rel: txt ACD¹FIbℵ¹17 Orig Bas-mss (-λειπον ACFIbL) επιδιορθωσῃς A επανορθωσης D¹: δειορθωσης F: txt CD³KLℵ rel Orig Chr Thdrt

6 ανηεγκλητος (but η marked and erased) ℵ¹.

5—9.] *Reason stated for Titus being left in Crete—to appoint elders in its cities. Directions what sort of persons to choose for this office* 5] **For this reason I left thee behind** (reff.: ἀπέλ gives the mere fact of leaving behind when Paul left the island;—κατέλ would convey the idea of more permanence cf Acts xviii 19; xxiv. 27. This difference may have occasioned the alteration of the reading from ecclesiastical motives, to represent Titus as permanent bishop of Crete) **in Crete** (on the island, and the whole matter, see Prolegg) **that thou mightest carry forward the correction** (already begun by me: ἐπι implying the furtherance, addition of διορθώματα The middle voice, as so often, carries only so far the subjective sense, that whereas the active would state the *mere fact* of διόρθωσις, the middle implies that the subject uses his own agency: *facit per se* see Kruger, Griechische Sprachlehre, p 363, who calls this the *dynamic* middle. So Polybius, xxx. 5 13, τὰ μὲν οὖν κατὰ τοὺς Καυνίους . . . . . ταχέως οἱ Ῥόδιοι διωρθώσαντο) **of those things which are defective** ('quæ ego per temporis brevitatem non potui expedire,' Beng ὁ γὰρ τῆς εὐσεβείας λόγος παρεδίδοτο πᾶσι παρ' αὐτοῦ, ἐλείπετο δὲ οἰκονομῆσαι τὰ κατὰ τοὺς πεπιστευκότας, καὶ εἰς ἁρμονίαν αὐτοὺς καταστῆσαι ταῖς ἐκκλησιαστικαῖς διατυπώσεσι. Theodr-Mops in Huther), **and** (καί brings out, among the matters to be attended to in the ἐπιδιόρθωσις, especially that which follows) **mightest appoint city by city** (reff) **elders** (see 1 Tim iv 14 note on Acts xx 17 Thl. remarks, τοὺς ἐπισκόπους οὕτως ἐνταῦθά φησιν, ὡς καὶ ἐν τῇ πρὸς Τιμόθεον· κατὰ πόλεις δέ φησιν οὐ γὰρ ἐβούλετο πᾶσαν τὴν νῆσον ἐπιτετράφθαι ἑνί, ἀλλ' ἑκάστην πόλιν τὸν ἴδιον ποιμένα ἔχειν· οὕτω γὰρ καὶ ὁ πόνος κουφότερος, καὶ ἡ ἐπιμέλεια ἀκριβεστέρα), **as I prescribed** (reff) **to thee** ("διεταξάμην refers as well to the *fact* of appointing elders, as to the *manner* of their appointment,—which last particular is now expanded in directions respecting the characters of those to be chosen." De W.) 6] **if any man is blameless** (see 1 Tim iii. 10 No intimation is conveyed by the εἴ τις, as Heinr and Heydenr. suppose, that such persons would be rare in Crete see besides reff Matt. xviii 28, 2 Cor. xi 20), **husband of one wife** (see note on 1 Tim. iii. 2), **having believing children** ('nam qui liberos non potuit ad fidem perducere, quomodo alios perducet?' Beng and similarly Chrys, Thl. πιστοί implies that they were not only 'ad fidem perducti,' but 'in fide stabiliti'), **who are not under** (involved in) **accusation of profligacy** (see Eph v 18, note) **or insubordinate** (respecting the reason of these conditions affecting his household, see 1 Tim iii 4. I have treated in the Prolegg. ch vii. § i, the argument which Baur and De W. have drawn from these descriptions for dating our Epistles in the second century) 7 ff] **For it behoves an** (τόν, as so often [reff], generic, *the*, i e. every our English idiom requires the indefinite article) **overseer** (see note, 1 Tim. iii 2; here most plainly identified with the presbyter spoken of before. So Thdrt: ἐντεῦθεν δῆλον, ὡς τοὺς πρεσβυτέρους ἐπισκόπους ὠνόμαζον) **to be blameless, as God's steward** (see 1 Tim iii. 15, to which image, that of a responsible servant and dispensator [1 Pet iv. 10] in the house of God, the allusion perhaps is, rather than to that of 1 Cor iv. 1 There is clearly no allusion to the ἐπίσκ's *own household*, as Heydenr supposes Mack well remarks, meaning perhaps however more than the words convey, "*God's steward*,—consequently spiritual superiors are not merely servants and commissioned

[k] τὸν [l] ἐπίσκοπον [c] ἀνέγκλητον εἶναι ὡς θεοῦ [m] οἰκονόμον,
μὴ [n] αὐθάδη, μὴ [o] ὀργίλον, μὴ [p] πάροινον, μὴ [q] πλήκτην,
μὴ [r] αἰσχροκερδῆ, 8 ἀλλὰ [s] φιλόξενον, [t] φιλάγαθον, [u] σώφρονα, δίκαιον, [v] ὅσιον, [w] ἐγκρατῆ, 9 [x] ἀντεχόμενον τοῦ
κατὰ τὴν [y] διδαχὴν [z] πιστοῦ [za] λόγου, ἵνα δυνατὸς ᾖ καὶ
[b] παρακαλεῖν [c] ἐν τῇ [d] διδασκαλίᾳ τῇ [d] ὑγιαινούσῃ καὶ

k = Matt xiii 3 xv 20 bis John xii 24 xv 6 al freq
l Acts xx 28 (Paul) Phil i 1 1 Tim iii 2 1 Pet ii 25 only 4 Kings xi 15 Job xx 29 Isa. lx 17
m = 1 Cor iv 1 1 Pet iv 10 (Gal iv 2 Esth viii 9) n 2 Pet ii 10 only Gen xlix 3, 7 Prov xxi 24 only o here only Prov xxi. 29 xxii 24 xxix 22 only p 1 Tim iii 3 only† q 1 Tim iii 3 only† Ps xxxiv 15 Symm r 1 Tim iii 8 only† (-ῶς, 1 Pet v 2) see ver 11 s 1 Tim iii 2 1 Pet iv 9 only† (-ία, Rom xii 13) t here only† Wisd vii 22 only u 1 Tim iii 2 ch ii 2, 5 only† v 1 Tim ii 8 reff w here only† Sir xxvi 15 al (-τεια, Gal v 23 -τεύεσθαι, 1 Cor vii 9) x Matt vi 24 Luke xvi 13 1 Thess v 14 only Prov iii 18 y pastl epp., 2 Tim iv 2 (reff) only z = 1 Tim i 15 reff a Acts xviii 15 2 Tim i 13 ch ii 8 al b absol, 1 Cor iv 13 2 Tim iv 2 al c = 1 Thess iv 18 2 Cor vii 6, 7 d 1 Tim i 10 reff

9 aft ινα ins και F 17. 73. for εν τη διδασκ. τη υγιαιν, τους εν παση θλιψει

agents of the Church According to the Apostle's teaching, church government does not grow up out of the ground"), **not self-willed** (*ἐπίσκοπος ἑκόντων ἄρχων, οὐκ ὀφείλει αὐθάδης εἶναι ὥστε αὐτογνώμως καὶ αὐτοβούλως καὶ ἄνευ γνώμης τῶν ἀρχομένων πράττειν. τυραννικὸν γὰρ τοῦτο*, Thl *σεμνότης δ' ἐστὶν αὐθαδείας ἀνὰ μέσον τε καὶ ἀρεσκείας, ἔστι δὲ περὶ τὰς ἐντεύξεις ὅ τε γὰρ αὐθάδης τοιοῦτός ἐστιν οἷος μηθενὶ ἐντυχεῖν μηδὲ διαλεγῆναι, ἀλλὰ τοὔνομα ἔοικεν ἀπὸ τοῦ τρόπου κεῖσθαι ὁ γὰρ αὐθάδης αὐτοάδης τίς ἐστιν, ἀπὸ τοῦ αὐτὸς αὑτῷ ἀρέσκειν*, Aristot Magn Moral i 29 see also Theophr Char c xvi [*αὐθάδειά ἐστιν ἀπήνεια ὁμιλίας ἐν λόγοις*] Suicer, i p 572 and Ellic's note here), **not soon provoked** (*οἱ μὲν οὖν ὀργίλοι ταχέως μὲν ὀργίζονται, καὶ οἷς οὐ δεῖ, καὶ ἐφ' οἷς οὐ δεῖ, καὶ μᾶλλον ἢ δεῖ παύονται δὲ ταχέως ὃ καὶ βέλτιστον ἔχουσι*, Aristot Eth. Nic iv 5 this meaning, and not Thdrt's, *ὀργίλον δέ, τὸν μνησίκακον*,—must be taken), **not a brawler, not a striker** (for both these, see 1 Tim iii 3, notes), **not greedy of gain** (1 Tim iii 8, note), **but hospitable** (1 Tim iii 2, note, and 3 John 5), **a lover of good** (cf the opposite *ἀφιλάγαθος*, 2 Tim iii 3 It is hardly likely to mean a lover of *good men*, coming so immediately after *φιλόξενον* Thl explains it, *τὸν ἐπιεικῆ, τὸν μέτριον, τὸν μὴ φθονοῦντα* Dionys Areop, Ep viii 1, p 597, calls God *τὸν ὑπεράγαθον καὶ φιλάγαθον*—and Clem. Alex, Pæd iii 11, p 291 P, classes together *ἀνδρία, σωφροσύνη, φιλαγαθία*), **self-restrained** (see 1 Tim ii 9, note I am not satisfied with this rendering, but adopt it for want of a better "discreet is perhaps preferable" See Ellic. on 1 Tim as above), **just, holy** (see on these, and their distinction, in notes on Eph. iv. 24. 1 Thess ii 10), **continent** (*τὸν πάθους κρατοῦντα, τὸν καὶ γλώττης καὶ χειρὸς καὶ ὀφθαλμῶν ἀκολάστων τοῦτο γὰρ ἐστὶν ἐγκράτεια, τὸ μηδενὶ ὑποσύρεσθαι πάθει*, Chrys, and id Epist ii ad Olympiad, vol. iii p 560 (Migne), *ἐγκρατεύεσθαι ἐκεῖνόν φαμεν. τὸν ὑπό τινος ἐπιθυμίας ἐνοχλούμενον, καὶ κρατοῦντα ταύτης* See Suicer i p 998 ff, for a full explanation of the subsequent technical usages of the word Here, the sense need not be limited to sexual continence, but may be spread over the whole range of the indulgences), **holding fast** (see reff.. constantly keeping to, and not letting go,—*φροντίζοντα, ἔργον τοῦτο ποιούμενον*, Chrys

Then how are we to take the following words? Is **τοῦ κατὰ τὴν διδαχὴν πιστοῦ λόγου** equivalent to (1) *τοῦ λόγου τοῦ κατὰ τὴν διδαχὴν πιστοῦ*, or (2) *τοῦ πιστοῦ λόγου τοῦ κατὰ τὴν διδαχήν*? (1) is taken by Wiesinger and Conyb [*the words which are faithful to* (?) *our teaching*]. (2) by Chrys, Thl, and almost all Commentators, and I believe rightly. For (α) it is hard to believe that even in these Epistles, such a sentence could occur as *ἀντεχόμενον [τοῦ-κατὰ-τὴν-διδαχὴν-πιστοῦ] λόγου* had this been intended, it would certainly have stood *τοῦ λ τοῦ κατὰ τὴν διδ. πιστοῦ*· (β) the epithet **πιστός**, absolute, is so commonly attached to *λόγος* in these Epistles [1 Tim i. 15, iii 1, iv. 9 2 Tim. ii 11 ch iii 8] as to incline us, especially with the above reason, to take it absolutely here also I therefore render accordingly) **the faithful** (true, trustworthy, see note on 1 Tim i 15) **word** (which is) **according to** (measured by, or in accordance with) **the instruction** [**which he has received**] (*διδαχή* may be *active*, as Calv, 'qui in ecclesiæ ædificationem sit utilis' Luth, 'daß lehren kann' But thus we should

τοὺς [e] ἀντιλέγοντας [f] ἐλέγχειν. 10 εἰσὶν γὰρ πολλοὶ ACDFI$_b$ KLℵ
[καὶ] [g] ἀνυπότακτοι [h] ματαιολόγοι καὶ [i] φρεναπάται, [k] μά- a b c d e f g h k l
λιστα [lm] οἱ [l] ἐκ [m] περιτομῆς, οὓς δεῖ [n] ἐπιστομίζειν, 11 [o] οἵ- m n o 17
τινες ὅλους [p] οἴκους [q] ἀνατρέπουσιν διδάσκοντες [r] ἃ μὴ δεῖ
[s] αἰσχροῦ [t] κέρδους [u] χάριν. 12 εἶπέν τις ἐξ αὐτῶν [v] ἴδιος

e Acts xiii 45 xxviii 19 Rom x 21 Hos iv 4 f 1 Tim v 20 reff g ver 6 reff h here only (-γία, 1 Tim i 6) i here only† (-τᾶν, Gal vi 3) k 1 Tim iv 10 reff l Rom ii 8. iii 26 iv. 14 al m Acts x 45 xi 2 Rom iv 12 Gal ii 12 Col iv 11 only n here only† o = Acts x 41, 47 Paul, freq p = Acts x 2 1 Cor i 6 2 Tim i 16 al q 2 Tim ii 18 only Prov. x 3 r so 1 Tim v 13 s 1 Cor xi 6 xiv 35 Eph v 12 only P Gen xli 3, &c only see ver 7 t Phil i. 21 reff u Eph iii. 1 reff v = 1 Thess ii 14 al (ὡς προφ, ib ver 15 v r)

A om τῃ υγιαινουσῃ I$_b$ Lucif τῃ υγιαιν διδ in 106 8-12 aft ελεγχειν ins μη χειροτονειν διγαμους μηδε διακονους αυτους ποιειν μηδε γυναικας εχειν εκ διγαμιας, μηδε προσερχεσθωσαν εν τω θυσιωστηριω λειτουργειν το θειον, τους αρχοντας τους αδικοκριτας, και αρπαγας, και ψευστας, και ανελεημονας ελεγχε, ως θεου διακονος 96 109-gr

10 om 1st και (*as unnecessary, and appearing to disturb the sense*) ACI$_b$ℵ a k 17 am[2](with demid) syrr copt goth Clem Ambrst-ed Aug ins DFKL rel vulg Chr Damasc Lucif Hil Jer. ins και bef ματαιολ F Syr copt æth Œc Jer$_1$. aft μαλιστα ins δε CD demid Thl Jer$_1$. ins της bef περιτομης CD[1] Frag-tisch.

11 aft χαριν ins τα τεκνα οτι τους ιδιους γονεις υβριζοντες η τυπτοντες επιστομιζε και ελεγχε, και νουθετει ως πατηρ τεκνα και ειρηνης επισκοπος 96. 109-gr

have a tautological sentence, in which the practice, and the result of the practice [ἵνα κ τ.λ.], would have the same power to instruct predicated of them besides that ἀντεχόμενον would require some forcing to make it apply in this sense of 'constantly *using.*' The passive acceptation of διδαχή is therefore preferable and the meaning will be much the same as in 2 Tim iii 14, *μένε ἐν οἷς ἔμαθες,*— cf 1 Tim iv 6, *οἱ λόγοι τῆς πίστεως καὶ τῆς καλῆς διδασκαλίας ᾗ παρηκολούθηκας.* So Ellic. also), **that he may be able both to exhort** (believers) **in** (the element of his *παράκλησις*) **healthy teaching** (the teaching which is healthy), **and to reprove** (see ver 13 below) **the gainsayers**

10—16] *By occasion of the last clause, the Apostle goes on to describe the nature of the adversaries to whom he alludes, especially with reference to Crete*

10] **For** (explains *τοὺς ἀντιλέγοντας* of ver. 9) **there are many** [**and**] **insubordinate** (ver. 6 above The joining *πολύς* with another adjective by *καί* is a common idiom. So Herod viii 61, *πολλά τε καὶ κακὰ ἔλεγε* Aristoph. Lys 1159, *πολλῶν κἀγαθῶν* Plat Rep x p 325, *πολλά τε καὶ ἀνόσια εἰργασμένος* Xen. Mem. ii 9 6, *συνειδὼς αὑτῷ πολλὰ καὶ πονηρά* Matthiæ, § 444) **vain talkers** (see 1 Tim i 6, and ch iii 9) **and deceivers** (see Gal vi 3 deceivers of men's minds), **chiefly** (not *only*—there were some such of the Gentile converts) **they of the circumcision** (i e not Jews, but Jewish Christians. for he is speaking of seducers within the Church · cf ver 11. On the Jews in Crete, see Jos Antt xvii. 12 1 B J ii 7 1 Philo, Leg ad Cai. § 36, vol ii p 587), **whose mouths** (*ἐλέγχειν σφοδρῶς, ὥστε ἀποκλείειν αὐτοῖς τὰ στόματα,* Thl) **it is necessary to stop** (we hardly need introduce here the figure of a bit and bridle, seeing that *ἐπιστομίζειν* is so often used literally of '*stopping the mouth,*' without any allusion to that figure. e g Aristoph, Eq. 811, *ἐμοὶ γάρ ἐστ' εἰργασμένον τοιοῦτον ἔργον ὥστε | ἀπαξάπαντας τοὺς ἐμοὺς ἐχθροὺς ἐπιστομίζειν* Plat Gorg, p. 329 d,—*αὐτὸς ὑπὸ σοῦ ἐμποδισθεὶς ἐν τοῖς λόγοις ἐπεστομίσθη αἰσχυνθεὶς ἃ ἐννοεῖ εἰπεῖν* and see other examples in Wetst And Plut, Alcib 2, speaks of *τὸν αὐλὸν ἐπιστομίζειν καὶ ἀποφράττειν* Cf Palm and Rost's Lex). **such men as** ("*inasmuch as they,*" Ellic . which perhaps is logically better) **overturn** (ref. 1 Tim so, literally, Plat. Rep. v p 471 b, *οὔτε τὴν γῆν ἐθελήσουσι κείρειν αὐτῶν, . . . οὔτε οἰκίας ἀνατρέπειν* and fig, Demosth 778. 22, *ἀνατρέψειν οἴει τὰ κοινὰ δίκαια,* and so often) **whole houses** (cf. Juv. Sat x. 5. "evertere domos totas optantibus ipsis | Di faciles." Here it will mean, "pervert whole families" Thl. says, *μοχλοὶ γάρ εἰσι τοῦ διαβόλου, δι' ὧν καθαιρεῖ τοὺς τοῦ θεοῦ οἴκους*), **teaching things which are not fitting** (on the use of *ἃ οὐ δεῖ* [things which are definitely improper or forbidden], and *ἃ μὴ δεῖ* [things which are so either in the mind of the describer, or which, as here, derive a seeming *contingency* from the mode in which the subject is presented], see Ellic 's note here and his references to Herm. on Viger, 267,

Ib ACDF KLℵab cdefg hklm no17

αὐτῶν προφήτης Κρῆτες ἀεὶ [w] ψεῦσται, κακὰ [x] θηρία, [y] γαστέρες [z] ἀργαί.
13 ἡ [a] μαρτυρία αὕτη ἐστὶν ἀληθής. [b] δι'
ἣν αἰτίαν [c] ἔλεγχε αὐτοὺς [d] ἀποτόμως, ἵνα [e] ὑγιαίνωσιν ἐν
τῇ πίστει,
14 μὴ [f] προςέχοντες [g] Ἰουδαικοῖς [f] μύθοις καὶ
ἐντολαῖς ἀνθρώπων [h] ἀποστρεφομένων τὴν ἀλήθειαν.

w 1 Tim i 10 reff. x met, here only see 1 Cor xv 32. y — here only (1 Thess v 8 reff). z 1 Tim v 13 reff. a 1 Tim iii 7 reff. b 2 Tim i 6 reff. c ver 9. d 2 Cor xiii 10 only † Wisd v 22 only. e 1 Tim. i 10 reff. f 1 Tim i 4 reff. g here only † (-κῶς, Gal ii 14). h 2 Tim. i 15 reff.

12 aft ειπεν ins δε F ℵ[1] copt. om εξ 67[2]. om (2nd) αυτων F Clem.
13 αληθ. bef εστ. D vulg lat-ff. om εν ℵ[1] 219 ins ℵ-corr[1].
14. ενταλμασιν F Thdrt.

and Kruger, Sprachlehre, § 67 4. 3) **for the sake of base gain** (cf 1 Tim vi 5).

12.] **One of them** (not, of the πολλοί spoken of above,—nor, of the οἱ ἐκ περιτομῆς · but of the inhabitants of Crete, to which both belonged), **their own prophet** (see below) **said, "The Cretans are always liars, evil beasts, slow bellies"** (Thl says ὁ μὲν οὖν εἰρηκώς, Ἐπιμενίδης ἐστίν, ἐν τοῖς μάλιστα τῶν παρ' Ἕλλησι σοφῶν θειασμοῖς καὶ ἀποτροπιασμοῖς προσέχων, καὶ μαντικὴν δυκῶν κατορθοῦν. And so also Chrys, Epiph, and Jer. But Thdrt ascribes the verse to Callimachus, in whose Hymn to Zeus, ver 8, the words Κρῆτες ἀεὶ ψεῦσται are found. To this however Jer [as also Epiph] answers, "integer versus de Epimenide poeta ab Apostolo sumptus est, et ejus Callimachus in suo poemate usus est exordio" EPIMENIDES was a native of Phæstus in Crete (Ἐπιμ. ὁ Φαίστιος, Plut Solon 12 or Cnossus, Diog Laert i 109, Κρὴς τὸ γένος, ἀπὸ Κνώσσου He makes his *father's name* to have been Φαίστιος —πατρὸς μὲν ἦν Φαιστίου, οἱ δέ, Δωσιάδου, οἱ δὲ Ἀγησάρκου), and lived about 600 B C He was sent for to Athens to undertake the purification of the city from the pollution occasioned by Cylon (see artt 'Epimenides' and 'Cylon,' in the Dict of Biogr and Mythol), and is said to have lived to an extreme old age, and to have been buried at Lacedæmon (Diog Laert i 115). The appellation '*prophet*' seems to have belonged to him in its literal sense see Cicero, de Divin. i. 18,—"qui concitatione quadam animi, aut soluto liberoque motu futura præsentiunt, ut Baris Bœotius, ut Epimenides Cres" so also Apuleius, Florid ii 15 1,—"necnon et Cretensem Epimenidem, inclytum fatiloquum et poetam" see also id. Apol 449 Diog Laert. also gives instances of his prophetic power, and says, λέγουσι δέ τινες ὅτι Κρῆτες αὐτῷ θύουσιν ὡς θεῷ. On the character here given of the Cretans, see Prolegg to this Epistle, § ii 9 ff. As to the words,—**κακὰ θηρία** is abundantly illustrated out of various writers by Wetst, Kyphe, and Raphel **γαστέρες ἀργαί** is said of those who by indulging their bodily appetites have become corpulent and indolent so Juv Sat. iv 107, "Montani quoque venter adest abdomine tardus")

13] **This testimony is true Wherefore** (ἐπειδὴ ἦθος αὐτοῖς ἐστιν ἰταμὸν καὶ δολερὸν καὶ ἀκόλαστον, Chrys) **reprove them sharply** (ὅταν ψεύδωνται προχείρως καὶ δολεροὶ ὦσι καὶ γαστρίμαργοι καὶ ἀργοί, σφοδροῦ καὶ πληκτικοῦ τοῦ λόγου δεῖ προσηνείᾳ γὰρ οὐκ ἂν ἀχθείη ὁ τοιοῦτος, Chrys **ἀπότομος**, 'cut off,' '*abrupt*' hence, met, 'rugged,' 'harsh,' so Eur Alcest 985, οὐδέ τις ἀποτόμου λήματός ἐστιν αἰδώς Soph Œd Tyr. 876, ἀπότομον ὤρουσεν εἰς ἄναγκαν), **that** (in order that De W. takes ἵνα κ τ λ., for the substance of the rebuke, as in παραγγέλλειν ἵνα and the like (?) but there appears to be no sufficient reason for this) **they may be healthy in the faith** (not, '*in faith*,' as Conyb · even were no article expressed after ἐν, it *might* be 'in the faith' when that article *is* expressed, the definite reference can never be overlooked. The Κρῆτες indicated here, who are to be thus rebuked in order to their soundness in the faith, are manifestly not the false teachers, but the ordinary believers cf ver. 11),

14] **not giving attention to** (ref) **Jewish fables** (on the probable nature of these, see 1 Tim. i 4 note. and on the whole subject, the Prolegg to these Epistles, § i 12 ff They were probably the seeds of the gnostic mythologies, already scattered about and taking root) **and commandments** (cf 1 Tim. iv 3 Col ii. 16, 22 and our next verse, by which it appears that these commandments were on the subject of abstinence from meats and other things appointed by God for man's use) **of men turning away** (or the pres. part may express habitual character—

15 πάντα καθαρὰ τοῖς καθαροῖς· τοῖς δὲ [i] μεμιαμένοις καὶ
[k] ἀπίστοις οὐδὲν καθαρόν, ἀλλὰ [i] μεμίανται αὐτῶν καὶ
ὁ νοῦς καὶ ἡ [l] συνείδησις. 16 θεὸν [m] ὁμολογοῦσιν εἰδέναι,
τοῖς δὲ ἔργοις [n] ἀρνοῦνται, [o] βδελυκτοὶ ὄντες καὶ [p] ἀπειθεῖς καὶ [q] πρὸς [q] πᾶν ἔργον [q] ἀγαθὸν [r] ἀδόκιμοι.

H ἀπιστοις ουδεν

ACDFH KLℵ a b c d e f g h k l m n o 17

i here bis John xviii 28. Heb xii 15 Jude 8 only Ezek xiv 11
k = 1 Tim v. 8 reff
l 1 Tim i 5 reff ii 2
m = John ix 22 Rom x 9
n = 1 Tim v 8 reff
o here only Prov xvii 15 Sir xli 5 vat 2 Macc i 27 only (-σσεσθαι, Rev xxi 8.)
p Luke i 17 Acts xxvi 19 (Paul) Rom i 30 2 Tim iii 2 ch iii. 3 only L P Num xx 10
q 2 Tim. ii 21 (reff)
r 2 Tim iii 8 reff

15 rec aft παντα ins μεν, with D[3]KLℵ[3] rel syr γαρ Syr copt (Orig): txt ACD[1]Fℵ[1] 17 67[2] latt Orig Tert Jer Aug Ambrst-ed Fulg Pelag rec μεμιασμενοις, with D[3], and (accg to our edd) Clem Orig all txt ACD(μεμιανμ) F(μεμειαμ) KLℵ(μεμιαμμ) d f Chr.

16 om και ℵ[1]. om αγαθον ℵ[1]: ins ℵ corr[1].

whose description it is that they turn away—in idiomatic English, the participial clause being merely epithetal, not ratiocinative [agst Ellicott], "who turn away") from (ref) the truth 15] *The Apostle's own answer to those who would enforce these commandments* **All things** (absolutely—all things with which man can be concerned) **are pure to the pure** (οὐδὲν ὁ θεὸς ἀκάθαρτον ἐποίησεν· οὐδὲν γὰρ ἀκάθαρτον, εἰ μὴ ἡ ἁμαρτία μόνη ψυχῆς γὰρ ἅπτεται καὶ ταύτην ῥυποῖ, Chrys 'Omnia externa iis qui intus sunt mundi, munda sunt,' Bengel Cf. Matt xxiii 26. Luke xi 41 There is no ground whatever for supposing this to be a maxim of the false teachers, quoted by the Apostle, any more than the πάντα μοι ἔξεστιν of 1 Cor vi 12, where see note. The maxim here is a truly Christian one of the noblest order τοῖς καθαροῖς is the dat. commodi,—'for the pure to use,' not, as often taken, 'in the judgment of the pure.' This is plainly shewn by the use of the same dative in Rom xiv. 14, where to render it 'in the judgment of' would introduce an unmeaning tautology τῷ λογιζομένῳ τι κοινὸν εἶναι, ἐκείνῳ κοινόν—'to him [for his use] it is really κοινόν.' As usual in these Epistles [see Prolegg. § i 38], *purity* is inseparably connected with soundness in the faith, cf. Acts xv. 9,—and 1 Tim. iv. 3, where our τοῖς καθαροῖς is expanded into τοῖς πιστοῖς καὶ ἐπεγνωκόσιν τὴν ἀλήθειαν), **but to the polluted and unbelieving** (cf the preceding remarks) **nothing is pure, but both** (or '*even*,' as E V. —but the other seems preferable, on account of the close correspondence of καὶ ὁ νοῦς with καὶ ἡ συνείδ) **their mind** (their rational part, Eph. iv. 17, which presides over and leads all the determinate acts and thoughts of the man) **and their conscience is polluted** (cf Dion Hal. de Thucyd. 8.—κράτιστον δὲ πάντων τὸ μηδὲν ἑκουσίως ψεύδεσθαι, μηδὲ μιαίνειν τὴν αὐτοῦ συνείδησιν. And therefore, uncleanness tainting their rational acts and their reflective self recognitions, nothing can be pure to them: every occasion becomes to them an occasion of sin, every creature of God an instrument of sin, as Mack well observes, "the relation, in which the sinful subject stands to the objects of its possession or of its inclination, is a sinful one" Philo de legg spec ad 6 et 7 dec cap § 337, vol ii p 333 f., has a sentence which might be a comment on our verse —ἀκάθαρτος γὰρ κυρίως ὁ ἄδικος καὶ ἀσεβὴς . . . . πάντα φύρων καὶ συγχέων διά τε τὰς ἀμετρίας τῶν παθῶν καὶ τὰς τῶν κακῶν ὑπερβολάς· ὥστε ὧν ἂν ἐφάψηται πραγμάτων πάντα ἐστὶν ἐπίληπτα τῇ τοῦ δρῶντος συμμεταβάλλοντα μοχθηρίᾳ καὶ γὰρ κατὰ τὸ ἐναντίον αἱ πράξεις τῶν ἀγαθῶν ἐπαινεταί, βελτιούμεναι ταῖς τῶν ἐνεργούντων ἀρεταῖς, ἐπειδὴ πέφυκέ πως τὰ γινόμενα τοῖς δρῶσιν ἐξομοιοῦσθαι Here again, the reference of the saying has been variously mistaken—ἡ ῥυπαρὰ διάνοια κακῶς περὶ τούτων λογιζομένη ἑαυτῇ συμμιαίνει ταῦτα, Œc. and similarly Chrys, Thl, al: 'non placent Deo quæ agunt etiam circa res medias, quia actiones tales ex animo Deus æstimat,' Grot· 'iis nihil prodest externa ablutio et ciborum dierumque observatio,' Baldwin, Croc in De W).

16] *Expansion of the last clause, shewing* (cf Dion Hal above) *their ἑκουσίως ψεύδεσθαι* **They make confession** (openly, in sight of men but not so only—their confession is a true one so far, that they *have the knowledge*, and *belie* it not 'they *profess*,' as E V ὁμολογοῦσιν necessarily contains an implication of the subjective truth of the thing given out) **that they know God, but in** (or, by) **their works they deny** (Him) (not '*it*' see 2 Tim ii 12), **being abominable** (cf βδέλυγμα ἐνώπιον τοῦ θεοῦ, Luke xvi. 15. In ref. Prov βδελυκτὸς παρὰ θεῷ is

II. [1] Σὺ δὲ λάλει ἃ [s] πρέπει τῇ [t] ὑγιαινούσῃ [t] διδασκαλίᾳ, [2] [u] πρεσβύτας [v] νηφαλίους εἶναι, [w] σεμνούς, [x] σώφρονας, [t] ὑγιαίνοντας τῇ [y] πίστει, τῇ [y] ἀγάπῃ, τῇ [yz] ὑπομονῇ·
[3] [a] πρεσβύτιδας [b] ὡσαύτως ἐν [c] καταστήματι [d] ἱεροπρεπεῖς,
[e] μὴ [f] διαβόλους, [e] μηδὲ οἴνῳ πολλῷ [g] δεδουλωμένας,
[h] καλοδιδασκάλους, [4] ἵνα [i] σωφρονίζουσιν τὰς νέας [j] φιλάν-

s Matt iii 15 1 Cor xi 13. Eph v 3 1 Tim ii 10 Heb ii 10 vii 26 only Ps xcii 7
t 1 Tim i 10 reff
u Luke i 18 Philem 9 only Job xxix 8
v 1 Tim iii 2, 11 only † (-φειν, 2 Tim iv 5)
w Phil iv 8 1 Tim iii. 8, 11 only Prov xv 26.
x 1 Tim iii 2 ch i 8 ver 5 only †
y 1 Tim vi 11 2 Tim iii 10 2 Pet i 6, 7
z Col i 11 reff
a here only †
b = 1 Tim ii 9 reff
c here only † = Jos Antt xv 7 5, ατρεμαιῳ τῳ καταστηματι
d here only †. Jos. Antt xi 8 5
e John iv 15 xiv 27 Acts iv 18
f = 1 Tim iii 11 2 Tim iii 3 only
g Acts vii 6, from Gen xv 13 1 Cor vii 15 only constr, Rom vi 18, 22 1 Cor ix 19. Gal iv 3. 2 Pet ii. 19
h here only †.
i here only † (-ισμος, 2 Tim i 7)
j here only †

Chap II. 1. aft δε ins α ℵ

3 κατασχηματι F. ιεροπρεπει CH[2] m 17 latt syrr copt arm Clem Bas Thdrt Ambrst Pelag Jer Sedul. for μηδε, μη DFHKLℵ[3] rel txt ACℵ[1].

4 rec σωφρονιζωσι, with CDKLℵ[3] rel txt AFHℵ[1] o

joined with ἀκάθαρτος) and disobedient, and for (towards the accomplishing of) every good work worthless (ref).

Ch. II. 1—III 11.] *Directions to Titus, how to exhort the believers of various classes, and how to comport himself* For intermediate divisions, see below

1.] **But** (contrast to the persons just described: 'on the other hand') **do thou speak** (not what they speak, ch. i 11· but) **the things which befit the healthy teaching** (that teaching which is sound and wholesome, not teaching ἃ μὴ δεῖ) viz, **that the aged men** (not = πρεσβυτέρους, which implies eldership, and not old age only) **be sober** (see note on 1 Tim. iii 2), **grave** (1 Tim iii 4, note), **self restrained** (a better word for σώφρων would be a valuable discovery see above on ch. i 8, and 1 Tim. ii 9 '*discreet*' is good, but not adequate), **healthy in their faith, in their love, in their patience** (see ref. 1 Tim, where the same three are joined together The datives are of the element or condition the same was expressed with ἐν, ch i. 13 ἵνα ὑγιαίνωσιν ἐν τῇ πίστει The articles should not be overlooked. The occurrence of τῇ ἀγάπῃ and τῇ ὑπομονῇ prevents us from rendering τῇ πίστει objective as in ch i 13, and compels us to take the subjective and reflective meaning) **3**] **The aged women** (= πρεσβύτεραι, 1 Tim v. 2, there being in this case here no official term to occasion confusion) **likewise** (after the same general pattern, to which the separate virtues above mentioned belong) **in deportment** (cf. Porphyr de abst in Wetst,—τὸ δὲ σεμνὸν κὰκ τοῦ καταστήματος ἑωρᾶτο πορεία τε γὰρ ἦν εὔτακτος, καὶ βλέμμα καθεστηκὸς ἐπετηδεύετο, ὡς ὅτε βουληθεῖεν μὴ σκαρδαμύττειν γέλως δὲ σπάνιος, εἰ δέ που γένοιτο, μέχρι μειδιασμοῦ. ἀεὶ δὲ ἐντὸς τοῦ σχήματος αἱ χεῖρες The κατάστημα would thus include *gesture and habit*, — more than καταστολή of 1 Tim ii. 9), **reverend** (two examples, of those given by Wetst., seem nearest to touch the meaning of the word here as connected with outward deportment·—the one from Jos. Antt xi 8 5, describing the High Priest Jaddus going forth to meet Alexander the Great,—πυθόμενος δ' αὐτὸν οὐ πόῤῥω τῆς πόλεως, πρόεισι μετὰ τῶν ἱερέων καὶ τοῦ πολιτικοῦ πλήθους, ἱεροπρεπῆ καὶ διαφέρουσαν τῶν ἄλλων ἐθνῶν ποιούμενος τὴν ὑπάντησιν . . . . . τὸ μὲν πλῆθος ἐν ταῖς λευκαῖς ἐσθῆσι, τοὺς δὲ ἱερεῖς προεστῶτας ἐν ταῖς βυσσίναις αὐτῶν, τὸν δὲ ἀρχιερέα ἐν τῇ ὑακινθίνῃ καὶ διαχρύσῳ στολῇ: the other from Plato, Theages, § 3, p. 262, Θεαγὴς ὄνομα τούτῳ, ὦ Σώκρατες Καλόν γε, ὦ Δημόδοκε, τῷ υἱεῖ τὸ ὄνομα ἔθηκες καὶ ἱεροπρεπές), **not slanderers** (see reff 1 Tim. and note), **nor yet enslaved** (so προσέχοντας, 1 Tim iii 8) **to much wine** (this vice may be included in the character given of the Cretans above, ch i 12), **teachers of that which is good, that they school** (see on σωφρονισμός, 2 Tim i. 7

The occurrence of ἵνα here with a pres indic in the best MSS is remarkable—especially as the only other instances of this construction in St Paul, 1 Cor. iv 6 and Gal. iv 17 [see notes there], may be accounted for on the hypothesis of an unusual [provincial] formation of the subjunctive, being both verbs in -όω If this reading is to stand, it would shew that that hypothesis is unnecessary, and that St Paul did really write the indic pres. after ἵνα see also 1 John v 20 Cf. Winer, edn 6, § 41 b. 1 c. If he did thus write it, it may be questioned whether he intended to convey any sense very distinct

δρους εἶναι, ˡφιλοτέκνους, 5 ᵏσώφρονας, ˡἁγνάς, ᵐοἰκουρ-
γούς, ⁿἀγαθάς, ᵒὑποτασσομένας τοῖς ἰδίοις ἀνδράσιν, ἵνα
μὴ ὁ λόγος τοῦ θεοῦ ᵖβλασφημῆται. 6 τοὺς νεωτέρους
ᵇὡσαύτως ᵠπαρακάλει ʳσωφρονεῖν, 7 ˢπερὶ πάντα ᵗσεαυτὸν
ᵗπαρεχόμενος ᵘτύπον ᵛκαλῶν ᵛἔργων, ἐν τῇ ʷδιδασκα-
λίᾳ ˣἀφθορίαν, ʸσεμνότητα, 8 ᶻλόγον ᵃὑγιῆ, ᵇἀκατά-

.. αγαθας H

ACDF KLℵ a b c d e f g h k l m n o 17

k ver 2. l = 2 Cor xi 2. 1 Pet iii 2. Prov xix 13. m here only †. n = Matt xx 15. Rom v 7. 1 Pet. ii 18. 1 Kings xxv 15. o Eph i 22 reff. p = 2 Pet ii 2 al. see 1 Tim vi 1 reff. q = and constr., Rom xii 1. 2 Cor ii 8. vi 1 al. r Mark v 15 | L. Rom xii 3. 2 Cor v 13. Tit ii 6. 1 Pet iv 7 only †. s = Luke x 41. Acts xix 25. Phil ii 23. 1 Tim i 19. vi. 4, 21. t refl pron aft mid voice, John xix 24. Isa. vii 11. Xen. Cyr viii 1. 30, παραδειγμα τοιονδε ἑαυτον παρειχετο. Winer, edn 6, § 38 6. u = Phil iii 17. 1 Thess i 7. 2 Thess iii 9. 1 Tim iv 12. 1 Pet v 3. v 1 Tim iii 1 reff. w ver 1. x here only. y 1 Tim ii 2 reff. z = 2 Tim i 13 reff. a = (and Paul) here only. see ver 1 reff., and Prov xxxi (at end of xxiv) 8. b here only †. 2 Macc iv 47 only.

5 rec οικουρους, with D³HKLℵ³ rel Clem txt ACD¹Fℵ¹. aft θεου ins και η διδασκαλια C 5 syr arm. υποτασσομεναι ℵ¹: txt ℵ corr.

7 for σεαυτον, εαυτον D¹ 37 Chr Damasc.—παντας εαυτον m¹ n 1 Thdrt Damasc. (So *might* the words in AC be divided, but vulg Syr read them as in text.) τυπον bef παρεχ ℵ¹ 120. rec αδιαφθοριαν, with D³I ℵ³ rel Chr. αφθονιαν F. txt ACD¹Kℵ¹ 17 Damasc Œc-comm. aft αφθορ ins αγνειαν C h² 73 80 syr arm Jer Chrom Steph. aft σεμνοτητα ins αφθαρσιαν, with D³KL rel syr Chr-ms Thdrt. om ACD¹ℵ 17.

from the pres. subj: perhaps more immediate and assumed sequence may be indicated: but it is hardly possible to join logically in the mind a causal particle with a pres. indic.) **the young women to be lovers of their husbands, lovers of their children, discreet** (this term certainly applies better to women than *self-restrained*: there is in this latter, in their case, an implication of *effort*, which destroys the spontaneity, and brushes off, so to speak, the bloom of this best of female graces. See, however, note on 1 Tim. ii 9. The word is one of our greatest difficulties), **chaste, workers at home** (the word is not found elsewhere, and has perhaps on that account been changed to the more usual one οἰκουρούς. It is hardly possible that for so common a word οἰκουργούς should have been substituted. If the rec. is retained, 'keepers at home' will be signified: so Dio Cass lvi p 391 [Wetst.], πῶς οὐκ ἄριστον γυνὴ σώφρων, οἰκουρός, οἰκονόμος, παιδοτρόφος, see Elsner's note on the word, in which he shews that, as might be expected, the ideas of 'keeping at home' and 'guarding the house' are both included: so Chrys.: ἡ οἰκουρὸς γυνὴ καὶ σώφρων ἔσται· ἡ οἰκουρὸς καὶ οἰκονομική· οὔτε περὶ τρυφὴν, οὔτε περὶ ἐξόδους ἀκαίρους, οὔτε περὶ ἄλλων τῶν τοιούτων ἀσχοληθήσεται), **good** (Thl joins this with οἰκουρούς—οἰκουρὸς ἀγαθή. So also Syr. But it seems better to preserve the series of single epithets till broken in the next clause by the construction. As a single epithet [reff.] it seems to provide, as Heydenr., that their keeping, or working, at home, should not degenerate into churlishness or niggardliness), **in subjection to their own** (inserted to bring out and impress the duties they owe to them—so in Eph. v. 22) **husbands, that the word of God** (the Gospel) **be not ill-spoken of** (τὸ γὰρ προφάσει θεοσεβείας καταλιμπάνειν τοὺς ἄνδρας, βλασφημίαν ἔφερε τῷ κηρύγματι, Thdrt.). 6 ff.] **The younger men in like manner exhort to be self-restrained** (see above ver 5, and 1 Tim ii. 9, note), **shewing thyself** (the use of σεαυτόν with παρέχεσθαι is somewhat remarkable, but borne out by Xen. in reff. The account of it seems to be, that παρέχεσθαι τύπον would be the regular expression for 'to set an example,' the personal action of the subject requiring the middle [see Kruger, p 363]: and, this being so, the form of such expression is not altered, even where ἑαυτόν is expressed in apposition with τύπον. Cf Ellic.'s note) **in** ('*about*,' '*in reference to*' [reff.]: a meaning of περί with the acc. derived from its local meaning of '*round about*:' see Winer, edn 6, § 49, i.) **all matters** (not masc. sing.) **an example** (κοινὸν διδασκαλεῖον καὶ ὑπόδειγμα ἀρετῆς ἡ τοῦ σοῦ βίου λαμπρότης ἔστω, οἷόν τις εἰκὼν ἀρχέτυπος πᾶσι προκειμένη τοῖς βουλομένοις ἐναπομάξασθαι τῶν ἐν αὐτῇ καλῶν, Thl.) **of good works** (reff.),—**in thy teaching** (παρεχόμενος) **incorruption** (it is difficult exactly to fix the reference of **ἀφθορία** [or ἀδιαφθορία, which means much the same]. It may be objective, of the *contents* of the teaching—that it should set forth purity as its character and aim: or subjective, that *he should be, in his teaching*, pure in motive, uncorrupted: so Wiesinger, comparing 2 Cor xi 3, μή πως . . φθαρῇ

γνωστον, ἵνα ὁ [c] ἐξ [cd] ἐναντίας [e] ἐντραπῇ μηδὲν [f] ἔχων
λέγειν περὶ ἡμῶν [g] φαῦλον. 9 δούλους [h] ἰδίοις [h] δεσπόταις
[i] ὑποτάσσεσθαι, [k] ἐν πᾶσιν [l] εὐαρέστους εἶναι, μὴ [m] ἀντιλέγοντας, 10 μὴ [n] νοσφιζομένους, ἀλλὰ [o] πᾶσαν [p] πίστιν
[q] ἐνδεικνυμένους ἀγαθήν, ἵνα τὴν [w] διδασκαλίαν τὴν τοῦ
[r] σωτῆρος ἡμῶν [r] θεοῦ [s] κοσμῶσιν [k] ἐν πᾶσιν. 11 [t] ἐπ-

c Mark xv 39 only 4 Kings ii 7. d 1 Thess ii 15 reff. e = 1 Cor iv 14 2 Thess iii 14 only (Luke xviii 2 al) Ps xxxiv 26. f constr, Luke vii 40 Acts xxiii 17, 18, 19 Eph iv 28. g Paul, Rom ix 11 only John iii 20 v 29 James iii 14 only Prov xxii 8. h 1 Tim vi 1 Prov xxii 7. i ver 5. k 2 Tim iv 5 reff. l Eph v 10 reff. m ch i 9 Acts xiii 45 Rom x 21 (from Isa lxv 2) al L P, exc John xix 12. n Acts v 2, 3 only Josh vii 1 2 Macc iv 32 only. o Phil i 20 reff. p = Matt xxiii 23 Rom iii 3 al Prov xii 22. q Rom ii 15 2 Cor viii 24 al Paul only, exc Heb vi 10, 11 Gen i 15, 17. r 1 Tim i 1 reff. s 1 Tim ii 9 reff. t Luke i 79 Acts xxvii 20 ch iii 4 only Num vi 25. (-νεια, ver 13)

8 rec περι [ ]μων bef λεγειν, with K rel Chr Aug txt ACDFLℵ m 17 latt syrr Thdrt Ambrst —rec υμων, with A h copt Thdrt txt CDFKLℵ rel latt syrr gr-lat-ff.
9 δουλοι D[1], servi subditi sint D-lat. δεσποταις bef ιδιοις AD latt syrr copt. txt CFKLℵ rel Chr Thdrt Damasc
10. μηδε C[2]D[1]F 17 rec πιστιν bef πασαν with KL rel copt Chr Thdrt Damasc: om πιστιν ℵ[1] 17 txt ACDℵ[3] m syr lat-ff.—πασ ενδεικν. πιστιν F. rec om 2nd την, with KL rel Damasc ins ACDFℵ 17 Chr Thdrt.

τὰ νοήματα ὑμῶν ἀπὸ τῆς ἁπλότητος τῆς εἰς τὸν χριστόν. Huther takes it of the *form* of the teaching, that it should be pure from all expressions foreign to the character of the Gospel This is perhaps hardly satisfactory and the first interpretation would bring it too near in meaning to λόγον ὑγιῆ which follows), gravity, a discourse (in its contents and import) **healthy, not to be condemned, that he of the opposite part** (τὸν ἐξ ἐναντίας φησὶ καὶ τὸν διάβολον καὶ πάντα τὸν ἐκείνῳ διακονούμενον, Chr. But the former idea is hardly before the Apostle's mind, from ver 5, in which *the Gospel being evil spoken of* was represented as the point to be avoided. Cf. also 1 Tim vi 1, and v. 14 2 Tim ii. 25 It is rather the heathen or Jewish adversaries of the Gospel, among whom they dwelt) **may be ashamed** (reff), **having nothing** (μηδέν, because, following the ἔχων, it is subjective to him, the adversary We should say, οὐδέν ἐστιν ὅ τι ἂν λέγῃ,—but μηδὲν ἔχων λέγειν in the former the objective fact, in the latter the subjective deficiency, is brought out) **to say of us** (Christians not 'me and thee') (that is) **evil** (in our acts φαῦλος is never used with λέγειν, nor of words, in the N. T., but always of *deeds*: 'having no evil thing to report of us'—no evil, whether seen in our demeanour, or arising from our teaching) 9.] (παρακάλει) **Slaves to be in subjection to their own** (see above on ver 5) **masters,—in all things to give satisfaction** (this, the servants' own phrase among ourselves, expresses perhaps better than any other the meaning of εὐαρέστους εἶναι. '*To be acceptable*' would seem to bring the slave too near to the position of a friend), **not contradicting** (in the wide sense, not merely in words, see especially ref. John), **not purloining** (ref νοσφιζόμενον, ὑφαιρούμενον, ἰδιοποιούμενον, Suid τὸ δ' αὐτὸ καὶ σφετερίζεσθαι, Eustath), but **manifesting** (see ref 2 Cor) **all** (possible, reff) **good faith, that they may adorn in all things** (not '*before all men,*' as Heydenr, al cf. ἐν πᾶσιν above) **the doctrine of our Saviour, God** (see on 1 Tim i 1 Not Christ, but the Father is meant in that place the distinction is clearly made On this '*adorning*' Calvin remarks, "Hæc quoque circumstantia notanda est [this is hardly worthy of his usually pure latinity], quod ornamentum Deus a servis accipere dignatur, quorum tam vilis et abjecta erat conditio, ut vix censeri soliti sint inter homines Neque enim famulos intelligit quales hodie in usu sunt, sed mancipia, quæ pretio empta tanquam boves aut equi possidebantur. Quod si eorum vita ornamentum est Christiani nominis, multo magis videant qui in honore sunt, ne illud turpitudine sua maculent" Thl strikingly says, κἂν γὰρ τῷ δεσπότῃ διακονῇς ἀλλ' ἡ τιμὴ εἰς θεὸν ἀνατρέχει, ὅτι καὶ ἀπὸ τοῦ φόβου ἐκείνου ἡ πρὸς τὸν δεσπότην εὔνοια τὴν ἀρχὴν ἔχει) 11—15] *Ground of the above exhortations in the moral purpose of the Gospel respecting us* (11—14) *and consequent exhortation to Titus* (15)

11] **For** (reasons for the above exhortations from ver 1. not as Chrys, al, only for vv. 9, 10 The latter clause of ver 10,

ἐφάνη γὰρ ἡ χάρις τοῦ θεοῦ [u] σωτήριος πᾶσιν ἀνθρώποις,
12 [v] παιδεύουσα ἡμᾶς, ἵνα [w] ἀρνησάμενοι τὴν [x] ἀσέβειαν
καὶ τὰς [y] κοσμικὰς ἐπιθυμίας, [z] σωφρόνως καὶ [a] δικαίως

ACDF KLℵ a b c d e f g h k l m n o 17

u here only † Wisd i 14 only (-ιον, Eph vi 17) v 1 Tim i 20 reff. w 1 Tim v 8 reff. x 2 Tim ii 16 Rom i 18. xi 26 Jude 15, 18 only Jer v 6 (-βεῖν, -βής Jude 15) y Heb ix 1 only † z here only † Wisd ix 11 only a Paul, 1 Cor xv 34. 1 Thess ii 10 only 1 Pet ii 23 Luke xxiii 41 only Deut i 16

11 rec ins ἡ bef *σωτηριος* (*to fill out the construction*), with C³D²³KL rel Clem Cyr jer-mss Nyssen Chr Thdrt Procl Damasc om AC¹D¹ℵ syrr for *σωτηριος*, *σωτηρος* ℵ¹ *του σωτηρος ημων* (*see ch* iii 4) F vulg copt æth Epiph.
12. om *τας* D¹.

it is true, gives occasion to this declaration, but the reference of these verses is far wider than merely to slaves) **the grace of God** (that divine favour to men, of which the whole process of Redemption was a proof: not to be limited to *Christ's Incarnation*, as Œc. and Thdrt: though certainly this may be said for their interpretation, that *it* may *also* be regarded as a term inclusive of all the blessings of Redemption. but it does not follow, that of two such inclusive terms, the one may be substituted for the other) **was manifested, bringing salvation** (not, 'as bringing salvation.' *σωτήριος* is not predicate after *ἐπεφ.*, but *παιδεύουσα* which follows: *σωτήριος* is still part of the subject, and to make this constructionally clearer, the art. ἡ has been inserted) **to all men** (dat. belonging to *σωτήριος*, not to *ἐπεφάνη*, which verb is used absolutely, as in ch. iii. 4. cf. *σωτὴρ πάντων ἀνθρώπων*, 1 Tim. iv 10 see also ib ii. 4), **disciplining us** (see note on 1 Tim. i. 20. There is no need to depart from the universal New Testament sense of *παιδεύουσα*, and soften it into '*teaching*' the education which the Christian man receives from the grace of God, is a discipline, properly so called, of self denial and training in godliness, accompanied therefore with much mortification and punitive treatment Luther has well rendered *παιδεύουσα ἡμᾶς* by 'und züchtiget uns' Corn-a-Lap [cited in Mack] explains it also well "tanquam pueros rudes erudiens, corrigens, formans, omnique disciplina instituens et imbuens, perinde ut pædagogus puerum sibi commissum tam in litteris quam in moribus hoc enim est *παιδεύειν*, inquit Gell. i 13 13"), **that** (by the ordinary rendering, "*teaching us, that,*" we make ἵνα introduce merely the *purport* of the teaching and so, following most Commentators, De W, and I am surprised to see, Huther, although I suppose representing in some measure the philological fidelity of Meyer, under whose shelter his commentary appears There must have been some defect of supervision here. Wiesinger only of the recent Commentators, after Mack and Matthies, keeps the telic meaning of ἵνα. The Greek Commentators, as might be expected, adhere to the propriety of their own language. So Chrys [*ἦλθεν ὁ χριστός, ἵνα ἀρνησώμεθα τὴν ἀσέβειαν*], Thl [*παιδεύει γὰρ ἡμᾶς, ἵνα τοῦ λοιποῦ σωφρόνως ζήσωμεν*], Thdrt [*τούτου χάριν ἐνηνθρώπησεν . . . . ἵνα* .] The truth is, that **παιδεύειν** is one of those verbs, the purpose and purport of which mutually include each other. The form and manner of instructive discipline itself conveys the aim and intent of that discipline So that the meaning of ἵνα after such a verb falls under the class which I have discussed in my note to 1 Cor xiv 13, which see Our English 'that,' which would be dubious after '*teaching*,' keeps, after 'disciplining,' its proper telic force), **denying** (not, 'having denied' the aor part *ἀρνησάμενοι* is, as so often, not prior to, but contemporaneous with, the aor. *ζήσωμεν* following [This, against Ellic, requires pressing here. The whole life being summed up in *ζήσωμεν*, aor, not *ζῶμεν*, pres, the aor part. *ἀρνησάμενοι* must be so rendered, as to extend over all that sum, not as if it represented some definite act of abnegation anterior to it all.] *διὰ τοῦ ἀρνήσασθαι*, says Thl, *τὴν ἐκ διαθέσεως ὁλοψύχου ἀποστροφὴν σημαίνει.* "Has [cupiditates] abnegamus, cum eis consensum negamus, cum delectationem quam suggerunt, et actum ad quem sollicitant, abnuimus, imo ex mente et animo radicitus evellimus et extirpamus." S Bernard, Serm. xi [Mack]) **impiety and the lusts of the world** (the *τάς* gives universality—'*all* worldly lusts' **κοσμικάς**, belonging to the *κόσμος*, the world which *ἐν τῷ πονηρῷ κεῖται*, and is without God see 1 John ii. 15—17 and Ellicott's note here), **we might live soberly** (our old difficulty of rendering *σώφρων* and its derivatives recurs 'Soberly' seems here to express the *adverb* well, though 'sober' by no means covers the meaning of the *adjective*. The fact is, that the peculiar

καὶ [b] εὐσεβῶς ζήσωμεν ἐν [c] τῷ νῦν [c] αἰῶνι, 13 [de] προσδεχό-
μενοι τὴν [f] μακαρίαν [eg] ἐλπίδα καὶ [h] ἐπιφάνειαν τῆς δόξης

b 2 Tim iii 12 only † Xen Mem ii 2 13 (see 1 Tim ii 2 reff)

c 1 Tim vi 17 2 Tim iv 10 only see 1 Tim iv 8 d = Mark xv 43 Luke ii 25, 38 al Paul, — here & Acts as below (e) only see Rom xvi 2 Phil ii 29 e Acts xxiv 15 f of things, Acts xx 35 only elsw (passim) of persons see 1 Tim i 11 reff g = Gal v 5 Heb vi. 18 al. h 1 Tim i 10 reff

meaning which has become attached to 'sober,'—so much so, as almost to deprive it of its more general reference to life and thought,—has not taken possession of the adverb) **and justly** (better than '*righteously*,'—'righteous,' by its forensic objective sense in St Paul, introducing a confusion, where the question is of moral rectitude) **and piously in the present life** ("Bernard, Serm xi : *sobrie* erga nos, *juste* erga proximum, *pie* erga Deum, Salmer p 630 f dicimus in his verbis Apostolum tribus virtutibus, sobrietatis, pietatis et justitiæ, summam justitiæ Christianæ complecti Sobrietas est ad se, justitia ad proximum, pietas erga Deum . sobrie autem agit, cum quis se propter Deum diligit juste, cum proximum diligit pie, cum charitate Deum colit" Mack Wolf quotes from Lucian, Somn p. 8, the same conjunction τὴν ψυχὴν . . κατακοσμήσω . σωφροσύνῃ, δικαιοσύνῃ, καὶ εὐσεβίᾳ . ταῦτα γάρ ἐστιν ὁ τῆς ψυχῆς ἀκήρατος κόσμος These three comprising our παιδεία in faith and love, he now comes to *hope*) **looking for** (this expectation being an abiding state and posture,—not, like ζήσωμεν, the life following on and unfolded from the determining impulse co-ordinate with the ἀρνήσασθαι,—is put in the *pres*, not in the *aor*) **the blessed hope** (here, as in reff Gal and Acts, Col. i. 5 al, nearly objective,—the hope, as embodying the thing hoped for · but keep the vigour and propriety both of language and thought, and do not tame down the one and violate the other, with Grot, by a metonymy, or with Wolf, by a hypallage of μακαρία ἐλπίς for ἐλπιζομένη μακαριότης) **and manifestation** (ἐλπίδα κ. ἐπιφ. belong together) **of the glory** (δύο δείκνυσιν ἐνταῦθα ἐπιφανείας· καὶ γάρ εἰσι δύο· ἡ μὲν προτέρα χάριτος, ἡ δὲ δευτέρα ἀνταποδόσεως, Chrys. Nothing could be more unfortunate than the application here of the figure of hendiadys in the E V.: see below) **of the great God** (the Father see below) **and of our Saviour Jesus Christ** (as regards the sense, an exact parallel is found in Matt. xvi. 27, μέλλει γὰρ ὁ υἱὸς τοῦ ἀνθρώπου ἔρχεσθαι ἐν τῇ δόξῃ τοῦ πατρὸς αὐτοῦ, compared with Matt. xxv. 31, ὅταν ἔλθῃ ὁ υἱὸς τοῦ ἀνθρώπου ἐν τῇ δόξῃ αὐτοῦ. See also 1 Pet. iv 13 The glory which shall be revealed at the appearing of our Saviour Jesus Christ is *His own* glory, *and* that of *His Father* [John xvii 3; 1 Thess iii 13] This sense having been obscured by the foolish hendiadys, has led to the asking [by Mr. Green, Gr Test Gram, p. 216], "What intimation is given in Scripture of a glorious appearing of God the Father and our Lord *in concert?*" To which the answer is, that no such appearing is even hinted at in this passage, taken as above. What is asserted is, that the δόξα shall be that τοῦ μεγάλου θεοῦ καὶ σωτῆρος ἡμῶν Ἰησοῦ χριστοῦ. And we now come to consider the meaning of these words Two views have been taken of them. (1) that τοῦ μεγάλου θεοῦ καὶ σωτῆρος ἡμῶν are to be taken together as the description of Ἰησοῦ χριστοῦ,—'*of Jesus Christ, the great God and our Saviour*' (2) that as given above, τοῦ μεγάλου θεοῦ describes the Father, and σωτῆρος ἡμῶν Ἰησοῦ χριστοῦ the Son. It is obvious that in dealing with (1), we shall be deciding with regard to (2) also (1) has been the view of the Greek orthodox Fathers, as against the Arians [see a complete collection of their testimonies in Dr Wordsworth's "Six Letters to Granville Sharp on the use of the definite article in the Greek text of the N T." Lond. 1802], and of most ancient and modern Commentators. That the former so interpreted the words, is obviously not [as it has been considered] decisive of the question, if they can be shewn to bear legitimately another meaning, and that meaning to be the one most likely to have been in the mind of the writer. The case of ἵνα in the preceding verse [see note there], was wholly different. There it was contended that ἵνα with a subjunctive, has, and can have, but one meaning · and this was upheld against those who would introduce another, *inter alia*, by the fact that the Greek Fathers dreamt of no other. The argument rested not on this latter fact, but on the logical force of the particle itself. And similarly here, the passage must be argued primarily on its own ground, not primarily on the consensus of the Greek Fathers. No one disputes that it *may* mean that which they have interpreted it and there were obvious reasons why they, having licence to do so, should choose this interpretation. But it is our

i here only. Neh. ix. 32. Dan. ii. 45. ix. 4 al.
j ch. i. 4 reff.

τοῦ [i] μεγάλου [i] θεοῦ καὶ [j] σωτῆρος ἡμῶν Ἰησοῦ χριστοῦ,
14 ὃς [k] ἔδωκεν ἑαυτὸν ὑπὲρ ἡμῶν, ἵνα [l] λυτρώσηται ἡμᾶς

ACDF KLℵ a b c d e f g h k l m n o 17

k Gal. i. 4. 1 Tim. ii. 6. 1 Macc. vi. 44. (= παραδιδ., Gal. ii. 20. Eph. v. 25.) l Luke xxiv. 21. 1 Pet. i. 18 only. Ps. cxxix. 8.

13. χριστου bef ιησ. ℵ[1].
14. υπερ ημων bef εαυτον D Lucif. αυτον ℵ[1] 238.

object, not being swayed in this or any other interpretation, by doctrinal considerations one way or the other, to enquire, not what the words *may* mean, but what they *do* mean, as far as we may be able to ascertain it. The main, and indeed the only reliance of those who take (1), is the omission of the article before σωτῆρος. Had the sentence stood τοῦ μεγ. θεοῦ καὶ τοῦ σωτῆρος ἡμῶν Ἰ. χ., their verdict for (2) would have been unanimous. That the insertion of the article would have been decisive for (2), is plain: but is it equally plain, that its omission is decisive for (1)? This must depend entirely on the nature and position of the word thus left anarthrous. If it is a word which had by usage become altogether or occasionally anarthrous,—if it is so connected, that the presence of the article expressed, is not requisite to its presence in the sense, then the state of the case, as regards the omission, is considerably altered. Now there is no doubt that σωτήρ was one of those words which gradually dropped the article and became a quasi proper name: cf. 1 Tim. i. 1 [I am quite aware of Bp. Middleton's way of accounting for this, but do not regard it as satisfactory]; iv. 10; which latter place is very instructive as to the way in which the designation from its official nature became anarthrous. This being so, it must hardly be judged as to the expression of the art. by the same rules as other nouns. Then as to its structural and contextual connexion. It is joined with ἡμῶν, which is an additional reason why it may spare the article: see Luke i. 78: Rom. i. 7: 1 Cor. i. 3 [1 Cor. ii. 7; x. 11]: 2 Cor. i. 2, &c. Again, as Winer has observed [edn. 6, § 19, 5 b, note 1], the prefixing of an appositional designation to the proper name frequently causes the omission of the article. So in 2 Thess. i. 12: 2 Pet. i. 1: Jude 4: see also 2 Cor. i. 2; vi. 18: Gal. i. 3: Eph. i. 2; vi. 23: Phil. i. 2; ii. 11; iii. 20 &c. If then σωτὴρ ἡμῶν Ἰησοῦς χριστός may signify 'Jesus Christ our Saviour,'—on comparing the two members of the clause, we observe, that θεοῦ has already had its predicate expressed in τοῦ μεγάλου; and that it is therefore natural to expect that the latter member of the clause, likewise consisting of a proper name and its predicate, should correspond logically to the former: in other words, that τοῦ θεοῦ καὶ σωτῆρος ἡμῶν Ἰη. χρ. would much more naturally suit (1) than τοῦ **μεγάλου** θεοῦ καὶ σωτῆρος ἡμ. Ἰη. χρ. In clauses where the two appellative members belong to one expressed subject, we expect to find the former of them without any predicative completion. If it be replied to this, as I conceive on the hypothesis of (1) it must be, that τοῦ μεγάλου is an epithet alike of θεοῦ and σωτῆρος, 'our great [God and Saviour],' I may safely leave it to the feeling of any scholar, whether such an expression would be likely to occur. Let us now consider, whether the Apostle would in this place have been likely to designate our Lord as ὁ μέγας θεὸς καὶ σωτὴρ ἡμῶν. This must be chiefly decided by examining the usages of the expression θεὸς ὁ σωτὴρ ἡμῶν, which occurs six times in these Epistles, once in Luke [i. 47], and once in the Epistle of Jude. If the writer *here* identifies this expression, 'the great God and our Saviour,' with the Lord Jesus Christ, calling Him 'God and our Saviour,' it will be at least probable that in other places where he speaks of "God our Saviour," he also designates our Lord Jesus Christ. Now is that so? On the contrary, in 1 Tim. i. 1, we have κατ' ἐπιταγὴν θεοῦ σωτῆρος ἡμῶν, καὶ χριστοῦ Ἰησοῦ τῆς ἐλπίδος ἡμῶν: where I suppose none will deny that the Father and the Son are most plainly distinguished from one another. The same is the case in 1 Tim. ii. 3—5, a passage bearing much [see below] on the interpretation of this one: and consequently in 1 Tim. iv. 10, where ἐστιν σωτὴρ πάντων ἀνθρώπων corresponds to θέλει πάντας σωθῆναι in the other. So also in Tit. i. 3, where the σωτὴρ ἡμῶν θεός, by whose ἐπιταγή the promise of eternal life was manifested, with the proclamation of which St. Paul was entrusted, is the same αἰώνιος θεός, by whose ἐπιταγή the hidden mystery was manifested in Rom. xvi. 26, where the same distinction is made. The only place where there could be any doubt is in our ver. 10, which possible doubt however is removed by ver. 11, where the

ἀπὸ πάσης [mn] ἀνομίας καὶ [mo] καθαρίσῃ ἑαυτῷ [m] λαὸν [p] περι-
ούσιον, [q] ζηλωτὴν [r] καλῶν [r] ἔργων. 15 ταῦτα λάλει καὶ

m Ezek xxxvii 23 n Paul R m iv 7 vi 19 2 Cor vi 14 2 Thess ii 7 Matt vii 23 al Exod xxxiv 9 o = Acts xv 9 Eph v 26 James iv 8 Sir xxxviii 10 p here only Exod xix 5. Deut. vii 6 xiv 2 xxvi 18 (alw w λαός, and never occ elsw, exc Mal iii 17 Aq σιασμος, Ps cxxxiv 4 Eccles ii 8) q = Acts (1 13) xxi 20 xxii 3 1 Cor xiv 12 Gal i 14 al 1 Pet iii 13 (Luke vi 15) only (Exod xx 5 al) 2 Macc iv 2 r 1 Tim iii 1 reff

15 for λαλει, διδασκε A.

same assertion is made, of the revelation of the hidden grace of God [the Father]. Then we have our own ch. iii. 4—6, where we find τοῦ σωτῆρος ἡμῶν θεοῦ in ver. 4, clearly defined as *the Father*, and διὰ Ἰησοῦ χριστοῦ τοῦ σωτῆρος ἡμῶν in ver. 6 In that passage too we have the expression ἡ χρηστότης καὶ ἡ φιλανθρωπία ἐπεφάνη τοῦ σωτῆρος ἡμ. θεοῦ, which is quite decisive in answer to those who object here to the expression ἐπιφάνειαν τῆς δόξης as applied to the Father. In the one passage of St. Jude, the distinction is equally clear for there we have μόνῳ θεῷ σωτῆρι ἡμῶν διὰ Ἰησοῦ χριστοῦ τοῦ κυρίου ἡμῶν It is plain then, that the usage of the words '*God our Saviour*' does not make it probable that the whole expression here is to be applied to the Lord Jesus Christ And in estimating this probability, let us again recur to 1 Tim ii 3, 5, a passage which runs very parallel with the present one We read there, εἷς γὰρ θεός, | εἷς καὶ μεσίτης θεοῦ καὶ ἀνθρώπων, ἄνθρωπος χριστὸς Ἰησοῦς, ὁ δοὺς ἑαυτὸν ἀντίλυτρον κ τ λ. Compare this with τοῦ μεγάλου θεοῦ | καὶ σωτῆρος ἡμῶν Ἰησοῦ χριστοῦ, ὃς ἔδωκεν ἑαυτὸν ὑπὲρ ἡμῶν ἵνα λυτρώσηται κ τ.λ Can there be a reasonable doubt, that the Apostle writing two sentences so closely corresponding, on a point of such high importance, would have in his view the same distinction in the second of them, which he so strongly lays down in the first? Without then considering the question as closed, I would submit that (2) satisfies all the grammatical requirements of the sentence: that it is both structurally and contextually more probable, and more agreeable to the Apostle's way of writing and I have therefore preferred it. The principal advocates for it have been, the pseudo-Ambrose [i e. Hilary the deacon, the author of the Commentary which goes by the name of that Father. whose words are these, "hanc esse dicit beatam spem credentium, qui exspectant adventum gloriæ magni Dei quod revelari habet judice Christo, in quo Dei Patris videbitur potestas et gloria, ut fidei suæ præmium consequantur Ad hoc enim redemit nos Christus, ut" &c], Erasm. [annot. and paraphr], Grot., Wetst, Heinr., Winer [ubi supra, end], De W, Huther [the other view,—not this as stated in my earlier editions, by inadvertence,—is taken by Ellicott]. Whichever way taken, the passage is just as important a testimony to the divinity of our Saviour according to (1), by asserting His possession of Deity and right to the appellation of the Highest: according to (2), even more strikingly, asserting His equality in glory with the Father, in a way which would be blasphemy if predicated of any of the sons of men), **who** (our Saviour Jesus Christ) **gave Himself** ("the forcible ἑαυτόν, 'Himself, His whole self, the greatest gift ever given,' must not be overlooked cf Beveridge, Serm 93, vol iv. p 285." Ellicott) **for us** ('on our behalf,' not '*in our stead*' reff), **that He might** (by this assertion of the Redeemer's purpose, we return to the moral aim of verses 11, 12, more plainly indicated as in close connexion with Christ's propitiatory sacrifice) **redeem** (**λυτροῦσθαι**, '*to buy off with a price*,' the *middle* including personal agency and interest, cf. καθαρίσῃ ἑαυτῷ below So in Diod. Sic. v 17, of the Balearians, ὅταν τινὲς γυναῖκες ὑπὸ τῶν προσπλεόντων λῃστῶν ἁλῶσιν, ἀντὶ μιᾶς γυναικὸς τρεῖς ἢ τέτταρας ἄνδρας διδόντες λυτροῦνται. Polyb. xvii 16 1, of King Attalus and the Sicyonians, where only personal *agency* is implied in the middle, τὴν ἱερὰν χώραν τοῦ Ἀπόλλωνος ἐλυτρώσατο χρημάτων αὐτοῖς οὐκ ὀλίγων See note, 1 Tim ii. 6: and cf ref. 1 Pet, where the price is stated to have been the precious blood of Christ) **us from all lawlessness** (see reff. and especially 1 John iii 4, ἡ ἁμαρτία ἐστὶν ἡ ἀνομία) **and might purify** (there is no need to supply ἡμᾶς, though the sense is not disturbed by so doing. By making λαόν the direct object of καθαρίζῃ, the purpose of the Redeemer is lifted off from our particular case, and generally and objectively stated) **to Himself** ('dat. commodi') **a people** (object: not, as De W, Wies, al, predicate, '(us) for a people') **peculiarly His** (see note on Eph i 14, and cf the reff here in the LXX, from which the expression is borrowed See also 1 Pet. ii 9, and Ellicott here The

ˢπαρακάλει καὶ ᵗἔλεγχε ᵘμετὰ ᵛπάσης ʷἐπιταγῆς· μη- ACDF
δείς σου ˣπεριφρονείτω. III. 1 ʸὑπομίμνησκε αὐτοὺς KLℵ a b c d e f g
ᶻἀρχαῖς ᶻᵃἐξουσίαις ᵇὑποτάσσεσθαι, ᶜπειθαρχεῖν, ᵈπρὸς h k l m n o 17
πᾶν ᵈἔργον ᵈἀγαθὸν ᵉἑτοίμους εἶναι, 2 μηδένα ᶠβλασφη-
μεῖν, ᵍἀμάχους εἶναι, ʰἐπιεικεῖς, ⁱπᾶσαν ʲἐνδεικνυμένους
ᵏπραΰτητα πρὸς πάντας ἀνθρώπους. 3 ἦμεν γάρ ποτε

s = 1 Tim vi 2. t 1 Tim v 20 reff. u = Mark iii 5. 1 Chron xxix 22. Paul, passim. v = Phil i 20 reff. w 1 Tim i 1 reff. x here only†. περιφρονῶ, ἴσον τῷ καταφρονῶ, Schol. Aristoph. Nub. 225. see 1 Tim iv 12. y 2 Tim ii 14 reff. z Eph i. 21 reff. a = Rom xiii 1. b ch ii 5, 9. Eph v 22 reff. c Acts v. 29, 32. xxvii 21 only†. Esdr viii 94 (90). Sir xxx (xxxiii) 28 only. d see 2 Tim ii 21 reff. e Paul, 2 Cor ix 5. x 6, 16 only. 1 Pet iii 15 al. Ps xvi 12. f = Rom iii 8 al. 4 Kings xix 6 F. g 1 Tim. iii 3 only†. h Phil iv 5. 1 Tim iii 3. James iii 17. 1 Pet. ii 18 only. Ps lxxxv 5 only. i ch ii 15. j ch ii 10 reff. k Gal v. 23. vi 1 reff.

CHAP III 1 aft *υπομιμνησκε* ins *δε* A Syr arm. rec aft *αρχαις* ins *και*, with D³KL rel: om ACD¹Fℵ 17. aft *πειθαρχειν* ins *και* A: pref F: in both places arm. *αγαθους* ℵ¹ k.
2 for *μηδενα*, *μη* F. G lat has both. *μηδεν* K. *ενδεικνυσθαι* ℵ¹. rec *πραοτητα*, with DFKL rel: txt ACℵ³ 17. 67². *σπουδην τα*(sic) ℵ¹.

ἐξειλεγμένον of Chrys., though expressing the fact, says too much for the word,—as also does the *acceptabilis* of the Vulg: *egregium* of Jerome, too little. the *οἰκεῖον* of Thdrt. is exact. that which *περίεστιν αὐτῷ*), **zealous** (an ardent worker and promoter) **of good works.** 15.] gathers up all since ver. 1, where the general command last appeared, and enforces it on Titus. In ch. iii. 1, the train of thought is again resumed. **These things** (the foregoing: not, the following) **speak and exhort** (in the case of those who believe and need stirring up) **and rebuke** (in the case of those who are rebellious) **with all imperativeness** (*μετὰ αὐθεντίας καὶ μετὰ ἐξουσίας πολλῆς*, Chrys.—*τουτέστι, μετὰ ἀποτομίας*, Thl.). **Let no man despise thee** (addressed to Titus, not to the people, as Calv. ['populum ipsum magis quam Titum hic compellat'] 'so conduct thyself in thine exhortations, with such gravity, and such consistency, and such impartiality, that every word of thine may carry weight, and none may be able to cast slight on thee for flaws in any of these points'). III. 1, 2.] *Rules concerning behaviour to those without.* **Put them in mind** (as of a duty previously and otherwise well known, but liable to be forgotten) **to be in subjection to governments, to authorities, to obey the magistrate** (*πειθαρχεῖν* here probably stands absolutely, not, as Huther, connected with the dat. *ἀρχαῖς ἐξ.* So Xen. Cyr. viii 1. 4, *μέγιστον ἀγαθὸν τὸ πειθαρχεῖν φαίνεται εἰς τὸ καταπράττειν τὰ ἀγαθά.* The other construction has however the reff. in its favour), **to be ready towards every good work** (the connexion seems to be as in Rom xiii 3, where the rulers are said to be *οὐ φόβος τῷ ἀγαθῷ ἔργῳ, ἀλλὰ τῷ κακῷ.* Compare also the remarkable coincidence in the sentiment of Xen. quoted above. Jerome in loc., Wetst., De W., al., suppose these exhortations to subjection to have found their occasion in the insubordination of the Jews on principle to foreign rule, and more especially of the Cretan Jews. In the presence of similar exhortations in the Epistle to the Romans and elsewhere, we can hardly perhaps say so much as this: but certainly Wetst.'s quotations from Diod. Sic., al., seem to establish the fact of Cretan turbulence in general. The inference drawn by Thdrt., al., from these last words,—*οὐδὲ γὰρ εἰς ἅπαντα δεῖ τοῖς ἄρχουσι πειθαρχεῖν*, does not seem to be legitimately deduced from them), **to speak evil of no one** (these words set forth the *general* duty, but are perhaps introduced owing to what has preceded, cf. 2 Pet ii 10. Jude 8), **to be not quarrelsome** (ref. and note), **forbearing** (ib., and note on Phil iv 5. "The *ἐπιεικής* must have been, it is to be feared, a somewhat exceptional character in Crete, where an *ἔμφυτος πλεονεξία*, exhibited in outward acts of aggression, *καὶ ἰδίᾳ καὶ κατὰ κοινόν* [Polyb. vi 46—9], is described as one of the prevailing and dominant vices." Ellicott), **manifesting all meekness towards all men** (from what follows, *πάντας ἀνθρ.* is evidently to be taken in the widest sense, and especially to be applied to the heathen without: see below.)

3.] **For** (reason why we should shew all meekness, &c: *οὐκοῦν μηδενὶ ὀνειδίσῃς, φησί· τοιοῦτος γὰρ ἦς καὶ σύ*, Chrys. *ὃ καὶ ὁ λῃστὴς πρὸς τὸν ἕτερον λῃστὴν ἔλεγεν, ὅτι ἐν τῷ αὐτῷ κρίματι ἐσμέν.* Thl.) **we** (Christians) **also** (as well as they) **were** (emphatically prefixed) **once without understanding** (of spiritual things, see Eph iv 18), **disobedient** (to God, ch i. 16: he is no longer speaking of *authorities*,

καὶ ἡμεῖς [l] ἀνόητοι, [m] ἀπειθεῖς, [n] πλανώμενοι, [o] δουλεύοντες
ἐπιθυμίαις καὶ [p] ἡδοναῖς [q] ποικίλαις, ἐν [r] κακίᾳ καὶ [s] φθόνῳ
[t] διάγοντες, [u] στυγητοί, μισοῦντες ἀλλήλους. 4 ὅτε δὲ ἡ
[v] χρηστότης καὶ ἡ [w] φιλανθρωπία [x] ἐπεφάνη τοῦ [y] σωτῆρος
ἡμῶν [y] θεοῦ, 5 οὐκ [z] ἐξ ἔργων τῶν [a] ἐν δικαιοσύνῃ ἃ ἐποι-

l Luke xxiv 25. Rom i 14. Gal iii 1, 3. 1 Tim vi 9 only. L.P. Prov xvii 28. m ch i 16 reff. n 1 Cor vi 9. xv 33. Gal vi 7. 2 Tim iii 13. Heb v 2. James v 19. Hos iv 12. o Gal iv 8, 9 reff. p Paul, here only. Luke viii 14. James iv 1, 3. 2 Pet. ii 13 only. Numb xi 8. Prov xvii 1. Wisd vii 2. xvi 20 only. see 2 Tim iii 4. q 2 Tim iii 6 (there also w. ἐπιθ.) reff. r Eph iv 31 reff. s Phil i 15 reff. t 1 Tim ii 2 only †. 2 Macc xii 38. u here only † (-γεῖν 2 Macc v 8). v Eph ii 7 reff. w Acts xxviii 2 only †. 2 Macc vi 22. xiv 9 only. (-πως, Acts xxvii 3.) x ch ii 11 reff. y 1 Tim i 1 reff. z = Rom iii 20 al fr Paul. a so ἐν θεῷ, ἐν κυρίῳ, John iii 21. 1 Cor vii 39. xi 11 al.

3. aft ανοητοι ins και D Syr vulg(but not am) aft δουλευοντες ins εν ℵ[1](ℵ[3] disapproving) for στυγητοι, μισητοι D[1] στυγηται ℵ[1] at end ins αποστερουντες μισθον μισθωτου, και εκχυνομενοι αιμα ιδρωτων αυτων, ων η κρισις ανιλεως τω μη ποιησαντι ελεος 96. 109.

5 rec for ἅ, ὧν (*correction for elegance*), with C[2]D[3]KL rel Ath(many mss) Cyr-jer Ps-Ath Chr Thdrt$_3$ txt AC[1]D[1]Fℵ 17 Clem Cyr$_{sæpe}$. [C is deficient from εποιησαμεν

but has passed into a new train of thought), **led astray** (so Conyb the passive sense should be kept, as best answering to N. T. usage, ref. 2 Tim. reff. Heb. and James, which Huther quotes for the neuter sense, are both better rendered passive Ellic. advocates the neuter '*going astray*'), **slaves to divers lusts and pleasures** (see reff an unusual word in N. T., though so common in secular Greek), **passing our lives** (in ref 1 Tim βίον is expressed) **in malice** (reff) **and envy,—hateful, hating one another** (the sequence, if there be any, seems to be in the converse order from that assumed by Thl, ἄξιοι μίσους ἦμεν, ὡς ἀλλήλους μισοῦντες It was our natural hatefulness which begot mutual hatred. Or perhaps the two particulars may be taken separately, as distinct items in our catalogue of depravities) **4.] But when the goodness** (reff) **and love-towards-men** (I prefer this literal rendering of φιλανθρωπία to any of the more usual ones. cf. Diog. Laert Plat iii 98, τῆς φιλανθρωπίας ἐστὶν εἴδη τρία ἓν μὲν διὰ τῆς προσηγορίας γινόμενον, οἷον ἐν οἷς τινὲς τὸν ἐντυγχάνοντα πάντα προσαγορεύουσι καὶ τὴν δεξιὰν ἐμβάλλοντες χαιρετίζουσιν· ἄλλο εἶδος, ὅταν τις βοηθητικὸς ᾖ παντὶ τῷ ἀτυχοῦντι· ἕτερον εἶδός ἐστι τῆς φιλανθρωπίας ἐν ᾧ τινὲς φιλοδειπνισταί εἰσι. The second of these is evidently that here intended, but Huther's view of the correspondence of this description of God's kindness to us with that which we are required [ver. 2] to shew to others, appears to me to be borne out and thus His φιλανθρωπία would parallel πραΰτητα πρὸς πάντας ἀνθρώπους above, and the fact of its being 'love *toward men*' should be expressed Bengel's remark also is worth notice "Hominum vitia plane contraria enumerantur versu 3" The junction of χρηστὸς, -ότης, with φιλάνθρωπος, -ία, is very common see the numerous quotations in Wetst) **of our Saviour, God** (the Father cf διὰ Ἰησ. χρ below, and see note on ch ii 13), **was manifested** (viz in Redemption, by the Incarnation and Satisfaction of the Redeemer),—**not by virtue of** (ἐξ, as the ground out of which an act springs Cf besides the frequent ἐκ πίστεως, ἐξ ἔργων,—Matt xii 37 bis: Rom i 4 2 Cor xiii 4) **works wrought in** (I have thus represented the τῶν ἐν — ἔργων [general, '*any works*'] τῶν ἐκ δικ. [viz '*which were*,' particularizing out of those, '*in righteousness*'] ἐν δικ *in* righteousness, as the element and condition in which they were wrought) **righteousness which we** (emphatic) **did** (not, '*have done*,' as E. V., nor '*had done*,' as Conyb.,—which in fact obscures the meaning. for God's act here spoken of was a definite act in time—and its application to us, also a definite act in time [see below] and if we take this ἐποιήσαμεν pluperfect, we confine the Apostle's repudiation of our works, as moving causes of those acts of God, to the *time previous to those acts*. For aught that this pluperfect would assert, our salvation might be prompted on God's part by future works of righteousness which He foresaw we should do Whereas the simple aoristic sense throws the whole into the same time,—"His goodness, &c was manifested . . not for works which we did . . . . He saved us,"—and renders the repudiation of human merit universal On the construction, cf. Thl ἔσωσεν ἡμᾶς οὐκ ἐξ ἔργων ὧν ἐποιήσαμεν, ἀντὶ τοῦ οὔτε ἐποιήσαμεν ἔργα δικαιοσύνης, οὔτε ἐσώθη-

ήσαμεν ἡμεῖς, ἀλλὰ κατὰ τὸ αὐτοῦ ἔλεος ἔσωσεν ἡμᾶς
διὰ [b] λουτροῦ [c] παλιγγενεσίας καὶ [d] ἀνακαινώσεως πνεύματος ἁγίου 6 [e] οὗ [f] ἐξέχεεν ἐφ' ἡμᾶς [g] πλουσίως, διὰ

ACDF KLℵ a b c d e f g h k l m n o 17

b Eph. v. 26 only. Cant. iv. 2. Sir. xxxi. (xxxiv.) 25 only. c Matt. xix. 28 only†. Jos. Antt. xi. 3. 9. Philo passim. d Rom. xii. 2 only†. (-νοῦσθαι, Col. iii. 10.) e attr., Eph. i. 6 reff. f = Acts ii. 17, 18 (from Joel ii. 28, 29), 33. x. 45. Jer. xiv. 16. g Col. iii. 16. 1 Tim. vi. 17. 2 Pet. i. 11 only†.

to εσωσεν] rec τον αυ. ελεον, with D³KL rel Chr: txt AD¹Fℵ 17 67² Clem Max Ath Cyr-jer Thdrt Damasc.—τ. ελ. bef αυτ. DF. ins του bef λουτρου A. om CDFKLℵ rel Orig$_{sæpe}$ Ath Cyr-jer. ins δια bef πνευματος D¹F.
6. for οὗ, ὅ D¹ lect-17.

μεν ἐκ τούτων, ἀλλὰ τὸ πᾶν ἡ ἀγαθότης αὐτοῦ ἐποίησε), **but according to** (after the measure of, in pursuance of, after the promptings of: see Ellic.'s note) **His compassion He saved us** (this ἔσωσεν must be referred back to the definite objective act of God in Redemption, which has been above mentioned. On the part of God, that act is one—in the application of it to individuals, it is composed of many and successive acts. But this ἔσωσεν, being contemporaneous with ὅτε ἐπεφάνη above, cannot apply, as De Wette, to our individual salvation alone. At the same time, standing as it does in a transitional position, between God's objective act and the subjective individual application of it, it no doubt looks forward as well as backward—to individual realization of salvation, as well as to the divine completion of it once for all in Christ. Calvin, h. l., refers the completeness of our salvation rather to God's looking on it as subjectively accomplished in us: "De fide loquitur, et nos jam salutem adeptos esse docet. Ergo utcunque peccato implicati corpus mortis circumferamus, certi tamen de salute nostra sumus, si modo fide insiti simus in Christum, secundum illud [Joh. v. 21]: 'Qui credit in filium Dei, transiit de morte in vitam.' Paulo post tamen, fidei nomine interposito nos re ipsa nondum adeptos esse ostendit, quod Christus morte sua præstitit. Unde sequitur, ex parte Dei salutem nostram impletam esse, cujus fruitio in finem usque militiæ differtur." The ἡμᾶς here is not *all mankind*, which would be inconsistent with what follows,—nor *all Christians*, however true that would be,—but the same as are indicated by καὶ ἡμεῖς above,—the particular Christians in the Apostle's view as he was writing—Titus and his Cretan converts, and himself) **by means of the laver** (not '*washing*,' as E. V.: see the Lexx., but always a vessel, or pool in which washing takes place. Here, the baptismal font: see on Eph. v. 26) **of regeneration** (first, let us treat of **παλιγγενεσία**. It occurs only in ref. Matt., and there in an objective sense, whereas here it is evidently subjective. There, it is the great second birth of heaven and earth in the latter days: here, the second birth of the individual man. Though not occurring elsewhere in this sense, it has its cognate expressions,—e. g. ἀναγεννάω, 1 Pet. i. 3, 23: γεννηθῆναι ἄνωθεν, John iii. 3 &c. Then, of the *genitive*. The font is the 'Laver of regeneration,' because it is the vessel consecrated to the use of that Sacrament whereby, in its *completeness* as a Sacrament [see below], the new life unto God is conveyed. And inasmuch as it is in that font, and when we are in it, that the first breath of that life is drawn, it is the laver *of*,—belonging to, pertaining to, setting forth,—regeneration. Observe, there is here no figure: the words are literal: Baptism is taken as in all its completion,—the outward visible sign accompanied by the inward spiritual grace; and as thus *complete*, it not only represents, but *is*, the new birth. Cf. Calvin.: "Solent Apostoli a Sacramentis ducere argumentum, ut rem illic significatam probent, quia principium illud valere debet inter pios, Deum non inanibus nobiscum figuris ludere, sed virtute sua intus præstare quod externo signo demonstrat. Quare Baptismus congruenter et vere lavacrum regenerationis dicitur. Vim et usum Sacramentorum recte is tenebit qui rem et signum ita connectet, ut signum non faciat inane aut inefficax: neque tamen ejus ornandi causa Spiritui sancto detrahat quod suum est." The font then, the laver of regeneration, representing the external portion of the Sacrament, and pledging the internal;—that *inward and spiritual grace*, necessary to the completion of the Sacrament and its regenerating power, is not, as too often, left to follow as a matter of course, and thus baptismal regeneration rendered a mere formal and unmeaning thing, 'ex opere operato,'—but is distinctly stated in the following words) **and** (understand **διά** again: so Thdrt apparently,—Bengel ['duæ res commemorantur: lavacrum regenerationis, quæ baptismi in Christum periphrasis,—

Ἰησοῦ Χριστοῦ τοῦ [h] σωτῆρος ἡμῶν, 7 ἵνα [i] δικαιωθέντες
τῇ ἐκείνου [k] χάριτι [l] κληρονόμοι γενήθωμεν κατ' [m] ἐλπίδα

h ch i 4 reff. i = Acts xiii 39 (Paul) Rom ii 13 al Paul pas sim elsw, Luke xviii 14 James ii 21, 24, 25 only Ps cxlii 2 k = Rom xi 6 al. l = Rom iv 13, 14 viii 17 Gal iii 7 James ii 5 m ch i 2 reff

7. δικαιωθεντος(sic) ℵ rec (for γενηθωμεν) γενωμεθα, with D[3]KLℵ[3] rel Cyr-jer txt ACD[1]Fℵ[1] (o) 17 Chr Ath

et renovatio Spiritus sancti'], al On the other hand, most Commentators [see Ellic here] take ἀνακαινώσεως as a second gen. after λουτροῦ and for the purpose of making this clearer, the τοῦ seems to have been inserted before λουτροῦ [see var readd] The great formal objection to this is, the destruction of the balance of the sentence, in which παλιγγενεσίας would be one gen, and ἀνακαινώσεως πνεύματος ἁγίου the other The far greater contextual objection is, that thus the whole from παλ. to ἁγίου would be included under λουτροῦ, and baptism made not only the seal of the new birth, but the sacrament of progressive sanctification) the **renewal** (ἀνακαίνωσις, see reff, is used of the gradual renewal of heart and life in the image of God, following upon the new birth, and without which the birth is a mere abortion, not leading on to vitality and action. It is here treated as potentially involved in God's act ἔσωσεν We must not, as Huther, al, for the sake of making it contemporaneous with the λουτρόν, give it another and untenable meaning, that of mere incipient spiritual life) **of** (brought about by, genitive of the efficient cause) **the Holy Spirit** (who alone can renew unto life in progressive sanctification. So that, as in 1 Pet. iii. 21, it is not the mere outward act or fact of baptism to which we attach such high and glorious epithets, but that complete baptism by water and the Holy Ghost, whereof the first cleansing by water is indeed the ordinary sign and seal, but whereof the glorious indwelling Spirit of God is the only efficient cause and continuous agent 'BAPTISMAL REGENERATION' is the *distinguishing doctrine of the new covenant* [Matt iii 11] but let us take care that we know and bear in mind what '*baptism*' means· not the mere ecclesiastical act, not the mere fact of reception by that act among God's professing people, but that, completed by the divine act, manifested by the operation of the Holy Ghost in the heart and through the life), 6] **which** (attr, not = ἐξ οὗ, as Heydenr. οὗ, viz the Holy Spirit, not λουτροῦ, as even De W. confesses, who yet maintains the dependence of both genitives on λουτροῦ) **He poured out** (reff) **on us richly** (again, it is mere waste of time to debate whether this pouring out be the one general one at Pentecost, or that in the heart of each individual believer· the one was God's objective act once for all, in which all its subjective exemplifications and applications were potentially enwrapped) **through** (as its channel and medium, He having purchased it for us, and made the pouring out possible, in and by His own blessed Sacrifice in our nature) **Jesus Christ our Saviour** (which title was used of the Father above of Him,—ultimately· of our Lord, immediately "Pater nostræ salutis primus auctor, Christus vero opifex, et quasi artifex," as Justiniani in Ellicott, whose own remarks are well worth consulting),

7.] **in order that** (this ἵνα, in the *form* of the sentence, *may* express the aim either of ἔσωσεν [Beng, De W, Huther, Ellic] or of ἐξέχεεν more naturally, I believe, of the latter [Wiesinger] and for these reasons, that ἔσωσεν seeming to have its full pregnant meaning as it stands, (1) does not require any further statement of aim and purpose. but ἐξέχεεν being a mere word of action, is more properly followed by a statement of a reason *why the pouring out took place* and (2) that this statement of aim and purpose, if it applies to ἔσωσεν, has been already anticipated, if ἔσωσεν be understood as including what is generally known as σωτηρία Theologically, this statement of purpose is exact the effusion of the Spirit has for its purpose the conviction of sin and manifestation of the righteousness of Christ, out of which two spring justifying faith) **having been justified** (the aor part. here [expressed in English by 'having been'] is not contemporaneous with the aor. subj below. Ordinarily this would be so but the theological consideration of the place of justification in the Christian life, illustrated by such passages as Rom. v 1, δικαιωθέντες οὖν ἐκ πίστεως εἰρήνην ἔχωμεν πρὸς τ. θεόν, κ τ λ, seems to determine here the aor part to be antecedent to γενήθωμεν) **by His** (ἐκείνου, referring to the more remote subject, must be used here not of our Lord, who has just been mentioned, but of the Father and

n 1 Tim i 15 reff. o = 1 Tim ii 8. v 14. p 1 Tim i 7 only†. q here only. Prov xxxi 21. r 1 Tim iii 1 reff.

m ζωῆς m αἰωνίου. 8 n Πιστὸς ὁ λόγος, καὶ περὶ τούτων ACDF KLℵ a b c d e f g h k l m n o 17
o βούλομαί σε p διαβεβαιοῦσθαι, ἵνα q φροντίζωσιν r καλῶν
r ἔργων s προΐστασθαι οἱ t πεπιστευκότες t θεῷ. ταῦτά ἐστιν
καλὰ καὶ u ὠφέλιμα τοῖς ἀνθρώποις. 9 v μωρὰς δὲ ' ζητή-

s Rom xii 8. 1 Tim iii 4 al. P. Prov xxvi 17 — ver 14 only. t Acts xvi 34 Gal iii 6 (from Gen xv 6). 1 John v 10. u pastl epp only 1 Tim iv 8 bis. 2 Tim iii 16†. v 2 Tim ii 23 (reff)

8 for πιστος, αληθης 67? rec ins τω bef θεω, with rel om ACDFKLℵ Thdrt Damasc Thl (17 defective) rec ins τα bef καλα, with D¹ rel Thdrt. om ACD¹FKLℵ m Chr Damasc (17 def)

so, usually, χάρις θεοῦ [Acts xi 23; xx. 24, 32. Rom v 15. 1 Cor i 4, &c.] is the efficient cause of our justification in Christ) grace, **we might be made** (perhaps passive, see however on 1 Thess i 5) **heirs** (see especially Gal iii 29) **according to** (in pursuance of, consistently with, so that the inheritance does not disappoint, but fully accomplishes and satisfies the hope, not '*through*' (?) as Conyb., referring to Rom. viii 24, 25, where, however, the thought is entirely different) **the hope of eternal life** (I cannot consent, although considerable scholars [e g. De W., Ellic.] have maintained the view, to join the gen **ζωῆς** with κληρονόμοι, in the presence of the expression, in this very Epistle, ἐπ' ἐλπίδι ζωῆς αἰωνίου, ch. i. 2. The objection brought against joining ἐλπίδα with ζωῆς here is that thus κληρονόμοι would stand alone. But it *does* thus stand alone in every place where St Paul uses it in the spiritual sense, viz Rom iv. 14, viii. 17 bis [θεοῦ is a wholly different genitive]. Gal. iii 29, iv. 1, 7: and therefore why not here? Chrys.'s two renderings, both of which Huther quotes for his view, will suit mine just as well. κατ' ἐλπίδα, τουτέστι, καθὼς ἠλπίσαμεν, οὕτως ἀπολαύσομεν, ἢ ὅτι ἤδη καὶ κληρονόμοι ἐστέ. The former is the one to which I have inclined the latter would mean, "we might be heirs, according to the hope"—i e in proportion as we have the hope, realize our heirship—"of eternal life")

8—11] *General rules for Titus.* 8] **Faithful is the saying** (reff viz the saying which has just been uttered, ὅτε ἡ χρηστότης κ τ λ This sentence alone, of those which have gone before, has the solemn and somewhat rhythmical character belonging for the most part to the "faithful sayings" of the apostolic church quoted in these Epistles), **and concerning these things** (the things which have just been dwelt on, see above) **I would have thee positively affirm** ('confirmare,' Vulg., 'asseverare,' Beza cf Polyb xii 12 6, διοριζόμενος καὶ διαβεβαιούμενος περὶ τούτων The διά implies persistence and thoroughness in the affirmation), **in order that** (not, 'that,' implying the *purport* of that which he is διαβεβαιοῦσθαι, nor is what follows the πιστὸς λόγος, as would appear in the E. V.. what follows is to be the result of thorough affirmation of vv 4—7) **they who have believed** (have been brought to belief and endure in it. the present would perhaps express the sense, but the perfect is to be preferred, inasmuch as πιστεύειν is often used of the hour and act of commencing belief cf Acts xix. 2: Rom xiii. 11) **God** (trusted God, learned to credit what God says: not to be confounded with πιστ. εἰς, John xiv. 1, 1 Pet i. 8, 21—or πιστ ἐν, Mark i. 15 [not used of God], or πιστ. ἐπί, Rom. iv 5 There appears no reason for supposing with De W that these words describe merely the Gentile Christians) **may take care to** (φροντίζειν with an inf. is not the ordinary construction. it commonly has ὅπως, ἵνα, ὡς, εἰ, μή, or a relative clause We have an instance in Plut. Fab. Max c 12, τὰ πραττόμενα γινώσκειν ἐφρόντιζεν See Palm and Rost, sub voce) **practise** (a workman presides over, is master and conductor of, his work and thus the transition in προΐστασθαι from presiding over to conducting and practising a business was very easy Thus we have, tracing the progress of this transition, οὗτοι μάλιστα προειστήκεισαν τῆς μεταβολῆς, Thuc viii 75. πῶς οὐ φανερὸν ὅτι προστάντες τοῦ πράγματος τὰ γνωσθένθ' ὑφ' ὑμῶν ἀποστερῆσαί με ζητοῦσιν, Demosth 869, 2. 'Ασπασία οὐ κοσμίου προεστῶσα ἐργασίας, Plut Pericl 24. τέχνης προΐστασθαι,— ὦ τοῖσιν ἐχθροῖς . προὐστήτην φόνου, Soph El 968. χειρὶ βιαίᾳ προστῆναι τοῦ πανουργήματος, Synes Ep 67, p. 211 d See Palm and Rost, sub voce) **good works: these things** (viz. same as τούτων before, the great truths of vv 4—7, this doctrine; not, as Thl, ἡ φροντὶς καὶ ἡ προστασία τῶν καλῶν ἔργων, ἡ

σεις καὶ ʷ γενεαλογίας καὶ ˣ ἔρεις καὶ ʸ μάχας ᶻ νομικὰς
ᵃ περιΐστασο· εἰσὶν γὰρ ᵇ ἀνωφελεῖς καὶ ᶜ μάταιοι. 10 ᵈ αἱρε-
τικὸν ἄνθρωπον μετὰ μίαν καὶ δευτέραν ᵉ νουθεσίαν ᶠ παραιτοῦ, 11 εἰδὼς ὅτι ᵍ ἐξέστραπται ʰ ὁ τοιοῦτος, καὶ ἁμαρτάνει ὢν ⁱ αὐτοκατάκριτος.
12 Ὅταν πέμψω Ἀρτεμᾶν πρός σε ἢ Τυχικὸν, ᵏ σπούδασον ἐλθεῖν πρός με εἰς Νικόπολιν· ἐκεῖ γὰρ ˡ κέκρικα
ᵐ παραχειμάσαι. 13 Ζηνᾶν τὸν ⁿ νομικὸν καὶ Ἀπολλὼ
ᵒ σπουδαίως ᵖ πρόπεμψον, ἵνα μηδὲν αὐτοῖς ᵠ λείπῃ.

H Ζηναν … ACDFH KLℵ a b c d e f g h k l m n o 17

w 1 Tim i 4 (reff) only †. x Phil i 15 reff. y 2 Cor vii 5. 2 Tim ii 23. James iv 1 only. — Gen xiii 7. z Matt xxii. 35. Luke vii 30. x 25. xi 45, 46, 52. xiv 3. ver 13 only †. a = 2 Tim ii 16 (John xi 42. Acts xxv 7) only ‡. b Heb vii 18 only. Prov xxviii 3. Jer ii 8. c Acts xiv 15. 1 Cor iii 20 (from Ps xciii 11). xv 17. James i 26. 1 Pet i 18 only. d here only †. e 1 Cor x 11. Eph vi 4 only †. Judith viii 27 (23) Ald. Wisd xvi 6 only. f = 1 Tim iv 7 reff. g here only. Deut xxxii 20. see 1 Tim i 6 reff. h Paul, 1 Cor v 5. 2 Cor ii 6, 7. xii 2, &c. i here only †. k 2 Tim. ii 15 reff. l = Acts xx 16 (of Paul). 1 Cor v 3. vii 37 al. 2 Macc xi 25. m Acts xxvii 12. xxviii 11. 1 Cor xvi 6 only †. n ver 9 reff. o Luke vii 4 only †. Wisd ii 6 only. (-ος, 2 Tim i 17.) p Acts xv 3. xx 38. xxi 5. Rom xv 24. L P, exc 3 John 6 †. 1 Macc xii 4. Jos Antt xx 2. 5. q ch i 5 reff.

9 for γενεαλ, λογομαχιας F. for ερεις, εριν D¹Fℵ¹.
10 νουθεσιαν bef και δευτεραν DF syr Chr Thdrt₁ txt ACKLℵ rel vulg(and F-lat) Eus Ath (17 def.)—for και, η F.—for δευτεραν, δυο D copt Iren-int₁ Jer₁(remarks, *in mss latt legi Post unam et alteram corrept.*).
13 απολλωνα F. απολλων D²H¹. for σπουδ, ταχεως F. λιπη D¹ b g² m Thdrt-ed.

αὐτὰ τὰ καλὰ ἔργα, which would be a tautology: see 1 Tim ii 3) **are good and profitable for men.** 9] Connexion—maintain these great truths, **but foolish questionings** (ref. and note), **and genealogies** (ref. and note, and ch. i. 14, note), **and strifes** (the result of the genealogies, as in 1 Tim. i. 4) **and contentions about the law** (see again 1 Tim. i. 7. The subject of contention would be the justification, or not, of certain commandments of men, out of the law: or perhaps the mystical meaning of the various portions of the law, as affecting these genealogies) **avoid** (stand aloof from, see 2 Tim ii 16, note): **for they are unprofitable and vain** ("ματ. is here and James i 26, as in Attic Greek, of two terminations: the fem. occurs 1 Cor xv. 17; 1 Pet i. 18." Ellicott). 10] **An heretical man** (one who founds or belongs to an αἵρεσις—a self-chosen and divergent form of religious belief or practice. When St. Paul wrote 1 Cor., these forms had already begun to assume consistency and to threaten danger: see 1 Cor xi 19. We meet with them also in Gal v 20, both times as αἱρέσεις, divisions gathering round forms of individual self-will. But by this time, they had become so definite and established, as to have their acknowledged adherents, their **αἱρετικοί**. See also 2 Pet. ii 1. For a history of the subsequent usage and meanings of the word, see Suicer, vol i pp 119 ff. "It should be observed," says Conyb., "that these early heretics united moral depravity with erroneous teaching: their works bore witness against their doctrine"), **after one and a second admonition** (reff. and note on ref. Eph.), **decline** (intercourse with: ref. and note: there is no precept concerning excommunication, as the middle παραιτοῦ shews: it was to be a subjective act), **knowing that such an one** (a thoroughly Pauline expression: see reff.) **is thoroughly perverted** (ref. Deut. and compare 1 Tim. i. 6, v. 15. 2 Tim iv 4), **and is a sinner** (is living in sin: the present gives the force of habit), **being** (at the same time) **self-condemned** (cf. 1 Tim iv 2, note,—with his own conscience branded with the foul mark of depravity: see Conyb. above).

12—14.] Various directions. 12.] **Whenever I shall have sent** (πέμψω, not fut. ind. but aor. subj.) **Artemas** (not elsewhere named: tradition makes him afterwards bishop of Lystra) **to thee, or Tychicus** (see Eph vi. 21, note: Col. iv. 7), **hasten** (make it thine earnest care) **to come to me to Nicopolis** (on the question which of the three cities of this name is here meant, see Prolegg. to Pastoral Epistles, § ii. 30, note): **for there I have determined to spend the winter.** **Forward on their journey** ([see below] the word here has the sense of 'enable to proceed forward,' viz. by furnishing with necessaries for the journey: so in ref. 3 John)

14 ʳ μανθανέτωσαν δὲ καὶ οἱ ˢ ἡμέτεροι ᵗ καλῶν ᵗ ἔργων
ᵗ προΐστασθαι ᵘ εἰς τὰς ᵛʷ ἀναγκαίας ʷˣ χρείας, ἵνα μὴ ὦσιν
ʸ ἄκαρποι. 15 ᵛ Ἀσπάζονταί σε οἱ μετ' ἐμοῦ πάντες.
ἄσπασαι τοὺς ᶻ φιλοῦντας ἡμᾶς ᵃ ἐν πίστει. ἡ ᵇ χάρις μετὰ
πάντων ὑμῶν.

ACDFH KLℵ a b c d e f g h k l m n o 17

ΠΡΟΣ ΤΙΤΟΝ.

r — and constr, 1 Tim v 4 Phil iv 11 s — here only t ver 8 u — Phil iv 16 v — 1 Cor xvi 22 Phil i 24 al † Wisd xvi 3 w Demosth p 608 end x Phil iv 16 reff plur, Acts xx 34. Rom xii 13 Sir xxxviii 1 y Paul, 1 Cor xiv 14 Eph v 11 (reff) only — 2 Pet i 8 z Paul, 1 Cor xvi 22 only Matt x 37 al fr a 1 Tim i 2 reff b Col iv 18 reff

15. for ασπασαι, ασπασασθε A aft η χαρις ins του κυριου D τ θεου F Ambrst Pelag rec at end ins αμην, with D³FHKLℵ³ rel om ACD¹ℵ¹ 17 fuld æth-rom Ambrst Jer Pelag

SUBSCRIPTION rec προς τιτον της κρητων εκκλησιας πρωτον επισκοπον χειροτονηθεντα εγραφη απο νικοπολεως της μακεδονιας, similarly HKL rel syr: no subscr in k l m· πρ. τιτ. εγραφη απο νικοπολεως A txt C 17, and D(addg επληρωθη) F(prefg ετελεσθη επιστολη) ℵ(adding στιχων ϟϛ)

with zeal Zenas the lawyer (Ζηνᾶς = *Ζηνόδωρος* Probably a Jewish scribe or jurist [Matt xxii 35, note] who had been converted, and to whom the name of his former occupation still adhered, as in the case of *Ματθαῖος ὁ τελώνης* Hippolytus and Dorotheus number him among the seventy disciples, and make him to have been subsequently bishop of Diospolis There is an apocryphal 'Acts of Titus' bearing his name Winer, RWB) **and Apollos** (see on Acts xviii 24 1 Cor i 12; xvi 12), **that nothing may be wanting to them** 14] **Moreover** (connexion of *δὲ καί* the contrast in the *δέ* is, 'and I will not that thou only shouldest thus forward them, though I use the singular number, *but* see that the other brethren *also* join with thee in contributing to their outfit'), **let also our people** (our fellow-believers who are with thee) **learn to practise** (see note, ver 8) **good works, contributions to** (*εἰς*, for the supply of) **the necessary wants which arise** (such is the force of *τάς*. such wants as from time to time are presented before Christians, requiring relief in the course of their Father's work in life), **that they may not be unfruitful** (implying, that in the supply by us of such *ἀναγκαῖαι χρεῖαι*, our ordinary opportunities are to be found of bearing fruit to God's praise)

15] SALUTATIONS GREETINGS APOSTOLIC BENEDICTIONS. **All that are with me salute thee Salute those that love us in the faith** (not '*in faith*' see note, 1 Tim. i. 2 This form of salutation, so different from any occurring in St. Paul's other Epistles, is again [see on ch i 1] a strong corroboration of genuineness An apocryphal imitator would not have missed the Apostle's regular formulæ of salutation). **God's** (*ἡ*) **grace be with all of you** (of the Cretan churches It does not follow *from this* that the letter was to be imparted to them but in the course of things it naturally would be thus imparted by Titus) On the subscription in the rec, making our Epistle date from Nicopolis, see in Prolegg. § ii. 30 ff.

ΠΡΟΣ ΦΙΛΗΜΟΝΑ.

DFK a h e f g l m o 17

1 Παῦλος [a] δέσμιος [b] χριστοῦ Ἰησοῦ καὶ Τιμόθεος ὁ
ἀδελφὸς Φιλήμονι τῷ [c] ἀγαπητῷ καὶ [d] συνεργῷ ἡμῶν
2 καὶ Ἀπφίᾳ τῇ ἀδελφῇ καὶ Ἀρχίππῳ τῷ [e] συνστρα-

a Acts xxiii 18 (of Paul) Eph iii 1 iv 1 2 Tim i 8 ver 9 b gen, Matt xxv 34. John vi 43. Winer, edn 6, § 30 2 c Acts xv 25 Rom i 7 xvi 5, 8 al d ver 24 Phil ii 25 e Phil ii 25 only† Xen Anab i 2 26.

TITLE. rec παυλου του αποστολου η προς φιλημονα επιστολη: παυλου (pref του αγ. αποστ L al) επιστ. πρ φιλ. KL παυλος επιστελλει ταδε βεβαια φιλημονι πιστω f: txt Aℵ h m n o 17, and (prefg αρχεται) DF.

CHAP I 1 for δεσμ., αποστολος D[1]. ιησ bef χρ D[1]L a d f h k syrr arm Chr Thl Thdrt Damasc Ambr Cassiod aft αγαπητω ins αδελφω D[1] Ambrst
2 αφφια D[1]: αμφια F. rec (for αδελφη) αγαπητη, with D[3]KL rel Syr Thdor-mops$_{expr}$ Chr Thdrt Damasc syr (pref αδελφη w. ob) txt AD[1]Fℵ 17 am(with tol harl[1]) copt arm Hesych Jer. (*It seems much more prob that the transcriber shd have carelessly written αγαπητη again, than that αδ. shd have been substd to avoid repetn.*)
[συνστρατιωτη, so ADFℵ 17]

VV 1—3] ADDRESS AND GREETING 1] δέσμιος χ. Ἰ., prisoner of Christ Jesus, i. e one whom He (or His cause) has placed in bonds cf. τοῖς δεσμ. τοῦ εὐαγγελίου, ver 13 He does not designate himself as ἀπόστολος, or the like, as writing familiarly, and not authoritatively Τιμόθ.] see Prolegg. to 1 Tim § i. 10 συνεργῷ] for construction, see Rom. xvi 3, 9, 21. We cannot say when or how, but may well infer that it was at Colossæ, in building up the church there, while the Apostle was at Ephesus: see Prolegg to Col § ii 7 ἡμῶν] Storr (cited in Koch) remarks, "In epistolarum inscriptione, quamvis pronomina et verba tertiæ personæ usitatiora sint, interdum tamen etiam pronomina et verba primæ personæ ut ἡμῶν l. n., et ver. 2 (cf 1 Tim i 1), ἡμῖν 2 Pet i 1 ἐμοί Gal. i 2 et ἐλάβομεν Rom i. 5 (cf Tit. i 3) reperire licet Cf. Cic epp ad diversos lib iv. ep 1, et lib iii. ep 2. Nempe verbum, quod ad omissum vocabulum χαίρειν intelligi debet, cum in tertia, tum in prima persona accipi potest, ut in laudatis inscriptionibus latinis S P D et L D. legere licet '(ego) M T C et Cicero *meus* salutem plurimam *dicimus*,' et '(ego) M. T. C. Appio Pulchro, ut spero, censori, salutem *dico*' cum legamus alias, v c, lib. xvi. ep 3, lib. xiv. ep 14, *dicunt*, vel v. c, ep. 1—5, *dicit*." Ἀπφία is the Latin name Appia, also written Ἀππ., see Acts xxviii 15 cf Kuhner, Gramm. § 44. She appears to have been the wife of Philemon (Chrys, Thdrt), certainly, as well as Archippus, she must have belonged to his family, or they would hardly be thus specially addressed in a private letter concerning a family matter. Ἀρχίππῳ]

f Col iv 15 reff
g Rom i 8 1 Cor i 4 Phil i 3 1 Thess i 2 2 Thess i 3 (2 Macc i 11.)
h Eph i 16 reff
i Rom i 10 Eph i 16 1 Thess i 2 only. ἐπὶ τῶν δείπνων, Diod Sic iv 3
k constr, Matt xi 2 Acts xxiii 16 Gal i 13 Eph i 15 Col i 4
l gen subj., Phil. i 9 reff
m 1 Tim i 19 reff
n = Col ii 5 reff πρός, 1 Thess i 8
o Eph. i 1 reff
p = Phil ii 1 (reff)
q 1 Cor xvi 9 Heb iv 12 only† Polyb xi 23 2
r = Phil i 9
s = Eph i 17 reff

τιώτῃ ἡμῶν, καὶ τῇ f κατ' οἶκόν σου f ἐκκλησίᾳ. 3 χάρις C. ACDF KLℵ a b c d e f g h k l m n o 17
ὑμῖν καὶ εἰρήνη ἀπὸ θεοῦ πατρὸς ἡμῶν καὶ κυρίου Ἰησοῦ
χριστοῦ.
4 g Εὐχαριστῶ τῷ g θεῷ μου πάντοτε h μνείαν σου
h ποιούμενος ἐπὶ τῶν i προσευχῶν μου, 5 k ἀκούων l σου τὴν
l ἀγάπην καὶ τὴν m πίστιν ἣν m ἔχεις n εἰς τὸν κύριον Ἰησοῦν καὶ εἰς πάντας τοὺς o ἁγίους, 6 ὅπως ἡ p κοινωνία
τῆς πίστεώς σου q ἐνεργὴς γένηται r ἐν s ἐπιγνώσει παντὸς

3. om ημων ℵ[1].
5 πιστιν και την αγαπην (see *Eph* i. 15, *Col* i 4, 1 *Thess* i. 3) D m 73 116 Syr arm Ambrst rec for εις, προς (*see note*), with D[3]FKLℵ rel syr G lat(*ad dominum .. et in omnes*). txt ACD[1] 17 copt. aft ιησ. ins χριστον D[1] æth
6 for διακ, κοινωνια ℵ[1]. ins εργου bef αγαθου F b[2] c e g l[2] vulg(with fuld, agst

Cf Col iv 17 **συνστρατιώτῃ**] see reff. and 2 Tim ii 3 He was perhaps Philemon's *son* (so Michael, Olsh, al.). or a family friend (ἕτερόν τινα ἴσως φίλον, Chrys. so Thl) or the minister of the family (ὁ δὲ Ἄρχιππος τὴν διδασκαλίαν αὐτῶν ἐπεπίστευτο, Thdrt) the former hypothesis being perhaps the most probable, as the letter concerns a family matter but see on next clause To what grade in the ministry he belonged, it is idle to enquire nor does Col iv 17 furnish us with any data **τῇ κατ' οἶκ σ. ἐκκλ.**] This appears to have consisted not merely of the family itself, but of a certain assembly of Christians who met in the house of Philemon see the same expression in Col iv 15, of Nymphas and in Rom xvi. 3–5; 1 Cor xvi 19, of Aquila and Prisca. Meyer remarks the *tact* of the Apostle in associating with Philemon those connected with his *house*, but not going *beyond* the limits of the house. The former part is noticed also by Chrys. συμπαραλαμβάνει κ. ἕτερον (-ρους) μεθ' ἑαυτοῦ ὥστε κἀκεῖνον ὑπὸ πολλῶν ἀξιούμενον μᾶλλον εἶξαι κ. δοῦναι τὴν χάριν

4—7] RECOGNITION OF THE CHRISTIAN CHARACTER AND USEFULNESS OF PHILEMON 4] See Rom i 8 1 Cor i 4 πάντοτε belongs to εὐχαριστῶ (Eph i. 16), not to μνείαν ποιούμενος The first part, **ποιούμενος**, expands εὐχαριστῶ,—the 2nd, **ἀκούων**, gives the ground of the εὐχαριστία—**for that I hear ....**

5] It is far better (with Thdrt, Grot, De W, all) to take **ἀγάπη** and **πίστις** as to be distributed between εἰς τὸν κύριον Ἰησοῦν and εἰς πάντας τοὺς ἁγίους, than, with Meyer, to insist on the ἣν as a bar to this, and interpret πίστις in the wider sense (?) of '*fidelity*,' or with Ellic to split up πίστις into spiritual faith towards the Lord, and practical faith towards the saints ἣν is naturally in concord with the nearest subst. The πρός of the rec. has perhaps been a correction for reverence sake εἰς is '*towards*,' but more as contributing to—'towards the behoof of' whereas πρός is simple direction · cf. ver 6.

6] **ὅπως** belongs, as usually constructed, to the former clause, εὐχαριστῶ—προσευχῶν μου The mixing of prayer and thanksgiving in that clause does not exclude the idea of intercessory prayer, nor does (as Meyer maintains) the subsequent clause make against this the ἀκούων κ τ λ was the reason why he ηὐχαρίστει ἐπὶ τῶν προσευχῶν αὐτοῦ, and ὅπως κ τ λ the aim of his doing so. To join ὅπως κ τ λ with ἣν ἔχεις is flat in the extreme, and perfectly inconceivable as a piece of St Paul's writing **In order that the communication of thy faith** (with others) **may become effectual in** (as the element in which it works) **the thorough knowledge** (entire appreciation and experimental recognition [by us]) **of every good thing** (good gifts and graces,—cf Rom. vii. 18, the negation of this in the carnal man) **which is in us, to** (the glory of, connect with ἐνεργὴς γένηται) **Christ [Jesus].** This seems the only simple and unobjectionable rendering. To understand **ἡ κοιν τῆς π. σου**, 'fides tua quam communem nobiscum habes,' as Bengel (and indeed Chrys, Thl, al), is very objectionable to join **εἰς χρ ['Ιησ.]** with **πίστεως** (Calv., Est, al) still more so. to render ἐπίγνωσις passively, '*recognition by others*' ('παθητικῶς sumitur

ἀγαθοῦ τοῦ ἐν ἡμῖν ᵗ εἰς χριστὸν [Ἰησοῦν]. 7 ᵘ χαρὰν
γὰρ πολλὴν ἔσχον καὶ ᵛ παράκλησιν ἐπὶ τῇ ἀγάπῃ ʷ σου,
ὅτι τὰ ˣʸ σπλάγχνα τῶν ᶻ ἁγίων ʸᵃ ἀναπέπαυται διὰ
σοῦ, ἀδελφέ. 8 διὸ πολλὴν ἐν χριστῷ ᵇ παῤῥησίαν ᶜ ἔχων
ᵈ ἐπιτάσσειν σοι τὸ ᵉ ἀνῆκον, 9 διὰ τὴν ἀγάπην μᾶλλον
ᶠ παρακαλῶ. ᵍ Τοιοῦτος ὤν, ᵍ ὡς Παῦλος ʰ πρεσβύτης
νυνὶ δὲ καὶ ⁱ δέσμιος ⁱ χριστοῦ Ἰησοῦ, 10 ᶠ παρακαλῶ σε
περὶ τοῦ ἐμοῦ ᵏ τέκνου, ὃν ˡ ἐγέννησα ἐν τοῖς ᵐ δεσμοῖς,

t w ἐνεργέω, Gal ii 8 bis
u χαρ ἔχειν, 3 John 4
v — 2 Thess ii 6 reff
w gen subj, ver 5
x — vi 12, 20 2 Cor vi 12 vii 15 Phil i 8 Prov xii 20
y ver 20
z ver 5
a — Matt xi 28 1 Cor xvi 18 2 Cor vii 13 2 Chron xxii 9, 18
b Eph iii 12 reff
c 1 Tim iii 13
d Mark i 27 vi 27, 39 ix 25 Luke iv 36 viii 25, 31 xiv 22 Acts xxiii 2 only Esth i 8 w acc, here only
e Eph v 4 Col iii 18 only † 1 Macc xi 35 al
f — Eph iv 1 reff
g not as Acts xxvi 29
h Luke i 18. Tit ii 2 only Job xv 10 al
i ver 1
k — 1 Tim i 2 reff
l — 1 Cor iv 15
m Phil. i 7 reff

am F-lat) Pelag om του AC 17. rec υμιν (*from a tendency, Meyer thinks, in transcribers of epp to use the 2nd person*), with Fℵ rel syrr copt Thl Jer om εν ημ am(with demid) txt ACDKL a b d e f g k l n fuld(with tol harl[2] mar[2] hal) syr-marg arm Chr Thdrt Œc Pelag-comm Ambrst. om ιησ ACℵ[1] 17 copt æth-rom Ambrst Jer · ins DFKLℵ[3] rel latt gr-lat ff (bef χρ, Syr)

7 Steph χαριν, with KL rel Chr-ms Thdrt Damasc Thl(χαριν, τουτεστι χαραν simly Hesych and Erotianus see also 2 Cor i. 15) · txt ACDFℵ a o 17 vss Chr lat-ff rec (for πολλην εσχον) εχομεν πολλην, with D[3]KL rel syrr Chr Damasc Thl Œc · πολλην εσχομεν D[1] Jer. πολλην εχομεν m: πολλην εχω n · txt ACFℵ 17 vulg copt arm Thdrt Ambrst Pelag om και παρακλησιν ℵ for επι, εν D[1] 115.

8 πολλ παρρ εχω εν χριστω ιησ D[1] vulg Jer.

9. for αγαπην, αναγκην A. for νυνι, νυν A 67[2] 73 Thl rec ιησ bef χρ, with D[3]FKL rel om ιησ. D[1] txt ACℵ 17 copt æth Ambrst Jer Ambr

10 ins εγω bef εγεννησα A m 68 Chr[1] om CDFKLℵ rel (*εγω may, as Meyer, have been omd from similarity of εγω εγεν., but εγε- may also have occasioned its* insertion) rec aft δεσμοις ins μου, with CD[3]KLℵ[3] rel vss gr-ff. om AD[1]Fℵ[1] 17 latt Ambrst Jer Ambr Pelag

habetque innotescendi significationem,' Grot.: so Erasm., Beza, Est., all.) worst of all The interpretation given above, I find in the main to be that of De W., Meyer, and Koch. 7] If we read χάριν with the rec., it will be best interpreted by 2 Cor. i 15, as a benefit,—an outpouring of the divine χάρις—not χάρ. ἔχειν in the sense of 1 Tim. i 12 2 Tim i 3, '*to give thanks,*' for then it seems always to be followed by a dative. The γάρ gives a reason for the prayer of ver 6 as De W., not, as Meyer, for the thanksgiving of ver 4 see above ὅτι κ τ λ] further specification of τῇ ἀγάπῃ σου, whose work consisted in ministering to the various wants and afflictions of the saints at Colossæ. ἀδελφέ is skilfully placed last, as introducing the request which follows.

8—21] PETITION FOR THE FAVOURABLE RECEPTION OF ONESIMUS 8] διό relates to διὰ τ. ἀγάπ below, and refers back to the last verse; it is not to be joined to the participial clause as Chrys., al it was not on account of ver 7 that St Paul had confidence to *command* him, but that he *preferred beseeching* him ἐν χριστῷ as usual, the element in which the παῤῥησία found place. τὸ ἀνῆκον, a delicate hint, that the reception of Onesimus was to be classed under this category—**that which is fitting** (reff.) 9 τὴν ἀγάπην] is not to be restricted to '*this thy love*' (of ver 7 so Calv., al.), or '*our mutual love*' (Grot., al.), but is quite general—'that Christian love, of which thou shewest so bright an example' ver 7 τοιοῦτος ὤν] reason for the μᾶλλον—'I prefer this way, as the more efficacious, being such an one, &c.' The 'cum *sis* talis' of the Vulgate is evidently a mistake I believe Meyer is right in maintaining that τοιοῦτος cannot be taken as preparatory to ὡς, '*such an one, as . . .*' as in E V., and commonly I have therefore punctuated accordingly, as has Ellic The rendering will be **Being such an one** (as declared in διὸ . . . παρακαλῶ),—**as (1) Paul the aged and (2) now a prisoner also of Christ Jesus** (*two* points are made, and not *three* as Chrys., all — Παῦλος πρεσβύτης going together, and the fact of his being a prisoner, adding weight [καί] The fact of πρεσβύτης is interesting, as connected with the date

Ὀνήσιμον, 11 τὸν ⁿ ποτέ σοι ᵒ ἄχρηστον, νυνὶ δὲ σοὶ
καὶ ἐμοὶ ᵖ εὔχρηστον, ὃν ᑫ ἀνέπεμψά σοι, 12 αὐτόν,
ʳ τουτέστι τὰ ἐμὰ ˢ σπλάγχνα, 13 ὃν ἐγὼ ἐβουλόμην ᵗ πρὸς
ἐμαυτὸν ᵘ κατέχειν, ἵνα ὑπὲρ σοῦ μοι ᵛ διακονῇ ἐν τοῖς
ʷ δεσμοῖς τοῦ ʷ εὐαγγελίου, 14 χωρὶς δὲ τῆς σῆς ˣ γνώμης

ACDF KLℵ a b c d e f g h k l m n o 17

n — Gal i 13 reff. o here only Hos viii 8. p 2 Tim ii 21. q — Luke xxiii 11 (7, 15 Acts xxv 21) only †. r Matt xxvii 46 Mark vii 12 Rom vii 18 al. s ver 7. t — Matt xiii 56 Mark ix 19 a Luke ix 41 John i 1. 1 Cor xvi 6, 7 al. u — Luke iv 42 Gen xxiv 56 xlii 19. v — Matt xxvii 55 Acts xix 22 Rom xv 25. Heb vi 10. w gen, see ver 1 reff. x — Acts xx 3 2 Macc iv 39.

11. ins και bef 2nd σοι Fℵ(ℵ[1] marked it for erasure but removed the marks) b vulg Syr for ανεπ., επεμψα D d 17 91 Chr rec om 3rd σοι, with D[3]FKLℵ[3] rel am(with fuld) syr goth: ins ACD[1]ℵ[1] 17 Syr copt arm Jer Pelag, προς σε demid Chr Ambrst

12. rec at beg ins συ δε (see above), with DFKLℵ[3] rel vss: om ACℵ[1] 17 rec at end ins προσλαβου (corrn to supply the sense, which is completed in ver 17 cf varr of posn), with CDKLℵ[3] rel vulg also aft συ δε in 73 116 copt. also aft αυτον G-lat arm Thdrt om AFℵ[1] 17

13 ηβουλ. ℵ rec διακονη bef μοι (transposn to avoid concurr of σου μοι), with KL rel syrr copt Chr[h 1] txt ACDFℵ 17 latt goth Thdrt Thl Jer Ambrst Pelag

of this Epistle and those to Eph and Col see Prolegg. to Eph. § iv), I beseech thee, &c. If we read ἐγώ before ἐγέννησα, the repetition of ἐμοῦ—ἐγώ will serve, as Meyer remarks, to mark more forcibly the character of his *own* child, and ἐν τοῖς δεσμοῖς gives more weight still to the entreaty. Ὀνήσιμον is not (with Erasm.-Schmid) to be treated as if it were a play on the name, ὃν ἐγένν . . . ὀνήσιμον, '*profitable to me*' but simply to be regarded as an accusative by attraction. 11.] Here there certainly appears to be a play on the name—'quondam . . parum suo nomini respondens,—nunc in diversum mutatus.' Erasm. (No play on χριστός [as Koch, al.] must be thought of, as too far-fetched, and because the datives σοί and ἐμοί fix the adjectives to their ordinary meanings.) He had been ἄχρηστος in having run away, and apparently (ver 18) defrauded his master as well. Meyer quotes from Plat., Lys. p. 204 B. φαῦλος κ. ἄχρηστος and from ib. Rep. p. 411 B. χρήσιμον ἐξ ἀχρήστου ἐποίησεν. On account of the σοὶ καὶ ἐμοί, **εὔχρηστον** must not be limited to the sense of outward profit, but extended to a spiritual meaning as well—profitable to me, as the fruit of my ministry,—to thee as a servant, and also as a Christian brother (ver 16). 12.] There does not appear to be any allusion to the fact of sonship in τὰ ἐμὰ σπλάγχνα, as Chrys. Thdrt (ἐμός ἐστιν υἱός, ἐκ τῶν ἐμῶν γεγέννηται σπλάγχνων), al: for thus the spiritual similitude would be confused, being here introduced materially. But the expression more probably means, **mine own heart**—'as dear to me as mine own heart.' Meyer compares the expressions in Plautus,—'*meum corculum*,' Cas. iv. 4. 14,—'meum mel, *meum cor*,' Pœn. i. 2. 154. Cf also, 'Hic habitat tuus ille hospes, mea viscera, Thesbon,' Marius Victor, in Suicer, Thes. ii. 998, and examples of both meanings in Wetst., Suicer, and Koch. The construction (see var. readd.) is an anacoluthon: the Apostle goes off into the relative clause, and loses sight, as so often, of the construction with which he began: taking it up again at ver 17. 13.] ἐγώ, emphatic, **I, for my part.** ἐβουλόμην, nearly as ηὐχόμην, in Rom. ix. 3 (though in that place there certainly is, as Ellic. remarks, a more distinct reference to a suppressed conditional clause),—**was wishing,—had a mind, = could have wished,** in our idiom. ἠθέλησα, ver 14, differs from ἐβουλόμην, (1) in that it means simply **willed**, as distinguished from the stronger **wished**, (2) in that it marks the time immediately preceding the return of Onesimus, whereas the imperfect spreads the wish over the period previous. **I was** (long) **minded . . . . but** (on considering) **I was not willing.** ὑπὲρ σοῦ] **For,** wert thou here, thou wouldst minister to me. I was minded therefore to retain him in thy place. διακονῇ, pres. subj., representing the ἐβουλόμην as a still continuing wish. ἐν τοῖς δεσμ. τοῦ εὐαγγελίου] explained well by Thdrt, ὀφείλεις μοι διακονίαν ὡς μαθητὴς διδασκάλῳ, κ. διδασκάλῳ τὰ θεῖα κηρύττοντι: not without allusion also to the fetters which the Gospel had laid on himself. 14.] **But without thy decision** (= consent: so χωρὶς τῆς αὐτοῦ γνώμης, Polyb. iii. 21. 7, xxi. 8. 7. μετὰ τῆς τοῦ Δ. γνώμ., id. ii. 11. 5) **I was willing** (see above) **to do nothing** (general expression, but meant to

οὐδὲν ἠθέλησα ποιῆσαι, ἵνα μὴ [y] ὡς [z] κατὰ [a] ἀνάγκην [a] τὸ
ἀγαθόν σου ᾖ, ἀλλὰ κατὰ [b] ἑκούσιον· 15 [c] τάχα γὰρ
διὰ τοῦτο [d] ἐχωρίσθη [e] πρὸς [e] ὥραν, ἵνα [f] αἰώνιον αὐτὸν [g] ἀπέχῃς, 16 οὐκέτι ὡς δοῦλον, ἀλλ' [h] ὑπὲρ δοῦλον,
[i] ἀδελφὸν [i] ἀγαπητόν, [k] μάλιστα ἐμοί, [l] πόσῳ δὲ [l] μᾶλλον
σοί, καὶ [m] ἐν σαρκὶ καὶ [n] ἐν κυρίῳ. 17 εἰ οὖν με [o] ἔχεις
[p] κοινωνόν, [q] προσλαβοῦ αὐτὸν ὡς ἐμέ. 18 εἰ δέ τι [r] ἠδί-
κησέν σε ἢ [s] ὀφείλει, τοῦτο ἐμοὶ [t] ἐλλόγα· 19 [u] ἐγὼ [u] Παῦλος

y = Rom ix 32 (see note). z here only (see note). ἐξ ἀν., 2 Cor ix 7 Heb vii 12. a Gal vi 10 reff. b here only. καθ' ἑκ., Num xv 3 see Thucyd viii 27. c Rom v 7 only†. Wisd xiii 6 xiv 19 only. d absol., 1 Cor vii 11, 15 bis. e John v 35. 2 Cor vii 8. Gal ii 5 only. see 1 Thess ii 17. f constr., Mark iv 28. John viii 7. Acts xii 10 al. Ps xiv 2. Winer, edn 6, § 51. 2. g = Matt vi 2. Phil. iv 18. Gen xliii 23. h = Matt x 37. Acts xxvi 13. i Eph vi 21. Col iv 7, 9. k 1 Tim iv 10 reff. l Rom xi 12, 24. Heb ix 14 al. m 1 Tim iii 16 reff. n = Rom xvi 2, &c. Phil ii 29. o = Phil ii 29 reff. p 1 Cor x 18, 20. 2 Cor i 7 al. Isa i 23. q = Acts xxviii 2. Rom xiv 1, 3. Ps xxvi 10. lxxii 24. r = Matt xx 13. 1 Cor vi 8. s = Matt xviii 28, &c. Luke xvi 5, 7. Deut xv 2. t here only. -γεῖν, Rom v 13 only†. u Gal. v 2 reff.

14. om 2nd κατα D latt Ambrst Jer, Ambr Pelag (κατ', 1st, DF; 2nd, F.)
16. αλλα D ℵ m 17. om αλλ' υπερ δουλον (*homœotel*) F. om αδελφον ℵ[1]: αγαπ bef αδελφ. 174.
17. rec (for με) εμε, with AK n f. txt CDFLℵ rel Chr Thdrt Damasc Thl Œc.
18. rec ελλογει, with D[2, 3]KL(ℵ[1?] but txt restored) rel: txt ACD[1]Fℵ 17.

apply only to the particular thing in hand, = 'nothing in the matter'), **that thy good** (service towards me: but not in this particular only: the expression is general—the particular case would serve as an *example* of it) **might be not as** (appearing as if it were: 'particula ὡς, substantivis, participiis, totisque enuntiationibus præposita, rei veritate sublata aliquid opinione, errore, simulatione niti declarat.' Fritz on Romans, ii. p 360) **of** (after the fashion of, according to: ᾔδει ὅτι πάντες κατ' ἀνάγκην αὐτῷ κοινωνήσουσι τῶν πραγμάτων, Polyb. iii. 67. 5) **necessity, but of free will**. 15.] **τάχα** is delicately said, to conciliate Philemon: so Chrys., καλῶς τὸ **τάχα**, ἵνα εἴξῃ ὁ δεσπότης· ἐπειδὴ γὰρ ἀπὸ αὐθαδείας γέγονεν ἡ φυγὴ κ. διεστραμμένης διανοίας, κ. οὐκ ἀπὸ προαιρέσεως, λέγει **τάχα**. And Jerome says, 'occulta sunt quippe judicia Dei, et temerarium est quasi de certo pronunciare.' He refers to Gen. xlv. 5, where Joseph suggests the purpose which God's providence had in sending him down into Egypt. **ἐχωρίσθη**] εὐφήμως καὶ τὴν φυγὴν χωρισμὸν καλεῖ, ἵνα μὴ τῷ ὀνόματι τῆς φυγῆς παροξύνῃ τὸν δεσπότην, Thl.: similarly Chrys. **πρὸς ὥραν**] much has been built upon this as indicating that the Epistle was written not so far from Colossæ as Rome: but without ground: the contrast is between πρὸς ὥραν and αἰώνιον. **αἰώνιον** agrees with αὐτόν: see reff: and imports οὐκ ἐν τῷ παρόντι μόνον καιρῷ, ἀλλὰ κ. ἐν τῷ μέλλοντι, as Chrys. **ἀπέχῃς**] see reff., and note on Matt. vi. 2—**mayest have him for thine own—possess him fully, entirely.** So Antonin., xi. 1, says that the λογικὴ ψυχή does not bear fruit for others to reap, &c., but ὅπου ἂν καταληφθῇ, πλῆρες κ. ἀπροσδεὲς ἑαυτῇ τὸ προτεθὲν ποιεῖ ὥστε εἰπεῖν, Ἐγὼ **ἀπέχω** τὰ ἐμά.

16.] And that, in a different relation from the one before subsisting. But οὐκέτι ὡς δοῦλον does not imply his manumission; rather the contrary: the stress is on **ὡς** and **ὑπέρ**—'no longer *as* a slave (though he be one), but *above* a slave.' **μάλιστα**, 'of all other men,' of all those without thy house, with whom he has been connected: but πόσῳ μᾶλλον σοί, with whom he stands in so near and lasting a relation. 17.] takes up again the sentiment (and the construction) broken off at the end of ver. 12. The κοινωνία referred to is that shewn by the ἀγάπη of him, common to both, mentioned in the last verse: but extending far wider than it, even to the community of faith, and hope, and love between them as Christian men: not that of goods, as Bengel: 'ut tua sint mea et mea tua.' 18.] **δέ**, in contrast to the favourable reception bespoken for him in the last verse. 'Confessus erat Onesimus Paulo, quæ fecerat,' Bengel: οὐκ εἶπον, εἴ τι ἔκλεψεν ἀλλὰ τί; εἴ τι ἠδίκησεν: ἅμα κ. τὸ ἁμάρτημα ὡμολόγησε, καὶ οὐχ ὡς δούλου ἁμάρτημα ἀλλὰ ὡς φίλου πρὸς φίλον, τῷ τῆς ἀδικίας μᾶλλον ἢ τῷ τῆς κλοπῆς ὀνόματι χρησάμενος, Chrys. **ἢ ὀφείλει** is said of the same matter, and is merely explanatory of ἠδίκησεν: τοῦτο referring to both verbs. The weight of MS. testimony to **ἐλλόγα** overbears the mere assertion of Fritzsche (on

v Gal vi 11 reff
w here only Exod xxi 19
x here only † Herod vi 59 (Schweigh.) Xen Cyr iii 2 7 Hell i 5 1 Demosth 6,0 21
y Phil iv 3
z here only † Sir xxx 2 only Xen Anab iii 1 38
a ver 7 reff
b Rom xvi 7, 9, 10 al fr
c constr., Phil i 14 reff
d Rom i 5 al[6] 1 Cor vii 15 x 5, 6 Heb v 8. 1 Pet i 2, 14, 22 only 2 Kings xxii 36 only.
e ver 16.
f 2 Tim ii 21 1 Cor ii 9 Heb xi 16 Gen xxiv 31
g Acts xxviii 23 only † Ælian Var Hist iii 37
h = Rom xii 3. Gal i 18
i = Acts iii 14. xxvii 24 1 Cor ii 12 L P † 2 Macc iii 33 al
k Rom xvi 7 Col iv 10 only †

[v] ἔγραψα τῇ ἐμῇ [v] χειρί, ἐγὼ [w] ἀποτίσω· ἵνα μὴ λέγω
σοι ὅτι καὶ σεαυτόν μοι [x] προςοφείλεις. 20 [y] ναί, ἀδελφέ,
ἐγώ σοῦ [z] ὀναίμην ἐν κυρίῳ· [a] ἀνάπαυσόν μου τὰ
[a] σπλάγχνα [b] ἐν χριστῷ. 21 [c] πεποιθὼς τῇ [d] ὑπακοῇ σου . πεποιθως F
ἔγραψά σοι, εἰδὼς ὅτι καὶ [e] ὑπὲρ ἃ λέγω ποιήσεις. 22 ἅμα (and also G)
δὲ καὶ [f] ἑτοίμαζέ μοι [g] ξενίαν· ἐλπίζω γὰρ ὅτι [h] διὰ τῶν ACDK
προςευχῶν ὑμῶν [i] χαρισθήσομαι ὑμῖν. LℵA b c d e f g
23 Ἀσπάζεταί σε Ἐπαφρᾶς ὁ [k] συναιχμάλωτός μου ἐν h k l m n o 17

19 for αποτισω, αποδωσω D[1] scholl (*reddam* latt). at end ins εν κυριω D[1].

20. rec (for χριστω) κυριω (*repetn from foregoing*), with D[3]K rel txt ACD[1]FIℵ a m 17 latt syr copt æth arm Chr Œc-comm Thdrt ms Thl Ambr Jer Ambrst Pelag.

21 rec ὃ (*appy corrn to suit circumstance, only one request having been made*), with DKL rel vss gr-lat-ff· txt ACℵ 17. 73 syr copt

23. rec ασπαζονται, with D[2,3]KL rel. txt ACD[1]ℵ m vulg Syr copt æth arm Chr Thdrt Thl Jer Ambrst Pelag

Rom v. 13)— λογᾶν est *dicturire* (Luc. Lexiph, p 15), sed ἐλλογᾶν vox nulla est.'—that reckon, or impute to me. hardly perhaps, notwithstanding the engagement of the next verse, with a view to actual repayment, but rather to inducing Philemon to forego exacting it.

19] The inference from this is, that the whole Epistle was autographic for it would be most unnatural to suppose the Apostle to break off his amanuensis here, and write this engagement with his own hand. ἵνα μὴ λέγω] "est σχῆμα παρασιωπήσεως sive reticentiæ, cum dicimus nos omittere velle, quod maxime dicimus," Grot ἵνα μή does not exactly, as Meyer, give the purpose of St. Paul in ἔγραψα—ἀποτίσω but rather that of an understood clause,—'yield me this request, lest I should have to remind thee, &c' Ellic paraphrases, 'repay yes I say this, not doubting thee, but not wishing to press on thee all the claim that I might justly urge' καὶ τοῦτο ἀπὸ ἀγάπης καὶ κατὰ τὸν τῆς φιλίας λόγον, καὶ τοῦ σφόδρα θαῤῥεῖν ἦν, Chrys And this may well be the right view. καὶ σεαυτόν] οὐ τὰ σαυτοῦ μόνον, Chr. δι' ἐμοῦ γάρ, φησί, τῆς σωτηρίας ἀπήλαυσας καὶ ἐντεῦθεν δῆλον, ὡς τῆς ἀποστολικῆς διδασκαλίας ἠξιώθη ὁ Φιλήμων, Thdrt.

20] ναί, as so often when we make requests, asserts our assent with the subject of the request · so Phil iv 3, al ἐγώ and σοῦ are both emphatic—and the unusual word ὀναίμην, thus thrown into the background, is an evident allusion to the name Ὀνήσιμος. "The form ὀναίμην is similarly used by Ignatius (Polyc 1, 6, pp. 720, 725; Magn 12, p 672, al),—once (Eph. 2, p 645), curiously enough, but apparently by mere accident, after a mention of an Onesimus." Ellicott (Lobeck, on Phryn, p 12, gives a complete account of the forms and tenses of this verb which are in use.) The sentiment itself is a reference to σεαυτόν μοι προσοφείλεις·—this being so, let me have profit of thee. ἐν κυρίῳ,—not in worldly gain, but in the Lord—in thine increase and richness in the graces of His Spirit ἀνάπαυσον] refresh (viz by acceding to my request) my heart (as above—the seat of the affections τὰ σπλάγχνα μου must not for a moment be imagined, with Jer, Est, Schrader, al., *to designate Onesimus*, who was so called in ver. 12 · which would be most unnatural) in Christ (as ἐν κυρίῳ above).

21] Serves to put Philemon in mind of the apostolic authority with which he writes: and hints delicately (perhaps: but this may be doubtful compare Ellic here) at the manumission of Onesimus, which he has not yet requested καί, also, besides doing *what* I say

22 ἅμα δὲ καί] But at the same time (as thou fulfillest my request), also . . . We may, perhaps, take this direction as serving to secure the favourable reception of Onesimus for the Apostle would himself come and see how his request had fared: πολλὴ γὰρ ἦν ἡ χάρις κ ἡ τιμὴ Παύλου ἐνδημοῦντος, Παύλου μετὰ ἡλικίαν, Παύλου μετὰ δεσμούς, Chrys Or it may be, as

χριστῷ Ἰησοῦ, 24 Μάρκος, Ἀρίσταρχος, Δημᾶς, Λουκᾶς,
οἱ [l] συνεργοί μου.
25 ἡ [m] χάρις τοῦ [m] κυρίου ἡμῶν Ἰησοῦ χριστοῦ μετὰ
τοῦ [n] πνεύματος ὑμῶν.

l Rom xvi 3, 9, 21. 1 Cor iii 9 al[8] Paul only, exc 3 John 8†. 2 Macc viii 7. xiv 5 only
m see Col iv. 18 reff
n Gal vi 18. Phil iv 23. 2 Tim iv 22

ΠΡΟΣ ΦΙΛΗΜΟΝΑ.

25 om ημων ℵ 17. 31 47. 116 rec at end ins αμην, with CD³KL ℵ rel · om AD¹ 17 arm Jer.

Subscription rec adds εγραφη απο ρωμης δια ονησιμου οικετου, with K al. FG are deficient after ver 20 but G (not F) after a vacant space notes προς λαουακησας (*Laudicenses* G-lat) αρχεται επιστολη· του αγιου αποστ παυλ επ. πρ φιλημ. και απφιαν δεσποτας του ονησιμου και προς αρχιππον τον διακονον της εν κολοσσαις εκκλησιας εγραφη απο ρωμης δια ονησιμου οικετου L b om l: A deficient. εργ απ. ρ. δ ο. οικ h k m: txt C 17, and D(addg επληρωθη), ℵ(adding στιχων, without numeral).

Ellic., that Philemon was not to consider the Epistle as a mere petition for Onesimus, but as containing special messages on other matters to himself ὑμῶν and ὑμῖν refer to those named in vv 1, 2

23—25] Conclusion See on Col. iv. 10, 12, 14, where the same persons send greeting. Ἰησοῦς ὁ λεγόμενος Ἰοῦστος (Col iv. 11) does not appear here

25] For this form of salutation, see reff On all matters regarding the date and circumstances of writing the Epistle, see the Prolegomena

END OF VOL III

LONDON:
GILBERT AND RIVINGTON, PRINTERS,
ST. JOHN'S SQUARE.

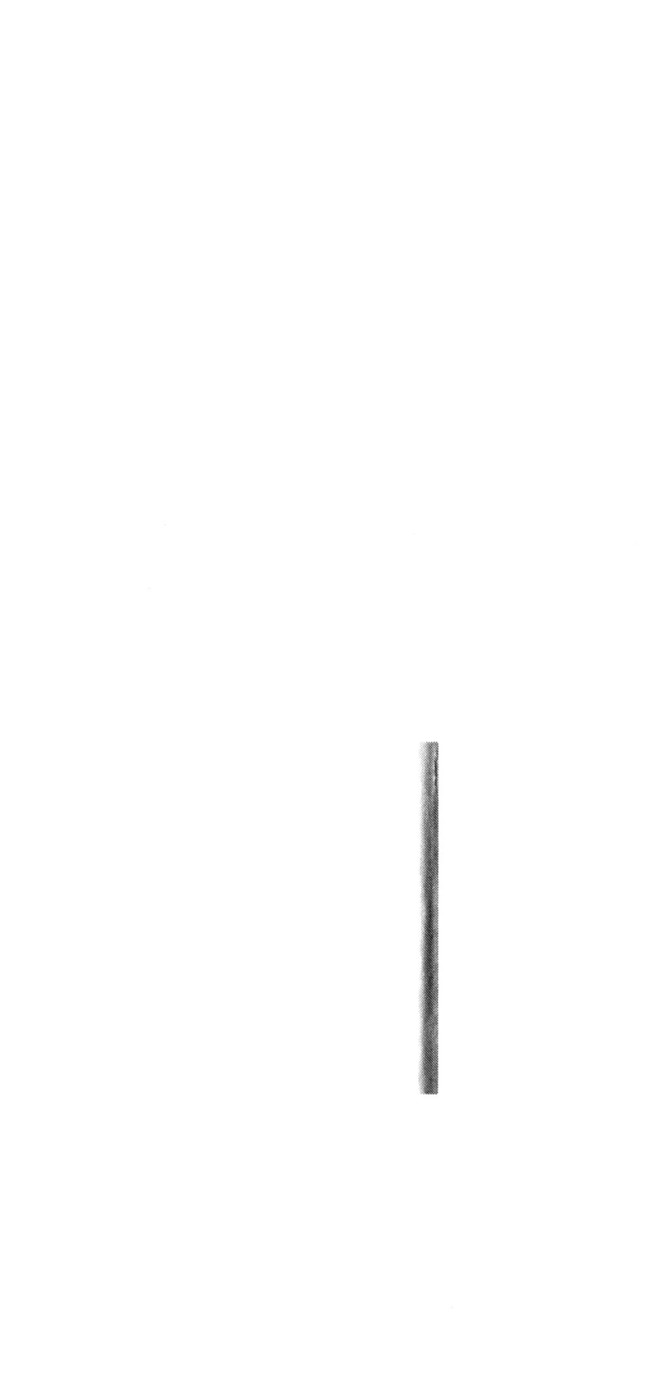

Lightning Source UK Ltd.
Milton Keynes UK
UKHW022336060520
362900UK00006B/49

9 781342 295361